CHRISTIAN LITURGY

CHRISTIAN LITURGY

Catholic and Evangelical

Frank C. Senn

FORTRESS PRESS

MINNEAPOLIS

CHRISTIAN LITURGY
Catholic and Evangelical

Scripture quotations, unless otherwise noted, are from the New Revised Standard Version Bible © 1989 Division of Christian Education of the National Council of the Churches of Christ in the United States of America. Used by permission.

EDITOR: Frank Stoldt
COPY EDITORS: Kari Kloos and William Congdon
PRODUCTION EDITOR: Linda Parriott
COVER AND INTERIOR DESIGN: Ellen Maly
COVER ART: Last Supper: Early Christian mosaic. S. Apollinare Nuovo, Ravenna, Italy. Photo copyright © Scala/Art Resource. Used by permission.

Library of Congress Cataloging-in Publication Data

Senn, Frank C.
    Christian liturgy : Catholic and Evangelical / Frank C. Senn.
      p. cm.
    Includes bibliographical references and index.
    ISBN 0-8006-2726-1 (alk. paper)
    1. Liturgics 2. Catholic Church—Liturgy—History. 3. Lutheran Church—Liturgy—History. 4. Liturgical churches—History. 5. Protestant churches—History. I. Title.
BV186.5.S46 1997
264'.009—dc21

97-6205
CIP

The paper used in the publication meets the minimum requirements of American National Standard for Information Sciences.

Manufactured in the U.S.A.   ISBN 0-8006-2726-1   01-2726
05   04   03   02   01   00   99   98   2   3   4   5   6   7   8   9

Contents

PART TWO: REFORMATION LITURGICAL TRADITIONS

List of Abbreviations

Bek.   *Die Bekenntnisschriften der evangelisch-lutherischen Kirche*. Göttingen: Vandenhoeck und Ruprecht, 1954.

Br.   *Martin Luthers Briefwechsel*. See WA.

CR   *Corpus Reformatorum*. Halle and Braunschweig: C. A. Schwetschke und Sohn, 1834ff.

LW   *Luther's Works*. Ed. by Jaroslav Pelikan and Helmut T. Lehmann. 55 vols. St. Louis: Concordia Publishing House and Philadelphia: Fortress Press, 1955–86.

PG   *Patrologiae cursus completus*. Series Graeca. Ed. by J.-P. Migne. Paris, 1886ff.

PL   *Patrologiae cursus completus*. Series Latina. Ed. by J.-P. Migne. Paris, 1878ff.

Sam. Sk.   *Olavus Petri Samlade Skrifter*. 4 vols. Uppsala: Almqvist och Wiksells Boktryckeri A-B, 1914–1917.

WA   *Martin Luthers Werke*. Kritische Gesammtausgabe. Weimar: Böhlau, 1883ff.

A WORD OF APPRECIATION

Regrettably, but not atypically, there were a number of small errors in the first printing of this book. My thanks to several readers who helped me locate them. Most especially I express my appreciation to Dr. Carl Heinrich A. Schmutzler, pastor of Old Zion Lutheran Church in Philadelphia, who worked with me on-line to spot these errata, mostly in foreign language names and titles. A few minor revisions or additions have been inserted in this second printing, but not enough to warrant a "revised edition." My thanks to Frank Stoldt and Augsburg Fortress for their continuing commitment to this book.

Frank C. Senn

Preface

THE HISTORY OF CHRISTIAN liturgy has been written many times by many competent liturgists. Why write it again? Two reasons come to mind.

First, good stories cannot be told too often or in too much detail. As we approach the end of the twentieth century and the second millennium of the Christian era, the world and the church are experiencing rapid change. Liturgy is the church's public presentation of its beliefs and enactment of its life. Pressures of social and cultural change tug at the liturgy because they tug at the church's life in society. Because the church's mission is to proclaim and celebrate the gospel of Jesus Christ, crucified for our offenses and raised again for our justification, this good news of forgiveness, reconciliation, and new life in a new creation under God's reign must be communicated in ways that make it accessible to those to whom it must be proclaimed and who are called to celebrate it. As the church proclaims and celebrates the gospel in changing social situations or new cultural settings, the natural tendency is to discover and experiment with new forms and expressions indigenous to local settings by which the gospel can be proclaimed and celebrated with fresh relevance. Customs encrusted with age that no longer seem relevant to the contemporary Christian community need to be evaluated in terms of their usefulness to the proclamation and celebration of the gospel. The study of the history of liturgy helps in the process of sorting out what is essential and what is peripheral in the church's practice of worship in word and sacrament.

We must also remember that the gospel of Jesus the Christ is rooted in history: in the history of Israel and of the nations grafted onto Israel by virtue of the turn Israel's history took with the appearance of Jesus the Christ at a specific time and place. Certain historical givens serve as an anchor for the ongoing mission of the church of God in world history as the community of faith in Jesus Christ crucified and risen again passes through various societies and cultures. A loss of historical memory would endanger the gospel itself. Liturgy must provide for the remembrance of this history of salvation as well as embody the ongoing history of the proclamation and celebration of the gospel in words and signs. The historical study of liturgy is a probing of changes that have occurred in the service of God, which frees us to make the changes that are needed today. The historical study of liturgy also reminds us of features of the divine service that have endured and must be maintained today. We are not at liberty to change anything we like. Some texts and practices from the past continue to inform our proclamation and celebrations today.

The second reason for writing the history of Christian liturgy again is to tell it from a different angle. I have been among the growing number of liturgical scholars who have been telling the story of Christian liturgy from the point of view of its cultural setting.[1] One of the most interesting aspects of liturgical studies has been its utilization of nontheological fields of expertise such as the social sciences, the humanities, architecture, and the arts. The appeal to cultural studies has differentiated liturgical studies from more traditional ecclesiastical disciplines, although one observes a recent willingness among biblical exegetes and church historians also to derive insights from historical-cultural studies. The consequence of this is to demonstrate the human provenance of liturgical forms and content; these are seen to be culturally conditioned and historically contingent.

At the same time, it is necessary to attend to the theological meanings of liturgy and of sacramental worship in particular, precisely in order to attend to the reality of liturgy as the divine service—the service rendered by God to the congregation and the congregation's service offered to God.[2] Liturgy (*leitourgia*) is the public work performed by a particular community under the leadership of its liturgists (*leitourgoi*) to enact its view of reality and commitments. It may very well draw upon symbols that are regarded as natural in that they are shared by many groups of people in different times and places (e.g., rites of washing and sacred meals), but the community of faith also gives expression to its own worldview and values by use of these symbols. Symbols convey meanings, often variously perceived by the beholders, but they are also employed in the service of expressing particular meanings. The church fathers held that there is a reciprocal relationship between prayer and belief, between the *lex orandi* and the *lex credendi*. This has provided a methodology for contemporary liturgical theology.[3] Anthropologist Roy Rappaport has also held that ritual "is not simply an alternative way to express certain things. . . . Certain things can be expressed only in ritual."[4] This is especially true of the sacramental means of grace: the "visible words" of Holy Baptism and Holy Communion.

---

[1] See my *Christian Worship and Its Cultural Setting* (Philadelphia: Fortress Press, 1983), which combined elements of an introduction to liturgical study with pastoral liturgics.

[2] See Peter Brunner, *Worship in the Name of Jesus*, trans. by M. A. Bertram (St. Louis: Concordia Publishing House, 1968).

[3] See Alexander Schmemann, *Introduction to Liturgical Theology* (London: The Faith Press, 1966) and Aidan Kavanagh, *On Liturgical Theology* (New York: Pueblo Publishing Co., 1984).

[4] Roy Rappaport, "The Obvious Aspects of Ritual," in *Ecology, Meaning, and Religion* (Richmond, Calif.: North Atlantic Books, 1979), 174.

One important consequence of attending to the cultural setting and symbolic performance of liturgy has been to wean liturgical scholars away from textual preoccupation. It may be that we American liturgists sometimes lack the linguistic ability to do competent textual analysis (although for doctoral dissertations this has usually been required). But we have come to see liturgy expressing meaning at least as much through actions or ceremonies as through texts, and even confessional identity is derived more from participation in the liturgical action than from a grammatical or historical understanding of a text. For example, a person may not understand or even be aware of the christological controversies that lie behind the Nicene-Constantinopolitan Creed; yet as Rappaport suggests, the person who attends the public liturgy and recites the creed cannot do otherwise than to indicate publicly an acceptance of what is implied in that liturgy and its confession of faith.[5] As Mary Douglas has suggested, this is already a meaning of ritual; it provides a means of expressing identity with the community that performs the rites.[6] Liturgical theologians would point out that this was the original purpose of the creed: it was a means by which baptismal candidates expressed identification with the community of faith in Jesus Christ dead and risen again.

The churchly or ecclesial context of liturgy is thus also important. The story of liturgy is inseparable from the community that performs liturgical orders as its public work. Liturgiology is really a subdivision of ecclesiology. The church is convened in an assembly by the public proclamation of the word of God, constituted as the priestly people of God in baptism, and manifested as the body of Christ in the world in the eucharist. Where there is no assembly for the proclamation of the word of God and the celebration of the sacraments of Christ, there is no "church," no matter what other kind of religious or spiritual activity is taking place. So the story of Christian liturgy is also the story of the church in its public mode.

Of course, this story is complicated by the fracturing of the body of Christ into different confessional communities, which in North America takes the form of denominationalism. I cannot avoid the fact that I am a member of and have a primary interest in a particular community of faith. Therefore I give this telling of the story of Christian liturgy a different center of gravity than other renditions might do. This has a certain practical benefit. The scope of liturgical history is so vast that it is not possible to give equal emphasis to its performance in every time and place, or to attend to every detail of liturgical evolution; nor have standard histories of the liturgy attempted to do this. Something is inevitably omitted or truncated. For example, Theodore Klauser[7] ignored Byzantine and Reformation liturgy as he brought his story of Western liturgy to a climax in the liturgical reforms of the Second Vatican Council. Gregory Dix[8] brought his story of liturgy to a climax in the Anglican Reformation and the tradition stemming from that.

---

[5] Ibid., 173–221.

[6] Mary Douglas, *Natural Symbols: Explorations in Cosmology* (New York: Random House, 1970; Vintage Books, 1973), especially chapter three on "The Bog Irish."

[7] Theodore Klauser, *A Short History of the Western Liturgy* (London: Oxford University Press, 1969).

[8] Gregory Dix, *The Shape of the Liturgy* (London: Dacre Press, 1945; reprinted New York: Harper and Row, 1982, with an afterword by Paul V. Marshall).

Alexander Schmemann, in his *Introduction to Liturgical Theology*,[9] virtually ignored Western liturgical developments as he probed the Byzantine liturgical synthesis. Herman Wegman[10] paid attention both to Eastern and Western liturgy, but only summarized post-Reformation liturgical rites and life. Only the multi-authored Oxford University *The Study of Liturgy*[11] has come close to telling the whole story, and only James F. White, in his *Brief History of Christian Liturgy*,[12] has given equal attention to all historical periods, including what has happened in North America.

It is important to devote attention, as all histories of Christian liturgy do, to the origins of liturgy and to its synthesis or coming together during the so-called patristic age. Our common roots are to be found in the first several centuries, although even in the New Testament data it is apparent that there were differences in liturgical practice and polity between Palestinian and non-Palestinian and between Jewish and Greek Christian communities.[13] But then separate developments of liturgy take place, beginning with the demarcation between the Chalcedonian and Non-Chalcedonian churches, continuing with the separation of the Eastern Orthodox and Western Catholic churches, and culminating in the schism in the Western church resulting from the Protestant Reformation, with further splintering among the Reformation traditions.

These developments in different times and places are so diverse that one author cannot possibly manage to do justice to the various details of the full story of Christian liturgy. So this author has focused on liturgy that is *catholic*—in continuity with the whole historic tradition—and *evangelical*—gospel-centered in its forms of proclamation and celebration. Accordingly, I have made the Reformation in the sixteenth century the center of gravity in Part Two. That has dictated that attention be given to the Western medieval liturgical developments that prompted reform, and to post-Reformation developments that have bequeathed to posterity the enduring legacy of the Reformation. Indeed, a case can be made that post-Reformation attitudes toward worship derived from the periods of orthodoxy, rationalism, and romanticism affect our liturgical assumptions and sensibilities more than do Reformation faith and practice. For this reason each of the chapters in Part Three ends with theological/pastoral reflections on issues that logically follow from the emphases of each of these historical periods, because these are issues that still concern us in our ordering of public worship.

My journey through liturgical history brings me finally to my home in North America where I regularly perform Christian liturgy within a particular community. I want to affirm that this is a terminus for me, but not for the ongoing evolution of Christian liturgy. Indeed, liturgical developments in the younger churches of Africa and

---

[9] Op. cit.

[10] Herman Wegman, *Christian Worship in East and West*, trans. by Gordon Lathrop (New York: Pueblo Publishing Co., 1985).

[11] *The Study of Liturgy*, rev. ed., ed. by Cheslyn Jones, Geoffrey Wainwright, Edward Yarnold, S.J., and Paul Bradshaw (New York: Oxford University Press, 1992).

[12] James F. White, *A Brief History of Christian Worship* (Nashville: Abingdon Press, 1993).

[13] See Ferdinand Hahn, *The Worship of the Early Church*, trans. by David E. Green; ed. with an introduction by John Reumann (Philadelphia: Fortress Press, 1973).

Asia indicate that the story of Christian liturgy continues in exciting ways. I would have liked to conclude this story among the liturgical traditions in Africa and Asia. But my base as a parish pastor keeps me confined to my place without firsthand access to the global church, and I believe it would be exceedingly foolhardy to comment on contemporary developments with which one has little firsthand experience.

My localization, however, does not preclude exploring Christian liturgy from an ecumenical perspective and context. Graduate programs in liturgical studies and liturgical professional associations have become ecumenical. In the situation of confessional or denominational pluralism, ecclesial communities cohabiting the same territories often share a common cultural context. So even (especially!) in the post-Reformation period, it is not possible to tell the story of the liturgy in, for example, the Evangelical Lutheran community without looking over one's shoulder at comparable developments in other faith communities (e.g., Roman Catholic, Reformed, Anglican, Free Church). A comparative approach to liturgy is required. Indeed, I hope that enough of the comparative approach is present in this book to make it of interest and value to those in ecclesial traditions other than my own. This ecumenical agenda will also explain to Lutheran partisans why I have not dealt in greater detail with our own more recent history, as Luther D. Reed did in his classic book, *The Lutheran Liturgy*.[14] Reed had the advantage of having served in the inner circles of liturgical committees and commissions for more than a half century; I have not had such experience.

A comparative approach to liturgy was already practiced by Reed. The idea for writing this book was generated by a publisher's inquiry to Philip H. Pfatteicher and me as to whether Reed's magnum opus could be profitably updated in the light of more recent liturgical studies and the publication of *Lutheran Book of Worship* (1978). We concluded that it was best to let Reed's work stand as the classic it is, but to undertake a new history and commentary that would be no less thorough than Reed's book. As work and discussion with the publisher proceeded, it was determined that two separate volumes were needed that would provide the history and commentary Reed included in one volume. Pfatteicher proceeded with *Commentary on the Lutheran Book of Worship* and finished first.[15] This present work is intended to be the companion to that commentary, although each volume can stand on its own. Hence, Pfatteicher abbreviated the historical and theological background, and I will refrain from a detailed analysis of the orders and texts in *Lutheran Book of Worship*.

Reed was well aware that Lutheran liturgy is but a variant of the Catholic liturgy of the Western church, and he made numerous ecumenical references. He rooted Lutheran liturgy in the ancient sources, East and West, and in medieval developments.

---

[14] A number of colleagues have suggested that the story of the Inter-Lutheran Commission on Worship (ILCW) should be written down for posterity, just as Luther Reed described the workings of the Joint Commission on the Common Liturgy that led to the *Service Book and Hymnal* in his book *The Lutheran Liturgy* (Philadelphia: Fortress Press, Revised Edition, 1960). I agree that this should be done; but it would probably be done best by someone who was a member of the ILCW and knew its innerworkings.

[15] Philip H. Pfatteicher, *Commentary on the Lutheran Book of Worship: Lutheran Liturgy in an Ecumenical Context* (Minneapolis: Augsburg Fortress, 1991).

He devoted full attention to Scandinavian as well as German Lutheran liturgies. He noted the Calvinist and Anglican liturgical developments at the time of the Reformation and afterward. But even more than Reed, Pfatteicher and I have endeavored to imbue our studies with ecumenical references that reflect the context in which Lutheran liturgy has evolved and in which *Lutheran Book of Worship* came into existence.[16]

Even to attempt to tell the story of Christian liturgy today, no matter how narrowly delineated, seems a foolhardy venture. The unearthing of new data and the proposing of fresh interpretations seems infinite. A general history such as this can only make sweeping interpretations of an array of information, and with the realization that a single new piece of evidence or a fresh insight can change the entire impression of origins and development.[17]

Furthermore, even as there are fresh contributions in the field of liturgiology, so there are fresh contributions in such ancillary fields as anthropology, biblical studies, general history, church history, historical theology, and musicology. If one realizes the extent to which one is dependent on the scholars in one's own field to help provide a comprehensive picture, one is even more humbled to realize how much one must rely on the insights of those in other fields in which one may have only a secondary competence. And just as there are conflicting theories and opinions in the field of liturgiology, so the liturgist needs to realize that theories and opinions in these ancillary fields are not value-free. So, for example, the liturgist who draws on the anthropological insights of Victor Turner needs to realize that Turner's view of the transformative purpose of ritual is not shared by all ritual experts.[18]

A liability in writing a book of this scope is that I have not made my living as a professional scholar and teacher in fifteen years. I have served as a parish pastor whose research and writing is limited to a few hours on a weekly day off or late at night. I started writing this book in the mid-1980s after I was no longer pursuing a professional academic career. I had much material to draw upon at that point: the copious notes and duplicated articles I had accumulated during my days as a graduate student at the University of Notre Dame; my doctoral dissertation[19] (some portions of which have been incorporated

---

[16] It is unfortunate that *Lutheran Book of Worship* was not given a name such as *The Book of Worship according to the Use of the Lutheran Church*, as many previous Lutheran service books were styled, e.g., *Common Service Book of the Evangelical Lutheran Church*, *Service Book and Hymnal of the Lutheran Church in America*. This would have reflected the catholic character of the liturgical rites used in the Lutheran churches.

[17] See, for example, the theory of the origins of Christmas from calendrical calculations rather than from competition with winter solstice festivals in Thomas Talley, *Origins of the Liturgical Year* (New York: Pueblo Publishing Co., 1986), or the theory of the origin of confirmation in the rite of the solemn dismissal of the catechumens in Aidan Kavanagh, *Confirmation: Origins and Reform* (New York: Pueblo Publishing Co., 1988).

[18] Ronald Grimes, "Liturgical Supinity, Liturgical Erectitude: On the Embodiment of Ritual Authority," *Studia Liturgica* 23:1 (1993) has challenged the assumptions of many ritualists and liturgists that ritual is inherently structured, formal, invariant, repetitive, canonical, and authoritative (the "erectitude" school) by showing that it can also be creative, playful, innovative, "unauthorized," sometimes subversive, often informal and relatively unstructured (the "supine" school).

in this book—James White has repeatedly prodded me to publish it in some form); and lecture notes from courses in liturgy that I taught at the Lutheran School of Theology at Chicago. But as time marched on (and the writing of this book was frequently suspended to write other books and articles), I found it necessary to update my notes in the light of new publications and interaction with colleagues at the annual meetings of the North American Academy of Liturgy (NAAL). Lack of regular access to an academic library often made checking references a daunting task.

Nevertheless, it is characteristically Lutheran to "sin boldly." There is a practical consequence to this effort that makes its risks worth taking. That is to persuade evangelical Christians to be respectful toward the catholic tradition, which has served as a cradle of the gospel; and to remind catholic Christians that sometimes so much has been put into the cradle that the gospel has been smothered. Accumulation was not just characteristic of the Gothic age; it is a perennial human habit. The church must always be reformed, and that includes the church's performance of its public work—its liturgy. But there is a danger of throwing out the baby with the excess quilts and toys. There are instances, especially in but not limited to the age of rationalism, when the liturgy itself was mutilated or destroyed in the interests of promoting a message essentially alien to the gospel. Hence comes the title of this book: *Christian Liturgy: Catholic and Evangelical.* It alludes to the storytelling path through the catholic tradition and into the evangelical Christian community. As the term "catholic" can mean several things, so can the term "evangelical." So by "catholic" I mean an ecclesial commitment to the received tradition, and by "evangelical" I mean an ecclesial commitment to the gospel of Jesus Christ, as articulated in the ecumenical creeds. My interest is in the liturgies of communities that make both kinds of commitment.

Finally, I must express my thanks to Frank Stoldt of Augsburg Fortress for pushing this project through to completion and to Linda Parriott for performing a work of supererogation on the editing. My thanks must also be expressed to Phil Pfatteicher for his occasional long-distance calls urging me toward completion of this project on which we embarked together at an NAAL meeting so long ago. My thanks also to the supportive members of Immanuel Lutheran Church who have felt that a pastor should be involved in intellectual pursuits, who have delighted in my sharing with them of insights and theories gleaned from my reading of historical sources, and who have accompanied me on the journey that leads up to the considerations of doing liturgy in the postmodern situation with which this book thankfully ends.

Frank C. Senn
Evanston, Illinois, June 29, 1996
The Feast of the Holy Apostles Peter and Paul,
also marking the 27th anniversary of my ordination
to the Holy Ministry of the Word and the Sacraments

---

[19] Frank C. Senn, "Liturgia Svecanae Ecclesiae Catholicae et Orthodoxae Conformis: An Attempt at Eucharistic Restoration during the Swedish Reformation" (Ph.D. diss., University of Notre Dame, 1978).

The Ritual of Christian Worship

CHAPTER 1

The Repertoire of Rites

THIS IS A STUDY of Christian liturgy: its history and the meanings that have been associated with its forms, content, and practices. *Liturgy* is what Christians have performed in their public assemblies. *Worship* is both more and less than liturgy. It is more in that it includes the devotional practices of individuals and households as well as public praise and common prayer; it is less in that liturgy is not only prayer but ritual. Ritual has to do not only with what a community does before God but also with what the members of a community do in interaction with one another. It is a pattern of behavior that expresses and forms a way of life consistent with the community's beliefs and values.

There has long been a bias against ritual in Western intellectual and religious thought. Rationalism denigrated ritualistic behavior as obsessive and regressive—as a need to impose order on a chaotic world and rooted in infantile strategies for managing conflict and stress. Rationalists, of course, operate with a worldview that posits an orderly universe. They believe, with Sigmund Freud, that conflict and stress would disappear if human beings would leave their infantile compulsions behind. Against such a view a more positive assessment of the role of ritual in human development has been posited, for example, by the psychologist Erik Erikson.[1] Also, biogeneticists have posited a biogenetic source of the human capacity for ritual and mythmaking located in the complex relationships between the left and right hemispheres of the brain and in the older (reptilian) and

---

[1] See Erik Erikson, "Ontogeny of Ritualization in Man," *Philosophical Transactions of the Royal Society of London*, Series B, No. 772, Vol. CCLI (1966), 337–50.

newer (new mammalian) strata of the evolution of the brain.[2] Unlike the older scientists, who tended to reduce all human experiences to material/physical (e.g., biochemical) causes, the newer scientists like Eugene d'Aquili and his structuralist colleagues take seriously the "spiritual capacities" of human beings.[3]

As the whole of human life and endeavors is a system of rituals, so is the life and mission of the Christian community a system of rituals. Educating our young, bringing new members into the community, looking after the needs of the most vulnerable members of church and society, and worshiping God are all ritual activities. But as Ronald Grimes has said, "The Liturgy of a ritual system is often, but not always, its most paradigmatic, most central, most valued rite."[4] The liturgy is the activity in which the life and mission of the church are paradigmatically and centrally expressed. As there is no development in human life without ritualization,[5] so there is no unritualized Christian life. Since every Christian church has an act of gathering in which its corporate life and mission are expressed, there are no Christian churches without liturgy. The distinction commonly made between "liturgical" churches and "nonliturgical" churches is not helpful. Even Quakers, who admit no texts or sacraments into their meetings, nevertheless observe certain patterns of behavior in their meetings. What they do in their meetings is their *leitourgia*, their "public work." Their liturgy is a ritual that comprises gathering, communal silence, sharing insights, and developing a sense of the meeting. What Quakers may lack in their meetings, but which some other churches have plenty of in their liturgies, are ceremonies. Ceremonies are the particular actions that constitute a ritual, such as carrying a flag at the head of a parade and saluting it as it passes by or carrying a cross in procession and bowing as it passes down the aisle of the church.

Not surprisingly, Christian ritual forms are not dissimilar from the ritual forms of other religions or social groups. After all, there are a limited number of ways in which human beings may express themselves. This was already noticed by ancient church fathers such as Justin Martyr, who regarded pagan rites of washing and sharing meals as diabolical imitations of Christian sacraments.[6] The rites of washing (baptism) and eating and drinking together (eucharistic meal) that Jesus instituted and commanded to be done had a prehistory in Judaism and corollary rites in other religions. These acts are also imbued with natural meanings. Natural symbols are ones that have meanings rooted in ordinary life. For example, washing is a form of cleansing, and eating and drinking are ways of receiving nourishment. So baptism has been spoken of as a washing away of sin and Holy Communion has been spoken of as spiritual nourishment. Theological meaning draws on the natural associations of these symbolic acts and expands on them in evocative ways.

---

[2] See Eugene d'Aquili and C. D. Laughlin, Jr., "The Neurobiology of Myth and Ritual," in *The Spectrum of Ritual* (New York: Columbia University Press, 1979), 152–82.

[3] See Frank C. Senn, "Being Human and Being Liturgical," *Lutheran Forum* 18:3 (1984), 19–23.

[4] Ronald Grimes, "Emerging Ritual," *Proceedings of the North American Academy of Liturgy 1990* (Valparaiso, Ind.: NAAL, 1990), 31.

[5] See Aidan Kavanagh, "The Role of Ritual in Personal Development," in James Shaughnessy, ed., *The Roots of Ritual* (Grand Rapids: William B. Eerdmans Publishing Co., 1973), 145–60.

[6] Justin Martyr, *First Apology*, 62, 64, 66.

🍇 THE ROLE OF SYMBOL

The theological tradition has wanted to distinguish between signs that signify or point to something other than themselves, and symbols that make present or provide participation in that which is represented (*sum-ballein*, "to throw together"). Sometimes it has been suggested that signs serve functions whereas symbols serve meaning. For example, a stop sign points to the necessity of stopping and often employs the word "stop" on its octagonal shape. But the sign is painted red because red is understood to be a symbolic color of danger. Or again, the bread and wine of the eucharist are called signs of the body and blood of Christ in those traditions in which there is an exact correlation between bread and wine and the body and blood of Christ. But the way Holy Communion is administered is symbolic because it suggests the meanings of receiving these sacramental signs. These examples also indicate the difficulty of distinguishing between signs and symbols. In reality, they coalesce.[7]

It may be more convenient to regard symbols as aspects of the general category of signs. All signs convey meaning but symbols expand rather than limit meaning. This is especially important in the use of words, which are both signs and symbols. For example, the verb "to eat" usually designates a bodily function and the act of taking nourishment. But the same term can be used metaphorically, as in "to eat your words." The Christian liturgy, like the Bible on which it is largely based, makes ample use of symbolic and metaphorical language simply because sacred reality can only be expressed in images and symbols. This is why we must be on our guard against the Western demotion of symbolic language, as when it is said, "This is only a symbol." Western thought has sometimes driven a wedge between "symbol" and "reality." But the language of liturgy, like the language of the Bible, does not know of such a differentiation. Reality is expressed in symbolic language. Human beings use words (which are also symbols) to express concepts that are within the realm of revelation and their experience in order to articulate the inexpressible.

Paul Ricoeur defines "symbol" as "any structure of signification in which a direct, primary, literal meaning designates, in addition, another meaning which is indirect, secondary, and figurative and which can be comprehended only through the first."[8] This alerts us to the double meanings of symbols. For example, the ceremonial breaking of bread in the celebration of the eucharist is already a symbolic act signifying the fellowship created by the meal. But symbolic interpretations of the Lord's Supper also see the fraction pointing to the sacrifice of Christ, the benefits of which are conveyed to the communicants.

The double meaning of symbols easily fosters allegorization, in which what is seen or said is neglected in favor of what is thought or imagined. Allegory turns every

---

[7] See David N. Power, *Unsearchable Riches: The Symbolic Nature of Liturgy* (New York: Pueblo Publishing Co., 1984), 62ff.

[8] Paul Ricoeur, "Existence and Hermeneutics," in *The Conflict of Interpretations* (Evanston, Ill.: Northwestern University Press, 1974), 12.

word and object into an instruction, often with a precise meaning or designation. Of course, allegorical interpretations of words and actions are deeply embedded in the theological tradition, and at its best allegory has stimulated the religious imagination. One finds a sophisticated form of allegory in the writings of the ancient church fathers, especially in the Alexandrine school, in which theologians like Clement and Origen deepened spirituality by drawing attention away from things in themselves to the contemplation of higher mysteries. But a crude form of allegory can be found in the expositions of the mass (*expositiones Missae*) during the Middle Ages in which everything was made to represent whatever the commentator chose. For example, when the priest washed his hands at the offertory, this was said to represent Pontius Pilate washing his hands of responsibility for Jesus at his trial. Allegorical interpretation turned the mass into a reenactment of the passion of Christ. The practical result was that the laity were left as spectators of a clerical performance as the priest offered the sacrifice of the mass. Representation in the sense of dramatic portrayal was substituted for symbolism in the true sense. This served to arouse devotion, but did not foster participation.

Allegory has not been preferred as much as typology in the best liturgical commentaries. Typology suggests that there is a pattern in God's redemptive activity. So, for example, baptism is seen as a type of the exodus crossing of the sea or as a type of the flood in which God rescued his people from destruction. Typology has served the biblical and liturgical acts of remembrance (Hebrew: *zakar;* Greek: *anamnesis*). The cultic rituals are not an intellectual act of recall but the emotional act of entering into a relationship with God whose earlier deeds imply a promise for the present and the future. This is clearly expressed in Deuteronomy 5:2–4: "The LORD our God made a covenant with us at Horeb. Not with our ancestors did the LORD make this covenant, but with us, who are all of us here alive today. The LORD spoke with you face to face at the mountain, out of the fire." Typology connects the past and the present on the basis of promise and fulfillment. Typology in the service of remembrance of past redemptive acts can perhaps best be seen in the text of the Exsultet in the Easter Vigil. Here it is proclaimed that "this is the night" of the passover, the exodus, the resurrection of Christ, and baptism—all experienced anew and simultaneously "this night."

> It is indeed right and salutary
> that we should with full devotion
> of heart and mind and voice
> praise the invisible God,
> the Father Almighty,
> and his only Son,
> our Lord, Jesus Christ;
> who paid for us the debt of Adam
> to the eternal Father,
> and who by his precious blood
> redeemed us from the bondage to the ancient sin.
> For this indeed is the Paschal Feast
> in which the true Lamb is slain,
> by whose blood

the doorposts of the faithful are made holy.
This is the night in which,
in ancient times,
you delivered our forebears,
the children of Israel,
from the land of Egypt;
and led them, dry-shod,
through the Red Sea.
This, indeed, is the night
in which the darkness of sin has been purged away
    by the rising brightness.
This is the night
in which all who believe in Christ
are rescued from evil and the gloom of sin,
 are renewed in grace,
and are restored to holiness.
This is the night in which, breaking the chains of death,
Christ arises from hell in triumph.
For it would have profited us nothing to be born
had we not also been redeemed.[9]

Many commentators have pointed out that modern Western people have difficulty apprehending symbolic meaning. We are a literal-minded people for whom signs work better. This also explains why people have difficulty with the historic liturgy of the church. For this liturgy is freighted with archetypal and primordial symbols of light and darkness, inclusion and exclusion, feasting and fasting that serve to open us to a sense of the sacred. The historian of religions, Mircea Eliade, likened the loss of the sacred to a second fall of humankind—the fall into secular, desacralized existence. For many people life is no longer centered in or determined by an overarching sacred reality. Yet an awareness of absence also suggests the possibility of a past—and therefore a future—presence. As Eliade wrote, "In his deepest being, man still retains a memory of [the sacred], as, after the first 'fall' his ancestor, the primordial man, retained intelligence enough to enable him to rediscover the traces of God that are visible in the world."[10]

Where there is memory, there is the possibility of retrieval. This retrieval may be facilitated through the performance of ritual actions, since the sacramental signs connect us with life and the world, and the sacramental celebrations connect us with the memory of the past (*anamnesis* = reactualization) and hope for the future (*prolepsis* = anticipation of eschatological reality). What we are suggesting is that the obedient performance of rituals that have lost their meaning because of our symbolic amnesia may help in the recovery of meaning, precisely because of the evocative power of symbols.

---

[9] *LBW*, Ministers Edition, 144.

[10] Mircea Eliade, *The Sacred and the Profane*, trans. by Willard R. Trask (New York: Harper Torchbooks, 1961), 213.

❦ THE ROLE OF RITUAL

Ritual is necessary in any society as a means of facilitating both continuity with the past (the conserving aspect of ritual) and an orderly process of change (the renewing aspect of ritual). Roland Delattre has identified four aspects of ritual, two that serve a conserving function and two that serve a renewing function.[11] The two that serve a conserving function are anchorage—going through the motions (e.g., toilet-training for children, Christian catechumenate) and articulation (e.g., human arts, baptism and eucharist). The two aspects of ritual that serve a renewing function are negotiation (e.g., writing memoirs, confession and absolution) and passage (e.g., marriage, vocation). The rituals of a community, if sound, will provide for both stability and change, conservation and reformation. They can move members of a society through the large rhythms of the life-cycle (birth, maturation, vocation, death) and the psychological microbes, or "little pieties," as Erving Goffman called "interaction ritual."[12]

Eliade has sorted through the repertoire of rites and categorized them according to their use in the sanctification of life, time, and space, in both *The Sacred and the Profane* and *Patterns in Comparative Religion*. This provides a convenient way of categorizing the repertoire of rites available to the Christian community. Rites that sanctify *life* deal largely with passage through various crises. They are by definition *occasional*. Such rites include:

- initiation (baptism, confirmation, first communion)
- penance (confession and forgiveness, reconciliation)
- vocation (ordination, commissionings, installations)
- marriage
- childbirth
- sickness
- anniversaries
- death and burial

Rites that sanctify *time* are *cyclical* or periodically recurring. These include:

- daily prayer offices
- weekly celebrations of word and eucharistic meal
- festivals and seasons of the church year, with special customs

Rites that sanctify *space* may be either occasional or cyclical. These include:

- consecration of churches; blessing of dwellings
- homecomings; pilgrimages
- groundbreakings; anniversaries

Rituals can decay, no longer conveying the force or meaning in personal or social life they once had. But what threatens ritual depends on the kind of rituals. Rituals that serve a conserving purpose are threatened when the very function of ritual is despised,

---

[11] Roland A. Delattre, "Ritual Resourcefulness and Cultural Pluralism," *Soundings* 41:3 (1978), 281–301.

[12] Erving Goffman, *Interaction Ritual: Essays on Face-to-Face Behavior* (Garden City, N.J.: Doubleday and Company Anchor Books, 1967).

along with the authority structures and hierarchies such rituals depend on and reinforce. Mary Douglas has written that "one of the gravest problems of our day is the lack of commitment to common symbols. . . . But more mysterious is a widespread, explicit rejection of rituals as such. Ritual has become a bad word signifying empty conformity. We are witnessing a revolt against formalism, even against form."[13]

On the other hand, authoritarianism and elitism are precisely the conditions that threaten rituals of renewal. Rites of passage, for example, depend for their effectiveness on a playfulness and risk-taking that pits novices against authority figures and builds up a sense of camaraderie among the initiates. It is necessary to give free play to these dynamics to create an authority that is not authoritarian and a hierarchy that is not elite but servile. In the community of Jesus' disciples, "whoever wishes to become great among you must be your servant, and whoever wishes to be first among you must be slave of all. For the Son of Man came not to be served but to serve, and to give his life as a ransom for many" (Mark 10:43–45).

✤ RITES OF PASSAGE

Rites of passage attempt to deal creatively with the unavoidable fact that, as anthropologist Arnold van Gennep put it, "For groups, as well as for individuals, life itself means to separate and to be reunited, to change form and condition, to die and to be reborn. It is to act and to cease, to wait and rest, then to begin acting again, but in a different way." For individuals and societies, "there are always new thresholds to cross: . . . the thresholds of birth, adolescence, maturity and old age; the threshold of death and that of afterlife."[14]

Van Gennep compared the structure of rites of passage to that of taking a journey: there is leave-taking, passage, and arrival. He wrote that "a complete scheme of rites of passage theoretically includes preliminal rites (rites of separation), liminal rites (rites of transition), and postliminal rites (rites of incorporation)."[15] The term "liminal" is derived from the Latin *limen* (threshold).

This scheme should alert us to the fact that the rites of passage involve a *process* that is marked out by different stages. Initiation, for example, involves being separated from a former status (such as childhood), passing through a novitiate (such as adolescence with all its excruciating experiential learnings), and being incorporated into a new status (such as adulthood with all its privileges and responsibilities). In some societies the liminal stage of transition is compressed into a few weeks as one moves quickly from childhood to adult responsibilities. In many traditional societies adolescence happens so quickly as to be practically nonexistent. In other societies, such as those of western

---

[13] Mary Douglas, *Natural Symbols: Explorations in Cosmology* (New York: Random House Vintage Books, 1973), 19.

[14] Arnold van Gennep, *The Rites of Passage*, trans. by Monika B. Vizedom and Gabrielle L. Caffe (Chicago: University of Chicago Press, 1960), pp. 189–90.

[15] Ibid., 11.

Europe and North America, the need for universal literacy, compounded by the technological information explosion and the need for complex skills to serve its sophisticated apparatus, have pushed the time of childhood back and the time of adulthood forward, thus prolonging the period of adolescence, that ambiguous betwixt and between stage when one no longer has the liberties of childhood but has not yet fully assumed the restrictive responsibilities of adulthood. The rites of passage to adulthood in such a society as ours are diffuse, prolonged, and subtle, including rituals of dating, getting a driver's license, graduating from high school and college, and establishing independence from one's family over a long period of time.

The ancient rites of Christian initiation can easily be analyzed in terms of van Gennep's tripartite scheme of the rites of passage. Whether Christian baptism is understood in terms of a co-death and burial with Christ (as in the letters of Paul) or in terms of adoption by God the Father (as in the model of the baptism of Christ in the Synoptic Gospels), it assumes a demarcation between the old life of sin and death and the new life in Christ. This entails ritualizing the transition between one state and the other. By the time of the *Apostolic Tradition* of Hippolytus of Rome, written early in the third century, Christian initiation involved being separated from the life of this world (marked by enrollment into the catechumenate), being taught and engaged in the values and lifestyle of the divine kingdom (marked by the catechumenate), and being incorporated into the fellowship of the eschatological community (marked by the water bath, the laying on of hands, the kiss of peace, and participation for the first time in the eucharistic meal of the Christian community).

It is clear that the center of gravity in this ritual process was the water bath, as the terms *baptizein* and *baptisma* indicate. The fact that Paul could construe baptism as a symbolic burial with Christ (Rom. 6:4; Col. 2:12) suggests an immersion in water. That was the case with the usual Jewish rite of purification (the *tebilah*), which may have been one of the antecedents of Christian baptism. Mosaics on early Christian baptistery walls suggest that the candidates were baptized naked, which was also the case with the Jewish rite. Taking off and putting on one's clothes for a bath is certainly a natural action; but it was compared metaphorically to putting off the old nature and taking on the new and the rather common ethical figure of taking off bad habits and putting on virtuous ones.

For these reasons the center of gravity in the Christian rites of initiation was not preceded by a washing, but *was* the washing. The significance of this fact is apparent if we compare Christian initiation to its nearest analogies: the Jewish immersion of proselytes and initiation into the pagan mysteries. In the mystery cults, lustration rites were preparatory for admission into the mysteries proper.[16] The same was true in Judaism: the water rites served the purpose of purification before entering a sacred time or place. For this reason they were often associated with the temple cult. The extension and democratization of the concept of purity and the means of attaining or restoring it by being loyal to the commandments brought about, among the Pharisees, the innovation of the immersion

---

[16] See George F. Mylones, *Eleusis and the Eleusinian Mysteries* (Princeton: Princeton University Press, 1961).

pool.[17] Yet, among the Pharisees, there was no thought that one could pass from the impure world into a pure community; purity had to be continually reestablished. So the immersions were frequently repeated. But Christianity accepted only one baptism for the forgiveness of sins. Baptism became, for Christianity, a permanent threshold between the impure world and the pure group, between those who remain in the world and those who have been initiated, between those who were outside the church's fellowship and those who have been brought inside to the gathering around the table.

Yet it is evident already in Paul's letters that the church was not totally a pure group (see especially 1 Cor. 5–6). Paul's baptismal teaching was often in the context of problems that arose in church life. He was constantly exhorting his readers to remember in what state they were before they were baptized and to behave in ways appropriate to their baptism (Rom. 6; 8:12–17; Gal. 3:26—5:6; 1 Cor. 1–4; and much of Colossians and Ephesians). It was in this context that rites of penance emerged in the church. Those who grossly failed to demonstrate the signs of their formation into the new life in Christ had to be re-formed by means of participation in a process similar to the catechumenate—the order of penitents. As time went on it became customary to call on the whole church to be characterized by a sense of holiness, unity, love, equality, humility, and so forth during the time of Christian initiation (what has become the season of Lent). Thus Lent became a time when the whole church returned, as it were, to the catechumenate, and in which the whole church, as it were, entered the order of penitents. This return bequeathed to this season of the church year its enduring catechetical and penitential emphasis.

Christian initiation can be related to the theory of ritual in terms of Victor Turner's understanding of liminality.[18] He has shown that the liminal, or betwixt and between stage, is the center of gravity in rites of passage. The liminal or transitional stage relates to the moments of separation and incorporation—death and rebirth—without ignoring the chaos that lies between them. Indeed, the purpose of the liminal stage in rites of passage is to use that chaos in a creative way. Rites of passage move from sense to sense via nonsense. There is a playful mood in the liminal mode that might seem to belie the seriousness of what is happening in these crisis rites; but play is serious business. It is a component part of such important animal and human functions as learning and mating. Play becomes very serious when it moves to the point of becoming game, where rules and patterns are decided that affect all the participants.[19]

Turner regards play as a liminal phenomenon, a threshold activity. Like other liminal phenomena it is, he says, in the subjunctive mood. "Subjunctivity is possibility. It refers to what may or might be."[20] In the liminal stage of rites of passage, candidates going through a novitiate are given a vision of the purposes and destiny of the group into which they will be incorporated. This vision can become a blueprint for a wished-for state

---

[17] See Jacob Neusner, *A History of Mishnaic Law of Purities: Studies in Judaism in Late Antiquity* 6. Part 22: "The Mishnaic System of Uncleanness" (Leiden: E. J. Brill, 1977).

[18] Victor Turner, *The Ritual Process: Structure and Antistructure* (Chicago: Aldine Publishing House, 1969).

[19] See J. Huizinga, *Homo Ludens: A Study of the Play Element in Culture* (Boston: Beacon Press, 1955).

[20] Victor Turner, "Body, Brain, and Culture," *Zygon* 18 (1983), 235.

of affairs, such as an ideal society. This is why Christian initiation without a viable cate-chumenate, ordination without a period of apprenticeship (e.g., seminary education, in-ternship), or marriage without a period of engagement cannot produce what is maximally hoped for, even though the rites themselves are "validly" performed. But questions of va-lidity are by nature reductionist. They are concerned with what one can minimally get by with and still have a valid rite. The real pastoral question should be, What conditions will allow the rites to work most effectively? Concerns about validity have constituted the sacramental history of the Western church since the Middle Ages, whereas the Eastern churches have been concerned about fullness *(pleroma)*. Precisely this marks the differ-ence in liturgical and sacramental attitude and practice between Eastern and Western Christianity. Eastern Christianity has understood that the ritual process simply cannot be hurried; it must pursue its full course to arrive at its desired end *(telos)*.

In addition to whatever visions or hopes are communicated to novices in the lim-inal stage of rites of passage, bonds of community are formed with others who are going through the ordeals of initiation. This is most evident in military boot camp and on col-lege campuses. Victor Turner calls this experience *communitas* and says that it is an ex-pression of antistructure. That is to say, communitas is spontaneous, immediate, and concrete, as opposed to norm-governed, institutionalized, and abstract (the nature of so-cial structure). Those who experience communitas at the margins of social structure will inject an element of renewal into the society when they are incorporated into it.

Because the learnings and experiences of liminality and communitas are so vital to human society, certain aspects of what is learned and experienced in rites of passage are repeated periodically in the regular gatherings of the community, such as gatherings to rehearse the myths that tell the stories of the community's origins and destiny and the sacred meals that celebrate one's incorporation into the community. As E. Norbeck points out, the crisis rites tend to define and shape the community because they articulate the values and purposes of the community.[21]

It is not surprising that a liminal quality pervades all ritual, cyclical rites as well as rites of passage. This is evident in the tenacity with which liturgical rites retain archaic forms. As Turner has suggested, "If ritual is not to be merely a reflection of secular social life, if its function is partly to protect and partly to express truths which make men free from the exigencies of their status incumbencies, free to contemplate and pray as well as to speculate and invent, then its repertoire of liturgical actions should not be limited to a direct reflection of the contemporary scene."[22] Turner listened to songs and prayer for-mulae in dead languages at the initiation rites of the Ndembu and Lunda in Central Africa, and saw persons thoroughly immersed in a modern money economy taking part wholeheartedly in ritual actions hallowed by antiquity. He commented:

> I do not believe such actions are hallowed merely because they are old but
> because they are metaphors for something most precious to all 'modernities,'
> to every living, viable society. They represent the chalice in which truth is

---

[21] E. Norbeck, *Religion in Primitive Society* (New York: Harper and Row, 1961), 138ff.
[22] Victor Turner, "Passages, Margins, and Poverty: Religious Symbols of Communitas," *Worship* 46 (1972), 391.

conveyed, the symbolic inversion of the utilitarian, of the currently fashion-able, and indeed, of the ensemble of institutionalized status-roles which com-poses the social structure. In other words, always and everywhere ritual *ought* to have a pervasive archaic, repetitive, formal quality if it is to be a vehicle for values and experiences which transcend those of status-striving, money-grub-bing, and self-serving.[23]

The historic liturgy of the church retains elements hallowed by antiquity, and in this way provides access to the liminal mode of existence. Liminality celebrates transition rather than status, and therefore provides the most appropriate mode of worship for Christians who are "strangers and pilgrims" in this world following the Christ who had "no place to rest his head." In other words, ritual that has "a pervasive archaic, repetitive, formal quality" is best able to provide that access to transcendence that an eschatological community requires. The ancient Christian catechumenate provided an institutionaliza-tion of liminality and communitas during the fourth and fifth centuries when the church was settling down into its new historical status as a licensed cult in the Roman Empire. It is not surprising that the monastic movement emerged in the church on the heels of the dissolution of the catechumenate, nor that the mendicant orders originated in the twelfth and thirteenth centuries when the monasteries had become wealthy and secularized (i.e., worldly). A community like the Christian church, which regards transition as its perma-nent condition in "this world," will find ways and means of institutionalizing liminality and straining to discover and preserve instances of communitas.[24]

THE ROLE OF MYTH

Myth and ritual belong together, although there has never been agreement on the nature of their relationship. A view of myth developed in the eighteenth-century Enlightenment and in nineteenth-century positivism, which regarded myths as untrue stories. To some extent, this can be blamed on Christianity, which regarded anything not in the Bible as a fable. To the myths of the world Christianity contrasted its historical gospel. Myth was contrasted with historical fact.

Nevertheless, anthropologists began to analyze the role and value of myth. Operating under the influence of scientific positivism, pioneering anthropologists, such as Bronislav Malinowski, described myth as a story that served to justify the present situa-tion of a society and thereby contributed to social stability. Claude Lévi-Strauss refined this point of view to show how myths can be reactivated to legitimize a view of history that is useful to the present generation.[25] Myths, like rituals, therefore, may bolster a view of origins or destiny that may serve either conservative or innovative ends. Mircea Eliade noted, however, that whatever purpose is served by telling the myth or sacred story, it is regarded as "absolutely true." "Being *real* and *sacred*, the myth becomes exemplary, and

---

[23] Ibid., 392.

[24] See Turner, *The Ritual Process*, 106ff.

[25] See Claude Lévi-Strauss, *Structural Anthropology*, trans. by Claire Jacobson and Brooke Grundfest Schoepf (New York: Basic Books, 1963), 206ff.

consequently *repeatable*, for it serves as a model, and by the same token as a justification, for all human actions. In other words, a myth is a *true history* of what came to pass at the beginning of Time, and one which provides a pattern for human behavior."[26]

Understood in this way, the Christian gospel serves the function of myth in that it relates a story that is regarded as absolutely true and that is intended to provide a pattern of behavior in those who hear it. The reading and telling of the gospel in Christian liturgy serves the same purpose as the ritual reenactment of myth in other communities and societies. Studying stories of the founding fathers in Fourth of July celebrations in nineteenth-century America will show the same purpose being served in the interests of a civil or secular religion. There are no societies without mythic stories that instill values and worldviews or that are bereft of the ritual means of reenacting them.

Victor Turner refined this theory of myth to suggest that "myths treat of origins but derive from transitions. . . . Myths relate how one state of affairs became another; how an unpeopled world became populated; how chaos became cosmos; how immortals became mortal; how the seasons came to replace a climate without seasons . . . and so on. Myths are *liminal* phenomena: they are frequently told at a time or in a state that is 'betwixt-and-between.'"[27] Thus the Gospels, which relate the mythic story of Jesus, are read on Sunday, the Lord's Day, also known as the "eighth day," the day that straddles this age and the age to come. The Gospels also serve as the essential content of that most liminal of Christian institutions, the catechumenate.

Mythic stories themselves often come out of a liminal or transitional situation (e.g., in the Gospels, Jesus' journey to Jerusalem and passion; in American civil religion, the transition from colony to sovereignty marked by the Declaration of Independence). Biogeneticists Eugene d'Aquili, C. D. Laughlin, Jr., and J. McManus have proposed that mythmaking is a neurological attempt by the human organism, when faced with an unknown or unexplained stimulus or crisis, to organize it within a known conceptual framework.[28] Communities tell and ritually enact their mythic stories in order to account for how crises or limitations can be overcome. By telling or reenacting myth in ritual drama, worshipers transcend their own time, fraught with crisis or limitation, by entering into primordial or eschatological time. It is necessary that myths take place in primordial or eschatological time so they can escape the defects and limitations of the present time. This does not mean that myth takes place outside of time, because then it would be of no relevance to us. Rather, myths tell the stories of gods or heroes who share our vicissitudes but surmount them. In this way myths, which are transparent to the sacred and the eternal, kindle in us a hope of transcending the secular and the temporal, not as something that humankind can achieve through a Promethean effort, but as something that can be received by obediently performing the rites.

---

[26] Mircea Eliade, *Myths, Dreams, and Mysteries*, trans. by Philip Mairet (New York and Evanston, Ill.: Harper and Row, 1967), 23.

[27] Victor Turner, "Myth and Ritual," in *The International Encyclopedia of the Social Sciences*, ed. David Sills (New York: Macmillan, 1968–1979), Vol. 10, 576.

[28] See Eugene d'Aquili, C. D. Laughlin, Jr., J. McManus, *Brain, Symbol and Experience: Toward a Neurophenomenology of Human Consciousness* (Boston: Shambala, 1990).

Of course, the stories that tell about the origin and destiny of the Jewish and Christian communities are historical events, and are, by definition, unrepeatable. There is also a sense in which the Bible, which is the language of liturgy, has demythologized myths. A well-known example is the first creation story in Genesis 1:1—2:4a, in which the celestial bodies—sun, moon, and stars—divinities in the Babylonian worldview, are put in their place as lights in the firmament by the God who created them. In the last book of the Bible, in Revelation 4, the four living creatures, who represent the cosmos, never cease to sing "Holy, holy, holy, the Lord God the Almighty, who was and is and is to come." Again, the cosmos that has been worshiped as divine is reduced to the status of creatures worshiping the true God.

Thus, while the Bible demythologizes myths, it does not abandon mythical language. For example, the Canticle of Moses in Exodus 15:1–21, which celebrates the escape of the Israelite slaves from Egypt through the sea, expresses this event as if it were about the conquest of the primordial chaos and the birth of a new creation. The event of the exodus is unrepeatable, but it was reinterpreted and applied to new situations, such as the return of the Jews from exile in Babylon. The Lord whose arm slew the ancient dragon and dried up the sea is besought as the source of a new exodus through the wilderness in Isaiah 51:9–11. The image of the exodus, interpreted in mythical language, is applied to new situations. These images of deliverance and rebirth are rehearsed in the readings of the Easter Vigil, which lead to the action at the baptismal font, which becomes a new sea through which a new people is led to be delivered from sin and reborn as God's people.

While the Bible demythologizes, it does not demythicize. Liturgy retains the Bible's mythical language. This is a language of images and stories, which are heard in the readings, sung in the psalms and canticles, and unpacked in sermons. Modern worshipers can no longer take myths literally—hence the need for demythologization. Nor can they afford to ignore mythic reality, because the images and stories connect us with the awesome and the transcendent, which provide meaning in life. The speaking snake of Genesis 3 did not really exist, but we are always listening to that snake because it has something to tell us that we want to hear. So the story of the snake, and the tragic consequences of listening to it, must be told. Sermons may suggest where the voice of the snake is speaking today, but even in the act of unpacking the story, the sermon cannot avoid mythical language. And to the extent that the sermon draws upon, applies, and reiterates the mythical language, it has a liturgical quality. It does not stand as something separate from or outside liturgy. It is itself a liturgical act whose purpose is to connect our stories with the stories of the people of God down through the ages, so that their faith or unbelief becomes our faith or illumines our unbelief. Such an act of preaching builds up the community of faith in the faith, and usually does so in a style of delivery that is less propositional than it is a form of incanting. In fact, in African American liturgy the preacher not infrequently breaks into chant as he gets more emotionally involved in retelling the story in the sermon. The people are also brought into the act of incantation by chanting responses to the stories heard in scripture, since the scripture readings and the preaching are surrounded by singing in the forms of psalmody and hymnody.

☘ THE ROLE OF MUSIC

It may seem strange to insert at this point a word about music. But historically the function of music in liturgical rites is traced to a point where we hardly look for it today: to the chanting of sacred texts. Music has acquired a role in worship for reasons both utilitarian and spiritual.

A basic reason for chanting is that singing texts aids in memorization, which was very important before the time of printed worship books and widespread literacy. For example, the hymns of the great Indian Sanskrit collection, the *Rigveda*, were intoned. The musicologist Gerald Abraham suggests that "owing to the frightful consequences of even slight error, . . . it is possible modern intonation of Rigvedic texts has not been much modified in the course of three millennia."[29] And yet the Hindu did not regard music only as a useful aid in the memorization and recitation of texts; chanting also fostered a state of meditation that enabled the person to break away from the endless cycle of birth, death, and rebirth and be absorbed into the spirit of the universe *(nirvana)*.

Even in a literary society there are utilitarian reasons for employing music in worship. Chanting makes the recitation of texts by a group more effective because the rhythm keeps the group together. For example, 1 Chronicles records that the Levites were "put in charge of the service of song in the house of the LORD" (1 Chron. 6:31), and what they sang in the Temple were the texts of the psalms. The verse structure of the psalms suggests that they were probably sung to short melodic patterns repeated over and over again with the necessary variations. Some of the psalms may have been sung antiphonally—two groups alternating back and forth from verse to verse—and others may have been sung responsorially—a group responding to a soloist. These different ways of singing the psalms suggest that there was also a concern to heighten or bring out the meaning of the text (or to employ a text in such a way as to bring out or heighten the meaning of the action or event for which the psalm was accompaniment or commentary). It is clear from Chronicles that the singing was supported by instruments.

In many ancient cults, instrumental music was employed in conjunction with sacrifices. Johannes Quasten pointed out that this was not just to drown out the noises of animals about to be immolated, since music also accompanied unbloody sacrifices such as incense offerings. Rather, flute playing and dancing were supposed to call down the good gods, while the blowing of horns and the sounding of gongs and bells were supposed to ward off evil gods and demons.[30] The church fathers condemned the use of instrumental music in Christian worship precisely because instruments had been employed in pagan cults.

Nevertheless, Christian worship has employed singing throughout its history to serve the word and to engender a sense of ecstasy in worship. There are liturgies in the

---

[29] Gerald Abraham, *The Concise Oxford History of Music* (New York and Oxford: Oxford University Press, 1985), 558–9.

[30] Johannes Quasten, *Music and Worship in Pagan and Christian Antiquity*, trans. by Boniface Ramsey (Washington, D.C.: National Association of Pastoral Musicians, 1983), chapter one.

Eastern and Western Christian traditions in which everything is sung—all prayers, psalms, readings, dialogical responses, except possibly the homily. Yet, as we said above, in some traditions even the preacher breaks into chant during the course of the sermon. And in the Western Christian tradition, instruments were introduced into liturgical performance once they no longer evoked associations with pagan cults.

🍇 SACRED MEALS AND SACRIFICES

At the conclusion of initiation rites and at periodic intervals, communities have offered sacrifices and participated in sacred meals. Sacrifices and meals serve the purpose of forming the bonds of community. Roman Catholics and Protestants have divided over the question of whether the eucharist is primarily a sacrifice or a meal. But R. K. Yerkes has shown that what we call by the Latin word *sacrifice* is a sacred meal. "The word *sacrifice*, which means 'to make a thing sacred' or 'to do a sacred act,' was used in Latin to describe various rites which arose from the common meal when that meal was held, not for the ordinary purpose of satisfying hunger, but for the sake of entering into union with the mysterious Power or powers which men felt within them and about them as life itself, and which they recognized in all their environments as both menacing and strengthening the life which they loved and to which they longed to cling."[31]

Thus, sacrifices are primarily meals of the gods in which human beings participate by paying for them, preparing them, or even eating them (as in the communion sacrifices). The Christian eucharist is, phenomenologically considered, both a sacred meal and a sacrifice. It is a sacrifice because bread and wine are offered, consecrated, and eaten and drunk with the understanding that the communicants enter into fellowship with the One who is both priest and victim. Put another way, sacrifice has served as a metaphor describing communion in Christ, who is our Passover sacrifice (1 Cor. 5:7).

Protestant aversion to works-righteousness (the attempt to wring a blessing from God apart from trust in God's word of promise) has blinded us to the reality of sacrifice generally, but especially to those sacrifices of the *do ut des* variety in which it appears that the meeting between the god and the human in the sacrificial rite takes the form of a business transaction. But, as Gerhard van der Leeuw has observed, we should not be misled by imposing our own modern way of thinking on the attitudes of primitive people.[32] When we think of a business transaction, we understand a purely material exchange with no spiritual overtones. For the primitive, business relationships implied some sort of fellowship. Furthermore, to interpret any kind of sacrifice as though it were purely profitable to the offerer and manipulative of the deity is to miss the point. Sacrifice was an act of fellowship or communion between the divine and the human, and therefore involved food to eat and drink such as grain, meat, and wine. Because our thinking about sacrifice

---

[31] R. K. Yerkes, *Sacrifice in Greek and Roman Religion and Early Judaism* (London: A. and C. Black, 1953), 25ff.

[32] Gerhard van der Leeuw, *Religion in Essence and Manifestation*, II, trans. by J. E. Turner (New York and Evanston: Harper and Row, 1963), 350ff.

tends to be confused, it might be helpful to list the six ways in which Yerkes claims that the ancient idea of sacrifice differs substantially from ours.

1. Sacrifice in the ancient world had no secular connotations whatever; it was a sacred act involving the divine-human relationship.
2. Sacrifices were occasions of joy and festivity, and the highest forms of sacrifice were the sacrifices of thanksgiving.
3. Because sacrifices were occasions of joy and festivity the offerings were as large as possible—often because the eating and drinking was a communal activity.
4. Sacrifices were offered *to the gods*. The emphasis was on the *gift given*, not on giving up something in the sense of experiencing a loss.
5. Sacrifices were more frequently thanksgivings for blessings received than petitions for divine favor. Therefore there was little sense of a "business transaction" in most sacrifices.
6. The death of the victim was not the sacrifice itself. Yerkes says that "no significance was ever attached to the fact that the animal had died. We never hear of death qua death effecting anything."[33] The sacrifice consists in the *offering* of the victim. Yerkes believes that the confounding of death and sacrifice is the starting point of most of our difficulties in understanding sacrifice. The death was simply a means to an end; the end was the necessity of providing food for a sacred meal.

What about the *sin offerings* in ancient Israel? Was there not a suggestion that they served the purpose of atonement or propitiation? The sacrifices related to sin, including the *chatta'th* or *'asham*, as well as the liturgy of Yom Kippur (the Day of Atonement), were offered by the priests themselves and not by the people. One who had committed a sin could not offer a sacrifice because such a person would not be in the state of ritual purity that was required of those who offered sacrifices. The sacrifices offered by the priest alone served to remove the ritual impurity of the individual or of the nation as a whole. In the sin offerings a part of the sacrificed victim was eaten by the priests, and the remainder was consumed by fire. In the Yom Kippur liturgy, the ritual purification of the whole nation of Israel was accomplished by the blood of the victim being sprinkled on the priests and on the Holy of Holies, but the animal slaughtered (the scapegoat) was not offered to the Lord. It was hauled outside the camp and burned.

There is a notion of sin here that is very ancient. Such sin is religious rather than moral, and had to be dealt with ritually rather than ethically. In most cases the sin was unavoidable and involuntary, such as childbirth or leprosy. The sin offering after childbirth was not for the purpose of removing any moral lapse, but simply to reinstate the mother in the community of the faithful. Likewise, the true offering of the leper was not a petition to remove the sin that caused the disease, since it could not be offered until after the leper was cleansed. Rather, it was a thankoffering for healing. As H. H. Rowley has written, "Where 'sin' was unwittingly or unconsciously or wholly ritual there could not be any true repentance, and the ritual cleansing could only be thought of as automatic. This could only tend to make men think of all sacrificial acts automatic in their effects. This

---

[33] Yerkes, 4ff.

was the attitude which the great pre-exilic prophets condemned, and it was equally far from the mind of the framers of the Priestly Law."[34]

Behind the ancient understanding of sin as ritual contamination, for which ritual purification was the antidote, was the idea that contact with the holy exposed the human being who had the temerity to approach it with a consciousness of oneself as a sinner. Isaiah in the Temple cries out, "Woe is me! I am lost, for I am a man of unclean lips, and I live among a people of unclean lips; yet my eyes have seen the King, the LORD of hosts" (Isa. 6:5). This text expresses a very profound appreciation of the divine-human relationship. As Louis Bouyer put it, "The sacral, ritual root of the idea of sin is the feeling which man has of God's radical transcendence whenever he is moved to have recourse to Him. It is practically the counterpart of that holy familiarity to which man is called in sacrifice, and it is that which keeps this familiarity from becoming sacrilegious."[35]

🍇 SACRED TIMES AND FESTIVALS

A sacrifice is fundamentally a meeting with God in a sacred meal. Because God is the source of life for the individual and the community, it is desirable that such a meeting take place on a regular basis. But the times of the meeting are not arbitrary; they have special significance. It is not surprising that the natural calendar determines these special times for many religions. Daily assemblies and sacrifices are clustered around the alternating of day and night. But the solar year also provides an essential framework for ritual celebrations. The return of the year with the rebirth of life gave the appearance of a genuine repetition of the creative act where the divine work is seen again in every new birth. Times of planting and harvesting have been laden with sacred significance.

On a lesser scale the rhythms of the moon with its succession of months constitutes a different hierophany or mode of sacred revelation, one that is maternal rather than paternal since it is often connected with female menstrual cycles. Thierry Maertens writes that "as early as three thousand years before the birth of Christ most of the religions of the East were regulated according to the lunar cycle."[36] The Jews observed the new moon like their pagan neighbors by offering a clan sacrifice, although they played down the fertility aspects of the celebration and emphasized instead the renewal of the covenant with Yahweh. The new year was simply a more solemn new moon feast. It was a time of purification, of the expulsion of sins, of demons, or of a scapegoat. Eliade explains that "it is not a matter merely of a certain temporal interval coming to its end and the beginning of another (as a modern man, for example, thinks); it is also a matter of abolishing the past year and past time."[37] And as the new moon feasts served as occasions for re-

---

[34] H. H. Rowley, *Worship in Ancient Israel: Its Forms and Meaning* (Philadelphia: Fortress Press, 1967), 131.

[35] Louis Bouyer, *Rite and Man: Natural Sacredness and Christian Sacraments*, trans. by M. Joseph Costelloe (Notre Dame, Ind.: University of Notre Dame Press, 1963), 88.

[36] Thierry Maertens, *A Feast in Honor of Yahweh*, trans. by Kathryn Sullivan (Notre Dame, Ind.: Fides Publishers, 1965), 24.

[37] Eliade, *The Sacred and the Profane*, op. cit., 78.

newal of the covenant among the Jews, so the New Year's Festival was also a time of covenant renewal.[38] The acclamations or trumpet blasts of Rosh Hashanah have raised the question of whether Israel also celebrated the new year as a feast of Yahweh's enthronement as King of Creation.[39]

The final step in calendrical calculations seems to have been taken by the Babylonians, whose astronomical observations led them to introduce the week. Their astrological interests led them to cease from work on the seventh, fourteenth, twenty-first, and nineteenth days (the latter was the forty-ninth day after the beginning of the preceding month) because these were "unlucky days" on which one could risk the wrath of the gods. The Jews developed the concept of the Sabbath from these unlucky days, but transformed the whole concept. Their day of rest was not a matter of astrological caprice but a proclamation of their liberation from slavery in Egypt (Deut. 5:12–15). Even the later Priestly documents in the Pentateuch emphasize the theology of election in connection with the Sabbath observance. The chosen people of God are privileged to unite themselves to the life of God by participating in his rest (Exod. 20:11; 31:12–17).[40]

The Sabbath became the primary day of worship for the Jews, especially after the Babylonian exile. It was observed by meetings in the synagogues to read and study the Torah. It is arguable whether the ancient Christian Sunday meeting was a transference of the Old Testament Sabbath from the seventh day of the week to the first day (the day of the resurrection of Jesus). It is certain that elements of the Jewish Sabbath were later absorbed into the Christian Lord's Day (*dies Dominica*), and that Christian worship was also held on this weekly fixed day. It should also be noted that the Sabbath and the Lord's Day are essentially affirmative rather than negative like the Babylonian unlucky days. The Sabbath affirms the goodness of God's creation and the Lord's Day affirms the redemption of the world in the resurrection as God's work of new creation. The philosopher Josef Pieper asserts that "festivity lives on affirmation." He adds that to "celebrate a festival means: to live out, for some special occasion and in an uncommon manner, the universal assent to the world as a whole." He also asserts, "Festivity is impossible to the nay-sayer."[41]

The element of affirmation, and the experience of rejuvenation or renewal that is the fruit of celebration, can be seen in the three great commemorative festivals in Judaism: the Feasts of Tents (*Succoth*)—sometimes referred to as Booths or Tabernacles; Unleavened Bread (*Pesach*); and Weeks (*Shavuoth*). The origins of each of these festivals lie in an agrarian or nomadic rite; but each was transformed into a historical commemoration.[42]

---

[38] See Artur Weiser, *The Psalms*, trans. by H. Hartwell. The Old Testament Library (Philadelphia: Westminster Press, 1962), introduction.

[39] See Sigmund Mowinckel, *The Psalms in Israel's Worship*, 2 vols., trans. by D. R. Ap-Thomas (New York and Nashville: Abingdon Press, 1962).

[40] Maertens, 152ff.

[41] Joseph Pieper, *In Tune with the World. A Theory of Festivity*, trans. by Richard and Clara Winston (Chicago: Franciscan Herald Press, 1973), 21, 23, 21.

[42] See Roland de Vaux, *Ancient Israel*, Vol. II (New York and Toronto: McGraw-Hill Book Co., 1961), 484ff.

The Feast of Unleavened Bread, originally a spring harvest festival, was combined with the nomadic rite of offering the firstborn lamb to form the Passover festival. As such it lost its agricultural and nomadic associations and became the celebration of Israel's liberation from slavery in Egypt. The Feast of Weeks, so called because it was held seven weeks after the Feast of Unleavened Bread, became a historical commemoration of the promulgation of the Torah on Mount Sinai. The Feast of Tents, with its retention of the ancient custom of living in temporary huts while dressing the vines, became a historical commemoration of Israel's journey through the wilderness and conquest of the promised land. After the Babylonian exile, eschatological motifs were easily grafted onto the Feast of Tents so that it became a celebration of Israel's destiny as well as its origin.

Not one of these feasts continued in the practices of the Christian community. Yet all of them were regarded as fulfilled in the person of Jesus the Christ. We can see this personification of the festival in Jesus' participation in the Feast of Tents, in which the Gospel of John records: "On the last day of the festival, the great day, while Jesus was standing there, he cried out, 'Let anyone who is thirsty come to me, and let the one who believes in me drink. As the scripture has said, "Out of the believer's heart shall flow rivers of living water"'" (John 7:37–38). On the last day of the feast there was, in Jesus' day, a procession to bring water from the pool of Silo to the Temple, where it was poured on the altar in memory of the rock of living water that followed Israel in the wilderness. During this procession Jesus apparently presented himself as the new rock of living water. In a similar way the apostle Paul proclaimed: "For our paschal lamb, Christ, has been sacrificed. Therefore, let us celebrate the festival, not with the old yeast, the yeast of malice and evil, but with the unleavened bread of sincerity and truth" (1 Cor. 5:7–8). Finally, according to Acts 2:1–4, on the morning of the Feast of Pentecost the apostles were assembled like their contemporaries to meditate on the Torah, when suddenly the phenomena of Sinai were renewed for them. As Yahweh had come down on Sinai in fire, amidst thunder and lightning (Exod. 19:16–18), so the Spirit of God came as tongues of fire resting on each of the apostles. The Pentecost of the Spirit fulfilled the Pentecost of the Law. Because the events commemorated in these three great festivals were personified in Jesus the Christ and his Spirit, there was no need for Christians to continue celebrating the old festivals. But the content of these festivals was spiritualized and elements of their meaning were retained and transformed in the new Christian festivals that celebrated the person and work of Jesus the Christ and his Spirit.

The connections between Passover and Easter and the Jewish and Christian Pentecost are easily recognizable. The content of the Feast of Tents has been scattered throughout several Christian observances. This festival was important to early Christian writers because of the eschatological perspective that it acquired in Judaism. Zechariah 14:16 prophesies a day on which "all who survive of the nations that have come against Jerusalem shall go up year after year" to Zion to worship the Lord at the Feast of Tents. This was an exuberantly celebrated festival which drew pilgrims to Jerusalem from throughout the Diaspora. On their way up to the city they sang the songs of ascent (Pss. 120—134). The libations with water and the torchlight processions around the Temple were striking. Priests sang the words of Isaiah 12:3, "With joy you will draw water from the wells of salvation." The trumpets sounded as the people moved in procession, waving *lulab* and *trod*. In the evening a ceremony of light was held in the forecourt before the burning golden candlestick in which the people sang antiphonally and danced. The Gospel of John, which is actually structured around the three Jewish pilgrim feasts, devotes chapters 7–9 to events that took place during the Feast of Tents. It was in this context that Jesus invited the thirsty to come to him and drink (John 7:37–38) and, in connection with the torchlight illumination of the Temple, proclaimed himself as the "light of the world" (John 8:12). The Gospel of John begins with the idea of the Feast of Tents by announcing that "the Word became flesh and tabernacled among us" (John 1:14; my translation). The book of Revelation gives an eschatological vision of God dwelling with his people (Rev. 21:3). It is not surprising that Jean Daniélou found parallels between the Feast of Tents and Christmas (the gospel for Christmas Day is John 1:1–14), Palm Sunday (procession with palms and reference to Zechariah), the Transfiguration (Peter wanted to build booths for Jesus, Moses, and Elijah), and the September Ember Days in the old Roman liturgy (which contains references in all the readings to the Jewish autumnal observances).[43]

🍇 SACRED PLACES

The community that meets to rehearse its myths, offer its sacrifices, and celebrate its festivals needs a meeting place. The meeting place is often a location where divinity has revealed itself, or, lacking a theophany, a location that serves as a sign pointing to divinity. Altars and poles can demarcate a sacred space; mountains or trees can point to divinity. The sacred space is a place from which to acquire orientation. It can be the center of a territory or a threshold place (i.e., "a gate of heaven"). It is the whole creation on a microscopic scale, and the community takes possession of it—that is, consecrates it—by repeating the cosmogony or paradigmatic work of the gods.[44]

Many sacred spaces were marked out by the erection of temples or shrines. The temple precinct itself was the *fanum* (sacred space); stretching around it was the *profanum*, the space of ordinary life that derived meaning from the sacred. The Greek word *Temenos* (temple), derives from the verb *temno*, "to cut out" or "separate." The temple itself was usually small because it was a house for the god, not the people. Only the priests went into the sanctuary; the people gathered in the courtyard or plaza in front of the temple.

At first Israel had no temple. The God of the patriarchs disclosed himself in places along the way in their journey to "the land that I will show you" (Gen. 12:1). The patriarchal journeys were dotted with wayside shrines, but not permanent places of orientation. When Israel was led out of Egypt, the people assembled before the holy mountain

---

[43] Jean Daniélou, *The Bible and the Liturgy* (Notre Dame, Ind.: University of Notre Dame Press, 1956), 333ff.; see also E. H. van Olst, *The Bible and the Liturgy*, trans. by John Vriend (Grand Rapids: William B. Eeermans Publishing Co., 1991), 41–6, 79.

[44] See Eliade, *The Sacred and the Profane*, 20ff.; Van der Leeuw, *Religion in Essence and Manifestation*, I, 393ff.

of Sinai to receive a theophany—Israel's revelation of God's will in the Torah, God's Commandments. The stone tablets on which the Commandments were inscribed were carried in a portable box called the Ark of the Covenant. It went ahead of the host of Israel, the cloud above it both revealing and hiding the presence of Yahweh. Once Israel settled in the promised land, Israelites were attracted to the fertility rites of the surrounding populations. To prevent a wholesale slide into idolatry, together with his desire to shore up his political leverage among the people, King David centralized the Israelite cult in Jerusalem, his capital city. His son Solomon built a temple there that became the center of the sacrificial cult. The temple was destroyed by the Babylonians under Nebuchadnezzar in 587 B.C.E. It was during the Babylonian exile that the religion of Israel was transformed into what would become Judaism as we have come to know it. The scribes wrote down the sacred stories into sacred scriptures, and pious Jews assembled in meeting places (synagogues) to study and meditate on the Law (Torah) and the prophets (Haftorah). After the Exile a second temple was built at Jerusalem under the leadership of Ezra and Nehemiah, but it never equaled the glory of the first temple. And the final Isaiah announced the ruin of the temple because it was too small for Yahweh. "Heaven is my throne and the earth is my footstool; what is the house that you would build for me, and what is my resting place? All these things my hand has made, and so all these things are mine" (Isa. 66:1–2).

In the Synoptic Gospels Jesus also foretold the destruction of the Jerusalem Temple (Mark 13:2; Matt. 24:2). The event that precipitated the events of the passion of Jesus in the Synoptic Gospels was Jesus' cleansing of the Temple after his entry into Jerusalem (Matt. 21:12–17; Mark 11:15–19; Luke 19:45–48). In the Fourth Gospel, Jesus' cleansing of the Temple occurs at the outset of his ministry (John 2:13–22), and he proclaims himself as the new Temple. "'Destroy this temple, and in three days I will raise it up.' . . . But he was speaking of the temple of his body" (John 2:19, 21). Jesus told the Samaritan woman, "the hour is coming when you will worship the Father neither on this mountain nor in Jerusalem. . . . the hour is coming, and is now here, when the true worshipers will worship the Father in spirit and truth, for the Father seeks such as these to worship him" (John 4:21, 23).

The anti-Temple polemic in the Gospels reflects the fact that they were written in close proximity to the time of the destruction of the Second Temple by the Romans in 70 C.E. Especially in Mark there was a concern to wean Jewish Christians away from reliance on the Temple or on Jerusalem itself as the center of Christian mission. In the deutero-Pauline letters there is also a tendency to transfer loyalty from the Temple to Christ himself, and to the church as the body of Christ. In Ephesians, Christ is the cornerstone, the apostles and prophets are the foundation, and all Christians are part of the building—"a dwelling place of God in the Spirit" (Eph. 2:19–22; RSV). Christians are the temple of God because the Spirit of God dwells in the community (1 Cor. 3:16). This is the reason given for avoiding any syncretism with pagan beliefs. "What agreement has the temple of God with idols? For we are the temple of the living God" (2 Cor. 6:16). In 1 Peter, Christ is called the living stone rejected by humankind, and Christians are called living stones of the temple of the Spirit (1 Peter 2:4–5).

The church itself, therefore, is the temple of God in which the Holy Spirit dwells. Any building erected for Christian worship is not a temple for deity but a meeting place or a house for the church. To be sure, after the Edict of Milan in 313, when Christianity became a legal cult in the Roman Empire, and the church could erect meeting places for worship, the church buildings acquired a sense of orientation: they were built on an east-west axis because Christians faced west to renounce the devil at baptism and faced east to pray to Christ, the sun of righteousness. Nevertheless, the consecration of church buildings served to proclaim the use of that building. As Bouyer wrote, "this place is sacred only because it is the place for the Eucharistic celebration, toward which the preaching of the Word leads, inviting us at the same time to advance toward the east, that is, to the *parousia* of the glorious Christ."[45]

The orientation of the church building is simply to accommodate the eschatological community that assembles in it. The community itself is the new cosmos in which Christ is Lord of all (Pantocrator), the place of light that is only reached by turning away from darkness (note the symbolism of the Easter Vigil in which the congregation processes into the dark church building with the light of Christ, the paschal candle). For this reason there is need of a decisive passage through the waters of death to the new life in Christ. The real consecration of the church—which is the new people of God, the body of Christ, and not a building—is baptism itself.

❧ SACRED PERSONS

In ancient cultures there were persons invested with sacral character. A typical example is a king who discharges a divine role by maintaining order in the state. The sovereign came to be regarded as a son or daughter of the gods, as happened in Egypt, China, and Japan. In Rome, too, the development of imperial dignity was accompanied by divinization. It became a public obligation to offer incense to the emperor's statue, and no one was exempt except the Jews. Naturally, Christians would not accept the divinity of the emperor or offer incense to his effigy. This often led to martyrdom.

In Israel itself the kingship was resisted precisely because of the aura of divinity that accrued to the office and person of the king. When kingship was accepted, and Saul and then David were anointed, the king did not assume the role of high priest, as was the case in other societies. Nor were his opinions regarded as oracles. God's oracles were the prophets, not the sovereign, and the little tribe of Levi was given the priestly dignity. The prophets and priests of Israel antedate the monarchy by several centuries, tracing back to Moses and Aaron respectively, who were regarded as the archetypal prophet and priest. Even so, neither the prophets nor the priests were more sacred than the kings. The three together partook of the sacredness of the whole people. As God said to Moses on Mount Sinai at the time of the promulgation of the covenant with Israel,

> Thus you shall say to the house of Jacob, and tell the Israelites: You have seen what I did to the Egyptians, and how I bore you on eagles' wings and brought

---

[45] Bouyer, *Rite and Man*, 186.

you to myself. Now therefore, if you obey my voice and keep my covenant, you shall be my treasured possession out of all the peoples. Indeed, the whole earth is mine, but you shall be for me a priestly kingdom and a holy nation. (Exod. 19:3–6)

We cannot study a particular tradition of worship without understanding the worshipers in that tradition. Liturgy is done by a people who constitute a liturgical assembly. Therefore this first chapter concludes by considering the character of the people of God, described in the above passage as "a priestly kingdom and a holy nation," who do liturgy.

John H. Elliott has devoted considerable attention to this passage and to its textual tradition in the Old and New Testaments. He points out that this pericope lays down both the conditions and the promise of the covenant.[46] The conditions are that Israel should do what humanity has not done: "obey my voice." The promises are that "you shall be for me a priestly kingdom and a holy nation." The parallelism of "priestly kingdom" and "holy nation" suggests the elements of sanctity and collectivity. Israel is to be "holy as priests are holy," and this applies to the nation as a whole and not just to individuals. The great age of this text makes it unlikely that it is a veiled polemic against the Levitical priesthood. For the same reason it is difficult to see in this text the idea of Israel exercising a priestly role as mediator between God and the nations. The idea embedded in this text is much simpler: Israel belongs to and serves Yahweh alone.

This basic idea was not to receive further textual expression until much later in Israel's history when the crossing of the Jordan, the conquest of Canaan, the time of the judges, the period of the kings and the divided monarchy, and the experience of exile and dispersion were past. It is after the Babylonian captivity, when the exiles were preparing for a second exodus and wilderness wandering experience as they prepared to return to the land of promise, that we find echoes of Exodus 19:6 in Isaiah 61:6.

> [Y]ou shall be called priests of the LORD,
>   you shall be named ministers of our God;
> you shall enjoy the wealth of the nations,
>   and in their riches you shall glory.

The context of this verse in Isaiah 61 is the prophecy of Israel's restoration. It is a time of the Lord's favor and vengeance (61:2). In a reversal of fortunes, Israel will exchange mourning for gladness (61:3) and shame for everlasting joy (61:7). The Lord is reestablishing with Israel an everlasting covenant (61:8). The weight of verse 6 is the restoration of Israel's honor and dignity before the eyes of the nations (*goiim*). The parallelism of "priests of the Lord" and "ministers of our God" suggests much more the Levitical priesthood than the general vocation to holiness in Exodus 19:6. The Jewish scholar, I. W. Slotki, picked up on this idea with the suggestion that "as the priests subsisted upon what the Israelites allocated to them, so the priestly nation will be supported

---

[46] John H. Elliott, *The Elect and the Holy. An Exegetical Examination of I Peter 2:4–9 and the Phrase basileion hierateuma.* Supplements to Novum Testamentum, XII (Leiden: E. J. Brill, 1966), 50ff.

by the other people since it is dedicated to the Divine Service."[47] The idea is that as the Levites were supported by the other eleven tribes of Israel, so Israel would be supported by the other nations. This is a way of describing Israel's eschatological destiny. The metaphor of "priesthood" relates also to Deutero-Isaiah's idea that Israel's vocation is to be "a covenant to the people, a light to the nations" (42:6; 49:8; 59:21; 60:1–3). A significant difference, therefore, between this passage and Exodus 19:6 is that the covenant formula was concerned with Israel's relationship to Yahweh while Deutero-Isaiah is concerned with Israel's relationship to the world.

In spite of the last prophecies added to the book of Isaiah, and perhaps because of the hopes fanned by the oracles of Deutero-Isaiah and Ezekiel, the restoration of Israel seemed far from realization. Jerusalem and the Temple were rebuilt; a cult enlightened by the scribal teaching that had developed during the exile was instituted there; and there was even an attempt to restore the monarchy. Yet Haggai could assert that this restoration on the material level was only a faint shadow of the former glory of Zion. Nevertheless, the vision of Ezekiel and Deutero-Isaiah continued to excite expectation of a future Jerusalem whose light would shine on the nations. To its cult would be brought the offerings of the whole world. A new priesthood would be consecrated in which not only the dispersed of Israel would have a place but perhaps even the goiim. "For from the rising of the sun to its setting my name is great among the nations, and in every place incense is offered to my name, and a pure offering; for my name is great among the nations, says the LORD of hosts" (Mal. 1:11). The church fathers picked up this text from the last of the prophets and proclaimed that it pointed to the pure offering of the Gentiles in the messianic age: the eucharistic sacrifice.

Under the Seleucids, Persian tolerance gave way to a fanatical attempt to assimilate the Jews to the hellenistic culture of their own country. The apocryphal writings that emerged during this time of cultural imperialism and political persecution emphasized the unique identity of Israel. The revolt of a priestly family, the Maccabees, put a stop to this direction of cultural assimilation and reestablished a kind of priestly monarchy under the Hasmoneans. Second Maccabees is primarily a Greek composition by an Alexandrian Jew whose intention was to foster reverence for the Temple in Jerusalem and also strict observance of the Maccabean festivals as a way of cementing the bonds of unity between Palestinian and Egyptian Jews. In 2 Maccabees 2:16–18, there is an allusion to the ancient covenant formula of Exodus 19:6:

> Since, therefore, we are about to celebrate the purification, we write to you. Will you therefore please keep the days? It is God who has saved all his people, and has returned the inheritance to all, and the kingship and the priesthood and the consecration, as he promised through the law. We have hope in God that he will soon have mercy on us and will gather us from everywhere under heaven into his holy place, for he has rescued us from great evils and has purified the place.

---

[47] I. W. Slotki, *Isaiah* (London: Soncino Books, 1949), 299.

Reference to "the kingship and the priesthood and the consecration" is made in connection with the celebration of the Feast of the Purification of the Temple. The author shows awareness of the covenant context of Exodus 19 by referring to the promise given through the law. 2 Maccabees 2 thus presents an optimism not grounded in a political messiah but in the faithfulness of God to the chosen people.

The problem with the success of the Maccabean revolt was that the priesthood was secularized because it was politicized. And because the priesthood was politicized, its members found ways of compromising first with the Greek and then with the Roman conquerors of Palestine. Their business involvements with the foreign occupiers of their country, despite their ritual and doctrinal conservatism, earned for the members of the priestly families (the Sadducees) the disdain of pious Israelites. As a reaction there appeared the party of the Pharisees (the separated ones), who were recruited from the leading laity and from whose ranks came the teachers of the law, the rabbis. The rabbis were seen as the genuine spiritual successors of the ancient priestly scribes. They saw in the strict observance of the ritual prescriptions of the Torah the dam they needed to preserve the identity of Israel from being flooded by assimilation to pagan customs, morals, and ideas. The rabbis developed a genre of oral and written tradition known as *Halakah*, whose casuistic punctiliousness was designed to reach the inner person through the outward discipline of obedience to the Torah.

Out of all the groups that flourished and competed for the soul of Israel during the latter days of the Second Temple, only Pharisaic Judaism and Christianity survived its destruction to reconstitute the religion of Israel. Neither Pharisaic Judaism (the party of the synagogue) nor the messianic sect known as Christianity depended on the Temple, its priesthood or sacrificial cult, as the focus of their devotion. Rather, both of these groups gathered around the study of the scriptures, a domestic meal, a lustration rite, and a concept of prayer as spiritual sacrifice. The antagonism between Jesus and the Pharisees in the Gospels undoubtedly reflects the competition between the local synagogue community and the local Christian community. The Christians were distinguished from the Pharisees by their devotion to Jesus as Israel's Messiah and the universal claims they made for this Christ. In both of these claims they depended on an apocalyptic mood and antinationalist perspective that put them at odds with the religion of the Pharisees. In reversing (or hastening?) the expectation of Isaiah that the nations shall come to the light of God's glory on Mount Zion, the Christians went to the nations with the light of the gospel of Christ.

In all respects the church worked out its identity and mission in terms of continuity and discontinuity with Israel. The church understood itself to be the community that recognized and followed the Messiah of Israel, so long expected, to the verge of the *eschaton*. It is a community that assembles to proclaim and celebrate Christ's passage from death to life, and to anticipate that passage for itself. As the barriers of time and space have been overcome in the resurrection of Christ, so that all times and places can become the times and places of encounter with God and salvation, so all the people baptized into the life, death, and resurrection of Christ constitute a new society, a new people of God, in which barriers between people are overcome. There is no longer male or female, Jew or Greek, circumcised or uncircumcised, barbarian or Scythian, slave or free, but only Christ in all (Col. 3:11). A new people is formed whose ties are not based on blood, class, or geography, but only on faith in the risen Christ. What applied to ancient Israel now applies a fortiori to the church. "[Y]ou are a chosen race, a royal priesthood, a holy nation, God's own people, in order that you may proclaim the mighty acts of him who called you out of darkness into his marvelous light. Once you were not a people, but now you are God's people; once you had not received mercy, but now you have received mercy" (1 Peter 2:9–10).

This text has served as the locus classicus for the Protestant doctrine of the priesthood of all believers, and this has tended to influence its interpretation. Elliott points out that it is important to see the long list of Old Testament quotations or allusions in this passage, and also to see it as the climax of the entire paraenetic section of 1 Peter 1:13—2:10. Maertens has exegeted it as a Christian paschal homily, and there are indeed many allusions to the Passover story in Exodus.[48] The salvation foretold by the prophets has been accomplished in the passion and glorification of Christ. "Therefore prepare your minds for action; discipline yourselves; set all your hope on the grace that Jesus Christ will bring you when he is revealed" (1:13). The hearers/readers are to turn from their former way of life and lead an obedient life as God-fearers because they have been redeemed by Jesus the sacrificial "lamb without defect or blemish. He was destined before the foundation of the world, but was revealed at the end of the times for your sake" (1:19–20). Sanctifying themselves in obedience, the newly born in Christ are to practice "genuine mutual love" (1:22). They are to abstain or separate themselves from hypocrisy and guile and, as newborn babies, yearn for the "pure, spiritual milk" of the word, that they might "grow into salvation" (2:1–2). For the word that gave them birth is that which nourishes and affords growth—the word of Jesus the Lord (2:3).

This is exactly the kind of exhortation that a bishop or presbyter of the church would give to those about to be or just baptized. The emphasis of this sermon is on the personal relationship between the believer and Jesus. That emphasis continues in verses 2:4ff. By coming to Jesus in faith believers are made alive as Jesus has been made alive. They have been elected by God as he was elected. They grow, are built, are united into a community of God's people (2:5). They have become precious (2:7) because they have believed in the Precious One (2:4, 6, 7). Having obeyed the word, they participate in God's mighty deeds of salvation and have been made heirs of the covenant of mercy (2:9f.). Proclamation of this word now becomes their task, for through Jesus Christ they have become the covenant people, "a spiritual house, to be a holy priesthood, to offer spiritual sacrifices acceptable to God" (2:5).

Elliott concludes: "The form and content of 1 Peter 2:4–10 reveal that this section was an attempt to describe via the motif of *election* the character and responsibility of the eschatological People of God, her bond with Jesus Christ, her infusion with the Spirit, her holiness, and her task of witness through the holy life and the proclamation of

---

[48] Maertens, *A Feast in Honor of Yahweh*, 126ff.

the saving deeds of God."[49] As Exodus 19:6 had no connection with the Levitical priest-hood, and certainly was not a polemic against it, so 1 Peter 2:9 had no connection with the special ordained ministry that emerged in the church and was certainly not a polemic against it. In fact, 1 Peter 5 presupposes the existence of elders or presbyters in the church, and the author of 1 Peter writes as one presbyter to others. Thus, 1 Peter 2:9 does not depict the rights and privileges of individuals, such as have been emphasized in the Protestant doctrine of the priesthood of all believers; but rather the text is concerned with "the electedness and holiness of the corporate people of God."[50] What Krister Stendahl notes concerning the significance of election generally in the New Testament applies to 1 Peter: "Election in Christ not only constitutes a new society; its meaning is to be found in the new society, and not in the status of individuals."[51]

This does not mean that the concept of a priestly people is without cultic con-tent. Israel, like other Middle Eastern nations, had a sacrificial cult and a special priest-hood to preside at sacrifices. But lay Israelites also had a role in the sacrificial worship. In the "democratization" of the restored temple after the Exile, the institution of the *Ma'amad* ensured the participation of representatives from local communities in the daily sacrifices of the temple. While these sacrifices were being offered in Jerusalem, the rest of the congregation of Israel met in local synagogues for daily prayer services that, as a consequence, acquired the sense of being spiritual sacrifices. This development had a profound influence on Christian liturgy and the understanding of the eucharist as a spiri-tual or "unbloody" sacrifice, the sacrifice of praise and thanksgiving.

A representative or ordained priesthood also emerged in the church that was given responsibility for presiding at this eucharistic sacrifice. But the participation of the priestly people was also expected and ensured, at least by the use of the word of assent, "Amen," to the Great Thanksgiving, by means of which the people made this central prayer of the liturgy their own. There are also prayers that the faithful offer on their own in intercession and thanksgiving, often through their representative, the deacon. The sense of belonging to a priestly community is preserved by the development of distinct liturgical roles within the liturgical assembly, and no study of Christian liturgy can ignore this communitarian way in which the liturgy is celebrated by a holy people.

[49] Elliott, 225.

[50] Ibid., 225.

[51] Krister Stendahl, "The Called and the Chosen. An Essay on Election," in *The Roots of the Vine. Essays in Biblical Theology*, ed. by A. Fridrichsen (Philadelphia: Westminster Press, 1953), 69.

CHAPTER 2

The Incarnational Reality of Christian Liturgy

T HE CHRISTIAN CHURCH SHARES with all human societies a symbolic discourse and a repertoire of rites. There is almost nothing among the great natural symbols of the world that Christians have not been able to assimilate. The reason for this is not difficult to understand. Natural symbols possess an archetypal power that appeals to the realm of human instinct that is not so much logical as emotional, not so much propositional as evocative. Since these symbols are employed in different religions and societies, they speak with primitive power and evoke depths of association with other human beings. The profound water symbolism of baptism appeals to something aboriginal in human nature. Eating and drinking in the eucharist employ our most primal appetites.[1] The image of the God-human may be at least five thousand years old, and the symbol of the trinity may be even older.[2] Likewise, such images as marriage feasts, parenthood and childhood, of breath figuring spirit, the rhythms of life and death and of light and darkness, and the hero struggling against adversaries all hold prototypal religious meanings. Christians share with all other human beings this intuitive way of apprehending reality, even though we have given these rites and symbols particular theological meanings. In light of this we have to believe that God took this basic human way of apprehending reality into consideration when deciding to communicate with us.

---

[1] See R. S. Lee, *Psychology and Worship* (London: SCM Press, 1955), chapter five.
[2] See Carl-Gustav Jung, *Psychology and Religion* (New Haven: Yale University Press, 1938), 56ff.

🍇 VISIBLE WORDS

Augustine of Hippo spoke of the visibility of the word: "The word comes to an element, and so there is a sacrament, that is, a sort of visible word."[3]

Augustine's dictum is not only an affirmation of the essential role of the word of God—the divine communication—in Christian life and understanding. It is also an observation of the general role of symbol and ritual in human life. Human beings desire their experiences of life, of time, and of place to be related to the sacred. Christians, like other peoples, have ways of ritualizing such passages in life as initiation, penance, marriage, childbirth, vocation, sickness, and death so as to make sense of these experiences. Christians, like other peoples, come together at regular intervals and on special occasions to have their identity as a community reaffirmed by hearing sacred stories, sharing a sacred meal or communion sacrifice, and engaging in prayer to the Source and Sustainer of all things. Christians also gather in especially appointed places that are more transparent of the sacred than other places because they are places in which the word has been proclaimed, the sacraments celebrated, and holy people have assembled.[4]

It is noteworthy that Augustine referred to many of these rites, times, and places as *sacramenta*. To be sure, he regarded baptism and the eucharist as sacramental rites distinct from other rites and symbols that he also called sacraments. His use of the term *sacramentum* lacks the precision of the medieval scholastic use of the term. So he is able to call sacraments such things as the sign of the cross, the salt of exorcism, the penitential garment, Easter Day and its octave, penance, the laying on of hands, reconciliation, the creed, the Lord's Prayer, the baptismal font, and other things.[5] What all these things have in common is that they are spiritually significant and externally visible.

Why are such "visible words" needed? They are needed because human communication is more than the transmission of propositions. The gospel is not proclaimed by stating propositions; it is proclaimed by the acts of preaching and ministering sacraments. Preaching is not giving a lecture; it is an incanting, a posturing, a storytelling, a proclaiming. The forgiveness of sins is not promised only by sentences, but by sentences joined to a bath, the laying on of hands, and communal eating and drinking. It is interesting to consider that the words that accompany these sign-acts can be changed, but the visible elements cannot be changed. No matter what words surround the baptismal rite, its central feature will still be washing with water. No matter what words of prayer and proclamation are said over the bread and cup, there is still no Holy Communion without eating the bread and drinking from the cup. This is exactly why repetition is a common feature of ritual, because the visible words at the heart of the rites are irreplaceable.

If we ask why we need such visible words, there is also a standard answer in the Christian tradition. Thomas Aquinas summarized it when he noted that human beings

---

[3] Augustine, *Treatise on the Gospel of John*, LXXX, 3 (c. 416).

[4] See Marion Hatchett, *Sanctifying Life, Time, and Space. An Introduction to Liturgical Study* (New York: Seabury Press, 1976).

[5] See Frederick van der Meer, *Augustine the Bishop*, trans. by B. Battershaw and G. R. Lamb (London: Sheed and Ward, 1961), 280–1.

are "composed of body and soul, to whom the sacramental medicine is proportioned, that through a visible thing touches the body and through a word is believed by the soul."[6] It is by its visibility, its sign-value, its sacramentality, that God's word to us is no mere transmission between pure spirits, but communication between persons. In our communion with God and with one another, we communicate through our bodies. Our bodily selves are our real selves. God takes that into account when communicating with us. The God whose word to us is sacramental is the God who comes to us to be spoken to and to speak. This is the God who has body and blood, the God who can enter deeply into our own flesh. The encounter with such a God makes Christian worship an incarnational event.

❧ The Sacramental/Sacrificial Duality of Liturgy

In Augustine's definition of a sacrament, God's word comes to an outward rite or symbol and makes it a means of God's communication with human creatures. Yet it is obvious that the use of the symbol or the performance of the rite is also an act of human communication both to God and to one another. Robert W. Jenson has said that "the life of the church, by Augustinian lights, is an antiphony of our words for God, which if true are God's words to us, and our words to God."[7] This is the way we understand the dialectic of the two directions of communication in liturgy: from God to the people, and from the people to God. Theology has classically described these as the "sacramental" and "sacrificial" dimensions of worship.

Philipp Melanchthon, co-worker of Martin Luther and author of the Augsburg Confession, devotes a lengthy section of Article XXIV of the Apology of the Augsburg Confession (1531) to a differentiation of *sacrament* and *sacrifice*. "A Sacrament is a ceremony or act in which God offers us the content of the promise joined to the ceremony; thus Baptism is not an act which we offer to God but one in which God baptizes through a minister functioning in his place."[8] When using the term "sacrifice" one must distinguish between the propitiatory sacrifice *(sacrificium propitiatorium)* and the thankoffering or eucharistic sacrifice *(sacrificium eucharistikon)*. The propitiatory sacrifice "is a work of satisfaction for guilt and punishment that reconciles God or placates his wrath or merits the forgiveness of sins for others."[9] There has only been one true propitiatory sacrifice: the atoning sacrifice of Christ, which was foreshadowed by the sacrifices of the Old Testament and which has now replaced them. The thrust of Melanchthon's polemic is that the mass could not be that kind of a sacrifice. The eucharistic sacrifice, on the other hand, is the means by which "those who have been reconciled give thanks or show their gratitude for the forgiveness of sins and other blessings received." Among the eucharistic sacrifices, or sacrifices of praise, Melanchthon lists "the proclamation of the Gospel, faith,

---

[6] Thomas Aquinas, *Summa Theologia*, III, 60, 6.

[7] Robert W. Jenson, "The Praying Animal," Zygon 18 (1983), 314. See also his *Visible Words. The Interpretation and Practice of Christian Sacraments* (Philadelphia: Fortress Press, 1978).

[8] *Apology* 24; *The Book of Concord*, ed. and trans. by Theodore G. Tappert, in collaboration with Jaroslav Pelikan, Robert H. Fischer, and Arthur Carl Piepkorn (Philadelphia: Fortress Press, 1959), 252.

[9] Ibid.

prayer, thanksgiving, confession, the afflictions of the saints, yes, all the good works of the saints."[10]

The examples of eucharistic sacrifice given by Melanchthon show that one cannot mechanically divorce the sacramental aspect of worship from the sacrificial aspect. He calls the preaching of the gospel a sacrifice of praise—which it undoubtedly is from the perspective of the one doing the preaching; yet it is also an act in which God addresses the people of God through the words of the preacher. Likewise, while Christ is present in Holy Communion to bestow the gifts of forgiveness, life, and salvation, the sacramental celebration is also an expression of the congregation's sacrifice of praise and thanksgiving. As Peter Brunner has argued, "one dare not divorce these two sides of worship actively and mechanically assign them to individual parts of worship." The reason is that "in worship the Lord becomes present to His congregation only by man's proclamation of the Gospel and the administration of Holy Communion in obedience to the command of institution."[11] In the same vein, we cannot rigidly separate prayer and proclamation, even though they designate two different directions of communication in worship. A hymn, psalm, or canticle may be both an act of prayer and an act of proclamation. The creed has been both a dogmatic and a devotional text. The eucharistic prayer includes the narrative of the institution of the Lord's Supper, and often other citations of or allusions to biblical texts, and thus is an act of proclamation even as it is being offered by the presiding minister on behalf of the whole congregation as the chief prayer in liturgy addressed to God.

This duality of prayer and proclamation characterizes what happens in the event during which God addresses the people through the words of scripture and the sign-acts of washing and sharing a meal, and the congregation addresses God with prayers of confession, petition, praise, and thanksgiving. The term "worship," therefore, does not adequately describe what this event is all about. "Worship" is said to derive from the Anglo-Saxon word *weorthscripe*, which means literally "to ascribe worth." Magistrates in England are still addressed as "your worship." The term suggests ascribing supreme worth to God. But the impression can be given that it is humankind that recognizes and ascribes worth, whereas it is really God who ascribes worth to humankind by deigning to enter into communion with fallen humanity.[12]

There is no doubt that the congregation does ascribe worth to God when it gathers in God's presence. The psalmist says, "Ascribe to the LORD the glory due his name" (Ps. 96:8); the Revelation canticle sings out, "Worthy is the Lamb . . . to receive . . . honor and glory and blessing!" (5:12). Yet this constitutes only one side of the duality of this sacramental/sacrificial event of encounter: it expresses the sacrifice of praise.

A theology of worship requires that we recognize the divine initiative in the divine-human encounter. The only basis on which we can ascribe to God "the glory due

---

[10] Ibid.

[11] Peter Brunner, *Worship in the Name of Jesus*, trans. by M. H. Bertram (St. Louis: Concordia Publishing House, 1968), 124.

[12] See Paul W. Hoon, *The Integrity of Worship* (Nashville: Abingdon Press, 1971), 91–4 for a theological critique of the category of "worthship."

his name" is that God is already glorified in humanity by the incarnation of the Word. Worship is not only what the congregation does; it is also what God does through the proclamation of the word and the ministration of the sacraments. Archaic people would concur with this insistence on the priority of the divine initiative, because the reason for assembling at certain times and places is that a hierophany or theophany has already made such times and places sacred.

So "worship" is not the most adequate word to describe the event of divine-human encounter that occurs in the assembly of God's people. The word used in the New Testament which most closely means "worship" is *latreia*. Romans 9:4 and Hebrews 9:1, 6 refer to the Jewish worship in the Temple. Romans 12:1 describes spiritual worship *(logike latreia)* in ethical terms. Logike latreia was an important concept in ancient Christian worship, doctrine, and life. But it is still not adequate to include the divine participation in the event we call worship.

A word that comes closer to incorporating both the divine and the human participation in worship is *leitourgia*. Originally this term came out of the realm of law and politics. It meant a service that was rendered on the people's behalf by a representative; hence it is composed from words for work *(ergon)* and public *(leïtos)*. In ancient Athens "leitourgia" referred to the legislative work of the citizen assemblies.[13] In subsequent use "leitourgia" referred to religious rites performed for the public good. The one who performs these services is a liturgist *(leitourgos)*. Paul speaks of the Roman authorities as "liturgists of God" (Rom. 13:6) and of himself as a "liturgist of Christ Jesus to the Gentiles" (Rom. 15:16). The term "liturgy" was also used by Paul to describe the collection of charitable gifts by the congregations in Macedonia and Greece for the relief of the poor in Jerusalem as a token of gratitude for their receipt of the gospel (2 Cor. 9:12), and also the gifts that were gathered for Paul's needs by the congregation in Philippi and delivered by Epaphroditus, who thereby became a liturgist to the apostle's needs (Phil. 2:25, 30). Elsewhere in the New Testament the term "liturgy" is used, as it had been used in the Septuagint (the Greek translation of the Hebrew scriptures), to refer to the sacrificial service performed in the tabernacle by the priests (Heb. 9:21; 10:11). This leitourgia does not have a direct continuation among Christians on earth, because Christ's sacrifice has superseded the sacrifices of the old covenant. Nevertheless, there is a direct continuation of this leitourgia in heaven where Christ the high priest offers his eternal sacerdotal service before God on behalf of the people (Heb. 8:1, 6). Thus, "leitourgia" describes the high priestly work of Christ as well as the work of the people of God on earth.

Just as Paul was a leitourgos to the Gentiles, and Epaphroditus was a leitourgos to Paul, and just as the church from an early date appointed ministers (bishops, deacons, as in *Didache* 15:1) who could render the leitourgia to the congregation, so there is a venerable tradition that regards Christ as the true leitourgos to the people, their true high priest or presiding minister. The liturgical role of Christ in the church has been given

---

[13] See Herman Strathmann, *leitourgeo*, in Gerhard Kittel, ed., *Theological Dictionary of the New Testament* 4 (Grand Rapids: William B. Eerdmans, 1976), 215–31.

focus in the sacramental celebrations. Thus, Ephesians 5:25–32 uniquely states that Christ gave himself up for the church "in order to make her holy by cleansing her with the washing of water by the word, so as to present the church to himself in splendor, without a spot or wrinkle or anything of the kind—yes, so that she may be holy and without blemish." The church's holiness and glory are those of Christ who gives himself for and to the church. He makes the church his own by cleansing it "with the washing of water by the word." Christ is the baptizer; the church and its ministers are only the instruments of his will.

The doctrine that Christ is the true minister of his sacraments was maintained with great difficulty during the Donatist controversy. Against those who questioned the validity of a baptism performed by an unworthy minister, Augustine argued that it didn't matter whether it was Peter or Judas who baptized since it was really Christ who baptized.[14] Thomas Aquinas appealed to this tradition, arguing that a valid baptism may be performed even by an unbaptized person, if it is done according to the church's rites: "The one who baptizes offers only his outward ministration; whereas it is Christ who baptizes inwardly, who can use all men to whatever purpose he wills."[15] Representatives of the ekklesia perform the rites, but the people experience through the rites the self-giving of Christ. So the human being who renders the leitourgia does so at the command and in the stead of Christ himself. Martin Luther affirmed this tradition in *The Babylonian Captivity of the Church* (1520) when he wrote, "For man baptizes, and yet does not baptize. He baptizes in that he performs the work of immersing the person to be baptized; he does not baptize, because in so doing he acts not on his own authority but in God's stead. Hence, we ought to receive baptism at human hands just as if Christ himself, indeed, God himself, were baptizing us with his own hands."[16] It is really Christ who baptizes, though human beings say the words and use the water. Luther said the same thing with regard to confession and absolution. He held that confession consists of two parts: "The first is my work and act, when I lament my sin and desire comfort and restoration for my soul. The second is a work which God does, when he absolves me of my sins through a word placed in the mouth of a man."[17] The same thing may be said about the eucharist: a minister of the church presides over the Lord's Supper, but it is the Lord's Supper in which Christ himself is both the host and the meal, both the priest and the victim. Seen in this way the liturgy of the church is not only the work offered by the people to God before the world; it is also the work of God who, in Christ and through his Spirit, pursues the mission of reconciling the world to God through the preaching of the gospel and the administration of the sacraments.[18]

---

[14] Augustine, *On Baptism Against the Donatists*, IV, 11ff.

[15] Thomas Aquinas, *Summa Theologia*, III, q. 67, art. 5, ad 1.

[16] *Luther's Works*, Vol. 36 (Philadelphia: Fortress Press, 1959), 62.

[17] Luther, The Large Catechism, V; Tappert, *The Book of Concord*, 458–9.

[18] See Frank C. Senn, *The Witness of the Worshiping Community. Liturgy and the Practice of Evangelism* (Mahwah, N.J.: Paulist Press), chapters 4 and 5.

❦ THE LITURGICAL ROLE OF CHRIST

Central to this act of sacramental encounter between God and the people of God is the role of Christ. As the high priest appointed by God from among his brethren (Heb. 2:11–18), who has made the sacrifice of obedience to the Father (Heb. 10:9f.) and has appeared in heaven as our forerunner (Heb. 6:19f.), Christ is our way of access to the Father (Eph. 2:18). Our worship is offered to God not only on account of what Christ has already done but also by his continuing mediation. "There is . . . one mediator between God and humankind, Christ Jesus himself human" (1 Tim. 2:5).

In a definitive study of *The Place of Christ in Liturgical Prayer*, Josef A. Jungmann demonstrated that the understanding that Christ is the mediator of Christian worship governed the public prayers of the church from the earliest days.[19] Thus, in the prayer over the eucharistic bread in the *Didache* 9:4, a church manual dating from the end of the first century or the beginning of the second, we find the doxological conclusion: "For yours is the glory and the power through Jesus Christ forever."[20] We may also note the eucharistic prayer uttered by Polycarp before he was burned at the stake, in the remarkable Acts of his martyrdom, which has a similar doxological conclusion: "I praise you, I bless you, I glorify you, through the eternal and heavenly High Priest, Jesus Christ, your beloved Servant, through whom be glory to you with him and the Holy Spirit both now and unto the ages to come. Amen."[21] And as a final example from the early period of Christianity we may note the beginning of the eucharistic prayer of Hippolytus in his *Treatise on the Apostolic Tradition* (c. 215 C.E.):

> We render thanks unto you, O God, through your beloved child Jesus Christ,
> whom in the last times you did send to us [to be] a Savior and Redeemer and
> the angel of your counsel.[22]

This prayer indicates that Christ not only mediates human worship to God, but also mediates the divine blessings to humanity. Already in the New Testament, Christians give thanks to God on account of what has been done for them in Christ Jesus (Eph. 1:3–14; 1 Peter 1:3).

Jungmann also showed how anti-Arian concerns prompted the church to shift the role of Christ from mediator of worship to object of worship. This is seen especially in the doxological conclusion of prayers. We have seen examples of early Christian prayers which are addressed to God the Father "through Jesus Christ, your Son, our Lord." The Arians, who held that the Son is subordinate to the Father, could justify their position by appealing to the public prayers of the church. The result was that prayer formularies were changed to stress the co-equality of the Father, the Son, and the Holy Spirit. So, if we may

---

[19] Josef A. Jungmann, *The Place of Christ in Liturgical Prayer*, Eng. trans. (Collegeville: The Liturgical Press, 1989).

[20] *Early Christian Fathers. The Library of Christian Classics*, Vol. I, ed. and trans. by Cyril C. Richardson in collaboration with Eugene R. Fairweather, Edward Rochie Hardy, and Massey Hamilton Shepherd (Philadelphia: Westminster Press, 1953), 175.

[21] Ibid., 155; alt.

[22] *The Treatise on The Apostolic Tradition of St. Hippolytus of Rome*, ed. and trans. by Gregory Dix (London: S.P.C.K., 1968), 7; alt. Words in brackets are the translator's.

take this one formula as an example, a doxology such as "Gloria Patri per Filium in Spiritu Sancto" (Glory to the Father *through* the Son *in* the Holy Spirit) was changed to "Gloria Patri et Filio et Spiritui Sancto" (Glory to the Father *and* the Son *and* the Holy Spirit).[23] In a similar way, Catholics in Spain during the fifth century, in reaction to the Arian Visigoths, began adding to the termination of Latin collects, "through Jesus Christ, your Son, our Lord," the expansion "who lives and reigns with you in the unity of the Holy Spirit, one God, forever and ever." The result of these changes, according to Jungmann, was that "stress was now placed not on what unites us to God (Christ as one of us in his human nature, Christ our brother), but on what separates us from God (God's infinite majesty)."[24]

Yet already in the New Testament, Christ was confessed as Lord *(Kyrios)*—particularly at baptism (Rom. 10:8–13). Christ was invoked as Lord in the Christian assembly (see the *maranatha*, "Our Lord, come!" in 1 Cor. 16:22 and Rev. 22:20). He was already *worshiped* as Lord by Christians, in anticipation of the day when every knee should bow and every tongue confess him as such (Phil. 2:5–11). The title "Lord" had been substituted for the divine name Yahweh in the Septuagint. It was used in many Jewish synagogues of the Diaspora as the equivalent of Adonai, since the divine name would not be spoken. The Jewish scholar, Alan Segal, commenting on the hymn quoted in Philippians, in which "the name that is above every name" (2:9) is bestowed on Jesus who is worshiped and confessed as Lord, wrote, "For a Jew, this phrase can only mean that Jesus received the divine name Yahweh, the tetragrammaton YHWH, translated as the Greek name *kyrios*, or Lord."[25]

The adoration and worship of Christ was also expressed in the Gospels where petitioners knelt before him in a gesture of entreaty asking to be healed of leprosy (Matt. 8:2) or imploring healing for a family member (Matt. 9:18; 15:25). The Samaritan leper whom Jesus cleansed with the other nine returned to thank Jesus and prostrated himself at Jesus' feet (Luke 17:16)—an act of utter adoration and worship. The disciples in the boat acclaimed Jesus as the Son of God when he came to them walking on the water (Matt. 14:33). On his entrance into Jerusalem he was hailed as the Son of David with shouts of "Hosanna" (from the Hebrew, meaning "Lord, save") and "Blessed is the one who comes in the name of the Lord!" (Matt. 21:9). The disciples' worship of Jesus reached a climax of awe and fear at his resurrection, as they fell on their knees before him (Matt. 28:9, 17). In the highest confessional statement in the Gospels, Thomas exclaimed to the Risen One, "My Lord and my God!" (John 20:28). This should alert us to the possibility that when we find prayers and hymns addressed to Christ in the ancient Christian tradition, it is not just an expression of anti-Arianism, as Jungmann suggested. It is also a way of articulating more clearly, in the face of heresy, what the Christian community had originally experienced and come to confess.

---

[23] See Josef A. Jungmann, *The Early Liturgy to the Time of Gregory the Great* (Notre Dame, Ind.: University of Notre Dame Press, 1959), 193.

[24] Ibid., 195.

[25] Alan F. Segal, *Paul the Convert. The Apostolate and Apostasy of Saul the Pharisee* (New Haven and London: Yale University Press, 1990), 62.

Beginning in the second century we find hymns in praise of Christ (as in the Letter of Ignatius to the Ephesians 7:2; 18:2; 19:2f.). By the third century there are hymns actually addressed to Christ. One of these, "Phos Hilaron," has come to have a place in the Service of Evening Prayer (Vespers).

> Joyous light of glory:
> of the immortal Father; heavenly, holy, blessed Jesus Christ.
> We have come to the setting of the sun, and we look to the evening light.
> We sing to God, the Father, Son, and Holy Spirit:
> You are worthy of being praised with pure voices forever.
> O Son of God, O Giver of life: The universe proclaims your glory. (*LBW*, p. 143)

This kind of devotion to Christ may have been more freely expressed in popular circles than in official liturgical prayers. Particularly in the Roman church, which was relatively unaffected by Arianism and the Nicene struggles over christology, prayer formularies continued to stress the mediatorial role of Christ. In the Eastern church, however, the struggle for the eventual triumph of the *homoousion* doctrine opened the way for even presidential prayers to be addressed to the Son. Also in the East, a number of hymns addressed to Christ became a standard part of the liturgy. One of these is "O Monogenes," which secured a position in the entrance rite of the Byzantine liturgy.

> Only begotten Son and Word of God, immortal as you are, You condescended
> for our salvation to take flesh from the Holy Mother of God and ever-virgin
> Mary, and without undergoing change, You became Man; You were crucified,
> O Christ God, and crushed death by your death; You are One of the Holy
> Trinity, equal in glory with the Father and the Holy Spirit: save us.[26]

The Gloria, imported from the East, secured a position in the entrance rite of the Roman liturgy. The second section of this hymn is addressed to the second Person of the Trinity.

> Lord Jesus Christ, only Son of the Father, Lord God, Lamb of God:
> You take away the sin of the world; have mercy on us.
> You are seated at the right hand of the Father: receive our prayer. (*LBW*, p. 59)

Western Matins includes the Te Deum, whose second section is also addressed to the second Person of the Trinity.

> You, Christ, are the king of glory, the eternal Son of the Father.
> When you became man to set us free, you did not spurn the virgin's womb.
> You overcame the sting of death, and opened the kingdom of heaven
>   to all believers.
> You are seated at God's right hand in glory. We believe that you will come
>   and be our judge.
> Come, then, Lord, and help your people, bought with the price of your own
>   blood, and bring us with your saints to glory everlasting. (*LBW*, p. 140)

---

[26] *Byzantine Daily Worship*, ed. by The Most Reverend Joseph Raya and Baron Jose de Vinck (Allendale, N.J.: Alleluia Press, 1969), 265. *LBW* # 375 is based on this Greek text.

In western Europe, the number of collects addressed to the Son in Gallican and Mozarabic sacramentaries indicates the concern of Catholics to score against the persistent Arianism of the Visigothic rulers in Gaul and Spain.

Prayer could be addressed to Christ the Kyrios because trinitarian dogma proclaimed the threefoldness of the one true God. Otherwise, of course, Christians would be committing an act of idolatry and offense against the first commandment. Yet here too the motive for developing the dogma of the Holy Trinity was the impact of Jesus Christ on the early Christians. They came to name as "Father" the God they had known in Judaism because this same God was revealed to them as the Father *(Abba)* of the Son, who was also designated as "Son" by the voice from heaven in both the baptism and the transfiguration of Jesus; and they named as "Holy Spirit" the divine presence that bore them toward the Son who brings them into communion with the Father of all.

The Spirit is the link, as it were, between the divine community of God in three persons and the human community, comprised of persons created in the likeness of this God and then recreated in the likeness of the Son in Holy Baptism. The Spirit is the source of mission because the Spirit works through the preaching of the gospel of Jesus Christ and the administration of the sacraments of Christ to bring the disobedient, hostile, and recalcitrant world into a new and redeemed community, the church, the body of Christ on earth.[27] The Spirit is, in Geoffrey Wainwright's words, "the enabler of worship"[28] because the Spirit enables the worship of the earthly church to participate in the eternal adoration and praise of the Holy Trinity. A true theology of Christian liturgy must be rooted in a theology of the Holy Trinity.[29] For the whole of Christian worship is a Spirit-enabled act of communion with the crucified and risen Lord Jesus Christ who now lives and reigns with the Father. Yet the process of addressing devotion *to* the Holy Spirit never developed to the same degree as the worship of the Son of God. Classical Christian prayers, especially at the eucharist, were offered "in the Holy Spirit." Baptisms were performed "in the name of the Father, and of the Son, and of the Holy Spirit." There were addresses of praise to the three divine hypostases before the eruption of the Arian controversy. In the eucharistic epiclesis in the Eastern churches, the Father was asked to send the Holy Spirit on the bread and wine. Not until the Middle Ages do we find addresses directly invoking the Holy Spirit. We may mention such classic hymns as "Veni, Creator Spiritus" *(LBW 472)* from before the tenth century and "Veni, Sancte Spiritus" from the thirteenth century. The paucity and lateness of this development may be ascribed, as Wainwright suggests, to the fact that "the 'place' of the Holy Spirit, in terms both of divinity and of personality (in a technical trinitarian sense), was recognized less by popular devotion than by theological reflexion; and it may be that the notorious cinderella position

---

[27] See Roland Allen, *The Ministry of the Spirit*, ed. by David M. Paton (Grand Rapids: William B. Eerdmans, 1960).

[28] Geoffrey Wainwright, *Doxology. The Praise of God in Worship, Doctrine and Life* (New York: Oxford University Press, 1980), 93ff.

[29] See Jean Corbon, *The Wellspring of Worship*, trans. by Matthew J. O'Connell (New York/Mahwah: Paulist Press, 1988) and Edward J. Kilmartin, S.J., *Christian Liturgy*, I. *Theology* (Kansas City, Mo.: Sheed and Ward, 1988), 100ff.

of pneumatology even in theology is due to the relatively poor place occupied by the Holy Spirit as an object of living worship."[30]

This lack of devotion to the Holy Spirit in liturgical history may be explained by the fact that the New Testament and Christian experience has usually understood the nature of the Holy Spirit through Christ's person, work, and presence. In the earliest New Testament strata, Gregory Dix reminds us, the Spirit is the power or presence of the risen and ascended Jesus energizing his body, the church. "'To walk after the Spirit' and for 'Christ to live through me' means for St. Paul the same thing."[31] Of later formulas, Oscar Cullmann adds that all elements connected with the Holy Spirit are named as functions of Christ.[32] Worship "in spirit and in truth" is bound up with the new life Christ brings into the midst of the old life through the work of the Spirit. The Spirit's function is to link the believer with the first and last comings of Christ and to constitute the church as the eschatological community, the first fruits of the new creation.

THE STUDY OF CHRISTIAN LITURGY

If Christian liturgy is both the work of God the Father, Son, and Holy Spirit (the sacramental aspect) and the work of the people of God (the sacrificial aspect), then the study of Christian liturgy must be concerned to describe each dimension using the appropriate tools. The tools for studying the meaning of Christian liturgy are theological: the revelation of God's being and work in the holy scriptures as refracted through biblical exegesis and systematic theological reflection. Theology is concerned with language because God communicates with people in, with, and under the languages we use (visible words as well as spoken words). Thus liturgical theology is also concerned with the language we use to address God and one another in the liturgical assembly.[33] The tools for studying the activities of the liturgical assembly are those of the behavioral sciences: anthropology, comparative religion, psychology, and sociology. These disciplines enable us to attend to the empirical task of describing and analyzing what is actually going on in the liturgy from the viewpoint of human behavior.[34] This phenomenological approach should remind us that it is insufficient simply to reconstruct in an abstract way the evolution of liturgical rites and the development of church dogma. We must also attend to the sociocultural context of the evolution of rites and the development of dogma. The history of liturgy is not just the history of rites; it is also the history of the people who used these rites to express their relationship with God and with one another.

In addition to the theology and phenomenology of worship, there is a liturgical theology that attends to the forms or structures of worship, and to the interrelatedness of

---

[30] Ibid., 102–3.

[31] Dix, *The Shape of the Liturgy*, 200.

[32] Oscar Cullmann, *The Christology of the New Testament*, trans. by Shirley Guthrie and Charles A. M. Hall (Philadelphia: Westminster Press, 1959), 2.

[33] See Geoffrey Wainwright, "A Language in Which We Speak to God," with Responses by Aidan Kavanagh, Leonel L. Mitchell, David N. Power, and Frank C. Senn, *Worship* 57 (1983), 309–32.

[34] See Mark Searle, "New Tasks, New Methods: The Emergence of Pastoral Liturgical Studies," *Worship* 57 (1983), 291–308.

all the individual liturgical texts and orders. Robert Taft points out that in the history of liturgy, "structure outlives meaning. Elements are preserved even when their meaning is lost (conservatism), or when they have become detached from their original limited place and purpose, acquiring new and broader meanings in the process (universalization). And elements are introduced which have no apparent relationship to others (arbitrariness)."[35] The elements added for arbitrary reasons, whether they are texts, actions, gestures, or accoutrements, are especially troublesome for liturgical theology, because they usually serve to highlight or illustrate some particular theological interpretation that is imposed on the liturgy (e.g., explaining the mass as the reenactment of the sacrifice of Christ and interpreting the rendering of prayers, the movement of ministers, manual acts, and priestly vestments as symbolic aspects of a dramatic reenactment). Taft observes that, beginning in the Middle Ages, commentators attended more to the symbolic meaning of liturgical units than to the structures themselves.[36] Lost in the detailed allegorical interpretations of each ceremonial action and manual gesture in the medieval commentaries was the sense that the shape of the liturgy itself also conveys meaning. So, for example, the presentation and arrangement of the bread and wine on the altar at the offertory represents the self-offering of the people of God, while in medieval allegory it represented the burial of Christ. The fraction (breaking of bread) signifies the unity of the one and the many in the sacrament and in the church, while in medieval allegory this action represented the breaking of Christ's body on the cross. The elevation signifies the summoning of the faithful to the adoration of Christ who is truly present in the sacrament; in medieval allegory this represented the raising up of Christ on the cross. The chasuble signifies continuity with the church down through the centuries from the earliest times; in medieval allegory it represented the seamless robe of Christ. In fact, the fundamental meaning of liturgy is that it is the public work of the church in which the gospel of Jesus Christ is publicly proclaimed; adoration, praise, and thanksgiving are offered to God the Father along with petitions and supplications for the life of the world; and the Lord's Supper is celebrated in anticipation of the banquet of the kingdom of God. The doing of liturgy therefore also says something about the identity and mission of the church.

Also lost in the Middle Ages was the patristic understanding of the sacramental economy, that is, the interrelatedness of the various liturgical orders. What is the relationship between the word and the table? There has always been "table talk" at the eucharistic meal. Does not the joining together of the liturgies of the word and the meal mean that there is always a proclamation of a particular aspect of the mystery of redemption and a concrete application of the mystery in the administration of the sacrament? What is the relationship of the occasional services—baptism, ordination, marriage, burial—and the eucharist to one another? These occasional orders were early celebrated in the context of the eucharist, and the sacrament was taken to the absent, including the sick, the

---

[35] Robert F. Taft, "The Structural Analysis of Liturgical Units: An Essay in Methodology," in *Beyond East and West: Problems in Liturgical Understanding* (Washington, D.C.: The Pastoral Press, 1984), 152.

[36] For a summary of some of the allegorical interpretations of the mass in the medieval *Expositiones missae* see John P. Dolan, *History of the Reformation* (New York and Toronto: The New American Library, A Mentor-Omega Book, 1965), 195ff.

imprisoned, and the dying. Is not baptism the initiation into the fellowship of the church, which is manifested at the Lord's Table? Is not ordination the ordering (i.e., arranging) of the eucharistic ministry? Is not life sanctified by recourse to the presence of the Christ who comes to the people in Holy Communion? What is the relationship of the daily prayer offices to the chief liturgy of the word and the eucharistic meal? Does not the liturgy of the hours serve to sanctify the time of this world between celebrations of the divine liturgy? What is the relationship of the seven days of the week to the Lord's Day? Is not each Lord's Day an "eighth day" that projects beyond the time of this world into the dimension of the kingdom of God but that is demarcated as such only by reference to the time of this world in which we still live? What is the relationship of the Sundays of the year to the annual Pasch? Is not each Lord's Day a little celebration of the resurrection of Christ and the annual Pasch a big Sunday? What is the relationship of catechetical instruction to the ritual bath? Is it not the case that the ritual bath is initiation into a community "called out" of the world (an *ekklesia*), so that the instruction, or catechesis, provided must be relevant to this eschatological vocation? What is the relationship of the Office of the Keys to the eucharistic fellowship? Must not the eschatological community whose fellowship is expressed at the Lord's Supper be in a state capable of withstanding the scrutiny of the Lord Christ who comes again as judge? It is the task of liturgical theology to sort through these relationships and to propose their meanings.[37]

The liturgical forms by which the community of faith addresses God constitute the church's rule of prayer *(lex orandi)*. The liturgical content by which the community of faith professes its faith (including the commemorations in the calendar as well as the readings, the items in the creed as well as the parts of the eucharistic prayer) constitutes the church's rule of belief *(lex credendi)*. There has been great confusion in the discussion about the relationship between these two "rules" as a result of claims made for the primacy of one over the other and arguments for the influence of one on the other.[38] One could argue for the primacy of prayer over belief in that what one says *to* God is of more ultimate concern than what one says *about* God. But there is a difference between what one says about God in the presence of God in acts of proclamation and what one says about God in the classroom. We have come to understand this as the difference between "first order" and "second order" theology.[39] "First order" theology is what is practiced—but practiced in the specific sense that it is what one says to God in prayer—whereas "second order" theology is reflection on such practices. But profession, too, can be first order theology. Reciting a creed, delivering a sermon, or offering a eucharistic prayer is first order theology with a primacy about it because it is done before God in acts of public testimony. There is, thus, a *practice and profession* of praying a collect, confessing the faith, or interpreting the Bible in a sermon before there is *reflection* in the form of liturgical theology, dogmatic theology, or biblical hermeneutics. These practices of prayer and

---

[37] See Alexander Schmemann, *Introduction to Liturgical Theology*, op. cit., 52ff.; also Gordon Lathrop, *Holy Things: A Liturgical Theology* (Minneapolis: Fortress Press, 1993), chapters 1–3.

[38] See Geoffrey Wainwright, *Doxology*, 218–83; also Frank C. Senn, *Christian Worship and Its Cultural Setting*, op. cit., 79ff.

[39] See Aidan Kavanagh, *On Liturgical Theology* (New York: Pueblo Publishing Co., 1984), 73ff.

professions of belief become rules or laws when they are embraced by the community of faith as ways of unifying and regulating its common prayer and public profession.

Such rules as govern the church's liturgy are also called canons, and there are several.[40] There is the canon of scripture. Canonical scripture is composed of writings that are discerned to be *of* God (i.e., inspired) and not just *about* God. Only these writings are read in public worship. There is also a baptismal canon in the form of a creed by which the candidates for baptism profess their faith and ever renew their baptism by recourse to this statement. There is the eucharistic canon that provides both a framework and the content for what is to be said at that meal which expresses the community's fellowship and nurtures it for its mission. There is an order of service *(ordo)* that is canonical in that it specifies a particular rhythm or sequence to be followed with regularity.

Because of the canonical character of liturgy, its ordered development in time, both the empirical task of describing the rites and ritual processes of the community of faith and the theological task of interpreting the meanings of the rites and symbols and their interrelatedness in the sacramental economy, must be anchored in historical study. We can only describe and interpret what the community of faith has said and done and what it has understood God to have said and done, as this is known to us from documents and artifacts. Historical study remains the primary tool of liturgiology because it establishes the *what* to which phenomenology addresses its *how* and theology addresses its *why*. By accepting the normativity of the historical tradition, liturgical study affirms the incarnational character of the economy of salvation. The incarnational understanding of Christian liturgy requires that we do not separate the divine from the human, the theological from the anthropological, and also that we do not confuse them. The autonomy of each discipline needs to be respected, and each needs to be heard for what it contributes to our total understanding of liturgy. Liturgy is a human activity, and its execution can be evaluated by helpful recourse to anthropological research, ritual studies, communication theory, and other behavioral sciences.[41] At the same time we dare not forget that God also works through these means of grace. Just so, it is the task of liturgical theology to explore the divine service for its theological, christological, and pneumatological aspects. Liturgical theology is finally about what all theology is about: God.[42]

🍇 THE FREEDOM AND NECESSITY OF LITURGICAL FORM

Upholding the canonical character, and therefore the historical normativity of liturgy, does not mean that it is absolutized as a legal requirement for the contemporary Christian community. Indeed, the historical study of liturgy bears witness to instances of decay, of superstitious abuse, of heretical malformations, and of flinty incrustations that require reform and renewal. This in itself should tell us that the elements of liturgy can have nothing to do with salvation. Furthermore, the forms of worship used in the

---

[40] Ibid., 140ff.

[41] A list of works in these human sciences that liturgists have found helpful is included in the bibliography at the end of this book.

[42] See David W. Fagerberg, *What Is Liturgical Theology? A Study in Methodology* (Collegeville: The Liturgical Press, 1992).

Christian community come out of particular cultural contexts, and differences in ethnic, economic, political, social, and cultural backgrounds are transcended in Christ. Liturgical forms are used in the service of the gospel of Jesus Christ. This message of good news is celebrated and proclaimed in Christian liturgy in scripture, preaching, prayer, and sacramental celebrations, as well as in songs and ceremonies. Liturgical forms must be judged according to their effectiveness in communicating the gospel and their appropriateness to the liturgical assembly. In evangelical freedom the Christian community is at liberty to develop new forms of worship that will meet the criteria of effective communication of the gospel and edification of the fellowship in the gospel.

On the other hand, there are areas in which Christian liberty is restrained. The word of God must be proclaimed and the sacraments of Christ must be celebrated, according to Christ's institution, in the community that assembles in the name of the Father and of the Son and of the Holy Spirit. To be sure, there is a great deal of latitude in how the word shall be preached and the sacraments ministered. Minimally, however, these criteria of what is commanded suggest that the sacred scriptures of the Old and New Testaments will be read and expounded in the Christian assembly, that baptism by water will be administered in the name of the Father and of the Son and of the Holy Spirit, and that bread and wine will be taken with thanksgiving in remembrance of the crucified and risen Lord and his instituting meal, distributed to the faithful and consumed. In summary, nothing will be done in the Christian assembly that is contrary to the sacred scriptures and scripture's gospel. Christian worship will be thoroughly evangelical, that is, imbued with the gospel of the life, death, resurrection, and ascension of Jesus Christ.

Furthermore, historical study that pays attention to the forms or structures of worship—the shape of the liturgy—demonstrates the remarkable uniformity in the evolution of Christian liturgical rites. Textual, musical, ceremonial differences between one Christian community and another, and from one time to another, abound; but Christian communities of vastly different place and time have shown a remarkable propensity for doing things in a similar way. And what Christians have done in worship have endured. Peter Brunner has observed that "there is perhaps no creation in the cultural realm which has shown such a puzzling constancy to date as the worship of the Christian church."[43]

Because the forms of worship have endured as vehicles for the proclamation of the word and the celebration of the sacraments in Christian communities located in different times and places, a particular Christian community would have to have good reasons for setting aside these forms in favor of new or different ones. There would have to be some sense that the forms in use were blurring the communication of the gospel or alienating people before such forms should be abandoned. Christian worship has yearned to be catholic—expressive of the whole church in its historical continuity and witness—as well as evangelical—faithful to the proclamation of the gospel. Liturgy that is the object of this study is at once catholic and evangelical.

---

[43] Brunner, op. cit., 229.

❧ LITURGY—CATHOLIC AND EVANGELICAL

Liturgy that is catholic is that which serves the public proclamation of the gospel in word and sacraments as celebrated by the whole people of God in Christ Jesus. The adjective *katholikos* refers to "the whole." It was applied to the church for the first time in literature in the letter of Ignatius of Antioch *To the Smyrnaens* (c. 110): "Wherever the bishop is, there his people should be, just as, where Jesus Christ is, there is the catholic Church" (8:2). In this context, "catholic" means quite straightforwardly "the whole church."

How could the local assembly lay claim to catholicity? It was only one of numerous similar local assemblies of Christians gathered to proclaim and celebrate the gospel of Jesus Christ. The answer was in the office of bishop. He became not just the leader of the local church; he represented the whole church (the church catholic) to the local church. This was expressed in *The Apostolic Tradition* of Hippolytus of Rome (c. 215), which provides that three neighboring bishops should participate in the ordination of a local bishop elected by his people. The bishop of a province even came to be called *catholicos*. "Catholicity," therefore, implies territoriality: the catholic church embraced the whole people of a land and their culture. Wider expressions of catholicity were framed in terms of provincial churches being in fellowship or communion with patriarchal churches. The whole Western church, up to the schism of the sixteenth century, was in communion with the bishop and church of Rome. Through ecumenical councils the patriarchal communions expressed fellowship with one another.

With or without bishops, the Churches of the Reformation (Lutheran, Reformed, Anglican) were also concerned with catholicity. They embraced whole peoples of territories and nations in established or state churches, and in that sense, they were not sects. Sects had a difficult time finding "space" in which to exist because it was inconceivable that there would be more than one church in a territory. Even in early America, the Anglican and Congregationalist churches enjoyed establishment status in several colonies and states. The Congregationalist church was not disestablished in Connecticut until 1818; in New Hampshire, not until 1819; and in Massachusetts, not until 1833. Establishment broke down only under the liberal tolerance and then affirmation of religious pluralism. But it is noteworthy that far from extolling some kind of rugged individualism, the Puritans in New England were almost totally preoccupied with "the Church in history, its form and membership and government."[44] Nor were the Puritans satisfied with the idea of a "pure," "invisible church." Their concern, like Calvin's, was the formation of a "pure," "gathered church." There was great debate in the latter seventeenth century about this, and one telling essay written by Samuel Stone was entitled, "A Congregational Church Is a Catholike Visible Church."

Liturgy that is catholic is that which expresses the faith and way of life (i.e., culture) of a whole people, but within an ecumenical shape by which it maintains a sense of

---

[44] Robert Middlekauf, *The Mathers: Three Generations of Puritan Intellectuals, 1596–1728* (New York: Oxford University Press, 1971), 99.

continuity with catholic churches of other times and places.[45] Thus liturgies of churches that embrace Middle Eastern, Slavic, or western European peoples express the cultures of those peoples; yet they also share a common shape or structure. This shape includes an entrance rite, a service of readings interspersed with psalmody, general intercessions, the collection and presentation of gifts (offertory), a great thanksgiving over the gifts of bread and wine, communion, and dismissal. We shall see that various reforms of the mass-liturgy in the sixteenth century generally retained the catholic shape of liturgy. Even among the Puritans who eschewed *The Book of Common Prayer,* this ecumenical order was followed. John Cotton's *The True Constitution of a Particular Visible Church Proved by Scripture* (London, 1642) provided an order of worship that included the following: opening prayers of thanksgiving and intercession, the singing of psalms, reading and expounding the Word of God in sermons, exhortation to the congregation, questioning of the preacher by the laity, and celebrating the Lord's Supper "once a month at least." The shape of Holy Communion followed the seven actions in the New Testament institution texts: taking the bread and cup, giving thanks over them, breaking the bread, distributing the elements, and singing a psalm or hymn of thanksgiving after the meal.

Obviously this ecumenical order could be overlaid with many particular details that so attract attention to themselves that the overall structure is obscured. Among these details of texts and practices are elements that set the churches against one another for confessional reasons. Following a catholic form is insufficient grounds for establishing the orthodoxy of a church. Nor is the quality of the community's act of worship grounds for recognizing its orthodoxy. Augustine of Hippo complained that the Donatists down the street outsang his Catholic congregation; they probably outnumbered the Catholics too. Since the third century, therefore, the term "catholic" has taken on the sense of "orthodoxy" in doctrine. Vincent of Lérins defined "catholicity" as that "which is believed everywhere and always by all."[46] The implication is that that which is catholic is also that which is orthodox.

Orthodoxia means "right praise" or "true worship" as well as "right opinion." But, of course, the praise and worship is "right" only if it is directed to the right God. Orthodox liturgy is that which prays to and worships the Holy Trinity. Thus, while the relationship between praying and believing, the lex orandi and the lex credendi, is a reciprocal one, the priority of right praise is such that the lex orandi establishes the lex credendi. Prosper of Aquitaine wrote in the heat of the Semi-Pelagian controversy, "legem credendi lex statuat supplicandi" (Let the rule of prayer establish the rule of belief).[47] From the apostolic injunction to pray for the whole human race (1 Tim. 2:1–4), and the example of the petitions in the bidding prayer of the Good Friday liturgy, he argued that one should *believe* with the Roman See that all faith, good will, and spiritual growth is, from start to finish, a work of grace, against those who allowed for human cooperation with God's

---

[45] See Gregory Dix, *The Shape of the Liturgy,* chart inserted between pp. 432 and 433.

[46] Vincent of Lerins, *Commonitorium* 1:2; P.L. 50: 640.

[47] The so-called *Capitula Coelestini* annexed to a letter of Pope Celestine I (432–42) but now attributed to the lay monk Prosper of Aquitaine; P.L. 51:205–12.

grace. Prosper's mentor, Augustine of Hippo, had also appealed to the lex orandi of the exorcism in the baptismal liturgy as proof that even infants are under the power of sin and the devil against those who held that infants are born without sin. "Why have recourse to the remedy if the ailment is absent?" he asked.[48]

Thus the content of liturgy is as important in establishing its catholicity as the fact that liturgy is used by the whole people of God. This content has to do with the gospel *(evangelion)*. Liturgy is the public work of the community called and gathered by the Spirit of the crucified and risen Christ to proclaim and celebrate the death and resurrection of Christ in word and sacrament. The gospel is "good news" in the sense that the passover of Christ from death to life has application and consequences; therefore "repentance and forgiveness of sins is to be proclaimed in his name to all nations, beginning from Jerusalem" (Luke 24:47). Whatever the sense of the good news may be, whether justification or sanctification or new life or deification or liberation or empowerment, these are predicates of the particular story of Jesus of Nazareth. The story of Jesus is composed of a set of narratives that identify Jesus as the Son of the God who is therefore Jesus' Father as well as Israel's Lord; the Jesus who was born of the Virgin Mary, crucified under Pontius Pilate, died, and was buried; and on the third day rose again from the dead; and ascended into heaven to rule at the right hand of the Father, from whence he will come again to judge the living and the dead; whose Spirit, in the meantime, has been sent to gather and form a people who shall be his "body" in the world.

This story is the evangelical content of Christian worship; and it is manifested not only in scripture readings, of which the gospel reading is the principal selection, but also in preaching, hymns, and prayers. The eucharistic prayer especially is a recital of the story of God's involvement in the history of Israel and Jesus long before the creed became a standard item in the eucharistic liturgy (sixth century in Constantinople; eleventh century in Rome).

The evangelical content of liturgy has served sometimes as a corrective of the catholic tendency to root liturgy in the culture of a people. Words and ceremonies derived from indigenous cultures are not always shorn of their heathen connotations. Symbolic actions and objects can be a source of superstition among Christians, and their multiplication can lead to a ceremonial pomp that is foreign to the spirit of Christianity. It is difficult to reconcile "chancel prancing" with worship done in spirit and in truth. The evangelical principle has served as a critique of the catholic substance of Christian liturgy.[49]

Thus, catholic liturgy has conveyed a sense of the continuity of God's people down through the centuries—Vincent's "ubique, semper, ab omnibus" (that which has been held "everywhere, always, by all"). The evangelical critique reminds us that the true continuity of the people of God is found in the living faith of its members. Catholic liturgy

---

[48] Augustine of Hippo, *Sermo* 174; P.L. 38:943–5.

[49] See Jaroslav Pelikan, "Luther and the Liturgy," in *More About Luther* (Decorah, Iowa: Luther College Press, 1958), pp. 3–62 for an analysis of "catholic substance" and "protestant principle" in Luther's liturgics, and in Christian worship generally.

has served as a link between the gospel of Jesus Christ and the cultural contexts in which that gospel is proclaimed and celebrated. The evangelical critique reminds us that when liturgy is too much shaped by cultural vitalities, it loses its ability to transcend culture or to transform the culture it seeks to address.

Yet human beings are creatures of their cultures. They inevitably form a way of life by being together in community and by passing on their knowledge and customs from one generation to another. The only way to transcend a particular culture, therefore, is to replace it with another. Ironically, it is precisely by recourse to the catholic tradition that cultural particularities are transcended, since the historic liturgy is a depository of the many cultures through which it has passed in its historical journey. The doing of liturgy forms its own way of life (a church culture) that is never absorbed by the particular culture that serves as its local setting.[50]

Moreover, catholic liturgy has not always fully embraced historical cultures; sometimes it has resisted them. For example, it has sometimes preferred a sacred language over the vernacular in order to maintain a sense of continuity and universality. This was the case with liturgical Latin both in the medieval Catholic church and in the Roman Catholic church after Trent and up to the mid-twentieth century, and in the Lutheran churches in the Reformation and post-Reformation periods (although in Lutheran practice, Latin and the vernacular language were both used). The church has sometimes "baptized" pagan festivals and at other times tried to "exorcise" them. The response of the church to any given situation will be dictated by its sense of pastoral need and mission strategy.[51]

Culture is a varied phenomenon with many layers or component parts, including a religious layer. It would be dangerous to the truth of the gospel to plant the gospel in the religious layer of a culture. This may be the reason why early Christians adopted secular rather than religious terms to describe the church itself (*ekklesia* = assembly), its jurisdictions (*diocesis, paroikia* = district, colony), its ministers (*episkopoi, presbyteroi, diakonoi* = overseers, elders, servants), its functions (*leitourgia, baptisma, deipnon* = public work, bath, meal) instead of sacred terms (such as cult, temple, sacrifice, priesthood). The strategy was precisely to avoid certain connotations embedded in pagan cults. Inculturation has been a cautious endeavor wherever the mission of the church has taken the gospel, precisely because it has been necessary to discern whether sacred meanings lie behind certain words, gestures, and ceremonies before those are embraced by the church in the service of the mission of the gospel.

On the other hand, the mission of the gospel always requires some degree of inculturation, and this needs to be approached with the same freedom with which Paul embraced Greek practices and allowed the seed of the gospel to germinate and flourish in the soil of Hellenistic culture—including men leaving their heads uncovered, an indifference to circumcision, an openness to ecstatic phenomena, and celebrating the eucharist

---

[50] See Frank C. Senn, *Christian Worship and Its Cultural Setting*, chapter 3.

[51] See S. Anita Stauffer, ed., *Worship and Culture in Dialogue*. Reports of the International Consultations at Cartigny, Switzerland, 1993, and Hong Kong, 1994 (Geneva: Lutheran World Federation, 1994).

in the context of a meal confraternity. So today, in parts of Asia and Africa, issues of liturgical inculturation are crucial because the historic liturgy comes in the dress of Western culture, and some liturgical practices are confusing or inscrutable in the local culture. In central Africa (to take one example), it is considered a sign of respect to remain seated and an indication of belligerence to stand up. Consider the effect of the rubric to stand for the reading of the gospel in this cultural context! Or, in China and Japan most public ceremonies begin by passing around tea or some other drink and end with a toast. If sacred connotations do not lie behind such ceremonies, or are no longer apprehended as such, the possibilities are open for the inculturation of these practices in Christian liturgy.[52]

The incarnational character of Christian liturgy is such that the risk of inculturation will usually be taken unless there is a good reason for the church to assume a countercultural stance. Such a stance would usually be taken for the sake of witnessing to the gospel in a particular situation that calls for confession (*status confessionis*). The core narrative of the gospel remains the same and is not exchangeable, and the visible words of the gospel proclamation are irreplaceable; but the implications of the gospel are too large to admit only one expression. Indeed, we have only to look to the New Testament itself to see that four different versions of the same story are embraced within one canon. That is the catholic principle of embracing the whole testimony of faith in Jesus Christ. Yet we are also aware of other (gnostic) gospels that were not admitted into the canon. That is the evangelical principle of knowing what kind of message is truly "good news."

In the best of situations, both the catholic tradition and the evangelical principles of orthodox Christian liturgy are held together in balance; or at least they exist together in creative tension. Sometimes one or another of these principles is emphasized by the community of faith as it forms a strategy for the mission of the gospel in a particular time or place. This is what makes the history of liturgy so scintillating and so enduringly relevant to Christian communities today. For communities must still find ways of proclaiming and celebrating the story of Jesus of Nazareth in words and sign-acts that make this story universally accessible. At the same time, the story and sign-acts of Jesus generate a church culture that the community of faith in Jesus Christ, crucified and risen, must pass on to new generations and into which new generations must be initiated.

---

[52] See Anscar J. Chupungco, *Cultural Adaptation of the Liturgy* (New York: Paulist Press, 1982); also G. A. Arbuckle, "Inculturation not Adaptation: Time to Change Terminology," *Worship* 60 (1986), 511–20 and Peter Schineller, S.J., "Inculturation of the Liturgy," in Peter Fink, ed., *The New Dictionary of Sacramental Worship* (Collegeville: The Liturgical Press, 1990), 598–601.

PART ONE

From Meal to Mass

CHAPTER 3

Early Christian Liturgy

ALTHOUGH LITURGY MAY BE defined etymologically as a public service, we must recognize that early Christian liturgy was not a public event. Christianity did not enter the world as a religion, as that word would have been understood by the early church's pagan contemporaries. Christians of the first several centuries lacked the publicity of the pagan cults. They had no shrines, temples, statues, or sacrifices. They staged no public festivals, dances, musical performances, or pilgrimages.[1] Their central ritual involved a meal that had a domestic origin and setting inherited from Judaism. Indeed, Christians of the first three centuries usually met in private residences that had been converted into suitable gathering spaces for the Christian community. So far as we know, the public was not invited. Newcomers, seekers, strangers, and visitors had to be vouched for by sponsors. In fact, early Christian writers were at pains to point out the differences between their assemblies and the pagan cults. This indicates that the ritual bareness of early Christian worship should not be taken as a sign of primitiveness, but rather as a way of emphasizing the spiritual character of Christian worship. Minucius Felix, writing at the end of the second century, says:

> Do you think that we hide the object of our worship because we have no shrines and altars? What image am I to contrive of God, since logical reasoning tells you that man himself is an image of God? What temple am I to build for Him, since this whole world, fashioned by His hand, cannot hold Him? Am I to

---

[1] See Ramsey MacMullen, *Paganism in the Roman Empire* (New Haven and London: Yale University Press, 1981), 1–48.

confine so vast and majestic a power to one little shrine, while I, a mere mortal, live in a larger place? Are our mind and heart not better places to be dedicated to Him?[2]

This is a bit disingenuous. A persecuted minority was not likely to establish a public cult. Furthermore, it belies the fact that Christianity had no more but also no less than contemporary Judaism by way of communal rituals. It had a sacred meal celebrated in the domestic setting of a house church as well as a regular gathering together to study the scriptures and to pray, using ritual forms inherited and adapted from Judaism.

The relations between Christians and Jews were complicated from the very beginning, because included in the church were Jewish Christians who observed ritual practices mandated by the Torah, Jewish proselytes who were God-fearing Gentiles converted to faith in Jesus as the Messiah, and Gentiles who came into Christian churches with no prior relationship to or experience of Judaism. The apostle Paul ran into trouble with Jewish leaders precisely because he saw all of these groups as "Israel," and traveled freely between Gentile house churches, Diaspora synagogues, and the Temple in Jerusalem. His offense was to see a single community of faith that included uncircumcised, nonkosher-observing Gentiles along with the Jewish members—an ideal that was finally not realized. In the Gospels, especially Matthew, there is a polemic against the "hypocrites" and a concern that the disciples of Jesus practice a Torah-based righteousness that "exceeds [the righteousness] of the scribes and Pharisees" (5:20). The Epistle to the Hebrews regards the new covenant and the sacrifice of Christ as "better" than the old covenant and the Mosaic sacrifices (7:22). As late as the *Didache* (c. 100) Christians were defining their practices over against Jewish practices precisely because the practices were so similar. Yet in the fourth century there was a resurgence of Gentile interest in the synagogue, as is evident in the synagogal-inspired prayers in the Syrian *Apostolic Constitutions*.

Thus, while Christians did not enter the arena of the Roman Empire with a public cultus entailing sacrificial rites, they did have a sacred meal to which one was admitted only through a rite of initiation (baptism); and they had a synagogal gathering to read the scriptures and to engage in common prayer which was at some point joined with the liturgy of the Lord's Supper. Both Jews and Christians lacked access to the Jerusalem temple after its destruction by the Romans in 70 C.E. Yet the psalmody that had been a feature of temple liturgies found its way into both Jewish and Christian synagogal gatherings. Other hymns and spiritual songs, many quoted in the New Testament, also found a place in Christian devotion. And the rich liturgical symbolism in the Apocalypse, or the Revelation to John the Seer, suggests that early Christian liturgy was not quite as barren as the letter of Minucius Felix suggests.

---

[2] Minucius Felix, *Octavius*, 32; in *Fathers of the Church*, ed. by J. Deferrari *et al.*, Vol. X (New York: Herder, 1950), 389.

❦ THE JEWISH RELIGIOUS MEAL

The most typical Jewish religious meal is the one which welcomes the Sabbath on Friday evening. Special meals were also held in celebration of the great festivals, especially the Passover. We cannot be sure whether the last meal that Jesus shared with his disciples "on the night on which he was betrayed" was the Passover. The Synoptic Gospels are certain that it was, but the Fourth Gospel says with equal certainty that the supper was held "before the festival of the Passover" (John 13:1). It is clear that John's intention was to have the crucifixion of Jesus take place at the same time that the lambs for the Passover sacrifice were being slaughtered in the Temple. Hence, the trial and crucifixion of Jesus took place on "the day of Preparation for the Passover" (John 19:14). Efforts have been made to reconcile these different chronologies in the Gospel traditions,[3] but all that can be said with certainty is that the passover context was important in the interpretation of Jesus' death. In any event, no specific use of the food peculiar to the Passover meal, such as the lamb and bitter herbs, was made by Jesus in instituting his sacramental meal. Rather, he focused on the blessing of the bread and wine common to any meal *seder* (order).

The Sabbath eve meal that has been observed by Jews for many centuries begins with the lighting of the table candles, typically done by the mother at sundown, when the Sabbath begins. When all are seated, a cup of wine is poured and the *qedush* (sanctification) is recited. This is a blessing of the Sabbath or festival day. A different prayer form is used for each festival and for ordinary sabbaths. We cannot be sure how old these prayers are, but a rabbinic controversy in the Mishnah, the second-century C.E. collection of rabbinic discussions about traditions, centered over whether it is proper to say the blessing of the day or the blessing over the cup first.[4]

It is possible that the Gospel according to Luke has this first cup in mind when it says of Jesus, "And he took a cup and when he had given thanks he said, 'Take this and divide it among yourselves; for I tell you that from now on I will not drink of the fruit of the vine until the kingdom of God comes" (Luke 22:17–18). In Luke's Gospel the sequence of the eucharistic narrative is cup-bread rather than bread-cup, such as we see in the Gospels according to Matthew and Mark and in 1 Corinthians. In Matthew and Mark this saying of Jesus also comes after the ministration of the cup, but it is the final cup of the meal rather than the first cup. The fact that Luke placed this saying after the first cup of the meal lends weight to his intention to place the cup in this position.[5] In some manuscripts of the New Testament there is also a "second" or final cup in Luke's eucharistic narrative, which harmonizes Luke's account with the other eucharistic traditions and also

---

[3] Annie Jaubert, *The Date of the Last Supper* (Staten Island, N.Y.: Alba House, 1965) argued that Jesus could have followed the solar calendar used by the Essenes, in which the 14th of Nisan fell on a Tuesday night and that the various trials of Jesus took place during the next few days before he was put to death on Friday, the actual 14th of Nisan in the traditional Jewish lunar calendar.

[4] *The Mishnah*, trans. with an introduction by Herbert Danby (Oxford: Clarendon Press, 1933), *Berakoth* 8:1, 8.

[5] See Arthur Vööbus, *The Prelude to the Lukan Passion Narrative* (Stockholm: Estonian Theological Society in Exile, 1968), 77ff.

relates it to the structure of the Jewish religious meal. This is an issue taken up in the next section.

In today's Jewish meals the blessing of the cup precedes the qedush, but since this was the subject of the rabbis' dispute we cannot know for certain the custom of the first century. The text of the *berakah* (blessing) of the cup is quite simple:

> Blessed are you, O Lord our God, King of the universe, who creates the fruit of the vine.

This is followed by the blessing of the bread, which is the formal beginning of every Jewish religious meal.

> Blessed are you, O Lord our God, King of the universe, who brings forth bread from the earth.

The male head of the household holds the bread in his hand while he says the blessing, and then breaks and distributes pieces of the bread to those at table, eating a piece himself. There can be no reasonable doubt that this was the point during the ritual at the last supper when Jesus said of the bread, "This is my body." There was conversation as well as prayer in the Jewish religious meal, and both were equally sacred. There was no dichotomy between sacred and profane in Jewish religious life, and the table talk could be about the events of daily life as well as edifying discourses or pious commentaries by the elders.[6] This lack of distinction between sacred and profane is also seen in the attitudes toward the food expressed in the blessings, which clearly proclaim the bread and wine as gifts from God even though human hands have obviously made them and put them on the table.

The chief prayer of the meal, the *Birkat ha-Mazon* (blessing for the food), is recited over the final cup of wine at the end of the meal. It is the oldest and most important Jewish blessing, because it was the only one commanded in the Torah: "You shall eat your fill and bless the LORD your God for the good land that he has given you" (Deut. 8:10).[7] The rabbis claimed that this blessing went back to the time of Moses, although it was probably only as old as the Second Temple (the time of Jesus). This blessing of the final cup became "the cup of blessing" mentioned by Paul (1 Cor. 10:16). It is introduced by a dialogue given in the Mishnah, *Berakoth* 7:3, and does not vary in wording according to the number of participants involved.

> V/ We will bless him of whose bounty we have partaken.
> R/ Bless him of whose bounty we have partaken.

The Birkat ha-Mazon follows, the earliest surviving text of which is from the *Seder Rav Amram Gaon*, the eighth-century C.E. collection of prayers.[8] The prayer collections of the *Gaonim*, to which Rabbi Amram belonged, do not claim any originality. The purpose of

---

[6] See Frank Gavin, *The Jewish Antecedents of the Christian Sacraments* (London: S.P.C.K., 1928; reprinted New York: Ktav, 1969), 68.

[7] See Carmine DiSante, *Jewish Prayer: The Origins of Christian Liturgy*, trans. by Matthew J. O'Connell (Mahwah, N.J.: Paulist Press, 1985), 145.

[8] *Seder R. Amram Gaon*, Part I, ed. by David Hedegård (Lund: Lindstedts, 1951), 147.

his *Seder* was to fix an immemorial tradition whose origins were considered to be inspired. The distinguished Jewish scholar Louis Finkelstein (1895–1991) sought to establish the first-century text of the Birkat ha-Mazon by comparing it with equivalent Christian eucharistic prayers in chapter ten of the *Didache,* a late first-century church manual.[9]

> Blessed are you, O Lord, our God, King of the universe, who feeds the whole world with goodness, with grace and with mercy. Blessed are you, O Lord, who feeds all.
>
> We thank you, O Lord, our God, that you have caused us to inherit a goodly land, the covenant, the Torah, life and food. For all these things we thank you and praise your name forever and ever. Blessed are you, O Lord, for the land and for the food.
>
> Have mercy, O Lord, our God, on your people Israel, and on your city Jerusalem, and on your Temple and your dwelling-place and on Zion your resting-place, and on the great and holy sanctuary over which your name was called, and the kingdom of the dynasty of David may you restore to its place in our days, and build Jerusalem soon. Blessed are you, O Lord, who builds Jerusalem.

The petition to rebuild Jerusalem presupposes that Jerusalem and its temple had been destroyed. This could have been after the Roman-Jewish War of 66–70 C.E., but it could also have been composed during the Maccabean struggle when the Temple and the Altar were under the control of the heathen. Finkelstein discerns a form of the Birkat ha-Mazon in the *Book of Jubilees* 22:6–9, the date of which can hardly be later than 100 B.C.E., which attributes to Abraham a prayer of thanks after he had eaten. The author of Jubilees did not commit the gross anachronism of having Abraham recite the Birkat in the form in which it was known in Hasmonean Judaism, but, like the Birkat, Abraham's prayer is in three parts: God is thanked for food and drink, praised for other blessings, and petitioned for mercy on Israel.[10]

We can assume that this three-part form of prayer was known by Jesus, although we cannot assume that we can establish the text he might have used. Indeed, many of these prayer texts were fixed only after the destruction of the Second Temple, and even that took time. Moreover, like the qedush at the beginning of the meal, the content of this prayer, especially in the third part, could vary according to the festival by means of the insertion of embolisms (added material) at certain points in the prayer. A significant embolism in the passover form of the Birkat ha-Mazon is found in the *Seder Rav Amram Gaon:* "And may Elijah and the Messiah, the son of David come in our lifetime, and let the kingdom of the house of David return to its place."[11] In the time of Jesus it was expected that Elijah would appear before the advent of the Messiah. If Jesus had prayed such a prayer at the last supper, taking the final cup—the cup reserved for Elijah—would have been significant. In any event, it is certainly in connection with this final cup that Paul relates in 1 Corinthians 11:25,

---

[9] Louis Finkelstein, "The Birkat ha-Mazon," *Jewish Theological Quarterly*, n.s. 19 (1928–29), 211–62.

[10] Ibid., 219.

[11] *Seder R. Amram Gaon*, 147f.

> In the same way he took the cup also, after supper, saying, "This cup is the new covenant in my blood. Do this, as often as you drink it, in remembrance of me."

And also in connection with this cup it is reported in Mark 14:23–25,

> Then he took a cup, and after giving thanks he gave it to them, and all of them drank from it. He said to them, "This is my blood of the covenant, which is poured out for many. Truly I tell you, I will never again drink of the fruit of the vine until that day when I drink it new in the kingdom of God."

It should be noted that Mark and Matthew retained a distinction between the blessing *(eulogesas)* of the bread and the giving thanks *(eucharistesas)* over the cup at the end of the meal, thus preserving the distinction between two types of Jewish prayers: the simple berakah and the *berakoth* in a series that includes thanksgiving.[12] Paul, on the other hand (and the so-called long text of Luke 22:19b–20), by the adverb "likewise" or "in the same way," refers to Mark's and Matthew's mention of the thanksgiving over the bread as being over the cup as well. There is no doubt, however, that "the cup of blessing" is the source of the eucharistic chalice in the Christian tradition, and the prayer of thanksgiving said over it is the antecedent of the Christian eucharistic prayer.

❧ THE LORD'S SUPPER IN THE NEW TESTAMENT

On the night of his betrayal, Jesus celebrated a meal with his disciples. We have indicated the conflicting chronologies between the Synoptic and Fourth Gospels concerning whether this "last supper" was a Passover meal. The passover context is important for understanding the meaning of Jesus' death, even though the specific ingredients of the passover meal did not enter into Christian sacramental usage. Rather, Jesus focused on the broken loaf at the beginning of the meal and the shared cup of blessing at the end of the meal. He gave this bread and cup a profoundly new level of meaning by declaring, "This is my body. . . . This is my blood." After the meal Jesus went to his betrayal, arrest, trial, and execution. Thereafter, whenever his disciples celebrated this meal it would be, in Paul's view, a proclamation of "the Lord's death until he comes" (1 Cor. 11:26).

In the New Testament, there are four accounts of the institution of the Lord's Supper at this last supper: Mark 14:22–24; Matthew 26:26–29; Luke 22:17ff.; and 1 Corinthians 11:23–25. Joachim Jeremias has shown the influence of the developing Christian liturgy on the transmission of these gospel traditions.[13] This is seen already in the earliest recension of the institution narrative in 1 Corinthians, which Paul refers to as a "tradition" (11:2), in which he relates that "the Lord Jesus on the night when he was betrayed . . ." (11:23) celebrated a supper.

Paul adds the rubric, not found in Mark or Matthew, "Do this in remembrance of me" (11:24), over both the bread and the cup. If this was an original word from Jesus,

---

[12] See Thomas J. Talley, "The Eucharistic Prayers of the Ancient Church According to Recent Research: Results and Reflections," *Studia Liturgica* 11:3/4 (1976), 138–58.

[13] Joachim Jeremias, *The Eucharistic Words of Jesus*, trans. by Norman Perrin (Philadelphia: Fortress Press, 1977), 106ff.

Jeremias argues that the Palestinian background of such an expression as "Do this in remembrance of me" would suggest a reference to God. Thus, Jesus would be asking "that God remember me."[14] Why would Jesus ask God to remember him? Jeremias suggests that the rubric refers to the Passover embolism in the third part of the Birkat ha-Mazon: "And may Elijah and the Messiah, the son of David come in our lifetime." Jesus is asking God to remember the Messiah. As Jeremias puts it, "God remembers the Messiah in that he causes the kingdom to break in by the parousia."[15] Paul has interpreted this as reminding God of the unfulfilled climax of the work of salvation whenever the bread and cup are taken in remembrance of Jesus. They become a visible proclamation of the Lord's death until the parousia.

Paul is not alone in this eschatological interpretation of the anamnesis-commandment. In chapter ten of the *Didache,* the third part of the eucharistic prayer is a petition for eschatological fulfillment, and the prayer ends with verses that are completely directed toward the parousia, including the Aramaic word "maranatha" (Our Lord, come), which Paul himself utters in 1 Corinthians 16:22:

> May the Lord come and this world pass away.
> Amen.
> Hosanna to the house of David.
> If any one is holy, let him come; if any one is not, let him repent.
> Maranatha.
> Amen. (*Didache* 10:6)

Thus, the Lord's Supper is a memorial meal; but the memorial is directed toward the future as well as the past; it anticipates Jesus' parousia as well as remembering his death.

In Matthew and Mark the death of Jesus is interpreted as a redemptive sacrifice in which Jesus laid down his life out of love for his fellow human beings. Jesus speaks of his blood to be "poured out for many for the forgiveness of sins" (Matt. 26:28), and declares that he has come to give his life as "a ransom for many" (Mark 10:45). The early church, too, made sense of the suffering and death of Jesus by describing it as a sacrifice: "[O]ur paschal lamb, Christ, has been sacrificed" (1 Cor. 5:7). God bought the church "with the blood of his own Son" (Acts 20:28). The blood of the lamb clearly signifies a sacrifice, but even the metaphoric character of this language disappears in the stark and simple reference to Christ as one who "gave himself up for us, a fragrant offering and sacrifice to God" (Eph. 5:2).

In Matthew and Mark the words "this is my blood" are amplified by "the blood of the covenant." Covenant (*diatheke*) is not to be understood as "testament." The author of the Letter to the Hebrews connected the ideas of will and death and inheritance with covenant (Heb. 9:15ff.). In Hebrews the sacrifice of Christ is related to the sacrifices performed in the Temple under the provisions of the covenant. But in Matthew and Mark the "blood of the covenant" refers to the blood that sealed the covenant between Yahweh and Israel.[16]

---

[14] Ibid., 237ff.
[15] Ibid., 252.

The words "this is my blood of the covenant" were softened by Paul and in the long text in Luke to read: "This cup is the new covenant in my blood" (1 Cor. 11:25; Luke 22:20). The emphasis here becomes "covenant" rather than "blood." It is possible that the alteration of the formula (if we assume Mark and Matthew to be more original) was occasioned by the need to ward off Greek misunderstanding that the Lord's Supper was a Thyestian meal in which blood was drunk.[17]

In Luke this cup disappears, if we accept the authenticity of the short text. (Note that in the Revised Standard Version, the long text, Luke 22:19b–20, is placed in a footnote.) In spite of the fact that scholars of the reputation of Jeremias have thrown their support behind the long text,[18] the manuscript evidence is such that, in the words of Arthur Vööbus, "Quality . . . washes out quantity."[19] While the long text has the support of the Greek manuscripts, the short text is attested to in Codex Bezae, the Sirus Sinaiticus, and the old Latin Codex Vercellensis. The Old Syriac and Old Latin versions push the textual evidence back into the second century. So we must come to terms with the fact that Luke presented us with a eucharistic order in which the cup precedes the bread. This same order is in chapter 9 of the *Didache* and is comparable to the Jewish Sabbath meal. That both orders appear in 1 Corinthians 10 and 11 should alert us to the fact that the place of the cup in the eucharistic celebration was not always settled in the same way. In coming to terms with Luke's presentation of the Lord's Supper, what leaps to the eye in the short text is that a eucharistic word of Jesus is given only to the bread: "This is my body." What Jesus is saying in this logion is, "This is myself which I am giving to you." The bread becomes the vehicle of Jesus' presence. That presence is more important for Luke than the sacrifice or covenant motif associated with the eucharistic cup.

The presence of the risen Christ is again manifested in the Emmaus episode in Luke 24:28–35, in which two disciples recognized Jesus "in the breaking of the bread." One cannot miss the eucharistic allusion in v. 30, "When he was at the table with them, he took bread, blessed and broke it, and gave it to them." The post-resurrection meal fellowship was as important to the disciples, if not more so, as the meal fellowship they experienced with Jesus during his earthly ministry, of which the most significant meal was the last supper. As Norman Perrin has pointed out, this table fellowship after the resurrection "provided the focal point for the community life of the earliest Christians, and was the most direct link between that community life and the pre-Easter fellowship of Jesus and his disciples."[20] What the disciples, who failed to follow Jesus at the moment of the cross, experienced in this post-resurrection table fellowship was the forgiveness of sins, a power that Luther rightly associated with "life and salvation."

---

[16] See the article on *diatheke* in Gerhard Kittel, ed., *Theological Dictionary of the New Testament*, II, trans. by Geoffrey W. Bromiley (Grand Rapids: William B. Eerdmans Publishing Co., 1964), 106ff.

[17] See Gustav Dalman, *Jesus-Jeshua*, Eng. trans. (New York: KTAV, 1971), 161.

[18] Jeremias, 139ff.

[19] Vööbus, *The Prelude to the Lukan Passion Narrative*, 88.

[20] Norman Perrin, *Rediscovering the Teaching of Jesus* (New York: Harper and Row, 1967), 107.

Whenever the community assembled for "the breaking of bread," as this fellowship meal was called in Acts, its members experienced the presence of the Risen One who offers "forgiveness of sins" (Acts 10:34–43). How often did the Christian community assemble to participate in this meal? Does Acts 2:46 suggest that the disciples "day by day" attended the Temple *and* broke bread in their homes, or does "day by day" refer only to attendance at the Temple? One might infer a Sunday gathering is implied in Acts 20:7–12 and 1 Corinthians 16:2, and we note a parallelism between "the Lord's supper" and "the Lord's day" in 1 Corinthians 11:20 and Revelation 1:10.[21] The picture of Sunday as the day of celebration of the Lord's Supper does not clearly emerge until the second century, but as with most later traditions, some previous development must have contributed to it.

Distinguishing between the sacramental meal and the ordinary community meal would not have been important to the earliest generation of Christians. The Lord's Supper was clearly instituted within the context of an actual meal, whether this was the Passover meal or not. There is evidence to suggest that already in 1 Corinthians a distinction was being made between the eucharistic meal and the community meal. There the conflict at the Lord's Supper is revealed: "when you come together, it is not really to eat the Lord's supper. For when the time comes to eat, each of you goes ahead with your own supper" (1 Cor. 11:20–21). Gerd Theissen suggests that the idea of every person individually having his or her own meal should not be pressed, because some "have nothing." Rather, he suggests that the source of the conflict lies in the social customs of Greco-Roman society in which the well-to-do, who were the benefactors of the congregation's place of assembly and the meal, provided one fare for the ordinary members of the congregation and a richer fare for those members who were their social equals. This would have been socially acceptable, but in Paul's view it failed to distinguish between the "private meal" and the Lord's Supper that belonged equally to the whole community. In this way the celebration of the Lord's Supper accentuated social differences rather than the common bond of all the members in the body of Christ, and Paul's practical solution was to confine the private meal to private homes.[22] This interpretation suggests that as early as 56 C.E., at least in Gentile congregations like that at Corinth, the Lord's Supper was separated from an actual community meal (if Paul's solution was accepted). On the other hand, it is clear that the community meal served as the context for the eucharist at least until the end of the first century, as we see in the Jewish Christian church manual known as the *Didache*.

🍇 A First Century Celebration: The *Didache*

Reference has been made to the *Didache* several times in this chapter. The discovery of this church manual by Metropolitan Bryennios of Nicomedia in 1873 must rank as one of the most important discoveries in the area of early Christian literature. However, we should note that the *Didache* (Teaching of the Twelve) was known in the

---

[21] See Willy Rordorf, *Sunday*, trans. by A. A. K. Graham (Philadelphia: Westminster Press, 1968), 205–6.

[22] See Gerd Theissen, *The Social Setting of Pauline Christianity*, ed. and trans. by John H. Schütz (Philadelphia: Fortress Press, 1982), 145–74.

ancient church. It forms the basis of Book VII of the Syrian *Apostolic Constitutions* and is quoted in the *Euchologion* (Prayer Book) of Bishop Serapion of Thmuis in Egypt, both from the fourth century.

How old is the *Didache* is the oldest of a genre of literature known as "church order." Church orders cover such aspects of church life as initiation, worship, discipline, polity, charitable organization, and so forth. This is exactly what we have in the *Didache*. Chapters 1–6 comprise a catechetical handbook called "the two ways . . . of life and of death." This is followed by instructions concerning baptism (ch. 7), fasting (ch. 8), eucharist (chs. 9–10), apostles and prophets (ch. 11), hospitality (ch. 12), the material support of prophets (ch. 13), confession of sin and reconciliation (ch. 14), the election of bishops and deacons (ch. 15), and some final exhortations (ch. 16).

How old is the *Didache*? A *terminus ad quem* is not difficult to establish. The polity embedded in chapters 11 and 15 reflects a time when the charismatic ministries of apostles and prophets were still flourishing, but the church is also instructed to elect bishops and deacons whose ministry "is identical with that of the prophets and teachers."[23] If, as is widely held, the *Didache* originated in the vicinity of Antioch, then the letters of Bishop Ignatius of Antioch c. 110 C.E., which indicate his very high regard for the ministries of bishops, presbyters, and deacons, but do not mention the charismatic apostles and prophets, would date the *Didache* before the second century.

Where is the manual's place of origin? There is no question that the *Didache* is the church order of a Jewish Christian community. Such communities flourished in Palestine, Antioch in Syria, and Alexandria in Egypt. The *Didache* seems to make use of the Gospel of Matthew,[24] and all three places have been suggested by various commentators as the provenance of that Gospel. J. P. Audet[25] and Robert Grant[26] have followed the majority line of proposing Antioch as the most likely place of origin. But there are several facts supporting Alexandria as the place of origin: Clement of Alexandria included the *Didache* in a list of "sacred scripture";[27] Athanasius used it as a catechetical manual;[28] and there is a complete absence of any reference to Paul (for whom Antioch was the center of his missionary enterprise, whose letters were first collected in Antioch and were known by Bishop Ignatius). This makes Egypt an equally likely candidate as the *Didache's* place of origin.[29]

Questions of date and origin are not the only ones that have vexed commentators. There has been a reluctance to accept the meal in chapters 9 and 10 as the eucharist. Liturgiologists of the stature of Henri Leclerq,[30] Anton Baumstark,[31] and Gregory Dix[32]

---

[23] *Early Christian Fathers, The Library of Christian Classics*, I, 178.

[24] R. Glover, "The *Didache's* Quotations and the Synoptic Gospels," *New Testament Studies* 5 (1958–1959), 12ff. suggests the possibility that not the Gospel of Matthew but its sources were used.

[25] J.P. Audet, *La Didachè. Instructions des Apôtres* (Paris, 1958), 208ff.

[26] Robert M. Grant, *The Apostolic Fathers*, I (London, New York, Toronto, 1964), 74.

[27] Clement, *Stromata*, I, 20, 100.

[28] Athanasius, *Epistula* XXXIX.

[29] See Arthur Vööbus, *Liturgical Traditions in the Didache* (Stockholm: Estonian Theological Society in Exile, 1968), 14.

[30] H. Leclerq, "Didachè," in *Dictionnaire d'archéologie chrétienne et de liturgie* (Paris, 1924ff.), IV, col. 782ff.

[31] A. Baumstark, *Comparative Liturgy*, Eng. trans. (London, 1958), 46.

[32] Dix, *The Shape of the Liturgy*, 91.

have asserted that chapters 9 and 10 represent an *agape* (love) feast, while the eucharist proper is described in chapter 14. In chapter 14 we are told that the eucharist is celebrated on the Lord's Day, that it is preceded by a confession and reconciliation so that the sacrifice would be pure, and that it is presided over by bishops and deacons. It has been argued that the explicit details of this eucharist were not disclosed because the *disciplina arcani* (secret discipline) forbade the public disclosure of sacramental formulas. Audet has proposed that chapters 9 and 10 represented a "minor eucharist," such as a vigil, while chapter 14 represents a "major eucharist" on the Lord's Day, for which formularies are not provided.[33] The validity of this hypothesis depends on how early the celebration of baptism and the eucharist after an all-night vigil became commonplace (it is described in the *Apostolic Tradition* of Hippolytus at the beginning of the third century), and when the disciplina arcani was first practiced (since we have no evidence of it before the fourth century). Audet's theory suffers from a reluctance to accept the possibility that what we see in chapters 9 and 10 of the *Didache* really was the way this community celebrated the eucharist: in the context of an actual community meal, in part because of the lack of an institution text.

The *Didache* itself calls this meal a eucharist. The introduction to the prayers in chapter 9 says, "About the eucharist." And at the end of the first prayer there is a clause that refers to the eating and drinking "of your eucharist" (9:5). The first prayer in chapter 10 gives thanks for "the spiritual food and drink for eternal life through Jesus, your Servant" (10:2). An admission requirement is laid down in 9:5: "no one shall eat or drink of your eucharist except those baptized in the name of the Lord." Furthermore, portions of these prayers entered into the later eucharistic tradition in the *Apostolic Constitutions* VII, 25–26. The prayer in 9:4 is reproduced almost verbatim in the Anaphora of Serapion of Thmuis in fourth-century Egypt. The prayers in 9:2 and 4 appear in the eucharistic fragment known as the *Der Balizeh* fragment discovered in Egypt. Thus the ancient sources clearly considered these prayers to be eucharistic. Chapters 9 and 10 are as follows:

> [9:1]Now concerning the eucharist: this is how to give thanks: First in connection with the cup:
>
> [2]We give thanks to you, our Father, for the holy vine of David thy servant, which you have made known to us through Jesus your servant; to you be the glory for ever.
>
> [3]Then concerning the broken bread: We give thanks to you, our Father, for the life and knowledge which you have made known to us through Jesus thy servant; to you be glory for ever.
>
> [4]As this broken bread was scattered on the top of the mountains and gathered together became one, so let your Church be gathered together from the ends of the earth into your Kingdom: for the glory and the power is yours through Jesus Christ for ever.
>
> [5]You must not let anyone eat or drink your Eucharist except those baptized in the Lord's name. For in reference to this the Lord said, "Do not give what is sacred to dogs."

---

[33] Audet, 414.

^{10:1}After you have finished your meal, give thanks in this way:

²We give thanks to you, holy Father, for your holy Name, which you have made to dwell in our hearts, and for the knowledge and faith and immortality which you have made known to us through Jesus your servant. To you be glory for ever.

³Almighty Master, you have created all things for your Name's sake; food and drink you have given human beings for enjoyment, that they might give Thanks to you; but to us you have graciously given spiritual food and drink, and life eternal through your Servant.

⁴Before all things we give thanks to you because you are mighty. To you be glory for ever.

⁵Remember, O Lord, your Church to deliver it from all evil, and to perfect it in your love, and to gather it from the four winds, the hallowed one, into your Kingdom, which you have prepared for it. For the power and the glory is yours for ever.

⁶Let grace come and let this world pass away.
Hosanna to the house of David.
If you are holy, come forward; if you are not, repent.
Maranatha. Amen.

⁷In the case of prophets, however, you should let them give thanks as much as they will.

The prayers in chapter 9 unfold a pattern that we have already seen in the Jewish meal prayers called "qedush" (sanctification) and that are described in the Mishnah *Berakoth* tractate 6. The first prayers in the Mishnah and the *Didache* make reference to "the vine." In the Christian prayer "the fruit of the vine" becomes "the holy vine of David your servant" made known "through Jesus your servant."[34] In the second prayer, the bread of the Jewish prayer is not mentioned at all in the prayer text, only in the rubric. Thus, the visible object of the Jewish blessing, the gift of earthly produce, has been transformed into a thanksgiving for spiritual gifts. The third prayer in chapter 9 is based on a theme prominent in several Jewish prayers probably emanating from the time after the destruction of Jerusalem. Among them are the *Qibbus galuyoth* (Benediction 10) from the *Amidah* or *Tefillah* of the synagogue liturgy:

> Blow the great horn for our liberation, and lift a banner to gather our exiles.
> Blessed are you, O Lord, who gathers the dispersed of your people Israel.

Vööbus notes, however, that there are other Jewish prayers which express this same theme.[35] One is the *mussaf* prayer from the Liturgy of Expiation (*Yom Kippur*):

> Unite our dispersed from the midst of the nations, and gather our dispersion from the ends of the earth, and lead us back into Zion your city.

---

[34] The Greek term translated here as "servant" is *pais*, which could be more literally rendered "child."
[35] *Liturgical Material in the Didache*, 16ff.

Another is the blessing before the *Shema* in the synagogue liturgy:

> Let peace come over us from the four corners of the earth and cause us soon to
> go upright to our land, for you have chosen us from all peoples and tongues and
> hast brought us near unto thy great Name in love.

Chapter 10 of the *Didache* is modeled on the Jewish thanksgiving after meals,
the Birkat ha-Mazon, but rearranged and adapted to Christian use. The Jewish grace consisted of four benedictions, all of which are mentioned in the Babylonian Talmud, where
the first is ascribed to Moses, the second to Joshua, the third to David, and the fourth to
the rabbis of Jamnia. The fourth benediction was also said to have been added after the
fall of Bethel in 135 C.E., where Bar-Kohkba made his gallant stand. Since the Didachist
did not use the fourth benediction, it has been suggested that he did not know it. The
Jewish prayers may be compared to the prayers of the *Didache* as Louis Finkelstein has
done.[36] We see that the benedictions in the Jewish grace were rearranged by the
Didachist in the order II, I, and III. They were freely adapted to Christian use. In the
second benediction, "Thou hast caused us to inherit a goodly and pleasant land" becomes
in the *Didache* the holy Name dwelling in "our hearts"—doubtless with reference to the
shekinah (presence of God). The mention of the Torah suggests to the Didachist "life"
and "knowledge . . . made known to us through Jesus your servant." The prayer for
Jerusalem, the Temple, and its restoration in the third benediction becomes in the
Didache a prayer for the church that it may be delivered from evil.

The inversion of the first and second prayers has the effect of subordinating the
theme of creation to that of redemption.[37] We note this because a whole way of eucharistic praying will enter into the Western church via Hippolytus and the Roman canon that
begins with thanksgiving for redemption in Christ rather than the praise of God for the
creation. The result is that the theme of creation falls out of the Western eucharistic
prayer tradition entirely. In contrast, in the Antiochene-Byzantine tradition after the
fourth century, a type of eucharistic prayer evolved in which interest in expressing trinitarian theology had the effect of restoring the sequence of the Jewish thanksgiving: praise
of God for the work of creation, remembrance of God's work of salvation culminating in
the Christ-event, and supplication for the Holy Spirit to bring about the fruits of communion in the life of the church.

It has also been noted, and caused perplexity, that there is no accounting for the
institution narrative in the *Didache*. Louis Bouyer has proposed that the narrative could
have been used in the eucharistic celebration of the *Didache* as a *haggadah* (narrative)
outside of the context of the eucharistic prayer.[38] This hypothesis is attractive because of
the similarities between the Christian eucharistic meal described in the *Didache* and the

---

[36] Finkelstein, *art. cit.*, 215–6.

[37] See Thomas J. Talley, "The Eucharistic Prayer of the Ancient Church according to Recent Research: Results
and Reflections," *Studia Liturgica* 11 (1976), 138–58, which appeared in slightly expanded form as "From
Berakah to Eucharistein: A Reopening Question," *Worship* 50 (1976), 115–37.

[38] Louis Bouyer, *Eucharist*, trans. by Charles U. Quinn (Notre Dame, Ind.: University of Notre Dame Press,
1968), 157.

Jewish religious meal. Certainly the Jewish meal-celebrations combined narrative, material elements, blessings, and thanksgivings. There is reason to believe that the Christian tradition in some places developed the use of the narrative outside of the anaphora or eucharistic prayer. In the Syrian tradition, for example, there is the paschal homily of Melito of Sardis that shows resemblance to the Jewish Passover Haggadah. But this can only remain a hypothesis since textual evidence is nonexistent for such a haggadic use of the institution narrative. Louis Ligier suggests that the institution narrative could have come into the eucharistic celebration like the narrative embolisms inserted in the meal prayers on festival days.[39] This theory at least has the evidence of the institution narrative finding a place in the eucharistic prayer, beginning with the anaphora of Hippolytus. On the other hand, we shall see that an institution narrative was also lacking in the third-century East Syrian anaphora of Addai and Mari, which also retains traces of a Semitic culture. The fact is that eucharist, the very name preferred for the sacramental meal, after Paul's use of the term *Lord's Supper,* indicates the importance of thanksgiving—grateful acknowledgment of a gift—as the form in which bread and wine are taken and received as communion in the body and blood of Christ.

There is a problem with the text in 10:6. It seems to join an admonition with liturgical acclamations: "If you are holy, come forward; if you are not, repent. Maranatha. Amen." Hans Lietzmann understood this text to be an invitation to come to the Lord's table, and therefore felt that it was dislocated from its proper position before 9:5.[40] A simpler solution, which does not require doing violence to the text, is to see this not as a liturgical acclamation but as a general admonition. The compiler of the *Didache* has also done this in the instructions after the Lord's Prayer in 8:3.

What are we to make of the fact that the eucharist is discussed again in chapter 14?

> [14:1]On every Lord's Day—his special day—come together and break bread and give thanks, first confessing your sins so that your sacrifice may be pure. [2]Anyone at variance with his neighbor must not join you, until they are reconciled, lest your sacrifice be defiled. [3]For it was of this sacrifice that the Lord said, "Always and everywhere offer me a pure sacrifice; for I am a great King, says the Lord, and my name is marveled at by the nations."

It has been pointed out that the requirement for participation in the meal in chapters 9–10 is baptism, but the requirement in chapter 14 is confession of sins.[41] This distinction can be maintained only if one ignores that what is required in chapters 9 and 10 is holiness and repentance (*metanoia*). We shall see that Christian initiation in the ancient church was a process that facilitated a complete change of life. The eucharistic meal was the eschatological feast at which the sanctified ones gathered in fellowship. There was also a need to maintain the life of sanctification, for which there developed a ministry of

---

[39] See Louis Ligier, "The Origins of the Eucharistic Prayer: From Last Supper to Eucharist," *Studia Liturgica* 9 (1973), 111–85.

[40] Hans Lietzmann, *Mass and Lord's Supper*, Eng. trans. (Leiden, 1953ff.), 192.

[41] Leclerq, col. 782.

reconciliation. We do not know what forms and structures of confession and reconciliation existed in the church of the first century, but it probably had more to do with the process of reconciliation and church discipline described in Matthew 18 than with a liturgical act of confession, since structures of reconciliation continue to be delineated in the church orders while no prayers of confession are extant.

It has also been noted that the eucharist is called "sacrifice" (*thusia*) in chapter 14, but that this term is not mentioned in chapters 9–10.[42] The prayers in chapters 9–10 may have been collected by the compiler of the *Didache*, and would therefore be older than the *Didache* itself, while chapter 14 is commentary by the compiler. The concept of sacrifice here is related to the "pure offering" of the Gentiles in the messianic age as prophesied in Malachi 1:11, as quoted in 14:3. As such, this concept relates back to the confession of sins in 14:1 and reconciliation with one's neighbor in 14:2, and therefore probably denotes the self-offering of the church as a pure oblation when it participates in the eucharist. The church is a pure oblation when it is at peace with itself.

Finally, it has been noted that 10:7 allows the prophets to give thanks as much as they will, while chapter 14 is followed by a chapter that instructs the church to elect bishops and deacons.[43] Some have presumed that the meal in chapters 9–10 stands under the presidency of the prophets while the bishops preside over the eucharist in chapter 14. However, nothing is said about the bishops presiding at the celebration of the eucharist. We may presume that they normally did (since Ignatius of Antioch emphasizes this in his letters, c. 115), but that where prophets were visiting, they were accorded this honor. Thus, we may conclude that there is no dichotomy between the eucharist in chapters 9–10 and the eucharist referred to in chapter 14. On the whole, the thrust of chapter 14 concerns less the eucharist than the discipline of the community that is related to the integrity of the eucharistic fellowship. If any distinction is to be made at all between chapters 10 and 14, it concerns the fencing of the table. The ones in need of repentance in 10:6 are probably the unbaptized; the ones in need of confessing their sins in 14:1 are probably the faithful. Chapter 14, then, is concerned with maintaining the purity of the eucharistic fellowship.

❧ FROM SYNAGOGUE SERVICE TO SYNAXIS

The early Christians assembled not only to celebrate the eucharist. "When you assemble," wrote Paul to the Corinthians, "each has a hymn, a lesson, a revelation, a tongue, or an interpretation" (1 Cor. 14:26). Both Colossians 3:16–17 and Ephesians 5:18–20 speak of "psalms, hymns, and spiritual songs," indicating that chanting and singing were a normal part of Christian meetings. New Testament form critics have discerned a number of hymns embedded in the texts of New Testament books, among them: the Lukan canticles (Luke 1:46–55, known as the "Magnificat," or Song of Mary; Luke 1:68–79, known as the "Benedictus," or Song of Zechariah; and Luke 2:29–32, known as

---

[42] Dix, 91.
[43] Leclerq, col. 782.

the "Nunc dimittis," or Song of Simeon);[44] John 1:1–16;[45] Philippians 2:5–11;[46] Colossians 1:15–20;[47] as well as the many songs and acclamations in the book of Revelation.[48] Colossians 3:16 mentions also "instruction" and "admonition." While Christians would "admonish" and "encourage" one another (as in Rom. 15:14; 1 Cor. 14:31; 1 Thess. 4:18; 5:11, 14), this was also a function of local leaders who "labor," and "have charge of" and "admonish" (1 Thess. 5:12).

Historians of liturgy commonly assume that early Christian assemblies were patterned on the model of the Jewish synagogue. Wayne Meeks properly warns that "we must be careful, however, not to explain one unknown quantity in terms of another, equally unknown."[49] He points out that references to synagogue worship contemporary with early Christianity are found only in the New Testament and alluded to in the writings of Philo and Josephus. We can only vaguely ascribe the origins of the synagogue to the period of the Babylonian exile and the Diaspora, when Jews were not able to attend the Jerusalem temple and offer the Mosaic sacrifices.[50] Certainly the synagogue existed long before the beginning of Christian worship, and it provided a model for Christian worship. But information about synagogue worship contemporary with the New Testament and early Christianity is sketchy at best, and the Gospel according to Matthew indicates an overt hostility between the Jewish synagogue and the Christian congregation.

Nevertheless, the shape and content of the synagogue liturgy of the early common era can be pieced together from information in the Mishnah. This book from the second century codified Jewish law as it had been discussed among the rabbis of Palestine during the period of relative peace and tranquillity 70–130 C.E. (between the destruction of Jerusalem, the Temple and its sacrificial cult, and the outbreak of the Bar-Kokhba rebellion), and thus reflects practices that are antecedent to the time when the oral tradition was written down.

The basic form of the synagogue liturgy as it emerged in the common era is as follows:

1. Invocation. "Bless the Lord who is to be blessed."
2. The *Shema Israel* ("Hear, O Israel") and its Blessings. The Shema, composed of Deuteronomy 6:4–9, 11:13–21 and Numbers 15:37–41, was the basic Jewish confession of faith. There are indications that it could have emerged during Maccabean times.[51] Two berakoth (blessings) accompany

---

[44] See Raymond E. Brown, *The Birth of the Messiah* (New York, 1977), 346–66.

[45] See Rudolf Schnackenburg, *The Gospel According to St. John*, I (London, 1968/New York, 1980), 229–30.

[46] See R. P. Martin, *Carmen Christi* (Cambridge, 1967; 2nd ed. Grand Rapids: Wm B. Eerdmans, 1983).

[47] See the bibliography in W. G. Kummel, *Introduction to the New Testament* (London, 1966/Nashville: Abingdon, 1975), 343.

[48] See E. Cothenet, "Earthly Liturgy and Heavenly Liturgy According to the Book of Revelation," in *Roles in the Liturgical Assembly*, Papers of the Twenty-Third Saint Serge Liturgical Conference, trans. by Matthew J. O'Connell (New York: Pueblo Publishing Company, 1981), 115–35.

[49] Wayne A. Meeks, *The First Urban Christians. The Social World of the Apostle Paul* (New Haven and London: Yale University Press, 1983), 146.

[50] See H. H. Rowley, *Worship in Ancient Israel: Its Forms and Meaning* (Philadelphia: Fortress Press, 1967), 213ff.

[51] See W. F. Albright, "A Biblical Fragment of the Maccabean Age: The Nash Papyrus," *Journal of Biblical Literature* 56 (1937), 145–76.

the recitation of the Shema at both morning and evening services. The first one, "Ma'ariv aravim" (who brings on the light), deals with the theme of light and darkness (because the services were held at sunset or sunrise). It praises the creator who orders the times and seasons. The second blessing, "Ahavat 'olam" (With abiding love [have you loved your people Israel]), praises God for the gift of the Torah as the tangible token of God's abiding love for Israel, and leads to the recitation of the scriptural texts that immediately follow. C. W. Dugmore adduces evidence that the Decalogue was recited before the Shema during the first century.[52] The blessing immediately following the scriptural recitation, "Emet ve'emunah" (True and trustworthy [are God's words and promises]), begins by acknowledging the truth and reliability of the divine words and concludes by recalling Yahweh's paradigmatic redemption of Israel from bondage in Egypt and anticipating Israel's ultimate redemption. A fourth blessing, "Hashkivenu" (Cause us to lie down in peace), is said in the evening to petition God's protection through the night.

3. The Eighteen Benedictions (*Shemoneh Esreh*), also known as the Amidah (Standing Prayer) or simply Tefillah (The Prayer). This series of berakoth probably grew out of the Ma'amad service, in which members of the community gathered for prayer and study, while their representatives were taking their turn in priestly service offering sacrifices in the Jerusalem temple. As a consequence, these prayers came to acquire the meaning of spiritual sacrifices. The first three blessings are called "praises," and the last three are called "thanksgivings." The petitions in between were originally variable and remained fluid for a long time. They have a supplicatory character. It became customary to omit the supplicatory petitions on the Sabbath as inappropriate (God must also have a day of rest). On the Sabbath, they are replaced by a single blessing dealing with the sanctification of the Sabbath (*Qedushat hayyom*). The invariable first three petitions of Tefillah are *Avot*, invoking the memory of the ancestors; *Gevurot*, invoking God's power to restore life; *Qedushat hashem*, invoking God's holiness; the last three petitions are '*Avodah*, a petition for the acceptance of prayer; *Hoda'ah*, a thanksgiving that acknowledges God's bounties; and *Shalom*, a prayer for peace. Dugmore provides the texts of the Palestinian '*Amidah*, compares them with a modern version, and suggests dates for the origins of these petitions.[53] Of special interest is the Palestinian text of the twelfth blessing (*Birkat ha-Minim*, dated 90–117 C.E.), written so that Christians and Gnostics could not recite it: "For apostates let there be no hope . . . ; and let Christians and heretics perish as in a moment, let them be blotted out of the book of the living and let them not be written with the righteous."[54] While this prayer was later softened and the specific references to Christians eliminated, it does reflect the definitive break between Christianity and Judaism brought about by the excommunication of Christians from the synagogues sometime after c. 90 C.E.

4. The priestly blessing (Num. 6:24–26). According to the Mishnah, the pronouncing of the Aaronic Benediction over the people originated in the Temple in connection with the daily sacrifices (*Tamid* 7:2). In the synagogue

---

[52] C. W. Dugmore, *The Influence of the Synagogue Upon the Divine Office* (Westminster, England: Faith Press, 1964), 21.

[53] See the appendix in ibid., 114ff.

[54] Ibid., 119–20.

it was given after the Tefillah but before the readings. This suggests that the Great Prayer and the Aaronic Benediction were viewed as a single liturgical unit, and that the Prayer was regarded as a substitute for the material sacrifices—a sacrifice of prayer and praise offered by the people.

5. Readings from the Torah and the Prophets. On Sabbaths and holy days, readings were added to the prayers. The principal reading was from the Torah, or "Instruction" (the Five Books of Moses). There were also readings from the Torah on Mondays and Thursdays. The Babylonian Talmud (completed c. 500–600) required reading through the Five Books of Moses continuously in one year, except on festivals that had prescribed pericopes. The earlier Palestinian Talmud (compiled by c. 400) was different; scholarly opinion held that it specified a three-year lectionary cycle.[55] There were readings from the Prophets (*Haftorah*) at least on the Sabbath, although how pericopes from the Prophets related to the Torah remains a mystery.

6. Homily given by the resident or visiting rabbis.

7. Psalms, which were originally part of the temple liturgy. They are sung at the beginning of the synagogue service and between readings. But how early psalmody secured a place in the synagogue service is uncertain. Both church and synagogue had to adopt the canonical psalter from the temple liturgies.

8. Since the thirteenth century C.E., every synagogue service has concluded with "Alenu leshabeah" (We must praise [the Ruler of all]), a prayer originating in the Rosh Hashanah (New Year) liturgy that anticipates God's rulership over the whole creation and petitions the speedy coming of God's eschatological reign. This prayer is followed by the *Qaddish*, recited by mourners.

At the heart of synagogue worship on Sabbaths and festivals was the reading of sacred scripture. This is what made the synagogue liturgy different on these days from others. Indeed, the synagogue was first a school for the study of scriptures before it became a place of worship, and its spiritual leader was a teacher (rabbi) rather than a priest. It is likely that the reading of certain writings in the synagogue had a profound influence on the development of the canon of Hebrew scriptures, called "the Old Testament" by Christians. That the Old Testament writings were also read in the early Christian assemblies is suggested by the numerous references to Old Testament texts and stories in the letters of Paul. Public reading of scripture is mentioned explicitly in 1 Timothy 4:13; that this scripture refers to the Old Testament is shown unequivocally in 2 Timothy 3:15f. Ferdinand Hahn also makes some interesting suggestions about the liturgical influence on the New Testament canon.[56] This includes not only the factor of authoritative weight accruing to writings read in the assemblies, but also the composition of certain New Testament texts for use in the liturgy before they were incorporated into the Gospels. For example, a written passion narrative may have existed even before it was included in Mark's Gospel, presumably to be read at annual paschal observances.

---

[55] This theory was first advanced by Adolph Büchler, "The Reading of the Law and the Prophets in a Triennial Cycle," *Jewish Quarterly Review* 5 (1893), 420–68; 6 (1894), 1–73.

[56] Ferdinand Hahn, *The Worship of the Early Church*, trans. by David E. Green, with an introduction by John Reumann (Philadelphia: Fortress Press, 1973), 92ff.

The influence of liturgical use can be seen in many instances in Matthew's Gospel (e.g., the Lord's Prayer). Liturgical responses, prayer formulas, and hymn fragments are cited profusely throughout the Pauline and deutero-Pauline letters and the Revelation of John the Seer. So one thing that is common both to Jewish and to Christian experience is that liturgy is "the cradle of scripture." Further discussion of this comes in a section about the mid-second-century *Apology* of Justin Martyr.

Just as the reading of scripture occupied a central place in synagogue and early Christian liturgy, so did the exposition and application of the readings. Evidence for this form of "teaching" in the synagogue is seen in the example of Jesus in the synagogue at Nazareth (Luke 4:16ff.). He was invited to read from the scroll of Isaiah and then took the teaching position of sitting in the chair to give an exposition of this text. His comment that "today this has been fulfilled in your hearing" suggests a christological interpretation of Old Testament texts in Christian preaching. While we have no reference to preaching as such in Christian worship before the witness of Justin Martyr, a number of ancient Christian writings are regarded as homilies, including 1 Peter and 2 Clement.

It would be pressing parallels too far to see verbal similarities between prayers of the synagogue liturgy and Christian prayers. In fact, the prayers of the Eighteen Benedictions come from different periods—some even from the Common Era.[57] But there are certainly parallels between the subjects of prayer. The directive in 1 Timothy 2:1–2 that "supplications, prayers, intercessions, and thanksgivings be made for everyone; for kings and all who are in high positions," and the prayers for kings and rulers that Polycarp urged Christians to offer, was an established Jewish practice. 1 Maccabees 7:33 indicates that sacrifices had been offered for foreign rulers; and the cessation of this offering in 66 C.E. was, as Josephus observed, tantamount to a declaration of war.[58] The rabbis also taught that a man is duty bound to offer a blessing for his enemies as well as his friends. The Mishnah states that "man is bound to bless [God] for the evil even as he blesses [God] for the good."[59]

The use of psalms and hymns was taken over into Christian assemblies (Col. 3:16; Eph. 5:19). Once again, there is no explicit reference to singing psalms in early Christian literature, but the psalms are frequently quoted, and by the time of Tertullian (c. 200 C.E.) the custom was established of intercalating refrains or antiphons in the course of the psalms, to be sung by the whole congregation after each verse or pair of verses, probably sung by a cantor.[60] Noncanonical songs were certainly being composed in the Jewish community and used in some way in corporate devotion.

Synagogue etiquette was also enjoined on Christians. The men and women were separated; and the men were to be bareheaded while the women were to have their heads veiled (1 Cor. 11:6–7). The posture for prayer was standing (Phil. 1:27; Eph. 6:14;

---

[57] See Dugmore, 114ff.

[58] See G. F. Moore, *Judaism*, II (Cambridge: Cambridge University Press, 1927–1930), 115.

[59] *Berakoth* tractate 9:5; Danby, 10. This stands in contrast with the malediction against Christians and heretics inserted in the Amidah about 90 C.E. See Dugmore, 121. Words in brackets are the translator's.

[60] Tertullian, *De oratione* [Concerning Prayer], 27; P.L. 1:1194.

1 Tim. 2:8). Tertullian also testifies that Christians stood for prayer on the Lord's Day and festivals.[61]

The times of gathering in the synagogue were morning, afternoon, and evening. The Sabbath morning service was simply an expansion of the daily morning service. The *Didache* perhaps reflects this custom in its instruction that Christians recite the Lord's Prayer three times a day (8:3). Tertullian also recommended prayer at the third, sixth, and ninth hours of the day,[62] although these hours do not correspond the times of prayer in the synagogue, and Tertullian specifies that these are in addition to the gatherings for prayer at the beginning and end of the day. The prayer offices, as they developed in the church, owe little to the synagogue liturgy as such. Indeed, from the fourth century on the fathers compare morning and evening prayer to the morning and evening sacrifices of the Temple. The liturgical use of the psalter also derives from the Temple. We may assume that the use of certain psalms at certain times of prayer was also inspired by the Temple. From the earliest texts and on through the patristic tradition, Psalm 63 was the principal psalm at Matins and Psalm 141 was the principal psalm at Vespers. To these could be added the *Hallel* (Praise the Lord) psalms at Matins: 148, 149, 150; and the candlelight psalms at Vespers: 15, 142, 132, 130. Supplicatory prayer also formed a basic ingredient of morning and evening prayer in the church, and this may have been inspired by Tefillah.

Dugmore has proposed the hypothesis that the synagogue services inspired the daily prayer services of the church; and that as the Sabbath morning service in the synagogue was only an extension of the daily morning service (with the addition of the readings), so Matins and Vespers formed the first part of the eucharist on the days of its celebration, but were independent offices on other days. But the office to which the eucharistic meal was joined, already in the second century, was the liturgy of the word. The office of the word has a character entirely different from that of the prayer offices: it is instructional rather than devotional; it is dominated by readings from scripture and preaching rather than psalms and supplications.

The liturgy of the word has also been called the liturgy of the catechumens, to distinguish it from the liturgy of the faithful (the eucharistic meal) because its synagogal features were well suited to the task of instruction. There is evidence that in Alexandria, Egypt, where a renowned catechetical school developed, the liturgy of the word or Proanaphora was celebrated daily. Origen speaks of the catechumens attending "daily to the hearing of the Law of God."[63] The Law and the Gospels were read by readers or lectors who held an esteemed office in the ancient church. The readings were read from a desk called a *pulpitum*, which Cyprian of Carthage described as "the tribunal of the church."[64] Also called an *ambo*, this desk was located in the center of the worship space on a platform called a *bema*, which was like the *almemar* of the synagogue.

---

[61] Ibid., 10; P.L. 1:1165.

[62] Ibid., 23; P.L. 1:1299.

[63] Origen, *Homily on Jesus' Nativity* 4:1; P.G. 12:843.

[64] Cyprian, *Epistle* 34:4; P.L. 4:331.

There was some influence of synagogal architecture on the spatial plan of early Christian churches. But in the private houses that were often used for worship, an interesting transformation took place. Synagogues often had adjacent rooms, which could be used for the celebration of the *Qedush*, or sacred meal, by a rabbi and his disciples (*chaburah*) or by a pious family. The earliest Christian church buildings excavated in Syria in the third century, which are not just converted private residences, show all the features of the Jewish synagogue: the ark containing the sacred books, with its veil; the *menorah*, or seven-branched candlestick; the ambo on the bema in the middle of the assembly; and the "chair of Moses," now occupied by the bishop, surrounded by his presbyters or elders in the apse. But in the middle of the apse is the table for the Lord's Supper, moved from an adjoining room to the focal center of the hall. The private or domestic meal has become the focal point of the liturgical gathering.

✤ THE UNIFIED LITURGY OF WORD AND MEAL

In the New Testament and post-apostolic literature, we find many references to liturgical forms and practices, but no coherent overview of a complete liturgy. One of the earliest complete descriptions of Christian worship comes not even from a Christian source, but from a Roman governor—Pliny the Younger, Governor of Bithynia and Pontus, who reported in a letter dated c. 111–112 to the Emperor Trajan his dealings with Christians. The information is admittedly relayed secondhand from lapsed Christians who had been taken prisoner; and therefore it is sketchy at best. But Pliny informed Trajan that these informants

> assured me that their fault or their error amounted only to this, that they regularly on a fixed day (*stato die*) came together before light to sing antiphonally a song to Christ as to a god (*carmen . . . Christo quasi deo*) and to bind themselves by an oath (*sacramento*) not for any criminal purpose, but to abstain from theft, brigandage, adultery, breach of faith and misappropriation of trust. With this complete, it had been their custom to separate, and to meet again to take food—but quite ordinary, harmless food; and even this, they said, they had given up after my edict, by which in accordance with your commands I had forbidden the existence of clubs.[65]

What can be gleaned from this source is that Christians in Asia Minor met before dawn for a service that included singing and possibly for the recitation of the Law (Ten Commandments) and prayer—in other words, a Christian synagogue service—and then came together for an evening meal. But the objection of the Roman government to evening meetings of "clubs" and "associations" had caused them to abandon their evening gathering. The prohibition on evening meetings may have led Christians to include the eucharistic meal—shorn of its context in an actual meal—in the morning gathering or *synaxis*, in which only the bread and cup of wine mixed with water remained of the meal. In any event, a unified morning service of word and meal is what Justin Martyr reports to the Emperor Antonius Pius and Senate of Rome in his *First Apology* (c. 150).

---

[65] Pliny, *Epistle* X, 96; trans. by J. Stevenson in *A New Eusebius* (London: S.P.C.K., 1968), 14.

Justin actually provides two descriptions of Christian worship. We cannot be sure whether he is reporting the actual usage of the Roman church or just giving a generic description of Christian worship. In chapter 65 he portrays the celebration of baptism that culminates in the celebration of the eucharist. Following the baptism, the neophytes are led into the assembly of the brethren where common prayers are offered for "the one who has been illuminated and all others everywhere."

> On finishing the prayers we greet each other with a kiss. Then bread and a cup of water and mixed wine are brought to the president of the brethren and he, taking them, sends up praise and glory to the Father of the universe through the name of the Son and of the Holy Spirit, and offers thanksgiving at some length that we have been deemed worthy to receive these things from him. When he has finished the prayers and the thanksgiving, the whole congregation present assents, saying, "Amen." "Amen" in the Hebrew language means, "So be it." When the president has given thanks and the whole congregation has assented, those whom we call deacons give to each of those present a portion of the consecrated [literally, "eucharistized"] bread and wine and water, and they take it to the absent.[66]

A description of the Christian understanding of the eucharist follows in chapter 66, including the words of institution quoted from the Gospels. The very fact that Justin relays this information to the Roman authorities, freely and without coercion, casts doubt on the existence at this early date of a disciplina arcani (secret discipline) that forbade the disclosure of sacred texts.

In chapter 67 Justin provides a description of a normal Sunday morning *synaxis* that makes reference to a liturgy of the word, which is lacking in the description of the baptismal eucharist in chapter 65.

> There is a meeting in one place of those who live in the cities or the country, and the memoirs of the apostles or the writings of the prophets are read as long as time permits. When the reader has finished, the president in a discourse urges and invites [us] to the imitation of these noble things.[67]

Justin mentions the reading of the writings (*syngrammata*) of the prophets. There has been much discussion about the influence of the Jewish method of reading the scriptures in the synagogue on Christian practice. This involved a *lectio continua* (continuous reading) of the Torah, interrupted by pericopes for festivals, and specific pericopes from the writings of the prophets to correlate with the Torah readings. Unfortunately, there is no documentary evidence to show that Jewish lectionaries (in whatever state of development they may have been in at the time) had any bearing on the practice of reading scripture in Christian liturgy.

Justin also witnesses to the "memoirs of the apostles" (*apomnemoneumata ton apostolon*) being read in the Sunday assemblies. These are identified in chapter 66 as the Gospels, from which he immediately quotes the eucharistic institution narrative. During the second century, the Gospels were being accepted as sacred scripture and were read in

---

[66] *First Apology of Justin Martyr*, in *The Library of Christian Classics*, I. *Early Christian Fathers*, 285–6.
[67] Ibid., 287.

the Christian assemblies. Toward the end of the century (c. 185) Irenaeus of Lyons argued for the acceptance of four canonical Gospels in *Against the Heresies* III, 11:8. Among the heresies, Marcion accepted only a mutilated form of the Gospel of Luke; the Ebionites used only Matthew; the Montanists did not accept the Gospel of John or the epistles of Paul; and Irenaeus said that the Valentinians "possess more gospels than there are" (III, 11:9). We may also assume the reading of epistles under the category of "the memoirs of the apostles." 1 Thessalonians 5:27 and 1 Corinthians 16:20–23 indicate that Paul expected his letters to be read in the eucharistic assembly. Colossians 4:16 directs the exchange of letters among congregations.

The juxtaposition of the prophets and apostles suggest a hermeneutic for Christian preaching, to which Justin also testifies. The prophetic promises and the apostolic tradition of the Christ are brought together in one sweep that does not see an either/or between the Old and the New Testaments.

Following the readings and sermon, Justin states that "bread is brought, and wine mixed with water, and the president similarly sends up prayers and thanksgivings to the best of his ability." Justin does not comment on the content of the thanksgiving, which obviously an *ex tempore* prayer, in his *Apology*. However, in his *Dialogue with Trypho* 41:1ff. he indicates that the presider gives thanks to God through the eucharistic bread "for creating the world and all that is in it for humanity's sake, for delivering us from the evil in which we were born and for fully destroying the Dominions and Powers through him who according to his will undertook to suffer." In this dialogue with a Jew, Justin not only speaks of the eucharist as the fulfillment of the prophecy of Malachi concerning the "pure offering" of the Gentiles (Mal. 1:11); he also calls the eucharist a sacrifice (thusia) (*Dialogue* 41:3; 117:1).

A few decades later Irenaeus of Lyons developed some of these same eucharistic themes in *Against the Heresies*, except that they were colored by his polemics against the Gnostics and their devaluation of the material creation. So, while Justin speaks of "bringing bread and a cup of wine mixed with water" to the president of the feast, Irenaeus speaks of Christ's instruction to his disciples

> to offer up to God the firstlings of all creation, not because he needs these things, but that they themselves may not appear barren and ungrateful. Therefore he took the bread (which comes from his creation) and gave thanks and said: This is my body; and in like manner he spoke of the chalice . . . as his blood and so taught the new sacrifice of the new covenant, that sacrifice which the Church has received from the apostles and which she offers to God throughout the world (IV:17, 5).

Later in this treatise Irenaeus also castigates the Ebionites who "reject the mixture of the heavenly wine, and wish to be only the water of the world, not receiving God into their mixture, but remaining in that Adam who was conquered and driven out of paradise" (V:1, 3). Many of the Gnostics would not use wine in the eucharist, and Irenaeus here argues that by not following the dominical institution and taking a cup of wine they do not "receive God into their mixture;" that is, they have no sacrament of the new covenant. (The reason for mixing wine with water was to follow common custom in

Greco-Roman society of diluting strong wine for what we would call "social drinking.") However, in this emphasis on offering the bread and wine as "the firstlings of all creation," Irenaeus has signified a shift in the name of the sacrament from "Eucharistia" to "Oblatio." The new emphasis on offering the natural gifts of bread and wine developed into a ceremonial presentation of the church's oblation to God, and so gave a stronger expression to the sacrificial element that was at the center of the eucharist.[68] Nevertheless, the oblation is still interpreted in terms of the fulfillment of the "pure offering" prophesied in Malachi 1:11. Thus Irenaeus states that "the sacrifice does not hallow the man, for God does not require sacrifice, but the conscience of the offerer, if it is pure, hallows the sacrifice and effects God's accepting it as from a friend" (IV:18, 3). We "show ourselves grateful to God our Creator" when we offer our sacrifice "in purity of mind, in faith without delusion, in steadfast hope, in ardent love" (18:4). Gifts offered to God in such a state of purity are returned to us by God with God's benefits (18:6).

Again, as in chapter 65, Justin states in chapter 67 that "the distribution, and reception of the consecrated [elements] by each one, takes place and they are sent to the absent by the deacons." The social ministry of the congregation also found expression in the liturgical gathering.

> Those who prosper, and who so wish, contribute, each one as much as he chooses to. What is collected is deposited with the president, and he takes care of orphans and widows, and those who are in want on account of sickness or any other cause, and those who are in bonds, and the strangers who are sojourners among us, and, briefly, he is the protector of all those in need. We all hold this common gathering on Sunday, since it is the first day, on which God transforming darkness and matter made the universe, and Jesus Christ our Saviour rose from the dead on the same day.[69]

There is a "shape of the liturgy" discerned in the two descriptions of Christian liturgy outlined in Justin's report, which has remained intact throughout the history of liturgy. It is:

gathering
readings
preaching
intercessory prayers
kiss of peace
presentation of bread and wine
great thanksgiving
distribution and reception of eucharistic gifts
extended distribution to the absent

We also notice a differentiation of liturgical roles that became standard in the tradition. The readings are read by a lector. The president (probably the bishop, but now referred

---

[68] See Joseph A. Jungmann, S.J., *The Mass of the Roman Rite: Its Origins and Development* (originally *Missarum Sollemnia*), trans. by Francis A. Brunner, C.S.S.R. (Westminster, Md.: Christian Classics, Inc., 1986), I, 26f.; II, 1ff.

[69] *First Apology of Justin Martyr*, in *Early Christian Fathers*, 287.

to by his liturgical function) preaches the homily and offers the eucharistic prayer. This is the only place where the minister of the word and the sacrament is called a "president" in early Christian literature. We cannot know whether this was a customary designation of the liturgical minister or a term Justin deliberately chose because it would be intelligible to his pagan readers. The congregation's role is to assent to the prayers with its "Amens" and to contribute offerings. The deacons administer the sacrament and take it to those who are absent. Thus we see in the testimony of Justin Martyr a fact that will recur in other sources as well: that the diversity of ministers exercising particular roles in and for the assembly was an important fact of life for the early church, and one that the modern liturgical movement has sought to recover. It fostered the sense of the liturgy as the work of the people.[70]

🍇 THE EUCHARISTIC PRAYER

The only words in the liturgy that articulate the meaning of the eucharistic meal, according to the witness of Justin Martyr, are those uttered by the presiding minister as he "sends up prayers and thanksgivings to the best of his ability." The eucharistic prayer had to express the meaning of the Lord's Supper, and Justin is clear that this was the president's prayer. There are no eucharistic formularies before the third century other than the meal graces in the *Didache*. Probably the oldest eucharistic prayer text is that provided by Hippolytus of Rome, in the *Apostolic Tradition*, c. 215.

The *Apostolic Tradition* is probably the most important document on the life and practice of the early church to have survived from the early centuries of Christianity. It is a complete manual for church life, including prayers for ordination and descriptions of the ordering of ministries; a detailed portrayal of the processes and rites of Christian initiation; and miscellaneous church observances ranging from the agape meal to daily prayer. This work survived anonymously in Latin, Coptic, Arabic, and Ethiopic versions, and in the nineteenth century was called *The Egyptian Church Order*. E. Schwartz (1910) and R. H. Connolly (1916) identified it as the work of Hippolytus, a Roman presbyter who was generally conservative and critical of church practices in Rome, and even went into schism with the bishop of Rome, Pope Callixtus, although both Callixtus and Hippolytus died as martyrs in the salt mines of Sardinia.

In this light we can see that the *Apostolic Tradition* was an unsolicited work, probably written on the occasion of the ordination of a new bishop as a way of offering advice. It purports to represent "the tradition which has remained until now." This very self-description of the work means that we must be cautious about saying that it was "written" by Hippolytus; some of it undoubtedly was, but some texts may have existed before the time of Hippolytus's codification. The eucharistic prayer is a model prayer included in the description of an ordination of a bishop as a sample of how the bishop should offer the Great Thanksgiving.

---

[70] See several papers in *Roles in the Liturgical Assembly*, op. cit. Also: *Liturgy: We Proclaim* (The Liturgical Conference, 1993).

The Canon of Hippolytus

Some scholars have regarded the so-called Canon or eucharistic prayer of Hippolytus as the earliest example of the Roman canon. This is unlikely since only the preface dialogue and concluding doxology are the same between the two prayers. The following text is provided by Gregory Dix in his edition. It is a reconstruction from a number of textual materials. This translation follows the Latin version.[71]

Bishop: The Lord be with you.
People: And with your spirit.
Bishop: Lift up your hearts.
People: We have them with the Lord.
Bishop: Let us give thanks unto the Lord.
People: It is meet and right.
Bishop: We render thanks unto you, O God, through your beloved
    child Jesus Christ, whom in the last times you did sent to us [to
    be] a Savior and Redeemer and the Angel of your counsel; who is
    your Word inseparable [from you] through whom you made all
    things and in whom you were well pleased; [whom] you did send
    from heaven into [the] Virgin's womb and who conceived within
    her was made flesh and demonstrated to be your Son being born
    of the Holy Spirit and a virgin; who fulfilling your will and
    preparing for you a holy people stretched forth his hands for
    suffering that he might release from suffering them who have
    believed in you.
Who when he was betrayed to voluntary suffering
    that he might abolish death
    and rend the bonds of the devil
    and tread down hell
    and enlighten the righteous
    and establish the limit
    and demonstrate the resurrection:
Taking bread [and] making eucharist [i.e., giving thanks] to you said:
    Take, eat; this is my Body which is broken for you [for the
    remission of sins]. Likewise also the cup, saying: This is my Blood
    which is shed for you.
When you do this [you] do my "anamnesis."
Doing therefore the anamnesis of his death and resurrection
    we offer to you the bread and the cup
    making eucharist to you
    because you have made us worthy to stand before you
    and minister as priests to you.
And we pray that you would send your Holy Spirit upon the oblation
    of your holy church [and] would grant to all [your saints]
    who partake to be united [to you] [Latin text: to gather and unite
    all who receive it] that they may be fulfilled with the Holy Spirit
    for the confirmation of [their] faith in truth.

---

[71] *The Treatise on the Apostolic Tradition of St. Hippolytus of Rome* (London, 1937; reprinted S.P.C.K., 1968), 6–9; alt. Words in brackets are the translator's.

> That we may praise and glorify you through your[beloved] child
>> Jesus Christ through Whom glory and honor [be] unto you
>> with the Holy Spirit in your Holy Church now and forever and
>> world without end. Amen.

The primitive character of this prayer is seen not only in the angel christology in which Christ is seen as a "messenger of the Father" as well as the *Logos* proclaimed in the Fourth Gospel; but also in the lack of two features that became standard in later anaphoras or eucharistic prayers: the Sanctus and the intercessions and commemorations of the saints.[72] The content of this prayer reflects the tradition of the apostolic preaching (*kerygma*)—the same events that found a place in the later Apostles' Creed (an embryonic form of which Hippolytus includes in his description of baptism). Like the meal grace in chapter 10 of the *Didache,* this prayer begins with thanksgiving for redemption in Christ, but in a narrative recital that culminates in a narrative of the institution of the Lord's Supper. This is the first time an institution narrative has been included in a eucharistic prayer. In fact, it is the first indication of the use of the institution narrative within the eucharistic rite. The narrative in this prayer serves a pivotal purpose: first, it provides the motive for the thanksgiving, and secondly, it serves as a bridge to the second part of the prayer, which begins with the anamnesis.

Anamnesis has become a technical term. Dix has translated *Memores* as "doing the anamnesis or memorial." It is done when the bread and cup are taken in remembrance of Christ's death and resurrection and offered in an act of thanksgiving. This is the first coupling of anamnesis and oblation in the eucharistic tradition: "Memores . . . offerimus" (Remembering . . . we offer). But the memorial is the content and the motivation for the thanksgiving, and the oblation is still linked with the thanksgiving. The oblation passes immediately to an *epiclesis* (calling down) of the Holy Spirit on the gifts of the church, the bread and cup—although in this early text there is no suggestion that the consecration is associated with either the institution narrative or the epiclesis. Rather, the communicants receive the fruits of Holy Communion through the operation of the Holy Spirit: unity with God, being filled with the Spirit of Christ, and being confirmed in true faith.

It is ironic that the eucharistic prayer drafted by the schismatic Hippolytus should have become an ecumenical text in the twentieth century. The anaphora of Hippolytus has served as the basis of Eucharistic Prayer II in the reformed Roman Catholic Mass after the Second Vatican Council and as an influence on Eucharistic Prayers A and B in Rite II of *The Book of Common Prayer* of the Episcopal Church (1976, 1979). A translation of the anaphora of Hippolytus was provided in the *Worship Supplement* of the Lutheran Church—Missouri Synod (1969), and a fresh translation by Gordon Lathrop has been provided as Great Thanksgiving IV in *Lutheran Book of*

---

[72] Among several uses of the anaphora of Hippolytus in contemporary worship books, only in *Lutheran Book of Worship*, Ministers Edition, where it appears as Great Thanksgiving IV, is it used in its primitive form without the interjection of the Sanctus or other acclamations. In *With One Voice* (Minneapolis: Augsburg Fortress, 1995), this primitive usage was overturned by making the Prayer of Hippolytus (an optional eucharistic prayer in Setting 5) a post-Sanctus prayer. Its opening extended recital of God's work of salvation in Christ is therefore duplicated in various seasonal prefaces.

Worship: Ministers Edition (1978). The Lutheran difficulty with eucharistic sacrifice made it necessary in *LBW* to translate "offerimus" as "we lift up" rather than as "we offer." This complicated development in the understanding of eucharistic sacrifice makes it unlikely that we today can simply go back to the early Christian concept of sacrifice as an interior or moral disposition that accompanied the offering of gifts from the creation to God the Creator in gratitude for all of God's gifts. Such an understanding of the offerer as the "pure sacrifice offered to God" can only follow from an understanding of what was accomplished in the conversion processes of Christian initiation and baptismal identification with Christ and his obedient sacrifice to the Father.

In spite of the ecumenical popularity of this prayer, it is important to realize that it is not the only example of eucharistic prayer to survive in textual form from the ancient church. A search for an Ur-anaphora (original form of the eucharistic prayer), such as seventeenth- and eighteenth-century Anglican liturgists searched for (and thought they found in Book VIII of the *Apostolic Constitutions*),[73] is methodologically mistaken. But liturgical scholars have inquired as to how Jewish prayer traditions were assimilated into Christian practice. More light is shed on this kind of research from the East Syrian tradition. Hippolytus is an artificial text, in the sense of not being a prayer actually used in a worshiping community but a sample prayer. But another ancient text that has been used in worshiping communities is the East Syrian Anaphora of the Apostles Addai and Mari. It is still used by the Syro-Chaldean (Nestorian) and Syro-Malabar (Uniate) Christians, although with an institution narrative not found in the oldest text.

The Anaphora of Addai and Mari (Mar Esaya Text)

The East Syrian Anaphora or Eucharistic Prayer of Addai and Mari is the oldest text of a developed eucharistic prayer in continual use in a Christian community. It is as early as the third century, since its theology is pre-Nicene. The oldest manuscript is in Syriac, and was discovered by W. F. Macomber in the Mar Esaya church (Mossul), dating from the tenth or eleventh centuries. The following translation is by Macomber.[74] The material in parentheses is in the text as given in the Mar Esaya manuscript, but is from the anaphora of Theodore of Mopsuestia and was probably not original with Addai and Mari. The translation is sense-lined to demonstrate the Semitic parallelism of the text.

> *Priest:* The grace of our Lord (Jesus Christ and the love of God the Father and
>   the fellowship of the Holy Spirit be with us now and always and forever
>   and ever).
> *People:* Amen.
> *Priest:* Let your minds be on high.
> *People:* To you, O God (of Abraham, Isaac and Israel, O glorious King).

---

[73] See *The Search for an Apostolic Liturgy*. Alcuin Club Pamphlet No. 18 (London, 1963), 3–5; also W. Jardine Grisbrooke, *Anglican Liturgies in the Seventeenth and Eighteenth Centuries*. Alcuin Club Collection No. 40 (London, 1958).

[74] "The Oldest Known Text of the Anaphora of the Apostles Addai and Mari," *Orientalia Christiana Periodica* 32 (1966), 335–71.

Priest: The oblation is offered to God, Lord of all.
People: It is fitting and right.

Priest: Worthy of glory from all mouths
and thanksgiving from all tongues
is the adorable and glorious Name
(of the Father, the Son, and the Holy Spirit),
who created the world in his lovingkindness
and its inhabitants in his clemency;
who redeemed humankind in his compassion
and effected great grace toward mortals.

Thousands upon thousands of celestial beings and
myriads upon myriads of angels adore your majesty;
hosts of spiritual beings,
servants of fire and spirit with the holy cherubim and seraphim
    glorify your name,
acclaiming and glorifying
(unceasingly crying out one to another and saying):
Holy, holy, (holy, mighty Lord, of whose praise
    heaven and earth are full;
Hosanna in the highest.
Blessed is he who comes and is coming in the Name of the Lord.
Hosanna to the Son of David.)

And with these heavenly hosts,
we too give you thanks, O Lord,
we your lowly, weak and miserable servants,
for you have effected in us great grace that cannot be repaid;
in that you have clothed yourself in our humanity
so as to enliven us with your divinity;
you have lifted up our lapsed state
and righted our fall;
you have raised up our mortality
and remitted our debts;
you have justified our sinfulness
and enlightened our knowledge.
Our Lord, our God,
you have defeated our enemies
and made victorious the lowliness of our feeble nature
in the abundant mercy of your lovingkindness.
And for all (your help and graces towards us,
we may offer you praise and honor,
now at all times and ever and ever.)

In your (great and) unspeakable mercy,
O Lord, make a gracious remembrance
of all the just and righteous forebears
who have been pleasing in your sight
in the commemoration of the Body and Blood of your Christ,
which we offer you upon the pure and holy altar
according as you have taught us;

and give us your peace and tranquillity
all the days of the world,

so that all the inhabitants of the earth may know you
that you alone are the true God, Father,
and that you sent our Lord Jesus Christ,
your beloved Son,
and that He, our Lord and God,
has taught us in his life-giving Gospel
all the purity and holiness
of the prophets, the apostles,
the martyrs, the confessors, the bishop, the priests, the deacons
and all the children of the holy catholic church,
who have been signed with the sign of holy baptism.

We, too, O Lord,
your lowly, weak and miserable servants
who are gathered and stand before you at this time,
and have received by tradition
the example that comes from you,
rejoicing, glorifying, exalting,
commemorating and praising,
we perform this great and dread mystery of the passion, death and resurrection
of our Lord Jesus Christ.

O Lord, may your Holy Spirit come
and rest upon this oblation of your servants,
and may bless and hallow it
so that it may be unto us, O Lord,
for the remission of sins,
for the great hope of resurrection from the dead,
and for new life in the kingdom of heaven
with all who have been pleasing in your sight.

And for all your marvelous dispensation towards us
may we give you thanks,
and praise you without ceasing openly
and with trustful countenance in your church
redeemed by the precious blood of your Christ,
offering up (praise, honor, confession and adoration
to our living and life-giving name
now at all times for ever and ever.)

This text is laden with difficulties. E. C. Ratcliff, one of the first scholars to study this anaphora, concluded that the Sanctus is not original.[75] It is an intrusion, just as it is in the Roman anaphora.[76] Against this view we must reckon with the facts that the Sanctus

---

[75] E. C. Ratcliff, "The Original Form of the Anaphora of the Apostles," *Journal of Theological Studies* 30 (1912), 23–32.

[76] E. C. Ratcliff, "The Sanctus and the Pattern of the Early Anaphora," *Journal of Ecclesiastical History* 1 (1950), 29–36.

is in the oldest extant text and that the anaphora has a developed angelology. Ratcliff also regarded the epiclesis as an interpolation, although Bernard Botte regarded it as an ancient redaction.[77] But Botte was disturbed by the lack of an institution narrative, which was apparently not added to the Malabar liturgy until the sixteenth century under the influence of the Portuguese Jesuits.[78] Botte held fast to the notion that the presence of an anamnesis should indicate the presence of an institution narrative. H. Engberding attacked this presupposition, and added that, in any event, the so-called anamnesis in the anaphora of Addai and Mari is not a proper anamnesis but part of the intercessions.[79]

But perhaps the biggest problem of all is the question of to whom the prayer is addressed. The first part is addressed to the name of the Trinity, while the second part is addressed to the Son who "righted our fall." Here we must note that the original form of this anaphora predates Nicene trinitarian theology, and that other Syrian anaphoras such as those of Gregory and in the *Acts of Thomas* are addressed to Christ.[80]

This anaphora has undoubtedly gone through a considerable evolution. It has been a living prayer in the East Syrian tradition, still recited today (with the later additions of the Sanctus and the institution narrative) in the Syro-Malabar church. In its original form, it was probably composed of several prayers that were put together and that also indicate the place of the ministration of communion in the celebration.[81] It is possible to see in the present structure of the prayer a blessing of the bread and wine before the communion (paragraphs 1–8) and a thanksgiving after the communion (paragraph 9), as follows:

1. Blessing addressed to the Father (pars. 2–3)
2. Thanksgiving addressed to the Son (par. 4)
3. Commemoration and intercessions (par. 5–7)
4. Epiclesis of the Holy Spirit (par. 8)
5. Ministration of Holy Communion
6. Final thanksgiving (par. 9)

This arrangement is dependent on the argument of G. Rouwhorst, who maintains that the East Syrian tradition preserved the distinction between blessings before the meal and thanksgiving after the meal that we have seen in the Jewish meal prayers and in chapters 9 and 10 of the *Didache*.[82] That distinction can still be discerned in the anaphora of Addai and Mari, although presumably one eucharistic prayer is said over both the bread and the cup simultaneously. It is possible that East Syrian Christianity developed an

---

[77] "Próblemes de l'anaphore syrienne des Apôtres Addai et Mari," *L'Orient Syrien* 10 (1965), 98–100.

[78] Bernard Botte, "L'Anaphore chaldéene des Apôtres," *Orientalia Christiana Periodica* 15 (1949), 275.

[79] H. Engberding, "Zum anaphorischen Fürbittgebet der ostsyrischen Liturgie Addaj und Mar(i)," *Oriens Christianus* 41 (1957), 102–24. Bouyer, *Eucharist*, op. cit., 151–2 simply ignored Engberding's objection.

[80] W. F. Macomber, "The Maronite and Chaldean Versions of the Anaphora of the Apostles," *Orientalia Christiana Periodica* 37 (1971), 67.

[81] See E. J. Cutrone, "The Anaphora of the Apostles: Implications of the Mar Esa'ya Text" *Theological Studies* 34 (1973), 624–42.

[82] G. Rouwhorst, "Bénédiction, actions de grâce, supplication; les oraisons de la table dans le Judaisme et les célébrations eucharistiques des chrétien syriaques," *Questions Liturgiques* 61 (1980), 211–40.

anaphora tradition that had more in common with the first Jewish blessing than with the Birkat ha-Mazon. We find in the fourth-century Syrian church order, *The Apostolic Constitutions*, Book VII, 25, a eucharistic prayer which was based on the first Jewish blessing.[83] The prayer modeled on the Birkat ha-Mazon in VII, 26 is a prayer of thanksgiving after communion. This suggests the possibility that the final paragraph in Addai and Mari was a post-communion thanksgiving, and that the actual communion occurred after the epiclesis.

Here is a tradition that brings us closer to the Jewish background of the Christian eucharist than do many others. Another anaphora with many affinities to Addai and Mari is the Third Anaphora of the Apostle Peter, which is preserved in the Maronite church.[84] A third prayer of great interest in the East Syrian tradition is in the *Acts of Thomas*.[85] Whatever the Gnostic influences on this work, the eucharistic passages clearly reflect early Christian usage.

As in the *Apostolic Constitutions* VII, 25, the eucharistic prayer in *Acts of Thomas* 133 is a blessing rather than a thanksgiving, but one which has the character of an epiclesis in that it blesses the bread by invoking "the name of the mother of the ineffable mystery of the hidden dominions and powers, we name over you the name of Jesus." Such a formulation is striking not only because it refers to Jesus in feminine terms (invocations of divine dyad Father/Mother were common in Gnostic circles, as in *Acts of Thomas* 50: "Come, you fellowship of the Masculine . . . Come, secret Mother"), but also because it testifies to the primitive Jewish-Christian understanding that consecration takes place by pronouncing the name of God over the person or object. The one named takes possession of the object and uses it according to his or her purposes. Odo Casel proposed in 1923 that the epiclesis consisted in naming the divine name upon the person or object to be blessed; therefore the eucharistic prayer itself was epicletic.[86] F. Nötscher claimed that such a notion is to be found in the Old Testament.[87] J. Betz saw in this understanding of epiclesis the pre-Nicene concept of the "real presence": the naming of the name of God implies a calling upon God or Christ or the Holy Spirit to be present now, to take possession of these elements and fill them with power.[88] Understood in this way, it was logical that the epiclesis should come at the end of the prayer and be connected with the communion. As Bouyer has suggested, after recalling the wonderful works of God in the Christ-event, it is natural to petition the fulfillment of these works in the gift of

---

[83] *Didascalia et Constitutiones Apostolorum*, ed. F.X. Funk (Paderborn, 1905), I, 410–3. See A. Verheul, "Les prières eucharistiques dans les Constitutiones Apostolorum," *Questions Liturgiques* 61 (1980), 129–43.

[84] See *Prayers of the Eucharist: Early and Reformed*, ed. by R.C.D. Jasper and G.J. Cuming, 3rd ed, revised and enlarged (New York: Pueblo Publishing, 1987), 45–51.

[85] See *Prex Eucharistica: Textus e Variis Liturgiis Antiquioribus Selecti*, ed. by Anton Hänggi and Irmgard Pahl (Fribourg: Éditions Universitaires Fribourg Suisse, 1968), 76–9.

[86] Odo Casel, "Zur Epiklese," *Jahrbuch für Liturgiewissenschaft* 3 (1923), 100–2.

[87] F. Nötscher, "Epiklesis in biblischer Beleuchtung," *Biblica* 30 (1949), 401–4.

[88] J. Betz, *Die Eucharistie in der Zeit der griechischen Väter 1/1: Die Actualpräsenz der Person und des Heilswerkes Jesu im Abendmahl nach der vorphesinischen griechischen Patristik* (Freiburg, 1955), 320–8.

Christ's presence in Holy Communion.[89] Ligier, too, sees the epiclesis directed toward the gathering together of the people of God around the shekinah, or presence of God.[90] As John H. McKenna has observed, on the basis of these studies of the epiclesis in the primitive Christian tradition, "definitions of the more developed epiclesis which limit themselves to the appeal for the transformation of the gifts hardly do justice to the liturgical data."[91] The early liturgical tradition was simply uninterested in pinpointing a "moment of consecration" and identifying that either with the words of institution or with the invocation of the Holy Spirit. There are early Christian traditions that had neither an institution narrative nor a consecratory epiclesis, without thereby losing a sense of communion with Christ in, with, and through the bread and cup.

The Sanctus

The lack of the Sanctus in the anaphora of Hippolytus, but in Addai and Mary, also merits comment because it has much to do with the joining together in one unified liturgical order the liturgies of the word and of the meal. We have shown the Jewish provenance of the eucharistic prayer tradition. The Sanctus was clearly a Jewish prayer, although its place was in the synagogue liturgy in the berakah before the Shema. While the Sanctus was not a part of all third-century anaphoras, it is present in all of the fourth-century anaphoras we shall look at in the next chapter. How did it become such a standard item in the eucharistic prayer? Bouyer suggests that at some point the prayers of the synagogue service, which include the two berakoth before the Shema and the Tefillah, were merged with the meal graces based on the Birkat ha-Mazon.[92] This was possible because the content of the two sets of prayers was formally identical, even if the texts were different, as the following chart indicates.

Synagogue	Meal	Content
First ber. before Shema	1st meal prayer	Blessing for creation
Second ber. before Shema	2nd meal prayer	Blessing for redemption
Tefillah	3rd meal prayer	Supplication for eschatological fulfillment

Bouyer believed, like other Jewish and Christian scholars before him, that the Jewish prayers were already fixed by the first century. He held that the eucharistic prayers in the *Didache* represent a primitive eucharist, that Addai and Mari also represented "an archaic formula of indisputable authenticity," and that the anaphora of Hippolytus was "the work of an archaizer." According to his line of reasoning, the synagogal and meal prayer formularies were merging already during the third century as a result of the unified liturgy of word and meal, and he claimed that they first appear fully merged in the Alexandrian Anaphora of Mark because of the presence of both the Sanctus and copious

[89] Bouyer, *Eucharist*, 177, 183–4, 310–3.

[90] L. Ligier, "De la Cène de Jésus à l'Anaphore de l'Eglise," *La Maison Dieu* 87 (1966), 44–5.

[91] John H. McKenna, *Eucharist and Holy Spirit: The Eucharistic Epiclesis in 20th Century Theology*, Alcuin Club Collections No. 57 (Great Wakering: Mayhew-McCrimmon, 1975), 101.

[92] Bouyer, *Eucharist*, 89–90.

intercessions. He even tried to correlate the themes of the particular intercessions in Mark with those of the Jewish Tefillah.[93]

Bouyer's theory is breathtaking in its ingenuity. It has won few loyal adherents because it tries to prove too much with too great a precision with data that is sketchy at best. This does not mean that he is not pointing in the right directions. Gregory Dix[94] and Georg Kretschmar[95] had long ago proposed that the Sanctus made its first appearance in Alexandria, in the writings of Origen early in the third century. Alexandria was a community in which Jewish synagogal traditions probably influenced Christian practice the most because relations between the Jewish and Christian communities seemed more cordial there than in Antioch. Geoffrey Cuming suggested that the Alexandrian Anaphora of Mark might have developed out of the fragment of a eucharistic prayer in the Strasbourg papyrus 254 (fourth or fifth century), which contains only a praise of God for the work of creation through Christ, a thankoffering of "this reasonable and bloodless service" (with a quotation of Mal. 1:11), extensive intercessions, and a concluding doxology. He thereby proposed that the Sanctus was added as a conclusion to the prayer, replacing the original doxology; and that later on, an epiclesis, institution narrative and anamnesis, and a second epiclesis petitioning the change of the elements into the body and blood of Christ and the fruits of communion were appended to the Sanctus. [96] This created an unusual arrangement in which the Sanctus followed intercessions. Other eucharistic prayers (such as those of Antioch) incorporated the Sanctus, but located it after the opening act of praise where it acquired a more integral position within the whole anaphora. Cuming and others have explored the idea of whether the Egyptian and Antiochene anaphoras could have been influenced and shaped by a common original, such as Papyrus 254.[97] Bryan Spinks has agreed that the Sanctus could have been taken over by Christians from the synagogue, but points out that it could just as likely have come from the influence of Babylonian Merkavah mysticism (which often concluded prayers with *qedushah*) or been taken over from biblical material without Jewish influence.[98] It might be that it originated in different ways in different places, just as the received texts of eucharistic prayers reflect an original diversity resulting from *ex tempore* praying in the early centuries that only later (perhaps as a result of doctrinal controversy) acquired more standardized forms and content.

 ## SABBATH AND LORD'S DAY

The day on which the early Christians gathered to celebrate the eucharist was more fixed than the textual formularies they might have used for their celebrations. We

---

[93] Ibid., 192ff.

[94] Dix, *The Shape of the Liturgy*, 165.

[95] Georg Kretschmar, *Studien zur frühchristlichen Trinitätstheologie* (Tübingen, 1956), 180–2.

[96] G. J. Cuming, "The Anaphora of St. Mark: A Study in Development," *Muséon* 95 (1982), 115–29.

[97] See Paul Bradshaw, *The Search for the Origins of Christian Worship: Sources and Methods for the Study of Early Liturgy* (Oxford University Press, 1992), 119.

[98] Bryan D. Spinks, *The Sanctus in the Eucharistic Prayer* (Cambridge University Press, 1991), 111–6.

have already seen in the letter of Pliny that Christians gathered on a "fixed day," and Justin Martyr clearly designated that day as the Day of the Sun in the Roman calendar. He specified Sunday because it was the day of the Lord's resurrection. Hence it was called the "Lord's Day" (*kyriake hemera*, Rev. 1:10). The *Didache*, certainly written close to the time of the book of Revelation (if not earlier), enjoined Christians to assemble on the Lord's Day for the breaking of bread and thanksgiving. But in the Greco-Roman world, Sunday was a work day, not a day of rest. There was a growing practice of observing Saturn's Day (Saturday) as a day of rest, perhaps under the influence of the Jewish sabbath observance.[99] This raises the question of when the eucharist was celebrated.

Acts 20 relates that Paul gathered with the Christians of Troas to break bread "on the first day of the week." There Paul, "since he intended to leave the next day," preached until midnight (20:7). Still later, after the hapless Eutychus's fall from the window and restoration, the apostle broke bread with the assembly and continued with them until daybreak. Is the timeframe of this gathering from Saturday to Sunday or from Sunday to Monday? According to the Jewish reckoning of the day, the first day of the week could begin at sunset on Saturday. But the Greeks reckoned a day from dawn to dawn, and the Romans from midnight to midnight. Willy Rordorf proposed that the time frame in Acts 20 is the Roman reckoning, so that the night in question is from Sunday to Monday.[100] This is consistent with his emphasis on the post-resurrection appearances of Christ on the evening of the resurrection (John 20:19), and again eight days later (John 20:26), as laying the foundation for observing the Lord's Day as a deliberate substitution for the Jewish Sabbath. The eucharist would then have been celebrated on Sunday evening.

While Rordorf's argument has enjoyed a wide following, there is the equally attractive hypothesis of Massey Shepherd that Christians gathered at the end of the Jewish Sabbath for their supper-rite. This would not have disturbed Jewish Christians who continued to observe the Sabbath, and Gentiles, who reckoned the day from sunrise to sunrise, might even think they were observing the Sabbath.[101] Shepherd's suggestion gains attraction because (1) there were Christians who continued to celebrate the Sabbath; (2) the popular designation of Sunday as "the eighth day" depends on understanding its meaning in juxtaposition with the Sabbath; and (3) Sunday was widely regarded as a "little pascha" or Easter, and there were, later on, all-night vigils that ended with an early morning celebration of the eucharist.

The evidence for the early church's observance of the Sabbath as well as the Lord's Day is scanty in the first few centuries, but it is there. *Didache* 8:1 retains the Jewish name for Friday as "day of preparation." While this could have been mere convention, since the *Didache* provides no information on Sabbath-observance, the substance of the *Didache* is preserved in Book VII of the *Apostolic Constitutions*, which does teach

---

[99] F. J. Dölger, "Die Planetenwoche der griechisch-römischen Antike und der christliche Sonntag," *Antike und Christentum* 6 (Münster, 1941), 217–22.

[100] Rordorf, *Sunday*, op. cit., 205.

[101] Massey Hamilton Shepherd, Jr., *The Paschal Liturgy and the Apocalypse* (Richmond: John Knox Press, 1960), 31.

about Sabbath-observance. The *Martyrdom of Polycarp* 7:1 also uses this name for Friday, while 8:1 relates that the day of Polycarp's trial was a "great Sabbath." The Coptic version of Hippolytus's *Apostolic Tradition* (known as the *Statutes of the Apostles*), preserves an instruction that slaves were to work only five days a week so that on the Sabbath and Lord's Day they could "devote themselves to the church that they may be instructed in piety." This passed into the *Apostolic Constitutions* VIII, 33:2 (Book VIII is based on the *Apostolic Tradition*).[102] Thus, it is clear that in the Eastern churches (especially in Asia Minor, Syria, and Egypt) there was a tradition of celebrating the Sabbath.[103]

Another source of evidence for early Christian sabbath-observance is from a polemic against it. Ignatius of Antioch, at the beginning of the second century, writes in *Magnesians* 8, "if we still go on observing Judaism, we admit we never received grace." Those who "arrived at a new hope . . . ceased to keep the Sabbath and lived by the Lord's Day" (9:1).[104] The *Epistle of Barnabas*, which reflects the situation around Alexandria a few years later, condemns "the present (Jewish) Sabbaths" as unacceptable and exhorts the readers to "observe the eighth day with gladness, on which Jesus also rose from the dead and, when he had been manifested, ascended to heaven." (15:9).[105]

Conversely, where the Sabbath was observed by Christians, they were exhorted not to practice it Judaistically, that is, in idleness, but for study of the word. Canon 16 of the Synod of Laodicea (c. 380) specified that "the Gospels along with other scriptures be read on the Sabbath," and exempted both the Sabbath and the Lord's Day from fasting during Lent.[106] The *Apostolic Constitutions* are also clear that one is not to fast on the Sabbath, except at Pascha/Easter time in commemoration of the Lord's death and burial (V, 14:20; 18:1; 20:19; VII, 23:3f.)—an attitude that is widely expressed by a number of church fathers ranging from Tertullian to Augustine of Hippo. It would appear that the origin of fasting on the Sabbath can be traced to the Roman church, from where it spread to the West. Possibly the annual paschal fast was being extended to become a weekly observance, as Tertullian seems to have thought (*On Fasting* 14)—a practice that he opposed because it destroyed the character of the Sabbath as a day of rest and rejoicing. Indeed, one wonders if the celebration of the eucharist on the Sabbath in the third and fourth centuries was not simply a way of preserving this character of the Sabbath Day. But, if so, it also helped to undermine the special relationship between the Lord's Day and the Lord's Supper.

An early and popular designation of Sunday was "the eighth day." This highlighted the eschatological character of this day. Rordorf suggests that it came about

---

[102] Funk, 539.

[103] See W.B. Bishai, "Sabbath Observance from Coptic Sources," *Andrews University Seminary Studies* [*AUSS*] 1 (1963), 25–31, and the rejoinder by Robert A. Kraft, "Some Notes on Sabbath Observance in Early Christianity," *AUSS* 3 (1965), 18–33, with the additional reply and commentary by Kenneth A. Strand, "Some Notes on the Sabbath Fast in Early Christianity," *AUSS* 3 (1965), 167–73. Seventh Day Adventist scholars have been especially attuned to data on sabbath-observance by early Christians.

[104] *Early Christian Fathers*, 96.

[105] Cited in Kraft, *art. cit.*, 28.

[106] Cited in ibid., 23–4.

through a typological comparison between circumcision on the eighth day and Christian baptism celebrated on Sunday—a theme expounded by Justin Martyr in his *Dialogue with Trypho* 41.[107] The earliest reference to Sunday as the eighth day is in the *Letter of Barnabas* (cited above). Clement of Alexandria, in *Stromata* VI, 1, emphasized the eschatological and cosmological dimensions of the "eighth day" by characterizing it as the day on which the sacrifice is offered that fulfills the promise of the completed creation.[108] But this put the Lord's Day into competition with the Sabbath as the day of fulfillment. Perhaps because of this duplication, the designation "the eighth day" dropped out of use, although Sunday continued to be treated homiletically as the eighth day in the sermons of the fathers.[109]

The designation of Sunday as the eighth day served a useful purpose in indicating that the Lord's Day was not a substitute or an equivalent of the Sabbath. The Sabbath remained a day of rest, commemorating the creation of the world. The Lord's Day was a day of messianic fulfillment, the day on which Jesus the Christ rose from the dead and inaugurated the new creation.

For this reason Sunday was the day of baptism as well as the day of the eucharist. This tradition had immense importance for the development of the Christian calendar. It helped to establish the Christian pasch or Easter on a Sunday, and not on the day of the Jewish Passover. We have become used to calling Sunday a "little Easter." But in the light of the developed patristic tradition, it would be more appropriate to call Easter a "big Sunday."

🍇 PASSOVER AND EASTER

The testimony of the Synoptic Gospels seems clear enough that Jesus ate the passover meal with his disciples on the night before his death (Mark 14:14; Matt. 26:18; Luke 22:8). The Fourth Gospel, on the other hand, places Jesus' crucifixion on 14 Nisan, at the time the lambs for the feast were being slaughtered in the Temple. The identification of Jesus with the passover lamb is already reflected in Paul (1 Cor. 5:7). Paul's testimony, earlier than any gospel tradition, is important. Writing around 55–56 C.E. from Ephesus in Asia Minor, Paul told the Corinthians that he planned to remain in Ephesus until Pentecost (1 Cor. 16:8). These references to Passover and Pentecost indicate that these times of Jewish festivals were important to Paul, and he assumed that they were also significant times for the Corinthian Christians to whom he wrote.

Clear testimony of the Christian observance of Pesach (Passover) appears only in the second century from Asia Minor, where the Johannine chronology was followed. The *Epistula Apostolorum* (preserved only in Ethiopic, but written originally in Greek), indicates that the celebration on 14–15 Nisan is a memorial of the Lord's death as the climax

---

[107] Rordorf, 275ff.

[108] See Jean Daniélou, *The Bible and the Liturgy*, Eng. trans. (Notre Dame, Ind.: University of Notre Dame Press, 1956), 260.

[109] Ibid., 262ff.

of salvation history.[110] The observance took the form of an all-night vigil ending at dawn. It seems that these Christians waited until the Jewish passover was over at midnight before beginning their celebration of the passover fulfilled in Christ. While the Jewish celebration was an evening of feasting, the Christian pascha was a night of fasting ending with the morning eucharistic feast.

The problem was that the Jewish lunar calendar did not equal the Greco-Roman solar calendar, and once Christians were cut off from the synagogue at the end of the first century, they no longer had access to the rabbinic authorities to help in the computation of the calendar with its periodic adjustments. The Christians in Asia Minor, who insisted on celebrating Christ's passion on the very day of the Passover (who were therefore known as the *Quartodecimans*, or "fourteenthers"), had to find an equivalent day in the Julian calendar. Sozomen, in his *Historia Ecclesiastica* VII:18, notes that the Montanists of Asia Minor set the Pascha on April 6. August Strobel has suggested that this was the practice of the Quartodecimans as well.[111]

Efforts to establish the exact date of Christ's crucifixion in the year of his death resulted in focusing on March 25. Hippolytus accepted this date, and the Johannine chronology along with it, as did Tertullian in *Adversus Iudaeos* VIII:18. March 25 coincided with the spring equinox in the Julian calendar, and it is noteworthy that it had some bearing on the establishment also on the date of Christ's birth. On the basis of the Jewish tradition that Passover occurred at the same time as the creation of the world (in the spring), Christians believed that the world's redemption also occurred in the spring at Passover time. It was believed that Christ was conceived and died on the same date, since the incarnation of the Word began the process of the redemption of the world. In spite of this importance for March 25, there was no concern in the third century to shift the date of the Pascha to the equinox itself. Later writers place the resurrection on March 25, but earlier writers associate it with Christ's passion. The *Peri Pascha* of Melito of Sardis (c. 165) maintains that the name "Pascha" derives from the Greek verb *paschein*, meaning "to suffer." But, as in John's Gospel, there was no sense of divorcing Christ's passion from his glorification.

> He came on earth from heaven for suffering man, becoming incarnate in a virgin's womb from which he came forth as man; he took on himself the sufferings of suffering man through a body capable of suffering, and put an end to sufferings of the flesh, and through his spirit incapable of death he became the death of death which is destructive of man. . . . This is he who in the virgin was made incarnate, on the cross was suspended, in the earth was buried, from the dead was resurrected, to the heights of heaven was lifted up.[112]

In the meantime, the churches of the West followed the lead of Rome in celebrating the Pascha always on a Sunday, the first day of the week, rather than on 14 Nisan

---

[110] See Thomas J. Talley, *The Origins of the Liturgical Year* (New York: Pueblo Publishing Co., 1986), 5–6.

[111] August Strobel, *Ursprung und Geschichte des frühchristlichen Osterkalendars, Texte und Untersuchungen* 121 (Berlin, 1977), 373.

[112] *The Paschal Mystery*, trans. by Thomas Halton from the French trans. of A. Hammann. Alba Patristic Library 3 (Staten Island, N.Y.: Alba House, 1969), 33f.

no matter on which day of the week it fell. Pope Victor I (+ ca. 200) took the lead in marshaling interest throughout the whole church for a common celebration of the Christian pascha. The Asians resisted, Bishop Polycrates claiming apostolic authority for the Quartodeciman practice in a remarkable letter that has been preserved in Eusebius's *Ecclesiastical History* (see chaps. 23–25 on the Quartodeciman Controversy). Upon receipt of this letter, Victor issued letters to all the churches excommunicating the province of Asia. Many bishops opposed Victor's precipitous action, Irenaeus of Lyons among them. Irenaeus pointed out that Victor's predecessor Anicetus did not wish to quarrel over this matter when Polycarp visited Rome and even gave him the honor of presiding at the eucharist. Of course, lurking behind this issue was the larger issue of continuity versus discontinuity between the old and the new covenants, and perhaps also the Roman church's growing sense of primacy and leadership among the churches.

The paschal controversy was not resolved until the Council of Nicea (325), which prescribed that Easter should always be celebrated on the first Sunday after the first full moon of spring. This decree, it would seem, had the effect of preventing the quartodeciman practice from recurring, because if 14 Nisan (the day of the first full moon of spring) should fall on a Sunday, Easter would still be observed on the following Sunday. This arrangement also meant that Easter could fall within a five-week period between March 22 and April 25.[113] Even with this settlement, there remained a disagreement between the Greek and Roman churches over whether Easter should be celebrated only *after* the Jewish Passover. Since the Orthodox churches observe this distinction, there remains a fundamental calendrical difference between the Eastern and Western churches.

🍇 CHRISTIAN INITIATION AND PENANCE

Easter was important not only because it celebrated the central Christian affirmation of the resurrection of Jesus the Christ, but also because it became the time of solemn initiation into the Christian community. Baptism was practiced as a way of participating in Christ's passover from death to life (Rom. 6:3–5). The celebration of baptism in this paschal context made it a new type of exodus (and the exodus a type of baptism). While there are some similarities between Christian initiation and initiation in the mystery cults that flourished in the Greco-Roman world, it is more common now to see the background of Christian baptism in Jewish lustration rites.[114]

When Hebrews 6:1–2 speaks of "baptisms" in the plural, it is referring to a genre of ritual acts that were well known in Judaism.[115] Some of these involved processes of ritual purification by which contact with impure objects or loathsome diseases was washed away. The practice of proselyte baptism, which seems to have developed primarily outside of Palestine early in the common era, was part of an initiatory process that included

---

[113] See Adolf Adam, *The Liturgical Year: Its History and Meaning After the Reform of the Liturgy*, Eng. trans. (New York: Pueblo Publishing Co., 1981), 59.

[114] See Jones, Wainwright, Yarnold, *The Study of Liturgy*, op. cit., 73–6.

[115] See G. Beasley-Murray, *Baptism in the New Testament* (New York: Macmillan, 1962), 1–44.

instruction in the Torah, circumcision for males, and washing for all.[116] Information in the Mishnah and Talmud indicate that candidates were probably immersed in the water as parts of the Torah were recited over them. But this could reflect the influence of Christian baptism on Jewish practice. Jewish sources also prefer washing in "living water" (i.e., cold running water) where it is available—a preference also expressed in *Didache* 7, although both Jewish and Christian sources show flexibility about this due to semi-arid conditions.

The importance of baptism for Christianity is seen in the four Gospels. Each Gospel begins with the ministry of John the Baptist, and the ministry of Jesus begins with his baptism by John in the Jordan River. The water-purification rites of the sectarian Essene community may lie behind John's baptismal practice. They regarded their lustration rites as a means of moral and religious cleansing that, when combined with penitence, nurtured their ardent eschatological expectation and their sense of a vocation to prepare the way of the Lord.[117]

Nevertheless, Christian baptism was more than a rite for the forgiveness of sins. Although the evidence of the Fourth Gospel indicates that even Jesus and his disciples baptized (John 3:22ff., 4:1–4), and there was some seeming competition between the disciples of Jesus and the disciples of John, the fullness of Christian baptism involved rebirth by "water and Spirit" (John 3:5). John the Baptist pointed to a messiah who would baptize not with water only but also with the Holy Spirit (John 1:33). There can be little doubt that the Spirit-baptism on the first Christian Pentecost (Acts 2) profoundly influenced the early church's understanding of the baptism of Jesus by John and its own initiatory practice. The Synoptic Gospels relate the dove-like descent of the Spirit on Jesus at his baptism. In Luke 4:18 Jesus applies the text of Isaiah 61:1–2 to himself: "The Spirit of the Lord is upon me, because he has anointed me." Acts 10:38 refers to Jesus as the One whom God "anointed . . . with the Holy Spirit and with power."

The Spirit-moment in Christian baptism came to be associated with the rite of baptismal anointing. It is not surprising that the practice of anointing arose as an integral part of Christian initiation, as in 1 John 2:20 ("you have been anointed by the Holy One") and possibly even in 2 Corinthians 1:22 ("God establishes us . . . by putting his seal on us and giving us his Spirit in our hearts as a first installment"). Some commentators, of course, have regarded these allusions to anointing as figurative and not referring to an actual rite of anointing.[118] On the other hand, if the actual practice of anointing is discounted, it is difficult to account for the sudden appearance of such rites in the second century. We need to remember that apart from the common use of oil in bathing in the Greco-Roman world, anointing had an even more recognized place in the Jewish ritual repertoire than water rites (e.g., the anointing of prophets, kings, and priests in the Old

---

[116] See J. Delorme, "The Practice of Baptism in Judaism at the Beginning of the Christian Era," in *Baptism in the New Testament: A Symposium*, trans. by D. Askew (London: Geoffrey Chapman, 1964), 25ff.

[117] See the careful exegesis of the baptism practiced by John the Baptist in Beasley-Murray, 45–67.

[118] Thus G. W. H. Lampe, *The Seal of the Spirit* (London: S.P.C.K., 1967), 81; G. R. Beasley-Murray, *Baptism in the New Testament* (New York: Macmillan, 1962), 234–5; B. Neunheuser, *Baptism and Confirmation*, trans. John J. Hughes (New York: Herder and Herder, 1964), 50–1.

Testament). So it is not surprising that the church adopted anointing as an integral part of baptism.[119] On the other hand, the use of such rites as explications of the Spirit's presence and work in Holy Baptism need not lead to the conclusion that such rites actually "gave" the Spirit to the newly baptized, as Dix and others maintained.[120]

With the exception of the *Didache*,[121] which could be the unique witness of a Jewish Christian community, a Spirit-moment did develop in the Christian baptismal rites of the second century. It is present in the Syrian *Acts of Thomas*, in which we see the pattern of anointing/water bath/eucharist that was to become normative in the Syrian Orient. This pattern is also evident in the *Didascalia Apostolorum* and in the Armenian liturgy and is commented on by John Chrysostom and Narsai of Nisibis.

In the Greco-Roman pattern of baptism described in Justin Martyr's *First Apology*, chapters 61 and 65, the newly baptized are received into the assembly of the faithful for the kiss of peace, the prayers, and the eucharist after being baptized "in a place where there is water." What this reception amounted to half a century later can be seen in Tertullian's treatise *On Baptism* and in Hippolytus's *Apostolic Tradition*.[122] Both authors were very conservative and opposed novelty, especially in sacramental practice. According to both authors, the reception of the newly baptized included a post-baptismal anointing with chrism (Tertullian) or the oil of thanksgiving (Hippolytus), the imposition of hands by the bishop with an invocation of the grace-gifts of the Holy Spirit, a sealing on the forehead, and the eucharist. It should be noted that the prayer accompanying the laying on of hands after baptism in the *Apostolic Tradition* actually associates the Holy Spirit with the water-bath and petitions for the newly baptized not the Holy Spirit but the "grace" of the Holy Spirit to serve God.

> Lord God, you have made them worthy to receive remission of sins through the laver of regeneration of the holy Spirit; send upon them your grace, that they may serve you according to your will, for to you is glory, to the Father and Son with the holy Spirit in the holy Church, both now and to the ages of ages. Amen.[123]

Hippolytus's description of the catechumenate and the rites of initiation is the fullest and most detailed up to that time. He reports a catechumenate that usually lasted three years, although "it is not the time that is judged but the conduct." The catechumens are to give up any professions that involved them in idolatry (e.g., actors, idol makers, practitioners of magic or sorcery), killing (e.g., gladiators, military), or immorality (e.g., pimps, prostitutes). The content of the catechetical instruction was primarily ethical and

---

[119] See Leonel L. Mitchell, *Baptismal Anointing* (London: S.P.C.K., 1966), 25.

[120] G. Dix, *The Theology of Confirmation in Relation to Baptism* (London: Dacre Press, 1946).

[121] An ointment prayer is found at the end of chapter 10 in a Coptic papyrus fragment of the *Didache*, which was previously known via the *Apostolic Constitutions*. See G. Horner, "A New Fragment of the *Didache* in Coptic," *Journal of Theological Studies* 25 (1924), 225ff. For extended commentary on this text see Vööbus, *Liturgical Material in the Didache*, 41ff.

[122] For English excerpts from these works see E.C. Whitaker, *Documents of the Baptismal Liturgy*, 2nd ed. (London: S.P.C.K., 1970), 2ff.

[123] Eng. trans. from G.J. Cuming, *Hippolytus: A Text for Students*, Grove Liturgical Study 8 (Nottingham: Bramcote, 1976), 20.

ministerial, and the candidates *(electi)* were examined or scrutinized before their baptism to see "whether they lived piously while catechumens, whether they 'honored the widows,' whether they visited the sick, whether they fulfilled every good work."[124]

The rigorous catechumenate described by Hippolytus is explainable in the light of that into which the catechumens were being initiated: the eschatological body of Christ. On the night of the Lord's Passover from death to life the catechumens assembled at the font while the faithful kept a solemn vigil waiting for the Lord's appearing. The catechumens received a final exorcism, renounced the devil, confessed their faith in God the Father, his Son Jesus Christ, the Holy Spirit and the holy church (an embryonic form of the Apostles' Creed), were stripped, anointed, and immersed. They emerged from the pool in the same way in which they emerged from the womb: naked. As a sign of their new birth they were clothed in new white garments. They were then led into the assembly of the faithful, still damp and aromatic from their anointing. The bishop laid hands on them, asking for the grace-gifts of the Holy Spirit, and sealed them with the sign of the cross. He then extended to them the greeting of peace, and for the first time the neophytes exchanged the kiss of peace with the faithful. For the first time they joined the prayers of the faithful and offered their gifts as members of the royal priesthood. For the first time they received communion, and the baptismal communion included cups of water and milk and honey as well as wine. The cup of water symbolized the internal cleansing of the eucharist. The cup of milk and honey symbolized the promised land to which the neophytes have now come. It was precisely in order to prepare persons capable of living and celebrating the divine kingdom in the midst of this world that the institution of the catechumenate developed as an inseparable part of Christian initiation.

The rigors of the catechumenate suggest that the baptized were expected to live as though they were reborn as new creatures in the waters of baptism. Yet already in the earliest Christian writings it is evident that backsliding was possible, and that the old creature lived alongside the new. In 1 Corinthians 5:13, Paul exhorted the congregation to "drive out . . . from among you" a "wicked person" who had been guilty of the gross immorality of an incestuous relationship. More than one specific case was being referred to here; a general principle was involved. Paul is "writing to you not to associate with anyone who bears the name of brother or sister who is sexually immoral or greedy, or is an idolater, reviler, drunkard, or robber. Do not even eat with such a one" (1 Cor. 5:11). Paul makes it clear that he is referring to actual church members, not to worldly people who are the objects of evangelization. This can only mean that Paul is recommending excommunication, since eating and drinking included the Lord's Supper that was celebrated in the context of an actual meal at which table fellowship was practiced.

Was it possible to forgive and restore to fellowship those church members who committed grave sins after baptism and were expelled from the church? Hebrews 6:4–6 refuses repentance and forgiveness to apostates. On the other hand, the Gospel of Matthew establishes a structure of church discipline by which the Office of the Keys can

---

[124] Dix, *The Apostolic Tradition*, 31.

be exercised (Matt. 16:19). The church had the right to bind and loose sins (Matt. 16:19). Matthew's Jesus even establishes a procedure by which reconciliation could be achieved among disputing or offended parties in the church (Matt. 18:15–18). The Gospel of John also sees the power of absolution granted to the apostolic leaders of the church: the power to retain and remit sins (John 20:22f.) 1 John 1:8—2:2 encourages confession of sins and expects forgiveness from God because "we have an advocate with the Father, Jesus Christ the righteous."

The early church vacillated between rigor and laxity on this issue, but pastoral realism finally won out. This is evident in the solution of *The Shepherd of Hermas*, an allegorical document from the Roman church c. 140 C.E.[125] This document recognized a limited opportunity for post-baptismal forgiveness and reconciliation. The author spoke of a "jubilee period" during which time baptized sinners were invited to do penance and seek reconciliation with the church.

It is not until Tertullian early in the third century that we have details of a rite of penance. In his *De Poenitentia* (On Penance) he witnesses to an outward rite called *exomologesis*, after the manner of the Greeks. Penitents are to engage in "conduct which attracts mercy" that is manifested even "in matters of dress and food." During the time of penitence the penitents, wearing sackcloth and ashes, are "to nourish prayer by fasting, to weep and groan to the Lord our God day and night, to throw oneself at the feet of the presbyters, and kneel to God's dear ones, to enlist all the brethren as intercessory legates of one's prayerful petitions."[126] This "second penance" could be granted only once.

These procedures were grim, and it is clear from Tertullian that many Christians disregarded them altogether and preferred to keep their sins to themselves and God. His purpose in writing *De Poenitentia* (On Penitence) was to encourage Christians to make use of the prayers of the church. Even in the treatise from his Montanist period, *De Pudicitia* (On Purity), in which Tertullian denied that the church had authority to forgive sins, he still taught that the church could pray for the penitent and the penitent could take confidence in the fact that the prayer of Christ does not go unheard.

This system was far from developed c. 200, and other avenues of forgiveness were available. Those going to martyrdom could grant a swift absolution, and sinners could turn to them. Clement of Alexandria, writing to rich Christians c. 200, recommended that they adopt holy persons from among the poorer brethren who could serve as "friends of God" to advise them and pray for them. Nevertheless, the idea of one, and only one, repentance was quickly gaining acceptance. As we move into the fourth century, it became a principal cause of persons delaying baptism until they reached an advanced age or even their deathbed. But in the third century, the full consequences of this were not appreciated. Tertullian, however, saw the problem in the practice of baptizing infants.

---

[125] See Bernhard Poschmann, *Penance and the Anointing of the Sick*, trans. and rev. by Francis Courtney, S.J. (New York: Herder and Herder, 1964), 26ff.

[126] Tertullian, *De Poenitentia* 9:2–5; in *Corpus Christianorum, Series Latina* I: *Tertulliani Opera*, I, 336. See Tertullian, *Treatises on Penance*, trans. by William P. LeSaint, *Ancient Christian Writers* (New York: Newman Press, 1959).

"Why," he complained, "should the age of innocence hasten to the forgiveness of sins? If the burden of baptism is understood, its reception will be feared more than its delay."[127] Nevertheless, Hippolytus witnessed the children of Christian parents being baptized.

Apart from children of Christian parents, where did new Christians come from? Both Paul, in his epistles, and Luke, in the Acts of the Apostles, credited the force and guidance of the Holy Spirit for the early church's rapid growth. Nevertheless, apart from episodes recorded in Acts we do not have reports of public speeches, and there were certainly no mass meetings to evangelize Jewish or pagan crowds. Compared with teachers of philosophy in Greco-Roman society, Christians kept a low profile. Probably the most public form of advertisement was martyrdom. Although most people in the crowds that witnessed the execution of Christians might simply have regarded these persons as stubborn and misguided, others might have wondered what exactly was this "atheism" of which they were charged that led harmless old people, and even women and girls, to face death. Judging by the Acts of the Martyrs, they were capable of giving impassioned speeches that were probably not all lost on their hearers. But martyrdoms were rare occasions—far rarer than the histories written by Christians would lead us to believe. Persecution was sporadic and local before the first Empire-wide persecution ordered by the Emperor Decius in 250. So most evangelism probably occurred informally between individuals: among friends, between merchants in the marketplace, and within families when Christians married pagans.

In any event, the process of the catechumenate meant that prospective members were not rushed into full church membership. Catechumens were watched and scrutinized and instructed over a long period of time. This thorough preparation may have been one of the faith's particular appeals. But it is estimated that by the year 250 only about two percent of the population of the Roman Empire was christianized, and this mostly in the urban centers.

❧ THE LITURGICAL ASSEMBLY AND ITS ROLES

The rites of Christian initiation and penance emerged in the church as a way of protecting the eschatological vocation of the church. It was an assembly called out of the world (*ekklesia*) in order to demonstrate proleptically the life of the world to come. The fact that this community also experienced periodic persecution from the Roman state made it necessary to maintain tight discipline in the ranks. Yet from the very beginning it was apparent that while the church could strive for perfection in its ranks, it could not achieve it. It came as a shock to Paul, for example, to discover that there was backsliding from the grace of baptism. To the Corinthians, whom he admonished to excommunicate the person living in an incestuous relationship, he expressed his surprise at the scandals of their life together: "But you were washed, you were sanctified, you were justified in the name of the Lord Jesus Christ and in the Spirit of our God" (1 Cor. 6:11).

---

[127] Tertullian, *On Baptism* 18; trans. in Whitaker, *Documents of the Baptismal Liturgy*, 8.

The problems Paul had to address in the church of Corinth prompted him to re-flect on the nature of the Christian assembly from both a practical and a theoretical point of view. The church established in the city of Corinth represented the cutting edge of Christian mission and church life. The city of Corinth was a great commercial center that attracted people and ideas from all over the Roman Empire. It had a large Jewish popula-tion, temples to many of the Greco-Roman deities, a special devotion to Poseidon, and cults devoted to Artemis and Isis.[128] A Christian community was planted in the midst of this welter of cults and lifestyles. The Jews had learned to live in an uneasy truce with pa-ganism, and apparently, Christians in Corinth were prepared to do the same. Paul's First Letter to the Corinthians (c. 56 C.E.) had to deal with such issues as the threat of schism caused by rival leadership and class rivalry (1:10–4:21); scandals such as incest, Christians suing one another, and prostitution (5:1–6:20); problems concerning marriage (7:1–40); eating food offered to idols (8:1–11:1); the attire of women in public worship (11:2–16),; divisiveness at the Lord's Supper (11:17–34); and the use and abuse of extraordinary spir-itual gifts (12:1–14:40).[129]

Much of Paul's teaching in 1 Corinthians is contextual and problem-related. He does not develop a comprehensive ecclesiology or sacramentology. Thus, his teaching on the Lord's Supper concerns two quandaries: the question of table fellowship with pagan deities and divisive behavior at the Lord's Supper itself. These two problems were related at a deeper level. It seems that the Corinthians regarded the sacrament as miraculous food for the individual and were ignoring its social dimensions. They ate food offered to idols with no consideration of the impact such an action had on weaker brethren, and they tolerated blatant inequities at the Lord's Supper. Paul brought two texts to bear on these problems: the formula in 10:16 and the tradition *(paradosis)* of institution of the Lord's Supper (11:23–25).

The order of the bread and cup in these texts is different, and this presents cer-tain problems of interpretation because both orders are rooted in early Christian tradi-tions of the Lord's Supper. The order "cup-bread" in 10:16 is the same as in the so-called short text of Luke 22:17–19 and in the *Didache* 9. This reflects the Jewish custom of blessing first the cup and then the bread at the beginning of a meal. However, in the Synoptic tradition Jesus identified his blood of the new covenant with the final cup of blessing *after* the meal, and Paul does the same with his tradition in 11:23–25. So it is pos-sible that Paul has deliberately inverted the order in 10:16 in order to connect the one-ness of the sacramental body of Christ with the oneness of the ecclesial body of Christ.

> The cup of blessing that we bless, is it not a sharing in the blood of Christ? The bread that we break, is it not a sharing in the body of Christ? Because there is one bread, we who are many are one body, for we all partake of the one bread.

---

[128] See H. S. Robinson, *Corinth: A Brief History of the City and a Guide to the Excavations* (Athens: American School of Classical Studies, 1964), and *The Urban Development of Ancient Corinth* (Athens: American School of Classical Studies, 1965).

[129] See *The Anchor Bible: I Corinthians*, Commentary with Eng. trans. by William F. Orr and James Arthur Walther (Garden City, N.Y.: Doubleday and Co., 1976).

Sharing in the *species* of the bread/body makes the participants one body. If the Corinthian Christians belong to that one body in Christ, it raises serious questions about their casualness in eating food offered to idols in the homes of pagans.

If the concern in chapter 10 is the oneness of the church's *witness*, the concern in chapter 11 is to realize the oneness of the church's *life*. Paul brings the tradition of the institution of the Lord's Supper to bear on the problem of divisiveness in the congregation because the very meaning of the Lord's Supper as fellowship with the crucified and risen Lord is undermined when the members do not "wait for one another" (11:33). This meal is to be a "[proclamation of] the Lord's death until he comes" (11:26). The Lord who comes again in glory comes as judge. His presence in the eucharistic meal includes his presence as judge. Therefore, those who participate in the Lord's Supper should be those who are able to withstand the eschatological judgment. Apparently there were some communicants who could not do this: "For this reason many of you are weak and ill, and some have died" (11:30). The exhortation to "examine yourselves" (11:28) relates directly to this concern that the Lord's Supper be a sign and foretaste of the eschatological banquet. It is that to the extent that an alienated and estranged humanity is brought into the new fellowship (*koinonia*) of the people of God manifested at the eucharistic meal. This fellowship is not just a consequence of the meal; it is a precondition for the meal. That is why only those who have been incorporated into Christ in baptism are allowed to share in it. The unity of an otherwise fractured humanity at the Lord's Table is a powerful sign of the new creation in Christ. The more diverse the eucharistic assembly, the more powerful a sign it is of the new creation.

In order to emphasize the fellowship dimension of the Lord's Supper, Paul developed the image of the church as the body of Christ. He already found this image in the traditions he cites: "This is my body," said Jesus as he broke the bread and shared it with his disciples. Because many partake of the one bread that Jesus proclaims to be his "body," the many become one body. This is the root of the Pauline conception of the church as "the body of Christ" (1 Cor. 12:27) and "one body in Christ" (Rom. 12:5). Fellowship with the Lord is at the same time fellowship with one's brothers and sisters in Christ, and this fellowship is a powerful witness to the reality of the gospel of forgiveness and reconciliation in Christ. Thus, there can be no divorce between liturgy and social conduct, between worship and ethics.

Paul's theology has some far-reaching practical consequences. It puts a brake on the exercise of one's individual freedom, because one who is a member of Christ must exemplify Christ's self-emptying in service to others. Thus, Christians have a witness to make to others that may abridge their social freedom. "You cannot drink the cup of the Lord and the cup of demons. You cannot partake of the table of the Lord and the table of demons" (1 Cor. 10:21). And the well-to-do Christians who can get to the eucharistic feast early will simply have to wait for the slaves and the poor to get off work and arrive before they begin to eat. Moreover, the well-to-do, who may be hosting the congregation in their homes, cannot make a distinction at table and in what they serve between their peers and those who might be regarded as their clients. Otherwise, it is their own supper they eat, not the Lord's Supper (11:20).[130] Those who do not "discern the body"—that is, the fellowship of reconciled humanity that is the church of Jesus Christ—can only eat and drink judgment upon themselves at the Lord's Table (11:29).

The same solution—self-restraint—is applied to the problem of the exercise of spiritual gifts in the assembly. There were a variety of spiritual gifts among the members of the Corinthian church, but the one Spirit of the crucified and risen Lord Jesus inspires them all in the one body of Christ. Paul's analogy of the relationship between the oneness of the body and its individual parts in 1 Corinthians 12:12–26 is both suggestive and somewhat obvious, but if Paul was the first to use it he performed quite an intellectual feat. Diversity of race and social class does not prevent incorporation into one body by means of Holy Baptism. Conversely, the unity of the body does not eliminate the differences between people. Jews are still Jews and Greeks are still Greeks; slaves are still slaves and freemen are still freemen; women are still women and men are still men. But they are all made into a new people by the one Spirit of Christ, so there can be no differentiation of status among them in the assembly where the Lord is present because that is an eschatological presence—especially manifested at the Lord's Supper.

At the same time the diversity of spiritual gifts indicates that different members have different functions to perform, and some of these are hierarchically ordered. "God has appointed in the church first apostles, second prophets, third teachers; then deeds of power, then gifts of healing, forms of assistance, forms of leadership, various kinds of tongues" (12:28). Not everyone can be apostles, prophets, and teachers; not all speak in tongues; and not all who speak in tongues can interpret what they are saying. The whole body is dependent on its individual parts. Therefore there can be no pride of place; each must humbly rely on the other members. This is undoubtedly why Paul inserted an excursus on love as the highest of the gifts in the middle of the section of the letter dealing with spiritual gifts (12:31b—14:1a). Without love (agape), all of the other gifts are worthless.

Nevertheless, some gifts are higher than others, and the highest of all are the ones that build up the church—such as prophecy. It is obvious that speaking in tongues had become a problem in the Corinthian church. Whatever theological claims the tongue-speakers may have been making, it is clear that they regarded themselves as spiritually superior to others. There was also some concern about glossolalia in public worship. Paul's discussion of the problem is a delicate attempt to avoid schism in the church. He does not denigrate glossolalia. Indeed, he claims that he can speak in tongues with the best of them. "But in church I would rather speak five words with my mind, in order to instruct others also than ten thousand words in a tongue" (14:19). Paul's concern is both to edify the faithful who have gathered for public worship and also to bring a word of judgment to unbelievers who may be present in the assembly. Glossolalia may make either a positive or a negative impression on unbelievers. Non-Christians may be impressed

---

[130] See Gerd Theissen, *The Social Setting of Pauline Christianity: Essays on Corinth*, ed. and trans. by John H. Schutz (Philadelphia: Fortress Press, 1982), chapter 4: "Social Integration and Sacramental Activity: An Analysis of I Cor. 11:17–34," 145ff.

by the phenomenon. They may also think Christians are mad. Therefore, it would be best to restrain the practice of glossolalia and emphasize the prophetic word. The prophecy that was meant as an edification for the faithful may even turn out to be a sign for unbelievers. For in the prophetic word the unbeliever may feel the presence of God reaching into his innermost being, and will respond to this by worship and public confession (14:22–25). For the same reason, there should be only one speaker at a time. Prophets should yield to those who have received the most urgent messages, but all speakers should restrain their urgent impulses (14:26–33a). Even the exhortation for wives to be silent in church (14:33b–36) is an attempt to interdict situations in which wives publicly contradict their husbands, thus causing embarrassment. This can hardly be a put-down of women in general, since in 1 Corinthians 7 Paul emphasized women's rights in the marital relationship and also recognized their right to prophesy and pray publicly in church. Once again, this was a specific problem Paul was addressing, and it has its place in this chapter that ends with the summary exhortation that "all things should be done decently and in order" (14:40).

This vision of the church, developed in order to deal with particular problems in a particular local church, is transposable to any church. In a more irenic and systematic way, Paul developed the same image of the church as the body of Christ in his epistle to the Romans. He begins by appealing to the sacrificial character of Christian life (Rom. 12:1–2), and immediately translates this "spiritual worship" (12:1) into that humility that comes from the fact that all have received the grace of God. It is at this point that Paul introduces his "body" metaphor: "For as in one body we have many members, and not all the members have the same function, so we, who are many, are one body in Christ, and individually we are members of one another" (12:4–5). This mutual belonging together in the body of Christ will regulate the exercise of the variety of gifts, which are to be used for the edification of all (12:6–8). Once again, Paul holds up love as the highest of the gifts and as the principle that allows all of the gifts to be properly exercised (12: 9–16). In both 1 Corinthians and Romans love is the highest gift. It subordinates all the other gifts, which remain in its service.

Modern Christians have tended to polarize charisms and ministries (i.e., official public functions). Paul is not aware of such a distinction. He is interested in showing that all of the charisms and ministries are gifts of the Holy Spirit that serve to build up the body of Christ. No charism is given except as a ministry and there is no ministry that does not suppose a particular charism. Furthermore, this in no way excludes an order of ministry with its particular charisms which guides all of the other ministries and charisms: that of the apostolate. Paul the apostle wrote to the churches precisely because he presumed that the office of apostle gave him the authority to do so. If the question is asked, Who was the leader of the Corinthian church? the answer, in a real sense, is Paul the apostle.

At the end of the first century there was another schism in the Corinthian church in which some young men had succeeded in deposing the ruling presbyters. Clement, bishop of Rome, wrote an epistle to the Corinthians c. 96 C.E. to address this dissension. While this uninvited intrusion into the affairs of a local church by the leader of another local church might be explained in terms of the close economic and political ties between Rome and Corinth, it is also a witness to a collegiality of the local churches and to the close sense of "succession" from the apostles that the bishops had. The apostolic prerogative exercised by Paul was also exercised by the author of the seven letters in Revelation, by Bishop Ignatius of Antioch, by Bishop Polycarp of Smyrna, as well as by Bishop Clement of Rome and others. Clement developed the idea that "Christ is from God and the apostles from Christ" and that the apostles "appointed their first converts, after testing them by the Spirit, to be the bishops and deacons of future believers."[131] The apostles "knew that there was going to be strife over the title of bishop," and therefore they made provision that "other approved men should succeed to their ministry."[132] Appealing to the sense of order manifest in this apostolic succession, Clement spoke of the "sin" of ejecting "from the episcopate men who have offered the sacrifices with innocence and holiness." Far from being opposed to the "charisms" of the Holy Spirit, this order is essential to the harmony of love which should characterize the body of Christ.

Clement appeals to the order inherent in the sacrificial worship in the Old Testament: the high priest, priests, Levites, and laity (ch. 40). He sees this as a principle that also applies to the people of God of the new covenant. The church acts as one body, moved by one Spirit, but this in no way means that everyone does the same thing or that anyone can fulfill any function. On the contrary, each member of the church has his or her own "liturgy" to perform, and each of these liturgies is but a part of the whole and loses its meaning outside this totality. The choice of the term *leitourgia* (public service) is significant. We have seen that in origin it is a secular term derived from the political structure of the Greek city-states. It is applied here specifically to Christian worship in the sense of a service performed by an individual or a group for the whole community. For Clement, everyone in the church had a liturgy to perform that no one else could perform, and without which the whole was but partial.

Clement derived this sense of liturgical order from the worship of the old covenant, where the term *leitourgia* was used in the Greek translation of the Old Testament (Septuagint) to refer to the public sacrificial cultus. It is interesting to see how he conceives of its correspondence with the liturgical order of the new covenant. The bishop corresponds to the high priest and the deacons to the Levites. But what corresponds to the ancient priests (*hiereis*)? There is no doubt that for all of Christian antiquity the term *hiereus* was never applied to those whom the Middle Ages called "the priests of second rank," the presbyters. "Hiereus" was applied to the Christian laity (*laos*). Here is the concrete working out of the "royal priesthood" metaphor in 1 Peter 2:9. All the Christian laity are priests and they exercise the function of priesthood in offering prayers and gifts. The bishop is the high priest (*archiereus, sacerdos magnus*) in that he presides over the eucharistic sacrifice of the people of God of the new covenant. In the performance of the various liturgies of the clergy and people there is a development of the exercise of the various charisms apportioned to the members of the body of Christ, as

---

[131] *I Clement* 42; in *Early Christian Fathers, The Library of Christian Classics*, op. cit., 62.
[132] Ibid., 63.

described by Paul. The division of liturgical roles is a working out of Paul's exhortation that "all things should be done decently and in order" in a church that had settled down for the long haul through history even though it still expected history to end in that triumph of grace already heralded in the resurrection of Jesus from the dead.

THE ORDERING OF MINISTRY

The question of liturgical roles and order in the liturgical assembly leads to the question of ordered or ordained ministries. This development within early Christianity is important in a history of Christian liturgy, since the differentiation of ordained ministers pertains especially to different liturgical roles.

A number of special ministries are mentioned in the New Testament. The most important of these is the apostolate because the apostles have a direct commission from Jesus himself, who is the envoy of God the Father: "As the Father has sent me, so I send you" (John 20:21). The New Testament is not completely clear concerning the specific role of the Twelve in relation to the missionary apostles such as Barnabas and Paul. It is likely that the idea of the Twelve is connected with Jesus' eschatological message and constitutes a symbolic embodiment of the new Israel. "Truly I tell you, at the renewal of all things, when the Son of Man is seated on the throne of his glory, you who have followed me will also sit on twelve thrones, judging the twelve tribes of Israel" (Matt. 19:28; see also Rev. 21:14). Nevertheless, all of the apostles are eyewitnesses of the resurrection and have a commission from Jesus himself to "make disciples of all nations" (Matt. 28:18).

The prophets are frequently mentioned together with the apostles (Luke 11:49; 1 Cor. 12:28f.; Eph. 2:20, 3:5, 4:11; Rev. 18:20). Their service is charismatic in the sense that their gift is received directly from the Holy Spirit without a mediating rite such as the laying on of hands. The teacher also played an important role in the early church (Acts 13:1; 1 Cor. 12:28f.; Eph. 4:11; James 3:1). It is unclear whether the teacher was a charismatic or a trained scholar or scribe.

Alongside these ministries, three others emerged that relate directly to the institutional life of the church. These ministries concern the tasks of oversight of the church's life and work, counsel to the "overseer," and service to the members. These functions developed into the offices of bishop (*episcopos* 'overseer'), presbyter (*presbyteros* 'elder'), and deacon (*diaconos* 'servant'). The offices of bishop and presbyter are not clearly distinguished in the New Testament. In Acts, the Pastoral Epistles, James, and 1 Peter the function of *episcope* is assigned to the elders (*presbyteroi*). Ephesians 4:11 lists the offices of apostle, prophet, evangelist, pastor, and teacher, which build up the saints for the work of ministry (*eis ergon diakonias*). It is possible that the office of pastor is the same as the office of bishop. In any event, the presbyter-bishops and deacons are ministers who come into their offices through a specific rite of public designation that includes the laying on of hands and prayer (Acts 6:6, 13:3; 1 Tim. 4:14; 2 Tim. 1:6).

While modern scholarship has paid a good deal of attention to the emergence of these offices in the church, relatively few studies have been devoted to the origins and development of the rites by which these offices were ordered or ordained. Nor is there much agreement on the meaning of the laying on of hands in the New Testament texts. The laying on of hands was used in blessings and in baptism, the healing of sickness, and the reconciliation of sinners (1 Tim. 5:22). It would seem that the meaning of the act in such instances is that God's power to bless, to claim persons as his own, and to heal is invoked and imparted. In Acts 13:3, Paul and Barnabas are commissioned to their missionary work with the laying on of hands. It is interesting that they were already included in the company of "the prophets and teachers" (Acts 13:1), and that Paul, who was later recognized as an apostle, was the recipient rather than the bestower of the laying on of hands. In Acts 6:6 the laying on of hands is used to set apart the first seven "deacons" of the church. The term *diaconos* is not actually used in this text; but clearly an office in the church is being designated and the function is that of service or *diakonia*. In 1 Tim. 4:14 and 2 Tim. 1:6, presbyters are appointed by the laying on of hands. According to 2 Tim. 1:6, Paul ordained Timothy. According to 1 Tim. 4:14, the college of presbyters so ordains, and they do "through prophecy."

It has been assumed, since the work of J. Behm early in this century[133] and amplified in the thorough study by E. Lohse,[134] that Christian ordination was modeled on the Jewish ordination of rabbis. There was almost complete scholarly consensus that the early Jewish ordinations included the laying on of hands (*semikah*) in imitation of Moses' "ordination" of Joshua in this way (Num. 27:22–23; Deut. 34:9). One immediate problem with the thesis of Christian adoption of the Jewish practice is that the offices of presbyter and rabbi are not parallel, except for the teaching function that accrued to presbyters who exercised the office of episcope (1 Tim. 5:17–18). A second problem is that we don't know about a comparable Jewish rite of ordination. We need to remember that post-Old Testament Judaism was in as fluid a state of development as early Christianity. There is no doubt that Judaism developed a rite of ordination based on the laying on of hands. Such a rite is mentioned in the Babylonian Talmud. But there is no evidence of it in the tannaitic literature (i.e., before 200 C.E.). The Palestinian Talmud uses the term *minuy* (appointment) to designate the recognition of a rabbi. This term is used in the Mishnah in the sense of a civil appointment, and it is applied to many office-holders and functionaries. But it is applied to rabbis, such as Hillel, only after 70 C.E. In view of this, Rabbi Lawrence A. Hoffman concluded that there is no evidence of a liturgical rite of ordination of rabbis in the early Jewish tradition. He even hints at a Christian influence on Jewish ordination.[135]

The evidence does not allow us to claim that Jewish ordination practice influenced Christian ordination practice. A. Ehrhardt was unconvinced that semikah was used in Palestinian Judaism before 70 C.E., but he conjectured that the example of Moses laying hands on Joshua influenced both Jewish and Christian ordination.[136] E. Ferguson found this argument unconvincing and tried to show, instead, a direct continuity between Jesus' use of the laying on of hands in blessing and similar use by the apostles in post-

[133] J. Behm, *Die Handauflegung im Urchristentum* (Leipzig: Deichert, 1911).
[134] E. Lohse, *Die Ordination im Spätjudentum und im Neuen Testament* (Berlin: Evangelischer Verlag, 1951).
[135] Lawrence A. Hoffman, "Jewish Ordination on the Eve of Christianity," *Studia Liturgica* 13 (1979), 36.
[136] A. Ehrhardt, "Jewish and Christian Ordination," *Journal of Ecclesiastical History* 8 (1954), 125–38.

baptismal and commissioning rites.[137] Edward Kilmartin found Ferguson's sharp distinction between "transferring of authority" and "conferring a blessing" irrelevant, but he
picked up on the possibility of a direct influence of the post-baptismal laying on of hands
on ordination rites.[138] The post-baptismal laying on of hands is directly associated with
the charisms of tongue-speaking and prophecy in Acts 19:6. It is likely that Luke saw the
laying on of hands as a bestowal of the charisms of the Spirit for specific tasks as well in
Acts 6:6 (the setting aside of deacons) and in Acts 13:3 (the setting aside of Barnabas and
Saul as missionaries).

The origin of the laying on of hands in the Pastoral Epistles is even more problematic. Kilmartin finds attractive the proposal of Georg Kretschmar that it can be traced
back to the solemn seating of members of the Jerusalem Sanhedrin in the Pharisaic tradition.[139] The Mishnah Sanhedrin Tractate 4:4 states: "Three rows of sages sat before them.
Each one knew his place; if they needed to *smkh*, they did so, starting with the first."
Kretschmar proposed that this rite of semikah was used by the Jewish Christians as a way
of recognizing their prophets. After the fall of Jerusalem in 70 C.E., Jewish Christians fled
Palestine and settled in the Pauline communities, bringing this practice with them. This
rite of appointment with the laying on of hands commended itself to these communities,
which were faced with the task of securing the teaching of Paul in the face of Gnostic
heresies (2 Tim. 2:8). It thus became a way of commissioning officials for the ministry of
the word and other institutional responsibilities. The attraction of this theory is that the
Christian presbyterate resembled much more the Jewish Sanhedrin than it did the rab-
binate. Ignatius of Antioch referred to the presbyters as being like the divine council of
God (*Trallians* 3:1). Indeed, as a body of elders, their role was to give counsel to the
bishop, who, by the time of Ignatius (c. 115 C.E.), had emerged as the sole leader or
"monarch" of the local church. Moreover, there is the suggestion in 1 Tim. 4:14 of the
presence of prophets at the ordination of presbyters.

It is clear from the letters of Ignatius and the *Didache* that the ministries of
bishops, presbyters, and deacons were established by the beginning of the second century C.E. The *Didache* reflects a situation in which the charismatic apostles and prophets
existed side by side with the bishops and deacons elected by the local community
(*Didache* 15). A century later, in the *Apostolic Tradition* of Hippolytus, there is still a
recognition of charismatic ministry. "If any one among the laity appear to have received a
gift of healing by a revelation, hands shall not be laid upon him, because the matter is
manifest."[140] We do not find a dichotomy between ordained ministers and charismatics in
the early church. Problems arose only when the hierarchy or the charismatics failed to
use their gifts in the service of love and unity.

---

[137] E. Ferguson, "Laying on of Hands: Its Significance in Ordination," *Journal of Theological Studies* 26 (1975), 2.

[138] Edward J. Kilmartin, "Ministry and Ordination in Early Christianity," *Studia Liturgica* 13 (1979), 52.

[139] Georg Kretschmar, "Die Ordination im frühen Christentum," *Freiburger Zeitschrift für Philosophie und Theologie* 22 (1975), 62–3.

[140] *The Treatise on The Apostolic Tradition of St. Hippolytus of Rome*, ed. Dix, 22. Further citations of AT are indicated by page references in the Dix edition.

In Part One of the *Apostolic Tradition* we have the early Christian ordination prayers for the offices of bishop, presbyter, and deacon, as well as the recognition of confessors, and the appointment of widows, lectors, virgins, and sub-deacons. The rubrics tell us a great deal about church order, and the prayers tell us a great deal about the responsibilities of these various ministerial offices.

The bishop is "chosen by all the people" (p. 2). On the appointed Lord's Day of the ordination the people and presbyters assemble with "such bishops as may attend" (p. 3). The intent here was to indicate that the bishop is elected by the local church but receives the recognition of the whole church through the participation of the neighboring bishops. All the bishops lay hands on the bishop-elect, the presbyters standing by in silence, while all pray silently "for the descent of the Spirit." Then one of the bishops prays the ordination prayer, which is in trinitarian form. It begins with a blessing of God for his gracious provision of rulers and priests for Israel; it invokes a pouring out of the "ruling Spirit" on the bishop-elect, which Christ bestowed on his apostles; and it beseeches the Father, who has chosen this candidate "to feed Thy holy flock and serve as Thy high priest, that he may minister blamelessly by night and day . . . and offer to Thee the gifts of Thy holy Church, and . . . have authority to forgive sins according to Thy command" (pp. 4–5). The bishop's status as leader of the local church is suggested by reference to the "princely" or "ruling Spirit" who is invoked on the candidate. The references to the bishop's functions as "high priest" also indicate that the episcopal office is understood primarily in liturgical terms. The bishop serves as the "presiding minister."

It is in conjunction with the ordination of a bishop that we have the famous eucharistic prayer of Hippolytus. The first act of the new bishop is to greet the people and celebrate the eucharist. It is possible that the phrase in the anaphora, "making eucharist to Thee because Thou hast made us worthy to stand before Thee and minister as priests to Thee," is a reference to the ordination that has just taken place. The petition for unity among the communicants may also be occasioned by the fact that representatives of other churches—at least in the persons of their bishops—have come together for this event.

The presbyter is ordained by the bishop laying hands on his head, "the presbyters also touching him" (p. 13). The bishop speaks the ordination prayer, which follows the same form as that for the ordination of a bishop. It is noteworthy that "the spirit of grace and counsel" is invoked on the candidate "that he may share in the presbyterate and govern Thy people in a pure heart" (p. 13). Then there is a reference to Moses' choosing of presbyters. It is clear that the presbyterate is a corporate body responsible for the administration of the local church (hence all the presbyters participate in the laying on of hands). What is not clear is the extent to which the presbyter shares the liturgical responsibilities of the bishop. It is certainly the case that liturgical imagery does not find a place in the ordination prayer for presbyters as it does for that of a bishop. On the other hand, the presbyters do not lay hands on the candidates for the office of deacon because the deacon "is not ordained for a priesthood, but for the service of the bishop that he may do only the things commanded by him" (p. 15).

The duties of the deacon are spelled out further: "he is not the fellow counsellor of the clergy, but (is) to take charge of property and to report to the bishop whatever is necessary" (p. 15). The actual prayer for the ordination of deacons is less specific: "whom thou hast chosen to minister to thy church." On the other hand, the prayer does indicate the deacon's liturgical function: "to bring up in holiness to thy holiness that which is offered to thee by thine ordained high priests" (pp. 17–18)—a reference to the distribution of the eucharistic elements.

A confessor who "has been in chains in prison for the Name" is regarded as a charismatic as far as the offices of presbyter and deacon are concerned. He may come into these offices without laying on of hands. "But if he be appointed bishop, hands shall be laid on him" (p. 18). The gifts a confessor might bring to the ministries of counsel or service he does not necessarily have for the ministry of oversight or supervision.

Widows and lectors are not ordained, but are appointed by the bishop. Widows are appointed by announcement. Lectors are appointed by the bishop's handing to them the book of scriptures. Virgins and sub-deacons are neither ordained nor appointed, but are simply named.

Two general comments may be made about these prayers and rubrics. First, the biblical typology employed in the prayers suggests the lack of any conscious distinction between the Old and New Testaments. Salvation history is of one piece. The community of Jesus Christ simply lives "in the last times." The eucharistic prayer over the bread and cup begins with thanksgiving to God "through Thy beloved Child Jesus Christ, Whom in the last times Thou didst send to us to be a Savior and Redeemer and Angel of Thy counsel." The church that lives in the "last times" has leaders who are in succession with the leaders God provided for Israel. The church's leaders receive the Holy Spirit originally bestowed on Christ and the apostles.

Secondly, the church order in the *Apostolic Tradition* is hierarchically structured. It is in line with the development seen at the beginning of the second century in the letters of Ignatius of Antioch. Ignatius expressed the view that there could not be a church without bishops, presbyters, and deacons, who are earthly icons of God the Father, the apostles, and Jesus Christ in the heavenly church (*Trallians* 3). The bishop preserves the unity of the local church, and therefore no eucharist or other service is to be held, nor is any other action to be taken, without his permission (*Smyrnaeans* 8:2, *Trallians* 7:2). This is not just an effort to organize the church for its long haul through history with strong institutional leadership, although the episcopal government and threefold ministry of the church has proven very durable and serviceable. Rather, as Frank Hawkins has suggested, "This is not a view based ultimately on a desire to magnify the priestly role: it is the natural consequence for the second-century Church of belief in God as Creator of all."[141] In other words, church structure reflects cosmology or worldview, and Christians viewed the universe as hierarchically ordered under the lordship of Christ. The church on earth is to reflect the cosmic order created, redeemed, and sanctified by God the Father, through his Son, in their Spirit who binds heaven and earth together by creating on earth a new community that reflects the life of God.

---

[141] Frank Hawkins, "The Tradition of Ordination in the Second Century to the Time of Hippolytus," in *The Study of Liturgy*, op. cit., 355.

❦ THE EARTHLY AND THE HEAVENLY LITURGIES

The idea that earthly worship approximates heavenly worship was well established in the ancient Near East and in the Bible. The representational images of deity served as "sacramental signs" of the presence of the deity on earth. The earthly temple and its cult thus became a reflection of the heavenly worship. For ancient Israel the real presence of the Lord was experienced in the Tent of Meeting during the days of the sojourn in the wilderness and in the Temple erected on Mount Zion by King Solomon. This presence was specifically identified with the ark of the covenant, since no image of the Lord was allowed. In Solomon's prayer of dedication of the Temple in 1 Kings 8, he acknowledged that the highest heaven could not contain the LORD God, but prayed that God would nevertheless watch over the Temple where he promised that God's Name would dwell (1 Kings 8:29) and hear the prayers offered there. Prayers were directed to God in the Temple and God was experienced in the Temple (e.g., Isa. 6:1ff.; Ps. 24:3–6).[142] After the Babylonian exile and the loss of the ark, the sacrifices became more important as sacramental means of the presence of God with the grace of forgiveness. The destruction of the Second Temple and its sacrificial cult was devastating to Israel, and emerging Judaism located the presence of the Lord in the gatherings of his people rather than in a specific place.

In the New Testament notions of the divine presence in Israel took on new meaning and significance in the incarnation of the Word and the gift of the Holy Spirit. The liturgy of Jesus Christ occurs simultaneously in heaven, by virtue of his ascension into the heavenly sanctuary (Heb. 9:11–12), and in the earthly assembly, by virtue of his sending of the Spirit. The Spirit enables the worship of the earthly church to be joined to the heavenly worship by creating faith through the preaching of the gospel and the administration of the sacraments, since the liturgy of Christ in its earthly mode can only be done by faith and not by sight (Heb. 11:1). The central mystery of faith celebrated in the earthly liturgy is the commemoration of Christ's passover from death to life, from suffering to glory. But, as Massey Shepherd suggests, Revelation projects the paschal liturgy of the earthly church into the heavenly worship, so reciprocal is the correlation between the earthly and the heavenly liturgies.[143] It is not that the Apocalypse is a liturgy; but the paschal liturgy seems to have served as a basis for the structure of the book, even if it does not provide all the symbolism. Thus, in Shepherd's analysis, the seven letters to the churches in Asia Minor in chapters 1–3 corresponds to the scrutinies of the elect; the assembly before the throne of God in chapters 4–5 corresponds to the assembly for the paschal vigil; the six seals in chapter 6 correspond to the readings of the vigil; the sealing of the white-robed martyrs in chapter 7 corresponds to the baptismal initiation; the seventh seal, censing, trumpets, woes, the little scroll, the witnesses, the struggle of Christ and Anti-Christ, and the hallelujahs of chapters 8–19 correspond to the synaxis with its

---

[142] See R. E. Clements, *God and Temple: The Presence of God in Israel's Worship* (Philadelphia: Fortress Press, 1965).

[143] Massey H. Shepherd, Jr., *The Paschal Liturgy and the Apocalypse*, op. cit., 77ff.

prayers, readings from the law and the prophets, gospel and psalmody; and the marriage supper of the Lamb in chapter 19 corresponds to the eucharist. This comparison of the Apocalypse with the paschal liturgy seems plausible. At the same time one must realize that there is no evidence for a full-blown paschal liturgy, such as the one described by Hippolytus a hundred years later, that was contemporary with the Apocalypse or that "such a standardized paschal initiation liturgy existed anywhere before at least the fourth century."[144]

A liturgy and symbolism as complicated and rich as that which served as the basis for the Apocalypse could not be as barren or as primitive as the letter of Minucius Felix claims. Even so, it was the content of the commemoration that connected the earthly and the heavenly liturgies, not the ambiance in which the earthly liturgy was celebrated. The liturgy of Christ commemorated his incarnation, historical ministry, suffering, death, resurrection, ascension, reign in glory, and promise to come again as judge of the living and the dead. The eschatological consciousness that pervaded the earthly liturgy was maintained only with great difficulty as the church settled in for the long journey through history. Yet it was maintained as Christians initiated into the passover of Christ found new ways of participating in his self-offering to God the Father.

---

[144] Paul E. Bradshaw, *The Search for the Origins of Christian Worship*, 35–6.

CHAPTER 4

The Patristic Liturgical Synthesis

T HE PREVIOUS CHAPTER ENDED with a discussion of the correlation between the heavenly and earthly worship in early Christian liturgy. This was certainly not dramatized in any mimetic way in the actual earthly assemblies of Christians. Christians met in the domestic setting of private homes, often donated to the church and renovated into space for the assembly. Like Jews in the synagogues of the same period, Christians gathered around the study of the word. They offered their prayers as a spiritual sacrifice, shared a meal, and practiced a rite of initiation that was centered on a ritual bathing. In no sense can Christian worship in the first three centuries be viewed as public. A persecuted community would not likely be grateful for publicity.

An event happened early in the fourth century, however, that made it possible for the worship of the earthly church to visually approximate heavenly worship. In fact, the public worship of the church actually came to be called "the divine liturgy." The worship of the earthly church could be joined with the praise and adoration of "the angels and archangels and all the company of heaven." In 313, after a decade of the fiercest persecution of Christians and the suppression of the church under the Emperor Diocletian, his successor, the Emperor Constantine, promulgated the Edict of Milan by which he secured for the church the privileges of a *religio licita* (licensed cult) in the Roman Empire.[1]

---

[1] On the provisions of the Edict of Milan and their implications see Charles Norris Cochrane, *Christianity and Classical Culture* (Oxford: Clarendon Press, 1940; reprinted Oxford University Press, 1957), 177ff.

The conversion of Constantine did not mean the immediate conversion of the Roman Empire; indeed, the old paganism resisted Christianity for more than a century after Constantine's reign (306–337).[2] But Christianity was now clearly a public cult. Especially because of the emperor's favoritism toward it, many sought membership in the church. Bishops, who had adjudicated cases between Christians, gained a notoriety for fairness even among pagans, and were granted the dignities of civil magistrates; and great public meeting halls (basilicas) had to be erected to house Christian assemblies.

All of this had a profound impact on the liturgy of the church. The dignities accorded the bishops because of their new social status—courtly greetings, bands of singers to greet their arrivals, lights and incense to precede them in processions—were imported into the liturgy. The logistics of celebrating liturgy in a large public hall required an increase in ceremonies with a complicated system of entrances and exits. New interest in the history of Jesus and places in the Bible encouraged pilgrimages to Palestine, and enterprising local bishops developed rituals at pilgrimage sites that served as dramatic reenactments of events in salvation history. Pilgrims took these stational liturgies home with them. The divine liturgy itself acquired a more dramatic quality, and, with the aid of allegorical interpretation, began to be seen as a reactualization of the saving acts of God in Christ that benefited the devotees of the "mystery of faith" just by their attendance and participation. The church building itself took on the characteristics of a temple—a place where God's glory dwells—almost independently of the liturgies performed in them.[3]

It has long been thought that the Christian cult was influenced by pagan practices, which survived in such instances as mysteriological interpretations of the sacraments, the civic observance of holy days, the cult of the martyrs, and funeral practices. At the same time, Christianity brought profound changes to Greco-Roman society. As Robin Lane Fox has written, "Its forms of worship distorted town plans of established cities and created new centers which showed a new type of hospitality to a broad clientele. Christianity taught the ideal of charity and the spiritual worth of the poor, teachings which did lead to new practice, though never to so much as idealists hoped."[4] What we see developing in the fourth through the sixth centuries is a synthesis of early Christianity, which was so unlike a religion in the minds of Greco-Roman pagans that Christians could be regarded as "atheists," and a Christianity that accommodated itself to and transformed the requirements of a religion for the sanctification of life, time, and space.

The changes that occurred in Christian liturgy during this period were so profound and lasting, as they fed into the cultural entity known as Christendom, that it has not been truly possible until the secular breakdown of Christendom in the twentieth century to finally get behind the fourth century to an earlier (and more eschatologically oriented) Christian piety.

---

[2] See Pierre Chuvin, *A Chronicle of the Last Pagans*, trans. by B.A. Archer (Cambridge: Harvard University Press, 1990).

[3] See the splendid analysis of the profound changes in liturgical practice and piety in the fourth century in Schmemann, *Introduction to Liturgical Theology*, op. cit., 73ff.

[4] Robin Lane Fox, *Pagans and Christians* (New York: Alfred A. Knopf, 1987), 22.

🍇 SOURCES OF LITURGICAL DATA

In spite of the revolutionary character of liturgical change in the fourth century, there was also a continuity between the earlier period and this time of late antiquity in terms of the shape and content of the liturgy. Nothing shows this continuity more than the primary sources of liturgical data: the church orders. We have already looked at the two most important church orders from the early period of Christianity: the *Didache* and the *Apostolic Tradition* of Hippolytus. What is noteworthy is that portions of these church orders are actually preserved intact in the major church orders of the fourth century.

The *Didascalia*, or *The Catholic Teaching of the Twelve Apostles and Disciples of Our Savior*, is thought to have originated in Syria in the first half of the third century. Its original language was Greek, but it survives fully only in a Syriac version, though parts of a Greek and a Latin version have survived in other collections.[5]

The *Apostolic Constitutions* is also of Syrian origin, dating from the second half of the fourth century. The original Greek text survives. Books 1–6 are a reworking of the above-mentioned *Didascalia*; Book 7 includes a version of the *Didache* followed by other liturgical prayers; Book 8 begins with a treatise on charisms, followed by an elaboration of the *Apostolic Tradition*, and concluding with 85 *Apostolic Canons*. The earlier books include several versions of the rites of Christian initiation, and Book 8 includes a full text of the Antiochene eucharist, including the eucharistic prayer. C. H. Turner wrote a series of articles earlier in the twentieth century arguing that the liturgies have an Arian character.[6] While theological differences often affect the texts of prayers, they do not significantly affect the shape of the rites. Thus, the rites of initiation can be compared with those of the orthodox churches, and the eucharistic prayer is clearly a type of the West Syrian eucharist. Moreover, heretical groups such as the Arians often preserved older rites and ceremonies against what they considered to be innovations.

The final church order is the *Testamentum Domini*. This is another elaboration of the *Apostolic Tradition* roughly contemporary with the *Apostolic Constitutions*, and also of Syrian origin. Its original text was probably Greek, but it survives fully only in Syriac. It outdoes the other two church orders, which place their instructions on the lips of the apostles, by placing its instructions on the lips of Christ himself.[7]

The church orders are primary liturgical sources because they provide directions, orders, and texts of liturgies. Another primary liturgical source is the *Euchologion* (Prayer Book) of Bishop Serapion of Thmuis in Egypt (c. 339–363), with whom

---

[5] For an English translation see R. H. Connolly, *Didascalia Apostolorum: The Syriac Version translated and accompanied by the Verona Latin fragments, with an Introduction and Notes* (Oxford: Clarendon Press, 1920). The surviving Greek text is in F. X. Funk, *Didascalia et Constitutiones Apostolorum* (Paderborn, 1905).

[6] C. H. Turner, articles in the *Journal of Theological Studies* 15 (1913–1914), 53–65; 16 (1914–1915), 54–61, 523–38; 31 (1929–1930), 128–41.

[7] For an English translation see *The Testamentum Domini: A Text for Students*, trans. by Grant Sperry–White. Alcuin/GROW Liturgical Study 19 (Nottingham: Bramcote, 1991). For a discussion of the relationship of all the church orders see B. Botte, *La Tradition Apostolique de Saint Hippolyte* (Münster, 1963), xvii–xxviii.

Athanasius corresponded on the issue of the divinity of the Holy Spirit. This book includes prayers to be used in the rites of initiation as well as a full eucharistic prayer, or anaphora, which can be compared with other Alexandrian and Egyptian anaphoras. These thirty prayers ascribed to Bishop Serapion are contained in an eleventh-century manuscript discovered by A. Dimitrijewsky in the library of the Monastery of the Great Lavra on Mount Athos and published by him in 1894. F. E. Brightman wrote a series of articles proposing a more logical arrangement of the prayers.[8] John Wordsworth, in the only English translation available, agreed with Brightman's rearrangement of the prayers but nevertheless followed the order in which they appear in the manuscript.[9] Bernard Botte argued that what survives is an Arian modification of the prayers done fifty years after the time of Serapion.[10] In a more recent analysis, Maxwell Johnson has contended that the prayers are a collection, and not the work of one author; the prayers appear to be substantially orthodox.[11]

The bishops not only presided over the liturgies and often composed their own prayers, but they also commented on liturgical rites and texts in their homilies and sermons. The most important of these for the study of the liturgy is a *genre* of homilies or instruction known as the mystagogical catecheses. These were delivered by bishops during the week after Easter to instruct the newly baptized about the meaning of the sacramental rites in which they had just participated. The most important of these were given by or attributed to Cyril of Jerusalem, Ambrose of Milan, John Chrysostom, and Theodore of Mopsuestia.[12]

Cyril of Jerusalem's catechetical homilies are divided into three sections: the Procatechesis preached to those who are enrolled for baptism; the eighteen catecheses preached to those who were preparing for baptism; and the five mystagogical catecheses that explained the ceremonies of baptism and the eucharist to the newly baptized and communing Christians.[13] While all scholars accept Cyril's authorship of the Procatechesis and the catechetical lectures, they dispute his authorship of the mystagogia because of differences in style and theology and the dating of the eucharistic liturgy described by Cyril. The first two sets were composed around 348 C.E. It is possible that the mystagogia were composed at a time closer to his death in 387.

---

[8] F. E. Brightman, in *Journal of Theological Studies* 1 (1899–1900), 88–113, 247–77. Brightman's order was followed by F. X. Funk in *Didascalia et Constitutiones Apostolorum*, op. cit., 158–95.

[9] For an English translation with an introduction see John Wordsworth, *Bishop Serapion's Prayer Book*, 2nd ed. (London: S.P.C.K., 1910).

[10] B. Botte, "L'Eucologe de Sérapion est-il authentique?" *Oriens Christianus* 48 (1964), 50–6.

[11] Maxwell Johnson, "A Fresh Look at the Prayers of Serapion of Thmuis," *Studia Liturgica* 22 (1992), 163–83. This article is based on Johnson's doctoral dissertation on "The Prayers of Serapion of Thmuis," written at the University of Notre Dame, which is published as *The Prayers of Serapion of Thmuis: A Literary, Liturgical, and Theological Analysis* in Orientalia Christiana Analecta 249 (Rome, 1995).

[12] For English translations see Edward Yarnold, S.J., *The Awe-inspiring Rites of Initiation* (Slough, England: St. Paul Publications, 1971).

[13] See F. L. Cross, *St. Cyril of Jerusalem's Lectures on the Christian Sacraments* (London: S.P.C.K., 1951), which also contains the Greek texts of the Procatechesis and the Mystagogia.

Scholars have accepted the authenticity of Ambrose's *De Mysteriis*, but his authorship of *De sacramentis* has been disputed.[14] Again, the concern is about discrepancies of detail in liturgy and theology. But it is possible that *De sacramentis* represents six spontaneously delivered mystagogia taken down in shorthand by a stenographer, and that *De Mysteriis* represents the shortened version published without those elements that would fall under the disciplina arcani, the secret discipline with regard to certain texts and practices that was observed in the fourth century. The probable date of both works is 391, so the rites described are close to what Augustine experienced at his baptism in 387.

There are three sets of baptismal homilies by John Chrysostom.[15] Of the twelve homilies in all, the second and eleventh describe the rites of baptism. But unlike the mystagogia of Cyril and Ambrose, these were preached before baptism. It is possible that Chrysostom delivered these homilies while he was a presbyter in Antioch before he became bishop of Constantinople.

There are sixteen extant baptismal homilies of Theodore of Mopsuestia, of which the last four describe the rites of initiation. While all of the catecheses concentrate on the symbolic meaning of the rites, Theodore focused especially on the allegorical significance of the liturgy. His catecheses survive only in a Syriac version of the original Greek.[16]

All of these homilies give us insight into the liturgies of the churches of their authors. The catecheses of Cyril are especially important because of the influence of the liturgy of the Jerusalem church on the other churches during the fourth and fifth centuries. Jerusalem in particular, and Palestine in general, gained new prominence during the reign of Constantine because of the magnificent shrines and basilicas he and his family caused to be built at the sites of events in the life of Christ. These drew pilgrims from all over the Roman world. Bishops like Cyril were able to exploit this opportunity by devising special pilgrimage rites at these shrines, which became important in the development of the customs and propers of the church year festivals and days of devotion. Pilgrims, impressed with these practices, took them home and adapted them in their own local churches.

One pilgrim who left a written record of her journey was the Spanish nun Egeria. Her *Itinerarium (Diary)* dates perhaps to the years 381–384, although some scholars have placed it twenty years earlier.[17] Her account of Holy Week and the rites of initiation in Jerusalem is especially interesting and supplements what we know of these practices from Cyril's *Catecheses*. A document that also corroborates the witness of Cyril and Egeria to the organization of the church year, its proper readings, and the buildings

---

[14] See B. Botte, ed., *Des Sacrements, Des Mystères. Sources chrétiennes* 25 (Paris, 1961).

[15] See the English translation with introduction and notes by P. W. Harkins, in *Ancient Christian Writers* 31 (New York: Newman Press, 1963).

[16] See the Syriac text with English translation in A. Mingana, ed. and trans., *Woodbrooke Studies* 6 (Cambridge, 1933).

[17] The best English translation, with a wealth of illustrative material, is John Wilkerson, *Egeria's Travels* (London: S.P.C.K., 1971). See also the English translation by George E. Gingras, *Egeria's Diary*, in *Ancient Christian Writers* 38 (New York and Paramus: Newman Press, 1970).

in which the liturgies were celebrated is the Armenian Lectionary, which testifies to the Jerusalem liturgy about 420–450 C.E.[18]

In addition to her descriptions of the special services that were arranged primarily for tourists and the great buildings in which the liturgies were celebrated, Egeria provides confirmation of three conclusions about the liturgy in the fourth century. First, it was both hierarchical and communal. The bishop was an honored figure accorded great respect. He was assisted by presbyters and deacons carrying out specific liturgical roles. These ministers were constantly in the midst of the people, who had their own role of responding to the litanies and prayers with "Kyrie eleison" and "Amen."[19]

Second, worship is in the process of becoming monasticized. Egeria mentions the *monazontes et parthenae* (male and female monks) who prayed the psalms during the vigils and remained in church after morning prayer for communal prayer until the celebration of the eucharist. As we shall see, the early monks were hermits who lived far away from centers of population. But Egeria witnessed the presence of monks in the city. The early monks had their own prayers and attended the eucharist in the town church. In the fourth century, they began to acquire a liturgical role in the church. This had enormous consequences for the development of the liturgy in both the East and the West.[20]

Third, there was no break with the liturgy of the period before Constantine. There was a continuous development, albeit an accelerated one in the fourth century. Morning and evening prayer were still popular offices consisting of short responses and well-known hymns that could be easily memorized by the congregation, but the monks were slowly introducing their own ideal of prayer with continuous recitation of the psalms. The pre-Constantinian church celebrated the Pasch and commemorated the martyrs, but other days celebrating the life of Jesus were being introduced in the fourth century. Specific readings at particular shrines in Palestine gave impetus to the development of propers for the festivals of the church year. In this development we see a historicizing of the economy of salvation; or, as Alexander Schmemann put it, "an unwavering tendency to detailization."[21]

In the eucharist itself, the essential shape of the liturgy was still clearly discernible. But over it was being laid devotional material (primarily psalmody in this period of liturgical history) to cover movement at certain points, such as at the entrance of the ministers, the procession with the gifts, and the ministration of Holy Communion, which took a considerable amount of time in the throng-filled basilicas. We see these same developments occurring in all of the families of rites ranging geographically from the far east (Persia and India) to the far west (Britain and Spain). This can only suggest similar antecedents for all of these liturgies, similar causes of ceremonial development, and a

---

[18] See the text and French translation in A. Renoux, *Le Codex arménien Jérusalem*, *Patrologia Orientalis* 163, 168 (Paris, 1969, 1971). See also Wilkerson, 253–77.

[19] See Charles Renoux, "Liturgical Ministers at Jerusalem in the Fourth and Fifth Centuries," in *Roles in the Liturgical Assembly*, trans. by Matthew J. O'Connell (New York: Pueblo Publishing Co., 1981), 221–32.

[20] See Schmemann, *Introduction to Liturgical Theology*, 101–13, 146–66.

[21] Ibid., 97.

great deal of cross-cultural influence made possible by the commerce and mobility that flourished within the vast Roman Empire with its highly developed infrastructure of highways and sea lanes.

🍇 THE FAMILIES OF RITES

Christianity flourished primarily, though not exclusively, in the Roman Empire during its first centuries of existence. The Empire constituted an enormous free trade zone embracing all the lands around the Mediterranean sea as far as Syria to the east, Spain and Britain to the west, the Danube and Rhine rivers and Britain to the north, and the expanse of North Africa from Egypt to Gibraltar above the Sahara. Christian missionaries since Paul and Barnabas had used the trade routes on land and sea to spread the gospel. A common Greco-Latin culture spread over this vast Empire, but indigenous cultures also flourished. Part of the wisdom of Roman political administration was to govern each province in the manner in which the local people were most accustomed. Thus, along the borders, especially along the Rhine and Danube Rivers to the north, where German tribes threatened Roman stability, there was a military administration. Towns such as Cologne and Vienna grew up around camps where soldiers settled down and married local women. In the provinces of Gaul, Spain, and Britain, there were few towns or political traditions, so the Roman machinery of government was imported. In the Greek city-states and in the Phoenician city-states of North Africa, a measure of self-government was retained. Outside of the cities in North Africa there were enormous estates owned by emperors or Roman colonists. In Egypt and the Middle East, where people were used to autocratic rule, Roman governors ruled autocratically. In Palestine there had been an effort to maintain a satellite kingdom under Herod the Great, which was one of Rome's more unsuccessful ventures. This experiment ended with the Roman-Jewish War and the siege of Jerusalem in 70 C.E.

The *Pax Romana* lasted for nearly two centuries, from the time of Augustus (31 B.C.E.–C.E. 14) to Marcus Aurelius (161–180). Aurelius was succeeded by his own son, Commodus (180–192), who showed no talent for governing and was assassinated. This was followed by a period of instability and civil war that was not ended until the reign of Diocletian (284–305). Diocletian was an army veteran who began a series of reforms to make the Empire more governable and restore the classical values of republican Rome. It was in connection with the resurgence of pagan devotion that he unleased the severest persecution of Christians. Of more lasting consequence was his attempt to transform the Empire into a centralized autocracy of the eastern type. He insured the loyalty of governors by doubling the number of provinces from fifty to one hundred, thereby reducing the military forces each governor had at his disposal. He instituted a supervisory office between the emperor and the governors called *vicarius* (the emperor's deputy), and each vicar governed a group of provinces called *dioceses*. This elaborate administrative machinery was completed by a reorganization at the top. There were co-emperors, called Augusti, each assisted by a junior emperor, or Caesar. Each Augustus and Caesar had his own capital, and thus began the process of relocating imperial government away from

Rome in cities such as Milan and Byzantium, which Constantine later renamed Constantinople in 330.[22]

The result of this division of the Empire was that local cultures were able to flourish more than they had under Roman rule in the past. Most especially, while ancient republican values continued to be idealized in the West, the more autocratic style of government flourished in the East. These cultural differences had an impact on church life. While the church became almost a department of state in the East, bishops fought to preserve the church's autonomy in the West. A telling symbol of this is that while the Emperor Theodosius was accustomed to standing at the altar with the clergy in Constantinople, Bishop Ambrose had a deacon escort him from the sanctuary in Milan.

Another consequence of imperial reorganization is that it determined the organization of the churches allied with the Roman state. Local churches (i.e., dioceses) began to be grouped into provinces headed by metropolitan bishops, and provinces were related to the great patriarchal churches of Rome, Alexandria, Antioch, Constantinople, and (in the fifth century) Jerusalem. The federation of local churches in provinces encouraged standardization of rites, but also had the effect of accentuating differences between the federations (even though there continued to be borrowing from one ritual family to another).[23]

A summary of the liturgical forms of the different Christian ritual families, moving from East to West, appears below. The major families of rites include the East Syrian, West Syrian, Alexandrian (Egyptian), Roman, and Gallican-Mozarabic (Visigothic).[24]

East Syrian

The ritual family called "East Syrian" flourished on the eastern border of the Roman Empire, centered around the city of Edessa. This was the least Hellenistic of the Eastern rites, and this church tended to look and move even farther eastward. Already in the third century there were Christian communities in Persia. Syrian Christians settled in the Indian province of Kerala by the middle of the fourth century. Syrian missionaries reached western China by the twelfth century. This church used the Aramaic language, now known as Old Syriac, rather than Greek. This semitic Christianity emphasized the humanity of Christ and embraced Nestorianism after the Council of Ephesus in 431. Embracing this "heresy" was also an expression of cultural, political, and ecclesiastical independence from Constantinople and the Byzantine (Eastern Roman) Empire. The East Syrian Christians thrived especially outside of the Byzantine Empire in Mesopotamia and Iran.

Of particular interest is the liturgy of the Syro-Malabar church of India. The Christians of Kerala are descendants of a colony of Syrian Christians that arrived about

---

[22] See Michael Grant, *The Roman Emperors. A Biographical Guide to the Rulers of Imperial Rome, 31 B.C.–A.D. 476* (New York: Charles Scribner's Sons, 1985), 203ff.

[23] See Robert Taft, *Beyond East and West,* 167ff.

[24] See Louis Bouyer, *Eucharist,* 136ff.

345 C.E. Their version of the East Syrian liturgy may have been influenced by Antioch. It developed its own devotional prayers that were said by the priest or the people during liturgical actions. It was further influenced by the Portuguese Catholics who arrived after 1498 and who brought the Malabar church into union with Rome. There was pressure for Latinization of formulas, the calendar, and customs, especially after the Council of Trent.[25]

In spite of this kind of development, the ancient shape of the East Syrian rite can still be discerned in the present-day Syro-Malabar liturgy. Its outline is as follows:

Preparation
Glory to God in the highest (thrice repeated)
Our Father (with embolism)
Psalmody
Hymn to the risen Lord and incensing

Liturgy of the Catechumens
Trisagion
Epistle
Alleluia
Gospel
Litany of Supplication while the sacramental vessels are prepared and
    incensed
Dismissal of the catechumens and the unworthy

Liturgy of the Faithful
Offertory (prayers for worthiness)
Entrance with the gifts
Nicene Creed
Greeting of Peace
Anaphora of Addai and Mari (with words of institution, added under Roman
    Catholic influence)
Fraction and consignation
Litany of forgiveness
Our Father
P/ Holy things befit perfectly the holy people, O Lord.
R/ One Holy Father; one Holy Son; one Holy Spirit.
Ministration of Holy Communion
Thanksgiving prayer
Last Blessing

There are features of this liturgy similar to the West Syrian rite: the entrance with the gifts, the use and location of the Nicene Creed, "Holy things befit . . . the holy people" at the elevation. Other elements are uniquely Semitic, especially the anaphora or eucharistic prayer. The Anaphora of Addai and Mari was discussed in the previous chapter. Other eucharistic prayers in this tradition include the anaphoras of Theodore of

---

[25] See Jacob Vellian, *History of the Syro-Malabar Liturgy* (Kottayam, 1967). The Catholic Malabar Christians are centered at Kottayam. Other Syrian Christians, who did not enter into union with Rome, are centered at Chingavanam.

Mopsuestia and Nestorius, and the Third Anaphora of the Apostle Peter, which is used in the uniate Maronite church in Lebanon.[26]

Some commentators have seen in the Third Anaphora of the Apostle Peter a text that, like Addai and Mari, dates back to the third century. There is in the initial dialogue an invitation to lift up "minds . . . to heaven" and "hearts in purity." We will also see this double lifting up of minds and hearts in the West Syrian Anaphora of James. But the response in Apostle Peter is purely Semitic: "To you, Lord, God of Abraham, Isaac, and Israel, O King glorious and holy forever."

There is a structural as well as a verbal and theological similarity between Addai and Mari and Apostle Peter. We will see in the West Syrian anaphoras a tripartite structure of praise to the Father, remembrance of the Son, and supplication of the Holy Spirit. In the East Syrian anaphoras there is a bipartite structure: praise—supplication. The praise section begins:

ADDAI AND MARI	APOSTLE PETER
Worthy of glory from every mouth	Glory to you,
and thanksgiving from every tongue	
is the adorable and glorious name	adorable and praiseworthy name
of the Father and of the Son	of the Father and of the Son
and of the Holy Spirit.	and of the Holy Spirit.

In both anaphoras the praise-section leads to the Sanctus. The thanksgiving continues after the Sanctus, and it is addressed to the Son rather than to the Father or to the Trinity as a whole.

ADDAI AND MARI	APOSTLE PETER
Lord, we also,	We confess to you, Lord,
your lowly, weak and miserable servants	we your sinful servants,
give you thanks because you have	that you have given
brought about in us a great grace	your grace
which cannot be repaid.	which cannot be repaid.
For you put on our human	You put on our human
nature to give us life	nature to give us life
through your divine nature,	through your divine nature;
you raised us from our lowly state,	you raised our lowly state;
you restored our fall;	you restored our fall;
you restored our immortality;	you gave life to our mortality;
you forgave our debts;	you justified our sinfulness;
you justified our sinfulness;	you forgave our debts;
you enlightened our intelligence.	you enlightened our intelligence,
	conquered our enemies,
	and made our weak nature to triumph.

This thanksgiving for the saving dispensation of grace granted to weak and sinful humanity leads to the petition: "You, Lord, be graciously mindful of all the holy and righteous

---

[26] See Hänggi and Pahl, *Prex Eucharistica*, 381ff., 387ff., 410ff., and Jasper and Cuming, *Prayers of the Eucharist*, 29ff. for the Third Anaphora of the Apostle Peter.

forbearers, when we commemorate your body and blood, which we offer to you on your living and holy altar, as you, our hope, taught us in your holy gospel and said, 'I am the living bread who came down from heaven that mortals may have life in me'" (similar words in Addai and Mari). It is noteworthy that this prayer of commemoration continues to be addressed to Christ. It expresses a gathering of the whole family of Christ around the eucharistic table. It also serves as a prelude to the anamnesis and institution narrative (much elaborated beyond the biblical texts) which is clearly embedded in the supplicatory section of the prayer (as it is also in the Alexandrian and Roman anaphoras).

The anaphoras in this tradition are more condensed than later texts. Scholarly opinion has turned against earlier views that the Sanctus is typically lacking.[27] There is little emphasis on sacrifice except for the offering of the gifts of bread and wine. The epiclesis is underdeveloped by later standards, and is missing entirely in Apostle Peter. But the glorification of the Name may be a form of invocation, making the whole anaphora an epiclesis. Odo Casel suggested that the primitive form of the epiclesis was a naming of God over the event or object of blessing.[28] The earliest development of the epiclesis, therefore, would have been to specify the objects of blessing with reference to the benefits the faithful might receive from sharing in these blessed objects. This happens for the first time in the Anaphora of Hippolytus, in which the institution narrative sums up the wonders for which God is praised, and introduces the memorial, in the context of which the gifts of bread and wine are offered to God for blessing. The blessing is accomplished by calling down the Holy Spirit with a petition for the benefits of communion. This seems to be less a "resurgence of the archaic type" of eucharistic prayer (L. Bouyer) than a development of a tradition. The East Syrian anaphoras themselves are survivals of the archaic table graces.

West Syrian

The West Syrian tradition had its center in Antioch, but was also linked with Jerusalem and Constantinople. Antioch was a Greek city in Syria, but was commonly regarded in the Roman Empire as the capital of the eastern world. It was an early center of Christian life and mission. After the christological confession of the Council of Chalcedon in 451, the church of Antioch divided. The orthodox party, called "Melkite" (followers of the emperor), retained their connection with Constantinople. The other party, called "Jacobite" after Bishop Jacob Baradai, embraced monophysitism, in part as a form of resistance to Byzantine cultural imperialism. It was among the Jacobites that the old Antiochene tradition lived on, embodied in the Liturgy of James. The Maronites, originating in 681 in connection with monotheletism, also maintained the old Antiochene tradition.[29]

The importance of the Jerusalem church during the fourth and fifth centuries has been mentioned. The Antiochene Liturgy of James also became the rite of Jerusalem,

[27] See Bryan Spinks, *The Sanctus in the Eucharistic Prayer*, 57–61.

[28] See Casel, "Zur Epiklese," *Jahrbuch für Liturgiewissenschaft* 3 (1923), 100–3.

[29] See M. Hayek, *Liturgie maronite* (Paris, 1963).

although G. J. Cuming has noted Egyptian elements in the rite described by Cyril in his Catechetical Homilies.[30] It would not be surprising that a church which exported so many of its practices also imported liturgical ideas from other churches through the many prominent visitors who made pilgrimages to the Holy Land.

It is possible to see the primitive shape of the West Syrian liturgy from two major sources. The *Apostolic Constitutions* provides a liturgy of the word that consisted of readings from the Old Testament, psalm singing, epistle and gospel, homily, dismissal of the catechumens, and prayers of the faithful. From Cyril's *Catecheses* we know that the liturgy of the eucharist included the anaphora, the Lord's Prayer, the invitation to communion ("Holy things for the holy people"), and communion from the bread and cup. This simple rite was expanded at several points, as was the case in all the classical liturgies. These were primarily at points of action: the entrance, the offertory, and the communion, at which there was movement of clergy and people.

The Liturgy of James was a conflation of the rites of Antioch and Jerusalem that emerged around 400.[31] The oldest full text of James is the ninth-century Vatican ms. gr. 2282, originating from the area around Damascus. This liturgy may be outlined as follows:

> Prothesis (Preparation—two prayers)
> Enarxis (five prayers)
> Little Entrance:
>   Prayer and Synapte (litany)
>   Antiphon
> Epistle
> Alleluia and two prayers
> Gospel
> Prayers of the Faithful
> Great Entrance with the gifts:
>   Cherubic Hymn
>   Five Prayers
> Nicene Creed
> Kiss of Peace
> Two offertory prayers and two prayers of the veil
> The Anaphora of James
> Prayer and the Lord's Prayer
> Prayer of Inclination (heads bowed during petition for worthy reception and
>   the benefits of communion)
> Prayer of Elevation
>   *Bishop (raising the gifts):* The holy things for the holy people.
>   *People:* One is holy, one is Lord, Jesus Christ, to the glory of God the
>   Father, with the Holy Spirit; to him be glory for the ages of ages.
> Communion

---

[30] G. J. Cuming, "Egyptian Elements in the Jerusalem Liturgy," *Journal of Theological Studies*, n.s. 25 (1974), 117–24.

[31] See F. E. Brightman, *Liturgies Eastern and Western* (Oxford, 1896; reprinted 1965), 31–68 (Greek text), 69–110 (Syriac text).

Two prayers behind the ambo
Thanksgiving for Communion
Dismissal

A law of liturgical development is that as some parts of the liturgy become over-burdened (particularly the points of action) with text and ceremonial, other parts get cut back (particularly elements from an earlier stage of development, such as the Old Testament lessons and the responsorial psalmody). It should also be noted that the anaphora is the telltale sign of a particular liturgy, since the shape of the liturgy tends to be similar in all the Eastern rites.

It should also be noted that there were two kinds of liturgical material developed in the East that aided congregational participation: the litany and antiphonal psalmody. These were the kinds of devotional material that often filled in moments of action when the clergy were otherwise involved. The litany is a series of prayer bids announced by the deacon with the people responding to each one, "Kyrie eleison" (Lord, have mercy). It is also a kind of prayer that could be sung in procession from one station to another. Antiphonal psalmody in the East was not at first two choirs singing alternately with each other, but the people responding to the singing of the psalm by a cantor with a repeatable refrain (the antiphon). These forms came to be employed in all the eastern liturgies.

The West Syrian eucharistic prayers display an order and logic that finds no equal elsewhere. These anaphoras have a trinitarian structure so conspicuous that it can only be regarded as the achievement of people imbued with the theology of the end of the fourth century. Each prayer has an introductory section that praises God for his work of creation, which leads to the Sanctus. A bridge from the Sanctus, such as "Holy are you," leads to a recital of salvation history culminating in the Christ-event and the institution narrative of the Lord's Supper. An anamnesis, often picking up from the last line of the institution text, "Do this in remembrance of me," leads to the oblation and epiclesis ("remembering . . . we offer . . . and petition"). The epiclesis is a petition for the Holy Spirit to manifest or transform *(metabole)* the gifts into the body and blood of Christ, and to bestow on the faithful the gifts of communion. This leads to an expression of the *communio koinonia* (community) of the church in the intercessions for the living and the commemoration of the departed. There is a concluding trinitarian doxology. The schema looks like this:

Father	Preface
(creation)	Sanctus
Son	Recital of salvation history
(redemption)	Institution narrative
	Anamnesis and oblation
Holy Spirit	Epiclesis
(sanctification)	Intercessions and commemorations
Holy Trinity	Doxology

Outlining the prayers in this way is not meant to suggest a modalism by which the work of one member of the Godhead is not the work of the whole God (for example, that the Son and Spirit are not involved in the work of creation, or that the Father and the

Spirit are not involved in the work of redemption). Indeed, the orthodoxy of the Byzantine liturgy is such that prayer is always addressed to the Trinity as a whole (e.g., We praise and glorify you, Father, Son, and Holy Spirit) rather than the Roman pattern of addressing prayer to the Father, through the Son, in the Holy Spirit. Nor is it meant to imply that all of the prayers in the West Syrian tradition routinely embody a trinitarian theology as Nicene as that of the Cappadocian fathers. The grandest of these prayers, from the so-called Clementine liturgy in Book VIII of the *Apostolic Constitutions*, may in fact have been put together by Semi-Arians. And the Liturgy of James came to be used, after 431, only by Monophysites. What contributed to the trinitarian structure may be have been less theology than the recovery of liturgical roots. Louis Bouyer propounds the thesis that the tripartite structure of the Jewish meal thanksgiving, the Birkat ha-Mazon, has been fleshed out by amalgamation with the three berakoth of the synagogue: the two blessings preceding the Shema (the second of which includes the qedushah, or Sanctus) and Tefillah of the eighteen benedictions.[32] This fusion of synagogue and meal-berakoth resulted in the expansion of the creation theme and the inclusion of the Sanctus from the two blessings preceding the Shema, and the expansion of the intercessions from the influence of Tefillah. The proof of the recovery of Jewish roots in the fourth century can be found in Book VII of the *Apostolic Constitutions*, where Christian prayers of a very Hellenistic cast are directly based on synagogue prayers, some of which are taken over into the anaphora in Book VIII.[33]

The so-called Clementine Anaphora in Book VIII of the *Apostolic Constitutions* is an impressive prayer in length, content, and style. It expresses as completely as possible everything that ancient Christians could think to put into a eucharistic prayer. There are many references to Hippolytus, as there are throughout this church order. But the invitation, "Lift up your hearts," from which the name "anaphora" derives (the "lifting up"), has been changed to "Lift up your minds" *(ton noun)*. In the Greek mind *nous* was the soul, the most spiritual aspect of the human being, whereas "heart" was only the seat of the emotions. This already alerts us to the Hellenistic character of this prayer, which nevertheless retains many Semitic expressions.

The introductory section transforms the "knowledge"-theme of the berakah leading to the qedushah into a Logos-theme, the "living Wisdom" through whom all things were made. This is the one proclaimed as "the firstborn of all creation, the Messenger of thy great Counsel [an allusion to Hippolytus], the High Priest, the King and Lord." It projects a great vision of all creation tending toward humanity created in the image of God, which evokes Genesis 1 and Psalm 103 as well as the first three prayers of Tefillah. The evocation of the angelic world as part of God's creation leads to the Sanctus. This is followed by a neat transition into the post-Sanctus recital of salvation history, which includes Christ in the work of creation and redemption.

> Truly you are holy and all-holy, most high and exalted above all forever. Holy also is your only-begotten Son, our Lord and God Jesus Christ, who ministered

---

[32] Bouyer, *Eucharist*, 88–90.
[33] Ibid., 119–35, 250–68.

to you, his God and Father, in all things, in the varieties of creation, and in appropriate forethought. He did not overlook the race of men as it perished.[34]

This leads to a fulsome account of salvation history in both the Old and the New Testaments in which the work of Christ is described by a series of paradoxes: humanity's creator becomes a man, the law-giver submits to the law, the priest makes himself a victim, the shepherd becomes a sheep, the Word becomes flesh, the author of all things is born of a virgin, the fleshless takes on a body, the eternal is born in time, the Judge is judged, the Savior is condemned, the Impassible is nailed to the cross, the immortal dies, and the Life-giver is buried.

After the institution narrative and anamnesis, the Holy Spirit is invoked on the oblation to manifest *(apophene)* the bread and wine as the body and blood of Christ. The foundation of this epiclesis is the curious formula in which the Holy Spirit is called "the witness of the sufferings of the Lord Jesus" (see 1 Peter 5:1). The second part of the epiclesis asks for the benefits of the sacrament and then passes into a litany of intercessions for the whole church and the whole world and a commemoration of all the forbearers and saints.

Antiochene creativity was not exhausted with this prayer. Equally impressive is the Anaphora of James, which was disseminated in Syriac, Arabic, Greek, Ethiopic, Armenian, Georgian, and Slavonic versions, even though it was quickly supplanted by the two abridged prayers attributed to Basil and John Chrysostom. We note at the outset a compromise of the Hellenistic and Semitic spirits in the anaphoral invitation, "Lift up your minds and hearts." The introduction is considerably briefer than the Clementine liturgy. Of special note is the summing up of all creation in the heavenly Jerusalem (this was, after all, the liturgy of the Jerusalem church): the festal assembly of the elect, the church of the firstborn whose names are written in heaven, the spirits of the righteous and the prophets, to whom are joined the souls of the martyrs and the prophets. The institution narrative and anamnesis are incorporated into the chronology of salvation history. The institution text becomes a part of the passion account, and the anamnesis introduces the resurrection, ascension, and promise to come again as judge of the living and the dead. This last thought leads to the offering of "this awesome and bloodless sacrifice, that you deal not with us after our sins nor reward us according to our iniquities, but according to your gentleness and [unspeakable] love for man to [pass over and] blot out [the handwriting that is against us] your suppliants."[35] This moves on to an epiclesis that contains as full a *Heilsgeschichte* (salvation history) of the Holy Spirit as will be found in any liturgical text. The Holy Spirit is extolled as "the Lord and giver of life, who shares the throne and the kingdom with you, God the Father and your (only-begotten) Son, consubstantial and coeternal, who spoke in the law and the prophets and your new covenant." The Spirit's descent as a dove on Jesus in the Jordan River and as tongues of fire on the heads of the apostles on the day of Pentecost are recalled before invoking the Spirit on the bread and wine to "make" them the body and blood of Christ. As in the Clementine

---

[34] Jasper and Cuming, 109.
[35] Ibid., 63.

liturgy, but in a more developed form, there follows a whole Christian Tefillah in which each petition is connected with the "memorial" by the words "Remember, Lord." There are twenty-one remembrances, the longest intercession in any patristic eucharist.

Despite its popularity for a time, James was soon replaced with other, briefer anaphoras that were adopted by the church of Constantinople, and that were soon used by the whole orthodox East, while James became the liturgy of the Syrian Monophysites. It should be added that a factor causing the abandonment of James was the feeling among the orthodox (and therefore the imperialist party in Syria) that it was a sign of local particularism, and therefore they readily embraced the liturgies of the imperial capital.

The third center of the West Syrian rite was the city designated as the "new Rome" by the Council of Constantinople in 381, Constantinople itself. All of the traditions of the East were filtered through this church, with orthodoxy prevailing over all heresies condemned by ecumenical councils. The great bishops of the imperial capital brought with them the theology of Cappadocia (Gregory of Nazianzus, 379–381) and the liturgy of Antioch (John Chrysostom, 398–404). The prestige of this patriarchal diocese enabled it to influence and eventually supplant other local rites. This is why we see Byzantine influences on the Liturgies of James (Antioch and Jerusalem) and Mark (Alexandria). The Byzantine rite also spread beyond the Empire into the countries Christianized by missionaries from Constantinople, especially the Slavic peoples to the north who were evangelized by the Greek brothers Cyril (827–869) and Methodius (c. 825–885).

Two liturgical rites were used for the eucharist in Constantinople: those bearing the names of John Chrysostom (349–407) and Basil of Caesarea (c. 329–379). The names of these bishops apply particularly to the anaphoras. Indeed, among the major liturgies influenced by Constantinople, development is so similar that only the anaphora texts distinguish one liturgy from another. What we see in the post-Nicene era is the "canonization" of eucharistic prayers, whereas in earlier times the eucharistic prayer was as much the work of the bishop or presiding minister as the homily.

It is thought that at least the core of the Anaphora of John Chrysostom can be attributed to one which he brought with him from Antioch. The Anaphora of John Chrysostom can be compared to the Anaphora of the Twelve Apostles, which is extant only in Syriac.[36] A Coptic version of the Anaphora of Basil testifies to a version of this prayer lacking post-Nicene/Constantinopolitan theological formulations (i.e., pre-381 C.E.).[37] It has been thought that an early form of this anaphora was brought from Cappadocia to Alexandria, and that the later version was amplified by Basil himself.[38]

---

[36] See Georg Wagner, *Der Ursprung der Chrysostomliturgie, Liturgiewissenschaftliche Quelle und Forschungen* 59 (Münster, 1973), 1–138; Hänggi-Pahl, 223–9, 265–8; Jasper-Cuming, 124ff., 129ff.; Bouyer, *Eucharist*, 280–90.

[37] See J. Doresse and E. Lanne, *Un témoin archaïque de la liturgie copte de S. Basile, Bibliotheque du Muséon* 47 (Louvain, 1960).

[38] See H. Engberding, *Das eucharistische Hochgebet der Básileiosliturgie* (Münster i.W., 1931); Hänggi-Pahl, 230–43; Jasper-Cuming, 34ff.; Bouyer, 290–303.

The main evidence for both of these liturgies is the Codex Barberini ms. gr. 336, from about 800, although a full description of the Byzantine liturgy of the seventh century is also given by Maximus the Confessor in his *Mystagogia* (c. 630).[39] The outline of these liturgies is as follows:

Prothesis
Enarxis
Little Entrance Prayers
Trisagion
Epistle
Psalm/Alleluia
Gospel
Ektene (Prayer of Supplication)
Dismissal of the Catechumens
Prayers of the Faithful
The Great Entrance/Cherubic Hymn
Proskomide (Offertory Prayer)
Kiss of Peace
Nicene Creed
The Anaphora
Lord's Prayer
Prayer of Inclination
Prayer of Elevation:
> P/ Holy things for the holy people.
> R/ One is holy, one is Lord, Jesus Christ,
> to the glory of God the Father.
Communion
Thanksgiving for Communion
Dismissal (prayer behind the ambo)

The most exhaustive critical studies of the Byzantine liturgy are by Juan Mateos and Robert Taft.[40] The Byzantine liturgy is the eucharistic service (typicon) of the Great Church of the Holy Wisdom (Hagia Sophia) in Constantinople, built by the Emperor Justinian in 532–37. It was for centuries the largest worship space in Christendom. What was done in this space was imitated by others, just as what was done in the stational liturgies of Rome was imitated by the churches across the Alps.

The *Prothesis* is the preparation of the eucharistic elements in the sacristy before the liturgy begins. The prayers accompanying this action may have been the original offertory prayers before the Great Entrance. The Prothesis itself originated only in the eighth century as a result of monastic influence.

---

[39] See *The Study of Liturgy*, 254ff.; also Juan Mateos, "The Evolution of the Byzantine Liturgy," *John XXIII Lectures* 1 (New York: Fordham University, 1965), 76–112.

[40] J. Mateos, "Evolution historique de la liturgie de saint Jean Chrysostome," *Proche-Orient Chrétien* 15 (1965), 333–51; 16 (1966), 3–18, 133–39; 17 (1967), 141–76; 18 (1968), 305–35; 19 (1969), 97–122. In these articles Mateos carried his commentary from the initial blessing to the gospel. The commentary was continued by his student, Robert Taft, in "Toward the Origins of the Offertory Procession in the Syro-Byzantine East," *Orientalia Christiana Periodica* 36 (1970), 73–107, and expanded in *The Great Entrance* OCP 200 (Rome: PIO, 1978).

The *Enarxis* is a series of three psalms and antiphons that were probably sung at stations during processions on certain days in Constantinople. In Chrysostom's day the actual liturgy began with the entrance of the clergy and people into the church. The bishop went to his throne in the apse and greeted the people with the words, "Peace be with you." The *Trisagion* became the entrance hymn. This was first mentioned at the Council of Chalcedon in 451, where it was used as an anti-Monophysite battle cry. Taft believes that the text is actually the incipit (beginning) and finale of an antiphonal psalm. The psalm has fallen out of use, leaving only the refrain—much like the Kyrie in the later Roman rite. This might also account for the inclusion of the Gloria Patri in the text. The text of the hymn is as follows:

> Holy God. Holy Mighty One. Holy Immortal One. Have mercy on us.
>   [three times]
> Glory to the Father and to the Son and to the Holy Spirit,
>   now and always and forever and ever. Amen.
> Holy God. Holy Mighty One. Holy Immortal One. Have mercy on us.

Similar developments in the liturgy of the word occurred in the liturgies of both the new and the old Rome. The Old Testament lesson with its responsorial psalm fell out of use, so that the readings were reduced from three to two. The general intercessions in litany-form were moved from the place for the prayers of the faithful after the dismissal of the catechumens to the entrance rite, where in the Byzantine liturgy it became the Litany of Peace and in the Roman liturgy it became the Kyrie. The *Ektene*, or insistent litany, sometimes called the "ecumenic prayer," was added after the gospel or sermon. It was originally a stational litany used on rogation days, or days of penitence. Its corollary would be the so-called Great Litany that developed in the Western church to be used on penitential days (see *LBW*, pp. 168ff.) This is followed in the Byzantine liturgy by the prayers for the catechumens and their dismissal.

The most splendid moment in the Byzantine liturgy is the Great Entrance with the gifts. In today's use, the priest and deacons bring the vessels and bread and wine from the table of prothesis in the sacristy into the nave, where they process through the nave to the royal doors in front of the sanctuary. There is a pause for commemorations before they proceed to place the vessels and elements on the altar. What made this procession necessary was the fact that originally the sacristy was a separate building, and the deacons had to fetch the gifts and bring them into the church. The size of Hagia Sophia made a ceremonial development necessary, and this was undoubtedly imitated in other local churches. But the theological undergirding for such a development had already been provided by Theodore of Mopsuestia (d. 428) in his mystagogical catecheses. There he summons the imagination of the faithful to behold in the liturgy a dramatic reenactment of the mystery of our salvation.

> It is indeed evident that [this eucharistic food] is a sacrifice, but not a new one and one that [the priest] performs as his, but it is a remembrance of that other real sacrifice [of Christ]. Because the priest performs things found in heaven through symbols and signs, it is necessary that his sacrifice also should be as their image, and that he should represent a likeness of the service of heaven. . . .

We are ordered to perform in this world the symbols and signs of the future things so that, through the service of this Sacrament, we may be like men who enjoy symbolically the happiness of the heavenly benefits, and thus acquire a sense of possession and a strong hope of the things for which we look. . . .

[This sacrament] contains an image of the ineffable Economy of Christ our Lord, in which we receive the vision and the shadow of the happenings that took place. This is the reason why through the priest we picture Christ our Lord in our mind, as though in him we see the One who saved us and delivered us by the sacrifice of Himself; and through the deacons who serve the things that take place, we picture in our mind the invisible hosts who served with that ineffable service. It is the deacons who bring out this oblation—or the symbols of this oblation—which they arrange and place on the awe-inspiring altar, [an oblation] which in its vision, as represented to the imagination, is an awe-inspiring event to the onlookers.[41]

Thus, the people were taught to regard the earthly liturgy as a representation of the heavenly worship. The splendid entrance procession during the singing of the so-called Cherubim Hymn sensually reinforced this image.

The Cherubic Hymn was introduced by Justin II in 574 to accompany the Great Entrance.

We who mystically represent the cherubim singing the thrice-holy hymn to the life-giving Trinity, let us cast aside all earthly cares that we may receive the King of all invisibly escorted by the angelic hosts. Alleluia.[42]

This hymn makes it clear that the offertory is the welcome extended to Christ the Ruler of all things (Pantocrator); at no other point is the earthly liturgy so explicitly the image of the heavenly liturgy. This awesome character of this moment in the liturgy led to the anaphora being said silently in the sanctuary to which only the ordained ministers had access. In time, a wall (iconostasis) was erected between the nave and the sanctuary that further screened out the people. It should be noted that already by the end of the fourth century, the stress on the holy and awesome character of the consecrated elements, plus the rigor of the pre-communion abstinence (including refraining from the marriage act), played a role in the decline in frequent reception of communion among the people. When the people no longer received communion, they focused their devotion elsewhere. The flow of the liturgy became interrupted by the addition of devotional materials, such as prayers and hymns and even the Nicene Creed. The Creed was inserted in 476 as a Monophysite practice to emphasize their loyalty to the Council of Nicea. Its introduction into the rite of Constantinople by Patriarch Timothy (511–17) separated the anaphora from the Great Entrance with the gifts, thus obscuring the original shape and flow of the liturgy at this point.

The Great Thanksgivings of the Byzantine rite are the anaphoras of John Chrysostom and Basil. The latter has come to be used only on the Vigils and Festivals of Christmas and Epiphany, the Feast of Saint Basil (January 1), the Sundays in Lent (except

---

[41] Trans. in Yarnold, *The Awe-Inspiring Rites of Initiation*, op. cit., 177. Words in brackets are the translator's.

[42] The hymn, "Let all mortal flesh keep silence" (LBW 198), is based on the "Cherubic Hymn."

Palm Sunday), Maundy Thursday, and Holy Saturday, although it was used more frequently in ancient times. John Chrysostom is used at other times.

The Anaphora of John Chrysostom is characterized by a use of verbatim quotations of Scripture, beginning with a salutation that follows the Pauline text in 2 Corinthians 13:14. Differences with "Twelve Apostles" are as follows:

TWELVE APOSTLES	JOHN CHRYSOSTOM
The love of God the Father,	The grace of our Lord Jesus Christ,
the grace of the only-begotten Son	and the love of the God and Father,
and our Lord and great God	
and Savior Jesus Christ,	
and the fellowship of the Holy Spirit	and the fellowship of the Holy Spirit
be with you all.	be with you all.

In view of this use of scriptural quotations, it is striking that the anamnesis in John Chrysostom is not dependent on the Pauline text, "Do this in remembrance of me" (1 Cor. 11:24), which is missing. Twelve Apostles even includes the Pauline amplification (1 Cor. 11:16, "For as often as you eat this bread and drink the cup . . ."). But it is placed on the lips of Christ, as indeed the anamnesis, like Addai and Mari, is addressed not to the Father but to the Son. John Chrysostom corrects this and also substitutes a sacrificial formula for the simple invocation of the divine mercy, as follows:

TWELVE APOSTLES	JOHN CHRYSOSTOM
While, therefore, we remember,	We, therefore, remembering
Lord, your saving command	this saving commandment
and all your dispensation	and all things
which was for us,	which were done for us:
your cross,	the cross, the tomb,
your resurrection from the dead	the resurrection
on the third day.	on the third day,
your ascension into heaven	the ascension into heaven,
and your session at the	the session
right hand of the majesty	at the right hand,
of the Father,	the second and glorious
and your glorious and second coming,	coming again;
in which you will come in glory	offering your own
to judge the living and the dead,	from your own,
and to repay all people	in all and through all:
according to their works	*People:* We hymn you,
in your love for humankind—	[we bless you,
for your church and your flock	we give you thanks,
beseech you, saying through you	O Lord, and pray to you,
and with you to your Father,	our God.]
"have mercy on me."	
People: Have mercy on us,	
God, almighty Father,	
have mercy on us.	

Priest: We also, Lord, give thanks and confess to you on behalf of all humanity for all things.[43]	*Priest:* We offer you also this reasonable service.[44]

The epiclesis in John Chrysostom introduces for the first time in the anaphoras the specification that the Holy Spirit makes the bread and wine the body and blood of Christ, "changing them (*metaballon*) by your Holy Spirit." This marks the first time that a technical term in sacramental theology has come into a eucharistic prayer. It is also found in the Byzantine version of the Anaphora of Basil.

The Anaphora of Basil of Caesarea was brought into Egypt at an early date. Whether this is an earlier version of the later expanded by Basil, as Dom Engberding thinks, we cannot say. But it is certain that the "Alexandrian Basil" is one of the oldest anaphoras known to us. It has captured the imagination of twentieth-century liturgists as a text to emulate, second only to Hippolytus. It serves as the basis of Roman Eucharistic Prayer IV in the 1970 *Roman Missal* and of the so-called Common Eucharistic Prayer composed by an ecumenical committee and included in *The Book of Common Prayer* of the Episcopal Church in the U.S.A. and in several Protestant worship books.

Because of the importance of this prayer in our contemporary use, and the antiquity of the Egyptian version, we provide here a translation of Engberding's reconstruction of the Greek original, supplemented by Doresse's and Lanne's Coptic text (which lacks the first third of the anaphora). A comparison of the versions shows that the later additions are of little importance. They are mainly rhetorical amplifications, explanatory formulas, or extensions of biblical quotations. The Egyptian text is striking for its sobriety by West Syrian standards (especially the pre-Sanctus section), and may lie behind the developed anaphora of James as well as the Byzantine anaphora of Basil.[45]

The Alexandrian Anaphora of Basil

It is indeed right and proper to give thanks to you who are the Master, the Lord, the God of truth, who are before time began and who reigns forever and ever: You live in the heights and search the depths; you have made the skies and the earth and the seas, and all that they contain; you are the Father of our Lord and Savior Jesus Christ, through whom you did create all things, visible and invisible.

You are enthroned in royal glory, and before you all heavenly powers bow down: the angels and archangels, the principalities and powers, the thrones and dominions; around you stand the many-eyed cherubim and six-winged seraphim, forever singing and crying aloud:

Holy, holy, holy, Lord of hosts . . .

---

[43] Jasper and Cuming, 125.

[44] Ibid., 133.

[45] See J. R. K. Fenwick, *Fourth-century Anaphoral Construction Techniques*. Grove Liturgical Study 45 (Bramcote, 1986), based on his doctoral dissertation.

You are truly holy, Lord our God, who fashioned us and placed us in the paradise of pleasure. But when we transgressed your command, under the temptation of Satan, we fell from eternal life and were driven out of that paradise. But still you did not neglect us. For in your concern for us, you did send us your holy prophets; and in the fullness of time you did reveal yourself to us, who were sitting in darkness and the shadow of death, through your only Son, our Lord and Savior Jesus Christ, who through the Holy Spirit took flesh of the virgin Mary and became man.

He showed us the way of salvation, and brought us the grace of rebirth from on high, through water and the Holy Spirit. He made of us a people for himself, sanctified by the Holy Spirit. He who loved his own who were in the world, for us gave himself over to death, which held us captive because of our sins.

He descended into hell by way of his cross. The third day he rose again from the dead, ascended into heaven, and is seated at your right hand. He has appointed the day when he will judge the world with justice and render to each person according to one's works.

And he has left for us this great and holy mystery. For when he was about to give himself over to death for the life of the world, he took bread, blessed and hallowed it, broke it and gave it to his holy disciples and apostles, saying: Take and eat this, all of you; This is my Body, which is given for you and for many for the forgiveness of sins. Do this in remembrance of me.

In like manner, after the supper, he mixed wine and water, blessed and hallowed it, gave thanks, and gave it to them, saying:

Take and drink this, all of you; for this is my blood, which is shed for you and for many for the forgiveness of sins. Do this in remembrance of me.

For as often as you eat this bread and drink this cup, you proclaim my death until I come again.

Remembering, therefore, his holy sufferings, his resurrection from the dead, his sitting on the right hand of the Father, and his coming again in majesty and awe, we have set before you from among your gifts this bread and this cup; and acknowledging your kindness and good will towards us, O God, we your sinful and unworthy servants beg you that your Holy Spirit come down upon us and upon these gifts now set before you; that he sanctify them and show them as holy things for your holy people.

And make us worthy so to partake of these holy mysteries that our souls and bodies may be sanctified, that we may become one body and one spirit, and may have our portion with all the saints who have found favor with you since time began.

[Here follow the intercessions and commemorations.]
[Then the deacon reads the diptychs.]

Give them rest in your presence; and on our journey there, keep us in faith and lead us to your kingdom, ever bestowing your gracious peace upon us through Jesus Christ and the Holy Spirit. The Father in the Son, the Son in the Father, together with the Holy Spirit in your one, holy, catholic, and apostolic church.

This anaphora is clearly in the West Syrian tradition in terms of its structure and use of scriptural allusions and quotations. It is clearly a fourth-century text in terms of its use of historical narrative; yet it shares with Addai and Mari a typical Semitic contrast between human weakness and the need for grace, which is only accentuated in the full text of Basil. We also note an undeveloped epiclesis in the Egyptian text. This is amplified in the full Byzantine text, yet it is to be noted that in his *Treatise on the Holy Spirit* Basil himself never once mentions any part played by the Holy Spirit in the consecration of the eucharistic gifts, even though he makes much of the work of the Holy Spirit in baptism. There is reference to baptism and the role of the Holy Spirit in forming the church in this anaphora. Finally, while Cyril of Jerusalem refers to the use of the Lord's Prayer as a preparation for communion, its earliest appearance in a eucharistic text may be in the Coptic manuscript of Basil. The Lord's Prayer could be regarded as a summing-up of the eucharistic prayer.[46]

The anaphora and Lord's Prayer in the Barberini manuscript are followed by a greeting from the priest, "Peace be with you," and the invitation of the deacon, "Let us bow our heads." The prayer of inclination follows—a different one in the two Liturgies of Basil and John Chrysostom. This is a prayer for worthy reception and the benefits of communion. After the elevation with its traditional formula, a portion of the consecrated bread is put in the chalice. It would seem that by the beginning of the ninth century, Holy Communion was being administered by a spoon to facilitate reception. We shall see in Rome that the device of the fistula was also designed to facilitate the communion of large numbers of people while still preserving the symbol of participation in one bread (broken at the fraction) and the one cup.

Communion was accompanied by a chant called the *koinonikon*. It is now a variable psalm verse with triple alleluia. This is the exact parallel of the Roman *Communio*, or *Antiphona ad communionem*. Thomas Schattauer's analysis of these communion verses in the tenth-century Typicon shows that these were originally antiphons or refrains for whole psalms.[47] This would agree with the earliest evidence in Cyril's *Catecheses* V, 20, *Apostolic Constitutions* VIII, 13, 16–17, and John Chrysostom's *Exposition of Psalm 144* that a psalm was sung during communion at Jerusalem and Antioch.

The Prayer of Thanksgiving after communion parallels the *Postcommunio* in the Roman liturgy. The prayers are different in Basil and John Chrysostom. This is followed by the dismissal

P/ Let us go forth in peace.
R/ In the name of the Lord.

and the prayer before the ambo. The ambo was the reading desk on the bema or platform in the middle of the nave. This was a stopping point for the clergy as they recessed from the sanctuary down the solea or processional path on their exit from the church. The same prayer is in both liturgies; it is a final supplication and praise. Later a prayer was said in the *keuophylakion* at the consumption of the remaining communion elements, thus

---

[46] See W. E. Pitt, "The Origin of the Anaphora of the Liturgy of St. Basil," *Journal of Ecclesiastical History* 12 (1961), 1–13.

[47] Thomas H. Schattauer, "The Koinonicon of the Byzantine Liturgy: An Historical Study," *Orientalia Christiana Periodica* 49 (1983), 91–129.

rounding out the prayers said at the preparation for the communion elements in the Prothesis.

Thus, by the ninth century the Byzantine liturgy was filled out to its present structure. What remained to be added were the same kind of affective devotional elements that found entrance into the Western medieval liturgy: ceremonial details in the preparation of the elements *(Proskomide),* private prayers said by the clergy as vestments were donned, the washing of hands before the icon screen, and devotions before communion.

The third great Byzantine liturgy is the Liturgy of the Pre-Sanctified, named after Gregory the Great, or the Theologian. This liturgy developed to satisfy the desire for communion on fast days when the eucharist would not be celebrated. The Typicon of the Great Church (tenth century) gives us a system of the eucharist being celebrated every Saturday and Sunday of the year, every day from Pascha through Pentecost, and on festivals of our Lord and our Lady and on some saints' days. But no eucharist is to be celebrated on the ferial days of Lent, on Monday through Wednesday of Holy Week, or on Wednesdays and Fridays throughout the year (the traditional fast days). On these days the Liturgy of the Pre-Sanctified, or previously consecrated gifts, could be celebrated.[48]

This scheme became the pattern of all the Eastern churches except the Coptic, which joined Roman practice in allowing the eucharistic feast on fast days. But the Byzantine practice is much older. It is testified to already at the Council of Laodicea (360–90), whose canons 49 and 51 prohibit commemorations of martyrs in Lent except on Saturdays and Sundays. As Taft points out, "The two go together: one cannot celebrate a feast, because to do so requires a Eucharist."[49]

The present Liturgy of the Pre-Sanctified is the Office of Vespers followed by communion from the reserved sacrament. The gospel reading is included as a reading in Vespers, followed by the Ecumenic Prayer and the dismissal of the catechumens. From the fourth week of Lent are added prayers for those who are ready for illumination (baptism). There is an entrance with the sacrament, although not the usual offertory prayers since these are the consecrated gifts. The priest says the usual pre-communion devotional prayers and the people are invited to come forward to receive communion.

> P/ Come up in fear of God with faith and with love.
> R/ Amen. Blessed is he who comes in the name of the Lord. The Lord is God
> and He has revealed Himself to us.

After communion there is a thanksgiving, the dismissal, a prayer for the keeping of a holy Lent said before the icon of our Lord, and concluding psalmody.

The practice of the Liturgy of the Pre-Sanctified has all but passed out of memory in the Western church because of the increase of daily masses. Only on Good Friday is there a Mass of the Pre-Sanctified in the Roman rite, in which the ministration of Holy Communion follows the liturgy of the word and the special devotions for this day known

---

[48] See Juan Mateos, ed., *Le typicon de la Grande Eglise, Orientalia Christiana Periodica* 165, 166 (Rome: PIO, 1962–63), II, 189, 315–6.

[49] Taft, *Beyond East and West,* 67.

as the Veneration of the Cross. The Pre-Sanctified in the Roman rite has the same structure as in the Byzantine rite: entrance with the sacrament, typical communion devotions before the distribution and reception of communion, the administration of the sacrament, a post-communion prayer, and dismissal.

We have devoted this attention to the Syro-Byzantine liturgy because of its importance and prominence in liturgical history. It is the rite used by Orthodox churches ranging from Syria to Russia. It has left its influences on both the East Syrian and Alexandrian rites. Texts in the Roman Latin rite, such as the Kyrie, the Gloria, and the Trisagion in the Good Friday liturgy, have been imported from the Greek Byzantine rite. There are also structural similarities between West Syrian and Gallican-Mozarabic eucharistic prayers. The Syro-Byzantine rite is clearly one of the most important ritual families in Christianity.

Alexandrian

Alexandria was both the metropolis of Egypt and an important center of church life and mission. It was second only to Antioch in the early days of Christianity. Its famed catechetical school produced such early Christian apologists as Clement and Origen. Its celebrated bishop of the fourth century, Athanasius, was one of the premier champions of Nicene theology. In the ensuing period it became the chief rival of Constantinople in the East. Yet the church in Egypt was severely divided by the christological controversies of the fifth century. As in Syria, theology became a way of preserving cultural distinctiveness. The Orthodox forfeited their independence from Byzantine domination and remained conformed to Constantinople. The Copts maintained their cultural particularity, but fell under the influence of the Syrian Monophysites. When the Muslims swept across Egypt and North Africa in the seventh century, the Greek-speaking Orthodox were allowed to leave the country if they wished, so that Egyptian Christianity became exclusively Monophysite. Nubia (the modern Sudan) and Ethiopia remained for a time independent Christian empires with a Monophysite population.

The old Alexandrian tradition was maintained among the Monophysite Copts. This was the Liturgy of Mark, which was also the rite of the Ethiopians. The oldest complete manuscript of the Liturgy of Mark was written in southern Italy in the thirteenth century.[50] An outline of it is as follows:

> Enarxis (three prayers)
> Little Entrance: Prayer, Hymn, Prayer of the Trisagion
> Epistle
> Alleluia and Prayer of Censing
> Gospel
> Prayers of the Faithful (Litany)
> The Great Entrance: Cherubic Hymn
> Kiss of Peace
> Nicene Creed
> Prayer of Prothesis

---

[50] See Brightman, *Liturgies Eastern and Western*, 113ff. (Greek), 144ff. (Coptic).

> The Anaphora of Mark
> Prayer and Lord's Prayer
> Prayer of Inclination
> Elevation
>> *Bishop:* The holy things to the holy people.
>> *People:* One Father is holy, one Son is holy, one Spirit is holy, in the unity of the Holy Spirit. Amen.
> Communion
> Thanksgiving and Prayer
> Dismissal

The centerpiece of this liturgy, as with the other ones we have looked at, is the anaphora. In spite of Byzantine influences, the unique characteristics of the Alexandrian anaphora are easy to discern, both in the Greek Liturgy of Mark and in its more or less equivalent, the Coptic Liturgy of Cyril of Alexandria.[51] The Coptic translation was made soon after 451, the year of Chalcedon. It lacks certain elements that are found in the Greek Mark, but it comports with earlier anaphoras such as that in the *Euchologion* of Serapion,[52] and the early Egyptian fragments known as the Strasbourg Papyrus, the British Museum Tablet, the Der Balyzeh Papyrus, and the Louvain Coptic Papyrus.[53]

Perhaps the chief characteristics of this tradition are intercessions located in the introductory part of the anaphora (preface) and an epiclesis linking the Sanctus with the institution narrative. The logic of this is clear. The invitation to give thanks to the Lord proceeds into a thanksgiving in which the prophecy of the "pure sacrifice" offered to God by all the nations in Malachi is recalled. Justin Martyr, in his *Dialogue with Trypho,* 116–117, and *Didache* 14, had already associated "pure sacrifice" with the Christian eucharist. The tangible expression of this eucharistic sacrifice is the offering of the bread and wine. The bread and wine are offered by the people, but sometimes by or for particular persons. The names of these persons are read in the diptychs, the list of people who are especially commemorated or remembered before God. Then comes a recommendation of the offerings and a supplication for the acceptance of this eucharistic sacrifice, which leads to a particularized series of intercessions for those for whom the offering is made: the bishops and clergy, the people, and the whole city. After a general recapitulation, there is a return to the act of thanksgiving and the invocation of the divine Name, which leads to the Sanctus.

The prayer that follows the Sanctus resumes the theme of the recommendation of the sacrifice, this time with a formal petition that God himself consecrate it. This is the first epiclesis in the Alexandrian anaphora. There is a second epiclesis after the institution narrative and anamnesis, in which the benefits of communion in the body and blood of Christ are petitioned.

---

[51] Hänggi-Pahl, 101–15 (Greek), 135–9 (Coptic); an English trans. of the Greek anaphora is in Jasper-Cuming, pp. 48ff. See the discussion in Bouyer, pp. 209–14.

[52] Hänggi-Pahl, 128–33; Jasper-Cuming, 39ff.

[53] See Hänggi-Pahl, 116–9, 120–3, 124–7, 140. See M. Andrieu and P. Collomp, "Fragments sur papyrus de l'anaphore de saint Marc," *Revue des Sciences Religieuses* 8 (1928), 489–515.

In Mark the first epiclesis picks up on the line in the Sanctus, "heaven and earth are full of your glory."

> Full in truth are heaven and earth of your holy glory through [the appearing of] our Lord and God and Saviour Jesus Christ: Fill, O God, this sacrifice also with a blessing from you through the descent of your [all-] Holy Spirit. For our Lord and God and King of all, Jesus the Christ, in the night when he handed himself over for our sins, and underwent death [in the flesh] for all men . . . took bread . . .[54]

The epiclesis is thus the only material between the Sanctus and the institution narrative. The narrative concludes with the Pauline text amplified and placed on the lips of Christ (as it is also in the Coptic Basil): "proclaim my death and confess my resurrection [and ascension] until I come." The anamnesis takes off from the verb "proclaim": "Proclaiming, [Master,] Lord, Almighty, [heavenly King] the death of your only-begotten Son, and [confessing] his blessed resurrection . . . and his ascension into heaven and his session at your right hand, . . . and looking for his second [and dread and awesome] coming, in which he will judge the living and the dead in righteousness." As usual, it leads to the formal offering and the supplication for the Holy Spirit "to sanctify and consecrate" the gifts and make the bread the body and the cup the blood of Christ, that those who receive them may also receive the fruits of the sacrament. This second epiclesis in Mark includes an extended extolling of the person and work of the Holy Spirit, comparable to what we saw in James. Indeed, this whole section—the invocation of the Holy Spirit, the elaboration of the Spirit's role, the fruits of communion—most betrays the influence of the West Syrian eucharist on the Alexandrian. But since the intercessions had been copiously included in the preface, there are no concluding commemorations or intercessions. The second epiclesis leads to the final doxology.

The Anaphora of Serapion is a full Egyptian prayer that does not betray West Syrian influences. Indeed, this anaphora must date from a period when the intercessions were not included in the eucharistic prayer. Nevertheless, it shares with the other Egyptian anaphoras the double epiclesis, the first one following the Sanctus and, like Mark, picking up on the words "full" and "fill" from the Sanctus; the second one following the institution narrative without any intervening anamnesis.

There are many peculiarities in this text. There is no mention of the Holy Spirit in either epiclesis. The first simply asks the Father to "Fill also this sacrifice with your power and your partaking." It speaks of the bread as the "likeness" (*to homoioma, similitudinem*) of the body, and then recounts the words of Christ over the bread. This is followed by a semblance of an anamnesis and oblation, which cites *Didache* 9:4.

> Therefore we also, making the likeness of his death, have offered the bread, and beseech you through this sacrifice: be reconciled to us all and be merciful, O God of truth. And as this bread was scattered over the mountains, and was gathered together and became one, so gather your holy Church out of every nation

---

[54] Jasper-Cuming, 64. Words in brackets are the translator's.

and every country and every city and village and house, and make one living catholic Church.[55]

This is followed by the offering of the cup, which Serapion calls "the likeness of the blood," and the words of Christ over the cup. The whole institution text is concluded with an invocation of the Word (logos) on the bread and cup, "that the bread may become the body of the Word" and that "the cup may become blood of the truth." This is followed by the petition for the fruits of communion and a general intercession before the final doxology.

From what we know about Serapion, the lack of a Spirit-epiclesis is an important datum. He was concerned with fighting the Arians, and had sought the advice of Athanasius about the divinity of the Holy Spirit. His concern about this undoubtedly led him to mention the Holy Spirit four times in this relatively brief anaphora. If there had existed a tradition of invoking the Holy Spirit on the gifts, Serapion would have been the last person to ignore it in favor of an invocation of the Logos. We can only conclude that the Alexandrian anaphoras of his time (the middle of the fourth century) did not mention any divine person in the epiclesis, and that Serapion had the idea of attributing the work of transformation to the divine Word.[56] This is a position championed later, theologically, by Ambrose of Milan in his *De Mysteriis* and *De Sacramentis*, in which he taught that consecration is by the word of Christ (*sermo Christi*). This would certainly not be the only parallel between the Alexandrian and the Roman-Milanese traditions.

Roman and North African

Christianity was established from its early years in the capital of the Roman Empire. After the peace of the church in 313, the bishop of Rome was granted a unique dignity by the emperor. Political events were to make the bishop of Rome an especially important and powerful patriarch (pope). Barbarian invasions of the western Roman Empire weakened the political structure. Theodosius I (379–95) was the last emperor to rule both the eastern and western portions of the Empire. He was succeeded in the West by a series of weak emperors who could not ward off the barbarians, and finally the city of Rome was sacked in 410 by Alaric the Hun. As barbarian kingdoms were carved out of the western Roman Empire by the Visigoths, the Ostrogoths, the Vandals, the Huns, the Burgundians, and the Lombards, the bishop of Rome came to be regarded more and more as the embodiment of those Roman certainties and values that were being threatened. From time to time the eastern emperors tried to reassert imperial control over the West, the most successful being Justinian I (527–565). But by the time of Pope Gregory the Great (590–604), after Italy had been laid waste in an effort to defeat the Lombards, the papacy more frequently chose to side with the barbarian kings than with the eastern

---

[55] Ibid., 77.

[56] Unseen by myself at the time of writing is the article by Maxwell Johnson, "The Archaic Nature of the Sanctus, Institution Narrative, and Epiclesis of the Logos in the Anaphora Ascribed to Serapion of Thmuis," in *Seventy-Fifth Anniversary of the Pontifical Oriental Institute*, Orientalia Christiana Analecta 250 (Rome, 1996).

emperors. Thus, the patriarch of the West became the champion of those nations that were emerging in the place of the old Empire.

The cultural and political importance of the papacy should not obscure the theological claims made by the incumbents of "Peter's chair" to primacy over the whole church. The student tracing the Arian, Donatist, Pelagian, and christological controversies cannot fail to be impressed by the skill and persistence with which the Roman bishops advanced their claim to primacy and played a determining role in establishing the orthodox confession.[57] The Tome of Pope Leo I played an influential role in the christological settlement at Chalcedon.[58] It is not surprising that the papal liturgy of the city of Rome, as contrasted with the parochial liturgy, became a norm and model for other churches. We will see this in the next chapter.

The Roman rite was adapted in North Africa as it developed in Rome, even as Africa itself was one of the most Roman of Rome's provinces. We need to remember that Africa in the first five Christian centuries was not a place of exile. It was rich in agriculture, populous along the Mediterranean coast, an excellent area for real estate speculation, and almost a carbon copy of Roman culture and government.[59] Yet the church of North Africa was not merely derivative. Tertullian was the father of Latin theology. Cyprian of Carthage had done as much to champion Roman primacy as any pope. And Augustine of Hippo was to become the most important theologian in the Western church, to be appealed to by all sides in theological disputes for more than a thousand years after his death in 430. The African liturgy flourished as an independent variant of the Roman rite.

A direct source for the Roman liturgy is the *Sacramentarium Veronense*, a book of prayers to be used by the presiding minister of the eucharist, baptisms, and ordinations.[60] With this Verona Sacramentary, a full prayer book was compiled out of the *libelli* or little books that contained one or two mass-formulae (i.e., the prayers spoken by the presider: an opening prayer, a prayer over the gifts, a proper preface for the eucharistic prayer, and a post-communion prayer). It is probable that several libelli were needed for the various festivals and Sundays. Leo I was formerly thought to have brought together these libelli into the sacramentary, and it was accordingly known as the Leonine Sacramentary for many centuries.

This Verona Sacramentary, dating from c. 600 C.E., is not complete (January through early April mass-formulae are missing, and with them the prayers for Easter). It is also a private collection, unlike the sacramentaries we shall look at in the next chapter, with formularies that go back to the fifth-century popes (e.g., Vigilius, Gelasius). But this

---

[57] See J. N. D. Kelly, *Early Christian Doctrines*, rev. ed. (New York: Harper and Row, 1960, 1978), 417ff.

[58] See *Christology of the Later Fathers*, ed. Edward R. Hardy, *The Library of Christian Classics* (Philadelphia: Westminster Press, 1954), 359ff.

[59] See Peter Brown, *Augustine of Hippo: A Biography* (Berkeley and Los Angeles: University of California Press, 1969), chapter one.

[60] *Sacramentarium Veronense*, ed. L. C. Mohlberg, 2nd rev. ed., *Rerum Ecclesiasticarum Documenta*, Series Maior, Fontes I (Rome, 1966). See also D. M. Hope, *The Leonine Sacramentary: A Reassessment of Its Nature and Purpose* (Oxford 1971).

book takes us as far back in the history of Roman liturgy as it is possible to go, and lets us see the distinction between *preces* (consecratory formulae), *orationes fidelium* (intercessions), and *orationes* (short prayers, or "collects," said after a canticle or a reading). The Verona Sacramentary lacks the chief prayer of the mass: the anaphora, or "canon," as it came to be called in the West. The text of the Roman canon is first found in the old Gelasian Sacramentary, *Codex Reginensis* 316, probably written at Chelles near Paris c. 750 C.E., which we shall consider in the next chapter.

Because the basic liturgical books available to us for the Roman rite—the sacramentaries and ordos—are products of Gallican importation, it is not easy to isolate the original features of the Roman liturgy and get at its spirit or "genius," as Edmund Bishop called it.[61] Bishop analyzed the developed Roman mass as follows. The purely Roman elements are:

> Collect
> Epistle
> Blessing before the Gospel
> Gospel
> Orate Fratres (offertory prayer) and Secreta (collect)
> Preface and Canon
> Our Father
> Embolism: Libera nos ("Deliver us . . . from all evil")
> Pax Domini
> Post-communion collect
> Ite missa est

The follow parts are non-Roman in origin:

> Asperges and psalm verses and prayers said by the priest when he ascends to the altar (all medieval additions)
> Kyrie eleison (imported from the East in the second half of the fifth century)
> Gloria in excelsis (imported from the East in the sixth century)
> Credo (added in the eleventh century under German influence)
> Prayers accompanying the offertory actions, the psalm at the lavabo, and the Suscipe sancta Trinitas (all late medieval additions from France)
> Agnus Dei (seventh century; origin obscure)
> Prayers accompanying communion (medieval additions from France)
> Four items of chant: the Introit, Gradual, Offertory, and Communion. These did not originate in Rome, but were adopted in Rome as soon as they began to appear elsewhere and quickly spread from Rome.

Thus, as Bishop summarizes in his classic essay:

> Nothing, then, can possibly be more simple than the composition (mind, I am not now speaking of ceremonies) of the early Roman mass, say about the middle of the fifth century. The singing of a psalm, the "introit," by the choir at the beginning, on the entry of the clergy; a prayer or collect said by the celebrant;

---

[61] See Edmund Bishop, "The Genius of the Roman Rite," in *Liturgica Historica. Papers on the Liturgy and Religious Life of the Western Church* (Oxford, 1962; originally published 1899), 1–19.

followed by readings from the Bible, separated by a psalm sung by the choir which we call the "gradual." After the collection of the offerings of bread and wine from the people, during which the choir sings another psalm—our "offertory"—the celebrant reads a second collect having reference to the offered gifts, which collect we call the "secret." Next comes, as an introduction to the great action of the sacrifice, what we call the "preface," said by the celebrant, and followed by a solemn choral song of praise to God, the Sanctus. Then follows the great act of sacrifice itself embodying the consecration, viz., the prayer called the Canon. As a preparation for the communion of the priest and people, the celebrant says the Lord's Prayer, adding a few words, which are, as it were, the echo of that holy prayer, our *Libera nos, quaesumus*. Then comes the communion of the people, during which a psalm is sung by the choir, which we call the "communion." Finally the celebrant says a third collect, our "post-communion," and the assembly is dismissed.

It is to be observed that these collects are extremely short; three or four lines, as we have them in our missal today.

What can be more simple? It is the mass reduced to its least possible expression. There is not a single element that is not essential—unless, indeed, it were contended that the readings from the Bible, and the preface and *Sanctus*, together with the singing of psalms at the entry of the clergy, before the gospel, and during acts of collecting the offerings and the communion, are superfluous.[62]

This was all an argument leading up to Bishop's famous conclusion: "If I had to indicate in two or three words only the main characteristics which go to make up the genius of the Roman rite, I should say that those characteristics were essentially soberness and sense."[63] This can be contrasted with the more rhetorical texts and ornate ceremonies of the Eastern and Gallican rites. Perhaps the principle of variable propers for the church year helped to insure simplicity. Unlike the Eastern liturgies, which had standard prayers for the whole church year, the Roman liturgy had different ("proper") prayers for every Sunday, festival, and day of devotion.

Perhaps nothing shows the simple character of the Roman rite more than the prayer form known as the collect. Actually, in the Verona Sacramentary, this prayer form, used in the introductory part of the liturgy and after communion, is called *"oratio."* In the later mixed Gallican-Roman sacramentaries it is called "collectio." But the form is usually the same, and may be outlined as follows:

a. address to God
b. a *qui*-clause stating some appropriate attribute of God
c. a petition or request
d. sometimes a reason or result of the request
e. a concluding "through Jesus Christ our Lord" (later expanded to a full trinitarian conclusion in order to counter the Arianism of the Visigoths)

The term *collect* suggests that the presider "collects" the prayers of the people. It is thus a communal prayer preceded by the presider's greeting, "Dominus vobiscum."

---

[62] Ibid., 7–8.
[63] Ibid., 19.

R/ "Et cum spiritu tuo" (The Lord be with you. R/ And with your spirit). The word "Oremus" (Let us pray) is an invitation for every member of the assembly to join in silent prayer before the celebrant gathers up the prayers in a spoken petition. The intention that the people should actually join in the prayer, at least silently, is made clear in the ancient Roman form of the intercessions known as the "bidding prayer." While the general intercessions fell out of use in the Roman liturgy, they were preserved in the Good Friday liturgy, which is an ancient form of the liturgy of the word. A bid or petition is announced by the deacon. Then the people are invited to kneel *(Flectamus genua)* and pray (Oremus). After a period of silent prayer they are bidden to stand *(Levate)*. Then the collect is offered. Here we see the authentic character of the collect as a conclusion to the silent prayer of the people.

We have said that the anaphoral prayer of the Roman rite does not exist in a full text before the old Gelasian Sacramentary of the eighth century.[64] This does not mean that it is impossible to establish an older origin of the Roman canon. Scholars have certainly ruled out the possibility that the Anaphora of Hippolytus is that older form, since nothing survived of it into the Roman canon except the introductory dialogue and the concluding doxology. The earliest text that seems to be similar to the Roman canon is quoted in *De Sacramentis* of Ambrose of Milan (d. 397), Books 4:13–27 and 6:24.

Ambrose says that at the eucharist "praise is offered to God, prayer is made for the people, for kings, for others; when the time comes for the venerated sacrament to be accomplished, the bishop no longer uses his own words, but the words of Christ."[65] It would seem that the praise to which Ambrose refers is the canon's preface *(Praefatio*, meaning "the prayer uttered aloud"—i.e., sung). The post-Sanctus supplication section ("prayer . . . for the people, for kings, for others") leads to the words of institution ("the words of Christ"). Ambrose then goes on to quote portions of the prayer known to him that are similar to equivalent parts of the Roman canon.

ROMAN CANON	DE SACRAMENTIS
Quam oblationem . . .	Fac nobis hac oblationem . . .
Qui pridie . . . (institution)	Qui pridie . . .
Unde et memores . . . (anamnesis)	Ergo memores . . .
Supplices te . . . (epiclesis)	. . . uti hanc oblationem
iube haec perferri manus	suspicias in sublime
angeli tui in sublime altare	altare tuum per manus
tuum in conspectu divinae	angelorum tuorum . . .
maiestatis tuae . . .	

Ambrose's text is not exactly in verbal agreement with the Roman canon, but clearly he is citing a prayer that follows the same structure and expresses similar ideas.

Gregory the Great indicates that the Roman canon was composed some time after the Roman liturgy began to be celebrated in Latin rather than in Greek, perhaps

---

[64] See *Liber Sacramentorum Romanae Aeclesiae Ordinis Anni Circuli (Sacramentarium Gelasianum)*. Rerum Ecclesiasticarum Documenta, Series Maior, Fontes IV, ed. L. C. Mohlberg (Rome: Herder, 1968), 183, introduced by "Incipit Canon Actionis."

[65] *De Sacramentis* IV, 14; Jasper-Cuming, 98.

under Pope Damasus (366–85). It was obviously a text under evolution, which would explain why there is not verbal agreement between Ambrose and the Gelasian Sacramentary. The two sections of the prayer that include lists of saints to be commemorated, the *Communicantes* and the *Nobis quoque peccatoribus*, were added to the canon sometime before Leo the Great.[66]

The patristic provenance of the canon is also evident in structural similarities between the Roman and Alexandrian anaphoral traditions.[67] In both traditions the initial praise and thanksgiving is followed by a commendation of the oblation. In both traditions intercessions and commemorations are intertwined with the thanksgiving rather than separated from the thanksgiving and remembrance, as in the West Syrian and Gallican prayers. In both traditions appeal is made to God's acceptance of the sacrifices of the old covenant: Abel's and Abraham's, and Rome adds Melchizedek's. In both traditions there are two epicleses. In both traditions there is a petition that the gifts may be received on the heavenly altar. It is not surprising that there would be some borrowing from Egypt, "the bread basket of Rome," since Rome and Alexandria were also sometime theological allies. Interpreted in the light of these ancient structural similarities, it is even possible to see a fundamental unity in the canon, which Ralph Keifer outlined,[68] and which may be amplified as follows:

We praise you	Vere dignum
with angelic beings.	Sanctus
We offer for the whole church,	Te igitur
for particular persons,	Memento
in union with (saints)	Communicantes
and for special needs.	Hanc igitur
Accept our offering	Quam oblationem
because Christ commanded it.	Qui pridie
As his memorial, we offer.	Unde et memores
Accept our offering	Supra quae
as you did those of the patriarchs.	
Make it pleasing to you	Supplices te
and beneficial to us,	
in spite of our unworthiness.	Nobis quoque
Through him from whom	Per quem
all good gifts come.	

In addition to this structural similarity with other patristic texts, the influence of the classical Roman pagan cults can be seen in the language of the Roman canon. A. Stuiber has shown that in pagan cultic practice an offering was inconceivable unless it was for something. Thus, the notion of votive offering influenced Roman understanding

---

[66] See E. Mazza, *Le odierne preghiere eucaristiche*, I (Bologna: Edizione Dehoniane, 1984), 78–80.

[67] See Bouyer, *Eucharist*, 214ff.

[68] Ralph Keifer, "Oblation in the First Part of the Roman Canon: An Examination of a Primitive Eucharistic Structure and Theology in Early Italian and Egyptian Sources." Ph.D. diss., University of Notre Dame, 1972. See the article based on this dissertation: "The Unity of the Roman Canon: An Examination of Its Unique Structure," *Studia Liturgica* 11 (1976), 39–58.

of the eucharistic oblation.[69] There is also the influence of the Roman court on Roman liturgical language. The term *Prex* was used to describe petitions to the emperor, and this became the name of the anaphora during the fifth and sixth centuries. V. Fiala even shows verbal similarities between petitions to the emperor and the *Te igitur* (post-Sanctus prayer) of the canon.[70] A petition addressed to the Emperors Honorius and Theodosius in 418 begins, "Petimus clementiam vestram, piissimi et clementissime imperatores" corresponds to "Te igitur clementissime Pater, per Jesum Christum, Dominum nostrum, supplices rogamus ac petimus uti." Thus, there is no question that in the Roman canon we are dealing with a patristic rather than a medieval text, even though no text of the canon exists before the eighth-century sacramentary manuscript. This means that it is also possible to interpret the language of oblation in the Roman canon according to patristic rather than medieval concepts of the eucharistic sacrifice.

Does the African rite also give us a glimpse of an ancient form of the Roman rite? It was an accepted opinion before the twentieth century that the African rite was a derivative of the Roman.[71] Against this, W. C. Bishop proposed that the African rite was closer to the Mozarabic (Visigothic) rite.[72] Yet he does admit that it was romanized under Augustine's influence. What is more likely the case is that liturgical influences were exerted on the rite of Carthage from different geographical directions, since Carthage was an important seaport and center of commerce. In any event, few concrete facts are available. Most of the sources that help to reconstruct the African rite are sermons and homilies, mostly those of Bishop Augustine of Hippo. As Hammon points out, these most often point in the direction of Rome.[73] If Bishop is correct that simplicity, soberness, and sense are characteristics of Roman liturgy, this is even truer of the African rite, which, if Augustine's sermons are any reliable indication, could even have been characterized as puritanical.[74]

Bishop's study enabled him to put together the following order for the African liturgy as used by Augustine:

> Salutation (Pax vobiscum)
> Lesson (usually Old Testament)
> Epistle
> Psalm
> Gospel (with Alleluia in Paschaltide)
> Sermon
> Dismissal of the catechumens

---

[69] A. Stuiber, "Die Diptychon-Formel für die Nomina offerentium im römischen Messkanon," *Ephemerides Liturgicae* 68 (1954), 127–46.

[70] V. Fiala, "Les prières d'acceptation de l'offrande et le genre littéraire du canon romain," in *Eucharistes d'Orient et d'Occident*, 2 vols. *Lex Orandi* 46, 47 (Paris, 1970), 117–33, especially 130–3.

[71] See Louis Duchesne, *Christian Worship: Its Origin and Evolution*, trans. M. L. McClure (London: S.P.C.K., 1923), 88, 572.

[72] W. C. Bishop, "The African Rite," *Journal of Theological Studies* XIII (1912), 250–77.

[73] A. Hammon, *La vie quotidienne en Afrique du Nord au temps de Saint Augustin* (Paris, 1979).

[74] See Ferdinand van der Meer, *Augustine the Bishop*, trans. by B. Battershaw and G. R. Lamb (London: Sheed and Ward, 1967), 317ff.

Prayers of the faithful
Diptychs and Oratio post nomina
Offering with offertory psalm
Oratio super oblata (Prayer over the gifts)

Eucharistic Prayer (including Sursum corda and words of institution;
epiclesis uncertain)
Fraction
Our Father
Kiss of peace
Blessing
Communion with psalmody
Thanksgiving
Dismissal

Unlike the Byzantine and Roman liturgies, there is no elaborate entrance rite. The bishop simply goes to his seat in the basilica and greets the people. The liturgy of the word is similar to most of the orders we have seen. There was powerful preaching on the readings by the great bishops of the era, and the situation was no different in North Africa. References in Augustine's sermons also indicate occasional emotional outbursts by his people, who constituted a racially mixed congregation of Roman landowners, Berber peasants, and the mixture of humanity who worked in the port of Hippo.[75] In the early fifth century the Old Testament reading had not yet dropped out of use, as references in Augustine's sermons indicate. There may also have been a custom of preaching through Old Testament books, as well as epistles and gospels. The prayers of the faithful were more like a litany than like the bidding prayers. The use of the diptychs and the prayer after the names *(post Nomina)* are characteristic of the Mozarabic rite, although the secret prayers of the Roman rite may also derive from the custom of reading of the diptychs (names of offerers). The eucharistic prayer would be a telltale sign of ritual affinity, but there is little information from Augustine about it except for reference in Sermon CCXXVII to the Sursum corda and the words of Christ, to which he, like Ambrose, attributed consecratory power. In *De Trinitate* III, 4:10 Augustine speaks of the "invisible operation of the Holy Spirit" *(operante invisibiliter Spiritu Dei)* in the sacrament, but we cannot deduce from this the use of a Spirit-epiclesis. The place of the kiss of peace is before communion, as in the Roman rite, rather than before the offertory, as in the Eastern and Mozarabic rites. But the rite of Milan, which belongs more to the Gallican family than to the Roman, also places the *Pax* in this position, and Augustine had been greatly influenced by Ambrose.

There is no doubt about the close ties between Rome and North Africa. Rome was also the only patriarchal see in the West, and yet not all the Latin rites show evidence of the influence of Rome. In fact, Rome had ceased to be the political center of the western Empire by the end of the fourth century; the seat of government had been moved to Milan. Milan's political position, and the great personal influence of its bishop, Ambrose,

---

[75] See Van der Meer, 388ff., for a picturesquely drawn description of "A Sunday in Hippo."

created two centers of ecclesiastical authority to which local churches could appeal and relate. This is the context of the famous letter written by Pope Innocent I to the bishop of Gubbio in 416. This local Italian bishop was tempted to introduce non-Roman practices. The practices that interested him are those that were conventionally called Gallican.[76]

Gallican and Mozarabic

The Gallican and Mozarabic rites constitute a second family of Latin liturgies in ancient Christianity. This ritual family is not as definable as the others, in part because it lacked an ecclesiastical center such as Edessa, Antioch, Constantinople, Alexandria, or Rome. We have seen that Ambrose is a witness to the Roman liturgy and even to the Roman canon before we have documentary evidence of it. Yet Milan was a see that absorbed influences from several directions: from Rome when it was a seat of government in the western Roman Empire, from Constantinople when Ravenna was a seat of Byzantine imperial government, and from Gaul since Milan was a terminal of departure to trans-Alpine Europe.[77]

Milan was not the only see that lent a cross-cultural character to the Gallican rite. The city of Lyons in southern Gaul (France) was Latin in origin, but as a commercial center at the head of navigation on the Rhone it also had a sizeable Greek-speaking population. The church of Lyons was Greek-speaking in the time of Irenaeus (late second century). Irenaeus himself is a witness to the contact between the churches of Gaul and those of Asia Minor. The church historian Eusebius quotes a lost letter of Irenaeus in which he relates his personal memories of the great martyr, Bishop Polycarp of Smyrna.[78]

Another problem in the study of Gallican liturgy is the paucity of extant textual evidence due to the Gallican penchant for variety. Varied propers for the days of the church year were even more prevalent in Gaul than in Rome. Not only were there collects and litanies for every day in the church year calendar, but the eucharistic prayers also were varied according to the church year. The "preface" or introductory section was called *Contestatio* or *Immolatio*, and it led to the Sanctus. A post-Sanctus prayer led to the institution narrative, called *Secreta* or *Mysterium*. This is assumed because the prayer after the institution narrative was called *post Secreta* or *post Mysterium*.[79]

There are a number of features unique to the Gallican liturgy. One is the tendency to address prayers to Christ rather than to the Father through Christ. The Song of Zechariah (Benedictus) was sung as the entrance canticle of praise rather than the Gloria in excelsis. The Song of the Three Young Men in the apocryphal addition to Daniel 3 (*Benedicite, opera omnia*) was sung between the lessons and the gospel. The prayer for the acceptance of the gifts was part of the offertory, at which the names of offerers were read (the diptychs) and a prayer was said after this reading (post Nomina). The kiss of

---

[76] See Duchesne, 87.

[77] See J. Schmitz, *Gottesdienst im altchristlichen Mailand* (Cologne and Bonn, 1975).

[78] Eusebius, *Ecclesiastical History*, V, 4.

[79] See Hänggi-Pahl, 467–8; Jasper-Cuming, 105–8; Bouyer, 315–37.

peace was exchanged between the offertory and the eucharistic prayer. The benediction was given before communion, presumably so that those among the faithful who were not receiving the sacrament could leave.[80]

A liturgy similar to this developed in Spain under the Visigoths (Western Goths) who settled there in 416. The Goths were converted to Christianity by Arian missionaries from Constantinople, and it is possible that they retained traces of Byzantine influence in their liturgy but also picked up Gallican influences as they migrated across the Rhine, through southern Gaul, and into Spain. What the pre-Visigothic liturgy in Spain might have been we cannot say—except to note that the cultural ties between Spain and Rome had been very strong in the earlier days of the Empire. Toledo became the capital of the Visigoth kingdom in 573, and a rich church life flourished beginning in the reign of King Recared (572–601), who embraced Catholicism in 587, until the conquest of Spain by the Moslems (Moors) in 711.

Before the end of the seventh century the brothers Leander and Isidore of Seville, who followed one another as archbishops (579–637), were ardently promoting the Mozarabic rite from Seville; and their enthusiasm was carried on from Toledo by Bishops Hildefonsus and Julian (657–690). In *De Ecclesiasticus Officiis*, Isidore provided an orderly account of the Mozarabic liturgy and its eucharistic center, outlined in seven points:

> An admonition to the people stimulating them to prayer
> Invocation to God for acceptance of the prayers and oblations of the faithful
> Begging mercy through the sacrifice for the offerer, or for the departed
> For love, as exhibited by the kiss of peace, that all being united in mutual love,
>   may be worthily knit together by the Sacrament
> The "illatio" in sanctification of the offering, wherein heaven and earth are
>   called to the praise of God, and "Hosanna in Excelsis" is sung
> The "conformation" of the sacrament, that the offering which is offered to
>   God, being sanctified by the Holy Spirit, may be conformed to the Body
>   and Blood of Christ
> Lord's Prayer, with a comment on each clause

These are the Seven Prayers of the sacrifice commended by the teaching of the gospel and of the Apostles. "Seven" represents either the sum of the holy Church or the seven-fold grace of the Spirit, by whose gifts the things brought are sanctified.[81]

The seven prayers mentioned by Isidore suggest the following component parts of the Mozarabic liturgy of the eucharist:

> Admonition, leading to the intercessions
> Prayer for the acceptance of the prayers and gifts
> Reading of diptychs and oratio post Nomina
> Oratio ad Pacem (prayer for peace) and kiss of peace

---

[80] See W. S. Porter, *The Gallican Rite* (London: S.P.C.K., 1958).
[81] Quoted in Walter H. Frere, *The Anaphora of the Great Eucharistic Prayer* (London: S.P.C.K., 1938), 101.

Preface (Illatio), leading to the Sanctus
Post-Sanctus prayer, Secreta (institution narrative—Qui pridie) and
    post-Pridie (which seems to be an epiclesis)
Lord's Prayer[82]

There is an orderliness in the Mozarabic eucharist that is comparable in structure to the West Syrian eucharist. The texts, however, were so variable (like the Gallican) that few survive. Isidore leads us to believe that there was a tripartite structure to the anaphora, easily demarcated by three rounded off but interconnected prayers: the *illatio* (Gallican contestatio) praising God for his work of creation and leading to the Sanctus; the post-Sanctus reference to salvation history leading to the institution narrative and the memorial of the Last Supper and the cross; and the *post-Pridie* invocation of God's blessing on the gifts (without always specifying the role of the Holy Spirit) leading to the concluding doxology.

In the liturgy of the word the Mozarabic liturgy was similar in structure to the Gallican liturgy, except that it provided an entrance psalm (Introit or *Intrada*) and used the Gloria as the canticle of praise rather than the Benedictus. One additional feature was the insertion of the Nicene Creed after the anaphora and fraction and before the Lord's Prayer, by decree from the Council of Toledo in 589, as a measure to counter the earlier Arian confession of the Visigoths. This was the earliest instance of the use of the Creed in the liturgy of the Western churches.

Because of Moorish occupation of Spain, the Mozarabic liturgy survived longer than the Gallican. It was the rite of the suppressed Christian people of Spain throughout the Middle Ages. After the expulsion of the Moors in 1492 by their Catholic majesties, King Ferdinand of Castile and Queen Isabella of Aragon, and the introduction of the Roman Catholic liturgy, the Mozarabic liturgy continued to be used in the cathedral of Toledo. It lives on in the Corpus Christi chapel of the cathedral in Toledo, where it is celebrated even today—albeit in mutilated form.

One final Western liturgy is the Celtic, but there is even less certainty about the features of this rite. It was probably a version of the Gallican liturgy mixed with Celtic customs. The Celtic contribution to the use of the Bible, the cult of saints, the divine office, and the confession of sins will be considered in the next chapter.[83]

❦ THE AWE-INSPIRING RITES OF CHRISTIAN INITIATION

There is a wealth of information concerning the practice and rites of Christian initiation in the fourth century from the homilies preached by the bishops to the newly baptized, which are known as mystagogic catecheses, or instructions in the mysteries (sacraments). Compared to the information in the church orders and conciliar decrees of the fourth and fifth centuries, it amounts to a fulsome description of what John Chrysostom called "the awesome mysteries about which it is forbidden to speak [before

---

[82] See Hänggi-Pahl, 497–8; Jasper-Cuming, 151–4; Bouyer, 315–37.
[83] See M. and L. de Paor, *Early Christian Ireland* (London, 1978).

one is baptized and communed]," "this awesome rite of initiation," and "the awesome and holy rite of initiation."[84]

The person who was the subject of these rites would probably have agreed as to their awesomeness after experiencing the almost daily fasts, instructions, exhortations, exorcisms, and prayers of his or her sponsors and the faithful during the weeks before Pascha (Easter). Finally on Holy Saturday night, the candidate would hear the voice coming out of the darkness commanding him or her to renounce the devil, swear allegiance to Christ, and strip off all clothing before having his or her body anointed and then immersed in water three times at the profession of belief in God the Father, God the Son, and God the Holy Spirit. The candidate was then dressed in a new white robe, led into the assembly of the faithful to be greeted by the bishop with the laying on of hands, a "sealing"-anointing, and the kiss of peace. And at last, he or she was allowed to participate for the first time in the hitherto off-limits (for the unbaptized) rite of the eucharistic meal by offering gifts and receiving Holy Communion.

It is remarkable how similar these rites of initiation were throughout the churches of the Roman Empire and beyond, so that a common "shape of baptism" is discernible.[85] Evidence for the practice of Christian initiation comes from all the centers of the families of rites we have delineated: Edessa, Antioch, Jerusalem, Constantinople, Alexandria, Rome, Milan, North Africa, and Spain. Without homogenizing the details that make practices different from one time and place to another, it is possible to construct a pattern of Christian initiation that shows an evolution from the third to the fourth and fifth centuries.

Sponsorship, which probably arose during the time of persecution, continued to be a custom. Whoever wished to become a Christian went to the bishop's residence along with sponsors from among the faithful. The bishop, or a presbyter or deacon, would write down the names of the inquirers and inquire as to their reasons for wanting to become Christians. As Ferdinand van der Meer notes in his book, *Augustine the Bishop*,

> People sought to be received from motives of pure time-serving, some came because they wished to please their master or protector, others from fear of their landlords, others, again, in order not to lose the custom of Church folk. Yet others appeared because they wished to marry a Christian girl. Finally, there were those who had studied the Scriptures and had come to think for themselves.[86]

After an address by a catechist laying out the contours of the faith, the supplicant was asked if he or she accepted what was presented and was prepared to live in accordance with it. If the answer was "yes," there followed a rite of enrollment into the catechumenate that included four little ceremonies: the sign of the cross on the forehead, the laying

---

[84] See Edward J. Yarnold, S.J., introduction in *The Awe-inspiring Rites of Initiation*, and *The Study of Liturgy*, 95–110.

[85] See Aidan Kavanagh, *The Shape of Baptism: The Rite of Christian Initiation* (New York: Pueblo Publishing Co., 1978).

[86] Van der Meer, *Augustine the Bishop*, 353.

on of hands in blessing, an exorcism (sometimes eating the bread of exorcism), and the "sacrament of salt." The meaning of the salt was explained by John the Deacon in his letter to Senarius, a Roman nobleman, written around 500.

> The catechumen receives blessed salt also, to signify that just as the flesh is kept healthy by salt, so the mind which is drenched and weakened by the waves of this world is held steady by the salt of wisdom and of the preaching of the word of God.[87]

Augustine did not hesitate to regard these four sacramenta as shadows or prefigurations of the actual sacraments of initiation, as a kind of conception within the womb of Mother Church that precedes the actual birth. The signing with the cross on the forehead foreshadowed baptism, the laying on of hands prefigured the post-baptismal rites, and the reception of the blessed salt and the bread of exorcism anticipated Holy Communion.

From this point the catechumen attended the liturgy of the word and heard the sermon, along with the faithful, Jews, and even pagans who were curious to hear about Christian teachings. The only subjects off limits in general Christian preaching were baptism and the eucharist—which is why special sermons were preached on the sacraments after Pascha. After the sermon all but the faithful were dismissed; the doors were closed and a porter stood guard to allow entry to no one except the baptized. It is understandable that during the third century the church had to be cautious about police spies. But by 400 most of the candidates for baptism were coming from Christian families in a society that was becoming Christianized. This very fact makes the practice of closing the doors all the more precious. It suggests, at least, that until one has received the gift of the Holy Spirit in baptism one cannot discern what the Lord's Supper is all about. Augustine compared the state of the catechumenate with that of the man born blind, whose eyes Jesus had touched with spittle, but who had not yet entered the Pool of Siloam.

> The catechumen has . . . been anointed by the Anointed One and he has this ointment upon his blind eyes. The catechumens themselves hear me speak these things, but all that is not sufficient for that for which they have been anointed. They must hurry to enter the bath if they will have sight in their eyes.[88]

The catechumenate was the customary state of nominal Christians who straddled the demands of the world and the call to discipleship. If, however, towards the time of fasting (Lent) a catechumen sought baptism, things became serious. They were presented by their godparents as candidates for baptism. Their lives were scrutinized (Egeria notes that the bishops would even question the neighbors of those who were presented) and, if they were not in need of amendment of life, they were publicly enrolled as candidates for baptism. The *competentes*, or elect, as such persons were called, stood apart in a special section of the church where they could be seen by all. The preaching was especially directed toward this group, but in the hearing of all so that the catechumens would

---

[87] Cited in Whitaker, *Documents of the Baptismal Liturgy*, op. cit., 155.
[88] Cited in van der Meer, 357.

be challenged and the faithful would be reminded of the essentials of Christian belief and lifestyle. Indeed, bishops did not confine themselves to the skeleton of Christian doctrine, but lashed out in moral exhortation. Nearly two centuries after Hippolytus, Augustine was still reminding his hearers that actors, stage managers, pimps, prostitutes, and gladiators would under no circumstances be received into the church. In some cases a total change in one's way of life was expected as a sign that the elect comprehended what the new life in Christ entailed. During the scrutinies the lifestyles of the catechumens were publicly examined, and they were subject to constant exorcisms. Unlike the public penitents who were clothed in garments of sackcloth or goatskin, the elect stood barefoot on top of their tunics, repudiating, as it were, the fall of our first parents who made repentance necessary.

About the third Saturday or Sunday in Lent, the elect were taught the rule of faith phrase by phrase in a process called the *Traditio symboli* (Handing over the Creed). A week later they had to recite it back *(Redditio symboli).* Then they were taught the Our Father in a similar manner. The Traditio took place in the baptisteries or other secluded places because the texts were not publicly used, and the catechumens were told not to write them down but to learn them by heart. These texts had not yet received a place in the liturgy. When they did come into liturgical use the Creed was located after the offering in the Eastern rites and the Lord's Prayer was used before communion. In both cases only the faithful would be present. In the West the Apostles' Creed was used at baptism in the seclusion of the baptistery; in the East the Nicene Creed was used for baptism. The Our Father was used primarily in private devotion. Egeria describes the ceremony of the Redditio as she witnessed it in Jerusalem.

> When the seven weeks [of Lent] have gone by and there remains only Holy Week, which is called the Great Week, the bishop comes in the morning to the major church, the Martyrium. To the rear, at the apse behind the altar, a throne is placed for the bishop, and one by one they come forth, the men with their godfathers, the women with their godmothers. And each one recites the Creed back to the bishop.[89]

Augustine, in his *Confessions*, Book IX, relates his own nervousness in having to do this before his baptism in Rome, even though he was a trained orator. He was therefore empathetic with his catechumens, but also insistent that this testing must be done.

On Maundy Thursday the candidates were permitted to break their fast and take a bath, so that they wouldn't leave an unpleasant odor in the baptismal pool. On Good Friday the whole church fasted and assembled to commemorate the passion of Christ by singing the psalm of the passion, listening to the reading of the gospel passion narrative, listening to sermons on this text, and praying for all sorts and conditions of people. On Holy Saturday, as evening fell, innumerable lamps flared up in the basilicas and in the homes of the faithful. This was the greatest *lucernarium* (light service) and vigil of the year. The faithful assembled in the basilicas to hear Old Testament readings that rehearsed the

---

[89] *Egeria: Diary of a Pilgrimage*, Ancient Christian Writers 38, trans. by George E. Gingras (New York and Paramus: Newman Press, 1970), 124.

history of salvation and to meditate on how these readings related to the pascha of Christ and to Holy Baptism. The elect assembled in the baptistery for the water-bath.

From here on the patristic sources vary in detail, although the basic shape of baptism is the same. In the West the rites began with the *Apertio* or "opening" of the ears and nose with the words "Ephphatha . . . be opened" (Mark 7:34). In all sources, the candidates faced west to renounce the devil and all its works and pomp. Then they faced east to declare their commitment or adhesion to Christ. They removed their clothing and there were anointings of the body, sometimes before, sometimes after, and sometimes both before and after the water-bath. Pre-baptismal anointings carried exorcistic connotations; post-baptismal anointings were much like putting on perfume after a bath. In every case there was a blessing of the water, with mention of the Holy Spirit who moved over the waters of the precreated world to bring order out of chaos, and often (especially in the Eastern prayers) an invocation of the Holy Spirit on the water.[90]

After the blessing of the water the candidates went down into the font one by one for the triple confession of faith in God the Father, God the Son, and God the Holy Spirit, with immersion after each profession, "I believe." Archaeological evidence suggests that immersion did not necessarily involve submersion, because most of the pools were only about two to three feet deep (although, as we shall see below, there were references to submersion in some patristic texts). Nevertheless, it was necessary to step down into the pools and then to step up again. Many of the pools were octagonal in shape, suggesting by the number eight the eschatological reality into which the candidates were being initiated (as in the eighth day).[91] The baptizing minister (often a deacon for men and a deaconess for women) poured water over the head of the candidate who was standing knee-deep in it. Upon emerging from the pool the neophyte put on a new white garment. The symbolism of the white robe varied in the discourses of the fathers. Cyril of Jerusalem quoted Isaiah 61:10, "He has clothed me with the garment of salvation, and with the robe of gladness he has covered me." John Chrysostom compared the white robe to a uniform that should be an external sign of having "put on" Christ. The white garment reminded Ambrose of the transfigured Christ, while John the Deacon saw a connection with the wedding garment.

After donning the white garment the neophytes were led into the assembly. Most of the fourth and fifth century sources follow the progression described by Hippolytus: invocation of the Holy Spirit with the laying on of hands; sealing with oil on the forehead in the sign of the cross; the kiss of peace; and the eucharistic liturgy. Aidan Kavanagh has offered the explanation that this sequence of actions derives from a *missa*—the solemn dismissal at the end of a liturgical unit.[92] The dismissal of the catechumens before baptism was an example of such an act. It would have been an act with which the catechumens were familiar, except that now the neophytes were not dismissed out of

---

[90] See E. G. Cuthbert F. Atchley, *On the Epiclesis of the Eucharistic Liturgy and in the Consecration of the Font* (Oxford: Oxford University Press, 1935).

[91] See S. Anita Stauffer, *On Baptismal Fonts: Ancient and Modern* (Bramcote: Grove Books, 1994).

[92] See Aidan Kavanagh, *Confirmation: Origins and Reform* (New York: Pueblo Publishing Co., 1988), especially chapter 2.

the assembly but into the ranks of the faithful. The invocation was a remembrance of the gift of the Holy Spirit that the neophytes received in baptism, and the anointing by the bishop was a public sealing of the baptism that had taken place in the relative privacy of the baptistery. This act of dismissal, now restructured as a rite of welcome, was still a kind of dismissal into the mission of the church. The connection between the Holy Spirit and mission is caught in the *Catecheses* of Cyril of Jerusalem, who compared Christian baptism with the baptism of Christ in the Jordan.

> He also bathed himself in the river Jordan, and having imparted of the fragrance of his Godhead to the waters he came up from them. And the Holy Spirit in substance rested upon him, like resting on like. In the same manner to you also, after you had come up from the pool of the sacred streams, was given the unction, the emblem of that wherewith Christ was anointed; and this is the Holy Spirit.[93]

We should also remember that the Syrian tradition lacked a post-baptismal anointing and laying on of hands. John Chrysostom follows this tradition by not mentioning these ceremonies in his mystagogical catecheses. It has been said that Chrysostom held that the Holy Spirit is bestowed on the candidate when the bishop lays his hands on the candidate's head in the baptismal pool. Actually, Chrysostom knew of a tradition in which the presbyter (priest) did the baptizing; and what the candidate received was forgiveness of sins and filial adoption into the life of the Holy Trinity. In the Stavronikita Series of Homilies delivered in Antioch c. 390, Chrysostom said,

> When the priest says, "So-and-so is baptized in the name of the Father, and of the Son, and of the Holy Spirit," he puts your head down into the water three times and three times he lifts it out again, preparing you by this mystic rite to receive the descent of the Spirit. For it is not only the priest who touches the head, but also the right hand of Christ, and this is shown by the very words of the one baptizing. He does not say: "I baptize so-and-so," but "So-and-so is baptized," showing that he is only the minister of grace and merely offers his hand because he has been ordained to this end by the Spirit. The only fulfilling all things is the Father and the Son and the Holy Spirit, the undivided Trinity. It is faith in the Trinity which gives the grace of remission from sin; it is this confession which gives us the gift of filial adoption.[94]

In the rite known by Chrysostom the neophytes are immediately greeted by the faithful with the kiss of peace when they enter the assembly. He does not witness to any rite that Western fathers might call the perfecting or strengthening or confirming of baptism. Nor did a rite of confirmation develop in the Eastern churches as it did in the Western churches.

Some of the sources mention the giving of a lighted candle to the newly baptized. Gregory of Nazianzus and Gregory of Nyssa seem especially interested in the candle and the theme of light, probably because they witness to the custom of baptizing on the Feast of the Epiphany (the Feast of Lights), which commemorated the baptism of

---

[93] Cyril, *Mystagogical Catechesis* 3; Cited in Whitaker, 30 (text slightly modernized).
[94] Cited in Whitaker, 41.

Jesus. Gregory of Nazianzus preached a great sermon on January 6, 381, in Constantinople, in which he developed the idea of baptism as illumination and employed almost every reference to light in the Bible to develop his emphasis on baptism as the source of the transformation of the baptized.

> Let us be made light, as it was said to the disciples by the Great Light, *you are the light of the world (Matt. 5:14)*. Let us be made lights in the world, *holding fast the Word of Life (Phil. 2:15–16)*; that is, let us be made a quickening power to others. Let us lay hold of the Godhead; let us lay hold of the First and Brightest Light. Let us walk towards him shining, *before our feet stumble upon dark and hostile mountains (Jer. 13:16)*. While it is day *let us walk honestly as in the day, not in rioting and drunkenness, not in chambering and wantonness (Rom. 13:13)*, which are the dishonesties of the night.[95]

In all of the patristic liturgies baptism led directly to first communion. Holy Communion was the goal of Christian initiation. The fellowship of the church was and is eucharistic fellowship.[96] Holy Communion was, and has remained, "closed" at least to the extent that no unbaptized person could partake of it. The eucharistic community was and is coterminous with the community of faith, since the baptismal profession of faith is the basis of the eucharistic koinonia.

Obviously Holy Communion was closed to the unbaptized. There has never been a question about this as long as it has been understood that inclusion in the eucharistic fellowship was the goal of Christian initiation and the sacramental economy was intact. Even the communion of heretics first became a special problem in terms of the question of the recognition of baptisms administered by heretics. The African church had been inclined not to recognize any heretical baptism; but the Council of Arles (314) and then the Council of Nicea (325) decided to recognize baptisms in the name of the Trinity even if performed by a heretic (except in the cases of heretics such as Paul of Samosata who were regarded as denying the doctrine of the Trinity). Augustine later tried to reconcile this more lenient view with the stricter practice of the African church by saying that the baptisms performed by heretics were inoperative because heretics lacked the Holy Spirit. This was proven by their lack of love in not seeking unity with the one, holy, catholic, and apostolic church. This view helped to solidify the practice of receiving Christians who had been baptized by heretics with the laying on of hands through which the Holy Spirit would be imparted.[97] This became the basis of receiving Christians from other (heretical) churches by confirmation, once this later rite came to be identified with the episcopal laying on of hands and began to be called by this term.

So intrinsically connected were baptism and the eucharist in the sacramental economy that Augustine even developed his view of eucharistic transformation by reference to baptismal transformation. In one of his mystagogical sermons he said:

---

[95] Cited in André Hamman, ed., *Baptism: Ancient Liturgies and Patristic Texts*. Alba Patristic Library 2 (Staten Island: Alba House, 1967), 115.

[96] See Werner Elert, *Eucharist and Church Fellowship in the First Four Centuries*, trans. by Norman Nagel (St. Louis: Concordia Publishing House, 1966).

[97] Ibid., 79.

You who are reborn to a new life, above all you who see his thing for the first time, hear the explanation which we have promised you—and you too of the faithful who are used to the sight, hear me, for it is good to be reminded, lest you fall into forgetfulness. What you behold upon the table of the Lord is that which, so far as its outward appearance is concerned, you see upon your own tables; yet only the appearance is the same, not the power. Similarly, you yourselves have remained what you were; you did not return to us with new faces when you returned from the baptismal pool. Yet you have been made anew; your fleshly form is the old one, but you are new through the grace of holiness. In exactly the same way this is something new; for what you see, what stands here, is bread and wine, but once the consecration has taken place, the bread becomes the body of Christ and the wine his blood. The name of Christ brings this about, the mercy of Christ brings this about, namely, that though one sees what one saw before, it no longer counts for what it counted for before.[98]

During the Octave of Easter, the newly baptized attended church every day, wearing their new white garments and standing together in a special place. The bishops delivered their mystagogical homilies explaining the meanings of the sacraments during the eucharistic celebrations of this week. This means that the bishops were instructing the newly baptized in what they had just experienced. It was also in this arena of the liturgical assembly that the bishops of the ancient church developed their sacramental theology. It seems that one of the peculiarities of these sessions was that the faithful were allowed to ask questions of the bishops as they delivered their homilies.

On Low Sunday (the Second Sunday of Easter) the neophytes were allowed to remove their white garments and mingle with the faithful. Augustine the bishop admonished the neophytes for one last time that, lamentably, the great mass of Christians no longer form a distinguishable band of the elect in this world; the new Christians had better decide whether they will be in the party of the sheep or of the goats. As Van der Meer commented, after this Sunday the newly baptized "laid aside their eight-day old skins in the *secretarium* [church office] and disappeared into the crowd in that curious sheepfold in which sheep, goats, and wolves are all indistinguishable from one another."[99]

CANONICAL PUBLIC PENANCE

The mixed quality of Christian life also raised questions about the eucharistic fellowship, which, as we have seen, go back to the First Letter to the Corinthians. When "anyone who bears the name of brother or sister" is guilty of gross immorality, the others are not to eat with him (1 Cor. 5:11). This social ostracization amounted to excommunication. But not all sins were equally grave. So structures of discipline evolved in the early church that involved the exercise of the Office of the Keys (Matt. 16:19), or the right of the church to bind or to loose sins (Matt. 16:19; 18:18) or to retain or remit sins (John 20:22f.). The possibility of loosing, remitting, forgiving, or absolving sin led to the establishment of penitential processes, which Tertullian called "exomologesis." These processes

---

[98] Cited in Van der Meer, 374.
[99] Ibid., 382.

developed further during the third century out the need to deal with the question of those who had lapsed from the faith during the persecution under the Emperor Decius (c. 250). Bishop Cyprian of Carthage objected to the reconciliation of lapsed Christians by confessors who had been made presbyters in honor of their sufferings. He believed that the bishop should supervise the reconciliation of the lapsed, which would include suitable forms of penance.[100]

The structure of penance recommended by Cyprian is presented in more systematic form in the *Didascalia Apostolorum*. The bishop is instructed to examine the penitents to see if they are sincere in their repentance. Only then are they formally excommunicated and engaged in fasting and prayer. The period of separation from Holy Communion is left to the discretion of the bishop. When this time of penance was over the bishop laid hands on the penitents and restored them to the eucharistic fellowship. This act of reconciliation was compared with the condition of the Christian after baptism. Like baptism, it could only be administered once.[101]

One can see the need to maintain discipline during a time of persecution. This explains the concerns of Cyprian. The Syrian "Teaching of the Apostles" discusses martyrdom and conduct during persecution and urges charitable assistance for Christians who are incarcerated or condemned to work in the mines. This suggests that the *Didasacalia Apostolorum* was written before the Edict of Gallienus in 260, which ended the general persecution of the church and inaugurated a period of peace that lasted more than thirty years. On the other hand, this document shows a humaneness that was trying to counter the rigorous attitudes of many Syrian Christians who taught the merits of sexual abstinence and extreme self-denial. It is important to place the *Didascalia*'s teaching on penance into this wider context so that we don't view it merely as an expression of rigor during a time of persecution when the church had to shore up discipline. It could just as well be the articulation of a tradition of discipline during a time when the church was able to relax after 260.[102]

This system of penance was honed by the church of the fourth century after the Edict of Milan. The patristic church knew of only two forms of penance: the daily, personal penance done by Christians for lesser sins; and the once-in-a-lifetime penance imposed by the church for more serious sins. Over time the differentiation between these two forms of penance, and the specification of what sins were grave enough to require the rigors of public penance, were articulated by conciliar and synodical legislation. This is why public penance was called "canonical." The canons of the Council of Elvira (c. 305) suggest that in Spain only the sins of apostasy, adultery, and murder required public penance. Those guilty of lesser sins could be reconciled after a period of abstention (but not formal excommunication) from the eucharist.[103]

---

[100] See Paul Palmer, ed., *Sources of Christian Theology*, II: *Sacraments and Forgiveness* (Westminster, Md.: Newman Press, 1959), 43.

[101] See R.H. Connolly, ed. and trans., *Didascalia Apostolorum* (Oxford: Clarendon Press, 1929), 52, 56, 104.

[102] See Fox, *Pagans and Christians*, op. cit., 549ff., especially 557ff. on the "Apostles."

[103] See Bernhard Poschmann, *Penance and the Anointing of the Sick*, trans. by Francis Courtney (New York: Herder and Herder, 1964), 94.

One important aspect of canonical public penance was its largely voluntary nature. Only on rare occasions were some Christians required to go through it. It was usually recommended by pastors and left to the individual to follow through on this counsel. Many entered the *ordo poenitentium* (order of penitents) completely on their own volition. The sinner had to present himself or herself to a bishop or presbyter in sackcloth and ashes, which amounted to a kind of public confession of sins. Jerome (d. 420) provides a case study of this in his account of the Roman lady, Fabiola, who had divorced her first husband and remarried, but presented herself as a public penitent after the death of her second husband. In view of "the whole city of Rome," in Jerome's account, "she put on sackcloth to make public confession of her error." With "disheveled hair, a ghastly countenance, soiled hands and sordid neck," she prostrated herself before "the bishop, the presbyters, and all the people" to ask for their prayers. She then confessed her sin to all those present. Thereafter she sat outside the church until the day when she received reconciliation in the sight of the whole congregation. Jerome testifies that this day of reconciliation was "the day before the Pasch."[104]

The fathers of the church were at pains to keep the scrupulous from entering into the order of penitents over sins less grave than the ones mentioned above. John Chrysostom never ceased to exhort his listeners to repent and confess their sins, but to God alone. There are homilies both from his days as a presbyter in Antioch and as bishop of Constantinople in which he makes this appeal.[105] This does not mean that public penance was unknown in Antioch and Constantinople; rather, that the bishops wanted to reserve public penance for sins that were truly grave, since it could be done only once.[106]

Nevertheless, public penance was available, and in Asia Minor there was even a differentiation between four classes of public penitents. The "hearers" were dismissed before the liturgy of the faithful without a blessing. The "kneelers" were dismissed before the liturgy of the faithful with a blessing from the bishop, like the catechumens. The "bystanders" (attested by Gregory the Wonderworker) were allowed to remain for the liturgy of the faithful, but could not participate in the offering or receive communion. The "mourners" (attested by Basil the Great) were not even allowed in the church building, but sat on the porch imploring the intercessions of the faithful.[107]

Those enrolled in the order of penitents dressed in sackcloth and ashes, and were required to engage in the ascetic disciplines of prayer and fasting. The length of time of penance was determined by the bishop. It could last several years, depending on the gravity of the offense and the sinner's previous status in the church. Clergy, for example, were required to do penance for a longer period of time than lay persons, and were

---

[104] Jerome, *Epistula 77, ad Oceanum*; P.L. 22:692–3.

[105] John Chrysostom, *Hom. contra Anomaeos* 5; P.G. 48:745; and *Hom. in Heb.* 9:5; P.G. 63:81; both cited in J. Quasten, *Patrology* III (Utrecht and Antwerp, 1963), 478–9.

[106] See Franz van de Paverd, "Testimonies from the Christian East to the Possibility of Self-Reconciliation," in *Concilium: The Fate of Confession*, ed. by Mary Collins and David Power (Edinburgh: T. and T. Clark, 1987), 96–104.

[107] See Poschmann, 90–1.

usually stripped of their ecclesiastical offices. When the assigned period of penance was over, the penitents were normally reconciled and restored to the eucharistic fellowship.

What emerged in the patristic church was a structure of penance that paralleled the structure of the catechumenate. Both were onetime processes that could not be repeated. Both involved enrollment in an ecclesiastical order (the *ordo catechumenorum*, the ordo poenitentium). Both involved learning or relearning the Christian way of life through the practice of ascetic disciplines and works of charity. Both involved ritual acts of dismissal from the assembly and blessings with the laying on of hands. Both led to the eucharistic fellowship: the catechumens for the first time and the penitents through restoration. Both orders were under the supervision of the bishop because the bishop was the chief minister of the eucharist and Christian initiation and penance were gateways to the eucharistic fellowship.

In the church of Rome the parallels between the orders of catechumens and penitents were further accentuated by making Maundy Thursday the stated day of public reconciliation of the penitents just as the Easter Vigil was the stated time of baptism and first communion. Thus both the catechumenal and penitential processes ended during Lent and Holy Week, bequeathing to this season its enduring catechetical and penitential character. Pope Innocent I (d. 417) was the first explicit witness to this practice, but he implied in his famous letter to Decentius that it was a practice of long standing in Rome. "But on the matter of penitents, whether they are doing penance for more weighty or for lighter offenses, the custom of the Roman Church makes it clear that they are to be reconciled (*remittendum*) on Holy Thursday."[108]

The problem with canonical public penance was its pastoral impracticality. Christians avoided seeking penance because of its onetime character as well as the social ostracization that it entailed. Many deferred penance until they were seriously ill, and there were many deathbed reconciliations so that penitents could receive communion (*viaticum*) to send them on their way to eternal life. The drastic changes required in one's social, marital, and economic status by public penance caused many, like Fabiola, to receive it only in widowhood. And some scrupulous Christians entered the order of penitents in order to engage in an ascetic spirituality. It flourished during the fourth and fifth centuries, but by 600 it had declined almost to the point of extinction.[109]

☙ THE SANCTIFICATION OF TIME

Both the continuity and the discontinuity of Christian liturgy from the third to the fourth centuries is seen in calendrical developments. Sunday continued to be observed as the day of the weekly assembly to celebrate the resurrection of Christ and the principal day of the eucharist. But in 321 Constantine made Sunday an official day of rest intended to make it easier for Christians to assemble on the Lord's Day. This inevitably brought Sabbath ideas to bear on the Lord's Day. Indeed, keeping Sunday as a day of

---

[108] Pope Innocent I, *Epistula 25, Ad Decentium*, 7:10; P.L. 20:559.

[109] See Nathan Mitchell, *The Rite of Penance: Commentaries*, III: *Backgrounds and Directions* (Washington: The Liturgical Conference, 1978), 28–32.

worship and rest became proof of good Christian behavior, with failure to observe the Lord's Day included in the catalogue of sins.[110]

Ordinary Sundays have come to be marked by the scripture readings of the liturgy of the word. It has been argued that the ancient church followed a lectio continuo approach to scripture readings, as the Jews did in the synagogue with the Law (though not with the Prophets). We know that during the paschal season there were continuous readings from certain books, such as Deuteronomy and the Gospel according to John, with sermons based on these from such noted preachers as John Chrysostom and Augustine of Hippo. Readings came to be fixed on festivals and days of devotion in the church year, as the sermons of the fathers also indicate. But we have no evidence of continuous readings on ordinary Sundays, and the sermons of the fathers are not helpful in determining what kind of sequence of readings there may have been. There was common agreement that at the eucharistic liturgy, the time, place, and occasion suggested the advisability of having shorter selections from the Old and New Testaments. This accounts for the pericope (cutout) selections that emerged in the lectionaries of the Eastern and Western churches. The fact that the Eastern and Western churches did develop significantly different lectionaries suggests that the pericope choices of great bishops could have been influential.[111]

Fourth-century developments that had a profound impact on the evolution of both calendar and lectionary were the popular interest in the life of Christ and pilgrimages to sites in the Holy Land. Constantine's own interest in these things caused him to erect great basilicas as shrines at the sites at which events were reported to have taken place in the Gospels. Along with general interest and devotion, these brought hordes of pilgrims to Palestine. Readings from pilgrimage offices at various shrines and from the celebration of events in the life of Christ on the day on which they supposedly occurred contributed to the development of the lectionary. By the beginning of the fifth century there was a complete festival pericope system in the Armenian Lectionary.[112] It is to this development that we owe the origins of Pentecost as a feast day in its own right with its own vigil rather than as the "great and last day" of the Fifty Days of Easter; the Ascension on the fortieth day after Easter rather than as part of the celebration of Christ's resurrection and exaltation (observed in the Church of the Ascension, or Imbomon, built in c. 375 by the Roman matron Poemenia); the individual days of Holy Week (especially Maundy Thursday and Good Friday) rather than just as part of the fast in preparation for paschal initiation;[113] and the fortieth day after the Epiphany (e.g., the Presentation of Jesus in the Temple and the Purification of Mary).[114]

The whole forty-day period of Lent developed as a way of preparing the catechumens for their baptism at the Easter Vigil. It was a time of fasting in which the whole congregation participated as a way of renewing their own baptism and life of penitence.

---

[110] See Rordorf, *Sunday*, op. cit., 162ff.

[111] See G. G. Willis, *St. Augustine's Lectionary*. Alcuin Club Collections 44 (London: S.P.C.K., 1962).

[112] A. Renoux, *Le codex arménien Jérusalem 121*, Patrologia Orientalis 35:1; 36:2.

[113] See Thomas J. Talley, *The Origins of the Liturgical Year* (New York: Pueblo Publishing House, 1986), 40ff.

[114] *Egeria: Diary of a Pilgrimage*, ch. 26, 96–7.

Sunday was never a fast day. Wednesdays and Fridays had been standard fast days for Christians. By the mid-third century a fast was begun on the Monday of Holy Week. This six-day fast extended the original two-day fast on Friday and Saturday in preparation for the Pascha. The earliest evidence for this six-day fast is a letter of Dionysius, bishop of Alexandria, in 247.[115] There is also evidence of the six-day fast in the Syrian *Didascalia*.[116]

On what has come to be called Palm Sunday, the gospel of the triumphal entry of Jesus into Jerusalem was read from Matthew 21:1–11. Shortly before 5 P.M. there was a reenactment of the event with a procession with palm and olive branches from the Mount of Olives in which, according to Egeria, "the bishop is led in the same manner as the Lord once was led."[117] There was nothing special on Monday except for the additional service. On Tuesday all assembled in the Eleona Church on the Mount of Olives where the bishop read Matthew 24:3–26:3, the long discourse delivered by Jesus on that mount. On Wednesday the people gathered in the Church of the Resurrection (the Anastasis) for the reading of Matthew 26:14–16, the agreement between Judas and the chief priests to betray Jesus for thirty pieces of silver. On Thursday the people gathered in the great Church of the Martyrium—built near the site where the Empress Helena, Constantine's mother, was reputed to have discovered the true cross—to hear the reading of Matthew 26:20–39, the account of the Last Supper. This was followed by a vigil on the Mount of Olives, at which the passage concerning Jesus' betrayal and arrest was read. On Friday the passion and death of Jesus was commemorated with a three-hour service at the place of the cross, at which psalms of the passion, the prophecies of the suffering servant, and the Gospel passions were read, ending with a reading at 3:00 P.M. of John 19:30. A voluntary vigil followed in the Anastasis church. On Holy Saturday the customary services were held at 9:00 A.M. and noon, but the 3:00 P.M. service was cancelled in order to prepare the great Church of the Martyrium for the Paschal Vigil. Egeria strangely provides no information on the vigil at Jerusalem, but it can be pieced together from Cyril's *Mystagogical Catecheses* and the Armenian Lectionary.[118]

The Vigil began in the Anastasis with the reading of Matthew 27:62–66, the account of the Jews' request of Pilate that the body of Jesus be sealed in the tomb lest it be stolen, and Psalm 88, which was interpreted as Jesus' descent to the place of departed spirits. Then the bishop lit three candles from a single stem, and a candlelight procession took the throng to the Martyrium. There a vigil service was held with twelve readings interspersed with psalms. The readings given in the Armenian Lectionary are: Genesis 1:1—3:24; Genesis 22:1–18; Exodus 12:1–14; Jonah 1:1—4:11; Exodus 14:24—15:21; Isaiah 60:1–13; Job 38:1–18; 2 Kings 2:1–22; Jeremiah 31:31–34; Joshua 1:1–9; Ezekiel 37:1–14; and Daniel 3:1–90 (Septuagint). Then the bishop, clergy, candidates for baptism and their sponsors left the Martyrium and went to the baptistery for the baptisms. After

---

[115] P.G. 10:1275f.

[116] R. H. Connolly, *Didascalia Apostolorum*, 183.

[117] *Egeria: Diary of a Pilgrimage*, ch. 31, 105.

[118] See J. G. Davies, *Holy Week: A Short History*. Ecumenical Studies in Worship 11 (Richmond: John Knox Press, 1963), 23ff.

the baptisms the newly baptized were led back to the Martyrium for the eucharist, which included the readings of 1 Corinthians 15:1–11 and Matthew 28:1–20. A second celebration of the resurrection took place at the Anastasis, where the gospel of the resurrection was read and the bishop celebrated the eucharist. But Egeria reported that "for the sake of the people, everything is done rapidly, lest they be delayed too long."[119]

This historical treatment of Holy Week in Jerusalem spread throughout the whole church. Egeria, the nun from Spain, was but one pilgrim among thousands who was impressed by what she saw there and carried ideas back home. In the Western churches there developed the Palm Sunday procession, the washing of feet (in Milan) and the evening celebration of the Lord's Supper on Maundy Thursday, devotions before the cross on Good Friday (for which purposes pilgrims tried to carry pieces of the "true cross" back home, and deacons had to be stationed by the cross in Jerusalem to prevent pilgrims from biting off pieces when they kissed it), and the candlelight procession at the beginning of the Easter Vigil. From the Gallican church come two texts for the rites of Holy Week that have great rhetorical power: the Reproaches on Good Friday and the Exsultet at the beginning of the Easter Vigil.[120] The Eastern influence on the Reproaches is seen in the singing of the Trisagion as a response, in both Greek and Latin. The Exsultet was the great thanksgiving for light in the style of the thanksgivings in the *Apostolic Tradition* and the *Apostolic Constitutions* for the greatest lucernarium (light service) of the year.[121]

The celebration of Christ's birth also became popular in the fourth century. The Eastern and Western churches differed in their computation of Christ's nativity. It has been thought that the Roman Christmas and the Eastern Epiphany originated from Christian efforts to offset the pagan Roman winter solstice festival, which was observed as the *dies natalis Solis Invicti* (day of the birth of the Invincible Sun) proclaimed by the Emperor Marcus Aurelius in 274.[122] There is no doubt that the months of November and December, being times of harvest and the thinning of herds for the winter enclosures, were times of excessive feasting and commemoration of the dead in Europe long before the coming of Christianity,[123] and that the festival of the sun's returning splendor was an occasion for special rejoicing in the Mediterranean and northern cultures.[124] It was easy to layer the festival of Christ's nativity over these preexistent holidays with their emphases on foods and drinks, green boughs and lights, family gatherings (including the dead), and

---

[119] *Egeria: Diary of a Pilgrimage*, 114.

[120] See John W. Tyrer, *Historical Survey of Holy Week: Its Services and Ceremonial*. Alcuin Club Collections 29 (London: Oxford University Press, 1932), 130ff, 151ff.

[121] An excellent translation of the text of the Exsultet is provided in *Lutheran Book of Worship*, Ministers Edition, 144–5.

[122] See Josef A. Jungmann, *The Early Liturgy to the Time of Gregory the Great*, trans. by Francis A. Brunner (Notre Dame: University of Notre Dame Press, 1959), 147–9.

[123] On the influence of the dead on agriculture and the inclusion of the departed in harvest festivals see Sir James Frazer, *The Belief in Immortality*, I (London, 1913), 247ff. and *The Fear of the Dead in Primitive Religion* (London, 1933–6), 51ff., 82ff.

[124] See Mircea Eliade, *Patterns in Comparative Religion*, trans. by Rosemary Sheed (Cleveland and New York: Meridian Books, 1963), 138ff.

gift-giving.[125] "Baptizing" or transforming these pagan holiday celebrations into fitting Christian celebrations was no easy task, and the church fathers expended much homiletical energy in countering the birthday of the Invincible Sun with the birthday of the Sun of Righteousness. Especially notable are the sermons of Pope Leo the Great, who injected the theme of eschatological judgment into a sermon delivered during the December harvest thanksgiving in Rome.

> When the Saviour would instruct His disciples about the Advent of God's Kingdom and the end of the world's times, and teach His whole Church, in the person of the Apostles, He said, "Take heed lest haply your hearts be overcharged with surfeiting and drunkenness, and care of this life." And assuredly, dearly beloved, we acknowledge that this precept applies more especially to us, to whom undoubtedly the day announced is near, even though hidden, for the advent of which it behooves every man to prepare himself lest it find him given over to gluttony, or entangled in cares of this life.[126]

Just because the celebration of Christ's nativity coincided with harvest and solstice festivals, however, does not mean that it was a festival invented to compete with paganism. Thomas Talley has championed the theory of Duchesne that the date of December 25 as Christ's nativity was reached by independent calendrical calculation on the part of Christians. On the basis of the passover connection with the passion, they believed that Christ must have died on or near the vernal equinox (March 25 in the Western calendar). They believed further that the world was redeemed on the same day on which it was created, and that the new creation began with the incarnation of the Word in human flesh (the Day of the Annunciation, also on March 25). Thus, the date of the nativity would have been calculated from the date of the annunciation (nine months later), which was also the date of the passion.[127]

These same theories serve as the hypothesis for the origin of Epiphany. The history of religions theory holds that January 6 was celebrated as the winter solstice in the Asian recension of the Julian calendar. The theophany of the sun god among human beings became a celebration of light, of water, and of wine. Hence the confluence of the themes of the visit of the Magi, the baptism of Christ, and Jesus' sign of changing water into wine at Cana in Galilee. The calendrical calculation theory propounded by Duchesne and Talley holds that the Eastern paschal date revolved around April 6. By the same theological calculation process used for Christmas in the West, the Eastern church set January 6 as the Epiphany of Christ. The custom of celebrating Christ's baptism on Epiphany may stem from the custom of the Egyptian church of beginning the reading of

---

[125] See Clarence A. Miles, "Pre-Christian Winter Festivals," in *Christmas in Ritual and Tradition Christian and Pagan* (London: T. F. Unwin, 1912; reprint, Detroit: Omnigraphics, 1990), 171–80 for a discussion of the Germanic Yule, the Celtic *Samhain*, and the Roman feasts of *Saturnalia* and *Kalends*.

[126] Leo the Great, Sermon XVII; *Nicene and Post-Nicene Fathers of the Christian Church*, Series II, ed. by Philip Schaff and Henry Wace, XII (reprint Grand Rapids: William B. Eerdmans, 1983), 127.

[127] L. Duchesne, *Christian Worship: Its Origin and Evolution. A Study of the Latin Liturgy up to the Time of Charlemagne*, trans. by M. L. McClure (London: S.P.C.K., 1923), 261ff; Talley, 91ff.

the Gospel of Mark at the beginning of the solar year, since this Gospel begins with Jesus' baptism.[128]

It is not certain just when the Eastern and Western churches adopted each other's festivals. *Apostolic Constitutions* V, 13 provides both feasts in its festal list. John Chrysostom preached a sermon on Christmas Day in 386 in which he notes that this date had been celebrated in Antioch for ten years.[129] We know that Christmas was introduced in Constantinople at the beginning of the reign of Theodosius I (379). The emphasis on the incarnation of the Word was a way of ending that church's flirtation with Arianism. A sign of the resurgence of orthodoxy was the call to Gregory of Nazianzus to become archbishop (379–381). During his brief patriarchate he preached on the nativity (which he called "Theophany") and on the Feast of Christ's Baptism (which he called "the Feast of Lights"). We find the same nomenclature for these feasts used by Gregory of Nyssa and Basil the Great at this time. The December festival was resisted until well into the fifth century in Jerusalem and Alexandria, with the latter retaining the memory that the reading of the Gospel of Mark was begun on January 6.

In terms of the acceptance of Epiphany in the West, we see another link between the Gallican and the Eastern churches. There is evidence that Epiphany was celebrated in Gaul by the end of the fourth century, and that the Roman December 25 festival was not known there. The themes clustering around January 6 were the same as in the East: the visit of the Magi, Jesus' baptism, and the miracle at Cana. There were some unique features in Milan's observance. The transfiguration was substituted for the miracle at Cana and the competentes were enrolled for baptism at Easter on Epiphany, which was observed as the Baptism of our Lord. In Spain, as in the East, Epiphany became the second great day for public baptism. The victory over Arianism at the Council of Constantinople in 381 may have prompted Rome to adopt the Epiphany as a way of emphasizing the incarnation. The theme of the Epiphany in the Roman propers was the visit of the Magi, as the counterpart to the visit of the shepherds on December 25. Thus, the two nativity stories framed the Twelve Days of Christmas in Rome.[130]

Where baptism was celebrated on Epiphany, a period of preparation of the candidates comparable to Lent was required. This was the origin of the season of Advent in Gaul and Spain. Since Spain followed the Eastern tradition of not fasting on Saturdays, getting a comparable forty-day period *(quadragesima)* pushed the time of fasting back to early November. The Feast of Saint Martin of Tours (November 11) became the time to begin the season of fasting in Gaul; hence it was called "Saint Martin's Lent" *(quadragesima Sancti Martini)*.[131] The earliest reference to the fast that has become identified with the Advent season may be a reference to fasting in the documentation of the Council of Saragossa in Spain in 380. Bishop Perpetuus of Tours (d. 490) called for three days of fasting each week from Saint Martin's Day until Christmas, adding Mondays to the usual

---

[128] Talley, 135ff.
[129] Ibid., 135–6.
[130] Ibid., 141ff.
[131] See John Gunstone, *Christmas and Epiphany* (London: The Faith Press, 1967).

Wednesday and Friday fasts. The Synod of Tours in 567 established this fast for monastics, and the Synod of Macon in 581 established one for the laity.[132]

Earlier than this, however, there is evidence of a December fast in Rome. This was one of the four times of fasting during the year known as the "Ember Days" (*quattuor tempora anni*; in German, *Quatember*). The precise dates associated with these days varied over the years. The oldest traditions associate them with the first week of Lent, the week following Pentecost, and, since medieval times, the Wednesdays, Fridays, and Saturdays following Holy Cross Day (September 14) and Saint Lucia's Day (December 13).[133] Wednesdays and Fridays were usual fast days throughout the year; but in the Ember weeks these fasts were extended over into Saturday and ended with a Saturday vigil.

The origin and purpose of these times of fasting remain veiled in obscurity. Germain Morin, at the end of the nineteenth century, suggested that they were established in the late fourth century as a way of relating to the three pagan agricultural *feriae conceptivae*.[134] Certainly Leo the Great (d. 461) connected the Ember Days with the four seasons of the natural year. He saw the December fast as an expression of gratitude for the harvest of that year. In the sermon quoted above he connected the themes of thanksgiving with purification from sin, gratitude for God's providence with alms-giving, and the earthly harvest with the heavenly harvest at the end of the age.[135] What is noteworthy in Leo's sermon for this occasion is that while he uses the term *Advent,* he makes no reference to the festival of Christ's nativity. However appropriate its placement at the end of the agricultural and civil year, there is no hint from Leo that the December fast was a preparation for Christmas. The full development of the Advent season as a time of preparation for Christmas awaits the next period in history and the next chapter of this book. But the pieces are in place for the conflation of the Gallican Saint Martin's Lent, with its penitential preparation for baptism (recalling, among other themes, the ministry of John the Baptist) and the Roman December Embertide with its eschatological note.

One final piece in the development of Advent comes from Spain. The fathers at the Council of Toledo in 656 were concerned that such a major feast as the Annunciation should occur very often in Holy Week, and therefore be suppressed. So they decreed that it should be celebrated one week before the nativity festival on December 18.[136] Such a decree does reveal, in their own minds, the difference between Advent and Lent. Advent never did acquire the somber character of Lent.

The church had not only a temporal cycle of seasons—Advent and Christmas–Epiphany, Lent and Easter–Pentecost—but also a "sanctoral cycle": that is, a calendar of commemoration of saints. This calendar began to be filled in already in the second century. The *Martyrdom of Polycarp* tells how the Christians took up the bones of the martyred bishop

---

[132] See F. Cabrol, "L'Avent liturgique," *Revue Bénédictine* 22 (1905), 484–95.
[133] Talley, 148.
[134] G. Morin, "L'origine des quatre-temps," *Revue Bénédictine* 14 (1897), 337–46.
[135] Leo the Great, Sermon XVII; *Nicene and Post-Nicene Fathers*, XII, 125–6.
[136] Talley, 152–3.

and laid them away in a suitable place. There the Lord will permit us, so far as possible, to gather together in joy and gladness to celebrate the day of his martyrdom as a birthday, in memory of those athletes who have gone before, and to train and make ready those who are to come hereafter.[137]

The commemorations of martyrs, including Polycarp, are the oldest days in the Christian calendar apart from the Pascha. The second-century *Martyrdom of Polycarp* testifies that martyrs were commemorated on the day of their death, which was their birthday into eternal life. Originally, the cult of the martyrs was practiced only at the site of their tomb or where Christian communities possessed relics of the martyrs.[138] At an early stage similar veneration was also accorded the apostles and evangelists, most of whom were also remembered as martyrs. Once the great persecution of Christians was ended, ascetics and virgins, who offered their lives as a kind of bloodless martyrdom, were also venerated.[139]

While Mary the Mother of our Lord figured prominently in devotion, sermons, and christological debates, days in the calendar honoring her memory were slow in coming. Mary's role in salvation history was recalled on the feasts of the Annunciation and Christmas. The day of her dormition (falling asleep) was first celebrated in the East on August 15 in the middle of the fifth century; the Emperor Maurice (582–602) extended it to the whole Byzantine Empire. Not until later would it be called "the assumption" of Mary into heaven.[140]

❦ THE SANCTIFICATION OF SPACE

Constantine's erection of shrines and basilicas to house Christian liturgy has been alluded to several times. These were often built at important sites in the history of Jesus and over the graves of the martyrs. In terms of the architectural setting for Christian liturgy, there was a great difference between the third and the fourth centuries. Before Constantine Christian places of assembly were modest. A house church has been excavated at Dura-Europas in the Upper Euphrates Valley. It was a decent-sized house that, in the 240s, had been enlarged to include a place of assembly by knocking out a wall to create a room that might hold about sixty people. Another room was used for teaching and a third as a baptistery.[141] The last persecution under Diocletian witnessed the destruction of Christian basilicas in three North African towns. The fact that they could be razed so easily suggests that they were modest in size.[142]

---

[137] "The Martyrdom of Saint Polycarp, Bishop of Smyrna, as Told in the Letter of the Church of Smyrna in the Church of Philomelium," in *Early Christian Fathers*, op. cit., 156.

[138] See Theodore Klauser, *Christlicher Märtyrerkult, heidnischer Heroenkult und spätjüdische Heiligenverehrung* (Cologne: Opladen, 1960.)

[139] See Adolf Adam, *The Liturgical Year: Its History and Meaning after the Reform of the Liturgy*, trans. by Matthew J. O'Connell (New York: Pueblo Publishing Co., 1981), 206ff.

[140] Ibid., 215f. See Frank C. Senn, "Mary in Ecumenical Dialogue and Liturgical Convergence," *dialog* 31 (1992), 251–8, and Robert W. Jenson, "An Attempt to Think about Mary," ibid., 259–64.

[141] See Fox, op. cit., 269–70.

[142] Ibid., 587.

Constantine was limited in ways he could serve the church. He could not abolish the pagan cults, but he could extend great privileges to the bishops. He could not destroy the pagan temples, but he could build impressive buildings for Christian cultic activities. Some of these buildings were privately financed; others, like the basilica on Golgotha in Jerusalem, were erected at public expense. Constantine's interest in this project was indicated by his request that construction progress should be reported to him personally.

Christian places of worship could not be like the pagan temples. Pagan temples were houses for the god or goddess, into which only the priests entered. These temples were not adequate as places of Christian assembly in which all the people entered the worship space. Hence the choice of the basilica or "royal hall." These buildings were used as covered market-halls or public law-courts. They were usually oblong rectangular halls with narrower, lower aisles on the sides and a circular dais at one end where the chairperson of the meeting or the magistrate could take a seat. The Christian basilica used the side aisles for the movement of the people during the offertory procession and during the distribution of communion. The bishop sat on his throne in the apse surrounded by presbyters. The colonnades that divided the nave from the aisles also supported brick walls that raised the roof of the nave. Small windows in these higher walls admitted light into the nave. This is the plan of such notable basilicas as Saint Peter's and Saint John Lateran in Rome.

Constantine's architects also employed a centralized plan that created a round, polygonal, or cruciform shape.[143] Diocletian's palace at Salonae had been a centralized structure, and the imperial builders extended the concept. The Church of the Holy Apostles in Constantinople had the shape of a cross with a conically shaped roof. This building combined the functions of a martyrium for the twelve apostles and a mausoleum for Constantine, who thereby suggested himself as a thirteenth apostle. Another centralized building was the Golden Octagon built on an island in the Errands River in Antioch. This church, dedicated to the divine Harmony or Concord, was capped by a gilded, wooden dome and flanked by a circular colonnaded aisle in two stories. The Grotto of the Nativity in Bethlehem and the Church of the Holy Sepulchre (Anastasis) in Jerusalem combined both rectangular and centralized concepts. It is unfortunate that so few of these original basilicas survive today. Saint Sabina in Rome is a superb example of a surviving fifth-century basilica in the Roman style.[144]

The Byzantine development of erecting a circular cupola on a square, octagonal, or rectangular base freed Christian worship space from the three bays of nave, aisles, and apse. In the typical basilica the placement of the bema or platform from which the scriptures were read always posed a problem. In the Byzantine church it could be left in the middle of the assembly space under the dome, and the people could gather around it. We know that in the greatest Byzantine church, Hagia Sophia (the Church of Holy Wisdom) in Constantinople, the bema was a raised structure that also held the bishop's throne,

---

[143] See Italo Furian, "Early Christian and Byzantine Art," in *The History of Art* (New York: Gallery Books, 1988), 139ff.

[144] See picture in ibid., 146; also the sketch of Hagia Sophia, 150–1.

seats for the presbyters, an ark for the sacred books, and the ambo for the readings and the sermon. On either side to the north and south, two smaller cupolas could shelter two divisions of the choir, which could then sing antiphonally to each other. The apse in the east came to be the room for the altar. This liturgical arrangement was almost the opposite of the Roman basilica, in which the altar itself was farther out into the nave and the bishop's seat was in the apse.

The question of how to decorate these buildings was controversial because the whole issue of the use of images caused violent disputes; none more so than the iconoclastic controversy that tore apart the Byzantine Empire in the eighth century.[145] Christians were generally agreed not to use statues for two basic reasons. First, graven images were condemned in the Decalogue. Second, to place a figure of Christ or the saints at some focal point would have been misleading to pagan converts who would have thought that these statues "represented" Christ or one of the saints, just as a statue by Pheidias was thought to represent Zeus. But many Christians had no objections to less lifelike paintings. Portrayals of biblical scenes, stories, and personages could serve a teaching purpose for the illiterate. More than mere visual aids, icons of Christ and the saints were windows to eternity. Most pictures in the church buildings were stone or glass mosaics that yielded bright and deep colors, and lent the interior of the church an appearance of solemn splendor that gave the impression of heaven and earth.[146]

The old cosmic symbolism of the cupola emerged anew to portray a vision of Christ the Ruler of All Things (Pantocrator), holding all things together above his people, enfolding the worship of the earthly church into the worship of heaven. However, in the Italian basilicas in Rome, Milan, and Ravenna, the figure of the Pantocrator was painted in the apse, so that he appeared as the one to whom worship was directed.[147] We should note that the apse of many secular basilicas contained a statue of the emperor, so that the icon of Christ the Pantocrator replaced it. We should also note that emperor worship made the place of the emperor's image a sacred place, so it is not surprising that the apse end of the church building continued to have an aura of sacrality about it. The altar was often positioned on the line that separated the apse from the nave, without yet being located in the apse itself. A canopy erected over the altar gave it the appearance of a throne.

The basilica as a type of building was the exponent of official architecture. Its public character is reflected in the use of the column, which in antiquity was often employed in the public sphere. Emperors preferred the basilican model for Christian church buildings because it was a monumental form of architecture that made visible the new religious foundation of the renewed Roman Empire under Constantine and his successors. It was also a public-type building suitable for a public cultus; the Christianity of this period was no longer entirely a private matter.

The Christian basilicas also expressed a sacred orientation. They were built so that worshipers could face east for prayer. To prevent worshipers from having to turn

---

[145] On the iconoclastic controversy, see essays in *Dumbarton Oaks Papers* 7 (1953).

[146] See E. H. Gombrich, *The Story of Art* (London: Phaidon, 1955), 92ff.

[147] See Bouyer, *Rite and Man*, 179–80.

their backs on the altar during prayer, there was a desire to locate the altar at the east end of the building. The altar in the Western basilica was protected by low railings called *cancelli* (from which we derive the term "chancel"). Sometimes curtains were hung around it from the beams of the canopy *(ciborium)*.[148] As yet there was no move to push the altar completely into the apse. This was the case, however, in the original Saint Peter's Basilica in Rome, allowing entry into the crypt *(confessio)* of the martyr under the altar.

❦ THE SANCTIFICATION OF LIFE

The connection between the altar in the church building and the relics of the saints was only an extension of the practice of celebrating the eucharist on the graves of the faithful departed in the earlier period. There is good reason why the covers of Roman graves were called *mensae*: they were tables on which feasts in honor of the dead were celebrated. It was an act of devotion *(pietas)* to keep alive the memory of the dead. People who died were washed, dressed in festive garments, and carried in torchlight processions to the cemeteries, which were located outside the towns and cities. Objects that the dead had liked during their lives were buried with them. A last meal for the dead *(viaticum)* was shared. Burial was usually within twenty-four hours. Relatives would come to the cemetery on the third day after death to mourn and share a feast *(refrigerium)*. This would be repeated on the ninth day. On the thirtieth day after death not only relatives but also friends and associates of the dead would attend the commemoration. All the dead were called to mind during the month of February, the month of the dead. On February 22 the *caristia* or *cara cognatio* was celebrated, in which all relations met together for a meal in honor of the dead.[149]

The ordinary Christian of antiquity was far from abandoning these customs, which belonged to the very stuff of civil life. Christian bishops tried to transform the pagan rites so that psalms and alleluias replaced lamentations and dirges. The church fathers inveighed against rich grave clothes and sumptuous trappings, and recommended instead a simple shroud and the giving of alms. There were also efforts to replace the *vestes sordidae* of paganism, usually black or red garments, with the white garments of Christian hope. Most significantly, the eucharist was substituted for the refrigeria, which sometimes degenerated into drunkenness and carousing.[150]

That the refrigeria continued among Christians is evident in that the bishops had to forbid them. As far as we know, Ambrose was the first on record to forbid holding the feasts in honor of the dead inside churches.[151] Ambrose also made a passing remark that the seventh and fortieth days were observed by the Christians of Milan as days of commemoration because of sabbath connotations, rather than the ninth and thirtieth

---

[148] See the architectural figures in *The Study of Liturgy*, 481–7.

[149] See A. C. Rush, *Death and Burial in Christian Antiquity* (Washington: Catholic University of America Press, 1941).

[150] See Geoffrey Rowell, *The Liturgy of Christian Burial*. Alcuin Club Collections 59 (London: S.P.C.K., 1977), 22ff.

[151] See F. van der Meer, 515ff.

days,[152] although other Christians continued to observe the customary days. There was clearly much discussion in the patristic church concerning the extent to which Christians should or should not continue to observe customs established in a pagan culture. Converts were not weaned away from these customs overnight. As late as 567, the Second Council of Tours had to prohibit Christians in Gaul from putting food on the graves of relatives.

Another aspect of life where pagan practices had to be transformed in Christian usage was in marriage rites. Unfortunately, there is a paucity of references to marriage rites in the writings of the church fathers. We need to remember that in its first centuries the church had no authority to solemnize marriages or to regulate the institution of marriage. At most the bishop replaced the pagan *auspex nuptiarum* in praying for and blessing the Christian couple, and the eucharist was substituted for the offerings to the gods and goddesses of marriage and of the hearth. Among pagan practices that survive to this day in customary Western marriage rites are the betrothal at the home of the bride (engagement), the placing of rings on the fourth finger, the joining of hands, the bridal veil (usually flame-colored among pagans rather than white), a floral crown, a solemn declaration before witnesses, a wedding banquet, and the husband carrying the bride over the threshold of her new home.[153]

If wedding rites are lacking in the patristic period, the theology of marriage is fully developed in the thought of such fathers as Augustine of Hippo. The North African bishop bequeathed to the Latin church a theology of marriage that served for centuries as the basis of the church's teaching. Against heretics who held that sexuality and marriage were evil, he held that sexuality and marriage were gifts created by a good God. Even in the fall marriage cannot lose its basic goodness. The goodness of marriage is seen in spousal fidelity, the generation of offspring, and the sacramental character of marriage, by which he meant its indissolubility.[154]

❧ THE DAILY PRAYER OF THE CHURCH

The daily prayer of the church has usually been considered under the category of the sanctification of time. The liturgy of the hours, as it is sometimes called, sanctifies the times of the day, especially sunrise and sunset. The liturgical day in both Judaism and Christianity is regarded as beginning with the evening (Vespers), so that the night does not fall out of the picture altogether, which would be the case if the day began with morning praise (Lauds). We are considering the daily prayer here because it forms a bridge to the ecclesial reality with which we shall end this chapter: the rise of monasticism. The "divine office" (as the liturgy of the hours is also called) came to be associated with the discipline of monastic communities and religious orders. But it is important to emphasize that

---

[152] Ambrose, *De Obitu Theodosii*, 3; P.L. 16:1448.

[153] See Marion J. Hatchett, *Sanctifying Life, Time, and Space. An Introduction to Liturgical Study* (New York: Seabury Press, 1976), 39–40.

[154] See Pope John Paul II, *Theology of Marriage and Celibacy: Catechesis on Marriage and Celibacy in the Light of the Resurrection of the Body*, preface by Donald W. Wuerl (St. Paul Editions, 1986).

in the patristic church the daily prayer offices were popular liturgies celebrated communally by at least some portion of the people with their ministers.

We saw in the last chapter that Tertullian advised Christians to pray at various times during the day: for example, at the ringing of the forum bell at the third, sixth, and ninth hours. These were times of private prayer and were not obligatory. "The prescribed prayers *(legitimae orationes),*" he wrote, "are, of course, an exception. Without any admonition they are obligatory *(debenter)* at the approach of day and night."[155] Though Tertullian did not specify the content of these gatherings for prayer, he did write in the same treatise of Christians singing psalms together in common.[156]

Eusebius of Caesarea (d. 339) may be the earliest witness to the content of the pivotal morning and evening prayer offices. In his commentary on Psalm 65:10 he wrote: "The very fact that in God's churches throughout the world hymns, praises, and truly divine delights are arranged in his honor at the morning sunrise and in the evening is surely no small sign of God's power. These 'delights of God' are the hymns sent up in his church throughout the world both morning and evening."[157] The *Apostolic Constitutions* II, 59 specifies:

> When you instruct the people, O Bishop, command and exhort them to make it a practice to come daily to the church in the morning and evening, and on no account to cease doing so, but to assemble together continually. . . . Nor should you place the needs of this life before the word of God; rather each day gather together in the morning and evening singing and praying in the Lord's house, in the morning saying Psalm 62 (63) and in the evening Psalm 141.[158]

John Chrysostom invoked the example of the Old Testament as the basis of daily prayer in the church in his commentary on Psalm 141. Praying at these times

> "was ordered and laid down by law for the priests, that . . . each morning and evening they sacrifice and burn a lamb; the former was called the morning sacrifice, the latter, the evening sacrifice. God had ordered this to be done, signifying through it that it is necessary to be zealous in praising him both at the beginning and at the end of the day."[159]

Appeal to the Old Testament cult probably inspired the introduction of an incense oblation in both the morning and evening offices already in the fourth century in Syria and in the fifth century in Palestine.

Putting together the various clues provided in patristic sources, including Egeria's *Diary,* chapter 24, as well as the *Apostolic Constitutions* and the above-mentioned commentaries, the morning and evening prayer offices of antiquity can be reconstructed as follows:[160]

---

[155] Tertullian, *De oratione* 25:1–3; *Corpus Christianorum, series Latina* I (Turnholt, Belgium), 272.

[156] Ibid., 253.

[157] P.G. 23:640B

[158] Funk, 171–3.

[159] P.G. 55:430

[160] See Juan Mateos, "The Morning and Evening Office," *Worship* 42 (1968), 31–47.

Morning Prayer includes:

> Psalm 63 (penitential)
> > Old Testament canticle (paschal in spirit)
> Light hymn: "Lux orta est iustis" in the Chaldean office; various hymns for
> > different days of the week in the Roman, Milanese and Spanish offices
> Incense oblation (done during the singing of the New Testament canticle, the
> > Benedictus [Song of Zechariah])
> Laudate psalms (148–150)
> Supplicatory Prayers (on Sundays the Gloria could take the place of the suppli-
> > cations and serve as a bridge from Lauds into the eucharistic liturgy)

Evening Prayer includes:

> Lighting of lamps with thanksgiving for light (the Lucernarium; texts of the
> > thanksgiving are provided in both the *Apostolic Tradition* and the *Apostolic
> > Constitutions*)[161]
> Phos hilaron (Joyous Light of Glory)—the evening hymn in Byzantine Vespers;
> > a third-century text[162]
> Psalm 141 (penitential)
> Incense oblation (accompanied in the East with Psalm 141; in the West with
> > the Magnificat [Song of Mary])
> Evening supplication (called "Preces" in the Roman Rite; Egeria mentions a
> > litany with "Kyrie eleison" as the response in Jerusalem)
> A solemn blessing by the bishop (according to Egeria)

It is clear from various descriptions that these services of morning and evening prayer were public, communal, and almost entirely invariable.[163] The content (psalms and hymns) was related to the time of the day at which the particular office was being celebrated. Because these offices were celebrated in the great basilicas of antiquity, they have come to be called "cathedral offices" to distinguish them from the monastic offices.[164] The designations "cathedral" and "monastic" can also delineate two different styles of worship: one suitable for lay devotion (repetitive and ceremonialized) and the other suitable for religious professionals (changeable in content and meditative).[165] Recapturing the spirit of the cathedral office has been one of the accomplishments of the modern liturgical movement. This has required getting behind the monastic appropriation of the divine office.[166]

---

[161] Translations of both are in *Lutheran Book of Worship*, Ministers Edition, 95.

[162] See *Lutheran Book of Worship*, Pew Edition, 143; see Timothy J. Keyl with Frank C. Senn, "Phos Hilaron: Joyous Song of the Light," *Currents in Theology and Mission* 13 (1986), 354–7.

[163] See William G. Storey, "The Liturgy of the Hours: Cathedral versus Monastic," *Worship* 50 (1976), 55–7.

[164] See W. Jardine Grisbrooke, "The Formative Period—Cathedral and Monastic Offices," *The Study of Liturgy*, 358–69.

[165] See Senn, *Christian Worship and its Cultural Setting*, op. cit., 105ff.

[166] See Senn, *The Pastor as Worship Leader: A Manual for Corporate Worship* (Minneapolis: Augsburg Publishing House, 1977), chapter 2.

🍇 THE MONASTIC REVOLUTION

In 305 an illiterate Coptic Christian named Anthony went into the desert to live a solitary life, encouraging others to follow him. In 313 he retreated still further. These dates are significant. The last great persecution of Christians ended in 304 and the Edict of Milan was promulgated in 313. The first hermits (anchorites) went into the desert to practice a discipleship through asceticism that was no longer available through martyrdom. They offered their own *martyria* (witness) not to the world but to the church that was, in their eyes, accommodating itself to the world. The aim of these ascetics was to cultivate perfection. Their efforts were encouraged by the fact that far-from-perfect Christian people had as great a need as ever for intercessors and agents of blessing and forgiveness once the confessors of the age of persecution were no longer available.[167]

This kind of ascetic life was not new in the fourth century. Syrian Christians were already familiar with wandering "sons of the covenant" in the early third century.[168] Perfectionism had been a constant theme in Christian spirituality, and in Syria and Egypt it lost none of its urgency. The years of the Great Persecution also saw the first teachings of the heretic Arius, whose theology included not only an abstract view of Christ's two natures but also the human capacity for perfectibility.[169] While Arius did not encourage a life of rigor in pursuit of perfection, the Manichees did. Their elect lived a life as austere as any Christian monk, and by c. 300 their presence in Egypt's Christian centers was well recognized.[170]

Not long after Anthony went into the desert, a fellow Egyptian named Pachomius, who had been pressed into the Roman army and had been converted to Christianity through the example of Christians' charity during a time of adversity, organized the first community of hermits (cenobites). It is not important to describe here the whole history of asceticism or of monasticism,[171] but it is important to note that early monasticism was a lay movement with no liturgical life of its own. The hermits and monks had to come into town for the eucharist, since the eucharistic presidency was vested in the bishop and his presbyters who were not numbered (at first) among the monks.

In the writings of Cassian, a Gallican monk who lived for a time in Egypt, we find the first traces of what might be called a "monastic rite." What is most notable—and fateful to the development of the liturgy of the hours—is the tailoring of the prayer offices to the monastic discipline. Not only were litanies and special prayers eliminated

[167] See H. J. Drijvers, in *The Byzantine Saint*, ed. Serge Hackel (Birmingham, UK: University of Birmingham Press, 1980), 25ff.

[168] See also Arthur Vööbus, *Celibacy as a Requirement for Baptism in the Early Syrian Church*. Papers of the Estonian Theological Society in Exile (Stockholm, 1951).

[169] See R. C. Gregg and D. E. Groh, *Early Arianism* (Philadelphia: Fortress Press, 1981), 88.

[170] See Peter Brown, *Augustine of Hippo* (Berkeley and Los Angeles: University of California Press, 1967), chapter 5.

[171] See Louis Bouyer, *A History of Christian Spirituality*, I. *The Spirituality of the New Testament and the Fathers*, Eng. trans. (New York: Desclee, 1960), 303ff.

(since these required clerical leadership in cathedral practice), but also the psalms appropriate to Lauds and Vespers (63 and 141) were eliminated in favor of a recitation of the whole psalter in sequence.[172]

The next fateful step was the movement of monks into the cities. In Cappadocia, instead of living apart and remote from civilization, the ascetics lived in their own communities in town. Basil, bishop of Caesarea, was one of the first bishops to recognize the potential usefulness of these communities within the local church. They could be centers of prayer, study, and charity. In his *Greater Rule* it is clear that Basil regarded the monks as the elite members of his congregation. The liturgy of the hours was celebrated by the monks. At first it was practically identical with the cathedral usage, except that ordinary Christians did not participate in the prayer offices to the same extent as the monks.[173] This is the same situation Egeria describes in Palestine. Perhaps under the influence of Constantinople (through the influence of Basil) monks were living in the cities as well as in the wilderness areas. In these urban centers, such as Jerusalem, the monks took over the ministry of praying the daily offices on behalf of the whole church. They inevitably put their own stamp on the liturgy of the hours.[174]

As Schmemann pointed out, the monastic prayer offices are not a liturgical act at all; they are a devotional act within a whole spiritual discipline designed to lead the monk toward the goal of "spiritual freedom." "The purpose of the liturgical ordo," wrote Schmemann, "is to make worship the expression of the faith of the Church, to actualize the Church herself; the purpose of the monastic devotional rules is to train the monk in constant prayer."[175] Consequently, the liturgy of time—the sanctification of the hour, the day, the week, the season, the year—is largely disregarded. "In monasticism . . . times and hours as such have no great significance. What is important is the division [of psalms and readings] in such a way that it will fill up the whole of life, and for this reason it is set in a framework of time. But time itself has no meaning at all other than as the 'time of prayer.'"[176] Time is not, for example, the time of the beginning or ending of the day. The great variation in monastic rules involving the recitation of the psalms and the reading of scripture is a result of the practical concern to help the monk's spiritual growth, not to relate one's daily life and activities in the world to God's word and Christian discipleship.

Monastic communities also had an influence on the sacraments. From the beginning the desert fathers had to practice private reservation of the eucharistic elements in order to receive communion, because they could not always be in the town churches and their communities were lay communities. This was no different from other lay Christians taking the sacrament to their homes in order to commune themselves after a

---

[172] See Alexander Schmemann, *Introduction to Liturgical Theology*, op. cit., 147.

[173] See J. Gribomont, "Le monachisme au IVs siècle en Asie Mineure," in K. Aland and F.L. Cross, *Studia Patristica*, II (Berlin, 1957), 409ff.

[174] See Pierre Salmon, *The Breviary Through the Centuries*, trans. Sr. David Mary (Collegeville: The Liturgical Press, 1962), 28ff.

[175] Schmemann, 108.

[176] Ibid.

period of fasting (a kind of delayed reception).[177] From this practical arrangement evolved a new kind of eucharistic piety: not celebrating the eucharistic meal to build up the fellowship of the church, but using the eucharistic elements as an aid to personal devotion. Monks and others could let the "exposed" elements stimulate meditation. The roots of the veneration of the sacramental elements are in the eucharistic liturgy itself, in the practice of showing the elements to the people (as a kind of elevation) at the invitation to communion: "Holy things for the holy people."[178] But there is a difference between exposing the elements for the purpose of consuming them and exposing the elements as a stimulus to contemplative prayer.

Perhaps the most fateful consequence of monastic spirituality for the whole life of the church was its implicit attitude toward baptism. As the ascetic and the monk took the place of the martyr and confessor, so the monastic noviate took the place of the catechumenate; monastic profession became an equivalent of baptism. The end result was the implication that there are two levels of Christians—a view that had long been held on the popular level, but that was brought to bear with force with the return of the monks from the desert to the city.

On the other hand, it is difficult not to see a providential development in the triumph of monasticism in the church. Here was an order of earnest, prayerful, and sometimes learned Christians poised to carry on the mission of the church in the wake of the social and ecclesiastical upheaval which followed the collapse of the western Roman Empire. Contemplative monks actually became the missionary force behind the evangelization of the peoples who moved into the territory of the western Roman Empire and who lived to its north. The disciplines and spirituality learned in Egypt, Palestine, Syria, and Asia Minor proved useful when adapted to the cultures of western and northern Europe, Great Britain, and Ireland.

---

[177] See Archdale A. King, *Eucharistic Reservation in the Western Church* (New York: Sheed and Ward, 1965), 3ff.

[178] See Nathan Mitchell, *Cult and Controversy: The Worship of the Eucharist Outside Mass* (New York: Pueblo Publishing Company, 1982), 47ff.

CHAPTER 5

The Franco-Roman Liturgy

THE PREVIOUS TWO CHAPTERS surveyed Christian liturgical development in the world of classical antiquity. The focus now narrows to liturgical development in the Western church from the period of late antiquity into the Middle Ages. This field affords a remarkable case study in liturgical adaptation as the Roman rite was imported into western Europe by local political rulers and church authorities and was transformed in the process. Liturgical adaptation also led to indigenization or inculturation as liturgical development was affected by the political and cultural history of western Europe in the period after the decline and fall of the western Roman Empire.

Since Edward Gibbon wrote his monumental *Decline and Fall of the Roman Empire*, people have had a view of a tottering edifice that finally crashed in a shower of debris. To some extent, Gibbon, who blamed the fall of Rome on "the triumph of barbarism and religion," may have been dependent on a view perpetrated by Christians like Jerome and Augustine of Hippo. In the wake of the crisis in confidence brought on by the sack of Rome by Alaric in 410, they portrayed the event in apocalyptic terms as the collapse of the pagan classical culture, exulted in the triumph of the church and the Christianized tribes that were overtaking the Roman Empire, and reoriented Christians from placing their confidence in the city of man to questing after the city of God.[1] Moreover, the "barbarians" were not pagans; they had been converted by Arian missionaries from Constantinople. So the successive waves of peoples—Vandals, Visigoths,

---

[1] See Jaroslav Pelikan, *The Excellent Empire: The Fall of Rome and the Triumph of the Church* (San Francisco: Harper and Row, 1987).

Ostrogoths, Burgundians, and Lombards—were not enemies of Christianity. Most likely, the Roman Empire never "fell" in the conventional sense of the word. It was simply worn away by tides of barbarian immigration it could no longer hold back, weakened by the increasing reliance of the army on Germanic troops and commanders to provide manpower for legions stretched out along a long and unstable frontier, and ill-served by a bureaucracy that was unable to deal efficiently and effectively with a rapidly changing situation.[2]

Furthermore, the ethnic identity of the Goths, who gathered around military leaders or "kings" as they fought their way from the Oder-Vistula region to the Dnieper, the Black Sea, across the Danube and into Italy over a period of forty years, has been debated. "The Goths" simply means "the men" (a Germanic equivalent of the Latin *gens*, or "people"). To join a Gothic, or Gutonic king, one did not have to belong to a certain ethnic group, nor even be a free man; all one had to be was a warrior who followed the king faithfully.[3] German warriors had already shown themselves willing to attach themselves to Roman emperors, and by the fifth century they were serving as military commanders within the territory of the Roman Empire and were even ruling over peoples within the Empire as kings. The Roman government permitted large groups of Germanic peoples to establish a permanent and powerful presence inside the Empire, with all the potential for misunderstanding and mischief that could bring.[4] In 418, eight years after the sack of Rome, Italy itself was ceded to the Goths; thereafter the peninsula became a football in the hands of several Ostrogothic (Eastern Goth) leaders. Independent kingdoms were carved out of Italy by Odoacer (476–493) and Theodoric (493–526). In spite of their glorification of the warrior, it seems that the Ostrogoths were content to live in peace with the Romans and even assimilate Roman ways and institutions. Theodoric the Great sought accommodation between Catholic Romans and Arian Goths, and even a better relationship between the Roman pope and the Byzantine emperor, since he craved the recognition of both. After the deposition of Romulus Augustulus in 476, there was no further emperor in the West until Charlemagne in 800. But the Germanic commanders and kings still regarded themselves as nominal subjects of the Roman Emperor enthroned in Constantinople. From time to time the eastern Roman (Byzantine) emperors reestablished imperial control over Italy and parts of the West, as Justinian did in the sixth century. The imperial exarch was seated at Ravenna, which had previously been the capital of Theodoric's Ostrogothic kingdom. This accounts for the presence of Byzantine architectural style in the churches of Ravenna.

In the sixth century these Gothic kingdoms were overrun by the Lombards, although the newcomers were not able to conquer either Rome or Ravenna. The Italian peninsula was ruined by wars between the Lombards and the eastern Roman Emperors, who tried to reclaim Italy as a part of the Roman Empire. They did not succeed. Only the

---

[2] Among recent explanations see Ramsey MacMullen, *Corruption and the Decline of Rome* (New Haven: Yale University Press, 1988), and Thomas S. Burns, *Barbarians Within the Gates of Rome* (Bloomington, Ind.: Indiana University Press, 1995), whose titles provide clues to the authors' respective theses.

[3] See Herwig Wolfram, *History of the Goths*, trans. by Thomas J. Dunlap (Berkeley: University of California Press, 1988), 12.

[4] See Thomas S. Burns, *Barbarians within the Gates of Rome* (Bloomington: Indiana University Press, 1995).

pope remained as a representative of the old culture, and the popes increasingly sided with the Gothic kings against the Byzantine emperors. This independent position of the papacy was firmly established when King Pippin of the Franks compelled the Lombards to surrender the territories of the Byzantine exarchate and turned them over, not to the emperor, but to the see of St. Peter as a papal state in 756. Pope Stephen II made Pippin, his wife and sons, "patricians of the Romans."

While the popes accommodated themselves to the successive waves of new peoples settling in western Europe and North Africa, there was an intense theological struggle against the Arianism of the Vandals, the Goths, the Burgundians and the Lombards. Byzantine reconquest of North Africa and Italy terminated the Arian kingdoms of the Vandals and the Ostragoths. The Burgundians abandoned Arianism in 517, and in 532 were absorbed by another Germanic people moving into Gaul—the Franks, whose chieftain Clovis (481–511) had married the Burgundian Clotilda in 493 and declared for Catholicism in 496. The rivalry of creeds ended in Spain when the Visigothic (western Goth) King Recared renounced Arianism in 587. The Catholicism of the Visigothic kingdom was reaffirmed at the Third Council of Toledo in 589. The conversion of the Lombards to Catholicism began at about this time, but was not complete until about 660.[5] In chapter two we commented on the liturgical ramification of this struggle against Arianism in terms of the termination of liturgical prayers.[6] This confessional struggle in the West also inspired the doxological and creedal texts, the *Te Deum Laudamus* ("We praise you, O God") and *Quicunque vult* ("Whoever wishes to be saved"—the so-called Athanasian Creed). The Te Deum was being sung at the monastery of Saint Honorat at Lérins off the coast of Cannes as far back as 498 when Caesarius of Arles joined the community. Quicunque vult comes from the same time.[7]

The Visigothic Kingdom of Toledo lasted for several centuries, but was finally terminated by the Arab invasion of Spain in 711. Islamic advance into Europe was finally halted by the Frankish king Charles Martel at the Battle of Poitiers in 732. The Franks, originating in the Lower Rhineland, were able to carve out a vast kingdom that included the present-day Low Countries, the Rhineland, and France. The Roman church had looked favorably on the Franks since the conversion of King Clovis (481–511) to Catholic Christianity (whether from Arianism or paganism is not clear).[8] The Carolingian dynasty of Charles Martel, Pippin the Short, and Charlemagne succeeded, step by step, in consolidating power and commanding the loyalty of chieftains. The prospects of political and ecclesiastical stability under this dynasty were blessed by the church in the anointing of Pippin as king by Boniface and the crowning of Charlemagne as emperor at Saint Peter's Basilica on Christmas Day, 800, by Pope Leo III. In the interests of shoring up law and order in their unruly realm, the Carolingians imported Roman books and practices into

---

[5] See Williston Walker, *A History of the Christian Church*, rev. ed. (New York: Charles Scribner's Sons, 1959), 119–23.

[6] See Josef A. Jungmann, *The Early Liturgy to the Time of Gregory the Great*, 192ff.

[7] See Arthur Carl Piepkorn, *Profiles in Belief*, I (New York, Hagerstown, San Francisco, London: Harper and Row, 1977), 148–51.

[8] See Edward James, *The Franks* (Oxford: Basil Blackwell, 1988), 121ff.

their court and churches, but inevitably they put their own stamp on them in the transmission of texts and the development of praxis.

The Irish church, in the meantime, developed around monasteries and powerful abbots who were able to exert a discipline that was lacking in the Frankish church.[9] Irish monks went as missionaries to Great Britain and the continent of Europe, and brought with them an ascetic form of church life. At the same time, Pope Gregory the Great sent Benedictine monks to England. At first there was rivalry between the Irish and Roman missionaries, but eventually they colluded to form an Anglo-Saxon church with a unique culture and a practical energy. Pippin and Charlemagne harnessed the energy and learning of Anglo-Saxon monks such as Boniface and Alcuin to evangelize tribes within and around their Empire and to foster literary efforts within the Frankish church that contributed to the Carolingian renaissance. Out of this latinized Roman-Frankish culture emerged the medieval liturgy.

❧ SACRAMENTARIES AND ORDINES

The Carolingian renaissance was, to a great extent, a liturgical renaissance. The books that were needed were primarily for the celebration of the liturgy: the Bible, prayer books, music books, manuals, and so forth. Carolingian rulers were concerned to unify their realm by means of a more unified, romanized cultus. Roman liturgical books had to be imported into their kingdom, copied and circulated. Several kinds of books were needed to perform the liturgy in a communal and public way.

Sacramentaries were the celebrants' books that contained the necessary texts for celebrating the eucharist: the collect (prayer of the day), the prayer over the offerings, the proper eucharistic preface (if one was necessary), and a post-communion prayer. We have seen that forerunners of the sacramentaries were the small collections of mass-formularies called "libelli." We have also seen the earliest example of a Roman sacramentary: the Verona Sacramentary, which for a long time was misleadingly called the Leonine Sacramentary, after Pope Leo the Great. Other popes gave their names to types of sacramentaries, particularly Gelasius I (the Gelasian) and Gregory the Great (the Gregorian). As we shall see, it is difficult to see these books going back to these popes, since the extant copies of these types of sacramentaries come from a century or two later than these popes reigned.

Lectionaries were the readers' books that contained the scripture readings for the masses of the church year. Sometimes lectionaries were only lists of readings, which were read from the Bible. Passages were marked "beginning" (incipit) and "end" (explicit). Later on there were separate books for the epistles and gospels of the church year (Epistularies and Gospelaries).

Antiphonaries were the choirs' books that contained those parts of the mass and divine office that were sung, especially the antiphons that introduced the psalms. (Most of the monks or canons who sang the Divine Office knew the psalter from memory, but needed the antiphon to announce the psalm or canticle.) It was not until the tenth century

---

[9] See Michael Richter, *Medieval Ireland: The Enduring Tradition* (New York: St. Martin's Press, 1988), Part II.

that melodies were written in *neums* (notes). Antiphonaries were usually of great size, so that all the members of a choir could read them together. Of great interest and importance is the Bangor Antiphonary, written at the Irish monastery of Bangor toward the end of the seventh century. This manuscript is now in the Ambrosian Library in Milan.[10]

Ordines were booklets containing the instructions (rubrics) concerning the performance of the liturgical rites. Originally describing the liturgical rites performed in the churches of Rome, these ordos were copied and used as guides in other churches as well.

All of these books—sacramentary, lectionary, antiphonary, and ordo—were needed for the complete celebration of the mass. While this may seem complicated, it ensured a variety of liturgical roles well into the Middle Ages: celebrant, deacons, lector, cantor, and choir, as well as acolytes, sacristans, and porters. Some of these books have enduring importance in the history of the Western liturgy.[11]

One of the earliest and most important of these books is the original Gelasian Sacramentary.[12] It is divided into three books, and the prayers are of mixed Roman and old Gallican origin. The book survives in the manuscript known as *Codex Reginensis 316* (from the library of Queen Christina of Sweden in the seventeenth century). This manuscript was copied in a monastery at Chelles near Paris about 750. The Roman material probably goes back to around 650. It represents a pre-Carolingian romanizing effort, and is important because it contains some of the oldest texts we have of the Roman liturgy, including the canon of the mass.

Other Gelasian sacramentaries of the eighth century (not as pure, because they are mixed with Gregorian material) include the sacramentaries of Gellone, Angoulème, and Gall. These were copied in monasteries during the reign of Pippin (751–768). The visit of Pope Stephen II (754–760) to France occasioned a great deal of interest in the Roman liturgy. The object may have been to unite the old Gelasian tradition with the more recent papal (Gregorian) tradition, and at the same time to unify Roman and Frankish practices.

There are three main subtypes under the Gregorian sacramentary tradition: the Paduensa, the Hadrianum, and the Hadrianum with the Supplement.

The Sacramentary of Padua was compiled in Liege around 850.[13] Like the old Gelasian, it was probably brought into Gaul by a pilgrim. The Roman prototype may stem from around 680. Material from other sacramentaries was added to it in the intervening 150 years, mostly of Gallican origin.

The impure character of the sacramentaries impeded the program of romanization and standardization in the Frankish kingdom. Charlemagne mandated Paul the

---

[10] See the critical edition by F. E. Warren, *The Bangor Antiphonary*. Henry Bradshaw Society Collections Nos. 4 and 10 (London: Harrison and Sons, 1893–94).

[11] See Cyrille Vogel, *Introduction aux Sources de l'Histoire du culte chrétien au Moyen âge* (Spoleto: Centro Italiano di Studi Sull'alto Medioevo, 1966). See the English trans. of Vogel by William G. Storey and Neils Krogh Rasmussen, *Medieval Liturgy: An Introduction to the Sources* (Washington, D.C.: The Pastoral Press, 1987).

[12] *Liber Sacramentorum Romanae Aeclesiae Ordinis anni circuli*, ed. by L. C. Mohlberg (Rome: Casa Editrice Herder, 1968).

[13] Ed. L. C. Mohlberg (Munster, 1927).

Deacon to ask Pope Hadrian I (772–795) for a pure Roman book without extraneous additions. Not until 785 did Hadrian send to Charlemagne a "sacramentary of Pope Gregory in pure form." Unfortunately, it was an incomplete book lacking many of the propers for Sundays of the church year. It is possible that Hadrian did not understand the nature of Charlemagne's request and simply sent one of the most beautifully written of the papal books. It survives in the Cambrai Codex 164.[14]

It was necessary to supplement the Hadrianum. The Supplement, known as *Hucusque* ("Up to this point"), was until recently ascribed to the work of Alcuin of York. More likely it was the work of Benedict of Aniane. There was a careful distinction between the material found in the *Sacramentarium Hadrianum* and the material that filled in the gaps. This material was probably taken from the *Gelasiana* of the eighth century, which probably goes back to Pope Honorius or even Pope Gregory the Great, and also from Gallican books for Sundays not in the Roman books (e.g., the Sundays of Advent). And so, by way of the Supplement, mixed Roman and Gallican material became official in the Frankish church and were preserved in the Western medieval tradition.[15]

With this plethora of mass-books it is obvious that there is a plethora of mass-texts in the early Middle Ages. Indeed, in the Gelasian Sacramentary alone there are three books of masses: masses for Christmastide and the Paschal season; masses of saints in calendar sequence; and some sixty mass-collects for votive masses (masses for various occasions such as weddings, anniversaries, times of affliction and illness, times of epidemic or war, for good weather, for undertaking a journey, for the sick, and for the dead). The older Gelasian has fifty-four eucharistic prefaces; the later Gelasian in the Gall manuscript has no fewer than 184 prefaces (although still not as many as the Verona Sacramentary with 267!). The number of prefaces was reduced in the Gregorian Sacramentary.

The older Gelasian Sacramentary *(Codex Reginesis 316)* has a supplement that contains mass-formularies for Advent and for the Advent ember days. Here we see the hybrid Roman-Gallican origins of the medieval mass as well as the mysterious provenance of this Sacramentary. Advent materials are clearly Gallican, since this season was not celebrated in Rome. On the other hand, the Ember Days are uniquely Roman observances. Is it possible that not only Gallican but also newly found Roman material was added to the basic core of Roman mass-formularies taken into France?

The same situation exists with regard to the Gregorian Sacramentary. The manuscripts are, for the most part, Frankish, and, except for a few fragments, no earlier than the ninth century. But comparative study makes it possible to reconstruct the exemplary sacramentary sent by Pope Hadrian to Charlemagne in 785–786. The conviction has been growing in recent years that Pope Gregory the Great may even have had a hand in producing the sacramentary tradition that bears his name.

---

[14] Ed. H. Lietzmann (Münster, 1911).

[15] See the discussion of the relationships of the various sacramentary traditions of the old Roman and Gallican texts in A. Chavasse, *Le sacrementaire Gélasien* (Paris and Tournai, 1958) and J. Deschusses, *Le sacrementaire Gregorien*, 2 vols. (Fribourg, 1971, 1979). See the chart showing these relationships in Vogel, *Introduction aux Sources*, 95.

The Gregorian Sacramentary was not a book for ordinary parishes; it was a papal book for feast days and station masses at which the pope would preside. This explains the many omissions in the Gregorian—including the ordinary Sunday mass, which the Gelasian is so careful to provide. But because so many ordinary Sunday and festival formularies were missing from the copy sent to France, a supplement was added by Alcuin to provide for ordinary parochial needs. At this point Gallican traditions were mixed with the Roman.

The sacramentaries provided the prayers needed for the celebration of mass— the collect for the day, the offertory prayer, and the post-communion prayer, as well as the canon (which first appears in Cod. Reg. 316) and the eucharistic prefaces (which were not considered part of the canon). A lectionary was needed for the scripture readings. Actually, until far into the Middle Ages the lessons were read from the Bible or book of Scriptures itself. Various methods were used to indicate the pericopes for the Sundays, festivals, days of devotion, and weekdays. Pericopes could be indicated in the margins of the Bible, noting the day in the church year and making the beginning and ending of the reading. Or a list of readings could be written out. Or the pericopes could be copied out in a separate book. These separate books of readings are the lectionaries properly so-called.[16] The principal lectionary manuscripts that are extant are the *Epistolarium* of Wurzburg, which provides the epistle readings from about the time of Pope Gregory I, and the *Comes* of Alcuin, which is thought to be a Roman pericope system dating from about 625 that was known to Alcuin and edited by him.[17] The Lectionary of Murbach is a Roman-Frankish book from the eighth century that, for the first time, places the epistles and gospels for the church year side by side in the same book.[18]

One of the most creative contributions to the Western liturgy from the early Middle Ages was the development of the pericope system. The ancient lectio continuo for the "ordinary Sundays" of the church year was breaking up, but vestiges could be seen in the Sundays after Pentecost in which the epistles of Paul are covered with little interruption, and in the Sundays in Lent and during Easter on which the gospel readings are taken from John. Another vestige of the continuous type of reading is evident in the formula for announcing the gospel reading: "Sequentia sancti evangelii" (The continuation of the reading of the Gospel according to . . .).

The third book needed for the celebration of mass was the antiphonary. This contained the sung texts and was the book provided for the choir (*schola cantorum*). The early antiphonaries contain the texts and notations for the entrance or introit psalm with Gloria Patri, gradual psalm and Alleluia, and offertory and communion antiphons and psalms. Like other Roman books, Roman antiphonaries were introduced into France during the time of Pippin and Charlemagne.[19] Critical studies push the Roman song

---

[16] See W. H. Frere, *Studies in Early Roman Liturgy*, II: *The Roman Gospel Lectionary* (London, 1934); *The Roman Epistle Lectionary* (London, 1935); A. Chavasse, "Les plus anciens types de lectionaire et de l'antiphonaire romain de la messe," *Revue bénédictine* 62 (1952), 1–91.

[17] See G. Morin, "Le plus ancien comes ou lectionaire de l'église romaine," *Revue bénédictine* 27 (1910), 41–7; A. Wilmart, "Le lectionaire d'Alcuin," *Ephemerides Liturgicae* 51 (1937), 137–97.

[18] See A. Wilmart, "Le Comes de Murbach," *Revue bénédictine* 30 (1913), 35–69.

[19] The texts are collected in the critical edition of *Antiphonale sextuplex*, ed. R. Hesbert (Brussels, 1935).

books back to Pope Honorius I (625–638). Medieval traditions regarded Pope Gregory I as the author or originator of Gregorian chant, although Gregory commented very little on music in his own writings and did not think that music should be the concern of the higher clergy (not even of deacons!).[20]

Finally, the ordo provides the rubrics governing the celebration of the mass and other rites. The most critical edition of the Roman ordos (*Ordines Romani*) is the extensive collection by Michel Andrieu,[21] although earlier uncritical editions were published by Jean Mabillon[22] and J. P. Migne.[23] The following chart gives the title, origin, and date of all fifty ordos in Andrieu's collection.

# in Andrieu	Title	Origin	Date
I	Papal Mass[24]	Roman	c. 700
II	Stational Liturgy by Bishop	Roman	c. 700
III	Variations in Papal Mass	Roman	c. 700
IV	Ordo of St. Amand[25]	Frankish	end 7th c.
V	Roman Mass Rite	Frankish	pre-8th c.
VI	Revised Ordo I	Frankish	
VII	Canon of the Mass	Frankish	end 9th c.
VIII	Vestments	Frankish	850–950
IX	Ordinary Bishop's Mass	Frankish	c. 850
X	Bishop's Mass in Cathedral	Frankish	900–950
XI	Baptismal Ordo	Roman	650–700
XII	Antiphonal Ordo	Frankish	775–850
XIIIa	Readings for Night Office	Roman	700–750
XIIIb	XIIIa with Added Feasts	Frankish	
XIIIc	Abridged XIIIa	Frankish	10th c.
XIIId	Modified XIIIa	Frankish	11th c.
XIV	Lectionary for St. Peter's	Roman	650–700
XV	Church Year, Mass, Baptism	Frankish	750–850
XVI	Benedictine Office and Calendar	Frankish	750–775
XVII	Abridged XV and XVI	Frankish	750–800
XVIII	Distribution of Hours	Frankish	end 8th c.
XIX	Monastic Meals	Frankish	750–780
XX	Purification of Mary	Frankish	end 8th c.
XXI	Greater Litany Procession	Frankish	end 8th c.
XXII	First Days of Lent	Frankish	795–800

[20] See G. Morin, *Les véritables Origines du chant Grégorien*, 2nd ed. (Rome and Tournai, 1904).

[21] *Les ordines romani du haut moyen âge*, 5 vols. (Louvain: Spicilegium Sacrum libri tres, 1931–1961).

[22] *Museum Italicum*, 2 vols. (Paris, 1687–1689). Mabillon's numeration of the Ordines does not follow Andrieu's. In fact, Mabillon includes only twelve Ordines or parts thereof from among the fifty published by Andrieu.

[23] P.L., Vol. LXXVIII.

[24] For an English trans., see E. G. Cuthbert F. Atchley, *Ordo Romanus Primus, with Introduction and Notes* (London, 1906).

[25] The *Ordines Romani* from the ms. of St. Amand is included in the appendix to L. Duchesne, *Christian Worship: Its Origin and Evolution*, trans. by M. L. McClure (London: S.P.C.K., 1923), 455–80 (Latin text). This "Gallicanized" collection, probably compiled under Pippin, and first published by Duchesne, includes Ordines 4, 30b, 21, 39, and 20.

# IN ANDRIEU	TITLE	ORIGIN	DATE
XXIII	Thurs.—Sat. of Holy Week	Frankish?	700–750
XXIV	Wed.—Sat. of Holy Week in Suburban Rome		750–800
XXV	Blessing of Paschal Candle	Frankish	early 9th
XXVI	Holy Thursday—Easter (I) in Suburban Rome		750–775
XXVII	Holy Thursday—Easter (II)	Frankish/Roman	8th c.
XXVIII	Passion Sun.—Easter Octave	Frankish	c. 800
XXVIIIa	Blessing of Baptismal Fonts	Frankish	early 9th
XXIX	Last Four Days of Holy Week	Frankish	870–890
XXXa	Holy Thursday—Easter Saturday	Frankish	end 8th c.
XXXb	Holy Thursday	Frankish	end 8th c.
XXXI	Passion Sun.—Easter Octave	Frankish	850–900
XXXII	Triduum of the Passion	Frankish	end 8th c.
XXXIII	Outline of Triduum	Frankish	pre-11th c.
XXXIV	Ordinations	Roman	c. 750
XXXV	Ordinations, Consecrations	Roman	900–925
XXXVa	Episcopal Consecration by Pope	Roman	850–900
XXXVb	Episcopal Consecration w/Exam	Frankish	975–1000
XXXVI	Ordinations, Consecrations	Frankish	c. 897
XXXVIIa	Ordo for Ember Days	Frankish	800–813
XXXVIIb	Later Version of XXXVIIa	Frankish	c. 825
XXXVIII	Ordinations on Saturdays of Ember Weeks	Frankish	c. 950
XXXIX	Ordinations at St. Peter's on Ember Saturdays	Frankish	end 8th c.
XLa	Ordination of Pope	Roman	6th c. (?)
XLb	Ordination of Pope with Prayer from Hadrianum	Frankish	c. 950
XLI	Dedication of a Church	Frankish	775–800
XLII	Placing relics in a Church	Roman	pre-750
XLIII	Transportation and Placing Relics in a Church	Frankish	end 8th c.
XLIV	The Diligentia at St. Peter's	Roman	end 8th c.
XLV	Blessing of Emperor at Coronation	Roman	888–915
XLVI	Blessing of Emperor	Frankish	1050–90
XLVII	Blessing of Emperor without Anointing	Frankish	pre-953
XLVIII	Mass for Emperor	Frankish	c. 950
XLIX	Funeral Rites	Roman	end 8th c.
L	Collection of Ordos for Various Ceremonies	Frankish	c. 950

❦ CHURCHES IN ROME AND STATION MASSES

The Ordines Romani provide directions for celebrating liturgies that were conducted at certain churches in Rome. Neither the churches nor the liturgies celebrated in them were all of one kind. There were, in fact, four kinds of church buildings in Rome.

First, there were the basilicas that served as the cathedral churches of Rome: Saint John Lateran, Saint Mary Major, Holy Cross in Jerusalem, Saint Peter at the Vatican, Saint Paul on the Ostian Way, Saint Lawrence over the tomb of the martyr, the Holy Apostles, and Saint Sebastian by the Catacombs. The pope's church was Saint John Lateran; suffragan bishops resided at each of the other basilicas, which were located roughly in each of the seven political jurisdictions of the city of Rome. Then there were the *tituli*, titles of properties which had been given to the church. These were located in the various neighborhoods of Rome, usually with a presbyter in charge. Next there were the deaconries, facilities administered by deacons from which charity was dispensed. Finally, on the outskirts of the city were the suburban cemetery churches. As early as the fifth century, monasteries were established near the great basilicas so that the monks could carry out the daily prayer offices, thus freeing the clergy for other pastoral responsibilities.[26]

These different kinds of church buildings served different purposes. The basilicas were the primary places of celebration of the liturgies of the word and the eucharist on Sundays and festivals. While the eucharist eventually came to be celebrated at the tituli, the original purpose of these buildings was for catechetical and penitential services, as well as for burial in various parts of the city. The deaconries were not liturgical centers at all, but centers in which the charitable work of the diocese was carried out. A deaconry was located in each of the seven ecclesiastical-political regions of Rome.

The pope himself made the rounds of the various churches, celebrating the eucharist at these places. His presence at particular churches was associated with specific days in the church year calendar, especially saints' days if the relics of the saints were deposited at those sites. The masses celebrated by the pope came to be called "station masses," and in theory the whole local church gathered around its bishop. Since the presbyters who served at the tituli could not be with the pope at most of these celebrations, he sent to each of them a piece of consecrated bread, called *fermentum*, which was carried by acolytes in linen bags and placed in the chalice by the celebrant at the words, "Pax domini sit semper vobiscum." This may be a reason why the greeting of peace came to precede the communion in the Roman mass instead of preceding the offertory, as it did in other liturgical traditions. By this means the bishop's eucharist was extended to portions of the congregation assembled in other parts of the city.

The papal station masses were the most solemn type of liturgy. As many clergy of the city as possible joined the pope at these liturgies. This included the suffragan bishop, presbyters, deacons and the archdeacon of Rome, subdeacons, and acolytes. The choir, or schola cantorum, was always present. The communal nature of this type of liturgy is striking: as far as possible the whole city was present. Rubrics in the Ordines concerning communion envision the administration of the sacrament to a large number of people.

Nevertheless, not all the clergy and people of the city were present at the papal station mass. On Sundays the presbyters assigned to the tituli were at those worship centers with the portion of the bishop's flock that worshiped there. Yet there was concern to

---

[26] See G.G. Willis, "Roman Stational Liturgy," in *Further Essays in Early Roman Liturgy*. Alcuin Club Collections No. 50 (London: S.P.C.K., 1968), 53ff.

include these presbyters and people in the bishop's eucharist. These churches were not parishes in the modern sense; nor were they autonomous congregations. The diocese itself was the congregation, and the bishop was its pastor. According to Pope Innocent I's decretal to Bishop Decentius of Gubbio (416), the pope sent the fermentum to all the title churches within the city in order to unite their eucharistic celebrations with his own.[27]

The diocese extended outside the city walls, and this part of its jurisdiction was called *parrochia*. The presbyters who served the churches outside the city were called "parish priests" (*presbyteri parochiales*). Innocent states that the fermentum was not sent to them. These presbyters had the right to celebrate mass without receiving the pope's fermentum, as well as to baptize and to administer penance.[28]

The worship in these rural parishes constituted a third type of liturgy. A pontifical liturgy was almost never celebrated in them, and they lacked the diversity of liturgical roles found in the urban churches. There may not have been any deacons in these parishes, and undoubtedly there was no schola cantorum. At most, there may have been a cantor and some acolytes in addition to the presbyter in charge. He was the real pastor to the people and had a degree of autonomy from the bishop not experienced by his urban counterparts.

Stational liturgies were celebrated in the Eastern patriarchates as well as in Rome, and a stational organization was maintained in the Frankish cities of Augsburg, Mainz, Cologne, Trier, Metz, Tours, and Angers. But most of the trans-Alpine areas were rural, with few urban centers, and the types and names of churches were different than in Rome. In Frankish nomenclature *ecclesiae* were places of liturgical assembly while *basilicae* were temples in which were deposited the relics of saints. Basilicas were located in monasteries and rural areas as well as in cities. As in Rome, there could be several basilicas in a city. The most important one was called basilicae senior; it was usually the cathedral, although not always. Gregory of Tours called the cathedral "ecclesiae liturgica" and referred to other churches as "basilicae."[29]

These places of worship, which were of good size, must be distinguished from the *cellula* or *oratoria*, many of which were on a feudal lord's estate and were usually served by a single cleric. The primary purpose of these smaller churches was to increase the places of worship and ministration of the sacraments, though often with the exception of baptism. There was still a concern to celebrate baptism at the bishop's church and to celebrate the principal festivals there as well. Only gradually did these rural sanctuaries acquire greater temporal, spiritual, and liturgical autonomy and become parishes in the modern sense.[30]

Well into the Middle Ages, even in the chaotic situation of the Frankish church, there was an effort to maintain the ancient pattern of the whole local church gathered around its bishop for the celebration of a "single eucharist," as Ignatius of Antioch had

---

[27] Innocent, *Epistula ad Decentium Eugubinum*, 5; P.L. 56:516–17.

[28] Willis, 8–9.

[29] M. de Laugardière, *L'Église de Bourges avant Charlemagne* (Paris: Tardy, 1951).

[30] See Pierre Salmon, *The Breviary Through the Centuries*, trans. by Sister David Mary (Collegeville: The Liturgical Press, 1962), 32.

called it. The Roman church went to great lengths to maintain this tradition under considerably different conditions than those known in the second century. By the Middle Ages, however, a system that was preserved and expanded in order to maintain a eucharistic ecclesiology was being interpreted as a jurisdictional ecclesiology.

❦ THE ROMAN BISHOP'S MASS

The archetypal description of this episcopal celebration is in *Ordo Romanus Primus*, which describes the station mass celebrated by the bishop of Rome at the end of the seventh century.[31] It cannot come from a time earlier than the pontificate of Pope Sergius I (687–701), since it refers to the Agnus Dei, which he inserted into the Roman liturgy. The Ordo describes the papal mass celebrated at Saint Mary Major on Easter Day.[32]

The Ordo begins with a description of the clerical offices in Rome and their assignments according to region. On festivals such as Easter, the acolytes of the third region and the *defensores* of all the regions were to assemble at the papal residence at the Lateran and walk in front of the pope to the stational church, while the *stratores* walked on either side of the pope's horse in case it stumbled. Also preceding the pope on horseback were the deacons, two regional notaries, the regional defensores, and the regional subdeacons. Other civil officials followed the pope. Books and vessels needed for the celebration were carried in procession by the acolytes. These were placed where they were needed in the church when the entourage arrived. The regional subdeacons assisted the pope with vesting and informed him concerning who was doing what in the liturgy.

The procession into the church was quite elaborate. The schola cantorum sang the Introit psalm while the pope entered, accompanied by the archdeacon and a deacon. The pope was preceded by a subdeacon bearing incense and seven acolytes holding lighted tapers. All of these ceremonial trappings—the choir of singers, the assistants on either arm, the lights and incense—were influences from imperial court protocol, now acquiring spiritual significance.

The procession divided at the altar, which the pope reverenced. When the pope reached the altar, the schola broke off singing the psalm and ended it with the Gloria Patri while the pope bowed to the altar and kissed the gospel book placed upon it. The schola took up the Kyrie while the pope went to his throne. Perhaps already by this time the petitions had fallen out of the Kyrie, leaving only the sung responses. At the throne, the pope faced the congregation and intoned the hymn, "Gloria in excelsis Deo," which was taken up by the choir. This served as the opening hymn of the mass, after which the pope greeted the people ("Pax vobiscum") and bid them pray ("Oremus"). He turned to the east for the collect, as he did for all the prayers.

These descriptions show the processional character of the Roman liturgy. In the

---

[31] *Les 'Ordines Romani'*, ed. Andrieu, II, 65–108.

[32] For full descriptions of the content of Ordo I see Willis, op. cit., 16ff. and Theodore Klauser, *A Short History of the Western Liturgy*, trans. by John Halliburton (London: Oxford University Press, 1969), 59ff.

order of mass the Introit and Kyrie were processional pieces, the Gloria was the opening hymn, and the salutation was the opening greeting.

The collect was followed by the epistle and gospel, read respectively by the subdeacon and deacon. Cantors sang the Alleluia verse between the readings and to cover the procession with the gospel book from the altar to the ambo. The gospel book was preceded by two subdeacons with incense and two acolytes with tapers. No sermon was specified in the Ordo. It may be that the sermon was omitted on this occasion because of the length of time it would take to commune so many people, and that the papal address was given at a different time and place, as is customary today. There is also no mention of the Creed, because this did not come into the Roman liturgy until the eleventh century under Franco-Germanic influence. There is no dismissal of the catechumens, which indicates that by this time baptism of infants had become normative. Also to be noted is the absence of the general intercessions or prayers of the faithful. This had disappeared two centuries earlier, and its function was taken by the litany form of the Kyrie. But, as we have indicated, by the time of Ordo I the petitions had dropped out of the Kyrie. This left intercessions only in the eucharistic prayer.

The offering was very complex because everyone in the great throng of worshipers brought gifts that needed to be collected. Apparently there was no longer an offertory procession of the faithful to the altar. Rather, the gifts were collected from different stations by the suffragan bishops, the pope himself receiving the gifts of the aristocracy. Nevertheless, the schola sang the *offertorium* (psalm and antiphon) to cover the collection of gifts, which must have taken some time. Most of the gifts were loaves of bread, which were put in large linen cloths (*sindones*) held by the acolytes, and flasks of wine, which were emptied into a large two-handled vessel (*scyphus*). When all was ready, the pope placed his own offerings of bread and wine on the altar and said the prayer over the gifts (*oratorio super oblata*), and then offered the eucharistic canon. The only elevation occurred at the concluding doxology, "Per quem haec omnie . . .," at which the archdeacon held up the chalice by its handles while the pope held the oblations on the edge of the chalice. After the Pater noster and "Pax domini sit semper vobiscum," the pope immersed a particle of bread from the previous day's mass in the chalice and broke off a piece of bread to serve as fermentum for the next celebration. He then returned to his seat and the consecration of the remaining elements was by commixture (mixing the consecrated elements in with the unconsecrated). Wine from the chalice was poured into the scyphus. The pope was communed (note that there was no self-communing, not even by the pope), and the next papal station mass was announced for the benefit of those who would leave before communion. A dismissal of the noncommunicants just before the ministration of the sacrament, which had become common in the Byzantine liturgy by the end of the fifth century, never found its way into the Roman liturgy.

If the entrance, the gospel reading, and the offertory constituted three processions, communion was the fourth. It required the pope, the suffragan bishops, the presbyters, and deacons to commune one another and all the people. The bread was taken from the acolytes' sack and the wine was poured into chalices from the scyphus. In former times the people would have come forward using the ample center and side aisles of the basilica. By the time of Ordo I they were probably communed at stations throughout the basilica. During this whole time the schola sang the *communio* (psalm and antiphon). The communion service ended abruptly with a post-communion collect (*oratio ad complendum*) and a dismissal:

> *Deacon:* Ite missa est.
> *People:* Deo gratias.

The pope then processed back to the sacristy, giving a solemn blessing to each section of the congregation on his way out.

There is no ordo, and almost no information, concerning the celebration of mass at the titular churches. These masses were not considered the regular form of the liturgy because they were not celebrated by the bishop. They had, therefore, what Klauser calls a "makeshift" character. This had a profound consequence on the fate of the Roman mass in France, since presbyteral liturgies were more normative and the only model provided from Rome was the papal liturgy. A sentence at the end of Ordo II states quite clearly: "Episcopi qui civitatibus praesident ut summus pontifex ite omnie agant" (The bishops who preside over congregations in towns must perform everything in the same way as the pope).[33] Lacking specific instructions to the contrary, it is reasonable to expect that town and country priests imitated their regional bishops, who were imitating the bishop of Rome, or else to rely on older Gallican practice. This helps to explain what might be called the high church character of Frankish liturgy. Complicated rubrics in Rome, apart from ceremonies taken over from the imperial court, were designed to keep a simple flow to a liturgy celebrated in a large public space with thousands of people present. In the scaled-down settings of Frankish churches, complicated rubrics meant complicated ceremonies.

❦ THE ROMAN MASS IN FRANCE

There were very few additions to the Roman liturgy in Rome after the time of Pope Gregory the Great (590–604) . The singing of the Agnus Dei during the fraction was an Eastern influence and the insertion of the Creed after the gospel was a Germanic influence. Development of the mass in the Frankish realms was not arrested, however. Here the Roman liturgy was not simply being imposed by Frankish rulers but was being adapted to the culture of the people. The restlessness of the Celts and the passionate aestheticism of the Germans also made an impact on the liturgy. Jungmann sees the Frankish contribution in terms of the dramatic buildup of the mass-ceremonies, the multiplying of prayers, the content of the prayers, and the use of Latin as a sacred language.[34]

The Roman mass made use of incense only at the entrance of the clergy and the gospel procession. In France the number of incensations increased, and objects such as the altar and the gospel book were incensed. The gospel book was not just carried to the

---

[33] Andrieu, II, 116, no. 10.

[34] See Joseph A. Jungmann, *The Mass of the Roman Rite*, I, trans. by Francis A. Brunner (Westminster, Md.: Christian Classics Reprint, 1986), 74ff.

ambo, but was carried in a triumphal procession through the midst of the people. Its announcement was greeted with acclamations: "Gloria tibi Domini and "Laus tibi Christe (Glory to you, O Lord. Praise to you, O Christ). The ambo was reserved for the reading of the gospel only. The other lessons were read from the steps (*Gradus*) of the altar. The gradual and sequence developed as psalmodic and poetic texts between the epistle and gospel to accompany the elaborate gospel procession.

Only one collect was said in the introductory rite of the Roman liturgy. In the Frankish mass up to seven collects were allowed. But this was not the only multiplication of prayers. Prayers of a personal and devotional character were inserted to be recited silently by the celebrant. The Sacramentary of Amiens provided such prayers to be said by the priest while vesting, when approaching the altar at the beginning of mass, during the offertory (beginning with the *Suscipe sancte Trinitas* and ending five prayers later with the *Orate fratres*), during the singing of the Sanctus within the eucharistic prayer, and before communion.[35] The prayers to be said before and after receiving communion acquired a long career in the Western liturgy, and were given secure places in the Missal of Pius V (1570). Before communion the priest prays:

> Lord Jesus Christ, Son of the living God, by the will of the Father and the work of the Holy Spirit, your death brought life to the world. By your holy body and blood free me from all my sins, and keep me from every evil. Keep me faithful to your teaching, and never let me be parted from you.

After receiving communion the priest prays:

> What we have received with our mouth, O Lord, may we also bear in our mind: so that this temporal gift may become an everlasting remedy.[36]

Most of these new prayer texts were couched in the singular "I" rather than the plural "we." They were often addressed to Christ rather than to God the Father through the Son, as the above example, "Domine Jesu Christi, Fili Dei vivi," illustrates. And they are of an apologetic nature, petitioning God's mercy. Jungmann attributes this development to the Gallican tendency to confuse God and Christ, which also obscured the concept of salvation by grace alone. The background for this may have been the anti-Arian struggle in France and Spain during the migration of the Gothic tribes. The concern was to express the equality of the members of the Trinity, as is stressed in the Athanasian Creed, which originated in the same context.

More profoundly affecting the fate of the liturgy was the retention of the Latin language at a time when the Romance languages were developing. This state of affairs can be contrasted with the evangelization of the Slavs by the Greek brothers Cyril and Methodius, who rendered both the Bible and the Byzantine liturgy into the Slavonic language, even developing an alphabet using Greek characters. Neighboring German clerics were most critical of these efforts at vernacularization, since Boniface had established such strong ties between the German tribes and Rome. The result was the retention of

---

[35] See Victor Leroquais, "L'Ordo Missae du sacramentaire d'Amiens," *Ephemerides Liturgicae* 41 (1927), 435–45.

[36] Ibid., 444.

Latin as the liturgical language in the West, and this reinforced the perception that the liturgy was a clerical preserve. Popular participation in the liturgy was difficult at best and the people's role had to be taken over by acolytes and choirs. Efforts to instruct the people in the mysteries of the mass led to the allegorical *Expositiones missae*, which we will consider in the next chapter.

The Western medieval rite emerged out of the adaptation of Roman liturgical forms in the Frankish kingdom. It was sharply outlined in structure and richly ceremonial in style. It secured permanent definition when it returned to Rome in force with the ascendancy of powerful German emperors in the tenth century.

🍇 THE FRANCO-ROMAN CALENDAR

The church year calendar as it is known today in the Western churches came to full development in the period of the sacramentaries. Sunday had been firmly established since early times as the fixed day of Christian assembly. Not until the ninth century were saints' days allowed to take precedence over the Lord's Day, with propers for the lesser festival replacing those of the Sunday in the eucharistic liturgy.

Easter, too, was well established since early Christian times, and since the end of the fourth century, especially through the influence of Jerusalem, Holy Week was also well established. The dramatic features of these days of devotion as developed in Jerusalem were especially popular in western Europe. The Palm Sunday procession was imitated in Spain in the fifth century (was Egeria's account influential?) and in Gaul by the seventh. It was known in England by the beginning of the eighth century, but not in Rome until the twelfth. The procession typically began outside the church building with the blessing of palms. At Canterbury the procession began at Saint Martin's Church and made its way to the cathedral. At Salisbury the presiding minister wore a red silk cope and the procession was headed by the veiled cross. Matthew 21:1–9 was read at the church door. Then the procession made its way around the church with an unveiled cross.[37] At York the hymn *Gloria laus et honor* ("All glory, laud, and honor") was sung by the choir during the procession. This hymn is attributed to Theodulph of Orleans (c. 760–821). The singing of the Passion on Palm Sunday is known only in the later missals.

Maundy Thursday liturgies in the Gelasian Sacramentary commemorated the reconciliation of penitents, the blessing of oils for baptisms at the Easter Vigil (*Missa Chrismatis*), and the Evening Mass of the Lord's Supper (*Missa ad Vesperum*), although the Gregorian has only the Chrism Mass. In the Gelasian and in *Ordo Romanus Primus* a rubric directs the sacramental elements from the Chrism Mass to be reserved for communion on Good Friday. Not until the twelfth century is there a procession to the altar of repose. But we do find directions for the stripping and washing of the altar in Isidore, *De ecclesiasticis officiis*, I, 29.[38] The Seventeenth Council of Toledo (694) also ordered the *Mandatum*, or footwashing, to be done. This was spread through various medieval missals.

The eucharist was not celebrated on Good Friday. In its absence emerged the

---

[37] See John W. Tyrer, *Historical Survey of Holy Week*, op. cit., 57.
[38] Ibid., 128ff.

paraliturgical veneration of the cross. Such devotion was aided by the dissemination of relics of the true cross in the West. The Gelasian gives very little information about it, and mixed it up with the Mass of the Pre-sanctified. Ordo I, however, does describe the veneration with its antiphon, "Behold the wood of the cross on which hung the salvation of the world; O come, let us worship," along with Psalm 118. From other ordines we have the texts of the Reproaches. From the Gallican books we have the Trisagion sung in Greek and Latin. And from the Mozarabic books we have the stirring hymn of Verantius Fortunatus, "Pange lingua gloriosi" (Sing, my tongue, the glorious battle).[39]

The lucernarium of the Easter Vigil became quite developed in the Western churches. The blessing of the paschal candle was popular in the churches of Africa, Spain, Gaul, and Italy already in the fourth and fifth centuries. The text of the Exsultet ("Rejoice, now, all heavenly choirs of angels") comes from the Gallican church, along with the blessing proper. Two phrases in the text of the blessing—"O certe nessarium" (O necessary sin of Adam) and "O felix culpa" (O happy fault)—were omitted in some churches on grounds of questionable theology; and the long eulogy of the bees who made the wax was sometimes left out.[40] The new fire may have come from the Jerusalem celebration, since Egeria mentions a fire being carried from the Holy Sepulchre into the basilica. But the ceremonial blessing of the fire on Easter Eve comes from northern Europe. Some even credit it to Saint Patrick.[41]

The Gelasian Sacramentary witnesses to a forty-day Lent beginning on Ash Wednesday, which is called *Caput jejunii*. By the time of Gregory the Great the three Sundays before Lent, Septuagesima, Sexagesima, and Quinquagesima, had emerged in Rome. The reason for this extended penitential season is not known. There may have been influence from the Byzantine church, which did not have fasting on Saturdays or Sundays, and so had an eight-week Lent. The repeated attacks of the Goths and Lombards may also have readied the people for additional penitence and prayer.

There were no major developments in the Christmas season during this period, except that Christmas was definitively established as a twelve-day season ending on the Feast of the Epiphany. But the pre-Christmas season of Advent owes its origins exclusively to the merging of Gallican and Roman traditions. The second half of December had been a celebration of the conclusion of the agricultural year in Rome, and a theme of thanksgiving pervaded the days of the Roman Saturnalia (December 17–23). Pope Leo I brought eschatological themes into his sermons at this time of the year in order to warn Christians against the excesses of the Roman festivities, but nowhere does he refer to the coming festival of the nativity of Christ.

It has been postulated that the season of Advent evolved in Spain and Gaul as a season of preparation for baptism at Epiphany, although documentation to substantiate this claim is minimal, if not nonexistent.[42] There is no doubt that Epiphany was a day for

---

[39] Ibid., 128ff.

[40] Ibid., 150ff.

[41] Louis Gougaud, *Christianity in the Celtic Lands* (New York: Sheed and Ward, 1932), 279ff.

[42] Terrance W. Klein, "Advent and the Evangelical Struggle for Cultural Symbols," *Worship* 60 (1995), 538–55, connects Advent more with pre-Christian agricultural observances than with baptism.

solemn baptisms (so was Christmas!), but the earliest secure date for a preparatory fast comes from the sixth-century synods at Tours (567) and Macon (581). This fast lasted from the feast of Saint Martin of Tours (November 11) until Christmas. Although it came to be called "Saint Martin's Lent," it only added Mondays to the normal fast days of Wednesday and Friday.[43] This period, comprising forty-two days, produced a six-week period of Sundays for which lectionaries of the sixth to eighth centuries provided appropriate readings.[44] In scanning such important sources as the eleventh-century manuscript of Silos in Spain known as the *Liber comicus*, the ninth-century Bible of Alcala, the Lectionaries of Luxeuil and Würzburg, and the Bobbio Missal, ten different gospel readings for Advent masses can be identified.[45] These cover four different themes:

> The end of the world and the signs of the times—
>   Luke 21:25ff.; Matthew 24.37–44; 25:1–13
> The triumphal entry of Christ into Jerusalem (a type of messianic arrival)—
>   Matthew 21:1–9
> The mission of John the Baptist—
>   John 1:19ff.; Luke 3:1ff.; Mark 1:1–8; Matthew 11:2ff
> The Annunciation and Visitation of the Blessed Virgin Mary—
>   Luke 1:26–38; 1:39–56 (with Magnificat)

Only the themes of the Annunciation and the Visitation relate to the historical nativity of Jesus. The Annunciation was celebrated in Milan on the last Sunday of Advent and at Toledo on December 18. While this celebration was considered inappropriate during Lent or Holy Week (March 25), it was regarded as appropriate to Advent. Advent thus took on the themes of eschatological vigilance, fasting and calls to repentance, and anticipation of the birth of Christ once the western European and Roman traditions were merged.[46]

There was a prolific development in the sanctoral calendar during the early Middle Ages. If in the earlier period the martyrs and confessors were the great heroes of the faith, in the Middle Ages wonderworkers were singled out for special veneration. The belief in and obsession with miracles was concentrated especially in the cult of the saints, and devotees appealed to the saints for miraculous intervention in their own lives. This is the source of the Roman Catholic practice of canonizing as saints only those to whom miracles could be attributed. The veneration of relics of the saints as pledges of help from them became an important aspect of the cult of the saints, although we note that from earlier times shrines and basilicas had been erected over the graves of the saints. Now it was standard to include relics of the saints in every altar, which necessitated a proliferation of relics. This was a practice that Rome resisted because Roman law considered the remains of the dead inviolable. Pope Gregory the Great refused to send to the empress Constantina, wife of the emperor Mauricius, the head of Paul or another part of his body

---

[43] See Thomas Talley, *The Origins of the Liturgical Year*, op. cit., 150ff.

[44] See Allan McArthur, *The Evolution of the Christian Year* (London, 1953), 75.

[45] See the chart in F. Cabrol, *art. cit.*, 494–5.

[46] See Frank C. Senn, "The Meaning of Advent: Implications for Preaching," *Concordia Theological Monthly* XLII (1971), 653–9.

as a relic for the new basilica built in honor of the apostle at Constantinople. She received only some *brandea* (certified artifact)that had touched his tomb.[47] But under pressure from the East, which regularly exhumed the bodies of the martyrs and divided pieces of them among the churches, Roman custom could not hold out against this desire for physical contact with the saints any longer. So great was the desire to collect the relics of saints that no means were spared to procure them.

As the number of saints commemorated in the calendar grew, the specialization of the saints and the particular roles assigned to them also grew. The feasts and memorials of Mary, the Mother of our Lord, constitute a special aspect of the cult of the saints. Remarkably, considering the devotion to Mary in the Middle Ages, Marian days came only slowly into the calendar. Around 700 there was already an observance of the Conception of Mary by Saint Ann in the East on December 9. Nine months later the Birth of Mary was celebrated on September 8. These feasts entered the West through Sicily and southern Italy when these territories were under Byzantine control. In France and England, however, the emphasis shifted from Mary's conception to her "immaculate conception" (being conceived without sin), an idea to which even as ardent a Marian devotee as Bernard of Clairvaux objected. Likewise, the idea of Mary's assumption into heaven was slow to gain acceptance. It grew out of the Feast of the Dormition (Falling Asleep) of Mary, celebrated in the East already in the sixth century. It was introduced into the Roman church by Pope Sergius I (687–701), the Syrian pontiff who did much to introduce Eastern practice into the church of Rome. The biblically based Feast of the Visitation of Mary was first taken up by the Franciscans under Bonaventure, and was introduced on July 2, 1263.[48]

The origins of a festival of all the saints are uncertain, although general memorial days exist in many societies. A hymn composed by Ephraim (c. 359) suggests that a commemoration of all the martyrs was held on May 11 in Eastern Syria. By 411 in East Syria a Festival of All Martyrs was held on the Friday after Easter, suggesting a parallel with Good Friday and the imitation of the passion of Christ. On May 13, early in the seventh century Pope Boniface IV dedicated the Pantheon in Rome to Mary and all the martyrs with much pomp and circumstance. As a result, the *Natale Sancte Mariae ad Martyres* was entered into the Roman calendar for May 13. It was the first time in which a nonmartyr was commemorated at the same time as the martyrs. This idea was sealed when Pope Gregory III dedicated a chapel in the old Saint Peter's Basilica in honor of "The Redeemer, his holy Mother, all the apostles, martyrs, and confessors, and all the just and perfect who are at rest throughout the whole world."[49]

Also, by the eighth century November 1 was listed as a day of commemoration of all the saints in England, and Alcuin of York brought it with him to Germany when he

---

[47] See Gabriel M. Braso, *Liturgy and Spirituality*, trans. by Leonard J. Doyle (Collegeville: The Liturgical Press, 1971), 37.

[48] See Adams, *The Liturgical Year*, op. cit., 212ff.; also Frank C. Senn, "Mary in Ecumenical Dialogue and Liturgical Convergence," *dialog* 31 (1992), 251–58, and other articles in this issue of *dialog*.

[49] See Thomas J. Talley, "For All the Saints: A Brief History," *Liturgy: All Saints Among the Churches* 12/2 (Fall 1994), 43.

came to work for Charlemagne.[50] The custom of commemorating all the saints on November 1 could have originated in Ireland, since the Irish assigned important feasts to the first day of the month. The fact that Alcuin mentions a vigil on the Eve of All Saints may have been an attempt to counter the impact of the Celtic *Samhain*, a night on which the boundary between the living and the dead was violated by the visits of the spirits of the departed at the threshold of winter.[51]

Because of the emphasis on sanctity or holiness promoted in large part by the monastic ideal that dominated medieval spirituality, and of the concomitant notion of two levels of Christian believers, a distinction was made between saints who were recognized as such and the faithful departed generally. The idea of remembering all the faithful departed on one day is first met in Isidore of Seville (d. 636). A Feast of All Souls was ordered by Abbot Odo of Cluny in 998. This idea spread quickly through France, Germany, and England. In the British Isles it found a natural place in conjunction with the Feast of All Saints, and was observed on November 2—also under the influence of pre-Christian notions of the visitation and presence of spirits in the mists and fogs of late autumn.

🍇 BAPTISM AND CONFIRMATION

"Disintegration" is the only term that can adequately describe what happened to the rites of Christian initiation after the fifth century. It is not intended here as a pejorative term but as a descriptive one. It suggests that the unified rites of sacramental initiation described in the preceding chapter were broken up, over the course of centuries, into separate rites, each accorded its own particular efficacy. This happened in the Western church, but not in the Eastern, and for reasons that are more peculiar to the West than to the East.

Both in the Eastern and the Western churches by the end of the fifth century, infant baptism was becoming a more usual practice. Already in the Letter of John the Deacon to Senarius there is reference to the scrutinies being performed in a classroom instead of in the church, and the emphasis is on the exorcisms rather than on the handing over and delivery of the Creed. This was probably because the majority of candidates for baptism were infants who were not capable of responding to instruction but only of receiving apotropaic acts performed on them. It would not be as profitable for the faithful to participate in rites of exorcism as in catechetical instruction. That same consideration led to the relocation of the scrutinies to weekdays in the Gelasian Sacramentary and Ordo Romanus XI (which represent Roman practice between the sixth and eighth centuries), when the faithful would not even have to be present. While the term *infantes* is ambiguous (the fathers regularly applied it to all those who were reborn in baptism), Ordo XI specifically directs an acolyte to hold the candidate on his left arm during the Traditio symboli (Delivery of the Creed). After the delivery of the Creed and the Our Father the parents are directed to take their "infants" out of the church. Another interesting rubric

[50] See Gerard Ellard, *Master Alcuin, Liturgist* (Chicago: Loyola University Press, 1956), 91–2.
[51] See Clarence A. Miles, "Pre-Christian Winter Festivals, in *Christmas in Ritual and Tradition Christian and Pagan*, op. cit., 171–80.

specifies that the newly baptized should not be put to the breast or receive any other food before they commune.[52]

It is the reason for the move toward the greater frequency of infant baptisms which distinguishes the Western from the Eastern development. To be sure, in both situations public penance was falling into decline by the end of the fifth century, which removed a major reason for delaying baptism. But in the West Augustine's doctrine of original sin proved very influential. Augustine did not originate this doctrine; it emerged over a period of centuries in North African Christianity. But Augustine appealed to it in his controversy with Pelagius, whose views of human potential seemed to undermine the redemptive effects of Christ's atonement and to render the Christian life into little more than a form of moral stoicism. Augustine held that people are born into the service of the devil and need exorcism to rid them of the influence of the demonic and open their lives to the influence of the Holy Spirit. In a typical patristic appeal to the lex orandi to establish the lex credendi, Augustine pointed out that the exorcism was performed on infant candidates for baptism as well as adults, indicating that children are not born innocent of the effects of the fall. This appeal to what sometimes happened tended to place an emphasis on it happening normally. This, combined with the high infant mortality rates in the early Middle Ages in the West, prompted parents to rush their children to the font for fear that they might die and go to hell.

Emergency baptisms had been performed for centuries; now they were becoming the usual way to perform initiation, thus undermining the paschal context of Christian initiation, since many infants were baptized at times other than Easter. The lessening of the interval between birth and baptism had the effect of reducing the rites of the catechumenate to ceremonies performed just prior to the baptism on the church porch or in the vestibule. These ceremonies consisted of the following: "What do you seek of the church? R/ Faith. What does faith give you? R/ Eternal life"; an exhortation to keep the commandments and believe in the Trinity; the signing of the candidate on the forehead and breast; the prayers of exorcism; the giving of the salt of exorcism; the recitation of the Lord's Prayer and Apostles' Creed by the priest and the godparents; and the procession to the font, where the *Effata* (using spittle) and renunciation of Satan took place; followed by another anointing and the order of baptism. The exact details of these ceremonies varied from one church province to another.

J. D. C. Fisher argues that in Rome there was an effort to maintain the unity of the initiation rites up to the twelfth century, with the post-baptismal ceremonies being performed by suffragan bishops as well as the pope himself.[53] Aidan Kavanagh argues that this episcopal anointing and laying on of hands is a survival of solemn dismissals of the catechumens in the ancient church, and that this is what we see reflected in the post-baptismal ceremonies in the *Apostolic Tradition* of Hippolytus.[54]

In the Frankish church these post-baptismal ceremonies were either performed by a priest or omitted. Charlemagne's interest in importing Roman liturgical books and

---

[52] See Whitaker, *Documents of the Baptismal Liturgy*, op. cit., 166ff.

[53] J. D. C. Fisher, *Christian Initiation: Baptism in the Medieval West* (London: S.P.C.K., 1965), 23–4.

[54] Aidan Kavanagh, *Confirmation: Origins and Reform* (New York: Pueblo Publishing Company, 1988).

practices into Frankish territories served to create more confusion than order because Roman practices inevitably had to be adapted to conditions in trans-Alpine Europe. Roman standards meant that the preferred time for Christian initiation was Easter or Pentecost, with the bishops presiding over a unified rite. But the fewer bishops in France and Germany administered geographically larger dioceses with more scattered parishes than did the more numerous bishops of central Italy. Moreover, Carolingian imperial expansion meant bringing whole pagan tribes into the "Christian empire" by means of mass baptism. In these rites, as Fisher notes, we sometimes find the episcopal imposition of hands occurring *after the communion*. This reflects what was becoming the usual practice in the Frankish churches, namely, that children baptized in scattered parishes by the parish priests, and communed at the time of their baptism, were being brought later to the bishop for confirmation. The lengthening of the interval between baptism and confirmation created a need to appeal to a theological rationale for this modest ceremony as a way of encouraging parents to see that their children were confirmed. There is no question that confirmation was, from its very beginning, "a practice seeking a theory."[55]

There were two sources for the theology of confirmation. First is in the letter of Pope Innocent I to Bishop Decentius of Gubbio (c. 416), to which we have already referred. On the post-baptismal ceremonies Innocent asserts: "it belongs solely to the episcopal office that bishops consign and give the Paraclete Spirit."[56] He cites the example of the apostles in Acts 8 going to Samaria to confirm the work done there by Philip the deacon by laying their hands on the newly baptized and giving them the Holy Spirit. There are no contemporary texts to indicate the formula that the bishops might use, although the text in the Gelasian Sacramentary has the bishop petitioning the Holy Spirit for his sevenfold gifts.[57] It should be noted that Jerome, who had served as secretary to Pope Damasus until the latter's death in 384, and who knew Innocent and was supported by this pope in his monastic endeavors in Palestine after 401, lampooned the notion that "from the bishop alone proceeds the calling down of the Holy Spirit" on the baptismal candidates.[58] Indeed, the Eastern churches did not know of a post-baptismal laying on of hands by the bishop and contented themselves with a post-baptismal anointing by a presbyter using oil that had been consecrated by a bishop.

Secondly, church councils in Spain and southern Gaul in the fourth and fifth centuries directed the bishops to "perfect," "complete," or "confirm" the baptisms performed by presbyters or deacons as a matter of pastoral oversight, although again Gallican and Hispanic books provide no references to a distinct episcopal post-baptismal rite.[59] The origin of these synodical decrees was probably the disciplinary need to oversee emergency situations, to ascertain what liturgical orders had been followed, or to reconcile heretics; in other words, to regularize irregular situations.

---

[55] Gerard Austin, *Anointing with the Spirit. The Rite of Confirmation: The Use of Oil and Chrism* (New York: Pueblo Publishing Company, 1985), 23ff.

[56] Ep. 25:3; P.L. 56:515.

[57] Whitaker, 178.

[58] See G. W. H. Lampe, *The Seal of the Spirit*, 2nd ed. (London, 1967), 199.

[59] See A. Winkler, "Confirmation or Chrismation? A Study in Comparative Liturgy," *Worship* 58 (1984), 2–17.

The term "confirmation" was used for the first time in a Pentecost sermon attributed to Faustus of Riez (c. 450), where the rite received theological justification. "In baptism," he said, "we are born anew for life, after baptism we are confirmed for battle; in baptism we are washed, after baptism we are strengthened."[60] This interpretation of the rationale for the rite of confirmation was used by medieval canonists, who made it the theological basis of a separate sacrament of confirmation. It acquired importance because in the middle of the ninth-century Pseudo-Isidore, the anonymous compiler of the False Decretals attributed parts of this sermon to the martyr pope Melchiades, who lived before the peace of the church under Constantine. This lent to Faustus's interpretation an authority it never would have had on its own.[61]

Thus we see in western Europe in the early Middle Ages the beginning of the process of separating the Spirit-moment from its baptismal context and the development of a separate sacrament of confirmation that came to be related to the disciplinary and educational needs of the church. The effort to specify the role of the Spirit, of course, only succeeded in limiting the role of the Spirit. Bishops and theologians had to make sense out of a rite whose original purpose was no longer evident. As Nathan Mitchell observed, even the most perceptive theologians no longer understood the relationship between the gift of the Spirit in confirmation and baptismal incorporation into Christ. "The 'law of accumulated symbolism,'" he wrote, "has done its work: the heavy symbolism of Christian initiation has, under the influence of declining catechesis and theological misunderstanding, forced the original architecture of the rite to collapse into two 'separate and distinct sacraments' with 'separate and distinct effects.'"[62]

🍇 THE EMERGENCE OF PRIVATE PENANCE

If the ancient church's process of Christian initiation disintegrated into separate and distinct sacramental moments in the early medieval West, the ancient church's process of penance languished in search of new and different ways to reconcile sinners to the communion of the church. The ancient canonical public penance entailed, as we have seen, the enrollment of penitents into an order, most often at the beginning of Lent, with reconciliation on Maundy Thursday. The strictures placed on penitents were severe: they were forbidden to marry or remarry, to assume public responsibilities in church or state, to take legal action, or to enter into commerce. There is little wonder that the faithful avoided penance, and most often asked for it only on their deathbeds. This system led to what Cyrille Vogel called a "penitential void" and a "spiritual desert."[63]

---

[60] Cited in ibid., 16.

[61] See J. D. C. Fisher, *Confirmation Then and Now*. Alcuin Club Collections No. 60 (London: S.P.C.K., 1978), 132–6.

[62] Nathan Mitchell, "Dissolution of the Rite of Christian Initiation," in *Made, Not Born. New Perspectives on Christian Initiation and the Catechumenate*, The Murphy Center for Liturgical Research (University of Notre Dame Press, 1976), 71–2.

[63] Cyrille Vogel, *Pécheur et pénitence dans l'Eglise ancienne* (Paris: Le Cerf, 1966); also Vogel, *Le Pécheur et la pénitence au Moyen âge* (Paris: Le Cerf, 1969).

A new form of penance emerged in the monastic communities of the fourth and fifth centuries. This form provided repeated opportunities of confession of sins to a spiritual director, although it did not entail formal ecclesiastical excommunication and reconciliation. But it did provide for private confession. This model was taken up by monasteries in Britain and Ireland. Because the monasteries in the Celtic lands provided the anchor of church life, a private form of penance developed in the Celtic church in the sixth century. By the seventh century, missionary-monks were bringing these new penitential forms to the continent of Europe.[64]

Perhaps because the Celtic church flourished in the British Isles, and particularly in Ireland and Scotland, which had been uninfluenced by Roman occupation, this church was largely cut off from the rest of the Christianized world. Moreover, unlike the Greco-Roman churches of the Mediterranean basin, which were organized around urban centers, the Celtic church flourished in areas that were totally rural. Church life was not organized around great basilicas, which had the atmosphere of a public place, but around monastic communities, where the most important kind of spiritual development took place within the privacy of the individual soul. Within the monastery, however, spiritual direction occurred and sin had to be dealt with, as it did in the lives of all the baptized. Spiritual directors could be anyone with whom a monk could establish a relationship. Brendan and Columban seem to have gone to women for spiritual direction, although Columban definitely reserved the duty of being a confessor to priests. Monks who seemed to have a gift for serving as confessors were assigned by their abbots to serve as such to lay Christians who worshiped in the monastery churches. But not all monks were ordained priests, and it meant that lay persons as well as ordained monks could serve as confessors (as was also the case in the Eastern church, which also relied on monks to serve as confessors and spiritual directors). The extreme privacy of the transaction between confessor and penitent was the unique feature of the Celtic practice of penance, especially when contrasted with the canonical public penance of the Roman church.

Our information about the Celtic practice of penance comes from manuals for confessors, known as Penitentials. These provide a wealth of information about penances but almost no information about rites of excommunication and reconciliation. It is likely that a penitent simply stopped receiving communion during the period of penance and resumed participation in the sacrament when the period of penance was ended.[65]

This system of penance was introduced on the continent of Europe through the missionary activities of Irish and British monks, and the establishment of Celtic monasteries throughout western Europe. It was generally accepted in the Frankish lands, as is evident in the rise of Frankish penitentials.[66]

---

[64] See O. D. Watkins, *A History of Penance*, 2 vols. (London, 1920); B. Poschmann, *Penance and the Anointing of the Sick*, op. cit., 131ff.

[65] For critical editions and translations of these materials see Ludwig Bieler, *The Irish Penitentials*. Scriptores Latini Hiberniae, Vol. V (Dublin: The Dublin Institute for Advanced Studies, 1963); John McNeill and Helena Gamer, *Medieval Handbooks of Penance* (New York: Columbia University Press, 1938).

[66] See Cyrille Vogel, *Les "Libri paenitentiales"* (Tournai: Casterman, 1978).

That this private type of penance clashed with the old canonical public penance is evident in the Carolingian reform synods of the ninth century. That it provided an actual way of dealing with the sins of the baptized is evident in the fact that its use was sanctioned by these synods along with the use of public penance for public sins or in cases of church discipline. The penances imposed on penitents by the monk-confessors applied the principle of *contraria contrariis*. That is, the manuals imposed fasting on the glutton, work for the idle, chastity on the lecherous, and so forth. Unlike the public penance, one could come to private penance as many times as one chose to do so, and reconciliation could be effected as many times as one made a confession—although the pardon was granted only when the penances had been performed. It was the performance of the penance that resulted in the name "tariff penance." How this worked out can be seen by looking at some specific examples.

The Penitential of Pseudo-Theodore (c. 690–740) recommended four years of fasting for an act of fornication, forty days of fasting for the desire to do the act, ten years of strict fasting for a homicide resulting from a fight, and eleven years of the same for perjury. If all four of these sins were confessed, the result would be twenty-five years and forty days of fasting. Obviously, such punishments could not be realistically applied. So, following the model of the German *Wehrgeld*, equivalences were sought. For example, a one-year fast could be bought off through thirty-six days of continuous fasting, or by the recitation of the psalter three times, or by a certain number of lashings, or by a certain amount of hard cash, or by a certain number of penitential masses that had a set price. Obviously, the rich could buy off their penances while the poor had to perform the satisfactions. Moreover, the system of penance by tariff paid more attention to actual offenses than to intentions, and to concrete expiation for sins more than contrition. Tariff penance thus had its own liabilities. This exacerbated the situation of pastoral care when tariff penance was the only alternative to canonical public penance, which was put back on the books during the Carolingian Renaissance when Roman forms were being imported and imposed in the Frankish kingdom. The approach taken by synods and councils was that public penance would be used for public sins and private penance would be used for private sins. But the private form of penance would win out as a result of spiritual evolutions that took place in the monastic milieus of the ninth to eleventh centuries.

🍇 MONASTICISM AND THE CANONICAL HOURS

Just as monastic discipline greatly influenced the practice of penance in the church, so monastic devotion greatly influenced the church's daily common prayer. The study of the Divine Office is complicated by the fact that every local church and every monastic community developed its own form of the prayer offices, although a course of psalmody, proper office hymns, a lectionary, and concluding prayers are common to all of them. Among the most noteworthy sources for descriptions of the Divine Office in the Western monastic traditions are the Ordo Monasterii attributed to Alypius of Thegaste in North Africa (c. 395), which was later incorporated into the Rules of Augustine and Caesarius of Arles; and the Rule for Monks written by Isidore of Seville while he was serving as abbot of a monastery in Betica (Andalusia) between 590 and 600.[67] But as interesting as the prayer offices in North Africa and Spain may be, the two traditions that contended for the soul of the Western church were the Gallican-Celtic and the Roman-Benedictine. These are the office traditions on which we must necessarily focus attention in this survey.

The Gallican-Celtic monastic rules claim a spiritual lineage that goes back to the desert fathers of Egypt, as communicated to Western Christians through John Cassian. He is thought to have been born around 360 in Scythia Minor (present-day Romania) near the delta of the Danube. He went to Egypt as a young monk and encountered hermetic monasticism, possibly including the Rule of Pachomius to which he refers in the Preface to his *Institutes*. In this famous and influential work, written between 417 and 425, Cassian is not giving a history of Egyptian monasticism, but is drawing on his memory of it to reform and establish on a sounder basis Gallican monasticism.[68]

The diocese of Apt, forty miles north of Marseilles in Gaul, had never had a monastery. Its bishop, Castor, desired to establish one. Around the year 420, he wrote to Cassian, a noted authority on Palestinian and Egyptian monasticism, for help. There exists a letter of request from Castor, but it seems to be spurious. The form of the answer, however, shows that he asked for advice on the Eastern or Egyptian rules for monks, and also for guidance on the interior ethics of the monastic life.

Cassian's reply to Castor's request was the *Institutes* (*De institutis coenobiorum*). This book, and Cassian's *Conferences*, constitute some of the most valuable sources of early monastic rule and spirituality.[69] The *Conferences* deal especially with spirituality; they purport to give summaries or reports of discussions or discourses given by various hermits in Egypt, twenty-four in all. They reflect the ascetic ideals of the desert fathers that Cassian wished to pass on to Western monks. The other-worldliness of these ascetics became popular in the early fifth century as a result of the catastrophic barbarian invasions in western Europe and the collapse of the Roman Empire. Cassian's *Conferences* was designed to help Western monks work out these ideals during this critical period in history. The *Institutes* is a quiet and sober treatment of the structure of monastic life.

The sobriety of the *Institutes* may even have disappointed some monks in southern Gaul who may have expected something more exciting out of Egypt. "I shall make no attempt," wrote Cassian in his preface, "to relate tales of miracles and prodigies. I have heard from my elders of amazing marvels, and have seen some with my own eyes. But I have wholly omitted them. They contribute nothing but astonishment and do not otherwise instruct the reader in the life of holiness." The life of the monk was the apostolic life. Cassian shared the belief of the early monks that their way of life was founded by the

---

[67] See Robert Taft, S.J., *The Liturgy of the Hours in East and West* (Collegeville: The Liturgical Press, 1986), 93ff.

[68] See E. C. S. Gibson, *The Works of John Cassian*. Nicene and Post-Nicene Fathers, Series 2, Vol. 11 (Grand Rapids: William B. Eerdmans, 1964).

[69] See Owen Chadwick, *John Cassian, A Study in Primitive Monasticism* (Cambridge, 1950). The *Conferences* are edited and trans. by Dom E. Pichery in *Sources chrétiennes* 42 (1945), 54 (1958), 64 (1959). Cassian's works are collected in Migne, PL 49 and 50.

apostles in the church of Jerusalem, which shared all things in common. Although a large part of the church had fallen away from these ideals, there were always some (he believed) who retained them. The monastic life of common property and personal holiness was the true life of the church; the novelty of Egypt was not the monk but the hermit. Hermits, like Paul and Anthony, wanted to fight demons face to face in open war. So they went to the desert (which was believed to be the headquarters of the demonic), like John the Baptist or Elijah, and became true solitaries. And Christianity rejoiced in these two vocations, cenobite (communal asceticism) and hermit (solitary asceticism).

Cassian's little history is intended to prove that monks are traditional Christians, perhaps because there were still plenty of vocal critics of monasticism in the Western church. But he also wanted to show that monasticism was, by the fifth century, a long-established tradition in the East. The Gauls wish to have monks; but they do not know how to be monks. All they need to do is to conform to a long-established and well-tested manner of ascetic life that has nothing in it of novelty.

Yet here lay the first of Cassian's difficulties. To imitate Egypt invited trouble in Gaul. The climate of Provence and the character of its people prevented the austere life that prevailed in Egypt. For Cassian, Egypt was heaven on earth; but he must temper Egyptian practices where they are unsuitable with customs from less rigorous sources. As he wrote in the introduction to the *Institutes*,

> I do not believe that any way of life, that might newly be designed in Gaul, could be better or more reasonable than the institutes which began in the age of the apostles and have been kept in the monasteries of Egypt and Palestine to this day. But I shall take this liberty: that if I think anything in the rules of Egypt are by climate or by difference of habits impossible or hard in this country, I shall temper the Egyptian customs by those of Palestine and Mesopotamia.

This difficulty touched off a bigger difficulty, which troubled the monastic movement for its first 200 years. In Palestine Cassian lived as a cenobite. In Egypt he lived in a hermit congregation. He believed the hermit society to be a higher way than the *coenobium*. He compared the coenobium to the kindergarten of ascetic life and solitude to the senior school. This created a problem for the early monastic legislators. To make the common life of a monastery the monks must be able to see the community as their true vocation. If they were led to aspire to leave the monastery on the ground that the monastery was a lower form of religious life, the monastery would hardly be conducive to religious contentment. Cassian stood within the authentic Egyptian tradition. The solitude that was higher than the community was not naked solitude, the lone man in the desert, but the society or congregation of hermits with a common worship and discipline. In Egypt the *coenobium* was the training school for beginners. Only as the monk purged his soul by practicing virtue in the community might he go out to the hermit's life. Only perfect men could go to the desert. If imperfect men took their faults out there, those faults would grow unseen.

This doctrine, as Cassian expressed it, pulled curiously in different directions. In theory he accepted the common Egyptian view that the eremitic life was superior, for the hermit could contemplate God in the undisturbed silence of prayer. In practice Cassian discouraged monks who wanted to become hermits. Only perfect men ought to go out to the wilderness. Who will declare himself perfect? Not Cassian; he considered himself a beginner writing for beginners. Like Benedict, he founded schools for beginners, corporate monasteries at Marseilles and Apt. The *Institutes* are thus like the Rule of Benedict, "written for beginners."

Cassian's description of the monastic office concerns us here. We have already noted Cassian's witness to the tenacity of morning and evening prayer in Egypt. If Cassian was a trustworthy reporter, the Egyptians kept an office of Vespers and another nocturnal office (later called Matins). At each of these hours they had twelve psalms, with prayers between each psalm. There were also two lessons at each office, from the Old and New Testaments. The psalms were not chanted by the whole community, but only by cantors. Each cantor chanted three psalms, so four cantors were required for each office. In a long psalm the Superior stopped the cantor after ten verses to allow for silent meditation upon the verses just sung. At the end of the psalm, after standing for some moments in silent prayer, all prostrated themselves in adoration; but the prostration could not last too long lest sleep overcome the prone worshipers, who must rise with the leader to pray with arms outstretched.[70]

Cassian was inclined to think that the Egyptian custom of two formal offices each day was best, for the Egyptians thereby kept the day free for their private and unceasing meditation. He thought that an increase in the number of offices might be a weakness and an interruption. Yet he confessed that weaker men needed more frequent times of set prayer. Therefore, he described the services of Terce, Sext, and Nones as they were celebrated in the monasteries of Palestine. Unlike Vespers and Matins with their twelve psalms, these had three psalms each.

Here were five hours of prayer for his monks. A century and a half later, Benedictine Rule 16 ordered eight offices that henceforth became canonical in monasteries: Lauds, Prime, Terce, Sext, Nones, Vespers, Compline, and the nocturnal office of Matins. The three daytime offices have their origin in the devotions that Christian writers like Tertullian recommended to the faithful at the common divisions of the Roman working day: the third, sixth, and ninth hours (9 A.M., noon, and 3 P.M.). Naturally, the monastic communities could observe these hours communally, together with the additional office in the middle of the night, which is distantly modeled on the Vigil office. Finally, private devotions on rising and retiring at the beginning and end of the day were also turned into communal offices—Prime and Compline.

The difficult question is how the morning office became divided into two: Lauds at dawn and Prime at the first hour of the day.[71] In chapter 4 of Book III of the *Institutes* Cassian describes the invention of a new morning office of prayer. This was started in Cassian's own monastery near the Cave of the Nativity at Bethlehem while he was a monk there. It is believed that Matins and Lauds had already been divided. So there was an office at dawn, but then no other office until Terce. The idler monks therefore started to

---

[70] See Taft, 97ff.

[71] On the debate over the origins of Prime see J. Froger, *Les origines de Prime* (1946) and Owen Chadwick, "The Origins of Prime," *Journal of Theological Studies* (1948), 178–82.

oversleep and miss their work and stay in bed until Terce. The more fervent monks complained to the elders. Therefore it was ordered that the monks might rest until sunrise. But then they should be summoned for an office like Terce, Sext, and Nones, consisting of three psalms and prayers, and this office should mark the end of sleep and the beginning of work.

This new office, said Cassian, makes up the number seven, according to Psalm 119:164: "Seven times a day I praise you." Though this new office started in Bethlehem, some of the ancient monasteries in the East refused to accept it. But in the West it was already widely used.

If this opinion is well-founded, it is possible to construct the following timetable for Cassian's monastery at Marseilles:

> Nocturns or Matins: twelve psalms with prayers between each psalm, followed
>   by two lessons chosen from the Old and New Testaments. (On Sundays
>   both lessons were chosen from the New Testament.) The time of the office
>   is not stated, but it finished before dawn.
> Dawn office (Lauds) followed the end of Nocturns either immediately or after
>   a short interval. Psalms 148–150. No lessons in any office copied from
>   Palestine.

Here followed a period of sleep in Palestinian houses, which Egyptian houses condemned as lax.

> Morning office (Prime) to mark the beginning of the day's work Psalms 51,
>   63, 90.
> Terce: three psalms, no lesson
>   Sext: three psalms, no lesson
>   Nones: three psalms, no lesson
>   Vespers: twelve psalms with two lessons, as at Nocturns

Cassian gives no instruction, such as we find in the Rule of Benedict, that the monks should recite the whole psalter every week. But even if there were as few as five daily offices (Dawn, Terce, Sext, Nones, and Vespers), the custom of twelve psalms at Nocturns and Vespers every day would mean that 150 psalms were chanted during the week even without the three midday offices. There were two ways of ordering psalmody that were combined to constitute the later system of monastic hours. Probably the older method, based on the cathedral office, was to use psalms appropriate to the time of day at which prayer was held. The other was to take the psalms in the order in which they are arranged in the Bible. Cassian stood closer to the latter arrangement. According to his text, the only special psalms were those set for Lauds and Prime, the old penitential and morning psalms of the morning office.

On Saturday evenings there was a vigil from Vespers until the fourth cockcrow, followed by a short sleep. Here the psalms were not said or chanted by a single voice, but communally in order to diminish the risk of sleep. The vigil was relieved by a variety of methods and postures. Three psalms were said antiphonally while the monks stood, then three psalms, each led by a different monk, with the rest responding from their stools, and then three lessons.

We have devoted this attention to Cassian's *Institutes* because of its immense influence on Western monasticism. This influence is no less evident in the development of the Divine Office in the Western monastic tradition. When we compare, for example, the Celtic or Irish office, adopted by Columban, with that described by Cassian, the general resemblance is at once apparent.[72] In fact, a tradition was preserved in Ireland that the office in vogue there had originally come from the region of the Nile. The author of an eighth-century Cottonian tract on the six principal arrangements of the hours held that the *cursus Scottorum*, or Irish arrangement, owed its origin to the evangelist Mark. That evangelist, the writer asserted, preached the gospel not only in Egypt but also in Italy. Gregory Nazianzus and the Eastern monks, Basil, Anthony, Macarius, John, and Malchus adopted his system. Cassian introduced it into Gaul. It was accepted at the island monastery founded by Honoratus at Lérins off the coast of Provence, and also by such Gallican monks as Caesarius of Arles, Germanus, Porcarius, and Lupus. Germanus and Lupus taught Patrick, and he, in turn, brought the cursus to Britain and Ireland. Thus it became the cursus Scottorum, and was reintroduced to the continent by Columban and his twelve missionary companions. The role ascribed to Mark in this tract is imaginary, and there is no proof for the personal references to the other saints. However, the four links—Egypt, Lérins, Britain, and Ireland—hold together, and the chain of transmission is substantially sound.

What we know of the Celtic office comes primarily from chapter seven of the Rule of Columban, "De cursu." In 590 Columban and his missionary companions came to the continent and established monasteries throughout France, southern Germany, Switzerland, and northern Italy. The best known of these were Luxeuil, Bobbio, Saint Gallen, and Ratisbon. The similarity with the office described by Cassian can be seen in the fact that Columban emphasized the two offices of Vespers and Nocturns (each of which were given twelve psalms), the night Vigil of Matins (for which Columban prescribed a special arrangement of psalms), and especially the weekend vigil on Saturday and Sunday nights. The daytime offices of Prime, Terce, Sext, and Nones were each provided with three psalms. As in Egypt, there were acts of humiliation after each psalm in the Celtic office. At the end of each psalm the brothers bowed in silence, then went to their knees while the collect was said. Then all rose together after reciting three times in silence, "Deus in adiutorium meum intende, Domine ad adiuvandum me festina" (O God, make haste to save me: O Lord, make haste to help me). On Sundays and during Paschaltide the brethren did not kneel, but only bowed. This, too, was typical of Eastern custom, which held that it was inappropriate to kneel on Sunday or during the Easter season; one remained standing during these times in honor of the resurrection. We also notice that, in accordance with Egyptian practice, there was a collect at the end of each psalm. Collects for psalms and canticles are provided for this purpose in the Bangor Antiphonary.[73] According to Bangor rubrics, the Te Deum was sung on Sundays and the Gloria at Vespers and Matins. Other hymns and canticles were assigned to the night office,

---

[72] See John Ryan, *Irish Monasticism, Origins and Early Developments* (London, 1931), 333ff.

[73] See *The Antiphonary of Bangor*, ed. F. E. Warren. Henry Bradshaw Society Collection No. 4 (London, 1895).

the festivals of martyrs, and the Matins of Saturdays and Sundays. But we would be hard-pressed to put together the exact structure of the various offices. We do know, however, that the daytime offices concluded with a series of six petitions in versicle form:

> *pro peccatis nostris* (for our sins);
> *pro omni populo christiano* (for all Christian people);
> *pro sacerdotibus,* and so on (for priests and other persons consecrated to God);
> *pro eleemosynas facientibus* (for those who give alms);
> *pro pace regnum* (for the peace of kings); and
> *pro inimicis* (for our enemies)

The most distinctive feature of the Celtic office is the arrangement of psalms at the night office.[74] Perhaps because the Irish monks were less capable of contemplation than their Eastern counterparts, they showed an exceptional zeal in reciting psalms and other vocal prayers. This is evident in Columban's arrangement of the night office. He divided the night office into three parts: *ad initium noctis, ad medium noctis, ad matutinam.* These offices correspond to first nocturn (at 9 P.M.), second nocturn (at midnight), and Matins with Lauds (at 3 A.M.). Following Cassian, Columban prescribed twelve psalms for nocturn, but with double nocturns he had double psalmody. But a lack of variation in the number of psalms prescribed for Matins seemed to Columban to be an imperfect arrangement; it imposed too light a task on the monks during the long winter nights and too heavy a task during the short summer nights. He therefore proposed a variation principle based on the seasons in his Rule.

It is not easy to decipher Columban's Latin in every instance, but it seems that he intended twelve *chori*[75] (thirty-six psalms) to be sung on the "holy nights" of Saturday and Sunday during the months of May through July. These were increased by three per week from August through October to the maximum number of seventy-five psalms per night, including twenty-five antiphons, during the winter months of November through January. These were then decreased by three per week from February through April until returning to the lighter load of summer with its shorter nights. Meanwhile, on other nights of the week twenty-four psalms were sung between March 25 and September 24, and thirty-six psalms were sung between September 25 and March 24.

Columban thus imposed on his monks the recitation of a quota of seventy-two psalms at the minimum and one hundred twenty-three psalms at the maximum, each day. It is possible that this cursus was adopted in other Irish monasteries. The Bangor Antiphonary likewise divides the night office into three sections: ad initium noctis, ad medium noctis, ad matutinam.

The Irish missionaries, with their strict rules, were not popular with the more lax Gallican clergy. Nor was the severe Celtic monastic rule compatible with the Gallicans who joined the Irish monasteries. Columban had tried to adapt, in the hills and forests of Burgundy and Austrasia, the monastic and liturgical usages of Egypt and Palestine which

---

[74] See Patrice Cousin, O.S.B., "La Psalmodie Chorale dans la Règle de Saint Colomban," *Melanges Colombaniens* (Paris, 1950), 179–91.

[75] Each "chorus" is a group of three psalms, in which the first two are sung "direct" (*psalliti*) and the third is sung "antiphonally" (*antifona*).

had been transmitted to Great Britain and Ireland. But malcontents among the Gallican monks forced Walbert, abbot of Luxeuil (630–635), to introduce the Benedictine Rule. It spread quickly from there to other Celtic-founded monasteries in western Europe.

Cassian was also incorporated into the Benedictine Rule. In chapter 1, Benedict instructs one of the brothers to read aloud the *Conferences*, or the *Lives* of the (Egyptian) Fathers, or any other edifying book, immediately after supper and until the time for Compline.[76] In chapter 73 (the last), Benedict declared that his Rule was only a little Rule for Beginners. Those who wished to advance toward heaven should meditate on the Bible or the Fathers. He specifically mentions Cassian's *Conferences* and *Institutes* and the *Lives* of the (Egyptian) Fathers. Cassian's disciplinary guidance is incorporated into the Benedictine Rule; his psalmic cry, "O God, make haste to save me: O Lord, make haste to help me," is appointed by Benedict to be said at the beginning of all offices. But it is in the structure of the offices that Benedict displayed his independence.

It is certain that he introduced the public office of Compline; he may also have introduced Prime, depending on what one thinks of the development of that office. He followed Cassian in appointing three psalms for the daytime offices. But he displaced the center of gravity of the Divine Office: the nocturnal vigil. Lauds ceased to be the important office: it comprised no more than five psalms with a scripture canticle. Vespers contained no more than four psalms in place of the dozen that were traditional in the East. It was composed of the psalms, a short epistle lection, a brief responsory, a hymn, the gospel canticle, and the supplication of the Litany. In the Benedictine office forty psalms were recited each day; twenty-two of them were included in the night offices. Benedict thus preserved far greater balance and more equal proportions between the night and the daytime offices. The suitability of Benedict's Rule for the western European temperament is evident in the fact that it eventually became the dominant Rule of Western monasticism.

It also ensured the triumph of the Roman office, because there is no doubt that the two greatest influences on the office in the Benedictine Rule were *Rule of the Master*, probably from Campania, southeast of Rome, in the early sixth century, and the Roman office of Benedict's time.[77] It is virtually impossible to determine the content of the Roman cathedral office since, beginning in the fifth century, the Roman basilicas were served by small monastic communities, and their office became that of the people of the city. Even the Roman monastic office is difficult to reconstruct, so triumphant has been the Benedictine recension. Pope Gregory the Great learned of the Benedictine Rule from a refugee monk from Monte Cassino, and he championed it. Later he sent a Benedictine monk, Augustine, as a missionary to England. The Benedictine office was established for use in England at the Synod of Clovesho (747) on the grounds that it was the Roman office.

This was the office that Boniface took with him to the continent and, with papal support, propagated first in Germany and then in France. With the connivance of Pippin

---

[76] *The Rule of St. Benedict*, trans. with introduction by Anthony C. Meisel and M. L. del Mastro (Image Books, 1975), 82.

[77] See Taft, *The Liturgy of the Hours in East and West*, op. cit., 121ff.

and Charlemagne, Boniface led the way in the elimination of the Gallican rite and its replacement by the Roman. Pippin's uncle, Chrodegang of Metz, went to Rome to collect Roman books and returned to found a community of canons regular, priests who would live together under a rule to serve cathedral churches like the monastic communities of Rome. And as early as 789 Charlemagne was insisting that all candidates for the ministry should study Roman (that is, Gregorian) chant for both the mass and the office. The Benedictine office triumphed throughout the Western church, and with it the monastic form of the office. The history of the Divine Office in the West has been the story of the establishment, the adaptation, and the reassertion of the monastic form of the office. Only in the cathedrals of Milan and Toledo, where the Ambrosian and Mozarabic rites were preserved, did the basic features of the cathedral office survive.

Monasticism and the monastic form of the Divine Office had an enormous influence on another development in the Western church: the institution of clerical celibacy and the ideal of a choral office. Augustine had already established a common life for the clergy of his diocese of Hippo. This idea was implemented in the basilicas in the Frankish kingdom around which a *domus basilicae* or *monasterium basilicae* was established to accommodate all the personnel serving these great churches and to provide hospitality to pilgrims. The head of these "houses" or "monasteries" was called an *abbas*, although he did not have to be the head of a religious community. A new impetus was given to this idea when Bishop Chrodegang of Metz, about 760, required his clergy to live *canonici*, that is, in a regulated life.[78] Like monks, the canons not only lived together but prayed together. Chapter four of the Rule of Chrodegang of Metz states:

> All should come to the divine office at all the canonical hours. At the hour for the divine office, as soon as the signal is heard, those who are close enough to the building to be able to get there for the office must drop whatever they have in hand and hurry there with all possible speed. And if anyone is far from the church, so that he cannot get there for the canonical hours, and the bishop or the archdeacon agrees that such is the situation, he shall perform the work of God right where he is at that time, with reverence dear. And the archdeacon or the head or guardian of the church shall see to it that the signals are sounded at the proper time.[79]

What we see here is the monasticizing of the secular clergy, with rules of clerical celibacy beginning to be imposed. The prayer office they used was taken over from the monasteries, with all of its hours of the day and the night. And just as Benedict required that monks who were unable to be present in choir nevertheless had to recite that part of the office in private, so the office obligation on secular clergy required that they recite in private what they could not gather in choir in recite.

This new mode of life for clergy spread quickly and widely. It was most easily implemented in the cathedrals, to which a number of priests were attached, rather than in the towns and villages where only a single priest might serve. The cathedral canons

---

[78] See H. Leclercq, "Chanoines," *Dictionnaire d'Archéologie chrétienne et de Liturgie* III (1913), 223–48.

[79] Cited in Pierre Salmon, *The Breviary through the Centuries*, trans. by Sister David Mary (Collegeville: The Liturgical Press, 1962), 9.

formed a *collegium* called a chapter. At a great synod held at Aachen in 817 the *vita communis* was made a general rule for all the clergy, as far as possible. As new cathedrals were formed, colleges of clergy lived together as canons with an obligation to participate in the choral celebration of the office. When this rule of communal life began to disintegrate a century later, and canons were living in their own houses, owning their own property, they still had the obligation of joining with the other canons to recite the office.

The fact that monks or canons had responsibility for the Divine Office also meant that it ceased to be a popular form of prayer. This is evident in the fact that the psalms and canticle were sung antiphonally (two groups facing each other) rather than responsorially (a large group responding to a cantor). Also, in the absence of printed books (or even multiple copies of books), the people were left out of singing the psalms since they usually knew only a few psalms or psalm verses. However, in the early Middle Ages the people still joined in singing the Gloria Patri which terminated each psalm. Cassian is a witness to this form of popular participation as early as c. 420 in his *Institutes*. In the time of Charlemagne the people were required to know the Gloria Patri and to join in singing it.[80]

🍇 GREGORIAN CHANT AND LATIN HYMNODY

Monasteries and cathedrals, as centers of church life in much of western Europe, ensured that liturgy would be sung because they provided communities of monks and canons who could be taught the chants and hymns. Sung portions of the mass included the proper introits, graduals, offertory and communion antiphons, plus the Kyrie, Gloria, Credo, Preface, Sanctus and Benedictus, and Agnus Dei. The sung portions of the Divine Office included versicles, psalms, office hymns, and canticles. This amount of singing had tremendous consequences for the development of Western music.[81]

Frankish authorities attributed the cycle of chants of the church year for the mass and the office to several popes, including Leo I, Gelasius I, and especially to Gregory the Great. A myth emerged within a couple of centuries after Gregory's death that he not only instituted a musical order but actually composed the body of tunes that came to be called Gregorian chant. Several illuminators of medieval manuscripts depicted Gregory, with a dove representing the Holy Ghost at his ear, dictating to a scribe (musical notation had been developed by this time). But Gregory's own writings seldom touch on music. A decree of 595 makes clear that music exists only as a vehicle of the text, that it was not the concern of the higher clergy, but that deacons should be chosen for their chanting ability.[82]

The earliest reference to Gregory's musical activity is found in the *Historia Ecclesiastica* IV, 2 and V, 20 of the Venerable Bede, dating from 731. This tells of Bishop

---

[80] See Josef A. Jungmann, S.J., *Public Worship: A Survey*, trans. by Clifford Howell, S.J. (Collegeville: The Liturgical Press, 1957), 42.

[81] See Gerald Abraham, *The Concise Oxford History of Music* (Oxford and New York: Oxford University Press, 1958), 56ff.

[82] See Amedee Gastoue, *Les Origines du chant romain* (Paris, 1907), appendix A.

Putta of Rochester, who was skilled in chanting in the manner of the Romans, and says that he had learned this from the *discipuli* of Pope Gregory in Kent. The *discipuli* were not Gregory's musical students, however, but Augustine and the band of monks Gregory had sent to England. Incidentally, they had been impressed by some Gallican usages and had been expressly granted permission by Gregory to make use of whatever local practices they thought fit. But Bede's insistence on the Roman provenance of church practices was due to the contest between the Celtic and the Roman customs, with the Roman practices winning over the Celtic only twelve years after Bede's death. The chances are great that the chants named "Gregorian" were no more composed by Pope Gregory than the prayers of the sacramentaries also named after him.

Nevertheless, there was as much borrowing back and forth between Rome and the Frankish church in musical matters as in prayer books. When Pippin, who was in the process of rescuing the papacy from the Lombards, sent Bishop Chrodegang of Metz as one of his envoys, Chrodegang became interested in Roman church music. In 754 a grateful Pope Stephen II came to Saint-Denis to anoint his rescuer as King of the Franks. Pippin requested additional Roman resources, including musical books and teachers. The Byzantine emperor, Constantine V, on hearing about Pippin's musical interests, sent an organ to him in 757 (an instrument that had been forgotten in western Europe since Roman times). About 760 a singing teacher who had studied in Rome was brought to Metz to establish a schola cantorum; and the *secundus* of the Roman schola was sent to Rouen where one of the king's brothers was bishop. The pope also sent to Pippin an antiphonary and responsorial that contained the chants for the mass and the office, respectively.

Amalarius of Metz first noted some discrepancies in the office books deposited in Metz since Chrodegang's time. He went to Rome in 831 to study the sources and ask Pope Gregory IV for an authentic antiphonary that he might take home. The pope was unable to provide this but suggested that Amalarius might consult the four office books given a few years earlier to the Abbot of Corbie near Amiens. Amalarius did so, and discovered that the order and texts sometimes differed from the books used at Metz, that there were many antiphons and responsories with which he was unfamiliar, and that, according to a notation in one of the volumes, all this was the result of a revision undertaken under Pope Hadrian I (772–795). Realizing that there was no single authoritative source, as he had supposed, Amalarius set about compiling a new antiphonary for use at Metz, drawing on the old Metz versions, the Corbie version, and the things he had learned in his youth from Alcuin at Tours. The Antiphonary of Metz became the model for church music in the Frankish realms. It was later imposed on Rome itself with the revival of the Empire of the Romans under the German Emperor Otto the Great and the subjugation of the papacy itself to Germanic influence.[83]

The influence of this northern musical spirit on Roman or Gregorian chant had important consequences. Roman chant was hardly even Roman. Rome had received

---

[83] A significant collection of facsimiles of Latin chant has been published in the series *Paleographie Musicale* by the monks of Solesmes (Solesmes, 1887ff.).

from the Byzantine East both a method for musical notation and the eight chant modes that became the basis of Gregorian melodies.[84] The musical style received from the East was, like the Byzantine icons, an impersonal art, unaffected by moods or passions. A much greater range of expression was desired north of the Alps. This was accomplished musically by introducing skips, especially of a third, fourth, or fifth, in the melodic line rather than proceeding strictly in stepwise intervals. During Carolingian times the first attempts were also made to sing in "harmony." An accompanying voice sang at intervals of a fourth or a fifth to the melodic line. This was a style known as *organum*. These developments in chants and chant-singing became important in the evolution of Western music generally.[85]

It should not pass unnoticed that the hymns that survive in actual use from this period come not from Rome but from northern Italy, Spain, France, Germany, England, and Ireland. Among the great Latin hymn writers can be listed Ambrose of Milan (340–397), the Spanish-born lawyer Marcus Aurelius Clemens Prudentius (348–c.413), Verantius Honorius Fortunatus, Bishop of Poitiers (530–608), Theodulph, Bishop of Orleans (760–821), and the German Hrabanus Maurus (776–856), who studied under Alcuin at Tours and served as Abbot of Fulda and Archbishop of Mainz. Hymns are also attributed to Patrick ("Saint Patrick's Breastplate," *LBW* 188) and the VenerableBede (*LBW* 157). Although Rome was slow to adopt the strophic hymn, such hymns eventually came into the Roman office and Pope Gregory the Great even made some contributions himself to Latin hymnody.[86]

The following are hymn texts and some tunes (indicated by °) that survive from this period and are still regularly sung in worship, some of which are included in *Lutheran Book of Worship*, with indicated hymn numbers.

TITLE	AUTHOR/PERIOD	HYMN
Aeternum rerum conditor	Ambrose	
Aeterna Christi munera	Ambrose	
O lux beata Trinitas	Ambrose	LBW 275
Splendor paternae gloriae	Ambrose	LBW 271°
O solis ortus cardine	Sedulius	LBW 64°
Corde natus ex Parentis	Prudentius	LBW 42°
O sola magnarum urbium	Prudentius	LBW 81
Jam lucis orto sidere	5th–6th c.	LBW 268
Lucis creator	5th–6th c.	

---

[84] See Egon Wellesz, *Eastern Elements in Western Chant* (Oxford: Oxford University Press, 1947). The standard study of Gregorian chant has been that of Willi Apel, *Gregorian Chant* (Bloomington, IN: Indiana University Press, 1958). A newer comprehensive study is that of David Hiley, *Western Plainchant* (Oxford: Clarendon, Press, 1993).

[85] See Donald Jay Grout and Claude V. Palisca, *A History of Western Music*, 5th ed. (New York: W. W. Norton and Co., 1996), 32ff.

[86] See M. Alfred Bichsel, "Greek and Latin Hymnody," in Marilyn Kay Stulken, *Hymnal Companion to the Lutheran Book of Worship* (Philadelphia: Fortress, 1981), 3–18.

TITLE	AUTHOR/PERIOD	HYMN
Rex Christe, factor omnium	Gregory	*LBW* 101
Nocte surgentes vigilemus omnes	Gregory? Alcuin?	*LBW* 267
Vexilla regis prodeunt	Fortunatus	*LBW* 125°
Pange, lingua, gloriosi proelium	Fortunatus	*LBW* 118
Lucis creator optime	6th c.	
Conditor alme siderum	6th c.?/9th c.	*LBW* 323°
Te lucis ante terminem	7th c.	*LBW* 277°
Urbs beata	7th c.	
Gloria, laus, et honor	Theodulph	*LBW* 108
Veni, Creator Spiritus	Maurus	*LBW* 472°

The tunes from this period that are often married with these texts are a style of music known as "plainsong." They are characterized by a one-note to one-syllable relationship. The texts of the hymns are liturgically specific: They all belong to the morning or evening offices (including "Vexilla Regis," which was sung at Vespers during Passion Week, and "Veni, Creator Spiritus," which was sung at Vespers during the week of Pentecost). The one exception is "Gloria, laus, et honor", which was sung in the Palm Sunday procession. It was in the Divine Office, rather than in the mass, that hymnody flourished in the Western church.

Finally, it should be noted that the content of these hymns is christological and trinitarian. The morning hymns celebrate Christ as the "splendor of the Father's light" (Ambrose) that enlightens Christians in their daily work; the evening hymns celebrate the Trinity as a "blessed light" (Ambrose) that remains with Christians in the darkness and dangers of the night. They are grounded in the biblical stories and narrate salvation history (Fortunatus). From the time of Ambrose, Western hymn writers concluded their hymns with a trinitarian doxology. "Splendor Paternae Gloriae" closes with,

> Deo Patri sit gloria,
>   Ejusque soli Filio,
> Cum Spiritu Paraclito,
>   Nunc et per omne saeculum.

At the same time, these Western hymns are also sensitive to the natural world: from the fiery sun of Ambrose to the whiteness of the moon at evening, the flashing lightning, the whirling wind, the stable earth, and the deep salt sea of Patrick, to Fortunatus's comparison of the cross with trees of foliage.

A splendidly performed liturgy that was doxological from beginning to end, and imbued with orthodoxia (right praise) to correct any lingering Arianism or paganism among semi-barbarian peoples, yet sensitive to the down-to-earth empirical outlook and sensual perception of the Western peoples, served the purpose of channeling the great practical energy of the western European peoples into the service of God. Yet the outward exuberance of liturgical celebration ran the constant risk of smothering the inner spirit, or of making the liturgy and its setting always more dramatic and more splendid precisely in order to evoke a spiritual response. Over the course of many centuries the theological bases of the liturgy were lost sight of, while the employment of everything that arouses the feelings increased, so that eventually what was sought was not so much participation in the sacramental life as the kind of devotion that affects the emotions. That was not yet the case in the early Middle Ages. From the standpoint of the liturgy this period does not constitute a "dark ages"; the spirit of the liturgy as the public and corporate work of the people of God was still intact. But the seeds of division were being planted that would become a deep separation of liturgy and piety in the Western liturgical experience.

CHAPTER 6

Medieval Liturgical Deteriorization

THE CHURCH OF THE early Middle Ages was in continuity with the church of antiquity in placing an emphasis not on personal piety but on the solemn offering of the liturgy. But a more introspective and affective spirituality was developing in the monasteries of the ninth through the eleventh centuries, especially in the new monastic orders that emerged in the wake of the monastic reforms of this period.[1] Particularly among the Cistercians there are examples of this subjective religiosity. These included the devotion to the crucified Lord focused on the crucifix (which Aelred of Rievaulx considered the only appropriate form of decoration in a monastery), the devotion to the Blessed Virgin Mary (who was regarded as a gracious lady and a loving mother), and an outpouring of lyrical hymns written in the first person singular (a form of expression seldom encountered in the ancient church). "Jesu, dulcis memoria" (Jesus, the very thought of you) is the opening line of an extended poem attributed to the great Cistercian Abbot Bernard of Clairvaux (1091–1153).[2]

This kind of piety resulted in what Abbot Gabriel Braso called a "decadence of liturgical spirituality."[3] Instead of providing the basis for personal devotion, the liturgy

---

[1] On the reforms of Benedict of Aniane, the "second founder" of Western monasticism, of Hildebrand, of Cluny and the Cistercians, and the Canons Regular see Herbert B. Workman, *The Evolution of the Monastic Ideal*, with a new forward by David Knowles, O.S.B. (Boston: Beacon Press, 1962), 219ff.

[2] Three hymns in *Lutheran Book of Worship* are derived from this poem: 316, 356, 537.

[3] Gabriel M. Braso, *Liturgy and Spirituality*, op. cit., 39.

was placed in the service of personal devotion. Devotional elements intruded into liturgical orders and texts, especially in the forms of tropes and secret prayers, which sometimes resulted in the breakdown of liturgical structure. Liturgy was performed for devotional purposes rather than as an action of the whole people of God engaged in their public work. Different groups cultivated their own forms of devotion, including clergy, convent communities, and the laity. The laity themselves were divided according to economic class even in their involvement in the liturgy. Each group had its own niche in the worship space; nobility, trade guilds, and peasants or the urban proletariat each had their own place in the church building. The great Romanesque and Gothic church buildings that dominate the medieval landscape reflected this liturgical development. They are among the highest expressions of the Gothic culture now "come of age." They are also a pristine example of the architectural motto that "form should follow function." But the function they were forming was the scattering of the congregation into various subunits and the diffusion of liturgical expression into a multitude of masses often being celebrated simultaneously, but not communally, at side altars in numerous chapels.

This period in Western liturgical history is very important because it fostered a spirituality that remained more or less intact until the liturgical movement of the twentieth century. As the lay people were systematically excluded from overt participation in the liturgy of the church, they ceased to cultivate a liturgical spirituality, a way of conceiving and expressing a relationship to God taught by the liturgy. It is not surprising that by the end of the Middle Ages people turned to paraliturgical forms to express their devotion to God. This chapter documents the slow but inexorable deteriorization of solid liturgical piety.

🍇 ROMANESQUE AND GOTHIC CHURCH BUILDINGS

Economic life in western Europe began to flourish in the eleventh century and reached a climax in the twelfth and thirteenth centuries. Agriculture was stimulated by new methods of farming. Roads were improved and rivers were used for transportation. Trade flourished, leading to the development of market towns and then cities. Wealth was therefore spread throughout society and was no longer concentrated in the hands of the landed nobility. Wealth needs an outlet, and one of these was the erection of great church buildings in the towns and monasteries. Indeed, there was often competition between towns in the building of great cathedrals (e.g., York versus Canterbury) or to become the site of a cathedral (e.g., Wells versus Bath).

The memory of the Roman-styled basilicas from Christian antiquity was by no means blotted out during the early Middle Ages. There was, in fact, a revival of such buildings in the Carolingian Renaissance of the ninth century. In architecture, as in liturgy and law, Charlemagne made his architects study the churches and palaces of Rome and Ravenna (the last imperial capital in the West). These buildings were copied in the new emperor's capital at Aachen, and spoils from Italy were deposited in them. The most important surviving Carolingian building is the Royal Chapel, which was consecrated in 805. It is a domed octagon with vaulted aisles and galleries on two levels, similar to Saint Vitale in Ravenna.[4]

The floor plans of early medieval church buildings followed those of the ancient basilicas: a central nave leading to an apse or a choir, with side aisles. The major difference is that the altar was pushed farther into the apse, sometimes butting up against the east wall, in order to accommodate a choir section in which monks or canons could gather to sing the divine office. In cathedrals this also displaced the bishop's throne to the side. Thus, the defining liturgical characteristic of the basilican plan—the centrality of the bishop's chair with the surrounding benches of the presbyters—was lost in the medieval churches.

The buildings of the tenth and eleventh centuries are called "Romanesque" to indicate their stylistic dependence on the Roman basilica.[5] The earliest appearance of this architectural style was in northern Italy where the new concepts were first employed in the basilica of Sant'Ambrogio in Milan, which was begun in the tenth century and completed in the eleventh. In England this architecture is called "Norman" after the Norman conquerors who brought the style with them from Normandy, where the most influential architectural model was the Cathedral at Durham.[6]

In typical Romanesque architecture, the classical columns of the Roman basilicas gave way to massive piers supporting rounded stone arches. There are few decorations and very small windows, giving the impression of a medieval fortress (which, indeed, the church sometimes was). The cathedral at Worms in Germany, built c. 1182–1234, actually has four massive towers, one at each corner. What added to the massiveness of the walls and columns was the concern to build stone roofs. The timber roofs over the old basilicas, it was thought, lacked dignity and could easily be destroyed by fire. But the Roman art of vaulting such large buildings demanded a technical knowledge that had largely been lost. As a result, the eleventh and twelfth centuries became times of ceaseless experimentation. It was no easy matter to span the whole breadth of the main nave by a vault. The solution was to bridge the two walls as a river would be bridged by stone arches. In order to accomplish this, tremendous pillars were erected on both sides to carry the weight of those arches. In time, architects discovered that the roof did not need to be so heavy. It was sufficient to have firm arches spanning the distance and to fill in the intervals with lighter material. It was further discovered that the easiest way to fill in sections was to have the bridges or ribs crisscross between the arches, and then to fill in the triangular sections. The innovation of a ribbed vault in stone was achieved in the Durham Cathedral early in the twelfth century on a larger scale than had been seen before.[7]

In France, Romanesque churches began to be decorated with sculptures. The porches and doorways were used especially to portray theological ideas, such as Christ

---

[4] See Gloria Fossi, "Carolingian and Ottonian Art," in *The History of Art*, op. cit., 180.

[5] The term was first employed in 1818 by the French historian M. de Gerville.

[6] See David L. Edwards, *The Cathedrals of Britain* (Wilton, CT: Morehouse Publishing, 1989), 88ff.

[7] See Italo Furian, "Romanesque Art," in *The History of Art*, 186.

the Pantocrator surrounded by symbols of the four evangelists (an angel for Matthew, a lion for Mark, an ox for Luke, and an eagle for John, based on a vision in Ezek. 1:4-12) as carved on the façade of Saint Trophime at Arles. The walls of many small village churches, which could not afford sculptures, were painted with pictures depicting biblical scenes. A wonderfully restored example of this folk art is seen in the Vendel Church in the Swedish province of Uppland. This church was completed during King Birger Magnusson's time, consecrated in 1310 by Archbishop Nils Allesson, and painted after 1451 by Johannes Iwan.

The Romanesque style was actually short-lived. A new idea was born in northern France, in the construction of the new Abbey church of Saint-Denis under Abbot Suger, that made all the Romanesque churches look clumsy. Suger was chaplain to the king of France, and the Benedictine Monastery of Saint-Denis was already a regal establishment. Suger decided to rebuild the west front of the church so that it would be more imposing. Then, between 1140 and 1160, he had the choir rebuilt using the revolutionary architectural concepts that had already been experimented with at Sens (1130–1140). It was recognized that a big building did not need thick walls with tiny windows, provided the weight of the arches and rib-vaulting was distributed precisely on a load-bearing skeleton. The rest of the building could be light stonework and glass. It was further discovered that pointed arches helped to support themselves more than rounded arches did. Moreover, pointed arches allowed for greater height. These still required support, but then it was discovered that the vaulting of a nave by means of crisscross girders required less massive pillars if there were other means of buttressing the arches and vaulting, the weight of which pushed outward as well as downward. As one would do in erecting scaffolding, builders introduced flying buttresses on the outside of the buildings. This made heavy stone pillars unnecessary. More space between the pillars could be filled in with larger windows, which gave a lightness and a brightness to the new buildings that the old Romanesque buildings lacked. The windows could be filled with stained glass, which could tell the biblical stories or employ the theological symbols that were previously painted on the walls.[8]

Once this architectural concept was established, it spread quickly and universally throughout Europe—but beginning in the Île de France, which had not been greatly affected by or committed to the preceding Romanesque style (and perhaps also because, under Abbot Suger's influence, the new Gothic style was supported by the French monarchy). No one building reflects perfectly the French Gothic style, but there are several striking examples. Chartres (1194) is probably the most splendid in all its details of design, Reims (1210) is the most imposing, and Amiens (1220) is the most majestic in the dignity of its lines.[9] German church buildings also aspired to height (see the Gothic cathedrals at Cologne and Ulm); notwithstanding the French-influenced Westminster Abbey, the English preferred length to height.

---

[8] For an imaginative evocation of the excitement of these new ideas see the historical novel by Ken Follet, *Pillars of the Earth* (New York: William Morrow and Company, 1989).

[9] See Richard Fremantle, "Gothic Art," *The History of Art*, 202ff.

The Gothic church was arguably the highest artistic expression of the Gothic Age. It spoke of a new and exciting time in the history of western Europe. As E. H. Gombrich has written, the older Romanesque churches "in their strength and power may have conveyed something of the 'church militant' that offered shelter against the onslaught of evil. The new cathedrals gave the faithful a glimpse of a different world"—the church triumphant in the heavenly city. "The walls of these buildings were not cold and forbidding. They were formed of stained glass that shone like precious stone. The pillars, ribs and tracery were glistening with gold. Everything that was heavy, earthly, or humdrum was eliminated. The faithful who surrendered himself to the contemplation of all this beauty could feel that he had come nearer to understanding the mysteries of a realm beyond the reach of matter."[10] These comments reflect the inscription of Abbot Suger himself, who saw mystical meaning in the new style of architecture embodied in Saint-Denis, which he consecrated in 1140:

> Bright is the noble work; but being nobly bright, work
> Should brighten the minds, so that they may travel, through the true lights,
> To the True Light where Christ is the true door.[11]

If these new buildings pointed to heaven, it was nevertheless a heaven on earth. If their artwork drew the beholder beyond matter, it was accomplished by taking matter seriously. While the old Romanesque master at Arles made his figures of saints look like solid pillars firmly fitted into the architectural framework, the master artist who worked on the northern porch of the Gothic cathedral at Chartres made each figure come to life. They seem to move and look at each other and hint of a real body beneath their flowing robes. They are no longer stereotypes, but individuals whose personalities can be recognized. Indeed, one might recognize friends and neighbors in these stone figures.

Whether Romanesque or Gothic, the worship space was designed to facilitate the kind of liturgical, devotional, and public activity that was conducted in these buildings. That is to say, these churches were not built to provide atmosphere, but to accommodate the uses for which they were intended. The principle that "form follows function" can be clearly seen in medieval church buildings. They are all multi-roomed facilities because different kinds of activities occurred in different spaces. The church porch and the nave were gathering places for the laity for both sacred and secular purposes. Candidates for baptism were met on the church porch and there couples exchanged marital vows. Notices were often posted on the church doors and fairs could be held in the plazas in front of the church (often spilling into the nave itself). A pulpit for preaching was usually wrapped around one of the columns in the nave, around which people could gather to hear the speaker. (Pews were first added in the fourteenth century.) Sometimes an altar was placed at the head of the aisle in the nave, in front of the choir screen, to facilitate the communion of the people on great feast days. However, the high altar was probably not easily seen from the nave. A choir screen was located between the nave and the chancel

---

[10] E. H. Gombrick, *The Story of Art*, op. cit., 134.

[11] *De Administratione* XXVII–XXVIII, trans. by Erwin Panofsky, *Abbot Suger on the Abbey Church of St. Denis and Its Art Treasures*, 2nd ed. (Princeton: Princeton University Press, 1979), 47.

to keep conventual communities, collegiate choirs, or cathedral canons from being distracted while singing the Divine Office. In conventual churches (abbeys, monasteries, convents) the choir section could be quite long. At the east end of the building, in the apse, was the high altar. However, in bays surrounding the nave, the chancel, and the apse were side chapels with altars so that several masses could be said simultaneously. These altars were necessitated by the proliferation of private votive masses, which led in turn to the need for more "mass-priests." But clericalization alone does not explain the compartmentalization of the medieval church building. Some side chapels were given over to noble families or trade guilds. Thus, the typical medieval abbey or cathedral church was a space with a number of self-contained compartments that did not so much gather the congregation as scattered it.[12]

The compartmentalization of churches contributed to the constant building of additions. Often construction began with the chancel or choir so that the divine services could be celebrated in buildings that took generations to build. Then transepts were added, which could become gathering places for the laity; then the nave was extended. In some collegiate chapels, like Merton and Magdalene in Oxford, naves were never added to transepts because the number of noncollegians gathering for offices was not that great. More typically, college chapels were one long choir. Then side chapels were added on, including an often richly endowed "Lady chapel" in honor of the Virgin Mary appended to the apse.

Canterbury Cathedral is a striking example of a church building constructed and reconstructed over a long period of time. From about 595 Canterbury in Kent was the seat of an archbishop—that is, the first or primatial diocese in a missionary territory. Pope Gregory the Great had dispatched Augustine and a band of Benedictine monks to Britain to evangelize and replant Christianity in this former Roman colony. As the first archbishop of Canterbury, Augustine dedicated the first cathedral to Christ about five years after baptizing Ethelbert, king of Kent, in 597. That cathedral was enlarged in the eighth century. After a convenient fire, a larger one was built by the Normans under Archbishop Lanfranc, who apparently modeled it after the great church of Saint Etienne in Caen, where he had been abbot. The dimensions of the nave were the same as Canterbury's present nave. The northwest tower survived until 1834, when it was demolished in order to build a duplicate of the fifteenth-century southwest tower. The east end of Lanfranc's church was pulled down by his successor, Anselm, in order to build a more spacious choir. A crypt under the choir was begun in 1096. A fire in 1174 made possible the construction of the cathedral as it is known today. The master mason, William of Sens, was put in charge of construction; and he imported stone from Caen in France. He also built in the newer, lighter style that had been experimented with in his hometown, carrying this early Gothic design further. However, in order to preserve Norman chapels, he

---

[12] See James F. White, *Protestant Worship and Church Architecture* (New York: Oxford University Press, 1964), chapter 3.

needed to conserve the old Norman walls along the side aisles, which gave the east end of the cathedral a shape like a wasp's. When William of Sens was incapacitated by a fall from scaffolding, the work was handed over to William the Englishman, who proved to be as innovative as the Frenchman. He raised the east end of the apse by sixteen feet to make way for a new crypt. Here the Trinity Chapel, in the apse of the cathedral, led into the final chapel, which served as the *corona* (crown) of the cathedral. The large stained glass windows, which admitted much light into the chapel, were supported by outside flying buttresses, which had not before been seen in England. The windows in the corona of Canterbury compare with those of Chartres, from where the original glass probably came. The tomb of the martyr-archbishop, Thomas à Becket, was relocated from the crypt to an ornate tomb in the just-finished Trinity Chapel in order to accommodate the hordes of pilgrims who were journeying to Canterbury to visit the site of the saint. An additional hall was built to receive upper-class pilgrims, and a covered walkway was built in 1390 to shelter the more privileged pilgrims on their way to better lodgings. The old central tower of the cathedral was demolished in 1430, and its replacement (the present-day "Bell Harry" tower) had to wait another sixty years to be built. Building the tower required the addition of large stone girders at the crossing of the nave and the transepts to augment the ability of the piers to hold the weight. An outstanding example of this kind of structure are the scissor arches or strainer girders in Wells Cathedral. The architect who built the 235-foot tower was John Wastell, who also achieved another masterpiece in the vaulting of King's College Chapel in Cambridge. The history of Canterbury Cathedral certainly continues on through the Reformation and into modern times, when it became the "mother church" of the worldwide Anglican communion. But this sketch is enough to indicate how such a building is a living structure, constantly undergoing change. Part of that evolution, and actually necessitating it, was the need to accommodate a variety of uses for different liturgical, devotional, and public purposes. Christ Church Cathedral at Canterbury was at once a monastic church, a seat of an archbishop, and a pilgrim church.[13]

Not all churches were abbeys, cathedrals, or pilgrimage sites. But even the most modest parish church had at least two rooms: a nave and chancel. And by the fifteenth century, many of these had become complex structures. To the nave were added chapels and a porch and a tower. The chancel had been extended so that it was about two-thirds the length of the nave. The nave provided the gathering place for the people and the chancel provided the worship space for the clergy. The chancel was separated from the nave by a rood screen, so called because a crucifix or a rood adorned the top of the screen. This crucifix often had figures of the Virgin Mary and John the Apostle on either side of it. The rood was often the most visible object in the late medieval parish church. The rood screen played the role of providing some measure of privacy to the clergy for the purpose of praying the office or reciting private masses. The high altar was actually obscured from

---

[13] See A. E. Henderson, *Canterbury Cathedral, Then and Now* (London: S.P.C.K., 1938).

the view of the laity and the only action of the mass that they might see was the elevation of the host at the eucharistic consecration, accompanied by the ringing of bells and genuflection. This dramatic action was mandated by rubrics after 1200 as a way of reconnecting the people with the eucharist at the moment of consecration.[14]

In these developments we see two simultaneous tendencies in medieval liturgical evolution: on the one hand the tendency to exclude people from the central action of the liturgy (they were outside the choir and had only a partial view of the high altar), and, on the other hand, the pastoral desire to draw people into the central action of the liturgy by dramatic gestures. Dramatic gestures included not just ceremonies in the mass, but commentaries inserted into the texts, narrative elements in liturgical songs, and finally drama itself.

🍇 TROPES, SEQUENCES, AND LITURGICAL DRAMAS

The Gothic Age saw the development and refinement of musical arts in the West as well as that of architecture and the plastic arts. There was a musical development in western Europe that was unparalleled elsewhere: several voices singing simultaneously, resulting in polyphony, and generating, as a consequence, the development of harmony. The earliest form of polyphony is having two voices singing the same melody simultaneously, separated by an interval of a fourth or fifth. This is called "organum." Sometimes the polyphony consisted of a sustaining tone while a florid melody was sung above it. Slowly this accustomed ears to intervals of a second, third, and sixth as Western music pressed toward a harmonic organization by thirds and the development of the major and minor scales to largely replace the old church modes.[15] This was a development that stretched out over centuries. It required the training of singers, which could be done in monastery, cathedral, and collegiate choir schools.

Professional singers and choirs look for challenges, so in addition to the development of polyphony, we find the amplification of music and texts in the form of tropes. In late Latin *tropare* means "to sing" and a *tropus* is a song. More specifically a trope became an addition to the music or text or both of an official text. The earliest examples of this would be the wordless *jubilus* of the Alleluia about which Augustine speaks. This was the use of a florid melody to express the jubilation of the Alleluia. It was not long before the affective devotion of the Middle Ages inspired the addition of words to liturgical texts, as, for example, in the Kyrie, "Lord, omnipotent Father, God, creator of all, have mercy on us." While Kyrie tropes such as this were the most common tropes, all parts of the mass except graduals and tracts, and all parts of the office except the psalms could be troped.[16] Here is an example of a troped Gloria. The italicized words are troped expansions of the text.

---

[14] See G. H. Cook, *The English Mediaeval Parish Church* (London: Phoenix House, 1954).

[15] Examples of early polyphony may be seen in Archibald T. Davidson and Willi Apel, eds., *Historical Anthology of Music* (Cambridge: Harvard University Press, 1950), Vol. 1.

[16] An important edition of tropes is P. Evans, *The Early Trope Repertory of St. Martial de Limoges* (Princeton: Princeton University Press, 1970).

> Gloria in excelsis Deo, *cuius reboat in omni gloria mundo*. Et in terra pax, *pax perennis*. Hominibus bonae voluntatis, *Qui Deum timent in veritate*.

Even scripture readings could be interspersed with commentary, which was a form of troping. Thus, an epistle reading for the Feast of the Holy Innocents begins this way:

> Lectio libri Apocalipsis Johannis apostoli, *Qui testimonium perhibet de his*. In diebus illis, Ecce ego Iohannes Vidi supra montem Sion Agnum stantem, *qui tollit peccata mundi*, Et cum eo centum quadraginta quatuor millia . . .

The better known tropes have even given their names to the masses, usually from the Kyries; thus: "Missa orbis factor" or "Kyrie Fons bonitatis." The result was a burdening of the liturgy, obscuring its basic shape and confusing its direction.

A sequence was a special kind of trope associated with the troping of the alleluias. From the Latin *sequor* (to follow), a *sequentia* was a text (called *prosa* in France) that followed the Alleluia. How this practice developed is a matter of debate. One theory is that the addition of words to the melismatic alleluias made the memorization of the notes easier. The earliest descriptions of the sequence are found in the *Liber Hymnorum* of Notker Balbulus (c. 850). He describes how a monk who fled from a monastery near Rouen, when it was destroyed by the Normans, brought to Saint Gallen an antiphonary in which words had been set to a previously wordless sequentia. Notker felt he could do better; his *Liber*, which is well preserved in manuscripts of the tenth and eleventh centuries, contains forty such sequences, some to existing melodies, others to new ones.

The standard sequence pattern has two strophes sung to the same melodic segment, which is repeated; the first and last strophes are exceptions, and do not have parallels. This pattern can be illustrated thus: a bb cc dd ee ff g. This pattern is plainly evident in the most celebrated sequence, "Victimae paschali laudes" (Praises to the paschal victim), ascribed to Wipo, chaplain to the Emperor Henry III in the first half of the eleventh century. Its popularity is evident in that adaptations of the text and tune came into Lutheran hymnody through Luther's hymn, "Christ lag in Todesbanden," and in the organ chorales, preludes, motets, and cantatas based on this sequence, culminating in the cantata by J. S. Bach of this name.[17]

Hundreds of sequences were produced all over western Europe from the eleventh to the thirteenth centuries and even later. Popular sequences were imitated and adapted to secular tunes; and, indeed, sometimes a secular tune, such as a carol, made its way into the sequence. Sacramentaries and missals included tropes and sequences as parts of the mass-liturgies. Among the liturgical reforms initiated after the Council of Trent were the abolition of tropes and sequences from the official liturgical books. Only four sequences survived Tridentine reform: "Victimae paschali laudes" at Easter; "Veni, Sancte Spiritus" (Come, Holy Spirit) on Pentecost; "Lauda Sion" (Zion, praise), by Thomas Aquinas, for the Feast of Corpus Christi; and the "Dies irae" (Day of wrath) for funeral or requiem masses. A fifth sequence, "Stabat Mater" (By the Cross the Mother

---

[17] *LBW* 137 is a translation of the *Victimae paschali* sequence. The carol, "Christ is arisen," c. 1100 (*LBW* 136) is based on the tune of the sequence, as is Luther's hymn "Christ Jesus lay in death's strong bands" (*LBW* 134).

Standing), ascribed to the thirteenth-century Franciscan monk Jacopo da Todi, was officially added in 1727.

In all of these surviving sequences, it is apparent that a feeling for dramatic expression came into the liturgy (and into music) after the eleventh century. Just as the great dramas of ancient Greece had grown out of religious rites, so Western drama grew out of liturgical rites—the tropes and sequences, to be exact. The earliest of the Saint Martial codices, Bibl. Nat. lat. 1140, c. 900, contains an Easter mass trope of tremendous importance, "Quem queritis in sepulchro, O Christicole?" This is a dialogue between the angel at the empty tomb and the three Marys:

> Whom do you seek at the sepulchre, O followers of Christ?
> Jesus of Nazareth who was crucified, O heavenly one.
> He is not here, he is risen as he foretold; go and tell that he is risen, saying:
> Alleluia, the Lord is risen today, the strong lion, Christ the son of God. Thanks
>   be to God. Sing "eia."
> Come and see the place where the Lord was laid. Alleluia. Alleluia.
> Go quickly and tell the disciples that the Lord is risen. Alleluia. Alleluia.
> The Lord is risen from the sepulchre, who hung for us on the cross. Alleluia.

Then follows the cue, "Resurrexi," from the Introit for the mass: "Resurrexi, et adhuc tecum sum." There is no doubt that the trope was sung antiphonally before the beginning of the mass. Within half a century it was moved from this place to Easter Matins, and was not only sung but was acted out dramatically. This was done first at Fleury-sur-Loire and Ghent, and then was taken to Winchester where, in the *Concordia Regularis* issued by Ethelwald, Bishop of Winchester (c. 970), we have not only the text and musical notes but also the "stage directions." The directions indicate that one monk, dressed in white and carrying a palm, enters the chancel unobtrusively during the third lesson and sits by the "sepulchre." During the third responsory, three other monks, dressed in copes and bearing censers, appear to search for something, enter the "sepulchre" and approach the "angel." The dialogue then begins. When the "angel" sings "Venite et videte locum," he shows the "women" the cloth in which the Lord had been wrapped on Good Friday. They, in turn, putting down their censers, show it to the other clergy. When they sing "Surrexit Dominus," they lay the cloth on the altar, at which point the prior begins the Te Deum Laudamus and "all the bells chime out together." The purpose of this little play, according to Bishop Ethelwald, was "to fortify the unlearned people in their faith."[18]

This Easter play became extremely popular and was duplicated all over Europe, sometimes with dramatic embellishments. Not surprisingly, other plays were developed for other festivals in the church year. In fact, two Saint Martial codices, Bibl. Nat. lat. 903 and 1084, have tropes beginning "Quem queritis in presepe, pastores?" (Whom do you seek in the manger, shepherds?).[19] This led to Epiphany plays with even greater dramatic elements based on King Herod, which were finally taken outside of the church building

---

[18] A complete translation of the Latin text is in E. K. Chambers, *The Mediaeval Stage* (London, 1903), II, 6. See also Gustave Reese, *Music in the Middle Ages* (London, 1941), 194.

[19] See LBW 68, "He Whom Shepherds Once Came Praising," for a hymn version of the *Quem pastores.*

itself and were no longer liturgical plays but religious plays.[20] Thus, an interest in liturgical drama entered the Western liturgy that even the Reformation was not able to eschew. Indeed, nativity and passion plays became popular in seventeenth-century Catholicism and Lutheranism[21] and, in spite of Puritan suppression, have returned with new force in American Protestantism.

🍇 PRIVATE PRAYERS IN PUBLIC CELEBRATIONS

Sequences and tropes were not the only textual insertions that stretched the shape of the liturgy. During the Carolingian era private prayers to be said by the priest were inserted to cover the actions of the priest while vesting, approaching the altar, at the offertory, during the singing of the Sanctus by the choir, and before and after receiving communion. The previous chapter cited the private communion prayers in the Sacramentary of Amiens. Similar prayers were included in the Prayerbook of Charles the Bald (d. 877), which were then incorporated into other sacramentaries such as those of Tours, Fulda, and Chartres.[22]

The fact that these prayers were for the use of the priest shows the relationship between the priest and the eucharist that was emerging in the ninth century, and that had an impact on the developing views of ordination The relationship of priestly power to the eucharistic sacrifice will be considered in the next chapter. Here it is worth to noting the efforts to preserve the communal character of the mass, such as those of Archbishop Herardus of Tours, who instructed his priests that they "should not begin the secret prayer (i.e., the canon) until the Sanctus is finished; rather, they should sing the Sanctus with the people."[23] However, the Sacramentary of Amiens reflects more the emerging pattern: "While the Sanctus is slowly being sung, the priest quickly leaves off his singing, and says [this] prayer: God, you desire not the death of sinners but their repentance; in your great pity, do not reject me, a weak and miserable sinner."[24]

The architectural setting of worship in the High Middle Ages reflects the liturgical reality in its scattering of the people. The priest was separated from the choir, engaged in his private devotions while the choir was singing extended chants of the mass. The choir was separated from the people who, as shall be seen, were also engaged in their own devotions while mass was being offered. Thus, all were gathered in separate spaces within one building, separately pursuing their own devotions. The notion of liturgy as a communal public work was becoming very tenuous indeed.

---

[20] See W. L. Smoldon, *The Music Drama of the Medieval Church* (London, 1980). Smoldon has transcribed several of the plays into modern rhythmic values: see *Officium pastorum*, *Peregrinus*, *The Play of Herod*, *Sponsus*, and *Visitatio sepulchri* (London, 1964–1972).

[21] See the description of Christmas Vespers in Moser's *Die evangelische Kirchenmusik in volkstümlichem Überblick* (Stuttgart, 1926), trans. into English in Theodore Graebner, *The Borderland of Right and Wrong* (St. Louis: Concordia Publishing House, 1945), and incorporated into Carl Halter and Carl Schalk, eds., *A Handbook of Church Music* (St. Louis: Concordia Publishing House, 1978), 66–8.

[22] See A. Wilmart, "Preces pour la Communion," *Ephemerides Liturgicae* 43 (1929), 320–8.

[23] Cited in Thomas F. Simmons, ed., *The Lay Folks Mass Book*, Early English Text Society, 71 (London, 1899), xxiv.

[24] Cited in V. Leroquais, "L'Ordo Missae du sacramentaire d'Amiens," *Ephemerides Liturgicae* 41 (1927), 442.

❧ THE EMERGENCE OF THE PRIVATE MASS

It was one thing for the devotional prayers of the priest to be inserted into the public celebration; it was something else to privatize what should be celebrated by the whole community. Since early days the eucharist had been celebrated in less than public places (e.g., private homes at sickbeds and deathbeds, cemeteries, etc.). The ordination of monks also introduced the celebration of mass in monasteries with religious communities in attendance rather than the whole body of the church. But the strongest source of the development of the private mass was, according to Jungmann, "the desire of the faithful for Votive Masses; that is to say, for Masses which took care of their earnest concerns (*vota*), not the least important of which was regard for the dead."[25]

The concept of the votive mass goes back to the fourth century. Masses in memory of the faithful departed were celebrated on the seventh and thirtieth days after death. By the sixth century, priests were celebrating series of masses for the repose of the souls of the dead. By the ninth century, it was common to have priests celebrating two or three masses per day. By the thirteenth century, a new increase in the number of masses can be attributed to the sheer growth of the number of clergy in the monasteries, universities, and cities. No church could make do with only one altar; churches with thirty-five to forty-five side altars were not uncommon. In Romanesque churches a series of side chapels surrounded the chancel; in Gothic churches the use of buttresses as part of the inner structure produced a number of altar-niches in the aisles of the nave.[26]

The most extreme form of the private mass was celebrated in the eighth and ninth centuries: the so-called *missa solitaria*, without even a server in attendance. Jungmann notes the number of mass formularies from this period that are written in the first person singular. But in the ninth century new legislation was aimed at stopping priests from celebrating alone. The concern was that someone would have to be present to respond to the dialogues and versicles of the mass. For example, someone must respond to "Dominus vobiscum" or "Sursum corda" or utter the "Amens" to the prayers to which the Oremus invites. This did not have to be a serving deacon or acolyte. It had to be anyone who could maintain the corporate character of the mass—someone who could respond to "Dominus vobiscum" with "Et cum spiritu tuo." Only in the course of time did this representative of the whole people of God become a cleric. This was a consequence of legislation that, beginning in the thirteenth century, specified that "no priest may presume to celebrate mass without a cleric responding" (Synod of Trier, 1227, Canon 8).[27]

Various rubrics in the thirteenth century specify the obvious: that the priest should read the sung portions rather than sing them. If the celebrant speaks his words, the servers in attendance would also speak their dialogical responses. Thus, out of the private mass grew the spoken liturgy—what has come to be called the low mass. It cannot be emphasized too strongly that this was an utter liturgical novelty. In the first ten or eleven centuries of Christian liturgy a worship service without singing was inconceivable.

---

[25] Jungmann, *The Mass of the Roman Rite*, op. cit., I, 217.

[26] Ibid., 224.

[27] Ibid., 227.

"Psalms, hymns, and spiritual songs" are taken for granted already in the New Testament as standard ingredients in Christian worship (Col. 3:16). Music is employed to reinforce the corporate character of liturgy as well as to inject an element of ecstasy into the celebration. The distinction between the high mass and the low mass was the inclusion or exclusion of singing. Nevertheless, it happened that the low mass or spoken liturgy also came to be used when the congregation was present. Thus the style of the private mass replaced the public mass as the normal form of celebration. It is the origin of the practice of spoken masses in the Roman Catholic Church and the loss of the practice of solemn celebrations in the Western church generally.

EUCHARISTIC WORSHIP OUTSIDE OF THE MASS

Even though masses were being celebrated virtually every hour of every day, the faithful were no longer receiving communion. Various ascetical practices, such as fasting and abstinence, and disciplinary fencing of the table by means of the requirement of confession and absolution, had so discouraged the faithful from receiving communion that the Fourth Lateran Council (1215) had to decree that the faithful must receive communion at least once a year at Easter, after first going to confession. In this same period eucharistic devotion spawned the development of a eucharistic cult outside of the mass. Nathan Mitchell delineates its four principal categories as follows:

> Devotional visits to the reserved sacrament;
> Processions in which the sacrament, concealed in a container or exposed to
> public view, was carried about;
> Exposition of the sacrament to the gaze of the faithful;
> Benediction, in which a solemn blessing with the eucharistic bread was
> imparted to the people, often at the conclusion of a procession or a period
> of exposition.[28]

The idea of reserving the consecrated eucharist for the communion of the sick or dying goes back at least to the second and third centuries.[29] Justin Martyr relates in his *First Apology* 67 that the deacons took the consecrated elements to the absent after the celebration. The first textual reference to the Viaticum, that is, taking the sacrament to the dying, comes from Bishop Dionysius of Alexandria (247–264). Obviously, having the sacrament in readiness for this purpose required that it be kept in some convenient place. Places of reservation in the early church would have been private homes (Tertullian is the first witness to this). Once public basilicas were built for Christian worship, a special room such as a sacristy could be built in which to store vessels and elements. On special days, communion could be received after mass in the sacristy. In the twelfth century it was customary for the Archbishop of Milan and his clergy to receive communion in the sacristy at the end of the Good Friday liturgy, in which the eucharist was not celebrated.[30]

---

[28] Nathan Mitchell, O.S.B., *Cult and Controversy: The Worship of the Eucharist Outside Mass* (New York: Pueblo Publishing Co., 1981), 163.

[29] See Archdale A. King, *Eucharistic Reservation in the Western Church* (New York: Sheed and Ward, 1964).

[30] Ibid., 60.

In the eucharistic devotion of the thirteenth century, in which the elevation of the host and chalice at the words of institution, accompanied by the ringing of bells and genuflection, became the high point of the mass, the desire to see the visible part of the sacrament intensified. This led people to the place of eucharistic reservation and to provision of devotional prayers addressed to the Blessed Sacrament.

The popularity of visiting the place of reservation led to reserving the eucharist not in the sacristy but on or near the high altar. When reserved in the sacristy, the eucharist might be placed in a special cupboard or recess in the wall called an aumbry. Wall tabernacles abound in Italy from the thirteenth century, although not until the sixteenth were they erected on altar itself. When reserved on the altar, the eucharist could be placed in a standing pyx. Or, it could be suspended above the altar in a hanging pyx. The hanging pyx was common in England and France throughout the middle ages. In Germany and the Low Countries, a sacrament house, often sculptured in the form of a monumental Gothic tower, was located to the side of the altar. It had the advantage of allowing the people to gaze at the reserved host through a door of metal lattice work, which facilitated the adoration of the Blessed Sacrament outside of the eucharistic celebration.

The next step was to carry the sacrament in procession. Various items came to be carried in the Palm Sunday procession, and Lanfranc of Canterbury is a witness that the eucharist was one of them. This became popular in England, and the fifteenth-century Sarum Missal stated that during the procession with palms "a bier be prepared containing the relics, together with the Body of Christ suspended in a pyx."[31]

The most popular procession with the Blessed Sacrament was on the Feast of Corpus Christi. Nathan Mitchell locates the background of this festival in the changing social conditions of the thirteenth century.[32] An important economic shift was taking place in the transition from a largely agrarian culture centered on the feudal estate to an urban and industrial culture centered in towns. Perhaps as a result of the profound socio-economic changes, producing such undesirable consequences as unemployment and vagabonds, social mobility and lack of the security of a recognized place, Europe experienced the emergence of dissenting groups such as the Cathari, which disseminated anti-clerical and anti-sacramental ideas among the people. In reaction to the antisacramental enthusiasts, there were proposals for the reform of clerical life, the simplification of Christian life, but also a devotion to the Blessed Sacrament. The Franciscans were one of these reforming groups; another was the Beguines in Liege. Lambert le Begue, in the late twelfth century, reputedly organized a way of life for "holy women" at his church whose devotion centered on the eucharist and the passion of Christ. In such an atmosphere, Juliana of Liege (1193–1258), abbess of the Augustinian canonesses of Mount Cornillon, promoted devotion to the Blessed Sacrament with the proposal of a Feast of Corpus Christi. This was really a celebration of the Octave of Maundy Thursday delayed until the Thursday after Trinity Sunday because of the intervening Easter season. The idea of the

---

[31] *Processionale ad usum insignis ac praeclarae ecclesiae Sarum*, ed. F. H. Dickinson (Leeds, 1882; reprinted Gregg International Publishers, 1969), 49.
[32] Mitchell, 172ff.

festival was championed by Jacques Panteleon, canon of Saint Lambert and archdeacon of Liege. Later, as Pope Urban IV, his bull *Transiturus* officially approved the feast for celebration by the universal church (although it had first spread on the merits of its own popularity to other cities and monasteries).[33]

The most popular feature of the Corpus Christi feast was the procession with the Blessed Sacrament. As Mitchell points out, the background for this and other processions with the sacrament lies in the practice of eucharistic exposition.[34] Before the twelfth century the only point at which the people were invited to gaze at the eucharist was just before communion when the priest lifted up the bread and cup and said, in the Eastern liturgies, "Holy things for the holy people" or, in the Western liturgy, "Behold the Lamb of God, who takes away the sins of the world." With the introduction of the eucharistic elevation around 1200 the people were also invited to gaze at the eucharist in conjunction with the consecration. This became very popular and church leaders often complained that people dashed from church to church in an effort to witness the miracle of transubstantiation several times a day. Admittedly not an unbiased witness, Thomas Cranmer, the Reformation archbishop of Canterbury, wrote:

> What made the people to run from their seats to the altar, and from altar to altar, and from sacring [as they called it] to sacring, peeping, tooting and gazing at that thing which the priest held up in his hands, if they thought not to honour the thing which they saw? What moved the priests to lift up the sacrament so high over their heads? Or the people to say to the priest "Hold up! Hold up!"; or one man to say to another "Stoop down before"; or to say "This day have I seen my Maker"; and "I cannot be quiet except I see my Maker once a day"? What was the cause of all these, and that as well the priest and the people so devoutly did knock and kneel at every sight of the sacrament, but that they worshipped that visible thing which they saw with their eyes and took it for very God?[35]

If the hierarchy complained about devotional excess, local conditions fostered it. Priests were known to receive larger stipends for holding up the host longer at the elevation. Choir doors in monastic churches were opened at the consecration so that the faithful could see the host when it was elevated. In some places a dark curtain was erected behind the altar so that the white host could be seen in clearer relief. In dark churches a candle was held aloft so that people could better see the host. From about the thirteenth century, apparently first practiced in Cologne, a bell was rung to signal the people's attention that the consecration was taking place.[36]

The stage was therefore set for the further exposure of the sacrament in the Corpus Christi procession. In his papal bull, *Transiturus*, Urban IV expressed the desire to increase participation in the eucharist by means of this feast. Therefore he proposed

---

[33] See Ernest W. McDonnell, *The Beguines and Beghards in Medieval Culture* (Rutgers University Press, 1954), 306ff.

[34] Mitchell, 176ff.

[35] Thomas Cranmer, *A Defence of the True and Catholic Doctrine, etc.*, IV, 9; in H. Jenkyns, ed., *The Remains of Thomas Cranmer, D.D., Archbishop of Canterbury* (Oxford, 1833), 442. Words in brackets are in cited source.

[36] Jungmann, *The Mass of the Roman Rite*, II, 208f.

one hundred days indulgence to all who would attend Matins, mass, and Vespers on the Feast of Corpus Christi, and an additional forty days to all who assisted at the lesser hours. Not until 1316 did Pope John XXII make the procession obligatory. But it had been gaining in popularity before that time. The eucharist would be exposed in the monstrance all through the parade route of the procession.

It was not a large step from this to continuous exposition of the eucharist, for example, in a sacrament house, or Solemn Benediction of the Blessed Sacrament at the conclusion of Vespers during the singing of Marian hymns.[37] Solemn Benediction consisted of the blessing of the people at the end of a service with the host in the monstrance, as in earlier times they had been blessed with such objects as a cross or the relic of a saint. It was originally, therefore, a solemn way of dismissing worshipers. But in Baroque Catholicism it became a devotion in and of itself complete with kneeling or genuflection, incensation of the sacrament, and hymns of adoration addressed to the Christ present in the eucharist. Many of the faithful attended Sunday Vespers just to be present for Solemn Benediction.

Thus, we have seen a long and complicated process by which people were content to gaze at the sacrament rather than to eat or drink it. At the same time, however, there was a further disconnecting of the people from the eucharist by the withholding of the cup from lay communicants and the de facto excommunication of children.

First Communion Separated from Baptism

We have seen in the previous chapter the process by which the post-baptismal ceremonies of the episcopal laying on of hands and anointing became separated from baptism and came to be regarded as a separate sacrament of confirmation. This became one factor that led to the separation of first communion from baptism, and thus completed the disintegration of the rites of Christian initiation.

We have seen that the theologians of the church provided meanings for the separate sacrament of confirmation. Among the reasons given for such a rite were: (1) baptism is incomplete in itself. It is completed by receiving the seal of the Holy Spirit upon what was done earlier. (2) While we do receive the Spirit in baptism, confirmation strengthens the gift of the Spirit to equip us to do battle with sin. (3) While in baptism we receive the Spirit, in confirmation we receive special gifts of the Spirit to enable us to fulfill our ministry as members of the body of Christ.

If confirmation is this important, should not parents and godparents be compelled to present their children to the bishop for this sacrament? The Council of Lambeth in 1281 decreed that unconfirmed persons could not receive communion. The intention was not to keep people away from Holy Communion but rather to shore up confirmation by imposing a penalty of great magnitude if it were neglected. Of course, it was still possible for a bishop to preside at baptism, perform the anointing at that time, and administer communion to the infant immediately. In England this was done for royal children as late as the time of the birth of King Henry VIII's children, Elizabeth in 1533

---

[37] Mitchell, 182ff.

and Edward in 1537. But most children, by this time, were not communed until later when they made their first confession or were confirmed.[38]

The separation of first communion from baptism was the result of the decision to withhold from infant communicants the only element they could receive: the wine. Infants were not able to swallow the bread. Appealing to the doctrine of concomitance (that the whole Christ is received under either species), infants were given the wine only. Priests usually dipped their finger into the chalice and then place their finger in the infant's mouth and let them suck. As the doctrine of transubstantiation took hold, the administration of the cup became more of a practical problem in the case of adults. The priest could prevent the desecration of the bread by placing it directly upon the tongue of the communicant while an assistant held a vessel under the chin lest the priest accidentally drop the bread or the communicant involuntarily ejected it. But there was the danger that in administering the chalice some of the wine would be spilled or that it would drip down the chin or remain in a mustache or beard. Therefore it was deemed wise that only the celebrating priest should receive the wine.

Now again we see evidence of the tendency for a practice that begins for one set of reasons to be perpetuated for another set of reasons. What was intended as a practice in the case of adults (who could still receive the bread) came to be applied to infants also, even though the danger of desecration was negligible since the priest administered wine to them from his finger rather than from the chalice directly. Since the infants were not given the bread, the withdrawal of the wine from them resulted in de facto excommunication, if not until confirmation then at least until they could eat bread—and ultimately until they could make their first act of penance. For penance also had come to be regarded as a gateway to the eucharist and apart from confession communion was not to be given. This requirement was laid upon all who had reached an "age of discretion" (around age seven), which provided a rationale for ending the communion of infants and young children altogether.

CONTRITION, CONFESSION, AND ABSOLUTION

We have seen the emergence of the private form of penance in the Celtic monasteries of the early Middle Ages. Private penance caught on and became the ritual basis for further development of the sacrament of penance, to the neglect of public penance altogether. In the period of the ninth to eleventh centuries, preachers of the *contemptus mundi* (contempt for the world), including Nilus, Romuald, and Peter Damian, emphasized a dramatic and thoroughgoing conversion that stressed self-examination. By the twelfth century, Abelard, Anselm, and Hugh of Saint Victor emphasized the role of conscience, willful intention, and needful shame in the process of penance. These theologians of contrition, who highlighted a sense of responsibility for sin, were also, quite logically, philosophers of human liberty.[39]

---

[38] J. D. C. Fisher, *Christian Initiation: Baptism in the Medieval West*, op. cit., 101–8.

[39] See J. C. Payen, *Le Motif du repentir dans la littérature française médiévale (des origines à 1230)* (Geneva: Droz, 1968), 36–69.

Abelard especially must be singled out as one who moved the center of gravity in the penitential process from the exterior penalty toward interior contrition, thus contributing to the development of the field of modern psychology. Against Abelard stood the more traditionalist Bernard of Clairvaux, who also emphasized the role of salutary remorse in the penitent, but who also declared that the sinner is inexcusable and that ignorance does not diminish the offense.[40] But Peter Lombard, the master of *The Sentences*, followed in Abelard's footsteps by holding that contrition or remorse is, in fact, the moment of forgiveness. "From the moment that anyone with contrite heart professes to confess, God forgives, because confession of the heart if not of the lips is present, in virtue of which the soul is interiorly cleansed of the stain and contagion of sin committed, and the debt of eternal death is cancelled."[41]

By the twelfth century, however, the pendulum was swinging back from the interior disposition of the penitent to an outward act: that of making a confession of sins. The Cluniac monk, Pierre de Celle (d. 1183), onetime bishop of Chartres, said that tears are the bread of the repentant soul: they quench the fires of passion, smother vices, cleanse sins, soften the heart, spread good speech and action, disseminate virtues, and inspire God's mercy and benevolence.[42] This piety moved the center of gravity in penance from the attitude of contrition to the act of confession. Against the practice of tariff penance, in which the acts of satisfaction were deemed the most important feature, the idea was now promoted that the penitent's inherent shame and humiliation constituted expiation for sin. Under this teaching, absolution was given upon confession, with acts of satisfaction to follow if required by the confessor. The regular and frequent practice of confession led to an abandonment of the emphasis on contrition. While monks, clergy, and persons of cultivated religious sensibility might be able to develop a sense of contrition, anyone could, by an act of will, make a confession of sins. Thus the pendulum swung back from the interiorization of the penitential process to the outward ritual form, and the church once again had a penitential practice that could be recommended to all Christians. This was done, in fact, by the legislation of Canon 21 of the Fourth Lateran Council, in 1215, which imposed on the faithful a practice that was undoubtedly already being implemented in many places: an annual obligation to make a confession to the parish priest, particularly before receiving communion at Easter.[43] The opening portion of the decree is as follows:

> Every fideles of either sex shall after the attainment of years of discretion separately confess his sins with all fidelity to his own priest at least once in a year: and shall endeavor to fulfill the penance imposed upon him to the best of his ability, reverently receiving the sacrament of the Eucharist at least at Easter: unless it happen that by the counsel of his own priest for some reasonable cause, he hold that he should abstain for a time from the reception of the

---

[40] Ibid., 63–9.

[41] *Sent. Lib. Quat.*, IV, d. 17, c. 2; P.L. 192: 881.

[42] Payen, 38, n. 92.

[43] See P. M. Gy, "Le Précepte de la confession annuelle et la nécessité de la confession," *Revue des sciences philosophiques et théologiques* 73 (1979), 529–48.

sacrament: otherwise let him during life be repelled from entering the church, and when dead let him lack Christian burial.[44]

The decree of Lateran IV had the effect of aggrandizing the power of the priest, since he alone could give absolution, and also of emphasizing the role of absolution in the penitential process. When Thomas Aquinas inquired into the "form" and "matter" of the sacrament of penance, it was clear, on the basis of developed tradition, that the three parts of contrition, confession, and satisfaction constituted the "matter" but that absolution constituted the "form." It was also clear to Aquinas that the efficacy of the sacrament came from the form while the function of signifying the use of the sacrament came from the matter.[45]

Two developments in the practice and theology of penance paved the way for the evangelical use of the Office of the Keys: the opportunity for catechesis in the transactions of the confessional and the emphasis on absolution within an opus operatum view of sacramental efficacy.

The authority given to parish priests by the legislation of 1215 also gave them the opportunity to catechize in the course of interrogatory dialogue with the penitents. A whole genre of literature emerged in the form of confessors' handbooks and confession manuals. These didactic manuals taught priests how to administer penance and worshipers how to receive the sacrament of penance. Penitential doctrine and spiritual formation were provided within a framework that encompassed three phases in the sacramental act: the preparation of the penitent (e.g., through the use of exhortations), the articulation of the sinner's confession, and finally the consequences (the penances to be performed). The examination of conscience and the expression of confession was conducted through recourse to memorizable categories such as: the seven deadly sins, the Ten Commandments, the use of the five senses, and occasionally the twelve articles of the Creed.

The literature that developed to enable people to examine their consciences in preparation for confession made an important contribution to what Jean Delumeau described as "the emergence of a Western guilt culture."[46] Symptomatic of this is the great literary masterpiece of the Middle Ages, Dante's *Divine Comedy*, which portrays the provisional punishments of Purgatory and the definitive punishments of Hell as based on the sins resulting from Satanic temptations, and the rewards of Paradise for those who resisted such temptations. In a somewhat different vein, the final tale in *Canterbury Tales* (this one not always attributed to Chaucer) is a strongly didactic treatise on penance placed in the mouth of the village parson. The path of salvation, according to this tale, passes through penance, which resembles a tree in which the roots are contrition, the branches are confession, and the fruit is atonement, with the understanding that repentance involves not only deeds but intentions. "Contricion destroyeth the prison of helle,

---

[44] Trans. in Watkins, *A History of Penance*, op. cit., II, 748.

[45] IV *Sent.*, d. 22, q. 2, a. 1, sol. 2.

[46] Jean Delumeau, *Sin and Fear: The Emergence of a Western Guilt Culture, 13th–18th Centuries*, trans. by Eric Nicholson (New York: St. Martin's Press, 1990), 198ff.

and maketh the wayk and fieble alle the strengthes of the develes, and restoreth the yiftes of the Hooly Goost."[47]

While Thomas Aquinas tried to emphasize a single unitary operation in the sacrament of penance, later scholastic theologians such as Duns Scotus held that absolution constituted the real essence of the sacrament of penance while sorrow, confession, and satisfaction were only the necessary condition for its efficacy.[48] This placed the center of gravity in the penitential process on the formula of absolution. The position of the Scotist school held many inconsistencies and did not endure, especially in the wake of the revival of Thomism in the sixteenth century. On the other hand, it laid the groundwork for the reinterpretation of penance in Luther's thought in which the word of absolution received emphasis and the very name of the sacrament of penance was changed to the sacrament of absolution. Such a reinterpretation was necessary in view of the uncertainty of forgiveness if it depended on a human act or feeling rather than a word of God. Even the Council of Trent held, in its Decree on Justification, chapter 9, "No one can know with the certainty of faith . . . that he has attained the grace of God." This statement may have been asserted against the evangelical view that the certainty of forgiveness can be known by faith in God's word of promise. It was also a realistic assessment of the very uncertainty with regard to sin and forgiveness that led the young Luther to look for certainty in the first place.

❦ THE MISSAL AND THE BREVIARY

We have seen in this chapter the systematic exclusion of the people from the liturgy of the church. This did not happen all at once, but over a very long period of time. Nor did it occur through intention. But with the scattering of the congregation in a church building composed of different rooms, the overburdening of liturgy with tropes and sequences and dramatic gestures, the insertion of private prayers by the celebrant into the public celebration, the offering of the mass for special intentions, often with only the priest and a server in attendance, the increasing practice of venerating the eucharist outside of the mass itself, the excommunication of children, and the imposition of a penitential discipline on all the baptized as a condition for receiving communion, the exclusion of the people from the sacramental liturgy is exactly what took place. In the previous chapter we also saw the monasticizing and clericalizing of the divine office. It is not surprising that liturgical books began to reflect this reality.

The private mass would not have been possible without a new kind of liturgical book: the *Missale Plenum*, or complete missal. The celebration of the liturgy had previously required several books and several ministers. By the thirteenth century all the liturgical texts were brought into one book so that the mass could be celebrated by one priest alone. What had at first been practiced only in the monasteries now became the rule

---

[47] Geoffrey Chaucer, "The Parson's Tale," *Canterbury Tales*, in *The Complete Poetry and Prose of Geoffrey Chaucer*, ed. by J. H. Fisher (New York: Holt, 1977), 347ff.

[48] See Robert Hancock and Robert Williams, "The Scholastic Debate on the Essential Moment of Forgiveness," *Resonance* 1–2 (St. Meinrad School of Theology, 1966), 63–74.

throughout the church.[49] The ministers needed to read the lessons—subdeacon and dea-con—could be dispensed with, and both the epistle and gospel could be read by the priest. The chant texts, too (Introit, Kyrie, Gloria, Gradual, Credo, Sanctus, Agnus Dei), which might be sung by the choir at high mass, could be read by the priest alone. It was expressly ordered for the first time around the middle of the thirteenth century that the priest would recite these texts in a low voice even if the choir were singing them. Jungmann commented that it was really a step forward to replace the *apologiae*, with which the celebrant had filled every pause, with these biblical and liturgical texts.[50]

The principles first developed for the private mass were extended to all masses. The people who were excluded in private masses were rendered totally passive in all masses. They were spectators witnessing a drama, and the allegorical interpretations of the mass that flourished throughout the Middle Ages in the form of Expositiones missae, beginning with Amalarius of Metz, were designed to help the people understand the drama taking place at the altar. Because the mass became a spectacle to be seen rather than an act of proclamation to be heard, the visual aspects of the celebration were in-creased. Everywhere the Gothic principle of accumulation, the heaping up of the same detail, had its affects on kissing the altar, making the sign of the cross over the bread and cup, bowings and genuflections. In this dramatic-mimetic sense, the enactment of the canon of the mass became a reenactment of Calvary, with every gesture given the assign-ment of portraying some aspect of the Lord's passion. For example, the celebrant's wash-ing of his hands at the offertory became an enactment of Pilate washing his hands at the trial of Jesus. The celebrant's striking of his breast while saying the concluding "Nobis quoque peccatoribus" of the canon in a loud voice seems to have been introduced as a vivid presentation of the impression the Lord's death made on bystanders, such as the centurion. Commentators looked for allegorical significance in every detail of the mass. As is common with allegory, there were ever new interpretations. Anselm of Canterbury, for example, in a pastoral letter chided priests for leaving the chalice uncovered during mass with the argument that Christ had hung naked on the cross and that this dishonor should not be perpetuated.[51] The impact of the collusion of dramatic reenactment with eucharistic realism will be explored in the next chapter.

The Breviary was a book that gathered all the material needed for the celebra-tion of the Divine Office between two covers, just as the Missal was a book that gathered all the material needed for the celebration of mass into one book. The Breviary devel-oped as a way of making it possible for pastorally active secular clergy to pray the Divine Office. It was a conflation of the cathedral and monastic office traditions, although the monastic tradition eventually predominated. The background of the Breviary tradition lies in the office obligations of clergy attached to local churches, and in order to under-stand its development it is necessary to understand the organization of the clergy at-tached to local churches beginning in the early Middle Ages.[52]

---

[49] Jungmann, op. cit., I, 106f.
[50] Ibid., I, 107.
[51] *Ad Waleranni querelas* 3; P.L. 158: 553f.
[52] See Pierre Salmon, *The Breviary Through the Centuries*, op. cit., 28–41.

We have seen in chapter four the organization of the churches in the See of Rome in four different types and noted that these different kinds of churches did not all have the same kind of liturgical offices. The churches in Italy tended to follow the Roman pattern on a reduced scale. This model called for the division of liturgical responsibilities, including the recitation of the Divine Office, among the various worship centers of the city.

In Gaul there was also a division between churches: the simple ecclesiae, at which most usual liturgies were conducted, and basilicas, which were temples in which the bodies of the saints reposed. There were three types of basilicas: (1) urban basilicas, which were the principal sanctuaries of the city; (2) monastic basilicas, which formed an integral part of the monasteries; and (3) rural basilicas, some of which were the parish churches of the towns in which they were built.

These types of sanctuaries were all of good size. They are to be distinguished from the cellula or oratorium, which was only a *memoria* of a saint, or from the *vilis aedicula*, which was a small oratory or chapel belonging to a feudal lord usually served by a single cleric. Christianity in Gaul, as elsewhere, spread from the towns to the countryside. Consequently, ecclesiae were often built on the lands of a great feudal lord and in the small market towns. But their purpose was quite restricted; they existed only to increase the places of worship. The eucharist could be celebrated at these churches; but baptisms were often held at the urban basilicas. Even the solemn celebrations of the great feasts were held in the urban basilicas. There is no ancient precedent for the notion that every local church should be able to do every liturgy.

We have seen that around the urban basilicas and centers of pilgrimage, there was a domus basilicae, or monasterium basilicae, to accommodate all the persons serving these great churches and to provide hospitality for pilgrims. The clergy attached to the basilicas, as well as the cathedral chapters, were canons with an obligation to join in the choral recitation of the Divine Office. It was primarily in the great basilicas that the office was celebrated. The Council of Orleans in 538, speaking of urban and rural basilicas, provided for sending urban clergy into the countryside to celebrate the office. Canon 25 of the Council of Épaone ordered that the relics of the saints should not be placed in the oratories of *villae*; in other words, these chapels should not be consecrated as basilicas except near an episcopal city where there would be clergy available to celebrate the Divine Office at them.

This organization of churches and clergy must be kept in mind when we study the celebration of the office in the Middle Ages. It demonstrates that the office was *not* observed in every church by every cleric. It was celebrated in the cathedrals, where there was a sufficiently important *presbyterium*, and then in churches that had an endowment sufficient enough to support a chantry (clerics whose primary responsibility was to carry out the daily round of offices). There is also evidence of the clergy of several churches taking part in a single celebration. Texts of this period that speak of an obligation to recite the office do not refer to personal recitation, but to the participation of the various ranks of clergy in the responsibility that fell upon them to maintain the public prayer of the church. The Council of Agde, in 506, for example, reminded bishops and priests of their duty in the daily celebration of the offices. The Council of Tarragonda, in 516, ordered clerics serving the rural churches to take turns in the church service so that each day Lauds and Vespers could be celebrated solemnly. On Sunday all were to be present at the offices. This is an indication of the Spanish church's concern to maintain the old Cathedral Office.

We have also seen in the clericalization of the office a monasticizing of it. Its content was less concerned with the time of day at which a particular office was celebrated than with getting through the cursus of psalmody and readings as a matter of spiritual discipline. This is evident in the reform that Boniface sought to bring about in the lands of Germany and France. The second council of Clovesho, over which he presided in 747, tried to tighten up the lax discipline of the clergy and people in these regions. The liturgical ordinances enacted at this synod give evidence of a very profound Roman (i.e., Benedictine) influence. Canon 15 of this council asserted: "The seven Hours for the canonical prayer must be regularly celebrated with psalmody and chant, in a uniform manner and according to the usages of the Roman church."[53] Among the edicts of the Capitulary of 802, promulgated under the authority of the Emperor Charlemagne, was the eighth, which decreed

> That all priests ring the bells of their churches at the proper hours of the day
> and night and pray the sacred offices to God at those times, and that they teach
> their people how God is to be adored, and at what hours.[54]

It does not follow, of course, that all the clergy submitted immediately to these requirements; nor is it likely that all the churches of the Carolingian Empire had from that time on one uniform, complete, solemn, daily office. Yet these promulgations by the emperor exerted tremendous influence on the conscience of the clergy. An echo of this is heard in a form of confession attributed to Alcuin, the great liturgical scholar at Charlemagne's court:

> I have rushed through the canonical offices, prayers, psalms and readings care-
> lessly and irreverently in the sight of God, and I have failed to fulfill many of my
> obligations. . . . I have sinned in being negligent . . . and with regard to my min-
> istry, which I have not kept in an orderly way.[55]

Within the general reform of canonical life, a movement was taking shape in favor of making up in private for the offices in which one could not take part. This, too, represented a monastic influence. Peter Damian (d. 1072), in his treatise on the Dominus vobiscum, bears witness to the general practice, in monastic circles, of reciting the office in private, and to the value set on the office in itself apart from its celebration. We possess tangible proof of this development: The first breviaries date from the eleventh century. These were the first volumes to contain in a single, portable collection all the elements of the office that were otherwise distributed among the psalter, the antiphonary, the hymnal,

---

[53] Ibid., 8.
[54] Ibid., 9.
[55] Ibid., 10.

the lectionary, the responsorial, the book of the Gospels, and the book of homilies. Such a practical collection was necessary for monks of the Cluniac type who were often working far away from the monastery in the fields, or who were on journeys. The Breviary, recited in private, was bound to make a favorable impression on secular clergy who found the solemn celebration of the office burdensome, or who were so occupied with other duties that they could not always celebrate the office in choir.

Salmon notes two influences in the thirteenth century that aided and abetted the private recitation of the office: (1) the Friars Minor and (2) the universities. The Franciscans, because of their lifestyle, could not always celebrate the solemn choral office. Outside of their large friaries (i.e., houses of formation and study) they were by necessity led to the expediency of reciting the office privately wherever they happened to be. In the same period, the frequenting of the universities by thousands of clerics raised a problem that was solved in the same way. Students living away from their church had to be excused from the obligation to participate in the choral office. The more fervent among them made up for it through private recitation.

Theology is always wont to provide a rationale for practice, and the private recitation of the office was no exception. Thomas Aquinas provided the theological rationale to sanction the practice of private recitation, and later he even justified its obligation. He developed this in several of his *Quodlibeta*, written between 1269 and 1272. In *Quodlibet* I, art. 13, in answering the question of "whether one who has two churches is obliged to say both offices," he distinguishes a two-fold duty: one towards God, and the other towards the church from which the cleric receives a benefice. The obligation toward the church is governed by canon law, which is set up in order to insure decency and good order. The obligation towards God can only be fulfilled by the person himself; and it matters little to God whether one kind of office is said or another, as long as the cleric is obeying his superiors. In *Quodlibet* III, q. 12, art. 29, "Whether one who has omitted the recitation of a divine office is to be compelled to make it up," he lays down this principle: "It has been wisely established that God be praised in different ways, which are suitable to different times and places." This is a matter of what is appropriate. In *Quodlibet* V, q. 23, art. 28, Thomas takes up the question of anticipating the Hours. He approves of the recitation of Matins the evening before where there is a reasonable cause, as, for example, the need of an instructor to prepare his lectures, "Because it is better to render both to God, namely the praises that are due Him and the other honorable duties, than to have one prevented by the other." To do this without justifiable reason, however, would be to commit a sin.

The growth of the practice of private recitation led to synodical decisions concerning the celebration of the office. Perhaps the most important of these are decisions decreed in the twenty-first session of the Council of Basel in 1435. Among the relevant decrees are the following:[56]

> the third: in all cathedral and collegiate churches the canonical hours are to be
> recited in common, slowly and reverently;

---

[56] Ibid., 18.

the fourth: all those obliged to sing the hours are to be present at them from
beginning to end and the same with processions. Monitors are to be
appointed to check on absentees;

the fifth: beneficiaries who cannot sing the office in choir must recite it, slowly
and becomingly, in some place where they will not be disturbed;

the sixth: any holder of a benefice who walks around during the Divine Office,
even inside the church, or who engages in conversations, loses not only the
allotments attached to that hour but also those for the whole day.

It is well known that by the fifteenth century many clerics were nonresident at their benefices. Many of the more important clergy accumulated benefices, and it was impossible to reside at several places at the same time. Most of these clerics spent more time at the court of some prince than in their parishes. Even the private recitation of the office must have posed a hardship on them.

Nevertheless, in addition to this practical consideration, two factors favored the private recitation rather than the public celebration of the Divine Office. The first was the new trend in spirituality that began in the fifteenth century and continued through the seventeenth century. This new spirituality marked an abandonment of monastic-asceticism in favor of a *devotio moderna* based on a wholly interior piety of self-examination leading to confession of sins. Outwardly, it cultivated the life of poverty and self-abasement in imitation of the Savior. The result of the "modern devotion" was disastrous to worship. It led to an abandonment of solemn celebrations of the liturgy, which were regarded as too external and too distracting to meditation, in favor of a more personal and intimate form of prayer.

This religious sensibility was fostered by a second factor, which we have already discussed: the liturgy was being burdened with tropes and sequences. This affected not only the mass but also the Divine Office. Even in monasteries the prayer offices were burdened with the multiplication of psalms that were added according to the intention of relatives, friends, or benefactors. Among the common groups of psalms added to those of the office were the fifteen psalms of ascent (or psalms of degree, or gradual psalms), Psalms 120–134; and the seven penitential psalms (6, 32, 38, 51, 102, 130, 143). A special Office of the Dead began to be recited daily from the ninth century on, which developed into three offices of Vespers, Nocturns, and Lauds, recited in addition to the normal course of the Liturgy of the Hours. From the eleventh century on the Little Office of Our Lady—a briefer but nevertheless complete cursus of the canonical hours to be said in addition to the regular offices—became very popular in the monasteries. These devotions added to an already lengthy schedule of daily worship in churches and monasteries. It is no wonder that the laity sought sustenance in paraliturgical devotions. Yet even here, as we shall see, we are not dealing with devotions that are irrelevant to the public liturgy of the church. Rather, these devotions attempted to distill the essence of the mysteries of the faith and the essential content of the faith celebrated in the church's official liturgy.

🍇 POPULAR DEVOTIONS AND POPULAR LITURGY

Devotions are understood here in the sense of *pia* or *sacra exercitia*, "exercises of piety." The liturgy of the church was not developed as a vehicle for personal devotion but as the public celebration of the faith of the church. Liturgy was breaking down during the Middle Ages precisely because it was being used as a means of exercising personal piety or of expressing a subjective religiosity. We have seen this in the insertion of private prayers said by the priest during the public rite and then in the practice of performing the church's liturgy in a private setting. Even in high masses, the Latin language and the use of choirs effectively excluded the people from more overt participation. But we should not think that they were totally excluded.

We have already indicated ways in which there was popular participation in cultic life during the Middle Ages. The great church buildings that housed Christian liturgy were community projects. Trade guilds could build their own chapels or sponsor windows in the Gothic churches with their emblems as vintners or butchers displayed in them, although an offer from the prostitutes of Paris to dedicate a window to Mary Magdalene was declined. While these opportunities applied more to the privileged or mercantile classes, the church recognized the need to appeal to different social groups. Special masses were offered and sermons preached to specific groups such as knights, crusaders, merchants, housewives, and peasants. For ordinary Christians there were liturgical dramas and processions.[57] Through participation in the ceremonies at the great shrines ordinary Christians would learn the stories of the Bible and the legends of the saints. The friars—Dominicans and Franciscans—were especially helpful in bringing devotional expressions to the lower classes. Perhaps the most famous example of this is the legend of Francis of Assisi making a Christmas crib or creche to illustrate the nativity of the Savior.[58]

The humanizing of Jesus along realistic lines is a part of the revolution in spirituality that occurred in the twelfth century. Crucifixes became a prominent feature in church decorations. No longer was the Lord shown as the triumphant and vested ruler of all things; now a dying man, naked and in agony, was offered for the compassion of the beholders who were invited, especially in Franciscan preaching, to share in the sufferings of the Savior. At the same time devotion to the Virgin Mary as the sorrowing mother increased and was popularized by the Little Office of the Blessed Virgin (a nonclerical liturgy of the hours), Marian hymns such as "Salve Regina," litanies, and prayers. The Hail Mary (Ave Maria) originated toward the end of the eleventh century and was included in the most common of popular devotions, the rosary.[59]

The rosary was, in Carl Dehne's words, "a kind of poor man's Marian psalter."[60] It also served the catechetical purpose of fixing in the mind of its devotee the essential

[57] See B. Hamilton, *Religion in the Medieval West* (London, 1986).

[58] See Arnaldo Fortini, *Francis of Assisi*, trans. by Helen Moak (New York: Crossroad, 1981), 531–3.

[59] See Joseph A. Jungmann, *Christian Prayer Through the Centuries*, Eng. trans. (New York, 1976), 124–6.

[60] Carl Dehne, S.J., "Roman Catholic Popular Devotions," in John Gallen, ed., *Christians at Prayer* (Notre Dame, Ind.: University of Notre Dame Press, 1977), 89.

mysteries of the faith. The fifteen mysteries of the rosary are arranged in sets of five, following the sequence of the life of Christ and his Blessed Mother. Each item in the rosary is composed of one Our Father, ten Hail Marys, and a concluding Gloria Patri. Each chaplet (five decades of Hail Marys) is preceded by the Apostles' Creed and three Hail Marys for the virtues of faith, hope, and charity. It was also customary to sing or recite one Marian antiphon. The mysteries of the rosary are as follows:

THE JOYFUL MYSTERIES

1. The Annunciation of the Angel Gabriel to Mary
2. The Visitation of Mary to Elizabeth
3. The Birth of Jesus in Bethlehem of Judea
4. The Presentation of Christ in the Temple
5. The Finding of Christ in the Temple

THE SORROWFUL MYSTERIES

1. The Agony of Jesus in the Garden of Gethsemane
2. The Scourging of Jesus at the Pillar
3. The Crowning of Jesus with Thorns
4. The Way of the Cross
5. The Crucifixion and Death of Jesus

THE GLORIOUS MYSTERIES

1. The Resurrection of Christ
2. The Ascension of Christ into Heaven
3. The Gift of the Holy Spirit
4. The Falling Asleep and Assumption of Our Lady
5. The Coronation of Our Lady and the Glory of All the Saints

As the rosary was a lay person's breviary, the Way of the Cross, with its fourteen pictures of the journey of Christ on the *via dolorosa* (some stations were biblical and some were extrabiblical), became a poor person's pilgrimage. Those who could not join the relatively well-to-do on a pilgrimage to Jerusalem and the Holy Land, or to Rome with its shrines of Peter and Paul, or to such Spanish pilgrimage sites as Compostela, Zaragoza, and Guadelupe, could perambulate their parish church building, where the stations of the cross would be displayed in statuary or paintings along the aisles or in stained glass windows. Yet increasingly, ordinary people joined the nobility on pilgrimages. In the British Isles, such pilgrimage sites as Canterbury (Thomas à Becket), Our Lady of Walsingham, and Saint Patrick's Purgatory in Lough Derg in County Donegal were, as Victor and Edith Turner note, "frequented increasingly by the poor."[61] But pilgrimages were also becoming pleasure trips on which people found opportunities to see the world and stray from the straight and narrow, just as attending church services provided occasions for amorous liaisons. Small wonder that the serious champions of the devotio moderna had little use for either, and turned instead to meditation and mysticism. Thomas à Kempis, the author of the devotional classic, *The Imitation of Christ,* asserted

---

[61] Victor and Edith Turner, *Image and Pilgrimage in Christian Culture* (New York: Columbia University Press, 1978), 6. See especially pp. 104–39 on St. Patrick's Purgatory.

that those who went on pilgrimages rarely became saints. Better to stay home and to re-cite and meditate upon the mysteries of the rosary!

In many ways people contemplated the saving deeds of God recounted in scrip-ture (even if they couldn't read it) and the lives of the saints (which unfortunately were marred by too many unfounded legends). The whole social life of the Middle Ages was saturated with the mystery of God revealed in Christ, and on the teachings of Christ transparent in the lives of the saints. The church was often energized by pastoral concern to connect the gospel personally with the lives of people. This kind of pastoral concern animated one of the greatest popes of the High Middle Ages, Innocent III (1198–1216). Innocent undermined heretical movements such as the Cathari, whose preaching of the life of poverty appealed to many uneducated Catholics, by putting his blessing on Dominic's order and Francis's "little brothers."[62] The Fourth Lateran Council, over which Innocent presided (with 71 archbishops, 412 bishops, and 800 abbots participating as full voting members), was a reforming council (although its decree that Jews should wear special garb to distinguish them from Christians was reprehensible). But even the decree requiring auricular confession of all Christians before receiving communion was more than a means of exercising social control. It had the intention of making spiritual counseling available to all. The council also approved a new catechism, reflecting recent theological developments, which was intended to provide material for the teaching of the laity. A program of this sort required the general improvement of the learning of the clergy, especially in the country places, for few of them had the ability to give advice in the confessional or to teach the basics of the faith. The teaching of the catechism was very basic: the Apostles' Creed, the Lord's Prayer, the Hail Mary.

In fact, however, the general level of lay devotion was raised during the four-teenth and fifteenth centuries, as is evident in the genre of popular devotional literature known as the Prymers. In his careful study of the background of the material included in the typical Prymer, or "Lay-Folks Prayer Book," Edmund Bishop shows that it is based on accretions to the Divine Office since the time of Benedict of Aniane.[63] Material com-monly included in prymers are special, gradual, and penitential psalms, and the Litany; and the offices of the dead and of the Blessed Virgin Mary (patterned after the hours of the Divine Office with psalms and canticles, antiphons, hymns, a sequence of readings, and collects)—although there is only one office, to be used each day of the week. As Bishop concludes,

> The perplexing intricacies of the Breviary, with its continually varying texts, apart from its size, put an adaptation of the old daily office for common use out of the question. But the accretions, now by this time popularly looked on as an integral part of the office, afforded just the material that was wanted. They were, with the exception of the office of the Blessed Virgin, invariable.[64]

---

[62] See Adolf Holl, *The Last Christian: A Biography of Francis of Assisi*, trans. by Peter Heinegg (Garden City: Doubleday, 1980).

[63] Edmund Bishop, "On the Origins of the Prymer," in *Liturgica Historica*, op. cit., 211–37.

[64] Ibid., 236.

The most characteristic feature of popular devotions such as the rosary and the Way of the Cross is that they are repetitious and unvarying.[65] The penchant for variety, which characterizes the religious professional (e.g., the monk or member of a religious order), does not excite the ordinary layperson. It may be that one of the features of Eastern Christian worship that has ensured its popular character is that, unlike Western liturgy, it is not only highly ceremonial but almost unvarying throughout the church year. The consequence is that in the Eastern church, there was no rift between liturgical spirituality and popular piety such as occurred in the Western church during the Middle Ages.

Eastern liturgy remained "the public work of the people" in practice as well as in theory. However, the eastern churches experienced conditions that ensured that the liturgy would remain both the object of devotion and the subject of theology—"the melody of theology," in the words of Patriarch Nicephorus of Constantinople (d. 829).[66] Those conditions were that one after another the patriarchal churches of the East fell under Moslem domination. Even several centuries before the final fall of Constantinople to the Ottoman Turks in 1453, many of the bishoprics under the jurisdiction of the "ecumenical patriarch" of Constantinople were in territories occupied and governed by Moslem or Latin Christian rulers. The Moslems (e.g., Arabs, Mamelukes, Turks) tended to be tolerant of the Christian people, but many of the educational and social institutions of the church could not flourish under conditions of cultural and polictical suppression. The liturgy could and did flourish as the means of faith expression and faith formation. It continued to be performed in the church buildings allowed to Christians under the direction of the church hierarchy, whose task was also to secure the obedience of their people to an infidel state.[67]

Because of the energy devoted to preserving the liturgy, it remained intact in the East both ritually and spiritually and with no tension between outward observance and inward contemplation. The veneration of icons, for example, allowed by the Second Council of Nicea in 787 in settling the iconoclastic controversy, provided for both sensual engagement and mystical absorption. The people did not need to find devotional outlet outside of the liturgy. The liturgy was more or less in the language of the people (e.g., Syriac, Greek, Slavonic). Singing remained an integral part of the celebration and the people's role was never completely taken over by a cantor or choir. Different books were needed by the different ministers with roles in the liturgy and for different liturgies, much like in the early Medieval West.[68] This too ensured a communal celebration such as had existed in the West before the invention of the missal and breviary with their encouragement of liturgies of convenience. Thus, the divorce of liturgy and piety that occured in the West by the end of the Middle Ages was not experienced in the East.

---

[65] See William G. Storey, "The Liturgy of the Hours: Cathedral Versus Monastery," *Worship* 50 (1976), 55–57.

[66] See Jaroslav Pelikan, *The Christian Tradition*, Vol. 2. *The Spirit of Eastern Christendom* (Chicago: University of Chicago Press, 1974), 133ff.

[67] See Steven Runciman, *The Great Church in Captivity* (Cambridge: Cambridge University Press, 1968).

[68] For an overview of sources and editions of books in the various eastern rites see Anton Baumstark, *Comparative Liturgy*, 214–35.

CHAPTER 7

The Real Presence and the Sacrifice of the Mass

P ROFOUND CHANGES TOOK PLACE in the forms of worship, in the styles of celebration, and in liturgical piety during the Middle Ages in western Europe. Great abbey and cathedral churches employed the plastic arts in sculpture on the stones, frescoes on the walls, and colored glass in the windows. There was a development in church music that led to polyphonic choir music and the use of organs. The allegorical interpretation of the Bible and the liturgy that began in the Carolingian period helped to transform liturgical rites into ritual dramas. These in turn spawned the miracle and mystery plays of the fifteenth and sixteenth centuries. These developments contributed to the outward splendor of worship in the High Middle Ages. But they were products of a cultural perspective that also had a profound influence on theology, especially on sacramental theology. The Gothic Age operated with an empirical outlook on the world that was interested in seeing reality. There is a correlation between the desire to see the sacrament of the altar, which led to practices of eucharistic reservation and exposition, and the retrieval of Aristotle and the development of the natural sciences at the same time in Western society. This empirical approach to reality had a profound affect on the theology of as well as practices associated with the doctrine of the real presence of Christ in the eucharist; and the doctrine of the real presence had a profound affect on the theology of and practices associated with the sacrifice of the mass.

🍇 AN EMPIRICAL WORLDVIEW

Western Europe was coming of age during the eleventh and twelfth centuries. The crusades against the Moslems to recapture the Holy Land, while of questionable religious motivation, were important for the cultural development of western Europe for two main reasons. First, they represent the Gothic society stretching itself. A society that had been surrounded by hostile powers and plagued with economic poverty and political weakness was stretching its muscles and asserting its newly acquired self-confidence. Secondly, the crusades gave Westerners access to the Greek and Arab worlds, with its learning that had been previously inaccessible. It is unlikely, for example, that Gothic architecture would have been possible without contact with the Arabic sciences, geometry, and mathematics.[1] Lynn White put it this way: "The emergence of Gothic art reflects a fundamental change in the European attitude toward the natural environment. Things ceased to be merely symbols, rebuses, *Dei vestigia*, and became objects interesting and important in themselves, quite apart from man's spiritual needs."[2] In the world of late antiquity and in the early Middle Ages, people lived "not in a world of visible facts but rather in a world of symbols."[3] The symbolic pointed to and participated in the unseen spiritual reality; but in the worldview of the Western Middle Ages there was a desire to see reality. It was an empirical worldview. It was not such a giant step to the next position: that what is visible—that is, what can be demonstrated or documented—is what is really real. It is not surprising that even the allegorical interpretation of the Bible and the liturgy took on a new factual and graphic quality. Contemplative interest shifted toward the events in the life of the historical Jesus. This is reflected in the efforts at realistic or lifelike portrayals of Jesus, the biblical characters, and the saints in the plastic arts and ritual dramas. Christmas crèches (under Franciscan influence) and crucifixes showing the body of Jesus contorted with pain are examples of this, as are the use of props and costumes rather than accoutrements and vestments in the liturgical dramas. As White commented,

> At the end of the twelfth century Catholic piety suddenly concentrated itself upon an effort to bring God down to earth and to see and touch him. It was as though Europe had become populated with doubting Thomases eager to thrust their fingers into the very wounds of Christ. To an extraordinary degree the new eucharistic cult was empirical in temper, permitting the constant seeing and handling of God. . . . Superficially the new piety might seem to be a development and expansion of the traditional sacramentalism, and as such a buttressing of the older symbolic and mediate view of nature. But, as the more conservative Eastern Church suspected, this was a sacramentalism of a new flavor, suffused with a spirit alien to that of the first Christian millennium. It seemed that the Latin Church, in centering its devotion upon the actual physical substance of its deity, had inadvertently deified matter.[4]

---

[1] See Paul Frankl, *Gothic Architecture*, trans. by Dieter Pevsner. The Pelican History of Art (Baltimore: Penguin Books, 1962), 17–30.

[2] Lynn White, Jr., "Natural Science and Naturalist Art in the Middle Ages," in *Medieval Religion and Technology: Collected Essays* (Berkeley: University of California Press, 1978), 33.

[3] Ibid., 27.

[4] Ibid., 33–4.

We have looked at the architectural feats that made Gothic church buildings possible. It needs to be recognized that the ambience of the Gothic church also served to emphasize the centrality of the mass and the eucharistic celebration. The stained glass windows not only provided artisans with ways of portraying the biblical characters and stories; they also admitted enormous amounts of light into the building. The apses of these churches were especially luminous. The main sanctuary with its high altar was ringed with side chapels. While the windows of the nave and apse provided ample light for saying mass at the side altars, the light streaming in from the rear windows was pointed to the central mystery celebrated at the high altar. For Abbot Suger of Saint-Denis, the play of light from stained glass windows bouncing off jeweled vessels and colorful vestments led to a spiritual vision that he deemed superior to the spoken or written word. It fostered contemplation and wonder. Georges Duby has summed up Abbot Suger's architectural ambition and theological vision in this way:

> The basilica of Saint-Denis stands for a form of Christianity no longer expressed solely in terms of liturgy and music, but also in those of a theology, a theology whose leitmotif is the Incarnation. This is why Suger's work opened up a new dimension, that of [the human being] illuminated by the *verum lumen*.[5]

In other words, the building itself erected under Abbot Suger's meticulous supervision, and copied and refined by numerous other master builders, expressed a devotion to Christ that focused on the humanity of the Word, whose glory shines in the works of his flesh and in the celebration of his sacrament, in which he is mysteriously present. The display of the eucharistic host at the elevation during the words of institution, which was deemed by many to be the high point of the mass, fits naturally into this architectural and theological context. The spiritual satisfaction derived from gazing upon the host in contemplation was certainly one reason for the growing infrequency of reception of Holy Communion, along with the rules of abstinence before receiving the sacrament and the sense of personal unworthiness in the presence of Christ himself in his sacramental body.

It is important to take this empirical worldview—that what is real is what is seen—into account as background for the most important issue in sacramental theology during the Western Middle Ages: the real presence. The questions raised about the eucharist during the twelfth and thirteenth centuries indicate a growing fascination with the eucharistic elements as natural species open to empirical analysis. If we are receiving the body and blood of Christ in Holy Communion, why do the species of bread and wine remain? Does a change occur in the species? If so, what kind of a change is it and when does it occur? The groundwork for such questions was laid in the eucharistic debates of the ninth through the eleventh centuries. But the background for such questions lies in the theories of consecration that were being proposed in the writings of the church fathers already in the fourth and fifth centuries.

---

[5] Georges Duby, *History of Medieval Art*, Part 2: *The Europe of the Cathedrals 1140–1280* (New York: Rizzoli, 1986), 17–9.

❧ THE "MOMENT" OF CONSECRATION

The witness of the church fathers is unequivocal that what the faithful receive in Holy Communion is the body and blood of Christ, even if they variously refer to the bread and wine as figures *(figurae)*, types *(typoi)*, antitypes *(antitypoi)*, or signs *(sacramenta)* of the body and blood of Christ. The earliest discussion of an act or formula by which the bread and wine are changed (metabole, *metarruthmizo, convertere*) into the body and blood of Christ can be traced to the fourth century. The developed eucharistic prayers of this period served to state the meaning of the eucharistic action. In typical patristic fashion, the lex orandi (the law of prayer) served to established the lex credendi (the law of belief), since the fathers interpreted the meanings of the eucharist from the eucharistic prayer in their mystagogical catecheses. These catechetical homilies on the mysteries or sacraments were preached to the newly baptized during Easter week. Because their purpose was to explicate the meaning of the initiatory rites in which the newly baptized had participated, it is not surprising that the eucharistic theology of the great teaching bishops of the ancient church was developed on the basis of the eucharistic rite that they used, especially the Great Thanksgiving or anaphora. Indeed, the exegesis of the anaphoras in these catechetical homilies even helps us to reconstruct the evolution of the classical eucharistic prayers. Not surprisingly, the fathers began to locate within the prayer the form of the consecration by which the bread and wine were "manifested as" or "changed into" the body and blood of Christ.

Also not surprisingly, those who were accustomed to the old Syrian rites focused on the operation of the Holy Spirit rather than the words of Christ because these prayers presumably lacked an institution narrative. In his famous *Mystagogical Catecheses*, Cyril of Jerusalem (d. c. 386) attributes the change in the elements to the work of the Holy Spirit. In his commentary on the eucharistic rite he says:

> Next, after sanctifying ourselves by these spiritual songs [the Sanctus], we implore the merciful God to send forth his Holy Spirit upon the offering to make the bread the body of Christ and the wine the blood of Christ. For whatever the Holy Spirit touches is hallowed and changed.[6]

Since Cyril's *Catecheses* contains the earliest references to the work of the Holy Spirit in "making" the sacrament, it has been argued that he may be an innovator here. But if, as Atchley suggests, Cyril worked on the *Catecheses* around 347–348, he was only a junior presbyter in the Jerusalem church and would not have been in a position to be making substantive changes in the rite of that church. "It may safely be concluded, therefore, that the epiclesis given by him was not new in his days, but, at any rate in his opinion, was of long standing and traditional."[7]

John Chrysostom (d. 407), the fiery Antiochene, has been taken as a champion of the consecratory force of both the words of institution and the epiclesis. In the

---

[6] Text in Hänggi-Pahl, *Prex Eucharistica*, op. cit., 206.

[7] E. G. Cuthbert F. Atchley, *On the Epiclesis of the Eucharistic Liturgy and in the Consecration of the Font.* Alcuin Club Collections No. XXXI (London: Oxford University Press, 1935), 51.

anaphora named after him, and in other West Syrian anaphoras, there is both an institution narrative and a developed epiclesis that petitions the Holy Spirit to "change" the bread and wine into the body and blood of Christ. Not surprisingly, Chrysostom does refer both to the words of Christ and to the work of the Holy Spirit in the transformation of the eucharistic gifts. Atchley proposed that in Chrysostom's view the words of Christ, spoken once, are eternally efficacious, so that in the last analysis it is Christ who consecrates the bread and wine. As Christ's minister, the priest speaks the words of Christ but it is God who gives them their power through the invocation of the Holy Spirit.[8]

This view of the transformative power of the Holy Spirit is even more pronounced in the *Catechetical Homilies* of Theodore of Mopsuestia (d. 428). For example, in *Cat. Hom.* 5:76 he says, "We ought not to regard the elements merely as bread and cup, but as the body and the blood of Christ, into which they were so transformed by the descent of the Holy Spirit."[9] But two factors should color the interpretation of the texts in Theodore's homilies in which he speaks of the transforming work of the Holy Spirit in the elements. One is the consistent incarnational view of many of the fathers that drew a parallel between the incarnation of the Word in the womb of the Virgin Mary and in the eucharistic gifts. As the Holy Spirit brought about the union of the divine Logos and human flesh in the incarnation, so the Holy Spirit brings about the sacramental union of the body and blood of Christ with the bread and wine. Second, Theodore engaged in an allegorical interpretation of the liturgy as the drama of redemption in his explanations of the eucharistic rite to the newly baptized and the faithful. He explains the eucharistic rite, from the offertory on, as a reenactment of the passion, death, burial, and resurrection of Jesus Christ. So, for example, when the deacons spread cloths on the altar-table, Theodore compares this action with preparing the tomb to receive the body of Christ. This whole ritual allegory culminates at the epiclesis, which Theodore interprets as the resurrection. The resurrection, of course, is the new creation brought about by the vivifying work of the Holy Spirit (which the newly baptized, to whom these homilies were addressed, had themselves just experienced). The ritual actions to which Theodore points as an illustration of this interpretation are the priest's gestures of backing away from the altar and bowing his head at the words invoking the Holy Spirit, since no human agency was involved in the resurrection of Jesus from the dead.[10] Considering the nature of allegorical interpretation, it would be pushing Theodore's texts too far to see in them anything as precise as a "moment" of consecration.

Turning to Ambrose of Milan (d. 397), the focus of the consecration is more exclusively on the words of Christ, and we are closer to identifying a "moment" of consecration. This is probably because the eucharistic prayer tradition known and commented on by Ambrose lacked a specific invocation of the Holy Spirit. In *De Mysteriis* IX, for example, in the midst of arguing that if God could work wonders through the words of the

---

[8] Ibid., 67–8.

[9] For a number of the texts in Theodore's *Catechetical Homilies* see John H. McKenna, *Eucharist and Holy Spirit*. Alcuin Club Collections No. 57 (Great Wakering: Mayhew-McCrimmon, 1975), 60ff.

[10] See Edward Yarnold, *The Awe-inspiring Rites of Initiation*, op. cit., 245–6.

prophets, if he could create the world from nothing with his word, and therefore it would be reasonable to suppose that he could change bread into Christ's body also by the power of the word, Ambrose states:

> For the sacrament which you receive, is effected by the words of Christ. . . . The Lord Jesus himself declares: "This is my body." Before the benediction of the heavenly words another species is mentioned; after the consecration the body is signified. He himself speaks of his blood. Before the consecration it is mentioned as something else; after the consecration it is called blood.[11]

John H. McKenna points out other writings of Ambrose that stress the Holy Spirit's equal sanctity with the Father and the Son.[12] But when commenting on the liturgical text to the newly baptized, Ambrose is quite clear that the *sermo Christi* consecrates the bread and wine. As he states in *De Sacramentis* IV, 14,

> By whose words and by whose speech does the consecration take place? By those of the Lord Jesus. For all the rest that comes beforehand is spoken by the priest: God is praised, prayer is offered, he prays for the people, for kings, and so on. Then it happens that this venerable sacrament is consecrated. Then the priest no longer uses his own words. Instead, he uses the words of Christ. Therefore the word of Christ confects the sacrament.[13]

He goes on to ask his hearers, "Do you want to know by what divine words it is consecrated?" And then he quotes the institution narrative. Nothing could be more explicit: consecration is by the words of Christ. What is not clear is whether Ambrose is referring to the words of Christ once spoken, and recorded in the institution narratives of the New Testament, or to the recitation of these words by the bishop or priest in the eucharistic rite.

Augustine of Hippo (d. 430) followed the lead of Ambrose in identifying the words of Christ as the form of the consecration. In Sermon 227, preached to the newly baptized, the bishop of Hippo states: "That Body which you see on the altar, consecrated by the Word of God, is the Body of Christ. That chalice, or rather, what the chalice holds, consecrated by the Word of God, is the Blood of Christ."[14] Or again, in Sermon 234, also preached at Easter, Augustine says: "The faithful understand what I am saying; they know Christ in the breaking of bread. For, not all bread, but only that which receives the blessing of Christ becomes the Body of Christ."[15] McKenna properly urges caution in jumping to conclusions about Augustine's consecration theory. As with Chrysostom and Ambrose, we must ask whether by *Verbum Dei* (Word of God) Augustine means the eternally efficacious words of Christ spoken once for all time or the recitation of the words of institution by the celebrant.

---

[11] *De Mysteriis* IX, 52–54. English version from *The Fathers of the Church*, ed. by J. Deferrari *et al.* (New York, 1947–60; Washington, 1961f.), XLIV, 25–6.

[12] McKenna, 63.

[13] Text in *Des Sacrements, Des Mystères*, ed. by Bernard Botte. *Sources Chrétiennes* 25 (Paris, 1961), 108–10.

[14] English version from *The Fathers of the Church*, XXXVIII, 196.

[15] Ibid., 224.

Nevertheless, the identification of the consecration with the words of Christ, repeated in the institution narrative by the presiding minister, contributed to the view of the "moment of consecration" that developed in western Europe during the early Middle Ages. Paschasius Radbertus (d. after 856), in line with Ambrose and Augustine, contrasted Christ's all-powerful and authoritative words of institution with all other words and authorities. Only by means of his words does Christ in his omnipotence effect that bread and wine become his body and blood. "All else spoken by the priest or sung by the clergy is nothing other than praise and thanksgiving, or pertains to invocations, prayers, and supplications of the believers."[16] The more fully developed doctrine of transubstantiation stressed the exclusiveness of Christ's authoritative words of institution even more. For Thomas Aquinas, just as all prayers can be dispensed with in an emergency baptism and the sacrament of baptism is still validly administered by means of the act of baptism in the trinitarian name, so too the sacrament of the altar may be validly administered when all else is omitted in the canon of the mass and only the words of institution are spoken, as long as the priest intends to confect the sacrament. The omission of the prayers of the canon would be, in Thomas's view, an infraction of the ritual of the church, and therefore a grave sin, but it does not annul the validity of the sacrament.[17] It would seem that, while Martin Luther's elimination of the entire canon except for the words of institution in his German Mass was an act of unprecedented liturgical radicalism, he was simply drawing to a logical conclusion the formulaic expression of the consecration theory that had developed in the Western tradition.[18]

Certain ritual gestures accompanying the words of institution added to the sense that this text was the formula of consecration. As we have seen, the canon (defined as that portion of the Roman eucharistic prayer after the Sanctus) was recited silently by the priest, often while the choir continued to sing the Sanctus and Benedictus. At more solemn celebrations a procession of clerics carrying lighted tapers entered the sanctuary during the singing of the Sanctus and arranged themselves symmetrically around the altar. At less solemn celebrations two Sanctus candles were lighted on the altar after the Preface. In some places two clerics swinging thuribles (incense pots) knelt to the right and left of the altar during the Sanctus. Other servers and the worshipers in attendance were also invited to kneel after the Sanctus.[19] This could create the impression that this section of the eucharistic prayer, with the institution narrative at its center, was the most sacred portion of the eucharistic rite.

From the beginning of the eighth century the celebrant was also directed by the rubrics to make the sign of the cross over the gifts at numerous places in the text of the canon after the Sanctus. The significance of the signs of the cross became a major point in the commentaries on the mass from the tenth century on.[20] In Franco-German territory

---

[16] *De corpore et sanguine Domini*, 15; P.L. 120: 132f.

[17] *Summa Theologica* III, q. 78, a. 1, obj. 4; ad 4.

[18] Brunner, *Worship in the Name of Jesus*, op. cit., 292.

[19] See Jungmann, *The Mass of the Roman Rite*, op. cit., II, 238–40.

[20] Ibid., 243.

the sign of the cross was increasingly regarded as a general form of blessing from the tenth century on, replacing the imposition of hands that had been the customary form of blessing in the first ten centuries.[21] The sign of the cross was made especially at words like "benedictam" and "benedicis," leaving no doubt that the signing was a gesture of blessing. Within this general usage, the sign of the cross at certain points in the canon underscored the importance of those words. In particular, the sign of the cross was made almost every time the gifts were mentioned in the canon. The sign of the cross was also made at the words "gave thanks" in the institution narrative as a way of imitating Jesus' blessing of the bread and the cup.

The words of institution were also recited with dramatic gestures by the celebrant so as to indicate their importance. The priest mimed the presumed gestures of Jesus at the last supper. So at the words "he took bread in his holy and venerable hands" and "he took the cup in his holy and venerable hands" the priest also took in his hands the bread and then the cup. In some places the priest cracked the bread at the words "broke it" (*fregit*), although he did not separate the parts until the later fraction of the bread and commingling of a piece of bread with the wine in the cup. The most affective action was the rubric directing the priest to look up at the words "lifted up his eyes to you, O God, his almighty Father." The most dramatic action of all was elevation of the host after the words, "This is my body," accompanied by the ringing of the Sanctus bells, incensing in the direction of the host, and genuflection.[22] Similar actions accompanying an elevation of the chalice do not seem to have been prescribed before the Missal of Pope Pius V in 1570, partly out of fear of spilling the content of the cup and also because the content of the cup could not be seen by the faithful.

The pinpointing of the moment of consecration at the words of institution, combined with the belief that the recitation of the words of Christ effect a change in the eucharistic species, also contributed to certain developments occurring elsewhere in the eucharistic rite. The offertory procession of the faithful continued into the Middle Ages and was even revived in the Frankish church. But it was less an opportunity for the faithful to offer bread and wine for the eucharist (which was increasingly restricted to clergy and religious, since the lay people were receiving communion less frequently and large supplies of bread and wine were not needed) or other gifts for use in the services of the church (which were increasingly restricted to royalty and nobility who alone had the jewels and other goods to contribute to the church) than to offer monetary gifts, most of which were mass stipends to pay for the offering of votive masses.[23] The concluding prayer of the Roman Canon ("Per quem haec omnia, Domine, semper bona creas . . .") had originally been a reference to all the gifts that had been offered, and the concluding doxology ("Per ipsum, et cum ipso, et in ipse . . .") had been an occasion for a grand elevation of the gifts of bread and wine. Now the elevation was a more limited action because missals specified that five signs of the cross be made over the elements—three over the

---

[21] Ibid., 145–6. See also Romano Guardini, *Sacred Signs* (Wilmington, Del.: Michael Glazier, Inc., 1979), 13–4.
[22] Jungmann, ibid., 208–10.
[23] Ibid., 1ff.

host and two over the chalice. And only the host and chalice were elevated, not the larger quantities of gifts as indicated in *Ordo Romanus Primus*. So, what is connected through a collusion of medieval faith and practice is the paying of stipends to the priest to offer the sacrifice of the mass for special intentions to benefit the living and the dead. What is offered to effect these benefits is the sacrament itself—the body and blood of Christ, into which the bread and wine have been changed at the words of institution. No text of the mass said this in so many words. Indeed, the Roman canon can be regarded as a patristic text. But medieval theory and praxis was laid over patristic words to give them a new interpretation. For example, nowhere does the Roman canon speak of offering the body and blood of Christ, only of offering the gifts of the church. But the only gifts in kind usually offered were the bread and wine that were changed into the body and blood of Christ at the words of institution and then offered in the anamnesis-prayer ("Unde et memores, Domini . . . offerimus . . ."). So the view of the real presence had a profound impact on the understanding of the eucharistic sacrifice.

❦ EUCHARISTIC CONTROVERSIES IN THE EARLY MIDDLE AGES

The issue of the real presence of Christ's body and blood in the sacrament of the altar was the dominant concern in sacramental theology during the Middle Ages in the West. This is because it became a controverted issue, and it became controverted to a great extent because of the difficulty of maintaining the worldview of classical antiquity embedded in the theology of the fathers in the increasingly empirical worldview of the Western Middle Ages. Ambrose and Augustine could hold that by virtue of the words of Christ the bread and wine become figures or images of the body and blood of Christ. *Figura* to them was no mere symbol. Indeed, the eucharistic bread was not treated like ordinary bread; it had to be eaten before other food was taken, and the African fathers are early witnesses to the practice of reservation.[24] But the understanding that the symbol participates in or points to the spiritual reality was increasingly difficult to maintain in Merovingian and Carolingian Gaul.

Questions of a moment of consecration that effects a change or transformation in the species can be regarded as flowing out of the texts and actions of the liturgy itself. But the questions raised by Paschasius Radbertus in *De Corpore et Sanguine Domini* (831)[25] dealt with issues that had no connection with the lex orandi. He asked about the relationship between the eucharistic body of Christ and the historical body of Jesus that lived, died, rose again, and ascended into heaven. If it can be affirmed that they are one and the same, how can the same Christ be present at different altars at the same time? Paschasius's answer was that God multiplies the natural body of Christ at each eucharist. That it is the natural body of Christ received in the sacrament cannot be disputed, because the words of Christ say, "This is my body, this is my blood." Moreover, Paschasius

---

[24] See Archdale A. King, *Eucharistic Reservation in the Western Church*, op. cit., 19ff.

[25] See *De Corpore et Sanguine Domini*, ed. by Beda Paulus. Corpus Christianorum, continuatio mediaevalis 16 (Turnholt: Brepols, 1969).

was able to back up this assertion by appealing to a number of miracle stories in which the body of Christ was seen as raw flesh or the host took the form of a child.[26]

Because the Emperor Charles the Bald found Paschasius's eucharistic theology excessively realistic, he urged another monk of Corbie, Ratramnus, to compose another treatise on the same subject. Ratramnus's work is also entitled *De Corpore et Sanguine Domini*.[27] Without denying the real presence of Christ in the sacrament, Ratramnus disagreed that the eucharistic body should be identified with the historical body of Jesus. He held that the presence of Christ is sacramental, not material or physical. In stating this view Ratramnus proved to be a faithful disciple of Augustine in not making any distinction between "sign" and "reality."[28] For Augustine "sign" belongs to the spiritual world even though it appears in the material world. The sign appears in the material world precisely to lead people to the spiritual world. It is in this sense that Augustine defined the sacrament as the union of the earthly and the heavenly, not because he had a materialistic approach to the sacrament but because he believed that the material sign participated in the spiritual reality to which it pointed and that it strengthened faith to lead people to that reality. For Augustine the really real was the unseen spiritual reality.

Gustave Martelet showed that this unseen spiritual reality was precisely what the medieval worldview increasingly resisted. In particular, he suggested that the chief obstacle for the followers of Augustine in the early Middle Ages lies in Augustine's localization of the glorified body of Christ in heaven.[29] Radbertus wanted to hold together as one reality the historical body of Christ in heaven and the "figurative" body of Christ in the sacrament. The problem was that the worldview of his time and place saw a difference between *figura* and *veritas*. The aversion to spiritual presence among the sacramental realists led to a different answer being given to another Augustinian theologian, Berengar of Tours, two centuries later: a "substantial change" takes place in the elements.

Berengar remained within the Augustinian tradition when he taught that the body of Jesus, born of the Virgin Mary, crucified, and raised from the dead, remains in heaven until the second coming, and so it cannot be physically present on the altar. The value of the sacrament *(signum)* is that it enables us to participate in the spiritual or heavenly reality. Berengar was also within the Augustinian tradition when he distinguished between the outward sacrament (signum), which could be taken orally, and the spiritual blessing *(res)*, which only believers could receive. But because "signum et res, figura et veritas" were no longer understood as a unity, the church of his time rose up to condemn him. In 1059 he was forced to recant by confessing a very crass view of the real presence. After renouncing as heresy his teaching that "the bread and wine which are placed on the altar remain *merely a sacrament* after consecration—and not the true body and blood of our Lord Jesus Christ," he went on to "confess with mouth and heart" that

---

[26] See Nathan Mitchell, *Cult and Controversy*, op. cit., 73–80.

[27] The text is in P.L. 121:125–70.

[28] See Mitchell, 80–6.

[29] Gustave Martelet, *The Risen Christ and the Eucharistic World*, Eng. trans. (New York: Alba House, 1976), 127.

the bread and wine which are placed on the altar are not merely a sacrament after consecration, but are rather the true body and blood of our Lord Jesus Christ—and that these are truly, physically and not merely sacramentally, touched and broken by the hands of the priests and crushed by the teeth of the faithful.[30]

Behind this view is the kind of teaching that influenced popular piety in the early Middle Ages, an example of which we find in the eucharistic miracle stories collected by Caesarius of Heisterbach in *The Dialogue on Miracles* (c. 1223).[31] Caesarius tells "Of Gottschalk of Volmarstein, who saw in his hands Christ under the form of an infant"; "Of Adolf, the priest who saw the host transform itself into the virgin and child and then into a lamb, and last of all into the crucified"; "Of the priest of Wickindisburg who felt a doubt in saying the Canon and beheld raw flesh," and so forth. Stories circulated about bees that built a gothic honeycomb over a fallen host, about a woman who suffered paralysis for taking home a host and spreading it over her cabbages, and about priests and deacons who saw blood in the chalice or on the corporal. A few missals gave directions about what to do in this latter eventuality.

In spite of the widespread and popular character of this piety and its influence on the developing doctrine of the real presence, the church hierarchy and its better theologians resisted too crass an understanding of the real presence. Hence, in 1079 the text of *Ego Berengarius*, which had been adopted in 1059, was replaced by another text, which can be regarded as the first dogmatic statement of the real presence. It held that

bread and wine . . . through the mystery of the sacred prayer and by the words of the Redeemer are substantially converted (*substantialiter converti*) into the proper and life-giving flesh and blood of our Lord Jesus Christ, and that, after consecration, they are the true body of Christ which was born of the Virgin Mary and hung on the cross for the salvation of the world and which now sits on the right hand of the Father, and the true blood of Christ which was shed from his side, not only as a sign and by virtue of the sacrament, but in their proper nature and true substance.[32]

This statement provided some parameters within which a definitive doctrine of the real presence could be worked out. It asserted the identity between Christ's body in heaven and Christ's body in the sacrament, and answered the question of how this could be by referring to the miracle of sacramental change or substantial conversion. To be sure, the use of the terms "substance" and "accidents" in this connection must not be understood in strict Aristotelian ideas, which did not enter theology until the twelfth and thirteenth centuries. But there were other questions left unanswered by this statement, such as: What kind of substantial change leaves the bread and wine unchanged? What is changed and what is not? These questions would be taken up in the twelfth and thirteenth

---

[30] Cited in Mitchell, 137.

[31] Caesarius of Heisterbach, *The Dialogue on Miracles*, trans. by H. von E. Scott and C.C. Swinton Bland (London: Routledge, 1929).

[32] Text in Hermann Sasse, *This Is My Body: Luther's Contention for the Real Presence in the Sacrament of the Altar* (Minneapolis: Augsburg Publishing House, 1959), 35.

centuries as the church promulgated the dogma of transubstantiation and explained it by recourse to Aristotle's categories.

❦ THE DOGMA OF TRANSUBSTANTIATION

The articulation of the real presence in *Ego Berengarius* was possible because between the two declarations of 1059 and 1079 Lanfranc, then abbot of Saint Stephen's Monastery in Caen, became involved in the debate. Against Berengar's view that the sacrament is destroyed if bread and wine are changed into something else, Lanfranc held that the sacrament is destroyed if the bread and wine are not changed into something else. Appealing to Ambrose, he demonstrated that God's word can change what exists into something else, and that such a change occurs at the consecration of the bread and wine. In his *Liber de Corpore et Sanguine Domini* (1063), written against Berengar, Lanfranc asserted:

> We believe that through the ministry of the priest, the earthly substances on the Lord's table are sanctified by divine power in a manner that is unspeakable, incomprehensible, marvelous; and that [these substances] are changed into the essence of the Lord's body, even though the appearances of earthly elements remain.[33]

Here Lanfranc articulated a distinction between outward appearances (the bread and wine) and hidden truth (the body and blood) that would be familiar in later scholastic theology.

After this the theologians began to speak regularly of a change in the elements. They did not always use the term "transubstantiation" to signify this change. Indeed, Peter Lombard, in his *Books of the Sentences*, which became the standard theological textbook up until the Reformation, spoke of the conversion (*conversio*) of the elements. But the Fourth Lateran Council in 1215, in the *Caput Firmiter* directed against the Albigensians and other antisacramental heretical movements in the twelfth and thirteenth century, did speak of the transubstantiation of the elements. It stated:

> There is one universal Church of the faithful, outside of which no one is saved. In this church Jesus Christ Himself is priest and sacrifice, whose body and blood are truly contained in the Sacrament of the Altar under the species of bread and wine, the bread having been transubstantiated into the body, and the wine into the blood by divine power.[34]

It should be noted that the conciliar decree did not go beyond the assertion that the bread and wine are transubstantiated into the body and blood of Christ. The term "accidents" is not used at all. It was left to Thomas Aquinas to add the clarity that came from the appropriation of Aristotelian metaphysics.

The "angelic doctor" held that the species of bread and wine are destroyed in the consecration, but the accidents (what is perceptible to the senses) are not affected by the

---

[33] P.L. 50:430; cited in Mitchell, 146–7.

[34] H. Denzinger and A. Schönmetzer, eds., *Enchiridion Symbolorum Definitionem et Declarationem*, 33rd ed. (Rome: Herder, 1965), 430. Cited in Sasse, 19.

change. Thomas knew that in this metaphysical system accidents could not exist without substance, so he appealed to Aristotle's second category, quantity, and suggested that quantity (appearance) replaced substance (essence). This too required a metaphysical miracle, but it is important to remember that Thomas was not trying to deny the miraculous; he was only attempting to explain the phenomenon. As Hermann Sasse points out, Thomas's doctrine of transubstantiation is not materialistic; *substantia* (essence) is a metaphysical concept, not a material reality. Moreover, transubstantiation is not magical; it appeals to the consecratory power of the Verba Christi.[35] Sasse does not find this objectionable from a Lutheran point of view. What he finds objectionable is that "the Roman Church did not stick with this conviction, but rather made the priest a partner of Christ in this most solemn act of the Mass."[36]

The doctrine of the real presence, articulated by the dogma of transubstantiation, had an impact on the understanding of the eucharistic sacrifice. The eucharist continued to be introduced by the Gratias agimus, but increasingly during the Middle Ages the offering was made as a petition for some special intention. The concept and practice of the votive mass had become so widespread by the tenth century that the following formula found its way into the ordination rite in the Pontificale Romano-Germanicum (c. 950): the ordaining bishop says to the newly ordained when presenting to him the chalice and paten, "Accipe potestatem offerre sacrificium Deo, Missamque celebrare tan pro vivis quam pro defunctis, in nomine Domini" (Receive the power to offer sacrifice to God, and to celebrate Mass, for both the living and the dead, in the name of the Lord).[37]

The *traditio instrumentorum* (handing over of instruments) came into ordination rites in the Middle Ages as an element of feudalism. It is true that handing over books and other objects of one's liturgical role is a custom that is already present in the *Apostolic Tradition* of Hippolytus, and it remained a practice in the conferring of "minor orders." But from the Investiture Controversy, in which bishops or priests were granted fiefs by kings and lords with a feudal rite, such a custom found its way into the ordination of candidates for "major orders" as well. Thomas Aquinas could say, as if it were obvious, "The conferring of a power is effected by giving to its subjects something which belongs to the proper exercise of that power."[38] The moment of authorization in ordination rites was shifting from the laying on of hands to the handing over of the instruments of office, and the priestly office was being defined as one that had "power to offer sacrifice to God for the living and the dead."

It is important to understand this development in order to understand that Luther's doctrine of the priesthood of all believers was not a polemic against ordained ministry as such, but against the sacrifice of the mass.[39] He did not object to the authority

---

[35] Sasse, 43ff.

[36] Ibid., 45.

[37] See Joseph A. Jungmann, *The Mass: An Historical, Theological, and Pastoral Survey*, trans. by Julian Fernandes, ed. by Mary Ellen Evans (Collegeville: The Liturgical Press, 1976), 146.

[38] In *IV Sent.*, XXIV, 2–3; see J. H. Crehan, "Medieval Ordinations," in *The Study of Liturgy*, op. cit., 326.

[39] See Carl F. Wisløff, *The Gift of Communion. Luther's Controversy with Rome on Eucharistic Sacrifice*, trans. by Joseph M. Shaw (Minneapolis: Augsburg Publishing House, 1964), 73–97.

of the minister of the word and sacraments to preside over and administer the sacrament of the altar; he objected to the idea that the ordained priest could offer the sacrifice of the mass for special intentions (vota). As we shall see in the next chapter, Luther objected to offering the mass to procure special benefits from God when Christ instituted the sacrament for the benefit of his people, chiefly as the gift of communion with himself. But here we would note that the benefits of such special intentions were dependent on the offering not just of the gifts of bread and wine, but of the body and blood of Christ. As we have said, the Roman canon did not say that the body and blood of Christ were being offered to God, in so many words. But for Thomas Aquinas, the "something done" in the mass that makes it a sacrifice is not the offering of the elements at all, either at the offertory or in the oblation of the anamnesis-prayer, but the consecration when the bread and wine are changed (transubstantiated) into the body and blood of Christ.[40] This is where the dogma of transubstantiation had a bearing on the eucharistic sacrifice: the sacrifice was the consecration (*sacrum facere*).

 ## THE UNDERSTANDING OF EUCHARISTIC SACRIFICE DURING THE MIDDLE AGES

Thomas Aquinas and Duns Scotus

The great schoolmen of the High Middle Ages actually devoted little attention to the understanding of eucharistic sacrifice. They were consumed with the issues of consecration and the real presence. When they did turn their attention to eucharistic sacrifice, they did not base their theology on the text of the eucharistic canon, which speaks variously of the people's gifts, of the offering of the bread and cup, and our offering of ourselves. They based it instead on the notion of sacrifice itself and how the sacrifice of Christ is represented in the celebration. They noted that the word "sacrifice" literally means "to consecrate," or "to make holy," from sacrum facere; it is not the same as "to offer."[41] So, for Thomas Aquinas, the *sacrificium* is not the *oblatio* but the *consecratio*.

The purpose of the consecration was to transform the bread and wine that are offered as the gifts of the church into the sacramental signs of the body and blood of Christ, which convey to the faithful the benefits that Christ won for his people by his atoning sacrifice of the cross. But the problem was to explain the relationship between the presence of that sacrifice in the mass and the benefits that accrued to the faithful because of the sacrifice of the mass, especially when the "fruits of communion" (which no commentators grew tired of enumerating) were extended to all manner of benefits for the living and the dead.

Francis Clark, in a massive work, set out to take up, one by one, the charges made by the Protestant reformers and, later, Anglican theologians against the medieval

---

[40] See John Jay Hughes, "Eucharistic Sacrifice: Transcending the Reformation Deadlock," *Worship* 43 (1969), 541.

[41] See Sebastian Moore, "The Theology of the Mass and the Liturgical Datum," *Downside Review* 69 (1951), 31–44.

understanding of the eucharistic sacrifice.[42] He sought to demonstrate that there was little development in the theology of sacrifice beyond what is found in the *Four Books of the Sentences* of Peter Lombard, and that even this was dependent on the patristic understanding bequeathed to the medieval church, especially from Ambrose and Augustine. But the passages quoted from these fathers have to do with the commemoration of the sacrifice of Christ, understood in the sense of anamnesis. The eucharistic sacrifice was understood by the fathers to be the memorial or reactualization of the sacrifice of Christ's life (actually the whole life of the incarnation, not just Christ's death on the cross). One celebrated passage that Lombard cites from Ambrose, although it is actually from John Chrysostom, is as follows:

> In Christ the saving victim was offered once. Then what of ourselves? Do we not offer every day? Although we do offer daily, that is done for the recalling of his death, and the victim is one, not many. But how can that be—one and not many? Because Christ was immolated once. For this sacrifice is what corresponds to that sacrifice of his: the same reality, remaining always the same, is offered and so this is the same sacrifice. Otherwise, would you say that because the sacrifice is offered in many places, therefore there are many Christs? No, but there is one Christ in all those places, fully present here and fully present there. And just as what is offered in all places is one and the same body, so there is one and the same sacrifice. Christ offered a victim and we offer the selfsame now; but what we do is a *recalling* of his sacrifice.[43]

The master of the *Sentences* comments on this and other patristic texts: "From these passages we gather that what is done at the altar both is called and is a sacrifice, and that Christ was offered once and is offered daily, but in a different manner then and now."[44] The "different manner" refers to the fact that the sacrifice of the mass is not a bloody sacrifice.

The great theologians of the High Middle Ages repeated these standard citations compiled in the *Sentences* of Peter Lombard or in the *Decretals* of Gratian. But the question is how they understood the language used by the fathers in the light of developments in theology and practice. In the light of the prevalence of allegorical interpretation in the medieval *Expositiones missae*, is the "representation of the Passion" in the eucharist understood in terms of anamnesis (liturgical reactualization) or mimesis (dramatic portrayal)? How does each understanding affect the relationship between the sacrifice of the cross and the sacrifice of the mass? If the two offerings are not related, for what can the sacrifice of the mass be offered that was not covered by the sacrifice of the cross?

Thomas Aquinas explained the idea of the mass as a sacrifice by reason of the fact that it is a representation of the passion of Christ. His understanding of *repraesentatio* was not that of reenactment in a mimetic sense, but a recalling in image and efficacy of the sacrifice of Christ. In *Summa Theologia*, Part III, Question 83, art. 1, he wrote: "Celebratio autem huius sacramenti . . . est imago quaedam est repraesentative passionis

---

[42] Francis Clark, S.J., *Eucharistic Sacrifice and the Reformation*, 2nd ed. (Oxford: Basil Blackwell, 1967).

[43] *Petri Lombardi Libri IV Sententiarum*, IV, d. 12, c. 5; cited in Clark, 75–6. The original passage is in P.G. 63: 131.

[44] Cited in Clark, 76.

Christi quae est vera ejus immolatio." This seems to suggest the patristic view that the eucharist is the reactualization of the sacrifice of Christ. Such a view would imply that the same benefits won in the atoning sacrifice are conveyed to the faithful through the sacrament.

But in Question 79 he seems to suggest that the devotion of those who offer the oblation is what finally determines the extent of the satisfaction received. He had to account for the prevalent practice of the votive mass. His problem was that he found it difficult to identify an offering by Christ in the mass because he saw the eucharist functioning primarily as a sacrament to convey the fruits of the passion in the person of Christ himself, really present in the sacramental species. The only act of offering he could identify was the people's oblation of bread and wine. So his statement in Question 79 seems to suggest that the offering of the mass is distinct from the offering of the cross. If this is so, then we are witnessing already in Thomas that historicization of the sacrifice of the cross that Ferdinand Pratzner called "the crisis of the sacramental idea"—the process by which the unity of the cross and the altar were rent asunder in the theology of the medieval schoolmen.[45] The "crisis" was that the sacrifice of Christ was confined to the atoning sacrifice on Calvary, which implied that some different sacrifice was being offered in the mass.

This "crisis" was carried further in the eucharistic theology of Duns Scotus. As in Aquinas, the material provided by Scotus on which to understand his views on eucharistic sacrifice is scanty. It is contained in only one of his *Quaestiones Quodlibetales*.[46] There he discusses it only incidentally while dealing with a casuistic problem concerning mass stipends. But how he conceives of the nature of sacrifice is clear enough. He held that the eucharistic oblation is the commemoration of the redemptive sacrifice of Calvary.

> The Mass consists both in representation of that offering made upon the cross and in pleading thereby: that is, pleading that through it God would accept the sacrifice of the Church. (When one pleads he usually does so by adducing something which is more acceptable to him whose favor is sought than is the entreaty of the petitioner himself.)[47]

The question is how Scotus understands "repraesentatio." It would seem that he viewed the "representation of that offering made upon the cross" as a ritual or liturgical reenactment rather than as a reactualization or making present of that offering. He opposed the opinion of some theologians that the mass was of equal efficacy with the sacrifice of the cross, and therefore was only of finite value in comparison with the infinite value of the atoning sacrifice.

> The Mass is not equal in worth to the passion of Christ, although it has a special worth inasmuch as it is a special commemoration of the oblation which Christ offered on the cross.[48]

---

[45] Ferdinand Pratzner, *Messe und Kreuzesopfer. Die Krise der Sakramentalen Idee bei Luther und in der Mittelalterlichen Scholastik* (Wien: Herder, 1970), 70–6.

[46] *Quodlibet* XX, in Duns Scotus, *Opera Omnia*, Vivès ed. (Paris, 1895), 26: 298–331.

[47] Ibid., 321.

[48] Ibid.

The "crisis of the sacramental idea" is clear here: the cross and the altar have been pulled apart. The sacrament is not viewed as a reactualization of the sacrifice of Christ, with the same benefits won in the atoning sacrifice being bestowed on the communicants: for example, forgiveness of sins, reconciliation with God, participation in the risen life of Christ, eternal salvation. This set the stage for confusion over the benefits or "fruits" of the mass in relation to the benefits of Calvary. If the sacrifice of the mass is a different sacrifice from that of Calvary, then it bestows different benefits.

Gabriel Biel and Cardinal Cajetan

In Clark's view, "there was no original speculation about the eucharistic sacrifice in the autumn period of medieval scholasticism."[49] But we are already alerted to the fact that the lack of speculation was more complicated, and that subtle theological changes were taking place. As representative of orthodox Catholic views on the eucharistic sacrifice on the eve of the Reformation, Clark takes the writings of Gabriel Biel (c. 1410–1495) and Tommaso de Vio (Cardinal Cajetan) (1469–1534). Biel, a Nominalist theologian, has been called the last of the medieval doctors (*Doctor profundissimus*). He held the position of preacher at the Cathedral of Mainz from 1462, and many of his sermons were circulated in printed editions. He was also a member of the Brethren of the Common Life, espousing the devotio moderna.[50] Martin Luther attended a school supported by the Brethren as part of his elementary education. Biel's *Expositio sacri canonis missae* was well known and Luther regarded it as the best book the Catholics possessed on the subject.[51] A copy of Biel's *Expositio* with Luther's own annotations is still extant. It is known that Luther read Biel's commentary before celebrating his first mass.[52] In his eucharistic theology Biel represented the Scotist school, which emphasized the representative or commemorative aspect of the eucharistic sacrifice. This position understood the sacrifice to be the ritual presentation of Christ, really present, before the Father in heaven in order to plead the merits of his passion for the benefits of the faithful in the church on earth.

Cardinal Cajetan, a Dominican theologian, was the leading Thomist theologian of his day. He was named a cardinal in 1517, and in 1518 was the papal legate to the imperial Diet of Augsburg. He came into direct confrontation with Luther at Augsburg in 1518, where he was mandated to examine Luther as part of the canonical procedure required by the accusations of error and heresy leveled against the Augustinian monk. He attempted to get Luther to recant his position on indulgences and on faith, but the Wittenberg theologian held to his positions. Later, in 1520, Cajetan drafted the bull of excommunication against Luther. Thereafter he played a leading role in the defense of Catholic faith and practice: in particular, on papal primacy (1521), on the eucharistic

---

[49] Clark, p. 78.

[50] See Steven E. Ozment, *The Age of Reform, 1250–1550: An Intellectual and Religious History of Late Medieval and Reformation Europe* (New Haven, 1980).

[51] See *Luthers Tischreden* III (Weimar, 1914), 192, no. 3146. *Gabrielis Biel Canonis missae expositio*, ed. by Heiko A. Oberman and William J. Courtenay, 4 vols. (Weisbaden, 1963–1967).

[52] Ibid., 564–5, no. 3722.

presence of Christ's body and blood (1525), the sacrifice of the mass (1531), and on justi-fying faith and good works (1532).[53] In 1530, Cajetan recommended to Pope Clement VII that he seek to heal the confessional differences between Rome and the Lutherans by conceding to the Lutherans communion under both kinds, the restoration of the chalice to lay communicants, and clerical marriage.

In comparing passages from these two theologians, Clark finds "substantial agreement" on the following issues:

1. The mass-sacrifice is a memorial of Calvary, but not a mere memorial.[54]
2. Although the mass is in a true sense one with the all-sufficient sacrifice of the cross, the manner of offering is different, for Christ does not die or suffer anew at the altar.[55]
3. The eucharistic sacrifice is the means through which the efficacy of the one redemptive sacrifice is mediated and applied to mankind.[56]

Clark has assembled an impressive array of primary and secondary sources in his study to document these theses on the late medieval teaching of the eucharistic sacrifice. His purpose was to show, contrary to the charges especially of Anglo-Catholic theolo-gians, that late medieval eucharistic theology is not the result of mere popular abuses or unorthodox teaching.[57] Rather, it represents the traditional Catholic view that prevailed throughout the whole of the Middle Ages and that was reaffirmed by the Council of Trent. Not even in the so-called baleful medieval bequest of Nominalism was there a de-parture from the traditional doctrine of sacrifice. There was, however, a considerable de-parture from the ancient Christian concept of Mysterium, the sense of the presence of the redemptive event in the sacramental celebration.

Clark's purpose was to show that the reformers understood the received doc-trine of sacrifice quite well, and that they rejected it because of their fundamental objec-tion to Catholic incarnational theology. "The Reformation hostility to the sacrifice of the altar is to be connected, in a coherent pattern, with the basic Reformation doctrines of grace, of justification, of the Church and the sacraments, and ultimately of Christology."[58] All of these Protestant doctrines are opposed, in Clark's view, to the Catholic conception of Christianity as incarnational religion "in the sense that the Church, transforming the

---

[53] See Jared Wicks, *Cajetan Responds: A Reader in Reformation Controversy* (Washington, D.C., 1978), an an-thology of texts in English from Cajetan's polemical works against Lutheran positions.

[54] Clark, 84.

[55] Ibid., 86.

[56] Ibid., 88.

[57] B. J. Kidd, *The Later Medieval Doctrine of the Eucharistic Sacrifice* (London, 1958; first published 1898), brought together charges made by Anglo-Catholics of the nineteenth century against the late medieval theology of the mass. His purpose was to show the orthodoxy of the English Reformation on this issue. This view was enormously influential on other Anglican scholars: e.g., Charles Gore, *The Body of Christ* (London, 1901; reprinted 1931); Darwell Stone, *A History of the Doctrine of the Holy Eucharist*, 2 vols. (London, 1909); E. J. A. Bicknell, *A Theological Introduction to the Thirty-Nine Articles of the Church of England* (London, 1919; 3rd ed., revised by H. J. Carpenter, 1955); F. C. N. Hicks, *The Fullness of Sacrifice* (London, 1953); E. L. Mascall, *The Recovery of Unity* (London, 1958); and C. W. Dugmore, *The Mass and the English Reformers* (London, 1958).

[58] Clark, 103.

world by the divine life of grace which flows to her from Christ her head, is a perpetual extension of Christ's incarnation."[59]

The sources amassed by Clark to document his contentions are impressive. He has made a case that the reformers did not deal with the best medieval theology on the eucharistic sacrifice. However, he has not adequately grasped the reformers' true concern about the eucharistic sacrifice, especially Luther's view (which we shall take up in the next chapter).[60] Nor has he dealt with the piety and practice of the mass which was so instrumental in shaping theological reflections. A scholastic theology operating from an Aristotelean basis would tend to be more phenomenological than speculative in approach, and would seek to provide a theological rationale for existing practices. So even if, as Clark rightly asserts, practical abuses do not adequately account for the reformers' attacks on the mass, theory and praxis still impact each other in a very complex way.

John Jay Hughes, in the most thorough analysis of Clark's work published to date, charges that Clark failed to take account of the possibility "that wrong theories are often developed in order to explain and justify bad practices."[61] It is impossible, for example, to study the late medieval concept of the eucharistic sacrifice without paying attention to the existence of a vast proletariat of "mass priests" who celebrated masses for special intentions. Apart from the question of simony raised by the buying and selling of masses, the very mechanical way in which these masses were celebrated caused the reformers to attack the concept of *ex opere operato*. As K. L. Wood-Legh wrote,

> The constant insistence on the daily performance of the appointed services with whatever additions to the established ritual, such as the sprinkling of the tombs at St. Giles's, Edinburgh, the founder had chosen to prescribe, and the recitation of prayers and psalms which if omitted on one day were to be made up on the next, appear to give a high, almost a magical, value to the mere repetition of formulae, reminiscent of the scribes of our Lord's day, who thought to be heard for their much speaking.[62]

Attendant on the multiplication of masses was the theory of the limited value of each mass. Here is a classic example of how this theory serves to justify the existing practice, and how the theory furthers the practice. The German Catholic scholar, Erwin Iserloh, explains the process in this way:

> In the fourteenth and fifteenth centuries the generally accepted theory was that the Mass had a limited value. A consequence of this theory was that a Mass that was offered for a single person benefitted him more than a Mass celebrated for him and others together. What produced this opinion was not so much the the-

---

[59] Ibid.

[60] For an Anglican critique of Clark's work see E. L. Mascall, "Eucharistic Sacrifice and the Reformation," *Theology* 64 (1961), 310–6. In the preface to the second edition of his work, Clark notes the research of Norwegian theologian Carl F. Wisløff, *The Gift of Communion*, op. cit., and expressions appreciation for the vindication of Catholic theology "from some time-worn misrepresentations;" but he does not allow Wisløff's study of Luther's attack on the sacrifice of the mass to affect any change in his understanding of the reasons for Luther's attack.

[61] John Jay Hughes, *Stewards of the Lord. A Reappraisal of Anglican Orders* (London and Syndey, 1970), 43.

[62] K. L. Wood-Legh, *Perpetual Chantries in Britain* (Cambridge, 1965), 312–3.

ology of eucharistic sacrifice—there was no such theology at this period—as the practice of the church, which allowed frequent Masses to be said for individuals, and which forbade a priest to accept several stipends for a single Mass.[63]

Gabriel Biel argues for the "commemorative representation" (*rememorativam repraesentationem*) of the sacrifice of the cross in the mass not only on the basis that Christ cannot die again, and hence the mass cannot be as efficacious as Calvary; but also on the basis that if the mass had the same efficacy as Calvary, one mass would suffice to redeem the whole world and release all the souls from purgatory. Then there would be no point in having so many mass-priests and so many masses for various intentions.[64] Since the value of each mass is limited, Biel argued that the "fruit" of each mass is also limited. Under this "quantitative" concept, a mass celebrated for one person is of greater value for that person than if it were celebrated for a large number of persons. In Hughes's view, such a "quantitative and materialistic conception of grace" would inevitably lead "to a radically false conception of the soul's relationship with God." Here is the basis, then, of the works-righteousness attacked by the reformers.

Such a view, however, also indicates that Biel does not seem to recognize the role of Christ as high priest in the eucharistic celebration, that is, that he is the high priest (*sacerdos principalis*) at the mass just as he was at Calvary. In this regard, writes Hans Bernhard Meyer, Biel has not overcome the position of the Scotist-Nominalist school.[65] A conception of Christ as sacerdos principalis in the mass would have enabled Biel to regard the eucharist as the representation or sign of the eternally valid sacrifice of Christ, such as Thomas had taught.

It would seem that for Biel the meaning of *commemoratio* was more the recollection of a distant historical event than the presence or reactualization of that salvation event with its benefits to the believers. This view of commemoration was reinforced by the allegorical interpretation of the mass characteristic of the medieval Expositiones missae. These commentaries tended to ignore the texts of the mass in any literal sense and concentrate instead on such external things as manual actions, ceremonial movements, vestments, altar appointments, and so forth, for the purpose of reminding the faithful of some aspect of Christ's passion. In this way the whole mass became a dramatic reenactment of Calvary. In some commentaries, each vestment worn by the priest represents some aspect of the passion: for example, the alb signified the gown given to Christ after his scourging, the amice symbolized the crown of thorns, the chasuble symbolized the cross of Christ (made more realistic by embroidering large crosses on the garment).[66] While some interpretations were widely accepted and taught, it should be remembered that the nature of allegorical interpretation is that there is no intrinsic connection between the object and what it is held to symbolize.

---

[63] E. Iserloh, "Der Wert der Messe in der Diskussion der Theologen vom Mittelalter bis zum 16. Jahrhundert," *Zeitschrift für katholische Theologie* 83 (1961), 66; cited and trans. in Hughes, op. cit., 49.

[64] Biel, Lectio 27, L; Oberman and Courtenay, I, 265.

[65] Hans Bernhard Meyer, *Luther und die Messe* (Paderborn, 1965), 155.

[66] See John P. Dolan, *History of the Reformation*, op. cit., 195ff.

Biel himself engaged in this kind of allegorical interpretation. He taught, for example, that the canon is recited silently to symbolize Christ hiding himself from the mul-
titudes, because the working of the canon is secret and hidden from the understanding of
reason, and so that the words of this great mystery are not cheapened by daily use and
public utterance.[67] To his credit, says J. H. Crehan, Biel did not develop interpretations
just according to his own fancy. Rather, he provided numerous explanations that he had
found in his sources and left it to his readers to sort them out.[68] Even so, these allegorical
explanations served to turn the mass into a drama. It may indeed be both a memorial and
a sacrifice; but the memores is no longer understood as the presence of God's redemptive
work in Jesus Christ, and the offerimus is no longer the self-offering of the faithful by
which they appeal to and surrender themselves to the effects of the saving mystery.

We must reckon with the fact that by the late Middle Ages the memorial of the
saving mystery had disintegrated into a multiplicity of mysteries called to mind by the various ceremonies of the mass. Repraesentatio was no longer understood in a sacramental
sense and the eucharistic sacrifice was no longer offered by the people. The oblation was
offered by the priest on behalf of the people while the people's money-offerings served as
means of paying for mass-stipends or buying indulgences. Luther rightly criticized this
kind of eucharistic celebration as a *monopolium sacerdotale*. As the people became *ad-
stantes* rather than *communicantes*, the corporate nature of Christian worship was lost
sight of. The multiplication of masses, altars, priests, and the privatization of masses contributed to the late medieval disintegration of eucharistic faith and practice. As Jungmann
wrote, the result was that

> The liturgy is no longer understood in its sacramental depth, and lies unused, in
> spite of the Eucharistic movement of the time, in spite of the tremendous re-
> gard of the Mass, in spite of the frequency with which Mass was celebrated—
> perhaps because of this frequency.[69]

This kind of liturgical situation was bound to have an effect on theology. Clark
advises us not to expect "to find in the late medieval period, when theological speculation
was at a less developed stage, a uniform and complete explanation of the unity of altar and
cross in the Christian sacrifice."[70] He admits that it is possible to find "two trends of
thought" on the eucharistic sacrifice at the beginning of the sixteenth century. One was
the Scotist viewpoint, which explained the mass as a liturgical representation before God
of Christ, really present, by a rite that commemorated his death on Calvary through
which the faithful could "plead" the merits of Christ. The other point of view was the
Thomist, which was more reminiscent of the Greek fathers. It held to "the permanence
of Christ's sacrifice in the 'sacramental mystery.'" [71] This interpretation must be qualified
by the recent discussion of "the crisis of the sacramental idea," to which we have referred.

---

[67] Biel, Lectio 15, E; Oberman and Courtenay, I, 123.
[68] J. H. Crehan, "Biel on the Mass," *The Clergy Review* 43 (1958), 606–17.
[69] Joseph A. Jungmann, *Pastoral Liturgy*, Eng. trans. (New York: Herder and Herder, 1962), 78.
[70] Clark, 260.
[71] Ibid.

Nevertheless, Thomas did speak of repraesentatio in a different sense than the Scotists, that is, as a "re-presentation" of Christ's redemptive sacrifice.[72] This Thomist point of view was represented by Cajetan, who wrote in *De missae sacrificio et ritu adversus Lutheranos*:

> The victim is one and the same, but there are two manners in which he is immolated. The first, the original, unique and proper manner of immolation, was by way of shedding of blood; that is, under natural appearances (*in propria specie*), when his blood was shed and his body broken on the cross. The second manner, which recurs every day, a manner which is extrinsic and accessory to the first (*externus accesoriusque*), is unbloody—re-presenting in an immolatory manner (*immolatitio modo repraesentans*), under the appearance of bread and wine, Christ offered on the cross.[73]

Here was an understanding of eucharistic memorial and sacrifice that could have profitably entered into dialogue with the reformers' views. Cajetan taught that the value of the mass is unlimited, and therefore the fruits of the mass are unlimited; that the merits of Christ's passion are imputed to the faithful through the mass, but that their beneficial reception is dependent on the faith of the recipient; that the efficacy of the mass celebrated for the dead is in relation to their own previous faith, and to the faith of those sharing in the mass here and now; that Christ is the only true offerer of the mass because he is the only true priest of the new covenant (although the priests of the church are his ministers); and that the mass is not an independent sacrifice, but a sacrifice in substantial unity with the sacrifice of the cross.[74] Here indeed is a formidable theology of the eucharistic sacrifice. But the findings of Notker Halmer suggest that it went largely without notice in its own day and exerted no influence in the following centuries.[75] Iserloh suggests that the Nominalist understanding of repraesentatio was the prevalent view on the eve of the Reformation and that it was strongly represented in the leading Catholic polemicist of the Reformation period, Johannes Eck,[76] with whom Luther debated at Leipzig in 1519.

The problem with the Nominalist understanding of repraesentatio was that it was not able to show the unity between the cross and the altar. Biel spoke of the mass as the representation of Christ's "testament," effected by his death on the cross. The benefits of that testament are distributed in the eucharist.[77] This is certainly the origin of the testament-idea developed by Luther, although for Biel the testament was the new law while for Luther it was the forgiveness of sins. In expressing the presence of the testament in the sacrament, Biel explicitly rejected the idea that the sacrifice of the mass is a

---

[72] Ibid., 264.

[73] Cited in ibid., 88.

[74] See the summary of Cajetan's eucharistic theology in Hughes, *Stewards of the Lord*, 93–6.

[75] Notker Halmer, "Die Messopferspekulation von Kardinal Cajetan und Ruard Tapper," *Divus Thomas* 21 (1943), 187–212.

[76] Erwin Iserloh, *Die Eucharistie in der Darstellung des Johannes Eck. Ein Beitrag zur vortridentinischen Theologie* (Münster, 1950), 92, 344.

[77] Biel, *Expositio*, Lectio 53, N.

repetition of the sacrifice of the cross in the sense of a "new slaying of Christ." Christ has offered himself on the cross once and for all, and that offering cannot be repeated. But, as Heiko Oberman suggests, Biel could have demonstrated the relationship between the two offerings if he had appealed to the high priestly role of Christ, as Luther did in his *Treatise on the New Testament* on the basis of Hebrews 9:24 and Romans 8:34.[78]

> From these words we learn that we do not offer Christ as a sacrifice, but that Christ offers us. And in this way it is permissible, yes, profitable, to call the mass a sacrifice; not on its own account, but because we offer ourselves as a sacrifice along with Christ. That is, we lay ourselves on Christ by a firm faith in his testament and do not otherwise appear before God with our prayer, praise, and sacrifice except through Christ and his mediation. Nor do we doubt that Christ is our priest and minister in heaven before God.[79]

An appeal to the high priestly role of Christ would have made it possible for Biel and other late medieval theologians to speak of the presence of the same benefits won on the cross in the sacrament (in Luther's terminology, "the forgiveness of sins, life and salvation"). There would have been no need to view the mass as another offering to receive other benefits.

The Middle Ages thus came to a close with a prevailing theology that was unable to demonstrate the presence of the sacrifice of the cross with all its saving benefits in the eucharist because it worked with an affective concept of commemoration rather than an effective one. Eck picked up the testament-idea and said that this implied the death of the testator, a death that was in this case a sacrifice. He could therefore argue that the presence of Christ's body and blood, which is his testament, also implies a sacrifice that is daily repeated in the commemoration of the mass—that is, a different sacrifice that applied to different needs than the sacrifice of the cross. Luther could not grant, on this premise, that a real sacrifice was taking place in the mass.[80] In part this was because Luther believed, like Eck, that a sacrifice required the death of the victim, and there was no such death in the mass. But also, *repraesentatio* had come to be understood to mean a "portrayal" of a reality rather than the presence of the reality itself.[81] On this basis the whole question could turn on the effectiveness of the commemoration, and Luther could argue that in the long run it would be better to hear sermons than to watch the dramatic spectacle of the mass.[82]

Thus, we have seen a very complex development in which, under the impact of an empirical worldview, the ancient Christian concept of Mysterium was lost in medieval theology. "Symbol" and "truth," "sacrament" and "reality" were torn asunder in the concern to defend and explain the real presence of Christ; speculation concerning the presence and effect of Christ's sacrifice was limited to consideration of the fruits of the mass;

---

[78] Heiko Oberman, *The Harvest of Medieval Theology* (Cambridge, Mass.: Harvard University Press, 1963), 279–80.

[79] Martin Luther, *Treatise on the New Testament*; LW 35:98–9.

[80] Iserloh, op. cit., 71–2.

[81] Ibid., 344.

[82] Ibid., 288.

and the dramatic features of the mass were exploited allegorically for the purpose of putting the faithful in mind of the passion of Christ for their sakes. The result was a "historicizing" of the sacrifice of the cross in both medieval and Reformation theologies. Any discussion of the mass as a propitiatory sacrifice could only suggest to the reformers that the all-sufficiency of Christ's once-for-all atoning sacrifice was being undermined and that the purpose of the sacrament as the gift of communion with Christ had been reversed to turn the sacrament into a sacrifice that the priest offers to God for benefits not covered by the sacrifice of Christ on the cross. Missing from this whole discussion is the biblical and patristic concept of anamnesis as the reactualization of the saving event, which might have averted the impasse between Catholic and evangelical theology. Such a concept would have enabled both sides to hold together the unity between the offering of Christ on the cross and the offering of the people of God in the eucharist. Gustav Aulén worked out this understanding of the commemoration of the sacrifice of Christ in the mass:

> The redemptive work of Christ continues through all ages and generations. This activity rests on the finished act of reconciliation and involves a continuous realization of the reconciliation which has been won. "The Sacrifice" of which we may speak in this connection is not an atoning sacrifice, but an expression of this indissoluble union between Christ and his church. The continuous, "high priestly" sacrifice testifies that the new life of the church issues from the life of Christ.[83]

This was a sense in which Luther too was reluctantly able to speak of the eucharist as a "sacrifice"—the real presence of the *totus Christus* in the celebration. Furthermore, because the presence of Christ is made tangible in the eucharistic elements, the gifts of the sacrament are real. The new relationship between God and humanity is accomplished by the sacrifice of Christ, and the benefits of this sacrifice are conveyed to the faithful in the sacraments. The sacraments are means of grace: they bring about this new relationship with God (in Holy Baptism) and nurture it (in Holy Communion).

---

[83]Gustav Aulén, *Eucharist and Sacrifice*, trans. by Eric H. Wahlstrom (Philadelphia: Muhlenberg Press, 1958), 99–100.

PART TWO

Reformation Liturgical Traditions

CHAPTER 8

Luther's Liturgical Reforms

M ARTIN LUTHER WAS NOT the first reformer to call for renewal of the church. Reform was, in fact, a medieval idea, particularly associated with a number of reform movements in the monasteries that produced new and more observant rules, houses, and orders of monks.[1] Two martyred reformers of the fifteenth century, Jan Hus of Bohemia and Savanarola of Florence, signaled to many the need of the late medieval church for reform in doctrine and in life. Two other towering fifteenth-century reformers, Jean de Gerson, chancellor of the University of Paris, and the German Cardinal Nicholas von Cusa, attempted to reform the church by curbing the excesses of piety and superstition and through conciliarism.[2] But they ultimately failed because they only tinkered with the educational and constitutional structures of the church. Luther's reformation attacked the heart of the medieval church—the sacramental system.

Yngve Brilioth remarked that "at no point was Luther so violently opposed to the medieval system as in his repudiation of the Roman doctrine of the Mass."[3] We have seen that there was no single "Roman doctrine of the mass" as much as theological rationales

---

[1] See Heiko A. Oberman, *Luther: Man Between God and the Devil*, trans. by Eileen Walliser-Schwartzbart (New York: Doubleday Image Book, 1989), 50ff.

[2] John P. Dolan, *History of the Reformation*, op. cit., 139ff.

[3] Yngve Brilioth, *Eucharistic Faith and Practice, Evangelical and Catholic*, trans. by A. G. Hebert (London: S.P.C.K., 1965), 137.

for a host of unevangelical practices. As Luther's theology developed in his search for a gracious God, his appreciation deepened for the means of grace by which God comes to humanity in Christ.[4] His reforms aimed at liberating the evangelical sacraments that communicate Christ from their captivity to misuse. In *The Babylonian Captivity of the Church (De Captivitate Babylonica Ecclesiae,* 1520), Luther denied that there were seven sacraments and accepted for the moment only the three that could claim dominical institution: "baptism, penance, and the bread."[5] Concerning the sacrament of the bread, he attacked the withholding of the cup from lay communicants, the doctrine of transubstantiation, and the notion that the mass is a good work and a sacrifice. It was the attack on the mass as a sacrifice that had radical liturgical consequences, but the nature of this critique has not always been understood. Unless Luther's critique of the sacrifice of the mass is understood in terms of what he attacked and why, it is not possible to move beyond the liturgical deadlock of the sixteenth century.

🍇 THE ASSAULT ON THE MASS-SACRIFICE

The "Roman doctrine of the mass" that Luther attacked was less related to theology than to practice, piety, and liturgical order. The removal of the cup from communicants had already been attacked by the Hussites in the fifteenth century, and the treatment of Jan Hus by the papacy still rankled Christians in central Europe a century later. (Luther's Saxony was situated geographically next to Hus's Bohemia.) Luther approached this issue, however, more in terms of disobedience to the dominical institution and denial of the right of the baptized to receive the full sacramental sign than because of any fundamental disagreement with the doctrine of concomitance.[6] While he repudiated the dogma of transubstantiation (and scholastic theology generally), he steadfastly embraced the doctrine of the real presence of Christ's body and blood in, with, and under the elements of bread and wine. His purpose was not to propose a new way of explaining the real presence by recourse to rational theology (e.g., with the doctrine of consubstantiation); his concern was rather to affirm the mystery of the presence of Christ without any recourse to scholastic constructs.[7] But Luther did have a theological point to raise that carried his critique beyond the efforts of Jean de Gerson and Nicholas von Cusa, among others, to curb the excesses of popular piety through church discipline and patient educational efforts.

Johan Huizinga characterized the popular piety of the late Middle Ages as dominated by "excitation" and "fantasy."[8] He portrayed graphically the emotional impact of popular preachers in the mendicant orders on the crowds who gathered in the towns to

---

[4] See David S. Yeago, "The Catholic Luther," in Carl E. Braaten and Robert W. Jenson, eds., *The Catholicity of the Reformation* (Grand Rapids: Wm. B. Eerdmans Publishing Co., 1996) 15–34.

[5] LW 36:18.

[6] Ibid., 97ff.

[7] See Hermann Sasse, *This Is My Body*, op. cit., 99ff.

[8] Johan Huizinga, *The Autumn of the Middle Ages*, trans. by Rodney J. Payton and Ulrich Mammitzsch (Chicago: The University of Chicago Press, 1996), 220.

hear them. In this state of agitation, normal practices that had a recognized and some-times venerable place in traditional Catholic piety were blown up into proportions that ceased to make sense, especially when indulgences were counted in millions of years and pilgrimages turned into epidemics of pilgrimages. As the Catholic historian Joseph Lortz wrote, "The somewhat insubstantial character of such piety was demonstrated both by the craze for miracles and visions, which accompanied the enthusiasm for pilgrimages, and by the numerous restraining prohibitions and warnings issued by German synods and theologians during the whole of the fifteenth century."[9]

A counterthesis has arisen, also in Catholic circles, which asserts that clerical corruption and abuses in piety existed more in the eyes of would-be humanist and Protestant reformers than in actuality; that practices that appear to have preyed in merce-nary fashion on the fears and superstitions of the simple laity—for example, flagellant processions, pilgrimages, the selling of indulgences, the veneration of relics, masses and offices for the dead, and so forth—were more an expression of the vitality of piety than of any deep illness in the church. For example, memorial masses and offices for the dead may have looked, to hostile reformers, like clergy "feeding" on the dead, but for pious laypeople they expressed love of family and friends and nurtured a consoling belief in the continuity between this world and the next. The worst Francis Oakley can find in late medieval piety is "waning convictions, spiritual sluggishness, and an unsteady sense of purpose."[10]

The extent of corruption or misguided piety is beside the point as far as Luther's critique is concerned. He termed the whole direction and effort of this piety "works-righteousness" (*Werksgerechtigkeit*) and pronounced it contrary to the word of God, which teaches justification by faith alone for Christ's sake.

Some Catholic theologians in the twentieth century, such as Jungmann and Iserloh, have taken Luther's critique seriously. John Jay Hughes has written that "if we were asked to identify the most serious charge which the sixteenth-century reformers brought against the church of their day we could find it exemplified in Luther's claim that in the monastery he and his brethren had been taught to hope for forgiveness of our sins and salvation from our good works."[11]

Seen in this light, it would seem that Luther's objection to the sacrifice of the mass was that the mass was being offered to God to procure God's favor apart from faith in the promises of God. The fact that German synods sought to keep practices within tra-ditional bounds, that Cardinal Nicholas von Cusa worked tirelessly during the fifteenth century to reform practice and enlighten piety, and that the Council of Trent later cor-rected a number of abuses would be irrelevant to Luther's charge of works-righteousness. Yet even Luther's attack on the mass as a good work has not been properly understood. It has been asserted over and over again, for example by Francis Clark, that Luther's

---

[9] Joseph Lortz, *The Reformation in Germany*, I, trans. by Ronald Walls (New York, 1939), 115.

[10] Francis Oakley, *The Western Church in the Late Middle Ages* (Ithaca, NY: Cornell University Press, 1979), 215–16. See also Lawrence G. Duggan, "The Unresponsiveness of the Late Medieval Church: A Reconsideration," *The Sixteenth Century Journal* 9 (1978), 3–26.

[11] John Jay Hughes, "Eucharistic Sacrifice: Transcending the Reformation Deadlock," *art. cit.*, 532.

"cardinal objection against the traditional doctrine of the sacrifice of the mass was that it was a 'work,' something which belonged to that whole order of instrumental mediation and of man's active participation in the economy of grace that was anathema to the Reformer."[12] But is it true that Luther's cardinal objection to the mass-sacrifice was that it was a "work?" We must inquire into what Luther meant when he charged that the mass had been turned into a "work." Clark understands "work" in a cultic sense: "something which belongs to that whole order of instrumental mediation and of man's active participation in the economy of grace." But another Catholic theologian, James F. McCue, notes that there is sufficient evidence in Luther's writings to indicate that the rejection of instrumental mediation was not at the heart of his sacramental theology. Rather, Luther believed that "in the sacrament what is signified is given."[13] The Norwegian theologian Carl F. Wisløff also disagrees that Luther understands "work" in a cultic sense.

> Now when Luther maintains that the mass had been made into a "work" he does not mean by this word simply an external, ritual action. His contention takes into account the religiously serious striving which aims to attain something with God, but without faith. The mass as *opus* is not simply superstition, but it is primarily *legalism*. With the term "work" reference is made quite inclusively to a spiritual attitude which does not stand face to face with God purely and simply to receive, but wants to present its piety to him.[14]

It is this basically wrong orientation in the relationship with God that produces works-righteousness. It is the attempt by the human being to find favor and acceptance with God by what he or she does rather than by what God has already done for us in Christ. This is a sin against the first Commandment, an act of idolatry and impiety.[15] If Luther's principal attack on the mass is that it is an act of works-righteousness, his violent campaign against the mass from 1520 on can be explained as an assault on the *piety* of the mass. This would account for the long list of abuses catalogued in the Smalkald Articles of 1537 which make the mass *der grosseste und schrecklichste Greuel* (the greatest and most horrible abomination) of the papal church for which no concession or compromise can be made.[16] As a work, the mass is equated with other activities which, from the Reformation's point of view, were human attempts to placate or manipulate God, such as monastic vows, pilgrimages, and the veneration of saints and relics. To use the mass as a good work means that it is used contrary to Christ's institution. Instead of being used as a means of strengthening faith and expressing the church's public witness, the mass was being used as a way of exerting an influence on God. In *Concerning the Private Mass and Consecration of Priests* (*Von der Winckelmesse und Pfaffenweihe*, 1533) Luther wrote:

---

[12] Clark, *Eucharistic Sacrifice and the Reformation*, op. cit., 106.

[13] James F. McCue, "Luther and Roman Catholicism on the Mass as Sacrifice," *Lutheran and Catholics in Dialogue*, III (U.S.A. National Committee of the Lutheran Federation and the Bishops' Committee for Ecumenical and Interreligious Affairs, 1967), 52.

[14] Carl F. Wisløff, *The Gift of Communion*, op. cit., 52.

[15] WA 8:417, 37. "Missas vero, quas sacrificia vocant, esse summam idolatrium et impietatem."

[16] Bek., 416–19; *The Book of Concord*, ed. and trans. by Theodore G. Tappert (Philadelphia: Fortress Press, 1959), 293–6.

> It is Christ's intention (as we have said) that the sacrament be dispensed to Christ's congregation, in order to strengthen its faith and to praise God publicly; but you have made a work of your own out of it, which is supposed to be yours and which you have accomplished without the assistance of any other person and such work you have dispensed to others and sold for money.[17]

When the mass is used as a form of works-righteousness it becomes a way of despising the work of Christ, and in this sense it can be charged that the papists crucify Christ anew.[18] The doctrine of justification by faith was brought to bear on the mass to expose its use in the service of works-righteousness. But is Luther's attack on the mass as a work his "cardinal objection against the traditional doctrine of the sacrifice of the Mass?" It would seem to be one thing to attack the mass as a work, and something else to attack it as a sacrifice.

In *Babylonian Captivity*, Luther charged that the mass had been turned into an *opus bonum et sacrificium* (good work and sacrifice). Vilmos Vajta suggests that these terms are used interchangeably and that they can therefore be regarded as synonyms.[19] To be sure, Luther frequently links up the mass with a distorted works-righteousness in this and other treatises. But in *Babylonian Captivity*, Luther is attacking more than just the opus bonum character of the mass. It is one offense when the mass is offered to God as a good work by which to please God or merit his favor. But there is a second offense *(alterum scandalum)*: it is that the mass is offered to God as a sacrifice. Luther points out that the canon of the mass clearly says that a sacrifice is being offered: "haec dona, haec munera, haec sacrificia;" and the canon also petitions God to accept the sacrifice of the church as he accepted the sacrifice of Abel.[20] Luther also points to the common expression in which Christ is called the *hostia altaris*. He understands that an identification between Christ and the host is required by the doctrine of the real presence of Christ in the sacrament.

So there is a second scandal in that the mass is believed to be a sacrifice offered to God.[21] From this Luther charged that the papists imagine that they are offering Christ himself to God the Father as an all-sufficient sacrifice.[22] The fact that this passage also speaks of the mass as an opus bonum illustrates how inseparable these two offenses were in Luther's mind. But it does seem, as Wisløff has pointed out, that Luther intends two different attacks on the mass: "(1) The mass is not an 'opus,' and (2) it is not a 'sacrificium.'"[23]

It is important to understand this second scandal for liturgical reasons. We reach the very heart of Luther's attack on the mass when we understand that he objects to the sacrament being called a sacrifice. Perhaps his most definitive statement in this regard

---

[17] WA 38:199, 23f.

[18] WA 15:766, 24f.

[19] Vilmos Vajta, *Die Theologie des Gottesdienstes bei Luther* (Stockholm, 1952), 105.

[20] WA 6:523, 8f.

[21] "Jam et alterum scandalum amovendum est, quod multo grandis est et speciossissimum, id est, quod Missa creditur passim esse sacrificium, quod offertur deo." Ibid.

[22] "Omnes imaginantur, sese offerre ipsum Christum deo patri tanquam hostiam sufficientissimam." WA 6:522, 24f.

[23] Wisløff, 41.

occurs in the *Admonition to the Sacrament* (*Vermanung zum Sakrament des leibs und bluts unsers Herrn*, 1530) when he says: "The memorial might well be a thankoffering, but the sacrament itself is not an offering, but is a gift of God."[24] The memorial (*das Gedechtnis*) can be regarded as a sacrifice according to "the teaching and faith of the fathers" (*die lere und glauben von der gnaden*).[25] It would seem that by "das Gedechtnis" Luther means the liturgical act; but by "the sacrament itself" (*das Sacrament selbs*), Luther means the consecrated elements: they cannot be offered to God because they are the gift of God to the people.[26] This is the witness of the institution narratives, which indicate that Christ did not offer himself at the last supper—nor did he perform a good work on behalf of others—but he set his testament before the disciples seated at table with him. It is Luther's fundamental proposition that

> the mass or Sacrament of the Altar is Christ's testament, which he left behind him at his death to be distributed among his believers. . . .
>
> A testament, as everyone knows, is a promise made by one about to die, in which he designates his bequest and appoints his heirs. A testament, therefore, involves first, the death of the testator, and second, the promise of an inheritance and the naming of the heir.
>
> You see, therefore, that what we call the mass is a promise of the forgiveness of sins made to us by God, and such a promise as has been confirmed by the death of the Son of God. For the only difference between a promise and a testament is that the testament involves the death of the one who makes it.[27]

Luther understands that in the early church it was customary for believers to bring collections with them, which were afterwards distributed among the needy, and that from this collection, bread and wine were taken and consecrated for sacramental usage.[28] Since all these gifts were sanctified by the word and by prayer, as in the Jewish rites, the anaphora (*ritus levandi seu offerendi*) has come down to us even though the gifts are no longer collected and used in this fashion. But this means that the terms "sacrifice" and "oblation" must be referred to the gifts that are collected and offered, not to the sacrament and testament.[29] Therefore, the priests should be careful that the words of the *Canonis maioris et minoris* be not referred to the sacrament, but to the bread and wine they consecrate.[30] Luther makes a distinction between the bread and wine that are offered and consecrated by the word and by prayer and the consecrated elements that are received in communion as the gift of God.[31] Therefore, by "das Sakrament selbs," Luther

---

[24] WA 30/2:614, 23. "Das gedechtnis sol wol ein danckopfer sein, aber das Sacrament selbs sol nicht eine opffer, sondern ein gabe Gottes sein."

[25] Ibid., 610, 13.

[26] This is contrary to Vatja, p. 292, who understands "Das Sacrament selbs" to refer to "the liturgical act."

[27] Luther, *The Babylonian Captivity of the Church*, LW 36:37–8.

[28] WA 6:524, 4ff.

[29] WA 6:524, 17.

[30] WA 6:524, 36.

[31] "Panis enim et vinum antea offeruntur ad benedicendum, ut per verbum et orationem sanctificantur. Postquam autem benedictus et consecratus est, iam non offertur sed accipiter dono a deo." WA 6:525, 1.

means not even the elements in general, but the elements that are received back as the gift of communion *after* the consecration. We will also have to come to terms with the fact that Luther accepted the "before-and-after" character of the consecration of the bread and wine by means of the proclamation of the words of Christ.

The liturgical consequences of this point of view were not lost on Luther's Roman opponents. Wisløff notes that it was of interest to Robert Bellarmine that Luther followed the usual liturgical order in his *Formula Missae* until the canon. He perceived that Luther took his starting point with the sacramental order (das Sakrament selbs) and that this affected of the shape of the sacramental *rite*.[32] This reshaping of the sacramental rite is also due to the consecratory weight that Luther and his followers accorded the Verba Christi in the institution narrative. Before the words of institution the bread and wine could be offered as the gifts of the church and blessed by prayer—providing that the gifts were not offered for inappropriate intentions that fell into the area of works-righteousness. But there could be no thought of offering the elements after the Verba consecrationis because now they are the body and blood of Christ. To offer them to God would be a blasphemous reversal of the direction of the sacrament and its institution as Christ's gift or testament to his people.

The Lutheran theologians theoretically insisted on the integrity of the entire eucharistic action; they did not narrowly focus only on a moment of consecration. The later Formula of Concord affirmed that the command of Christ—"Do this"—"comprehends the whole action *(totam actionem)* or administration of this sacrament (namely, that in a Christian assembly we take bread and wine, consecrate it, distribute it, receive it, eat and drink it, and therewith proclaim the Lord's death)." This action "must be kept integrally and inviolately, just as St. Paul sets the whole action of the breaking of bread *(panis frangitur)*, or of the distribution and reception, before our eyes in 1 Corinthians 10:16."[33] Nevertheless, in practice the Lutherans held that the sacramental union is accomplished in close temporal as well as causal connection with the words of institution.[34] Luther sometimes even spoke of a change *(wandeln)* in the elements at the consecration, that is, the bringing about of the sacramental union of the body and blood of Christ with the bread and wine.[35] After the words of institution, therefore, the elements are also the true body and blood of Christ. For this reason there could be no thought of offering the elements after the Verba, which was the traditional location of the oblation-text in the eucharistic prayer. The only proper use of the elements after the words of institution was to receive them as the gift of communion.

Consequently, the language in the *Unde et memores* section of the Roman canon was most offensive to Luther. It suggested that the very body and blood of Christ were being offered by the church to God the Father: "offerimus . . . hostiam puram, hostiam sanctam, hostiam immaculatam panem sanctum vitae aeternae et calicem salutis

---

[32] Wisløff, 58–9.

[33] Formula of Concord, Solid Declaration VII, 83–4; Tappert, 584; Bek., 1000.

[34] See Titus Verinus, "The Moment at Which the Sacramental Union Begins," *Una Sancta* (1961), 11–8.

[35] See WA 30/1:122. "Eucharistia est panis et vinum verbo conjunctum, mutatum in corpus et sanguinem Christi."

perpetuae." His argument against the sacrifice of the mass in *The Abomination of the Secret Mass* (*Vom Greuel der Stillmesse*, 1525) centers on the fact that in the Qui pridie (institution narrative), "the bread has become the body of Christ."[36] This governs what comes before the words of institution and what follows them. Clinging scrupulously to the text of the canon, Luther pointed out how meaningless it was in the Te igitur to speak of the bread and wine as though they were the body and blood of Christ. They had not yet been consecrated. So it is an abominable thing "to regard the wafer as so precious and worth so much that it may serve as a sacrifice before God on behalf of all Christendom." The text of the canon implies here "that bread and wine are regarded as highly as Christ's own blood."[37] But it is the ultimate abomination that in the Unde et memores "the priest offers up once again the Lord Christ, who offered himself only once."[38] The language of the canon compromised for Luther the uniqueness of the atoning sacrifice of Christ and obscured the gift of communion in which the benefits of that atoning sacrifice are given to and received by the faithful.

Hans Bernhard Meyer points out that

> Luther did not see, and perhaps would not or could not see in his polemical zeal, that the Canon prayers neither before nor after the consecration say that we take the divine-human person of Jesus Christ in our hands, as it were, in order to offer him to the Father. They speak rather of our gifts, of the bread and the cup and of our oblation, and what we offer are the gifts which we can comprehend with our senses.[39]

But this is not the interpretation that accompanied these prayers in medieval theology. The doctrine of the real presence, combined with the pinpointing of the moment of consecration at the words of Christ, probably already influenced the text of the Roman canon in terms of describing the *panem et calicem* in terms of their full value and significance as "panem sanctam vitae aeternae et calicem salutis perpetuae."[40] By the end of the Middle Ages, Gabriel Biel spoke of the priest offering the flesh and blood of Christ (or of Christ offering himself) in the *Unde et memores* and *Supra quae*.[41] In Luther's eyes, this could only confuse the sacramental gift with the oblation of the church. His liturgical solution was to eliminate any statement of oblation between the consecration (the proclamation of the words of Christ) and the communion. This utter lack of oblationary language, and often of a full eucharistic prayer, became the telltale mark of a Lutheran liturgy. In other respects, the order of service might deviate little from the pre-Reformation rite, and might even be celebrated in Latin. Other Reformation liturgical orders that departed more overtly from the pre-Reformation rite might nevertheless have a full eucharistic prayer. The excision of oblationary language and prayer was the most characteristic feature of the

---

[36] LW 36:320; see WA 18:22ff.

[37] LW 36:314.

[38] LW 36:320.

[39] Hans Bernhard Meyer, *Luther und die Messe* (Paderborn, 1965), 251–2.

[40] See Ralph A Keifer, "Liturgical Text as Primary Source for Eucharistic Theology," *Worship* 51 (1977), 186–96.

[41] Biel, *Expositio*, Lectio 54, E-F; Lectio 55, A-B; Oberman and Courtenay, II, 340–2, 345–7.

Reformation Lutheran liturgy. The restoration of a full eucharistic prayer has been the most controverted issue in contemporary Lutheran liturgical revision.[42]

 ## LUTHER'S REVISIONS OF THE ORDO MISSAE

Formula Missae et Communionis, 1523

It has been necessary to review Luther's polemic against the sacrifice of the mass at length because it was decisive for his reordering of the mass. The critique of the mass as a sacrifice in *The Babylonian Captivity* of 1520 found practical expression in Luther's revision of the form of the mass in 1523.

It should also be noted that the radicality of Luther's revision of the canon of the mass is in contrast with the conservatism of Luther's handling of the rest of the mass. This is explainable if we keep in mind the chronology of events that preceded the publication of the *Formula Missae et Communionis*. After Luther's trial at Worms in 1521 and the declaration of the Emperor Charles V making Luther an outlaw of the Empire, he was abducted by troops dispatched by Luther's prince, the Elector Frederick the Wise, and taken to the Wartburg in secret for safekeeping. During his sojourn in the Wartburg, Luther's older and more radical colleague Andreas Karlstadt took over the leadership of the reform movement in Wittenberg and went on an iconoclastic binge. This so aroused Luther that he left the safety of the Wartburg and returned to Wittenberg where he assumed leadership in the reformation. Much of 1523 was devoted by Luther to restoring order and providing practical leadership in the work of reform. The treatise on *An Order of Mass and Communion for the Church at Wittenberg* (*Formula Missae et Communionis pro Ecclesia Vuittembergensi*) appeared in December of that year.[43]

This treatise, written at the request of Luther's friend Nicholas Hausmann, bishop of the church in Zwickau, was a detailed commentary on the Latin mass, not a liturgical book. Pastors could follow Luther's treatise as a guide for editing the missal they were already using. Luther admitted that he had been "hesitant and fearful" to make changes, "partly because of the weak in faith, who cannot suddenly exchange an old and accustomed order of worship for a new and unusual one, and more so because of the fickle and fastidious spirits who rush in like unclean swine without faith or reason, and who delight only in novelty and tire of it as quickly, when it has worn off."[44] Luther may here have been thinking of radicals like Karlstadt, although it seems that the only innovations introduced by Karlstadt were giving communion in both kinds, omitting the canon,

---

[42] For a critique of eucharistic prayer in Lutheran orders see Gottfried G. Krodel, "The Great Thanksgiving of the Inter-Lutheran Commission on Worship: It Is the Christian's Supper and Not the Lord's Supper," *The Cresset* Occasional Paper No. 1 (Valparaiso University Press, 1976).

[43] WA 12:205-220; LW 53:19–40; Emil Sehling, ed., *Die evangelischen Kirchenordnungen des XVI. Jahrhunderts* (Leipzig, 1902–13; reprinted Aalen, 1970), I, 3–9; Aemilius Ludwig Richter, ed., *Die evangelischen Kirchenordnungen des sechzehnten Jahrhunderts* (Weimar, 1846; reprinted Nieuwkoop, 1967), I, 2–7; Joachim Beckmann, ed., *Quellen zur Geschichte des christlichen Gottesdienstes* (Gütersloh, 1956), 122–7.

[44] LW 53:19.

reciting the words of institution in German, and laying aside the traditional mass vestments.[45] There were several experiments going on in Germany with vernacular liturgy during 1522 and 1523. But Luther asserted in this treatise that "it is not now nor ever has been our intention to abolish the liturgical service of God completely, but rather to purify the one that is now in use from the wretched accretions which corrupt it and to point out an evangelical use."[46]

Thus, Luther's first effort at liturgical reform was a revision of the Latin mass for use in Latin. The content of the mass is determined by the propers, and these depend on the church year calendar and lectionary. Luther indicated that "we in Wittenberg intend to observe only the Lord's Day and the festivals of the Lord." He did not object if others wanted to observe apostles' days, feasts of the Virgin Mary, and other saints. But he felt that the many saints' days should be abolished (at least as holidays) and that the feasts of the Holy Cross should be anathematized. He retained the feasts of Purification (February 2) and Annunciation (March 25) as feasts of Christ, along with Circumcision (January 1) and Epiphany (January 6). For the most part the traditional propers for Sundays and festivals of the church year would be retained. These matters decided, the liturgy of the word took the following shape:

> Introit
> Kyrie
> Gloria
> Collect for the Day
> Epistle
> Gradual of two verses and Alleluia
> Gospel
> Nicene Creed
> Sermon

Where Luther makes no recommendation, we must assume that traditional practices remained intact. Thus, it is likely that the Introit was sung by a choir at a high mass, probably to a polyphonic setting, and that during the Introit the priest and his assistants prepared themselves for worship by silently confessing their sin (using the *Confiteor*). There is otherwise no mention of an act of confession of sins in Luther's *Formula Missae*. The Kyrie was to be sung three times instead of nine. There is no reason to suppose that troped versions of the Kyrie and Gloria were suppressed among the Lutherans, as they later were by the Council of Trent. Indeed, they made an appearance in the form of chorales based on the liturgical chants. These texts may also have been sung to plainsong or polyphonic settings by the choir. The Gradual between the epistle and gospel consisted of two psalm verses and the Alleluia, and could also be rendered by the choir in a polyphonic setting. The sequences, however, were to be abandoned, except for those for Christmas ("Grates nunc omnes") and Pentecost ("Veni, sancte Spiritus"). (The

---

[45] See Julius Smend, *Die evangelischen deutschen Messen bis zu Luthers Deutscher Messe* (Göttingen, 1896; reprinted Nieuwkoop, 1967), 3; Hermann Barge, *Andreas Bodenstein von Karlstadt* (Leipzig, 1905; reprinted Nieuwkoop, 1968), I, 361.

[46] LW 53:20.

Council of Trent also limited the number of sequences to five.) The Latin Credo followed the gospel. It could be sung in a polyphonic or plainsong setting by the choir or on a monotone by the priest. We mention these practices to indicate that there was very little provision for congregational participation through singing in early Lutheranism. That came later with the German Mass and Luther's call for poets to write congregational hymns.

The sermon followed the Creed in the medieval mass as celebrated in the German-speaking countries. Luther had no objection to keeping the sermon in this position, but he also argued that the sermon might be preached before the Introit of the mass since "the Gospel is the voice crying in the wilderness and calling unbelievers to faith."[47] The sermon was often placed in the Office of Prone, a late medieval pulpit office. This office was retained in some Lutheran territories such as Sweden. This little office would also have provided intercessions in connection with parish notices and a confession of sins and absolution. We shall see that it was the form of the liturgy of the word in the first liturgical reforms of the Swiss reformer, Ulrich Zwingli.

Then follows in the order of the mass "that utter abomination," the offertory. "From here on," wrote Luther, "almost everything smacks and savors of sacrifice. And the words of life and salvation [the words of institution] are embedded in the midst of it all, just as the ark of Lord once stood in the idol's temple next to Dagon. . . . Let us, therefore, repudiate everything that smacks of sacrifice, together with the entire canon, and retain only that which is pure and holy, and so order our mass."[48]

What Luther proposed was the elimination of all the offertory prayers and all of the prayers of the canon after the Sanctus. (The canon, in Luther's day, was thought to begin with the Te igitur, not with the Preface. This was a consequence of the way in which the canon was printed in missals and sacramentaries, often with an ornate "T" on the page beginning "Te igitur clementissime Pater.") Luther removed the words of institution from the middle of the canon and placed them in the Preface, in the place of the proper. This ensured that they would be sung or read aloud, since the Preface continued to be that part of the eucharistic prayer that was sung or read aloud.[49] Thus, after making ready the bread and wine "in the customary manner," the blessing (*Benedictio*) was as follows:[50]

P/ Dominus vobiscum	P/ The Lord be with you.
R/ Et cum Spiritu tuo.	R/ And with your Spirit.
P/ Sursum corda.	P/ Lift up your hearts.
R/ Habemus ad Dominum.	R/ We have, to the Lord.
P/ Gratias agamus Domino Deo nostro.	P/ Let us give thanks to the Lord our God.
R/ Dignum et iustum est.	R/ It is worthy and right to do.

[47] LW 53:25.

[48] LW 53:25–6.

[49] See Frank C. Senn, "Martin Luther's Revision of the Eucharistic Canon in the *Formula Missae* of 1523," *Concordia Theological Monthly* 44 (1973), 101–18.

[50] Text in Irmgard Pahl, ed., *Coena Domini* I. *Die Abendmahlsliturgie der Reformationskirchen im 16./17. Jahrhundert* (Universitätsverlag Freiburg Schweiz, 1983), 34.

P/ Vere dignum et iustum est,	P/ It is truly worthy and right,
aequum et salutare,	proper and salutary,
nos tibi semper et ubique	that we should always and everywhere
gratias agere: Domine,	give thanks to you, O Lord,
sancte Pater, omnipotens	holy Father, almighty,
aeterne Deus: per Christum	eternal God: through Christ
Dominum nostrum.	our Lord.
Qui pridie quam pateretur,	Who the day before he suffered
accepit panem gratias agens	took bread, and when he had given thanks,
fregit deditque discipulis	broke it and gave it to
suis dicens: Accipite, comedite,	his disciples, saying: Take, eat;
Hoc est Corpus meum,	This is my Body,
quod pro vobis datur.	which is given for you.
Similiter et calicem,	In the same way also the cup,
postquam caenavit, dicens:	when he had supped, saying:
Hic calix est Novi Testamenti	This cup is the New Covenant
in meo Sanguine, qui pro	in my Blood, which is shed for you
vobis et pro multis effunde-	and for many for the remission
tur in remissionem peccatorum.	of sins.
Haec quotiescunque feceritis,	This do, as often as you do it,
in mei memoriam faciatis.	in remembrance of me.

If this text of the institution narrative is compared with the text in the Roman canon, it will be seen that Luther has eliminated all extrabiblical words and phrases. If it is compared with the four institution narratives in the New Testament, it will be seen that Luther has drawn from all of them, but that he preferred the Lukan-Pauline versions more than the Matthean/Markan versions. It should also be noted that this institution narrative is still included within a eucharistic prayer, since it is introduced by a dependent Qui-clause. This eucharistic prayer concluded with the singing of the Sanctus. During the Sanctus the bread and cup were to be elevated "according to the customary rite for the benefit of the weak in faith who might be offended if such an obvious change in this rite of the mass were suddenly made."[51] The "customary rite" would have entailed the ringing of the Sanctus bells during the "Blessed is he who comes" (Benedictus qui venit) of the Sanctus, with the elevation of the bread and cup and genuflection. This occurred during the Sanctus and Benedictus because at high mass the celebrant began to recite the canon silently while the choir began to sing the Sanctus, often to long florid plainsong melodies and, by the time of the Reformation, to polyphonic settings. The celebrant would have reached the words of institution at about the time the choir got to the Benedictus. By re-taining the outward ceremonial act of the elevation at the place where it usually would have occurred, Luther was able to effect a radical change in the rite of the mass: the vir-tual elimination of the canon and the relocation of the Verba institutionis. No sense of change was conveyed to the ordinary worshipers. This was because the Verba institutionis would have been sung in Latin (like the proper prefaces) and the people would never

---

[51] LW 53:28.

have heard the rest of the "silent canon" anyway. This stroke of pastoral genius has to be unequalled in the history of liturgy: to have effected a radical revision of the heart of the mass without the worshipers necessarily noticing any outward change.

After this the Lord's Prayer was said, introduced by the usual invitatory, "Praeceptis salutaribus moniti, et divina institutione formati, audemus dicere . . ." (Taught by your saving precepts, and guided by your divine institution, we are bold to say . . .). But the embolism, *Libera nos* (Deliver us from every evil), was omitted. The Pax domini (The peace of the Lord) was to be said facing the people. Luther regarded this as "a public absolution of the sins of the communicants, the true voice of the gospel announcing remission of sins, and therefore the one and most worthy preparation for the Lord's Table, if faith holds to these words as coming from the mouth of Christ himself."[52] Luther consistently regarded the minister of the word and the sacraments as speaking and acting in the place of Christ, especially where the gospel of forgiveness of sins was being proclaimed.

The Agnus Dei was to be sung during the distribution of the bread and cup, the celebrant communing himself first and then the people. The administration formula was to be changed from singular to plural pronouns. During the ministration of the sacrament the choir could sing the Communio, an "anthem" (antiphon) consisting of one or two psalm verses. After the distribution either the prayer "Quod ore sumpsimus" or the prayer "Corpus tuum" could be said, once again changing the pronouns from singular to plural. Then, after the salutation and *Benedicamus domino,* the benediction is given—either the customary *Benedicat vos* or the Aaronic benediction from Numbers 6:24–27.

If no communicants were present, it became customary to abbreviate the entire liturgy after the sermon, often by using the Great Litany. Luther appreciated this prayer and in 1529 published a German translation and a corrected Latin version. He could report to Nicholas Hausmann, earlier that year, "We sing the Litany in church in Latin and in the vernacular."[53] But, of course, the greater concern was to increase the frequency of the reception of Holy Communion, which would have the effect of increasing the number of celebrations, since the reformers all disapproved of the celebration of the Lord's Supper without communicants.

A second part of the treatise on the *Formula Missae* dealt, in fact, with "The Communion of the People." This statement on communion practices was as important for the common life of the church as the ordering of the mass, and had more long-term consequences. Luther directed that the faithful were to request "in person" to the pastor to receive the sacrament. Upon registering for the sacrament, communicants should be examined for their faith and conduct. They should also be catechized, be able to recite the words of institution from memory, explain the benefits of the sacrament. Luther did not think this kind of examination would be necessary every time a person received communion; it should be left to pastoral discretion. Those who were to receive communion should be grouped together in the chancel so that they could be seen especially by those

---

[52] Ibid., 28–9.
[53] Ibid., 153.

who were not receiving communion. This could have had the effect of providing an encouraging witness to those who were not receiving. It more likely had the effect of providing a moral scrutiny of those who were receiving by those who were not. Luther himself said that those who are to receive communion should be seen publicly "in order that their lives may be better observed, proved, and tested."[54]

Private confession before receiving communion should still be encouraged, in Luther's view, although it should not be demanded. Likewise, fasting was still regarded by Luther as a useful discipline, although it was no longer obligatory. It is probable that obligations of fasting and abstinence, as well as requirements for confession, were among the factors that discouraged frequent reception of the sacrament all during the Middle Ages.

The whole style of celebration of mass assumed by Luther was close to the Roman tradition. Vestments, candles, and incense could be retained ("Let these things be free"), along with altars, crucifixes, and the sign of the cross. The people would not experience any outward changes in the celebration of the mass. Even the most conspicuous ceremony of the medieval mass—the elevation—was retained by Luther.

There was no place in this order of mass for the singing of vernacular hymns by the congregation. This was something that concerned Luther deeply. He wrote, "I wish that we had as many songs as possible in the vernacular which the people could sing during mass, immediately after the gradual and also after the Sanctus and Agnus Dei. For who doubts that originally all the people sang these which now only the choir sings or responds to while the bishop is consecrating? The bishop may have these [vernacular] hymns sung either after the Latin chants, or use the Latin on one day and the vernacular on the next, until the time comes that the whole mass is sung in the vernacular."[55]

A few vernacular hymns were available in 1523. It is a misconception that there was no popular hymn-singing in the medieval church. Luther mentioned "Let God be blest," a Corpus Christi *Leise* (a type of vernacular hymn which ended with a germanized "Kyrie eleison"—*Kyrieleis*) that was sung by the congregation between verses of the Latin sequence "Lauda Sion Salvatorem"; also "Now let us pray to the Holy Ghost," another Leise. In 1524 Luther altered and added verses to both of these.[56]

Luther mentioned these hymns and alerted people to the need for new vernacular hymns "to encourage any German poets to compose evangelical hymns for us."[57] As we shall see, Luther led the way in this regard. He engaged in a creative spurt of hymn writing in 1523–1524, the year in which the first evangelical hymnals were published. He also made known to people his desire for a German mass, but that would not be published until 1526. In the meantime, practices may have developed that became standard in later Lutheranism, such as reading the scripture lections in German immediately after they were sung in Latin, and adding the singing of vernacular hymns by the congregation (as these became available) after the singing of the Gradual and Agnus Dei by the choir, as Luther had suggested. In other words, practices that began as temporary measures

---

[54] Ibid., 34.
[55] Ibid., 36.
[56] Ibid., 252f., 263f.
[57] Ibid., 37.

acquired greater longevity than they should have had. This is a not unfamiliar pattern in the history of liturgy.

Deutsche Messe und Gottesdienstes, 1526

We have noted that at the time Luther was revising the Latin mass there were already experiments with German vernacular liturgies. Already in 1522 Wolfgang Wissenburger in Basel and Johann Schwebel in Pforzheim were holding services in German. That same year the Carmelite prior Kaspar Kantz prepared a German mass for the use of his monks.[58] In 1523–1524 Thomas Müntzer published a German mass, Matins, and Vespers all complete with an original plainsong setting for use in Alstedt.[59] An interesting German mass with a revision of the Roman canon was prepared for use in Worms in 1534.[60] In that same year, German services were introduced in Reutlingen, Wertheim, Königsberg, and Strassburg.

The Strassburg German Mass prepared by Diobald Schwartz in 1524 was a very conservative adaptation of the Roman rite.[61] That same year Martin Bucer published his *Grund und Ursach* in which he laid out an order for the celebration of the word and the Lord's Supper, as follows:

> Admonition to confession
> Prayer of confession (on behalf of the congregation)
> Prayer for pardon
> Declaration of forgiveness
> Congregational psalms or hymns
> A brief prayer
> Reading from the Apostles (Epistle), with brief explanation
> Congregational hymn
> Gospel
> Sermon
> Articles of Faith (Creed)
> Intercessory prayers
> Admonition to communicants
> Institution narrative
> Ministration of Holy Communion
> Hymn of Praise
> A thanksgiving prayer
> Blessing of the people
> Dismissal: "Go in the peace of the Lord."[62]

This order could have had some influence on Luther's German Mass. By 1525 Bucer was guiding the revision of the Strassburg German Mass. Eighteen revisions later, in 1539,

[58] Smend, 73–8; *Coena Domini*, I, 14–7.

[59] Smend, 99–105; Sehling, I, 497–504; *Coena Domini*, I, 21–4.

[60] See Peter Brunner, "Die Wormser Deutsche Messe," in Heinz Dietrich Wendland, ed., *Kosmos und Ekklesia. Festschrift für Wilhelm Stählin* (Kassel, 1953); *Coena Domini* I, 17–21.

[61] Smend, 125–38. See English trans. in William D. Maxwell, *An Outline of Christian Worship: Its Development and Form* (London: Oxford University Press, 1936), 88ff.

[62] See Bard Thompson, *Liturgies of the Western Church* (Cleveland: World Publishing Co., 1961), 161–2.

the definitive Strasbourg liturgy was published which became so influential on John Calvin's liturgical work.[63]

The multiplicity of German services presented a confusing situation, and Luther's friends prevailed on him to provide some guidance in this matter. Nicholas Hausmann, bishop of Zwickau, to whom the *Formula Missae* had been dedicated, even suggested that an "evangelical council" be called to establish some kind of liturgical order and uniformity. Luther himself was adamantly opposed to the use of legal compulsion. Evangelical freedom should not be used as a pretext for a new legalism. Already in the *Formula Missae* Luther had advised, "Let us approve each other's rites lest schisms and sects should result from this diversity in rites—as has happened in the Roman Church."[64] When Luther did get around to publishing the *German Mass and Order of Service* in 1526, he prefaced it with the admonition: "In the first place, I would kindly and for God's sake request all those who see this order of service or desire to follow it: Do not make it a rigid law to bind or entangle anyone's conscience, but use it in Christian liberty as long, when, where, and how you find it to be practical and useful."[65]

The first matter of evangelical freedom was that of language. Luther wrote that he arranged this German Mass "for the sake of the unlearned lay folk."[66] He wanted to give this liturgy a popular quality. But he would not change or abrogate the *Formula Missae*, "For in no wise would I want to discontinue the service in the Latin language, because the young are my chief concern."[67] In other words, the Latin mass should be continued where it made sense to use it, as in schools and universities where Latin was a language still in scholarly use. Luther also envisioned "a truly evangelical order" that would be used by those "who want to be Christians in earnest," who might "meet alone in a house somewhere to pray, to read, to baptize, to receive the sacrament, and to do other Christian works."[68] This was a suggestion taken up a century and a half later in the *collegia pietatis*, the pietistic cell groups, although not with the celebration of the sacraments included. Thus Luther himself did nothing to try to stop the multiplicity of experimental practices. Rather, he envisioned different kinds of liturgies being used in different kinds of communities and situations.

Luther's slowness at producing a German service was in part a concern for aesthetic integrity. He realized more than some of his eager colleagues that producing a good vernacular liturgy required more than merely translating the Latin texts and resetting the chants. As he wrote in his pamphlet, *Against the Heavenly Prophets* (1524), "I would gladly have a German mass today. I am also occupied with it. But I would very much like it to have a true German character. For to translate the Latin text and retain the Latin tone or notes has my sanction, though it doesn't sound polished or well done. Both the

---

[63] See Garrit Jan van de Pol, *Martin Bucer's Liturgical Ideas* (Assen, 1954).

[64] LW 53:31.

[65] Ibid., 61ff. See also WA 19:72–113; Sehling, I, 10–6; Richter, I, 35–40; Thompson, 123–37.

[66] See Frank C. Senn, "Luther's German Mass: A Sixteenth Century Folk Service," *Journal of Church Music* 18 (1976), 2–6.

[67] LW 53:63.

[68] Ibid., 63–4.

text and notes, accent, melody, and manner of rendering ought to grow out of the true mother tongue and its inflection, otherwise all of it becomes an imitation in the manner of the apes."[69] The style of the German Mass is characterized by German verse set to a popular musical style known as the *lied*, for which Luther enlisted the help of two leading musicians in the chapel of the Elector of Saxony, Conrad Rupsch (d. 1525) and Johann Walther (1496–1570).[70]

Among other matters, Luther advised the retention of vestments, altars, and candles, but suggested that "the altar should not remain where it is, and the priest should always face the people as Christ doubtlessly did in the Last Supper. But let that await its own time."[71] (This idea's own time was long in coming.)

The order of service still follows the historical shape of the liturgy, especially in the liturgy of the word. The outline of the German Mass is as follows:

> A hymn or German psalm in the first tone
> Kyrie, three times instead of nine
> A collect sung on a monotone
> The Epistle sung in the eighth tone
> A German hymn (e.g., "Now let us pray to the Holy Ghost," *LBW* 317)
> The Gospel sung in the fifth tone
> The German Creed ("In one true God we all believe," *LBW* 374)
> The Sermon on the Gospel for the Sunday
>   or festival paraphrase of the Lord's Prayer
> Admonition to the communicants
> The Words of Institution (sung)
>   Our Lord Jesus Christ, in the night in which he was betrayed, took bread;
>   and when he had given thanks, he broke it and gave it to his disciples,
>   saying, Take, eat; this is my body, which is given for you; this do in
>   remembrance of me.
>
>   After the same manner also, he took the cup, when he had supped, and
>   when he had given thanks, he gave it to them saying, Drink ye all of it; this
>   cup is the New Testament in my blood, which is shed for you, and for many,
>   for the remission of sins; this do, as oft as ye drink it, in remembrance
>   of me.
> Ministration of the bread after the words over the bread
>   The German Sanctus ("Isaiah 'twas the prophet who did see," *LBW* 528)
> Ministration of the cup after the words over the cup
> The German Agnus Dei ("O Christ, thou Lamb of God," *LBW* 103)
> Other songs during communion:
> "Let God be blest" (*LBW* 215)
> The hymn of Jan Hus, "Jesus Christ, our God and Savior"[72]
> Post-communion prayer:
>   We give thanks to you, almighty God, that you have refreshed us with this
>   your salutary gift; and we beseech your mercy to strengthen us through the

---

[69] LW 40:141.

[70] See the notes on the music of DM by Ulrich S. Leupold in LW 53:55–60.

[71] Ibid., 69.

[72] Ibid., 250–1.

same gift in faith toward you, and in fervent love among us all; for the sake
of Jesus Christ our Lord. Amen.
Aaronic Benediction

Luther's aversion to legalism of any kind may have influenced his reluctance to give specific rubrics. It is not clear who was intended to sing the introit psalm: the celebrant, the choir, or the congregation. Luther didn't much care whether the paraphrase of the Lord's Prayer and admonition to the communicants were read from the pulpit or the altar. If the elevation was to accompany the German Sanctus, and that was sung after the words over the bread, was there also an elevation of the cup after the words over the cup? Luther's directions are unclear.

This kind of rubrical indifference did not pertain to everything. Luther directed "that this paraphrase or admonition follow a prescribed wording or be formulated in a definite manner for the sake of the common people."[73] For the same reason Luther crafted the words of institution with symmetry between the bread-word and the cup-word to facilitate memorization. The didactic character of the German Mass has been noted by many commentators.

The musical provisions of the German Mass prevented it from becoming excessively didactic. Indeed, the German Mass provided an impetus for the development of Lutheran liturgical music and the chorale, since new reciting tones were provided that were congenial to the natural cadence of the German language, and congregational hymns were substituted for parts of the ordinary. The use of hymn-paraphrases facilitated congregational participation in the liturgy. As imprecise as Luther was in his ceremonial directions, he was very precise in his musical directions, even to the point of appending an "exercise of the melodies" as practice material. The chorale versifications had a long career in Lutheran liturgy and the Chorale Service of Holy Communion (LBW, p. 120) is based on the tradition of the Lied Messe (Song Mass).

The difficult question is whether Luther intended the eucharistic order of the German Mass to be a definitive development beyond that of the Formula Missae. There is no doubt that his concern to retain the Formula Missae was motivated by his desire to retain the use of the Latin language and not because he preferred the order that placed the words of institution within a eucharistic prayer. Bryan Spinks has emphasized Luther's desire to remove the canon of the mass entirely and to substitute a new composition. Spinks suggested that Luther's liturgical creativity is evident in the relationship between the Verba and the Sanctus. "Instead of trying to participate and enter into the sacrifice of Christ by lifting our hearts to the heavenly altar, we stand in awe with Isaiah as Christ speaks to us on earth, granting us pardon and therefore taking us up into his sacrifice."[74] This is a valid insight, but it could apply to *both* the Formula Missae and the German Mass since in both the Sanctus follows the Verba. Nevertheless, the majority of later Lutheran church orders followed the practice of the German Mass in separating the

---

[73] Ibid., 80.

[74] Bryan Spinks, *Luther's Liturgical Criteria and His Reform of the Canon of the Mass*. Grove Liturgical Study No. 30 (Bramcote: Grove Books, 1982), 37.

words of institution from eucharistic prayer, even when the proper prefaces were sung and these led to the Sanctus. But in these instances the Sanctus was followed by the Lord's Prayer and then the Verba, so that the Verba were no longer in juxtaposition with the Sanctus.

In the light of Luther's endorsement of many of the later church orders, it is too much to claim that he regarded his German Mass as a definitive eucharistic order. Rather, he regarded the German Mass as a liturgy with a limited value—something "arranged for the sake of the unlearned lay folk"[75]—and serving an interim purpose—"this or any other order shall be so used that whenever it becomes an abuse, it shall be straightway abolished and replaced by another."[76] The official church orders (*Kirchenordnungen*) of the territorial church supplanted Luther's own early efforts of 1523 and 1526. While they drew on Luther's liturgical models they were not slavish imitations, and Luther would have been the last person to think that they should be. It is most likely that, as a priest and pastor in the Evangelical Church, he himself used the Wittenberg and Saxon Church Orders of 1533 and 1539.

🍇 THE FLOWERING OF HYMNODY

In Luther's age music was a part of everyday life. It was integral to the daily prayer offices and the festivals of the church year, to secular celebrations and dances, to instruction in the schools, and to recreational life at home. Luther himself received the standard musical education of his time. As a clergyman he was expected to be something of an expert in music. As a pupil in the Magdeburg cathedral school in 1497, he probably sang as a choirboy in the services. As a pupil in the Latin schools in Mansfeld and Eisenach, he was probably taught music theory and sang as a *Kurrende-Knabe* (a schoolboy who sang with others in the streets for money and food). In his studies at the University of Erfurt he received instruction in music theory and in Aristotle's musical aesthetics. He apparently had a fine tenor voice and was an accomplished lute player. He was also capable of composing music—not only the hymn tunes ascribed to him but also a polyphonic motet based on Psalm 118:17, which has been handed down in Joachim Greff's humanistic school drama *Lazarus* (1545) as a work of Luther. His unbiased assessment of his own compositional skill in comparison with the greater gifts of Ludwig Senfl and Josquin des Prez indicate that Luther had a comprehensive knowledge of the music of his time. He appreciated the difference between his own modest efforts and the great composers of the age.[77]

Luther was not only musically gifted; he also integrated music into his theology. The principal source of his concept of music is the foreword he wrote to Georg Rhau's *Symphoniae jucundae* of 1538. There he wrote that music is a gift of God "instilled and implanted in all creatures . . . from the beginning of the world." "Nothing is without

[75] Ibid., 63.

[76] Ibid., 90.

[77] See Friedrich Blume, "The Period of the Reformation," in Friedrich Blume, ed., *Protestant Church Music* (New York: W. W. Norton, 1974), 5ff.

sound or harmony," but the human voice is the most wonderful gift of all. Therefore, "next to the Word of God, music deserves the highest praise."[78]

It is not surprising that Luther took a personal interest in the publication of hymns and hymnals, and even led the way in writing them. In the foreword to the first edition of Johann Walther's *Geistliches Gesangbüchlein* (1524), Luther wrote that "I, too, in order to make a start and to give an incentive to those who can do better, have with the help of others compiled several hymns, so that the holy gospel which now by the grace of God has risen anew may be noised and spread abroad."[79] Yet even his most prominent colleagues and successors could not compete with Luther in his role as a creator, arranger, and promoter of hymnody.

The first source of German songs for use in church, school, and home were pre-Reformation liturgical chants, German sacred songs, and German folk songs. Texts and tunes might be "improved in a Christian manner" or simply translated from the Latin and re-set to the tunes; or new texts might be written for well-known tunes; or texts might be translated and set to new melodies.[80] For example, the Pentecost sequence "Veni, Sancte Spiritus" was rendered in German in Thomas Müntzer's "Komm du Tröster, Heiliger Geist" (1524), in Michael Weisse's "Heiliger Geist, Herre Gott" (1544), and in Luther's "Komm, Heiliger Geist, Herre Gott" (*LBW* 163). Or again, the Easter song "Christ ist erstanden" (sung in the mass and in liturgical dramas since the twelfth century, and a standard item in the Easter liturgy in German territories by the fifteenth century) was "improved" by Luther in his chorale, "Christ lag in Todesbanden," which was also based on the tune of the Easter sequence, "Victimae paschali laudes."[81]

The second source of German songs were those procured through the contrafactum technique of supplying religious verse to a popular tune. The contrafactum technique was a craft already practiced by the Meistersingers, and therefore something of a German tradition. As an example we may cite Paul Speratus's "Es ist das Heil" (*LBW* 297), based on the melody of a pre-Reformation Easter song, "Freut euch, ihr Frauen und ihr Mann." Or again, Luther's Christmas song, "Vom Himmel hoch" (*LBW* 51), was set to an old village song, "Ich komm aus fremden Landen her." But the poetry too was arranged in the style of a song sung at the laying of a ceremonial wreath, and this particular song was probably intended to be sung as a round dance for the Christmas manger play that was popular in Catholic spheres and that Luther had no desire to discontinue. The tune that enjoyed the longest history as a contrafactum in Protestant church music was Heinrich Isaac's famous fourteenth-century melody, "Innsbruck, ich muss dich lassen," which was rendered in the sixteenth century as "O Welt, ich muss dich lassen" (probably by Johann Hess), in the seventeenth century with Paul Gerhardt's "Nun ruhen

---

[78] LW 53:312–24.

[79] Ibid., 316.

[80] Blume, 15ff.; Carl F. Schalk, "German Hymnody," in Marilyn Kay Stulken, ed., *Hymnal Companion to the Lutheran Book of Worship* (Philadelphia: Fortress Press, 1981), 19ff.

[81] In chronological order these three hymns are provided in *LBW*: 137 (the sequence), 136 (the song), and 134 (Luther's chorale).

alle Wälder" (*LBW* 276), and in the eighteenth century with Matthias Claudius's "Der Mond ist aufgegangen."

The third source of German songs were new texts and tunes. Luther's part in the creation of new melodies has been long debated. Although thirty-six songs have been credited to him, some were based on pre-Reformation sources or were created by the contrafactum technique. Among those tunes most likely written by Luther himself are "Nun freut euch" (*LBW* 299; the first hymn in the first Lutheran hymnal, the *Achtliederbuch*, 1524), "Vater unser" (*LBW* 310, 442), "Jesaia, dem Propheten" for the German Mass (*LBW* 528), and, of course, "Ein feste Burg" (*LBW* 228— the syncopated tune, not the "smoothed-out" melody in 229). "A mighty fortress is our God" was probably written between 1526 and 1528, perhaps in response to the persecution of some of Luther's followers in 1527. Luther himself is known to have sung it daily at Coburg while awaiting the outcome of the Diet of Augsburg in 1530. It is, in the words of Friedrich Blume, "one of the most magnificent examples of the perfect unity of word and tone and of compactness, achievement of an affect, and significance of melodic form—qualities that made Luther's lieder the mightiest source of strength for the Reformation and raised them into the immortality of great works of art."[82]

In the tenth chapter we shall look at the compilation of hymnals during the Reformation period. Here we simply note that Luther's own hymns formed the backbone of these collections. His original aim was to stimulate others who could improve on his work. For this reason, perhaps, no fewer than twenty-three of his thirty-six songs were written in the single year between 1523 and 1524. His song output after 1524 was nowhere near as abundant. Nevertheless, while some of his contemporaries matched him as a songwriter, no one surpassed his songs in durability and popularity. While the original purpose of these songs was to make congregational participation practical in evangelical liturgies, they became such a formidable means of disseminating doctrine that the Jesuits later said of Luther's songs that they "destroyed more souls than his writings and speeches."

THE REVISIONS OF THE ORDER OF BAPTISM

First Taufbüchlein, *1523*

Providing a vernacular Service of the Word and Lord's Supper and hymnody to facilitate congregational participation in this service was not the only task of liturgical revision Luther faced. Equally important for Christian life was the Order of Baptism. But Luther's critique of the medieval theology and practice of baptism was not as severe as his critique of the mass. Indeed, he began his section on "The Sacrament of Baptism" in *Babylonian Captivity* with the words,

> Blessed be God and the Father of our Lord Jesus Christ, who according to the riches of his mercy (Eph. 1:3, 7) has preserved in his church this sacrament at least, untouched and untainted by the ordinances of men, and has made it free

---

[82] Blume, 43.

to all nations and classes of mankind, and has not permitted it to be oppressed by the filthy and godless monsters of greed and superstition. For he desired that by it little children, who were incapable of greed and superstition, might be initiated and sanctified in the simple faith of his Word; even today baptism has its chief blessing for them.[83]

These sentences already alert us to two things about Luther's baptismal practice: first, he was not interested in a radical revision of the Order of Baptism; and second, he continued to practice and defend the baptism of infants, as did the other major reformers—Zwingli, Bucer, and Calvin. All of these reformers stressed the role of faith in the reception of the sacraments. Indeed, Luther wrote that "unless faith is present or is conferred in baptism, baptism will profit us nothing."[84] This element of personal appropriation of the sacrament was placed against the doctrine of ex opere operato, especially as taught by Duns Scotus, because it suggested that justification could be received by means of a ceremony without that faith which trusts and believes in the promise of God. This emphasis on faith might have led Luther and the other reformers to question the practice of infant baptism. But against Anabaptist assaults on this practice the reformers defended it. In fact, by the time Luther wrote his Catechisms at the end of the turbulent 1520s, he was ready to make a distinction between the word and command of God that *makes* the sacrament and faith that *receives* it.

> [W]e are not primarily concerned whether the baptized person believes or not, for in the latter case Baptism does not become invalid. Everything depends upon the Word and commandment of God. This, perhaps, is a rather subtle point, but it is based upon what I have already said, that Baptism is simply water and God's Word in and with each other; that is, when the Word accompanies the water, Baptism is valid, even though faith be lacking. For my faith does not constitute Baptism but receives it. Baptism does not become invalid even if it is wrongly received or used, for it is bound not to our faith but to the Word.[85]

This may represent a shift of emphasis in Luther's teaching between 1520 and 1529 as a result of the Anabaptist attacks on infant baptism, but it is also a further application of his original concern. For already in *Babylonian Captivity* Luther's principal critique was that the promise of God made in baptism was being ignored in favor of religious works in which Christians could put their trust.

> Now, the first thing to be considered about baptism is the divine promise, which says, "He who believes and is baptized will be saved" (Mark 16:16). This promise must be set far above all the glitter of works, vows, religious orders, and whatever else man has introduced, for on it all our salvation depends. But we must so consider it as to exercise our faith in it, and have no doubt whatever that, once we have been baptized, we are saved.[86]

Baptism, for Luther, was the ritual sign of justification; and therefore Christians should be taught always to return to their baptism and the word of promise made in it.

---

[83] LW 36:57.
[84] Ibid., 59.
[85] Large Catechism, IV, 52–3; Tappert, 443.
[86] LW 36:58–9.

Thus you see how rich a Christian is, that is, one who has been baptized. Even if he would, he could not lose his salvation, however much he sinned, unless he refused to believe. For no sin can condemn him save unbelief alone. All other sins, so long as the faith in God's promise made in baptism returns or remains, are immediately blotted out through that same faith, or rather through the truth of God, because he cannot deny himself if you confess him and faithfully cling to him in his promise.[87]

Baptism constitutes the basis of Christian life. It inaugurates a new relationship of forgiveness and reconciliation with God. It puts all the baptized on the same footing before God, and therefore constitutes the basis of the doctrine of the priesthood of all believers, which Luther articulated in his *Open Letter to the Christian Nobility of the German Nation* (1520). Because of the crucial importance of baptism for Christians, it was important that they understood it, and therefore Luther began the task of putting the Order for Baptism into the vernacular several years before he did this with the mass.

The first Baptismal Booklet (*Taufbüchlein*) appeared in 1523 between the publications of the pamphlets *Concerning the Order of Public Worship* and the *Formula Missae et Communionis*. It contained an Order of Baptism that was largely a translation into German of the late medieval Order of Baptism found in the Magdeburg Agenda of 1497. Luther followed this rite very closely. He slightly abbreviated and compressed the numerous exorcisms, moved the Creed from before the Our Father in the catechetical rites (which took place in front of the church) to the questions at the font, and replaced the prayer after the giving of salt (*Deus patrum nostrorum*) with his own Flood Prayer (*Sintflutgebet*):

Almighty and eternal God, who has through the flood, according to your righteous judgment, condemned the unfaithful world, and, according to your great mercy, has saved faithful Noah, even eight persons, and has drowned hardhearted Pharaoh with all his in the Red Sea, and has led your people Israel dry through it, thereby prefiguring this bath of your holy baptism, and through the baptism of your dear child, our Lord Jesus Christ, has sanctified and set apart the Jordan and all water for a saving flood, and an ample washing away of sins: we pray that through your same infinite mercy you will graciously look upon this N., and bless him[/her] with a right faith in the spirit, so that through this saving flood all that was born in him from Adam and all which he himself has added thereto may be drowned and submerged: and that he may be separated from the unfaithful, and preserved in the holy ark of Christendom dry and safe, and ever fervent in spirit and joyful in hope serve your name, so that he with all the faithful may be worthy to inherit your promise of eternal life, through Christ our Lord. Amen.[88]

---

[87] Ibid., 60–1.

[88] J. D. C. Fisher, *Christian Initiation: The Reformation Period* (London: S.P.C.K., 1970), 9ff. provides English translations of the Magdeburg Order of Baptism and Luther's Order in parallel columns. On the flood and passage through the Red Sea as types of baptism in the teachings of the church fathers see Jean Daniélou, *The Bible and the Liturgy* (Notre Dame, Ind.: University of Notre Dame Press, 1956), 70ff., 86ff.

The outline of Luther's Order of Baptism (1523) is as follows:[89]

A. CATECHETICAL RITES IN FRONT OF THE CHURCH

Exsufflation (exorcism of the eyes by breathing under them)
Signing with the cross on the forehead and breast
Exorcism prayers
Giving of salt (exorcism of the mouth)
Flood Prayer
Additional exorcisms
Prayer for enlightenment
Salutation
The Gospel (Mark 10:13–16)
Our Father (while the priest lays his hands on the head of the child)
Ephphatha (opening of the ears and nose with spittle)

B. BAPTISMAL RITES AT THE FONT

Procession to the baptistery
Renunciation of Satan
Profession of Faith (interrogatory form)
Anointing on breast
Immersion with invocation of the trinitarian Name
Anointing on the forehead with the sign of the cross
Peace
Presentation of the white robe (christening gown)
Presentation of the baptismal candle

It is evident that Luther's 1523 Order of Baptism was a very full rite, retaining many of the texts and ceremonies of the medieval Order of Baptism. In the epilogue to this Order, however, he cautioned:

> Now remember, too, that in baptism the external things are the least important, such as blowing under the eyes, signing with the cross, putting salt into the mouth, putting spittle and clay into the ears and nose, anointing the breast and shoulders with oil, signing the crown of the head with chrism, putting on the christening robe, placing a burning candle in the hand, and whatever else has been added by man to embellish baptism.[90]

The reformers contrasted the ceremonies that had been "added by man to embellish baptism" with the divine institution of baptism in the New Testament, which, in their view, required only dipping in water in the name of the Trinity. So much did Luther want the water-rite emphasized that he recommended and practiced immersion in the water (which is not the same as submersion). The medieval fonts were still large enough to dip a child into the water. In the view of the reformers, however, the other ceremonies lent themselves to superstition; it is not surprising, then, that these ceremonies were eventually suppressed. Luther and his colleagues grew more and more impatient with these

---

[89] See the text of the Order of Baptism (1523) in LW 53:96ff.
[90] Ibid., 102.

"embellishments," and in 1526 he yielded to the urging of Nicholas Hausmann and published a revised Order of Baptism.

Second Taufbüchlein, *1526*

The Order of Baptism Newly Revised[91] began with a preface that was simply the epilogue of the first *Taufbüchlein*, with the final paragraph deleted in which Luther had explained why he didn't want to make any marked changes in the order of baptism. In this revision almost all of the external signs except water were suppressed, and most of the exorcisms were omitted. However, the order still began with the powerful words of the exsufflation (without the breathing): "Depart you unclean spirit and make room for the Holy Spirit"; and the sign of the cross was still made on the forehead and breast with words to that effect (without the use of oil); and the custom of putting a christening gown on the child after the baptism was retained (probably for the practical reason that the child was dipped naked in the water and had to be clothed anyway; and perhaps the passing down of family christening gowns had already become a folk custom). The outline of this order is as follows:

A. THE CATECHETICAL RITES IN FRONT OF THE CHURCH

"Depart you unclean spirit . . ."
"Receive the sign of the holy cross . . ."
Prayer for the blessing of baptism (based on the text: "Ask, and ye shall receive . . .")
The Flood Prayer
Exorcism

> I adjure you, unclean spirit, by the name of the ✠ Father and of the ✠ Son and of the ✠ Holy Ghost that you come out of and depart from this servant of Jesus Christ, N. Amen.

Gospel (Mark 10:13–16)
Our Father (while the priest lays his hands on the head of the child)

B. BAPTISMAL RITES AT THE FONT

Procession to the font
Renunciation of Satan
Profession of faith
The immersion of the child with the invocation of the trinitarian Name
The giving of the white robe

> The almighty God and Father of our Lord Jesus Christ, who has regenerated you by water and the Holy Spirit, and has forgiven you all your sins, strengthen you with his grace unto eternal life.

This last prayer is the anointing prayer in the old Latin rite, but modified since there is now no anointing.

This revised Order of Baptism was very influential on subsequent Lutheran Church Orders, as we shall see in the next chapter. It is also very conservative when compared with the baptismal orders prepared by Zwingli and Bucer. Zwingli's order was one

---

[91] Ibid., 107ff.; Fisher, 23ff.

from which "all additions which have no foundation in scripture have been removed." It included a prayer resembling Luther's Flood Prayer, the gospel from Mark 10, the naming of the child, the water-bath, and the vesting of the child in the christening gown. Bucer's rite is distinguished by ample exhortation to the godparents, and the act of dipping in water in the trinitarian name is made to stand out as the only matter and form of baptism. Bucer did insist, however, that the baptism be celebrated at the Sunday eucharist of the congregation and not just any time in an almost empty church by private arrangement with the priest.[92] This was a reform Luther missed: to recover the ecclesial dimension of this rite of Christian initiation by providing that it be celebrated in the Christian assembly at the chief service. Nevertheless, baptism did come to be celebrated before the congregation in Lutheran as well as in Reformed churches. This is signified by the relocation of the baptismal font from the church door to a position in the chancel in front of the congregation.

❦ CONFIRMATION AND FIRST COMMUNION

We have seen that a separate rite and sacrament of confirmation developed in the Western church as a consequence of delaying the post-baptismal ceremonies of the laying on of hands, the invocation of the Holy Spirit, and the anointing with the sign of the cross until the baptized child could be taken to the bishop or the bishop could visit the parish to "confirm" the baptism of the child. We have also seen the problems attendant to this arrangement. In view of the history and practice of confirmation in the medieval church it is not surprising that Luther found it "amazing that it should have entered the minds of these men to make a sacrament of confirmation out of the laying on of hands."[93] It had been a practice in search of a theory, less tenuously connected with baptism as time went on, administered haphazardly by bishops and to children of vastly different ages ranging from infancy to adolescence. Luther denied that the sacramentality of confirmation can be proved from scripture, although he exclaimed: "Would that there were in the church such a laying on of hands as there was in apostolic times, whether we chose to call it confirmation or healing."[94]

Luther variously referred to the Roman sacrament of confirmation as "monkey business" (*Affenspiel*), "a fanciful deception" (*Lügenstand*), and "mumbo-jumbo" (*Gaukelwerk*), and strongly urged that it be avoided because it had no basis in scripture—although in a sermon in 1522 he conceded that he "would permit confirmation as long as it is understood that God knows nothing of it, and has said nothing about it, and that what the bishops claim for it is untrue."[95] "Nevertheless," he went on to say, "we do not find

---

[92] See J. D. C. Fisher, "Initiation: Lutheran, Anglican, and Reformed Rites," in *The Study of Liturgy*, op. cit., 120.

[93] *The Babylonian Captivity*, LW 36:91.

[94] Ibid.

[95] Quoted in Arthur C. Repp, *Confirmation in the Lutheran Church* (St. Louis: Concordia Publishing House, 1964), 15–7.

fault if every pastor examines the faith of the children to see whether it is good and sincere, lays hands on them, and confirms them."[96]

Luther had little interest in a rite of confirmation as such, but a great deal of interest in catechesis. The practice of infant baptism carried with it the obligation of parents and sponsors to see that the child was instructed in the basics of the Christian faith (the Ten Commandments, the Creed, and the Lord's Prayer). Luther frequently and regularly preached catechetical sermons and worked diligently to shore up the practice of parents catechizing their children at home. The official visitation of parishes in Saxony in 1528 revealed how little Christian education was actually taking place, either in the homes or from the pulpits. It was in response to that situation that Luther prepared his Small and Large Catechisms in 1529.

The great humanist scholar, Desiderius Erasmus (1466–1536), in his *Paraphrase of Matthew* (1522), proposed that during Lent baptized boys be required to hear catechetical sermons that explained to them their baptismal profession, and that they renew this profession in a solemn ceremony at Easter. This proposal had great influence on Martin Bucer and Philipp Melanchthon, both of whom provided a rite of confirmation at the completion of the catechetical instruction process. Luther himself never prepared a rite of confirmation, but seems to have taken up the idea of providing a period of catechetical instruction conducted by the pastor as a preparation for communion. It should be noted, however, that parents usually presented their children to be prepared for first communion when they deemed them ready, and that the average communicant became a catechumen each time he or she went to communion, to make up for poor instruction.[97]

CONFESSION AND ABSOLUTION

Throughout his life Luther encouraged the use of private confession and absolution, both as a preparation for Holy Communion and as an independent means of grace. It was a practice he had found helpful during his days of spiritual struggle in the monastery. When he returned to Wittenberg from his hideaway in the Wartburg in 1522 to restore order after Karlstadt's iconoclastic campaign, he preached eight sermons in eight days, the last of which concerned private confession (which Karlstadt had abolished). He agreed that no one should be forced to go to confession, and that one who had a strong, firm faith might confess to God alone. "But how many have such a strong faith? Therefore, as I have said, I will not let this private confession be taken from me. But I will not have anybody forced to it, but left to each one's free will."[98]

Nevertheless, he did not give up trying to teach people to use the confessional in an evangelical way. He prepared "A Short Order of Confession Before the Priest for the Common Man" in 1529,[99] which was included in the Small Catechism. In the 1531 edition of the catechism he gave a more detailed example of evangelical auricular confession

---

[96] Ibid.

[97] Ibid., 22ff.

[98] LW 51:99.

[99] LW 53:117–9.

under the title, "How One Should Teach Common Folk to Shrive Themselves."[100] Essential to his understanding of confession is that one should confess specifically only those sins that torment the conscience, and cling to the word of absolution as the declaration of forgiveness from God himself. He denounced the view that absolution is contingent on the performance of penances or works of satisfaction, but emphasized the need to trust and believe the word of absolution.

Thus, in the Small Catechism Luther taught:

> Confession consists of two parts. One is that we confess our sins. The other is that we receive absolution or forgiveness from the confessor as from God himself, by no means doubting but firmly believing that our sins are thereby forgiven before God in heaven.[101]

In a similar way, he wrote in his Large Catechism:

> Confession consists of two parts. The first is my work and act, when I lament my sin and desire comfort and restoration for my soul. The second is a work which God does, when he absolves me of my sins through a word placed in the mouth of a man. This is a surpassingly grand and noble thing that makes confession so wonderful and comforting.[102]

As with the Nominalists, Luther placed the emphasis in penance on the word of absolution. This was not because he was shoring up God's almighty power over human efforts, in Nominalist fashion, but because when the gospel is rightly proclaimed it is the word of forgiveness. In the Smalkald Articles, Part III, Article IV, on "The Gospel," Luther held that "the Gospel . . . offers counsel and help against sin in more than one way." He enumerated these ways as follows:

> First, through the spoken word, by which the forgiveness of sin (the peculiar office of the Gospel) is preached to the whole world; second, through Baptism; third, through the sacrament of the Altar; fourth, through the power of the keys; and finally, through the mutual conversation and consolation of brethren.[103]

In the order for private confession that Luther provided in the Small Catechism, he offered counsel in typical medieval fashion when he advised penitents to "Reflect on your condition in the light of the Ten Commandments."[104] This correlates with the kind of catechesis that accompanied auricular confession. But he placed the center of gravity in the rite of penance on the word of absolution when he instructed the confessor to ask the penitent: "Do you believe that the forgiveness I declare is the forgiveness of God?"[105] There is no point in declaring forgiveness to those who cannot accept or believe that they are forgiven. That would wreck the entire penitential process as a return to one's status as

---

[100] Ibid., 119–21. See also Tappert, 349–51.
[101] Tappert, 349, 16.
[102] Ibid., 458, 15.
[103] Ibid., 310.
[104] Ibid., 350, 20.
[105] Ibid., 351, 27.

a baptized child of God. If one is justified by grace, of which baptism is the ritual sign, then one is justified by grace. Faith's role is to hear the word of forgiveness and believe that God means it. Philipp Melanchthon wrote that from the sinner's side the "parts" of penance are not contrition, confession, and satisfaction, as the medieval scholastics had taught; but "contrition and faith"—sorrow for one's sins, when indicted by the law, and trust in the word of forgiveness, which one hears from the ministry of the gospel.[106] He went on to affirm in the Apology of the Augsburg Confession:

> We also keep confession, especially because of absolution, which is the Word of God that the power of the keys proclaims to individuals by divine authority. It would therefore be wicked to remove private absolution from the church. And those who despise private absolution understand neither the forgiveness of sins nor the power of the keys.[107]

In the face of such an emphasis as this, it may now seem strange that private confession has largely disappeared in the practice of the Lutheran churches. This did not happen immediately. Chapter ten reviews the reasons for its general demise. There have also been efforts to restore individual or private confession in the nineteenth and twentieth centuries, and a form of Individual Confession and Forgiveness modeled on the order in Luther's Small Catechism is included in *Lutheran Book of Worship*[108] and in *Lutheran Worship*.[109]

While Luther's reform of the confessional seems conservative, especially in comparison with those reformers who abolished auricular confession entirely, his teachings actually made a dent in what Jean Delumeau called "the Western guilt culture."[110] The doctrine of justification by faith had the effect of reassuring sinners that they remain sinners but are accepted by God anyway. The corollary of the doctrine of justification by faith is the doctrine of predestination, which assures sinners that they are chosen as children of God. It is worth recalling that Luther arrived at his views of justification and predestination via the path of despair. Luther observed that a clear-sighted and exacting conscience cannot help but be overwhelmed by the number and gravity of one's sins. When compared to such offenses, goods works "vanish like a breath of wind." It was precisely for these reasons that Luther clung to the practice of individual confession and absolution. Those burdened by particular sins and the pangs of a guilty conscience could make a confession, and thus lay those things that accuse the soul on the table; but then the penitent was taught to rely on the word of absolution on the lips of the confessor "as from God himself." Thus the evangelical practice of confession and absolution could actually be regarded as the most concrete form of proclamation of the gospel.

---

[106] Augsburg Confession, XII, 4–5.

[107] Apology, XII; Tappert, 197.

[108] *Lutheran Book of Worship*, 196–7.

[109] *Lutheran Worship* (St. Louis: Concordia Publishing House, 1982), 310–1.

[110] See Jean Delumeau, *Sin and Fear: The Emergence of a Western Guilt Culture. 13th–18th Centuries*, op. cit., 493ff.

❧ THE VOCATION OF CHRISTIANS

Marriage

There were other areas in which Luther's teachings had the effect of fomenting what Steven Ozment has called "a social revolution," none more so in than the doctrine of vocation. This was a consequence of his doctrine of the priesthood of all believers, in which Luther held that the practice of the Christian faith cannot be left to professionals alone. All Christians stand equally under the command and promises of God, and all Christians bear equal responsibility for their life and conduct before God. Luther believed that every Christian who is engaged in socially productive work is engaged in full-time Christian service. As William Lazareth has pointed out, this meant that the calling to marriage and family life was as great a vocation as the calling to monastic or religious life.[111]

Extending Lazareth's work on Luther's view of family life, Ozment has demonstrated the paradox that the reformer's denial of sacramental status to the rite of marriage and his suggestions about transferring the administration of marriage from the church to the state nevertheless exalted the married status and the home as the primary arena of Christian service to God. The abolition of required clerical celibacy also created a new relationship between pastor and people, and imposed (unwittingly) on pastors the further obligation of demonstrating an ideal Christian home life as once they had been expected to demonstrate ideal Christian ascetic disciplines.[112]

As in other areas, Luther was reluctant to get into the work of producing a liturgical order for marriage. His view of the secular character of marriage was expressed in the preface to the Order of Marriage for Common Pastors, which he wrote in 1529.

> Since marriage and the married estate are worldly matters, it behooves us pastors or ministers of the church not to attempt to order or govern anything connected with it, but to permit each city and land to continue its own use and custom in this connection.[113]

Nevertheless, because it had been the custom "to surround the consecration of monks and nuns with such great ceremonial display . . . how much more should we honor this divine estate of marriage and gloriously bless and embellish it and pray for it. . . . It should be accounted a hundred times more spiritual than the monastic state." Furthermore, having an impressive order of service would help young people "to take this estate seriously."[114]

In 1529, Luther published an Order of Marriage for Common Pastors to provide a simple and worthy rite to replace the nuptial mass. In this order he followed the traditional tripartite division of the medieval marriage rite: the publication of the banns at a time before the day of the wedding; the exchange of vows and rings on the church porch;

---

[111] William H. Lazareth, *Luther on the Christian Home* (Philadelphia: Muhlenberg Press, 1960).
[112] Steven Ozment, *Protestants: The Birth of a Revolution* (New York: Doubleday, 1992), 151ff.
[113] LW 53:111.
[114] Ibid., 112.

and the reading of scripture, an exhortation, and prayer for the couple in front of the altar. The publication of banns or announcement of the impending marriage was done several weeks before the wedding, and was a legal requirement. The exchange of vows and rings was also the legal part of the marriage rite and had, for centuries, been conducted on the church porch because of its civil character. The reading of Genesis 2:18, 21–22, the exhortation based on biblical texts pertaining to marriage, and the prayer for the couple replaced the nuptial mass before the altar. The most radical departure in Luther's rite was the elimination of the celebration of the eucharist, although weddings could take place on Sunday and the couple might receive communion at the public mass. Martin Bucer took the step of locating the marriage rite within the Sunday service of Holy Communion.

Ordination

Among the vocations exercised by Christians is the office of pastor. In his Address to the Christian Nobility (1520) Luther developed his view that the only difference between a priest and a lay person is one of office, not one of status before God.[115] The content of this office is the ministry of the word and the sacraments. Such a ministry, in Luther's view, was divinely instituted; but its incumbents were subject to call and election by the church. A crisis developed in the provision of ministers for congregations when the bishops would not ordain pastors for evangelical churches. At that point, in writings of 1522 and 1523, Luther argued that congregations had the right to call and ordain ministers and teachers.[116]

Nevertheless, the actual ordaining was done by ordained priests. Luther led the way when he ordained Georg Rörer in Wittenberg in 1525. But not until 1535 did the Elector John Frederick provide a definite order for the examination, calling, and ordination of ministers. Luther was a frequent ordinator (of bishops as well as pastors). He prepared his Order for the Ordination of Ministers of the Word for this purpose.[117]

Luther's order presumes the examination of candidates for ordination either on the same day or on the preceding day. The ordination rite itself begins with the choir singing "Veni, Sancte Spiritus" and the Collect for Pentecost. It continues with the reading of 1 Timothy 3:1–7 and Acts 20:28–31, an exhortation, and the consent of the candidate. "Then while the whole presbytery impose their hands on the heads of the ordinands, the ordinator says the Lord's Prayer in a clear voice." He may also add the following prayer:

> Merciful God, heavenly Father, you have said to us through the mouth of your dear Son our Lord Jesus Christ: "The harvest truly is plenteous, but the laborers are few. Pray therefore the Lord of the harvest, that he will send forth laborers into his harvest" (Matt. 9:37–38). Upon this divine command, we pray heartily that you would grant your Holy Spirit richly to these your servants, to us, and to all those who are called to serve your Word so that the company of us who publish the good tidings may be great, and that we may stand faithful and

---

[115] Martin Luther, *Three Treatises* (Philadelphia: Fortress Press, 1970), 17.

[116] See Hans Küng, *Structures of the Church*, trans. by Salvator Attanasio (Notre Dame, Ind.: University of Notre Dame Press, 1968), 107ff.

[117] LW 53:124ff.

firm against the devil, the world, and the flesh, to the end that your name may be hallowed, your kingdom grow, and your will be done. Be also pleased at length to check and stop the detestable abomination of the pope, Mohammed, and other sects which blaspheme your name, hinder your kingdom, and oppose your will. Graciously hear this our prayer, since you have commanded, taught, and promised, even as we believe and trust through your dear Son, Jesus Christ our Lord, who lives and reigns with you and the Holy Ghost, world without end. Amen.[118]

The rite ended with an exhortation based on 1 Peter 5:2–4, a blessing with the sign of the cross, and the congregational hymn, "Now let us pray to the Holy Ghost."

Absent from this order is any declarative formula, such as "receive the Holy Spirit."[119] Conspicuously absent are the explicatory rites that assumed such importance in medieval orders of ordination, especially the anointing of the hands of the candidate and the handing over of the instruments of office, such as the chalice and paten. These had come to be associated with the priest's reception of authority to offer the sacrifice of the mass for the living and the dead (as in the Romano-German Pontifical, c. 950). Luther clearly prepared a rite for the ordination of ministers of the word. Also absent, however, is a significant role for the congregation, a medieval fault that Luther retained and that has plagued Lutheran ordination rites ever since. However, the ordination did take place in the context of the mass or communion service and the ordinands were instructed to commune with the congregation.

---

[118] Ibid., 126; alt.

[119] See Ralph W. Quere, "'The Spirit and the Gifts are Ours:' Imparting or Imploring the Spirit in Ordination Rites?" *Lutheran Quarterly* 27 (1975), 322–46.

CHAPTER 9

Word and Sacrament in Luther's Reformation

How shall we assess the impact of Luther's liturgical reforms? They were of a conservative nature when compared with the more radical reforms of Zwingli and Calvin. Nevertheless, the principal reform resources taken together—liturgy, Bible, hymns, catechisms, and so forth—made a profound impact on the development of German culture, indeed on the culture of the whole of central and northern Europe. Luther D. Reed opined that Luther's work "eventually made possible congregational participation in worship in every land and established hymn-singing by the people as a characteristic and important feature of Protestantism."[1]

Nevertheless, congregational participation in worship and hymn-singing did not come about all at once; nor was this the most important concern of the Lutheran reformers. Rather, as Herman Wegman has suggested, "The great reformers of the church in the West ordered worship according to one important principle: the holy scripture, the word of God, which they placed again at the heart of church life."[2] Worship was to conform, in one way or another, to scripture; scripture was to be read in public worship in the language of the people; sermons were to be preached on the scripture readings; and liturgical practices were to be judged according to biblical norms. This was the great concern of liturgical reform among the reformers. If *sola fide* became the principle on

---

[1] Luther D. Reed, *The Lutheran Liturgy*, op. cit., 86.
[2] Herman Wegman, *Christian Worship in East and West*, op. cit., 297.

which personal life was based, *sola Scriptura* became the principle by which liturgical life was formed.

THE WORD AS TEXT

Luther's liturgical reforms, and even more so those of the other reformers, cannot be appreciated without attending to the cultural context in which they originated: western Europe's slide into textual preoccupation, stimulated by the invention of the printing press and the flowering of humanist scholarship in the Renaissance. This engendered a great deal of interest in the study of classical languages, and especially the study of the Bible in Greek and Hebrew. The study of scripture brought about new insights that raised questions about inherited beliefs and practices.

Gutenberg of Mainz is credited with the invention of movable type around 1440–1450. (Movable type should be distinguished from block printing, which was known in China already by the ninth century.) While printing revolutionized communication and caught on very quickly throughout Europe, book fairs were especially popular in Germany, France, and the Netherlands. Literary humanism was centered in northern Europe by the beginning of the sixteenth century, while aesthetic humanism was concentrated south of the Alps. It cannot pass unnoticed that the Reformation occasioned a North-South schism in the Western church, much as the East-West schism made final by the mutual excommunication of the pope of Rome and the patriarch of Constantinople in 1054 also reflected differences between Latin and Greek culture. Luther's profound insight into the gospel of justification by faith alone, defended on the basis of scripture alone, need not be minimized by Aidan Kavanagh's observation that "proponents of the Reformation were largely men of the north who fell as easily into textual obsession with the Bible as they did into mistrust of urbane aesthetes from south of the Alps."[3]

Most humanists were put off by the state of liturgical hypertrophy at the end of the Middle Ages. Printing made possible a thorough assault on this state of affairs. Texts could be pruned, revised, and cheaply mass-produced. There were a number of consequences of this. In both Reformation and Catholic churches mass production of liturgical books greatly accelerated liturgical change. It also made Christian liturgy easier to control by church law administered through central bureaucratic offices of church and civil government, something that was largely unknown until the sixteenth century. Printed church orders could now regulate liturgical rites and practices within principalities and city-states, and in Lutheran and Reformed territories these church orders were backed up by civil authority. The English Act of Uniformity of 1549 directed that the only liturgical use that would be tolerated throughout the whole realm was that contained in *The Booke of Common Prayer and Administration of the Sacraments, and Other Rites and Ceremonies of the Church, after the Use of the Churche of England*. Similar steps were taken by the Roman See as a consequence of the decree of the Council of Trent in 1563 that all churches under obedience to the Roman See should use the liturgical orders of the

---

[3] Aidan Kavanagh, *On Liturgical Theology* (New York: Pueblo Publishing Co., 1984), 103–4.

Roman See, unless they could prove that their own rites were at least two hundred years old. This decree was implemented with the publication of the archetypal Roman Breviary in 1568 and Roman Missal in 1570, and it was not completed until the publication of the *Rituale Romanum* in 1614.[4] The revolutionary impact of printing on liturgical uniformity can be seen by comparing the ease with which it was brought about in the sixteenth and seventeenth centuries to the chaos that ensued from the attempt to impose Roman books on the Frankish church in the seventh and eighth centuries.

But an even more profound consequence of printing was the divorce of word and rite. The holy could now be approached through texts put cheaply into the hands of worshipers rather than through events, symbols, ceremonies, sacred times and places. Indeed, as Kavanagh asserts, "Rite became less a means than an obstacle for the new textual piety. And once rite receded, so did the need for that kind of assembly whose common burden was the enactment of rite rather than attendance upon didactic exposition of set texts."[5]

Worshipers came together not to perform liturgical actions, for which the space had to be kept open to accommodate moving bodies, but to hear and read texts, for which pews were probably a welcome convenience and the reading desk an important piece of liturgical furniture. In the iconoclasm that naturally attended this shift of emphasis from rite to word, anything that detracted from concentrating attention on the word had to be removed. For the truth was perceived to lie in the text, not on the walls or in the windows or in the liturgical activity of those who occupied the churches. The conservative nature of Luther's reformation is evident in its willingness to retain the accoutrements of rite, such as bells, candles, paraments, and vestments. The visual arts were never developed to the same extent as the art of music in Lutheran church life. Music served the word by heightening, teaching, or interpreting the text.

Luther, like the other reformers, was vitally interested in the word as text. The chief text of the Reformation was the Bible as studied in the original languages of Greek and Hebrew, and as translated into various vernaculars so that it could be read by an increasingly literate populace. Luther's struggle to find a gracious God and his insight into the gospel came through his study of scripture. He was a professor of the Bible at the University of Wittenberg. The bulk of his literary output consists of exegetical commentaries and sermons on biblical texts. His most enduring literary achievement is the German translation of the Bible.

None of this could have been accomplished without humanist scholarship. For example, Luther made use of the critical Greek text of the New Testament produced by Erasmus of Rotterdam. Luther was no humanist, and while he relied on Erasmus's scholarship, he disputed Erasmus's views in *The Bondage of the Will* (1525). Luther's biographer Roland Bainton stated that "this man was no son of the Italian Renaissance, but a German born in remote Thuringia, where men of piety still reared churches with arches and spires straining after the illimitable. Luther was himself so much a gothic figure that

---

[4] See Theodore Klauser, *A Short History of the Western Liturgy*, op. cit., 117ff.
[5] Kavanagh, 104.

his faith may be called the last great flowering of the religion of the Middle Ages."[6] Yet the matter is not quite that simple.

Luther did not come from a peasant family, nor was he brought up in a piety where faith was mingled with superstition. His father, Hans Luder, was a miner who had become a superintendent of mines. His ambitions for his son are reflected in the kind of education he provided. Martin attended a school at Magdeburg operated by the Brethren of the Common Life and matriculated at the University of Erfurt, from which he received his Bachelor and Master of Arts in 1501 and 1502 respectively. He was prepared to enter law school when an incident, reputed to have been a thunderstorm in which he prayed to St. Ann for deliverance, drove him into the strict cloister of the Augustinian Hermits. It was the Observant branch of the Augustinians in which he professed his monastic vows, and this placed Luther in a tradition of reform at least within the monastic life.[7] He was ordained a priest and studied the philosophy and theology of the *via moderna,* the school of William of Ockham. Though he departed in many respects from this school of thought later on, especially on the matter of freedom of the will, he learned much from his "dear master" Ockham, especially the antithesis between reason and revelation. The God he came to know through his study of the Bible was both *Deus revelatus* and *Deus absconditus,* the God both "revealed" and "hidden" in Christ, in the Bible, in the sacraments, and in the church.

The impact of this background on Luther's liturgical reforms stands in clearer relief if Luther's background is contrasted with Ulrich Zwingli's. Zwingli never studied theology, but took holy orders as a secular priest after he had attained the degree of Master of Arts at Basel. At the University of Basel, he gained considerable knowledge of the *via antiqua,* the philosophical and theological schools of Thomas Aquinas and Duns Scotus, for whom revelation could not contradict reason. Unlike Luther, Zwingli never would have understood the word of God as that which contradicts and confounds human wisdom. Zwingli was also tutored in Erasmian humanism, from which he learned the separation of mind and matter and gained appreciation for the moral imperative of the Christian gospel and respect for the ethics of classical antiquity.[8]

We shall presently see how the difference in Luther's and Zwingli's backgrounds led to their disagreement over the presence of Christ in the sacrament of the altar. But here we note also the difference in their approach to the task of liturgical revision. Zwingli undertook a revision of the Latin mass in the same year that Luther did, his *De canone missae epicheiresis* of 1523. As the title of this work indicates, it was particularly the canon that was of concern to Zwingli. He was, like Luther, put off by the sacrificial emphasis on the mass, but he also had no patience with what he considered to be its barbarisms and incoherence. So he replaced the canon with four Latin prayers leading up to the institution narrative, completed by the Pauline sentence on the proclamation of the Lord's death in the sacrament (1 Cor. 11:26), and then the communion introduced by the

---

[6] Roland Bainton, *Here I Stand: A Life of Martin Luther* (Nashville: Abingdon Press, 1950), 25.

[7] See Heiko A. Oberman, *Luther: Man Between God and the Devil,* op. cit., 50ff.

[8] See Hermann Sasse, *This Is My Body,* op. cit., 116ff.

words of Christ: "Come to me that are weary and are carrying heavy burdens, and I will give you rest" (Matt. 11:28).[9] In contrast Luther simply omitted the prayers of the Roman canon after the Sanctus except for the words of institution.

It became a tendency in Reformed liturgies to have lengthy prayers, including the prayers of consecration. Prayers can express the sense of mystery, as the ancient Eastern anaphoras do. Prayers can also be used to explain away mystery—to articulate doctrine so precisely that there is no ambiguity left concerning the liturgical action or the attitude of worship. Luther shared with the other reformers a concern for *intelligibility* in worship, and the elimination of those ritual acts that too easily lent themselves to superstition. Unlike many of the other reformers, however, Luther also had an appreciation for *the mystery* of Christian worship—the sense that the reality being addressed in worship, or addressing the worshipers, is "beyond reason" and can only be apprehended by faith. The Roman Catholic (ex-Lutheran) liturgiologist Louis Bouyer said about the Reformation Lutheran mass: "Whatever its defects may have been, and they were . . . medieval defects pushed to their extreme, this Lutheran mass preserved for the faithful all that they had found best about the mass of the Middle Ages. . . . Along with the ceremonial, liturgical chant, sacred vestments, the crucifix and statues, incense and candles, the mass of devout Lutherans still found in their worship the whole atmosphere of adoration which the best Christians of the Middle Ages found in the holy presence and the evocation of the saving cross."[10]

It needs to be recognized, however, that the retention of the element of mystery in worship was the case not in spite of Luther's emphasis on the word, but because of his doctrine of the word, which Heinrich Bornkamm regards as one of the most creative and dynamic elements of Luther's theology.[11] For Luther the word of God, like God himself, is both hidden and revealed. It can be made known through the text of scripture, but it cannot be limited to a text. This dynamic understanding of the word was at the center of Luther's theology, and also of his understanding of worship and the sacraments. Perhaps because of his background as a professor of scripture, with a concentration on the Old Testament, Luther came to appreciate the fact that the word of God is first and foremost God's self-communication, and therefore God's self-disclosure. Therefore the word of God is always an event.

✱ THE WORD AS EVENT

For Luther, the word of God is not primarily a text; it is first and foremost an oral event—the act of preaching. The scriptures are the written form that the word has taken as a necessary aid in the ongoing proclamation of the church. But, as Luther stated, "the need to write books was a serious decline and a lack of the Spirit which necessity forced upon us; it is not the manner of the New Testament."[12] But the word is not just the equivalent of scripture. As the word of God can be recovered, so it can be lost.

---

[9] See Louis Bouyer, *Eucharist*, op. cit., 392.

[10] Ibid., 396–7.

[11] Heinrich Bornkamm, *Das Wort Gottes bei Luther* (München: Kaiser Verlag, 1933).

[12] "Sermon on the Gospel for the Festival of the Epiphany," LW 52:206.

Let us consider our former misery and the darkness in which we sat. Germany, I trow, has never heard so much of God's Word as now. . . . If we permit it to go by without thanks and honor, it is to be feared we shall suffer a still more dreadful darkness and plague. Buy, dear Germans, while the fair is at your door. . . . God's Word is but a passing rainstorm. . . . It came to the Jews, but it passed over; now they have nothing. Paul brought it to the Greeks, but it passed over; now they have the Turk. Rome and the Latins had it, too; but it passed over; now they have the pope.[13]

Luther's first and foremost critique of the state of liturgical life in the churches as he encountered it was that "God's Word has been silenced, and only reading and singing remain in the churches."[14] In its place had entered "a host of un-Christian fables and lies, in legends, hymns, and sermons" that had fostered superstition and works-righteousness. Luther's prescription, in his first essay on liturgical reform of 1523, was "that a Christian congregation should never gather together without the preaching of God's Word and prayer, no matter how briefly."[15]

He then spun out a program of reform based on this prescription. The daily masses should be completely discontinued (unless there was actually a desire on the part of the faithful to receive the sacrament), and in their place should be daily morning and evening prayer (Matins and Vespers). Books of the Bible should be read in a lectio continua fashion, the Old Testament in the morning and the New Testament in the evening, with preaching on all the readings even though these daily services might not be attended by the whole congregation. On Sundays there should be the mass and Vespers, with preaching on the gospel in the morning and on the epistle in the afternoon.[16] There can be no adequate presentation and assessment of Luther's liturgical reforms, and those of the Reformation generally, without attention to the act of preaching and the role of the sermon.

Roland Bainton gives a synopsis of the scope of preaching in Wittenberg as reforms were implemented. There were three public services on Sunday (Matins, the mass, and Vespers). In his treatise on the German Mass Luther set forth directions that prescribed preaching on the Pauline epistles at Matins, on the Gospels at mass, and in the afternoon at a variable hour a continuation of the morning's theme or a sermon on the catechism. During the week there were sermons on the catechism on Mondays and Tuesdays, on the Gospel of Matthew on Wednesdays, on the apostolic letters on Thursdays and Fridays, and on the Gospel of John on Saturdays. This preaching task was shared by the clergy of the city and the university, but Luther's share was prodigious. Bainton counts some 2300 extant sermons preached by Luther in his lifetime.[17] Many of these were transcribed by students, edited, and published later. However, in the interest of providing models of evangelical preaching, Luther himself prepared a series of sermons for Advent and Christmas while sequestered in the Wartburg in 1521–1522—the

---

[13] *Luther's Works*, IV (Philadelphia: Holman, 1931), 108.

[14] "Concerning the Order of Public Worship" (1523), LW 53:11.

[15] Ibid.

[16] Ibid., 12–3.

[17] Bainton, 348–9. See samples of Luther's sermons on pp. 350–7.

Wartburg Postil. These sermons were originally written in Latin and translated into German in the Postil with the suggestion that less competent preachers should read these sermons to the congregation. In 1525 his Lenten Postil was published.

Luther reformed the approach to preaching as well as the content of sermons. The medieval approach to biblical interpretation and preaching queried a biblical passage for its literal, allegorical, moral, and eschatological significance. Luther largely abandoned this approach in favor of a simpler and more direct approach. His sermons usually began with a brief introduction to the text (a grammatical approach), an exposition of the text in terms of its place and significance within the biblical story (a historical approach), and finally its application to the life of faith or the corporate life of the church. Many of Luther's sermons were concerned, of course, with the reformation of the church. But perhaps the most noteworthy aspect of Luther's sermons is that he took his examples from daily life both in his exposition of the text and in his application of the text. Here is a precious example of Luther setting the historical context of the nativity of Christ.

> Think, women, there was no one there to bathe the Baby. No warm water, nor even cold. No fire, no light. The mother was herself midwife and the maid. The cold manger was the bed and the bath tub. Who showed the poor girl what to do? She never had a baby before. I am amazed that the little one did not freeze. Do not make of Mary a stone. For the higher people are in the favor of God, the more tender are they.[18]

Luther then moves from the exposition to the application.

> Let us, then, meditate upon the Nativity just as we see it happening in our own babies. Behold Christ lying in the lap of his young mother. What can be sweeter than the Babe, what more lovely than the mother! What fairer her youth! What more gracious than her virginity! Look at the Child, knowing nothing. Yet all that is belongs to him, that your conscience should not fear but take comfort in him. Doubt nothing. To me there is no greater consolation given to [hu]mankind than this, that Christ became [hu]man, a child, a babe, playing in the lap and at the breasts of [a] most gracious mother. Who is there whom this sight would not comfort? Now is overcome the power of sin, death, hell, conscience, and guilt, if you come to this gurgling Babe and believe that he is come, not to judge you, but to save.[19]

Luther's method of preaching set a powerful example to his evangelical contemporaries. Reformation preachers were expected to deal with two contexts in their sermons: the context of the biblical text and the context of the contemporary congregation. The new humanist scholarship was quickly harnessed to help in the formation of evangelical preachers. They were expected to study the scriptures in the original languages. With the arrival of the humanist scholar Philipp Melanchthon, Wittenberg University became the first university to teach all three classical languages: Hebrew, Greek, and Latin. As Melanchthon was given more responsibilities for the reform of the university, rhetoric

---

[18] Ibid., 354.

[19] Ibid., 354–5. See *The Martin Luther Christmas Book*, trans. and arranged by Roland H. Bainton (Philadelphia: Fortress Press, 1948).

(declamation) was more strongly emphasized than formal logic (dialectics); scholastic lectures on logic and natural science were supplemented with the study of ancient sources, which led to the cultivation of the study of classical literature and history. The result was to give preachers knowledge of the actual human world in which they lived and which the word of God addressed. Melanchthon, "praeceptor of Germany," was kept busy serving as a consultant to other universities initiating similar reforms.[20] New Lutheran universities were established at Marburg (1527), Königsberg (1544), Jena (1558), and Helmstedt (1575).[21]

In all of the Reformation traditions it came to be expected that the preacher would be a man of learning. But evangelical preaching can never convey just facts, information, ideas, or teachings. It invites a response from the hearer because it brings a person before God—*coram Deo*. To use Old Testament imagery (as Luther often did), it moves David from behind the judge's bench to a position before the bar of justice, and then pronounces him justified. The word both indicts and pardons; it is at once law and gospel.

Luther was articulating a new understanding of the word. The word is as much a means of grace as the sacraments, but grace no longer understood in terms of substance but in terms of communication: address and response. In the Lutheran liturgy the hymn that came to surround the sermon or the pulpit office both furthered the proclamation of the word and provided a devotional response to it. However, the response sought by the preachers was the Spirit-gifted response of faith. As God's self-communication, the word of God is an encounter with the Person of God himself. One cannot encounter God without responding in faith and hope, in fear and love. The preaching of the word is sacramental, because it conveys Christ himself.

> Again, I preach the Gospel of Christ into your heart, so that you may form him within yourself. If now you truly believe, so that your heart lays hold of the Word and holds fast within it that voice, tell me, what you have in your heart? You must answer that you have the true Christ, not that he sits there, as one sits on a chair, but as he is at the right hand of the Father.[22]

It is noteworthy that this passage about the real presence of Christ in the preaching of the word is found in a treatise in which Luther was defending the real presence of Christ in the sacrament, *The Sacrament of the Body and Blood of Christ—Against the Fanatics* (1526). This should alert us to Luther's view that the word that bears Christ's presence comes through the sacramental signs as well as through the oral proclamation.

God's word always attaches itself to something created, even to something physical. As a form of self-communication from person to person, it is never disembodied. The word may be in the book or text of the Bible, the mouth of the preacher, or the

---

[20] The most definitive study of Melanchthon's reforms of the university is Karl Hartfelder, *Philipp Melanchthon als Praeceptor Germaniae* (reprint Nieuwkoop, 1972).

[21] See Lewis W. Spitz, "The Importance of the Reformation for the Universities: Culture and Confessions in the Critical Years," in James M. Kittelson and Pamela Transue, eds., *Rebirth, Reform and Resilience: Universities in Transition, 1300–1780* (Columbus: University of Ohio Press, 1984).

[22] LW 36:340.

earthly elements in the sacraments. The Word that was incarnated in Jesus the Christ, the divine Logos, is always taking on flesh not only in the way in which it is conveyed, but also in the life of the believer who receives it. The word of God is communication between persons, an "I" addressing a "you." But such communication is never only verbal. It is just as "real," just as "living," when it is conveyed through those sacramental signs that are also forms of the word of God, the divine self-communication. It was this incarnational understanding of the word of God for which Luther contended in his controversy over the real presence with Zwingli and the Swiss Reformers.

🍇 THE CONTROVERSY OVER THE SACRAMENT OF THE ALTAR

We have seen that the medieval church explained the real presence of Christ in the sacrament of the altar in terms of transubstantiation. Luther was slow in giving up this doctrine. He related his surprise, in *Babylonian Captivity*, at discovering the opinion of Peter d'Ailly of Paris that it would require fewer miracles to explain the real presence in terms of consubstantiation, since the bread and the wine would then remain on the altar *with* the body and blood of Christ after the consecration. From this Luther concluded that "the opinion of Thomas" on transubstantiation should have remained an opinion, and should not have been made an article of faith.[23] But it cannot be concluded from this that Luther held to the theory of consubstantiation. Neither here nor in any other passage does Luther use this term to describe his own views, and it was never accepted as a doctrine in the Lutheran Confessions—although the Formula of Concord does speak of the sacramental union of "the two essences [Latin: *substantiae;* German: *zwei Wesen*], the natural bread and the true, natural body of Christ" being "present together here on earth in the ordered action of the sacrament."[24]

Luther's defense of the real presence against the "sacramentarians" (e.g., Zwingli, Oecolampadius, Karlstadt) forced him to be more specific about the mode of Christ's presence. Zwingli opened the debate in 1524 by pointing out, in a letter to Pastor Matthäus Alber of Reutlingen, that the significance of the sacrament is a "spiritual eating" by which faith remembers the atoning death of Christ, that the idea of a bodily eating of Christ is a "most noxious and idolatrous opinion," that the word *est* in the words of institution is figurative, that "communion" (koinonia) in 1 Corinthians 10:16 does not mean eating but fellowship, and, in any event, Christ is present now at the right hand of God the Father in heaven and not in flesh and blood on the earthly altar.[25] The letter was circulated around southern Germany, where it caused some disturbance and was answered by Johann Bugenhagen and Johann Brenz. Martin Bucer and the Strassburgers felt a strong kinship to the Swiss view, but urged unity among the reformers. Luther did not join in the debate until 1526, when he published a treatise on *The Sacrament of the Body and Blood of Christ—Against the Fanatics*.[26] This was a pastoral view of the issues, edited from

---

[23] LW 36:28–9.

[24] *Formula of Concord*, Solid Declaration VII, 37; Tappert, 575–6.

[25] CR 90:335ff.

[26] LW 36:335ff.

three Easter sermons. Luther's most comprehensive discussion of the issues is found in two later treatises: *That These Words of Christ, "This Is My Body," Etc., Still Stand Against the Fanatics* (1527)[27] and the *Confession Concerning Christ's Supper* (1528).[28]

Refuting the denial of the real presence, Luther asserted that the body of Christ, though seated at the right hand of the Father, is "everywhere" (*ubique*) because "the right hand of the Father is everywhere." The humanity of Christ shares the omnipresence of his divinity. When Zwingli replied that the body of Christ would then be present in every piece of bread and even in every part of nature, Luther replied in *That These Words of Christ . . . Still Stand Firm Against the Fanatics*,

> Listen, now, you pig, dog, or fanatic, whatever kind of unreasonable ass you are: Even if Christ's body is everywhere, you do not therefore immediately eat or drink or touch him; . . . There is a difference between his being present and your touching. He is free and unbounded wherever he is, and he does not have to stand there like a rogue set in a pillory, or his neck in irons.
>
> See, the bright rays at the sun are so near you that they pierce into your eyes or your skin so that you feel it, yet you are unable to grasp them and put them into a box, even if you should try forever. . . . So too with Christ: although he is everywhere, he does not permit himself to be so caught and grasped; he can easily shell himself, so that you get the shell but not the kernel. Why? Because it is one thing if God is present, and another if he is present for you. He is there for you when he adds his Word and binds himself, saying, "Here you are to find me." Now when you have the Word, you can grasp and have him with certainty and say, "Here I have thee, according to thy Word."[29]

When his critics pointed out that this mode of existence is philosophically impossible, Luther called attention to the fact that the philosophers themselves recognized several modes of presence. From his "dear master," William of Ockham, Luther had learned the distinction between "circumscriptive" or local presence, *esse diffinitive*, and *esse repletive*, which Ockham used to describe the God's omnipresence.[30] Luther did not appeal to this distinction because he was relapsing into scholastic theology. He only related this "in order to show that there are more modes whereby an object may exist in a place than the one circumscribed, physical mode on which the fanatics insist."[31] The basis of Luther's belief in the real presence was not metaphysical theory, but the word of God. Even if the Swiss view of the presence of Christ was more logical, Luther couldn't get around the text of scripture: "This is my body."

Out of concern to maintain the unity of the Reformation, Prince Philip of Hesse brought the Wittenberg and Swiss reformers together at Marburg in 1529 to try to work out their differences over the sacrament. Throughout the entire colloquy Luther remained adamant that he would not depart from the literal sense of the text, "This is my body."

---

[27] LW 37:3ff.
[28] Ibid., 151ff.
[29] Ibid., 68–9.
[30] Ibid., 213ff.
[31] Ibid., 216.

Zwingli's argument against the real presence at Marburg was that one and the same body cannot occupy two places at once. Luther's various replies were: (1) How do you know so much about "the ways of God?" (2) If God or Christ says, "This is my body," the burden is on you to prove that he does not mean what he says. (3) You argue that Christ must mean "body" metaphorically because he has ascended and gone to heaven. But why cannot "ascended into heaven" also be a metaphor? (4) More to the point: "I confess that the body of Christ is in heaven, but I also confess that he is in the sacrament."[32] Luther kept pushing his opponents to show from scripture that the words of Christ, "This is my body," are to be understood figuratively. Zwingli and Oecolampadius kept insisting that John 6 was the key to the issue, since it refers to spiritual eating; indeed, both sides admitted that there is a spiritual eating. "Then why do we need bodily eating?" asked Oecolampadius. In reply, Luther clung to the command of Christ:

> We do not deny the spiritual eating; on the contrary, we teach and believe it to be necessary. But from this it does not follow that the bodily eating is either useless or unnecessary. It is not our business to judge whether it is useful or not. We have the command "Take, eat; this is my body." Christ gives himself to us in many ways: first, in the preaching of the Word; secondly, in baptism; thirdly, in brotherly consolation; fourthly, in the sacrament as often as the body of Christ is eaten, because He Himself commands us to do so. If he ordered me to eat dung, I would do it.[33]

But by "word of God," Luther always understood more than the text of scripture. The Word was also the divine Logos incarnated in human fleshly existence. What ultimately concerned him in his conflict with the "fanatics" was the fact that "they divide the two natures of the person of Christ." The sacramental question was really a christological question. This was also at issue at the Marburg Colloquy. Luther insisted that in the sacrament we receive Christ as a person, as he is in himself, and not just as we attune our spirits to Christ's Spirit. In one revealing exchange, Oecolampadius, the reform preacher of Basel, said: "You should not cling to the humanity and the flesh of Christ, but rather lift up your mind to His divinity." To which Luther replied: "I do not know of any God except Him Who was made flesh, nor do I want to have another."[34]

The crux for Luther was belief in a God in Christ who meets us "deep in the flesh." The two natures of Christ cannot be divided. Human nature shares the omnipresence, the ubiquity, of Christ's divine nature precisely in order to save us where we are in our human situation of sin and death. But even if Christ is present everywhere, Christ's omnipresence does not benefit us unless we have a specific word of promise: "Here you can find me." Luther found that word of promise in such texts as "This is my body," to which one responds by obeying the accompanying command: "Take and eat." Even though under certain circumstances the Lutherans could accept the idea of a "spiritual communion" (e.g., when Christians are deprived of the sacrament), one normally appropriated the promise of Christ by doing what was commanded.

---

[32] Sasse, *This Is My Body*, op. cit., 250.

[33] Ibid., 237.

[34] Ibid., 252.

The Lutheran position on the real presence, as developed in the course of the controversy with the Swiss reformers, ultimately depends on no philosophic explanation, neither consubstantiation nor even a doctrine of ubiquity. None of these can serve the Lutheran position. Rather, the Lutheran position depends on the mystery of the word, which is God's effective self-communication and self-disclosure. What is disclosed in the sacrament is the same reality that is disclosed in the incarnation: a God who meets us deep in the flesh in order to know us as we are, forgive us, share his own life with us, and save us. Only in the preaching of the gospel and in the performance of the sign-acts of the sacraments do we have any assurance by words of promise that God in Christ continues to come to us in a saving way.

❦ THE REAL PRESENCE IN LUTHERAN FAITH AND PRACTICE

In January 1530, Emperor Charles V summoned an imperial diet to convene in Augsburg in April to reconcile religious differences between the papal and Reformation parties and work out a united front against the Turks. The statement presented at the diet by the Lutheran princes and free cities was irenic, but also descriptive of what was being taught and practiced in the evangelical churches. With regard to the Lord's Supper, it was stated in Article X "that the true body and blood of Christ are really present in the Supper of our Lord under the form of bread and wine and are there distributed and received."[35]

After hearing the Lutheran Confession, the Roman party prepared a Confutation which was read publicly before the diet. The Lutherans undertook a reply to the Confutation, working under the handicap of not being allowed to see a copy of it. The emperor refused to accept the Lutheran Apology, prepared by Melanchthon, so on his way back to Wittenberg he revised and expanded it and published it in April or May of 1531. It is noteworthy that more of the articles of the Confession were actually accepted entirely or in part by the Roman Confutation than were rejected. Naturally, the greatest difficulties concerned the articles on justification, the role of good works, and the invocation of the saints, as well as the articles at the end dealing with practical abuses in the church. There was considerable agreement on the theology of the sacraments in the Augsburg Confession, including Article X on the Lord's Supper. Melanchthon writes,

> They approve the tenth article, wherein we confess our belief that in the Lord's Supper the body and blood of Christ are truly and substantially present and are truly offered with those things that are seen, the bread and the wine, to those who receive the sacrament.[36]

The real fight on this issue was not with the Roman church, but with the "Sacramentarians" and those Lutherans who tried to build a bridge to the Reformed camp. Martin Bucer was neither a Lutheran nor a Zwinglian on this issue. He taught that just as it is not the water of baptism but the Spirit who works regeneration, so it is not eating and

---

[35] Tappert, 34.
[36] Ibid., 179.

drinking bread and wine but faith in Christ that constitutes the real reception of the body and blood of Christ. He tried to convince Luther and the Wittenbergers that at the last supper Jesus could not have given his body to the disciples, and it is plain in scripture and to common sense that after the ascension Christ's body is in heaven. Yet there is a real communion between the believer and Christ in that while we receive the bread outwardly we receive the true body of Christ inwardly by faith. In this connection, Bucer was able to use the term *unio sacramentalis.* This expression meant for Luther that the connection between bread and wine and body and blood was so intimate that to receive one was to receive the other. But Bucer was not able to accept the test cases of the *manducatio oralis* (oral communion) and *manducatio impiorum* (communion of the unbelieving) which Luther accepted. Nevertheless, some sort of agreement was reached in the Wittenberg Concordat in 1536.

The Concordat was produced as a result of the political pressure to develop a united Reformation front against the Emperor and Pope Paul III, who wanted to convene a general council of the church in 1537. Zwingli had been killed in battle in 1531, and it was thought possible to bring Luther and Bucer together. Bucer had already worked tirelessly since Augsburg, 1530, to bring the south German cities into the united Protestant camp. The success of his work was the fact that they were able to join the Smalkaldic League, which Landgrave Philip of Hesse and Duke John of Saxony had organized as a mutual Protestant defense alliance. The Concordat is not to be seen as a confession, but as a declaration on the part of Luther and his colleagues stating what they understood Bucer and his colleagues to be able to confess and what would be regarded as a sufficient basis for church fellowship.[37] "They concede that through the sacramental union the bread is the body of Christ." It is because of this nature of the Concordat that it could be cited later on in the orthodox Lutheran Formula of Concord. Sasse suggests that the only concession made by Luther in this document was his willingness to permit the expression "*manducatio indignorum*" (communion of the unworthy) to replace "manducatio impiorum."[38] This change of expressions was allowed because Luther's concern was not what non-Christians would receive but what "hypocrites and evil persons" would receive if they communed. Put aside for the moment was the real concern behind any of these expressions: that what one receives is the body and blood of Christ because the word of God makes the sacrament, whether one receives it in faith or not. Nevertheless, the Concordat was important because it brought the south German evangelicals into the Lutheran church. But Bucer was not successful in bringing the Swiss into a situation of concord with the Lutherans.

Melanchthon, like Bucer, was an indefatigable ecclesiastical negotiator. This, more than anything else, explains his apparent vacillations on the issue of the real presence. Like Bucer, he worked hard to reach a consensus with the south Germans and the Swiss, using especially his cordial relationship with his fellow humanist,

---

[37] See James Kittelson and Ken Schurb, "The Curious Histories of the Wittenberg Concord," *Concordia Theological Quarterly* 50 (1986), 119–37.

[38] Sasse, 309.

Oecolampadius.[39] As a basis for further discussion with the Reformed on the divisive issue of the eucharist, Melanchthon prepared a revision of the Augsburg Confession in 1540, which has been subsequently called the *Augustana Variata*. It was only at a later date that the Lutherans discovered that the changes made in the Latin text of the Augsburg Confession were not as harmless as they seemed at first to be. The tenth article was changed to read:

> Concerning the Supper of the Lord they (i.e., our churches) teach that with the bread and wine the body and blood of Christ are offered to those who eat in the Lord's Supper.[40]

The problem is with the word "with" *(cum)*. It had been used in the Wittenberg Concordat and can mean the same as "in" or "under." But it can also be interpreted in the sense of *simul cum,* (simultaneously with). This is the sense in which it was understood by John Calvin. The words in the Wittenberg Concordat, "truly and substantially present" after "the body and blood of Christ," are missing in the Variata. Calvin was able to sign the Variata, and thereafter consider himself in substantial agreement with the church of the Augsburg Confession. This became politically important in the Peace of Augsburg in 1555, since that gave equal rights and protection within the Roman Empire to the Roman church and to the churches of the Augsburg Confession.

In his doctrine on the Lord's Supper, Calvin tried to work out a *via media* between Lutheran and Swiss theology. He consistently held that in the sacrament our souls are fed with the body and blood of Christ, even though the body of Christ is in heaven and not in the bread. But Calvin went beyond Zwingli by noting that Christ's Spirit is not limited, and the Spirit becomes the bond of the communicant's participation in Christ. "The Spirit feeds us with the substance of the flesh and blood of our Lord for immortality."[41] The Spirit does this by lifting up our minds by faith above the things of this world so that we may receive Christ who reigns in heaven. This idea, based on the Sursum corda of the mass, made it possible for Calvin to speak of a real participation (communio) in the body and blood of Christ. In subsequent years, Calvin could even speak of receiving the body "really," "truly," "essentially," and "substantially." He was convinced that he had found an answer to the problem, which could serve as a basis of union for the Protestant churches.

As Brian Gerrish has demonstrated, Calvin had a rich doctrine of the Lord's Supper.[42] With Luther, Calvin spoke warmly of the gift of communion, affirmed that this gift is Jesus Christ himself, and agreed that the gift is received through signs. He believed that he had bridged the gap between "sign" and "thing" in the Supper by pointing to the Spirit's role in lifting up the hearts of the faithful. He did not exclude the communion of

---

[39] See Ralph W. Quere, *Melanchthon's Christum Cognoscere: Christ's Efficacious Presence in the Eucharistic Theology of Melanchthon* (Nieuwkoop, 1977).

[40] Cited in Sasse, 317.

[41] Cited in Sasse, 323.

[42] See Brian A. Gerrish, *Grace and Gratitude: The Eucharistic Theology of John Calvin* (Edinburgh and Minneapolis, 1993).

the ungodly *(communicatio impiorum)*, since 1 Corinthians 11:29 clearly indicates that one can eat and drink without "discerning the body" and thereby eat and drink judgment upon oneself. Indeed, this Pauline admonition made it all the more important to eat and drink worthily, that is, in faith. Unfortunately, Calvin's very deep faith in the real presence of Christ in the sacrament was obscured by the naively geographical way in which he continued to locate the body of Christ in heaven at the right hand of God the Father. The Spirit still has to "lift up our hearts" to where Christ is. Christ is portrayed as the risen and ascended Lord who rules over creation rather than the suffering servant who meets us deep in our flesh.

The Lutherans sought to overcome this localization of Christ by a radical application of the ancient christological doctrine of the interchange of attributes between the human and divine natures of Christ *(communicatio idiomatum)*. What could be said about Christ's divine nature (e.g., omnipresence) could also be attributed to his human nature, and vice versa. In the Formula of Concord, Article VII in the Solid Declaration on the Lord's Supper is followed by Article VIII on the two natures of Christ, thus showing the connection between the sacramental and the christological issues in the Lutheran view of the controversies.

The Formula is primarily an intra-Lutheran document drawn up to resolve intra-Lutheran disputes. The Council of Trent is mentioned only once in the Solid Declaration and the Calvinists are mentioned only once in the Epitome. Calvin's name is not mentioned at all in the Formula, but Calvinism was clearly seen as a threat because of Calvinist inroads in the Palatinate and the "Crypto-Calvinist" views of certain Philippists (disciples of Melanchthon). This is clearly seen in the catalogue of views rejected by the Formula:

1. "The assertion that the words of institution are not to be simply understood in their strict sense";
2. "The denial of an oral eating of the body and blood of Christ in the Supper, and the contrary teaching that in the Supper the body of Christ is partaken of only spiritually through faith and that in the Supper our mouth receives only bread and wine";
3. "The teaching that bread and wine in the supper are no more than badges whereby Christians recognize one another";
4. "Or that they are figures, parables, and types of the far-distant body of Christ";
5. "Or that they are nothing more than symbols and reminders of the absent body of Christ";
6. "Or that in the Supper there is distributed to faith only the virtue, operation, and merit of the far-distant body of Christ";
7. "Or that the body and blood of Christ are only received and partaken of through faith, spiritually";
8. "Likewise, the teaching that because of his bodily ascension to heaven Christ is so confined and circumscribed by a certain space in heaven that he is neither able nor willing to be truly and essentially present with us in the Supper";
9. "Likewise, the assertion that Christ could not or would not have promised to have been able to achieve the true, essential presence of his body and

blood in his Supper because the nature and properties of his assumed human nature neither permit nor allow this";

10. "Likewise, the doctrine that it is not the words and the omnipresence of Christ but faith that achieves the presence of the body of Christ in the Holy Supper";

11. "Likewise, that according to the words of Christ's institution believers are not directed to seek the body of Christ in the bread and wine of the Supper, but to look away from the bread of the Supper and by their faith to look to that place in heaven where Christ is present with his body and there to partake of him";

12. "The doctrine that unbelieving, unrepentant, and wicked Christians . . . receive only bread and wine in the Supper and not the body and blood of Christ";

13. "The doctrine that worthiness does not consist in true faith alone but also in man's preparation";

14. "The teaching that even true believers who have and retain a true, genuine, living faith, but who fail to meet their own self-devised standard of preparation, may receive this sacrament for judgment, just like unworthy guests";

15. "The teaching that the elements (the visible forms of the blessed bread and wine) are to be adored"; and

16. "All presumptuous, scoffing, and blasphemous questions and expressions which are advanced in a course, fleshly, Capernaitic way about the supernatural and heavenly mysteries of this Supper."[43]

The acceptable Lutheran position is stated in this way:

> In addition to the words of Christ and of St. Paul (the bread in the Lord's Supper "is true body of Christ" or "a participation in the body of Christ"), we at times also use the formulas *"under* the bread, *with* the bread, *in* the bread." We do this to reject the papistic transubstantiation and to indicate the sacramental union between the untransformed substance of the bread and the body of Christ.[44]

With this formula, Lutheranism sought to set forth the sacrament as a mystery that is inaccessible to human reason, the mystery that Christ himself is present "in, with, and under" the earthly actuality.[45] In making himself available *in* an earthly vessel, Christ's divinity does not dissolve his humanity. *With* the bread and wine is mysteriously joined Christ himself, who feeds us with his true body and blood, which merited forgiveness of sins, life, and salvation for us on the cross. At the same time, this divine self-giving remains veiled in obscurity *under* the earthly signs. Even in the sacrament we are confronted with the Deus absconditus, "the hidden God." Even the sacrament is related to the *theologia crucis*. The church has not yet arrived triumphantly in heaven; it is on the way. A pilgrim people is more interested in receiving nourishment from the sacrament than stopping to adore the Christ who is present in, with, and under it.

---

[43] Tappert, 589–91.

[44] Ibid., 575.

[45] See Wilhelm Stählin, *The Mystery of God* (St. Louis: Concordia Publishing House, 1964), 23ff., 68ff.

For this reason, in spite of the confession of the real presence, Lutheranism has resisted an adoration piety (although the Formula states that "no one except an Arian heretic can or will deny that Christ himself, true God and man, who is truly and essentially present in the Supper when it is rightly used, should be adored in spirit and in truth in all places but especially where his community is assembled"[46]). The Lutheran church invites a believing reception, not an adoration of Christ in the sacrament.

Yet the matter is an ambiguous one, as is evident in the issue of the elevation. Luther knew instinctively that the elevation was a powerful proclamation of the real presence. It was finally dropped in Wittenberg in 1542 in order to express agreement in practice with other Evangelical churches. But in his *Brief Confession Concerning the Holy Sacrament* (1544), Luther related that he had retained it so long because of Karlstadt's ravings against it, and if provoked again, "I would still today not only retain the elevation but, where one would not be enough, assist in introducing three, seven, or ten elevations."[47]

The issue here is the "true use" of the sacrament. It became an axiom in Lutheran theology that "nothing has the character of a sacrament outside of the use instituted by Christ." The Formula of Concord defined "use" or "action" not just as oral eating, "but the entire external and visible action of the Supper as ordained by Christ: the consecration or words of institution, the distribution and reception, or the oral eating of blessed bread and wine, the body and blood of Christ."[48] Sasse argued that "since the word 'usus' is explained by 'actio' it cannot mean the same as 'sumptio.'"[49] This was apparently the position of Melanchthon, who held that the sacramental union ended with the service, or distribution of the sacrament.

Edward F. Peters has collected a number of instances which show that for Luther *vere usus* was not so limited.[50] In one instance (recorded in the Table Talk), Luther chided those who would deny that what is carried to the sick after the service is actually the body and blood of Christ.[51] Again, Pastor Simon Wolferinus raised the question of whether the sacramental action was completed with the end of the service. Luther's reply was that the pastor should see that there are no leftovers. What remains should be consumed by the ministers and communicants.[52] Finally, in the case of Pastor Adam Besserer, Luther castigated this careless curate for mixing the consecrated hosts with the unconsecrated.[53]

These examples, when considered in the light of Luther's whole theology of the Lord's Supper, suggest that he believed that the consecrated bread and wine, by virtue of the words of Christ, are the earthly bearers of the body and blood of Christ, and should

---

[46] Tappert, 591.

[47] LW 38:316.

[48] Tappert, 584–5.

[49] Sasse, 174.

[50] Edward F. Peters, "Luther and the Principle: Outside of the Use There Is No Sacrament," *Concordia Theological Monthly* XLII (1973), 643–52.

[51] WA, *Tischreden*, 5:55.

[52] WA, *Briefwechsel*, 10:336–9, 348–9.

[53] Ibid., 11:258–9.

therefore be treated with reverential care. Luther's devotion to the real presence was undoubtedly involved in this, but so was his awareness of what it means to call the sacraments "visible words." Words are forms of communication, and Luther had a sound pastoral instinct that every word, action, or gesture will communicate something to someone. The Lutheran tradition has usually not been willing to introduce or abandon ritual practices without considering the theological consequences. It is a deep-seated awareness that the lex orandi does establish the lex credendi, that practice influences profession.

This also meant that some practices that became confessionally identified with certain traditions had to be avoided in order to avoid communicating certain views. This was the case with the fraction. Since large loaves that required a utilitarian breaking for distribution were no longer used, any fraction of the wafers could only be done for significatory purposes *(causa signicationis)*. The fraction in the medieval mass had been the source of unending allegorical explanations. The fraction was retained in the Reformed traditions because of their concern (1) to follow the directions of the New Testament institution texts in the ceremony of the Lord's Supper; (2) to reenact in the ritual of the Lord's Supper the passion of Christ, of which the sacrament was a memorial; and (3) to emphasize the fellowship character of the Lord's Supper, in conformity with references to "the breaking of bread" in Acts 24:35 and 1 Corinthians 10:16. In spite of similar views in Luther's *Babylonian Captivity*[54] and the Formula of Concord that "the entire action" as Christ ordained it should be observed, Lutherans began to categorically exclude the ceremony of the fraction from their practice of the Lord's Supper. The Lutheran theologians made a distinction between the aorist verbs in the institution narratives, "took," "gave thanks," and "broke," and the imperatives "take" and "eat." They held that obedience to the divine command did not entail imitation of the Lord's actions at the supper.[55] A revival of any fraction in the Lutheran celebration of the eucharist other than one performed for strictly utilitarian purposes (i.e., to break a large loaf for distribution) would contend against a formible consensus on the issue in classical Lutheran theology. But just so, it would be totally inappropriate in the Lutheran tradition to break the bread at the words "he broke" in the words of institution, since this would be a kind of mimetic act that classical Lutheranism resisted. The only possibilities would be to break the bread before the beginning of the service, as the Byzantine churches do at the Proskomide, or to break the bread in the process of distributing it, which would be necessitated if the bread and wine were to be presented among the gifts of the faithful at the offertory.[56]

---

[54] Luther wrote: "The more closely our mass resembles that first mass of all, which Christ performed at the Last Supper, the more Christian it will be." *Three Treatises by Martin Luther* (Philadelphia: Muhlenberg Press, 1947), 162.

[55] See Oliver K. Olson, "Contemporary Trends in Liturgy Viewed from the Perspective of Classical Lutheran Theology," *Lutheran Quarterly* XXVI, 2 (1974), especially 125–34 for an analysis of the controversy over the fraction.

[56] Olson, ibid., 134–7, examines the offertory from a biblical and historical perspective and argues against the revival of the offertory procession of the faithful.

❦ THE MINISTRY OF THE WORD AND THE SACRAMENTS

The church is called and gathered by the preaching of the word, and constituted and built up by the administration of the sacraments. The acts of preaching and presiding at celebrations of the sacraments raise questions of order and authority. On what basis does there exist in the church a special ministry or office of word and sacrament? Who orders this ministry and authorizes persons to do these tasks?

Lutheran tradition has not always been clear about this. The confusion stems, first, from the fact that Luther dealt with different issues affecting ministry at different times in his career and came down on different emphases, and, second, that Luther's personal positions on the doctrine of the ministry (no matter how influential) are not identical in all respects with the understanding of ministry presented in the confessional documents.

Early in his career as a reformer Luther had to deal with the fact that the ecclesiastical authority was not responding to the call for reform. In his *Open Letter to the Christian Nobility of the German Nation* (1520) he proposed that the secular rulers take the initiative in reforming the church, which the spiritual rulers refused to do. But in order to make this proposal he had to break down the "three walls of the Romanists": (1) that the spiritual authority is above the temporal authority; (2) that no one can interpret the scriptures except the pope; and (3) that no one can call a council but the pope.[57]

Luther assaulted these walls with the doctrine of the priesthood of all believers. He held that all Christians are given equal authority by virtue of baptism into Christ to proclaim and live the gospel in their vocations in the world. Some Christians are chosen to proclaim and teach the gospel in a public and representative way. "Therefore when the bishop consecrates it is the same thing as if he, in the place and stead of the whole congregation, all of whom have like power, were to take one out of their number and charge him to use this power for the others."[58] In an emergency situation, for example, "If a little group of pious Christian laymen were taken captive and set down in a wilderness, and had among them no priest consecrated by a bishop," they could "choose someone from among themselves to baptize, say mass, absolve and preach, and such a man would be as truly a priest as though all bishops and popes had consecrated him. . . . That is why in cases of necessity anyone can baptize and give absolution, which would be impossible unless we were all priests."[59]

Luther was proposing a radical view in this *Open Letter*. Everyone is a priest and bishop by virtue of baptism; therefore the so-called spiritual rulers have no authority that is not possessed by the temporal rulers other than that given to them by and on behalf of the whole Christian community. So no ordained priest has any spiritual authority that a lay priest does not have; it is only for the sake of good order that no one pushes himself forward without consent and election. "For what is common to all, no one dare take upon

---

[57] *Three Treatises by Martin Luther*, op. cit., 13.

[58] Ibid., 14.

[59] Ibid., 14–5.

himself without the will and command of the community."[60] What the ordained priest exercises is an *office*, which is deserving of respect. But there is no *characteres indelibiles* (indelible character) given to the person who holds the priestly office.

It is important to see that what Luther was proposing in his *Open Letter* was a doctrine that would make it possible for the princes to undertake leadership in the reform of the church, which the bishops were not disposed to do. It would be too much to say that he was only calling for emergency measures in an emergency situation, because he continued to draw practical consequences from this view for the organization of congregations and the appointment of pastors.[61] He continued to insist that congregations have the right to judge and call, appoint and dismiss pastors and teachers, and he appealed to this doctrine when bishops would not provide pastors for evangelical congregations.[62]

To be sure, the failure of the bishops to take the lead in the reform of the church and their unwillingness to provide suitable ministers of the word and the sacraments constituted an emergency situation. So other measures had to be taken in order both to work for the reform of the church and to ensure that congregations would not be deprived of the ministry of word and sacrament because of their adoption of the Reformation. Luther believed that the gospel is the possession of all Christians. Therefore he felt free to urge the emperor to call a general council of the church and to call on the civil authorities to take the lead in the reform of the church, and to assert that congregations deprived of suitable pastors and teachers could appoint their own. The election and call of pastors by congregations became regularized in Lutheran church life.

Nevertheless, events from the middle of the 1520s on caused Luther to reconsider the value of the traditional episcopal polity and the need for wider supervision in the church. Already in 1523 he had to intervene against the activities of Karlstadt, Müntzer, and other radicals. In 1524 the peasants revolted, appealing to principles enunciated by Luther in his *Treatise on the Freedom of the Christian* (1520). In 1525, the first intimations appeared of a theological rift with the Swiss reformers and the need to provide for a teaching authority in the church to judge true doctrine. In 1526, the Diet of Speyer decreed that each territorial ruler could decide whether to implement the Reformation in his territory until such time as an ecumenical council could settle the religious differences. This provided an opportunity for evangelical princes to reorganize church life in their territories according to evangelical principles, and required, in turn, visitation of parishes to evaluate the conditions of church life and determine what practical reforms were needed. Parochial visitation was a duty of the bishop, but in Electoral Saxony it was undertaken under the authority of the Elector. Luther and Melanchthon prepared

---

[60] Ibid., 15–6.

[61] See *De instituendis ministries Ecclesiae*, 1523; WA 169–96.

[62] See "The Right and Power of a Christian Congregation or Community to Judge and to Call, to Appoint and to Dismiss Teachers, Established and Proved on the Basis of Scripture" (1528); WA 11:408–16.

[63] See Bernhard Lohse, "The Development of the Office of Leadership in the German Lutheran Churches: 1517–1918," in Ivar Asheim and Victor Gold, eds., *Episcopacy in the Lutheran Church?* (Philadelphia: Fortress Press, 1970), 51ff.

Visitation Articles for the visitors. But the visitors went out as electoral officials, and Luther was not slow to realize the danger of the princes taking over episcopal functions.[63]

The experience of the visitation caused both Luther and Melanchthon to give more thought to the need for oversight (episcope) in the church, whether that be exercised by a bishop, a superintendent, or a consistory. Melanchthon especially viewed with suspicion a church ruled by privy counselors. He was concerned over the prospects of a church supervised by the state. Consequently he tried to shore up the independence of the church by emphasizing the divine institution of the ministry of the word and the sacraments. This was even tied to the crucial article on justification by faith. Article IV of the Augsburg Confession proposed justification by faith for Christ's sake through grace as the way of understanding humanity's saving relationship with God. Article V went on to state: "To obtain such faith God instituted the office of the ministry, that is, provided the Gospel and the sacraments. Through these, as through means, he gives the Holy Spirit, who works faith, when and where he pleases, in those who hear the Gospel."[64] People do not acquire saving faith on their own; it is a gift given by the Holy Spirit working through the means of grace—the preaching of the gospel and the administration of the sacraments, for which the office of the word and the sacraments was instituted.

If one cannot acquire saving faith on one's own, neither can anyone take it upon himself or herself to preach or teach or administer the sacraments without a regular call. Article XIV states: "It is taught among us that nobody should publicly teach or preach or administer the sacraments in the church without a regular call."[65] The word "publicly" and the phrase "regular call" require some interpretation. All Christians proclaim the gospel to their neighbor by the witness of their lives. Any Christian can teach the gospel to others. Luther had already provided the Small Catechism so that the head of the household could teach the faith to the family. So the ordained minister is neither the only preacher nor the only teacher in the congregation; but the ordained minister has responsibility for the faithful and public proclamation and teaching of the gospel. The ordained minister preaches and teaches the gospel on behalf of the church and to the church. Authority to do so comes from a "regular call," which is understood to be mediated by the Holy Spirit operating on behalf of Christ, the lord of the church, and discerned by the church through its examining processes. While later Lutherans debated what constitutes a "regular call," there was no doubt in Melanchthon's mind that it is the rite of ordination (*ritus vocatio*). In the Apology of the Augsburg Confession he was even willing to call ordination a sacrament.

> If ordination is interpreted in relation to the ministry of the word, we have no objection to calling ordination a sacrament. The ministry of the word has God's command and glorious promises. . . . If ordination is interpreted this way, we shall not object either to calling the laying on of hands a sacrament. The church has the command to appoint ministers; to this we subscribe wholeheartedly, for we know that God approves this ministry and is present in it.[66]

---

[64] Tappert, 31.
[65] Ibid., 36.
[66] Ibid., 212.

God commands the appointment of ministers and is present in this ministry. By these statements Melanchthon placed the doctrine of the ministry on a firmer foundation than Luther had done ten years earlier in his *Open Letter*. The reason for this lies in further refection on the relation between the gospel and the church. The gospel is the message the church has been given to proclaim; but it is also that which calls and gathers the church, and so stands over it. In the same way, the ministry of word and sacrament is a function within the church; but the gospel-office also represents to the church the gospel's independence. The ordained minister serves the people of God by serving the gospel in the public acts of preaching and teaching and ministering the sacraments.[67]

One way to indicate the independence of the ordained ministry vis-à-vis the congregation is to emphasize the *sentness* as well as the *calledness* of this ministry. The minister of word and sacrament is ordained by the wider church rather than by the local congregation The minister is in some way recommended to the local congregation by an agency exercising wider ecclesiastical jurisdiction (bishop, synod) as well as called (accepted, elected) by the local congregation. Hence, Melanchthon indicated in the *Apology* "our deep desire to maintain the church polity and various ranks of the ecclesiastical hierarchy, although they were created by human authority." He testifies that this has not always been possible because of the "cruelty of the bishops" in actions taken against evangelical priests. Nevertheless, "We know that the church is present among those who rightly teach the Word of God and rightly administer the sacraments." Hence, "We want at this point to declare our willingness to keep the ecclesiastical and canonical polity."[68]

The *desire* to retain the traditional polity, even if this could not always be done in actuality because of the emergency situation, has a theological rationale. The gospel by its very nature creates a tradition. It is a story passed on from person to person, from community to community, from generation to generation. There is a succession of believers who possess the gospel, as the reformers rightly asserted. What was not so clearly asserted is the need for a succession of ordained ministers to represent the independence of the gospel over the church. This was the purpose of the *apostolic succession*: just as Christ was the *apostolos* (the "sent one") of the Father, so he sent out his disciples as apostles, and they, in turn, delegated others to carry on the proclamation of the gospel. The concern of the Reformation was that this succession in the task of gospel-proclamation had broken down. There were persons succeeding one another in office, but the gospel was not being transmitted. Hence, the reformers emphasized a *functional* view of the ministry: the function of preaching and teaching the gospel and administering the sacraments. But this function was not posited in an either/or fashion against what came to be called the "ontological" view of the ministry—the divine institution of the ministry of the word and the sacraments. The reformers also knew that a gospel that stood over the church required a ministry that was also, in some way, independent of the calling community.

---

[67] See Eric W. Gritsch and Robert W. Jenson, *Lutheranism: The Theological Movement and its Confessional Writings* (Philadelphia: Fortress Press, 1976), 119.

[68] Tappert, 214–15.

The office of the gospel, that is, the ministry of the word and the sacraments, exists prior to the church since it is instrumental in calling and gathering the church. The church, like its members, either lives by faith in the saving work of Christ, whose benefits are conveyed to the faithful through word and sacrament, or the church lives by its own good works. This is why the church was so clearly defined in Article VII of the Augsburg Confession as "the assembly of all believers among whom the Gospel is preached in its purity and the holy sacraments are administered according to the Gospel."[69] The pure preaching of the gospel and administration of the sacraments is exercised by a ministry called by but also sent to the local congregation. The ministry, like the gospel, is a possession of the congregation; but this ministry also, like the gospel that it serves, stands over against the congregation. Because of the potential for conflict between the ministry of the gospel and the congregation, it has been found necessary to have a structure beyond either the pastor or the congregation to which either can appeal for support or vindication. Episcope is needed in the church; and Melanchthon came to see that it is more appropriately exercised by bishops in the traditional polity than by governmental officials. The ministry of bishops was more securely preserved and provided in the Scandinavian churches than in the German churches. But even the German Lutheran churches were not without their superintendents (i.e., evangelical bishops).

What was lost in all the Reformation churches was the presence of orders in the church (e.g., monks, nuns, friars, etc.), which can serve as "shock troops" in the mission of the gospel. There was no intrinsic reason why monastic communities or religious orders could not have a place within Lutheranism. In the nineteenth and twentieth centuries there were revivals of such orders in the deaconess communities and Protestant communities such as that in Taizé, France. But in the sixteenth century the abuses of the monasteries had been so enormous, in the eyes of the reformers, that there was little inclination to develop a theory or practice of evangelical monasticism. Article XXVII of the Augsburg Confession pointed out that the monastic life was falsely believed to be a way of meriting God's grace, and that the religious were regarded as holier than secular Christians (clergy as well as laity). Worse than this, monastic vows were viewed as equal to baptism. These vows were not as irrevocable as the theologians maintained because persons had been regularly released from them by the pope and others in authority. These vows included celibacy; but God has permitted marriage to all and has blessed it as an institution. Furthermore such vows obscure the true service of God in faith and love and induce people to think that normal life and everyday duties are tainted by sin.[70]

As Steven Ozment has pointed out, in few areas of life were the social consequences of the Reformation more evident than in the areas of clerical and religious life. Churches and monasteries, priests and monks, had dominated medieval western European society. In comparing life in the cities of central Europe before and after the

---

[69] Tappert, 32.

[70] Tappert, 70ff.; see also Apology XXVII, Tappert, 268ff., in which Melanchthon deals not so much with the abuses of monasticism as with the doctrinal assumptions underlying monastic vows.

implementation of the Reformation, Ozment notes that at the end of the fifteenth century, clergy and members of religious orders made up "6 to 10 per cent of the urban population, and they exercise enormous political as well as spiritual power. They legislate and they tax; they try cases in their very own courts; and they enforce the laws of the church with penances and excommunication . . . Monasteries and nunneries are prominent and influential social institutions. The children of society's most powerful citizens reside there. . . . On the streets, Franciscan and Dominican friars from near and far beg alms from passersby."[71] But in those same cities in the 1540s and 1550s, writes Ozment, "Overall numbers of clergy and religious have dropped by as much as two-thirds. In some towns, the decrease is astonishing; Rostock, for example, has gone from more than two hundred to thirteen. . . ."[72] Monasteries are nearly totally empty. The lands and assets of many have been confiscated by princes and lords; others have been turned into hospitals or hospices or educational institutions. Those that have been converted to the care of the sick retain some aura of being Protestant monasteries; but the religious vows and habits are gone. A few cloisters continue unchanged; but with the pensioning off or deaths of the old monks and nuns who reside in them, these cloisters too will close and be converted to some other use. In the short time of a generation, the clerical ideal has shifted from celibate, cloistered priests, monks and nuns to a married, domestic pastoral ministry. Ozment notes that "an unmarried cleric is deemed strange; the reformers play cupid for one another in a rush to share the newly discovered bliss of married life and to make another public statement against Rome."[73]

There is no doubt that there were some unfortunate losses as a result of the Reformation, particularly an ecclesiastical polity that allowed a measure of independence to the church from the civil authorities and excluded the presence of religious orders that remind the whole church of its call to holiness. On the other hand, what emerged was a church life in which lay Christians assumed responsibility for their own faith and calling, both in their occupation and in their domestic settings, and in which clergy attended in a serious way to the tasks of preaching and catechizing. Because of the new sense of Christian vocation in the world, the faithful needed the spiritual nourishment provided through the preaching and teaching of the word of God and the administration of the sacraments. If anything, the preaching and teaching of the gospel and the administration of the sacraments were attended to with greater seriousness than they had been on the eve of the Reformation. The ironic consequence regarding the status of the clergy was that in spite of the denial of any special spiritual or social status (for the clergy were now on equal footing spiritually with the laity as Christians and as citizens), the most ordinary Protestant parish pastor acquired even more spiritual and social authority than the parish priest had had before the Reformation.[74] The Protestant parish pastor was a trained expert on the only authority that now mattered: the word of God in the Holy Scriptures.

---

[71] Steven Ozment, *Protestantism: The Birth of a Revolution*, op. cit., 24–5.

[72] Ibid., 26.

[73] Ibid., 27.

[74] On the low esteem in which the clergy were held in the late Middle Ages, see Johan Huizinga, *The Autumn of the Middle Ages*, op. cit., 204.

CHAPTER 10

The Emergence of Lutheran Liturgy

ARTIN LUTHER AND LUTHERANISM are not synonymous. Luther himself was rather diffident about applying his name to a church body. "I was not crucified for anyone," he wrote.[1] Nevertheless, Lutheranism did emerge as a movement and as an ecclesial reality that worked out the implications of Luther's teachings. Some of his teachings were enshrined as articles of faith. Justification by faith alone became the confessional article on which it was said that "the church stands or falls." Some of his writings acquired confessional status: the Large and Small Catechisms, the Smalkald Articles, and portions of his writings quoted in the Formula of Concord. His personal opinions on matters of faith and church practice carried great authoritative weight. Both as the dean of the theological faculty at Wittenberg and as the great prophetic figure of the Reformation, Luther often became the final arbiter on questions of a doctrinal or ecclesiastical nature. The force of his charismatic personality could be overwhelming. Yet no matter how great his intellectual or personal influence, once the reform movement was embraced by a whole territory or city, other forms of guidance and church order were also needed. This was provided not only by other reformers and theologians, but also by the secular authorities to whom Luther had appealed for help in the task of reforming the churches, beginning with the Saxon Visitation of 1527. It was precisely in this attempt to provide an alternative form of supervision or episcope of church life under civil authority,

---

[1] WA 8:685.

to produce catechisms and church orders to inculcate teaching in the home, and to regulate practices in the churches that Lutheranism as an ecclesial reality emerged.

THE EMERGENCE OF LUTHERANISM

The Smalkald League

The Emperor Charles V was not able to carry out the Edict of Worms (1521) because powerful German princes and imperial cities embraced Luther's reforms and the Elector of Saxony accorded Luther protection. An action of the Diet of Speyer in 1526 (which Charles could not attend) provided that each state should conduct its religious affairs in accord with its obligations to God and the emperor, which was expressed by the phrase, *"cuius regio, eius religio"* (whoever is the ruler, his religion). When Charles tried to get this provision repealed at a second Diet of Speyer in 1529, the Lutheran estates protested (whereupon they were called "Protestants"), and Charles was forced to call a diet at Augsburg in 1530 to hear the religious differences. It was at this diet that the Lutheran princes and representatives of the free cities presented their Confession (Augsburg Confession). The papal party drew up a Confutation of the Confession. Charles asserted that this answered and refuted the charges of the Confession. Melanchthon wrote the Apology of the Augsburg Confession (1531) in response to the Confutation. Charles, however, was determined to enforce the Edict of Worms to suppress Lutheranism, so he reconstituted the Imperial Supreme Court so that it would have less Lutheran influence, promised to call a general council of the church to settle the religious issues, and demanded that the Lutherans return to the Catholic fold by April 15, 1531.[2]

This vigorous action by Charles resulted in greater solidarity among the Protestants. The Protestant estates banded together in February of 1531 to form the Smalkald League (named after the Hessian town of Schmalkalden). This League became virtually an *imperium in imperio* (an empire within an empire)—a strong anti-Hapsburg European power capable of carrying on negotiations with other powers (e.g., with Henry VIII of England and Gustav I of Sweden). It originally comprised seven princes of northern Germany: the Elector of Saxony, the Landgrave of Hesse, the two Dukes of Brunswick-Luneburg, the Prince of Anhalt, and the two Counts of Mansfeld, as well as the cities of Magdeburg and Bremen.

These princes and magistrates had taken a considerable risk in leaguing together against the emperor. They were staunch personal believers in the Protestant cause. Landgrave Philip of Hesse (1504–1567) emerged as the fiery and headstrong leader of the League, and under his leadership the first large territory in southern Germany—Württemberg—was won over to Lutheranism, even though this duchy remained a fief of Austria. The League was also strengthened by the introduction of Lutheranism into other northern territories: Brandenburg in 1533, Hannover in 1534, and the combined kingdoms of Denmark and Norway in 1536 when Christian III of Schleswig and Holstein became king over all these territories.

---

[2] See Harold Grimm, *The Reformation Era 1500–1560* (New York: The Macmillan Co., 1954), 203ff.

Charles's attention, in the meantime, was diverted from the religious-political controversy in Germany because of conflicts with the Turks in the east, the Romans in the south, and France in the west. Not until 1546—the year of Luther's death—was Charles ready to resolve the religious problem in Germany by force of arms. He pretended, however, that he would not attack the Smalkald League for religious reasons, but that he would act only against those estates that had opposed him. Accordingly, he proclaimed an imperial ban against John Frederick of Electoral Saxony and Philip of Hesse. The League banded together to meet the attack. But in spite of superior military forces, it was handicapped by a lack of decision, for every military question had to be decided by a council of war. Duke Maurice of Ducal Saxony joined forces with the emperor and defeated John Frederick of Saxony at Mühlberg in 1547. Frederick was taken prisoner and forced to give up his electoral title to Duke Maurice. Philip of Hesse was induced by his son-in-law, Maurice, and by the Elector of Brandenburg to give himself up to Charles. With its two principal leaders imprisoned, Charles had defeated the Smalkald League and become master of Europe. And yet it was not a defeat of Lutheranism, because several Lutheran princes had sided with Charles in the conflict, and Charles felt bound to use the council that had just convened at Trent to reform the papacy as well as resolve the religious difficulties in Germany.

The Interims and the Adiaphoristic Controversy

Charles had aroused the opposition of the papacy because of his concern to place the papacy on a firmer spiritual foundation by lessening its temporal influence, and also the opposition of many Protestants because of a curious document drawn up in 1548 known as the Augsburg Interim. Although it affirmed basic Catholic doctrines and reimposed some Catholic practices on Lutheran territories, it made some concessions to the Protestants, such as permission for clerical marriages without papal dispensation, communion in both kinds, a statement on the doctrine of justification by faith, and recognition of the need for reforms.[3]

This document, drawn up by the Lutheran Johann Agricola, the humanist Julius von Pflug, and the historian Michael Heldin, was rejected by the Lutherans. Even though Charles was able to enforce it in most of the southern German territories, the northern territories, led by the city of Magdeburg, refused to abide by it. Fearing civil war, the Electors Maurice of Saxony and Joachim of Brandenburg urged Melanchthon to revise the Augsburg Interim in such a way as to maintain essential Lutheran doctrine while conceding as much as possible to Rome. The result was the Leipzig Interim of December 17, 1548. It affirmed justification by faith without meritorious works, but conceded the validity of the seven sacraments (thereby restoring episcopal confirmation and extreme unction among Lutherans) and agreed to regard many medieval rites and ceremonies as useful adiaphora (from the Greek *adiaphoron,* meaning "a thing that makes no difference").[4]

---

[3] Ibid., 256ff.; see CR 6:865–74.
[4] CR 7:260–64.

A stormy controversy erupted from the publication of the Interim. Lutheran theologians from Hamburg, Berlin, and Jena accused Melanchthon of betraying the Confession he had helped to write and Luther's Smalkald Articles. Melanchthon responded by insisting that Christian liberty consisted in the free confession of the gospel and not in the rejection of adiaphora. But the Gnesio-Lutherans (so-called from the Greek *gnesios,* meaning "authentic"), led by the Slavic theologian Matthias Flacius (Matija Vlacic, 1520–1575), were convinced that Melanchthon and his followers (the Philippists) had reverted to papal abominations.[5]

Flacius's arguments are contained in two major treatises of 1549: *Wider das Interim (Against the Interim)* and *De veris et falsis adiaphoris (Concerning True and False Adiaphora).* The first treatise asserted Flacius's basic contention that in a time of persecution adiaphora cease to be indifferent. As long as imperial edicts compel Lutherans to restore medieval practices, the rejection of these ceremonies and rites is mandated by the gospel. It is from this argument that the famous slogan emerged, "In statu confessionis nihil est adiaphoron" (In a situation of confession nothing is an indifferent matter). Flacius's second treatise underscored this position by arguing that the divine commandments to preach the gospel, to baptize, to observe the Lord's Supper, and to forgive sins are accompanied by divinely instituted ceremonies, and that these must not be violated. Liturgy and doctrine are correlative. Whatever rites and ceremonies a church observes will reflect the doctrine of that church. There are liturgical consequences of doctrinal decisions.[6]

Melanchthon remained cool, responding in an open letter to Flacius, dated October 1, 1549, that the article on justification, on which the church stands or falls, had been preserved; that the Interim had protected the Lutheran churches from wanton destruction; and that God should be trusted in these matters.[7] The later Formula of Concord tried to resolve the issue by establishing confessional norms with regard to adiaphora, and in the process gave more support to Flacius and the Gnesio-Lutherans than to the Philippists. It refused to consider as matters of indifference "ceremonies which are basically contrary to the Word of God," "ceremonies which give or (to avoid persecution) are designed to give the impression that our religion does not differ greatly from that of the papists," or ceremonies that "are intended to create the illusion (or are demanded or agreed to with that intention) that these two opposing religions have been brought into agreement and become one body." Furthermore, it held that "the community of God in every place and at every time has the right, authority, and power to change, to reduce, or to increase ceremonies according to its circumstances," and that "at a time of confession [Flacius's term], as when enemies of the Word of God, desire to suppress the pure doctrine of the holy Gospel, the entire community of God, yes, every individual Christian, and especially ministers of the Word as the leaders of the community of God, are obligated to

---

[5] For a sympathetic introduction to the contributions of Flacius see Oliver K. Olson, "The Importance of Matija Vlacic," *dialog* 15 (1976), 202–6.

[6] See Eric W. Gritsch and Robert W. Jenson, *Lutheranism: The Theological Movement and Its Confessional Writings,* op. cit., 195–6.

[7] CR 7:477–82.

confess openly, not only by words but also through their deeds and actions, the true doctrine and all that pertains to it, according to the Word of God." In such situations "we should not yield to adversaries even in matters of indifference, nor should we tolerate the imposition of such ceremonies on us by adversaries in order to undermine the genuine worship of God and to introduce and confirm their idolatry by force or chicanery."[8]

The adiaphorist controversy waned after 1552 when the Elector Maurice became the emperor's enemy and the Leipzig Interim was rescinded. But it had produced a reaction that hardened the Lutheran position on liturgical matters and led to the adoption of the above statements in the Formula of Concord. The importance of the Formula's statements is that they indicate that not all liturgical matters are adiaphora. Some are forbidden and others are commanded by the word of God. The exact status of adiaphora depends on the situation in which the church as a confessing fellowship finds itself. Therefore adiaphora can never be indifferent in the sense that it does not matter what is thought about them. They are indifferent matters only as far as salvation is concerned. But God accomplished salvation, and once the church has made clear the doctrine of the gospel, all that is left to deal with are adiaphora. The church gives diligent attention to these things precisely because what the church does matters.

It matters, for example, that a dominical mandate is attached to the institution of the Lord's Supper: "Do this for the remembrance of me." The content of the sacrament is the "remembrance" of Christ. But to what does "do this" refer? It can only refer to those things that are signified by verbs in the institution texts: that bread and wine must be *taken*, that thanks must be *given* over the bread and wine, that the bread must be *broken* (implying the sharing of the meal), and that the bread must be *eaten* and the wine *drunk*. Serious questions must be raised about any putative eucharist that does not include bread to be broken and a cup of wine to be shared, thanksgiving over the bread and cup, and the eating and drinking of the sacramental elements. As the Formula of Concord states:

> [T]his recitation of Christ's words of institution by itself, if the entire *action* of the Lord's Supper as Christ ordained it is not observed . . . does *not* make a sacrament. But the command of Christ, "Do this," which comprehends the whole *action* or administration of this sacrament . . . must be kept integrally and inviolably (Solid Declaration 7:83–84, emphasis added).[9]

Obviously, the interpretation of the institution texts is an exegetical matter; but the exegesis is required precisely because the Lutheran understanding of adiaphora implies that some matters are *not* a matter of indifference, and many of these matters are liturgical issues. So not all liturgical issues are indifferent or unessential. The confessional testimony about adiaphora helped to raise concern also about Lutheran church practice, not only the practices of other churchly traditions. The Formula of Concord dealt primarily with intra-Lutheran issues. Even when the Lutheran movement became a Lutheran church, its original character as a movement remained a source of continual call for reform and renewal—not least in areas of liturgical and sacramental life.

---

[8] *Formula of Concord*, Solid Declaration, X; Tappert, 611–2.

[9] Tappert, 585.

The Peace of Augsburg

The Interim ended because Duke Maurice took advantage of the German antipathy toward "the Spanish servitude" inflicted on them by the presence of Spanish troops serving Charles V, gained control of the Smalkald League, and concluded an alliance with Charles's enemy, King Henry II of France. The combined forces of France and the League forced Charles to sue for peace at Passau in 1552, then flee to Carinthia. The Council assembled at Trent, fearing a military solution to the religious questions, broke up without plans for reconvening. A diet was convened between February and September of 1555 in Augsburg to provide peace within the Empire.

It is significant that the diet proceeded without the presence or influence of the emperor and without able papal representation. Charles, fully aware that his hopes for religious unity under the protection of a strong Hapsburg empire were dashed, gave his brother Ferdinand the authority to conclude peace at Augsburg. Charles formally abdicated in 1556 and retired to a monastery. Pope Julius III died in March of 1555, and his successor, Marcellus II, elected in April, died in May. The summer was gone before Pope Paul IV could deal with the situation in Germany.

The Recess of Augsburg reflected the status quo between Lutherans and Catholics within the Empire. It (1) provided equal security for both Lutheran and Catholic estates within the Empire; (2) gave each estate the right to choose between Catholicism and Lutheranism, according to the principle "cuius regio, eius religio"; (3) decreed that all church lands seized by Lutherans before the Peace of Passau (1552) were to be retained by them; and (4) decreed that every ecclesiastical prince—archbishop, bishop, abbot—who became a Protestant would forfeit his title, lands, and privileges.[10]

The Peace of Augsburg can be viewed historically as a fait accompli in the Empire. The territorial division of religion had existed since the Diet of Speyer in 1526. The right of the territorial prince to exercise leadership in religion within his domain was a custom of long standing in Germany. The German princes had long been used to being "bishops" in their realms. They had controlled or influenced much public religious life from the appointment of clergy to important churches to the sale of indulgences (from which they took a share in the profits). In fact, a case can be made that the only way the hierarchy could exercise direct oversight of the churches was to be temporal lords themselves.[11]

The exact status of Calvinism was not clear from the language of the Recess. Legal recognition of non-Catholics depended on adherence to the Augsburg Confession (which is why Calvin supported the Variata edition). But the Recess did constitute a legal recognition of Lutheranism. Lutheranism was now recognized as an ecclesiastical reality and not just as a confessing movement within the Western church. As an ecclesiastical entity, Lutheranism needed constitution and polity. These were provided by the church orders and forms of church governance that had emerged since 1526.

---

[10] Grimm, 261–2.

[11] See Frank C. Senn, "The Office of Bishop in the Lutheran Reformation," *dialog* 24 (1985), 119–27.

🍇 THE PROLIFERATION OF CHURCH ORDERS

Church orders (Kirchenordnungen) are legal documents that mandated the church teachings and practices as canon and civil law. The first true Reformation church order was prepared for the principality of Hesse in 1526, by the former Franciscan Francis Lambert on the request of Landgrave Philip. The landgrave had already undertaken actions, such as the suppression of cloisters, as his way of fulfilling the edicts of the Diet of Speyer authorizing rulers to settle religious differences in their realms in a way pleasing both to God and to the emperor. This ordinance was adopted by a synod of clergy and laity at Hamburg. It provided for a democratic organization in which congregations elected their own pastors, elders, and deacons and sent their pastors and elected representatives to an annual synod or assembly. This synod was charged with overseeing the care of the whole territorial church and providing a superintendent (the Latin term for bishop) for each district. The landgrave was permitted only to take part in deliberations and to vote.[12]

When Landgrave Philip showed this church order to Luther, the reformer advised that it was not suited to the needs of Hesse, that some interim step was needed before Hesse could move to a representative or synodical form of church life, and induced the Hessians to adopt the model of the Saxon Visitation instead. The Elector of Saxony had taken up Luther's request that a visitation of parishes and church institutions be carried out and appointed a number of Visitors. The Elector had some basic guidelines for the Visitors prepared in "The Instruction and Mandate on the Basis of which the Visitors are to be Trained" (June 16, 1527). In the summer of 1527, on the basis of the experience of the Visitations, Melanchthon composed the treatise "Instructions for the Visitors of Parish Pastors in Electoral Saxony," for which Luther wrote the preface. It was published in 1528, and can be regarded as a church order (Kirchenordnung).

In his preface to the Instructions, Luther made it clear that the assistance of the Elector was viewed as a service of love and not as a rightful function of government. The Elector, however, had issued his own "Instructions" as a prince and granted the Visitors "power and authority" from himself.[13] Thus, the Saxon Visitation marked the beginning of the state control of the Lutheran churches in Germany. The model that emerged from Electoral Saxony had the prince as *summus episcopus,* appointing visitation committees to examine and evaluate church life, consistories to judge doctrine and practices, and superintendents to oversee pastoral care of the parishes.

The organization of the Reformation in the cities was often patterned after the organization in Wittenberg. The city council usually designated one of the city pastors to serve as superintendent or senior of the ministerium and made him responsible for the religious life of the entire city. The property and income from the monasteries, as well as

---

[12] See Grimm, 157.

[13] See Bernhard Lohse, "The Development of the Office of Leadership in the German Lutheran Churches, 1517–1918," in Ivar Asheim and Victor Gold, eds., *Episcopacy in the Lutheran Church?* (Philadelphia: Fortress Press, 1970), 55ff.

endowments for votive masses, were now used for educational purposes and for the care of the poor.

The church orders that regulated church polity, church administration, congregational life, charitable institutions, schools, and liturgy proliferated from 1528 as the Reformation was adopted in various cities and states. Many of Luther's colleagues were drawn into the task of preparing them. Johannes Bugenhagen (1485–1558), the senior pastor or superintendent at Wittenberg, was especially active in the preparation of these documents. He drafted church orders for Brunswick (1528), Hamburg (1529), Lübeck (1531), Pomerania (1535), Denmark (1537), Schleswig-Holstein (1542), and Hildesheim (1544). Bugenhagen's influence was also felt in the church orders prepared by his colleague Justus Jonas for Wittenberg (1533) and for Duke Henry of Saxony (1539). Melanchthon was involved in the preparation of church orders for Mecklenberg (1540 and 1552, with Aurifaber and Riebling) and Cologne (1543, with Bucer). One other early and important church order was that for Brandenburg-Nuremberg (1533), prepared by Johannes Brenz and Andreas Osiander.

The reformers who served as consultants and authors in the drafting of church orders had been pamphleteers in the cause of the Reformation, and their rhetoric was incorporated into the church orders as they castigated superstitious abuses that were to be abolished in favor of the pure gospel of faith in Jesus Christ. In the Brunswick church order, Bugenhagen criticized those in the old church who

> do not place their hearts and faith in God, but rather in cowls, special foods, holy water, holy candles, consecrated herbs, indulgences, prized little prayers, precious Friday fasting, confraternities, the pilgrimage of Saint James, the rosary, and observances, rules, and clothing, none of which God has ever commanded. . . . The more holy water we had, the more poltergeists; we warded off thunder with candles and herbs and practiced magic with herbs in our beds and in the cellar by the beer, unaware that all of these things were contrived against the grace of our Lord Jesus Christ, who alone takes away our sin, and also against Christian prayer, by which we should call out to our dear Father through Christ for all our bodily and spiritual needs. For that is what will help us, not water, candles, and herbs.[14]

The Brandenburg-Nuremberg church order also complained about confessing "false, fabricated sins," such as eating meat on Fridays, cutting wood on religious holidays, touching the consecrated eucharistic chalice, "and other such foolishness," while it dismissed as "unnecessary and childish" the elaborate memorial masses.[15]

While similar in their denunciations of pre-Reformation practices, the church orders differed in their prescriptions of new practices. Luther D. Reed recognized the classification of church orders according to three groups or types: the central Saxon-

---

[14] Johannes Bugenhagen, *Der erbarn Stadt Braunschwyg Christliche Ordenung* (Nuremberg, 1531), in *Die evangelischen Kirchenordnungen des 16. Jahrhunderts*, ed. A. L. Richter (Weimar, 1846; 2nd ed. Leipzig, 1871), I, 106ff.

[15] Johannes Brenz, *Kirchen Ordnung. In meiner genedigen Herrn der Margraven zu Brandenburg* (Nuremberg, 1533), in Richter, I, 182, 195–97.

Lutheran type, the ultra-conservative type, and the mediating or radical type. Among the Saxon-Lutheran types he includes those prepared by Bugenhagen, Melanchthon, and Osiander. Among the ultra-conservative, which retained as many of the pre-Reformation rites and ceremonies as possible, were Mark Brandenburg (1540), Pfalz-Neuburg (1543), and Austria (1570, prepared by Chytraeus). The mediating or radical group comprised those developed in southern and western Germany where Reformed influences were strong: Brenz's orders for Württemberg (1553 and 1559); Bucer's orders for Strasbourg; and the orders for Baden (1556), Rheinpfalz (1557), and Worms (1560). The orders for Hesse (1532), Cassel (1539), Marburg (1574), and Nassau (1576) also show Reformed influence, but possess strong individuality.[16]

A unique and important church order is that prepared for Archbishop Hermann von Wied of Cologne in 1543 by both Bucer and Melanchthon. Archbishop Hermann, an elector of the Holy Roman Empire, was determined to carry out the reform of the church of Cologne against the opposition of the influential Johann Gropper (1503–1559) and his Cathedral Chapter. Bucer and Melanchthon headed a team of Lutheran and Reformed theologians assembled at Bonn in July of 1543 to prepare a document to guide the reformation of Cologne. It was published in German that year under the formidable title, "A Simple and Religious Consultation of us to Hermann by the grace of God Archbishop of Cologne, and Prince Elector, etc., by what means a Christian reformation, founded in God's Word, of doctrine, administration of divine sacraments, of ceremonies, and the whole cure of souls, and other ecclesiastical ministries, may be begun among men committed to our pastoral charge, until the Lord grant a better to be appointed, either by a free and Christian council, general or national, or else by the states of the Empire of the nation of Germany, gathered together in the Holy Ghost." For convenience it is usually referred to as the "Einfaltigs Bedencken or Pia Deliberatio," after the Latin translation of 1545. This church order was never fully implemented in Cologne, because in 1546 Archbishop Hermann was brought before the emperor and pope on charges of heresy by his Chapter and was deposed and excommunicated. But in 1547 it was translated into English by John Daye (revised in 1548) and it became influential on the liturgical reforms in England carried out by Archbishop Thomas Cranmer.

The first scholarly collection of these church orders was that made by Aemilius L. Richter, *Die evangelischen Kirchenordnungen des sechzehnten Jahrhunderts,* two volumes (Weimar, 1846; second edition Leipzig, 1871). In the twentieth century a fifteen-volume (to date) critical edition was begun by Emil Sehling, *Die evangelischen Kirchenordnungen des XVI. Jahrhunderts* (Vols. I–V, Leipzig, 1902–1913; Vols. VI–XV, Tübingen, 1955–1970). Richter's two-volume collection arranges the church orders chronologically in terms of date of publication, although an index shows the relationships between them (II; 509). The work begun by Sehling (interrupted by both world wars) arranges the church orders in terms of the territories for which they were prepared and reproduces the entire texts with critical introductions.

---

[16] Luther D. Reed, *The Lutheran Liturgy,* op. cit., 89.

❦ THE DIFFERENTIATION OF LUTHERAN MASS-ORDERS

Among the important issues dealt with in the Kirchenordnungen are liturgical details, especially regarding the order of the mass and offices and sacramental practices. The church orders themselves are not liturgical books. Like Luther's *Formula Missae*, most of them give directions on what to use or not to use from the liturgical books inherited from the pre-Reformation church. Texts are provided only where they cannot be found in these other sources. Sometimes, as in the Brandenburg-Nuremberg Order 1533, chants are provided for these texts. Otherwise, reference is simply made to chant tones or to German hymns that could be found in the various hymnals that were published from 1524 on.

No fewer than 135 church orders appeared between 1523 *(Formula Missae)* and 1555 (Peace of Augsburg). They differ considerably in minor details, and yet their liturgical provisions show a remarkable similarity. This was due to the far-reaching influence of Luther and to the fact that many of the church orders were prepared by the same authors (Bugenhagen seven, Brenz five, Jonas four, Melanchthon four, Bucer three or four, etc.).

Since Bugenhagen prepared the largest number of church orders, his influence on the liturgical life of the Lutheran churches has been enormous. The following is an outline of the mass-order provided in the Brunswick Orders 1528, the first of the church orders prepared by Bugenhagen for north German cities and states and the kingdom of Denmark.

> Introit: Psalm 34 or another psalm
> Kyrie
> Gloria
> > *Minister intones:* Gloria in excelsis Deo
> > *Choir continues:* et in terra pax
> Collect
> Epistle
> Gradual *sung by the choir boys*
> > [Sequences were sung on Christmas, Easter, and Pentecost, with the choir
> > singing each strophe in Latin and the congregation repeating it in German.]
> Gospel
> *Minister intones:* Ich glaube an einen Gott
> *Congregation responds:* Wir glauben all an einen Gott (Luther's chorale)
> Sermon
> Announcements and Exhortation to Prayer for the State
> German hymn or psalm *sung as communicants enter the chancel, the men and
> > boys on the right, the women and girls on the left
> > The minister prepares the bread and wine, then gives an exhortation to the
> > communicants using a fixed form.*
> Preface *in Latin, with propers for festivals and Trinity preface for ordinary
> > Sundays*
> Sanctus *sung by the choir in Latin*
> Lord's Prayer *sung by the minister in German, with congregational "Amen"*
> Words of Institution

> Ministration of Communion *while German hymns are sung by the*
>   *congregation, including the Agnus Dei sung in German*
> Luther's Post-communion prayer
> Aaronic Benediction

If there are no communicants, the minister nevertheless wears the customary vestments, and the service concludes with the Preface, Sanctus, Lord's Prayer, and Benediction.[17]

In his introductory comments on the mass, Bugenhagen contrasted the Evangelical mass with the Roman mass, but insisted that traditional elements be retained where possible and that novelties not be introduced needlessly. He objected to the multitude of saints' days and other occasions and urged that there be one mass in German on Sundays so that the people could truly "hear mass." It can be seen, however, that he was not adverse to the retention of Latin texts where these could be sung according to the traditional chant tones. We see here a conflation of the two styles of worship provided by Luther in his *Formula Missae* and German Mass.

Another important and influential church order was that prepared for Brandenburg-Nuremberg in 1533. The state of Brandenburg-Anspach had been ruled by two brothers since 1515, the Margraves Casimir and George. In 1527 Casimir died and the following year Margrave George introduced the Reformation into Brandenburg. A committee prepared a church order that contained regulations concerning church polity, doctrine, and worship. Andreas Osiander (1498–1552), pastor of St. Sebaldus's Church in Nuremberg, and Johann Brenz (1499–1570), pastor in Schwäbisch-Hall, were the principal drafters. The material was initially prepared by Osiander, circulated among other pastors in Nuremberg and the theologians in Wittenberg for their reactions and responses, and then put into a unifying literary form by Brenz, who worked on the document for six weeks in Osiander's home. It contains more actual liturgical texts than any other church order up to that time and proved to be more influential than any other Reformation document of that period except the Saxon Visitation. It formed the basis of the revised church order for Mark Brandenburg in 1540, and Bucer drew extensively upon its commentaries on the sacraments for his work on Archbishop Hermann's *Consultation*. It should also be noted that Archbishop Thomas Cranmer, who married Osiander's niece while serving as Henry VIII's ambassador to the court of Charles V in 1531, obtained a copy of it for his library.[18]

Two orders of mass are provided: one mostly in Latin and the other mostly in German. Which mass-order was used depended upon the availability of a choir to sing the traditional Latin chant tunes. In Nuremberg this was possible, and Latin masses continued in that Lutheran city until the beginning of the nineteenth century. The Latin mass is as follows:

---

[17] Richter, I, 106ff.; Sehling, VI, 1:440–2; Reed, 92ff.

[18] Richter, I, 176ff.; Sehling, XI, 140ff.; Reed, 96ff. See Edward T. Horn, "The Reformation in Nürnberg," *The Lutheran Church Review* X (1891), 123–45. An impressively bound copy of the Brandenberg-Nuremberg CO is in the Rare Book Collection of the Krauss-Jesuit-McCormick Library at the Lutheran School of Theology at Chicago.

Minister recites the Confiteor, *or whatever his devotion suggests, at the altar*

Introit *sung by the choir*

Kyrie *sung by the choir*

Gloria *sung by the choir*

Salutation and Oremus ("Let us pray") *either in Latin or German collect (one or more)*

Epistle *in German (lectio continua)*

Gradual *sung by the choir*

Gospel *in German (lectio continua)*

Creed *sung in Latin*

Sermon

Exhortation to communicants *spoken in German from the altar*

Words of Institution *in German*

Sanctus *in Latin*

Lord's Prayer *in Latin, with traditional introduction*

Pax domini

Ministration of Communion

The celebrant administers the bread and the deacon the cup, while the choir sings the Agnus Dei in Latin. If time permits the choir also sings a Latin responsory and other texts.

Thanksgiving collect *in German*

Benediction *in German (either the Aaronic benediction or the following: "The blessing of almighty God the Father the Son and the Holy Spirit be with you and abide with us always.")*

The German Service is as follows:

German hymn or introit *sung while the minister says the* Confiteor *or some other devotion*

Kyrie and Gloria *read by the minister in Latin while the congregation sings the same in German*

Salutation and Collect

Chapter from an Epistle

Gradual *in Latin*

A chapter from the Gospels or Acts

Creed *said by the minister in Latin while the congregation says it in German*

Sermon

Exhortation to communicants *spoken from the altar*

Words of Institution

Sanctus

Lord's Prayer

Pax domini

Ministration of communion *during which the congregation sings German hymns*

Post-communion collect

Benediction *as above*

Electoral Brandenburg did not receive the Reformation until it was introduced in 1538 by the sons of Elector Joachim I, who divided his realm. The younger son, Johann, was an ardent supporter of the Reformation. Joachim II, who succeeded to the electoral dignity, appreciated its popular support and the income that accrued to his treasury from

the secularization of the bishoprics and monasteries. But he also sought the fullest retention of the traditional ceremonies in worship. He desired to be subservient neither to
Rome nor to Wittenberg. At the time a church order was being prepared for Electoral
Brandenburg, the elector's chaplain, Buchholzer, wrote to Luther about his prince's concern to retain such traditional vestments as alb and chasuble and also processions. Luther
wrote to Buchholzer on December 4, 1539:

> As to the matter that worries you . . . this is my advice: If your lord, the mar-
> grave and elector, will allow the gospel of Jesus Christ to be preached openly,
> clearly, and without admixture—and the two sacraments of baptism and the
> flesh and blood of Jesus Christ to be administered and given according to his in-
> stitution, and will let the invocation of the saints fall away, so that they are not
> patrons, mediators, and intercessors, and the sacrament be not carried about in
> procession, and will let the daily masses and the vigils and requiems for the
> dead fall, and not have the water, salt, and herbs consecrated, and will sing pure
> responsories and songs in both Latin and German during the march or proces-
> sion; then in God's Name, go along in the procession, and carry a silver or
> golden cross, and a chasuble or an alb of velvet, silk, or linen. And if one cha-
> suble or alb is not enough for your lord the elector, put on three of them, as
> Aaron the high priest put on three, one over the other. . . . and if his Electoral
> Grace is not satisfied with one circuit or procession, in which you go about and
> ring and sing, go around with him seven times, as Joshua and the children of
> Israel went around Jericho shouting and blowing with trumpets. . . . For such
> matters, if free from abuses, take from or give to the gospel nothing; only they
> must not be thought necessary to salvation, and the conscience dare not be
> bound to them.[19]

Elector Joachim II appointed a commission including Buchholzer, Bishop
Matthias von Jagow of Brandenburg, and the humanist George Witzel to prepare the
church order. The preface was written by the elector himself. The doctrinal sections were
taken largely from the Brandenburg-Nuremberg Order 1533 and the Church Order of
Duke Henry of Saxony of 1539. The liturgical section, or agenda, contained an unusually
rich provision for ceremonial usages.[20] The order of mass is as follows:

> *The minister and assistants, wearing customary vestments, go to the altar in
>   procession with lights.*
> Confiteor *recited by the minister in Latin*
> Introit, Kyrie, and Gloria *sung by the choir in Latin*
> Salutation, Oremus, Collect for the Day *in Latin*
> Epistle *sung in Latin, then read in German*
> German hymn *sung by the congregation*
> Gradual with Tract and Sequence *sung by the choir in Latin*
> Gospel *sung in Latin, then read in German*
> Nicene Creed *sung in Latin by the choir (In villages, the German versification,
>   "Wir glauben all," is sung by the congregation.)*
> Offertory Verse *sung by the choir*

[19] *Martin Luthers Briefwechsel*, XII:316f.; trans. in Reed, 99.
[20] Richter, II, 122ff.; Sehling, III, 39ff.; Reed, 98ff.

> Preface and Sanctus *in Latin*
>> *During the Sanctus the minister quietly offers four German prayers:*
>>> *for the emperor and civil rulers*
>>> *for the clergy*
>>> *for unity*
>>> *for forgiveness of sins (from Brandenburg-Nuremberg Order)*
> Words of Institution *with inclination and elevation*
> Latin responsory *sung by the choir* or a German hymn of praise
> Lord's Prayer and Pax domini *intoned by the minister*
> Agnus Dei *sung in Latin by the choir*
> Exhortation to communicants (from Brandenburg-Nuremberg Order)
> Ministration of Communion
>> *The celebrant administers the bread and the deacon the cup, while the choir sings a communion verse in Latin.*
> German hymn *sung by the congregation*
> Thanksgiving Collect *in German,* followed by several prayers from the pre-Reformation missal *said quietly by the minister in Latin*

When there are no communicants, as on weekdays, the order of mass is used up to the sermon, which follows the Creed. Then the German Litany or a metrical version of the Lord's Prayer is sung, followed by collects and the benediction. Sick persons may be communed in the church at another hour or the sacrament may be taken to their houses after the service. When the sacrament was taken to the sick, it was accompanied by acolytes with bells and tapers.

These three mass-orders show the similarity of the early Lutheran mass in the various church orders. The influences of both Luther's *Formula Missae* and German Mass are evident not only in the liturgical material (traditional Latin texts or German versifications and hymns), but also in the order itself in a very important respect. The most significant variation in Lutheran mass-orders concerns the relationship between the words of institution and the ministration of Holy Communion. In Luther's *Formula Missae,* it will be recalled, the words of institution were included in the Preface, and therefore were separated in time from the distribution of the sacrament. In the German Mass, however, the bread was to be distributed immediately after the words over the bread and the cup was to be distributed immediately after the words over the cup. Hans-Christoph Schmidt-Lauber developed the thesis that the Lutheran liturgy is differentiated according to the placement of the words of institution, or Verba Testamenti.[21] The Bugenhagen mass-orders follow the pattern of Luther's German Mass in juxtaposing the Verba Testamenti and the distribution, as follows:

> Offertorium *sung as the elements are prepared and the communicants move into the chancel*
> Eucharistic Dialogue, Preface, and Sanctus
> Exhortation to the communicants
> Paternoster and Pax
> Verba Testamenti *and* Communion

---

[21] Hans-Christoph Schmidt-Lauber, *Die Eucharistie als Entfaltung der Verba Testamenti* (Kassel: Johannes Stauda, 1957).

Agnus Dei *sung during communion*
Thanksgiving Collect
Benediction[22]

The Brandenburg-Nuremberg and Mark Brandenburg mass-orders follow the pattern of Luther's *Formula Missae;* the Verba are not juxtaposed with the Communion.[23]

BRANDENBURG-NUREMBERG 1533	MARK BRANDENBURG 1540
	Salutation
	Offertorium
Exhortation to the Sacrament	Eucharistic Dialogue and Preface
	Sanctus with intercessions
Verba Testamenti	*Verba Testamenti*
Sanctus	Song of Praise
Paternoster and Pax	Paternoster and Pax
Agnus Dei	Agnus Dei
	Exhortation to the Sacrament
Communion	*Communion*
Communio and other songs	Communio and other songs
Post-communion prayer	Post-communion prayer
	Corpus tuum, Quad ore
Benediction	Benediction

One other mass-order, the Pfalz-Neuberg 1543, follows the pattern of the *Formula Missae* in not juxtaposing the Verba and the Communion. Its scheme is as follows:

Exhortation
Epicletic offertory prayer
> O Lord Jesus Christ, the only true Son of the living God, who has given
> your body unto bitter death for us all, and has shed your blood for the
> forgiveness of our sins, and has bid all your disciples to eat that same body
> and to drink your blood whereby to remember your death; we bring before
> you divine Majesty these gifts of bread and wine and beseech you to hallow
> and bless the same by your divine grace, goodness and power and ordain
> (*schaffen*) that this bread and wine may be (*sei*) your body and blood, even
> unto eternal life to all who eat and drink thereof; who lives and reigns . . .[24]

Verba Testamenti
Sanctus *with intercessions (as in Mark Brandenburg)*
Paternoster and Pax
Agnus Dei and Communion prayer
Communion *with singing during the distribution*
Post-communion prayer
Salutation and Benedicamus
Benediction[25]

---

[22] Ibid., 115–6.
[23] Ibid., 121.
[24] Trans. in Reed, 753. The Pfalz-Neuburg CO, like many others, was published in Nuremberg.
[25] Schmidt-Lauber, 120; alt.

While the various church orders based their mass-orders on the examples of Luther's Latin and German masses, it is also evident that many of the mass-orders were textually and ceremonially fuller than what Luther had provided. Some retained the *confiteor* as the private prayer of the minister. The Strassburg German masses began with a general confession of sins and declaration of grace. We shall see that a form of confession and absolution intended to include the congregation was provided in the Swedish Mass of 1531. The form of the confession of sins and declaration of grace provided by Melanchthon in the Mecklenburg Order 1552 became the basis of the Confession of Sins in the Common Service of the Evangelical Lutheran churches in North America in the late nineteenth century.[26] While most mass-orders retained the traditional pericope system, Brandenburg-Nuremberg and some others instituted "in course" (lectio continua) reading of the epistle and gospel. A number added intercessions, either after the sermon as part of the pulpit office, as in Bugenhagen's orders, or as a part of the eucharistic office, as in Mark Brandenburg. Some retained the offertory verses and Pfalz-Neuburg even provided an offertory prayer with an epiclesis. It is apparent that the various church orders made their own contributions to the evolution of Lutheran liturgy, influenced by but also independent of the contributions of Martin Luther.

🍇 MATINS AND VESPERS

The same may be said of the provision for the traditional prayer offices in the church orders. These offices had been maintained primarily in the cathedrals and monasteries of the Middle Ages, although Sunday Vespers remained popular in parish churches as well. The Lutheran Reformation did much to restore these offices as congregational services because they were used to replace the daily masses in churches and schools. Edward T. Horn provided the following outlines and comments on these offices in the various Lutheran church orders.[27]

1. STRASBOURG-ERFURT KIRCHENAMPT 1525	2. GERMAN MASS 1526	
Vespers	*Matins*	*Vespers*
Psalms with Antiphon	Psalms with Antiphon	Psalms with Antiphon
Lections	Lections	Lections
Hymn	Antiphon	Magnificat
Magnificat	Lections	Antiphon
Salutation	Lord's Prayer	Lord's Prayer
Collect	Collect	Collects
Psalm 66	Benedicamus	Benedicamus
Benediction		

[26] See Reed, 258–9.

[27] Edward T. Horn, "The Lutheran Sources of the Common Service," *The Lutheran Church Review* X (1891), 261ff. Horn's meticulous research served as background for the offices of Matins and Vespers in the corpus of liturgical material comprising the Common Service of 1888.

3. PRUSSIA 1526	4. HESSE 1526	5. SCHWÄBISCH-HALL 1526
Matins	*Matins*	
O Lord, open thou,		
Venite (Ps. 95)	Venite	
Antiphon	1, 2, or 3 Psalms	
2 or 3 Psalms	Rhythmical Psalm	
Lesson	Lesson	
Explanation	Interpretation	
Response	Benedictus	
But, Thou, O Lord	Salutation	
Thanks be to God	Lord's Prayer	
Seasonal collect	Prayer	
Benediction	Benediction	
Vespers	*Vespers*	*Vespers*
Make haste	As in the morning,	Make haste
Gloria Patri	except omit Venite	Latin Psalm
1, 2 or 3 Psalms	and sing Magnificat	Antiphon
Lesson	or Nunc dimittis	Sermon
Explanation	instead of	Magnificat
Magnificat	Benedictus.	Prayer
Versicles	On Sundays sing both	Benediction
Collects		
Benediction		

6. SAXON VISITATION ARTICLES 1528	7. WITTENBERG 1533	8. SAXON 1539
Matins	*Matins*	*Matins*
Three Psalms		1, 2, or 3 Psalms with
Lesson	As in Vespers, singing	Antiphon
Te Deum or Benedictus	Te Deum, Benedictus,	Lesson
or Quincunque Vult	or Quincunque Vult	Benedictus with Antiphon
or Preces	Collect	
Lord's Prayer	(The Te Deum may be	
German Song	sung)	
Collect		
Vespers	*Vespers*	*Vespers*
Three Psalms with	2 or 3 Psalms with	1, 2, or 3 Psalms with
Antiphons	Antiphon	Antiphon
Hymns	3 Lessons	Responsory or Hymn
Responses	Hymn	Lesson
Lections	Magnificat on Sundays	Magnificat
Lord's Prayer	Sermon	Antiphon
German song	Collect	Collect
Collects	Litany	Benedicamus
	Versicle	
	Collect	
	Benedicamus	

9. NORDHEIM 1539	10. HAMBURG 1539	11. CALENBERG-GÖTTINGEN 1542
Matins	*Matins*	*Matins*
3 Psalms	Antiphon	Make haste, O Lord
Psalm	Invitatory and Venite	
Lesson	Lesson	3 Psalms with
		Antiphon
Responsory	Responsory	Lesson
Te Deum	Te Deum	Te Deum
		Lesson
Lesson	Kyrie	Benedictus with
		Antiphon
	Lord's Prayer	Collect
Benedictus	Benedicamus	Benedicamus
Collect		Da pacem
Vespers	*Vespers*	*Vespers*
Psalms	Antiphon	Make haste, O Lord
Antiphon	Psalm	Gloria Patri
	Lesson	Antiphon
Hymn	Responsory	3 Psalms
Magnificat	Hymn	Hymn de tempore
	Magnificat	Versicle
Catechism	Antiphon	Antiphon
	Nunc dimittis	Magnificat
	Kyrie	Lesson
	Lord's Prayer	Exposition
	Versus	Collect
	Collect	Benediction
	Benedicamus	

12. POMMERN 1542	13. REF. COLOGNE 1543	14. PRUSSIA 1544
Matins	*Matins*	*Matins*
Antiphon	3 Psalms	2 or 3 Psalms
Psalm	Te Deum	Lesson
Lesson	Benedictus with	Exposition
Responsory	Antiphons and	Responsory
Lesson in German	Responsories	Versicle: But Thou . . .
Te Deum		Collect of the Season
Collect		Benediction
Benedicamus		
Vespers	*Vespers*	*Vespers*
Antiphon	A pure Hymn and	Make haste
Psalm	theMagnificat	Gloria Patri
Responsory	instead of Te Deum	1, 2, or 3 Psalms
Hymn	Catechism	Lessons
Lesson	A Lection from holy	Magnificat
Catechism	scripture	Versicle
Antiphon	General Prayer	Collects

Vespers	*Vespers*	*Vespers*
Magnificat or	Song of praise	Benediction
Nunc dimittis	Benediction	
Da pacem	Te Deum	
Lesson	to be sung at early service	
Litany	on Sundays.	
Collect for the Church	Special Responsories	
Benedicamus	and Hymns may be sung	
Da pacem	on the Festivals	

15. BRANDENBURG-NUREMBERG 1533 provides that Vespers shall be at the usual time in the usual manner.

16. SCHLÜTER'S ROSTOCK GESANGBUCH 1531 gives us a picture of these services in process of development. Thus:

The German Vespers

Antiphon
Veni, Sancte Spiritus *or* Komm, heiliger Geist
Collect
Psalms 110–114
Magnificat
Collect

The German Completorium or Compline

Psalms 4, 25, 91, 134
Nunc dimittis
Two Collects

The German Matins

Psalms 1, 2, 3
Old or New Testament Lesson
Responsory: *Si bona suscepimus*
Te Deum

Lauds

Psalms 93, 100, 63, 67, 148
Benedictus
Collects

We have here outlines from sixteen church orders and other sources, which are repeated and reinforced by the abundant musical provisions of the choir books known as the Cantionales (see below). What do they teach us concerning the Lutheran Office tradition in the Reformation church orders? Edward T. Horn made these ten observations (misnumbered in his article):

1. That it was modeled on the familiar old service. 2. That the service of Lauds was combined with Matins, and Vespers with Compline? 3. That they consisted of Psalmody, Lections, Hymn and Prayer, and generally were given in that order.

4. That a Sermon or Exposition or Summary of the lessons was added to them by the Reformation. 5. The only serious question of Order is caused by the Sermon. Is it to follow the Canticle or to precede it? Is it to be put with the lessons or to form a separate and unassimilated part? 6. The parts were introduced, connected and interpreted by Antiphons, Responsories, Versicles. 8. The traditional opening versicles of the Matins Service (*Domine labia* and *Deus in adjutorium*) and of the Vespers (*Deus in adjutorium*) were not altogether discarded. 9. The Morning Service was distinguished from that of the Evening (a) in some cases, as formerly, by the Invitatory and *Venite* (Ps. 95) or by the *Venite* only; (b) by the use of the Te Deum and Benedictus instead of the Magnificat and Nunc dimittis; (c) sometimes by the use of Psalms 1–110 (*Dixit Dominus*) at Matins, 110–150 at Vespers; (d) sometimes by the use of New Testament at Matins and Old Testament at Vespers in the Lessons. 10. The characteristic ending is the *Benedicamus*, sometimes followed by the *Da pacem*. 11. We have for the prayer the traditional Kyrie, Lord's Prayer, Collect (Wittenberg 1533, Hamburg 1539), or pure *Preces* (*Vis. Art.* 1528), or the Litany, or a General Prayer, or simply Collects.[28]

Thus, it is evident that the historic offices of morning and evening prayer were retained in Lutheran use, and even received a kind of revitalization as congregational prayer.

❧ THE CHURCH YEAR CALENDAR

The content of the mass and the prayer offices was determined by the church year calendar. Each church order specified what seasons and days would be observed in the territorial church for which it was drafted. This means that there was potential for a great deal of variety in the observance of the church year, but a reading of the church orders indicates a remarkable consensus in the calendrical observances of early Lutheranism.[29]

As in the Roman church of the time, the church year in Lutheranism began with the four Sundays of Advent beginning on the Sunday closest to St. Andrew's Day (Nov. 30). The altars were arrayed in violet, and many church orders forbade marriages during Advent as well as during Lent. Christmas was retained with the solemn Matins or Nocturnes that has become the traditional candlelight service, although Holy Communion could also be celebrated on Christmas Eve and Christmas Day. Pfalz-Neuburg (1543) forbade the consecration of wine on Saint John's Day (December 27), along with plays in the church and the display of the crèche that had become customary Christmas practices during the late Middle Ages. Saint Stephen's Day (December 26) and Saint John's Day, plus Holy Innocents (December 28), were retained in some lands, abrogated in others. Even if these days were kept in the calendar, their specific content was usually ignored in favor of the Christmas celebration. The Circumcision of Our Lord continued to be observed on January 1 and the Epiphany on January 6 (also called the

---

[28] Ibid., 264.

[29] Edward T. Horn, *The Christian Year* (Philadelphia: Lutheran Book Store, 1876), 57ff. reconstructed the "Lutheran church year" from these early Reformation resources.

Day of the Three Kings, *Der Obere Tag*, and *Hohe Neujahr*). Luther expressed a preference that Epiphany be celebrated as the Baptism of Our Lord, as in the Eastern churches. The Sundays after the Epiphany were given specific content, as follows:

> First Sunday: Jesus' manifestation to the teachers in the Temple (Luke 2:41–52)
> Second Sunday: Jesus' first miracle at the wedding feast in Cana (John 2:1–11)
> Third Sunday: Jesus' manifestation to the crowds and the heathen centurion
>   (Matt. 8:1–13)
> Fourth Sunday: Jesus' power over nature in the stilling of the storm on the lake
>   (Matt. 8:23–27)
> Fifth Sunday: Jesus' wisdom and love in sparing the ungodly and caring for the
>   faithful (Matt. 13:24–30)
> Sixth Sunday: Jesus' glorification in the Transfiguration (Matt. 17:1–9)

The observance of Transfiguration on August 6 seems to be no earlier than 1456, when Pope Calixtus III proclaimed its observance in honor of a victory over Islam at Belgrade; but Bugenhagen and Veit Dietrich chose it as a sermon theme for the Sixth Sunday after the Epiphany, and it subsequently became generally observed on that day in the Lutheran churches.[30] The pre-Lenten Sundays of Septuagesima, Sexagesima, and Quinquagesima, which point toward Lent and Easter, were also observed in the Lutheran churches.

Lent was observed from Ash Wednesday through Easter Eve. Mark Brandenburg (1540) ordered the customary fasts on Friday and Saturday and on the forty days of Lent, but with the qualification that the peoples' consciences should not be bound by such times and distinctions of meat. Calenburg and Göttingen (1542), with the same proviso, nevertheless stated that "such fasts ought of right always be in use among us." The altars were arrayed in violet or black, songs of joy were omitted (such as the Gloria and Alleluia), the organs were silent, and weddings were forbidden. During Holy Week (called *Karwoche* in German) the Passion was read and preached on at Matins and Vespers. The Passion according to Matthew continued to be read on Palm Sunday and the Passion according to John continued to be read on Good Friday. Holy Communion was celebrated on both Maundy Thursday and Good Friday. In this way Good Friday was kept as a liturgical day and celebrated with less somberness in the Lutheran churches than in the Roman church, in which the altars were stripped bare and the organs and bells silenced. There were no special observances for Holy Saturday except for Saturday Vespers with communal confession.

Easter had been the great communion day in the medieval church. The reformers tried to prevent too many communions on this day, and instead urged the faithful to receive it on various Sundays throughout the church year. As the rite of confirmation developed in the Lutheran churches, it was sometimes celebrated on the First Sunday after Easter (named *Quasi modo geniti*, from its Introit: "As new-born babes desire the sincere milk of the Word . . ."). The Second Sunday after Easter (*Misericordia domini*, "Goodness of the Lord") became popularly known as "Good Shepherd Sunday" (which became a

---

[30] See Reed. 485–6.

popular devotion among Lutherans not unlike the devotion to the Sacred Heart among Roman Catholics). The Third Sunday after Easter was named *Jubilate* (Rejoice) and the Fourth *Cantate* (Sing ye). The Fifth Sunday was named *Rogate* (Pray ye), but the name derived from the Gospel rather than the Introit. In some Lutheran churches the Monday, Tuesday, and Wednesday after Rogate Sunday were kept as penitential Rogation days with litanies and prayers. Ascension Day was kept in all the church orders, and sometimes the theme of the ascension was repeated on the Sixth Sunday after Easter, *Exaudi* (Hear). Pentecost *(Pfingsten)* was also observed as a major festival, and sermons and hymns developed the role of the Holy Spirit in the church and in Christian life on the basis of the third article of the Creed.

Trinity Sunday was the octave of Pentecost and it formed a hinge between the so-called half-year of Christ and the so-called half-year of the church. Following the established custom in the northern European churches, the remaining Sundays of the church year were counted after Trinity. The Feast of Corpus Christi was retained in some Lutheran churches up until about 1600 because of its great pre-Reformation popularity, although Luther himself was hostile to it. In many Lutheran churches the last Sunday after Trinity was called "Judgment Sunday," and it became a feast of the dead to replace the Roman All Saints and All Souls Days. As on All Saints Day, the Beatitudes (Matt. 5:1–12) was read as the gospel. Luther chose to give the last Sundays after Trinity special content that would be observed no matter how many Sundays after Trinity there were in a given year. These Sundays were as follows:

> 25th Sunday: the abomination of desolation (Matt. 25:15–28)
> 26th Sunday: the last judgment (Matt. 25:31–46)
> 27th Sunday: remembrance of the faithful departed (Matt. 5:1–12)

However, a number of Lutheran churches continued to observe All Saints Day (November 1), although not All Souls (November 2), and by the end of the sixteenth century it became more customary to read the parable of the wise and foolish virgins (Matt. 25:1–13) on this last Sunday of the church year.[31]

Some feasts of the Virgin Mary were retained in Lutheran churches as feasts of our Lord. The Conception and Presentation of Mary were not kept at all, because they were judged to have no scriptural basis or dogmatic interest. Luther allowed the Feasts of the Nativity and the Assumption of Mary to be retained for a while on account of popular or civil customs connected with their observances. The Annunciation, Purification (Presentation of Our Lord), and Visitation were kept in Lutheran church orders. Some Marian hymns or Marian themes in hymns were retained in altered texts in early Lutheran hymnals.[32] Marian piety was very deep-seated during the fifteenth century, and it couldn't be obliterated immediately. An example of this piety given evangelical expression is found in Luther's 1521 Commentary on the Magnificat.[33] It should be noted that

---

[31] Ibid., 548.

[32] See Friedrich Blume, *Protestant Church Music*, op. cit., 28.

[33] LW 21.

the date of the Feast of the Visitation in earlier Lutheran calendars was July 2, in accordance with the Roman calendar.

Two feast days were widely celebrated because they enjoyed the status of serving as civil holidays as well: The Nativity of St. John the Baptist (June 24), and St. Michael and All Angels (September 29). Among the theologians of Lutheran orthodoxy, St. Michael's Day provided an occasion to preach on the doctrine of angels and to give thanks for their ministry.

Apostles' days and evangelists' days were also kept in Lutheran calendars, although the days were not always observed unless they fell on a Sunday. Some nonbiblical saints were commemorated in various local calendars. The church orders of Halberstadt (1539) and Nördlingen (1585) prescribed a special service of thanksgiving for the gospel on the Sunday after St. Ansgar's Day (February 3), the missionary through whom the gospel came to their land. The Schweinfurth Order (1543) ordered the commemoration of St. Elizabeth of Thuringia; Nördlingen (1538) of St. George; and many churches kept the days of St. Nicholas, St. Lawrence, St. Martin, and St. Mary Magdelene.[34]

Bugenhagen provided in his church orders that an annual service of thanksgiving would be held on the anniversary date on which the Reformation was implemented in the territories whose practices the orders regulated. This is the origin of a Festival of the Reformation, although there was no uniform date of such a festival in the sixteenth century. Some churches held it on the date of Luther's birth or death. In Württemberg and Baden the festival was observed on June 25, the date of the presentation of the Augsburg Confession. During the Thirty Years War the observance of a Reformation Festival was obliterated, but in 1667 Elector John George II of Saxony reestablished such a festival on the Eve of All Saints Day (October 31) to commemorate Luther's posting of his ninety-five theses to the door of the Castle Church in Wittenberg to challenge the sale of indulgences. This date, or the Sunday immediately preceding or following, became a generally accepted time for the Festival of the Reformation in most Lutheran churches.[35]

Finally, it remains to be noted that the Lutheran churches dropped the quarterly Ember Days. In Roman practice the Embertides were often times for ordination to ministry. However, quarterly examinations in the catechism were often introduced that coincided with the old Roman Ember Days: in December (Advent), March (Lent), June (Pentecost), and September. The concept of octaves of festivals and days of devotion was also dropped from Lutheran calendars, although many days were retained in the calendars that had originated as octaves.

The liturgical propers—the introits, graduals, readings, proper prefaces in the mass; choice of psalms, antiphons, and responsories in the prayer offices—are determined by the content of the church year calendar. While we have seen a few church orders that provided for continuous reading of epistles and gospels, the majority of them retained the historic one-year lectionary and pericope system. Continuous readings of biblical books and expository preaching on them tended to occur at Matins and Vespers.

[34] See Horn, *The Christian Year*, 75–6.
[35] See Reed, 569.

Some church orders also provided for the reading of the catechism and preaching on it during the weekdays.

Many of the popular customs that had accompanied some festivals and days of devotion—for example, blessing of candles on Candlemas (Feast of the Purification of Mary and Presentation of Jesus, February 2), the imposition of ashes on Ash Wednesday, and the blessing of palms on Palm Sunday—were suppressed after the Reformation. But the liturgies on these days were enriched by the prodigious musical offerings encouraged by the Lutheran Reformation. We turn now to the hymnals and cantionales that provided these musical resources.

🍇 HYMNALS AND CANTIONALES

We have seen that Luther led the way in writing vernacular hymns as a way of encouraging other poets and musicians to do the same. Others did pick up his challenge, and before 1550 a number of poets and musicians produced hymns of enduring quality. We may mention Nikolaus Decius's Low German songs "Allein Gott in der Höh" (*LBW* 166), "Heilig ist Gott der Vater," and "O Lamm Gottes unschuldig" (*LBW* 111), all based on Gregorian melodies; Justus Jonas's "Wo Gott der Herr nicht bei uns hält"; Elizabeth Cruciger's "Herr Christ, der einig Gottes Sohn" (*LBW* 86); Paul Eber's "Herr Jesu Christ, wahr Mensch und Gott" (*LBW* 124, tune only) and "Wenn wir in höchsten Nöten sein" (*LBW* 303, text); Lazarus Spengler's artful Meistersinger-like "Durch Adams Fall ist ganz verderbt"; and Paul Speratus's masterful setting of the doctrine of justification to verse with a simple and folk-like tune in "Es ist das Heil" (*LBW* 297). In the course of time a group of hymns were taken over from the Bohemian Brethren, especially the songs of Michael Weisse (c. 1480–1534).

From the beginning of the Reformation these hymns were collected into hymnals and given widespread circulation. The history of Protestant hymnals begins with the *Achtliederbuch* (*Eight Song Book*) of the Nuremberg printer Jobst Gutknecht (1523–1524). It contained four songs by Luther, including "Nun freut euch" (*LBW* 299), three by Speratus, including "Es ist das Heil," and one anonymous two-voice setting of "In Jesus Namen heben wir an." This book was followed in 1524 by two Erfurt *Enchiridia*, almost identical in content, from the printing firms of Maler and Loersfeld. The first systematically planned hymnal also appeared that year: Johann Walther's *Wittenberger Geystliche gesangk Buchleyn* (*The Wittenberg Spiritual Songbook*), with an introduction by Luther. It contained thirty-eight German and five Latin compositions for three to five voices, and became the model choral songbook for early Lutheranism. It is worth pondering what it means that the first music book to which Luther lent his authority was not a book of unison songs for the congregation but a book of polyphonic pieces for choir.

In 1525 new editions appeared of the Erfurt *Enchiridia*, as well as a Nuremberg *Enchiridion*, and songbooks from Breslau and Zwickau. These were only slight expansions of the earlier books. The most significant publication of 1525 was Wolf Köpphel's Strasbourg *Deutsch Kirchenamt*, in which the song repertoire was increased and enriched by some important new melodies, such as Luther's "Es wolle Gott uns gnädig sein"

(*LBW* 335) and "Aus tiefer Not" (*LBW* 295). The Strasbourg hymnals went through successive revisions every few years up through 1545. A series of Augsburg songbooks were also published between 1529 and 1539. The important Wittenberg Songbook published by Joseph Klug in 1529 is lost, but has been reconstructed through its reprints by Rauscher (Erfurt, 1531) and Gutknecht (Nuremberg, 1531). Luther wrote a foreword for this collection, and indeed it was organized into sections of Luther songs, songs "from others of us," "sacred lieder composed by pious Christians before our time," and "Varia." This arrangement was partly copied in the Bapst Songbook. 1531 was also the year in which the influential hymnal of the Bohemian Brethren (also know as the Unitas Fratrum) was edited by Michael Weisse and appeared in Jungenbunzlau.

The last of the songbooks bearing a connection with Luther was the Bapst Songbook (Leipzig, 1545). To the rather stock collection of eighty *lieder* and a few Latin songs was added an appendix of "Psalms and religious songs, which are made and read together by devout Christians." This appendix contained forty songs; by the edition of 1551 this was increased to seventy. The aging Luther knew that new reformatory voices were questioning the singing of songs not based entirely on biblical texts, and he began the Bapst Songbook with a warning:

> Many false masters now hymns indite,
> Be on your guard and judge them aright.
> Where God is building his church and word,
> There comes the devil with lie and sword.[36]

This same year the first comprehensive collection of the entire body of German and Latin hymns and chants sung in the Lutheran liturgy appeared in Johann Spangenberg's encyclopedic collection (Magdeburg, 1545), organized into *Cantiones ecclesiasticae* (Latin liturgical chants and songs) and *Kirchengesänge deutsch* (German liturgical chants and songs). Similar cantionales later in the century brought together the entire liturgical repertoire of chants and songs. Noteworthy collections are Johannes Keuchenthal's *Kirchengesänge lateinisch und deutsch* (Wittenberg 1573), Nikolaus Selnecker's *Christliche Psalmen . . .* (Leipzig, 1587) and Lucas Lossius's *Psalmodia, hoc est Cantica sacra veteris ecclesiae selecta* (1553, 1561, 1569, 1579), for which Melanchthon provided a foreword. As the title of the Lossius book indicates, its purpose was to present a selection of the liturgical chants of the old church for use in the new one. Originally planned as an agenda only for the Lüneburg churches, it influenced the liturgical usage of much of northern Germany. As Lossius himself stated in the foreword, the purpose of the collection was to counteract musically the decline of the Protestant liturgy. It was published at a time of reaction occasioned by the Augsburg Interim and the growing influence of Calvinism.

The scope of these cantionales was monumental. Spangenberg's was a large folio volume of 379 pages prepared, we are told, at the urging of Luther. It contained a *de tempore* arrangement of parts of the liturgy with the traditional melodies set to the Latin texts and adaptations of them to the German translation. Lossius's *Psalmodia* contained within

---

[36] LW 53:332.

its 800 pages a complete section of texts and melodies from the pre-Reformation *Missale, Graduale*, and *Antiphonarium*, adapted for use in Lutheran services. It provided plainsong melodies to fifty-six Introits, fourteen Alleluias, thirty-one sequences, 206 antiphons, forty-seven responsories, as well as settings of the Kyrie, Gloria, Credo, Proper Prefaces, Sanctus, Agnus Dei, the Litany, and full provision for Matins and Vespers. Keuchenthal's cantionale also contained a rich collection of musical settings for the liturgy, both de tempore and for saints' days (among which we find St. Lawrence). Following this are 212 congregational hymns set to 165 melodies, the Litany in Latin and German, psalms and canticles, numerous antiphons and responsories for Matins and Vespers, and a German Passion. Franz Eler's *Cantica Sacra* (1588) is a volume of 360 pages in octavo prepared for congregations and schools in the Hamburg area. It too provided traditional plainsong melodies for the Lutheran mass, the Litany, psalms and canticles for Matins and Vespers, along with 253 antiphons and seventy-one responsories.[37]

These hymnals and cantionales indicate that music had an essential role in emerging Lutheran liturgy. Unsung liturgies were a rarity in the Lutheran tradition. They also testify to the flexibility of early Lutheran liturgy. This is indicated somewhat in the statement in the Augsburg Confession, Article 24, that "no conspicuous changes have been made in the public ceremonies of the mass, except that in certain places German hymns are sung in addition to the Latin responses for the instruction and exercise of the people."[38] Actually, any liturgy could be held completely in Latin or completely in German. A German hymn could be substituted for any Latin or German prose text. A German hymn could be added to any Latin or German prose text. And German hymns were freely added before and/or after the sermon. Certain hymns came to be associated with the texts of the ordinary of the mass so that a *Lied Messe* in the style of Luther's German Mass became a Lutheran tradition. The liturgical hymns include:

> Kyrie: "Kyrie, Gott Vater" (*LBW* 168)
> Gloria: "All Ehr und Lob" (*LBW* 164, tune)
>   or "Allein Gott in der Höh" (*LBW* 166).
> Credo: "Wir glauben all" (*LBW* 374)
> Sanctus: "Jesaia, dem Propheten" (*LBW* 528)
> Agnus Dei: "O Lamm Gottes unschuldig" (*LBW* 111)
>   or "Christe, du Lamm Gottes" (*LBW* 103)

The cantionales also provided numerous traditional plainsong chants for these texts, and adapted the tunes to German translations of the Latin texts. These were sung by the choir while the congregation was responsible for the lieder (songs or hymns). The choir came to have an important place in Lutheran worship, and polyphonic as well as monophonic settings of texts were provided by various composers. Two early collections

---

[37] See Luther D. Reed, *Worship: A Study of Corporate Devotion* (Philadelphia: Muhlenberg Press, 1959), 166–7. I have been able to examine the Cantionales of Spangenberg and Lossius in the Newberry Library in Chicago. The Rare Book Collection of the Jesuit-Krauss-McCormick Library of the Lutheran School of Theology at Chicago holds original editions of the *Achtliederbuch*, the Erfurt Enchiridion, and other early Lutheran hymnals.

[38] Tappert, 56.

of polyphonic settings of lieder approved by Luther were the songbook of Johann Walther (1524) and the *Neue deutsche geistliche Gesänge* (1544) by the most important publisher of early Lutheranism, Georg Rhau. It is remarkable that among the principal composers of Rhau's collection were no fewer than five who definitely or probably were members of the Catholic church: Stoltzer, Ludwig Senfl, Arnold von Bruck, Stephen Mahu, and the Netherlander Lupus Hellinck. (Senfl carried on clandestine correspondence with Luther while he was in the service of Duke Wilhelm IV of Bavaria and later composed two motets for the reformer.) Rhau's anthology also included masters who were important Lutheran composers: Sixtus Dietrich, Benedictus Ducis, and Balthasar Resinarius.

Polyphonic settings of lieder were needed because the choir alternated with the congregation in singing the many stanzas of the hymns. The hymn texts were considered to be of a whole, and so it was unthinkable to omit stanzas. Consequently, a style of singing the hymns developed whereby the congregation sang some stanzas in unison and unaccompanied, the choir sang other stanzas in unaccompanied polyphonic settings, and the organ introduced the hymn with an improvised prelude and "spelled" the two singing groups by providing improvised interludes. This meant that a tradition developed in Lutheranism of granting the organ an equal place with the congregation and choir as an interpreter of hymns (although virtuoso performances by the organist were regarded as an objectionable assertion of individuality into the service during the sixteenth century).

Latin art music was also produced in great quantity by both Lutheran and Catholic composers. This provided not only motets and anthems that the choir could sing during communion, but also settings of the liturgical texts. Once again Georg Rhau led the way as he endeavored to provide for the early Lutheran churches a comprehensive repertoire for all their liturgical requirements. His *Opus decem missarum* (1541) contained ten four-voice settings of the ordinary of the mass; and his *Vesperarum precum officia* (1540) brought together all the material needed for Vespers. If this polyphonic collection is compared with Lossius's plainsong collection, the following structure of the choral offices can be reconstructed:

> Antiphon (which might be a motet)
> Three or four psalms (sung by the choir)
> The Lesson or Gospel sung in Latin, repeated in German
> Responsory (sung by the choir)
> One or more hymns (probably surrounding the sermon or homily)
> Canticle: Te Deum (Matins)
>   Magnificat (Vespers)
>   Nunc dimittis (Compline)
> Prayers
> Benedicamus Domino (sung by the pastor and choir)

This meant that the typical prayer office was a choral liturgy in which the people participated overtly only in singing some stanzas of the hymns, and which continued to be sung mostly in Latin. In Blume's opinion, the increasing performance of Latin art music in Lutheran services inserted a new division in the church. "The result was not . . . as in the Catholic church, the hierarchical separation into priesthood and laity, but rather the division, by the humanistic order of precedence of the intellectual aristocracy, into the educated and the noneducated."[39] Because of this division Lutheranism offered Calvinism the broadest field of attack; and to it the Reformed church owed its increasing success in Germany. It was able to represent more of a "low culture" appeal in comparison with Lutheranism's "high culture" appeal. Lutheranism's openness to and promotion of the highest expressions of culture has sometimes proven to be more than can be profitably absorbed by the ordinary members of the community of faith.

❧ BAPTISM AND CONFIRMATION

While the church orders, agendas, hymnals, and cantionales moved beyond Luther in terms of their provisions for mass-orders, prayer offices, the church year, hymnody, and music for the liturgy, Luther's order of baptism (*Taufbüchlein*, 1526) remained very influential. Osiander included it in the Brandenburg-Nuremberg church orders, and it was also authorized for use in the church orders for Göttingen (1530), Nordheim (1539), Duke Henry of Saxony (1539), Halle (1541), Schleswig-Holstein (1542), Pomerania (1542), Schweinfurt (1543), Ritzebüttel (1544), and Mecklenburg (1552).[40]

On the other hand, rites of confirmation developed in the Lutheran churches even though Luther never provided one. The first evangelical rite of confirmation (as distinct from catechesis leading to first communion) appeared in the Hessian church in 1538, where it was introduced by Bucer. Bucer had been influenced by Erasmus's proposal of a rite of renewal of baptismal vows. He was also put on the defensive by the Anabaptists who charged the Reformed church with spiritual laxity for permitting infant baptism. When given an opportunity by Philip of Hesse to prepare a church order for Cassel in 1538–1539, Bucer developed a rite that was marked by a public profession of faith and a vow of obedience to Christ and the "holy church." This rite was used to mark the completion of catechetical instruction and served as the gateway to the fellowship of the altar.[41]

Bucer also retained in this rite of confirmation a traditional element: the laying on of hands with the invocation, "Receive the Holy Spirit, protection and guard against all evil, strength and help to all goodness from the gracious hand of God the Father, Son, and Holy Spirit. Amen." There was a great deal of reaction to this practice, and Bucer had to defend himself by asserting that since Jesus and his disciples bestowed blessings with the laying on of hands, it was proper for the church to continue to do so. The Calenberg-Göttingen Order of 1542 retained the rite of the imposition of hands, with the stipulation that it be accompanied by instruction so that it would not revert to papal Affenspiel ("monkey business"—Luther's word for the rite of confirmation). It is clearly stated that the laying on of hands is an outward ceremony, but the Holy Spirit comes through the Word. The various theologians had different opinions of the value of this ceremony,

---

[39] Blume, 122.

[40] See J. D. C. Fisher, *Christian Initiation: The Reformation Period*, op. cit., 25.

[41] See Repp, *Confirmation in the Lutheran Church*, op. cit., 28ff.

which was complicated by Interims that reimposed the Roman rite of confirmation in Lutheran territories. Flacius was vehement in his opposition to it. Brenz believed that the time was passed when it could be employed without offense. Chemnitz, on the other hand, held that the ancient custom should be maintained if it could be done without superstition.[42]

There were, in fact, those Lutherans who wanted to retain as much of the old rite of confirmation as possible. The Mark Brandenburg Order of 1540 retained the name "confirmation," reserved the rite for the bishop when he came to examine the faith of the confirmands, and included the laying on of hands. This traditional rite of confirmation was also restored in many Lutheran territories during the Augsburg and Leipzig Interims, and for that reason it was resisted and rejected when the Interims were rescinded. Nevertheless, in the welter of church orders we see a practice of confirmation developing in the Lutheran churches that included catechesis, examination, a public profession of faith, a promise to remain in this faith and its community, and prayer for the strengthening of the gift of the Holy Spirit accompanied by the laying on of hands. Such were the elements Melanchthon included in the Wittenberg Reformation of 1545, and these elements have become somewhat standard in the Lutheran rite of confirmation.

🍇 CONFESSION AND EXAMINATION

Luther bequeathed to Lutheranism two forms of preparation for Holy Communion that became interrelated in the church orders: private confession and catechetical examination. Private confession, as a form of the Office of the Keys, could serve church discipline and spiritual growth independent of its use in preparation for Holy Communion; nor need private confession be required for Holy Communion. But it became linked in actual practice with a form of preparation for Holy Communion that was required: the catechetical examination. Communicants were to announce to the pastor their intention to receive the sacrament. They were then to be examined to see if they knew the words of institution and the benefits of the sacrament. The pastor could also examine the lives and conduct of the communicants, and this could lead to the application of church discipline in the use of the Office of the Keys. Article XXV of the Augsburg Confession witnesses to the conflation of confession and examination: "Confession has not been abolished in our churches, for it is not customary to administer the body of Christ except to those who have previously been examined and absolved."[43]

The danger was great that some people, especially the educated and noble classes, would be excused from both confession and examination, since the pastor could use discretion to decide who would have to undergo the catechetical examination and how often. Nevertheless, the church orders provided for private confession as well as the catechetical examination, and they could theoretically be distinguished even though they were usually joined in actual practice.

---

[42] See Fisher, 179–81; Repp, 41.
[43] Tappert, 61.

The Cologne Order (1543) provides a typical example of how confession and examination were actually practiced.[44] Those who had announced their intention to receive communion at the Sunday service attended Vespers on Saturday evening. The office included psalmody sung by the clergy and choir boys, a reading with responsory, a hymn, the Magnificat, and collects. Then the congregation sang a German psalm and the pastor read from 1 Corinthians 11 and John 6, after which he gave an exposition on the sacrament and an exhortation to the communicants. This was followed by the examination of the communicants individually, with individual confession and absolution as well. This service was called *Beichtgottesdienst* (Confessional Service).

As the number of communicants became larger (a result of the pastors always exhorting the people to receive the sacrament more frequently), the examination and confession became more perfunctory and absolution was given to several penitents at once. From this it was but a short step to replacing private confession with a general confession. Other factors that contributed to the demise of private confession in later Lutheranism included the revolt against the payment of the *Beichtpfennig* (confession penny) to the priest, and the Pietist dislike of unconditional absolution. Under Reformed influence, Lutheran pietists felt that spiritual direction should be provided and that this could not be done within the formal confines of the confessional service.[45] Nevertheless, this confessional service flourished in Lutheranism for about two centuries after the Reformation, and in some places for even longer. It was revived in the nineteenth century, beginning in the Bavarian town of Neuendettelsau, under Pastor Wilhelm Löhe.[46]

❧ MARRIAGE, MINISTRY TO THE SICK, AND BURIAL

The church orders gave directions for other occasional services. We have seen how Luther simplified the order of marriage. The marriage rites in the church orders tend to be fuller, and they followed the tripartite medieval process of the marriage ritual: publication of the banns before the day of the wedding; the betrothal at the church door; and the blessing before the altar in the church.[47] The rite prepared for Cologne, for example, specified that the couple and their parents should be examined and the banns be published on three successive Sundays. The marriage rite itself was to take place within the Sunday service, which meant that it could be included within the Holy Communion. The custom of having weddings at the Sunday Service of Holy Communion was taken into Anglican practice through the influence of the Cologne church orders and Bucer on the *Book of Common Prayer*.[48] The Cologne marriage rite begins with an exhortation based on scripture quotations. This was followed by the betrothal questions, the exchange of rings, the proclamation of the marriage, and the singing of Psalms 127 and 128 as the

---

[44] See G. J. van de Pol, *Martin Bucer's Liturgical Ideas*, op. cit., 138ff.

[45] See Laurentius Klein, *Evangelisch-Lutherische Beichte: Lehre und Praxis* (Paderborn, 1961), 185ff.

[46] See Gerhard Ottersberg, "Wilhelm Loehe," *Lutheran Quarterly* IV (1952), 180–91.

[47] See Philip Pfatteicher, *Commentary on the Lutheran Book of Worship*, op. cit., 459.

[48] See Marion Hatchett, *Sanctifying Life, Time, and Space: An Introduction to Liturgical Study* (New York: The Seabury Press, 1976), 120.

[49] Richter, II, 30ff.

couple processed to the altar. At the altar there was a blessing of the couple.[49] The blessing of rings was typically omitted in the Reformation church orders. Perhaps the most significant change in Protestant marriage services, beginning with the Brandenburg-Nuremberg Order 1533, was replacing the betrothal question with a declaration of intent ("I, N., take you N., as my wedded spouse and pledge you my troth"), which in later times evolved into an exchange of vows.[50]

The church orders also provided for ministry to the sick. The anointing of the sick, practiced in the medieval rites, was typically omitted because it had become identified only as the "last rites" or "extreme unction." But confession and absolution, scripture reading and exhortation, and the ministration of Holy Communion were customary practices. Mark Brandenburg 1540 provided an extended distribution of communion to the sick. At the conclusion of the Service of Holy Communion the minister, wearing a surplice and preceded by a sacristan carrying a lantern and bell, took the sacrament from the altar to the sick person's home and communed him or her there, after hearing his or her confession.[51]

Luther provided no model for a funeral service as he had of baptism and marriage. Perhaps for this reason there tended to be a greater variety in funeral and burial practices in the church orders.[52] The reformers were opposed to the doctrine of purgatory, since in their view it was based on flimsy biblical evidence and was a source of undermining the believer's confidence in the promise of Christ (John 14). Since requiem masses had been celebrated as vota for the release of the soul from purgatory and promoted fear of judgment (e.g., *Dies Irae*) more than comfort in the consolation of the promises of God to his people, they were abolished. But the evangelical funeral services in the church tended to be adaptations of the little office of the dead. In Mark Brandenburg 1540 this office included several psalms, two or more lessons (1 Thess. 4:13–18; John 11:21–28) with Latin responsories or German hymns between them, the Benedictus, the Lord's Prayer, other collects, and Luther's Nunc dimittis. The Burial of the Dead in Mark Brandenburg included a procession to the grave with cross and lights, while Luther's paraphrase of the medieval antiphon, "Media vita" (*LBW* 350), and his hymn based on De profundis (Ps. 130), "Aus tiefer Not" (*LBW* 295) were sung.[53] Wittenberg 1533 differentiated between the burial of common people (no bells), those of middle degree (singing by school children), and honorable and noble people (procession and bells).[54] Formal prayers of committal of the body were typically omitted, but hymn singing at the grave with the reading of appropriate scripture passages as the body was lowered into the ground were common elements in the practical of burial of the dead.

---

[50] Pfatteicher, 480.
[51] Richter, I, 307ff.; Sehling, I, 264ff.
[52] Pfatteicher, 480.
[53] Richter, I, 307ff.; Sehling, I, 264ff.
[54] Sehling, I, 195.

🍇 LUTHERAN "TRADITIONALISM"

What stands out in the Lutheran church orders, especially when compared with the orders and practices of other Reformation churches, is what Jaroslav Pelikan called "a critical reverence" for the received catholic tradition. The concern of Luther and other reformers was to make worship consonant with Holy Scripture. Sola Scriptura, as a principle of reform, was useful up to a point. The point at which it ceased to be useful was when there were several theological parties and ecclesial communities, each of them appealing to the authority of the Bible. A literal repristination of biblical practice led to scandal in some cases, as when the radical reformers advocated and practiced polygamy by appealing to patriarchal precedent in the Old Testament. (It will be recalled that Luther also brought scandal to the Smalkald League by recommending and defending the bigamy of Philip of Hesse, on the grounds that bigamy was sanctioned by scripture whereas divorce was not.) On theologically substantive issues, both Lutheran and Reformed had to admit, against attacks by the radicals, that infant baptism, though apostolic, was not expressly taught in scripture. Neither were the doctrines of the Trinity or the "satisfaction" theory of the atonement. In the face of all this, Lutherans had to probe the relationship between scripture and tradition, and give theological attention to the role of tradition in the faith and practice of the church.

The theologian who first developed a theory of tradition in Lutheranism was Philipp Melanchthon. Indeed, the historian of dogma, Otto Ritschl, suggested that Melanchthon's "traditionalism" differed in degree, but not in kind, from that of the Council of Trent.[55] Yet Ritschl maintained that it represents one of the major theological strands emanating from Wittenberg. (The other two strands, according to Ritschl, were Luther's soteriological interpretation of scripture as the book of the promises of God and Matthias Flacius's biblicism by which he sought to avert the corrupting influence of philosophy.)

As a humanist scholar, Melanchthon was interested in the publication of critical texts of patristic literature. This was not just a matter of disinterested scholarship. It was rather in the interest of demonstrating the doctrinal continuity between the teachings and practices of the evangelical churches and those of the ancient church, "in so far as the ancient church is known to us from its writers."[56] It was, after all, a commonly accepted definition of heresy that it is a "new teaching." Melanchthon was at pains to demonstrate that "nothing new" was being taught in "our Churches." So he studded the Augsburg Confession with copious patristic citations and aligned the evangelical churches on the side of catholic orthodoxy, as defined in the trinitarian and christological dogmas promulgated by the ecumenical councils of the undivided church. To be sure, under the Justinian Code of the Holy Roman Empire, the evangelical princes and free cities were compelled to accept the "Apostolicam disciplinam Evangelicamque doctrinam Patris et Filii et Spiritus."[57] Otherwise, they would not only lose their right to reform the churches

---

[55] Otto Ritschl, *Dogmengeschichte des Protestantismus*, I (Leipzig, 1908), 338.

[56] See Peter Fraenkel, *Testimonia Patrum. The Function of the Patristic Argument in the Theology of Philipp Melanchthon* (Geneva, 1961), 171ff.

[57] See Werner Elert, *The Structure of Lutheranism*, trans. Walter A. Hansen (St. Louis: Concordia Publishing House, 1962), 274ff.

within their territories; they would also lose the right to rule and could be deposed. But it would be a mistake to think that the confession of the trinitarian faith and the christological dogmas was motivated solely by political necessity. A theological principle was also at stake. This can be seen in the arrangement of the articles of the Augsburg Confession. The first three articles deal respectively with (1) the doctrine of God, (2) original sin, and (3) the doctrine of Christ—all accepted dogmas in the Catholic church. Then comes article IV with its proposal of justification by faith. As Jaroslav Pelikan has observed,

> If the Holy Trinity was as holy as the Trinitarian dogma taught; if original sin was as virulent as the Augustinian tradition said it was; and if Christ was as necessary as the Christological dogma implied—then the only way to treat justification in a manner faithful to the best of Catholic tradition was to teach justification by faith.[58]

Furthermore, justification by faith required what the catholic tradition preserved. How does one receive justifying faith? Article V says saving faith is received through the preaching of the gospel and the administration of the sacraments, through which the Holy Spirit works as through means. This requires a ministry of the word and the sacraments. The preaching of the gospel and the administration of the sacraments bring about a new obedience (article VI), and assembles a community in which the gospel is proclaimed and the sacraments are administered (article VII).

Furthermore, the reformers did not receive these catholic teachings just on an a posteriori basis, because they were judged consonant with scripture, but a priori, as something given and settled. The preface to the Book of Concord speaks of the place of "ancient and received symbols" (*veteribus receptisque symbolis*), and understands this reception as a fact to be accepted, not as a task to be worked out. The inclusion of the three ecumenical creeds (Apostles', Nicene, Athanasian) in the Book of Concord is indicative of the creedal orthodoxy of Lutheranism. So are the condemnatory clauses or anathemas in the Lutheran Confession, which disavow any affinity with the heresies condemned by the catholic tradition.[59] So far from teaching new doctrines, the confessors at Augsburg asserted that "there is nothing here that departs from the Scriptures or the catholic church or the church of Rome, in so far as the ancient church is known to us from its writers."[60] Again, it is asserted in conclusion:

> Only those things have been recounted which it seemed necessary to say in order that it may be understood that nothing has been received among us, in doctrine or in ceremonies, that is contrary to Scripture or to the church catholic. For it is manifest that we have guarded diligently against the introduction into our churches of any new and ungodly doctrines.[61]

Thus, the Augsburg Confession seems to regard tradition as a source and norm for faith and practice. The reformers have been careful not to teach or do anything "that

---

[58] Jaroslav Pelikan, *Obedient Rebels: Catholic Substance and Protestant Principle in Luther's Reformation* (New York and Evanston: Harper and Row, 1964), 47–8.

[59] See Hans-Werner Gensichen, *We Condemn: How Luther and Sixteenth-Century Lutheranism Condemned False Doctrines*, trans. Herbert J. A. Bouman (St. Louis: Concordia, 1967).

[60] Tappert, 47; *Bek.*, 83c.

[61] Tappert, 95; *Bek.*, 134.

is contrary to Scripture or to the church catholic." A concern is expressed to correlate teaching and practice with both sources and norms: scripture and the church catholic. Yet the *traditiones* seem to be referred to in a negative way. So how is tradition understood? The word *traditio* is used in the plural in the Confessions to translate *Menschensatzungen*, that is, *traditiones de cibis et diebus, etc.* (traditions concerning feasts and days, and so forth). Restricting the technical use of "traditio" to "rites and ceremonies instituted by men" gives the term what Pelikan calls "a predominantly pejorative connotation" that "is used to express the Protestant principle of biblical authority."[62] But we have seen the Confession's professed concern to uphold the received teaching and practice. So what is designated by the pejorative term "traditio" is not the creedal or liturgical substance of catholic Christianity, but "the opinion which holds that they justify."[63] Otherwise the Menschensatzungen are given a valuable place in the life of the church.

> We gladly keep the old traditions set up in the churches because they are useful
> and promote tranquility, and we interpret them in an evangelical way, excluding
> the false opinion which holds that they justify.[64]

In support of this assertion he points out how decently the mass is celebrated in "our churches" as opposed to the "papalist churches"; how the children chant psalms and the people sing hymns; how the young people are catechized; and how the gospel is preached regularly in sermons that are based on the Bible. "From this description of the state of our churches it is evident that we diligently maintain church discipline, pious ceremonies, and the good customs of the church."[65]

If, at Augsburg, the confessing princes and free cities could hold that "for the true unity of the church it is enough to agree concerning the teaching of the Gospel and the administration of the sacraments," and also that "it is not necessary that human traditions or rites and ceremonies, instituted by men, should be everywhere alike,"[66] this was because they could presume the continuing ideal of one Western Catholic church within which there could be varying theological positions and different local customs. But the hardening of theological and political positions, resulting in the Smalkald War, made it evident that the Western church had indeed been rent asunder. As various reforming movements solidified into churches, the situation of religious pluralism had to be taken seriously. Lutherans had to define their doctrines and practices over against other Protestant churches as well as the Roman church. In such a situation it was important to develop a more precise clarification of the relationship between the norm of scripture and the norm of tradition.

---

[62] Pelikan, 43.

[63] Apology XV, 38; Tappert, 230.

[64] Ibid.; *Bek.*, 304.

[65] Ibid., XV, 44; Tappert, 221; *Bek.*, 305.

[66] Augsburg Confession VII; Tappert, 32; *Bek.*, 61.

CHAPTER 11

The Spectrum of Reformations

Luther's reformation was neither the only reform movement in the sixteenth century, nor the first. Christian communities in Europe were dissenting from the doctrines, discipline, polity, and liturgy of the Roman church long before Luther. Documentation regarding the practices of the Hussites in Bohemia and the Lollards in England is scarce, but the Unitas Fratrum in Bohemia can be regarded as the oldest Reformation community, and the Anabaptists were organizing in central Europe at the same time as Lutheranism.

A second major reform movement that rivaled Lutheranism was led by Zwingli, Bucer, and Calvin. These reformers, more sophisticated than the men from Wittenberg, planted the Reformation in major commercial centers in Switzerland and the Rhineland, and in many cases succeeded in penetrating the government itself. Both Lutheran and Reformed influences were felt in England during the Reformation under King Edward VI, with a tilt toward the Reformed just before the ascendancy of Mary Tudor, although later under Queen Elizabeth I the Anglican church developed its own unique ethos.

Influencing both Protestant and Roman Catholic reformers were humanists, who in some instances mounted reform programs of their own. They were concerned about curbing superstition, recovering ancient Christian tradition, reestablishing the biblical basis of Christian worship, and making worship more intelligible to the worshiper.

Finally, there was the Roman Catholic response to all these movements, which received definitive articulation at the Council of Trent. It is to this spectrum of reformations, and their liturgical expressions, that this chapter turns.

🍇 UNITAS FRATRUM

The United Brethren, or Bohemian Brethren, or Moravians, as they have been variously called, were the sectarian offspring of the Hussite Movement. They lived from 1457 on in the remote forest regions of eastern Bohemia. The Brethren organized themselves in 1467 according to strict congregational rules, although they did have a bishop. Because of their discipline and literary activity, they continued to gain followers. In 1478, a group of Hussite Waldenses emigrated from Mark Brandenburg and settled east of Landskron (Bohemia) and Fulneck (Moravia) and founded the German branch of Unitas Fratrum.

The Brethren are to be distinguished from the Anabaptists in that they did practice infant baptism, except in the case of Roman Catholic converts. Even this limited practice of rebaptism was given up in 1534 (partly under political pressure). Their simple, extempore rite of baptism included much singing, as did their worship in general.

Their celebration of Holy Communion began with a three-week period of preparation that included both public and private confession. While printed orders are not available there are some descriptions of the Brethren's Communion Service, such as this one from the fifteenth century by Schweinitz:[1]

> A hymn
> Prayer
> Sermon
> Preparation of the table by the pastor and deacons while a hymn is sung
> An exhortation to repentance
> Our Father
> A hymn
> The absolution
> The chanting of the words of institution
> The ministration of Holy Communion while hymns are sung
> Thanksgivings and intercessions
> A blessing

It is evident that there was a generous amount of congregational singing among the Brethren. Hymnals with vernacular songs were published in 1501, 1505, 1519, and 1541, although only this last one survives. This book, edited by Johannes Horn (Jan Roh in Czech), contains 481 songs set to some 300 melodies, thus surpassing any Reformation songbook up to that time. The first official songbook of the Unitas Fratrum was prepared in 1555 by the Brethren Jan Cerny, Jan Blahoslav, and Jiri Sturm. It was completed in manuscript in 1560 and published in Poland a year later. This book was even bulkier than the 1541 hymnal.[2]

There were two main lines of songbooks produced by the Brethren: in Poland in 1561, 1569, and 1587; and in Germany. The Polish branch attained an excellence through

---

[1] See D. H. Tripp, "Protestantism and the Eucharist," in Jones, Wainwright, Yarnold, Bradshaw, eds., *The Study of Liturgy*, 250.

[2] See Walter Blankenburg, "The Music of the Bohemian Brethren," in Blume, ed., *Protestant Church Music*, 593.

the editorial work of the humanist Blahoslav, who was conversant with Reformation song development in both Wittenberg and Geneva. The German branch had its origin in *Ein Neue Gesengbuchlein*, edited by Michael Weisse in 1531. Weisse, according to the book's preface, was a native of Upper Silesia who ministered to Brethren congregations in Landskron and Fulneck. It was based on earlier Czech hymnals, but also bears the influence of Walther's *Geistliche Gesangbüchlein* (Wittenberg, 1524). With its 157 songs, not all with their own tune, it was also the most comprehensive Reformation songbook up to that time. It followed Luther's lead in making use of medieval sacred songs, many of which had already entered the Brethren's repertoire. A comparison of common tunes shows that Weisse retained the original melodic lines more faithfully than Luther did, because Luther often changed tunes for textual reasons.[3]

It should be noted that the use of hymns in worship by the Brethren was strictly liturgical. Hymns served either as responsorial pieces for the congregation or else to cover ritual actions.

Thus began a tradition of congregational singing and a repertoire of congregational songs that predated Luther's reformation and that enriched Lutheran hymnody. The hymnody of the Brethren was enriched in return by the hymns of Lutheran Pietism in the eighteenth century when the remnants of the Unitas Fratrum received shelter and leadership from the Lutheran pietist leader, Count Nicholas von Zinzendorf, and thereafter became known as the Moravian Brethren. A number of *Liturgien* (liturgy books) were published in the eighteenth and nineteenth centuries. These were hymnals with proper prayers and litanies for special seasons and purposes.

✤ THE ANABAPTISTS

The hymnals of the Unitas Fratrum provide a way of tracking the liturgical life of their community. Even this kind of source is lacking among the Anabaptists. Nor was Anabaptism a cohesive movement. It cropped up under various leaders in Switzerland, Germany, the Netherlands, England, northern Italy, and eastern Europe.

The term "Anabaptist" (Rebaptizer) was first used by Ulrich Zwingli, and the first clear rejection of infant baptism occurred in Zurich in the disputes in 1523 and 1525 between Zwingli and Balthasar Hubmaier (c. 1485–1528). The radicals found infant baptism unscriptural and unreasonable; those defending the traditional practice found it scriptural and reasonable. In the end the city council found Zwingli's views more persuasive, and the "rebaptizers" were expelled from the city.

Their contemporaries tended to lump Anabaptists together as subversives who needed to be exterminated. This was a result of the revolutionary fervor stirred up by the militants Thomas Müntzer, Andreas Bodenstein von Karlstadt, and Melchior Hoffmann in the early 1520s. Müntzer, in particular, preached that the elect would rise up and destroy the godless so that the second coming of Christ would take place and the millennium would begin. He tried to anticipate this by establishing a theocracy, the New

---

[3] Ibid., 594–7.

Jerusalem, in the city of Münster. This experiment was put down by Duke George of Saxony and Prince Philip of Hesse, who slaughtered between four and five thousand peasants at Frankenhausen, captured Müntzer, and had him beheaded. But pacifists such as Hubmaier, Conrad Grebel, Felix Mantz, Michael Sattler, Hans Denck, Ludwig Haetzer, Hans Hut, Pilgram Marpeck, and Menno Simons were also considered dangerous. Of this list, all but Marpeck and Simons were martyred in 1526–1528.[4]

Anabaptism was not a unified movement, but there were several motifs the Anabaptists held in common: a rejection of infant baptism, a memorialist view of the Lord's Supper, and an emphasis on cross-bearing. Their stress on righteous suffering and martyrdom was no doubt prompted by the ferocity with which Anabaptists were hounded and killed by Catholics, Lutherans, and Reformed.[5]

These emphases were all present in the writings of the learned layman, Conrad Grebel (1498–1526), a leader of the Swiss Brethren. These Brethren published their *Directory for Christian Living* in 1524, in which they resolved to live according to the teachings of the New Testament and held that baptism must be received in faith. The church should be known by the fruit of its faith, which will include a baptism in blood following the baptism in water. Cross-bearing is as much a sign of the true church as baptism and the Lord's Supper. The Supper was especially important for Grebel, because when celebrated properly it is a reflection of the brotherly love that should characterize all Christians and Christian communities. But it should be celebrated with simplicity and freedom, and while he regarded Müntzer as a brother in the faith Grebel criticized him for his liturgical reforms. Grebel believed that Müntzer's reforms, such as his German Mass and theocratic ideas, were contrary to scripture and in opposition to the ideal of the church as a voluntary body of committed believers.[6]

One of the best known of the Anabaptist martyrs was Michael Sattler (c. 1490–1527), a Benedictine who joined the Swiss Brethren in Zurich, was imprisoned and expelled from that city, and then went to Strasbourg, where he made a major contribution to the Schleitheim Confession. With an eschatological sense of living in the last days, Sattler joined together the themes of church discipline, the centrality of the Supper, and martyrdom. He wrote that

> The Lord's Supper . . . proclaim[s] the death of the Lord, and thereby warn[s]
> each one to commemorate, how Christ gave his life for us, and shed his blood
> for us, that we might also be willing to give our body and life for Christ's sake,
> which means for the sake of the brothers.[7]

One of the most highly trained Anabaptist theologians was Balthasar Hubmeier, who had been a student of Johannes Eck, and followed his mentor in professorships at

---

[4] See Peter C. Erb, "Anabaptist Spirituality," in Frank C. Senn, ed., *Protestant Spiritual Traditions* (Mahwah, N.J.: Paulist Press, 1986), 80ff.

[5] See H. S. Bender, "The Anabaptist Vision," in James M. Strayer and Werner O. Packull, eds., *The Anabaptists and Thomas Müntzer* (Dubuque, Iowa and Waterloo, Ont.: Kendall Hunt, 1980), 14.

[6] See Harold S. Bender, *The Life and Letters of Conrad Grebel* (Goshen, Ind.: The Mennonite Historical Society, 1950). On Müntzer's liturgical reforms see Sehling, I, 497–504 and *Coena Domini*, I, 21–4.

[7] Cited in John H. Yoder, *The Legacy of Michael Sattler* (Scottsdale, Pa.: Herald Press, 1973), 43.

Freiburg and Ingolstadt, where he earned a doctorate. He served as a parish priest in Waldshut, in Austrian-controlled territory in south Germany. There he became caught up in Zwingli's reforms in 1523, but with Grebel pushed reforms beyond what Zwingli would countenance or Zurich would tolerate. Unlike other Anabaptists, Hubmaier believed that the Brethren's ideal of a pure gathered church (a sect) could be reconciled with the idea of a territorial church (a catholic concept). Hubmaier experimented with this in the village of Waldshut, which also became a center of radical peasant protest. In his church laypeople were given the freedom to speak after the sermon, but the form of worship was determined by the pastor. Hubmaier provided "A Form of Christ's Supper" in 1527, which included the following elements:[8]

> Confession of sins, led by the priest, all seeking forgiveness together
> Exposition of the scriptures by the priest
> Opportunity to ask questions or impart revelations
> Self-examination in silent meditation on Christ's passion
> Catechesis about the Lord's Supper and exhortation to Christian life
> Thanksgiving over the bread and cup and the words of institution
> Reception of the bread and cup in silence
> Further exhortation after the meal and dismissal

The complexity of Anabaptist groupings, as well as their desire for extempore worship, makes it difficult to present a general picture of Anabaptist liturgy. Common features, however, included questioning the preacher and sharing insights in the assembly, much exhortation, and space for silent meditation. In Hubmaier's "Form of Christ's Supper," there is much exhortation concerning worthy partaking of the sacrament, personal self-examination to see if one is willing to suffer for Christ, exhortation to brotherly love, and further exhortation to live uprightly in the world—all of which concerned the purity of the gathered community. The wicked who blemished the purity of the community were excommunicated and banned from the assembly. Discipline was especially rigorous among the followers of Menno Simons (c. 1496–1561), who spent much of his time stilling controversies within the flock, especially over questions of marriage when shunning was involved.[9]

Local communities chose their own pastors to preside over gatherings for exposition of the word, prayer, and sacramental worship. One's previous status as a priest or monk was less important for this office than the quality of one's life. The Lord's Supper was celebrated only a few times of the year, but with great intensity of preparation. Baptism was obviously a major event for Anabaptists. The typical rite of baptism began with the candidate confessing his or her sins before the pastor and the congregation and asking for baptism. The preacher asked if anyone in the assembly had any objections. If there were none, the candidate knelt and water was poured "in the Name of the Father

---

[8] See John Rempel, art. on "Historic Models of Worship 170. Anabaptist: Hubmaier's 'A Form for Christ's Supper' (1527)," in Robert E. Webber, ed., *The Complete Library of Christian Worship*, Vol. 2: *Twenty Centuries of Christian Worship* (Nashville: Star Song Publishing Group, 1994), 216–25.

[9] See James F. White, *Protestant Worship: Traditions in Transition* (Louisville: Westminster/John Knox Press, 1989), ch. 5 on "Anabaptist Worship."

and of the Son and of the Holy Spirit." Baptism by immersion was rare until it became the practice of the English Baptists in the seventeenth century.[10] Mennonite worship in general was influenced by contact with Protestant Pietism and Puritanism in the seventeenth and eighteenth centuries.

REFORMED LITURGY

The radicality of Anabaptists such as Conrad Grebel can be measured by the fact that he did not consider Zwingli's reform of church life and liturgy to go far enough. Yet in contrast to the Lutherans, who permitted the retention of forms of the mass and the prayer offices, the church year calendar and lectionary, Latin texts and plain chant, vestments and "east wall" altars, candles and crucifixes, paraments and other accoutrements of worship, Zwingli changed the forms of liturgy, abolished holy days and much of the church year, abandoned the lectionary system of pericopes in favor of a lectio continua of whole books of the Bible, chapter by chapter, and generally retained, in his own words, "as little ceremony as possible."

Nevertheless, Zwingli's initial reforms, like Luther's, were conservative—"for the sake of the weaker brethren." His treatise *De canone missae epichiresis* (1523) specified the use of scripture reading in the vernacular and provided a eucharistic canon consisting of four prayers: a thanksgiving, an epiclesis petitioning the benefits of communion, an anamnesis, and a prayer for worthy reception.[11] Two years later he replaced this Latin liturgy with a German one: *Action oder Brauch des Herren Nachtmal* (1525).[12] This specified that communion would be administered four times a year. The ministers were not to wear any liturgical vesture except for cassock and gown. The altar was replaced with a communion table from which the bread and wine were administered to the people in their seats using wooden trays and cups. The order was as follows:

> Collect (prayer of preparation)
> Epistle: 1 Corinthians 11:20–29 (fixed)
> Gloria (read antiphonally)
> Gospel: John 6:47–63 (fixed)
> Apostles' Creed (read antiphonally)
> Exhortation to the communicants
> Our Father
> Communion prayer (that the communicants may give thanks rightly and live as
>   becomes members of the body of Christ)
> Words of institution (1 Cor. 11:23–26)
> Ministration of Holy Communion (accompanied by the reading of John 13)

---

[10] See H. S. Bender, art. on "Baptism," *Mennonite Encyclopedia* (Hillsboro, Kans., 1955), I, 224–8.

[11] See Bard Thompson, *Liturgies of the Western Church* (The World Publishing Co., 1961), 141ff.; *Coena Domini*, I, 185ff.; Yngve Brilioth, *Eucharistic Faith and Practice: Evangelical and Catholic*, trans. A. G. Hebert (London: S.P.C.K., 1965), 159ff.

[12] See Thompson, 149ff.; *Coeni Domini*, I, 189ff.; William D. Maxwell, *An Outline of Christian Worship: Its Developments and Forms* (London: Oxford University Press, 1936), 81ff.

Psalm 113 (read antiphonally)
Prayer of thanksgiving
Dismissal

Since the city council would not tolerate antiphonal reading of texts by the people, the only congregational participation was reception of communion and an occasional "Amen."

Zwingli's concern was not just to repristinate the original celebration of the Lord's Supper, since every celebration of the Lord's Supper is Christ's. Nevertheless, there was a sense in the Reformed churches that the more biblical or apostolic a practice was, the better it would be. We have already cited Luther's own early view in *The Babylonian Captivity of the Church*, that "the more closely our mass resembles that first mass of all, which Christ performed at the Last Supper, the more Christian it will be."[13] Among the Reformed leaders, however, there was more of an effort to conform contemporary practice with what they believed to be New Testament or patristic practice.[14]

Perhaps most fateful to the Reformed tradition was Zwingli's recommended practice of celebrating the Lord's Supper four times a year. Both Bucer and Calvin advocated celebration of the Lord's Supper every Lord's Day because that had been the apostolic practice. As early as the 1536 edition of the *Institutes of the Christian Religion*, Calvin wrote: "Now as far as the Lord's Supper is concerned, it would have been administered most becomingly if it were offered to the church quite often, and at least once a week."[15] Bucer was able to institute this practice in Strasbourg, at least at the cathedral, but Calvin was never able to institute it in Geneva. The authorities there wanted to maintain agreement with Zwingli's practice at Zürich, which had been accepted in the Reformed Swiss cities and cantons. However, it should be recognized that reception of communion four times a year was the maximum number of times that the most ardent Christians received communion during the Middle Ages. What was important to Zwingli was not the number of times Christians received, but that everyone in the congregation should receive together. The communal or fellowship character of Holy Communion received new emphasis in the Reformed churches, in contrast with the Lutherans who were willing to follow the medieval practice, as indicated in the Apology to the Augsburg Confession: "In our churches Mass is celebrated every Sunday and on other festivals, when the sacrament is offered *to those who wish for it* after they have been examined and absolved" (emphasis added).[16] In his review of the *Prayer Book* of King Edward VI (1549), Martin Bucer commented on the provisions that there must be at least one communicant besides the minister and that everyone shall communicate at least once a year:

> In their place there should be a weighty exhortation to pastors that they should
> teach and exhort their people that just as they should always live in Christ the
> Lord so particularly in the sacrament of the divine supper they should take this

---

[13] LW 36:52.

[14] See Hughes O. Old, *The Patristic Roots of Reformed Worship* (Zürich, 1975).

[15] Cited in Thompson, 185.

[16] Apology XXIV, 1; Tappert, 249.

life from the Lord as often as it is celebrated in the holy assembly; and they should show how great an insult they offer to Christ if they neglect to do this.[17]

The liturgy of the Lord's Supper was not the usual Sunday observance in Reformed Switzerland. Zwingli had developed a liturgy of the word out of the medieval office of Prone. This had been a pulpit office, used either during the mass or as a special office during preaching missions. In Zwingli's use (at least in the early years of the Reformation), Prone retained curious bits of late medieval liturgical piety. Its order was as follows:[18]

> The Our Father (Lord's Prayer)
> An Ave Maria
> A Sermon
> A remembrance of those who had died during the previous week
> Another Our Father
> Another Ave Maria
> The Apostles' Creed
> The Decalogue
> Confession and absolution (if the mass were to follow)

Bucer followed (and helped to mold) the Lutheran practice of celebrating the Ante-Communion (fore-mass or liturgy of the word) if Holy Communion was not to be celebrated. As a witness to his own conviction that Sunday worship without the Lord's Supper was a defective practice, the typical Sunday liturgy prescribed by Calvin for use in Geneva in 1542, under the title *La forme de prières et chantz ecclésiastique avec la manière d'administer les sacrements*, was also Ante-Communion. It began with the verse, "Our help is in the Name of the Lord," a congregational confession of sins, the singing of the Decalogue, a prayer for divine help, and a psalm. Then the minister went into the pulpit, offered a prayer for illumination, read a chapter of the gospels, and expounded on it. After the sermon there was intercessory prayer and the Lord's Prayer.

Under the heading, "La maniere de célébrer la cene," Calvin provided that on communion Sundays the Apostles' Creed would mark the transition to the celebration of the Lord's Supper. The Table was furnished during the Creed. There followed a prayer of humble access, a lengthy exhortation to the communicants, a reading of the institution narrative from 1 Corinthians 11 (as a warrant for the celebration, not as an act of consecration), the "fencing of the table" with the exclusion of immoral and irreligious persons, and an invitation to the rest to examine themselves, cling to the promises of Christ conveyed in this sacrament, and lift up their hearts "on high where Jesus Christ is in the glory of his Father." Communion followed, accompanied by psalms and readings. The service ended with a prayer of thanksgiving, the singing of the Nunc dimittis, and a benediction.[19]

---

[17] E.C. Whitaker, ed., *Martin Bucer and the Book of Common Prayer*. Alcuin Club Collections No. 55 (Great Wakering: Mayhew-McCrimmon, 1974), 30.

[18] Howard G. Hageman, *Pulpit and Table* (Richmond: John Knox Press, 1962), 17.

[19] Thompson, 197–210; *Coeni Domini*, I, 347ff. See William D. Maxwell, *The Liturgical Portions of the Genevan Service Book* (London, 1965).

Calvin adapted this order of service from the German liturgy used in Strasbourg while he was serving as pastor to the French-speaking congregation in that city. He brought it with him when he was recalled to Geneva in 1542 with few modifications. It was further translated and adapted by John Knox, who had experienced it at Geneva, for use in the Church of Scotland, where it supplanted the *Book of Common Prayer* in 1562 as the definitive Scottish rite under the title *The Book of Common Order*.

The Scottish liturgy was no slavish imitation of the Genevan liturgy, because Knox supplied new intercessions and a new prayer of consecration in the Service of Holy Communion, and the influence of the 1552 *Book of Common Prayer* is still detectable in the Exhortation to Communion and in the Order of Marriage. Calvin's influence is evident in the fact that Ante-Communion remained the chief Sunday service when Holy Communion was not celebrated. The first communion rubric in the *Book of Common Order* suggested that communion be celebrated once a month. In subsequent practice, however, the Church of Scotland celebrated Holy Communion four times a year as in Zürich and Geneva. Lest these communion Sundays be associated with the church year, which was abolished, the times tended to be fixed on the first Sundays of March, June, September, and December. However, the practice of quarterly communions did not imply a Zwinglian understanding of the Lord's Supper. The first Scots Confession said: "We utterly damn the vanity of those who affirm sacraments to be nothing else but naked and bare signs." The approved doctrine, set forth in the confession and in the exhortation, was Calvinist: "We spiritually eate the fleshe of Christ, and drinke his bloude; then we dwell in Christ, and Christ in us; we be one with Christ, and Christ with us."[20]

In spite of differences between the Reformed liturgies of Strassburg, Geneva, and Scotland, the similarities between them are striking.[21] The major difference between Bucer's liturgy and those of Calvin and Knox is the juxtaposition of the words of institution and the ministration of communion, which in Bucer's order is similar to Luther's *Deutsche Messe* and the 1552 *Book of Common Prayer*. The other liturgies moved the words of institution to a position in which they would serve as warrants for the celebration and not suggest an actual consecration. The following chart demonstrates the common order of these Reformed liturgies.

STRASSBURG GERMAN 1537	STRASBOURG FRENCH 1540 / GENEVA 1542	SCOTLAND 1562
	Verse: Psalm 124:8	
Confession of Sins	Confession of Sins	Confession of Sins
Words of Pardon	Words of Pardon (Prayer for Pardon 1542)	Prayer for Pardon
Absolution	Absolution	
Psalm, hymn, or Kyrie and Gloria	Metrical Decalogue with Kyrie response after each law (Kyrie deleted 1542)	Metrical Psalm

---

[20] Cited in Thompson, 291–2.

[21] See the chart comparing these orders of service in Maxwell, *An Outline of Christian Worship*, 114–5, 129–30.

Collect for Illumination	Collect for Illumination	Illumination
Lection (Gospel)	Lection	Lection
Sermon	Sermon	Sermon
Collection of alms	Collection of alms	Collection of alms
Preparation of the elements while Apostles' Creed is sung		
Intercessions and Consecration Prayer	Intercessions	Thanksgiving and Intercessions
Lord's Prayer	Lord's Prayer in paraphrase	Lord's Prayer
	Preparation of elements while Apostles' Creed is sung	Preparation of elements while Apostles' Creed is sung
	Consecration Prayer (1540 location)	
	Lord's Prayer (1540 location)	
Exhortation	Words of Institution	Words of Institution
Words of Institution	Exhortation	Exhortation
	Consecration Prayer (1542 location)	Consecration (new prayer)
Fraction	Fraction	Fraction
Ministration of Communion while psalm or hymn is sung	Ministration of Communion while psalm is sung	Ministration of Communion while Passion History is read
Post-communion collect	Post-communion collect	Post-communion thanksgiving
		Psalm 113 in meter
Aaronic benediction	Aaronic benediction	Aaronic benediction
Dismissal		

There are some instances of similarity between Lutheran and Reformed liturgy simply in terms of some shared Reformation ideas. But the dissimilarities between Lutheran and Reformed liturgies are striking. They were in obvious agreement on the centrality of the word in worship in terms of scripture and in preaching. But Lutherans were content to retain the historic lectionaries of the church and to preach on the pericopes. Only occasionally and on weekdays were biblical books read in course with sermons based on them. Both Lutheran and Reformed preaching tended to be a verse-by-verse exposition of the text. Luther's preaching style served as a model for his followers in his constant flow between the historical situation of the text and the contemporary situation of the believer. Zwingli blazed a more thoroughgoing path of reform for preaching. Already in 1519 he started preaching his way through the Gospel according to Matthew verse by verse, day after day for a whole year, and did so in a systematic expository fashion that followed the forms of classical rhetoric. He took as his model the great fourth-century preacher, John Chrysostom.[22]

---

[22] Hughes O. Old, *Worship That is Reformed According to the Scripture* (Atlanta: John Knox Press, 1984), 69.

The Reformed influence was great in the Rhineland between Strassburg and Basel. There had existed in this area a tradition of preaching, and endowed pulpits, going back to the fifteenth century. Johann Geiler von Kayserberg (1445–1510) preached regularly at the cathedral at Strasbourg. Johannes Heynlin von Stein (1430–1496), former rector of the University of Paris, retired to Basel's Carthusian monastery and preached regularly at Basel's cathedral. Johann Ulrich Surgant (1450–1503) preached at the Saint Theodore Church in the suburbs of Basel. In 1518 Johann Oecolampadius (1483–1531), a Christian humanist like Zwingli who had mastered Greek and Hebrew, was called as preacher for the endowed pulpit at Augsburg. He translated many of the great sermons of the church fathers from Greek to Latin, thus making them available to the Western church for the first time. In 1523, Oecolampadius was invited by the city council of Basel to preach on Isaiah. His scholarly preaching so completely won the city that by 1529 it officially embraced the Reformation.[23]

Another area where Lutheran and Reformed liturgy diverged even more strikingly was in public prayer. Lutherans were content to use the classical prayers of the church—collects and litanies. The Reformed sought a greater role for prayer in public worship. The recovery of a comprehensive intercessory prayer became an important feature of worship at Strassburg. In prayers composed by Martin Bucer, the influence of Paul's instruction to Timothy (1 Tim. 2:1–8) is transparent: petitions are offered for the civil authorities, for the ministry of the gospel, for the conversion of humankind, for the perfection of the saints, and for the afflicted. In addition to the general intercessory prayer, the Strasbourg liturgy included a congregational prayer of confession based on the medieval Confiteor. These two types of prayers were translated into French, and, as we have seen, became a part of the Genevan liturgy through Calvin's influence. John Knox (1513–1572) used these prayers as models for similar prayers in the *Book of Common Order* of the Church of Scotland. In addition, he composed a eucharistic prayer that is a thanksgiving for the works of creation and redemption. It celebrates both the grace we have received in this life and the life to which we look forward in the kingdom of heaven.[24]

In addition to written prayer texts, Reformed pastors were interested in developing extemporaneous prayer in public worship on the basis of Romans 8, that prayer is a sanctifying work of the Holy Spirit in human hearts. Calvin used to conclude sermons with extemporaneous prayers, hundreds of which have come down to us from stenographers who also recorded the sermons. For Calvin, hearing the word of God naturally led to prayer. Thus, in the Genevan tradition, there was a balance between written prayers and extemporaneous prayers. The later Puritans in England would emphasize extemporaneous prayers over the written prayers.[25]

Lutheran and Reformed liturgies also differed in the role of music in worship. As we have seen, Luther himself encouraged the adaptation of medieval hymns and the

---

[23] Ibid., 70.
[24] Jasper and Cuming, *Prayers of the Eucharist*, op. cit., 253–7.
[25] Old, *Worship That is Reformed*, 99–100.

composition of new hymns for congregational use in the liturgy. Gregorian chant and polyphonic music were also sung by the choirs. Organs and other instruments were used in the church, although these were not at first used to accompany congregational or choral singing, but to introduce and alternate with it. Zwingli, on the other hand, who had received a good musical education, forbade any music in the liturgy. This was a consequence of his peculiar understanding of prayer: "In your devotion you should be alone. Devotion is falsified by the participation of many."[26] He regarded singing and instrumental music as distracting to contemplation. The church organs in Zürich were accordingly sold. This point of view may have been the product of Zwingli's training in art music, and his lack of awareness of the realm of folk music and its role in the lives of people.[27]

When John Calvin came to Strasbourg, on the other hand, he was impressed by the congregation's singing of metrical versions of biblical texts. He made use of metrical psalms for his French-speaking congregation from Clement Marot's *Aulcunes pseulmes et cantiques my en chant* (Strasbourg, 1539), and took this practice with him to Geneva. He encouraged Marot to continue working on psalm translations, which were published as the *Pseulmes de David* (Antwerp, 1541). Marot died in 1544 and Theodore Beza completed the full Geneva Psalter (1551). Calvin also secured the services of the composer Louis Bourgeois in providing tunes for these psalms. The complete French Psalter, *Pseulmes de David* (Paris, 1562), contained 125 tunes, seventy of which were composed by Bourgeois. It was published in France because Calvin objected to the harmonizations Bourgeois wanted to include in it; the people were to sing an unadorned melody line.[28]

The production of the psalter, with Marot's and Beza's texts and Bourgeois's elegant tunes, was a significant achievement in the history of church music. Those English Protestants who fled to Geneva in 1553 to escape persecution under the reign of Mary Tudor were also captivated by it, and brought the concept of the metrical psalter back to England and Scotland. Following the example of the Geneva Psalter, each psalm and canticle was wedded to its own tune. Hence the name of the psalm tune takes the name of the psalm: for example, "Old Hundredth," "Old 124th." While this practice was not strictly adhered to in England, it was in Geneva and Scotland. This meant that once the psalter was collected, there was nothing further to do except to revise it periodically. By contrast, the great age of Lutheran hymnody was yet to come in the seventeenth century.

There are similarities and dissimilarities between the Lutheran and Reformed orders for Holy Communion. Bucer took over Luther's rubrics from the *Formula Missae* whereby the bread and wine were prepared on the table during the singing of the Creed. But the Reformed liturgies replaced the Nicene Creed with the Apostles'. Bucer also juxtaposed the words of institution and the administration of the elements, as in Luther's *Deutsche Messe*. But, as we have seen, Calvin pushed the words of institution away from the ministration so as not to suggest that the Verba are consecratory. They had been the

---

[26] See Walter Blankenburg, "Church Music in Reformed Europe," in Blume, *Protestant Church Music*, 510.

[27] See Eric Routley, *Music Leadership in the Church* (Nashville: Abingdon, 1967), 23ff. on the tension between art music and folk music in worship.

[28] See Carol Ann Doran, "Metrical Psalmody," in Marilyn Kay Stulken, ed., *Hymnal Companion to the Lutheran Book of Worship* (Philadephia: Fortress Press, 1981), 58–67.

moment of consecration (i.e., of transubstantiation) in the medieval scholastic theology, and Calvin was concerned to avoid this connotation. He also provided a consecration prayer that did not include the words of institution. The fraction preceded the ministration of Holy Communion; and often loaves of bread were used instead of the wafers. We have seen the Lutheran aversion to any fraction at all, especially a symbolic one. Lutherans continued to kneel to receive communion. Reformed practice varied considerably. In Zwingli's practice, the people sat while the bread and wine were passed through the pews. In Bucer's orders the people stood around the table to receive the elements. In Knox's Scottish order, communicants sat at tables set up in the chancel.

The Reformed were one with the Lutherans in defending the practice of infant baptism against the Anabaptists. Unlike the Lutherans, the Reformed insisted on the public nature of baptism and allowed private baptisms only in emergency situations. They rejected all ceremonies as superstitious (including the exorcisms, signations, blessing of the font, anointings, vesting of the baptized, and presentation of the candle) except for the use of water, which was administered by affusion (pouring). Their rites did typically rehearse the Apostles' Creed and Lord's Prayer and make use of the trinitarian formula, but their orders were provided with new prayers and exhortations. The use of godparents was not rejected, but there was a sense among the Reformed that the congregation is the real sponsor of baptism.

We have seen that Bucer retained a rite of confirmation as the conclusion of catechetical instruction, a renewal of baptismal vows, and an admission to Holy Communion. It consisted of examination of the candidates, the laying on of hands, and prayer. By the time he collaborated on the Cologne Church Order he felt that it should be conducted by the bishop or superintendent as a way of getting the overseer to visit the congregations and standardize instruction. While Calvin denounced the Roman practice of confirmation, especially the use of chrism, he retained the kind of ceremony envisioned by Bucer as a form of church discipline.

Bucer had developed a strong sense of church discipline as a result of his controversy with the Anabaptists. He proposed a rite of ordination that would be altered to fit the setting apart of bishops, presbyters, and deacons. The names of candidates for ordination were read out on the Sunday prior to the ordination. The rite of ordination included the liturgy of the word with readings and sermon, an exhortation and examination of the candidates, congregational silent prayer and the singing of "Veni, Sancte Spiritus," prayer and the imposition of hands, and the eucharistic rite beginning with the Creed. Among the Reformed, ministers were elected by the congregation, prayed for by both the people and the presbytery, and sometimes accomplished by the laying on of hands. A functional view of the ordained ministry led to the practice of reordaining ministers who received calls to different communities.[29]

This communal sense of liturgy among the Reformed influenced marriage rites as well. Weddings were typically conducted during the Sunday service, the banns having been published beforehand. But the blessing or giving of rings was typically rejected. The

---

[29] See Maxwell, *The Liturgical Portions of the Geneva Service Book*, 58–60, 165–74.

Reformed aversion to the blessing of material objects had a consequence on burial practice also: There was typically no rite of committal of the body other than the reverent burial. But burial was often followed by a service of psalms, readings, sermon, and prayers in the church building to comfort the bereaved and to edify the community.

THE ANGLICAN REFORMATION

The Reformation came later to England than to the countries of central Europe and it followed there a very different course. One feature of the English situation that differentiated it from other situations was the prestige and authority of the English monarchy. There was also a close bond between the crown and the church hierarchy, which stood Henry VIII in good stead when he initiated his divorce proceedings against Catherine of Aragon. On the other hand, Henry was not in a position to initiate the more radical ideas of the Reformation because, by and large, the English people were not disaffected from the church. The standard of outward observance of religion was relatively high in England, if attendance at mass and bequests to parish churches are any indication, even though the intellectual climate of religion in England was low, if measured in terms of the production and publication of books.[30]

Nevertheless, Lutheran books were entering the country all during the 1520s, and Lutheran ideas were being discussed in the lowland areas of southeastern England. A group of Cambridge dons met regularly at the White Horse Tavern to discuss these ideas. While there were efforts at suppressing these ideas with the exile of William Tyndale and later the burning at the stake of "little Bilney" (1531) and Friar Robert Barnes (1540), Lutheran influence continued in England up to the reign of Edward VI and the publication of the first *Book of Common Prayer*.[31]

Lutheran influence was evident in the personal life of Thomas Cranmer, archbishop of Canterbury (1533–1556), and principal leader of the English Reformation. He had been in the Lutheran city of Nuremberg in 1532 while serving as Henry's ambassador to the court of Emperor Charles V. He there observed Lutheran services, conversed with the city's celebrated pastor, Andreas Osiander, and married Osiander's niece. Upon his return to England, Henry nominated Cranmer to become archbishop of Canterbury, presumably because he was a trusted ally of the king and could be counted on for support in the complicated case of Henry's annulment from Catherine of Aragon. Indeed, two months after his consecration Cranmer fulfilled the king's desire by releasing him from his marriage to Catherine and crowning the Protestant Anne Boleyn as Queen of England. When Catherine appealed to the pope, Henry severed his ties with the papacy and was proclaimed supreme head of the church in England. But the king on whom the pope had previously bestowed the title "Defender of the Faith" because of his writings against Luther continued to display a steadfast religious conservatism, not unlike that of his people. Cranmer's position as a champion of reform was compromised by Henry's

---

[30] See T. M. Parker, *The English Reformation to 1558* (London: Oxford University Press, 1966), chapters 1 and 2.

[31] See Henry Eyster Jacobs, *The Lutheran Movement in England during the Reigns of Henry VIII and Edward VI, and Its Literary Monuments* (Philadelphia: Frederick, 1892).

promulgation in 1539 of Six Articles, which asserted transubstantiation, communion under one kind, clerical celibacy (Cranmer had to send his wife back to Germany), monastic vows, private masses, and auricular confession. At the same time Henry employed Protestant tutors for Prince Edward, and by his own intervention rescued Cranmer from charges of heresy on several occasions.[32]

In spite of Henry's traditional theological views, Cranmer was able to preside over a slow implementation of the Reformation. The first complete English translation of the Bible was completed by Myles Coverdale and published abroad in 1535. The revision of this translation in 1539 became known as the "Great Bible," and Cranmer wrote no fewer than five of the seven prefaces to succeeding editions. A new English Primer was published in 1534 under Cranmer's direction. There was also an attempt to formulate religious doctrine in Ten Articles of 1536 based on the Augsburg Confession. These articles were revised in 1537 in a document known as the Bishops' Book, but royal assent was never given. A third revision resulted from alterations made by Henry himself and in this form it became known as the King's Book.

What was implicit in this early body of work was soon made explicit in the revision of liturgical materials. Cranmer found ample excuse to undertake this work of liturgical revision in the general disarray of liturgical books throughout England. He revised the Sarum (Salisbury) Breviary and then set to work on an English Processional or Litany, which appeared in 1544.[33]

Real liturgical change occurred after the death of King Henry VIII on January 28, 1547. He was succeeded by the ten-year-old (and sickly) Edward VI. After Edward's coronation on April 11 liturgical and doctrinal reform proceeded more quickly. There was a royal visitation of parishes, much like the Saxon visitations. It resulted in the English translation of A Simple and Religious Consultation, the church order of Archbishop Hermann von Wied of Cologne, the joint work of Bucer and Melanchthon (revised in 1548). In 1548 Cranmer himself translated into English the Lutheran Catechism of Nuremberg, from a Latin edition by Justus Jonas, under the title, *Catechismus, that is to say a Shorte Instruction into the Christian Religion*. This was the year of the Grand National Debate on eucharistic faith and practice in Parliament. With this catechism in use, Cranmer himself had not advanced beyond a Lutheran understanding of the real presence.[34] Also in response to the visitations, thirty-seven Royal Injunctions were imposed, making significant changes in worship practices. The Epistles and Gospels were to be read and the Litany to be sung in English. A *Book of Homilies* was published in 1548 as a basis for uniform teaching. There were some initial experiments in rendering canticles, such as "Glory be to God on high," into English. In January of 1548, candles at Candlemas, ashes on Ash Wednesday, and palms on Palm Sunday were all suppressed. In March of 1548 an order known as The Order of Communion, based on material in the

---

[32] See J. G. Ridley, *Thomas Cranner* (Oxford University Press, 1962), 92–3.

[33] See E. C. Ratcliff, "The Liturgical Work of Archbishop Cranmer," *Journal of Ecclesiastical History* 7 (1956), 189–203.

[34] Ibid., 281.

Consultation of Archbishop Hermann, was interpolated before the distribution of Holy Communion in the Latin mass. It included two exhortations, an invitation to Holy Communion, a confession of sins, absolution, the "Comfortable Words," a "Prayer of Humble Access," the words of administration of the sacrament, and a blessing. Communion was to be administered under both species.

This period of experimentation came to an end with the publication of the First Prayer Book of King Edward VI in 1549, entitled *The Booke of Common Prayer and Administration of the Sacraments, and other Rites and Ceremonies of the Churche, after the Use of the Churche of England*. It was a remarkable achievement, containing the mass, the prayer offices, and other occasional services all in English. An Act of Uniformity passed by Parliament required its exclusive use throughout the realm by Whitsunday, June 9, 1549.[35] This Act of Uniformity was itself a departure from the pre-Reformation situation in England, in which there were at least six ritual uses. The most prevalent of these uses was that of Salisbury Cathedral, usually called by its Latin name *Sarum*. Since Thomas Cranmer depended heavily on the Use of Sarum as a model, this rite was given a wider influence through the *Booke of Common Prayer* than it may have had before the Reformation.

Nevertheless, the orders in the *Booke of Common Prayer* are not simply translations and revisions of the medieval Use of Sarum. The influences of German church orders on the Prayer Book are obvious, and have been noted by older scholars.[36] We may note the fusion of the offices of Matins and Lauds to form an Order of Morning Prayer and the fusion of Vespers and Compline to form an Order of Evening Prayer. This was inspired by several German church orders, especially Calenburg and Göttingen 1542. Cranmer also drew on the proposed revisions of the Roman Breviary by Cardinal Quinonez in 1536, which is reflected in the course of psalmody and the daily lectionary, as well as in the elimination of the antiphons and responsories. The Litany was based largely on the Sarum Processional and Luther's German Litany.

The communion service began with a whole psalm serving as the Introit, as Luther suggested in his *Deutsche Messe*. During the choral introit the priest said the Lord's Prayer and the Collect for Purity. The Collect for Purity is a prayer with roots in the Gregorian Sacramentary used in various places in medieval missals. It was used in the Sarum rite as part of the preparation for mass, and Cranmer continued this use in the English Prayer Book. Marion J. Hatchett has shown that in translating the collects Cranmer sometimes worked from the texts in the German church orders, not in the medieval English rites.[37] Phrases in the prayer "for the whole state of Christes church" are

[35] For a chronicling of liturgical change in England during the reigns of Henry VIII and Edward VI see Aidan Kavanagh, *The Concept of Eucharistic Memorial in the Canon Revisions of Thomas Cranmer, Archbishop of Canterbury 1533–1556* (St. Meinrad, Ind.: St. Meinrad Abbey Press, 1964), 1–45.

[36] See F. E. Brightman, *The English Rite: Being a Synopsis of the Sources and Revisions of the Book of Common Prayer with an Introduction and an Appendix*, 2 vols. (London: Rivington, 1915) and E. C. Ratcliff, *The Booke of Common Prayer of the Churche of England: Its Making and Revisions MDXLIX–MDCLXI* (London: S.P.C.K., 1949).

[37] Marion J. Hatchett, *Commentary on the American Prayer Book* (New York: Seabury, 1980).

derived from Archbishop Hermann's *Consultation*, as are the exhortations, invitation, confession, absolution, "Comfortable Words," "Prayer of Humble Access," and administration formulas of the communion rite. The institution narrative is similar to the one in the Brandenburg-Nuremberg Order. In a provision similar to communion directives in Luther's *Formula Missae*, those who were to receive communion were to move from the nave into the chancel during the offertory. The effect of this provision was to treat the nave as a room for the liturgy of the word, centered about the pulpit, and the chancel as a room for the liturgy of the Lord's Supper, centered about the altar.

Typically the third liturgical center was the font, located near the west door. The Order of Baptism in the 1549 Prayer Book was drawn from the work of Bucer in Archbishop Hermann's *Consultation*, which in turn had been drawn from the work of Osiander in the Brandenburg-Nuremberg Order, which in turn had utilized the Order of Baptism in Luther's Second *Taufbüchlein*. Not surprisingly, the Prayer Book's "Administracion of Publyke Baptisme" bears resemblances to Luther's order, including an English translation of Luther's "Flood Prayer." It also included a post-baptismal anointing, although this was done after the vesting in the christening gown rather than before the vesting (as in the medieval rites). A catechism modeled on that in the Consultation was also included in the Prayer Book, under the heading "Confirmation." Showing the influence of Bucer, the rite of confirmation began with a renewal of baptismal vows, followed by the laying on of hands and prayer. The apology for noncompulsory private confession for those whose consciences were not quieted by "their humble confession to God," and "the generall confession to the churche," were reminiscent of several German church orders. The Consultation and other German church orders are among the sources of the Order of Marriage in the Prayer Book. The 1549 Prayer Book also made provision for the Communion of the Sick from the reserved sacrament on days of a public communion, as in the Mark Brandenburg Order. The Order of the Burial of the Dead was also framed within the structure of a prayer office, as in Mark Brandenburg and other church orders.[38]

There are other influences and sources of the 1549 Prayer Book than these we have indicated, including the writings of the church fathers, Eastern liturgies, Gallican rites, and various medieval uses of the Roman rite. But the influence of the continental Reformation church orders has loomed in importance in modern studies of the *Book of Common Prayer*. If the 1549 *Book of Common Prayer* was not entirely a "Lutheran Book," it was, nevertheless, a Reformation prayer book closer in spirit to the Lutheran Reformation than to any other.

Aidan Kavanagh has demonstrated that the 1549 eucharistic prayer was a reworking of the Roman canon.[39] Yet even here there were models emanating from Strasbourg and Brandenburg that Cranmer could consult, and that themselves were reworkings of the Roman canon. For example, the eucharistic prayer in the 1549 *Book of*

---

[38] For texts see *The First and Second Prayer Books of King Edward VI*. Everyman's Library 448 (London: Dent and New York: Dutton, 1910).

[39] See Kavanagh, *The Concept of Eucharistic Memorial* . . . , 219ff.

Common Prayer begins with the preface with several seasonal propers and the Sanctus and Benedictus, and then proceeds into the intercessions and commemorations, which would have been comparable to the Te igitur, Memento, Communicantes, and Memento etiam of the Roman canon. Yet, as we have seen, the Mark Brandenburg Order 1540 also has proper prefaces, Sanctus and Benedictus, and four intercessory prayers that were recited silently during the singing of the Sanctus. The first of the four prayers in Mark Brandenburg was for the emperor and civil rulers, in lieu of the prayer for the pope in the Te igitur. Cranmer substituted intercession for the king in place of the prayer for the pope. The consecration prayers in the succession of German masses in Strasbourg began with allusions to biblical references admonishing Christians to assemble in Jesus' name and "pray for those with authority over us";[40] so does the 1549 eucharistic prayer. Alluding to 1 Timothy 2:1–6, the prayer begins: "Almightye and euerliuying God, which by thy holy Apostle haste taught us to make prayers and supplicacions, and to geue thankes for all menne."

There is no question that Cranmer followed the Roman canon more faithfully than did his German models. His tailoring of the text of the canon to make it acceptable to Reformation concerns is nothing short of ingenious. The commemoration of the saints is a praise and thanksgiving "for the wonderfull grace and vertue, declared in all thy sainctes, from the begynning of the world," rather than an invocation of the saints. The faithful departed are commended to the mercy of God in anticipation of "the day of the generall resurrecion," thus eliminating any idea of purgatory. Most famously, Cranmer added a gloss to the *Hanc igitur*'s petition for the fruits of the oblation by calling to mind Christ's "full, perfect, and sufficient sacrifyce, oblacion, and satysfaccyon, for the sinnes of the whole worlde" (comparable to Mark Brandenburg's prayer for the forgiveness of sins as the equivalent of the Hanc igitur). The consecratory epiclesis in the Roman canon is the *Quam oblationem,* in which God is asked to bless the oblation of the church. Kavanagh has suggested that Cranmer introduced something like an invocation of the Trinity by asking the Father to bless the gifts and "creatures" of bread and wine "with thy holy spirite and word."[41] However, by "word" Cranmer probably means not the Logos, or second person of the Trinity, but the word of scripture, since the institution narrative follows the epiclesis and it closely follows 1 Corinthians 11:23–25. In the equivalent of the Unde et memores, "Wherefore, O Lorde," it is made clear that what is done in the eucharist is not to offer Christ (implied in the offering of the bread of eternal life and the cup of eternal salvation), but to "celebrate and make here . . . the memoryall whyche thy sonne hath wylled us to make." Yet there is a sacrifice that the church makes. In place of the references to the offerings of Abel, Abraham, and Melchizedek, which could be associated with the sacrifice of the mass, the 1549 eucharistic prayer offers "this our Sacrifice of praise and thankes geuing" as well as "oure soules, and bodies, to be a reasonable, holy, and liuely sacrifice unto thee." In the *Supplices te,* the ministry of the angels is sought to carry not our oblations but "our prayers and supplicacions" to the heavenly tabernacle.

---

[40] See Maxwell, *An Outline of Christian Worship*, 95, 106.

[41] Kavanagh, 192.

In spite of the great care taken to express Reformation teachings within a Catholic order of service, it seemed that no one was satisfied with the First Prayer Book. Popular resentment had been building against religious changes since the fall of 1536 when the people of the north country embarked on the "Pilgrimage of Grace." The new Prayer Book became the occasion for further violence. The clergy of Oxfordshire refused to use it and riots broke out in twelve counties from north to south. In the western shires of Devon and Cornwall formidable rebellion was occasioned in part because of the fact that the vernacular language in these areas was a Celtic dialect and the Act of Uniformity imposed an English-language liturgy on the people. The result of all this unrest was a coup d'etat by conservative nobles that toppled the Lord Protector, the king's uncle, Edward Seymour, Duke of Somerset. But the radicals quickly regrouped and installed to the presidency of the Council of Regents the unscrupulous John Dudley, Earl of Warwick. Warwick was regarded as an ally by the more radical reformers because of his liquidation of the wealth of the monasteries and endowed chantries to fill the royal treasury. John Hooper, bishop of Glouchester and a radical Zwinglian, rose to a leadership position, and even Cranmer had to proceed with caution.

A new Ordinal was promulgated in 1550 that was based extensively on Bucer's *De Ordinatione legitima ministrorum ecclesiae revocanda*. It placed occupants of ecclesiastical office on the same spiritual plane as occupants of civil office, and removed the priest's sacrificial function entirely. In order to combat priests who would "counterfeit the popish mass" using the new communion service, the Council ordered the destruction of all altars throughout the realm on November 23, 1550. They were to be replaced with tables at which the Lord's Supper could be eaten rather than the sacrifice of the mass offered. The old service books were also to be destroyed, and in the course of doing this the royal bailiffs also confiscated a good deal of church plate. Princess Mary, the daughter of King Henry VIII and Queen Catherine of Aragon, the next in line to the throne and a Catholic, had been allowed to have the Latin mass celebrated in her private chapel. She was now subjected to such harassment that the Emperor Charles V laid plans to rescue her from England.

Conservative bishops who would not countenance such measures, such as Stephen Gardiner of Winchester and Edmund Bonner of London, were imprisoned and replaced by more radical bishops such as Hugh Latimer and Nicholas Ridley. Cranmer invited to England some of the leading reformers from the continent and gave them prestigious and influential positions. Martin Bucer was given a professorship at Cambridge and Pietro Vermigli (Peter Martyr) taught at Oxford. Philipp Melanchthon was also offered a professorship at Oxford, but declined because of the problems of the Interims in Germany. Lutheranism was not in a position to influence the course of the Edwardian Reformation, and it is not surprising that it took a more radical turn.

The presence of Reformed theologians at Oxford and Cambridge lent support to those who desired a more Reformed Prayer Book. The work of revision proceeded apace and the Second Prayer Book of King Edward VI was mandated for use throughout the realm by a second Act of Uniformity passed by Parliament, beginning on All Saints Day 1552.

There is much evidence that Cranmer himself regarded the First Prayer Book as transitional. He asked the visiting reformers for critiques of the book. Martin Bucer wrote an extended criticism of the Prayer Book entitled, *Censura super libro sacrorum seu ordinationis Ecclesiae atque ministerii in regno Angliae (1550)*. Peter Martyr also wrote a *censura* of the Prayer Book, which has not survived. The following chart indicates structural revisions of the communion service.

1549 PRAYER BOOK[42]	1552 PRAYER BOOK[43]
Preparation:	Preparation:
vesting	(table in middle of chancel)
Lord's Prayer (minister)	Lord's Prayer (minister)
Collect for Purity	Collect for Purity
Introite sung by clerks (Psalm)	
Kyrie ("Lorde have mercie")	Rehearsal of Decalogue
sung by clerks or said by priest	with "Kyrie" response
"Glory be to God on high"	
sung by clerks	
Salutation	
Collect for the Day	Collect for the Day
Collect for the King	Collect for the King
Epistle	Epistle
Gospel	Gospel
Creed sung by clerks or said by congregation	Creed said
Sermon or Homily	Sermon or Homily
Exhortation	
Offertory sentences	Offertory sentences
Procession with gifts	Collection of gifts
	Intercessions
	Exhortation
	Invitation
	Confession of sins
	Absolution
	Comfortable words
Sursum corda	Sursum corda
Preface	Preface
Sanctus	Sanctus
Intercessions, commemorations,	Prayer of Humble Access
epiclesis leading to institution narrative	
	Consecration prayer leading to
	institution narrative
Memorial and Oblatory Prayer	
Our Father	
Invitation	
Confession of sins	
Absolution	
Comfortable words	

---

[42] *The First and Second Prayer Books*, 212ff.
[43] Ibid., 377f.

Prayer of Humble Access
"Lamb of God" sung by clerks or said
Communion   Communion
Post-communion verse
Prayer of Thanksgiving   Oblatory Prayer or Thanksgiving
                                                             "Glory be to God on high"
Blessing   Blessing

The insertion of the Decalogue into the introductory rites was similar to the liturgies of Bucer and Calvin. The Kyrie was transformed into a response to the reading of the commandments: "Lord have mercie upon us, and encline our heartes to kepe this lawe." It has been suggested that the elimination of psalmody between the epistle and gospel was due to the fact that some of the offertory preparation associated with the sacrifice of the mass occurred at this point in the Use of Sarum.[44] One of the unique features of the Anglican Communion Service is that the priest initiated the offertory with scripture sentences addressed to the congregation. In the 1549 *Book of Common Prayer* this was the signal for the offertory procession to bring the bread and wine to the table. In the 1552 *Book of Common Prayer* the receiving of alms from the congregation received as much emphasis as the preparation of the bread and wine. In the 1551 *Book of Common Prayer* the prayer "for the whole state of Christ's Church militant here in earth" became a part of the offertory rite, thus effecting a transfer of the intercessions from the eucharistic prayer. The title of the prayer indicates the elimination of any prayers for the dead. Three options for the exhortation to the communicants were provided in the 1552 *Book of Common Prayer*: the first and third were revisions of the 1549 exhortations and the second one had been written largely by Peter Martyr. The invitation, general confession, absolution, and comfortable words were basically those of 1549 (derived from Archbishop Hermann's *Consultation*), and were relocated from before the administration of Holy Communion to before the eucharistic prayer.

Within the eucharistic action itself care was taken in the 1552 *Book of Common Prayer* to avoid any expression of the real presence of Christ in the bread and wine or of the presence of the sacrifice of Christ. "Blessed is he who comes in the name of the Lord" was eliminated from the Sanctus since Benedictus qui venit had been associated with the elevation, and the elevation had signaled the transubstantiation of the elements. The "Prayer of Humble Access" was inserted between the Sanctus and the consecration, with only one significant textual change.

> We doe not presume to come to this thy table (O mercyfull Lorde) trusting in our owne righteousnesse, but in thy manifolde and greate mercies: we bee not worthye, so much as to gather up the crummes under thy table: but thou art the same Lorde whose propertie is always to haue mercye: graunt us therefore (gracious lord) so to eate the fleshe of thy dere sonne Jesus Christe, and to drinke his bloud [in 1549: "in these holy Misteries"], that our synfulle bodyes

[44] See B. Wigan, *The Liturgy in English*, 2nd ed. (London: Oxford, 1964) and C.W. Dugmore, *The Mass and the English Reformers* (London: Macmillxan, 1958).

maye be made cleane by his body, and our soules wasched through his most precious bloud, and that we may euermore dwel in him, and he in us. Amen.

The fact that the phrase "in these holy Misteries" was dropped from the 1552 text is significant in that this appears to be contrary to Bucer's desire, expressed in the *Censura*, to see "real presence" emphasized more clearly at this point.[45] The obvious intent was to make the phrase "so to eate the fleshe of thy dere sonne Jesus Christe, and to drinke his bloud" seem more ambiguous. It suggests that there was less reliance on the guidance of Bucer in the preparation of the 1552 Prayer Book, perhaps due to the ascendancy of the radical party and the death of Bucer in 1551—a year before the appearance of the revised Prayer Book. The 1552 *Book of Common Prayer* also eliminated any formal anamnesis and epiclesis—the anamnesis because of its linkage with the oblation in the classical eucharistic tradition, and the epiclesis so as not to suggest any change in the elements. These significant changes can be seen by comparing the texts of the Consecration Prayer in the 1549 and 1552 Prayer Books.

1549	1552
O God heauenly father,	Almighty God oure heauenly father,
which of thy tender mercie	whiche of thy tender mercye
diddest geue thine only sonne	geue thine-onely sonne
Jesus Christ to suffre death	Jesus Christ, to suffre death
upon the crosse for our redempcion	upon the crosse for our redempcion,
who made there (by his one oblacion	who made there (by hys one oblacion
	of hymselfe
once offered)	once offered)
a full, perfect, and sufficient	a full, perfecte, and sufficiente
sacrifyce, oblacion,	sacrifice, oblacion,
and satisfaccyon,	and satisfaccion,
for the sinnes of the whole worlde,	for the sinnes of the whole worlde,
and did institute,	and dyd institute,
and in his holy Gospell commaund us	and in hys holy Gospell commaund us
to celebrate	to *continue*
a perpetuall memory of that	a perpetuall memory of that
his precious death,	hys precious death,
untyll his comming again:	untyll hys comynge agayne:
Heare use (o merciful father)	Heare us O mercyefull father
we besech thee;	wee beeseche thee;
and with thy holy spirite and worde,	
vouchsafe to blesse + and sanctifie +	
	and graunt that wee,
these thy gyftes,	*receyuing* these thy
and creatures of bread and wyne	creatures of bread and wyne,
that they maie be unto us	
the bodye and bloude of thy moste	
derely deloued sonne Jesus Christe.	*accordinge* to thy *sonne our*
	Sauioure Jesus Christ's holy

---

[45] See Kavanagh, *The Concept of Eucharistic Memorial . . .* , 202.

institucion, in remembraunce of his
death and passion, maye be partakers
of hys most blessed body and bloud:

Who in the same nyght that he	who, in the same night that he
was betrayed: toke breade,	was betrayed, tooke bread,
and when he had blessed,	and when he had
and geuen thanks . . . [46]	geuen thanks . . . [47]

The only change in the institution narrative was the omission of the word "blessed," perhaps because Bucer had taken exception to anything in the 1549 rite that could have been construed as implying a consecration or hallowing of an inanimate object.[48] On the other hand, the immediate juxtaposition of the words of institution and the ministration of Holy Communion accords with the German Masses of Luther and Bucer. The words of administration of the sacrament in 1552, however, contain no suggestion that the communicants are receiving the body and blood of Christ, and have been regarded as a pure expression of Zwinglian theology.

> Take and eate this, in remembraunce that Christ dyed for thee, and feede on him in thy hearte by faythe, with thanksgeuing.
>
> Drinke this in remembraunce that Christ's bloude was shed for thee, and be thankefull.[49]

While the posture for receiving communion remained kneeling, a rubric was inserted at John Knox's insistence, but over Cranmer's objections to deny any sense of veneration of the elements. This was called the "Black Rubric" because it was added at the last minute, and could not be printed in red (as rubrics are). It is also evident that this rubric expressed Zwinglian theology, unaffected by any of Calvin's nuances.

> Whereas it is ordeyned in the booke of common prayer, in the administracion of the Lord's Supper, that the Communicants knelyng shoulde receyue the holye Communion: whiche thynge beyng well mente, for a sygnificacion of the humble and gratefull acknowledgyng of the benefites of Chryst, geuen unto the woorthye receyuer, and to avoyde the prophanacion and dysordre, which about the holy Communion myght els ensue: Leste yet the same kneelyng myght be thought or taken otherwyse, we dooe declare that it is not ment thereby, that any adoracion is doone, or oughte to bee doone, eyther unto the Sacramentall bread or wyne there bodily recyued, or unto anye reall and essencial presence there beeyng of Christ's naturall fleshe and bloude. For as concernynge the Sacramentall bread and wyne, they remayne styll in theyr verye naturall substaunces, and therefore may not be adored, for that were Idolatrye to be abhorred of all faythfull christians. And as concernynge the naturall body and blood of our sauiour Christ, they are in heauen and not here. For it is agaynst

---

[46] *The First and Second Prayer Books*, 222.

[47] Italics added for comparison. Ibid., 389.

[48] See Van der Pol, *Martin Bucer's Liturgical Ideas*, op. cit., 151–2, who finds this notion expressed in Bucer's correspondence with Peter Martyr on the matter of the "epiklesis" in the 1549 BCP.

[49] *The First and Second Prayer Books*, 389.

the trueth of Christes true natural bodye, to be in moe places then in one, at one tyme.[50]

The ministration of Holy Communion is followed by the Lord's Prayer, a post-communion prayer (either the transferred oblation prayer "mercifully to accept this our Sacrifice of prayse and thanks geuing" or another prayer of thanksgiving), the Gloria (in a place typically occupied by a psalm in the Reformed rites), and the benediction.

It is debatable to what extent it can be claimed that the 1552 Communion Service was a Zwinglian rite, or that Cranmer's eucharistic theology was Zwinglian, as Dix charged,[51] thereby precipitating a stormy debate in which Dugmore took the view that Cranmer was really a Reform Catholic who belonged to the Augustinian "realist-symbolist school."[52] Aidan Kavanagh might be closer to the truth in suggesting that "the Archbishop was a master of ecclesiastical politics with a high sense of responsibility as a leader in the realm, and genuinely concerned that the Reformation be carried out without the upheaval of revolt and antinomianism which had dogged its course on the Continent."[53] If this is the case, it would seem likely, as Francis Clark suggested, that "the subtle and comprehensive language of Martin Bucer and the Strasbourg school had a special attraction for [Cranmer], language which should cover rather than expose the differences in Eucharistic belief between the Reformers of Switzerland, Saxony, and Alsace."[54] But the final thrust of the language of the 1552 Communion Service moved in a Zwinglian direction that did not accord with Bucer's own mediating views on the real presence, and this was no doubt due to the fact that Bucer was no longer a living presence who could wield enormous personal influence. Whatever Cranmer's personal views on the sacrament, it is also evident that he was not as singly responsible for the 1552 Prayer Book as he had been for the 1549 Prayer Book.

In any event, the 1552 Prayer Book was shortlived because the young King Edward died in 1553 and was succeeded by the Catholic Mary Tudor, who restored the Roman rite and the liturgical status quo that had existed during the last years of the reign of Henry VIII. The leading reform bishops were deposed. Cranmer, Hooper, Latimer, and Ridley were imprisoned, tried for heresy, and burned at the stake in Oxford. Other leaders of the English Reformation took refuge on the continent. None were welcome in the Lutheran territories, and this rejection affected future Anglican-Lutheran relationships. Those who settled at Frankfurt-am-Main continued to use the 1552 *Book of Common Prayer* with further revisions (thereby raising speculation about whether the 1552 Prayer Book should also be viewed as transitional to a still more radical prayer book). Those who settled in Geneva adapted Calvin's liturgy, and we have seen how Knox used it as the basis for the liturgy of word and meal in the *Book of Common Order* of the Church of Scotland.

---

[50] Ibid., 392–3.
[51] Dix, *The Shape of the Liturgy*, 646ff.
[52] Dugmore, *The Mass and the English Reformers*, op. cit.
[53] Kavanagh, 41.
[54] Clark, *Eucharistic Sacrifice and the Reformation*, op. cit., 167.

In 1558, upon the death of Queen Mary, the daughter of Henry VIII and Anne Boleyn succeeded to the throne as Queen Elizabeth I. With a Protestant sovereign on the throne, relations with the papacy were once again severed and in 1559 the *Book of Common Prayer* was restored and again imposed for use throughout the realm by an Act of Uniformity. The 1559 Prayer Book was essentially the 1552 *Book of Common Prayer*, but with some changes. The "Black Rubric" was deleted and the formula for the distribution of Holy Communion joined together the formulas from both the 1549 and the 1552 Prayer Books, thus making possible an expression of the real presence. The Elizabethan Primer or Catechism was modeled on that of Henry VIII rather than that of Edward VI, and in 1560 a Latin version of the *Book of Common Prayer* was prepared for use in the universities. Some traditional texts and formularies crept back into the *Book of Common Prayer* through this Latin version. Thus, Elizabeth embarked on the policy of "comprehension" that was designed to bring Catholics (non-Roman, of course) and Puritans (those desiring a purer Reformed church in England more closely resembling Geneva) into one national church. It was at best a precarious policy requiring that neither party gain undue ascendancy or influence. Nevertheless, the Anti-Calvinist party did achieve more influence in the latter days of Elizabeth's reign, paving the way for overt conflict with the Puritans in the seventeenth century.

☙ THE HUMANIST REFORMATION

One of the great figures of the Reformation period was the Dutch humanist scholar, Desiderius Erasmus of Rotterdam (1469?–1536). While it can no longer be held that Erasmus laid the egg that Luther hatched, he did nurture a reform movement that continued until the Council of Trent. No reformer, Catholic or Protestant, was unaffected by Erasmus's influence. All of them shared, to some extent, his vision of a church that lived according to the teachings of Jesus as articulated in the New Testament. He gave the reformers a suitable Greek text of the New Testament from which to work. His last great work, on ecclesiastical concord, *De Sarcienda Ecclesiae Concordia*, served as a platform for the mediating party that looked for a way to achieve reconciliation between Rome and the Reformation.[55]

George Witzel (1501–1573) best expressed and worked for this humanist program of reform. He studied at Erfurt and Wittenberg, where he was an early disciple of Luther, was ordained a priest in 1522, but married Elisabeth Krus the following year. Deprived of his vicarage because of his marriage, Witzel settled in Eisenach, the home town of his wife. This was the first of a long series of flights occasioned by his outspoken criticism of both Catholicism and Lutheranism.

In 1538 Witzel was appointed a religious advisor to Duke George of Saxony. In 1539 he attended a colloquy at Leipzig also attended by Bucer, which attempted to draw up a via media between Rome and the Reformation based on Justin Martyr's *Apology*. The program prepared by the Colloquy called for the abolition of private masses, a revision of the canon of the mass, the use of German as well as Latin, and a reduction in the

---

[55] See John P. Dolan, *History of the Reformation*, op. cit., 320–6 for translated excerpts of this work of Erasmus.

number of saints' days. It was the hope of the Colloquy that the emperor would call a national council and that the peace of the Empire could be preserved by means of religious compromise. Witzel put many of the ideas from this Colloquy into his *Typus Ecclesiae Catholicae* (1540). Like Erasmus, he regarded the ancient church as the ideal type of form for a renewed church. But he also saw the need for continuity with the whole church down through the ages and he felt that this could be accomplished only through communion or fellowship with the church of Rome. The Roman church should be purified, not abandoned.

Witzel was much in demand for consulting work on church orders. He contributed to the Mark Brandenburg Order 1540, about which Luther said that it smelled "Witzelish" because of its concern for ceremonies and vestments as signs of continuity with the church catholic. Witzel settled in Fulda as advisor to Abbot Johann von Henneberg, the temporal ruler who was preparing a new church order. This Fulda Order reflected Witzel's program of catechesis, communion in both kinds, the use of the vernacular as well as Latin, and the establishment of seminaries in which students would study the scriptures in Greek and Hebrew. Witzel's reformation agenda also influenced the church orders prepared for Mainz, Strassburg, and the Duchy of Cleves.[56]

Witzel spread his ideas by means of his voluminous writings. Like Luther, he had mastered a colloquial German, which made his works popular. His most popular book was *Methodius Concordiae Ecclesiasticae* (1539), which contained a general outline of his standard themes. He called for a reduction of scholastic jargon in theology, a standard translation of the Bible which could be used in the pulpit, a reduction in the number of monasteries, and an upgrading of the intellectual and moral lives of the clergy. He felt that abuses connected with the mass were the most pernicious. The very term "leitourgia," he said, shows that the Mass is a public, not a private, ministry. Masses for money, masses for the dead, and masses celebrated by priests living in concubinage must be abolished. Like Luther, he emphasized baptism as the basis of Christian life and urged Christians to participate in baptismal celebrations so that they could renew their own baptism and receive some sense of their incorporation into the body of Christ. Witzel saw the liturgy as an agent of unification since it was the center of Christian culture shared by both Catholics and Lutherans.

Because the outline of the *Methodius* followed that of the Augsburg Confession, Witzel was invited to the Diet of Augsburg in 1547 by the Emperor Charles V. Many of his ideas found their way into the Augsburg Interim. He continued to serve the Emperor until Charles's abdication in 1555. Witzel then took up residence in Mainz, where he polemicized against the reactionary tendencies evident in the Council of Trent. The arrival of the Jesuits in Mainz in 1561 introduced devotional practices and an educational system completely at variance with Witzel's liturgical piety and humanist ideals. Peter Canisius worked to reduce Witzel's reputation and reform proposals to historical oblivion.

---

[56] See John P. Dolan, *The Influence of Erasmus, Witzel and Cassander in the Church Ordinances and Reform Proposals of the United Duchies of Cleves during the Middle Decades of the 16th Century. Reformationsgeschichtliche Studien und Texte* 83 (Münster, 1953).

He died in 1573, still lamenting about Trent, "Would that this Council had been able to see what was really necessary."[57]

The other great Catholic humanist who tried to build bridges between papalists and reformers was George Cassander (d. 1566). A Flemish teacher who lived and worked in Cologne, Cassander developed the idea of achieving Christian unity through a return to the *consensus quinquasaeculorum* (the consensus of the first five centuries). He enunciated his famous phrase, "in essentials, unity; in nonessentials, liberty; in everything, charity."[58] But it remained to be determined how the essentials would be determined. As shall be seen in the next chapter, Cassander's approach to Catholic-Lutheran reconciliation was attempted in Sweden by King Johan III (1568–1592). We shall devote considerable attention to King Johan's mediating program, because of its ecumenical and liturgical interest.

🍇 THE CATHOLIC REFORMATION

As the ideas of humanism took hold among Lutherans and the Reformed, so there were leaders in the Catholic reform movement before the Council of Trent who epitomized humanistic ideals. Among these Catholic reformers were Johann Gropper, chancellor of the archdiocese of Cologne, and Gaspar Contarini, former ambassador of Venice to the imperial court.[59]

Gropper, born in Soest in 1501, attended the University of Cologne at the time Reuchlin and the humanists were exerting great influence there. The young Gropper rose fast and in 1524 became chancellor of the curia of the archdiocese of Cologne. Cologne was one of the title electorates of the Holy Roman Empire and the largest ecclesiastical province in Europe. Its archbishop-elector, Hermann von Wied, was a supporter of Erasmus and a leader in the Catholic reform movement. Largely at Gropper's urging, he convened a great synod in the city in 1536 that was attended by representatives of the bishoprics of Liege, Utrecht, Osnabrück, and Minden. In the face of papal obstructionism, the synod published a number of important decrees. It defined the church as a community of believers in Christ. It upheld the authority of scripture and emphasized the importance of biblical preaching. It admonished preachers against interspersing sermons with unfounded legends about the saints. It made an effort to place monasteries more directly under episcopal control in matters of preaching and administration of the sacraments. While it upheld the idea of the mass as a sacrifice for the living and the dead, it emphasized that it is a memorial of the one death of Christ. It recommended the celebration of mass in the vernacular and the restoration of the ancient public confession. It concluded with a section stressing the need of the church to be concerned for the poor and to establish and maintain hospitals and orphanages.[60]

---

[57] Dolan, *History of the Reformation*, 337.

[58] See Owen Chadwick, *The Reformation*. Pelican History of the Church, 3 (Baltimore: Penguin Books, 1964), 371.

[59] See Dolan, 337ff.

[60] Ibid., 338–9.

As a commentary and manual on these synodical decrees, Gropper published in 1538 his *Enchiridion Christianae Institutionis*. The popularity of this work may be judged by the fact that it went through fifteen printings between 1541 and 1555 in Verona, Venice, Paris, Antwerp, and Cologne. The *Enchiridion* provided explanations on the basics of the Christian tradition, including the Creed, the sacraments, the Lord's Prayer, and the Ten Commandments. It tried to evaluate Luther's teachings in the light of traditional Catholic dogma and formulated the doctrine of *iustitia duplex* (double justification). He moves away from the forensic view of justification by arguing that justification is an inner renewal of the forgiven sinner through the work of the Holy Spirit and the Spirit's gifts, including the infusion of charity. This inner renewal is not, as the scholastics held, a result of justification, but is conjoined with the divine act of forgiveness. With Luther, Gropper held that faith is trust in the promises of God; but he went on to emphasize that faith unites us with Christ and makes us members of his body. The gift of faith is an act of preparatory grace *(gratia praeveniens)*. After justification the Christian receives enabling grace *(gratia cooperans)*, which draws the Christian to love what God loves and to perform God-pleasing works.[61]

In 1541 a Diet was convened at Regensburg to work out religious differences within the Empire. Charles V appointed Gropper, along with Eck and Pflug, to represent the Catholic position, and Melanchthon, Bucer, and Pistorius to represent the Protestant position. It was the appointment of Gaspar Contarini (1483–1542) as the papal legate which raised hopes for this meeting. Contarini was from a distinguished patrician family of Venice and had served as Venetian ambassador to the court of Charles V and Pope Clement VII. He had urged the pope to give up the claims of the papacy on the Papal States in Italy as a condition for peace and also to effect moral reform in Rome. He was among those who believed that the Lutheran movement could be dissipated if the Roman church showed less interest in temporal advantage and devoted itself to "what is plainly set before us in the Gospels." As an Italian, he had little experience with the German concern for theology. There was general rejoicing among the reform Catholics when the renewal-minded Pope Paul III elevated Contarini, who was still a layman, to the college of cardinals in 1535. Even with the college of cardinals Contarini argued that reconciliation with the Lutherans could not be achieved until the head of the church was purified. *"Purga Romam, purga mundum"* (Purify Rome, purify the world) was his slogan.[62]

Contarini's arrival in Regensburg in March 1541, was enthusiastically greeted by Catholics and Protestants alike. The basis of the discussions in April and May formed the *Book of Ratisbon*. The foundation of this document was an earlier secret agreement worked out in Worms between Bucer and Gropper. Melanchthon stayed in the background of this discussion, because he was under orders from the Elector of Saxony to limit his positions to the teachings of the Augsburg Confession. The controversial article in the *Book of Ratisbon* was Gropper's on "double justification." Contarini informed the pope of this breakthrough, and the Elector of Brandenburg also greeted it with enthusiasm. But

---

[61] Ibid., 339–42.
[62] Ibid., 343–7.

this reaction proved to be premature. Cardinal Farnese informed Contarini that the Holy See would have to study it further before it could be approved. The efforts of the diet collapsed, and Contarini left Regensberg in sorrow and died the next year.[63]

In the absence of a call for a general council, there was widespread agreement that bishops could initiate reform measures within their own dioceses. Archbishop von Wied directed Gropper and Bucer to draw up a church order for Cologne in order to implement the Reformation in this province. Gropper broke with the archbishop on this, and when the archbishop proceeded with the project anyway with the collaboration of Bucer and Melanchthon, Gropper led the cathedral chapter into open revolt against the him. The struggle for Cologne lasted four years, and was broken only with the arrival of Spanish troops and the Jesuits under Peter Canisius. Von Wied was deposed and the humanist influence in Cologne was broken. Gropper attended the Council of Trent during its second convocation (1551–1552), but his position of leadership was clouded as a result of the suspicions of heresy that the Italian inquisitor Zacharias Delphinus raised concerning his *Enchiridion*.[64]

The Council of Trent was convened in 1545, a year before the outbreak of the Smalkald War. It was located in Trent, since that was a part of Italy within the boundaries of the Holy Roman Empire, but close enough to Rome to be controlled by the papal forces. It was hardly an ecumenical council. The Lutherans refused to attend because they did not regard it as a free council, such as the emperor might have convened. The aging Luther wrote one of his vilest treatises, *Against Roman Popery Founded by the Devil*, in response to it. By the end of the first session (1545–1547), only about seventy bishops were in attendance, mostly Italians. Its work was interrupted twice, between 1547–1551 and 1552–1562, so that what was begun in 1545 was not completed until 1563.[65]

Among the many matters brought to the attention of the Council were the desire for uniform liturgical books and the correction of abuses associated with the mass. Many provincial synods had undertaken reform of the missals and breviaries then in use in order to curb the great amount of variation in uses that existed by the sixteenth century. France and England (during the brief period of Mary Tudor) preferred internal regulation of liturgical books within each country. Spain and Portugal, emerging from centuries of Moslem domination, argued strenuously for a unified missal and breviary with appendices of special diocesan observances. It was not until 1562, in connection with discussions regarding the doctrine of the sacrifice of the mass, that the Council finally took up the matter of abuses connected with the mass. Among the abuses pointed out were: sequences and prefaces with legendary content; new mass-formularies of questionable origin; the system of stipends for votive masses; the relationship of votive masses to the liturgical calendar (e.g., the problem of setting aside propers for Sundays and festivals in favor of privately chosen formularies); and the superstitious arrangement of masses in series for the dead.[66]

---

[63] Ibid., 348–50.
[64] Ibid., 351.
[65] Grimm, *The Reformation Era*, op. cit., 396–7.
[66] Jungmann, *The Mass of the Roman Rite*, op. cit., I, 133–4.

A commission was appointed to deal with these matters, and it added issues of its own to the list, including the custom of saying private masses in churches while the high mass was being celebrated. The Council itself was not prepared to deal with such a catalogue of abuses, and the commission limited the actions taken by the Council. The *Decretum de observandis et evitandis in celebratione missae*, which was a supplement to the teaching and canons regarding the sacrifice of the mass, was passed on September 17, 1562, in the twenty-second session. Among its decrees were that bishops should regulate the system of mass-stipend; that masses should be celebrated only in consecrated places; that irreverent conduct and frivolous music should be banished; that the capriciousness of priests in choosing mass formularies should be curtailed; and that the superstitious observance of various numbers of masses in series should cease. Not until the twenty-fifth session in 1563, almost at the time of the Council's adjournment, was a decree passed that left the revision of the missal and breviary to the pope. While there were some council fathers in favor of more radical reforms, nothing was recommended concerning the use of the vernacular, a more active participation of the laity in the liturgy, and communion under both kinds.

Pope Pius IV set about immediately to carry out this decree of Trent. He appointed a liturgical commission, which was continued under his successor Pius V. Their work resulted in the publication of the *Breviarium Romanum* in 1568 and the *Missale Romanum ex decreto ss. Concilii Tridentini restitutum, Pii V Pont. Max. iussu editum* in 1570. By order of the accompanying papal bulls, these uses were made binding on the whole Western church, except in provinces or dioceses that could demonstrate a two hundred-year custom for their own usage. Exceptions to the rule of Rome, therefore, included certain medieval religious orders and the dioceses of Milan (the Ambrosian rite), Toledo (the Mozarabic rite), Trier, Cologne, Liege, Braga, and Lyons. This exception specifically did not include the rites and ceremonies of the Reformation churches, which the Augsburg Confession had argued "need not be everywhere alike" (Art. 7). It should not pass unnoticed that this was a revolutionary move in liturgical history. Provincial and national uniformity had been imposed before, but this was the first effort at international uniformity. It would not even have been possible without the printing press to disseminate standard editions.

The new Roman Missal was based on the *Missale secundum consuetudinem Romanae Curiae*—the book of the Roman Curia. Its calendar and propers agreed with the new breviary. Exact directions were provided in the choice of mass texts, whereas there had been a certain optional character in pre-Reformation missals in terms of which propers would be used, especially for votive masses. A book of general rubrics was provided in the *Ritus servandus in celebratione Missae*. These directions were taken from the *Ordo Missae* of John Burchard of Strasbourg (1502), the papal master of ceremonies. A certain pruning is evident in the limitation of the number of votive masses to those for each day of the week, and in the reduction in the number of saints' days, which left about 150 days in the calendar freed of feasts, not counting octaves. This was achieved by retaining only those feasts observed in the city of Rome itself. What the commission provided, and what the papal bull promulgated, was the liturgy of the city of Rome.

Nevertheless, the spirit of humanism was present in the quest for a purer, more unadultered form. This also explains why tropes and sequences of Frankish provenance were deleted, leaving only four out of thousands of sequences that had been in use throughout the Middle Ages: "Victimae paschali" for Easter; "Veni, Sancte Spiritus" for Pentecost; "Lauda Sion"; and the "Stabat Mater."[67] Finally, the commission did nothing to hinder polyphonic church music, which left the door open for the golden age of Renaissance polyphony that occurred at the end of the sixteenth century.

The spirit of humanism had initially guided the reform of the breviary as well. The Spanish cardinal Quiñones had issued a reformed breviary in 1535 (revised in 1536). This was commissioned by Pope Clement VII and authorized for use by Pope Paul III.[68] This breviary was a revolutionary break with tradition in that the Divine Office had always been regarded, in theory at least, as a choral office, a body of prayer to be sung publicly. Quiñones's breviary was intended for private use by clerics. It abandoned the old tradition of allocating certain psalms to certain hours of the day and certain feasts in the calendar in favor of an even distribution of three psalms per office. The night office of Matins was augmented with three lessons: one from the Old Testament, one from the New Testament, and one from a patristic or hagiographic reading. Hymns were placed at the beginning of each office. Lauds was combined with Matins, but the other canonical hours were all retained. But the supplementary Offices of the Dead and of the Blessed Virgin Mary were suppressed. This breviary was used for over thirty years, and exerted a profound influence on the *Book of Common Prayer*.[69]

Nevertheless, the liturgical commission of Pius V swept away Quiñones's breviary in favor of the old classical monastic office of the Roman basilicas. This restored office made a copious use of psalms, including eighteen psalms plus twelve lessons for Sunday Matins and twelve psalms plus three lessons for ferial Matins, six psalms and an Old Testament canticle for Lauds, and four psalms for Compline. The antiphons and responsories deleted in Quiñones's breviary were restored. Thus, it was clearly intended to be a choral office. But in the meantime a tradition of private clerical recitation had developed, and this new breviary was unmanageable for pastoral clergy who were to become far busier in the centuries after the Council of Trent than they had been before. For the ideal of choral recitation, only Sunday Vespers remained in cathedrals and parishes to connect the laity with the Divine Office, and this was never as popular as the popular devotions that emerged in Baroque Catholicism.

While the Holy See continued to show reserve in the matter of private recitation of the office, new religious orders appeared that no longer had an obligation to maintain a communal life of prayer, such as the Jesuits. Ignatius Loyola was himself undecided on this point, but the tendency toward private recitation grew stronger in the Society of Jesus and finally prevailed in spite of the interventions of Popes Pius IV and Pius V. The

---

[67] Ibid., I, 437–8.

[68] See *Breviarium Romanum a Francisco Cardinali Quignonio*, ed. by J. Wickham Legg (Cambridge, 1888; reprinted 1970).

[69] See G. J. Cuming, "The Office in the Anglican Community," in *The Study of Liturgy*. op. cit., 441–6.

suppression of the choral office in the Society was definitively ratified by Pope Gregory XIII in the Bull *Ex sedis apostolicae* of February 28, 1575.[70]

The Council of Trent had only provided for the revision of the missal and breviary. But the Roman Curia felt bound to produce revisions of the other essential liturgical books. Thus, in 1596 a revised *Pontificale Romanum* was issued under the authority of Pope Clement VIII for those sacraments and sacramentals reserved to the bishop. There followed in 1614 the *Rituale Romanum* containing forms for the administration of those sacraments and sacramentals not reserved exclusively for the bishop. These books also reflected uses of the diocese of Rome now imposed on the whole church in communion with the bishop of Rome. It cannot be emphasized too strongly that conformity to Roman use mandated by Rome (as opposed, say, by local rulers) was a new idea. It is in this sense that "Roman" Catholicism emerged.

Only by accident did these revised liturgical books reflect the liturgy of the ancient church. Nor did they address the changed social conditions of the post-medieval church. Nevertheless, these books served the liturgical life of Roman Catholicism until the middle of the twentieth century. This suggests that liturgy is meaningful not just when it reflects the constituting traditions of a community of faith or when it expresses the culture of the people who use the books, but when it provides a symbol of *identity* for the people whose public work it is. The Catholic Reformation sought essentially to regroup the church under the papacy with a uniform liturgy, a well-trained clergy, priests resident in their parishes, bishops resident in their dioceses, pastors fervent and self-sacrificing, trained as confessors and teachers, a priesthood uncorrupted and incorruptible, and religious orders obediently devoted to the Holy See. Such a renewed church was able to provide such a challenge to Protestantism that its efforts have been termed "the Counter-Reformation."

"Examination of the Council of Trent"

Lutheranism had to redefine itself over against this spectrum of reformations, including radical and Reformed reformations as well as Catholic. Part of the task of making this restatement fell to Martin Chemnitz (1522–86), a disciple of Melanchthon. It has been possible to distinguish at least three types of followers of Melanchthon, or Philippists. One type was the Cryptocalvinist, who was driven out of the Lutheran church and into the Reformed camp by the Formula of Concord of 1577, and who then exerted a modifying influence on the German Reformed church. The second type of Philippist was the humanist, exemplified by George Calixus, who combined a commitment to the Lutheran position with a tolerance that grew out of a genuine concern for the unity of the visible church. The third type of Philippist was exemplified by Chemnitz, who upheld the Lutheran position as a matter of principle but without the excesses of Gnesio-Lutherans, such as Matthias Flacius. Nicholas Selnecker and David Chytraeus, two of the other authors of the Formula of Concord, are also representatives of this type of the Praeceptor's

---

[70] See Pierre Salmon, *The Breviary through the Centuries*, op. cit., 21.

protégés. Chemnitz is also known for his contribution to the Formula, especially for the "Catalogue of Testimonies" appended to it (the mere presence of which refutes the claim of Otto Ritschl and others that the Formula of Concord was a repudiation of Melanchthon's traditionalism). In addition, Chemnitz is known for his *Treatise on the Two Natures of Christ* (1571) and, above all, for the monumental *Examen Concilii Tridentini* (1565–1573).[71]

Martin Chemnitz's *Examen* had a prehistory in a little diatribe that he wrote against the Jesuit Order. This was answered by the formidable Portuguese theologian Jacob Payva de Andrada, who tried to discredit Chemnitz's attack on the Jesuits, but really was defending the positions of the Council of Trent. Chemnitz's response was to undertake an examination of the canons and decrees of the Council, which eventuated in four books exhaustively analyzing the positions of Trent from the perspective of scripture and tradition. The first two extensive topics treated in the *Examen* concern Sacred Scripture and traditions. In the course of working out the formal principle of sola Scriptura, Chemnitz also clarified the Lutheran understanding of the role and meaning of tradition.[72]

Melanchthon's identification of traditio with Menschensatzungen (rites and ceremonies, instituted by men) confused the singular and plural usages, "tradition" and "traditions," which for many of his contemporaries and successors were two distinct entities. "Tradition" refers to doctrine, which is unchangeable, while "traditions" refer to church usages, which are changeable. Peter Fraenkel has observed: "As far as is known Chemnitz was the first to transpose his master's teaching of doctrinal continuity into the vocabulary of 'tradition.' "[73] It was also Pelikan's assessment that "Chemnitz's view of tradition, as defined in the *Examen*, went beyond Melanchthon's by including in the term 'tradition' much of what Melanchthon had said, in the *Apology* and elsewhere, under other rubrics."[74]

Chemnitz marked eight different senses in which the word *traditio* could be used in theology. For each of these senses he provided an abundance of patristic evidence. In so doing he was able to maintain that the Roman Catholic understanding of tradition, defined by the Council of Trent, was based on a confusion of the various senses of *traditio*. The first decree of the Fourth Session of the Council, which defined the role of tradition in the church, is quoted in Chemnitz's *Examen* as follows:

> The most holy Synod of Trent, perceiving that this truth and instruction is contained in the written books [of Sacred Scripture] and in the unwritten traditions, which, after they had been received by the apostles from the mouth of Christ Himself or from the apostles themselves, the Holy Spirit dictating, have

---

[71] For an excellent introduction and analysis see Arthur Carl Piepkorn, "The Genesis and Genius of the *Examen Concilii Tridentini*," *Concordia Theological Monthly* 37 (1966), 5–37.

[72] See Arthur L. Olsen, "Martin Chemnitz and the Council of Trent," *dialog* 2 (1963), 60–7.

[73] Peter Fraenkel, "Revelation and Tradition. Notes on Some Aspects of Doctrinal Continuity in the Theology of Philipp Melanchthon," *Studia Theologica* 13 (1959), 123.

[74] Jaroslav Pelikan, *Obedient Rebels. Catholic Substance and Protestant Principle in Luther's Reformation* (New York and Evanston: Harper and Row, 1964), 50.

come down to us, transmitted as it were from hand to hand; and following the example of the orthodox fathers, it receives and venerates with equal devotion and reverence all the books of the Old and New Testament (since God is the author of both) and also said traditions, both those pertaining to faith and those pertaining to morals, as dictated either orally by Christ or by the Holy Spirit and preserved in a continuous succession in the Catholic Church.[75]

Chemnitz discerned that this definition of tradition "is truly a Pandora's box, under whose cover every kind of corruption, abuse, and superstition has been brought into the church. For what fiction will not be allowed if once this postulate is granted, that proof and confirmation from the scriptures are not necessary."[76] He reminds his readers that when the reformers attacked certain abuses with the testimony of scripture, the papalists tried to shore up their position by arguing that such things as the reformers were attacking had been handed down orally from the apostles. This provided the papalists with an "authoritative" answer to every protestation. Therefore it was necessary to return *ad fontes* to see how the early Christian writers understood the role of tradition, especially in relation to the scriptures. But "because the word 'tradition' was not used by the ancients in one and the same way, and because the traditions of which mention is made in the writings of the ancients are not all of the same kind, the papalists sophistically mix together such testimonies without discrimination."[77] So Chemnitz proposed to distinguish between the various meanings of "tradition" in the writings of the early Christian writers and in doing so he differentiates eight senses of the term.

We shall set down as the first kind of traditions that the things which Christ and the apostles delivered by word of mouth and which were later committed to writing by the evangelists and apostles are often called tradition.[78]

The second kind of traditions is this, that the books of Holy Scripture were, as Augustine says, cared for in an unbroken span of time and by a sure unbroken succession and faithfully transmitted to posterity and to us, as it were, from hand to hand.[79]

We set down as the third kind of traditions that concerning which Irenaeus, in Bk. 3, and Tertullian, in *De praescriptione adversus haereticos*, speak. Both bestow high praise on the apostolic tradition.[80]

Chemnitz had in mind here the appeal to the unwritten tradition in the dispute with the Gnostics who would not accept the authority of the canonical scriptures and often appealed to their own gospels and writings instead. Nevertheless, said Chemnitz, the early Christian writers

---

[75] Cited in Martin Chemnitz, *Examination of the Council of Trent*, Part I, trans. by Fred Kramer (St. Louis: Concordia, 1971), 219. See *Examen Concilii Tridentini per Martin Chemnicium*, ed. E. Preuss (Berlin, 1861), Locus II: De Traditionibus, 69ff.

[76] Ibid.

[77] Ibid., 229.

[78] Ibid., 223.

[79] Ibid., 227.

[80] Ibid., 231.

do not bring forward or prove any other dogma of faith by tradition beside those which are contained in the Scripture; but they set forth and prove also by tradition those very same dogmas which are found in the Scriptures.[81]

The fourth kind of traditions is concerning the exposition, the true sense, or natural meaning of the Scripture. It is certain from Irenaeus and from Tertullian that their dispute with the heretics was not only concerning the Scripture but also concerning the exposition, or meaning, of the Scripture.[82]

We shall make this the fifth kind of traditions, that the fathers sometimes call those dogmas traditions which are not set forth in so many letters and syllables in Scripture but which are brought together from clear testimonies of Scripture by way of good, certain, firm, and clear reasoning.[83]

Such traditions include the doctrine of the Trinity and the practice of infant baptism.

As the sixth kind of traditions we set down what is said of the catholic consensus of the fathers. For it is a common form of speech to say: "The fathers handed it down this way."[84]

Here Chemnitz refutes the accusation of the Portuguese Jesuit, Jacob Payva de Andrada, that the Lutherans disregard the testimony of antiquity altogether and discount the authority of the Fathers. He took Andrada's commentary on the Council as the official view of the Tridentine fathers, published at their behest. As Piepkorn has indicated, "Chemnitz canonized for his readers as the authentic understanding of the Tridentine position the partisan interpretation of the Latin theologians of the extreme right."[85] The result was the foreclosure of a possible "evangelical" interpretation of the decrees and canons of the Council. Nevertheless, Chemnitz rejects the charge that the Lutheran position is novel on some issues. After citing a number of *testimonia patrum* from Melanchthon's *Loci Communes*, he points out "the public testimony of our churches, how reverently we think about the consensus of antiquity, about the testimonies of the ancients, and about the confession and examples of the ancient church."[86] Indeed, a Catalogue of Testimonies was appended to the Augsburg Confession, and the Confession itself cited numerous decrees of ancient councils and church writers.

The seventh kind of traditions is that where the ancients make mention of the unwritten traditions, they do not actually understand dogmas of faith without, besides, and beyond Scripture which are to be accepted even though they cannot be proved by any testimony of Scripture, but they speak of certain ancient rites and customs which they trace back to the apostles because of their antiquity.[87]

---

[81] Ibid., 236.
[82] Ibid., 244.
[83] Ibid., 249.
[84] Ibid., 256.
[85] Piepkorn, *art. cit.*, 18.
[86] Chemnitz, 257.
[87] Ibid., 267.

These are the kinds of traditions that Melanchthon treated under the category of Menschensatzungen. They are primarily liturgical and ritual traditions, such as the sign of the cross, turning to the east for prayer, "the words of the epiclesis when the bread of the Eucharist is shown," the blessing of the font in the baptismal liturgy, the baptismal anointing, the threefold immersion, the renunciation of Satan, the confession of faith, and so forth. Concerning these traditions Chemnitz writes:

> We do not simply reject and condemn all traditions which are of this kind. For we do not disapprove of what Jerome writes to Lucinius, namely, that the churchly traditions, especially such as do not harm the faith, are to be observed as they were handed down by the elders.[88]

The eighth kind of traditions are "the particular property of the papalists," and only this sense of tradition is rejected by Chemnitz. These are:

> traditions which pertain both to faith and morals and which cannot be proved with any testimony of Scripture but which the Synod of Trent nevertheless commands to be received and venerated with the same reverence and devotion as the Scripture itself.[89]

This understanding of "tradition" was rejected not because traditions that "cannot be proved with any testimony of Scripture" were to be rejected out of hand. That would be a biblicistic stance that was incompatible with the Lutheran approach. But what was rejected was the Council of Trent's teaching that such traditions were as normative for faith and practice as scripture. Chemnitz already understood scripture as a form of tradition. Scripture is the written apostolic tradition that the church canonized as Sacred Scripture. But by this action of canonization the church gave scripture an authority as a "norming norm."

When the Lutheran Formula of Concord held that "we believe, teach, and confess that the prophetic and apostolic writings of the Old and New Testaments are the only rule and norm according to which all doctrines and teachers alike must be appraised and judged,"[90] this could be regarded as a rejection of the Council of Trent's undifferentiated understanding of tradition. At the same time, in contrast with the more radical reformations, scripture is designated as "rule and norm," not as *source*. Traditions in the church, whether they are dogmas, ethical teachings, liturgical rites, or sacramental practices, are scriptural not if they can be found in the Bible but if they are consistent with or in harmony with scripture. Chemnitz helped to secure a more viable role for tradition in the Lutheran churches. Tradition in the form of patristic teaching, conciliar decision, and liturgical practice has a place of reverence in the life of the church. But it is a critical reverence, subject to reevaluation in the light of scripture as the final "rule and norm" by which faith and practices are judged.

---

[88] Ibid., 271.
[89] Ibid., 272.
[90] Tappert, *The Book of Concord*, 464; *Bek.*, 834.

CHAPTER 12

Scandinavian Liturgies

REFORMATIONS IN WHICH THE formal evangelical principle of *sola Scriptura* coexisted with reverence for the received catholic tradition occurred in the Scandinavian countries. The speed of implementation of reformation in these countries varied. Lutheranism made rapid inroads in Denmark, although less so in Norway and Iceland even though they were under Danish rule in the sixteenth century.[1] Reform ideas were being considered in Denmark from the beginning of the sixteenth century, and the country was able to embrace Lutheranism when that was made the official religion by royal decree in 1537. It was implemented with the help of one of the leading German reformers, Johannes Bugenhagen. The Reformation in Norway and Iceland was really decreed and implemented by an absentee ruler in Copenhagen, in the absence of a leading reformer, and it took a longer time for the people to embrace Lutheranism as a popular religion.[2] By contrast, there were reformers in Sweden and Finland who were advocating the adoption of Lutheranism, but, as in Norway and Iceland, Reformation ideas were not readily embraced by the populace. Sensitive to the conservative nature of their subjects, the Swedish kings of the House of Vasa gave free course to the reformers but adopted no Reformation confession of faith until a political crisis forced this decision in 1593—and then it was not the king but the Estates and the Synod of the National Church that

---

[1] The Republic of Iceland entered into a union with Norway under the rule of King Hakon the Old in 1262, and Norway passed under Danish rule, along with Sweden, by the Union of Kalmar in 1397, which united the Scandinavian countries.

[2] See Ole Peter Grell, *The Scandinavian Reformation: From Evangelical Movement to Institutionalization of Reform* (New York, 1995).

adopted the *Confessio Augustana*. The need to preserve the catholic tradition while slowly implementing evangelical theology and practices led to some creative liturgical endeavors on the part of Olavus Petri, the reformer of Sweden, his brother Laurentius, the first evangelical archbishop, and the "high church" King Johan III.[3] Even after the constitutional crisis of 1593 Sweden achieved a liturgical settlement that eschewed the more radical impulses of gnesio-Lutheranism. What developed in the five Scandinavian countries was a church life that was both catholic and evangelical, embracing the whole population of the country and maintaining continuity with pre-Reformation traditions, but centered in the Bible's gospel.

THE INFLUENCE OF BUGENHAGEN IN DENMARK

Within a few years after the historic events of 1517 in Wittenberg, news and views of Luther's reformation were being introduced into Scandinavia by the merchants of the Hanseatic League.[4] Lutheran ideas also infiltrated the duchies of Schleswig and Holstein, which were geographically adjacent to Denmark and which stood in a personal relationship to Denmark since their duke was usually also the Danish king. Denmark was an electoral monarchy, and by agreement of the Union of Kalmar (1397) the three Scandinavian kingdoms were ruled by one monarch.

In Denmark itself, reform ideas gained a hold during the reign of King Christian II (c. 1513–1523), who was married to the sister of Emperor Charles V. In spite of his interest in humanist ideas, King Christian had a reputation for brutality and terrorism in limiting the economic and political power of the higher nobility and clergy. The "Stockholm Bloodbath" in 1520, by which he tried to crush an insurrection in Sweden by using charges of heresy (since the uprising had begun with the deposition of the archbishop of Uppsala), was regarded with revulsion throughout western Europe. He began sweeping economic reforms in Denmark that would have limited the power of the nobility in favor of the peasants and burghers. In spite of his bloody suppression of what he considered heresy in Sweden in 1520, he began flirting with Lutheran ideas in the early 1520s. Finally, in 1523 he was forced into exile by an uprising of the nobles—a situation Sweden took advantage of by waging a war of national independence under the leadership of Gustav Vasa.

With the deposition of Christian II, Frederick I of Holstein was elected king. The upper nobility and clergy forced a provision that in his coronation oath Frederick would pledge not to allow the Lutheran heresy in Denmark and Norway (Sweden had won its independence from Denmark in 1523). Yet the new king was solicitous toward Lutheran cities and rulers because of his need to finance a large army to keep Christian II from reconquering the kingdom. (He made an attempt in 1531, but was arrested and

---

[3] See Rudolf Stählin, "Die Geschichte des christlichen Gottesdienstes, in *Leitourgia. Handbuch des evangelischen Gottesdienstes*, I (Kassel, 1954), 62ff for an excursus on the Swedish liturgy.

[4] A loose confederation of north German merchants and cities that was the dominant trading power in northern Europe in the fourteenth through the sixteenth centuries. The major Hanseatic cities included Bremen, Hamburg, and Lübeck, with outposts in Copenhagen, Bergen, Stockholm, Åbo/Turku, Visby, and Riga.

held in prison until his death in 1559). These were years of conflict between Catholic and evangelical Christianity as evangelical ideas took hold in the churches in all the larger market towns during the early 1530s. Frederick's own confessional position is hard to discern, but his policy of suppressing the archbishop and the bishops shows that his goal was a royally directed national church.

King Frederick died in 1533. The Catholic majority in the national council tried to establish a republic ruled by the nobility. Civil war broke out and lasted for three years until Duke Christian of Schleswig, Frederick's oldest son, emerged as victor and was elected king as Christian III. The Catholic nobility had supported his election in return for a guarantee of their economic and political privileges. But immediately upon his election, Christian III removed the bishops from office, blamed them in large measure for the civil war, placed them in prison, and confiscated church property for the crown. At a public meeting of the council in Copenhagen in October 1536, Christian declared that only evangelical Christianity and a reformed church would be allowed in the country in the future, and he brought in the German reformer, Johannes Bugenhagen, to implement the reformation in Denmark.[5]

Because there had already been experiments with evangelical practices, the church order Bugenhagen prepared for Denmark was easily implemented.[6] These experiments included efforts to preach on biblical texts, administer communion under both kinds, and read the scripture lessons in Danish. After some experimental translations, an adequate translation of the New Testament into Danish was made by Christian Pedersen in 1529. The first Danish Hymnal of ten hymns was published by Hans Mortensen in 1528. Additional hymn collections circulated until a definitive compilation was made by Bishop Hans Tausen in 1544.[7] Tausen had been the first evangelical pastor in Malmö (an area of modern Sweden that remained under Danish rule in the sixteenth century).

Tausen's own hymnal in 1528 included an order of service that blended features of Luther's *Formula Missae* and *Deutsche Messe*.[8] The order of service was as follows:

> Prayers at the foot of the altar:
>> Versicles: Adjutorium nostrum
>> Confiteor
>> Absolution
> Introit or a hymn
> Kyrie or a hymn
> Gloria
> Salutation and Collect
> Epistle

---

[5] See E. H. Dunkley, *The Reformation in Denmark* (London, 1948).

[6] See B. J. Kidd, ed., *Documents Illustrative of the Continental Reformation* (Oxford, 1967), especially the Seizure of the Bishops of Denmark, 12 August 1536 (in English); the Recess of the Diet of Copenhagen, 30 October 1536 (in Latin), no. 132; Ordinatio Ecclesiastica, 2 September 1537 (in Latin), no. 132a; the Manifesto of King Christian III, 30 October 1536 (in English), no. 133.

[7] See Edward A. Hanson, "Scandinavian Hymnody: Denmark," in Marilyn Kay Stulken, ed., *Hymnal Companion to the Lutheran Book of Worship* (Philadelphia: Fortress Press, 1981), 34.

[8] See F. J. Bergmann, "The Liturgy of the Icelandic Church," *Memoirs of the Lutheran Liturgical Association* IV (1901–2), 99.

Alleluia and Gradual
Gospel
Credo and a hymn as the preacher went to the pulpit
Sermon
Hymn
Luther's paraphrase of the Lord's Prayer (German Mass)
Sanctus (sometimes preceded by the Preface)
Words of institution
Agnus Dei
Luther's exhortation to the communicants (German Mass)
Ministration of Holy Communion
Hymn of thanksgiving
Salutation and Luther's post-communion prayer (German Mass)
Benediction
The Ten Commandments in versified form by Claus Mortensen

This order of service, for all its merits, did not satisfy everyone, and it lacked a fully developed calendar and lectionary. This may have contributed to King Christian's decision to request to the Elector of Saxony for the services of Bugenhagen, the premier editor of church orders in northern Germany, to prepare a church order for Denmark that would govern the whole sphere of liturgical observance and pastoral activity.

Bugenhagen did not arrive until the summer of 1537. In the meantime, a commission of twenty-nine pastors and theologians drafted a church order, using Bugenhagen's previous efforts as models. King Christian amended this and sent it to Wittenberg for review. As he wrote in his confirmatory document recommending the authorization of the church order by the church synod, he had sent a copy to "worthy Father Doctor Martin Luther, by whom God in His mercy and kindness, in these last times, has again sent Christ's holy and pure Gospel; thus he, with several other men highly learned in scripture, in Wittenberg, examined the same Ordinance and adjudged it to be good and right."[9] When Bugenhagen arrived, he revised it still further and it was published in Latin as *Ordinatio Ecclesiastica*. But it did not become law until it was published in Danish in 1539, at which time it was officially adopted by the Diet of Odense.

As a comprehensive church order, it delineated true doctrine; provided suggestions on how these doctrines could be developed in sermons; provided an order of service; designated church year festivals and their pericopes; provided a procedure for the calling of pastors, provosts, and bishops; and outlined their duties and privileges. It also gave guidance for the religious education of children, the management of church property, the care of the poor, and the preparation of candidates for the Holy Ministry.

To implement the provisions of this church order, the king appointed, on the very day the church order was adopted, seven new bishops or superintendents to replace the incarcerated Catholic bishops. The installation (not consecration) of these new bishops was performed by Bugenhagen, a priest, thus breaking the historical episcopal succession. It is noteworthy that before the installation of the new bishops, Bugenhagen

---

[9] Quoted in Edmund Belfour, "The History of the Liturgy of the Lutheran Church in Denmark," *Memoirs of the Lutheran Liturgical Association* II (1899–1900), 58–9.

presided at the coronation service for the king and his queen. Realizing the momentous nature of this undertaking (since usually an archbishop would have presided at a coronation), Bugenhagen addressed the congregation gathered for the coronation (before the entrance of the king and queen) saying that he was doing this only because he was the minister appointed to serve at the altar that day and the king and queen were coming to "his altar."[10] There is no indication that the people did not accept the king and queen and the new bishops. The new king also acted to make Norway a province of Denmark, both politically and ecclesiastically. So new bishops were installed for Norway at the same time as the installation of the new Danish bishops, although two of them were pre-Reformation bishops who had never been consecrated. This was a not uncommon situation in the medieval church, which saw episcopacy more in terms of juridical than of pastoral leadership. Bishops sometimes functioned for years by appointment before they were properly consecrated or ordained. A new bishop was also installed for Iceland, although the two older bishops on the island resisted the Reformation for another decade. Nevertheless, in spite of a few pockets of resistance, the Reformation was implemented in Denmark, Norway, and Iceland in one fell swoop under a new king with a new church order, new bishops, and a new liturgy.

Full liturgical provisions were missing from the church order. Ministers had to use pre-Reformation books and new evangelical hymnals, as these became available. A Handbook or Manual was prepared by Peder Palladius (1503–1560) in 1538 to provide some guidance. Palladius had been summoned back from studies at Wittenberg by Christian III to accompany Bugenhagen to Denmark and to become bishop (superintendent) of Zealand and professor of theology at the University of Copenhagen.[11] He became the spiritual leader of the Church of Denmark for the next twenty years, served as the principal theological advisor to King Christian III and was appointed superintendent of ecclesiastical affairs in Denmark, Norway, and the Faeroes. He took seriously the provision in the church order that there should be episcopal visitation of parishes, and provided a *Visitatsbog* to cover the whole range of parochial concerns from altar furnishings to the doctrinal positions of the parish pastor. This latter provision was made necessary by the fact that most pre-Reformation priests remained in their parishes in Denmark, Norway, and Iceland. While some had already embraced Reformation ideas, others had not. It took time to convince them of the evangelical faith and practices or for Lutheran priests to replace them as they died out.

A synod of the Danish church that met in Copenhagen in 1540 declared the usage of the Church of Our Lady in Copenhagen (*Frue Kirke*), where the royal coronation and episcopal installations had taken place, to be the liturgical norm for the realm, since in his two years of ministry in Copenhagen Bugenhagen had been able to influence practice in this "cathedral" church. Even so, a certain flexibility was built into the authorized order of service, reflecting the standard German Lutheran practice of using Latin in

---

[10] See Sven Børregaard, "The Post-Reformation Developments of the Episcopacy in Denmark, Norway, and Iceland," in Ivar Asheim and Victor Gold, ed., *Episcopacy in the Lutheran Church?* (Philadelphia: Fortress Press, 1970), 116ff.

[11] See Martin Schwartz Lausten, *Biskop Peder Palladius og kirken, 1537–1560* (Copenhagen, 1987).

town and collegiate churches and a service based on chorales in village churches. The use was as follows:

> The minister, kneeling before the altar in full vestments, said the versicles
>   and confiteor in Danish or Latin and prayed for the pardon of the people.
>   He then offered prayer for the word, the king, and the realm.
>   Then followed:
> The Introit or a Danish hymn
> Kyrie three times, sung by the deacon
>   or the hymn "Kyrie, Gud Fader alsomhøiste Trøst"
> Gloria sung by the choir in Latin or
>   Danish hymn sung by the congregation
> Salutation and Collect
> Epistle
> Halleluia sung by two children
>   and Gradual, or Danish hymn to the Holy Spirit,
>   or the traditional sequence on Christmas, Easter, and Pentecost
> Gospel
> Credo sung in Latin in the schools;
>   replaced by a hymn to the Trinity in towns and villages
> Hymn as the preacher mounts the pulpit
> Sermon
> Hymn
> General Prayer

Without communion the service terminated with the Lord's Prayer, the Aaronic benediction, and a hymn. When there were communicants, an exhortation followed the general prayer, and the order continued as follows:

> Lord's Prayer
> Words of institution
> Ministration of communion while the Agnus Dei was sung
> Communion blessing
> Hymn of thanksgiving
> Collect
> Benediction
> Hymn *pro pace* or *pro exitu*
> (Sometimes the versified Decalogue was sung)

Hymnody played an important role in the Danish liturgy. Collects, epistles, gospels, and the words of institution could also be sung. There was no provision for the Sanctus; but it could be sung before the words of institution on festivals. The synod of 1540 allowed a "decent elevation" and the use of the sign of the cross at blessings and benedictions. All sources indicate that the words of institution were to be said over additional supplies of bread and wine. The minister was allowed to commune himself.

In other provisions, the church order provided for morning and evening services that retained some features of the traditional Matins and Vespers, although they became chiefly occasions for rehearsing and preaching on the catechism. The instructions concerning baptism were filled out by a corresponding liturgical order in Palladius's Manual, which was not unlike Luther's orders, including the initial exorcism and "flood prayer" over the water. The rite of confirmation was abolished, although Bugenhagen made provision for the catechesis and admission of children to Holy Communion at about age eight. The liturgical resources compiled around 1540 lasted exactly a hundred years until a new church order was adopted in 1640. Bishop Palladius revised his Manual in his *Altarbog* (1556), and that remained in use as the official manual until 1685.

🍇 THE BEGINNING OF THE REFORMATION IN SWEDEN

In contrast with the swift implementation of the Reformation in Denmark, the Reformation in Sweden made very slow headway. The background for the Reformation was a war for national liberation precipitated by a typical late-medieval skirmish between church and state. The Swedes, under their regent, Sten Sture, had deposed the archbishop of Uppsala, Gustav Trolle, in 1515. The Swedish Estates declared Trolle a traitor, razed his castle to the ground, and swore to stand together.[12] Viewing this as a direct assault on the authority of both the church and the state, King Christian II of Denmark entered Sweden, rounded up many of the nobles (including some bishops who had sided with Sture), convened an ecclesiastical court (under the presidency of a Danish bishop), and summarily executed nearly a hundred people in the public square of Stockholm on November 8, 1520 (an event that has gone down in Swedish history as the "Stockholm Bloodbath").[13]

A young nobleman, Gustav Vasa, carried off by King Christian to Denmark in 1518, escaped, returned to Sweden, and led a resistance with economic assistance from the city of Lübeck. Civil war also erupted in Denmark at this time as the Danish nobility deposed King Christian II. The new King Frederick wanted to assert his claims on Sweden just as Christian had done, but he was in debt to Lübeck just as Gustav Vasa was, and Lübeck preferred to deal with a divided Scandinavia. Lübeck had made Frederick king in Denmark; they would make Gustav Vasa king in Sweden. The Swedes had no one else to whom to turn, so they offered the crown to young Vasa on June 6, 1523, and Stockholm surrendered to him on June 17.

Gustav thus achieved political power; but he also inherited the church-state clash that had erupted between Sten Sture and Archbishop Trolle. With both removed from the scene (Sture had been executed in the "Bloodbath" and Trolle was in Denmark), reconciliation between church and state might have been possible. But a new factor was injected: the importation of the Reformation. In 1523 the new king came into contact with two of the men who would figure most prominently in the Swedish Reformation: Olavus Petri and Laurentius Andreae (aka Olaf Pettersson and Lars Andersson).

Laurentius Andreae (c. 1470–1552) had studied in Skara and Uppsala and obtained his master's degree at the University of Rostock in Germany. He then studied

---

[12] See Michael Roberts, *The Early Vasas. A History of Sweden, 1523–1611* (Cambridge University Press, 1968), 12.

[13] John Wordsworth, *The National Church of Sweden* (London and Milwaukee: A. R. Mowbray, 1911), 178ff.

canon law in Rome and made two additional trips to that city. He returned from his last trip to Rome to become archdeacon in the diocese of Strängnäs. He took over the administration of the diocese when Bishop Mattias was executed in the Stockholm Bloodbath. He became an aide to Gustav Vasa during the war for national liberation. After Gustav's election as king, Andreae was made secretary (i.e., principal adviser) to the king, a member of the council of state (the *råd*), and archdeacon of Uppsala. He became the principal political engineer of the implementation of the Reformation in Sweden.[14]

Olavus Petri (1493–1552), the son of a blacksmith from Örebro, attended the University of Wittenberg between 1516 and 1518. These were the years in which Luther was formulating the formal and material principles of the Reformation: sola Scriptura and sola fide. Petri may also have studied languages briefly with Melanchthon, who arrived in Wittenberg in 1518. While these were years of great intellectual ferment and political excitement in Wittenberg, they were also years before any formal break with Rome had occurred. Luther had not yet had his debate with Eck at Leipzig, which was the first event to push Luther's reformation to a point of ecclesiastical impasse. Returning to Sweden, Olavus Petri was energized with the ideas of Luther but not with thoughts of a complete break with the pre-Reformation church. He settled down in Strängnäs, where he was ordained a deacon by Bishop Mattias. There he met Laurentius Andreae, the archdeacon of the diocese. Olavus Petri would emerge as the great preacher and literary figure of the Reformation in Sweden, putting a unique stamp on the reformed Church of Sweden.[15] He acquired the positions to influence the course of the Reformation by being appointed secretary of the city council of Stockholm (he was still a deacon at this time, not a priest) and by being appointed preacher of the Great Church *(Storkyrkan)* of Stockholm (this was the closest church to a cathedral in the capital city; Stockholm was not a bishopric).

The third person who would figure importantly in the Swedish Reformation was the younger brother of Olavus Petri, Laurentius (1499–1573). Laurentius (Lars) also studied at Wittenberg, but during the days in which the first efforts were being made in the practical reform of church life in the period after 1522. He would be the person to give leadership to the practical reform of church life as the first evangelical archbishop (1531–1573).[16]

Standing behind these three evangelical leaders was King Gustav Vasa, whose own theological ideas are difficult to measure but who was willing to use the Reformation to assist in the cause of national unity and economic development. In Olavus Petri he had an able theologian who could argue against the positions of the old guard, and in Laurentius Andreae he had an able canon lawyer who could use existing legal traditions to the advantage of the crown. Olavus had great influence on the archdeacon, whose

---

[14] See Peder Svart, *Gustav Vasas krönika*, ed. by Gunnar T. Westin (Malmö, 1964).

[15] See Nils Forsander, *Olavus Petri. The Church Reformer of Sweden* (Rock Island, Ill.: Augustana Book Concern, 1918) and Conrad Bergendoff, *Olavus Petri and the Ecclesiastical Transformation in Sweden* (Philadelphia: Fortress Press, 1965).

[16] See Eric E. Yelverton, *An Archbishop of the Reformation: Laurentius Petri Nericius, Archbishop of Uppsala, 1531–73* (London and Minneapolis: Augsburg Publishing House, 1959).

Lutheran sympathies were quickly manifested in a famous letter that he wrote to the celebrated convent at Vadstena. In this letter Laurentius Andreae maintained that the church belonged to the whole community of the faithful, that its resources were originally given to the convent to serve public needs, and that they may serve the common good now when needed. In short, the church's wealth is the people's wealth because the church is the people.[17] These ideas were clearly derived from Luther's "Open Letter to the Christian Nobility of the German Nation Concerning the Reform of the Christian Estate" (1520).

The implications of this assault on the economic immunities of the church were not lost on Gustav Vasa. The war of independence had proven costly and the dangers to national security required a standing army and navy. The debt payment to Lübeck had to be met as well. And there was no national treasury. As early as 1524 the new king was suggesting that the church, especially the wealthy monasteries, help bear some of the burden of this expense. At first the råd rejected the idea, but by 1525 they consented to the quartering of troops in the monasteries on the argument that the bishops had formerly billeted their own retinues in the cloisters. They also decreed that a portion of the tithe that went to the parish churches should this year be diverted to the national treasury to help defray defenses expenses.[18]

There was considerable local resistance to the confiscation of church property, funds, and treasures. A rebellion broke out in Dalarna. The result of these turmoils was the summoning of the Estates to Västerås in June 1527. The *riksdag* (parliament) was asked to consider the political unrest in Dalarna and deal with theological issues. King Gustav opened the meeting with a long address concerning the state of the nation. Roberts has commented that "it was a document of great political adroitness, masterly in its plainness, its forcefulness, its irony, its seductive logic, and in a certain roughhewn, popular quality which fitted it well to the tastes and understandings of most of the audience to which it was addressed."[19]

After a seemingly endless recital of the problems of government, especially the problem of insufficient revenue, Gustav played his trump card: the threat of abdication. The Estates were in a quandary. They could not afford to hope that another national leader would emerge to relieve them of the necessity of choosing between Frederick I and Christian II of Denmark. In terms of securing additional revenue there seemed no way out other than to dip into the resources of the church. Bishop Brask of Linköping led a vigorous opposition, and it took days for the Estates to come up with the resolution for which Gustav was waiting. The resistance was broken only with a timely burst of tears from the king and a new threat of abdication, which this time seemed definite.

The resulting resolutions were celebrated in Swedish history as the Recess of Västerås. The Recess provided (1) a mutual agreement to put down all revolts and punish all enemies of the king; (2) authorization for the king to appropriate all castles and

---

[17] See Wordsworth, 190.
[18] See Roberts, 66–7.
[19] Ibid., 73.

strongholds held by the bishops; (3) authorization for the nobles to resume that part of their inheritance that had been transferred to the churches and monasteries since 1454, if the heir could substantiate his claim; and (4) freedom for the preachers to proclaim the pure word of God.[20] This latter measure was passed after a disputation had been held, as requested by the king, between Olavus Petri and Peder Galle, who represented the anti-Reformation point of view.

The decisions at Västerås were a complete triumph for King Gustav, but they cannot be regarded as a definitive triumph for the Reformation in Sweden. In fact, says Roberts, what the Recess really did by implication was to exculpate Gustav Vasa "from the charge of Lutheranism." The commoners and the members of the råd urged him to preserve "good Old Christian customs," and there was no break with papal authority. What the Recess did was to insure was the future of the Reformation in Sweden. The reformers were exonerated of all charges of heresy and were given free rein to preach the doctrines based on the scriptures. There is no indication that Gustav Vasa was as yet a convinced Lutheran. He made use of the Reformation for political purposes and economic advantages. But he was a man who knew the power of the spoken word. He was himself a good "stump" politician, and he increasingly came to measure a priest's usefulness in terms of the assiduity of his preaching. Preachers who based their sermons on the Bible rather than on the doctors, councils, or popes had a sympathetic listener in Gustav Vasa. Anti-Reformation bishops saw their inevitable fate. Hans Brask left Sweden, never to return to his homeland, as did the archbishop-elect, Johannes Magnus, who lived in exile and wrote his celebrated *History of All the Kings of the Goths and Swedes.*

Vacancies on the episcopal bench gave the king an opportunity to appoint bishops who would be sympathetic to the Reformation. His impending coronation in 1528 required that properly consecrated and anointed bishops be installed to officiate at the coronation and lend validity to the reign of an elected monarch. In the absence of an archbishop, the senior bishop of the realm, Petrus Magni, was ordered to consecrate three new bishops on Epiphany 1528, and consented to do so provided that they would seek papal confirmation afterward. Similarly, in 1531 the king's impending marriage provided an opportunity to deal definitively with the complications of the abandoned archiepiscopal See of Uppsala and to have a proper archbishop to officiate at the royal wedding. The deposed Gustav Trolle was still in Europe arguing that he should be restored to his position. Johannes Magni had been elected archbishop in place of the deposed Trolle by the Uppsala chapter and had been confirmed by the pope but had not yet been consecrated. In view of this situation, Gustav set aside the rights of the cathedral chapter and convened an assembly of clergy from throughout the whole kingdom (171 in all), of whom 150 voted for Laurentius Petri. An additional three new bishops were consecrated on August 13, and the new archbishop on September 22, 1531, by Bishops Petrus Magni and Magnus Sommar, who deposited objections to the new doctrines and practices with the Chapter of Strängnäs on August 10.[21] The result of these episcopal

---

[20] See Wordsworth, 109.
[21] Wordsworth, 206–7.

consecrations without papal confirmation was an autocephalous church.[22] But the historic episcopate was preserved in the Church of Sweden, even though because Gustav later preferred superintendents to bishops and allowed bishoprics to remain vacant, the Swedish apostolic succession depended on Laurentius Petri alone.

🍇 THE LITURGICAL WORK OF OLAVUS PETRI

Olavus Petri provided Swedish Lutheranism with its fundamental literary monuments. Since fewer than ten books had been published in the Swedish language before 1526, he can be regarded as the father of Swedish literature as well as the Swedish church's foremost theologian. The year 1526 saw the anonymous publication of three small works that are now attributed to Olavus Petri and the translation of the New Testament into Swedish, for which Bergendoff credits Olavus a major role.[23]

The most important of the small books was a catechism or primer entitled, *A Useful Instruction (Een nyttwgh wnderwijsning)*.[24] It included instruction on man's creation and fall, the Ten Commandments, the Creed with an explanation of its twelve articles, the Pater Noster and Ave Maria with explanations, the Magnificat, "a right observance of our Lord's suffering and death," and an exposition of the seven penitential psalms. It has been assumed that this primer was based on Luther's *Betbuchlein* (Prayer Book) of 1522, but Bergendoff points out that the sections on man's creation and fall are independent, and that the Magnificat is not found in any edition of Luther's *Betbuchlein* before 1526.[25] The purpose of *A Useful Instruction* was probably to counter the influence of the Swedish Catholic Prayer Book (*Tideboken*, or *Horae*), which was printed in 1525.

In 1526, Olavus Petri was taken up with the translation of the New Testament into Swedish, for which he bore major responsibility. This was followed by several treatises dealing with practical matters of church life and A Useful Postil, which contained twenty-seven sermons and homilies translated from Luther's Church Postil.

Olavus Petri published his own Postil in 1530. It was, in part, an effort to carry out the decisions of the church council held in Örebro in 1529, which ordered the reading of scripture in churches and schools, enjoined faithfulness to the scriptures in preaching, and urged priests to carefully explain the rites and ceremonies of the church to their people.[26] The council aimed at compromise and did not want to unduly provoke the Catholic party. So the Latin mass was not abolished; but provision was made for a preaching service based on the medieval vernacular office of Prone. Petri's Postil was designed to help preachers with this service. That is why it not only contains sermons on seventy-two *de tempore* and eighteen *de sanctis* gospel texts, but also vernacular forms of

---

[22] See Theodor van Haag, "Die apostolische Sukzession in Schweden," *Kyrkohistorisk årsskrift* 44 (1944), 33; also Sven Kjöllerström, *Kräkla och mitra* (Lund, 1965), 20–3.

[23] Bergendoff, 91ff.

[24] *Sam. Sk.*, I, 1–120.

[25] Bergendoff, 88.

[26] Roberts, 85–6.

introductory and concluding prayers, the Pater Noster, Ave Maria, Credo, and Commandments.[27] To aid clergy with explanations for these texts, Petri appended to the Postil a catechism based on Luther's Large Catechism of 1529.

The office of Prone was also the place for congregational singing. The first collection of Swedish hymns was probably made in 1526, but the first Swedish hymnal of which we possess extant copies was published in 1530, the same year as the Postil.[28] This hymnal went through several augmented editions in subsequent years, of which *Swenske songer eller wisor* (*Swedish Songs and Ditties*) of 1536 is the oldest and best preserved.[29] Olavus Petri was apparently the editor of these first Swedish hymnals. They are primarily translations of German hymns with their tunes, although some Swedish originals were included, including two hymns written by Olavus Petri: "O Fadher waar barmhertigh och godh" (Our Father, merciful and good) and "O Jesus Christ som mandom togh" (Thou, Jesus Christ, didst man become).

Olavus Petri's work in the field of liturgics constitutes, in Bergendoff's view, his most important, influential, and lasting endeavor.[30] His Postils went far in creating a style of preaching in Swedish. The preaching service is still discernible in the pulpit office of the modern Swedish *Högmässa* (High Mass). His hymn collections form the basis of the Swedish *Psalmboken* (Hymnal). The Swedish Mass, prepared by him in 1531, remained in use, with few modifications, until the twentieth century. But of equal importance in Swedish liturgical history with the hymnal and the mass is the *Handbok* or *Manual: Een handbook paa Swensko* (1529). This work holds the distinction of being the first Protestant vernacular occasional services book. Eric Yelverton called it "the first rudiment in Europe of what we in England call a Book of Common Prayer,"[31] although it contains only occasional offices. (The eucharistic rite was treated two years later, and no vernacular choral office tradition developed in Sweden.)

A general church council had been held in Örebro in 1529, over which Laurentius Andreae presided in the absence of an archbishop. This council provided that the more learned clergy were to give lessons in biblical exegesis and preaching to the less learned clergy; loosened the laws regarding clerical celibacy; and required an explanation of ceremonies such as anointing.[32] Olavus Petri drew on the results of this council in preparing his *Manual*. As he wrote in his introduction:

> I have determined, through the grace that God hath given me, to set forth a little manual in Swedish, especially since at the Council which has met this very year at Örebro it was proposed that Baptism might well be administered in Swedish, and that some instruction should be put forth for the sake of sick people who desire preparation for their death, to the end that the unlearned clergy may have some guidance how they may teach those who lie on their death.[33]

---

[27] *Sam. Sk.*, III, 470ff.

[28] Ibid., II, 561–9.

[29] Ibid., II, 521–9.

[30] Bergendoff, 147.

[31] *The Manual of Olavus Petri*, trans. with an introduction by Eric Yelverton (London: S.P.C.K., 1953), ix.

[32] Wordsworth, 204–5.

[33] *The Manual of Olavus Petri*, 62. See *Sam. Sk.*, II, 314–5.

Thus the baptismal rite and the rites for the visitation of the sick form the nucleus of the *Manual*. Olavus relates that in addition to these two rites, which were dealt with at the Council, he worked out Orders for Marriage, the Churching of Women, the Hallowing of the Dead, Burial, and the Visitation of Prisoners under sentence of death. In these rites Olavus did not follow the Latin manual entirely, "since that manual doth not agree with the Scriptures, as it should."[34] But he admits that "in this my manual I have also retained in the main the Ceremonies and customs which have been hitherto observed, being in themselves not repugnant to the word of God."[35] These ceremonies included in the baptismal rite the sign of the cross, the major and minor exorcisms, the pre-baptismal anointing, the post-baptismal anointing (chrism), and the giving of the white robe and the lighted candle. In the marriage rite the ceremonies included the betrothal at the church porch, the nuptial preface said under the bridal canopy (a blessing of the couple, not the eucharistic elements), and the nuptial eucharist. In the visitation of the sick, they included auricular confession, communion from the reserved sacrament, and anointing "unto life, and not unto death."[36] (This last phrase suggests that Olavus Petri wished to restore the apostolic anointing of the sick in the Epistle of James rather than retain the medieval practice of extreme unction.)

Here, then, is a liturgical book which, like the Swedish Mass of 1531, followed a *via media* between the old and the new. Olavus Petri may have preferred to make more thoroughgoing changes in these offices than he did. But, as Bergendoff pointed out, "Olavus understood the power of ceremony, and knew the conservative nature of his countrymen."[37]

The *Manual* of 1529 was not promulgated on any official authority. Yet the ultimate success and worth of Olavus Petri's liturgical work in this book is evident in the fact that it has been revised only fourteen times since its publication; the first two revisions were by Olavus Petri himself (in 1533 and 1537), and the next three revisions (1541, 1548, and 1557) were written by Olavus's brother, Archbishop Laurentius.

Perhaps Olavus Petri's most enduring legacy was *Then Swenska Messan* (The Swedish Mass). The subtitle of this publication indicates its original limited purpose: "as it is now held in Stockholm with reasons why it is so held."[38] No liturgical change had been ordered by the Recess of Västerås, and unrest in the provinces of Småland and Västergötland in 1529, occasioned by liturgical change, militated against a kingdomwide change in the mass. The king's attitude was that official meetings of the Estates in 1527 and of the church in 1529 had neither commanded nor forbidden the use of vernacular masses, and such worship can be defended by God's word over which he had no authority. Moreover, many people in Stockholm (especially the Germans) thought the pace of reform was too slow. As secretary of the city council, Olavus Petri brought up several resolutions that the mass should be celebrated in Swedish in that city and the Latin mass

---

[34] Ibid.
[35] Ibid.
[36] Ibid., 76ff.
[37] Bergendoff, 176.
[38] *Sam. Sk.*, II, 405ff.

discontinued. Perhaps mindful of the proceedings at Augsburg that spring, the city council passed such a resolution in August, 1530. As Sven Kjöllerström notes, this resolution applied only to the city of Stockholm and not to the country as a whole.[39] Indeed, as late as 1536 Bishop Johannes Magni prepared a reformed Latin mass for use in his diocese of Linköping: the curious *Missa Lincopense*. This was simply the medieval mass with all objectionable references to the intercessions of the saints and the sacrificial language of the offertory and eucharistic prayers altered or removed.

Olavus had examples of evangelical mass-orders from which to work. The Swedish liturgist Oscar Quensel believed that the Swedish Mass was a critical reworking of the medieval Roman mass with some innovations derived, partly from *Formula Missae*, partly from *Deutsche Messe*.[40] Edvard Rodhe, however, showed that the Swedish Mass was more closely based on another evangelical mass, which also followed the structure of Luther's *Formula Missae*: the *Evangelische Messe* prepared by Andreas Döber for the New Hospital in Nuremberg in 1525.[41] This Nuremberg Mass found its way into a number of German song books. Conrad Bergendoff suggests that the one with which the Swedish Mass most agrees is Sluter's *Gesangbuch* (Rostock, 1531).[42] The order of the Swedish Mass follows:

1. Preparation for the mass:
   Invitation to "the supper of our Lord Jesus Christ"
   Confession of sins
   Absolution (in precatory form)

2. Entrance rite:
   Introit: may be a psalm or other song
   Kyrie three times
   Gloria

3. The Word:
   Salutation and Collect
   Epistle (a chapter or a half-chapter)
   Gradual: the hymn about God's commandments
   Gospel (read continuously)
   Creed: Apostles' or Nicene

4. Eucharist:
   Preface, expanded, leads to . . .
   Words of institution
   Sanctus
   Our Father, with traditional introduction
   The Peace of the Lord
   Agnus Dei
   Exhortation (if the priest deems it necessary)
   Ministration of Holy Communion

---

[39] Sven Kjöllerström, *Missa Lincopense: En liturgi-historisk studie* (Stockholm, 1941), 32.

[40] Oscar Quensel, *Bidrag til svenska liturgiens historia* (Uppsala, 1890–1893), II, 48.

[41] Edvard Rodhe, *Svenskt gudstjänstliv. Historisk belysning av den svenska Kyrkohandboken* (Stockholm, 1930), 30ff.

[42] Bergendoff, 152.

5. Post-Communion:
   A Swedish hymn or the Nunc dimittis
   Salutation and Benedicamus
   Aaronic benediction

The Swedish Mass follows Luther's *Formula Missae* in the tell-tale eucharistic structure of preface-words of institution-Sanctus, and it retains the historic structure of the mass generally. In other respects, however, Olavus Petri did not follow the *Formula Missae*. Most obviously, the Swedish Mass is entirely a vernacular liturgy whereas the *Formula Missae* was entirely in Latin. The exhortation and communion prayers are based on Döber's Nuremberg Mass, from whence also comes the Lutheran tradition of singing the Nunc dimittis after the ministration of communion.[43] This may have been a custom in some late medieval German missals as well, which explains why it was included in the Rostock Songbook.[44]

One area in which Olavus very conspicuously departed from Luther was in providing a confession of sins for the whole congregation. There is no such provision in either the *Formula Missae* or the German Mass, although Luther regarded the Pax Domini as a true absolution in which the communicants know that their sins have been forgiven.

The tripartite preparation office in the medieval mass was recast by Olavus into a simpler invitation, confession, and absolution in which the people joined the priest. The invitation and confession were the work of Olavus himself, although the confession was based on the one in the original Nuremberg Mass and in the Nuremberg Enchiridion of 1527.[45] This confession has remained a part of the Swedish Mass until the twentieth century. In English translation, it is:

> I, poor sinful man, who am both conceived and born in sin, and ever afterwards have led a sinful life all my days, heartily confess before you, almighty and eternal God, my dear heavenly father, that I have not loved you above all things nor my neighbor as myself; I have (alas!) sinned against you and your holy commandments in manifold ways both in thoughts, words and deeds, and know that for that cause I am worthy of hell and everlasting damnation, if you should judge me, as your stern justice requires and my sins have deserved. But now have you promised, dear heavenly father, that you will deal graciously and pitifully with all poor sinners who will turn themselves and with a steadfast faith fly to your incomprehensible mercy; with them you will overlook whatsoever they have offended against you, and nevermore impute to them their sins; in this I miserable sinner put my faith, and pray trustfully that you will after thy same promise vouchsafe to be merciful and gracious to me and forgive me all my sins, to the praise and honor of your holy name.[46]

---

[43] See Julius Smend, *Die evangelischen deutsche Messe bis zu Luthers deutscher Messe* (Göttingen, 1896), 246.

[44] See Jungmann, *The Mass of the Roman Rite*, II, 404, n. 31.

[45] Bergendoff, 152.

[46] Text in Eric Yelverton, ed. and trans., *The Mass in Sweden: Its Development from the Latin Rite from 1531 to 1917*. Henry Bradshaw Society, Vol. 57 (London: Harrison and Sons, 1920), 33; alt.

Quensel suggests that the absolution, which is properly sacramental (directed to the people as a word of grace), is cast in sacrificial form because the priest includes himself with the people.[47]

> The almightiest and eternal God of his great incomprehensible mercy forgive us all our sins and give us grace that we may amend our sinful life and attain with him eternal life. Amen.[48]

However, Olavus retained the properly sacramental form of the absolution by directing that it be said "over the people."

Following his Nuremberg models, Olavus abandoned the whole system of proper collects and lections in favor of a freer usage. An appendix to the Swedish Mass provided Swedish translations of the seven penitential psalms, which could be used for Introit material, and sixteen collects, from which a wider selection could be made for the collect of the day. No readings were assigned: Olavus preferred the lectio continua principle because it acquainted the people more thoroughly with the scriptures.

Also following the German models, the Apostles' Creed was proposed as an alternative to the Nicene, although only the Apostles' Creed was printed in the Swedish Mass. From the Creed, the order passed on to the preface, which led into the institution narrative, and which was followed by the Sanctus during which the bread and cup were elevated. The preface was one of the most original texts in the Swedish Mass. Yngve Brilioth suggested that it was freely based on the paschal preface in the medieval mass. Following Brilioth, we compare here the preface in the Nuremberg Mass with the *Praefatio communis* and the preface in the Swedish Mass with the *Praefatio paschalis*.[49]

PRAEFATIO COMMUNIS	THE NUREMBERG MASS
Vere dignum et iustum est,	Ja, wahrlich es ist billich
aequum et salutare, nos tibi	und recht, auch heylsam, das
semper et ubique gratias	wir an allen orten dir, herr,
agere: Domine sancte, Pater	heyliger vater, almechtiger
omnipotens, aeterne Deus:	ewiger Gott, dank sagen, durch
per Christum Dominum nos-	Christum, unsern herren. Amen.
trum. Per quem maiestatem	Welcher in der nacht, do er
tuam laudant Angeli . . .	verraten ward . . .

PRAEFATIO PASCHALIS	THE SWEDISH MASS OF OLAVUS PETRI
Vere dignum et iustum est,	Verily it is meet and right
aequum et salutare: Te quidem,	that we should in all places
Domine, omni tempore,	give thanks and praise to you,

---

[47] Quensel, II, 29.

[48] Yelverton, *The Mass in Sweden*, 34.

[49] Yngve Brilioth, *Nattvarden i evangeliskt gudstjänstliv* (Stockholm, 1951), 340. This work is known in the Eng. trans. of A. G. Hebert, *Eucharistic Faith and Practice: Evangelical and Catholic* (London: S.P.C.K., 1965), but the chapter on the Swedish Rite has been abridged in the English version.

sed in hac potissimum die
gloriosius praedicare, cum
Pascha nostrum immolatus
est Christus. Ipse enim
verus est Agnus, qui abstulit
peccata mundi. Qui mortem
nostram moriendo destruxit,
et vitam resurgendo
reparavit. Et ideo cum
Angel is . . .

holy Lord, almighty Father,
everlasting God for all your benefits,
and especially for that one that
you did unto us, when we all
by reason of sins were in so bad
a case that nothing but damnation
and eternal death awaited us, and
no creature in heaven or earth
could help us, then you did
send forth your only-begotten
Son Jesus Christ, who was of
the same divine nature as yourself,
did suffer him to become
a man for our sake, did lay
our sins upon him, and did
suffer him to undergo death in
stead of our all dying eternally,
and as he hath overcome death and
risen again into life, and now
dies nevermore, so likewise
shall all they who put their
trust therein overcome sins and
death and through him attain to
everlasting life, and for our
admonition that we should bear
in mind and never forget such
his benefit, in the night that
he was betrayed celebrated a
supper, in which he took the
bread in his holy hands . . .[50]

Brilioth criticized this pattern of the eucharistic preface that leads into the institution narrative for "missing its natural climax in the Sanctus."[51] Rather than lament the displacement of the Sanctus in these evangelical revisions of the mass, it would be more profitable to inquire into the meaning that could be ascribed to the Sanctus as a result of its relocation to the end of the eucharistic prayer. Eric Yelverton, recalling the Lutheran view that "the presence of Christ in the sacrament is effected by the consecration and reception, which are linked together as one indivisible whole," has suggested: "If we regard the Sanctus as a hymn of praise to the coming Christ, then from the Lutheran point of view the Sanctus is linked with the reception rather than with the Preface."[52] Luther had the German Sanctus sung during the distribution in his *Deutsche Messe*.

There is probably another reason for the placement of the Sanctus after the words of institution in the Lutheran mass. It was standard practice in the medieval high mass for the priest to start reciting the canon quietly while the choir sang the Sanctus.

---

[50] Text cited from Yelverton, *The Mass in Sweden*, 37–8; alt.

[51] Brilioth, *Eucharistic Faith and Practice*, 242.

[52] Yelverton, *The Mass in Sweden*, 30.

The elevation was timed to occur at the Benedictus qui venit. This was an arrangement with which Luther was familiar and which he retained in his *Formula Missae*. Olavus Petri retained the elevation of the bread and the cup after the words over each in his Swedish Mass. In his treatise, *De officiis ecclesiasticis* (1568), Laurentius Petri provided for a fully sung mass by having the traditional Latin chants interspersed with the Swedish texts. The Latin preface could be sung, leading into the Sanctus; then the words of institution were sung in Swedish, followed by the Benedictus qui venit.[53] The Sanctus was broken into two sections: the Ter Sanctus was sung before the words of institution and the Benedictus was sung after the Verba. The effect was to retain the association of the elevation with the Benedictus which had been known in the pre-Reformation mass-rite and continued as a practice in Baroque Catholicism.[54] In a sense, therefore, the Sanctus was not displaced or relocated in the Lutheran mass; rather, it was retained in the position where it had been known ceremonially before the Reformation. Outwardly there would have been little noticeable difference to the congregation because the canon had been recited silently anyway. The sequence of preface–words of institution–Sanctus thus provides another indication of Lutheran cultic conservatism.

Two other items deserve special notice in Olavus Petri's Swedish Mass. One is the absence of any reference to a sermon, either before the mass or as a part of it. The second item is the permissive rubric that allowed the Gradual, Sanctus, Agnus Dei, Communio (and the Introit by inference) to be sung or said. These considerations prompted Brilioth to suggest that, like Döber's Hospital Mass, "The first Swedish Mass was designed to take the place of the low mass at which the people made their Communion, not the high mass."[55] The Latin high mass continued to be sung on Sundays and festivals and the preaching would normally occur at those celebrations. But the people did not usually receive communion at the high mass. What Olavus Petri provided, therefore, was a "low mass" or a communion-mass.

If what Olavus Petri provided was a vernacular low mass, then this suggests a reconsideration of the point of view that Latin was gradually reintroduced in the Swedish Mass in its successive revisions. Rather, what was happening was that the Swedish low mass was being merged with the Latin high mass to provide for celebrations with all the ceremonial and music of the old rite. There was contemporary precedent for such a usage in some north German church orders such as Brandenburg-Nuremberg 1533 and Mark Brandenburg 1540. It is a well-known fact that Latin was retained in Lutheran services in many areas long after the Reformation, especially where there was a desire to retain the traditional Gregorian chants or polyphonic settings of the mass-texts sung by the choir.

It must also be kept in mind that the Swedish Mass was not an official rite. Except in Stockholm, where the Latin mass had been banned, Olavus Petri's Swedish Mass was, in the words of Sven Kjöllerström, "a private venture without ecclesiastical sanction."[56] Not until 1536 did the church council assembled in Uppsala give Olavus

---

[53] Yelverton, *An Archbishop of the Reformation*, 33, 114, 128.

[54] Jungmann, II, 137.

[55] Brilioth, 244.

[56] Kjöllerström, *Missa Lincopense*, 44.

Petri's *Manual* and Swedish Mass approval for use throughout the realm. Even then the use of the Swedish Mass was not compulsory, because there was no church order to regulate practice and the king withheld his official sanction. The Latin *Missa Lincopense* was the reaction of one diocese to the decision of the 1536 Council that the mass be reformed. Thus, it took time for the Swedish Mass to gain acceptance outside of Stockholm. It may be postulated that this acceptance came with successive revisions of the Swedish Mass which brought it more into conformity with the rubrics of the old rite. It is no accident that the tradition-minded archbishop was the one who guided the Swedish Mass through these revisions.

The revisions of the Swedish Mass in 1535 and 1537 were apparently the work of Olavus Petri because the style of the Swedish Mass is not severely altered. The 1537 revision increased the number of collects to thirty, including fifteen for particular festivals; limited the length of the Introit texts to six verses at most; and allowed the Gradual to be sung in Latin as long as the texts were from the Bible. These provision indicate efforts to make the Swedish Mass more usable as a high mass, especially on festivals.

This process was carried forward in the 1541 revision, which shows the hand of Archbishop Laurentius. His project was to gradually replace the Latin high mass without communicants with a Swedish sung mass or high mass with communicants. As Eric Yelverton suggests, "step by step he introduced a kind of macaronic rite, in which Swedish and Latin were deftly combined so as to 'highlight' the vernacular for the more important parts of the rite, that is, the Lections, the Prone, the Consecration Prayer, the Communion of the people, the Post-communion, and Solemn Benediction."[57] While the primary concern may have been to lead the people to an evangelical order of worship, a secondary concern must surely have been the practical problem of the lack of music for the Swedish texts. Thus, while the 1541 revision provided for a private prayer of confession of sins by the priest in Latin as an alternative to the public confession by the people in Swedish, the rest of the Latin in the mass is for the sung parts: the Introit, Gradual, and Apostles' Creed. At the same time, the archbishop restored the epistle and gospel pericopes for the day as an alternative to the free selection of texts recommended in the 1531 Mass. Equally important is the rubric placing the sermon after the Gospel, which also indicates an effort to move toward a Swedish high mass. Further evidence that this was the intention of the 1541 revision is the provision of musical settings for the preface and the Lord's Prayer, a new set of communion chants in place of the Nunc dimittis (now omitted), and the provision of three signs of the cross with the benediction.

The 1548 revision carried this direction even farther by printing the text of the Nicene Creed in Swedish; by introducing the Swedish hymn, "O Rene Gudz Lamb" (O pure lamb of God) from Olavus Petri's 1536 hymn collection after the Agnus Dei; and by providing four additional post-communion collects, three of them translated from Latin originals.

In 1557 the archbishop published what was to be his last revision of the Swedish Mass. Its main feature was the restoration of the traditional cycle of collects for the

---

[57] *An Archbishop of the Reformation*, 24.

Sundays of the church year, plus those for Christmas Day, Ascension Day, seven others for holy days (i.e., the Purification, the Annunciation, and other feasts of the Virgin Mary, the Nativity of Saint John the Baptist, angels' days, apostles' days, martyrs' days, and a general collect for saints' days), and a number of collects for special occasions. The interesting aspect of this restoration was the omission of the collect for the third Sunday after Trinity, which displaced the rest of the collects in the Trinity season by one Sunday. Laurentius also disapproved of the collect for the seventeenth Sunday after Trinity. Quensel suggested that the words *bonis operibus* and *liberis mentibus* smacked of Pelagianism to the archbishop.[58] So he omitted it and substituted a new one. Again, the collect for the twentieth Sunday displeased him and he substituted one from his brother's collection in the 1531 Mass-book. This turned out to be a rendering of the collect for the third Sunday. The result was that Laurentius omitted the collect on the third Sunday, moved all the rest up one week, and completed the cycle by writing new collect for the seventeenth, twentieth, and twenty-fifth Sundays after Trinity. This cycle of collects survived in the Swedish rite until the twentieth century.

Thus, by 1557, the Swedish *Högmässa* had been filled out with all its provisions and propers.[59] The preparatory office (*Beredelseakten*) consisted of the exhortation, general confession of sins, and absolution (together called *skriftermal*), as found in the Swedish Mass 1531. If the priest did not have skriftermal before the mass, he could place it after the sermon. Both positions had been well established in the tradition of the Swedish Mass. In the Swedish Mass 1531, Olavus Petri placed the confession before the Introit; in the *Postilla* 1531 he placed it after the sermon in the Office of Prone. As an alternative to the general confession, the Latin Confiteor and *Misereatur* were provided for the use of the priest.

The Introit is either a psalm in Latin or Swedish or a hymn of praise (*lovsang*). A third option is the *Introitus de tempore* in Latin from the medieval missals. This is followed by the Kyrie (three times) in Swedish and the Gloria in Swedish ("Ära wari Gudh i högden"). In the period after 1557, the Swedish church picked up the hymn, "Aleneste Gudh i himmelrik," as a substitute for the *Laudamus* in order to encourage more congregational singing. This was a translation of Nicholas Decius's German original, "Allein Gott in der Höh." In a circular letter of 1565, Laurentius Petri approved this practice and it has remained an option in the Swedish Mass ever since.

We have already discussed the arrangement of the cycle of collects in the 1557 Mass-book. Laurentius Petri encouraged the use of these collects for the church year. In addition, the standard collect from the Swedish Mass 1531, "Wij bidhie tich alzmechtuge gudh käre himmelske fadher," was printed in place in the mass-book. The alternative use of the pericopes assigned in the church year lectionary or the lectio continua plan begun in 1531 was continued in 1557. The epistle was followed by the Gradual, either the traditional Latin Gradual or a Swedish hymn. The sermon followed the Gospel, as in 1541. It is presumed that the sermon continued to be framed within the Office of Prone, in which

---

[58] Quensel, II, 69.

[59] See *Messan på Swensko 1557*. Facsimile edition with introduction by Sigtrygg Serenius (Uppsala, 1969).

case the general prayer came after the pulpit announcements, followed by the Lord's Prayer and the Creed. The Apostles' or Nicene Creed was to be spoken or sung in Swedish or in Latin.

No directions are provided regarding the preparation of the gifts on the altar. In Lutheran practice this was usually during the Creed. The eucharistic preface of 1531, including the words of institution, was set to music in the 1557 Mass-book. For a shorter form, the Praefatio communis could be used without the paschal expansion, in the style of Luther's Formula Missae and Döber's Nuremberg Mass. The Sanctus was sung after the words of institution as a conclusion to the act of consecration. The Lord's Prayer was then intoned with the traditional introduction. The communion commenced with the greeting of peace and the Agnus Dei ("O Gudz Lamb"), followed by the Swedish hymn, "O Rene Gudz Lamb," both sung during the distribution of the sacramental elements. As in 1531, the priest could read an exhortation before the ministration of communion if he deemed it appropriate. Following communion a collect was read from a selection of five. The mass concluded with the salutation, benedicamus, and Aaronic benediction.

❧ THE SWEDISH CHURCH ORDER

Kyrkoordningen, 1571

It was undoubtedly Laurentius Petri's desire to follow the publication of the 1557 *Messan på Swensko* with a church order to regulate the liturgical practice and ecclesiastical discipline of the Swedish church. The publication of such a church order had long been urged on Gustav Vasa by the reformers, but the king was unwilling to give the bishops the legal authority they needed to promulgate and enforce such a document.

The first sketch of a church order is found in the *Articuli ordinantiae* of 1540, authorized by the king's superintendent of church affairs, his German councilor George Norman, although it displayed the hand of the archbishop in its directives for the celebration of the church year. It did direct that the Roman canon was not to be used even in Latin masses; rather the words of institution were to be recited in Swedish after the preface and Sanctus.[60] Not until the Vadstena Articles of 1552 did directions indicate that the sung Swedish Mass was replacing the Latin high mass. The Music Book of 1553 provided the necessary settings for the sung Swedish Mass.[61]

With the death of King Gustav and the accession of his oldest son as King Erik XIV in 1561, Archbishop Petri hoped that a church order could be published. In July 1561, he presented a draft of a church order to the riksdag, but the new king was unwilling to accept it because of his Calvinist sympathies. The handsome and well-educated Erik considered himself a good prospective suitor for the hand of Queen Elizabeth I of England, and it served his purpose to present himself and the Swedish church as generally Protestant but not specifically Lutheran. Even though Laurentius Petri had not specified the mode of Christ's presence in the sacrament, the silent testimony of such

---

[60] Brilioth, *Nattvarden*, 351.
[61] Ibid., 353.

practices as the elevation of the host and chalice and kneeling for reception of the elements spoke loud enough of its Lutheran views. As Bergendoff wrote,

> the Swedish situation revolved around public practices which involved a theology, and the defense of elevation and veneration proclaimed the reality of Christ's presence as surely as any scholastic subtleties. The people understood little of *communicatio idiomatum*, but they did understand that the sacrament was more than a memorial or a symbol if the cup was elevated and the proper posture was kneeling.[62]

By 1568, Erik XIV, who was showing signs of insanity brought about by wild mood swings and acute paranoia, had entered into a contest against the nobility and was the suspected murderer of Nils Sture.[63] He was deposed by a coup d'etat of the nobles led by his brothers, Duke Johan of Finland and Duke Karl of Södermanland. This placed on the throne as King Johan III the second son of Gustav Vasa. Johan had been incarcerated in the Gripsholm Castle by his royal brother for carving out his own foreign policy in the eastern Baltic by his dealings with Russia, Livonia, and Poland. In the case of Poland, he had married Katarina Jagellonica, the sister of King Sigismund II Augustus of Poland, and a Roman Catholic. The nuptial agreement committed Johan to provide Catholic chaplains for his wife and to raise his son Sigismund as a Roman Catholic. Johan was an aesthete and intellectual like his brother Erik, but more interested in theology than in science. He was, in fact, a learned disciple of George Cassander and his "mediating theology," and was interested in ecclesiastical reconciliation on the basis of "the consensus of the first five centuries" *(consensus quinquasaecularis)*. The new king, with his architectural and liturgical interests, was sympathetic to many of the concerns of the old archbishop, and the church order (Kyrkoordningen) was finally authorized and published in 1571. It was substantially the same as the handwritten document submitted to the riksdag in 1561.[64]

The Swedish church order is unique in several respects. It contains a vigorous defense of the episcopal office. Laurentius Petri declared that the distinction between "bishop" and "priest" "proved itself useful and without doubt was inspired by God the Holy Spirit, from whom all good gifts come," so that "it was approved and accepted in all of Christendom. Thus it came to be, and must be as long as the world lasts."[65] The Swedish situation allowed for the preference of early Lutheranism "to keep the ecclesiastical and canonical polity and the various ranks of the ecclesiastical hierarchy, although they were created by human authority."[66] But Laurentius Petri undoubtedly felt a need to

---

[62] Conrad Bergendoff, "The Unique Character of the Reformation in Sweden," *Symposium on 17th Century Lutheranism* (St. Louis: Concordia Historical Society, 1962), 96.

[63] See Ingvar Anderson, *A History of Sweden*, trans. by Carolyn Hannay and Alan Blair (New York and Washington: Praeger Publishers, 1956), 148.

[64] See Emil Färnström, *Laurentius Petris handskrivna kyrkoording av år 1561* (Stockholm, 1956). For the text of the church order see *Den svenska kyrkoordningen 1571*, ed. with introduction by Sven Kjöllerström (Lund, 1971), published on the occasion of its 400th anniversary.

[65] Trans. Bergendoff, art. cit., 98. *Den svenska kyrkoordningen 1571*, 162.

[66] Apology XIV; Tappert, 214.

defend the office of bishop because in the last years of his reign Gustav Vasa had moved toward a presbyterian polity and had nearly allowed the episcopal succession to lapse.

In view of the Calvinist sympathies of King Erik XIV, the preface to the church order does not hesitate to call the Lord's Supper "the mass," "and use therein the mass vestments, altars and frontals, gold and silver chalices and patens, consecrate and elevate the sacrament, and have other such papistical customs, with crossing and signing."[67] Nor does the archbishop have any scruples about calling the sacrament "a sacrifice," "since that sacrifice which our High Priest Christ once made upon the cross is celebrated in the mass. So also the scripture calls the prayers and thanksgivings, such as are used in the mass, sacrifices."[68]

The chapters on the Lord's Supper and on the Order of the Mass are preceded by chapters "On Penance, Confession and Absolution," "On Private Confession," "On Public Confession," and "On Excommunication." Indeed, one is struck by the fullness of the emphasis on confession and absolution and on church discipline in the Swedish Order.

The Swedish Order teaches that there are two kinds of private confession: one made by the individual to God and the other made by the individual before a confessor. Priests are charged to be in the church at least a half hour, and preferably an hour, before the celebration of mass to hear confessions, but they are also to sit in a public place so as not to cause gossip. They should give advice to help people avoid sin, and not bind consciences as used to be done under the papacy. Priests should be especially cautious when dealing with youths and simple-minded people, so as not to frighten them away.

The Swedish Order also teaches that there are two kinds of public confession: a general confession by the whole congregation and the *poenitentia publica* prescribed for those who have committed gross sins. A list of such sins is provided along with directions guiding the confessor *(poenitentiarius)* on how to deal with such sins before giving absolution in the presence of the congregation. The chapter on excommunication begins with the assertion that "Excommunication is not an ordinance of man, for Christ himself has instituted and appointed it, as we see in Matthew 18 . . . Therefore it shall be neither despised nor set aside."[69] Archbishop Petri cautioned against a hasty use of excommunication. There should be a delay during which time the priest should try to persuade the sinner to repent. If this fails and the sinner is excommunicated, the person under the ban shall not attend church except to hear sermons. The *Forma excommunicandi,* however, is not to be used by a priest until he has consulted with the bishop or dean (senior minister of the diocese).[70]

The fact that these chapters on church discipline were placed before the chapters on the Lord's Supper and the Order of Mass indicates that they were regarded as integral to the proper use of the sacrament. These forms of confession and church

---

[67] Brilioth, *Eucharistic Faith and Practice*, 251; *Den svenska kyrkoordningen 1571*, 12.

[68] Ibid.

[69] *Den svenska kyrkoordningen 1571*, 81.

[70] Ibid., 84.

discipline, practiced in conjunction with the celebration of the mass and Lord's Supper, served to inject a penitential character into the eucharistic celebration that has lasted up until modern times in Swedish piety. Nevertheless, the Swedish Order encourages the frequent reception of communion.[71] Even though noncommunicant masses are disapproved,[72] the Swedish Order laments that daily communion, which was the practice of the ancient church, has fallen into disuse. It is a sign that the people have grown "cold and dull in heart" with regard to their sins and "this sublime comfort."

> For it is likewise easy to understand that whoever does not have a hearty desire
> for the Supper of our Lord Jesus Christ, so that he gladly and often comes to it,
> can neither have a right idea of and repentance for his sins, nor any true prayer
> and thanksgiving to God, and therefore no forgiveness of sins.[73]

The corrective to this is to instruct the people on the gravity of sin and the consolation of forgiveness. Where it happens that mass used to be celebrated but now none desire to receive the sacrament, then something should be put in the place of the mass: "namely some godly Psalms, Sermon and the Litany, whereby the folk may be awakened to godliness and so be made better."[74]

Following Lutheran precedent in Germany, Archbishop Petri recommended that "some Latin hymns" be used in the mass and at other services, especially in towns and schools on high festivals or apostles' days, "lest the Latin language seem to be entirely condemned or allowed entirely to disappear."[75] Nevertheless, in "country places" it would be best if the mass were always in Swedish.

The chapter on "The Order of the Mass" represents the final standardization of the celebration of the Swedish Mass. The priest may begin the mass by kneeling before the altar and reading the Latin Confiteor, but then the Swedish confession should be read to the people, either at the beginning of the mass or after the sermon.

According to the second chapter of the Swedish Order, "The Order with Preaching" (Ordning medh predican), when a sermon is preached at Matins, Evensong, or at the mass, it is to be set within the Office of Prone.[76] In Swedish usage this office consisted of:

> Optional exhortation to communicants
> Lord's Prayer
> A penitential psalm or hymn
> A prayer
> Sermon
> Invitation to confession
> General confession
> Absolution
> Intercessions

[71] Ibid., 85.
[72] Ibid., 86.
[73] Ibid., 87.
[74] Ibid., 88.
[75] Ibid., 90.
[76] Ibid., 34ff.

This was an order set within an order. It is important to note that this preaching office became an almost invariable part of the Swedish Mass. The inclusion of the intercessions in the Office of Prone insured the inclusion in the mass or chief service of the general prayer for all sorts and conditions of people, especially for the leaders of church and state, the sick and the dying, and for the comfort of the bereaved and the hope of eternal life with all the saints in light.

Some flexibility is allowed in "the manner and order" of the Swedish Mass, especially in the substitution of vernacular hymns for the choral parts of the mass. Specific hymns are suggested in place of the Introit and Gradual when these are not sung in Latin. The Kyrie may be sung three times or nine times, "yet on great Festivals it must be sung nine times with different tunes, as is customary, in Latin or Swedish."[77] Sequences may be sung after the Gradual on Christmas, Easter, Holy Thursday, and Pentecost, and the Tract during Lent. The Creed may sometimes be sung in Latin, especially on apostles' days, that "it be not forgotten." The exhortation concerning the sacrament may be used according to the circumstances either in Prone or before the communion.

The ceremonies of the mass are treated as befits their nature as adiaphora:

> Elevation, Mass Vestments, Altars, Altar Cloths, Lights, and whatsoever of these ceremonies there are, such as have been adopted here in the kingdom since God's pure Word hath been preached, may we freely retain as optional matters, albeit such things in other countries have been set aside through the same freedom.[78]

A long section in the chapter on the mass deals with the "fencing of the altar," developing ideas initially laid down by Luther in the section on "The Communion of the People" in the *Formula Missae* and widely implemented in the German Lutheran church orders. The priest should know how many people are coming to receive the sacrament in order to know how much bread and wine to prepare. The people should signify their intention of communing before the time of the celebration of mass. The priest should be careful not to commune any persons who are unworthy (e.g., those "confirmed in some manifest vice") or strangers (unless they present themselves to the priest first). Communicants should be able to give a reason for coming to the altar and be able to recite the Lord's Prayer, the Creed, and the Ten Commandments. Children younger than nine who cannot do this, and lunatics, "so long as they are out of their minds," are also to be excluded. No one should be compelled to receive the sacrament; but if some person neglects it for a long period of time he should be admonished and, failing that, excommunicated. Brides and grooms should be allowed to receive communion on their wedding day, if they are qualified, but they shall not be compelled to do so. Elements that remain after the communion should be kept in some convenient place until they are needed for the next communion. The priest should include himself in the communion; "nor can it do him any harm, if he should receive it even several times a day, that is, as often as he celebrates mass in his parish churches."[79]

---

[77] Yelverton, *An Archbishop of the Reformation*, 120.

[78] Trans. in ibid., 120–1.

[79] Ibid., 122.

The Swedish Order codified and stabilized liturgical use and sacramental practice in the Swedish church. It represented the lifetime achievement of the archbishop of the Swedish Reformation and Laurentius Petri's enduring legacy.

Nova Ordinantia Ecclesiastica, 1575

After the death of Laurentius Petri in the autumn of 1573, King Johan III began to embark on his own church policy. While the new king and the old archbishop shared many concerns and interests, Laurentius Petri was too identified with Lutheran orthodoxy to suit the ecumenically minded king. Nevertheless, he named the son-in-law and namesake of the old archbishop, Laurentius Petri Gothus, as his successor.

With the help of the *archielectus,* Johan presented plans for revising the Swedish Order to the riksdag in the spring of 1574. This led to the formulation of Seventeen Articles, which the king and his secretary, Petrus Fecht, presented at a meeting of the bishops in January 1575. The discussion with the bishops can be followed in the meeting minutes, which indicate that Johan III was present and participated in the debates. Roland Persson shows by comparing these minutes with the text of *Nova Ordinantia Ecclesiastica* that concepts discussed by the king and the bishops were incorporated into the new or revised church order, meaning that the revised church order was a compromise between the king and the bishops.[80] This is evident in its full title: *Nova Ordinantia ecclesiastica anno 1575 conscripta et unanimi episcoporum consensu approbata.*

Nevertheless, a comparison of the minutes and the text of the revised church order also indicate that in some instances Johan III went beyond the consensus of the bishops. For example, the minutes indicate an appeal to the church fathers as interpreters of the Bible while the *Nova Ordinantia* asserts their authority.[81] The minutes also name Luther, Melanchthon, and Brenz as "nostri saeculi scriptores," but the *Nova Ordinantia* warns that their writings should not be read uncritically.[82] In the same vein, the orthodox Lutheran doctrine of ubiquity is rejected. This doctrine was developed by orthodox Lutheran theologians out of Luther's arguments for the presence of the human nature of Christ with the divine nature, which is omnipresent, in refuting the sacramentarian denial of the bodily presence of Christ in the sacrament. Instead of this view, as Brilioth noted, the emphasis in the *Nova Ordinantia* "is laid on the centrality of the incarnation, in a way that is not familiar to Lutheran ears."[83] According to the *Nova Ordinantia*, our trust and consolation lies in that

> Christ has not laid aside our human nature which once he took, nor transformed it into another nature, but in that same flesh and blood, with infinite and unspeakable honour and glory, ordains and rules all things, our almighty King and Priest to all eternity. . . . For as he has left us the pledge and assurance of the Spirit, so he has taken from us the pledge and assurance of our humanity, the pledge of the perfection which it shall at last attain. Therefore, flesh and

---

[80] Roland Persson, *Johan III och Nova Ordinantia* (Lund: Gleerups, 1973), 18–9.
[81] Ibid., 28.
[82] Ibid., 30.
[83] Brilioth, *Eucharistic Faith and Practice*, 225.

blood, be of good courage, for you have entered heaven and the Kingdom in Christ Jesus.[84]

While the real presence of the body and blood of Christ in the sacrament is affirmed, the mystery is preserved and no magicality is attached to the words of institution. Transubstantiation is rejected along with ubiquity or any other philosophic attempt to explain the sacramental union. Yet the word "pledge," which is used several times, indicates that the words of institution are to be proclaimed because the sacrament's promise and assurance is attached to them.

According to Brilioth, "The king's patristic studies led him to a warm sacramental piety, in comparison with which the restrained language of the older Swedish reformers sounds almost chilly."[85] In a string of phrases lifted out of the writings of the fathers, the *Nova Ordinantia* proclaims with a sense of awe and wonder the "coeleste et venerabile Sacramentum, venerandum dominicam coenam, magnam et inscrutabile mysterium."[86] The benefits of this "heavenly and most venerable sacrament" include incorporation into Christ, "that he may be in us, and we in him."[87] "As he is lord over life and death, so I become the same also in him."[88] Here is language reminiscent of Irenaeus, whose words are cited in this connection, along with those of other patristic writers.

The *Nova Ordinantia* reasserts the positive view of eucharistic sacrifice held in the Swedish Order, but explicates it more fully. The idea of the mass as a propitiatory sacrifice is rejected, but the mass is a sacrifice: first, "because the true body and blood of Christ, which are given and received in the eucharist, which were once for all a sacrifice for us, and ever retain the name which they then received"; second, because the body and blood of Christ are the pledge that the fruits and power of the one sacrifice for sin are available for us; third, because the mass is celebrated in remembrance of Christ's passion and death; fourth, because "we thank, praise, glorify, honor and call upon God in the eucharistic act."[89] The eucharist is thus the presence of the sacrifice of Christ, the means of conveying the benefits of that sacrifice, the memorial of that sacrifice, which summons the thankoffering of the church.

The order of mass in the *Nova Ordinantia* does not differ much in detail from the rubrics and order provided in the Swedish Order. But the article on holy days, which follows the article on the mass, expands the sanctoral cycle to include Saint Mary Magdalene, Saint Lawrence, Corpus Christi, and the Marian feasts of the Assumption and the Nativity of Mary. Finally, the *Nova Ordinantia* expanded the intercessory character of the Swedish Mass by providing both a long and a short form of a general prayer of the church to be offered before the preface begins.

---

[84] Trans. in ibid., 256. See NO VII, 6–7 in *Handlingar rörande Sveriges historia*, Ser. II/2, 277ff.

[85] Ibid., 256.

[86] *Handlingar rörande Sveriges historia*, Ser. II/2, 269.

[87] Ibid., 310.

[88] Ibid., 311.

[89] Ibid., 314–6; see Brilioth, 256.

Among the liturgical instructions we find special insistence that the people are all to remain at mass until it is over so that they may share in the prayers and the eucharistic act even if they are not receiving the sacrament,

> that all may unitedly thank God for all his mercies, and especially for the redemption offered to us in Christ, and pray God that he will grant to them and to all others his grace, that they may always have a will and a desire for this most comfortable food and medicine of a troubled conscience, and that he will make it to be, for those who rightly use the sacrament, for the strengthening and confirming of faith, for trust and consolation, for the forgiveness of sins, for justification and eternal salvation. This act, at which a man may delight to be present, where the Lord's Supper is administered, is for those who fear God a glorious act of confession whereby they may let it be seen what they hold about the Lord's Supper, and so set to others a Christian example, and a sign that they show to this sacrament fitting honor and reverence, and that it is for their own good when they celebrate it in a right godly spirit. So also churches have not been built only in order that men may there hear sermons, but also that each and every Christian who goes there may together with others pray to God for all needs.[90]

If the liturgical movement in King Johan's reign had culminated with the *Nova Ordinantia*, viewed as a supplement to the Swedish Church Order, much might have been achieved in the revitalization of parochial worship in the Church of Sweden along evangelical catholic lines. The *Nova Ordinantia* added a profound patristic theological dimension to the orthodox Lutheran faith and practice already embedded in the Church Order of Laurentius Petri. But some contemporaries viewed the *Nova Ordinantia*, with justification, as a prelude to the introduction of the king's new "liturgy" in 1576. This liturgy precipitated a liturgical struggle between the king's liturgical and ecumenical policies and a vocal anti-liturgist party of gnesio-Lutherans. As Bishop John Wordsworth observed, "had the king been satisfied with the ground covered by the *Nova Ordinantia*, or even introduced his liturgy in a deliberate and ecclesiastical manner, he might have contributed much more to the final settlement than he actually did."[91] But the *Nova Ordinantia* was a springboard for further liturgical and ecclesiological advances. In July of 1575, Johan insisted on the use of unction in the consecration of the new archbishop and two other bishops. As Wordsworth commented, "This was an arbitrary act which naturally aroused suspicion of further changes in prospect, and suspicion was changed into conviction by the unfortunate publication of the new liturgy or Red-book of 1576, without any Church authority."[92] And yet, in spite of the hastiness with which the new liturgy was published and also the impatience with which it was enforced in parochial use, the Liturgy of 1576 does stand in continuity with the liturgical development we have chronicled thus far. It was not simply a "romanizing" aberration, as charged by older historians, but a considered attempt to reclaim more of the catholic and orthodox tradition within the parameters of evangelical theology. The Liturgy of King Johan III and the controversies

---

[90] Ibid., 319–20; trans. in Brilioth, 256–7.

[91] Wordsworth, 243–4.

[92] Ibid., 243.

surrounding it are worth examining as a case study of similar liturgical struggles that have occurred in subsequent history, including in our own time.

 ## Liturgia Svecanae Ecclesiae Catholicae et Orthodoxae conformis, 1576

The Publication of the Red Book and the Liturgical Struggle

When the archbishop-elect Laurentius Petri Gothus protested the king's order, not only to assume crook and mitre but also to submit to unction in the ceremonies of his archiepiscopal consecration, Johan III replied: "And you may as well realize that We, thank God, are quite well enough versed in God's Word to be able to judge that neither ceremonies nor gestures avail to salvation or damnation."[93] Ceremonies and gestures are, in the Lutheran view, adiaphora, "non-essential things." More specifically, they are things that are neither commanded nor forbidden by scripture, and which may therefore be freely used or not used. As we have seen, Matthias Flacius originally appealed to this concept in a polemical way during the Interims in Germany following the Smalkald War to lighten the burden of canon and cultic law on the consciences of believers. Flacius's negative principle that "nothing is an adiaphoron in a time of confession" would be enshrined in the Formula of Concord adopted in 1577, a year after the promulgation of King Johan's liturgy. So Johan III was actually out of step with the usual Lutheran use of the principle of adiaphora when he appealed to the concept to justify the *retention* of certain ceremonies and usages rather than the *rejection* of them.

As Sigtrygg Serenius has indicated, King Johan had not been secretive about his desire for a revised order of mass. He had made his desire known during the election of the new archbishop in June 1574.[94] During the Christmas season of 1575 the liturgy was completed and copies were shown to Archbishop Gothus and to Bishop Erasmus Nicolai of Västerås for approval. On March 8, 1576, a copy was delivered to the king's brother, Duke Karl of Sodermanland. The liturgy was published during the summer of 1576 and was used for the first time on the Feast of the Nativity of Mary, September 8, 1576.

Called *Den Röda Boken* (the Red Book) because of the color of its binding, the official title of the new mass was *Liturgia svecanae ecclesiae catholicae et orthodoxae conformis*. The preface bears the signature of Archbishop Laurentius Petri Gothus, but the liturgy itself was quite likely the work of King Johan III in collaboration with his secretary, Petrus Fecht, who had studied with Melanchthon at Wittenberg. The book was printed in Latin and Swedish, with the bilingual liturgical texts in parallel columns and copious marginal notes, rubrics, and commentaries in Latin.[95] The commentaries and notes consisted mostly of citations from the Greek and Latin fathers justifying particular usages. These commentaries were deleted from the 1588 edition of the book.

---

[93] Roberts, 281, n. 1.

[94] Sigtrygg Serenius, *Liturgia Svecanae Ecclesiae Catholicae et Orthodoxae conformis. En Liturgiehistorisk undersökning med särskild hänsyn till struktur och förlagor* (Åbo, 1966), 13.

[95] A facsimile edition of *Den Röda Boken* was published by J. Kroon in Malmö, 1953.

The preface states that the purpose of the liturgy was to steer a course between the scylla and charybdis of *superstitio* and *profanitas*. Undoubtedly echoing King Johan's sentiments, the archbishop asserted that at the moment profanitas was the more dangerous of the two extremes.[96] Nevertheless, it seemed to many of the "gnesio-Lutherans" in the realm that in its ceremonies the Red Book was falling into the danger of superstitio. They felt that King Johan's liturgy was forcing them into a status confessionis. Those who resisted the use of this liturgy came to be called Anti-Liturgists.[97]

No sooner was the Red Book off the press than the anti-liturgy party rallied against it. On September 7, 1576 (the day before the first use of the liturgy), Abraham Andrae Angermannus, principal of the Stockholm Grammar School, and Olaus Medelpadius (both of whom had received their education at the gnesio-Lutheran University of Rostock), were suspended from their posts for refusing to countenance the celebration of the liturgy.[98] The dissidents issued a paper, entitled *Rationes quaedam, cur Novum Liturgiam . . .*, which criticized the theological character of the Red Book. Its publication provoked the wrath of the king and brought about the immediate expulsion of its authors from Stockholm.

On Christmas Day, 1576, the archbishop celebrated mass in the cathedral at Uppsala using the new liturgy. The Anti-Liturgists at the university, headed by Petrus Jonae and Olaus Luth, immediately stirred up trouble, causing such a disturbance that the archbishop had both of them suspended from office. Angermannus and Medelpadius appealed to the riksdag, whose sanction for the use of the new liturgy had been sought by the king. Persuading the riksdag to sanction the Red Book was no problem, because the king and the commons had too much in common, including a basic liturgical conservatism, and the nobility were divided, some siding with the king and others with the king's brother, Duke Karl. But more opposition was expressed at the Ecclesiastical Convocation, over which the king presided. The bishops signed the resolution promulgating the use the liturgy (some with reservation), but the Anti-Liturgists refused to sign. They remained so adamant after two days of debate that Johan finally gave up the effort to persuade them. The less hostile clerics were allowed to return to their posts, and the more persistent critics were appointed to positions far removed from the capital.[99] A law was soon passed forbidding Swedish students to attend German universities of a "gnesio-Lutheran" persuasion, such as that at Rostock.[100] Instead, Johan founded the Royal College of Stockholm (*Collegium Regium Stockholmense*) at the old Grayfriars convent, staffed by secret Jesuits under the leadership of Laurentius Norvegus. This school provided a patristic-based program of theological studies.

Efforts to achieve consensus for his own religious policy were thwarted by Johan's brother, Duke Karl, a crypto-Calvinist who desired a more thorough reformation

---

[96] See the text in Pierre LeBrun, *Explication de la Messe*, IV (Paris, 1726), 142–4.

[97] On the liturgical struggle during the reign of Johan III see J. A. Hammargren, *Om den liturgiska striden under konung Johan III* (Uppsala, 1898).

[98] See Ragnar Ohlsson, *Abraham Angermannus. En biografisk studie* (Lund, 1946).

[99] See Hammargren, 62ff.

[100] Ibid., 69.

on the basis on the Bible. His travels in Germany in 1578–1579 had convinced him of the need for a united Protestant front against Rome, but he was not prepared to be bound by the *Confessio Augustana,* whether *Variata* or *Invariata*.[101] Like Johan III, Karl had ecumenical leanings, but he looked for unity on the left wing of the Reformation rather than on the right. He was ready to accept the 1571 Swedish Order, and he would reluctantly accept the *Nova Ordinantia*, but he would not acquiesce to the use of the Red Book. He was consistently one of its strongest critics and he gave sanctuary in his duchy to many of the Anti-Liturgists.

The success of Johan III's church policy was threatened by the existence of a nearly autonomous region within his own realm. To overcome this he summoned the riksdag to Stockholm early in 1582 and persuaded the Estates to sanction a decree that no part of the realm should be exempt from using the Red Book or its doctrinal counterpart, the *Nova Ordinantia*. Those clerics who opposed Johan III's liturgy now had no option except to leave the realm (although it might be noted that, unlike in England, no one lost his or her life because of disagreement with the king's religion).[102] A year later, the king induced the bishops to ratify the decision of the riksdag and pledge an oath to enforce the use of the Red Book in their dioceses. They also agreed to celebrate mass personally on the great feast days in full episcopal vesture, and to see that liturgy was recited in Latin in all cathedrals and large churches at least once a year. In addition, consecrated oils were to be used at ordinations and extreme unction was to be reintroduced. Lastly, the bishops were asked to pledge their oath of loyalty to the king and queen and to the crown prince Sigismund, who was being raised as a Roman Catholic and was a candidate for election as king of Poland as well as the heir-apparent of the kingdom of Sweden.[103]

Johan III was able to secure this agreement from the bishops because he had had an opportunity to stack the episcopal bench with his own candidates: Andreas Laurentii Björnram, appointed archbishop of Uppsala; Kristen Agricola, the Rector of the Åbo Academy in Turku, Finland, appointed bishop of Reval; and Nicolaus Stephani, dean of Växjö, appointed bishop of that diocese, all in 1583. In return, however, Johan promised to take stronger measures against Roman Catholics in Sweden, whose numbers had been revealed by the exposure of the Jesuit mission operating under the cover of the faculty of the Royal Theological College.[104] This episode is of interest not only because it added to the intensity of the liturgical struggle, but also because it represents an interesting chapter in the history of ecumenical negotiation.

The Missio Suetica

Toivo Harjunpaa has asserted that "Liturgical questions have never aroused wider public interest and more intense emotions in the history of Sweden and Finland

---

[101] Roberts. 289.

[102] Ibid., 291.

[103] See Hammargren, 173–4.

[104] See Oscar Garstein, *Rome and the Counter-Reformation in Scandinavia*, I (Oslo, 1963; distributed by Oxford University Press, 1964), 253.

than they did during the last quarter of the sixteenth century."[105] This was because the Anti-Liturgists regarded the Red Book as an overt move toward a return to Rome. Among the charges against it was the accusation that it had been written by Jesuits.[106] This view was encouraged by the fact that Johan III had allowed the Jesuit mission to enter Sweden during the time in which he was negotiating with the papacy in the matter of Queen Katarina's inheritance, which was tied up in legal disputes in Naples, and to explore the possibility of a reunion of the churches along the lines of Cassander's mediating theology.

Sensing the possibility of some kind of accord with the Swedish king, a Polish Jesuit, Stanislaus Warszewicki, was dispatched to Sweden under the supervision of Cardinal Hosius to negotiate with King Johan. In their discussion Johan was willing to compromise on some issues, but he refused to accept the dogma of transubstantiation, the propitiatory sacrifice of the mass, *Communio sub una specie*, and papal supremacy over the national church of Sweden, although some expression of fellowship with the Roman See would be desirable.[107] Warszewicki understood the nature of Johan III's "high church" theology, and raised the issue of whether the Swedish church had truly consecrated bishops and properly ordained priests. If the Swedish clergy were not in *Successio Apostolica*, the Swedish church lacked valid sacraments. This succeeded in raising doubts in Johan's mind, and when he sent a mission to Rome in 1576, headed by Petrus Fecht, one item on the agenda was to try to regularize the situation of the ministry in the Church of Sweden by persuading the pope to consecrate a bishop, possibly Fecht himself. Unfortunately for the future of Johan III's church policy, Fecht was drowned in a storm while crossing the Baltic and the mission to Rome was deprived of its theological expert.

The Roman Curia did not feel it was in a position to grant dispensations to Sweden regarding communion in both kinds, married clergy, and vernacular liturgy. This would only create a precedent for other dispensations and eventually break up the liturgical and pastoral uniformity so laboriously achieved by the Council of Trent. Nor could the Curia give a dispensation to Queen Katarina to receive communion at Lutheran altars from Lutheran priests. So the Curia embarked on another plan: the conversion of King Johan III. If this succeeded, the communion problem would disappear of its own accord, and the Swedish fleet might be enlisted against William the Silent in Holland.[108]

The person the Curia sent to carry out the conversion of the king was Laurentius Nicolai Norvegus, a Scandinavian convert to Roman Catholicism educated at Louvain, Douai, and Cologne. He had been involved in previous Jesuit missions to Norway and Denmark. Norvegus arrived in Stockholm just at the time that Johan III was undertaking the foundation of his theological college in Stockholm in the facilities of the old Franciscan Priory on the Island of Gråmunkeholmen (now Riddarholmen). Johan

---

[105] Toivo Harjunpaa, "Liturgical Developments in Sweden and Finland in the Era of Lutheran Orthodoxy," *Church History* 37 (1968), 14.

[106] Yelverton, *The Mass in Sweden*, 67.

[107] Garstein, 76.

[108] Roberts, 284.

appointed Norvegus *Professor sive Lector Theologiae* and principal of the new school, although his Jesuit identity was kept secret. As Garstein has reported,

> Contrary to what might have been expected, students of all ages made their way to the Theological College in such numbers that no less than sixty persons entered their names in the register. By the spring of 1577 the total had risen to more than seventy. Of these some thirty were Lutheran priests, the rest were scholars from the higher classes of the Stockholm Grammar School or the Schola Civitatis Stockholmensis.[109]

Known in Swedish history as *Klosterlasse,* Norvegus confined his public teaching and preaching to patristic theology and the ecumenical creeds. For all intents and purposes he was a learned Lutheran humanistic scholar of King Johan III's "high church" persuasion. He even participated in debates defending the Red Book. In private, however, he gave instruction to students interested in Roman Catholicism and arranged to send them to the Collegium Germanicum at Rome. How far Norvegus got with the king is not known. What is known is that after Easter 1577, Johan would not receive communion at a Lutheran service.[110] The situation seemed promising enough for the Curia to dispatch to Sweden Antonio Possevino, a former secretary-general of the Society of Jesus, to explore the possibilities of Johan's conversion and the reunion of the Swedish and the Roman churches.

The papal legate was warmly received by King Johan. Oscar Garstein believes that at this time Johan actually made a profession of faith and received communion from Possevino.[111] However, it would seem that Johan did this under the impression that only ecclesiastical-political problems remained barring the way to some expression of formal fellowship with Rome and that the Curia would grant certain concessions for the sake of reunion. Garstein also believes that in March 1578, Johan worked out a proposal for the gradual reintroduction of the Roman Catholic faith into Sweden in his essay, entitled, "Quae Rex Suetiae cupit ut a Serenissimo Domino Nostro obtineantur ut sine perturbatione Suetiae restituatur Religio Catholica."[112] However, far from showing Johan to be a secret Catholic or to be willing to allow for the introduction of the Counter-Reformation in Sweden, in the sense of the implementation of the Roman Catholic faith and practice defined by the Council of Trent, this document demonstrates the tenacity of Johan's own religious convictions. In it the king requested the pope to permit the mass to be celebrated in Swedish, to allow *communio sub utraque specie,* to place bishops guilty of political crimes under royal jurisdiction, not to discontinue the marriage of priests, not to forbid Roman Catholics in Sweden to attend Lutheran services (such as Queen Katarina), not to reintroduce holy water, and to allow the omission of the invocation of the saints by name and the prayers for the dead in the mass. There were also some non-doctrinal issues Johan wanted to negotiate with the pope, such as the ownership of lands belonging to the

---

[109] Garstein, 97.
[110] Ibid., 119.
[111] Ibid., 124ff.
[112] Ibid., 135.

church before the Reformation and the pope's promise to allow the tomb of Gustav Vasa in Uppsala Cathedral to remain unmolested.

Pope Gregory XIII answered in October 1578. While agreeing to negotiate the matter of allowing the present owners to retain land that had belonged to the church in pre-Reformation times and to leave intact the tomb of Gustav Vasa, the pope flatly refused all the theological issues. Moreover, while Johan might listen to Lutheran sermons if he had to, under no circumstances was he to attend a Lutheran mass.[113]

This was too much even for the ecumenically patient king. The pope had implicitly condemned the king's *Liturgia svecanae ecclesiae* since it was the authorized Lutheran mass in Sweden. Johan became disillusioned in his hope for reunion with Rome and by July 1579 he was again receiving communion at Lutheran altars.[114] Possevino took the gamble of blowing the cover off the Jesuit mission in order to force Johan's hand and to rally all the Catholic converts in Sweden to demonstrate the strength of their movement. While groups of converts did come together in Stockholm, Vadstena, and Linköping after the revelation of the Jesuit mission, there were ugly anti-Catholic riots throughout the realm.[115] The riksdag assembled in Vadstena and passed a resolution on February 19, 1580, aimed at severing the king's relationship with papal diplomats. Norvegus was deprived of his rectorship, and the Jesuit professor made his breach with Johan III irreparable by openly attacking the Red Book. There was no future left in Sweden for Norvegus, Possevino, or the *Missio Suetica*.

In 1581, Pope Gregory XIII made a belated effort to reconsider the matter of the cup for the laity, if France and Spain could be persuaded to agree; but Johan made no reply. For another three years the school at Gråmunkeholmen remained under Roman Catholic influence. But in 1583 Queen Katarina died, and thereafter Johan's interests shifted away from Rome. Shortly after the queen's death, he married the sixteen-year-old Gunilla Bielke, a Protestant who was out of sympathy with "the king's religion." Perhaps as if to signal his total severance of connections with the *Missio Suetica,* Johan revealed his plans to the bishops assembled in Uppsala in 1583 for seeking fellowship with the Greek church. There had already been contacts between the Lutheran Reformation and the patriarch of Constantinople, begun by Melanchthon in 1559[116] and continued over a decade later by the theologians at Tübingen, who sent to Patriarch Jeremiah II a Greek translation of the Augsburg Confession.[117] The patriarch examined the Confession in detail, but found that it repeated the usual "Latin errors" (e.g., the retention of the *filioque* in the Nicene Creed and the neglect of the epiclesis in the consecration of the eucharist) and in some respects it even diverged further from Eastern teaching than did medieval

---

[113] Roberts, 286.

[114] Ibid., 286.

[115] Ibid., 287.

[116] See "Epistola Philippi Melanchthonis scripta ad Patriarcham Constantinopolitanum, per Demetrium Thracem, anno salutis 1559 mense Septembri," CR 9:922–3.

[117] See Ernst Benz, *Wittenberg und Byzanz. Zur Begegnung und Auseinandersetzung der Reformation und der östlich-orthodoxen Kirche* (Marburg, 1949).

Latin teaching (e.g., the limitations placed on human free will).[118] King Johan III may have been aware of these theological exchanges, as well as of the long record of negotiations between Sweden and Russia that involved churchmen from both sides. In 1583, he authorized the Finnish bishop of Åbo (Turku), Ericus Erici Sorolainen, to translate the *Liturgia svecanae ecclesiae* into Greek and take it to Patriarch Jeremiah II. Nothing came of these plans, however, because of the temporary dismissal of Jeremiah II from office for political reasons during 1584–1585.[119]

While the Constantinopolitan mission was doomed to failure from the start because of Byzantine-Turkish problems, it demonstrates the consistency and tenacity of Johan's theological position. He thought that the theological impasses of the sixteenth century could be transcended by appealing to the "consensus of the first five centuries." While the *Liturgia svecanae ecclesiae* was conceived in an ecumenical spirit, it was in no sense a "romanizing" effort. Nor was it the product of the Jesuit mission, as Angemannus charged. It was mainly the work of King Johan III with the help of his secretary, Petrus Fecht, and it was intended to serve as the centerpiece of his church policy that was aimed, first and foremost, at the refinement and enrichment of parochial life in Sweden. The strict measures used to enforce the liturgy, however, might not have been so necessary if the agents of the Counter-Reformation had not been active in Sweden at the time of the publication and promulation of the Red Book. The exposure of the Jesuit mission only fanned the suspicions of Angermannus and other Anti-Liturgists that the liturgy was created by the Jesuits. This certainly contributed to the hostility with which the Red Book was greeted in some quarters, a hostility preserved today in the scathing comments written into the margins of a few copies of the Red Book in the university libraries of Sweden.

Four centuries removed from the passions of the liturgical controversy we should be able to analyze the content of the liturgy with some degree of objectivity and with an overview of the Reformation period not accessible to those living through it in order to determine how the Red Book fits into the chronology of the Swedish Mass in the sixteenth century.

The Structure and Sources of the Liturgy of King Johan III

Oscar Quensel represented the opinion of older Swedish scholars that the spirit and trend of the Red Book was un-Lutheran and that it marked an important step in King Johan III's journey back to Roman Catholicism. He asserted that the ceremonial richness of the liturgy, with its genuflections, consignations, lavabo, elevations, and so forth, combined with the reintroduction of offertory prayers and a silent canon, only served to alienate the sympathies of the people "who were daily growing more and more attached to the grand, simple, ardent spirit of Luther."[120] The evidence suggests, however, that Quensel's view of the widespread acceptance of the Reformation by the common people is sheer romanticism. In the backwoods areas of Sweden and Finland,

---

[118] See Jaroslav Pelikan, *The Christian Tradition*, vol. 2, *The Spirit of Eastern Christianity* (Chicago, 1974), 282.
[119] Roberts, 254.
[120] Quensel, II, 122.

pre-Reformation ways lingered on well into the seventeenth century,[121] and the Red Book was not without its partisan supporters.

Nevertheless, Quensel's opinions carried great weight. While J. A. Hammargren asserted that Johan III was never a Catholic in the Roman sense, but rather a disciple of Cassander who found the reactionary tendencies of the Council of Trent abhorrent, he nevertheless maintained Quensel's view that the liturgy was a conflation of two heterogeneous elements: the *Missale Romanum* 1570 and the *Messan på Swensko* 1557.[122] This view was repeated by Hjalmar Holmquist in his *History of the Swedish Church*.[123]

Setting the elements of the liturgy side by side with the Roman mass-order of the *Missale Romanum* 1570 published after the Council of Trent and the Swedish Mass-order of 1557, we can see that this opinion is somewhat justified. This comparison will also give us an overview of the structure of the liturgy.

MISSALE ROMANUM 1570	SWEDISH MASS 1557	RED BOOK 1576
	1. Preparation	
Priest's devotions		Priest's devotions
Vesting prayers		Vesting prayers
Confiteor (P)		Confiteor (P)
	Invitation	Exhortation
	Confession	Confession
	Absolution	Absolution
	Confiteor (P)	
	2. The Entrance Rite	
Introit	Introit or Hymn	Introit
Kyrie (9 times)	Kyrie (3 times)	Kyrie (3 times)
Gloria	Gloria	Gloria
	or hymn version	
Salutation and Collect	Salutation and Collect	Salutation and Collect
	3. Liturgy of the Word	
Epistle	Epistle	Epistle
Gradual and Tract	Gradual or Hymn	Gradual and Tract
Gospel	Gospel	Gospel
Nicene Creed	Nicene or Apostles' Creed	Nicene or Apostles' Creed
	Pulpit Office	Pulpit Office
	4. Offertory	
Offertorium		Offertorium
Lavabo		Lavabo
Offertory Prayers:		Offertory Prayers:
Orate fratres		Omnipotens aeterne Deus
Secreta		Te igitur
		Domine Deus

---

[121] As late as 1659, Bishop Samuel Enander of Linköping had to forbid the veneration of images, especially of the Virgin Mary, and to prohibit adorning these images with clothing and crowns of straw. See O. Hassler, *Linköpings Stift under Biskop Samuel Enander*, I (Lund, 1935), 124.

[122] Hammargren, 250.

[123] Hjalmar Holmqvist, *Svenska Kyrkans Historia*, III (Stockholm, 1933ff.), 56.

5. *Consecration*

Preface dialogue	Preface dialogue	Preface dialogue
Vere dignum	Vere dignum	Vere dignum
Proper preface	expanded paschal preface	8 proper prefaces
		2 common prefaces
	Words of Institution	Words of Institution
Sanctus	Sanctus	Sanctus
Post-Sanctus prayers:		Post-Sanctus prayers:
Te igitur		
Memento		
Communicantes		
Hanc igitur		
Qui pridie		
Unde et memores		Memores igitur
Supra quae		
Supplices te		Supplices te
Memento etiam		
Nobis quoque		Nobis quoque
Per Quem		Per Quem

6. *Communion*

The Lord's Prayer	The Lord's Prayer	The Lord's Prayer
	with embolism	with embolism
Pax Domini	The Peace	Pax Domini
Agnus Dei	Agnus Dei	Agnus Dei
	or Hymn version	
	(Exhortation)	(Exhortation)
Communion prayers		Communion prayers
Communion antiphon	Communion hymns	Communion antiphon

7. *The Post-Communion*

Collect (for each mass)	Collect (one of five)	Collect (one of five)
Dismissal	Salutation	Salutation
	Benedicamus	Benedicamus
Benediction	Benediction	Benediction

On the basis of this structural comparison it would seem that the *Liturgia sve-canae ecclesiae* is a "conflation of two heterogeneous elements." But an analysis of the content does not bear this out. It is evident that no text which is not also in the Swedish Mass had been received unaltered from the Roman mass into the liturgy. The question must therefore be asked: What are the sources for the revisions of the Roman texts? The further question must be asked: How have the meanings of the Roman texts been changed by their revisions in the Red Book?

Coincidentally, a Swedish scholar living in Johan III's former duchy of Finland provided a more balanced and penetrating analysis of the *Liturgia svecanae ecclesiae*. Sigtrygg Serenius dissociates himself from those who regard the liturgy as a step in the King's journey to Roman Catholicism or who hold that the agreement with the bishops in 1583 marked the high point in Johan III's church program. He is convinced that Johan III's aim was to return to the sources in the humanistic spirit of Cassander, and that this church program was basically laid out intact in the *Nova Ordinantia* 1575 and the *Liturgia svecanae ecclesiae* 1576. It simply took until 1583 to bring the bishops to agree to implement some of the features of this program. Serenius then explores the relationship of the liturgy to streams of tradition other than the *Missal Romanum* 1570. These non-Tridentine influences in the Red Book include: patristic sources; medieval Swedish missal traditions; German Lutheran church orders, especially Mark Brandenburg 1540 and Pfalz-Neuburg 1543; and the English *Book of Common Prayer*.

There are parts of the liturgy that are not different from the conservative Lutheran church orders. The Latin Confiteor for the preparation of the celebrant is found in several of them as well as in the Swedish Order. The exhortation, general confession, and absolution are the same as in the Swedish Mass. The Entrance rite[124] and liturgy of the word are also the same as the Swedish Mass, although the Red Book provides for the sequences for Christmas, Epiphany, Easter, Ascension, Pentecost, and Trinity to be sung after the gradual. The telltale structure of the Lutheran eucharist is maintained: preface-words of institution-Sanctus, even though the liturgy goes on to provide some post-Sanctus prayers. Among the proper prefaces is even the expanded paschal preface of Olavus Petri, which is provided for ordinary Sundays; and the simple Vere dignum is provided for weekday celebrations. The liturgy restores the proper prefaces for Christmas, Epiphany, the Annunciation, Passiontide, Easter, the Ascension, Pentecost, and Trinity—thus providing ten prefaces in all. The institution narrative follows the Roman version more closely than other Lutheran institution texts, but Johan took pains in the accompanying commentary to defend his text on the basis of scripture and the fathers. The communion and post-communion sections of the liturgy are the same as the Swedish Mass, except for the communion prayers. But these prayers, *Quod ore sumpsimus* and *Corpus tuum Domine,* were also used in Luther's *Formula Missae*, Mark Brandenburg 1540 and Pfalz-Neuburg 1543.

There are three sections in which the liturgy goes beyond the provisions of other Lutheran mass-orders: the preparation office, the offertory prayers, and the parts of the eucharistic prayer following the Sanctus (actually to be recited quietly by the celebrant while the choir sings the Sanctus).[125]

The preparation office may be viewed as part of the purpose of the liturgy to combat prophanitas. As the celebrant put on each vestment, he recited a prayer. This caused the celebrant to consider his office and ministry as one of serving *in persona Christi* (in the role of Christ) as he prepared to celebrate the liturgy. Some of the vesting prayers are the same as in the *Missal Romanum* 1570; but others are derived from various medieval Swedish missal traditions. In typical late medieval fashion, these prayers assign allegorical significance to each piece of vesture.

---

[124] In an unusual gloss in the Gloria in excelsis the liturgy adds the following italicized words to the standard text: "Domine Fili unigenite, *Salus nostra* Jesu Christe, *et sancte Spiritus.*"

[125] See Frank C. Senn, "*Liturgia svecanae ecclesiae*: An Attempt at Eucharistic Restoration during the Swedish Reformation," *Studia Liturgica* 14 (1980–81), 20–36.

Lutheran Reformation liturgies are characterized by the omission of the offertory (except for the occasional singing of the offertory antiphon or anthem). But three prayers are provided in the Liturgy of King Johan III in the offertory section, along with the ceremonial action of the washing of the celebrant's hands *(lavabo)*. The prayers are for grace to call upon God in spirit and in truth, a general intercession for the church and the government, and a prayer for worthy communion combined with an invocation of the Holy Spirit on the gifts of bread and wine.

Serenius shows that the Swedish text of the first prayer, "Almighty, eternal God," reveals verbal similarities with the introduction to one of the general intercessory prayers in the Swedish Order 1571.[126] It simply asks for grace "that we according to thy commandment and promise may call upon thee in spirit and in truth" and petitions: "Let thy holy Spirit rule our hearts, for without thee we cannot be pleasing to thee."[127]

The second prayer is based on Te igitur clementissime pater in the Roman canon. The words in italic show the changes Johan III made to the Roman text.[128]

ROMAN CANON	THE LITURGY
Te igitur clementissime pater	Te igitur clementissime pater
per Iesum Christum Filium tuum	per Iesum Christum Filium tuum
Dominum nostrum supplices	Dominum nostrum supplices
rogamus ac petimus, uti	rogamus ac petimus, ut
accepta habeas et benedicas,	*preces nostras acceptas habere*
haec dona, haec munera,	*easque exaudire digneris,*
haec sacrificia illibata,	
in primus, quae tibi	*imprimus,* quae tibi
offerimus pro Ecclesia tua	offerimus pro Ecclesia tua
sancta catholica,	sancta catholica,
quam pacificare, custodire,	quam pacificare, custodire,
adunare et regere digneris	adunare et regere digneris
toto orbe terrarum,	toto orbe terrarum,
una cum	una cum
famulo tua Papa nostro N.	*omni magistratu ecclesiastico*
et Antistite nostro N.N.	*et politico, euiuscunque*
	dignitatis praeeminentiae
	et nominis sint,
et omnibus orthodoxis atque	et omnibus orthodoxis atque
catholicae et apostolicae	catholicae et apostolicae
fidei cultoribus.	fidei cultoribus.

The "gifts" *(haec dona)* are replaced by "our prayers" *(preces nostras)* which are offered for the church and the government. Joseph Jungmann commented that the Te igitur of the Roman canon "is on the same footing as the offertory, or more precisely the *oratio super oblata*. . . ."[129] King Johan has transferred this prayer from the "major canon" to the

---

[126] Serenius, 198.

[127] See text in Yelverton, *The Mass in Sweden*, 101.

[128] See Serenius, 199–200.

[129] Jungmann, *The Mass of the Roman Rite*, II, 48.

"minor canon," from the eucharistic prayer to the offertory, where it is serves as a general intercession for the church.

The third prayer is the most interesting of all, since it contains what appears to be a consecratory epiclesis.

> O Lord God, who wills that your Son's holy and most worthy Supper should be unto us a pledge and assurance of your mercy: awaken our heart, that we who celebrate the same his Supper may have a salutary remembrance of your benefits, and humbly give you true and beholden thanks, glory, honour, and praise for evermore. Help us your servants and your people that we may hereby remember the holy, pure, stainless, and blessed offering of your son, which he made upon the cross for us, and worthily celebrate the mystery of the new testament and eternal covenant. Bless and sanctify with the power of your Holy Spirit that which is prepared and set apart for this holy use, bread and wine, that rightly used it may be unto us the body and blood of your Son, the food of eternal life, which we may desire and seek with greatest longing. Through the same your Son Jesus Christ our Lord, who with your and the holy Spirit lives and reigns in one godhead from everlasting to everlasting. Amen.[130]

The power of the Spirit is associated with the "right use" of the sacrament. The phrase *in vero usu* is a code phrase suggesting the axiom of Lutheran orthodoxy, "Nothing has the character of a sacrament outside the use instituted by Christ," which was an understanding condemned by the Council of Trent.[131] The whole formula, beginning "Bless and sanctify" (*Benedic et sanctifica),* is not intended as a consecration, but as part of an offertory prayer presenting the bread and wine for consecration. In a four-page excursus, entitled "De sanctificatione seu benedictione Sacramenti," Johan objected to the recitation of the *nuda narratio* on the basis of patristic practice and the weight of tradition. But he still associated the consecration with the Verba Christi, citing the authority of Ambrose, Chrysostom, and Augustine. A similar epicletic offertory prayer was provided in the Pfalz-Neuburg Church Order (1543),[132] and the 1549 *Book of Common Prayer* has a similar formula in its eucharistic prayer, as we have seen.[133] The Anglican connection here and in other texts of the liturgy is not far-fetched because Johan spent 1559–1560 in England trying to win the hand of Queen Elizabeth I for his brother, Erik, and was much interested in the Elizabethan Settlement of the Church of England, with its restored Prayer Book.

The offertory in the liturgy does not compromise Lutheran theology. The primary objection to the offertory was its association with the payment of mass-stipends to offer the sacrifice of the mass for the living and the dead. In the Liturgy of King Johan III the offertory prayers include a prayer for the grace of the Holy Spirit to "rule our hearts" in what we are doing, a prayer of intercession for the "holy catholic church . . . throughout the world" "together with all government, spiritual and worldly," and a prayer asking for a

---

[130] Yelverton, *The Mass in Sweden,* 102–3; alt.

[131] Session 13, Canon 4; see H. J. Schroeder, ed., *Canons and Decrees of the Council of Trent* (St. Louis: Herder, 1941), 79.

[132] Text in Luther Reed, *The Lutheran Liturgy,* 753.

[133] Text in *The First and Second Prayer Books of King Edward VI,* Everyman Edition, 222.

salutary remembrance of the benefits of Christ's sacrifice on the cross received in the sacrament of bread and wine, which are presented to God for his blessing that, rightly used, they may be received as the body and blood of Christ.

The Red Book continues the eucharistic prayer beyond the institution narrative. Just as Luther excised the silent canon without causing a stir, so Johan hoped to restore the *post-pridie* section of the canon by having it recited silently while the choir sang the Sanctus.

> Dum chorus canit Hymnum Sanctus, celebras sequentem legit orationem. Quando autem legendo sacra peraguntur Liturgiae officia, oratio illa continua lectione Hymno subijcitur.[134]

The only other evangelical church order to prescribe silent prayers during the singing of the Sanctus was Mark Brandenberg 1540, which directed the priest to offer four German prayers (for the civil rulers, for the clergy, for unity, and for the forgiveness of sins) during the Sanctus.[135]

The post-Sanctus prayer is, in Hammargren's words, "a reworking and fusion of no less than 4 prayers in the Roman Missal:"[136] the Unde et memores, the Supra quae and Supplices te, the *Nobis quoque,* and the *Per quem.* The first two prayer texts have been significantly altered and the *Memento etiam,* which should precede the Nobis quoque, has been entirely omitted. The net effect was to eliminate all reference to a mass-sacrifice and the commemoration of the faithful departed.

The Unde et memores required the most careful reworking because it is, as Jungmann writes, "the central sacrificial prayer of the entire Mass, the foremost liturgical expression of the fact that the Mass is actually a sacrifice."[137] Here is a comparison of the anamnesis-prayer in the Roman mass and the Liturgy of King Johan III, with text in italic type indicating what is common between them.

ROMAN CANON	THE LITURGY
Unde et *memores domine nos* servi tui, sed et plebs tua sancta, *eiusdem Christi Filii tui Domini nostri tam beatae passionis, nec non* ab inferis *resurrectionis, sed et in caelos* gloriosae *ascensionis: offerimus*	*Memores* igitur et *nos Domine* salutaris huius mandati, et tam *beatae passionis* et mortis *nec non* ex mortuis *resurrectionis, sed et caelos ascensionis* eiusdem filij tui Domini nostri Jesu Christi, Quem im mensa tua misericordia nobis *praeclarae maiestati tuae* de tuis
donis ac datis, *hostiam puram,*	donasti ac dedisti, ut victima pro peccatis nostris fieret, et una sui
immaculatam, Panem sanctum vitae aeternae, et Calicem salutis perpetuae.	*hostiam sanctam, hostiam* oblatione in cruce, solueret tibi pro nobis precium redemptionis nostrae,

---

134 *Den Röde Boken*, Facsimile edition, 53.

135 Richter, I, 326; Sehling, III, 68.

136 Hammargren, 49.

137 Jungmann, *The Mass of the Roman Rite,* II, 223.

et iusticiae tuae satisfaceret,
et impleret Sacrificium profuturum
electis ad finem usque mundi.
Eundem Filium tuum,
eiusdem mortem et oblationem,
hostiam puram, hostiam sanctam,
hostiam immaculatam, propitiationem,
scutum et umbraculum nostrum contra
iram tuam, contra terrorem peccati
et mortis, nobis prepositum fide
amplectimur, *tuae que praeclara*
Maiestati humilimus nostris precibus
offerimus, Pro tantis tuis beneficiis
pio cordis affectu, et clara voce,
gratias agens, non quantum debemus,
sed quantum possumus.[138]

> Therefore we also remember, O Lord God, this salutary command and the same your son our Lord Jesus Christ's holy passion and death, his resurrection and ascension. And this your son you have in your boundless mercy sent and given to us, that he might be a sacrifice for our sins, and by his one oblation on the cross pay the price of our redemption, fulfill your justice and make perfect such a sacrifice as might serve for the welfare of all the elect until the end of the world. The same your Son, the same sacrifice which is a pure, holy and undefiled sacrifice, set before us for our reconciliation, our shield, defence, and shelter against your wrath, against the terror of sins and of death, we take and receive with faith and offer before your glorious majesty with our humble supplications. For these your great benefits we give you fervent thanks with heart and mouth, yet not as we ought but as we are able.[139]

While there is some material from the Roman canon embedded in this prayer in the liturgy, it is the non-Roman material that gives away the character of this meaning of this anamnesis-prayer. It has been recast along the lines of the Eastern anaphoras. The opening phrase, "Memores igitur . . . salutaris huius mandati," is the Latin translation of the beginning of the anamnesis-prayer in the Anaphora of Saint John Chrysostom.[140] Several phrases from the Roman canon have been altered in Johan III's prayer with phrases that appear in Pamelius's Latin translation of the so-called Clementine Liturgy of the *Apostolic Constitutions* (the edition of the Eastern liturgies that Johan III probably used as a source), such as "ex mortuis resurrectionis" rather than "ab inferis resurrectionis" and the addition of "gloriosae" to "ascensionis."[141] The last phrase of the anamnesis-prayer, "gratias agimus . . . non quantum debemus, sed quantum possumus" ("we give thanks . . . not as we ought, but as we are able"), is also from the Clementine Liturgy, in Pamelius's translation. The central thought of this anamnesis-prayer is the "once for all

---

[138] *Röda Boken*, 63–4.

[139] Eng. trans. of Swedish text in Yelverton, *The Mass in Sweden*, 106–7. Because the one Swedish word offer can mean both "sacrifice" and "oblation," the distinction in the Eng. trans. depends on the Latin text.

[140] Serenius, 262.

[141] Pamelius, *Liturgica Latinorum* (1571), I, 115.

Sacrifice of Himself." This not only has the Epistle to the Hebrews to recommend it, but also similar formularies from the patristic era. In the post-Sanctus section of the Armenian anaphora we find the following:

> You who from of old in diverse manners did take care of and comfort man fallen in sin, by prophets, by giving the law, by priesthood and the typical offering of kine, but in these last days, having torn up utterly the sentence of condemnation touching all our debts, did give us you only-begotten Son, both debtor and debt, immolation and anointed, lamb and bread of heaven, high priest and sacrifice.[142]

The same thoughts are expressed in the post-Sanctus section of the Clementine Liturgy: "he, the Judge, was judged, the Savior was condemned, the Impassible was nailed to the cross, the essentially immortal died, and the Life-giver was buried that he might release from suffering and deliver from death those for whom he came, and might break the chains of the Devil, and rescue men from deceit."[143]

Thus, in the very anaphoras to which Johan III turned for sources for his own eucharistic prayer, he found ideas that were similar to atonement theories of Reformation theology, and that also were given memorable expression in the eucharistic rite of the *Book of Common Prayer*. We may compare the memorial prayers of the *Book of Common Prayer* with the Liturgy of King Johan III, conflating the 1549 and 1552 versions (with the 1552 text in brackets) of Cranmer's prayer.

> God [Almighty God oure] heauenly father, which of thy tender mercie didest geue thine only sonne Jesu Christ to suffer death upon the crosse for our redemcion, who made there (by hys one oblacion [of himselfe] once offered) a full, perfect oblacion, and satisfaction, for the synnes of the whole world . . .[144]

It is evident that King Johan tried to give expression to the evangelical emphasis on the uniqueness of the atoning sacrifice of Christ in the central sacrificial prayer of the eucharistic tradition. It was the expression of offering this sacrifice to the Father that prompted the charge that the Roman notion of the mass-sacrifice had been included in the liturgy. Offering to God the Father the sacrifice of Christ that had paid "the price of our redemption" fulfilled God's justice. It serves for "the welfare of all the elect until the end of the world," and which is "set before us for our reconciliation, our shield, defence, and shelter" against God's wrath and the terrors of sin and death. This expression can only be understood in the sense of presenting this perfect sacrifice to God in order to appeal to it as the basis on which we may come before God "with our humble supplications." It is an admirable expression of the *solus Christus* emphasis of Reformation theology. Of course, the same theological logic lies behind the offering of the sacrifice of the mass: the perfect sacrifice of Christ is offered to God the Father as the basis for pleading our special intentions or supplications. The difference is that in the Roman canon the impression

---

[142] *Liturgies Eastern and Western*, ed. by F. E. Brightman and C. E. Hammond, I (Oxford University Press, 1896), 436.

[143] Eng. trans. by R. H. Cresswell, *The Liturgy of "The Apostolic Constitutions"* (London, 1900), 62; alt.

[144] *The First and Second Prayer Books of King Edward VI*, 222, 389.

could be given that the sacrifice offered to God is the sacrament itself ("the bread of life and the cup of eternal salvation"), which God gives to us as the gift of communion, whereas in the Liturgy of King Johan it is clearly the atoning sacrifice of the cross that serves as the basis of our appeal. We shall return to this prayer and this seemingly intractable issue again in the next chapter after we have considered evangelical understandings of the eucharistic sacrifice.

The anamnesis-prayer passes over directly to the prayer, *Et supplices*. This prayer fuses together the Supra quae and the Supplices te of the Roman canon in a way reminiscent of the *Et petimus et precamur* prayer in Ambrose's *De sacramentis*.[145] The phrase "panem sanctum . . . salutis perpetuae," which had been omitted from the revision of the Unde et memores, is inserted in this prayer.

ROMAN CANON	THE LITURGY
Supra quae *propitio ac sereno vultu respicere digneris et accepta habere:* sicuti accepta habere dignatus es munera pueri tui iusti Abel et sacrificium patriarchae nostri Abrahae et quod tibi obtulit summus sacerdos tuus Melchisedech: sanctum sacrificium, immaculatam hostiam.	Et *supplices te* per eumdem Filium tuum unicum intercessorem nostrum in arcano consilio divinitatis a te constitutum, Dominum nostrum Jesum Christum rogantes, ut *propitio ac sereno* vultu ad nos nostrasque preces *respicere digneris*, easque *in* caeleste *altare tuum in conspectu divinae maiestatis tuae* suscipias, gratas *et accepta* clementer habeas faciasque *ut quotquot ex hac altaris participatione* benedictum et sanctificatum cibum et potum, panem sanctum vitae aeternae, et calicem salutis perpetuae *sacrosanctum Filii tui corpus et preciosum eius sanguinem sumpserimus omni benedictione caelesti et gratis repleamur.*[146]
Supplices te rogamus omnipotens Deus iube haec perferri per manus sancti angeli tui: in sublime *altare tuum in conspectu divinae maiestatis tuae, ut quotquot ex hac altaris participatione sacrosanctum Filii tui Corpus et Sanguinem sumpserimus, omni benedictione caelesti et gratia replemur.* Per eumdem Christum Dominum nostrum.	

And we humbly beseech you through the same your son, whom in your Godly and secret counsel you have set before us as our only Mediator, that you would look upon us and our prayers with mercy and pitying eye, and to let them come to your heavenly altar before your Divine majesty and be pleasing to you, that all we who are partakers at this altar of the blessed and holy food and drink, the holy bread of eternal life and the cup of eternal salvation, which is the holy body and precious blood of your Son, may also be filled with all heavenly benediction and grace.[147]

Roman liturgiologists have viewed the Supra quae and the Supplices te as the "second epiclesis" of the Roman canon on the basis of an external comparison with

---

[145] See Hänggi-Pahl, *Prex Eucharistica*, 422.
[146] *Röda Boken*, 63.
[147] Yelverton, *The Mass in Sweden*, 108.

Eastern and Gallican anaphoras. According to Jungmann, there is actually a plea here that the power of God touch the sacrificial gift, "but in reverse order, not by the descent of the Spirit, but by ascent of the gift."[148] In his revision of this section of the canon, Johan virtually passed over the Supra quae: omitted from the liturgy are the mention of the patriarchal sacrifices and the angel who carries the earthly gifts to the heavenly altar. He substituted for them the image of Christ the mediator interceding for us in the heavenly sanctuary. This image, derived from the Epistle to the Hebrews, also played a prominent role in Luther's *Sermon von dem Neuen Testament* (1520).

The second half of this prayer is nearly the same as the Supplices te except for the phrase transferred from the Unde et memores. The petition here is not that the "sacrifice" be accepted at the heavenly altar, but "us and our prayers." The prayers of the church have become the sacrifice brought to the heavenly altar. This prayer thus becomes a plea for the acceptance of the eucharistic sacrifice, which is here understood as our prayer, praise, and thanksgiving.

The Supplices is also a prayer for the fruits of communion, which is the thrust of the epicletic prayers in the ancient and Eastern anaphoras. The addition of the phrase "panem sanctum vitae aeternae, et calicem salutis perpetuae" (holy sacred of eternal life and cup of eternal salvation), preceded by the words "cibum et potum" (food and drink) spells out the meaning of "ex hac altaris participatione" (we who are partakers at this altar). The fellowship-character and meal-character of the Lord's Supper are emphasized. An attached note on the meaning of "participatione" calls attention to this explicitly: "Coena Domini est communio quia non est unius tantum personae propria, sed publica multorum in Ecclesia congregatorum."[149] Johan goes on to discuss the meaning of "participatione" (koinonia) in 1 Corinthians 10 and 11 and cites some relevant passages from John Chrysostom and Augustine.

The Supplices passes on to the Nobis quoque, omitting the Memento of the dead. The Nobis quoque continues the petition for the fruits of communion begun in the Supplices. The connection between the petitions for "all heavenly benediction and grace" and "may be received among . . . all your saints" is more apparent in the liturgy than in the Roman canon, where the Memento intervenes. Jungmann suggests that the Memento is a later addition to the Roman canon because there is nothing corresponding to it in the primitive eucharists and it is missing in a number of older manuscripts of the Roman mass (e.g., the sacramentary sent by Pope Hadrian I to Charlemagne).[150]

Except for the deletion of specific names of the martyrs and saints, Johan followed the text of the Nobis quoque just as it was found in the Uppsala missal tradition (*Manuale Upsalense* 1487, *Missale Upsalense Novum* 1513).[151]

ROMAN CANON	THE LITURGY
Nobis quoque peccatoribus de multitudine miserationum tuarum	Nobis quoque peccatoribus de multitudine miserationum tuarum

---

[148] Jungmann, *The Mass of the Roman Roman Rite*, II, 233.
[149] *Röda Boken*, 64.
[150] Jungmann, *The Mass of the Roman Rite*, II, 238.
[151] Serenius, 277.

sperantibus partem aliquam et	sperantibus, partem aliquam et
societatem donare digneris cum	societatem donare digneris cum
tuls sanctis apostolis et martyribus,	tuis sanctis apostolis et martyribus,
cum Ioanne, Stephano,	
Barnaba, Ignatio, etc. et cum	
omnibus sanctis tuis. Intra	et omnibus sanctis tuis. Intra
quorum nos consortium, non es-	quorum nos consortium nos aes-
timator meriti: sed uenie que-	timator meriti, sed venie quae
sumus largitor admitte	sumus largitor admitte.
per Christum Dominum nostrum.	Per Christum Dominum nostrum.

We likewise beseech you, O Lord God, that you would give us, poor sinful mortals *(syndiga menniskior)* who trust in your manifold mercies, that we may be received among your holy Apostles, Martyrs and all your saints, into whose number admit us, not through our merit, but by your mercy which forgives our sins and failings. Through the same Jesus Christ our Lord.[152]

The only difference between the *Missal Romanum* 1570 and the medieval Uppsala missal tradition is that the *Missal Romanum* 1570 adds "famulis tuis" after "Nobis quoque peccatoribus." A literary problem is raised by the omission of the Memento: to what does the "quoque" (likewise) refer if not the faithful departed? Jungmann suggests that Peccatores originally referred not to the whole congregation, but to the clergy. Using self-deprecatory expressions was common in the piety of late antiquity.[153] Undoubtedly, in the Red Book, however, it refers to the congregation as well as the celebrant.

All the classical anaphoras end with a trinitarian doxology. The Per quem is that doxology in the Roman canon, and it is closely akin to the doxology of the Anaphora of Saint Hippolytus.

ROMAN CANON	THE LITURGY
Per quem *haec* omnia Domine	Per quem Domine omnia bona
semper *bona* creas, sanctificas,	semper creas, sanctificas,
vivificas, benedicis	vivificas, benedicis,
et praestas nobis.	et praestas nobis.
Per ipsum, et cum ipso,	Per ipsum, et cum ipso,
et in ipso *est* tibi	et in ipso *sit* tibi
Deo Patri omnipotenti in unitate	Deo Patri omnipotenti in unitate
Spiritus sanctis	Spiritus sanctis
omnis honor et gloria.	omnis honor et gloria.
Per omnia saecula	Per omnia saecula
saeculorum. Amen.	saeculorum. Amen.

Through whom, O Lord, you do ever create, sanctify, quicken, bless and grant us every good thing *(alt gott)*. Through him, with him, and in him be all honour, glory and praise, *(all ähra, loff och prijs)* to you, almighty God, Father, and to the Holy Spirit, from everlasting to everlasting. Amen.[154]

---

[152] Yelverton, *The Mass in Sweden*, 108.

[153] Jungmann, *The Mass of the Roman Rite*, II, 265.

[154] Yelverton, *The Mass in Sweden*, 109.

The *Missal Romanum* "haec omnia bona" is rendered "omnia bona" (in Swedish "alt gott," every good thing) in order to neutralize the reference to the sacramental elements. We also note the change from the indicative "est" to the subjunctive "sit." Originally "haec" referred to all the gifts presented at the altar. Prayers of blessing over these gifts would have been inserted before the Per quem.[155] When these gifts were no longer blessed at the altar the haec naturally came to be associated with the gifts of bread and wine for the sacrament exclusively. An attached note draws attention to this fact and offers the following explanation: "Nihil tamen obstat, quo minus idem in genere de omnibus beneficijs tam spiritualibus quam corporalibus, omisso pronomine demonstrativo haec omnia bona, dici possit."[156] By omitting the pronoun "haec" King Johan was able once again to stress the general thanksgiving (eucharistic) character of the mass.

Thus, in his eucharistic prayer King Johan carefully avoided any sacrificial references to the sacramental gifts. The eucharistic sacrifice is that of prayer, praise, and thanksgiving. References to the sacramental elements are specifically to receiving the gift of communion.

The Structure of the Eucharistic Prayer

Analysis of the eucharistic prayer in the *Liturgia svecanae ecclesiae* shows that there was no slavish dependence on the Roman canon. Whatever canon prayers were used as sources of the liturgy were reworked to stress the evangelical understanding of the eucharistic sacrifice as a response in prayer, praise, and thanksgiving to the proclamation of the mighty acts of God in Christ. That proclamation is made in the preface of the prayer, which includes the institution narrative as the proclamation of the gospel. In remembrance of all that has been done for our salvation, the faithful present themselves and their prayers before the divine majesty, appealing to Christ their only mediator, petitioning for the benefits of the sacrament. The only portions of the canon prayers that were retained nearly verbatim in the liturgy are those concerned with the fruits of communion, and which constituted the communion prayers proper. (The devotional prayers recited before the reception of the sacrament are early medieval additions to the Roman mass, mostly of Gallican provenance.)[157]

Moreover, this whole revision has been done with a systematic appeal to the ancient and Eastern eucharists. This is evident not only in the actual quoting of prayer formularies, but in the structure of the eucharistic prayer itself. We can see this if we compare and contrast the shape of the eucharist in the Red Book with that of the Roman canon and the West Syrian anaphoral shape.

---

[155] Jungmann, *The Mass of the Roman Rite*, II, 260f.
[156] *Röda Boken*, 65.
[157] Jungmann, *The Mass of the Roman Rite*, II, 367ff.

ROMAN SHAPE	WEST SYRIAN SHAPE	THE LITURGY
Initial thanksgiving (preface) leading to the Sanctus	Initial thanksgiving leading to the Sanctus	Initial thanksgiving (preface) including the institution narrative
Prayer recalling the sacrifice (Te igitur)		
Intercessions/Commemoration		
Prayer for acceptance of the sacrifice (Quam oblationem)— the first epiclesis	Praise recalling salvation history leading to . . .	Praise leading to . . .
Institution narrative	Institution narrative	The Sanctus
Anamnesis (Unde et Memores)	Anamnesis	Anamnesis (Memores)
Second epiclesis (Supra quae and Supplices te)	Epiclesis	Epiclesis (Supplices and Nobis quoque)
Intercessions/Commemorations (Memento, Nobis quoque)	Intercessions/ Commemorations	
Doxology (Per quem)	Doxology	Doxology (Per quem)

A significant theological step has been taken by removing the institution narrative from the oblationary context it has in the Roman canon, to a salvation history context, such as it has in the West Syrian anaphoras. This enables the prayers that follow to serve as a response to the saving works of God whose benefits are received by the faithful in the sharing of the Lord's Supper. By contrast, in the Roman canon the words of institution serve as the basis for offering the sacrifice of the mass. The fact that material from the Roman canon has been used as one of the sources of King Johan's eucharistic prayer does not mean that the same meanings are employed if the structure has been altered. Theological meaning lies as much in the shape of the liturgy as in the texts. The meaning of the texts, whose terminology was common in patristic liturgies, is dependent on the context of words and phrases within the ordo.

There is another anaphoral structure to which the eucharistic prayer in the Red Book bears similarities, if the Sanctus were omitted and allowance were made for the lack of a Spirit-epiclesis: the Anaphora of Hippolytus. The structure of the Anaphora of Hippolytus is the thanksgiving for the saving deeds of God in Christ leading to the institution narrative, which introduces the anamnesis and oblation followed by the epiclesis and concluding doxology. Of course, the *Apostolic Tradition* has only been reconstructed in the twentieth century, so Johan III had no access to the Hippolytean anaphora. Nevertheless, it invites consideration that the one full eucharistic prayer of Lutheran Reformation provenance bears structural similarity to the third-century prayer that has been so influential on twentieth-century liturgical revision.

The eucharistic prayer in the Red Book is another viable way of giving thanks "in remembrance of me."[158] The retention of the proper prefaces assures the element of variability that Western liturgy has preferred. The movement from the preface to the

---

[158] See Frank C. Senn, "Toward a Different Anaphoral Structure," *Worship* 58 (1984), 346–58.

institution narrative makes the action of Christ in the upper room serve as the climax of the *mirabilia Dei* (wonders of God) for which praise and thanks is rendered to God the Father. The Sanctus has been something of an interruption, even in the Roman canon since the "igitur" (therefore) of the Te igitur presumably refers back to the mirabilia Dei in the preface as the motive for the church's act of oblation. E. C. Ratcliff has suggested that the Roman anaphora may originally have ended with the Sanctus.[159] Relocating the Sanctus to the doxological conclusion of the prayer would make the referent of "Blessed is he who comes" the Christ who is received in Holy Communion. In a certain sense it is the doxological conclusion in the Liturgy of King Johan III, since it is being sung by the choir while the celebrant prays the rest of the prayers silently. Of course, the Liturgy of King Johan III shares with other Western anaphoras a deficient role for the Holy Spirit, although King Johan appealed to the Spirit's role in the transformation of the elements in the offertory prayer. This epicletic prayer could be transferred to a place between the anamnesis and the concluding doxology. Thus, the eucharistic prayer in the Liturgy of King Johan III provides a model for eucharistic praying that is steeped in both ancient structure and Reformation theology. Like the eucharistic prayer in the 1549 *Book of Common Prayer* it is both fully catholic and evangelical.

❧ The Decisions of Uppsala Möte, 1593

We have seen that by 1583, King Johan III had achieved some measure of acceptance of his religious program. While the aesthetically minded king could rail against clergy who kept their churches "like sheepfolds or pigsties, so that a man would spew at the stink of them,"[160] much work was done to improve the quality of church life in the kingdom, not least of all in the area of architecture. Much renovation and construction of churches as well as castles was done, and ecclesiastical affairs in Sweden would have been tranquil had it not been for the theological convictions of the king's brother, Duke Karl.

Karl believed that in the provisions of Gustav Vasa's Testament, all powers not expressly reserved to the crown were transferred to the dukes, and he was jealous to preserve what he considered his own prerogatives. When the See of Strängnäs fell vacant in 1585, Karl influenced the appointment of Petrus Jonae (who was not only an Anti-Liturgist, but a fugitive from royal justice). King Johan refused his approval and no bishop could be found to perform the consecration, so Jonae remained unconsecrated until after Johan's death in 1593.[161]

In May 1587 the clergy of the duchy drew up the *Confessio Strengnesis*, which damned the errors of the liturgists in sharp terms. Karl, for his part, wrote to the Universities of Leipzig, Helmstedt, and Wittenberg for opinions of the Red Book and

---

[159] E. C. Ratcliff, "The Sanctus and the Pattern of the Early Anaphora," *Journal of Ecclesiastical History* 1 (1950), 29–36, 125–34. See also Bryan D. Spinks, *The Sanctus in the Eucharistic Prayer* (Cambridge University Press, 1991), 104ff.

[160] Roberts, 291.

[161] Ibid., 292.

received from these faculties the condemnatory answers he expected.[162] He was thus able to line up some of the leading German theologians against the liturgy.

The year 1587 also saw Prince Sigismund's election as King of Poland. His election meant that a semi-absent, Catholic king would eventually rule Sweden, and something had to be done on both counts. The råd (privy council) began making preparations for the administration of government during periods of the king's absence. These provisions were spelled out in the Statute of Kalmar, which further stipulated that the Lutheran religion was not to be interfered with. Unfortunately, even though Johan had a hand in preparing these proposals, they were never submitted to the Estates for ratification and therefore were never implemented.

The Polish crown proved more of a bane than a blessing for both Johan and Sigismund. Sigismund wanted to be rid of it, and Johan wanted his son back in Sweden during his declining years. But the råd was convinced that peace with Russia depended on an alliance with Poland. The other viable candidate, the Hapsburg Archduke Ernest, vacillated over whether he would accept the Polish crown, and the Polish Senate was unwilling to go through another election. When Johan urged Sigismund to abdicate in 1589, leading members of the råd publicly opposed him, thwarting their king's policy and rebuking his personal conduct. Stunned, Johan felt that he needed to consolidate his position against the råd. This led to temporary reconciliation and alliance with his brother Karl in 1590 and a new Succession Pact to prevent a relapse into electoral monarchy. This Pact extended the right of succession to the female line after the male. In the case of Sigismund's absence from Sweden, the nearest male kin was to be named regent—which in this case meant Duke Karl.

Johan died on November 17, 1592; as Roberts noted, "in charity with all men, save perhaps with those bitter-end Anti-Liturgists for whom the hour of opportunity was now to strike."[163]

Little had been settled before Johan's death concerning the future of Sweden, except that Sigismund would become king under the law of succession. For Karl, the Anti-Liturgists, and many of the aristocrats, the impending coronation of Sigismund was viewed catastrophically. In his will, Johan had expressed his desire that the Liturgy would continue to be used after his death.[164] The Anti-Liturgists never got over their feeling that the Liturgy had been the product of Jesuit influence. Now a Roman Catholic would be king of Sweden, and one committed to the Counter-Reformation at that. The fears of the Swedes had some grounding in fact, because a special commission for the return of Sweden to the papacy was appointed as soon as news of Johan's death reached Rome.

The only person the ruling Estates of Sweden could turn to in this moment of crisis was Duke Karl. Even though his Calvinist inclinations were known, that seemed a lesser threat at the moment. In January 1593, Karl and the members of the råd issued a public declaration that they would jointly govern Sweden in the absence of King

---

[162] Ibid., 293.

[163] Ibid., 326.

[164] Holmquist, *Svenska Kyrkans Historia*, III/2, 142.

Sigismund. They also declared that they would maintain the true religion based on the pure word of God as confessed in the Augsburg Confession. This was a significant move since up to this point no confession of faith had been adopted by the national church. The declaration further summoned the bishops and representatives of the clergy to a special church assembly *(möte)* in Uppsala to settle the disputes over doctrine and ceremonies and to fill the vacant sees.

This Assembly or Council was held in Uppsala in March 1593.[165] John Wordsworth has written concerning it:

> It is scarcely possible to exaggerate the importance of this council as a turning point in the history of Sweden. . . . It stands out as evidence of what a national church may do for the people when it is allowed to have a reasonable independence. There are very few if any parallels to be found to it in the religious history of mankind. The freedom and the unanimity of the action could only be possible in a nation so much accustomed to the idea and practice of self-government by a large popular assembly, and so ready to be swayed by enthusiasm in making great decisions at critical moments of its history.[166]

Wordsworth's assessment is not much overstated. It was a bold move for the government to call such a council and for the council to make its own decisions in the absence of the king. Duke Karl has been generally commended for standing in the background and allowing the council to do its work without undue interference. But actually, although Karl was the first citizen of Sweden by reason of his family position and personal wealth, he was not the king, nor as yet even the regent. He had wanted to call a meeting of the riksdag (all the Estates), but was voted down in the råd on the grounds that only the king can convene a parliament.[167] In spite of Karl's known theological convictions, the council voted to include Calvinists and Zwinglians on the list of heretics condemned. The fact that the actions taken could be so unanimous testifies more to the growing coalescence of theological persuasion and liturgical practice in the national church than to the self-governing practices of the Swedes. This is evident by the fact that the council was not nearly as iconoclastic as Karl and the most virulent Anti-Liturgists might have preferred.

The conclusions of the council may be summarized as follows:[168]

1. The church should abide by the word of God as contained in the Holy Scriptures of the Old and New Testaments. The Bible is the ultimate rule and authority for all matters of doctrine, faith, and morals, and needs no further interpretation by the Fathers or others. This stance was in conformity with the scripture principle in the Formula of Concord. Although the Book of Concord (1580) included an appended Testimonia Patrum, the Council was not adopting the full Book of Concord and the Uppsala Resolution was aimed specifically against the patristic ideal propounded in the theology of King Johan III that had served as the basis of his church policy.

---

[165] See Hans Cnattingius, *Uppsala Möte 1593* (Stockholm, 1943), 68ff.

[166] Wordsworth, 262.

[167] Roberts, 331.

[168] The text of the *Uppsala möte beslut* (Resolution) is appended to Cnattingius, 137ff.; see also Wordsworth, 259–60.

2. The church assented to the Apostles', Nicene, and Athanasian Creeds, the unaltered Augsburg Confession of 1530, and to the religion held in the time of Gustav Vasa and set forth in the Church Order of 1571. The council admitted that that church order contained certain ceremonies that had long since been abolished by other evangelical churches. But the council felt that representatives of the dioceses would need to discuss these matters at greater length in order to ascertain a consensus on ceremonial use at the present time. In the meantime the clergy should teach their people the proper meaning of such things as the use of salt and lights at baptism, the movement of the missal from one side of the altar to the other during the gradual, the elevation of the host and chalice at the consecration and the ringing of the sanctus-bells at the elevation.

3. Exorcism was held to be unessential to baptism, but it was also regarded as a suitable reminder of the condition of all people who come to baptism, and as such could be retained in the Swedish church. A sentence was added, however, that the council did not wish to cast any slur on foreign churches or "high personages here in the kingdom" who found it offensive.[169]

4. The Liturgy which had caused so much dissension in the realm was condemned as a *monstrum horrendum*, "superstitious and quite like the popish mass."[170] The council rejected the liturgy and all its implications for doctrine, ceremonies, and discipline, and strictly forbade its use. But the council also rejected the errors of the sacramentarians, Zwinglians, Calvinists, and Anabaptists, and all other heretics by whatever name they were known.

5. The council approved of the discipline set forth in the 1571 Church Order.

6. The council forbade those who held false doctrine or disagreed with the council's resolutions to hold public meetings in houses or elsewhere, upon pain of punishment.

The lack of dissent in the council caused Professor Nicolaus Bottniensis of Uppsala to proclaim, "Now Sweden is one man and we all have one God." But to ensure further consensus, copies of the resolutions were circulated in the provinces and almost 2,000 signatures were added to those who signed at Uppsala.

The uniqueness of this situation must be appreciated. In no other country up to that time was a situation set up in which the ruler's faith and practice would not be that of his subjects. The Swedes were prepared to accommodate their new king's religion as a matter of the king's private convictions, but not as a public faith. Before his coronation in February 1594 Sigismund was forced to sign an Accession Charter that guaranteed the religious freedom of his subjects according to the provisions of the Uppsala Council, but denied freedom of worship to others.[171] This put the king in an untenable position for a strong-willed Vasa, and after his coronation Sigismund made it clear that he had no intention of abiding by these conditions. He openly countenanced Roman Catholic worship in Stockholm. When he returned to Poland, Duke Karl convened a riksdag—which

---

[169] Roberts, p. 335, relates that Duke Karl would assert that he would chase out of his house with a poker any priest who tried to perform an exorcism therein. See also Bodo Nischan, "The Exorcism Controversy in the Late Reformation," *Sixteenth Century Journal* 18 (1987), 31–51.

[170] Holmqvist, III, 313.

[171] Roberts, 343.

he had been expressly forbidden to do—and this precipitated a constitutional crisis that paved the way for civil war in 1596, when Sigismund invaded Sweden with an army to reestablish his authority. He was defeated, given another chance to abide by the conditions of the Accession Charter, and only after great soul-searching was finally deposed as the lawful king in 1599. Duke Karl was now all-powerful in Sweden, but the need to shore up the new Swedish government's administration of Finland and Estonia, which were very loyal to King Johan III and King Sigismund, and foreign relations with Russia, Poland, and Denmark, which involved armed hostilities, delayed his coronation as King Karl IX until 1604.

INTO THE AGE OF ORTHODOXY

Roberts wrote that the "liturgical struggle is a good example of the power of a fanatically resolute and intellectually honest minority."[172] It is important to emphasize the word "minority." Throughout the 1580s the Anti-Liturgists clung tenaciously to their convictions in spite of persecution and hounding. There is no indication that most of the people and lesser parish priests were not content with the religious practices maintained by King Johan. But with the exception of Archbishop Björnram, whose death in 1591 deprived the liturgical party of its ablest champion, the Anti-Liturgists were among the best educated clergy in Sweden. Most of them had attended the leading universities in Germany, especially the "gnesio-Lutheran" University of Rostock. Their victory at Uppsala in 1593 was the victory of Lutheran orthodoxy. Indeed, Toivo Harjunpaa suggests that 1593 marks the beginning of the period of orthodoxy in the churches of Sweden and Finland.[173] The period of orthodoxy is characterized by a rigorous enforcement of Lutheran doctrine and practice as defined by the Lutheran confessions and the Reformation church orders.

But Harjunpaa also notes that the Uppsala Council had to warn against an undue disturbance of the people with regard to ceremonial changes. A marked liturgical conservatism flourished among the common people and the less well-educated clergy in Sweden and Finland. Well into the seventeenth century, salt, chrism, and lighted candles were used in baptism. The custom of lighting votive candles for men fishing out at sea was also practiced in some coastal and inland parishes.[174] In Finland, the Governor-General, Klas Fleming, was a loyal supporter of King Sigismund. He did not approve of the decisions at Uppsala and did what he could to thwart them. He wanted to preserve King Johan's concern for decency and good order in the churches. In a letter to Bishop Sorolainen of Åbo, he wrote that disorder and desecration resulted in parishes where the priests introduced changes too quickly. He reminded the bishop of one incident not far from Åbo where angry peasants had seized the reforming priest during the service and had thrown him over the church yard fence.[175]

---

[172] Ibid., 329.
[173] Harjunpaa, *art. cit.*, 18–19.
[174] Ibid., 20–21.
[175] Ibid.

Even those in the church hierarchy, now led by the stalwart anti-liturgist Archbishop Abraham Angermannus, were not prepared to go as far in the opposite direction as Duke Karl would have wished. To the Duke's great annoyance, Angermannus summoned a church council in 1595 on his own authority. As Roberts notes, "We are at the beginning of a period of strong, authoritarian bishops, men neither disposed to moderate their voices to the tender ears of royalty, nor willing to suffer usurpation of their authority by the laity in silence."[176] The council confirmed the decisions of Uppsala 1593 and made provision for a general visitation of the parishes. But the only ceremonial change countenanced by this council was the abolition of the elevation. It also recognized the need to revise the liturgical books and appointed a special commission to do this. But codification rather than the creation of new texts is one of the hallmarks of liturgy in the age of orthodoxy. Thus the liturgical books in Sweden at the end of the sixteenth century followed the order of the Swedish Mass in its 1557 revision, as specified by the 1571 Swedish Order. The major omission in the 1599 revision of the *Handbok* was the sign of the cross in baptism.

Karl did not think that the proposed changes went far enough. He argued against the adoption of the new *Handbok* at the 1600 Riksdag. He even put forward his own Services of Baptism and Holy Communion.[177] These proposed services met with strong condemnation from the clergy, who detected in them signs of Calvinism. Undaunted, Karl submitted his own *Handbok* to the Estates in 1602 and imposed its use in his own chapel. The archbishop publicly denounced it as doctrinally unsound. Karl retorted by condemning the official *Handbok* as superstitious and unscriptural. He did secure from the riksdag a resolution calling for further revision of the *Handbok*, and even managed to get consent for having lay representatives on the commission as well as clergy. But the clergy were in no hurry for further changes, and the revised *Handbok* was not submitted until 1608 when Karl, as king, demanded it. But that effort proved so unsatisfactory to the king that he stopped the project. Once Karl was dead, however, the revised version was submitted to the riksdag in 1611, won immediate approval, and was put into law in 1614 by Karl's son, King Gustaf II Adolf.[178] The 1614 *Handbok* remained in use until 1693, when a minor revision was carried out. This *Handbok* remained in use until 1811 in Sweden and 1886 in Finland.[179] However, the 1614 *Handbok* did omit the Introit and Gradual in favor of Swedish hymns and substituted the chorale "Allenaste Gud i Himmelrik" (All glory be to God on high) for the Gloria. While Gregorian chants for the Swedish texts were published in the *Liber Cantus* (Uppsala, 1620), these changes in the *Handbok* marked by beginning of the decline of plainsong settings of the liturgy and their replacement by congregational chorales, many of the tunes of which were imported from Germany.[180]

---

[176] Roberts, 413.

[177] See Yelverton, *The Mass in Sweden*, 127–46 for the communion office of Karl IX.

[178] Roberts, 418.

[179] Harjunpaa, 22.

[180] See Torben Schousboe, "Protestant Church Music in Scandinavia," in Blume, ed., *Protestant Church Music*, op. cit., 620.

The story of the Swedish liturgy demonstrates the remarkable consensus that developed in the national church of Sweden, a consensus that could be maintained even against the nation's rulers, if need be. It is the story of the preservation of catholic tradition within an evangelical church. Well into the seventeenth century many old customs were preserved. Altars, lights, and vestments flourished anew during the Baroque period when many new churches were built. Bells continued to be rung for liturgical purposes; funeral processions were held; some of the old church festivals were kept as public holidays; and the 1614 *Handbok* even restored the sign of the cross in baptism (although it had remained in use in the dioceses of Västerås and Strängnäs even during the reign of Karl IX). A record of church life in Sweden in the middle of the seventeenth century is preserved in this passage from the diary of the Puritan Whitelocke, an English ambassador to Sweden during the Cromwellian Commonwealth, noting what he saw in Skara Cathedral in 1653.

> In the choir are many pictures of saints and other images; and at the east end of it a high altar, and a stately crucifix upon it: there are also diverse other and lesser crucifixes in several places of the church and choir. In the vestry we saw the chalices and pyxes, with pieces of the wafer in them; and none could see a difference betwixt this and the Papists' churches.[181]

---

[181] Whitelocke, *Journal of the Swedish Embassy in the Years 1653 and 1654*, I, ed. by C. Morton (London, 1855), 187–8.

CHAPTER 13

Reconsideration of Eucharistic Sacrifice

WE HAVE SEEN THAT Lutheranism retained almost everything from the medieval mass except the offertory and full eucharistic prayers. The effort of King Johan III of Sweden to reconstruct offertory and eucharistic prayers from patristic models met with intense criticism from a party of gnesio-Lutheran Anti-Liturgists. The reason for the elimination of these prayers in the Lutheran mass-orders had to do with Luther's concern that the body and blood of Christ are God's gift to his people, to be received in faith, and therefore cannot be offered to God the Father for special intentions for the dead as well as the living. The oblation of the memorial prayer, coming after the consecratory words of Christ in the institution narrative, was especially condemned as blasphemous since the offering here could only suggest a reversal of the "direction" of the sacrament. The offertory prayers were regarded as misleading and contributing to that false piety branded as works-righteousness, although it should be noted that the offertory had become the point at which special intentions paid for by mass stipends were collected and proposed.

Any reconsideration of the role of a eucharistic prayer in Lutheran liturgy must deal with the issue of eucharistic sacrifice. There is not only the need to achieve some sort of ecumenical breakthrough that transcends the impasse of the sixteenth century on eucharistic sacrifice, but also the agenda of enabling Lutherans to reclaim with confidence the theologically richer tradition of the church catholic than is afforded by a "canon" reduced to preface, Sanctus, and words of institution at most. The concern of this chapter is to review the teachings of the reformers on eucharistic sacrifice to recover their positive views, sometimes buried beneath their negative polemics.

Luther's reserve about using the word "sacrifice" was not only "due to his reaction against the misuse of the word in the contemporary doctrine and practice of the mass," as Gustav Aulén has suggested.[1] Rather it was due to his concern that the elements—the hostia altaris—cannot be offered to God because that is the gift God gives to his people. But what if the starting point for understanding eucharistic sacrifice is not "the sacrament itself" (the elements), but the liturgical celebration? Or, in the words of Sebastian Moore, not "the theology of the mass" but "the liturgical datum?"[2] Does that suggest another way of viewing the eucharistic sacrifice?

We recall the thesis of John Jay Hughes that, for Thomas Aquinas, what makes the sacrament a sacrifice is not the offering but the liturgical/ritual act of consecration.[3] The words of Christ proclaimed by the presiding minister become the action of God in transforming the bread and wine into the body and blood of Christ. This understanding of sacrifice as consecration does suggest a collusion between the church's action in the liturgy and God's action in the sacrament, a simultaneity of sacramental and sacrificial dynamics, that might help break through the "Reformation deadlock" on eucharistic sacrifice. But it still does not deal with the liturgical datum that essential to the eucharistic meal are bread and wine, which are at least presented on the altar even if the word "offering" is not used, and that must be regarded as gifts from God's creation being returned to God for God's use; and that the act of eating and drinking is essential to the nature of the eucharistic meal, and many ancient sacrifices involved a communion meal. The dogmatic issues must be bracketed and the liturgical issues dealt with. When the *use* of the Lord's Supper rather than the ontology of the elements is considered, other possibilities open up for understanding eucharistic sacrifice. Some of these other possibilities are already present in the writings of the reformers.

❦ MELANCHTHON: *Apologia Confessio Augustana*, 1531

Philipp Melanchthon was the systematic theologian of the Lutheran Reformation. A humanist scholar who reformed the curriculum of the German university, he was the principal author of the Augsburg Confession and its Apology, or defense. Both were included in the Book of Concord (1580) as confessional or symbolical expressions of Lutheranism. His *Loci Communes* (1535) became the standard theological textbook in Lutheran universities. Even so, he has occupied an ambivalent place in the estimation of Lutheran scholars, as he did among his own contemporaries. Chief among the charges against him is that he intellectualized the faith. In an influential article, Richard Caemerer said that Melanchthon provides "a useful case study for the mind of the sixteenth century and its abridgment of the essential vitality of Luther's thought."[4]

---

[1] Gustav Aulén, *Eucharist and Sacrifice*, op. cit., 101.
[2] Sebastian Moore, "The Theology of the Mass and the Liturgical Datum," *Downside Review* 69 (1951), 31–44.
[3] John Jay Hughes, "Eucharistic Sacrifice: Transcending the Reformation Deadlock," *Worship* 43 (1969), 541.
[4] Richard Caemmerer, "The Melanchthonian Blight," *Concordia Theological Monthly* 18 (1947), 322.

Franz Hildebrandt suggests that this ambivalence stems from Luther's unqualified confidence in this humanist scholar who nevertheless was more conciliatory and systematic than Luther himself. In fact, Melanchthon was "the only humanist with whom [Luther] came to terms; and it must be said that in this strange alliance Melanchthon has proved the stronger influence in shaping the history of Lutheranism" (brackets added).[5] Melanchthon's theological method became the theological method of the post-Reformation Lutheran theologians. Yet the gnesio-Lutherans held the Praeceptor (Melanchthon) in suspicion of betraying Luther's "sola fideism" by his appeal to tradition and reason. Philippists were condemned in the Formula of Concord for their synergistic conception of free will and their crypto-Calvinist conception of the Lord's Supper. Moreover, in the confessional narrowing and scholastic rigorism that occurred in the post-Reformation generation the Praeceptor's central concern—How inclusive can the church be?—passed out of favor even as his theological method became standard in the universities.

It was surely this concern for comprehensiveness, at first between reformers and papalists, and then between various Protestant parties, that contributed to the so-called vagueness that Boussuet, among others, noticed in the Praeceptor's later eucharistic theology.[6] In an important article, Peter Fraenkel has suggested that this was due neither to the irenic reformer's timidity nor to his desperate attempts to achieve agreement among conflicting parties at any price. It was rather "connected with certain persistent themes of the Praeceptor's patristic argumentation in this context."[7] Melanchthon was simply unwilling to enter into discussion that went beyond the patristic consensus. This was the reason Melanchthon could take Oecolampadius seriously, because the Swiss reformer shared the same concern not to go beyond the patristic consensus.[8]

What Melanchthon saw in the patristic writers was an emphasis on the function or use of the sacrament rather than the ontology of the elements. This functional view clearly emerges in *Iudicium de Missa et Coelibatu*, probably written in 1526 during the controversy with Zwingli. In an interesting passage Melanchthon reports the view of John Fabri on the eucharistic sacrifice, against which Melanchthon argued that we do not "give" anything, but that it is God who "gives," and the mass can be called a sacrifice only because it is a means by which we can render thanks for the grace God gives in the sacrament.[9] Melanchthon's concern here is not with "the sacrament itself," but with the use and benefits of the sacrament. Because the principal use of the sacrament is as a means of grace, it cannot be only a human ceremony that celebrates mutual love among Christians, as John á Laski contended.[10] But it certainly is *also* a human ceremony, and Melanchthon will be concerned to say what the ceremony of the Lord's Supper does celebrate.

---

[5] Franz Hildebrandt, *Melanchthon: Alien or Ally?* (Cambridge University Press, 1946).

[6] Bousuet, *Histoire des Variations des Églises Protestantes*, VIII (Paris, 1688), 485ff.

[7] Peter Fraenkel, "Ten Questions Concerning Melanchthon, the Fathers and the Eucharist," in *Luther and Melanchthon. Referate und Berichte des Zweiten Internationalen Kongress für Lutherforschung* (Göttingen, 1961), 147ff.

[8] Ibid., 159–60.

[9] CR 1:843.

[10] Ibid., 846.

It is also of interest that Melanchthon argued against the use of the sacrament in private masses because he finds no evidence of private masses before the time of Gregory the Great. Chrysostom, Jerome, and Augustine are all cited to support Luther's view that private masses should be abolished.[11] In line with this consistent appeal to the patristic writers in the Praeceptor's writings, Fraenkel suggests that Melanchthon regarded the functional view of the presence of Christ in the sacrament as "the undoubted, obvious, well-known and pure biblical teaching of the Fathers."[12]

This observation is in agreement with the definition of the sacrament found in the Augsburg Confession and its Apology. In these documents, Melanchthon never referred to the elements used in baptism or in the Lord's Supper. As Holsten Fagerberg comments, "In so doing he connected the divine presence with the sacred acts as such, not with the water of Baptism or the bread and wine of the Lord's Supper."[13] This is evident in the cautious wording of Augustana X, that "the body and blood of Christ are truly present and are distributed to those who eat in the Supper of the Lord."[14] This formulation proved acceptable both to Luther and to the authors of the Roman Confutation of the Augsburg Confession. Yet it differed from Luther's insistence that the sacramental elements are the signs of God's saving presence. Luther wrote in the Smalkald Articles, "We hold that the bread and the wine in the Supper are the true body and blood of Christ and that these are given and received not only by the godly but also by wicked Christians."[15]

Melanchthon defined the "sacrament" not in terms of the elements but as a *ceremonia* or *opus* by which God gives us what the sacrament's *promissio* offers. "Sacrifice," on the other hand, is a ceremonia or opus by which we render glory to God. The Praeceptor expressed his famous distinction in Article XXIV of the Apology.

> The theologians make a proper distinction between sacrament and sacrifice. The genus common to both could be "ceremony" or "sacred act." A sacrament is a ceremony or act in which God offers us the content of the promise joined to the ceremony; thus Baptism is not an act which we offer to God but one in which God baptizes us through a minister functioning in his place. . . . By way of contrast, a sacrifice is a ceremony or act which we render to God to honor him.[16]

Melanchthon further distinguished two types of sacrifice: the propitiatory sacrifice that satisfies guilt and punishment, placates God's wrath and merits the forgiveness of sins, which is the atoning sacrifice; and the sacrificium eucharistikon by means of which thanks and praise is rendered to God for the reconciliation and forgiveness effected by the atoning sacrifice.[17] The mass cannot be a propitiatory sacrifice, because there has been only

---

[11] Ibid., 844, 845.

[12] Fraenkel, 152.

[13] Holsten Fagerberg, *A New Look at the Lutheran Confessions (1529–1537)*, trans. Gene L. Lund (St. Louis: Concordia, 1972), 191.

[14] Tappert, 34; *Bek.*, 64.

[15] SA III, VI, 1; Tappert, 311; *Bek.*, 450.

[16] Tappert, 252.; *Bek.*, 354.

[17] Ibid.

one true propitiatory sacrifice in the history of the world: the atoning sacrifice of Christ. The only sacrifice Christians can offer are the eucharistic sacrifices, which are called *sacrificia laudis* (sacrifices of praise), examples of which include: "the proclamation of the Gospel, faith, prayer, thanksgiving, confession, the affliction of the saints, yes, all the good works of the saints."[18] Among these sacrifices of praise is the ceremony of the mass, which is a eucharistic sacrifice if it is used *ad laudem Dei* (to the praise of God).

We have seen that Luther's attack on the sacrifice of the mass stemmed from his view of the presence of the body and blood of Christ "in, with, and under" the bread and the wine. With great consistency Luther interprets the words, "Hoc est corpus meum," in a literal sense, emphasizing the "est." Hence, his focus is on the elements. After the words of institution these can only be received as the body and blood of Christ; they cannot be offered to God. Since Melanchthon does not focus on the sacramental elements, he is less restrained in speaking about the mass as a sacrifice. We would expect, and do find, that he attacks the mass as a "good work," or, in the cultic sense, as an *opus operatum* (a work that is accomplished just by doing it). This relates to his concern for the proper *use* of the Lord's Supper, its use *in faith*.

Catholic theology employed the concept of opus operatum to stress the objective nature of the sacraments. They are "means" used by God, the "validity" of which is wholly independent of the personal qualifications of the minister or the communicants. Since the Lutheran Confessions also affirm the objectivity of the sacraments, they do not discuss this aspect of opus operatum. Rather, Melanchthon is concerned about the view that the mass is able to gain grace for those for whom it is offered ex opere operato, whether they are present or not, whether they are living or dead. Under a section in Article XXIV of the Apology, "De missa pro defunctis," Melanchthon charges that the opus operatum concept is an insult to the gospel.[19] As applied to the mass, the opus operatum doctrine teaches that the mass can be a human work in the service of "works-righteousness" performed without regard to God's promise and gift and without faith. It becomes a human attempt to draw near to God on the basis of one's own merits when God has already acted to draw near to humanity in a gracious condescension in the incarnation and cross of Christ.

This is where Melanchthon's distinction between sacramentum and sacrificium becomes fundamental. It picks up Luther's concern that the mass not be used in the service of works-righteousness. It tries to solve this spiritual problem by drawing what Holsten Fagerberg calls a "boundary line between two completely different acts of worship."[20] But this boundary line has sometimes been drawn between areas where it does not apply. As Peter Brunner points out, "Melanchthon's elaborations have also shown us that one dare not divorce these two sides of worship activity and mechanically assign them to individual parts of worship."[21] Melanchthon's distinction between the sacramental

---

[18] *Bek.*, 356.

[19] Ibid., 374.

[20] Fagerberg, 200.

[21] Brunner, *Worship in the Name of Jesus*, op. cit., 123–4.

and sacrificial dimensions of worship concerns what we might call the "internal-direction" of the liturgical action: Who is offering what to whom? His distinction concerns the *use* of the Lord's Supper rather than the ontological status of the elements. Carl Wisløff has observed,

> In light of history it would seem that Melanchthon's criticism of the mass has remained Lutheranism's actual objection to the Catholic teaching concerning the sacrifice of the Mass. And when Luther's criticism is described in such a way that it does not go beyond the complaint about the "Werkgerechtigkeit" of the mass, then in reality this fact constitutes a sign that Luther is being interpreted in the light of Melanchthon's exposition in the Apology.[22]

Be this as it may, the functional view of the mass and Lord's Supper opens up the possibility of a positive Lutheran interpretation of the eucharistic sacrifice. As one might expect, Melanchthon offers this view in the light of patristic teaching: "Quid patres de sacrificio senserint."[23] The Praeceptor points out that the patristic writers do not call the mass a sacrifice because it confers grace ex opere operato, but because it is a grateful response to the gifts of God. From the patristic point of view he speaks about *de usu sacramenti et de sacrificio*.[24] The sacrament was not instituted only as a *nota et testimonium professionis* (mark and testimony of profession), nor as a friendship meal signifying *mutuum inter Christianos coniunctionem atque amicitiam* (mutual unity and friendship among Christians); nor are the sacraments merely signs among people. They are primarily God's signs of good will toward us. The proper use of the sacrament, therefore, is in the worship (*cultus*) of the New Testament, the commemoration of what God has done for humanity's salvation in Jesus Christ. But this commemoration of Christ (*meminisse Christi*) is not like celebrating an heroic example as the ancient Greeks did in their tragedies; it is to receive Christ's blessings by faith so that these blessings enliven us coram Deo. The pastoral consequence of this insight is that terrified consciences (*perterrefactae conscientiae*) are the ones most worthy to receive the sacrament.[25]

Since one thing can have several meanings, one can also speak of a sacrifice in connection with the commemoration of Christ. When faith has been strengthened and the conscience has been liberated from terror, then it is really possible to give thanks for the blessings of Christ and to praise God through the ceremony of the mass. According to patristic teaching, in Melanchthon's view, the purpose of the sacrament is *de consolatione conscientiarum* (the consolation of consciences) and the purpose of the sacrifice is *de gratiarum actiones seu laudis* (thanksgiving and also praise).[26] It is from this response to the blessings of God that the term *eucharistia* arose in the ancient church and served as an ancient name of the Lord's Supper.

This brings Melanchthon to a philological discussion of the names of the mass. He points out that the term "leitourgia," as used by the Greeks, does not mean "sacrifice,"

---

[22] Wisløff, *The Gift of Communion*, op. cit., 57–8.
[23] *Bek.*, 368.
[24] Ibid., 369.
[25] Ibid., 370.
[26] Ibid., 371.

but "public service" (*publicam ministerium*). Melanchthon also suggests that *synaxis* might be used as a term for the celebration of the mass, since it shows that the mass was formerly a communion of many. But he is willing to use the term "liturgy" because it relates well to the evangelical understanding of a minister as one who "shows forth (*exhibet*) the body and blood of Christ to the people" and thereby renders a public service. Melanchthon is aware that this term arose in Greek secular usage, and that Paul, in 2 Corinthians 9:12, used it to refer to a collection. He also points out that it is a far-fetched etymology to derive the word "mass" from the Hebrew word for altar, *mizbeach,* and to argue from this that the mass is a sacrifice, especially since in Deuteronomy 16:10 the term applies to the collections of gifts of the people rather than the offering of the priest.[27] Melanchthon knew from the *Apostolic Canons* that it was also the custom of the early Christians to gather bread and wine and other offerings, part of which was consecrated and the rest of which was distributed to the poor.[28] For this reason the mass can also be called "oblatio," for what does this mean except that "prayers, thanksgivings, and the whole worship are offered here?"[29]

Melanchthon points out that the "Greek canon" also speaks of *oblatione,* but the term is not applied to the body and blood of Christ, but to "the whole service, the prayers and thanksgivings." As an example of the proper expression of eucharistic sacrifice he quotes from the so-called Clementine Liturgy: "And make us worthy to come to offer Thee entreaties and supplication and bloodless sacrifices for all the people."[30] This is not offensive because it prays that "we might be made worthy to offer prayers and supplications and bloodless sacrifices for the people." The "bloodless sacrifices" are the prayers. Melanchthon also cites the epiclesis from the Anaphora of John Chrysostom: "We offer thee this reasonable and bloodless service." This *rationalem hostiam* does not refer to the body of Christ since this canon speaks of "de toto cultu." Furthermore, "logike latreia" is Paul's designation in Romans 12:1 for "the service of the mind, fear, faith, prayer, thanksgiving, etc. *contra opus operatum.*"[31] All of this data is presented without prejudice as examples of the patristic and Greek Orthodox understanding of the eucharist. Melanchthon has thus opened the door to an evangelical understanding of eucharistic sacrifice primarily as the believers' response of prayer, praise, and thanksgiving to the saving work of God in Christ, given expression in the ritual ceremony of the Lord's Supper.

🍇 LUTHER: *Vermanung zum Sakrament,* 1530

If this positive interpretation of the eucharistic sacrifice is possible for Melanchthon because he deals with the sacrament only in terms of its ceremonial or liturgical use, then the same kind of view should be seen in Luther's works where his attacks on the

---

[27] Ibid., 372.

[28] Ibid. See *Apostolic Constitutions* VIII, 47; Funk, 565.

[29] Ibid.

[30] Ibid.; Tappert, 265. See Brightman, *Liturgies Eastern and Western,* 375.

[31] *Bek.,* 373; Tappert, 265.

mass as a sacrifice are bracketed. We find this in his *Admonition Concerning the Sacrament (Vermanung zum Sakrament des Leibes und Blutes Christi)* of 1530.[32]

The purpose of this treatise was "to provide clergy and preachers with the reasons to be used in admonishing their people and attracting them to the sacrament."[33] Luther's concern here is with the use of the sacrament, not the ontology of the elements. So we can expect to find the polemic against works-righteousness to figure prominently in the argument of the treatise. Indeed, Luther emphasizes that this is "a sacrament of faith" rather than "a work of merit." So "pastors should make the first reason [for going to the sacrament] quite clear to the people so that they might understand, and indeed believe, that this sacrament is God's gracious and fatherly ordinance, instituted for us human beings."[34]

The sacrament is to be honored, said Luther, not only because it is commanded by God, but because promises are attached to it: "it is full of benefit and salvation, as well as innumerable and unspeakable blessings."[35] God instituted this sacrament in remembrance *(gedechtnis)* of Christ so that we would not forget these benefits. This remembrance consists in praising, listening to, proclaiming, and thanking God, and honoring "the grace and mercy which he has shown us in Christ." Whoever celebrates the sacrament in this way renders two great honors to God: first, because the person uses the ordinance properly; and secondly, because the person preserves the remembrance "by preaching, praising and thanking God for the grace of Christ shown to us poor sinners in his suffering." This is the true *Danckopfer* (thankoffering), and it is "the most beautiful sacrifice, the supreme worship of God, and the most glorious work."[36]

The content of this thankoffering is the "remembrance of Christ," but it is not a remembrance that "consists of meditating on Christ's suffering, with which some have sought to serve God as with a good work and to obtain grace." Rather, the remembrance of Christ is to believe in "the power and fruit of his suffering."[37] Such a remembrance renders our work and merit insignificant because it brings to mind God's grace and mercy in Christ. This is a commemoratio that needs to be proclaimed as an objective reality and not enacted only as a figurative representation. The drama of the mass, with all its allegorical interpretations, was insufficient for the true remembrance of Christ: "This memorial requires a sermon."[38]

Luther's critics asserted that the celebration of the mass could be an effective proclamation of Christ's death. This argument was used by those who thought private masses, purged of meritorious notions, might be retained on weekdays because the act of thanksgiving would itself constitute a proclamation of Christ's passion. This was the style of the *Missa Lincopensis*, according to Kjöllerström's study. It is known that Melanchthon

---

[32] WA 30/2:595–626; LW 38:97–137.
[33] LW 38:102.
[34] Ibid., 104.
[35] Ibid., 105.
[36] Ibid., 111.
[37] Ibid., 116.
[38] WA 1:334, 8.

put such an idea before Luther, although we don't know whether the Praeceptor himself subscribed to such an idea or was merely relaying it.[39] But Luther was unwilling to make that concession because he was apprehensive that the opus bonum idea would revive again.[40] But, above all, he did not think that a silent mass could authentically proclaim God's saving act in Christ. In the *Vermanung zum Sakrament,* Luther recalled the teaching of Albertus Magnus that "a single contemplation of the suffering of Christ even in a superficial way" was better than a host of penitential exercises. But he regarded this as a work that even an ungodly person could perform because in this fashion one reaches only to "the history of the suffering of Christ"; one does not conform one's life to Christ's by meditating on a past event. No picture could compensate for the living Word by which the Holy Spirit brings the living Christ into the heart of the believer. Only the work of the Spirit through the word could bridge the gap between the Jesus of history and the Christ of faith.[41]

It is noteworthy that Luther places the fanatics' understanding of remembrance in the same category as those who espoused the commemorative interpretation of the mass. Andreas Karlstadt viewed the Lord's Supper as a "memorial feast" by means of which the believer should "with ardent fervor think of the Lord and his death on the cross."[42] Luther had no use for the "inward thoughts of the heart, as when one thinks of someone. For such a mind insists on making something inward and something spiritually internal that which God wants to be outward."[43] Thus, "Christ's remembrance . . . does not consist of meditating on his suffering."[44]

Vajta suggested that, in Luther's eyes, *Gedächtnis* in the papal church consisted of an external "presentation of the suffering of Christ in the sacrament," while for the fanatics it consisted of "a mental procedure." Actually, for Luther both the Roman and the *Schwärmer* interpretation of remembrance amount to the same thing: "the inward thoughts of the heart." The papalists engender the subjective contemplation of Christ's passion through the ceremony of the silent mass; the fanatics do it by means of their memorial service. In neither case is the reality of Christ's death effectively proclaimed and made objectively contemporaneous for the believer. Wisløff has pointed out that

> Luther places his tradition-minded foes and the enthusiasts on the same level. In other words, the situation is that his instinct has been to support a realistic interpretation of the *memoria Christi*—in opposition to the spiritualism which prevailed on both of the other two fronts. He maintained that the remembrance was an external act coinciding with the proclamation of the Lord's death—in the audible word of the sermon and through the obedient and believing performance of the ceremony of the Lord's Supper.[45]

---

[39] Br. 5:490, 12.

[40] Br. 5:498, 4.

[41] See WA 49:76, 24.

[42] See Hermann Barge, *Andreas Bodenstein von Karlstadt,* II (Leipzing, 1905), 172.

[43] WA 18:197, 8.

[44] WA 38:116.

[45] Wisløff, 95.

In this emphasis on the objective reality of the anamnesis, or remembrance, Luther had the same intention of preserving an effective memorial as do twentieth-century Catholic theologians who subscribe to Odo Casel's "mystery theology." The difference is that, for Casel, the *Vergegenwärtigung* (reactualization) of the saving event takes place through the ritual action, while for Luther the saving events are really present because of Christ's personal presence in his word mediated by the Holy Spirit. Heiko Oberman has suggested that "the genius of the Reformation is best described as the rediscovery of the Holy Spirit, the present Christ," in the preaching of the word.[46] The sermon, therefore, is the most effective anamnesis of Christ, although as we have seen in the case of the elevation of the host, Luther would not limit the anamnesis to the preaching; there are other forms of the proclamation, including "visible words." But since the remembrance is the chief content of the thankoffering, the sermon is also a eucharistic sacrifice. Wisløff has pointed out that for Luther the sacrifice can be a long succession of things: the sermon, the prayers, the liturgical chants, and so forth. Only it cannot be "that which primarily was called *hostia* up to now, Christ's body and blood," because that is God's gift to us.[47]

In the light of such considerations Luther was "ready to concede and to permit not the sacrament itself (*das Sacrament selbs*) but the reception or use of the sacrament, to be called a sacrifice."[48] Luther attached four qualifications to this concession: first, the sacrifice must be called *ein danck opffer* and not *ein deut opffer odder werck opffer*—a thankoffering and not an interpretative sacrifice or a sacrifice of works; second, when priests offer this sacrifice it only signifies that "they are in their own persons giving thanks to Christ in their hearts," just as other Christians do who receive the sacrament; third, "that henceforth they do not sell to anyone the sacrament or mass as a sacrifice of works nor offer it as a sacrifice for others"; and, fourth, that priests return all the goods and income they have received by selling the mass as a sacrifice of works.[49] If this was done, Luther was also willing "to concede that they may perform these sacrifices of thanksgiving for others, just as I can also thank God, apart from the mass, for Christ and all his saints, yes, for all creatures."[50] The priest could thank God in the mass "for ourselves, for all people, for all creatures, as Saint Paul teaches [1 Tim. 4:4]." But the "sacrament" and "sacrifice" must be completely separated as two different matters. "Das gedechtnis sol wol ein danckopffer sein, aber das Sacrament selbs sol nicht eine opffer, sondern ein gabe Gottes sein."[51]

> The sacrament is one matter, the remembrance is another matter. [Christ] says that we should use and practice the sacrament and, in addition, remember him, that is, teach, believe, and give thanks. The remembrance is indeed supposed to

---

[46] Heiko A. Oberman, "The Preaching of the Word," *Harvard Divinity School Bulletin* (October 1960), 7–18.

[47] Wisløff, 86.

[48] LW 38:120; WA 30/2:613, 5.

[49] Ibid.

[50] LW 38:121.

[51] WA 30/2:614, 20. "The remembrance might well be a thankoffering, but the sacrament itself is not an offering, but a gift of God."

be a sacrifice of thanksgiving; but the sacrament itself should not be a sacrifice
but a gift of God which he has given to us and which we should take and receive
with thanks.[52]

Luther added that it was for this reason that the ancients called this office *eucharistia* or
sacramentum eucharistiae, that is a *dancksagung* (thanksgiving). But when a person says,
"I want to go to the eucharist," this should mean "I want to go . . . to that office at which
one thanks and praises God in his sacrament, as it appears the ancients intended that it
should be done."[53] Luther believed that it was as a result of such an understanding that
the mood of praise and thanksgiving pervaded the mass from beginning to end: as, for example, in the Gloria, the Alleluia, the *Patrem* (Nicene Creed), the preface, the Sanctus,
the Benedictus, and the Agnus Dei. "In these various parts you find nothing about a sacrifice, but only praise and thanks. Therefore, we have kept them in our mass."[54]

What Luther did not keep was the canon. It remains manifestly curious that he
could see the elements of eucharistia and anamnesis pervading the whole mass, but that
he could not tolerate a reworking of the canon, such as was done by Zwingli, Bucer, and
Cranmer, and as we have seen in the *Liturgia svecanae ecclesiae*. Any reason for Luther's
reluctance to undertake a creative revision of the canon remains pure conjecture, since
he did not express himself on this issue. But it is evident that even his positive appraisal of
the eucharistic sacrifice is a concession grudgingly made. Perhaps Luther feared that objectionable ideas concerning the sacrifice of the mass might return if given an opportunity, say, in a revised eucharistic prayer. On the other hand, it would seem that Luther has
contributed to a positive evangelical interpretation of the eucharistic sacrifice.

🍇 CHEMNITZ: *Examen Concilii Tridentini*, 1565–1573

The term "Lutheran Orthodoxy" designated more a theological school than a
historical period. The great scholastic theologians of Lutheran orthodoxy took up the task
of systematizing the theology of the Lutheran Reformation. In this regard, Melanchthon
can be considered the "father" of Lutheran scholasticism, since his *Loci communes* provided the theological method employed by these theologians. A number of them took up
the issue of the sacrifice of the mass in controversy with Counter-Reformation theologians. Two theological works dealt at length with the eucharistic sacrifice in response to
the Council of Trent. One was a prolegomenon to his 1569 Commentary on Leviticus by
David Chytraeus (1531–1600), professor of biblical theology at the University of Rostock.
The other was the great four-volume *Examination of the Council of Trent* by Martin
Chemnitz (1522–1586), which appeared in print between 1565 and 1576.

The treatise by Chytraeus, *De sacrificiis,* dealt primarily with the understanding
of sacrifice in the Bible, but Chytraeus did draw a line between Catholic and Lutheran
understandings of *sacrificia eucharistica*. According to Chytraeus, the papalists maintain

---

[52] LW 38:122.
[53] Ibid., 122–3.
[54] Ibid., 123.

that in the sacrifice of the Mass the priest offers to God the body and blood of our Lord Jesus Christ and sets God's Son in the presence of His eternal Father. And they declare that this oblation of Christ's body and blood is the chief act of worship and the continual sacrifice of the church of the New Testament, and that by offering it for others, living or dead, one may apply to them the fruits and benefits of Christ's sacrifice on the cross.[55]

Against this view, Chytraeus set forth Luther's doctrine of the Lord's Supper as Christ's testament or promise of the remission of sins, which was sealed by Christ's death, and which believers lay hold of by eating and drinking Christ's body and blood in faith. Thus, in this treatise by one of the great orthodox Lutheran theologians of the post-Reformation period, "testament" is irreconcilably set against "sacrifice" in the Lord's Supper. This treatise is important because it set forth the views of the principal author of the section on the Lord's Supper in the Formula of Concord. Chytraeus was also one of the theologians who provided tutelage to the Swedish Anti-Liturgists who attended the University of Rostock, and his views were used to assault the Liturgy of King Johan III, especially its eucharistic prayer.

A more detailed response to the Council of Trent is provided by Martin Chemnitz in his *Examen Concilii Tridentini*. In Session 22, chapters one and two, the Council laid out a view of the sacrifice of the mass, which Chemnitz cites at the beginning of Locus VI.[56] Trent held that Christ offered himself on the altar of the cross in order to effect an eternal redemption. But this did not complete his priesthood. In order that he might leave his church a visible sign (as human nature requires), he instituted in his last supper a sacrifice by which his bloody sacrifice on the cross should be remembered (*repraesentaretur*) and his memory should remain until the end of the world along with its salutary power for the forgiveness of sins. As "priest forever after the manner of Melchisedek," Christ offered his body and blood under the species of bread and wine to God the Father. He delivered these symbols to the apostles, who constituted the priest-hood of the New Testament, and they delivered these things to their successors. The divine sacrifice offered by the priests of the Catholic church is the same sacrifice that Christ offered on the cross; so the Synod of Trent taught that it is a propitiatory sacrifice. Only the mode of offering is different, since the sacrifice of the mass is an unbloody one. Condemned, therefore, is (1) anyone who says that in the mass a true sacrifice is not offered; (2) anyone who says that Christ has not instituted the apostles as priests by his words, "Do this in remembrance of me," or has not ordered them and other priests to offer the body and blood ("ut ipsi aliique Sacerdos offerrent corpus et sanguinem"); (3) anyone who says that the sacrifice of the mass is solely an act of praise and thanksgiving or the mere commemoration of the sacrifice of the cross, but not a propitiatory sacrifice, or that it merely profits the partakers and should not be offered for the living and the dead, for sins, punishments and satisfactions, and so forth; (4) anyone who says that blasphemy

---

[55] *Chytraeus on Sacrifice*, trans. and ed. by John W. Montgomery (St. Louis: Concordia, 1962), 120.

[56] Chemnitz, *Examen Concilii Tridentini*, ed. Preuss, op. cit., 381ff.; Martin Chemnitz, *Examination of the Council of Trent*, Part II, trans. by Fred Kramer (St. Louis: Concordia, 1978), 439ff.

is afflicted to the most holy sacrifice of Christ brought on the cross, by the sacrifice of the mass. (These are the first four canons of Session 22.)

Chemnitz examines these canons in Part II, Locus VI, Section 1, by beginning in Article I with the meaning of the word "sacrifice" and how it can be applied to the mass.[57] He finds the word "sacrifice" used in eight different senses in biblical and patristic literature: (1) In the Old Testament there was a difference between animal sacrifices, cereal offerings, and libations. (2) There are different causes of the offerings in the Old Testament (e.g., the daily holocaust, propitiatory sacrifices, peace-offerings, first fruits). These were a foreshadowing of the sacrifice of Christ and of the true, inward, invisible, and spiritual sacrifices of the faithful, such as Augustine describes in *De civitate Dei*, Book 10, chapter 5. (3) The conversion of the Gentiles and the faith of those embracing the gospel is regarded as a sacrifice in Romans 15 and Philippians 2. (4) The prayers mentioned in Hebrews 5 and Apocalypse 5 and 8, are called sacrifices. (5) Hebrews 13 mentions sacrifices of praise and thanksgiving. (6) The gifts for the poor and for the support of the ministry in Hebrews 13 and Philippians 4 are regarded as sacrifices. (7) The mortification of the old man, when he is consecrated and devoted to God, that he may die to the world and live unto God (Rom. 12) is regarded as a sacrifice. (8) The entire Christian cult in its acknowledgment of God's benefits, together with abstention from sins and zeal for the new obedience, constitutes the "spiritual sacrifices" of 1 Peter (see also Pss. 4, 51, 145; Hosea 14; Micah 6; and Augustine in *De civitate Dei*, Book 10, chs. 5 and 6.).

Chemnitz then inquires, in Article II, "in which sense the liturgical act can, according to the scriptures, be rightly called a sacrifice."[58] The mass can be called a sacrifice because (1) the death of Christ is proclaimed in the word that is read and expounded at mass; (2) the praises of God are celebrated, declared, and chanted; (3) it includes the public prayers and common thanksgiving; (4) alms are contributed for the poor; (5) at mass the whole person consecrates himself to God, in repentance and faith, and the love of God and neighbor is kindled in the true use of the Lord's Supper; (6) the eucharist is blessed or consecrated (which is an act of gospel ministry, and Paul calls the whole ministry of the gospel a sacrifice in Rom. 15); and (7) the dispensing and partaking of the eucharist is done in commemoration of the one sacrifice of Christ.

The papalists, according to Chemnitz, understand none of these things to be the mass-sacrifice. What they understand by sacrifice is explained by Eck in his *De Missa* I, 10: The celebration itself is called a sacrifice because it is a representative figure of the passion of Christ, which had been a true immolation.[59] In Article III he explains that the Roman church not only uses the eucharist in memory of Christ's passion, but represents the sacrifice of Christ by means of the gestures, words, rites and vestments of the mass. By this liturgical action Christ is offered anew to God the Father. Chemnitz makes this point in the following remarkable sentence:

---

[57] Ibid., 383; Art. I, "De vocabulo sacrificii."

[58] Ibid., 383–4; Art. II, "Quo sensu actio liturgiae, juxta Scripturam, recte possit sacrificium appellari."

[59] Ibid., 384; Art. III, "Quid illud sit Missa, quod pontificii proprier intelligunt sacrificium."

Therefore the sacrifice of the Mass about which the papalists contend consists of this, that the priest uses (together with certain ornaments and vessels) various gestures, motions, and actions over the bread and wine of the Eucharist, such as genuflecting repeatedly, now bowing, now stretching out clenched hands, now drawing the arms back, now turning around, now being loud, now murmuring something very quietly, looking up high, then hanging forward, not standing still in one place, but moving, now to the right side, now to the left of the altar, pointing with the fingers, breathing on the bread and the cup, now elevating them, afterward putting them down, breaking the bread, casting it into the cup, smiting the breast with the fist, sighing, closing his eyes, representing sleep, waking up, showing the gilded patella to the people with outstretched arm, but with his back turned, moving it to his forehead and breast, kissing now the altar, now the little image inclosed in the metal, etc.[60]

By this kind of theatricalization, said Chemnitz, the papalists believe that they renew the sacrifice of Christ and offer his body and blood to God the Father. This is a description of the Scotist understanding of *repraesentatio* that was discussed in chapter seven.

In Article IV, "What kind of sacrifice the papalists understand the mass to be,"[61] Chemnitz notes that Gropper of Cologne suggested that the mass is called a sacrifice, not because it literally is one, but because it is a figure of the one propitiatory sacrifice of the cross, just as certain Old Testament sacrifices are called propitiatory because they prefigure the one true propitiatory sacrifice of Christ. The Council rejected this interpretation and held that the mass is a propitiatory sacrifice offered for the sins, punishments, and satisfactions of the living and the dead.

In Article V Chemnitz lists the arguments of the papalist writers in behalf of the sacrifice of the mass, most of which are based on allegorical interpretations of the scriptures.[62] The most serious argument is that the *Verba Testamenti* are present tense, "given and shed for you," indicating that Christ has sacrificed his body and blood not only on the cross but also in the supper. Chemnitz replies by noting first that the institution narrative in the *Canon missae* omits the words, "which are given for you," and in the second part puts them in the future tense, "shall be shed" *(effundetur)*. Second, how can the sacrifice of the mass be said to be unbloody, when in its offering at the first supper the effusion of blood has been made in the present? Third, scripture is very clear that Christ's body was broken and his blood shed on the cross, not in the upper room.

The most weighty part of Chemnitz's locus on the sacrifice of the mass concerns the arguments of the Tridentine Synod, which he enumerates and refutes in Article VI.[63]

1. Concerning Christ's perpetual priesthood: the Epistle to the Hebrews teaches what the offering of the priesthood of Christ is. It is rendered once and for all and cannot be repeated. But it is perpetual, not because Christ is

---

[60] Chemnitz, *Examination*, trans. Kramer, 446.

[61] Chemnitz, *Examen*, 384ff.; Art IV, "Quale sacrificium pontificii missae intelligant."

[62] Ibid., 387–9; Art. V, "Augmenta scriptorum pontificiorum pro missa."

[63] Ibid., 389ff.; Art. VI, "Argumenta Tridentinae Synodi pro missa."

offered again, but because he lives forever, because his one offering is eternally efficacious, because he intercedes for us, because we have access to the Father through him, and because he saves those who come to God through him.

2. Concerning the assertion that human nature demands a visible sacrifice and Christ has instituted this in the histrionic representation of his passion in the mass; religion and faith are not to be established from what blinded and corrupted human nature dictates, but by the voice of the apostles.

3. Concerning the assertion that Christ has instituted in his last supper a memorial of his bloody sacrifice that is to remain until the end of the world: It must be asked whether that memorial is that dramatic representation of the rites, gestures, and actions of the papal mass. Christ has commanded such a memorial, and has left it to human arrangements how it is to be held; but he has expressed and prescribed that the memorial be celebrated with thanksgiving, dispensing and eating and drinking of his body and blood, also with the proclamation of his death. This testament of Christ is inviolable.

4. Concerning the argument that Christ has given his sacrifice to the disciples as well as his body and blood: what we read in the New Testament does not at all allude to any form of sacrifice, and certainly not to Christ's offering of himself.

5. Concerning the argument that Christ has commanded that the priest should sacrifice the body and blood of Christ in the eucharist: "This do ye" means only that the ministers of the church should do what Christ did in the institution of the Last Supper, and it has already been established that he did not offer himself in the supper but on the cross. What the ministers are to "do" is what is established that Christ did at the last supper.

6. Concerning the argument that Christ has constituted the Apostles as priests of the New Testament and commanded them to offer his body and blood: the Old Testament priesthood is a prefiguration of the priesthood of Christ, not of the presbyters of the church. And if another or the same repeated sacrifice needs to be offered for sin, the sacrifice of the cross is not perfect, nor does it merit remission of sins and eternal life. The only royal priesthood mentioned in the New Testament (1 Peter 2:9) refers not to presbyters, but to the general priesthood of all believers who offer spiritual sacrifices. But even if the appellation "priests" can be applied to the ministers of the New Testament, nothing can be found in the New Testament to indicate that they must offer the body and blood of Christ as a propitiatory sacrifice for the sins of the living and the dead by a dramatic representation in the mass.

7. Concerning the argument that the paschal sacrifice was offered as well as eaten: The papalists deal with shadows and figures rather than with the sure and certain testimonies of scripture. But if they want to deal with figurative interpretations, then they should consider that the paschal lamb was not only offered, but slain in a bloody sacrifice, and not by the priests, but by the people, and not as a propitiatory sacrifice for sin, but in commemoration of the liberation from Egypt. The New Testament proclaims the figure of Christ as the lamb of God, but the paschal sacrifice has been fulfilled on the cross (John 19).

8. Concerning the argument that Malachi foretells the pure offering of the mass (1:11): Malachi cannot mean that the pure offering of the Gentiles must be the papal mass, with its gestures, rites, and actions. The true meaning of Malachi's prophecy can be seen in the New Testament passages that speak of spiritual sacrifice. In support of this interpretation, Chemnitz cites Tertullian, Chrysostom, Eusebius, Justin, Irenaeus and Augustine.

9. Concerning the argument that Paul, in 1 Corinthians 10:21, means "altar" by the expression "table of the Lord": this is again a figurative interpretation that in no way supports the papalist doctrine of the mass.

10. Concerning the argument that figures in the Old Testament should be completed in the New, including the sacrifices of the Old Testament that are fulfilled in the sacrifice of the mass: the New Testament clearly teaches that the Old Testament sacrifices are fulfilled in the sacrifice of Christ on the cross and in the spiritual sacrifices of the believers.

11. Concerning the argument that the mass is a propitiatory sacrifice because Christ is present in his Supper with his body and blood: it is required that the act as well as the essence of the sacrifice be present. In this case it must be an act prescribed by God, not thought up by men; that it be done by a person appointed to do this as prescribed by God in his word. These requirements were met only in the sacrifice of the cross. The body and blood of Christ are not present in the mass to be a sacrifice, but to be a sacrament imparted and taken.

12. Concerning the argument that the Catholic church has always taught this doctrine of the mass-sacrifice, and that such a rite as the mass has been in the church since the time of the apostles: it is necessary to check what the ancients say in their testimonies.[64]

In Article VII[65] Chemnitz takes up Eck's argument that the word "mass" is testified in the writings of the Fathers. He shows that where the word "mass" is used by the Greek authors (the Greek word is "leitourgia"), it is in Latin translation.

Then he shows, in Article VIII, in what sense the ancients called the mass (or, more properly speaking, the liturgy) a sacrifice: (1) Gifts of bread and wine and contributions for the support of the poor and the clergy were offered on the Lord's table, and the names of the offerers were commended to God by prayer. (2) The common and solemn prayers for all were usually held at the Lord's Supper, and because these prayers were called "sacrifices" in scripture the ancients also called them so. (3) The Lord's Supper is called "eucharist" by the oldest church fathers because in its celebration the many and various blessings of God were set forth, especially the blessing of redemption in Christ. The sacrifices of praise and thanksgiving are also scriptural. (4) The death of Christ is remembered in the liturgy, and Paul calls the whole ministry of the gospel a sacrifice in Romans 15. (5) Many exercises of the true piety are connected in the celebration and use of the Lord's Supper, that is, the "spiritual sacrifices" of 1 Peter 2:5. (6) The church and the individual believers consecrate and dedicate themselves wholly to the Lord and for

---

[64] Ibid., 398–9; Art. VII, "De vocabulo missae."
[65] Ibid., 398–9; Art. VII, "De vocabulo missae."

the sake of the neighbor, which is the Christian sacrifice of which Augustine speaks in *De civitate Dei*, Book 10, ch. 6.

If the papalists object that the eucharistic sacrifice is not only applied to those exercises of piety by the ancients, but also to the act of the Lord's Supper, Chemnitz would agree. But he would want to say that the Lord's Supper is called a sacrifice, oblation, and immolation of Christ because it conveys the benefits of the saving cross. If the patristic writers called the body and blood of Christ present in the Supper "a saving offering, a pure sacrifice, our truce, the price of our redemption, the price for the sins of the whole world, the sacrifice of propitiation and atonement," it is not because the body and blood of Christ are offered by the priest, but because that sacrificial victim offered once for our redemption and forgiveness, namely, the body and blood of the Lord, is present in the supper, is dispensed, offered, and received, so that the power and efficacy of that offering made once on the cross may be applied and sealed to the individual partakers through faith. So the statements of the patristic writers do not support the arguments of Trent, especially regarding that histrionic sacrifice of the papalists in which they dramatically portray the sacrifice of Calvary in the ceremonies of the mass. Nevertheless, those statements of the Fathers about offering the body and blood of Christ obscured, in the course of time, the true use of the Lord's Supper and introduced strange opinions about the merit of the acts of the priest. The anniversary day in memory of the blessed departed with the gifts offered on the altar became, in time, propitiations made for the sins of the dead. This shows, says Chemnitz, that it is better to eschew any designation of the Lord's Supper as "sacrifice," and to speak of it instead as "sacrament" to indicate its true use and proper meaning—receiving the benefits of the merits of the passion of Christ sealed with his body and blood. "The appellation sacrifice, however, leads us away from [the merits of Christ] to those which we offer and render to God in the act of the Lord's Supper."[66]

Finally, in Article IX Chemnitz asserts that the abomination of the papal mass consists in the following:[67]

1. It is idolatrous to institute a cultus outside of the word of God that purports to propitiate sin, remove the offense against God, and obtain his grace and blessings. The *theatrica repraesentatio* of the mass has no such testimony in scripture or in the patristic era. It is clear throughout this locus that what Chemnitz is reacting to is the Scotist-Nominalist understanding of repraesentatio as a ritual reenactment of Calvary that was so popular in the late Middle Ages and that was advocated by Johannes Eck. Other criticisms of the mass follow from this.

2. It is a sin to transfer the sacraments from the use instituted by Christ into that act which is entirely different, that is, to make the sacrament a sacrifice. Chemnitz is here suggesting that the "theatrical representation" of the mass obscures what God wills to give to human beings in favor of what human beings offer to God.

---

[66] Ibid., 403.
[67] Ibid., 403f.; Art. IX.

3. It is a crime to set anything over even a human testament when it has been ratified and confirmed, and the papal mass superimposes something over the testament of Christ. Chemnitz is here suggesting that the "theatrical representation" of the mass obscures the Verba testamenti, which should be proclaimed clearly and observed inviolately.

4. It is shameful that the papal mass conflicts in many ways with the one propitiatory sacrifice of Christ. Chemnitz is here asserting that what was accomplished by the true propitiatory sacrifice of the cross is all one needs for one's temporal and eternal welfare before God, and the benefits of this sacrifice are conveyed in the sacrament.

5. The papal mass conflicts with the perpetual priesthood of Christ, for only Christ can offer himself. Chemnitz is here suggesting that the papalists would not have had the need for an additional propitiatory sacrifice if they had recognized the high priestly function of Christ to offer his eternally valid sacrifice to God the Father in heaven on behalf of his faithful ones.

6. In conclusion, "The papal mass obscures and subverts those means of grace which the Son of God has instituted and ordained that through them the merit, power and efficacy of his death and passion for the remission of sins and eternal life, should be applied and received."[68]

While the character of the *Examen* is naturally critical in tone and manner, it does enable us to see what Lutheran theology is willing to affirm about eucharistic sacrifice. It is clear that Chemnitz would rather speak about God's sacramental action than about the church's sacrificial action. But there was much in the tradition that he was willing to affirm over against what he understood to be Trent's view of eucharistic sacrifice on the basis of scripture and the testimonia Patrum. The theologian who provided a balanced view of the role of tradition in church teachings and practice (in Part I of the *Examen*) uses that sense of tradition to good effect in discussing the theology of the sacrifice of the mass.

For Chemnitz, Trent's view of eucharistic sacrifice derives from the late medieval understanding of commemoration as dramatic reenactment of the passion of Christ. He has thus interpreted Trent on the basis of one Catholic position, that represented by Johannes Eck. At the first session of the Council, at Bologna, there were indeed those who spoke in terms of the Scotist-Nominalist understanding of commemoration. In later sessions, however, theologians and bishops moved away from this understanding and stressed the unity of the sacrifice of the cross and the sacrifice of the mass in terms of the "same Victim" offering himself in both, "the manner of offering alone being different," with the mass as a sacramental application of the benefits of the sacrifice of the cross. The influence of Cardinal Cajetan can certainly be seen here in terms of the unity of the cross and the altar. Nevertheless, the Council avoided identification with a particular theological school.[69]

---

[68] Ibid., 405.
[69] See Theodore Schneider, "Opfer Jesu Christi und der Kirche: Zum Verständnis der Aussagen des Konzils von Trent," *Catholica* 44 (1977), 51–65.

Lutherans could also speak of receiving the benefits of the atoning sacrifice of Christ in the faithful reception of the sacrament of the altar. These benefits include "forgiveness of sins, life, and salvation," as Luther wrote in his Small Catechism. Chapter II of the Decrees on the mass also speaks of the Lord, placated by the sacrifice of Christ, granting grace, penitence, and forgiveness of sins. The real issue between the Lutherans and those who attended the Council of Trent had to do with the application of grace for the remission of sins through the mass as a means of grace distinct from the use of the sacrament by the faithful. Trent and the Protestant reformers were at an impasse over whether the grace of the sacrament could be applied to those who were not physically present, such as the dead. The final sentence of chapter II of the Decrees of the Council of Trent on the mass states: "For this reason [the mass] is rightly offered, according to the tradition of the apostles, not only for the sins, punishment, satisfactions, and other necessities of the faithful who are living but also for those who have died in Christ and have not yet been fully purified." In other words, the mass can be offered for and its benefits applied to those in purgatory. The Tridentine theologians wanted to affirm that the eucharist gathers the living and the dead into one communion of grace. The Reformation theologians did not deny the communion of grace embracing both the church militant and the church triumphant, but they thought that the way it was taught by the papalist church and practiced in the Roman mass was offensive to the redemption won by Christ and to the freedom of God in bestowing grace to sinners.

Today we see more at stake in the deliberations of the Council of Trent than only the clarification and articulation of a theological system. As David Power has suggested, the practice behind the dogma "offered an integral and coherent social and cultural persuasion and a Christian identity to peoples and institutions."[70] The sacrifice of the mass was an integral part of a religio-cultural system which the Catholic reformers wanted to keep, freed from an overlay of superstition and popular ignorance, but which the Protestant reformers wanted to dissolve in the name of salvation through the merits and work of Christ alone. The clash between Tridentine and Reformation theologians was between a religio-cultural system and a recovered biblical principle that was challenging that system and establishing a new one. Transcending a confessional impasse becomes even more difficult if a whole worldview and communal identity are at stake. The concern of the Council of Trent to preserve, provide, and protect Catholic identity can be seen in its reluctance to extend the chalice to lay communicants and to consider the use of vernacular in the mass and other offices, even though it accomplished much to correct abuses and extend the instruction of priests and laity.

In Germany, where Lutherans and Catholics lived side by side in adjacent territories, this impasse in doctrine, worldview, and confessional identity proved to be finally so impossible to transcend that it was virtually impossible for Lutherans to speak of the

---

[70] David N. Power, "The Sacrifice of the Mass: A Question of Reception and Re-reception," *Ecclesia Orans* 1 (Rome 1985), 74. This point of view is more fully developed, along with its ecumenical ramifications, in David N. Power, *The Sacrifice We Offer: The Tridentine Dogma and Its Reinterpretation* (Edinburgh: T. & T. Clark; New York: Crossroad Publishing Company, 1987.)

sacrificial aspect of the mass or to develop a fuller expression of eucharistia beyond the preface and words of institution. We must turn again to the Swedish Reformation to see the positive development of doctrinal views and liturgical forms that admit an evangelical interpretation of eucharistic sacrifice.

🍇 EUCHARISTIC SACRIFICE IN SWEDISH REFORMATION THEOLOGY

In Sweden, where the Reformation had the luxury of developing at its own pace through internal discussion in the national church without the pressure of conflict with other confessional bodies, the possibility of transcending the catholic/evangelical impasse was achieved in an evangelical catholicism. This can be seen especially in the issue of the eucharistic sacrifice.

Sven Ingebrand has written a systematic study of Olavus Petri's theology.[71] He compares the writings of Olavus with those of Luther, Melanchthon, and the south German theologians (especially Andreas Osiander). One significant difference that Ingebrand notes between Luther and Olavus is that Luther's view of the word of God grew out of an intense personal experience that emphasized the work of Christ in such a way as to make human work for salvation meaningless. Olavus went through no such crisis, but he found in the word of God an authority for theology above all others.

In the section dealing with Olavus's eucharistic teaching, Ingebrand concentrates on Olavus's "positive teaching on the Lord's Supper," based largely on ideas found in the earliest eucharistic writings of Luther. This is seen most clearly in the polemical writings against Paul Helie in 1527 and in *Den svenska massan* 1531.[72] Like Luther, Olavus Petri based his interpretation of the sacrament on the words of institution. But whereas the polemics against the sacramentarians forced Luther to emphasize the words of Christ, "This is my body, this is my blood," Olavus Petri focused on the Pauline words, "This do for my remembrance" ("Göran detta till min åminnelse"). The Lord's Supper is a reminder of Christ's one sacrifice (offer). To try to repeat or renew this sacrifice makes it nothing *(intet)*. But when one eats Christ's body and drinks his blood, one is concretely reminded of Christ's life and death, of his body given and his blood shed for the sake of sinners. Ingebrand concludes, on the basis of Olavus Petri's preaching and catechizing, that "the remembrance-motif is constant in Olavus's presentation on the Lord's Supper."[73]

In the 1530 Postil, this remembrance-motif is found both in the Maundy Thursday sermon and in the communion exhortation following the catechism.[74] It is also emphasized in the exhortation preceding the communion in the Swedish Mass 1531.

> And chiefly has our Lord commanded us to use this sacrament for a remembrance of himself, namely that we should herewith remember his worthy death

---

[71] Sven Ingebrand, *Olavus Petris reformatorisk åskåding* (Uppsala, 1964).
[72] Ibid., 325.
[73] Ibid., 326.
[74] *Sam. Sk.* III:159, 23ff.; 466, 18ff.

and bloodshedding, and consider that this has been done for the remission of our sins. So now he wills herewith that we shall not forget such his great benefit, but steadfastly cleave unto it with all thanksgiving, that we may be free from sins.[75]

This act of remembrance is no mere subjective recollection. The sacramental signs convey what the words of institution promise, although the Pauline remembrance-motif is still, for Olavus, the dominant "word" that the communicant should latch onto "with a firm trust."

> Therefore whosoever now eats of this bread and drinks of this cup with a firm trust in the word that he hears here, namely that Christ has died and shed his blood for our sins, the same shall likewise assuredly find remission of sins, and therewith escape the death that he wages of sins, and lay hold on eternal life with Christ.[76]

This same theme is also prominent in the expanded eucharistic preface and it serves as the bridge into the institution narrative.

> So likewise shall all they who put their trust therein overcome sins and death and through him attain to everlasting life, and for our admonition that we should bear in mind and never forget such his benefit, in the night that he was betrayed celebrated a supper . . .[77]

It is evident that many of Luther's teachings on the Lord's Supper are found in the writings of Olavus Petri, especially the testament-motif. But as Brilioth points out, they are primarily Luther's early, positive, and unpolemical ideas that are reproduced in translation by the Swedish reformers. In an Easter sermon in the 1528 Postil (*En nyttog postilla*), Olavus dwells on koinonia as a fruit of communion.[78] This Pauline idea was best expressed by Luther in *Ein Sermon von dem hochwurdigen Sakrament* (1519),[79] which was translated by Olavus Petri and Laurentius Andreae in the same 1528 Postil.[80] Thus, from the outset, eucharistic doctrine in the Swedish Reformation was characterized by a positive rather than a negative evangelical thrust.

This positive thrust is even more evident in the eucharistic theology of Laurentius Petri, which has been the subject of a systematic study by Bo Ahlberg.[81] As archbishop, Laurentius became embroiled in controversy over the sacrament to a greater extent than his brother did, especially during the reign of King Erik XIV. Because these controversies concerned the use of the sacramental elements, Laurentius found it necessary to deal more precisely with the mode and manner of Christ's presence than Olavus did. Like his brother, Laurentius took his point of departure from the words of institution. But in the Liquorist Controversy of the early 1560s, he was compelled to focus on the

---

[75] Yelverton, *The Mass in Sweden*, 40; alt.

[76] Ibid., 41; alt.

[77] Ibid., 37–8.

[78] Brilioth, *Eucharistic Faith and Practice*, 233ff.

[79] WA 12:476ff.

[80] Ingebrand, 329ff.; Brilioth, *Nattvarden*, 325ff.

[81] Bo Ahlberg, *Laurentius Petris nattvardsuppfattning* (Lund, 1964).

mode of Christ's presence in the bread and cup as the referents of the word "this" in "this is my body, this is my blood." A shortage of wine in Sweden had led to the suggestions that communion be administered in one kind or that water be substituted for wine. Against the Reform Catholics the archbishop upheld the practice of *sub utraque specie;* against the Calvinists he upheld the *solum vinum.*[82]

Perhaps the most important source of Laurentius Petri's eucharistic views is the *Dialogus Om then förwandling som medh Messone (Dialogue Concerning the Changes in the Mass),* written in 1542 but not published until 1587. Four dialogues take place between two imaginary debaters, Simon, who represents the Roman point of view, and Petrus, who represents the evangelical point of view. The points of disagreement between Romans and Evangelicals concern the use of the vernacular versus the use of Latin alone and the function of the words of institution contrasted with the *Canon missae.* But even in this polemical document, the positive thrust of the Swedish Reformation is apparent. Laurentius points out, for example, that the consecration of the bread and wine is identified with the proclamation of the words of institution, and that the institution narrative in the Swedish Mass is in closer agreement with the Gospels than the form in the Latin mass. But he also sounds the notes of thanksgiving and memorial: the eucharistic act is a response to the redemptive act of God in Christ. Laurentius points to it in the eucharistic preface of the Swedish Mass:

> before these words of consecration we have a fitting prelude or godly address to the congregation, or more rightly to make a fine thanksgiving to God for the many and great benefits that he has assured to us, and especially that he has redeemed us by the death and passion of his dear Son and our Lord Jesus Christ, and given us the sacrament for a sure pledge thereof . . .[83]

In the eucharistic economy, sacrifice and memorial are interrelated. So once Laurentius mentions the eucharistic memorial, the eucharistic sacrifice cannot be far behind. Naturally, he joins the other reformers in attacking the Roman doctrine of the mass-sacrifice, especially as it is associated with the votive mass. This comes out in his comments on the "use and misuse" *(bruk och missbruk)* of the mass.[84] But a positive attitude toward the eucharistic sacrifice is also evident in the 1542 Dialogue. "Petrus" admits that Augustine, Ambrose, Cyprian, and other ancient church writers call the mass a sacrifice. But in what sense is it a sacrifice?

Laurentius reproduces Melanchthon's distinction between the once-for-all atoning sacrifice of the cross and "that other sacrifice which under many names is always one, which all Christian men can offer, as I said, to God's praise and glory for all the good that he hath shown them."[85] But beyond the idea of sacrifice as an act of thanksgiving for the mighty acts of God in Christ, "Petrus" concedes that the mass can also be called a sacrifice "because it signifies or represents the sacrifice which Christ made upon the cross."[86]

---

[82] Ibid., 53–79.

[83] Trans. in Brilioth, *Eucharistic Faith and Practice,* 249.

[84] Ahlberg, 255–60.

[85] Brilioth, 250.

[86] Ibid.

Laurentius spoke of repraesentatio not in the Scotist sense of ritual reenactment, but in the sense of "re-presentation" or "actualization." According to Ahlberg, Laurentius got at this understanding of "re-presentation" by speaking of the administration of the sacrament of the once-for-all sacrifice of the cross.[87] Moreover, it would be a misunderstanding of Laurentius's affirmation to speak only of a distribution of the fruits or benefits of that sacrifice. The connection between the sacrifice of the cross and the Lord's Supper is found in the nature of the Lord's Supper as a sacramental gift. In the sacrament, Christ himself is really present. Where Christ is present, his sacrifice is also present. This is the meaning of the *totus Christus* aspect of the real presence and the confession that the two natures of Christ are present in the sacrament.

Thus, for Laurentius Petri, the mass is not only a sacrifice of praise and thanksgiving that Christians offer to God, although it is that too. But "one may also well say that the aforementioned Doctors call the Sacrament a sacrifice because the priest and the people set it between their sins and the wrath of God as a token of peace."[88]

The 1542 Dialogue sheds valuable light on the treatment of the eucharist in the 1571 Church Order. There, as we have seen, Archbishop Petri also justified calling the mass a sacrifice. Against the more radical party in the Church of Sweden, he asserted that "we with the Papists call the Lord's Supper the mass."[89] The theory that the word "missa" means "sacrifice" in Hebrew does not bother his conscience, "for even if it were so, which yet is not fully sure . . . , so neither is it forbidden to call that Sacrament a sacrifice, as has always been done in Christendom, since that sacrifice which our High Priest Christ once made upon the cross is celebrated in the mass."[90]

It would seem that the ecumenical theology of Gustav Aulén in the twentieth century has its roots in the eucharistic theology of Laurentius Petri. The former bishop of Lund, like the sixteenth-century archbishop of Uppsala, represents a conscious return to biblical and patristic understandings of eucharistic sacrifice. In concluding his ecumenical study, *Eucharist and Sacrifice*, Aulén asserted that "the Lord's Supper combines the sacrifice and the real presence in an inseparable unity."[91] The Lord who is present in the eucharistic meal is the living and ascended Lord; but that risen Christ is none other than the Crucified One. "When he comes in the Holy Communion, he actualizes the sacrifice of the new covenant and makes it effectively present."[92] The benefits of Holy Communion depend upon the real presence of the body and blood of Christ, and therefore the presence of his eternally valid sacrifice. The liturgical question is how to articulate this belief. Here we turn to the Liturgy of King Johan III, who sought to give liturgical expression to the eucharistic theology that had been articulated in the writings of Sweden's leading reformers.

---

[87] Ahlberg, 299–301.
[88] Trans. in Brilioth, 250; see text in *Nattvarden*, 360.
[89] Brilioth, 251.
[90] Ibid.
[91] Aulén, *Eucharist and Sacrifice*, 203.
[92] Ibid.

❦ EUCHARISTIC SACRIFICE IN THE RED BOOK

We have seen that the Red Book of King Johan III contains a eucharistic prayer for which no Lutheran mass-order in the sixteenth century had an equivalent. The eucharistic sacrifice is expressed in the prayer following the words of institution, Memores igitur. This prayer, as we have seen, is the corollary of the Unde et memores of the Roman canon, but it is characterized more by what it added to the canon than by what it retained.

From the Eastern sources Johan III added the commemoration of *salutaris huius mandati* (his salutary command).[93] This commemoration is connected to Christ's command, "Do this in remembrance of me," in a way which is not apparent in the text of the Roman canon. Yet it does not follow, as Louis Bouyer charges, "that the memorial in fact becomes here a subjective commemoration of the Last Supper, before indirectly recalling the passion and the whole work of salvation."[94] We want to take up two of Bouyer's points: the "subjective commemoration" and the "indirect recalling" of the passion and salvatory work of God in Christ.

With regard to the "subjective commemoration," neither of the two principal points of contact in the liturgy, Lutheran sacramental theology and patristic liturgy, allow for a mere subjective or affective memorial. We have seen that the opening sentence of the Memores-prayer is a Latin translation of the beginning of the anamnesis-section in the Anaphora of John Chrysostom. Bouyer already called this anamnesis-prayer "a perfect expression of the original sense of the memorial."[95] He pointed out that the original meaning of the eucharistic memorial is found in the Hebrew concept of *zikkaron*. Concerning this, Bouyer writes in his discussion of the Jewish *Toseftah*-prayer, "The memorial here is not merely a simple commemoration. It is a sacred sign, given by God to his people who preserve it as their pre-eminent spiritual treasure."[96]

It is along these lines that we can tie in with Lutheran sacramental theology. When Jesus established a memorial of himself, he gave as signs of it his very body and blood. These are the signs *pro nobis* of his redeeming sacrifice. The sacrament therefore functions as a sign of God's will for us. This is so not only in terms of the sacramental elements, but also in terms of the whole sacramental action.[97] Christ is remembered by means of the proclamation in the mass from beginning to end, as Luther emphasized in his *Admonition Concerning the Sacrament*.

All of this is assumed in the Liturgy of King Johan III. The optional exhortation to the communicants speaks of our Lord's command "to use this sacrament for a remembrance of himself." In Lutheran theology, based on an interpretation of Paul in 1 Corinthians 11:26 (eating and drinking the bread and the cup as a proclamation of the

---

[93] *Röda Boken*, 49. Johan III cites the text of the Anaphora of St. John Chrysostom in Pamelius, *Liturgica Latinorum* (1571), I, 115.

[94] Bouyer, *Eucharist*, op. cit., 402.

[95] Ibid., 288.

[96] Ibid., 84.

[97] See Warren Quanbeck, "'Sacramental Sign' in the Lutheran Confessions," in *Lutherans and Catholics in Dialogue*, III: *The Eucharist as Sacrifice* (1969), 84.

Lord's death), the memorial is effected by the proclamation. This is the point of preaching at every mass.[98] It is also the point of proclaiming aloud the dominical words of institution, which are regarded as a summary of the gospel.[99] The memorial of Christ is proclaimed to awaken faith in the saving benefits of the sacramental gift. But the memorial is real (objective) whether it is apprehended in faith or not, because the signs convey what they signify—the body and blood of Christ—and eating and drinking them is itself a form of proclamation, of remembrance.

It is possible that the direction of the proclamation in Luther's theology is different from that in Paul's theology. According to Jeremias, the memorial in the Jewish prayers and in Paul is proclaimed first of all to God, to recall to him his promises with regard to his people.[100] For Luther, the proclamation is directed first of all to the people, to awaken in them a trust in the promises of God. Either way, the other party is listening in, and no matter what the direction of the proclamation, the memorial is objectively real because the signs of it are objectively real.

Thus, it is not clear, as Bouyer charges concerning the concept of anamnesis in the Red Book, that "we find ourselves in the context of the medieval and Protestant view of things."[101] The medieval view that Bouyer has in mind is the understanding of *repraesentatio* espoused, for example, by Gabriel Biel.[102] The Protestant view that Bouyer has in mind may be the Zwinglian, or even the Calvinist, but not the Lutheran. The concept of memorial is tied to the understanding of the presence of Christ. Lutherans obviously rejected the spiritualistic interpretation of the presence of Christ taught by the Zwinglians. As Quanbeck relates, the Lutherans also found Calvin's language about a *real, spiritual* presence unacceptable, "suspecting that it meant an unreal, ethereal presence."[103] No one has ever accused King Johan III of importing these Protestant ideas into the liturgy of the Swedish church. Even Serenius suggests that "Johan's anamnesis-teaching is closely connected with the medieval teaching."[104] But, in spite of the king's interest in ritual ceremonies known from the rubrics of late medieval missal traditions, we find no evidence of a purely symbolic, liturgical-dramatic understanding of commemoratio in the Red Book. Gabriel Biel does not have the same authority for King Johan III as Ambrose or Chrysostom. On the basis of what we know about Johan's personal theological convictions, it would seem more productive to see in the liturgy an attempt to correlate Lutheran teachings about the remembrance of Christ in the sacramental celebration with patristic teachings. The Memores-prayer suggests the idea that the saving benefits of the sacrifice of Christ are present in the mass through the proclamation of

---

[98] WA 6:373.

[99] Ibid.

[100] Jeremias, *The Eucharistic Words of Jesus*, op. cit., 237ff.

[101] Bouyer, 402.

[102] See Heiko Oberman, *The Harvest of Medieval Theology. Gabriel Biel and Late Medieval Nominalism*, op. cit., 274.

[103] Quanbeck, 87.

[104] Serenius, *Liturgia svecanae ecclesiae*, op. cit., 268.

the memorial, not simply through a liturgical reenactment of it. That is precisely why a fuller eucharistic text is needed rather than the preface and words of institution alone.[105]

Nor are "the passion and the whole work of salvation" only "indirectly" recalled in the liturgy. The benefits of Christ's sacrifice are received in the supper, whose institution is commemorated. But Christ's sacrifice comprehends the whole of his "holy passion and death, resurrection and ascension." It is all of "this" *(Quem, Hwilken)* that Christ has "sent and given unto us, that he might be an offering for our sins."[106] The "passion and the whole work of salvation" are directly recalled along with the dominical command to celebrate the meal because the one is contingent upon the other. The benefits of Christ's "holy passion and death, resurrection and ascension" are conveyed by receiving the sacramental signs. This is specified by proclaiming Christ's "holy passion and death, resurrection and ascension" before the ministration of the sacramental elements.

Since Bouyer is convinced that a subjective concept of commemoration lies behind the prayers in the Red Book, he is consistent in his analysis of the meaning of the sacrifice in these prayers. "The explanation given of this sacrifice, as if it were reduced to the Anselmian notion of penal satisfaction, is quite typical not only of Luther himself but of Lutheran scholasticism which took over this explanation precisely in order to set the whole redemption within the strict framework of the past."[107] But we must question whether such phrases as this "pure, holy, and undefiled offering, set before us for our reconciliation, our shield, defense, and covering against thy wrath, against the terror of sins and of death,"[108] do represent the medieval Latin concept of the atonement.

Throughout the Red Book, Johan has tried to set Lutheran theology in traditional liturgical forms. These phrases sound as if they could have been lifted straight out of Luther's writings. But Gustav Aulén has written an important study challenging the assumption that the Anselmian notion of "penal satisfaction" was Luther's concept of the atonement.[109] For one thing, Aulén shows that the doctrine of the incarnation was not as much a living idea for Anselm as it was for Irenaeus or Athanasius. Therefore, it is not connected with the atonement. For the Greek fathers, wrote Aulén,

> God enters into this world of sin and death that He might overcome the enemies that hold mankind in bondage, and Himself accomplish the redemptive work, for which no power but the Divine is adequate. But for Anselm the central problem is: Where can a man be found, free from sin and guilt, and able to offer himself as an acceptable sacrifice to God?[110]

Anselm thus teaches redemption by means of a freely offered work of satisfaction by Christ. "The Atonement is worked out according to strict requirements of justice; God

---

[105] A marginal note bears this out: "Memoria illa quae iuxta institutionem Domini coniungenda est cum manducatione continet praedicationem et applicationem beneficiorum mortis et resurrectionis Christi . . ." *Röda Boken*, 62 (misnumbered LXIII).

[106] Yelverton, *The Mass in Sweden*, 106–7.

[107] Bouyer, 402–3.

[108] Yelverton, 107.

[109] Gustav Aulén, *Christus Victor*, trans. by A. G. Hebert (New York: MacMillan, 1931; reprinted 1966), 87.

[110] Ibid., 90.

receives compensation for man's default."[111] But this juridical concept does not square with Luther's understanding of justification, which is more than a forensic declaration of forgiveness and acquittal. It is an ascription to human beings of the "alien" righteousness of Christ. Aulén cites, from among many passages, Luther's commentary on Galatians 3:13 (from the longer *Commentary on Galatians*): "When therefore we teach that men are justified through Christ, and Christ is the conqueror of sin, death, and the everlasting curse, then at the same time we testify that He is in His nature God."[112] Here Luther asserts that redemption is a divine operation, that the atonement is closely connected with the whole act of incarnation, and that there is a basic dualism or opposition to be overcome. That dualism is between God's wrath and God's love.

Common medieval teaching posited the wrath of God in the judgment to come; Luther set it forth in the present as lying even now on a sinful and guilt-laden humanity. To overcome God's wrath, God is necessary; God's love must triumph over God's own wrath. For Carl Wisløff, however, Aulén's interpretation at this point does not go far enough. Christ's victory over sin, death, and hell may express what redemption is, but this does not express the atonement. Wisløff proposes a substitutionary view of the atonement as a more adequate interpretation of Luther's thought.

> The moment God's wrath is taken seriously, and the moment the atonement becomes essentially (if not entirely) identical with the substitutionary suffering of punishment, the atonement is no longer a divine struggle or exclusively God's "bounteous mercy." For here we are dealing not merely with the relation between God and the powers of corruption, but with the relation between God and God.[113]

Christ suffered the punishment that we would all have endured under God's wrath. This is more than a penal *satisfactio*; it is the punishment for that sin for which no one could render satisfaction. God's wrath can be stayed only by the incarnate Son's sacrificial death on the cross. The Son who is beloved of the Father dies on behalf of those whom he loves, and thus stays God's wrath and wins forgiveness for his brothers and sisters who are joined to him by baptism into his death.

Wisløff's study is even more penetrating than Aulén's, but his liturgical conclusions are inadequate when he polemicizes against any sense in which the sacrifice of the cross can be present in the mass. How are we to receive the salutary benefits of the atoning sacrifice except through the proclamation of the word and the celebration of the sacraments? The presence of the sacrifice of the cross in the word and sacrament of the mass serves to bestow to the faithful the benefits of what Christ accomplished once and for all in his "obedience unto death."

Moreover, the sacrifice cannot be present without the victim. When the faithful grasp in faith the saving cross, they are also grasping the victim, who is present in, with, and under the signs of bread and wine. This is what the Red Book proposes when it says,

---

[111] Ibid., 90.
[112] Ibid., 105–6.
[113] Wisløff, *The Gift of Communion*, op. cit., 123.

"The same your Son, the same offering" is "set before us" and "proposed" to faith. What would be more Lutheran than this grasping of the one oblation of Christ by believers in the prayer of faith?

Yet it was the fact that the prayer said "we offer" which raised the suspicions of the Anti-Liturgists.[114] The object of offerimus is *Eundem Filium tuum, eiusdem mortem et oblationem* (the same your Son, his death and oblation). To the gnesio-Lutheran party this could only appear as a new sacrificing of Christ and therefore a compromise of the unique atoning sacrifice. Johan III was conscious of this problem, and in a marginal note he drew reference to Melanchthon's distinction between the sacrificium propiciatorium and the sacrificium eucharisticum.[115] He had an adequate grasp of the uniqueness of the propitiatory sacrifice. But somehow the idea of the sacramental presence of Christ and his sacrifice in the mass had to be integrated with the offering that the faithful can make, the sacrificium eucharisticum, their prayers of praise and thanksgiving that, in the Supplices-prayer that follows, are presented upon the heavenly altar for divine acceptance.[116]

From his reading of the Fathers, King Johan III had learned a more integrating concept of *mysterion* than was possible to implement in the polemical situation of the sixteenth century. The real presence of Christ and his sacrifice means that the saving events commemorated in the mass are the reality of the present as well as a part of the past; that the substance of all Christian sacrifice is the sacrifice of Christ; and that even our praise and thanksgiving to the Father becomes Christ's own that he presents to the Father in heaven on our behalf.[117] There is no other way in which our act of eucharistia could be acceptable to the Father. Luther had a grasp of this when he wrote in his Treatise on the New Testament,

> I will gladly agree that the faith which I have called the true priestly office is truly able to do all things in heaven, earth, hell, and purgatory; and to this faith no one can ascribe too much. It is this faith, I say, which makes us all priests and priestesses. Through it, in connection with the sacrament, we offer ourselves, our need, prayer, praise, and thanksgiving in Christ and through Christ; and thereby we offer Christ to God, that is, we move Christ and give him occasion to offer himself for us and to offer us with himself.[118]

While Luther had a grasp of this fuller concept of the eucharistic sacrifice, he never tried to integrate it into liturgical formularies. King Johan III attempted to do so. His clear intention was to recapture the patristic tradition and implement it without compromising Lutheran theology or surrendering the inherited Catholic forms. In the end he satisfied neither Evangelicals nor Catholics. Both were more thoroughly tied to the medieval

---

[114] See Holmqvist, *Svenska Kyrkans Historia*, op. cit., III/2:56.

[115] *Röde Boken*, 64. "Sacrificium propiciatorium est opus solius Domini Jesu Christi, placens iram Dei pro alijs, et satisfaciens pro culpa et poena aeterna, debita generi humano propter peccatum. Christus unicus et sempiternus est novi Testamenti Sacerdos, qui unica pro peccatis peccatorum invenit."

[116] Yelverton, 108.

[117] See Brilioth, *Eucharistic Faith and Practice*, 54–69.

[118] LW 35:101.

"deformations" of faith and practice than was this humanist king who believed in the possibility of reconciliation on the basis of the "consensus of the first five centuries." Yet, from the vantage point of our own more ecumenical age, it is an attempt worth considering. For there is no doubt that the sacrifice of Christ, the self-offering of Christians, the offering of the gifts of bread and wine, and communion in the body and blood of Christ were all held together and expressed in the historic eucharistic prayers that served as the models and sources of King Johan III's liturgy, and might still help us to overcome the impasse of the sixteenth century on the issue of eucharistic sacrifice.

🍇 AN ECUMENICAL IMPASSE

The sixteenth century came to an end with an impasse over the eucharistic sacrifice. The Reformation theologians repudiated the eucharistic sacrifice, and had an aversion to eucharistic prayer, because Catholic theology insisted on interpreting this sacrifice in a propitiatory sense. Even this might have been overcome if there had not been the belief that in the mass the priest offered to God the body and blood of Christ, and did this to plead special intentions. We cannot forget the fact that the most frequently celebrated form of the mass in the Catholic church at the time of the Reformation was the votive mass. As a result, the only sense in which eucharistic sacrifice could be retained was as "prayer, praise, and thanksgiving." Lutherans felt that this act of thanksgiving was best expressed *after* the ministration of Holy Communion so as to preclude any misunderstanding that might suggest a blasphemous reversal of the direction of the sacrament or foster works-righteousness. Indeed, Lutheran post-communion prayers have not been remiss to begin with a "thank you" for the gift received.

It is important to understand what the exact nature of this impasse is before any attempt can be made to penetrate it. The question is whether it is proper to use language in which the church, through its ministers, offers Christ himself, or Christ's body and blood, to God the Father. The Roman Catholic Church has deemed this language appropriate and in the new Eucharistic Prayer IV in the 1974 Roman Missal says quite flatly, "We offer you his body and blood, the acceptable sacrifice which brings salvation to the whole world."[119] The composers of this prayer were not loath to change the "bread and wine" of the Alexandrian Anaphora of Basil, on which Eucharistic Prayer IV is based, into "body and blood." On the other hand, Lutherans are so squeamish about eucharistic sacrifice that it was deemed necessary to change Hippolytus's "we *offer* this bread and cup" to "we *lift* this bread and cup before you," (italics added) in the translation of the Anaphora of Hippolytus that serves as Eucharistic Prayer IV in *Lutheran Book of Worship*, Ministers Edition.[120] And then a weak justification was provided for this mutilation of Hippolytus's text with the allusion to Luther's retention of the elevation at the

---

[119] International Committee on English in the Liturgy, *Eucharistic Prayers* (Washington, D.C.: ICEL, 1980), 27.
[120] *LBW*, Ministers Edition, 226.

words of institution.[121] Neither Roman Catholic nor Lutheran recent "reforms" of the mass were able to use patristic texts unaltered by their respective theologies.

The exact nature of this impasse was brought out in the Lutheran/Roman Catholic Dialogues. The Roman Catholic participants in the international dialogue upheld this kind of language of offering the body and blood of Christ as a proper interpretation of the teaching of the Council of Trent.[122] Taking a lead from the U.S.A. Lutheran/Roman Catholic Dialogue, they explained that by offering the body and blood of Christ, the church expressed its total reliance on the sacrifice of Christ, and at the same time expressed its self-offering by appealing to communion with Christ. Such an understanding could be reconciled with the sense in which Luther could say "We offer Christ" in his *Treatise on the New Testament,* cited above. The Lutheran partners in the dialogue expressed reservations about using this kind of language at all, lest this be understood in a propitiatory sense. The result of this view in Lutheran eucharistic prayers is that not only is Christ's sacrifice not offered, or at least proposed, to the Father; but not even the bread and wine are offered. The tragedy of this impasse is that both traditions are cut off from the earliest Christian eucharistic tradition in which effective memorial of the sacrifice of Christ, the oblation of bread and wine, and the self-offering of Christians are all held together and expressed in the act of eucharistia. While we may need to say more in our public prayers than ancient Christians said, we should at least be able to say no less.

 ## THE RELEVANCE OF THE STUDY OF EUCHARISTIC PRAYER IN TRANSCENDING THE ECUMENICAL IMPASSE OVER EUCHARISTIC SACRIFICE

The thrust of this chapter has been to see instances where the reformers and theologians of the Reformation period opened the door to an understanding of eucharistic sacrifice and the possibility of eucharistic prayer. The reformers did allow for the sacrifice of praise and thanksgiving and for the offering of themselves by the faithful, in union with Christ, whose one sacrifice once offered is commemorated in the eucharist. Catholic teaching held that the eucharist is a sacrifice, and that when it is offered by the priest in representation of Christ's sacrifice (understood in at least two different ways), it avails for the forgiveness of sins of the living and the dead. What eluded both sides was the connection between the sacrifice of thanksgiving and self-offering, on the one hand, and effective representation of Christ's sacrifice, on the other. Yet these ideas are all expressed within the framework of classical eucharistic prayers.[123]

What we do not find in the classical eucharistic tradition is an offering of the body and blood of Christ. Even in the ancient Roman canon, what is offered is the bread

---

121 See Paul V. Marshall, "The Eucharistic Rite of the Lutheran Book of Worship," *Worship* 54 (1980), 254f.

122 Lutheran/Roman Catholic Joint Commission, *The Eucharist* (Geneva: Lutheran World Federation, 1980), 20f.

123 See David N. Power, "The Anamnesis: Remembering, We Offer," in Frank C. Senn, ed., *New Eucharistic Prayers: An Ecumenical Study of Their Development and Structure* (Mahwah, N.J.: Paulist Press, 1986), 151ff.

and cup. True, it is the "bread of life" and "the cup of salvation," both elaborations using biblical references; and theologians of the sixteenth century and later could interpret this as the body and blood of Christ, especially since the change (transubstantiation) of the elements occurred at the words of institution before the anamnesis-oblation. But it is only when we come to the 1974 Roman Missal that we find in Eucharistic Prayer IV the bald statement, "we offer you his body and blood." This is a new development in the eucharistic tradition, and it might be challenged in the name of tradition, as Martin Chemnitz did in his Examination of the Council of Trent.

In the Anaphora of Basil, on which this prayer is based, there is only the offering of the bread and wine. In the early eucharistic tradition, however, the bread and wine offering expressed the self-offering of the church. Robert Daly points out that Christians are made a sacrifice through baptism into Christ's death and resurrection.[124] This was the consistent teaching of the church fathers. Augustine especially emphasized that this is the sense in which the eucharist is the celebration of the sacrifice of the totus Christus, members as well as head.[125] The body of Christ is not divisible. The offering of Christ is the offering of his members as well. The tokens of this self-offering, the bread and wine, which are offered for the needs of the liturgy as well as the needs of the community, are transformed by the word through the Spirit into the gift of communion in Christ. In eating and drinking the eucharistic bread and wine as the body and blood of Christ the faithful receive the forgiveness of sins, life, and salvation.[126]

There is no doubt that the study of eucharistic prayers could help to transcend the sixteenth-century impasse on sacrifice. On the other hand, the very sparseness of sacrificial language in traditions other than the Alexandrian and Roman should make one pause. Cesare Giraudo, in his study of the Jewish todah tradition, shows how some psalms of thanksgiving accompanied the offering of sacrifices in the Temple; but such prayers are also found in circumstances where there are no links to sacrifice (e.g., Isa. 51:3; Jer. 30:19; Ps. 42:5).[127]

The implication of this is that while Jewish prayers of blessing and thanksgiving informed Christian eucharistic prayers, they cannot be held accountable for the introduction of the theme of sacrifice into Christian eucharistic prayers. Even the early Christians' penchant for citing Malachi 1:11 when they spoke of their eucharist as a sacrifice of praise and thanksgiving may have arisen more out of a Gentile world, where the offering of sacrifices was viewed as a fundamental act of religion, than out of the Jewish heritage, where the possibility existed of understanding prayer as a spiritual sacrifice. David Power suggests that the language of sacrifice may have been laid over an earlier understanding of the eucharist "as a memorial representation of and participation in the

---

[124] Robert Daly, *Christian Sacrifice: The Judaeo-Christian Background before Origen* (Washington, D.C.: The Catholic University of America Press, 1978), 194.

[125] St. Augustine of Hippo, *The City of God*, Book X, chapter 6.

[126] See the studies on Ignatius of Antioch and Irenaeus of Lyons in R. Johanny and A. Hamman, *L'Eucharistie des Premiers Chrétiens* (Paris: Beauchesne, 1976).

[127] Cesare Giraudo, *La Struttura Letteraria della Preghiera Eucaristica* (Rome: Pontifical Biblical Institute, 1980), 266ff.

saving death and resurrection of Jesus Christ."[128] Understanding memorial to include Christ's incarnation, servant-ministry, resurrection, and ascension as well as his passion and death might lead to less emphasis on the language of sacrifice; or, conversely, it might broaden the understanding of Christ's sacrifice to include his whole work of redemption.

Lutherans need to understand that sacrifice is a polysemous concept in the eucharistic tradition that refers variously to the offering of bread and wine, the self-offering of the faithful, and the saving work of Jesus Christ. Roman Catholics need to remember that sacrifice is one metaphor for the saving act of Christ along with others, such as ransom and purchase, victory over sin, death, and the devil, and the restoration of immortality through the incarnation of the Word. All of this is present in the eucharistic tradition. Study of this tradition would go a long way in helping us to overcome the ecumenical impasse on eucharistic sacrifice in particular and on the eucharist in general.

---

[128] Power, art. in *New Eucharistic Prayers*, 164.

PART THREE

Liturgical Loss, Retrieval, and Renewal

CHAPTER 14

Liturgy in the Age of Certainty

IT IS DIFFICULT TO know what name to give to the post-Reformation era in Western history, especially as it affects liturgy. Culturally, it was a period of transition. At the beginning of the seventeenth century many Europeans were still partly medieval; by the end of the century they were practically modern. It is not surprising that we find, as Douglas Bush pointed out, "the clash and the fusion of old and new on every side, in science and religion, politics and economics, law and literature, music and architecture. It is the impact of modernism upon medievalism which gives the age its peculiar character."[1]

Carl J. Friedrich has accepted the common designation of this period as "The Age of the Baroque."[2] This label has stuck with architecture, art, and music. The term indicates the ornateness, the brilliance, the exuberance, sometimes the grotesqueness of expression. But although this might characterize the architectural design of Gianlorenzo Bernini (1598–1680) and the musical architecture of J. S. Bach (1685–1750), it does not so much characterize Sir Christopher Wren (1632–1723) or George Frederick Handel (1685–1759), who strove toward simplicity of line. Politically this post-Reformation era has been called the age of absolutism, with Louis XIV of France, the "Sun King," as the paradigmatic ruler. But the first modern experiments in republicanism also stirred in the

---

[1] Douglas Bush, *English Literature in the Earlier Seventeenth Century, 1600–1660. Oxford History of English Literature*, ed. by F. P. Wilson and Bonamy Dobree (New York: Oxford University Press, 1945), 1.

[2] Carl J. Friedrich, *The Age of the Baroque, 1610–1660* (New York and Evanston: Harper and Row, 1952).

seventeenth century. Theologically, it has been called the age of orthodoxy; Friedrich Blume called it "the age of confessionalism."[3] But in each orthodox tradition there was a formidable dissenting movement; and not every religious tradition was "confessional" in the strict sense of adhering to historical symbols of faith. I have therefore opted for "Certainty," a term that alludes to the philosophy of René Descartes (1596–1650), who, from a method of doubting everything arrived at certainty via the personal affirmation, "I think, therefore I am" (*Cogito, ergo sum*). This was an age of doubt as well as faith, of individualism as well as corporate identity. The giants of cosmology and physics, Kepler and Galileo, replaced the Ptolemaic universe with the Copernican, while Descartes and Pascal debated the impact of mathematics and mechanics on the total worldview, and Harvey's and Bacon's panegyrics over the inductive method in science had its parallel in the passion of the social sciences for statistics and natural observation, as is evident in the political theories of Hobbes and Spinoza. While these scientists had no intention of attacking the Christian faith or the Christian worldview, the new science did call everything into doubt. As John Donne expressed it in "An Anatomie of the World,"

> [N]ew Philosophy calls all in doubt,
> The element of fire is quite put out;
> The sun is lost, and th' earth, and no man's wit
> Can well direct him where to look for it.
> And freely men confesse that this world's spent,
> When in the Planets, and the Firmament
> They seek so many new; then see that this
> Is crumbled out againe to his Atomies.
> 'Tis all in peeces, all cohaerence gone;
> All just supply, and all Relation;
> Prince, Subject, Father, Sonne, are things forgot,
> For every man alone thinkes he hath got
> To be a Phoenix, and that then can bee
> None of that kind, of which he is, but hee.[4]

With the challenge of the "new Philosophy" offering a whole new worldview, people looked for certainty. Some sought it in personal mystical experience. A quietistic mysticism is evident in the writings of Sir Thomas Browne (1605–1682). His *Religio Medici* (1643) has been called a prose equivalent of Donne's poetry. He felt himself surrounded by oceans of mystery in an unfamiliar cosmos, but rather than frightening him it intensified his quiet piety. The note of mysticism was even more pronounced in the work of Jacob Boehme, a small shopkeeper in Silesia, who published his *Aurora* in 1612. Claiming the divine light as the source of his revelations, he drew upon the *Urgrund*, or "ground of grounds," to resolve all conflict, including the ultimate conflict between good and evil. In England, champions of "the inner light" influenced the Baptists and the Quakers, who looked for certainty within the soul.

---

[3] Friedrich Blume, "The Age of Confessionalism," in *Protestant Church Music*, op. cit., 127–315.

[4] *John Donne, Dean of St. Paul's. Complete Poetry and Selected Prose*, ed. by John Hayward (London: The Nonesuch Press, 1967), 202.

Against the potential chaos of individualism, as each person worked out for himself the meaning of the universe, communities of faith tried to establish the boundaries of belief and practice for their adherents. As faith clashed against faith, political absolutism, the consequence of the triumph of the state over the estates, teamed up with theological orthodoxy to impose uniformity of belief and practice on whole populations. The result was the persecution of dissenting minorities, such as the Separatists in England, the Reformed Protestants (Huguenots) and the Roman Catholic Jansenists in France, pietists in orthodox Lutheran lands, and, ironically, the orthodox Lutherans in Brandenburg-Prussia once toleration became a state policy under the Great Elector Friedrich Wilhelm I and his successors. The seventeenth century was an age of religious war, culminating in the Thirty Years' War on the continent and the English Civil War. The "madness of the theologians" (Melanchthon's term) affected even sensitive poetic souls, such as John Milton in England, who remained a nonconformist through changes of administration, expressing a Puritanical "contempt for the world" of the Established Church from the exile of his country estate; and Paul Gerhardt in Brandenburg, who would rather lose his pastoral post than admit that Calvinists were Christians.

In such a context liturgy became a mark of confessional identity, and departure from liturgical orders was not countenanced. In the period after the Council of Trent we find the Roman Catholic Church exercising doctrinal control over the liturgy. But even before the promulgation of Trent's decrees on the liturgy in 1562, the Act of Uniformity was enacted by the English Parliament upon adoption of the 1559 *Book of Common Prayer*. This required "uniformity" in ceremony for the sake of "common order" and "quiet discipline" (although for the sake of sister Protestant churches in other nations the preface to the Prayer Book declared that "in these doings we condemn no other Nations, nor prescribe anything but to our own people").[5] The state imposed uniformity of ceremony for its own purposes. Thus, in the state church situation in the Protestant countries we find not just doctrinal control over liturgy but political control over liturgy. In the expanded kingdom of Prussia in the eighteenth century, which included a minority Reformed population in an overwhelmingly Lutheran land, the Reformed King Friedrich Wilhelm I exercised his function as summus episcopus by forbidding candles, copes, chasubles, Latin hymns, and the sign of the cross (1733). "If any . . . wish to make it a matter of conscience . . . they can be relieved by dismissal from their parishes."[6]

The restrictions placed on liturgy by ecclesiastical and political authority (which certainly hampered liturgical creativity) may give the impression that the post-Reformation period was a low point in liturgical history. Indeed, the assessment made by twentieth-century Roman Catholic scholars would indicate that the whole period after Trent was deleterious to the flowering of Roman Catholic liturgy in its true sense as "the work of the people." Liturgical historians characterize this period as one of "rigid unification" and "rubricism" (Klauser), "unyielding uniformity" and "timelessness" (Jung-

---

[5] *Liturgical Services: Liturgies and Occasional Forms of Prayer Set Forth in the Reign of Queen Elizabeth*. Parker Society Edition, ed. by W. K. Clay (Cambridge: University Press, 1847).

[6] See James Hastings Nichols, *History of Christianity, 1650–1950. Secularization of the West* (New York: The Ronald Press, 1956), 47.

mann).[7] On the other hand, in spite of the emphasis on uniformity this period can be regarded as "the golden age" of Reformation and Counter-Reformation liturgy. The basic forms and orders of worship established in the Reformation experiments and solidified for Roman Catholicism by the decrees and revised books issuing from the Council of Trent were now enriched especially by music and architecture.

What makes this period so important for our contemporary consideration is that the reason theology was so concerned about liturgy was precisely because it recognized the lex credendi imbedded in the lex orandi. Liturgy in the age of certainty served as a confessional symbol. It was this for established churches as well as for dissenters. It was clearly understood that praying is an act of believing, although in the Western churches this led to a concern to regulate prayer out of concern for true doctrine, which produced dissenting movements in all of the mainline Christian traditions. We will look at the orthodoxy embodied in seventeenth-century Russian Orthodoxy, post-Tridentine Roman Catholicism, Lutheranism, and Anglicanism, and then also look at the dissenting movements in each of these establishment traditions: the Russian Old Believers, the Jansenists, Pietists, and Puritans. Even the Puritans, who themselves were dissenters from Anglicanism, had dissenters in their ranks in the form of Baptists and Quakers.

This is not an age in which new orders and texts were being produced. Nevertheless, worship in the Roman Catholic, Lutheran, Reformed, and Anglican traditions was greatly enriched by music and architecture. After looking at these artistic expressions of Baroque worship, we will pick up the concern for orthodoxy that characterizes this period in order to reflect on the idea of worship as primary theology or living dogma. This raises an issue that must be a constant concern of liturgical theology: the integrity of worship. Patterns and acts of worship both express and form the beliefs of the worshipers. A lesson from this "age of certainty" is the need for a theological custody of worship.

🍇 THE AGE OF ORTHODOXY

Liturgical Reform and Schism in the "Third Rome"

The center of gravity of this book has been the Protestant Reformation. Even Roman Catholicism became what it was in response to the experience of the Reformation. The Reformation eluded the Eastern churches entirely, and there is a sense in which it is like trying to squeeze a square object into a round hole to make Eastern Orthodoxy correlate with Western Christian history. However, the center of Eastern Orthodoxy was transferred from the Middle East to Russia with the progressive shrinkage of the Byzantine Empire as a result of Moslem conquest, and developments in the West had an impact on Russia.

By 1453, with the fall of Constantinople to the Ottoman Turks, every one of the four Eastern patriarchates existed only under Moslem sufferance. Only in the Slavic lands north of the Black Sea was Orthodoxy able to continue its historic development according

---

[7] See Theodore Klauser, *A Short History of the Western Liturgy*, op. cit., 117ff.; J. A. Jungmann, *Pastoral Liturgy*, op. cit. Even so, the mass was not totally unchanging, as J. D. Crichton amusingly points out in *The Once and Future Liturgy* (Dublin: Veritas, 1977), chapter one.

to its own genius. While many Eastern Christians regarded the fall of Constantinople as presaging the end of the world, Russian Christians saw it as a divine judgment on the patriarchate for its concessions to the Roman church at the Council of Florence in 1438–1439. In a last-ditch attempt to secure Western support against the Turks, the Patriarch acknowledged the Bishop of Rome as the chief bishop in the universal church and accepted the controversial filioque in the Western text of the Nicene Creed as non-heretical (although these concessions were later repudiated). The consequence of the destruction of the Byzantine Empire, in the Russian point of view, was that guardianship of Orthodoxy passed from Constantinople to Moscow. The monk Philotheos, at the beginning of the sixteenth century, formulated the theory that Moscow was the "third Rome." The first Rome had fallen because of heresy; the second Rome (Constantinople) had fallen because of unfaithfulness; "but a new third Rome has sprung up in the north, illuminating the whole universe like a sun . . . the third will stand till the end of history; a fourth Rome is inconceivable."[8]

Naturally, this ideology served the expansionist aims of the Dukes of Moscow, who became the caesars (czars) of the Third Rome. They encouraged Orthodox refugees from Moslem-dominated lands to seek refuge in Russia. Czar Alexei Mikhailovich, who reigned from 1645 to 1676, annexed the eastern Ukraine with its capital Kiev, which had been the entry point of Orthodoxy into Russian lands, in order to enhance his protection of Orthodox peoples bordering on Catholic Slavic countries. The "Third Rome" idea also served the purpose of gaining autocephalous status for the patriarchate of Moscow. In 1589 the fugitive Patriarch Jeremiah II of Constantinople, in gratitude for the protection provided by the Czar, was induced to preside over the consecration of an independent Patriarch of Moscow and All Russia.[9]

Syrians, Greeks, and Ukrainians, however, pointed out discrepancies in ritual between their rites and the Russians'. Czar Alexei became convinced that the Russian usage should be brought into conformity with the Byzantine *Typicon* if the Russian Czar were to serve as the protector of all Orthodox people, since this would require cordial relationships with the four historic Eastern patriarchates. He found a kindred spirit in Abbot Nikon of the Anzer Monastery on the White Sea. Alexei was instrumental in getting Nikon elected Metropolitan of Novgorod in 1649 and Patriarch of Moscow in 1652. Alexei and Nikon set out on a campaign to revise the service books. These revisions have traditionally been identified with Nikon, but Paul Meyendorff underscores that Nikon was the Czar's instrument in this effort, not the other way around.[10]

This effort was fraught with difficulties from the outset. While the Greeks regarded the Slavs as barbarians, the Russians were not impressed by the moral degradation of the Greeks, the infamous political intrigues of the Byzantines, and the potential of subjugated peoples to connive with the Moslem Turks or the Roman heretics. Simply put, many of the Russian faithful did not regard the Greeks as examples worthy of imitation.

[8] Quoted in Nichols, 20.

[9] See W. F. Adeney, *The Greek and Eastern Churches* (New York: Charles Scribner's Sons, 1908).

[10] See Paul Meyendorff, *Russia, Ritual, and Reform: The Liturgical Reforms of Nikon in The Seventeenth Century* (Crestwood, N.Y.: St. Vladimir's Seminary Press, 1991).

Moreover, Russia was largely an illiterate land, including the clergy. Many priests and deacons had to learn their liturgical roles from memory, and continual changes in the service books proved confusing and burdensome. Also there was little preaching or teaching. The faith was conveyed entirely by the liturgy and the icons. Consequently, any liturgical changes touched the core of the people's faith. Even seemingly little issues—such as making the sign of the cross with three fingers instead of two, singing a triple Alleluia in the style of the Latin liturgy instead of a double Alleluia, or shaving one's beard—became major controversies.[11]

Rationalistic Westerners have difficulty appreciating what it means for an Orthodox Christian to celebrate leitourgia. It is the "work of the people" in a sense that Western liturgy seldom has been. Eastern liturgies are truly indigenous in the culture of the people and therefore were "popular" in ways the Western liturgies seldom were. The liturgical life ensured the continuity of tradition. It engendered not only a communal spirit, but a communion that united heaven and earth. The icons are "windows to another world" in the sense of letting the light of heaven stream into the earthly assembly.[12] Eastern liturgy has indeed evolved, but slowly and through painstaking consensus. This was a consensus that had not been carefully cultivated by Patriarch Nikon. When the Czar encouraged his liturgical changes, and pan-Orthodox councils in 1666 and 1667 supported his "innovations," the Orthodox faithful rose up in horror. The last third of the seventeenth century in Russia was characterized by the schism of the "Old Believers" and by hysterical apocalyptic fervor. Many thought that the "apostasy" of the hierarchy was the beginning of the reign of the Antichrist, and many of the faithful spent their nights sleeping in white shrouds and coffins waiting for the day of judgment.[13]

Plots against Czar Alexei's son, Peter the Great, in 1699 caused this Westernizing czar to play the role of the Antichrist with relish as he amused himself for some days by cutting off the beards of the nobility. Once again there were reports of people lying in coffins, but the end did not come and the Old Believers had to decide about their future. The radicals decided that there was no church any longer and they waited quietly for a new dispensation. They denied the validity of any sacraments, except those available to the laity—baptism and confession. They formed the "priestless" wing of the Old Believers, and flourished primarily in the forests and swamps of the White Sea littoral or in Siberia. The less radical wing of the Old Believers, concentrated mostly in the Ukraine, would not do without priests and sacraments, but in the absence of priests they celebrated a Liturgy of the Pre-Sanctified, in which they continued to add supplies of bread and wine to the already consecrated bread and wine.[14] It is estimated that one-sixth of the

---

[11] Meyerdorff, ibid., devotes the second part of his book to an examination of the textual and ceremonial innovations of Nikon's reform, citing the 1602 *Euchologion* (published in Venice!) which served as the basis of Nikon's reforms, as well as the 1652 Moscow *Sluzhebnik* (issued before Nikon's intervention) and the revised 1655 Moscow *Sluzhebnik*. The texts cited are in Greek and Church Slavonic, untranslated.

[12] See Robert Taft, S.J., *Beyond East and West: Problems in Liturgical Understanding* (Washington, D.C.: The Pastoral Press, 1984), 111–26. For two recent books on icons see John Baggley, *Doors of Perception: Icons and Their Spiritual Significance* (Crestwood, N.Y.: St. Vladimir's Seminary Press, 1988) and Michel Quenot, *The Icon: Window on the Kingdom* (Crestwood, N.Y.: St. Vladimir's Seminary Press, 1991).

[13] See Nichols, 22ff.

[14] See S. Bolshakov, *Russian Nonconformity* (Philadelphia: The Westminster Press, 1950).

population could be counted as Old Believers; and their number would undoubtedly have been higher if they had not been subject to intermittent persecution. The Old Believers represented a kind of pietistic strain in Russian Orthodoxy comparable to other examples of dissent in the seventeenth century: the Jansenists in Roman Catholicism, the Pietists in Lutheranism, and the Nonconformists in Anglicanism.

The Roman Congregation of Rites

The Aftermath of the Council of Trent

In the Roman Catholic Church after the Reformation, liturgical rigidity characterized the central hierarchy more than the local priests and laity—although these were brought into conformity through the efforts of the Congregation of Rites. The Council of Trent entrusted the task of producing new liturgical books mandated by its decrees on the liturgy to the Roman Curia, which, in 1568 and 1570 respectively, promulgated the *Breviarium Romanum* and the *Missale Romanum*. The emphasis in the titles is on "*Romanum.*" As a way of solidifying adherence to the Roman See, all dioceses had to use the Roman books unless they could prove that their usages were more than two hundred years old. This allowed exceptions for Milan and northern Italy, Toledo in Spain, and many dioceses in France that could appeal to the old Gallican rite. Thus, portions of the three most ardent Roman Catholic countries did not have to conform to Roman use, while all the Protestant liturgies were, by fault of their newness, unacceptable.

As a way of ensuring conformity to the Roman rite, especially as the Jesuits showed success in reclaiming some territories to the papal church, the Roman Curia established a Congregation of Rites in 1588. This Vatican congregation became the arbiter of what was locally permissible, since no additions or alterations could be made without its permission.[15] It also continued the task of producing post-Tridentine liturgical books, promulgating the *Pontificale Romanum* in 1596, which contained those liturgical orders used by bishops exclusively (e.g., confirmation, ordination), and the *Rituale Romanum* in 1614, which contained orders for those sacramental acts not reserved for bishops (e.g., baptism, penance, marriage, ministry to the sick and dying, burial).

While these post-Tridentine liturgical books reflect ritual reform in terms of the pruning and simplification of orders, there was no thought of encouraging or facilitating the participation of the people. A decree of the Council of Trent had mandated the continued use of the Latin language: "The Latin language, which is used for the celebration of Mass in the Western church, is in the highest degree appropriate, seeing that it is common to many nations. . . . There would also be great danger of various errors arising in many translations, with the result that the mysteries of our faith, which are in fact one, would seem rather to differ."[16]

There was also concern about the musical settings of the mass-texts.[17] There had been complaints about secular elements in Catholic church music before the Council of

---

[15] See Theodore Klauser, 129ff., on "The Congregation of Rites and Its Working Methods."

[16] Quoted in H. A. P. Schmidt, *Liturgie et langue vulgaire: le probleme de la langue liturgique chez les premiers Reformateurs et au concile de Trente. Analecta Gregoriana* 53 (Rome: Gregorian University, 1950), 135.

[17] See Gerald Abraham, *The Concise Oxford History of Music*, op. cit., 244ff.

Trent. These complaints included the exhibitionism of organists, the use of tropes, and the obscuring of sacred texts by polyphony. The Tridentine ideal in church choral music was a kind of homophonic polyphony, which had developed in the Netherlands but was exemplified in the mass settings of Giovanni Pierluigi da Palestrina (c. 1525–1594), the choir master at Saint Mary Major Basilica in Rome.[18] Palestrina wrote more than a hundred masses. These were either based on a plainsong foundation or were freely composed, such as the *Missa Papae Marcelli* and *Missa brevis*. Second only to Palestrina was Tomas Luis de Victoria (c. 1548–1611), who came to Rome from Spain in 1565. Victoria's output of mass settings was smaller than Palestrina's, but eight of them were based on his own motets.

The people were allowed to attend to their own devotions while the mass was being sung or said. In Germany, however, communal songs could be sung, not so much as a part of the mass (as in Lutheran practice), but *while* mass was being celebrated. The Cantual of Mainz (1605) provided a fixed plan for singing German songs during mass. At high mass hymns could actually be inserted as propers of the liturgy in place of the gradual, offertory, or communion antiphons (the usual choir anthems). At low mass, on the other hand, singing simply continued throughout the mass except that the Cantual provided that singing should stop during the reading of the gospel, at the elevation, and at the final blessing.[19] This practice continued into the nineteenth century. Franz Schubert's *Deutsche Messe* (1826) was actually a collection of eight songs to be sung during the celebration of mass, which he provided for the student congregation of the Vienna Polytechnic Institute.

During the Baroque Era there was an elaboration of the musical forms used in or during the liturgy: Choirs, organs, and whole orchestras were employed. The place of the choir was moved from the chancel to a gallery, where a pipe organ was installed, often in the rear of the nave. The musical settings of the liturgy increased in scope, beginning with those by Claudio Monteverdi (1567–1643), who was already famous as a madrigalist and opera composer before turning to church music. His setting of Vespers especially went far beyond the chaste homophonic settings of Palestrina and de Victoria in its expression of human emotion. The operatic character of the mass-settings reached the apex of their development in the Austrian tradition of Mozart and the Haydn brothers, Franz Joseph and Johann Michael, to the point where what the choir was singing had no relation to what was going on at the altar. Thus, the celebrant could routinely proceed with the offertory while the choir was still singing the Credo or finish the canon while the choir was singing the Sanctus.

There was no need to be concerned about singing during the communion of the people because ministration of Holy Communion regularly took place *before or after* mass, but never as a part of the mass.[20] While the frequency of communion was actually increasing during the seventeenth century, there was little sense of connection between

---

[18] See K. G. Fellerer, "Church Music and the Council of Trent," *Musical Quarterly* xxxix (1953), 588.

[19] Jungmann, *The Mass of the Roman Rite,* op. cit., I, 147.

[20] Ibid., I, 148ff.

the mass and communion. The mass was not conceived as something that must include the people as anything other than spectators in the presence of Christ the King. And the heavenly King must be honored in a style and setting no less opulent than the court of any earthly king, which led to the ornate richness of the interiors of Baroque church buildings.

Louis Bouyer has suggested three factors that produced the Baroque mentality: the literary and aesthetic world of Renaissance neo-paganism; a reaction to medieval asceticism, and with it a rejection of the plainness of the traditional liturgy; and a loyalty to the church that was more a negative reaction to Protestantism and the "new philosophy" than a positive expression of genuine piety.[21] It is little wonder that the celebration of mass and its architectural setting came to resemble the great cultural creation of the Baroque era, and its most popular one, the opera. The faithful of this period came to expect in the liturgy a religious equivalent of the opera, with all its pomp, sensuousness, and artifice. Bouyer has also noticed certain architectural similarities between Baroque Catholicism and Lutheran orthodoxy (e.g., the Church of the Gesù in Rome and the Storkyrka in Stockholm).[22]

The Jansenist Critique and Neo-Gallicanism

Nevertheless, there occurred in France a renewal of piety and Christian learning that might have pushed forward the elements of the humanist reformation, if this renewal had not been obscured by the controversies of Jansenism and Quietism. The Jansenists (named after the Augustinian scholar, Cornelius Jansen [1585–1638], a professor of the University of Louvain and bishop of Ypres at his death) represented a reaction to the external religiosity of Baroque Catholicism in the middle of the seventeenth century. As a reforming movement of deep piety and ethical earnestness, Jansenism appealed especially to the rising middle class, the intellectuals, the Dominicans, and the Augustinians. It therefore aroused the concern of King Louis XIV and the Jesuits at his court. Jansenists shared with Lutheran Pietists an aversion to externality and a desire for more overt lay participation in worship. As part of a campaign against externality, the Jansenists urged the church to restrain the cult of the Blessed Sacrament. Benediction of the Blessed Sacrament after Vespers had become the most popular of Roman Catholic practices, and Baroque altars became veritable thrones for the sacrament reserved in the tabernacle or sacrament house now placed upon it in the style of the throne of Louis XIV, the Sun King. The fact that the Jansenists were opposed to this development prompted the Jesuits to promote it all the more.[23]

The Jansenists also became associated with neo-Gallican efforts to make the celebration of mass more communal by providing a translation of the Missal (Voisin's translation was condemned by a papal brief of Alexander VII in 1661), by having the canon of the mass prayed aloud, and by having the people respond with an "Amen" to each prayer

---

[21] Louis Bouyer, *Liturgical Piety* (Notre Dame, Ind.: University of Notre Dame Press, 1954), 5–6.

[22] Ibid., 44.

[23] See Klauser, 138.

in the canon. There were also efforts to not have the priest read the parts of the mass silently that the choir sang aloud.[24] Interestingly, these and other neo-Gallican efforts at liturgical reform were not opposed by the Holy See.[25]

Ironically, the Jansenists encouraged one development that worked against the recovery or a more communal celebration of the mass-liturgy. Antoine Arnauld (1612–1694) published *De la fréquente communion* in 1643, in which he argued that thorough preparation should precede the reception of Holy Communion. This book produced a storm of controversy: opponents saw it as a discouragement of more frequent reception of the sacrament and proponents saw it as a restoration of ecclesiastical discipline and as a deepening of piety. Certainly the unintended result was that the more pious Christians abstained from receiving communion for long periods of time.[26]

The reaction to Jansenism also put a brake on the development of diocesan liturgical books that sought to recover old Gallican liturgies, under the permission granted by the Council of Trent to retain liturgical usages that were more than 200 years old at the time. Nevertheless, some neo-Gallican liturgies were published and these recovered some genuinely ancient practices and added to the variety in regional and local liturgical usages.[27]

These neo-Gallican rites were encouraged politically by the policies of King Louis XIV. In the 1680s the theology faculty of the University of Paris affirmed the king's temporal rule over the Church of France in the *Articles gallicans* that were adopted by the Assembly of the Clergy in 1682, and remained in effect during the next 150 years.[28] These articles gave the bishops exclusive jurisdiction over the liturgies in their own dioceses. Even though some bishops maintained and promoted the missal and breviary of Pope Pius V, others created new diocesan liturgies known as "neo-Gallican." The most prominent of these neo-Gallican rites was the Ritual Use of Paris that originated in the liturgical reforms initiated by Archbishop Francois de Harley in the 1670s. With the breviary and missal published by his successor, Charles de Vintmille, in 1736 and 1738 respectively, the Parisian rite assumed the form it was to have until it would be replaced by the Roman rite under the influence of the Ultramontaine movement in the nineteenth century. The task of providing musical settings for the Parisian rite was entrusted to Abbé Lebeuf, canon of Auxerre and the foremost French musicologist of his time. His Paris Antiphoner (1737) and Paris Gradual (1738) contained a repertoire of new and traditional chant that remained the basis of Parisian liturgical music until the mid-nineteenth century.[29] The last editions of these chant books were published in 1829 and 1846, respectively.

---

[24] The defense of silent prayers was taken up by Pierre LeBrun, *Explication de la Messe* (Paris, 1716–1726), IV, 226–520, who thought that silent prayer could be found even in the earliest centuries of the church.

[25] See F. Cabrol, "Liturgies néo-gallicanes," *Liturgia* (Paris, 1935), 864–70.

[26] See Louis Cognet, *Le Jansénisme* (Paris: Presses Universitaires de France, 1964), 44.

[27] See F. Ellen Weaver, "The Neo-Gallican Liturgies Revisited," *Studia Liturgica* 16 (1986–87), 54–72.

[28] See Aimé-Georges Martimort, *Le Gallicanisme* (Paris: Presses universitaires de France, 1973), 79–103.

[29] See Benjamine Van Wye, "Organ Music in the Mass of the Parisian Rite to 1850 with Emphasis on the Contributions of Boëly," in *French Organ Music From the Revolution to Franck and Widor*, ed. by Lawrence Archbald and William J. Peterson (University of Rochester, 1995), 19ff.

The recovery of Gallican liturgical usages was made possible by the prodigious historical scholarship into the early sources of the liturgy which went on in France during this period. It would not be a mistake to see this as the first liturgical movement. The Renaissance interest in antiquarian research and historical scholarship continued into the seventeenth century. The certainty of liturgical tradition was shored up by means of the great historical discoveries and publications that advanced liturgical science. It is generally held that the father of this science is Giovanni Cardinal Bona (1609–1674). While editions of ancient Greek and Latin texts had been published throughout the sixteenth and seventeenth centuries (for example, Goar's *Euchologion*), it was Bona who brought them all together in an historical synthesis. The first of his principal two works, dealing with the divine office, is *De divina Psalmodia* (first published in Rome in 1653, under the title *Psallentis Ecclesiae harmonia*; and republished in Paris in 1663 under the auspices of the Maurist Benedictines). His second principal work, dealing with the mass, was *De sacrosancto Missae sacrificio disquisitiones historicae* (1671). The collected works of Bona were published in Antwerp in 1673, and in Cologne 1674, under the title *Rerum liturgicarum libri duo*. An important edition of these volumes was published by the Cistercian Robert Sala in Turin, from 1747–1753, with many new texts and some commentary spoiled by polemics.

Next we must mention the work of Giuseppe-Maria Cardinal Tommasi (1649–1713). His *Codices sacramentorum nongentis annis vetustiores* (Rome, 1680) includes texts of the Gelasian Sacramentary, the Gregorian Sacramentary, the *Missale Gothicum*, the *Missale Francorum*, and the *Missale gallicorum vetus*. These manuscripts had all been consulted by Bona, for they were in Roman libraries, but Tommasi was the first to publish them. He also published a critical study of the Roman Antiphonary in 1688 and a summarizing study of mass texts, *Antiqui libri missarum romanae ecclesiae* (1691).

Of greater importance in the publication of ancient liturgical texts was Dom Jean Mabillon (1632–1707), a French Benedictine of the Congregation of Saint-Maur. Two of his publications of immense importance for liturgical study are *De liturgica gallicani libri III* (Paris, 1685), which contains in Book II the Luxeuil Lectionary, which he discovered and edited; and *Museum italicum* (1687ff.), which includes in the first tome the Bobbio Missal, while the second contains the *Ordines romani* that he found.[30]

After Mabillon the following deserve mention:

- Dom E. Martene, *De Antiquis Ecclesiae Ritibus* (Rouen, 1700–1702), which gives many details about liturgical usages especially in French cathedrals and dioceses.
- Pierre LeBrun, *Explication des prieres et des ceremonies de la Messe* (Paris, 1716–1726), which makes available editions of old Roman and Gallican sacramentaries and also provides in Book IV, as we have indicated, a text of the *Liturgia svecanae ecclesiae catholicae et orthodoxae conformis* (1576), noting its provision of a silent canon.
- L. A. Muraturi, *Liturgia Romana Vetus* (Venice, 1748), which provides further texts of old Roman and Gallican sacramentaries.

---

[30] Mabillon's entire collection of the *Ordines romani* is reproduced in Migne, P.L. 78, cols. 837–1371,

- J. A. Assemani, *Codex liturgicus Ecclesiae universalis* in *XV libros distributus*, of which only thirteen volumes appeared (Rome, 1749–1765), which includes Eastern as well as Western texts.

The publication of Assemani's *Codex liturgicus* was the end of a prodigious period of scientific liturgical scholarship that, however, had little consequence on liturgical revision until the twentieth century. Indeed, it did not occur to these great historians and antiquarians that their work might have some impact on the forms and texts of the liturgies of the church. Apart from a few Jansenist and neo-Gallican efforts, it did not occur to these scholars to try to recover the sense of liturgy as "the work of the people." To whatever extent these ancient sources were drawn into actual church life, it was primarily to provide ammunition for use against Protestant doctrines and practices. Louis Bouyer may be right that a centralized liturgical authority maintaining the Tridentine consensus prevented a truly creative, but risky, adaptation of the Roman liturgy to Baroque or Enlightenment conceptions of liturgy, sacraments, and solemnity, since the contrast between Baroque and Classical spirituality and that of the ancient liturgy was so great as to set apart two different worlds.

Lutheran Church Orders and Agendas

The Impact of the Thirty Years' War

The post-Reformation period of orthodoxy in Lutheranism (from roughly the publication of *The Book of Concord* in 1580 through the early eighteenth century) did not witness any creative development of liturgical orders. Once the forms of worship achieved final shape in the various church orders of the sixteenth century, they tended to remain intact, with only modest changes in the direction of simplification as the age of orthodoxy wore on. To a great extent this reflected not only Lutheran conservatism in general, but Lutheran competition with Calvinism.

Politically, the Lutheran position within the Holy Roman Empire was secure, and Calvinist inroads in Germany were minimal. The Lutheran leaders were content to hold their own. But the sloth and intemperance of many of the Lutheran courts encouraged reformers among the princes to embrace the more ascetic attitudes of Calvinism, first by the Elector Palatine and later by the Elector of Brandenburg, as well as the Landgrave of Hesse-Cassel and the Count of Nassau. It was the animosity between Lutheran and Calvinistic princes that encouraged Duke Maximilian of Bavaria to form a Catholic League against the Protestants and the new Emperor Ferdinand to attempt to reorganize the Empire and restore Catholicism to at least its position in 1555.[31] This led to the Thirty Years' War, which had as profound an impact on Lutheran liturgy as it did on church life in general.

The immediate cause of the outbreak of the Thirty Years' War was the rebellion of the Bohemian Protestants against the election of Ferdinand as their king, and their turning to the Elector Frederick of the Palatinate as their rival candidate. Because of

---

[31] See David Kaiser, *Politics and War: European Conflict from Philip II to Hitler* (Cambridge: Harvard University Press, 1990), 83ff.

limited resources available to him as emperor, Ferdinand had to draw upon the military resources of the Spanish Hapsburgs, the wealthy and militantly Catholic Duke Maximilian of Bavaria, and military entrepreneurs within the Empire such as Tilly and Wallenstein to put down the rebellion. Duke Maximilian took the opportunity to seize the electoral dignity from his cousin Frederick of the Palatinate, and that drew the German Protestants to his defense. The arrival of Spanish troops in Germany, however, caused Catholic France under the leadership of Cardinal Richelieu to throw its support to the German Protestants. The military successes of imperial troops under Tilly and Wallenstein brought into the war, first King Christian IV of Denmark, who was also military governor of Holstein, and then King Gustav II Adolf of Sweden.[32] Rivalry between Denmark and Sweden (they had been at war with each other in 1611–1613) prevented unified action. In addition, Gustavus Adolphus had designs on Poland, whose king was his cousin Sigismund III, son of his uncle King Johan III. Sigismund's court had been a source of Counter-Reformation activity in Scandinavia.[33] Thus, Germany became a battleground in which Spaniards, Frenchmen, Austrians, Bohemians, Germans, Danes, and Swedes contended in a chaotic, protracted struggle. While the leading figures were looking out for their own political interests, this was sometimes merged with religious devotion and even fanaticism.

It is not true, as is sometimes claimed, that the war ended in a stalemate. The Peace of Westphalia in 1648 did not just restore the situation as it existed in 1618. While in other nations the centralized state was becoming more powerful, Germany became more decentralized. Each principality now declared itself a sovereign state with the right to wage war and make peace. Alsace, with the exception of the free city of Strasbourg, was ceded to France. Sweden acquired the western parts of Pomerania and the ports at the mouths of the major rivers emptying into the Baltic. The acquisition of territory within the boundaries of the Empire enabled France and Sweden to intervene in imperial matters at any time. Brandenburg added the eastern parts of Pomerania to its territory, along with the bishoprics of Magdeburg, Halberstadt, and Minden, and thus began its territorial expansion—and its need for religious toleration to accommodate territories with Calvinist populations. The electorate of the Palatinate was divided in two, so that the Duke of Bavaria acquired the electoral dignity of the Upper Palatinate and the Lower Palatinate was returned to the Count Palatine. Full sovereignty was given to the United Provinces of Switzerland. And perhaps most significantly, Calvinists, at the insistence of the Elector of Brandenburg, were given equal status with Lutherans and Roman Catholics in the Empire.[34]

Germany itself, however, was left in ruins by the war. Marches, countermarches, invasions, occupations, evacuations, sieges of towns and cities, and other military maneuvers converted whole regions into deserts. Whole populations were decimated

---

[32] A good brief narrative of the war can be found in *The New Cambridge Modern History*, IV (Cambridge: University Press, 1957–1979), 306–58. A leading study of the Thirty Years' War is the book of that title by Geoffrey Parker.

[33] See Michael Roberts, *Gustavus Adolphus: A History of Sweden, 1611–1632*, 2 vols. (London, 1958).

[34] Friedrich, *The Age of the Baroque*, op. cit., 192; Parker, *The Thirty Years' War*, 217.

by famine and disease if not by outright slaughter and the burning of towns and villages. The worst devastated lands were Bohemia, Wuerttemberg, Saxony, and Thuringia. In Wuerttemberg alone the number of men capable of bearing arms had dropped from 65,400 in 1623 to 14,800 in 1653. Half of all the buildings were destroyed. The total population of Germany had been reduced by between thirty and fifty percent.[35]

This had as deleterious an effect on church life as on civic life. Church buildings and books were destroyed, there was a shortage of pastors, and congregations were demoralized. Not only were church orders lost or destroyed, but so were medieval missals, breviaries, antiphonaries, and other liturgical books on which the full performance of Lutheran liturgy depended. It should be remembered that the church orders were not worship books as such; they were manuals that provided rubrical directions. Though they might prescribe the introits, collects, graduals, and so forth, the church orders did not provide the texts or music of these propers. As Luther Reed noted, "The clergy and the choirmaster were expected to find them in the older liturgical books."[36] The loss of these books meant that new books had to be published that would provide these texts and musical settings, and the inevitable result was simplification. Fewer options were made available in the new books and some pre-Reformation treasures were lost to Lutheranism.

Moreover, in the face of ignorance, lawlessness, and competition from Calvinism, church leaders sought to bring order into chaos by enforcing catechesis, attendance at worship, and doctrinal preaching. Fines were imposed for noncompliance and nonattendance. Relations between church and state were such that civil offenders were sentenced by the courts to go to confession and receive the sacrament. As Reed noted, "With the hardening and narrowing of its intellectual life went the externalization of worship and the neglect of spiritual quality in everyday life and conduct."[37] So while the forms of worship were generally restored, the spirit that characterized the first century of Lutheran church life was not restored.

Nevertheless, it would be a mistake to characterize this church life as "lifeless," as Reed and others have done. Theologians such as Johann Gerhard (1582–1637) rivaled Thomas Aquinas and John Calvin in the systematic scope of their work. Gerhard and others also produced a body of devotional writings that sought to recover a Pauline "Christ in us" mysticism without compromising the "Christ for us" proclamation emphasized in Lutheran theology.[38] The greatest devotional book was the *True Christianity* of Johann Arndt (1555–1621).[39] Arndt succeeded in recovering for Lutheran spirituality the Augustinian mystical tradition represented by Bernard of Clairvaux and Johann Tauler, a tradition also to be found in Luther's writings although undeveloped there.[40] We shall see that there was a prodigious outpouring of hymns that gave expression to a confident faith

---

[35] See Günther Franz, *Der Dreissigjährige Krieg und das deutsche Volk* (Stuttgart, 1961). Parker, *The Thirty Years' War*, pp. 210f. argues for a more conservative figure of fifteen to twenty percent.

[36] Luther Reed, *The Lutheran Liturgy*, op. cit., 143.

[37] Ibid.

[38] See Frank C. Senn, ed., *Protestant Spiritual Traditions* (Mahwah, N.J.: Paulist Press, 1986), 43ff.

[39] Johann Arndt, *True Christianity*, trans. with an introduction by Peter Erb (New York: Paulist Press, 1979).

[40] See Bengt R. Hoffman, *Luther and the Mystics* (Minneapolis: Augsburg Publishing House, 1976).

in the midst of trial and tribulation, especially in the verse of the great poet Paul Gerhardt (1606–1676). But generally speaking theology had become scholastic and polemical and the people were drilled in the catechism and required to attend worship by law rather than by evangelical persuasion.

The Pietist Reaction

There was bound to be a reaction to this. It came in the form of Pietism, a program of reform and renewal that sought "to convert the outward orthodox confession into an inner living theology of the heart."[41] The pre-history of Pietism is to be found in the efforts of Johann Arndt and other devotional writers to inject a mystical element into Lutheranism so that Christian moral life would be enlivened in a tradition that, by emphasizing the objective or forensic doctrine of justification, left human beings passive in their faith-relationship with God. The fundamental document of Pietism was the *Pia Desideria* of Philipp Jacob Spener (1635–1705).[42] This was originally published in 1666 as a long introduction to a collection of Arndt's sermons. It was republished as a separate piece in 1675. It contains all of the crucial themes of Pietism and its program of practical reform. Part I analyzes the defects in the civil authorities, in the clergy, and in the common people in terms of public morals, church teaching, and Christian witness. Part II offers six proposals to better conditions in the church: (1) "a more extensive use of the Word of God among us," including opportunities for the continuous reading of the Bible in church and a gathering of small groups to study the scriptures or discuss the sermons with a minister; (2) "the establishment and diligent exercise of the spiritual priesthood," including the provision of volunteer lay assistance for overburdened pastors; (3) a call for an emphasis on the practice rather than just the knowledge of the Christian faith, which included the suggestion that each Christian have a confessor or spiritual director; (4) a more loving and less polemical engagement with unbelievers and heretics; (5) a reform of the schools and universities in order to train men for the ministry "who, above all, are true Christians and . . . have the divine wisdom to guide others carefully on the way of the Lord;" and (6) the provision for practical experience in the training of candidates for the ministry.

We recognize almost contemporary ideas in these proposals for Bible study groups, lay ministries, practical Christianity, ecumenism based on Christian love rather than dogma alone, seminaries as places of spiritual formation, and seminary curricula that provide practical experience in ministry. It was Spener's disciple, August Hermann Francke (1663–1727), who organized Pietism into a movement with its characteristic *collegia pietatis* (conventicles), which functioned like Bible study or support groups. Both Spener and Francke were driven out of Saxony because of distrust of the pietistic conventicles. They were given asylum in Brandenburg by Elector Frederick III. Francke

---

[41] See F. Ernest Stoeffler, *The Rise of Evangelical Pietism* (Leiden: E. J. Brill, 1965). For a succinct survey of this movement see John Weborg, "Pietism: 'The Fire of God which . . . Flames in the Heart of Germany,'" in Senn, ed., *Protestant Spiritual Traditions*, op. cit., 188–216.

[42] Philip Jacob Spener, *Pia Desideria*, trans. with an introduction by Theodore G. Tappert (Philadelphia: Fortress Press, 1964).

especially became instrumental in developing the newly founded University of Halle and the charitable institutions and mission societies of that city. Unfortunately, Francke unleashed the more intolerant aspects of Pietism, including his disputes with Christian Thomasius of Leipzig, his struggle against the philosopher Christian Wolff that led to the latter's expulsion from Halle by King Friedrich Wilhelm I, the controversy with Valentin Ernst Loescher (1718), and the withholding of Holy Communion from the "unconverted."

The idea of an *ecclesiola in ecclesia* (little church in the church) was given specialized and spectacular form on the estate of Count Nicholas von Zinzendorf (1700–1760) at Berthelsdorf near Dresden, which he opened up to refugees from Moravia in 1722 and named *Herrnhut* (the Lord's Watch). To this community came Lutherans, Reformed, Brethren, Separatists, and even Roman Catholics. Zinzendorf became the de facto bishop of this community and eventually led his Moravians to North America. Johann Albrecht Bengel (1687–1752), as superintendent (bishop) and member of the Supreme Church Council of Württemberg, was able to domesticate Pietism and bring it into the parish system so that by the middle of the eighteenth century it was not uncommon to find evidence of Pietism in parish church life.

Pietism did not have a liturgical program of its own with which to replace that of orthodoxy, but its emphases did have a profound impact on public worship. Jeremiah F. Ohl has summarized the "destructive processes" unleashed on the public cultus by Pietism by noting that "the personal, subjective element and individual experience were struggling for expression."[43] In the various influences of Pietism we again see concerns that have surfaced in recent years. The personal character and spiritual maturity of the officiating minister were emphasized to an extent that undermined confidence in the efficacy of the word itself. Because Pietism emphasized the sincerity of faith, it unleashed a distrust of external ritual forms that are performed just for the sake of performing them. Pietists were not in a position to abandon or replace authorized worship books, but they were in a position to influence the conduct of public worship and the development of new resources. Thus, Pietist influences were evident at points in the liturgy where extempore prayer could be offered, as in the pulpit office, and where hymns could be selected. The old objective church hymns, which celebrated the saving acts of God in Christ, were set aside in favor of hymns that concentrated on the conditions of the soul. As new hymnals were published, they were arranged according to the theological order of salvation rather than the liturgical calendar and church year. New melodies, better suited to the emotional character of Pietist hymn texts, replaced the old chorales. And in church music a homophonic choral style replaced the old polyphonic choral music, and sentimental arias patterned after the popular operatic literature replaced the old recitatives (even though Pietist preachers would exhort their congregations not to attend the opera or the theater). As Ohl stated in his insightful essay,

---

[43] Jeremiah F. Ohl, "The Liturgical Deteriorization of the Seventeenth and Eighteen Centuries," *Memoirs of the Lutheran Liturgical Association* IV (1901–1902), 70.

in a word, what Pietism set out to do finally resulted not in bringing about again a proper union between the objective and the subjective, but in the overthrow of the former and the triumph of the latter. The sacramental and the sacrificial were divorced, and the sacrificial alone remained. Public worship ceased to be a celebration of redemption, and became only an act of edification. From one extreme of a frigid orthodoxy and its resultant formalism, the pendulum had swung to the other extreme of an emotional piety that regarded all fixed forms and churchly order as a detriment to spiritual life, and a hindrance to its expression.[44]

Not only was Pietism as rigid in its view of Christian life as was orthodoxy in its articulation of Christian doctrine, but the prescription may actually have been stronger than the disease warranted. There actually were numerous demands for reform in orthodox Lutheran circles. These were directed not toward the liturgical orders but toward the worshiper. According to Frederick Kalb, the "decisive theme of demand for reform of the divine service" in orthodoxy was to emphasize "the harmony of heart and deed," and this entailed "a demand directed not to the divine service but to *man* taking part in it."[45] In other words, the best of Lutheran orthodoxy sought a right relationship between "inner worship" and "outer worship." But this concern for "worship in spirit and in truth" required, in orthodox eyes, no need to alter or disrupt the forms and orders of public worship. Rather, one had to regard the "Spirit and truth" embedded in the historic orders and conform one's life to the testimony of the liturgy. Pietism, on the other hand, saw a need for forms that would make some impact on the spiritual formation of the worshiper.

Liturgical Life in Orthodox Leipzig

The most orthodox of Lutheran territories was Saxony. Orthodoxy flourished there well into the eighteenth century at a time when it had been abandoned elsewhere in favor of a full-fledged Pietism or an incipient Rationalism. Yet the picture of church life in Leipzig, in the heart of orthodox Saxony, belies the accusation of "lifeless" that is often attached as a modifier of "orthodoxy," in light of Günther Stiller's thorough examination of the liturgical life in that city at the time of J. S. Bach.[46] One of Stiller's main sources is the handwritten notebook kept by Johann Christoph Rost, who served as sexton of Saint Thomas Church from 1716–1739, during part of the time in which Bach served as cantor (1723–1750).[47] The sexton's notes scrupulously detail the types of services held on Sundays, weekdays, festivals, and days of devotion, and the provisions needed for those services. Successive sextons added to Rost's notes, so that we have a detailed picture of liturgical life in that city up to 1820, and may contrast the vigor of liturgical life in the

---

[44] Ibid., 70–1.

[45] F. Kalb, *Theology of Worship in 17th Century Lutheranism*, trans. by H. P. A. Hamann (St. Louis: Concordia Publishing House, 1965), 159.

[46] See Günther Stiller, *Johann Sebastian Bach and Liturgical Life in Leipzig*, ed. by Robin A. Leaver, trans. by H. J. A. Bouman, D. F. Poellot, and H. C. Oswald (St. Louis: Concordia Publishing House, 1984).

[47] Ibid., 35ff. An earlier attempt to investigate liturgical life in Leipzig was by Charles Sanford Terry, *Johann Sebastian Bach: Cantata Texts Sacred and Secular, with a Reconstruction of the Leipzig Liturgy of his Period* (London, 1926).

period of orthodoxy with its rapid decline at the end of the eighteenth century under a Rationalist pastor.

What we see in Leipzig was a full round of liturgical services coordinated among the churches of the city. On Sundays, Matins was sung by the choristers in Latin, followed by the Service of Holy Communion at 7:00 or 8:00 A.M. If the number of communicants was great, this Service could last three to four hours. This was followed by a Noon Service, which was apparently a preaching service. In mid-afternoon Vespers was sung in Latin by the choristers. There were prayer services with preaching on the catechism every day of the week at the various churches, with a communion service on Wednesday mornings at Saint Nicholas Church and on Thursday mornings at Saint Thomas Church to accommodate the people who were not able to receive the sacrament on Sundays. There was also a penitential service with sermon on Friday mornings at Saint Nicholas.[48]

The number of weekday services was considerably higher during weeks when the festivals or days of devotion of the church year were observed. These days included the three chief festivals of Christmas, Easter, and Pentecost with two or three special days following each one, as well as the days of Holy Week. They also included the following greater or lesser festivals that were observed either with the Communion Service, Vespers, or both: Saint Stephen the Proto-martyr (December 26), Saint John the Apostle (December 27), Holy Innocents (December 28), the Circumcision of Jesus on New Year's Day (January 1), the Epiphany (January 6), the Purification of Mary and Presentation of Jesus (February 2), the Annunciation (March 25), the Ascension, Holy Trinity, the Nativity of Saint John the Baptist (June 24), the Visitation of Mary (July 2), and Michaelmas (September 29). Vespers was sung on the eve of each of these festivals, in Latin and without a sermon, and Holy Communion was celebrated on the day of the festival, with a sermon but without catechetical instruction. We also note that the proper eucharistic preface was always sung on these days, as Bugenhagen had provided in his church orders.[49]

The orders of worship observed in Leipzig differed little from the Reformation church orders. The offices of Matins and Vespers included three psalms with antiphons, scripture reading with responsory, appropriate gospel canticle, and collects. The other prayer services during the week were more free-form, including hymns, scripture reading, sermon, and various prayer forms (e.g., litanies, collects, hymns, and prayers based on the catechism). The chief Service of Holy Communion, in typical Lutheran fashion, admitted of considerable variation of style in its individual parts:[50]

> Hymn sung by congregation or Introit sung by choir (to plainsong or
>   polyphonic setting)
> Kyrie sung by choir (to plainsong or polyphonic setting) or the hymn "Kyrie,
>   Gott Vater in Ewigkeit" sung by congregation
> Gloria sung by minister and choir (to plainsong or polyphonic setting) or the
>   hymn "Allein Gott in der Höh" by congregation

---

[48] Ibid., 48ff.
[49] Ibid., 55ff.
[50] Ibid., 108ff.

> Salutation and Collect
> Epistle
> The Hymn of the Day *(Hauptlied)*
> Gospel
> Cantata sung by choir, usually based on the Gospel and the Hymn of the Day
>   (note: Bach always provided a text for the congregation to follow)
> Nicene Creed and/or Creedal hymn, "Wir glauben all an einen Gott"
> Sermon
> Conclusion of Hauptlied or Cantata

There were two different forms of the liturgy of the sacrament:
On Sundays and Festivals:

> General Prayer
> Sung Preface (with proper) and Sanctus (polyphonic setting)
> Lord's Prayer (sung by the minister)
> Words of Institution (sung by the minister)

On weekdays:

> Lord's Prayer
> Words of Institution
> (During Lent: Exhortation to the communicants preceded the Preface)
> Ministration of Holy Communion during which hymns are sung
> Post-Communion Collect
> Benediction
> Closing Hymn

Ministers customarily wore a white ankle-length surplice over a black cassock. The celebrant at Holy Communion wore a chasuble in the color of the day or season throughout the service, although the liturgical color scheme is not one we would recognize (e.g., green on Palm Sunday and Maundy Thursday).[51] As we might assume during the cantorship of J. S. Bach, the church music was exceptionally rich. The services were well attended and the number of communicants was high, especially when contrasted with later Rationalism. During the period of Bach's cantorship (1723–1750) the yearly number of communions at Saint Nicholas and Saint Thomas Churches ranged from 14,000 to 18,000 each. These figures remained constant throughout the eighteenth century until the Rationalist Johann Georg Rosenmüller was installed as pastor in 1786, at which point they dipped to 10,000. By the end of Rosenmüller's tenure in 1815, yearly communions were down to 3,000—and this in spite of the fact that reception of communion was removed from private confession and the communion office was being detached from the service itself. In a few instances Holy Communion was even administered in the sacristy for the few communicants who registered to receive the sacrament.[52] This data belies any thought of a "lifeless" or "sterile" worship life during the age of orthodoxy in contrast with the more "relevant" worship of the age of rationalism.

---

[51] Ibid., 65.
[52] Ibid., 131–7, 164–5, 260–3.

Lutheran Liturgy in the North American Colonies

This orthodox Lutheran liturgical tradition was established in North America by Lutheran settlers, especially in the colony of New Sweden along the Delaware River. This colony was Sweden's attempt, during the reigns of Gustavus Adolphus and his daughter Christina, to assert Sweden's new role as a world power by entering the colonizing business. But Sweden's colony lasted only about twenty years before it was taken over, first by the Dutch from New Netherlands under its Governor, Peter Stuyvesant, and then by the British. But Swedish and Finnish settlers remained after their colony passed into the hands of the Dutch and then English, and they continued to maintain public worship, teach the catechism to their children, and call pastors. There was, in fact, a resurgence of interest in Sweden in providing pastors to the Swedish-speaking congregations at the end of the seventeenth century. The eventual drift of these congregations into the Anglican (later called the Protestant Episcopal) church may have had less to do with the issue of language (although the descendants of the Swedish immigrants were losing the use of their mother tongue and were increasingly using English, the language of the colonies) than with their concern to align themselves with the more orthodox, "church"-type groups. They were opposed to the pietistic, "meeting house"-type groups who were quickly populating Pennsylvania under the liberal settlement policies of the Quaker Proprietor, William Penn. The Church of England was having as difficult a time establishing and maintaining itself in Pennsylvania and Maryland as the Lutherans ministered to by the Church of Sweden, but Swedish immigration had pretty much stopped whereas Anglicans continued to settle.[53] Penn had encouraged dissenting and persecuted religious groups to settle in his colony. In addition to his Quaker friends this included the Mennonites, Amish, Brethren, Schwenkfelders, and other "Plain People" of Anabaptist persuasion, as well as the Zinzendorf Moravians and the German Reformed from the Palatinate.[54] With the revocation of the Edict of Nantes in 1685, large numbers of French Huguenots fled to the Palatinate and other parts of Germany where the Reformed faith flourished. With word of Penn's invitation, however, large numbers of them emigrated to Pennsylvania and also to New York, where the Dutch Reformed already flourished.[55] Lutherans came later for economic rather than religious reasons (except for the persecuted Salzburgers, who settled in Georgia[56]). The Lutheran position in the English American colonies was an advantageous one because of close connections with the Church of England. As early as 1692, Saint Mary's Church in the Savoy in London was established as a Lutheran chapel through the patronage of Prince George of Denmark, consort to Queen Anne. With the death of Queen Anne, the English monarchy passed to the Lutheran House of Hannover. A theological consultation at the time of the accession

---

[53] See Richard Hulan, "New Sweden and Its Churches," *Lutheran Quarterly* II/1 (1988), 3–33.

[54] See Frederic Klees, *The Pennsylvania Dutch* (New York: The Macmillan Co., 1952).

[55] See H. M. J. Klein, *The History of the Eastern Synod of the Reformed Church in the United States* (Lancaster, 1943).

[56] See the chapter on "The Salzburger Frontier" in Ted Morgan, *Wilderness at Dawn: The Settling of the North American Continent* (New York: Simon and Shuster, 1993), 165–92.

of George I found that, except on the issue of episcopacy, the Lutheran Confessions and the Anglican Articles of Religion were in substantial agreement. With the provision of episcopal ordination, German Lutheran pastors could serve Lutheran congregations in Anglican Virginia. One of these pastors, Peter Gabriel Muhlenberg, was the son of Henry Melchior Muhlenberg and later became a Revolutionary War general.

The work of the elder Muhlenberg, called the "patriarch of American Lutheranism," was remarkable. Educated in Göttingen, Henry Melchior Muhlenberg went to the Pietist center at Halle for training as a missionary to India. August Hermann Francke was in receipt of a request for a pastor from three congregations in Pennsylvania, who threatened to join the Moravians if a pastor was not forthcoming soon. Francke persuaded Muhlenberg to accept this "call." The three Pennsylvania congregations were not expecting him when Muhlenberg arrived in 1742. He had to gain their acceptance and also serve other congregations to save them from vagabond "pastors" or Zinzendorf's influence. We might note that while Muhlenberg was considered a Pietist, he had misgivings about the wisdom of Lutherans and Reformed from the same German homelands (such as the Upper Rhineland) erecting union church buildings for economic reasons. But to tend to all of these scattered Lutheran congregations, he had to travel by horseback hundreds of miles each week. He set up parochial schools and, in the absence of schoolmasters, often taught the children himself. Within six years, in 1748, he organized the first Lutheran synodical body in America, the Ministerium of Pennsylvania. The six pastors present (including the Swedish dean or provost, Carl Magnus Wrangel) and the lay representatives of nine congregations adopted a form of governance, participated in the dedication of Saint Michael's Church in Philadelphia (the largest church building in the English colonies at the time of its dedication), ordained a candidate for the ministry, and adopted a liturgy prepared by Muhlenberg.[57]

The liturgy presented and authorized was patterned after the old Lutheran use of the Savoy Chapel in London. Muhlenberg noted that "to adopt the Swedish liturgy did not appear either suitable or necessary since most of our congregations came from districts on the Rhine and the Main and considered the singing of collects to be papistical. Nor could we select a liturgy with regard to every individual's accustomed use, since almost every country town and village has its own."[58] The Order of Service included:[59]

> Hymn of invocation of the Holy Spirit
> Confession of sins: Exhortation, Confession, farsed Kyrie
> Gloria in metrical form: "Allein Gott in der Höh"
> Salutation and Collect for the Day
> Epistle (Marburg lectionary)
> Hymn of the Day
> Gospel

---

[57] See E. Clifford Nelson, *The Lutherans in North America* (Philadelphia; Fortress Press, 1975), 49ff.

[58] *The Journals of Henry Melchior Muhlenberg*, ed. by Theodore G. Tappert and John W. Doberstein (Philadelphia: Fortress, Press, 1942–1958), I, 193f.

[59] See Luther Reed, *The Lutheran Liturgy*, op. cit., 167–8.

Metrical Creed: "Wir Glauben All"
> (The Gospel and Creed were omitted on the occasion of a baptism, because the order for baptism included a gospel text and a creedal profession of faith.)

The Pulpit Office:
> Hymn
> Sermon
> General Prayer, with special intercessions, or Litany
> Lord's Prayer
> Announcements
> Votum: "The peace of God which passes all understanding . . ."
> Hymn

Salutation and closing collect
Aaronic benediction with Trinitarian invocation

Holy Communion was definitely appointed for Christmas, Easter, and Pentecost, and, of course, whenever a circuit-riding pastor could be present. When the sacrament was celebrated, the following order was observed after the pulpit office:

Preface and abbreviated Sanctus
Exhortation (from Luther's *Deutsche Messe*)
Lord's Prayer
Words of Institution
Invitation to communion (from the London liturgy)
Ministration
Versicle and post-communion collect (from Luther's *Deutsche Messe*)
Aaronic benediction with Trinitarian invocation

In addition to the German text of this Service, English orders of baptism and marriage were provided from the *Book of Common Prayer*. Muhlenberg himself may have been a convinced Pietist, but the orders of service he provided reflected the orthodox Lutheran liturgical tradition in his German homeland. His *Agenda* was circulated in handwritten form and was used for forty years among Lutherans who rubbed shoulders with Quaker, Anabaptist, and Pietist neighbors, and who often shared church buildings with the Reformed.

Anglican Liturgy through the Restoration

The Church of England in the age of orthodoxy sought comprehension. This should not be interpreted as a liberal policy. Comprehension was as hard-line a position in the Anglican tradition as transubstantiation was in the Roman Catholic tradition or justification by faith in the Lutheran. The political situation in England during the forty-five year reign of Queen Elizabeth I required it. The midland and eastern counties, the bustling port cities, and London itself were solidly Protestant. But from the beginning of Elizabeth's reign in 1558 a party of Catholic reaction, resting on the embers of feudal prerogative and local conservatism (especially in the northern and western counties), fanned by Spanish intrigue and secret missions undertaken by priests, kept the Protestants on edge. But the lessening of the Roman Catholic threat with the execution of the Catholic

Mary Queen of Scots in 1587 and the defeat of the Spanish Armada in 1588 emboldened those Protestants who felt that the English church was not sufficiently reformed according to the doctrines of John Calvin that they had learned while in exile in Geneva during the reign of Mary I.

Comprehension meant including in one church those with both Catholic and Puritan spiritualities. The threat of civil war, such as England had experienced in the fifteenth century, prompted most English people to pray for one church under one gracious sovereign. To that end there was widespread agreement that there should be one *Book of Common Prayer* and one English Bible as imposed by the Act of Uniformity at the beginning of Elizabeth's reign.

At the accession of James I, however, the Puritans presented a petition calling for the abolition of certain ceremonies and ornaments (such as the sign of the cross in baptism, the marriage ring, and the surplice), which led to the Hampton Court Conference between Puritan leaders and the bishops with the king presiding. While the Puritans called for a number of revisions, the 1604 Prayer Book, issued by royal proclamation rather than a parliamentary act, made few changes beyond stressing the desirability of an ordained minister to officiate at private baptisms and adding a section on the sacraments to the catechism. The Canons of 1604 called for a minimum of three communion services a year and presumed a minimum of ceremony.[60] Of more significance was the call for the revision of the English Bible, which led to the publication of the Authorized Version in 1611.[61] While the church warded off Catholic plots, keeping at bay Puritan criticism, a definite style of church life developed. Its most articulate teacher was Richard Hooker, who, in his monumental *Laws of Ecclesiastical Polity* (1594–1597), explicated a theology of the church, its place in society, and the value of participation in its life. A style of Anglican cathedral preaching was developed by Lancelot Andrewes, the bishop of Ely, and John Donne, the dean of Saint Paul's. The model of Anglican spirituality and devotion was the country priest and poet George Herbert (1593–1633), whose "many Spiritual Conflicts" are not unlike Luther's *Anfechtungen*.[62] Herbert's poetry also expresses the Anglican *via media*, especially in a poem with a sustained metaphor of two women (churches), one too gaudy and painted (Roman Catholic), the other naked and unkempt (Puritan).[63]

Maintaining a "middle road," even as a matter of conviction, is not always easy to do, and during the reign of the Stuart kings, James I and Charles I, a High Church party developed under the leadership of the Archbishop of Canterbury, William Laud (1573–1645). These High Churchmen could be as critical of the Prayer Book as the Puritans, although for opposite reasons. By and large, they were committed to the ideal of

---

[60] See "Canons of 1604" in J. V. Bullard, ed., *Constitutions and Canons Ecclesiastical 1604* (London: The Faith Press, 1934).

[61] For the records of the Hampton Court Conference see E. Caldwell, *A History of Conferences Connected with the Book of Common Prayer* (Oxford University Press, 1840).

[62] See such poems as "Affliction," "The Temper," and "The Collar." See also the commentary by Paul V. Marshall, "Anglican Spirituality," in Frank C. Senn, ed., *Protestant Spiritual Traditions* (Mahwah, N.J.: Paulist Press, 1986), esp. 139ff.

[63] "The British Church," in *The Works of George Herbert* (Oxford: Clarendon Press, 1964), 109–10.

corporate liturgy and one Prayer Book in one national church.[64] But as opportunity presented itself to recover the pre-Reformation heritage of the Anglican Church, their attempts to return to the old Catholic order often went too far and too fast. It is ironic, however, that when Laud was executed by the Puritans during the Civil War, he died claiming to be a good Protestant just as his predecessor Cranmer had died claiming to be a good Catholic. Among various measures undertaken during the tenure of Archbishop Laud were attempts to reorder the chancels of churches by placing the altar-tables once again in their east wall positions.[65] This became the source of the curious Anglican practice of presiding at the north end of the altar, since the rubric giving this direction in the 1552–1559 Prayer Book envisioned a table placed in the middle of the chancel parallel to the choir pews.

James I and Charles I were kings of Scotland as well as England, and under Charles I and Archbishop Laud there were attempts to unite the churches of these countries. As a step in that direction the king and the archbishop favored the preparation of a worship book for Scotland similar to the *Book of Common Prayer* to replace the *Book of Common Order*. This book was the work of two Scottish bishops and not the work of Laud, although at his trial during the Civil War he stated that he would "neither deny nor be ashamed of it." It was a book closer in order and content to the 1549 than to the 1552 Prayer Book. The lectionary was revised; some Scottish festivals were included; the Authorized Version of the Bible was used; the term "presbyter" replaced the term "priest"; and the communion table was consistently called the "Lord's Table" or the "Holy Table" (the result of Scottish influence). The communion service restored the offertory of the unconsecrated bread and wine; restored thanksgiving for the saints in the Prayer for the Whole State of the Church Militant; inserted the Prayer of Humble Access between the consecration and the distribution; reunited the Prayer of Oblation and the Lord's Prayer with the consecration; provided an epiclesis in the eucharistic prayer; retained only the 1549 formula of administration of the elements, without the 1552 additions; and provided rubrics governing the consecration and consumption of the consecrated elements.[66]

A riot broke out when this book was used in Saint Giles Cathedral in Edinburgh; and a National Covenant was drawn up to repudiate the king's Prayer Book and to call for the abolition of episcopacy. The Scottish Prayer Book of 1537 was never actually used until it was picked up by the Non-Jurors in the eighteenth century. But it was one of the events leading to the outbreak of the Civil War.

The *Book of Common Prayer* was abolished by the English Parliament in 1645, along with the monarchy and the episcopate, and was replaced by *A Directory for the Publique Worship of God.* When King Charles II and the episcopate were restored in 1660, it was inevitable that the Prayer Book would also be restored.

---

[64] See Harry Boone Porter, *Jeremy Taylor, Liturgist (1613–1667)* (Alcuin Club/S.P.C.K., 1979), 8ff.

[65] See G. W. O. Addleshaw and F. Etchells, *The Architectural Setting of Anglican Worship* (London: Faber, 1948), chapters. 4–6.

[66] See Gordon Donaldson, *The Making of the Scottish Prayer Book of 1537* (Edinburgh: University Press, 1954); text on 168ff.

It will seem more appropriate to discuss the English Civil War and the Commonwealth in the next section. Here it is important to note that revolution was in the air in the 1640s. Already in 1636–1637 there were peasant revolts in southern and western France, and in 1640 there were revolts of the Catalans, Portuguese, Neapolitans, and Irish—two years before the actual outbreak of Civil War in England. The Thirty Years' War was still raging in central Europe, and its cessation did not really bring peace to Europe. Civil war broke out in France, territorial war was waged in north Germany, and there was war between England and the Netherlands. This widespread unrest contributed to economic hard times, famine, and heavy taxes. There was inevitable reaction; people longed for the return of centralized royal authority. Even so, all was not lost. The condition for the restoration of the monarchy in England and Scotland was the Declaration of Breda, in which Charles II made it clear that the restored Stuarts would rely on a "free Parliament" under the new order.

The political balance between king and Parliament is also reflected in the content of the 1662 *Book of Common Prayer*. The High Church party would have liked a Prayer Book that was closer to the 1549 Prayer Book. Some of them, such as Jeremy Taylor, had worked privately on a liturgy during the Commonwealth and Protectorate that took the Liturgy of Saint James as an inspiration.[67] Taylor's eucharistic rite had a preface derived in large measure from the general thanksgiving after the communion, followed by a Sanctus that fused together Isaiah 6:3 and the "worthy is the Lamb" songs in Revelation 4:8–11 and 5:12–13. Interestingly, the preface and Sanctus were followed by the Lord's Prayer (as in some Lutheran mass-orders) and then the Cherubic Hymn. There followed a series of prayers, comprising an invocation of the Holy Spirit (epiclesis), a thanksgiving leading to the words of institution, a prayer of oblation, and communion prayers before the distribution of the elements. There was no attempt to form these prayers into a continuous eucharistic formulary.

All things considered, it was probably wise that these private ventures, with their idiosyncrasies, were not adopted at the Savoy Conference, which was convened in 1661 to work on the restored Prayer Book.[68] Neither were the Presbyterian and Puritan proposals accepted, many of which were similar to those presented in 1604. The Prayer Book as restored in 1662 was substantially what had existed before the Civil War. A nod to the Laudians was the commemoration of the faithful departed in the prayer of the church. In an effort to appease the Puritans, the "Black Rubric" from the 1552 Prayer Book was also restored, although in a slightly amended version that altered "real and essential presence" to "corporeal presence."[69] There was also a certain collusion of liturgical ideas between the High Church "Caroline divines" and the Puritans in that both regarded the liturgy as the "work of the people" rather than a public performance by specialists, and they were opposed to any rebuilding of the rood screens between the chancel and the nave that later enamored Anglo-Catholics. We shall see that Sir Christopher Wren provided the

---

[67] See Porter, *Jeremy Taylor, Liturgy*, op. cit., 71ff.

[68] See W. Jardine Grisbrooke, *Anglican Liturgies of the Seventeenth and Eighteenth Centuries* (London: S.P.C.K., 1958).

[69] See R. T. Beckwith, *Priesthood and Sacrifice* (London: Marcham, 1964), 63 and notes.

perfect architectural expression of this Restoration Anglicanism. His buildings were designed to accommodate, in an open space, the various liturgical functions of prayer, preaching, baptism, and eucharist. Since this Prayer Book remained in use in the Church of England up until the late twentieth century (the proposed revision of the Prayer Book in 1928 was never passed by Parliament), we provide here an outline of the Service of Holy Communion.[70]

> Lord's Prayer, said by the celebrant alone
> Collect for Purity
> Decalogue with English Kyries and response: "Lord, have mercy upon us, and incline our hearts to keep this law."
> Collect for the King
> Collect for the Day
> Epistle
> Gospel
> Nicene Creed (could be sung)
> Sermon or Homily
> Offertory:
>> Scripture sentences
>> Collection of alms
>> Preparation of the elements
>> Intercessions, with commemoration of the departed
> Preparation for Holy Communion:
>> Exhortation to the communicants
>> Invitation to the sacrament
>> General confession of sins
>> General absolution
>> Comfortable Words
> Sursum corda
> Prayer of Consecration:
>> Preface with common or five propers
>> Sanctus
>> Prayer of Humble Access
>> Commemoration of the Passion
>> Words of Institution with manual acts and fraction
> Communion
> Lord's Prayer with doxology
> Oblation or Post-communion thanksgiving
> Gloria
> Peace and Blessing

No introits, graduals, offertories or communion antiphons were provided in the Prayer Book, but in time and in some places hymns were substituted at these points. We note the location of the confession and absolution before the consecration rather than at the beginning of the mass, as a means of preparation for the celebration of the liturgy (although confession and absolution was provided at the beginning of Morning and

---

[70] See W. J. Grisbrooke, *Anglican Liturgies of the Seventeenth and Eighteenth Centuries* (London: S.P.C.K., 1958).

Evening Prayer). Even more than most typical Lutheran liturgies, Luther's recommendations in his *Deutsche Messe* concerning the juxtaposition of the words of institution and the distribution of the sacrament are followed in the English Prayer Book. It is also noteworthy that the Protestant concern that the sacrifice of praise and thanksgiving should properly be offered in *response* to God's grace receives expression in the prayer of thanksgiving and the singing of the Gloria *after* rather than before the ministration of Holy Communion.

It should be remembered, however, that this full Service of Holy Communion was typically celebrated only three or four times a year in most parish churches. An important rubric specified that the Ante-Communion should be celebrated on Sundays and festivals, if there were no communicants. Evensong was also typically held on Sundays, but there is not much evidence from this period that parish clergy observed the rubric calling for the daily recitation of Morning and Evening Prayer. However, it should be remembered that these prayer services had not been in use for fifteen years during the government of the Commonwealth; that many church buildings were in a deplorable state; that organs had been destroyed and choir schools abolished, which might have provided for a choral office; and that the Restoration occurred just at the beginning of the influence of Deism in England, when revealed religion and its cultus was increasingly despised, as we shall see in the next chapter.

Efforts to impose conformity to the situation of the Restoration saw the liturgy used for state purposes. The calendar of the Prayer Book included two political holy days: one for the martyrdom of Charles I and the other for the Restoration of Charles II. For the first time episcopal ordination was made an indispensable requirement of ministry in the Church of England. This forced ministers ordained during the Commonwealth to seek reordination; thousands of others, however, simply demitted or were deposed. Even the size of the exodus, or "Great Ejection," did not daunt those who tried to impose conformity to the state church. The Corporation Act and the Test Act required communication according to the liturgy of the *Book of Common Prayer* as a qualification for office in corporations, or civil and military functions. The University Test Acts required subscription to the Articles of Religion and compulsory attendance at the state's liturgies at the universities. Penalties under the Conventicle Acts included banishment and death for engaging in worship other than the state's. A generation of persecution was launched under the restored Stuarts. Thousands languished in prisons (the Baptist, John Bunyan, was imprisoned for twelve years); thousands of others emigrated or were exiled to America; the killings of dissenters in Scotland was as vicious as the persecutions of the French Huguenots under Louis XIV, and James II undertook the suppressions with frank enthusiasm. His efforts to model the English monarchy on the despotism of the French king finally came to disastrous conclusion when the appeal went to William of Orange, Louis XIV's worst enemy, and Europe's most ardent Protestant champion, to come to the throne of England.

The "Glorious Revolution" of 1689 finally brought religious toleration to England; but the implications of the failure of the Savoy Conference to achieve "comprehension" were now apparent. The Church of England was no longer the national church, but merely the largest and most governmentally favored denomination. It had to compete with other legal, self-governing, and self-supporting churches—the Presbyterian, Congregationalist, Baptist, and Society of Friends (Quakers). In Scotland, on the other hand, the accession of a Dutch Calvinist king established the Presbyterian Kirk as the state Church of Scotland, while the Scottish Episcopal Church became one denomination among others. While "Nonconformists" in England still suffered the civil and social disabilities of the Corporation and Test Acts, they were granted legal protection for public worship and freedom of the press to publish their writings. The English state, by the logic explained by John Locke in his *Letters on Toleration*, was on the road toward confessional neutrality.[71]

The Puritan Alternative

Throughout the whole period from the Reformation until the Restoration the *Book of Common Prayer* was attacked by a Puritan minority whose concerns, as James White notes, were primarily liturgical.[72] The controversy between the High Church and Puritan parties of the Church of England (the Puritans, except for the Separatists, were members of the Established Church until the time of the Restoration) was not over theology: all English Protestants were more or less Calvinists. But the Puritans were hyper-Calvinists operating with a biblicism Calvin himself might not have recognized. They wanted the scripture to serve as "the supreme liturgical criterion."[73] Anything else would be human invention and human presumption over against God's instructions. Of course, the Bible is not a liturgical manual, and the Puritans could never agree among themselves what examples and prescriptions in the Bible should be followed. For example, was the Lord's Prayer a text to be recited or a model for extempore prayer?

Perhaps of greater importance for the development of "Free Church" worship was the idea that liturgical decisions should be made at the grassroots level: the congregation. In this the Puritans and Separatists stood removed from the Reformation traditions (Lutheran, Reformed, Anglican), which gave an authoritative role in liturgical matters to wider judicatories or even national conferences, councils, or synods. But they argued that this made worship more relevant to the needs and concerns of the local congregation. This might make it seem impossible to discuss Puritan worship. But sharing occurred among congregations, perhaps above all in order to provide mutual consolation in times of persecution. This resulted in similar orders and even similar prayer forms among them.

One is struck by their concern for frequent celebration of the Lord's Supper. Indeed, Doug Adams begins his study of free church worship in America by stating that "from the landing of the Mayflower through the American Revolution, the majority of free church clergy probably spent more time interacting with worshipers around the

---

[71] See Nichols, *History of Christianity 1650–1950*, op. cit., 59ff.

[72] See James F. White, *Protestant Worship: Traditions in Transition* (Louisville: Westminster/John Knox Press, 1989), 117ff.

[73] Horton Davies, *The Worship of the English Puritans* (Westminster, Md.: Dacre Press, 1948), 49–56.

communion table than they did preaching from pulpits."[74] In this they took over Calvin's preference rather than his practice. They also insisted on the eucharistic presidency of ordained ministers. The Pilgrim Separatists in the Plymouth Bay Colony went without Holy Communion from the time of their arrival in 1620 until 1629, when an ordained minister settled in the colony.

The Pilgrims were in that branch of Puritans known as Separatists. They were, in White's words, "impatient reformers" who separated from the Established Church in their effort to separate themselves from a "corrupt world."[75] Their separation from the Anglican Church also led to their exile from England, and many of them established communities and congregations in the Netherlands. There they not only came into contact with the Dutch Reformed, but with the Anabaptists. The Pilgrims journeyed from Leyden in the Netherlands to Plymouth Bay in New England. That was a spiritual as well as a geographical journey, because practices were developed in Leyden that were taken to the new world. This included not only Answorth's *The Book of Psalms: Englished both in Prose and Metre* (1612), a practice of singing championed by the Dutch Reformed, but also lay exhorting, questioning the preacher, and prophesying, which suggests a Mennonite influence. These practices influenced the Anglican Puritans who settled in Salem and Boston in 1629 and 1630 and also the Baptists who separated from the Plymouth congregation.[76]

The main body of Puritans, however, were not Separatists. They worked within the Established Church to try to carry out a more thorough liturgical reformation than what had occurred during the Edwardian Reformation. Several Anglican bishops were Puritans, including Archbishop Edmund Grindal (1519?–1583) and Bishop Miles Coverdale (1488–1568), although Thomas Cartwright (1535–1603) and Edmund Calamy (1600–1666) contended for a presbyterian polity and John Cotton (1584–1652) and Thomas Nye (1596–1672) fought for a congregationalist polity.[77]

But liturgical issues were more hotly contested than polity issues. Already in 1550 a controversy had erupted over the use or nonuse of vestments in the consecration of Bishop John Hooper. The 1552 Prayer Book can be seen in many respects as a turn in a more thoroughgoing Reformation direction. But the Act of Uniformity of 1559, which restored the Prayer Book, also restored some provisions from the 1549 Prayer Book, including the use of "such ornaments of the church as were in use by authority of Parliament in the second year of the reign of King Edward VI."[78] This seemed to be turning back the clock. The Church Convocation in 1563 protested the use of vestments. Archbishop Parker ordered "a comely surplice with sleeves" at the eucharist instead of the traditional mass vestments, but this did not satisfy the Puritans.

---

[74] Doug Adams, *Meeting House to Camp Meeting. Toward a History of American Free Church Worship from 1620 to 1835* (Austin: The Sharing Company, 1981), 13.

[75] White, 120.

[76] See Adams, 57ff.

[77] White, 123.

[78] *The Book of Common Prayer 1559*, ed. John Booty (Charlottesville, Va.: University Press of Virginia, 1976), 48.

Failing to reform the church through ecclesiastical assemblies, the Puritans took their case to Parliament, where they had strong support. Under the leadership of Cartwright, the Puritans in Parliament in 1572 not only called for a reform of church government (since the bishops had proven resistant to reform), but also for the abolition of the use of wafers, kneeling for communion, the admission of papists to the sacrament, and vestments. Parliament was on the verge of amending the Act of Uniformity to direct it only toward papists while Puritans would be free to adopt continental Reformed liturgies in place of the Prayer Book when Elizabeth outmaneuvered the Puritans and squashed their efforts.

In the face of pamphlets such as the "Admonition to Parliament," Puritans assailed the moral, intellectual, and spiritual fitness of the clergy, including the bishops, attacked the unscriptural character of the Anglican liturgy, and called for a presbyterian form of government. As Puritans gained access even to the highest reaches of the Court, the Crown cracked down. Field and Newgate were sent to Newgate Prison and Cartwright fled to the continent. Edmund Grindal, who had spent the reign of Queen Mary in exile, became archbishop of Canterbury in 1576. He was prepared to curb Puritan excesses, not suppress them. Elizabeth had him sequestered until his death in 1583, when the see of Canterbury passed to John Whitgift, who lost no time giving battle to the Puritans. He demanded their subscription to three articles, the second of which was that "the Book of Common Prayer . . . containeth nothing in it contrary to the Word of God."[79]

The Puritans countered with an offensive to enact in Parliament a presbyterian system and a liturgy closely modeled on that of John Knox in Scotland, which was annotated with marginal references to document the scriptural warrant of each section. The Star Chamber restricted Puritan printing in 1586, and the publishing center of Puritanism was transferred to Middleburg, an English trading community in the Netherlands where Cartwright served as a pastor. There the amended Knox liturgy was published.[80]

The chief complaint of the Puritans was that the *Book of Common Prayer* had stopped short of a genuine reformation of the Church of England. Puritans were mostly middle-class folk whose championing of the authority of scripture alone had led them to stress literacy and an educated clergy. As people of the word, they had little use for ornaments, pictures, vestments. White points out that the three human ceremonies they most strenuously and consistently condemned were the sign of the cross in baptism, the exchange of rings in marriage, and kneeling for communion.[81] They believed in extempore praying, even in public services, and gatherings for Bible study in addition to the liturgical assembly. Their conventicles were considered subversive by the state church, and those who attended these meetings were persecuted. They were opposed to most holy days other than Sunday, which they observed as a sabbath in a rigorous Old Testament fashion. They objected to the chanting of the services and to the singing of hymns, which Elizabeth I had allowed before and after services. Only metrical paraphrases of biblical

---

[79] Bard Thompson, *Liturgies of the Western Church*, op. cit., 313.
[80] The Middleburg Liturgy of the English Puritans is provided in Thompson, 322ff.
[81] White, 125.

psalms could be sung, and were sung with relish. Most of all they objected to the reading of homilies and looked for ministers who wrote their own sermons. Most highly prized were preachers who studied the biblical texts in their original languages but also applied the scriptures to everyday life.[82]

The Puritan agenda was intact long before they had a chance to practice such worship legally. But they had an opportunity to put their ideas into practice in the Massachusetts Bay Colony in Salem in 1629 and in Boston in 1630. Unlike the Puritans in Plymouth, these were not Separatists; they considered themselves part of the Anglican Church. But they were Anglicans without bishops and without the Prayer Book. They were congregationalist in polity and free church in liturgical practice, but they were the Established Church. Congregationalism remained the Established Church until 1818 in Connecticut, until 1819 in New Hampshire, and until 1833 in Massachusetts.[83]

John Cotton, a pastor in Boston, described *The Way of the Churches of Christ in New England* (published in London, 1645, at the time of the Puritan victory in old England). In a previous publication, *The True Constitution of a Particular Visible Church Proved by Scripture* (London, 1642), Cotton provided a full description of Puritan worship. Although he minimized the influence of the Separatist Plymouth congregation on Boston Puritans, the Plymouth congregation's order of worship appealed to the Puritans because the Pilgrims' pastor in Leyden, John Robinson, had based each aspect of it on the Old or New Testaments.[84] The order of worship included:

> Opening prayers of thanksgiving and intercession (a literal application of
>   1 Tim. 2:1), offered extemporaneously
> Singing of psalms (lined out by a cantor)
> Reading, expounding, and preaching the word of God, a whole chapter at a
>   time. Reading of scripture without comment was not allowed in Puritan
>   churches.
> Exhorting the people by the elders and questioning the preacher by the laity

Cotton noted that the Lord's Supper was administered "once a month at least" in the Sunday morning worship. "Ceremonies we use none, but are careful to administer all things according to the primitive institutions."[85] There was a separate blessing and distribution of the bread and the cup, which was passed from the presiding minister sitting at the head table by deacons to people sitting at adjacent tables. After the distribution a psalm of thanksgiving was sung, followed by the dismissal.

In the afternoon the congregation came together again. At this service children were baptized, offerings were brought to the deacon's seat, members were admitted, admonished, or cast out; and the service ended with a psalm of praise and a prayer for God's blessing.[86]

---

[82] See Perry Miller and Thomas H. Johnson, *The Puritans*, I (New York: Harper and Row, 1963), 281.
[83] See Perry Miller, *Orthodoxy in Massachusetts, 1630–1650* (Boston: Beacon Press, 1959).
[84] See Adams, 19ff.
[85] Cited in ibid., 31.
[86] Ibid., 35ff.

Back in England, the religious situation had deteriorated as a result of the efforts of the Stuart kings and Archbishop Laud to suppress Scottish Presbyterianism and the Knox liturgy and place in the Church of Scotland bishops and a Prayer Book. As we have seen, the Scottish Prayer Book of 1637 was a return in spirit and content to the 1549 Prayer Book. The book had not been prepared by Laud, but Laud attempted to inject elements of the Scottish Prayer Book into the English Prayer Book under a warrant from Charles I. English bishops acquiesced to the policies of Laud and were unpopular throughout the realm. Scottish resistance to the royal policy invigorated the English Puritans, who had suffered heavily under the Stuart kings.[87] They had been politically disenfranchised by Charles I's royal governance and taxation without Parliament, which was not convened between 1629 and 1640. Charles had not had to call Parliament, because his avoidance of entanglements in Europe during this time of the Thirty Years' War kept spending and taxes down. But the Scottish resistance called for a military response. When Parliament was finally convened in 1640, Laud's ecclesiastical machinery was dismantled and the archbishop himself was sent to the Tower. Following the outbreak of civil war, the episcopacy and the Prayer Book were abolished.[88]

Parliament authorized a convention to reform the standards of the church in a manner "most agreeable to God's holy Word." This assembly convened in Westminster Abbey on July 1, 1643. The presbyterian Puritans were in the majority; but the independents or congregationalists were a strong minority (although these terms did not have the precise meaning they acquired later).[89] In an effort to establish closer political and religious bonds with the Scots, several Scottish commissioners were included in the Westminster Assembly and on the subcommittee that drafted the service book. To satisfy the independents, who believed in no formal liturgical prayer, the subcommittee was inspired by the idea of preparing a *Directory for Worship* rather than a worship book. It provided an outline for worship with a description of each element so worded that a minister could make a prayer out of the directions. Thus, the drafting subcommittee was able to produce a worship resource that was similar in its liturgical orders to the Scottish *Book of Common Order*, but also satisfy the free church congregationalists. The finished *Directory for the Publique Worship of God* was approved and authorized by Parliament in 1644.

The preface to the *Directory* reiterated the Puritan assessment that the *Book of Common Prayer*, while commendable in its day, had become a burden on "sundry good Christians." It had fostered a prayer-book idolatry to the depreciation of good preaching. The virtues of the *Directory* were that it conformed in all matters to the word of God, achieved uniformity in the sense and scope of public prayers, but did not stifle the gift of prayer.[90] The order of public worship provided in the *Directory* is as follows:

---

[87] David Kaiser, *Politics and War*, op. cit., 118 suggests that the real challenge to the prevailing theological orthodoxy in England came not from the Puritans but from the Arminians, led by Archbishop Laud, who challenged the Calvinist doctrine of predestination and emphasized the sacraments as means of grace.

[88] The bibliography on the English Civil War is extensive; but see especially Brian Manning, ed., *Politics, Religion, and the English Civil War* (London, 1973).

[89] See David Underdown, *Pride's Purge: Politics in the Puritan Revolution* (Oxford, 1971), 45–65.

[90] See Thompson, 354ff.

Call to worship

Opening prayer

Reading of scripture (ordinarily one chapter from each Testament)

Singing of the psalm

Public prayer before the sermon (a very long pastoral prayer for all sorts and
conditions of humanity)

The sermon (with directions on being faithful to the text)

Prayer after the sermon (the pastor is directed to "turn the chief and most
useful heads of the sermon into some few Petitions")

When Holy Communion is celebrated (how often is determined by the ministers and governors of each congregation), an exhortation, warning, and invitation are given to the communicants who sit "about" or "at" the table. "About the table" was a concession to the independents, who received communion in their pews, while "at the table" was a concession to the Scots, who received while sitting at table. The minister "set apart" the elements for "holy use" by "sanctifying" and "blessing" them by "Word and Prayer." The institution narrative was considered a warrant for the celebration, and was usually read before the prayer of blessing. The bread is then broken and the bread and cup are distributed to the communicants. In Congregationalist practice, everyone communed together; in Scottish Presbyterian practice the minister communed himself first and then the congregation.

The *Directory* was received with mixed reviews. The Anglicans found it odious and the independents considered it excessively precise. It was, nevertheless, as Thompson opines, "a monumental effort to comprehend the virtues of form and freedom."[91] However, it embodied the main characteristics of Puritan worship: long and exhortatory prayers and even longer and more didactic sermons. This all took place in a setting devoid of any appeal to the senses: no organs, little singing, no pictures, few stained glass windows. This kind of worship has its limitations in appealing to the whole person. It could not permanently appeal to the whole English people, and many longed for the restoration of the old Prayer Book, the customs of the church year, and music and art in the churches.

After the Restoration, the *Book of Common Prayer* was brought back. The failure of efforts at compromise led to the expulsion of over two thousand Puritan clergy when they refused to use the restored Prayer Book. Puritan hopes of reforming the Church of England were dead and after 1689 the dissenters became English Presbyterians, Congregationalists, and Baptists.[92]

The Puritans in New England presented a special situation after the Restoration; the Congregationalists were as much the Established Church there as the Presbyterians in Scotland. So they were not required to conform to episcopacy and the Prayer Book, only to tolerate other Protestants. This presumably meant especially Episcopal Anglicans, since while Baptists and Quakers were no more tolerated in Massachusetts than they were in old England before 1689, Episcopalians with their Prayer Book faced

---

[91] Ibid., 353.

[92] On Baptist worship orders in America see Adams, 66ff.

great difficulties in Massachusetts and New Hampshire and were only officially tolerated in Rhode Island and Connecticut.

Baptists represented an extreme form of Puritanism. They broke with other Puritans not so much over principles of worship as over who was eligible to participate in worship. Roger Williams (c. 1603–1683) protested compulsory attendance at worship in the established Congregationalist Church. But he objected to this because he was against having unregenerated persons polluting the "pure, gathered church." As a pastor, first in Separatist Plymouth and then in Congregationalist Salem, he could not impose such standards on the congregation. With his assistance, the first Baptist congregation was established in Providence, Rhode Island, in 1639 and it attracted refugees and rebels from the Massachusetts Bay Colony. A second Baptist congregation was established in Newport in 1641 by John Clarke. In spite of efforts by the Congregationalists to keep them out, Baptists also came to Massachusetts and established a congregation in Boston in 1665. In these early "Particular" Baptist congregations, only the regenerate were admitted to worship. Edmund Morgan called Williams's principle "the equality of worship," meaning that each part of worship was equally important because each was founded on a divine ordinance, and therefore eligibility to participate was treated equally for all rites and orders of worship.[93] A distinction could not be made, for example, between the liturgy of the word and the liturgy of the Lord's Supper, or the liturgy of the catechumens and the liturgy of the faithful. Appealing to Acts 2:42, Williams held that the word, prayer, and the breaking of bread were equally important parts of the Christian assembly.[94] Williams mediated to American theology and spirituality a radical biblicism, not unlike that of the continental Anabaptists, that eschewed any appeal to tradition in the interpretation of the biblical norm. But this meant that a personal interpretation of scripture replaced an ecclesial one; and the consequence of this is seen in the fact that Williams (like John Milton) became a sect of one when the Rhode Island congregations forsook the "Particularist" stance and embraced Arminianism in the 1650s. It is also seen in the splintering of Baptists into numerous denominations and sects.[95]

Baptists did not quibble with other Puritans over liturgical principles any more than the Puritans quibbled among themselves over particular issues. But Baptists did implement the most radical principles of Puritan worship. The problem in delineating elements of Baptist worship, as Doug Adams points out, is that the evidence is sketchy, and some of it is based on government witnesses in the trials of Baptist leaders who persisted in holding their own worship services.[96] So, for example, the absence of references to group singing in worship in the Boston Baptist Church may reflect a desire by the Baptists not to call attention to themselves since Baptists elsewhere engaged in singing.

---

[93] See Edmund Morgan, *Roger Williams, The Church and the State* (New York: Harcourt, Brace and World, 1967), 29–33.

[94] See "Queries of Highest Consideration" (1644), attributed by John Cotton to Roger Williams; in *The Complete Writings of Roger Williams* (New York: Russell and Russell, 1963), II, 272.

[95] See Arthur Carl Piepkorn, *Profiles in Belief: The Religious Bodies of the United States and Canada*, II (New York: Harper and Row, 1978), 395ff.

[96] See Adams, 67ff.

Obviously, since they believed in a fellowship of the regenerate, only baptized persons could participate in worship; and the baptism of children was precluded. The element of lay prophesying, already practiced in Puritan worship, continued to be emphasized in Baptist worship. As Harold Bloom has suggested, the great contribution of the Baptists to American religion was the idea of the competence of each believer to stand before God and to receive insight from the scriptures and inspiration from the Holy Spirit.[97]

This provided a major point of contention between Roger Williams, who invited Quakers into Rhode Island, and the Quakers. Williams held that this "soul competency" made possible the Puritan practice of questioning the preacher. The Quakers responded that an inspired word from the Holy Spirit should not be questioned, and therefore did not engage in this practice.[98] In fact, they allowed no speaking in public worship other than inspired speaking, which should even take precedence over scripture. In Quaker worship all set forms were eliminated so as not to quench the Spirit.[99] This may indeed be worship "in Spirit and in truth," but it goes beyond worship that is catholic or evangelical, since it cannot appeal to the whole of the Christian tradition and does not explicitly proclaim Christ according to the gospel of the scriptures.

CHURCH MUSIC AND HYMNODY IN THE BAROQUE PERIOD

Roman Catholic and Protestant Liturgical Art Music

We already commented above on the impact of musical settings on the Roman Catholic mass. The reforms of the Council of Trent had produced the chaste homophonic mass settings of Palestrina and da Victoria. Toward the end of their lives both Palestrina and Victoria became aware of the festive possibilities of the double-choir effect from Saint Mark's in Venice. This was exploited in brass and choral pieces by Andrea Gabrieli (c. 1515–1586) and his nephew Giovanni Gabrieli (c. 1557–1609). A musical style was developed under the Gabrielis in Venice that proved to be very appealing to musicians in Germany, since it lent itself to alternation between groups. Claudio Monteverdi's name is most associated with secular music—madrigals and the early development of opera. But his Vespers of 1610 was revolutionary since it added solo voices and instruments to the traditional choral medium for liturgical music. This was also a style that was adopted by Protestant composers for their church cantatas and sacred oratorios.

North of the Alps the most versatile composer of both sacred and secular music was the Netherlander Orlando Lassus (c. 1532–1594), who served the Dukes of Bavaria from 1556 until his death. Bavaria provided the leadership for the Catholic Counter-Reformation in Germany. The Elector Maximilian I provided the Jesuits with a base of power to develop a cultural and intellectual match for the Protestant *gymnasia* and universities in northern Germany. The church music of Lassus provided the tonal splendor for the Catholic resurgence. It carried on the pre-Reformation Dutch tradition of Josquin

---

[97] Harold Bloom, *The American Religion: The Emergence of the Post-Christian Nation* (Simon and Schuster, 1992), 191ff.

[98] Adams, 76.

[99] Ibid., 73ff.

des Prez, but was also influenced by Andrea Gabrieli. Lassus, in turn, influenced Giovanni Gabrieli, who sang under him in his Munich choir from c. 1575–1579.[100]

Lassus's music was well known in France, and may have influenced the French Huguenot composers who were primarily concerned with the settings of vernacular psalms from the Marot-Beze Psalter. Although Calvinist in origin, these psalm tunes were sung also by French Catholics in settings by the Catholic Jacques Mauduit (1557–1627), Claude Le Jeune (c. 1530–1600), and Pascal de L'Estocart (b. c. 1540). They were also sung by Lutherans in German translation.

Lutheran music also began to be influenced by Venice as well as by Lassus. In the case of Hans Leo Hassler (1564–1612), this was because he was long in the service of the banking family of Fugger in Augsburg, who were strict Catholics. Later in life he was ennobled by the Emperor Rudolf II. Only toward the end of his life, when he entered the service of the Protestant court in Dresden, was Hassler able to write music based on the Lutheran Reformation hymns. In the case of Michael Praetorius (c. 1571–1621), who wrote Lutheran church music throughout his career, and may be regarded as the most vigorous musical representative of Lutheran orthodoxy, the Venetian influence was calculated, as it was later on in the music of the greatest German composer of the seventeenth century, Heinrich Schütz (1585–1672). Schütz studied in Venice with Giovanni Gabrieli, wrote Italian madrigals, and returned there twenty years later to study with Monteverdi.

The Venetian style was noticeable in Latin liturgical music used in Lutheran services. This included settings of the ordinary of the mass (Kyrie and Gloria, but not usually the Credo, Sanctus, and Agnus Dei) as well as the propers (Introits, but not usually Graduals), and office canticles (the Magnificat and Te Deum). This style was also noticeable in settings of the psalms in Latin, such as those of Melchior Franck of Coburg. But after the sixteenth century, Latin liturgical music waned in Lutheranism except for settings of the Magnificat for Vespers. The new form of church music that developed in Lutheran lands was the lied motet, based on the songs or hymns that were being written in great abundance by the end of the sixteenth century. As the tradition of the Hauptlied (Hymn of the Day) became established in Lutheran liturgy, the motet (and later the cantata) secured a place in juxtaposition with the gospel reading and sermon. The motet might be sung after the gospel reading and before the sermon; or it could also be sung during the ministration of communion, since these are places in the liturgy where chorales, hymns, or church lieder were sung.

Between 1605 and 1611 Praetorius published 1,244 German chorale settings for two to twelve voices, thus providing a virtual encyclopedia of motet-like chorale settings. Further significant collections of motets were those by Johann Hermann Schein (1615), Samuel Scheidt (1620), and Heinrich Schütz (1625 and 1648). The motet as a form began to be replaced by church concertos based on the Italian model of Gabrieli (1615). This was a work of several movements that was sometimes divided before and after the sermon. Schütz collected church concertos in five volumes between 1629 and 1650. They are exceptionally lively pieces based on the Italian madrigal style in order to give better

---

[100] See Gerald Abraham, *The Concise Oxford History of Music*, op. cit., 254f.

expression to the biblical texts. Unlike other Lutheran composers, however, Schütz hardly ever based his concertos on the chorale or church lied. As the number of movements increased with recitatives and arias in the style of Italian opera, the concertos came to be called cantatas. An immense number of these were composed for Lutheran services, although relatively few of these survived or are performed today. For example, of hundreds of church cantatas written by Dietrich Buxtehude (1637?–1707), only about a hundred of them dating from the years 1675–1687 survive. After Buxtehude, more than 2,000 cantatas were written by Johann Philipp Krieger (1649–1725), and 1,500 each by Christoph Graupner (1683–1760) and Georg Philipp Telemann (1681–1767).[101] They are, for the most part, formula pieces that lack the dramatic content of the cantatas of Johann Sebastian Bach (1685–1750). Like Schütz, Bach found a musical-dramatic solution for each text; unlike Schütz, he continued to base his cantatas on the old chorales.

Lutheran composers also provided dramatic settings of the Gospel passions for use during Holy Week. This tradition began already with Luther's musical collaborator, Johann Walther, who composed settings of the Saint Matthew and Saint John passions as early as 1545. The Italian Lutheran convert who served as the Dresden court composer, Antonio Scandello (1517–1580), composed a Saint John passion in 1561. This tradition employed roles for three singers: the evangelist-narrator (baritone), Jesus (bass), and the other characters and crowds in the passion story (tenor). Already before the Reformation there had been dramatic elaborations with the choir singing the *turbae* (groups of disciples, soldiers, crowd). This development of the passion as a musical form continued in Lutheranism, and as time went on Lutheran passions included the congregational chorales and solo arias interspersed with the gospel text, until the form achieved the oratorio character of the immense *Saint John Passion* and *Saint Matthew Passion* of J. S. Bach.[102]

The situation in Great Britain was such that the strict Calvinism of the Church of Scotland would not tolerate music other than the singing of congregational psalms; but in Elizabethan England strict Calvinism was resisted and choral music was provided for the cathedrals.[103] Ironically, the greatest composer of post-Reformation Anglican cathedral music was the Roman Catholic William Byrd (1543–1623) and his pupil Thomas Morley (1557–1602), who may also have been a Roman Catholic. They continued a tradition of composing "English services" begun by Thomas Tallis (c. 1505–1585). Tallis's one note-per-syllable principle, devoid of verbal repetition, became the classic model of the English service and anthem style that was to persist up through the Victorian period. Two excellent examples of this style are Richard Farrant's "Hide not thou thy face" and the anonymous anthem, "Lord, for thy tender mercies sake," which breaks into only a slight polyphonic texture at the words "that we may walk."

---

[101] See Lowell Lindgren, "The Baroque Era," in Leonie Rosenstiel, ed., *Schirmer History of Music* (New York: Schirmer Books, 1982), 436ff.

[102] Blume, "The Age of Confessionalism," in *Protestant Church Music*, op. cit., 177ff.; *Schirmer History of Music*, 444–5; Abraham, *The Concise Oxford History of Music*, 400ff.

[103] See Watkins Shaw, "Church Music in England," in Blume, ed., *Protestant Church Music*, 701ff.

The chief musical services in the Church of England were Morning Prayer and Evening Prayer. So by "service" is meant a musical setting of the canticles prescribed for use in the various offices. At Morning Prayer these canticles included the Venite, the Te Deum or Benedicite, and the Benedictus or Jubilate. At Evening Prayer the canticles included the Magnificat or Cantate Domino and the Nunc dimittis or Deus Misereatur. Settings of the Kyrie, the Nicene Creed, the Sanctus, and the Gloria (in that order) were required for the communion service. Nevertheless, it was the anthem, a motet-like work usually based on psalm verses, that attracted the interest of most composers. Anthems (an anglicization of the word "antiphon") were sung in proximity to the sermon at the end of the prayer offices and at the offertory and during communion in the communion service (the place of the old offertory and communion antiphons in the Roman mass).

During the middle of the seventeenth century there was virtually no development of church music in England because of the Civil War and the Puritan Commonwealth. With the Restoration there was also a return of cathedral music and a momentary flourishing of service and anthem writing. Indeed, the best composers of the Restoration—John Blow (1649–1708) and Henry Purcell (1659–1695)—put their best church music writing into anthems rather than "services."[104] Charles II introduced a string band into his chapel, and anthems written during his brief reign include introductory symphonies and intermediary ritornellos. After the Glorious Revolution, the string bands were disbanded and anthems were accompanied only by organ continuo. Anthem-writing was carried on into the early eighteenth century by Blow's pupil, William Croft (1678–1727), and by the German immigrant, George Frederick Handel (1685–1759), who was very much influenced by Purcell in his splendid Anglican anthems for royal and state occasions. While the oratorios of Handel are his greatest contribution to choral literature, and are all based on biblical texts or stories, they were intended to be dramatic works performed in theaters (usually during Lent when the opera and theater season was suspended) and are not, strictly speaking, church music.

In parish churches throughout this whole period the basic musical element was the metrical psalm. The psalter tradition was common to all English and Scottish Protestants, and was brought to colonial America by Anglicans, Puritans, and Presbyterians. The first book of any kind published in the English colonies was the Bay Psalm Book, printed in Cambridge, Massachusetts in 1640 (although it contained no music, probably because no printer in the colonies was capable of doing the engraving). The first breakthrough toward hymnody was the experiments of Dr. Isaac Watts (1674–1784), who felt that the texts should relate more freely than literally to the biblical texts. What he called "Psalm Imitations," his detractors called "burlesquing" the psalter, but the higher quality of his hymns commended them to congregational use both in Britain and in America. They achieved immense popularity that has waned only slightly since the nineteenth century.[105]

---

[104] Abraham, 416.

[105] See Carol Ann Doran, "Metrical Psalmody," in Marilyn Kay Stulken, ed., *Hymnal Companion to the Lutheran Book of Worship* (Philadelphia: Fortress Press, 1981), 58–67.

After the Restoration there was a discernible spread of organs in parish churches, which increased the number of musicians working outside of cathedrals and choral foundations. Around these musicians in the West gallery organ lofts were assembled bands of amateur singers to lead the singing of the psalms. These bands of singers also appeared in churches without organs during the eighteenth century; and sometimes they were joined by instrumental bands. This amateur music-making in the West gallery became a significant social force in English life, especially in country churches.[106] Inevitably, more complicated musical settings were provided for these West gallery singers and it was not long before they arrogated to themselves the singing of the music of the services just as much as the surpliced choirs of the cathedral did.

Protestant Hymnody, Songbooks, and Organ Music during the Seventeenth Century

While congregational singing flourished in all Protestant worship, in the Reformed and Puritan traditions this was largely restricted to the singing of metrical psalms. This restriction on congregational song applied also in the Anglican Church of this period until Isaac Watts expanded the repertoire, although choirs and organs were allowed in Anglican worship. Thus for the production of congregational hymns for use in public worship, and organ music related to it, we must turn primarily to Lutheranism in this period.

The liturgical and doctrinal hymns of the Reformation era were supplemented with a more mystical type of hymn by the end of the sixteenth century. From this period we have hymns by Nikolaus Selnecker (1532–1592), one of Melanchthon's favorite students at Wittenberg and one of the writers of the Formula of Concord, including "Lass mich dein sein und bleiben" ("Let me be yours forever," *LBW* 490); Bartholomaeus Ringwaldt (1523–1599), who contributed, among others, "Es ist gewisslich" ("The day is surely drawing near," *LBW* 321); Ludwig Helmbold (1532–1598), whose metrical version of the Augsburg Confession has been forgotten, but whose "Von Gott will ich nicht lassen" ("From God can nothing move me," *LBW* 468) endures; and Martin Schalling's (1532–1608) masterful hymn of comfort "Herzlich lieb" ("Lord, thee I love with all my heart," *LBW* 325) served as the final chorale of Bach's *Saint John Passion*.[107] Philipp Nicolai (1556–1608) contributed two of the greatest hymns ever written: "Wie schön leuchtet" ("O Morning Star, how fair and bright!" *LBW* 76) and "Wachet auf" ("Wake, awake, for night is flying," *LBW* 31), which occasioned two of Bach's greatest church cantatas, Nos. 1 and 140. With their ardent profession of devotion to the "King and Bridegroom," Nicolai's hymns injected the same mystical warmth into Lutheran piety that was being recovered by his contemporary, Johann Arndt. Indeed, Nicolai is considered an ancestor of Lutheran Pietism along with Arndt.[108]

These hymns were sung in church, in schools, and at home, thus establishing a unity between public and personal devotion. The Thirty Years' War provided tremendous

---

[106] An almost idyllic picture of West gallery musical contribution to parish life was provided by Thomas Hardy's recollection of his boyhood days in Dorset in *Under the Greenwood Tree* (1894).

[107] See Carl F. Schalk, "German Hymnody," in *Hymnal Companion to the Lutheran Book of Worship*, 25.

[108] See Stoeffler, *The Rise of Evangelical Pietism*, op. cit., 197ff.

impetus to hymnwriting. The distress and deprivations of the war contributed signifi-cantly to the development of a new type of hymn. Among the hymns that were the prod-uct of the war years were: Martin Rinkart's (1586–1649) "Nun danket alle Gott" ("Now thank we all our God," *LBW* 533, 534), which has been called the Lutheran Te Deum; Johann Heermann's (1585–1647) passion chorale, "Herzliebster Jesu" ("Ah, holy Jesus," *LBW* 123); and Johann Franck's "Schmücke dich" ("Soul, adorn yourself with gladness," *LBW* 224) and "Jesu, meine Freude" ("Jesus, priceless treasure," *LBW* 457, 458), which served as the basis of Bach's unaccompanied funeral motet.[109]

The greatest hymnwriter and German poet of the seventeenth century was Paul Gerhardt (1607–1676), who suffered personally the ravages of the war and endured diffi-culties after the war because of his staunch defense of Lutheran orthodoxy. Gerhardt wrote 123 hymns, which are noteworthy for introducing a more personal and subjective element into Lutheran hymnody that became very appealing to Pietists. Among Gerhardt's enduring *Lieder* are the Advent hymn, "Wie soll ich dich empfangen" ("O Lord, how shall I meet you," *LBW* 23); the Christmas hymn, "Fröhlich soll mein Herze springen" ("Once again my heart rejoices," *LBW* 46), the Lenten hymn, "Ein Lämmlein geht und tragt die Schuld" ("A Lamb goes uncomplaining forth," *LBW* 105); the passion chorale, "O Haupt voll Blut und Wunden" ("O sacred Head, now wounded," *LBW* 116, 117), based on the Latin hymn of Saint Bernard of Clairvaux; the Easter hymn, "Auf, auf, mein Herz" ("Awake, my heart, with gladness," *LBW* 129); the morning hymn, "Die güldne Sonne" ("Evening and Morning," *LBW* 465); the evening hymns based on the ex-tended *Abendlied* (*LBW* 276, 282); and the intensely personal "Ist Gott für mich" ("If God himself be for me," *LBW* 454). Gerhardt had the good fortune of collaborating with Johann Crüger (1598–1662), the organist and choirmaster of the Saint Nicholas Church in Berlin where Gerhardt was pastor. Crüger did not consider particular texts to be mar-ried to particular tunes. Indeed, the texts and tunes could be interchangeable. Thus, "O Lord, How Shall I Meet You" could be sung to "Valet will ich dir Geben" (also known as "Saint Theodulph") as well as "Wie soll ich dich Empfangen." But Crueger's tunes helped to popularize Gerhardt's texts. Crüger also set the hymns of Johann Franck.

An important contemporary of Gerhardt's was Johann Rist (1607–1667). It might be noted that while nine of Gerhardt's 123 hymns are included in *Lutheran Book of Worship*, only one of Johann Rist's (1607–1667) 680-odd hymns is included: "Wie wohl hast du gelabet" ("O living Bread from heaven," *LBW* 197). Among those omitted from *LBW* was "Break forth thou beauteous heavenly light" (*SBH* 29), which is known only in the Bach harmonization.[110] Rist was more highly regarded than Gerhardt during their lifetime. He was perhaps a more irenic person who made it clear that he was prepared to sign the Great Elector's Declaration of Tolerance whereas Gerhardt lost his position as

---

[109] Ibid., 26ff.

[110] Bach harmonizations are not found in *LBW*. The hymn tune subcommittee of the Inter-Lutheran Commission on Worship obviously preferred the older syncopated rhythms of the chorales to the eigh-teenth century "smoothed out" versions. In a few cases both versions were provided. There also seems to have been a point of view on the committee that the Bach harmonizations were not intended for congre-gational singing.

provost of Saint Nicholas Church in Berlin because of his opposition to it. Yet both expressed many of the same thoughts and feelings in their hymns, Rist in a more erudite and Gerhardt in a more popular way.[111]

The large number of new hymns being written in the seventeenth century, added to the numerous Reformation chorales that still continued to be sung, resulted in hymnals of great size. Friedrich Blume reports: "In 1599 a hymnal appeared in Nuremberg containing 525 hymns, one in Frankfurt on the Main in 1600 with 535. The Gorlitz hymnal of 1611 increased the figure to about 700, the Fuhrmann hymnbook, appearing in Nuremberg in the same year, to 748, while a hymnal of 1626 even reached a total of 836."[112] All these numbers, it should be noted, refer only to texts; the cantionales, which provided the tunes and settings for the organist and the choirs, made it unnecessary to provide the tunes in the congregation's book. Another important development was that the state church took over the publication of the hymnals, which in the sixteenth century had been commercial publishing ventures. This made larger hymnals more feasible; it also led to the authorization of hymnals by state church authorities. But inevitably, judicious selections had to be made because by the end of the seventeenth century the corpus of Lutheran hymns in Germany had grown to about 10,000.

The "singer of orthodoxy" in Denmark was Thomas Hansen Kingo (1634–1703), bishop of Fyn. A prolific hymnwriter, King Christian V appointed Kingo in 1683 to prepare a new hymnal for Denmark, Norway, and Iceland, since the Thomissøn Hymnal of 1569 was well over a hundred years old. Kingo's commission included the directive to eliminate undesirable hymns, to revise antiquated rhymes and expressions, and to adopt two new hymns by himself or others for every pericope of the church year. He finished a draft hymnal in six years containing 267 hymns, of which 137 were his own. This draft was rejected for having eliminated too many familiar hymns. A committee continued the work Kingo had begun, and "Kingo's Hymnal" was authorized in 1699. Of its 297 hymns, eighty-five were by Kingo. *LBW* has four of Kingo's hymns: "All who believe and are baptized" (194), "O Jesus, blessed Lord" (220), "On my heart imprint your image" (102), and "Praise and thanks and adoration" (470).[113] In the same year a Gradual containing liturgical music replaced Jesperson's *Gradual and General Songbook* of 1573.[114]

The Pietistic movement gave new impetus to hymnwriting, including hymns from the pens of Spener, Francke, and Zinzendorf. The latter's "Jesus, still lead on" (*LBW* 341) and "Jesus, your blood and righteousness" (*LBW* 302) are still sung. However, the most significant hymnwriters of the period were the German Reformed hymnists Joachim Neander (1650–1680) and the mystical Gerhard Tersteegen (1697–1769). From Neander we have "Lobe den Herren" ("Praise to the Lord, the Almighty," *LBW* 543) and from Tersteegen we have "Gott ist gegenwärtig" ("God himself is present," *LBW* 249).

---

[111] Blume, *Protestant Church Music*, 237ff.

[112] Ibid., 147.

[113] Edward A. Hansen, "Scandinavian Hymnody: Denmark," in *Hymnal Companion to the Lutheran Book of Worship*, 34–5.

[114] See Torben Schousboe, "Protestant Church Music in Scandinavia," in Blume, *Protestant Church Music*, 614–5.

The most famous Pietist hymnal was Johann Anastasii Freylinghausen's *Geistliches Gesangbuch* (1704) and his *Neues Geistreiches Gesangbuch* (1714), which were combined in 1741 and known as the "Freylinghausen Gesangbuch" or the "Halle Hymnal" (after the Halle Orphanage that published and distributed it throughout Germany). Copies of this book were brought to America by many Lutheran and Reformed immigrants in the mid-eighteenth century. It contained 1,581 hymns with 597 different melodies and figured basses.

The figured basses in these hymnals leads to the question of when organs were used to accompany congregational singing. Organs were certainly used to introduce hymns; and they sometimes played between stanzas of hymns. During the course of the seventeenth century, organ accompaniments to congregational hymns came gradually into use. Musicologists, however, debate how early or how late this occurred.[115] In his Cantionale of 1627, Johann Hermann Schein (1586–1630) added a thorough bass to the melodies, and many hymnbooks followed his lead. However, it is not certain whether this accompaniment was intended for singing at home or in church.[116] Samuel Scheidt (1587–1654) is regarded as the father of German organ music. His *Tabulatura Nova* (1624) provided variations on standard chorale melodies (one variation for each stanza). It is assumed, however, that the organ variation was played between stanzas, or to introduce the hymn. This can be regarded as the origin of the chorale prelude that became part of the standard organ repertoire. It is possible that in conservative Leipzig the organ still did not accompany congregational singing when Bach arrived in 1723.

Nevertheless, the organ became an almost indispensable feature of Lutheran worship. Ironically, the Lutheran organ music tradition was founded by a Dutch Calvinist, Jan Pieterszoon Sweelinck (1562–1621). His many Lutheran students carried his tradition directly to Bach. Two of them, Jacob Praetorius (1586–1651) and Heinrich Scheidemann (1596–1663) secured employment in churches in Hamburg, as did two of their students: Matthias Weckmann (1619–1674) and Jan Adam Reinecken (1623–1722). The young Bach traveled to Hamburg to hear Reinecken play; twenty years later the aged Reinecken, on hearing Bach improvise at great length on a chorale prelude, declared that the art lived on in Bach.[117] All of these north German organists looked to Buxtehude, however, as their great master; whereas the leading organ composer in south Germany was Johann Pachelbel (1653–1706). Bach, of course, surpassed them all. It should be noted that the great organ preludes and fugues, toccatas, fantasies, and so forth were not usually used for worship services, unless they were played during communion. They were intended for church concerts, which sometimes followed services, or for the instruction of organ students. Organ music used within the service continued to be music that could be related to texts, such as the chorale preludes and variations that introduced hymns and provided organ "commentary" between stanzas of the chorales. Thus, even the purely instrumental organ music was placed in the service of the text.

---

[115] See Edwin Liemohn, *Organ and Choir in Protestant Worship* (Philadelphia: Fortress Press, 1968), 44–5.
[116] Blume, 245.
[117] *Schirmer History of Music*, 446.

The Church Music of J. S. Bach

The organ pieces of J. S. Bach are regarded by organists as among the best music written for that instrument, just as his church cantatas and passions are the highest expressions of Protestant church music. In fact, everything that Bach composed—including dance suites and concertos for the princely court as well as well-tempered exercises and instructional music—is as good as music can be. Bach is known by all music lovers (thanks to the Romantic recovery initiated by Mendelssohn) in a way that his predecessors, Pachelbel (except for the famous "Canon") and Buxtehude (except by organ students) are not known. The Bach revival in the nineteenth century did not originate with church musicians; it was championed also by Chopin and Schumann. Nor was it limited to Bach's church music. Not so surprisingly there has been a disinclination to see Bach within the setting of orthodox Lutheran liturgical life. Even where Bach's religious genius is admitted, as in innumerable concert program notes, it is seen from a more general and universal perspective or along humanistic lines. But this is to interpret Bach more in the context of the Enlightenment than the evidence warrants. As Joseph Sittler concluded already in 1943, "I have yet to find in Bach's confessions, either by word or by implications of his life or in the content of his music, any concern for religion save as that word meant to him the common faith of his people and church and time."[118]

Bach's career, to be sure, took him in and out of church work—from organist in Arnstadt and Muhlhausen in his early career, to service in the courts of Weimar and Cöthen, to cantor at the Thomasschule and Director of Music in the city of Leipzig.[119] His well-known disagreements with both city and church authorities in Leipzig (who were practically indistinguishable), the fact that he wrote no church cantatas during the last years of his life, and his constant search for other musical positions, prompted even Friedrich Blume to suggest (against the Romanticized religious nimbus painted around Bach by Philipp Spitta and others) that for Bach the writing of church music was a job to be done and "not an affair of the heart." According to Blume, Bach had been a court musician for many years and "only with great reluctance . . . resumed the cantor's gown" in Leipzig in 1723. This change of positions meant "a descent in social scale" that he accepted as a personal sacrifice because of the educational advantages Leipzig would offer to his sons.[120]

Günther Stiller has challenged Blume's contentions point by point. He emphasized the fact that from early childhood Bach was closely associated with church life of the strictest Lutheran orthodoxy.[121] The first ten years of his life were spent in Luther's own city of Eisenach in the shadow of Wartburg, where Luther translated the New Testament into German. Young Bach was enrolled in the lower classes of the old Saint George Latin School from whose upper classes Luther had graduated 200 years earlier.

---

[118] Joseph Sittler, in *The Cresset* (April, 1943), 23.

[119] See Werner Felix, *Johann Sebastian Bach*, foreword by Paul Henry Lang (New York and London: W. W. Norton and Company, 1985).

[120] Friedrich Blume, "Outlines of a New Picture of Bach," *Music and Letters* 44 (1963), 214–27.

[121] Stiller, op. cit., 173ff.

All of the teachers of this school were theologians under church supervision. Religious instruction was an integral part of the curriculum, and Bach learned the catechism, Bible history, chanted the psalms, and read the epistles and Gospels in Latin as well as German. Involvement in public worship in school and in the parish church was integrally related to the teaching of the Bible and theology in Lutheran orthodoxy.[122]

Stiller notes that when Bach left the Saint Michael School at Luneberg in 1702, and his financial situation precluded study at the university, he explicitly chose a career as a church organist. During his tenure at Arnstadt, he took a leave of absence to visit the great church organist Buxtehude at Lübeck to learn from him. His stay at Mühlhausen was a happy one in terms of the personal relationships he developed there and the support he received from the church and city councils, including permission to rebuild the organ in Saint Blase's Church according to Bach's specifications and the publication of his early cantatas by the town. Unfortunately Bach was caught in the pulpit wars between Lutheran orthodoxy and Pietism, and the latter was advanced in Mühlhausen by the town's leading pastor, Superintendent Frohne. In his request for dismissal from the Mühlhausen position, Bach testified: "I should always have liked to work toward the goal, namely, a well-regulated church music, to the glory of God. . . . yet it has not been possible to accomplish all this without hindrance."[123]

Bach saw the possibility of achieving that goal in Weimar "without further vexation." Duke Wilhelm Ernest of Saxe-Weimar was a champion of Lutheran orthodoxy. While he had forbidden the pulpit wars between orthodoxy and Pietism in his territory, he also had taken measures to retard the advance of Pietism. He ruled his tiny dukedom piously, and conscious of his responsibilities in both the civil and the ecclesiastical realms. Bach was brought to Weimar as the court organist, which meant that he had responsibilities for the chapel services. He also assisted the duke's aging *Kapellmeister*, Johann Samuel Drese, and provided a church cantata every four weeks. While Bach was highly valued at the court, and probably had input in decisions to renovate the court chapel and rebuild the organ, he was passed over for the position of kapellmeister when Drese died, in favor of the latter's son. This prompted Bach to apply for the position of kapellmeister in the court of Prince Leopold of Cöthen, the brother of the duchess of Saxe-Weimar, to which Duke Wilhelm Ernest released him after four weeks of incarceration for insubordination.

Prince Leopold was a Calvinist, although he provided a school and chapel for his Lutheran subjects. No church duties were required of Bach at Cöthen, and it was primarily "secular" music that Bach wrote and directed. He was also well-paid at Cöthen and reasonably happy. But this position was not advancing Bach's life-goal to produce "a well-regulated church music, to the glory of God," and he applied for positions in two cities that were regarded as citadels of Lutheran orthodoxy: Hamburg and Leipzig.

---

[122] Friedrich Kalb, *Theology of Worship in Seventeenth Century Lutheranism*, op. cit., maintained that liturgics was not separated from dogmatics in Lutheran orthodoxy, but that one informed the other.

[123] Hans David and Arthur Mendel, eds., *The Bach Reader* (New York: W. W. Norton, 1966), 60.

Contrary to Blume's assertion that the transition from Cöthen to Leipzig represented "a descent in the social scale," it should be noted that many prominent musicians applied for the position at Leipzig. It was a dual position that combined the posts of music director of the city of Leipzig and cantor of the Saint Thomas School. This combined position included responsibilities for music in the principal churches of the city. The fact that Bach's early flurry of musical production in Leipzig was for the churches may indicate not only the preponderance of need but also some sense of exhilaration at resuming his true vocation.[124] Unfortunately, Bach found inadequacies, including the fitness of the singers admitted into the boys' choir of the Thomasschule, the availability of necessary instrumentalists, and the lack of funds to secure outside help (on which, in fact, the city council had reneged). This prompted him to address the council in 1730 with his famous "Short but Most Necessary Draft for a Well-Appointed Church Music; With Certain Modest Reflections on the Decline of the Same."[125]

In this memo Bach outlined what would be required to maintain a flourishing liturgical life in the tradition of Lutheran orthodoxy and he described its current disarray, ending with the prognosis that "a still greater decline is to be feared."[126] The council's failure to respond to Bach's specifications put him in the position of merely maintaining the musical life that was already in place in the churches. It is no wonder that he directed his creative energies elsewhere after 1730. But there were two spectacular exceptions. One exception was the Kyrie and Gloria for what would become the *Mass in B Minor*. These movements were presented to the Elector Friedrich August II of Saxony in 1733 (who had scandalized his subjects by converting to Roman Catholicism), with the petition that Bach be awarded a *Praedicat con Dero Hoff-Capelle*. In so doing he obligated himself to compose church music, or music of any kind, upon the command of the Elector. Nothing came of this petition because the Elector died that year. But we might wonder whether this was a last-ditch effort to secure support for a "well-regulated church music, to the glory of God" by turning to the most powerful prince of the Saxonies, a man who was committed to the liturgical tradition at a time when it was disintegrating under the combined impact of a stagnant orthodoxy, a fanatical Pietism, and an incipient Rationalism that would call for an entire reorientation of cultic life.

Bach also had to contend with the gradual introduction of the Enlightenment in Leipzig. Between 1734 and 1736 the cantor came into serious conflict with the new rector of the Saint Thomas School, Johann August Ernesti. Ernesti was one of the founders of the science of biblical criticism and a leading theologian of the Enlightenment. As rector of the Saint Thomas School, he displayed a lack of enthusiasm for music in general, for church music in particular, and for Bach's brand of "old-fashioned" church music especially. Like other theorists of Rationalism, he had use only for the practical aspects of religion—those ideas and forms that could help to develop the moral life of the people.

---

[124] Stiller, 191ff.

[125] *The Bach Reader*, 120–4.

[126] See Mark Bangert, "Toward a Well-Regulated Church Music: Bachian Prescriptions with Enduring Shelf Life," *dialog* 24 (1985), 107–12.

Worship had to be, above all, an act of edification and moral formation. Ernesti had no use for Bach's view that worship be conducted *soli Deo gloria*.[127] One wonders whether this conflict with Ernesti did not provide the second major exception to Bach's apparent moratorium on the composition of church music after 1730: the *Christmas Oratorio* of 1734–35. This was, in reality, six cantatas presented in the Saint Thomas and Saint Nicholas Churches during the twelve days of Christmas in 1734–1735. They are the most grandiose of Bach's church cantatas, but were clearly intended as liturgical pieces since they strictly adhered to the liturgical hymns of the days for the first three days of Christmas, New Year's Day (Circumcision and Name of Jesus), the Second Sunday after Christmas, and the Epiphany.[128]

Perhaps as a final testimony to his view of worship and life, and at that time in his life when he was compiling examples of his art in encyclopedic fashion (e.g., *The Goldberg Variations*, *The Art of the Fugue*), Bach completed the Mass in B Minor with the addition of a Sanctus first composed in 1724, an Agnus Dei assembled by use of parodies from previous compositions, and finally the mighty Credo. This monumental work was completed with no hope or expectation of ever hearing a performance of the complete work. His son, Carl Philipp Emmanuel Bach, called it "the great Catholic Mass." It shares features with the *Magnificat in D*, and both inhabit the narrow border of interconfessional creativity. But perhaps it seemed to Bach that the Enlightenment challenged such basic notions of Christian faith and worship that a response to it had to be interconfessional: that is, catholic as well as evangelical.

Bach's relationship to the Enlightenment is a complicated one. Jaroslav Pelikan showed how Bach had to steer a course between theological Rationalism as represented by Ernesti, on the one hand, and Enlightenment aestheticism, or art for art's sake, as represented by King Frederick the Great, on the other.[129] It is beyond our task to assess the extent to which Bach's musical theory and the architecture of his compositions were influenced by aesthetic ideas current in the Enlightenment (although we would note that his musical style as well as his theological position came to be regarded as "old fashioned" before he was dead and buried). Nevertheless, in retrospect we can hear and appreciate how old Bach breathed creative life into the decaying liturgical forms of Lutheran orthodoxy, and allowed the finer mystical qualities to shine through pietistic texts in spite of his conflicts with a shallow Pietism, at a time of growing religious disintegration brought about by the advances of enlightened Rationalism when the institutional foundations of church music were in precipitous decline. Even the cantors of Saint Thomas had to fight a hopeless battle for medieval privileges and a theocentric view of music and learning that could not possibly stand up against the onslaught of the natural sciences and the new

---

[127] See Robert Stevenson, "Bach's Quarrel with the Rector of St. Thomas School," *Anglican Theological Review* XXXIII (1951), 219–30.

[128] Stiller, 234–7.

[129] Jaroslav Pelikan, *Bach Among the Theologians* (Philadelphia: Fortress Press, 1986), chapter 3.

[130] Jaroslav Pelikan, *Fools for Christ* (Philadelphia: Muhlenberg Press, 1955), chapter 6 on "The Beauty of Holiness."

humanism. Jaroslav Pelikan was certainly right to place Bach in the company of "fools for Christ."[130]

BAROQUE CHURCH ARCHITECTURE

The Reformation Experiments with Existing Church Buildings

We have seen that the basic problem with the late medieval church building from the point of view of Reformation liturgics was that it did not gather the congregation; it scattered it. The typical medieval church building had several "rooms" in which different activities were carried on by or for different groups within the body of Christ. Not only were the nave and the chancel two different rooms, often separated by a rood screen, but churches had numerous bays and chapels where side altars were placed at which private masses could be said. These side altars, bays, and chapels were protected from distraction by means of parclose screens. Thus, the typical late-medieval church was a series of compartments or self-contained rooms intended to meet the different devotional needs of clergy, canons, monks, guilds, noble families, and the laity in general.

These were the building arrangements that the reformers—both Protestant and Roman Catholic—inherited. Buildings tend to longevity, and the reformers had to experiment with the space available to make it work for renewed ideas of the church as the congregation of the faithful, laity and clergy together, as well as for new liturgical forms and emphases.

This was true of Roman Catholic as well as Protestant church architecture. The Council of Trent had called for a renewed emphasis on preaching.[131] New religious orders emerged that took on preaching as a special apostolate, such as the Capuchins, Oratorians, and Jesuits. This required pulpits that were acoustically well-placed and pews on which auditors could listen to sermons. The Jesuit Church of the Gesù, built in Rome from 1568 to 1575, reflected the reality that the Jesuits had no need of choir space and that the foci of their worship were both preaching (done from a pulpit that stood high in the middle of the north wall of the nave) and eucharistic devotion (centered on a high altar situated in the apse, on which was placed a tabernacle with the reserved sacrament). Obviously, no barriers such as a choir screen should block the congregation's view of the altar. James White notes that this new arrangement of liturgical space determined Roman Catholic architecture for the next several centuries. Even neo-Gothic churches in the nineteenth century retained the open view of the altar of Il Gesù.[132]

Lutheran architecture reflected the non-iconoclastic character of the conservative Reformation. Altars, candles, crucifixes, vestments, and organs were retained. In his *Deutsche Messe* of 1526, Luther recommended that "the altar should not remain where it is, and the priest should always face the people as Christ doubtlessly did in the Last Supper. But let that await its own time."[133] A form of "free standing altar" can be found in southern Germany (e.g., in Nuremberg, Rothenberg, and Ulm), which was placed in the

---

[131] *Canons and Decrees of the Council of Trent*, trans. H. J. Schroeder (St. Louis: Herder, 1941), 26, 195.

[132] James F. White, *Roman Catholic Worship: Trent to Today* (Mahwah, N.J.: Paulist Press, 1995), 7–8.

[133] LW 53:69

middle of the chancel and were often adorned with carved reredoses (note especially those created by the master wood carver, Tilman Riemenschneider) and surrounded by a small circular fence. Communicants gathered in the choir stalls. There would be only one altar table; the numerous side altars were demolished, and medieval side chapels were turned into burial chambers for royal and noble families and memorial rooms.

Experiments in Reformed churches in Strasbourg, Switzerland, the Netherlands, and Scotland were more radical. In the Grosse Kirche in Emden the chancel was turned into a room for the Lord's Supper with a table reaching down its length. In many cases, however, the chancel was abandoned entirely. The nave, as the place for gathering to hear the word of God, was all that was used for worship. Choirs and organs were abolished. But sometimes galleries were added to increase accommodation of people. A small wooden table was placed at the head of the central aisle in the nave from which Holy Communion was administered to the people sitting in their places. In Scotland communicants sat around tables placed in the aisles.[134]

In England a more conservative spirit prevailed. However, English churchmen reflected Martin Bucer's belief that the minister should lead the service "from a position from which the things said may by all present be apprehended abundantly."[135] Anglican reformers were guided by the desire to make the service audible and visible to all worshipers. During the reign of King Edward VI stone altars were demolished and replaced by movable wooden tables, in order, as Bishop Nicholas Ridley said, to put an end to sacrifices. The Lord's Table was to be put in some "convenient" spot. This sometimes meant detaching the altar from the east wall and placing it lengthwise in the chancel, in which communicants gathered as in Luther's directions. However, communicants continued to kneel to receive the sacrament. Under Queen Elizabeth I the roods were destroyed, although the screens were retained. And a reading desk or lectern was erected for the minister in the nave from which the service might be read.

Buildings Erected for Protestant Worship

The sixteenth century was a time when existing buildings had to be adapted for Protestant worship. The need arose for new buildings in the seventeenth century as a result of destruction during the Thirty Years' War or by fire. The growth of cities and the relocation of populations (e.g., to America) also created the need for new church buildings. Lutherans readily adopted the new Baroque forms, but also arranged their buildings to reflect and expedite the requirements of evangelical worship that had not been possible with a mere adaptation of existing medieval buildings.[136] There were many experiments in church design during the seventeenth and eighteenth centuries, but certain liturgical

---

[134] See George Hay, *The Architecture of Scottish Post-Reformation Churches, 1560–1848* (Oxford: Clarendon Press, 1957).

[135] See G. W. O. Addleshaw and Frederick Etchells, *The Architectural Setting of Anglican Worship* (London: Faber & Faber, 1948), 245.

[136] See Vereinigung Berliner Architekten, *Der Kirchenbau des Protestantismus von der Reformation bis zur Gegenwart* (Berlin: Kommissions-Verlag von Ernst Toeche, 1893) and Oskar Mothes and K. S. Baurath, *Handbuch des Evangelisch-Christlichen Kirchenbaues* (Leipzig: Tauchnitz, 1898).

features characterize most of them. In many Lutheran church buildings there was a desire to bring the altar and pulpit into close juxtaposition. In Germany this often meant that the pulpit was placed behind and above the altar like a canopy, although the altar was still dressed with crucifix, candles, and paraments, and an architectural conservatism favored the longitudinal arrangement with the altar at the end of a long central aisle. In the still more conservative Scandinavian churches the altar retained its traditional position in a shallow apse, and the pulpit was located to its right (facing the nave). The baptismal font was also removed from a baptistery near the entrance and was placed in the front so that the congregation could see the baptisms. Galleries were built (sometimes multi-tiered as in theatres and opera houses) so that people could see and hear the preacher; and the pulpits were correspondingly elevated (often to the level of the second story). The favored place for the organ and choir in the Lutheran church was in a gallery at the opposite end of the building from the altar. In this location musical forces could do what was required to support congregational singing and perform church music such as cantatas without creating too much disturbance or distraction to the worshipers.

There were some similarities but also differences between Lutheran and Reformed church buildings. Reformed churches mostly did without organs, choirs, and other instrumentalists; but the galleries were still built to accommodate those who came to church to hear sermons. The altar-table was not a principal liturgical need because communion was celebrated only four times a year. It could be brought out when needed and placed in or at the head of an aisle. Since preaching dominated the service, church buildings could be designed to bring people closer to the speaker. Hence, the pulpit might be located in the center of one of the long walls instead of at the head of the longitudinal axis of the building, as is seen in the Presbyterian Church of New Castle, Delaware, built in 1707. Church buildings might be square, round, or octagonal instead of rectangular, like the round church in Richmond, Vermont, built by William Rhodes in 1812. Some of these experiments thus also characterized Congregationalist meeting houses in New England, although by the eighteenth century a standard architectural design was established in which a tall (often wine glass-style) pulpit was placed in the center of a short wall at the opposite end of the room from the entrance. Good examples are the Congregationalist meeting houses in Lebanon, New Hampshire (1712); West Barnstable, Massachusetts (1717); and North Danville, New Hampshire (1760). By the nineteenth century the pulpits had become reading desks on an elevated platform, with stairs leading to the pulpit on both sides. An example of this is the Congregationalist Church in Old Bennington, Vermont, 1805, and many other churches throughout New England.

The Architectural Synthesis of Christopher Wren

Puritan meeting houses as well as most Anglican church buildings in Britain and America in the eighteenth century reflected the influence of Sir Christopher Wren (1632–1723). In 1666 a fire devastated a major portion of the city of London, destroying eighty-four city churches and Saint Paul's Cathedral. Wren was chosen as the architect for about fifty of the new church buildings, as well as the cathedral. He was in a position to start afresh, and he did so by combining an interest in the ancient Roman basilicas with the strong English preference for Gothic architecture and brought both to bear in a hall that was designed for public worship according to the rubrics of the *Book of Common Prayer*. Wren's buildings are only superficially Baroque. Saint Paul's Cathedral, the largest space for Protestant worship in the world at the time, has nothing freakish or fantastic in its decorations; it is restrained and sober compared with Catholic Baroque church buildings (or with Saint Peter's Basilica in Rome, with which it has often been compared). In spite of the requirements in a cathedral of providing a space in which the choir offices could be sung by choristers without distractions from the nave, Wren's Protestant cathedral still conveys the sense of the whole congregation being gathered together under its immense dome. Neither Saint Paul's, nor any of Wren's parish churches, are temples of the deity; they are meeting houses of the congregation.

Wren's parish churches are typically one-room halls. His primary consideration was that "all who are present can both hear and see," and he even calculated how close people had to be to or around the pulpit to "hear distinctly." Since the days of Archbishop Laud, altar-tables in Anglican churches had been returned to their east wall position and enclosed by altar rails on three sides at which communicants knelt to receive Holy Communion. The pulpit was usually placed to the north of the altar and the reading desk to the south, both closer to the congregation than the altar but not so as to suggest a separate chancel. Baptismal fonts remained at the entryways. Thus, although there was one room, there were different liturgical centers for baptism, the prayer offices, the liturgy of the word, and the celebration of Holy Communion. In contrast with Baroque Catholic churches, in which altars were the visible focus and were designed to suggest that the worship space was a throne room for Christ the King, altars do not dominate in Wren's churches. Rather, as Addleshaw and Etchells comment, "They are only fully and properly seen by the communicants when they draw near and kneel round the altar."[137] The worshiper does not see the altar until he or she has passed by the font, the reading pew for the prayer offices, and the pulpit for the sermon.[138]

In Wren's churches and Wren-inspired churches, Gothic-type steeples encased bells summoning people to worship; basilican domes or curved ceilings gathered the people in an open hall and amplified acoustics to enable them to hear the word; and tall, clear glass windows let in the light of the sun so that people could read their Bibles and prayer books. Wren's church buildings are the apotheosis of Protestant church architecture, and his auditory church plan became the norm for most Anglican churches in Britain and America until the middle of the nineteenth century. As in Lutheran churches, Wren's churches and Episcopal churches in general during the eighteenth century display a remarkable experimentation in the use of liturgical space. For example, Christ Episcopal Church in Georgetown, South Carolina, built in 1750, has the pulpit above the

---

[137] Addleshaw and Etchells, 58.

[138] It needs to be noted that many of Wren's parish churches in London were altered during the Victorian era to reflect Ecclesiological movement styles, with high altars and collegiate divided choirs. An example of this is Saint Bride's, whose spire has been called "a madrigal in stone." A number of other Wren parish churches have been restored since World War II. Two restorations most faithful to Wren's original designs are Saint James's Piccadilly (a basilican form) and Saint Anne and Saint Agnes (a square form with columns creating a Greek cross).

altar. Pohick Episcopal Church in Accotinck, Virginia, 1769, has the pulpit on a long wall and the altar table on a short wall. Saint Michael's Episcopal Church in Charleston, South Carolina, has the pulpit to the immediate right of the center aisle, and the boxed pews oriented toward the pulpit rather than toward the communion table. St. Peter's Episcopal Church in Philadelphia, 1761, has the pulpit on the west end and the communion table at the east end. The older Christ Church, Philadelphia, features a simple communion table at the east wall under large, clear-glass windows, a wineglass-shaped pulpit to the right (facing the nave), and an organ in the west gallery, a design that would also be congenial to any Lutheran congregation.[139]

A word on pews is in order here. The emphasis on preaching in Protestant worship required seats for the auditors. The benches were enclosed by high backs or even in boxes with doors. This was done for practical reasons: to keep out drafts of wind when the doors were opened. In the wintertime, footwarmers were placed in them to keep worshipers warm, and they served as "play pens" for small children during the service. The high backs cut down the view of objects or other worshipers, but this was considered a reinforcement to meditation. We have already said that it was not considered important to see the altar until one went to communion, and there was a great deal of experimentation with the location of the altar and the pulpit in Anglican churches. On the other hand, one of the reasons for high pulpits was to enable worshipers to see the preacher above the high boards surrounding the pews. Obviously, if the boxed pews are removed (as was often the case with later renovations), the pulpits seem imperiously high. But the same impression is not given with the pews intact. We should note that the seats in the pews faced in the direction of the pulpit, not the altar. We should also note that Wren himself would have liked to be rid of pews, but church leaders preferred to keep them as a source of income (they were rented or sold); and worshipers appreciated the fact that they kept out the draft.

❧ LITURGY AS A CONFESSION OF FAITH

It has been thought that worship in the age of orthodoxy was subservient to doctrine. This was true only in the sense that doctrinal concerns regulated liturgy, but in the case of each ecclesiastical tradition, the liturgy that was regulated was an order that existed before the age of orthodoxy. The actual concern was to keep the lex orandi in balance with the lex credendi. As understood in chapter two, both "rules"—prayer and belief—are expressions of what has come to be understood as "primary theology." Primary theology is the encounter with the living God in word and sacrament, prayer and church fellowship, upon which "secondary theology" reflects. As an expression of the encounter with God, orthodox theology understood that worship no less than doctrine had to be "certain" and intact. A group of nineteenth-century Swedish liturgical editors was getting at this understanding when they wrote that liturgy "is to be regarded as a congregation's

---

[139] See the plan of the Augustus Lutheran Church in Trappe, Pennsylvania, built in the 1740s and still used for public worship in the summer months. Muhlenberg served this church as pastor and is buried in the graveyard, along with several of his family members.

confession, one of its symbols, wherein the congregation, on the basis of the divine institution of grace, builds itself up in faith, and expresses the adoration which constitutes the innermost needs and the most glorious fruits of the true life of faith."[140]

Liturgy proclaims *God*, not ideas about God; and the God who is encountered in the liturgy is the God revealed in Christ who comes to us concretely through the means of grace. The liturgy begins with a procession into the very presence of God; but this is the God who is present in Christ. "The Father and I are one . . . the Father is in me, and I am in the Father" (John 10:30, 38). Christ himself promises his presence in the assembly: "wherever two or three are gathered together in my name, there am I in the midst of them." The first prayer of the liturgy, the Kyrie, is a reminder of the christological piety of Christian worship, for it is directed to *Kurios Christos*, the name by which the faithful down through the ages have invoked and proclaimed their Savior. The first song of the liturgy, the Gloria, also expresses the prayer to Christ who alone is worthy of worship:

> Lord Jesus Christ, only Son of the Father,
> Lord God, Lamb of God:
> you take away the sin of the world;
> have mercy on us.
> You are seated at the right hand of the Father;
> receive our prayer.
> For you alone are the Holy One,
> you alone are the Lord,
> you alone are the Most High,
> Jesus Christ,
> with the Holy Spirit,
> in the glory of God the Father.

So the liturgy proclaims not just ideas about Christ, but Christ himself in the fullness of his saving work. He alone is the savior who takes away the sins of the world. He alone is the glorified one who makes intercession for us before God the Father in heaven. So he alone is worthy of receiving the true worship directed to God the Holy Trinity.[141]

After an introductory prayer that "collects" the specificities of the particular liturgy and presents these to the Father, "through Jesus Christ our Lord," the scripture readings proclaim Christ in the Old and New Testaments. The Old Testament readings (only restored to the order of mass or service in the twentieth century) project human hopes and expectations that can only be fulfilled in Christ. The Epistles and Acts of the Apostles establish what the church's kerygma (proclamation) should be in the Spirit of Christ. The Gospels bring us Christ himself in word and deed, for which reason the assembly stands with shouts of acclamation at the announcement of the gospel. The annual cycle of festivals and seasons presents christological history. To be sure, the particularities of the church year calendar and lectionary have been shaped by cultural forces and should be adapted according to cultural factors. But the essential structure of the church year— Advent, Christmas, Epiphany, Lent, Easter, Pentecost, and the Sundays of "ordinary

---

[140] *Kyrko-Handbok* (Stockholm, 1854), 10.

[141] See Gordon Lathrop, *Holy Things: A Liturgical Theology* (Minneapolis: Augsburg Fortress, 1993), 135.

time"—rehearses sacred history. And preaching on these texts and singing songs related to these themes enliven the worshiper with the remembrance of Christ.

The congregation is further engaged in the sacred story of God's saving work in Christ through the Holy Spirit in the recitation of the Creed. Creeds have been used as statements of dogma; and the Nicene Creed especially was introduced into liturgy for polemical purposes. But Luther, in his *Formula Missae*, designated the Creed a sacrificium laudis, "a sacrifice of praise." He recaptured something of the original purpose of confessions of faith, which in the New Testament were expressions of praise before the lordship of Jesus the Christ.[142] Only by the end of the second century did creeds come to be regarded as summaries of belief, useful as a "rule of faith" for believers (Irenaeus) and as professions of faith for baptismal candidates (Hippolytus). While the Apostles' Creed is embryonically reported in Hippolytus's *Apostolic Tradition*, it did not receive its final form until the seventh century. But even the conciliar Nicene-Constantinopolitan Creed was based on the baptismal confessions of the churches, amplified with christological and pneumatological specificities to establish orthodoxia (true worship) against the false worship of the Arians (false because the Arians could not worship the true God if they could not worship Christ). As such, the Nicene Creed became a mark of catholic and orthodox identity; but it was also deeply evangelical because it summarized the gospel story of Jesus.

The Creed still reminds us of the relationship between baptism and Christian life and worship. For this reason it is most appropriate that baptism be celebrated within the liturgy at the place of the Creed, as the hinge between the liturgies of the word and the eucharistic meal. The Creed is in the "first order" language of primary theology. It says what needs to be said without elaboration, and it says it to God as well as about God. As Geoffrey Wainwright observed, "In this expression of the *fides quae creditur* [the faith that is believed], the force of the *fides qua creditur* [the faith by which one believes] is firmly felt."[143] It is hardly a coincidence that the Nicene Creed, a thoughtfully enunciated statement of essential Christian dogma, is also an instrument of devotion that has summoned the resources of church music to give it proper and glorious expression. Both Luther and Calvin agreed that it should be sung. It has been profoundly set to music in the great masses of J. S. Bach, W. A. Mozart, Franz Joseph Haydn, and Johann Michael Haydn.

The Creed is followed by the anaphora or Sursum corda—the lifting up of one's heart to God. The anaphora is thanksgiving accompanying offering. Elaborate offertory rites have been laid over the simple presentation of the bread and wine; and there may have been a simple dramatic force in the offering of these gifts during the recitation of the Creed in the classical Lutheran liturgies. Originally, the eucharistic prayer or Great Thanksgiving said all that needed to be said by way of exomologesis (confession of faith) and oblatio (offering of the gifts). The introduction to the eucharistic prayer is called, in

---

[142] See D. Gerhard Delling, *Worship in the New Testament*, trans. by Percy Scott (London: Dartman, Longman & Todd, 1962), 88; Oscar Cullmann, *Early Christian Worship*, trans. by A. Steward Todd and James B. Torrance (London: SCM Press, 1953), 23.

[143] Wainwright, *Doxology*, op. cit., 191.

the Western tradition, "praefatio" (from *prae* and *fari*, to speaker before [hearers]), and already in Roman times it was a form of public proclamation in both religious and civil spheres.[144] The preface, in the Roman tradition, is also christological proclamation; and with or without the intervening Sanctus it leads to the words of institution by which the bread and wine are declared to be the body and blood of Christ. To eat of this bread and to drink from this cup in the act of communion is, as Paul says in 1 Corinthians 11:26, "to proclaim the Lord's death until he comes."

This central act of proclamation ("take and eat, the body of Christ given for you"; "take and drink, the blood of Christ shed for you") and confession of faith (the elements are received with the word "Amen" [so be it], often with the further identifying sign of the cross given in baptism) is framed in the liturgy by what secondary theology might call utterances of transcendence and radical immanence. The Holy Communion takes place between highest heaven and deepest earth: the Sanctus and the Agnus Dei. When in the liturgy we join our voices "with angels and archangels and all the company of heaven" to sing "Holy, holy, holy Lord," this is an act of utter transcendence (signified by the Holy One's entourage of heavenly beings). This is the language of the pure adoration in eternity coupled in the Sanctus-hymn with the greeting-reception ("Hosanna!") of the eschatological one "who comes in the Name of the Lord." But that one who "comes again" in the meal in anticipation of the final coming in glory is the crucified one: the "Lamb of God who takes away the sins of the world." He alone can "grant peace" to sinners, because he has entered deeply into our alienation from God in his suffering and death.

This explication of the chief Christian liturgy of word and sacrament does not purport to be complete in all particulars. We have not mentioned the intercessions, by which we voice our concerns to God on behalf of the world and its needs, which might be included in the petitions of the Kyrie (e.g., the Litany of Peace in the Byzantine liturgy) as well as in connection with the pulpit office, the offering, and the eucharistic prayer. We have not mentioned psalmody, the words of which give expression to the full range of human emotion from praise to lament in response to the words/actions of God or of human beings. We have not mentioned elements of commitment, which might be expressed in recognitions accompanying the offertory or in the concluding rite of sending-forth from the assembly into the world. But we have focused on those elements in liturgy that serve as a confession of faith, and that provide the invariable order of the divine service. These parts especially remind us of the truth claims that liturgy makes as a form of primary theology.

Here, however, we must part company with many orthodox Protestant theologians. The truth claim of the liturgy is not, as Bishop Olof Herrlin said, that "the entire content of the liturgy shall agree with the Scriptures."[145] The historic liturgy is thoroughly grounded in the Bible. But its truth claim is, as Romano Guardini would have put it, that

---

[144] Josef Jungmann, *The Early Liturgy* (Notre Dame, Ind.: University of Notre Dame Press, 1959), 300.

[145] Olof Herrlin, *Divine Service—Liturgy in Perspective*, trans. by Gene J. Lund (Philadelphia: Fortress Press, 1966), 72.

God in Christ is encountered in the liturgy of word and sacrament.[146] Liturgy as a confession of faith can only be performed in the conviction of God's reality, since confession is made to and about God.

The basic parts of the "ordinary of the mass"—Kyrie, Gloria, Credo, Sanctus, Agnus Dei—are simultaneously acts of prayer and proclamation. They both address God in Christ and they proclaim the saving work of God in Christ, for which God is to be praised. There is a certain objectivity about such prayers and proclamations in that they focus on the reality of God rather than on human need. Liturgy that ignores the subjective element of human need (whether spiritual or material) is not worship "in Spirit and in truth." But without the focus on the reality of God that orthodoxy emphasized, the resources for truly dealing with human need are soon exhausted.

---

[146] See Romano Guardini, *The Church and the Catholic and The Spirit of the Liturgy*, trans. by Ada Lane (New York: Sheed and Ward, 1935), "The Spirit of the Liturgy," 119–211.

CHAPTER 15

Liturgy in the Age of Reason

WE HAVE SEEN IN the previous chapter how orthodox Christianity was challenged toward the end of the seventeenth century by a new current of personalized "religion of the heart" known as Pietism. At about the same time another movement
challenged orthodoxy in a different way. This was the religion of the Enlightenment
known as Rationalism. It was inevitable that there would be a reaction to religious wars
and the continuing persecution of religious minorities such as the French Huguenots,
the English Nonconformists and the Salzburg Lutherans. It was inevitable that the new
scientific discoveries would raise questions about the reliability of biblical revelation, that
a more positive (anti-Augustinian) anthropology would champion free will over predestination, and that a natural theology would be constructed on the foundation of the new
cosmology.

Rationalism did not emerge in all places at the same time. Holland was the first
bastion of religious tolerance, and the persecuted from many countries found refuge
there in the seventeenth century. There the great Jewish philosopher Benedict Spinoza
(1632–1677), whose family had fled persecution in Spain, constructed his rational system,
although he was excommunicated from the Dutch synagogue because of his pantheistic
ideas. Across the Channel in England, the Cambridge Platonists showed a development
of natural theology in late Puritanism. The representative figure in England was John
Locke (1632–1696), whose *Reasonableness of Christianity* (1695) argued that the essence
of Christianity lies in its ethics. This was echoed by "the prince of rhyme and the great
poet of reason," Alexander Pope, who wrote in his *Essay on Man* (1732–1734),

For modes of faith let graceless zealots fight.
His can't be wrong, whose life is in the right.
On faith and hope the world will disagree,
But all mankind's concern is charity.

Locke did not find a discrepancy between reason and biblical revelation. Deism, however, which flourished in England for more than a century from Lord Herbert of Cherbury (d. 1648) to David Hume (d. 1776), found this juxtaposition of reason and revelation untenable, and challenged the reliability of prophecy and miracles on the basis of natural law. David Hume's *Essay on Miracles* (1748) challenged the contention that every unexplained occurrence should be taken as a sign of God's intervention.[1] Hume's work constituted the high point of English Deism, because by the 1740s it was burning out in the fires of the First Great Evangelical Awakening. But this was not before Voltaire (1694–1788) had visited England and, with Rousseau (1712–1778), was popularizing Deism back in France, where it turned into a critique of tradition that prepared the way for the French Revolution.[2]

The Enlightenment came to Germany when it was practically over in England, perhaps retarded by the strong antihumanist strain in Lutheran theology.[3] But it was replicated there on a higher plane. Gottfried Leibnitz (1646–1716), and his popularizer Christian Wolff (1679–1754), provided a philosophic apologetic conceived as parallel to revealed theology. The same process was applied to the Bible itself by the first practitioners of historical criticism, Semler, Ernesti, and Michaelis. The doctrine of inspiration was retained, but it was argued that the Holy Spirit had accommodated himself to the world-view of the times. The popular poet Christian Fürchtegott Gellert affirmed "the spacious firmament on high" as the proclamation of the divine architect, and prepared the way for true Deism to flourish in Germany. The young King Frederick II (called "the Great") of Prussia brought Voltaire to his court at Potsdam, and German translations of English Deistic writings supplemented the original German works of Reimarus and Lessing.

Toward the end of the eighteenth century Immanuel Kant of Konigsberg (1724–1804) pushed the whole program of natural religion to a new phase with his *Religion Within the Bounds of Reason Alone* (1793). Kant himself had been the product of a thoroughly pietistic upbringing and education. Even though he eschewed both pietistic and orthodox religion, he always maintained a role for religion in society and seemed to draw inspiration for writing his books of philosophy by gazing at a church steeple.[4] *Religion* was written in a complicated context that may have influenced its line of thought. Kant had developed views both of the free exercise of individual reason and duty to society that had endeared him to Frederick the Great. Under King Frederick William II, who reacted against Rationalist assaults on orthodox Christianity, Kant experienced

---

[1] See John Hunt, *Religious Thought in England* (London, 1870ff.), Vol. II.

[2] See R. Wadinger, *Voltaire, A Reformer in the Light of the French Revolution* (Geneva, 1959).

[3] See Otto W. Heick, *A History of Christian Thought*, II (Philadelphia: Fortress Press, 1966), 94.

[4] See B. A. G. Fuller, *A History of Philosophy*, 3rd ed. revised by Sterling M. McMurrin (New York: Holt, Rinehart and Winston, 1963), 216.

royal censorship of his writings on religion. *Religion* was undoubtedly influenced by his need to personally work out of the corner into which he had trapped himself.[5] He therefore developed a view of Christianity as the perfect natural religion, needing no fulfillment in prophecy or justification in miracles. There were even ways in which *Religion* was allied with principles of Lutheran theology. First, like Luther, who rejected a "theology of glory," Kant did not believe that God could be known as God is in himself (*das Ding an sich*); this was a conclusion from his "critique of pure reason." Secondly, he taught that people should do what is right because it is their duty, and not for the sake of reward or fear of punishment; so his "categorical imperative" may at least be correlated with the Lutheran assault on works-righteousness. On the other hand, there is a thoroughgoing moralism in Kant that is the exact opposite of a religion of grace.[6] Indeed, Kant rejected faith in the means of grace along with faith in miracles and faith in mysteries as illusory.[7] Human life is conceived of as a struggle between good and evil; the good will triumph with the aid of a good society. For this reason Kant defended church attendance and the sacramental celebrations—not out of devotion to God but for the sake of cultivating good citizens. He regarded baptism as a "ceremonial initiation, taking place but once, into the church-community," and communion as "an oft-repeated ceremony . . . of a renewal, continuation, and propagation of this churchly community."[8]

The idea of a natural religion that emphasized ethics, allied with the Pietist emphasis on sanctification, had great impact on preaching, which dealt less with dogma or points of biblical exegesis than with reliance on divine guidance, the cultivation of the virtuous life, and finding meaning in everyday, practical life. William Nagel provides such examples of Enlightenment sermon topics: "On the value of human expressions of good wishes" (the "Hosanna" greeting of Jesus in Matthew 21:1–11, read on the First Sunday of Advent); "On the hardiness of shepherds and a warning against the use of fur-caps" (Luke 2:1–20, read on Christmas Day); or "On going for walks—Sermon for Hypochondriacs" (the Emmaus-story in Luke 24, read on Easter Monday).[9] That Rationalist clergy would find traditional worship books and sacramental practices objectionable was inevitable, since they could have no sympathy for a cultus embodying a faith they no longer accepted. What began as an anti-ritualistic bias in Pietism became an assault on the supernatural in Rationalism. But in the state churches, the regulation of prayer books, agendas, and hymnals retarded the alteration of worship materials so that liturgical changes could be realized only through compromise. The liturgical picture is thus complicated; liturgy did not undergo uniform "deteriorization" in all churches at the same time.

Worship books in some traditions, such as the Roman Catholic and Anglican, were only slightly affected by the Age of Reason. The Reformed and free church worship

---

[5] See the introduction by Theodore M. Greene and Hoyt H. Hudson to Immanuel Kant, *Religion Within the Limits of Reason Alone* (New York: Harper Torchbooks, 1960), xxxiiff.

[6] Ibid., 166.

[7] Immanuel Kant, *Religion within the Limits of Reason Alone*, trans. by Theodore M Greene and Hoyt H. Hudson (New York: Harper and Row, 1960), 182.

[8] Ibid., 187.

[9] W. Nagel, *Geschichte des christlichen Gottesdienstes* (Berlin: de Gruyter, 1962), 146–51.

traditions, which depended more on outlines of worship than on texts, could have been highly susceptible to the profound influence of Rationalism because so much "text" was left to the minister; but sometimes brakes were applied to Rationalism by theological orthodoxy, Pietism, or Revivalism. In the Age of Reason there was actually an enrichment of Reformed and Puritan worship with the lowering of restrictions against hymn singing, organs, and church music in the interests of "edifying" the congregation. Lutheran liturgy was most subject to changes influenced by Rationalism, either because local pastors were given the freedom to experiment with liturgical orders and texts or because new worship books reflected the spirit of the times. We shall see the impact of Rationalism on Lutheran liturgy both in Europe and in America. But we will also note the exceptions to Enlightenment religion in the initial proposals of John Wesley to his Methodist followers and among the Episcopalian Non-Jurors in Scotland who provided Episcopalians in America with episcopal succession and influenced the American *Book of Common Prayer*. We will review the changes that took place in church music during the Enlightenment, including the impact of this on Reformed churches. We will then look at the role of confirmation in the Age of Reason and its contribution to "culture Christianity." We will conclude this chapter with a reflection on the relationship between Rationalism and Revivalism in terms of the concern of Enlightenment religion for the edification of the worshiper, even though the impersonal God of the Rationalists and the personal God of the Revivalists could not be more diametrically opposite. Finally, we will offer a reflection on the role and validity of emotional experience in worship.

❦ THE BREAKDOWN OF LITURGICAL ORDER

The church leaders of the Enlightenment valued public worship only to the extent that it was edifying to the people. Some viewed the liturgy only as a concession to humanity's sensual, or nonintellectual, nature, although Friedrich Gottlieb Klopstock (1724–1803) found an important role for adoration and singing in his Introduction to Part I of his *Sacred Songs* (1758).[10] Even so, official liturgies, when revised, tended to become simpler and sentimental expressions found their way into prayer texts as well as hymns. In church music, the complexities of counterpoint were eschewed in favor of homophonic treatments. J. S. Bach, considered an anachronism already during his lifetime, was eclipsed by his sons, although Bach's contemporary, George Frederick Handel, remained a popular model for church music. His oratorios were studied even by Mozart, Haydn, and Beethoven. The environment for worship also took on a light and simple character, with whitewashed walls and clear glass windows. With the elevation of the sermon above the rest of the liturgy, pulpits were typically placed on a longitudinal wall or above the altar-table, with seating arranged around it on the ground floor as well as in several tiers of balconies so that the preacher could be seen as well as heard.[11]

---

[10] See Georg Feder, "Decline and Restoration," in Friedrich Blume, ed., *Protestant Church Music*, op. cit., 334.

[11] See Ulrich Leupold, *Die liturgischen Gesänge der evangelischen Kirche im Zeitalter der Aufklärung und der Romantik* (Kassel, 1933).

Developments were not the same everywhere. Some provinces remained conservative while others allowed ministers the freedom to experiment with liturgical orders. Sometimes all liturgy was abolished entirely and, as in the Reformed churches, free orders consisting of hymns, scripture reading, sermon, and prayer were devised. In keeping with the Rationalist notion that repetition breeds monotony, the "ordinary" of the liturgy was frequently replaced by hymns that provided more variety in public worship. Also to avoid repetitiveness the prayer offices were largely suppressed in favor of preaching services. The chanting of the lessons was abandoned completely and the pericope system was often abandoned in favor of freely selected preaching texts. The frequency of the celebration of Holy Communion was greatly reduced, both because there were fewer communicants and because it was not emphasized by pastors.[12] A common practice was to detach the celebration of Holy Communion from the main service entirely, so that it took on the character of an extra devotion for the especially devout or spiritually needy. The practice of private confession as a way of preparing for communion fell away almost completely. Only rarely was the preface sung; an exhortation, prayer of confession, declaration of pardon, the words of institution, the Lord's Prayer, a prayer of thanksgiving, and benediction were deemed a sufficient liturgical order for the celebration of Holy Communion.

The consistory in Hannover granted permission to pastors to make "alterations and improvements" in the service after consulting with the more cultured lay members of their congregations. Soon a flood of orders and texts were produced to supplement the authorized Agendas that, in Luther Reed's words, "ranged in character from empty sentimentality to moralizing soliloquy and verbosity."[13] Jeremiah F. Ohl provided English translations of a number of these texts in his article on "The Liturgical Deteriorization in the Seventeenth and Eighteenth Centuries."[14] Several of the texts are from the 1808 Agenda of Christian F. Sintenis. A sampling is provided here.

AN INVITATION
Let us do as the Apostles did, and not come to the Altar to receive a sacrament, but to bring our sacrament (!) thither, viz., the obligation to hold fast His teachings, which bring us so much happiness, and always and everywhere to show public spirit, as He did. (Agenda of Sintenis)

WORDS OF INSTITUTION
Let all hear the invitation of Jesus Himself to His supper! After this manner spake the Lord when He took bread, brake it praying, and distributed it: Take, eat, this is My Body, which shall soon be offered for your benefit. Repeat this in remembrance of Me! Thus spoke the Lord when He afterward also prayerfully passed the cup around: Take, drink, this is My Blood; which shall soon be shed for your benefit. Repeat this in remembrance of Me! (Sintenis, alt.)

---

[12] Günther Stiller, *Johann Sebastian Bach and Liturgical Life in Leipzig*, op. cit., notes the alarming drop in communion registrations in the city churches after the installation of the Rationalist Pastor Johann Georg Rosenmuller as Superintendent (1785–1815), 164.

[13] Luther Reed, *The Lutheran Liturgy*, op. cit., 148.

[14] Jeremiah F. Ohl, "The Liturgical Deteriorization of the Seventeenth and Eighteenth Centuries," in *Memoirs of the Lutheran Liturgical Association* IV (1901–1902), 75–8.

A RECONSTRUCTION OF THE LORD'S PRAYER

Most High Father; Let it be our supreme purpose to glorify you; Let truth thrive among us; Let virtue already dwell here as it does in heaven; Reward our industry with bread, And our forgiving disposition with grace; From severe conflicts preserve us; And finally let all evil cease; That you are powerful, wise, and good over all—let this forever be our confidence. (Sintenis, alt.)

A FORM OF DISTRIBUTION

Eat this bread; may the spirit of devotion rest upon you with all its blessings.
Drink a little wine; moral power does not reside in this wine, but in you, in the teachings of God, and in God.

OR

Use this bread in remembrance of Jesus Christ; he that hungers after pure and noble virtue shall be filled.
Drink a little wine; he that thirsts after pure and noble virtue shall not long for it in vain. (In Hufnagel: *Liturgische Blätter*, alt.)

A PRAYER OF THANKSGIVING

Before you, the Omnipresent One, have these admirers of Jesus professed their (!) Sacrament of the Altar. To you, Omniscient One, do they appeal with all confidence and joy, that they have done so with truly upright hearts. Therefore they beseech you, the All-powerful One, to enable them to be increasingly faithful. Not as if they would feel themselves weaker than they are (!); No! No! they can do much for themselves, but—the spirit is willing and the flesh is weak! Father! support them in their weakness, so that when tempted to be unfaithful to Jesus and their vows, and to depart from their Christian convictions and sentiments, their moral nature may always triumph over their carnal nature. Thou hast a thousand means to bring this about, and certainly also hast their hearts in your power in a manner incomprehensible to them. O be their stay, therefore, when they are in danger of wavering; and should the world by its sorrows endeavor to separate them from Jesus, then cause the world itself to disappear for them in spirit, and open heaven to them, that they may refresh themselves with the glory which all those shall there share, who remain in fellowship with Jesus to the end, and who suffer as He did!... My Beloved: May God, through His Son bless you more and more with holy thoughts. (Sintenis, alt.)

SAMPLES OF BENEDICTIONS

The Lord bless and cheer you with the happiness of a blameless heart and life.
The Lord bless and cheer you with the assurance of His good pleasure.
The Lord bless and cheer you with the joy-giving hope of everlasting life. Amen (Scheiz: *Kirchen-Agende*)

OR

May God, our Father, protect and prosper us.
May Jesus Christ teach and guide, comfort and encourage us.
May the Spirit of the Lord ennoble us. Amen. (Frosch: *Allgemeine Liturgie*)

OR

The Lord bless us with wisdom, with a heart and strength for good works.
The Lord keep our souls pure, our consciences quiet, and our hearts contented.
The Lord grant us a modest portion of this life's happiness, and at last the higher joy of the life eternal. Amen. (*Schleswig-Holsteinische Agende*, 1797)

The moralism and sentimentality of Enlightenment religion is apparent in these texts, as well as a not-so-veiled polemic against the doctrine of original sin, the existence of the reality of evil, and the sacraments as means of grace by which sins are forgiven and Christians are strengthened in their spiritual warfare against evil. An inability to articulate a clear need for Holy Communion as an antidote to the unholy trinity of the world, the flesh, and the devil (as Luther had explained in his Large Catechism) probably contributed to the drastic drop in the number of communions.

The Scandinavian worship books suffered considerably less from the Enlightenment than some of the German agendas, although some characteristic features of Pietism and Rationalism are evident. The Danish Ritual of 1685 and Altar Book of 1688 (also used in Norway and eventually implemented in Iceland) gave greater prominence to the sermon and to hymn singing, which now thoroughly replaced the chant-texts of the "ordinary." The Lord's Supper became more of an appendix to the service than the climax of it. But the typical liturgy in Denmark, Norway, and Iceland continued to provide a role for a deacon as well as a priest-celebrant, who wore an alb or ankle-length surplice and a chasuble over a black cassock and ruff. The epistle and gospel continued to be chanted at the altar and not from the pulpit. Baptisms were celebrated after the pulpit office; and the Holy Communion, while less frequently celebrated, was still a part of the service, although non-communicants could leave the church with a clear conscience before Baptism and Holy Communion since the Aaronic benediction was given at the end of the pulpit office.[15]

Conditions in Sweden were even more conservative. The Church Book of 1614 had stipulated that all future innovations should be taken from Lutheran sources only, so as to avoid the past experiences of the Catholicizing of King Johan III and the Calvinist tendencies of King Karl IX. A new edition of the Mass Book was published in 1693, but revisions were minimal since Karl XI positively prohibited ministers from making any alterations in the service. During the reign of Gustav III at the end of the eighteenth century, however, Rationalism and neology influenced the Church. There was a proposal to modernize the language of the Divine Service in 1789, and in 1793 a new Church Book appeared but failed to be adopted in its present form. After further examination and modification by the clergy it was ratified in amended form by the King in 1810, and was implemented in the parishes in the following year (with considerable dissension in northern Sweden).[16] The most characteristic trait of the new mass was its rhetorical style, expressed especially in the remarkable introduction sung or said by the pastor after the opening hymn, which combines phrases from the Sanctus and the Gloria and leads into the confession of sins. Since this text was abridged in the 1894 revision (and in the Liturgy of the Augustana Synod in America), we give the full text here.

> Holy, Holy, Holy, Lord God almighty! The heavens and the earth are full of
> your glory! We praise you: We worship you: We give thanks to you for your

---

[15] See the full description of worship during the nineteenth century in F. J. Bergmann, "The Liturgy of the Icelandic Church," in *Memoirs of the Lutheran Liturgical Association*, Vol. IV (1901–1902), 104–7.

[16] See N. Forsander, "The Swedish Liturgies," in *Memoirs of the Lutheran Liturgical Association*, Vol. II (1899–1900), 24–5.

wonders. O! Lord God, heavenly King. God, the Father almighty! O! Lord, the only-begotten Son of the All highest, Jesu Christ! O! Holy Spirit, Spirit of peace, truth, and grace!

All your works praise you, eternal God: Eternal, as you are, is your might, unchangeable your goodness. Look in mercy, eternal Father, upon a people, gathered in your holy house to worship you, to give thanks to you for your benefits and to beseech your favour for their spiritual and bodily welfare. Enlighten our understanding in the knowledge of you, and teach our hearts to present unto you your holy offering of a true obedience. Bowed beneath the burden of our sins, we fall down before you in the dust, and invoke your grace and deliverance. O God, our Saviour! You are gentle and good, mighty in grace and compassion. Graciously hear the cry, that is here lifted up with one accord to your throne.[17]

This is followed by the confession of sins and absolution, the three-fold Kyrie, and the Gloria in abridged or chorale version. The only other noteworthy features of the 1811 Mass are the omission of the Nicene Creed as an alternative to the Apostles' Creed and the relocation of the exhortation to the communicants from after the consecration to before the preface.

If Rationalistic influences were minimal in the Scandinavian liturgies, they were rampant in early American Lutheran liturgies. Not only was rationalistic theology imported to America, but the new republic was founded on the doctrines of Locke and Hume, Rousseau and Voltaire. Indeed, the revolutionaries regarded the emerging American Republic as the fulfillment of the hopes of the Enlightenment.[18] Lutherans in America participated in the ferment and spirit that led to the war for independence and the establishment of the new government. It is noteworthy that while the elder Muhlenberg remained politically neutral during the Revolutionary War, his sons put off their clerical attire for the vesture of soldiers and statesmen and joined other Lutheran lay persons in providing leadership both in the war for independence and in the emerging new government. Muhlenberg's oldest son, John Peter Gabriel Muhlenberg, resigned from his call in order to lead a regiment of Virginians under General Washington and rose to the rank of major general. After the war he served as vice president of the Commonwealth of Pennsylvania and as a U.S. Congressman and U.S. Senator. His brother, Frederick Augustus Conrad Muhlenberg, served in the Continental Congress, was twice speaker of the Pennsylvania legislature, served as president of the Pennsylvanian convention that ratified the U.S. Constitution, and was elected the first Speaker of the U.S. House of Representatives. The Swedish Lutheran layman, John Hanson of Maryland, helped organize pan-colonial resistance to the Stamp Act, was a member of the Continental Congress, signed the Articles of Confederation, and under that instrument in 1781 was elected the first "President of the United States in Congress Assembled."[19]

---

[17] In Eric E. Yelverton, *The Mass in Sweden*, op. cit., 151–2; alt.

[18] See Gordon S. Wood, *The Radicalism of the American Revolution* (New York: Alfred A. Knopf, 1992), 189ff.

[19] See Abdel Ross Wentz, *A Basic History of Lutheranism in America*, rev. ed. (Philadelphia: Fortress Press, 1964), 44ff.

Lutherans in America lived and breathed the ideologies of liberty and equality that became the hallmarks of American society. Early on, they developed lay leadership in congregations and in the years after the Revolution added lay delegates to the ministeria in synodical meetings. Moreover, thanks to the efforts of Henry Melchior Muhlenberg, Lutherans in America had their own church organization and were paying their own way long before the outbreak of the Revolution. The Dutch Reformed, Episcopal, Methodist, and Roman Catholic churches did not achieve independent American organizations until after the political ties with Europe had been severed. Lutherans owed nothing to Europe, and therefore it is not surprising that they felt no compulsion to follow the old Lutheran agendas in their worship practices. Muhlenberg's Agenda of 1748 was used by pastors in its handwritten form for about forty years after it was adopted by the Ministerium of Pennsylvania. It was finally published by synodical authorization in 1786, but with amendments. The rubrics indicating when the minister should face the altar or face the people were omitted. Any suitable opening hymn could be used, whereas Muhlenberg had specified a hymn of invocation to the Holy Spirit. The Gloria was omitted. An extemporaneous prayer or a morning prayer was substituted for the collect of the day. The formularies for announcing the epistle and gospel were omitted. The gospel was no longer read at the altar but from the pulpit, and the people were no longer directed to stand during the reading of the gospel. In fact, gospel texts other than the assigned pericope could be read, at the discretion of the minister. The hymn of the day no longer needed to be suitable to the day or season in the church year. The Creed was omitted. Another and much longer general prayer was provided.[20]

Muhlenberg's son-in-law, Dr. John Christopher Kunze, who served as president of the newly formed New York Ministerium, undertook an English translation of the Liturgy of 1786, in connection with his *Hymn and Prayer Book* of 1795. This was to meet the demands for worship in English, especially in New York City. This liturgy was apparently short-lived, perhaps because it paled in comparison with the language of the new *Book of Common Prayer* of The Episcopal Church in the United States, just authorized in 1789. The Swedish congregations along the Delaware were already adopting the *Book of Common Prayer* for worship in English, and a prominent New York City pastor, George Strebeck, who found Kunze's liturgy inadequate, after trying his hand at his own liturgy and hymn collection, defected to The Episcopal Church.[21] In 1806, an associate of Dr. Kunze, Ralph Williston, published a *Book of Hymns and Liturgy of the Lutheran Church*, which had the approval of Kunze as president of the Ministerium. It is a conflation of parts from the 1786 Liturgy with material from the *Book of Common Prayer*. Its order of Morning Service was as follows:

---

[20] See D. M. Kemerer, "Early American Liturgies," in *Memoirs of the Lutheran Liturgical Association* IV (1901–1902), 88.

[21] One of Muhlenberg's sons also defected to the Episcopal Church and became the father of William Augustus Muhlenberg, one of the leading figures in the Episcopal Church in the nineteenth century. In addition to his reorganization of the parish for urban mission, he worked toward the enrichment of liturgy and hymnody in the 1853 revision of the *BCP*. See A. W. Skardon, *Church Leader in the Cities: William Augustus Muhlenberg* (Phladelphia: University of Pennsylvania Press, 1971).

The minister addresses the congregation from the altar and leads them in a
confession of sins.

The salutation and response are followed by an extempore or standard prayer.

The gospel and epistle are read (in that order!).

A hymn is sung.

The minister offers an extempore prayer, followed by the Lord's Prayer.

The sermon follows.

The litany or the Te Deum may be sung.

A concluding hymn is announced and the pulpit office is ended with "The
peace of God, which passeth all understanding, keep your hearts and
minds, through Christ Jesus."

From the altar the salutation is followed by an extempore or general prayer
and the Aaronic benediction, with the Trinitarian invocation.

The Lord's Supper, when celebrated, followed the pulpit office and was similar to
the orders for 1748 and 1786, except that there was a separate prayer for the consecration
of the elements and the words, "Jesus said," were added to the forms of distribution.[22]

In 1817, at the insistence of the New York Synod, Drs. Quitman and Wacker-
hagen edited and published a *Hymn Book and Enlarged Liturgy for the Use of the
Evangelical Lutheran Church*. The liturgical portion of this book provided alternate and
optional texts to those already provided in 1806, most of them suffused with Rationalist
rhetoric whereby the Father in heaven may also be addressed as "Supremely Exalted and
Adorable Jehovah," "Infinite and Incomprehensible Jehovah," "Self-existent and Infinite
Jehovah." Communicants are invited to "this feast of love," and in the forms of distribution the words "Jesus said" must be used, but the minister could be free to substitute any
other words after these.[23]

In the heavily Germanic culture of Pennsylvania, the use of English in worship
was not such an urgent issue at this time. But the *Agende* published by the Ministerium
of Pennsylvania in 1818 was no improvement over the English language efforts. Almost
every vestige of congregational response is eliminated. The confession of sins, offered by
the pastor, is not followed by an absolution. The confessional prayer led to the Kyrie.
The salutation has no response. The gospel and epistle may be read (again, in that
order!), or any suitable scripture reading may be substituted. A hymnal was published in
the same year for joint use among Lutherans and Reformed, who were already sharing
church buildings and had cooperated in the joint founding of Franklin College in
Lancaster.[24] The Rationalist character of this hymnal is evident in the fact that it included only one of Luther's hymns, only eleven of Gerhardt's, while forty of Gellert's
hymns were represented.[25]

While there were subsequent revisions of agendas and hymnals after 1818, none
represented a significant departure from the 1818 *Agende* until the 1850s. But if Rationalism contributed to the disintegration of liturgical form, Revivalism contributed to the

---

[22] Kemerer, 89.

[23] Ibid., 90.

[24] On Lutheran cooperation with other denominations see Nelson, *The Lutherans in North America*, op. cit.,
91ff.

[25] See Reed, *The Lutheran Liturgy*, op. cit., 171.

deterioriation of hymnody. In the 1820s and 1830s especially, the influence of the Second Great Awakening began to be felt in many Lutheran congregations as their pastors adopted the "new measures" of Revivalism. Revival hymns and temperance hymns found a place in the hymnals of the time. Thus the General Synod's *Hymns, Selected and Original* (1828) included the following example:

> Round the temp'rance standard rally,
> All the friends of human kind;
> Snatch the devotees of folly,
> Wretched, perishing and blind:
> Loudly tell them
> How they comfort now may find.

LITURGICAL EXCEPTIONS

The Wesleyan Movement

Throughout the period of Rationalism there were voices raised that took exception to the Rationalist directions in theology and worship. The strongest movements against Rationalism were the Great Awakenings in Great Britain and then in America. Growing out of the First Great Awakening were the Methodist Societies founded by the Wesley brothers, John (1703–1791) and Charles (1707–1788). John Wesley's early influences all disposed him to follow a non-Rationalist direction. Coming out of a high Anglican parsonage, his convictions concerning the need for inward holiness of life were confirmed by his reading of William Law's *Christian Perfection* and *A Serious Call to a Devout and Holy Life* (London, 1729). This exposed Wesley to a High Church movement at Oxford University that emphasized a disciplined devotional life and frequent reception of Holy Communion, as well as a commitment to the practical works of charity among the urban poor, the illiterate, and the imprisoned.[26]

On a voyage to Georgia in 1735, John Wesley encountered the warmer piety of the Moravians. Convicted by them of a need for a genuine assurance of pardon, Wesley had his own such experience of grace when he related that his "heart was strangely warmed" at a meeting in Aldersgate Street in London in 1738, following the reading of Luther's Preface to the Epistle to the Romans.[27] Later that year he paid a visit to Zinzendorf's Herrnhut Community in Germany, where he reflected more seriously on the role of sanctification within the order of salvation and received inspiration for the development of the class meetings of the Methodist Societies.

There are ways in which Wesley's distaste for exclusivist dogma (e.g., his dislike of the Athanasian Creed), his theological Arminianism (belief in universal salvation) and his emphasis on sanctification (the role of perfection or holiness in Christian life) correlate with Rationalism's antidogmatic biases and emphases on free will and the ethical life.

---

[26] See David Lowes Watson, "Methodist Spirituality," in Senn, ed., *Protestant Spiritual Traditions*, op. cit., 217ff.

[27] See *The Bicentennial Edition of the Works of John Wesley*, ed. by Albert C. Outler (Nashville: Abingdon Press, 1984), I, 475–6.

But James F. White is right when he asserts that "Methodist worship was a countercultural movement in the midst of the English Enlightenment."[28]

Methodist worship was countercultural in two respects. First, it was enthusiastic, and this was frowned upon by the Anglican establishment. It was enthusiastic because it reached out to the poor, particularly the new urban proletariat, those persons displaced from farms and estates to work in "the dark satanic mills" of London, Bristol, Newcastle, Liverpool, and other emerging cities. John Wesley traveled incessantly by horseback from one city to another, often holding preaching services outdoors because the crowds could not fit or were not welcomed into church buildings. Charles Wesley provided the Methodist meetings with the greatest outpouring of hymnody in the English language— some six thousand hymns. It was John Wesley, in fact, who published the first Anglican hymnal, *Collection of Psalms and Hymns* (Charleston, 1737). The Wesleys encouraged hymn singing not only at the preaching services but also during communion, and their eucharistic hymns are the best source of Wesleyan eucharistic piety, with their accents on the eucharistic sacrifice, the role of the Holy Spirit in the sacrament, and the eucharistic meal as a foretaste of the feast to come.[29] The pleading of the atoning sacrifice of Christ and the confession of his "very presence" in the earthly eucharistic banquet is expressed in "Victim Divine, Your Grace We Claim" (*LBW* 202).

Second, Methodist worship was countercultural because it was sacramental; it emphasized baptism, the Lord's Supper, and prayer as "the means of grace."[30] At a time when Holy Communion was celebrated in Anglican practice three or four times a year, Wesley urged reception as frequently as possible.[31] The intense cultivation of the devout life in the small classes, with their more informal opportunities for worship with extempore prayer, fed into the larger societies. Indeed, one could not receive communion at a society meeting without a ticket from one's class. Wesley believed that only ordained ministers should preside at the Lord's Supper, so his provision of lay leaders of classes and lay preachers at society meetings was not extended to the eucharist. But the problem of finding Anglican clergy who would preside at the eucharist as frequently as Methodists preferred was solved only by Wesley himself ordaining presbyters to serve Methodist societies at first in American (where the Methodists became independent in 1784) and then in England (although the Methodists did not officially separate from the Church of England until after Wesley's death).

When the Methodist societies in the United States became independent, Wesley provided a revision of the *Book of Common Prayer* for their use. He accepted some of the Puritan exceptions to the *Book of Common Prayer* from 1661, and added a few amendments of his own. Most of these were in the interest of shortening the services on the Lord's Day in order to make the full communion service more tolerable so as to be celebrated more frequently. But it was essentially the Morning Prayer and Communion

---

[28] White, *Protestant Worship*, op. cit., 152.

[29] See J. Ernest Rattenbury, *The Eucharistic Hymns of John and Charles Wesley* (London: Epworth Press, 1948).

[30] This was the title of an important sermon by John Wesley. See *The Works of John Wesley*, I, 381.

[31] See his sermon on "The Duty of Constant Communion," in *The Works of John Wesley*, III, 428–9.

Service of the 1662 the *Book of Common Prayer* that Wesley provided for American Methodists, because he believed that "there is no LITURGY in the World, either in ancient or modern language, which breathes more of a solid, scriptural, rational Piety, than the COMMON PRAYER of the CHURCH of ENGLAND."[32] Methodists in Britain also continued using the rites of the *Book of Common Prayer*.

Conditions in America prevented Wesley's vision from being realized. The lack of pastors or ordained elders limited the frequency with which Holy Communion could be celebrated. This led to the substitution of the Love Feast, presided at by deacons, being celebrated as a substitution for, and eventually in preference to, the Lord's Supper.[33] But in addition to these conditions, it must be admitted that Bishop Francis Asbury, who was acutely attuned to the American situation, appreciated Wesley's pragmatism more than his traditionalism. While Asbury concurred with Wesley that unordained ministers should not preside at the Lord's Supper, it was more out of a sense of discipline than to defend a traditional approach to the sacrament. So little did the church year mean anything to Asbury that he scarcely even noted Christmas Day in his journals, much less other lesser festivals.[34] The year after John Wesley's death, in 1792, the 314 pages of his *Prayer Book* were quietly laid aside in favor of thirty-seven pages of "Sacramental Services, Etc." in the *Book of Discipline*. The Sunday service became more free-form in terms of the selection of lessons and extempore prayer (since Methodist worship leaders found that they could pray more earnestly with their eyes closed than with their eyes open, thus precluding the use of a book). All that survived was the communion portion of the Sunday service, when used, and the occasional services for the baptism of infants, the baptism of adults, marriage, burial, and the ordination of bishops, elders, and deacons.[35] Methodism in America was deeply affected by the individualistic piety of the frontier and the need to reach people in widely scattered settlements through circuit riders, so that the practices of revivalism and what White calls "frontier worship" replaced the class system of early Methodism as well as the liturgical life of the early Methodist societies. We shall propose that Revivalism was a variation of the Enlightenment emphasis that worship should have an impact on the worshiper. But we must also reckon with the fact that the emphasis on edification in Enlightenment religion contributed to or was modified by the ethos of pragmatism in American life.

The Non-Jurors and the American Prayer Book

One other major exception to Enlightenment religion that must be noted was the High Church party of Anglicans who refused to take the oath of allegiance to William of Orange. Archbishop Sancroft, ten bishops, and some 400 clergy suffered deprivation rather than take an oath that they regarded as inconsistent with the oath they had already

---

[32] Cited in Thompson, *Liturgies of the Western Church*, op. cit., p 416. The full texts are provided in Thompson, 417ff.

[33] See Frank Baker, *Methodism and the Love-Feast* (London: Epworth Press, 1957).

[34] See William N. Wade, "A History of Public Worship in the Methodist Episcopal Church" [unpublished doctoral dissertation] (University of Notre Dame, 1981), 146–52.

[35] White, op. cit., 158.

taken to the anointed King James II. These "Non-Jurors," as they were called, emphasized the apostolic succession of the episcopate, the catholicity of each episcopal church, and the authority of the church fathers in the interpretation of scripture. They were able to command a following in parts of England and Scotland for political as well as theological reasons, and in 1717 the government even suspended Convocation for more than a century for its opposition to certain Protestant ideas and because of the High Churchmen's efforts to gain control of the lower house.[36]

The influence of this party waned during the eighteenth century, only to experience resurgence in the Oxford Movement of the nineteenth century. In the meantime, they played a role in the establishment of the Episcopal Church in the United States of America. Anglicans had no bishops in the colonies, and while this had been discussed throughout the eighteenth century (and resisted both in the Privy Council, which feared the opposition of the dissenters, and also by parish vestries, which were not prepared to share their power with a bishop) it became critical after the American Revolution if the Episcopal Church were to survive.[37]

The Revolution left the Anglican Church in shambles. The Anglican Church had not been strong in the colonies outside of Maryland, Virginia, and the Carolinas, although it was making strong inroads in Connecticut during the eighteenth century. But beyond this the Anglican Church was looked upon with hostility by other Americans, for political as well as theological and liturgical reasons. Even though probably two-thirds of the signers of the Declaration of Independence were Anglicans, and Anglicans in the southern colonies were deeply committed to the cause of independence, most of the Loyalists who emigrated to Canada after the War were Anglicans; and American antipathy toward the crown included hostile feelings toward the Church of England. Once the Continental Congress declared independence, Anglican clergy were faced with the problem of what to do with the mandatory prayers for the king and the royal family included in the Prayer Book; and some closed their churches rather than omit them. Others simply omitted these prayers and some substituted new prayers for the new state.[38] There was no organization for all of the Anglican churches in the several states, and each proceeded on its own path toward reconstitution after the war. The first to act, however, was the Anglican Church in Connecticut, which dispatched to England the high churchman Samuel Seabury (who had been imprisoned during the Revolution for his Loyalist sympathies) to obtain consecration as a bishop. Existing laws prevented the archbishop of Canterbury from consecrating someone who could not take the oaths of allegiance and supremacy to the king. So Seabury applied to the Non-Juring bishops of Scotland and was consecrated by three of them on November 14, 1784.[39] But the condition of his consecration was that

[36] See Stephen Neill, *Anglicanism* (Baltimore: Penguin Books, 1958), 173–5.

[37] Ibid., 223–4. See also Carl Bridenbaugh, *Mitre and Sceptre: Transatlantic Faiths, Ideas, Personalities and Politics, 1689–1775* (New York: Oxford University Press, 1962), 27–8.

[38] See Piepkorn, *Profiles in Belief*, op. cit., II, 197.

[39] As relations with England thawed, William White and Samuel Provost were consecrated by the archbishop of Canterbury in Lambeth Palace in 1787. It is ironic that Seabury, the Loyalist, could not be consecrated by Church of England bishops while William White, who had served as chaplain to the Continental Congress, could be.

he would try to persuade the church in America to adopt the communion office of the Non-Jurors, which was largely based on the 1637 Scottish Prayer Book, which was styled in turn after the 1549 the *Book of Common Prayer*.

Marion Hatchett has documented the complicated history that led to the adoption of the first American *Book of Common Prayer*.[40] There was widespread agreement that an American Prayer Book was needed, but it was felt that the only way to gain consensus on one would be to make those changes in the current Prayer Book necessitated by political independence. Seabury too realized that the Scottish book would require revision in order to be acceptable to American Episcopalians, who tended on the whole to be Latitudinarian rather than High Church. A committee prepared such revisions and sent a draft of a Prayer Book to Episcopal churches in the various states. The committee received proposed revisions from these conventions and amalgamated them into a Prayer Book proposal that was submitted to a convention of all the state Episcopal churches outside of New England, held in Philadelphia in 1785. This draft was accepted and published in 1786. This book was adopted in all the states except New Jersey and Connecticut. Seabury, as bishop of a High Church and Tory diocese, had done an about-face and opposed the proposed book. This required further revision before the American Prayer Book was finally adopted at the General Convention of the Episcopal Church in the United States in 1789.

A number of sources fed into the 1789 Prayer Book (authorized in 1790): two anonymous collections of Non-Juror essays that had contributed to the 1786 version: *Free and Candid Disquisitions* (1749) and *The Expediency and Necessity of Revising and Improving the Publick Liturgy* (1749); ideas from Bishop Jeremy Taylor's *Holy Dying* and Bishop Edmund Gibson's *Family Devotions*; a manuscript notebook of Seabury's that described such varied sources as the Scottish Communion Office and the Liturgy of King's Chapel in Boston (a rite based on ancient Arian liturgies, since this chapel became Unitarian); as well as the existing Prayer Book of the Church of England. This book lasted, with supplemental pamphlets for mission use in the 1850s and an Armed Services edition in the 1860s and only minor revisions in 1892, until the more major revision of 1928. It must be regarded as a major worship resource for evangelical catholic liturgy in the United States. In the face of liturgically deficient American Lutheran agendas, the *Book of Common Prayer* represented a full liturgical resource to which Lutherans could turn, especially for prayers and occasional services in English. When Lutherans began working in earnest on a common service in English in the second half of the nineteenth century, they turned to the translations of texts in the *Book of Common Prayer* (including the Lord's Prayer, Nicene and Apostles' Creeds, and canticles).

The American Prayer Book provided a church year calendar and lectionary for daily prayer; orders for daily Morning and Evening Prayer; the Litany; a collection of prayers and thanksgivings; collects, epistles, and gospels for use throughout the church year; the Order for Administration of the Lord's Supper, or Holy Communion; orders for

---

[40] See Marion J. Hatchett, *The Making of the First American Prayer Book* (unpublished Th.D. dissertation) (New York: General Theological Seminary, 1972).

the Ministration of Baptism of Infants and Adults, in houses and in churches; a Catechism; the Order for Confirmation; the Form for the Solemnization of Marriage; the Order for the Visitation of the Sick; the Communion of the Sick; the Order for the Burial of the Dead; the Thanksgiving for Women after Childbirth, commonly called "The Churching of Women"; prayers for use at sea, in the visitation of prisoners, for harvest time, for use in families; and the Psalms of David.[41]

While the obligation to recite the prayer offices daily was not specified, they were called "Daily Morning Prayer" and "Daily Evening Prayer." The book provided for Morning and Evening Prayer a selection of scripture verses to use as a call to worship. This was followed by an invitation to confession, a general confession, and a "Declaration of Absolution." The Lord's Prayer followed the confessional office. The second of the opening versicles for Morning and Evening Prayer ("O God, make speed to save us . . .") was dropped out of Latitudinarian and Arian concerns. After the Gloria Patri, the *Venite exultemus* (Psalm 95) and other psalms followed in Morning Prayer, the psalms and the Gloria in Evening Prayer. Out of concern for repetition, the rubrics indicated that the Gloria Patri would not have to be recited after the psalms and canticles. There were two lessons, one each from the Old Testament and the New Testament. Canticles following the lessons were as follows:

MORNING PRAYER	EVENING PRAYER
Old Testament Lesson	Old Testament Lesson
Te Deum	Psalm 92:1–4, substituted for the Magnificat
or Benedicte, omnia opera	
New Testament Lesson	New Testament Lesson
Jubilate Deo	Psalm 103:1–4, 20–22, substituted for the
or Benedictus (first four verses)	Nunc dimittis

The readings and canticles or psalms were followed by the Apostles' or Nicene Creed. The state churches (conventions) were given permission to omit the phrase "He descended into hell" or to substitute "He went to the Place of Departed Spirits." Not all of the versicles and responses from the 1662 the *Book of Common Prayer* were retained. Several fixed collects were provided for each office:

Collect for the Day
Collect for Peace (different for Morning and Evening Prayer)
Collect for Grace in Morning Prayer ("O Lord, our heavenly Father . . . who
    hast safely brought us to the beginning of this day . . .")
Collect for Aid against Perils in Evening Prayer ("Lighten our darkness . . .")
Prayer for the President of the United States, and all in Civil Authority
Prayer for the Clergy and People
Prayer for all Conditions of Men
General Thanksgiving

---

[41] See W. McGarvey, ed., *Liturgiae Americanae: or the Book of Common Prayer As Used in the United States of America Compared with the Proposed Book of 1786 and with the Prayer Book of the Church of England, and an Historical Account and Documents* (Philadelphia: Philadelphia Church Publishing Co., 1907).

> Prayer of John Chrysostom ("Almighty God, who hast given us grace at this
> time with one accord to make our common supplications unto thee . . .")

Some of these prayers could be omitted, and other collects could be added. The Litany was said or sung in place of these prayers on Sundays. Wednesdays and Fridays were also Litany days, unless the Holy Communion were to follow Morning Prayer.

Holy Communion was being celebrated more than three or four times a year in many parishes when the 1790 the *Book of Common Prayer* was adopted. Ante-Communion could be used on Sundays and festivals when the sacrament was not celebrated. The communion office in the proposed 1786 book was retained substantially as it was in the 1790 book. It included the following:

> Lord's Prayer
> Collect for Purity ("Almighty God, unto whom all hearts are open . . .")
> Reading of the Decalogue or Summary of the Law
> Collect for the Day
> Epistle
> Gospel (with acclamation "Glory be to thee, O Lord")
> Nicene or Apostles' Creed (could be omitted on nonfestival days or if said in
>   Morning Prayer)
> Sermon
> Offertory Sentences
> Offering
> Prayer for the whole state of Christ's Church militant
> Exhortation
> Invitation, Confession of Sins, and Absolution
> Comfortable Words
> Sursum Corda
> Preface (proper prefaces provided for Christmas-day, and seven days after; for
>   Easter-day, and seven days after; for Ascension-day, and seven days after;
>   for Whitsunday and six days after; for Trinity Sunday). Permission was given
>   to omit the Trinity Preface or substitute a less metaphysical version of it.
> Prayer of Humble Access ("We do not presume to come to this thy Table,
>   trusting in our own righteousness . . .")
> Prayer of Consecration ("All glory be to thee, Almighty God . . .")
> Ministration of Holy Communion ("all devoutly kneeling")
> Lord's Prayer
> Thanksgiving Prayer
> Gloria or another hymn is sung
> Blessing

The Prayer of Consecration is noteworthy. It was substantially what Seabury had in his Notebook, derived from the Scottish Prayer Book. Some of the Scottish Episcopal ministers in America had been using the Scottish Prayer Book and had insisted on an epiclesis. This was passed by the Virginia and Pennsylvania conventions and incorporated into the 1790 Prayer Book.[42] The text of the epiclesis is as follows:

---

[42] See Marion J. Hatchett, *Sanctifying Life, Time, and Space: An Introduction to Liturgical Study* (New York: The Seabury Press, 1976), 152–3.

> And we most humbly beseech thee, O merciful Father, to hear us; and, of thy almighty goodness, vouchsafe to bless and sanctify, with thy Word and Holy Spirit, these your gifts and creatures of bread and wine; that we, receiving them according to thy Son our Saviour Jesus Christ's holy institution, in remembrance of his death and passion, may be partakers of his most blessed Body and Blood.

It is also noteworthy that if additional supplies of bread and wine were needed, the whole Prayer of Consecration from "All glory be to thee" through "partakers of his most blessed Body and Blood" was to be recited, not just the words of institution alone as in the 1662 *Book of Common Prayer.*

The 1790 book represents an impoverishing of the church year: black letter days and the observance of the eves of festivals were done away with. However, the observance of the chief festivals, days of devotion, and seasons of the church year was an exception in Calvinistic America. One state occasion, Thanksgiving Day, was added; and, of course, the four state commemorations in the *Book of Common Prayer* of the Church of England were dropped.

The occasional services of Baptism, Confirmation, Marriage, and Burial were retained with only slight emendations as they were received from the Prayer Book of the Church of England. We would note that these included the sanctifying of the water in baptism (using a version of Luther's "Flood Prayer") and the exchange of rings in marriage (although not their blessing). To the final exhortation to the sponsors of candidates for infant baptism (who could be parents) was added the admonition: "Ye are to take care that *this Child* be brought to the Bishop to be confirmed by him, so soon as *he* can say the Creed, the Lord's Prayer, and the Ten Commandments, and *is* sufficiently instructed in the other parts of the Church-Catechism set forth for that purpose." The catechetical component of confirmation was emphasized in a situation in which basic Christian education had to be provided in the home and the parish rather than in the schools.

Finally, it should be noted that the 1790 Prayer Book included the whole of the musical Psalter of Tate and Brady as well a small hymn collection, composed chiefly of the hymns of Isaac Watts, Philip Doddridge, and Joseph Addison. This gave hymnody a greater recognition than it had previously had in Anglicanism.

🍇 CHANGES IN CHURCH MUSIC AND HYMNODY

The previous chapter showed how Johann Sebastian Bach called attention to the decline of church music in his famous Memo to the Leipzig City Council of 1730. That his assessment was an accurate prophecy is validated by history. We would not want to paint a picture of a steady deterioriation in all places; there were regional differences. Nor did the call for confessional revival in 1817 lead to an immediate revival of church music. Indeed, as Georg Feder pointed out, "Viewed as a whole, the period of 'decline' shows even more originality than the period of restoration, not only in the music but also in the way it dealt with the ideas and problems of church music. Close scrutiny will show that the restoration failed to create a prominent place for Protestant church music in the general consciousness. Only the Bach revival, which did not come from within the church, accomplished this."[43]

Nevertheless, the existence of high quality and well-executed church music for public services, weddings, funerals and other special occasions depended on the institutions of the school choir, the cantorate, the town and court musicians who were obligated to participate in church music, and voluntary assistance from students and town musical organizations. As the old Latin schools were invaded by humanist educators of the Enlightenment, they lost their ecclesiastical connection. The regimen the boys' choirs were put through, their singing processions through the streets in all kinds of weather, their presence at funerals (and sometimes at executions), and their traditional forms of begging, were all considered unseemly by enlightened citizens. Demands escalated for the abolition of these choral foundations. Increasingly, their place was taken by amateur singing societies (*Singakademien*), at a time when the best musicians were finding employment outside the church in the burgeoning secular concert halls and opera houses that were flourishing by the late eighteenth century.[44] Changing notions of the creative artist toward the end of the eighteenth century also caused critics to look down on "official" composing, whether for the church, the court, or the city. It was considered superior to compose "for eternity" (Preussner's term) rather than for functions; C. P. E. Bach had this in mind when he composed his famous *Heilig* for double choir. Cantors and kapellmeisters (conductors) still provided functional music for church and court, and even composers who were free agents had to accept commissions for specific works; but the Enlightenment spawned an ideal of art for art's sake that gained momentum in the Age of Idealism and Romanticism.

Music composed "to the glory of God alone," as Bach inscribed many of his compositions, might actually have appealed to those enlightened aesthetes. But Enlightenment notions viewed church music, like liturgy generally, not so much to glorify God as to edify the congregation. This point of view worked against the polyphonic choral and organ music such as Bach had composed and in favor of more homophonic music. Handel's monumental works were imported into Germany and came to be regarded as the ideal for church music. In Catholic circles there was even a revival of Palestrina. The idealization of Handel and Palestrina influenced the church music of Wolfgang Amadeus Mozart (1756–1791), who applied for the position of unsalaried assistant to the kapellmeister of Saint Stephen's Cathedral in Vienna in 1791, with the hope of succeeding the elderly and feeble kapellmeister upon the latter's death. The position paid well; and Mozart was taking a serious interest in church music toward the end of his life. He

---

[43] Georg Feder, "Decline and Restoration," in Blume, ed., *Protestant Church Music*, op. cit., 319

[44] Among the celebrated examples are George Frederick Handel, who left the employment of the Elector of Hannover to be a free agent in London; Johann Christian Bach, who also took up residence in London and influenced the young Wolfgang Amadeus Mozart on a visit to London; Mozart himself, who early sought release from the court of the Archbishop of Salzburg to be a free agent in Vienna; and Franz Josef Haydn, who retired with a pension from the service of the Esterhazy princes and spent his last dozen productive years as a free agent in Vienna. Beethoven was never in the employment of any court or church.

composed for his friend Anton Stoll a motet for the Feast of Corpus Christi entitled *Ave, verum corpus,* which was performed at the Baden Parish Church in 1791. With this motet, written in the popular *(Volkstuemlichkeit)* style, as well as the Kyrie κ. v. 341 and the Requiem, Mozart was developing a musical style that was unadorned, devotional, direct, and easily understood by the public, in keeping with the Enlightenment views of Emperor Joseph II of Austria.[45] Unfortunately, while the City Council granted Mozart's petition, Herr Kapellmeister Hoffman survived Mozart by two years and church music was deprived of the potentially enormous influence Mozart could have made on it had he made a career of it. Mozart exerted some musical influence on his older friend and colleague, Franz Josef Haydn (1732–1809), but not, apparently, on his church music. The symphonic masses that Haydn resumed writing in 1796 after fourteen years of writing no church music display a contrapuntal texture that was not favored by the enlightened authorities in Austria.[46] Franz Josef's brother, Johann Michael Haydn (1737–1806), while music director at the court of the Prince-Archbishop of Salzburg, wrote church music that was much more in keeping with the simple, homophonic ideal of the Enlightenment.[47]

In Lutheran lands the decline in church music institutions went hand in hand with the revival of emphasis on chorale singing by the congregation. But the chorales themselves underwent changes. Many, especially the old Reformation catechetical hymns, were simply eliminated from hymnals as space was given to newly composed hymns. The texts of many other old chorales were revised. This was a task advocated by Friedrich Gottlieb Klopstock (1724–1803) in the appendix to Part I of his *Sacred Songs* (1758); and many others followed his example. The greatest and most popular hymn-writer of the Enlightenment was Christian Fuerchtegott Gellert (1715–1769). Of his fifty-four sacred songs, thirty-three were written to be sung to existing hymn tunes; but melodies had to be created for the meters of the remaining twenty-one. A number of composers leaped to the opportunity, including C. P. E. Bach (who in 1758 set Gellert's songs in their entirety, not as church songs but as art songs with piano accompaniment).[48] The old tunes that were retained were "smoothed out," their syncopated rhythms regarded as out of fashion with the desire for classical symmetry in the eighteenth century (a style already practiced in the chorale settings of J. S. Bach).

The church cantata continued to flourish throughout the eighteenth century. There were significant post-J. S. Bach contributions in this genre from Carl Heinrich Graun, kapellmeister at the Prussian court; J. S. Bach's oldest son, Wilhelm Friedemann Bach, while he served as musical director in Hannover (1746–1764); Carl Philipp Emmanuel Bach, who succeeded Georg Philipp Telemann as music director of

---

[45] See H. C. Robbins Landon, *Mozart's Last Year* (New York: Shirmer Books, 1988), 54. Mozart's church music is thoroughly discussed in K. Geiringer, *The Mozart Companion* (London, 1956). See also the article on the Requiem by F. Blume, "Requiem but no Peace," *Musical Quarterly* 47 (1961), 147–69.

[46] See C. M. Brand, *Die Messen von Joseph Haydn* (Wurzburg, 1941).

[47] See Abraham, *The Concise Oxford History of Music,* op. cit., 552–4.

[48] See Feder, 336ff.

Hamburg's principal churches (beginning in 1768); Gottfried August Homilius, cantor of the Kreuzkirche and music director in Dresden (beginning in 1755); and Johann Friedrich Doles, second cantor at Saint Thomas's after J. S. Bach (beginning in 1755).[49] As the old chorales passed more and more out of favor by the end of the century, cantatas came to be based on psalm texts rather than on the chorales. Felix Mendelssohn-Bartholdy represents the end of the line in the composition of church cantatas. Three of his five psalm-cantatas (written between 1830 and 1843) and the vocal parts of his symphony-cantata, *Lobgesang* (1840), are among the best achievements of the time; but they also represent a tradition that could not be continued except on festivals in the church year and other special occasions because of limited means. Cantors had at their disposal, by then, only amateur choirs and "curious combinations of instruments." In the face of inadequate instrumental resources, unaccompanied motets replaced the cantatas as the preferred form of church music by the end of the eighteenth century. In spite of the fact that hundreds were written, few of them are sung today.

The decline in church music in the Lutheran churches may be contrasted with the general enrichment of church music in the Reformed churches during this same period. This was occasioned by the increasing relaxation of the hitherto strict Calvinist principles regarding church music since the age of Pietism and the Enlightenment.[50] In the late seventeenth century there was a flourishing of pietistic Reformed poetry in the Lower Rhineland, including the writings of Joachim Neander, Gerhard Tersteegen, and Friedrich Adolf Lampe. The songbooks created by these poets (e.g., the Darmstadt Songbook of 1698) did as much for Reformed piety as the Freylinghausen Songbook (Halle, 1704) did for Lutheran piety. At first there were attempts to set these verses to tunes from the Genevan Psalter; but Neander was also a creator of tunes, and his influence was such that new tunes were admitted into the repertoire of Reformed church *lieder*. At first these songs were intended to be sung in domestic settings. But they found their way into both Lutheran and Reformed services. The practice of accompanying congregational singing on the organ was also being adopted in Reformed congregations as it was in Lutheran (although outside of Germany and the Netherlands restrictions on organ music remained in place until well into the nineteenth century).

As the Enlightenment had an affect on the old Lutheran chorales, so in every Reformed church throughout Europe there were attempts to change, revise, or eliminate altogether the Genevan Psalter and its offshoots in various countries. Sometimes, as in France, there was an attempt to update the two centuries-old texts of the metrical psalms. But altered texts affect the tunes to which they are set, and there was a preference to use new materials. Reformed hymnals toward the end of the eighteenth century (e.g., the Zurich Songbook of 1787) included fewer psalm lieder and more hymns. The Zurich book also provided four-part settings of the psalm lieder and hymns. This proved to be so

---

[49] Ibid., 347ff.

[50] See Walter Blankenburg, "Church Music in Reformed Europe," in Blume, ed., *Protestant Church Music*, 575ff.

popular that there were attempts to introduce it elsewhere, as in Wurttemberg, although unsuccessfully. But the development of singing societies in Lutheran lands saw a similar development in Reformed territories, beginning in Switzerland. At first these community singing societies met outside of the churches; but with the relaxation of restrictions on church music, church choirs also began to appear within the Reformed churches.

What we see happening quickly in the Reformed churches, although more slowly in the Lutheran churches, is the influence of popular culture on church music. As the old institutions of church music declined and theological restrictions on church music were loosened, popular practices derived especially from singing societies influenced the direction of church music. Since amateur groups take professional performances as their models and aspirations, the music of the concert halls (which were largely middle-class institutions) determined the type of music sung in the churches. The oratorios of Handel exerted considerable influence; the cantatas of Bach did not. But this meant that church music ceased to have any relationship to the liturgy. Its purpose was not to enrich the celebrations of the church year (which means chiefly to proclaim the saving work of God in Christ), but to edify the assembled congregation. To do this, it was believed, music must be accessible and intelligible to the worshipers. A Mozart might have made church music serene; in lesser hands it became simply sentimental. That is, it stirred the momentary emotions of the hearer without truly edifying or strengthening the enduring faith of the hearer. One wonders whether the works of a C. P. E. Bach might have been more lastingly edifying if his music had been composed less "for eternity" and more for "the Eternal One."

❧ THE RITE OF CONFIRMATION AND CULTURE CHRISTIANITY

It is not surprising that the Rationalists came to regard the rite of confirmation very highly. Their concern, articulated by Immanuel Kant, was the development of a virtuous society that required the formation of virtuous citizens. Confirmation came to be regarded as playing an important role in this process, and it therefore came into competition with baptism. Baptism, in the state churches of Europe, was a rite performed on an infant who was incapable of responding in any willful way to what was being said or done. Ever since Bucer in the Reformation era, however, Lutherans and Reformed were able to compensate for the problematic of a personal faith response in infant baptism by recourse to the rite of confirmation.[51]

We should remember that Luther himself had not favored the rite of confirmation. Some church orders, following Luther, made no provision for it. Under Olavus Petri and Johannes Bugenhagen, who were disciples of Luther in this matter, the rite of confirmation was eliminated in the Scandinavian churches. Other church orders, such as Mark Brandenburg, retained it out of a sense of tradition. The *Nova ordinantia ecclesiastica* (1575) in Sweden appealed to Mark Brandenburg in its restoration of the rite of confirmation; but it was abolished by the Uppsala Möte of 1593 when the Church Order (1571)

---

[51] Hastings Eells, *Martin Bucer* (New Haven: Yale University Press, 1931), 155.

of Laurentius Petri was restored.[52] The imposition of episcopal confirmation during the post-Smalkald War Interims, and the reactions to that by the gnesio-Lutherans, prompted more Lutherans to abandon confirmation (although not catechetical instruction). The general demise of church life and discipline during the Thirty Years' War also eliminated confirmation in some territories. On the other hand, Arthur C. Repp, in the most detailed study of the complicated history of confirmation in the Lutheran church, demonstrated the continuation of confirmation in many territories.[53]

Nevertheless, confirmation was continued, restored, or even instituted in many territories toward the end of the seventeenth century, for various reasons. The orthodox saw it as a way of shoring up doctrinal formation through catechetical instruction. The general catechetical instruction given to all the faithful in the form of catechetical sermons and at announcements for communion became intensified in classes for children; and confirmation became a prerequisite for first communion. In reaction to the shocking conversion of the Elector Friedrich Augustus II of Saxony (1670–1733) to Roman Catholicism, the confirmation of children of the nobility often included a solemn vow to remain faithful to the Lutheran church. Impressive ceremonies were introduced in connection with such confirmations.[54]

Among the Pietists, confirmation was promoted as an opportunity to elicit a personal renewal of the baptismal covenant. The great Pietist leader, Philip Jacob Spener, was exposed to this type of confirmation in the Hessian Church Order while serving as a pastor in Frankfurt. When he relocated to Dresden in Electoral Saxony, confirmation was not practiced. But when he moved to Berlin to serve at the Nikolai Church, he found confirmation observed there according to the Brandenburg Church Order. He modified the rite of confirmation in Berlin along Hessian lines by emphasizing the vow. But unlike Bucer, who had spoken about "remembering the baptismal covenant," Spener emphasized a "renewal of the baptismal covenant." The pre-confirmation catechetical instruction also changed emphasis from indoctrination to what might be called "conversion therapy." That is, it served the purpose of enabling young people to make a personal confession of faith. Only those who were so converted could affirm the confirmation vow. Confirmation was already a prerequisite for Holy Communion, so only the converted could theoretically become communicants. A further development occurred under August Hermann Francke, who replaced the Apostles' Creed as the form of the confession of faith to allow young people to express their faith in their own words. The consequence of this was that since not all children could do this, the common children continued to use the Apostles' Creed while the cultured children devised their own creeds. Furthermore, since the child was required to examine himself to determine whether he was truly a Christian, and be able to apply Christian doctrine to one's life, it became necessary to advance the age of confirmation.[55]

---

[52] See Carl-Gustav Andrén, *Konfirmationen i Sverige under medeltid och reformationtid.* Bibliotheca Theologiae Practicae, I (Lund, 1957), 291.

[53] Arthur C. Repp, *Confirmation in the Lutheran Church* (St. Louis: Concordia Publishing House, 1964), 62.

[54] Ibid., 64.

[55] Ibid., 68ff.

To a great extent, the Rationalists simply amplified the emphases in catechesis and confirmation already found in orthodoxy and Pietism. The orthodox emphasis on the transmission of communal identity and the Pietist emphasis on the personal experience of the Christian faith were both appropriated by the Rationalists. Their emphases can be seen in the sermons, examinations, addresses, and confession of faith. The sermons reached extraordinary lengths (one as long as fifty-three printed pages!), as did the examinations of the candidates. In fact, the examinations became so long that they began to be separated from the actual rite itself. A confession of faith was required, but following the tradition already established by the Pietists the confession was often written by the confirmands themselves. The making of vows or promises became a dramatic moment, often accompanied by a pastoral exhortation to take the vows seriously because they are being made to God and not to man. After the vows the pastor gave to each confirmand a special Bible passage, hymn stanza, or folk saying. The Schleswig-Holstein Agenda of 1797 listed thirty-three from various sources, including Bible passages as well as such moralistic sayings as: "Love Virtue: she is the soul's eternal fortune." Sometimes the children then left the chancel and went to their parents to ask their forgiveness and blessing.[56]

Other customs came to be associated with the rite to increase its significance and impact: antiphonal singing between the children and the congregation; flowers and floral arrangements; the ringing of church bells; and wearing a new suit or dress for the occasion. It was the occasion for a special family celebration. It was usually timed to coincide with the completion of elementary school, and was even used to enforce school attendance. This was usually during Holy Week, with confirmation on Palm Sunday and first communion on Maundy Thursday or Easter. Confirmation was one's admission to Holy Communion, and also the requirement for getting married in the church or serving as a baptismal sponsor. In not a few places in the early nineteenth century, it was also an admission into civil rights and privileges such as going to high school, joining a guild, getting a job, or (for upper-class girls) making one's debut in society (for which purpose confirmation was sometimes delayed).[57]

The 1808 Church Order of the Lutheran Church in Russia explicitly confirmed majority rights on the confirmand and therefore included instruction in civic duties as part of the catechetical program and solemn vows by the confirmands to live up to their duties as citizens in the confirmation rite.[58] Since Finland was transferred from Sweden to Russia in 1809, this Russian Church Order also exerted some influence in eastern Finland for a short time. Finally, under the influence of rationalism, confirmation was finally accepted in Sweden in 1811, although it was called "the rite of admission to the Lord's Supper." The Swedish rite reflected the rationalistic German orders of confirmation by including eight promises with an emphasis on the renewal of baptismal vows, an address to the confirmands, a prayer, but not the laying of hands. This Swedish Manual was translated into Finnish in 1817.[59]

---

[56] Ibid., 76ff.
[57] Ibid., 81–2.
[58] Ibid., 81–2, 84.
[59] Ibid., 83–4.

Was this practice influenced by theology, or (as we have seen in the earlier history of confirmation) did the practice influence the theology? In any event, the Pietist Georg Friedrich Seiler (1733–1807) regarded confirmation as the formal completion of the baptismal covenant. He was able to deflect any arguments against the practice of infant baptism by showing that in confirmation the instructed children of Christians made their own profession of faith. Friedrich Schleiermacher (1768–1834), the theologian of "feeling," went one step farther by declaring confirmation to be the second half of baptism, in fact, its necessary completion.[60] Thus, under Rationalism confirmation loomed in importance liturgically as "the festival of human nature," culturally as "the most important day of a child's life," and theologically as "really your first true baptismal day."[61]

It is noteworthy that the Reform movement in German Judaism, emerging at the beginning of the nineteenth century, also attached great importance to the rite of confirmation. It may be that this movement, which was interested in the greater assimilation of Jews into the general culture, might have latched on to confirmation as a way to help its young people advance in Prussian society. It is equally possible that the very personalist elements that the Rationalist Protestants found in the rite of confirmation were also appealing to Reform Jews of the Enlightenment. Just as Schleiermacher considered confirmation the second and more important part of baptism, so for Israel Jacobson, one of the founders of the Reform movement in Judaism, confirmation superseded bar mitzvah, and was available to girls as well as boys.[62]

❦ REASON AND REVIVAL: A RELATIONSHIP

It may seem strange to include in this chapter a section on Revivalism. As a movement that sought, usually through emotional manipulation, an act of commitment to a personal God, it seems the polar opposite of Rationalism, which sought to confine religion "within the bounds of reason alone." Ironically, as the Rationalist practice of confirmation illustrates, the Rationalists also constructed rites so as to make an emotional impact; and as the Rationalist theology of confirmation indicates, the personal response was emphasized more than the divine initiative. Under the rubric of edification, preaching and church music especially sought to speak to the soul. Edifying discourses (as sermons were sometimes called) often became emotional harangues and church music was not above employing theatrical devices such as operatic-styled arias and choruses to produce the desired effect. The difference between a confirmation service in Berlin in the Kingdom of Prussia and a camp meeting in Cane Ridge, Kentucky, was more one of cultural style rather than of ritual purpose.

It might also be noted that the great theorist of evangelical confirmation and the organizers of the camp meetings in Kentucky came out of the Reformed tradition. Schleiermacher was a leading theologian of the Prussian Union Church, and James

---

[60] Ibid., 77. See Friedrich Schleiermacher, *Der christliche Glaube nach den Grundsätzen der evangelischen Kirche*, 4th ed. (Berlin, 1843), II, 386–7.

[61] Sources cited in Repp, 78.

[62] See A. Z. Idlesohn, *Jewish Liturgy and Its Development* (New York: Schocken Books, 1960), 269.

McGready (c. 1758–1817) and Barton W. Stone (1772–1844) were Presbyterian ministers. The first camp meeting staged by McGready at Gaspar River, Kentucky, in the summer of 1800 was intended to be a "Communion season" meeting such as had been held in the highlands of Scotland for two centuries, in which people came from the whole surrounding territory to spend several days listening to sermons, singing psalms, confessing their sins, and finally partaking of a mass celebration of the Lord's Supper.[63] Successive camp meetings also included the celebration of the Lord's Supper, although once the meetings became ecumenical the sacramental celebrations of baptism and the Lord's Supper were conducted at the end of the meeting by different denominations. It should be noted that the one new denomination to come out of the camp meeting revivals, the Christian Church (Disciples of Christ), founded in 1832 by the Presbyterian ministers Thomas Campbell (1763–1854) and Alexander Campbell (1788–1866), had as one of its most distinctive features the weekly celebration of the Lord's Supper.[64] The camp meetings were originally held for the purpose of celebrating the sacraments, and the enthusiastic spirit of the camp meetings emphasized the outward manifestations of belief in the sacraments.

The Gaspar River Camp Meeting was so successful that a follow-up camp meeting was held at Cane Ridge, Kentucky, in 1801. Attendance was beyond all expectation (estimates range from 10,000 to 25,000). It ensured the future of the camp meeting as a form of mission, worship, and fellowship on the American frontier. The camp meetings were major social events, bringing together blacks, whites, and even some American Indians, and fostering the major social reform movements in early nineteenth-century America (abolition of slavery, temperance, and women's rights among them.)[65] The ecumenical character of the camp meetings (involving Baptists, Congregationalists, Disciples of Christ, Methodists, and Presbyterians) also ensured that the revival style of worship would have an impact on all the major American Protestant denominations. It was a style that did not remain on the frontier but was imported even into established congregations.

No one fostered this process of assimilating revival techniques more than Charles A. Finney (1792–1872). A Presbyterian minister, he preached in the revival meetings of upstate New York,[66] and then accepted a call to Second Presbyterian Church in New York City in 1832. Because of opposition from other Presbyterians, especially at Princeton Theological Seminary, he became a Congregationalist and accepted a call as pastor of the Broadway Tabernacle in New York City. In 1837 he moved to Oberlin, Ohio, where he served as a Congregationalist pastor and as a theology professor and president of Oberlin College. In 1835 he had published his *Lectures on Revivals of Religion* in which he extolled "new measures" learned from the camp meetings. Against those in the Reformed and Puritan traditions, which insisted on scripture as a norm or source of worship,

---

[63] See the discussion of "Communion Seasons" in Julius Melton, *Presbyterian Worship in America* (Richmond: John Knox Press, 1967).

[64] See Keith Watkins, *The Breaking of Bread* (St. Louis: Bethany Press, 1966), 48–67.

[65] See Timothy L. Smith, *Revivalism and Social Reform* (Nashville: Abingdon Press, 1957).

[66] See Whitney R. Cross, *The Burned-over District* (New York: Harper and Row, 1965) for a history of the great revivals that swept upstate New York for the first half of the nineteenth century.

Finney argued that there are no normative forms of worship in the New Testament; nor can historical traditions be regarded as normative. Just as "our present forms of public worship . . . have been arrived at by degrees, and by a succession of new measures,"[67] so ministers need not be constrained by historical practice; they need to be constrained by what works to save souls. Finney is an important figure in the history of American liturgy because he first articulated the principle on which American worship has been based ever since: pragmatism. Taking to a logical conclusion the Rationalist principle that worship must be edifying, Finney held that the test of authentic worship was what worked; and experience demonstrated what the "new measures" ought to be—what kind of singing should be encouraged, how one could preach for results, how to deal with those on the "anxious bench." As James White noted, a hundred years earlier Jonathan Edwards had expressed amazement over the Great Awakening in his *Faithful Narrative of the Surprising Work of God* (1737). In his *Lectures on Revivals* Finney packaged God's work and told ministers how to accomplish it.[68]

In *Protestant Worship*, White analyzes the characteristics of "Frontier Worship;"[69] they are remarkably faithful to Finney's "new measures." Revival worship begins with "preliminaries," which include the singing of many songs of a rousing character. The hymns of Isaac Watts were popular, but new songs were written for the occasions that were more subjective, personal, moralistic, and direct, optimistic about salvation but warning about hell. The refrain of one early American revival song, which has twenty stanzas, is:

> Shout, shout, we're gaining ground, Halleluia!
> We'll shout old Satan's kingdom down, Halleluia!

In the ecumenical but boisterous context of the camp meetings, the members of various denominations even sang dogmatic doggerel against one another.[70] The singing set the stage for the sermon, which was delivered away from a pulpit and without a script. The aim of preaching was the "harvest of souls," leading to expressions of commitment such as baptism.

Revivalism shared with Rationalism a concern, as Jerald C. Brauer put it, "to get results in the moral life."[71] It used direct techniques to get direct results: to lure rough-hewn people on the frontier away from drinking, gambling, womanizing, and other anti-social habits and into a respectable, responsible, settled life. It was not really interested in building up the life of the church; the community of faith served only as a prop to support the individual in the moral life, and people felt no hesitation to leave one church to seek out another one (or none at all, or to start one's own) when they no longer felt its

---

[67] Charles A. Finney, *Lectures on Revivals of Religion*, ed. William G. McLoughlin (Cambridge: Harvard University Press, 1960), 250.

[68] James F. White, *Christian Worship in Transition* (Nashville: Abingdon, 1976), 78–9.

[69] James F. White, *Protestant Worship*, op. cit., 177–8.

[70] See Kenneth G. Phifer, *A Protestant Case for Liturgical Renewal* (Philadelphia: Westminster Press, 1965), 101–3.

[71] Jerald C. Brauer, *Protestantism in America: A Narrative History* (Philadelphia: The Westminster Press, 1953), 114.

sustaining power. Revivalism fought the deistic theology of Rationalism, but in the process limited its message to a theology of the saved and the damned and "bound it to emotionalism."[72]

THE ROLE OF EMOTION IN WORSHIP

The question of the role of emotion in worship is a vexing one. It is vexing because few who are interested in worship in spirit and in truth (i.e., the integrity of worship) would want to turn worship into psychological manipulation. Most revivalists and others sincerely believe that what is happening in worship is the work of the Holy Spirit. And few revivalists or others would want to foster the idolatry of focusing on the emotional experience instead of God. It just happens that the element of emotion in worship is unavoidable. Preaching and church music will appeal to the emotions. To be sure, the emotional response is subjective (that is what makes it so vexing); one worshiper responds emotionally to a Bach chorale, another to a revival hymn. Furthermore, the extent of one's emotional response to what is presented in worship depends on the needs one brings to worship. Worship will be an emotional experience if a prayer publicly offered voices my existential petition, if a song stirs my soul, if a sermon addresses my dilemma, if the sacramental celebration satisfies my hunger.

The real question is not whether worship will be an emotional experience; it will be! The question is whether worship should be designed to elicit an emotional response. This question could not have been asked before Charles Finney's *Lectures on Revivals*; since Finney it cannot be avoided. Any realistic answer must take into account our contemporary sophistication in using the analytical tools of the behavioral sciences and the increasingly sophisticated techniques of mass communication. Modern worship leaders find themselves incapable of not inquiring into the psychological and sociological situation of the worshiping community, of the cultural influences that enable or disable people for participating in certain forms and styles of worship, and how the relation between worship and daily life is conceived (must it be incarnationally relevant or eschatologically irrelevant?). Any discussion about the role of emotion in worship must also take into account that God the Holy Spirit may indeed be acting, through the preaching of the word and the celebration of the sacraments, through the songs and prayers of the assembly, to convict and convert, to edify and instruct, to commission and empower the worshiper and the congregation. Jonathan Edwards was sincerely amazed at the surprising work of God in his congregation as he faithfully preached the word of God. This is the model for dealing with emotion in worship. It is one thing to plan worship with the primary intention of producing certain results. It is something else to obediently proclaim the word and administer the sacraments and to be surprised by the work of God, to see how the Holy Spirit works in, with, and through the means of grace to produce a faith response. What finally makes worship authentic is not human design but the presence of Christ in the proclamation of the gospel and in the celebration of the sacraments, whose Spirit works through these means to create, sustain, and awaken faith.

---

[72] Ibid., 116.

Things that are done in worship have an emotional impact on the worshiper. The revivalists emphasized altar calls, invitations to discipleship, going to "the anxious bench" to be prayed over by the ministers. Physical actions in themselves—gathering, standing, kneeling, walking, signing with the cross, genuflecting—produce an emotional response, which in turn forms belief. A different emotional response, and a different belief, is fostered by one's posture in receiving communion—whether standing, kneeling, or sitting. The Council of Nicea must have been aware of this when it forbade anyone to kneel on Sunday or during the Easter season, because only standing could declare the Christian's faith in the resurrection. The Rationalists emphasized postures in the rite of confirmation: standing to make one's profession of faith, walking to the communion rail and kneeling to receive the blessing with the laying on of hands, and then returning to one's place, so as to emphasize that one is not passive in renewing the baptismal covenant as one was in receiving baptism.

Just because bodily expressions, like ceremonies in general, are "a living commentary upon the Gospel,"[73] great care must be taken in the choice of actions. Actions not only have an emotional impact; they also suggest meaning. It makes a difference theologically as well as psychologically whether one stands or sits for the reading of the gospel; whether the gospel is read from the pulpit or from the midst of the congregation; or whether the minister presides at the eucharist facing the people or the east wall. J.A.T. Robinson suggested that presiding at the eucharist facing the east wall suggests a sense of transcendence, the westward or "basilican" position (facing the people across the table) suggests a sense of immanence.[74] While it is difficult to say that one position is right and the other wrong, physical expression powerfully interprets spiritual meaning. The decision one makes in terms of which position or posture to use will require some sense of the impact that expression is making on the worshipers vis-à-vis what one intends to communicate or proclaim.

Physical expression also has an impact on the spirit of the worshiper. Singing a hymn of praise when the spirit is low may reawaken joy. Confessing the Creed when faith is low may rekindle faith. It also may not; it could leave the worshiper in the doldrums or alienate one from belief even more. But there is bound to be some reflexive effect of bodily expression. This includes the moral effect of repeated actions. As the Free Methodist theologian, Paul Hoon, has suggested,

> A worshiper may bring more courage to the threatening changes of history if he has regularly knelt—as Luther advised us to do—at the words of Creed marking the invasion of the Divine into history: *homo factus est*. She will face the prospect of death with less fear if she has sung again and again the "Gloria:" "is now and ever shall be, world without end. Amen." He can appraise both the good and the evil of secular influences hourly beating upon his consciousness if he has regularly signed his existence with the sign of the cross. And she may

---

[73] Scott Francis Brenner, *The Art of Worship: A Guide in Corporate Worship Techniques* (New York: The Macmillan Co., 1961), 21.

[74] John A. T. Robinson, *Liturgy Coming to Life* (Philadelphia: Westminster Press, 1960), 27.

more likely stand for the Gospel in the ambiguous ethical decisions she must make in this life in the world if she has stood for the Gospel in his worship.[75]

Worship in spirit and in truth involves the totality of one's being. This must include human emotion. "Why are emotion and soul so intimately bound up?" James Hillman asks. "Mainly because . . . it is through emotion that we get the . . . sense of soul."[76] Jung spoke of the "feeling function" in personality as the mechanism by which we evaluate experience: "When we feel it is in order to attach a proper value to something."[77] The implications of this for worship are enormous. It has been expressed in this way by the Roman Catholic Daniel Callahan,

> It is just not—in the long run—enough that religion asks significant questions and has some interesting answers, or that it takes value and community seriously and offers some guidance for the ethical and communal life. What *is* necessary in the long run is that religion be able to make people *feel* the universe in a different way; that it provide them with a consciousness of themselves and of the world around them which is unique and compelling. That is why the question of religious experience seems to me central. . . . What people seem to want most of all from religion is a total way of being, in the world and in themselves. They do not only want to be intellectually convinced of the value of religion; they also want to *feel this value* in the depths of their being.[78]

Just as worship in the Age of Certainty fostered a kind of objectivity by focusing on the reality of God in orders and texts, so worship in the Age of Reason, by focusing on the human being and his or her needs, causes us to consider the role of subjectivity in the act of worship. Worship in spirit and truth, worship that is both catholic and evangelical, worship that emphasizes both the outward means of grace and the believer's response of faith, will maintain objectivity and subjectivity in polar tension and see the value of one informing the other.

---

[75] Paul Waitman Hoon, *The Integrity of Worship* (Nashville: Abingdon Press, 1971), 323–4.

[76] James Hillman, *Insearch* (New York: Charles Scribner's Sons, 1967), 53–4.

[77] Carl-Gustav Jung, *Modern Man in Search of a Soul* (New York: Harcourt, Brace and Co., 1933), 105.

[78] Daniel Callahan, "God in a Technological Society," *Yale Alumni Magazine* (June 1968), 21.

CHAPTER 16

Liturgy in the Age of Romanticism

THE IDEAS OF THE Enlightenment led directly to political revolution, first in America, then in France. The French Revolution in particular transformed life and thought not only in France, but throughout the Western world. It did so swiftly, with great violence and upheaval. After the storming of the Bastille on July 14, 1789 (done as a measure to protect the National Assembly), changes came quickly. The privileges of the feudal system were abolished, the Rights of Man were declared, the church was secularized, and the entire civil bureaucracy was restructured. The goals of the revolution were ruthlessly enforced, with some 300,000 people arrested and 17,000 executed as enemies of the revolution. The "reign of terror" began with the execution of King Louis XVI and Queen Marie Antoinette in January 1793, for "a multitude of crimes."[1] The Revolution was eventually codified under the administration of the First Consul of the Republic and later Emperor of the French, Napoleon Bonaparte.

There were those who exulted in the dynamism of this turbulence and had a sense, as Keats wrote in one of his sonnets, that "Great spirits now on earth are sojourning." He could look to Napoleon, who dominated the age; or to Goethe, Schiller, and Beethoven in Germany; or to his English contemporaries Wordsworth, Coleridge, Byron, and Shelley. But there were also those sensitive spirits who lamented the fact that the

---

[1] See John Paxton, *Companion to the French Revolution* (New York: Facts on File, 1988), 186. For a succinct summary of the events of the French Revolution see *The Columbia History of the World*, ed. by John A. Garraty and Peter Gay (New York, Evanston, San Francisco, London: Harper and Row, 1972), 763ff.

revolution had turned sour. At the news of Napoleon's self-coronation as Emperor of the French, Beethoven changed the title of his revolutionary Third Symphony from "Bonaparte," in tribute to the young hero of revolutionary France, to the generic *Eroica*. William Wordsworth, at about the same time, wrote in *The Prelude*, XI: 206–9, that revolutionaries have

> become oppressors in their turn,
> Frenchmen had changed a war of self-defense
> For one of conquest, losing sight of all
> Which they had struggled for . . .

Political reaction set in across Europe after the defeat of Napoleon at Waterloo in 1815. Governments that were set on maintaining the status quo ante were inattentive to the need to manage or regulate the economic changes that were taking place as a result of the Industrial Revolution. Real wealth and power were passing from the landed aristocracy into the hands of large-scale employers who put to work peasants who had been displaced by new agricultural methods and land uses and who had migrated into crowded urban centers in search of employment. The squalor that resulted from industrialization and urbanization was graphically depicted in the novels of Charles Dickens from the 1840s on.

Dickens's indignation at social conditions produced by the Industrial Revolution was shared by John Ruskin, who abandoned art criticism in order to expose the faults of Victorian industry and commerce, as in his history of architecture, *The Stones of Venice* (1855). In this prophetic work he extolled both the architecture of the Gothic Age and the kind of society that could produce such noble edifices. The Waverly novels of Walter Scott had already nurtured in England a nostalgia for the lost age of chivalry. Ruskin drew upon this interest in archaeology in "The Nature of Gothic," in which he explained that medieval architecture was the work of free, intelligent, and creative workmen, but that in the nineteenth century the powers of faith and creation alike were enslaved by industrialism. Developing the same ideas in a lecture in Edinburgh in 1853, Ruskin suggested a Gothic revival, which should extend also to domestic architecture (although he should not be blamed for Victorian houses and neo-Gothic college campuses). A year later he criticized the Crystal Palace in London because it used machine-made glass and steel instead of stone and mortar.[2]

Here is the archetypal expression of the Romantic sensibility: a yearning after an ideal golden age in the past, whether that was ancient Greece, the Middle Ages, or the Reformation. This more than anything else characterizes the art and literature of the mid-nineteenth century. Romanticism is an effort to bring one age to the rescue of another, which means that the leading romantics were also critics of their own age and culture. Sometimes it was a mythical age that was invoked to reform the present age. There was a resurgence of interest in Greek and Nordic mythology exemplified in Shelley's *Prometheus Unbound* and Wagner's operas on *Der Ring des Nibelungen*. The loss of the peasantry and the depletion of villages caused by the Industrial Revolution also brought

---

[2] See H. A. Ladd, *The Victorian Morality of Art: An Analysis of Riskin's Esthetic* (New York: Long, 1932).

about an interest in folk culture and village life. Various kinds of cultural revivals, folkloric and historical, became immensely important in terms of shoring up or generating ethnic and national identity during the second half of the nineteenth century. F.A. Munch, a Norwegian professor of history, practically "created" Norway by giving scholarly credibility to the notion of Norway as a great center of medieval civilization. This effort was replicated in other countries in Europe that were straining after national independence. In America too there was a nostalgic interest in the American past after the Civil War, perhaps as a way of reestablishing national identity.[3]

All this had its corollaries in the history of the liturgy. We shall see in this chapter efforts to retrieve historical liturgies, music, architecture, vestments, and ceremonies to serve as the centerpieces of movements in several major confessional traditions that sought to renew spiritual life, reform church practices, recover church dogmatics, and revive traditional polity. In opposition to the religion of the Age of Reason, romantic revivalists emphasized the Middle Ages or the Reformation as the Age of Faith. But as a part of this romantic retrieval liturgists were greatly interested in the externals of these periods. Hence we see in the Western churches revivals of Gothic buildings, Gothic vestments, and Gothic liturgical music (e.g., plainsong and Reformation chorales) that paralleled Gothic poetry and romance in literature. The fact that this represents a pan-cultural phenomenon is indicated by the ways Romanticism asserted itself in different confessional traditions.

ROMANTIC REACTIONS

Dom Guéranger and the Solesmes Movement

Modern Roman Catholicism is only in part the product of a reaction to the Reformation. It is as much, if not more so, a reaction to the French Revolution. The radicality of this revolution sent shock waves throughout Europe and to America. While the impact of the revolution was catastrophic on Roman Catholicism, other churches were not untouched.

With no real experience of democracy, but with the ideologies of "liberty and fraternity" in the air, the convening of the National Assembly by King Louis XVI to deal with a bankrupt state turned into a "reign of terror." The whole traditional social order was overturned. At first there was no thought of a France without a Roman Catholic state church, although Protestants were given freedom of worship, but bit by bit the Roman Catholic Church was disestablished. After the abolition of feudal dues (which deprived the pope of his annates), and the subsequent papal rejection of the Declaration of the Rights of Man and alignment with the traditions of absolutism and inherited rights of rule, the National Assembly nationalized church lands, placed restrictions on monasteries and religion orders, and made the clergy civil servants paid by the state.[4]

---

[3] See Michael Kammen, *Mystic Chords of Memory: The Transformation of Tradition in American Culture* (New York: Alfred A. Knopf, 1991), 93ff.

[4] See Nichols, *History of Christianity*, op. cit., 111ff.

Many of the French bishops and clergy, encouraged by the pope, refused to take oaths of allegiance to the new "Civil Constitution of the Clergy." Various measures were enacted to enforce the compliance of the clergy or to banish them, and it is estimated that 1,000 to 2,000 non-Juring priests were killed in the "September Massacres" of 1792 and another 40,000 non-Juring priests were driven out of France and became propagandists against the revolution outside of France. Thousands of others, however, Protestants as well as Roman Catholics, subscribed to the new religion of nationalism and renounced the Christian faith or resigned from their ecclesiastical positions. The religion of nationalism is evident in the efforts on the part of the Committee on Public Instruction to organize a national school system not under the control of the church, and in the efforts of Robespierre and the National Assembly to displace and replace the traditional church festivals and holidays with artificial festivals and holidays celebrating the themes of the revolution and the Enlightenment. These public celebrations included such events as the Festival of Freedom (held in Notre Dame Cathedral on November 10, 1793, which was converted into a Temple of Reason) and the deistic Festival of the Supreme Being (celebrated on June 8, 1794). Robespierre proposed some thirty-six new national festivals in his "anti-atheism" speech on May 4, 1794.[5]

Perhaps as a result of the very sterility of such artificial festivals, there was a religious revival in the winter of 1794–1795, especially among the peasants, and in the next few years churches were reopened and services were resumed. When a coup d'etat established Napoleon Bonaparte as First Consul of the French Republic in 1799, he set about to reconcile the ideas of the revolution with the traditional order—especially in religious matters. In 1801 he proposed a Concordat with the newly elected Pope Pius VII that regularized the alienation of church property and the government's responsibility to pay the salary of the clergy, and granted to the dictator the old royal prerogative of nominating bishops in return for the free exercise of religion. In addition to this, however, governmental permission was required for all church meetings, marriage was to be civically licensed prior to the ecclesiastical marriage service, and the monasteries were still radically curtailed. All this took place in what had been the largest and strongest Roman Catholic nation, which, through Napoleon's conquests, added territory to France and set up satellite nations all around it. In 1809 Napoleon also annexed the Papal States to France and spirited away the pope to France. The old pope put up such a strenuous moral resistance to pressure from the most powerful ruler in Europe (usually by refusing to exercise the papal office) that the papacy emerged from the fall of Napoleon in 1814 and 1815 with a prestige it had not had since the Reformation.[6]

Nevertheless, both the French Revolution and the Napoleonic administration of the church had taken their toll on church life. Many church buildings had been demolished or turned over to other uses. Marble and brass had been pillaged, and lead had been taken from roofs and windows to turn into ammunition. French church music was

---

[5] See Josef Pieper, *In Tune with the World: A Theory of Festivity*, trans. by Richard and Clara Winston (Chicago: Franciscan Herald Press, 1965), 47ff.

[6] Nichols, 123–34.

at a seriously low ebb as a result of the blurring of differences between sacred and secular styles. German and English musicians who visited France in the early nineteenth century found nothing good to say about the state of church music.[7] Even the one exception, the chapel of the Tuileries (which Napoleon had endowed as a showplace for his regime), provided a style of music that, however well performed, bore no relation to the mass or the office that was being prayed. Organ music performed at the offertory or the elevation tended to be grandiose and more than the moment really required (such as a whole movement of a sonata). Even this came to a halt in 1830 when Louis-Philippe took the throne and dismissed all the chapel musicians.

The "romantic reaction"[8] that set in after the fall of Napoleon moved in the direction of strengthening the papacy over the national churches and recapturing the whole spirit of medieval Christendom. This has been called the Ultramontane movement. Part of the Ultramontane program was to restore the monasteries. Dom Prosper Guéranger (1805–1875), after ordination to the secular priesthood, worked to restore the abbey of Solesmes in the Sarthe *département* in France as an outpost of a romantically conceived medieval Catholicism. A restored Benedictine monastery is inconceivable without a restored liturgy of the hours, a choral office, and Gregorian chant. Guéranger's critical scholarship of medieval manuscripts and his painstaking reconstruction of Gregorian chant are reflected in his two great works: *Les institutions liturgiques* and *L'Année liturgique* (1840).[9]

Dom Guéranger can be credited with the recovery of a solemn style of liturgical celebration which made use of the traditional church chant. This ideal form of solemn celebration received official endorsement, a *motu proprio* of Pope Pius X on church music (November 22, 1903), that called attention to the dignity of Gregorian chant and encouraged the participation of the people in its rendition. Guéranger had held up the church's prayer as superior to the popular devotions used by ordinary Catholic lay people, although without providing a form that would make the divine office accessible to popular use. He also retarded the incipient movement toward the vernacularization of liturgical language by an ultramontane reaction to Gallicanism and Jansenism. While Guéranger and the Solesmes revival is often regarded as the beginning of the liturgical movement (at least in the Roman Catholic Church), as Ernest B. Koenker points out, "his work did not involve bringing the liturgy to the masses as does the work of the modern movement."[10] We cannot regard the Solesmes movement as the beginning of the modern liturgical movement. But his work was part of a romantic program of liturgical retrieval that occurred in several ecclesial traditions.

---

[7] See Orpha Ochse, *Organists and Organ Playing in Nineteenth Century France and Belgium* (Bloomington and Indianapolis: Indiana University Press, 1994), 121ff.

[8] See Louis Bouyer, *Liturgical Piety*, op. cit., 10ff.

[9] See Henri Daniel-Rops, ed., *The Twentieth Century Encyclopedia of Catholicism. The Liturgical Movement*, trans by Lancelot Shepherd (New York: Hawthorn Books, 1964), 10–2.

[10] Ernest B. Koenker, *The Liturgical Renaissance in the Roman Catholic Church* (St. Louis: Concordia Publishing House, 1954), 11.

The Slavophile Movement

Russia, since the time of Czar Peter the Great, had flirted with Western culture and intellectual ideas. Czar Peter moved his capital from Moscow to Saint Petersburg to be closer to the West. He introduced Western dress (and shaving), a Western form of government bureaucracy, and a subjugation of the church to the state under himself as a Prussian-styled summus episcopus. He supervised the church through a Lutheran-type of consistory called the Holy Synod.[11] He had even suspended the Patriarchate for a time. He permitted Lutherans and Orthodox to marry so that he could retain the services of skilled Swedish miners in the Urals. These policies were continued and strengthened under the German-born Empress Catherine the Great, who also encouraged German Lutherans to settle in the Volga region in order to share their agricultural skills. While the peasants remained unaffected by the importation of Western ideas and practices, the nobility turned to French culture and embraced the ideas of the Enlightenment.

However, the long war against Napoleon, and especially the burning of Moscow, brought about a resurgence of Russian nationalism, which effected also a literary and a theological renaissance. This renaissance was influenced by the philosophical idealism of Hegel and Schelling and by the revival of patristic studies. The great novelists of nineteenth-century Russia, from Dostoyevsky to Tolstoy, focused on humanitarian reform and were critical of the Orthodox Church for its complicity in the oppression of the masses. In the "Legend of the Grand Inquisitor" in Dostoyevsky's *The Brothers Karamazov*, Jesus is portrayed as a social reformer persecuted by a despotic church hierarchy. But over against these Westernized humanitarians there emerged the so-called Slavophiles, who, although they lamented the actual life of the Orthodox Church, were convinced that a redeeming and transformative power lay within it. These thinkers turned to the peasants and their conception of the world as the source of regenerative power of the church.[12]

Kirievsky developed an apophatic approach to truth derived from such Orthodox fathers as Isaac the Syrian. To know the truth is to become a part of it, rather than to just have knowledge about it. He contrasted the mystical East with the rationalistic West, and thus emphasized a polarization that was perhaps unfair to both Eastern and Western Christianity.

Aleksei Khomiakov (1804–1860) developed a view of the kind of religious community in which this kind of truth can flourish. He turned to the ecclesiology of the Greek fathers, with their emphasis on "the body of Christ," and contrasted this with the juridical view of the church in Roman Catholicism and the institutional view of the church in Protestantism. Against the individualism of the West, he held that one can only be saved in community *(sobornost)*. Such community, however, cannot be coercive; it must be voluntary. He felt that Rome had unity without freedom, and Protestantism had freedom without unity. True community had to blend unity and freedom. He believed that

---

[11] See Evgenii V. Anisimov, *The Reforms of Peter the Great*, trans. by John T. Alexander (M. E. Sharpe, 1993), who sees in the "reforms" of Czar Peter the origins of Russian totalitarianism.

[12] Ibid., 341ff. See also F. C. Conybeare, *Russian Dissenters* (Cambridge: Harvard University Press, 1921).

Orthodoxy had the resources to develop this kind of community, particularly if it took as its model the village communities of the Russian peasants. Such communities might also realize sobornost in economic and political life.[13]

While the Slavophile movement was not a liturgical movement, it must be realized that the Orthodox faithful live from the liturgy and that this has colored their perspectives on truth, community, and spirituality. Liturgy is the depository of tradition, and the people who live from the liturgy are the custodians of tradition. Such liturgically informed people do not need to depend on hierarchical order or on academic theologians. Truth is found in the community itself, not in these "authorities." Indeed, Khomiakov turned the whole idea of authority upside down. "The church," he wrote, "is not authority; rather it is the truth."[14]

Ecclesiological concerns have been of paramount importance in the twentieth century, but already in the nineteenth century the doctrine of the church dominated the thinking of the Oxford Tractarians, King Friedrich Wilhelm III and the creation of the Prussian Union Church, Wilhelm Loehe in southern Germany, and Nikolai Grundtvig in Denmark.

The Oxford and Cambridge Movements

The French Revolution did not have the significance in the British Isles that it had on the continent, other than to retard the acceleration of social and political change. The revolution that struck Great Britain was the Industrial Revolution. This can be regarded as an extension of the Enlightenment since industrial technologies were the application of sciences developed during the seventeenth and eighteenth centuries, and they demonstrated humankind's ability to subject the physical world to its own purposes. But, as Dickens's novels illustrate, "progress" took its toll on the quality of human life.

The established church was not in a position to deal with the impact of this revolution in even the most basic ways. The number of clergy and buildings was not adequate to minister to the needs of the expanded urban populations. But even if the resources had been there, the dry rationalism of the established church would have been totally unappealing to the new working class. While the Evangelicals were more successful in reaching out to these elements in British society, so that the Nonconformist churches grew along with the population, many people were left untouched by any church.

As the Nonconformist churches gained in strength, constitutional changes were enacted that served to disestablish the established Church of England. First came the repeal of the Test Act in 1828, which made participation in Holy Communion a requirement for holding public office. Next came Roman Catholic Emancipation, which was enacted under threat of revolution in Ireland. Then the bitterly fought Reform Bill of 1833 was enacted, which extended the franchise and gave greater representation to members of the Nonconformist churches. The result was that non-Anglicans sitting in Parliament were in a position to govern the Church of England. The leaders of the

---

[13] See Nicholas Berdyaev, *Origins of Russian Communism* (New York: Charles Scribner's Sons, 1937).

[14] See N. Zernov, *The Russian Religious Renaissance of the Twentieth Century* (London: 1963).

Anglican Church and the University of Oxford opposed these measures and their consequences. John Henry Newman dated the beginning of the Oxford movement to John Keble's sermon of 1833 on "National Apostasy," which is how Keble characterized the eminently sensible reorganization of the Anglican Church in Ireland by Parliament. But from Keble's point of view, the crucial matter was that Parliament was "suppressing" bishoprics. Keble (1792–1866), Newman (1801–1890), Edward B. Pusey (1800–1882) and their fellow Oxonians felt that the independence of the church to regulate its own life was more important than the values of establishment. They put their anti-Erastian case before the Anglican clergy in a series of *Tracts for the Times* (so that the Oxford movement has also been known as the Tractarian movement).[15]

The posture of the tracts is defensive and even shrill, which is to be expected from those who believed they were sounding an alarm. The Swedish Lutheran scholar and churchman, Yngve Brilioth, saw in the Tracts a relationship between ecclesiology and sacramentality,[16] which has been further explored by Louis Weil.[17] Upon the centennial of the Oxford movement (1933), Brilioth commented on the central idea of the Tractarians: the church established on apostolic succession. Brilioth regarded this as a "static" rather than a "dynamic" concept of the church. The idea was that Christ had given authority over the church to his apostles, who had in turn transmitted that authority to their successors, the bishops of the church. This succession, the Tractarians maintained, remained intact throughout the whole history of the Church in England, including in the Reformation period. The Tractarians held a more rigid view of apostolic succession than the Church of England had held before. There had been no inclination on the part of older High Church Anglicans to regard the historic succession of bishops as so essential to the life of the church as to de-church continental Protestants whose episcopates were in an historically broken succession (Lutherans) or who even constituted church polity without an episcopate (Calvinists). But the implication of the Tractarian emphasis on apostolic succession as the basis for an authentic ministry was to question the validity of any sacraments administered by ministers not ordained by bishops in the historic episcopate.

It is not difficult to see in retrospect why the Tractarians fastened on this concept: it rooted the church in the authority of Christ, his apostles, and their successors, and disqualified Parliament to serve as governor of the church. But on the occasion of the one hundred and fiftieth anniversary of the Oxford movement (1983), Louis Weil faulted the Tractarians for isolating "one aspect of the meaning of Apostolic Succession from the rich complex ideas in which its full meaning is manifested."[18] He even points out that a richer and more dynamic understanding of "the sacramentality of the church" is evident in Newman's writings apart from the Tracts, and that this provides a more positive basis for their understanding of the individual sacraments such as baptism and the eucharist.

---

[15] See Owen Chadwick, *The Mind of the Oxford Movement* (London: A. & C. Black, 1960).

[16] Yngve Brilioth, *The Anglican Revival. Studies in the Oxford Movement* (London: Longmans Green, 1933).

[17] Louis Weil, *Sacraments and Liturgy: The Outward Signs. A Study in Liturgical Mentality* (Oxford: Basil Blackwell, 1983).

[18] Ibid., 28.

The Tractarians emphasized the sacraments as instrumental means of spiritual power. This set them at odds with the Evangelicals, who thought that the doctrine of baptismal regeneration undermined the doctrine of justification. Newman asserted in his *Lectures on Justification* that "the instrumental power of Faith cannot interfere with the instrumental power of Baptism" because "when . . . faith is called the sole instrument, this means the sole *internal* instrument" to which baptism is "the sole *external* instrument" of justification.[19] The Tractarians also developed a clearer view of the presence of Christ in the eucharist than had previously been the case in Anglicanism. Robert Wilberforce, in *The Doctrine of the Holy Eucharist* (1853), emphasized that while faith is necessary to perceive the grace of the sacrament, spiritual gifts are communicated through its instrumentality by God's act and not by subjective religious feelings.[20]

The Oxford movement has been popularly regarded as concerned with the importation of Roman ritual norms into Anglican worship. Actually the leading Tractarians, Keble, Newman, and Pusey, were not much concerned about rubrical details and ceremonial niceties. Their own liturgical practice fits more the model of the old high churchmen who observed the rubrics of the *Book of Common Prayer* and celebrated those liturgies "decently and in order."[21] For them it was more important that the eucharist be regarded as the central act of the church, and be celebrated more frequently, than that it be celebrated in the form of Solemn High Mass.[22] It was under the influence of John Mason Neale (1818–1866) and the partisans of the Cambridge Ecclesiological movement that the external aspects of the liturgy became major preoccupations. The Cambridge Camden Society was primarily concerned with church architecture and Christian aesthetics in the face of the explosion in new church construction taking place in the early nineteenth century.[23] Augustus Welby Pugin (1812–1852) regarded Gothic architecture not simply as one style among others available as a choice for the architect, but as *the* architectural expression of Catholic faith and worship. John Mason Neale, a founding member of the Society and eminent translator of ancient Greek and Latin hymns, expressed the opinion that the recovery of Gothic architecture would lead to an awareness of "the poverty of our present vestments." The "present vestments" probably included cassock or gown and surplice with scarf, the cope and stole having long since passed out of use. The ritualists were instrumental not only in the recovery of the cope and stole for solemn celebrations (and hence for use by bishops especially, along with mitre and crozier, whose presence usually indicated a solemn celebration), but also the alb and chasuble for the celebration of the eucharist. When Anglicans wanted to retrieve these usages, the simple fact is that the samples they were looking for were found in Roman Catholic usage. But it did occur to Anglicans that a recovery of Gothic architecture should be accompanied by a recovery of Gothic-styled vestments (full and ample) rather than the short cottas and fiddleback chasubles of Baroque Catholicism. Since the neo-

---

[19] Cited in ibid., 48.

[20] Ibid., 54.

[21] See G. W. O. Addleshaw, *The High Church Tradition* (London: Faber & Faber, 1941).

[22] See T. Dearing, *Wesleyan and Tractarian Worship* (London: Epworth Press, 1966).

[23] See James F. White, *The Cambridge Movement* (Cambridge: Cambridge University Press, 1979).

Gothic church buildings were equipped with chancels with divided choir stalls, surpliced choirs were installed in them that took up the singing of choral services, at least on Sundays. These well-scrubbed, well-rehearsed choirs displaced the more boisterous amateur choristers and instrumentalists, who had inhabited the west galleries in Anglican parishes. The consequences of this shall be taken up in later sections of this chapter.

Finally, we should note that the Anglo-Catholicism that resulted from the Oxford and Cambridge movements drew a connection between the sacraments and social action on the basis of the presence of Christ. Pusey drew this connection in a sermon entitled, "God With Us."

> If we would see Him in His Sacraments, we must see Him also, wherever He has declared himself to be, and especially in His poor. In them also He is "with us" still. And so our Church has united mercy to His poor with the Sacrament of His Body and Blood, and bade us, ere we approach to receive Him, to remember Him in his poor. . . . Real love to Christ must issue in love to all who are Christ's, and real love to Christ's poor must issue in self-denying acts of love towards them. Casual alms-giving is not Christian charity. Rather, seeing Christ in the poor, the sick, the hungry, the thirsty, the naked, we must, if we can, by ourselves, if not, by others, seek them out, as we would seek out Christ, looking for a blessing from it far greater than any they can gain from our alms. It was promised of old time, as a blessing, "the poor shall never cease out of the land," and now we know the mercy of this mysterious blessing, for they are the Presence of our Lord.[24]

We shall see the connection between liturgy and social action in other romantic liturgical movements as well. But it is not surprising that this connection was made by the Oxford and Cambridge movements, for these movements began as a social critique whose theological-ecclesiological aim was to challenge the authority of the state where it was unwanted and whose hope in architectural ecclesiology was to better the sense of social well-being.[25]

Confessional and Liturgical Revival in Germany and America

The aftermath of the French Revolution and the Napoleonic Wars required a reorganization of church life in Germany. The Congress of Vienna, in redrawing the map of Europe after the defeat of Napoleon, awarded more territory to the Kingdom of Prussia than it had lost during the Napoleonic Wars, including the predominantly Roman Catholic province of Westphalia. King Friedrich Wilhelm III now had substantial Lutheran, Reformed, and Roman Catholic populations in his territory. At the same time, the old Holy Roman Empire, which Napoleon had abolished in 1806, was never restored. Prussia began to embark on a policy that would lead eventually to a new German empire under Prussian (and Hohenzollern) leadership rather than under Austrian (and Hapsburg) leadership. Within this empire, as in the kingdom of Prussia itself, there would have to be a united Protestant (Evangelical) church that could embrace the whole population

---

[24] Quoted in Weil, 91.
[25] See A. G. Hebert, *Liturgy and Society* (London: Faber & Faber, 1935).

(thereby expressing one meaning of "catholicity"). There was considerable discussion of the concept of "evangelical catholicity," which was proposed as an intellectual application of Hegelian philosophy. Johann Peter Lange, a professor at Bonn, developed the proposition, based on Hegel's logical system, that the thesis of Catholicism, countered by the antithesis of Protestantism, would produce a new synthesis of evangelical catholicity. Ernst Ludwig von Gerlach and Heinrich Leo were two confessionally and politically conservative Lutherans who used this concept in the development of the Prussian Union Church (a union of Lutheran and Reformed churches), and Moritz August von Bethmann-Hollweg projected it on a future national German Protestant church.[26]

King Friedrich Wilhelm III declared his desire for the constituting of the Prussian Union Church at the celebration of the tercentenary in 1817 of Luther's Ninety-Five Theses. The desire for a Union Church was on a collision course with the confessional revival that was taking place in reaction to the religion of reason. The popular preacher, Klaus Harms, archdeacon of Saint Michael's Church in Kiel, had used the occasion of the Tercentenary to publish Luther's Ninety-Five Theses and he added ninety-five of his own that attacked Rationalism and indifferentism.[27] Thesis 32 stated, "The so-called religion of reason is without reason, or without religion, or both." But some of his theses also took aim at Lutheran-Reformed union. Thus, Thesis 71 stated, "If at the Colloquy at Marburg, 1529, the body and blood of Christ was in the bread and wine, it is still so in 1817." The Prussian King, however, proposed that the anniversary be marked by joint Lutheran-Reformed communion services. When the ministers agreed, the Friedrich Wilhelm presented his own liturgy, which produced almost unanimous disagreement on the part of the clergy, both Lutheran and Reformed. To which the king replied: "You have fallen into the error of all who have written new liturgies and agenda. You have forsaken the historic ground. . . . All the liturgies and agenda which have appeared in our time seem to have been shot out of a pistol. . . . If anything is to come out of this matter at all we must return to Father Luther."[28]

The king had studied the liturgical orders of the sixteenth century and believed that liturgy must be established on an historical foundation. His liturgy was first published in 1816, used in the anniversary celebrations of 1817, revised, and then issued in an official Agenda in 1822. It continued to meet with strong opposition, especially from his favorite theologian, Friedrich Schleiermacher. But during the next fifteen years it was widely introduced throughout the provinces of Prussia and was increasingly accepted by the Old Lutherans. Its order is as follows:[29]

> Hymn
> Invocation
> Versicle

---

[26] See Sven-Erik Brodd, *Evangelisk Katolicitet. Ett studium av innehåll och funktion under 1800– och 1900–talen* (Lund: CWK Gleerup, 1982), 59ff. (Lange), 82ff. (von Gerlach and Leo), 66ff. (von Bethmann-Hollweg).

[27] See Luther Reed, *The Lutheran Liturgy*, op. cit., 151–2.

[28] Cited in ibid., 152.

[29] Ibid., 152–3.

> Confession of sin and declaration of grace
> Gloria Patri (sung by the choir)
> Kyrie (sung by the choir)
> Gloria
> Salutation and Collect
> Epistle
> Halleluia
> Gospel
> Apostles' Creed
> Preface and Sanctus
> General prayer
> Lord's Prayer
> Benediction

The sermon could follow the Creed or the Lord's Prayer. When Holy Communion was celebrated, the General Prayer was followed by:

> Exhortation
> Words of institution
> Pax domini
> Prayer for worthy communion
> Agnus Dei (sung by the choir)
> Distribution
> Post-communion prayer
> Benediction

The resistance may have had less to do with the liturgy than with the circumstances under which it was introduced. The Reformed congregations resisted the imposition of the liturgy by the king under his authority as summus episcopus; they still retained their presbyterian and synodical structures. Furthermore, being surrounded by Roman Catholic populations, they did not share the king's enthusiasm for chanting, vestments, genuflexions, altars, and candles. On the other hand, the Lutherans resisted altar and pulpit fellowship with the Reformed. In areas of Silesia and Saxony now annexed to Prussia, the old orthodox Lutherans still regarded all Calvinists as heretics. Congregations could be closed down and pastors suspended or jailed for refusing to use the king's liturgy. Not until the accession of Friedrich Wilhelm IV in 1840 were they given permission to emigrate. These Lutherans moved to the United States and set up the Buffalo, Ohio, and Missouri Synods.[30]

Meanwhile, in areas unaffected by the Prussian Union, such as in Mecklenburg and Bavaria, a high church Lutheranism began to flourish that was not unlike the Tractarian movement in England. Theodor Kliefoth of Mecklenburg (1810–1895) engaged in historical liturgical scholarship and showed a related tendency toward the apostolic authority of the pastoral office and an emphasis on sacramentalism. His *Theorie des Kultus der evangelischen Kirche* (1844), *Die ursprüngliche Gottesdienstordnung in den deutschen Kirchen lutherischen Bekenntnisses* (1847), and *Liturgische Abhandlungen*, in eight volumes (1854–1861), were works of great erudition. With Otto Kade, the church

---

[30] See Nichols, 155–6.

musician, he also brought out the musically rich and beautifully printed *Cantionale* of the Duchy of Mecklenburg.[31]

Equally important was the liturgical and pastoral work of Wilhelm Loehe (1808–1872). As with the Tractarians, Loehe's concern was first of all ecclesiological. The Congress of Vienna had annexed the Lutheran territories of Swabia and Franconia to the former Duchy (now Kingdom) of Bavaria. The new constitution of Bavaria created a constitutional monarchy and gave the government control over the churches. A spirit of cooperation was deemed necessary in order to comprehend Lutherans and Roman Catholics in one kingdom. Loehe's neo-Lutheranism was viewed as confessionally rigid, and his concern for Christian discipline was considered excessively pietistic by the Evangelical Church authorities in Bavaria. So he was sent as pastor to the small town of Neuendettelsau in northern Bavaria. Here, removed from the close supervision of the church authorities, he attempted to establish an evangelical catholic cultus for the town and surrounding district. It called for more frequent celebrations of Holy Communion, combined with screening of the communicants by the pastor or by the deacons when they announced their intention to receive the sacrament on Saturday afternoons. Eventually Loehe also restored the Office of the Keys (private confession and absolution) as an independent means of grace.[32]

His *Drei Bücher von der Kirche* (*Three Books on the Church*, 1845) was offered to a wider public to promote discussion about the nature of the church as a universal fellowship gathered around the word and sacraments, the confessional divisions among the churches, and the character and contribution of the Lutheran church. He ended with an appeal for liturgical recovery as a defense of doctrine. "The true faith is expressed not only in the sermon but is also prayed in the prayers and sung in the hymns. In this way the liturgy will serve the church as a new defense against its enemies." The Lutheran church has lost its familiarity with its own historical forms of worship, but the use of these forms must be retrieved. "A habit must be developed again, and what has become unnatural must become natural through practice."[33]

Like the Tractarians, Loehe also saw connections between the church, its liturgy, and social ministry. He was one of the leaders in the establishment of the deaconess movement in Germany, with a motherhouse and other charitable institutions tended to by the deaconesses in Neuendettelsau. He was also interested in the fate of Lutherans emigrating to the United States and was instrumental in dispatching missionary pastors to Ohio, Michigan, and Iowa.[34] These pastors brought with them an *Agende für christliche Gemeinden* (*Agenda for Christian Congregations of the Lutheran Confessions*), prepared

---

[31] Reed, 153–4.

[32] See Kenneth Korby, *Loehe: Theology of Pastoral Case* (Th.D. Thesis, Concordia Seminary-in-Exile, St. Louis, 1976), 111ff., 188ff.

[33] Wilhelm Loehe, *Three Books About the Church*, trans., ed. with an introduction by James L. Schaaf (Philadelphia: Fortress Press, 1969), 178–9.

[34] A picture of the Bavarian community in Michigan (c. 1852) is provided in Carl F. Schalk, "Sketches of Lutheran Worship," in Carl Halter and Carl Schalk, eds., *A Handbook of Church Music* (St. Louis: Concordia Publishing House, 1978), 86–90.

by Loehe in 1844. According to Luther Reed, it greatly influenced the liturgical studies of Drs. Charles Porterfield Krauth, Beale M. Schmucker, and Henry E. Jacobs, who were working on a Lutheran liturgy in English that could be based on Reformation sources.[35]

These confessional and liturgical revival movements in Germany had an impact in the United States not only on the Lutheran community, but also on the Reformed. Philip Schaff (1819–1893) left the University of Berlin to accept a professorship at the German Reformed Seminary in Mercersburg, Pennsylvania. Inspired by the theologian of the Prussian Union at Berlin, Friedrich Schleiermacher, he was also interested in the "evangelical catholic spirit" that permeated German theological literature. In his *Principles of Protestantism* he envisioned the future development of an evangelical catholic church in America.[36] Because he had suggested that Protestantism derived from and was in continuity with medieval Catholicism, he was tried for heresy by the classis (ecclesiastical jurisdiction in the Reformed church) of Philadelphia (charges dropped).[37] At Mercersburg, Schaff joined John W. Nevin (1803–1886), a Scotch-Irish Presbyterian graduate of Union College and Princeton Seminary, who worked to revive Calvin's understanding and preferred practice of the sacraments. When the distinguished Presbyterian theologian at Princeton, Charles Hodge, read Nevin's *Mystical Presence: A Vindication of the Calvinistic Doctrine of the Eucharist*, he expressed surprise that Calvin could have written such stuff.[38] When the Dutch Reformed Church read the Mercersburg theologians, it broke off relations with the German Reformed Church on the grounds that it did not wish to have fellowship with a body so afflicted with "Romanizing tendencies."[39] In America, Protestant liturgical recovery in the nineteenth century not only went up against Puritanism, Pietism, and Revivalism, but also against that cultural-political expression of anti-Catholic bigotry known as "Know-Nothingism."

The revival of a Lutheran confessional consciousness in Germany, combined with the retrieval of old Lutheran forms, engendered a great interest in those Lutheran leaders in the eastern United States who were eschewing the "American Lutheranism" of Samuel S. Schmucker (1799–1873). Schmucker had been a driving force in the formation and leadership of the General Synod of the Lutheran Church in America, constituted in 1820. This Princeton-educated theologian was a founder and first president of Gettysburg Seminary in 1826 and the preparatory school that became Gettysburg College in 1832. He was an early American ecumenical leader who proposed a plan of union for evangelical churches in America, but believed that this required a reconsideration of Melanchthon's "Variata" edition of the Augsburg Confession.[40] In fairness to Schmucker, it must be pointed out that even his sense of subscription to the Augsburg Confession

---

[35] Reed, 153.

[36] See Brodd, 91ff.

[37] See Howard G. Hageman, "Reformed Spirituality," in Senn, ed., *Protestant Spiritual Traditions*, op. cit., 75.

[38] Ibid., 74.

[39] For a full discussion of the Mercersburg movement in general and John Nevin's work in particular see James H. Nichols, *Romanticism in American Theology*.

[40] See Samuel Simon Schmucker, *Fraternal Appeal to the American Churches, with a plan for Catholic Union on Apostolic Principles* (1838), ed. with an introduction by Frederick K. Wentz (Philadelphia: Fortress Press, 1965).

(which he required in the professors' oath at Gettysburg) was more than had been the case with Rationalists. Also, the "evangelical catholic" emphasis at the neighboring Mercersburg Seminary, the Broad Church movement in the Episcopal Church under the leadership of William A. Muhlenberg (the grandson of Henry Melchior Muhlenberg),[41] and the examples of denominational cooperation in missionary work on the frontier (e.g., the Plan of Union for Congregationalists and Presbyterians in 1801 for comity arrangements on the Western frontier) encouraged Schmucker to seek a basis of unity between evangelical denominations in his proposed Evangelical Alliance. But by mid-century, the wave of immigration was bringing many orthodox Lutherans or neo-Lutherans to America. Leaders among these groups included C. F. W. Walther (1811–1887) of the Missouri Synod (organized in 1839) and Johannes Andreas August Grabau (1804–1879) of the Buffalo Synod (also organized in 1839), both of whom had resisted the Prussian Union. These new arrivals had a sharper sense of confessional identity than did Schmucker and the "American Lutherans,"[42] and new Lutheran immigrants outnumbered by millions the half-million Lutherans already settled in the United States at mid-century.[43]

Folk Church in Scandinavia

Denmark suffered more in the settlements of the Congress of Vienna than Germany did because it had supported Napoleon to the end. Its punishment was the loss of Norway, which was given to Sweden to compensate for Sweden's loss of Finland to Russia in 1809. The Danish church had also imbibed from the cup of reason as much as the German church had done. The culture Christianity that was created in Denmark became the brunt of Søren Kierkegaard's *Attack Upon Christendom* (1854–1855). "What . . . is 'Christendom?'" he asked.

> Is not 'Christendom' the most colossal attempt at serving God, not by following Christ, as He required, and suffering for the doctrine, but instead of that, by 'building the sepulchers of the prophets and garnishing the tombs of the righteous' and saying, 'If we had been in the days of our fathers, we should not have been partakers with them in the blood of the prophets'? [Matt. 23:29–33][44]

Pietistic revivals occurred in Sweden under the leadership of Henrik Schartau (1752–1825), who laid great stress on worship and whose catechetical lectures drew great crowds; in Norway under the controversial leadership of the lay preacher, Hans Nielsen Hauge (1771–1824); and in Finland under the similar careers of lay preacher Pauvo

---

[41] See Edward R. Hardy, "Evangelical Catholicism: W. A. Muhlenberg and the Memorial Movement," *Historical Magazine of the Protestant Episcopal Church* 13 (1944), 155–92. In spite of Muhlenberg's interest in rituals for the urban church and weekly communion, he was more associated with the Evangelical Wing of the Episcopal Church than the Tractarian ovement. A thorough treatment of Muhlenberg's liturgical efforts was presented in a paper at an N.A.A.L. study group meeting by Paul V. Marshall, "William Augustus Muhlenberg's Quiet Defection from Liturgical Uniformity."

[42] See Clifford Nelson, *The Lutherans in North American*, op. cit., 154–9.

[43] See Syndey E. Ahlstrom, *A Religious History of the American People* (New Haven and London: Yale University Press, 1972), 756.

[44] Søren Kierkegaard, *Attack Upon "Christendom"*, trans. by Walter Lowrie (Boston: The Beacon Press, 1956), 121.

Routsalainen (1777–1852) and Pastor Lars Laestadius (1800–1861). These revivals formed a popular bulwark against the Enlightenment while at the same time nurturing a sense of the church as the community of the faithful. This kind of folk church development came later to Denmark under the leadership of Nikolai Frederik Severin Grundtvig (1783–1872).[45]

Young Grundtvig was shaped by the ideas current at the beginning of the nineteenth century: the Enlightenment, the French Revolution, and the incipient Romantic movement. After a dull academic career, he became intellectually alive through the cultivation of an interest in Nordic history and mythology and through a study of the philosophies of Locke and Schelling. In the 1820s, when in his forties, he experienced a typical pietistic conversion that, for Grundtvig, was a breakthrough to religious certainty and authority that pulled him away from Rationalism and toward a more traditional Lutheran theology. But the areas of Lutheran theology toward which he gravitated were ecclesiology and sacramentology. His experience of pastoral work and church life in general had been depressing. Now he developed a new sense of excitement about the prospects of personal and ecclesial renewal, which was memorably expressed in his great hymns such as "The bells of Christmas" (*LBW* 62), "Bright and glorious is the sky" (*LBW* 75), "O day full of grace" (*LBW* 161), and "Built on a rock the Church shall stand" (*LBW* 365). Ecclesiastical advancement came very slowly to Grundtvig as a result of his attacks on Rationalist professors and church leaders. Only as a result of his literary efforts (e.g., translations of Nordic sagas and his 1,500 hymns, some original and others adaptations of ancient, medieval, and Reformation hymns) and his establishment of folk schools (which helped to convert a depressed peasantry into a community of progressive peasants) was he awarded at the end of his life with the title of bishop (though without a diocese).[46]

Grundtvig founded a movement in the Danish church that was similar to the Tractarian movement in England, with its high church ecclesiology and emphasis on the role of the sacraments in Christian life, although the pietist in him eschewed any kind of clerical pretension. A unique aspect of Grundtvig's teaching was that the confession of faith by the individual and the congregation at baptism represents a word of salvation from God himself. This was interpreted by some as meaning that the Apostles' Creed was a word of the Lord. Grundtvig accepted this notion to the extent that the Creed is a summary of the scripture's gospel and that by rendering it back to God a mutual covenant is formed between God and the baptized. As Johannes Knudsen summarized: "Grundtvig repeatedly says that the signs of the Christian life are the confession of faith, the proclamation of the gospel, and the songs of praise, refusing to include the personal appropriation that was so central for Kierkegaard."[47]

---

[45] See Frank C. Senn, "Lutheran Spirituality," in *Protestant Spiritual Traditions*, op. cit., 46–7.

[46] See Johannes Knudsen in *Danish Rebel* (Philadelphia: Muhlenberg Press, 1955); also Noelle Davis, *Education for Life: A Danish Pioneer* (Liverpool: Williams & Norgate, 1931).

[47] Johannes Knudsen, Introduction to *N. F. S. Grundtvig: Selected Writings* (Philadephia: Fortress Press, 1976), 7.

Perhaps the most enduring legacy of Grundtvig is in his revolution of congregational song. His new hymns were first sung by the congregation of the Vartov Church in Copenhagen, of which Grundtvig became vicar in 1839. But there was a feeling that the strikingly metaphorical texts did not go well with the old chorale tunes. At first new melodies were provided by using known folk and patriotic tunes. But church organists, whose creativity was stirred by the vigorous singing of the Vartov congregation, began to provide new and appropriate tunes for Grundtvig's texts. One of these composers was A. P. Berggren, who was a leading figure in Danish musical life and the editor of a chorale book (1853, supplement, 1856) for the hymnal (1852, revised 1855), which included many of Grundtvig's hymns.[48] It is noteworthy that these books were intended to be used in both church and home, and became a way of building bridges between liturgy and popular devotion in Scandinavian Lutheranism.

Most of the two million Scandinavian immigrants to the United States after mid-century were nominally Lutheran. The first to arrive were the Norwegians, who began to settle in northern Illinois in the 1830s. The Norwegians, like most of the other Scandinavian groups, were represented in two contrasting types of groups: pietistic and confessional. The Norwegians were split between the followers of the lay preacher Hans Nielsen Hauge, who were organized into a synod by Elling Eielsen, and those who emphasized confessional theology and were organized into the Synod of Northern Illinois by J. W. C. Dietrichson. The largest Scandinavian immigrant group were Swedish Lutherans, who affiliated at first with the Synod of Northern Illinois (in Europe Norway had been joined to Sweden after the Napoleonic Wars; before that Norway had been under Danish rule). The affiliation of the Synod of Northern Illinois with the General Synod allowed the Swedes to establish a sentimental relationship with the older New Sweden Lutheranism. In 1860 these immigrants formed the larger Scandinavian Augustana Synod. Ten years later the Danish-Norwegian element in this synod went its own way.

Since the Scandinavian immigrant congregations could be either confessional or pietistic, they generally followed two different liturgical traditions. The confessional groups used versions of the liturgies of the state church from their country of origin. These included versions of the liturgies of the Church of Sweden of 1811 (adopted with some changes in 1870) and the Danish-Norwegian Liturgy of 1685 (as modified in 1887–1889). The pietistic groups regarded liturgy as a sign of formalism and preferred free-form worship orders, which generally left the form and content of worship up to the pastor.[49]

RESTORATION OF THE ORDO: THE COMMON SERVICE

The ecclesiastical and liturgical situation of Lutheranism in America in the middle of the nineteenth century was chaotic, although all of the Lutheran groups felt an

---

[48] See Torben Schousboe, "Protestant Church Music in Scandinavia," in Blume, ed., *Protestant Church Music*, op. cit., 622–3.

[49] A sketch of a typical Norwegian-American service as celebrated in Muskego, Wisconsin is provided in Schalk, 95–8.

obligation to develop as inclusive a Lutheran fellowship as possible and to seek intersynodical cooperation on the basis of confessional ties. The older ministeriums and synods on the east coast had formed a federation of synods called the General Synod in 1820. As new immigrants arrived in the Midwest they formed their own synodical organizations, sometimes existing independently and in some cases aligning with a federation like the General Synod or a looser conference such as the Synodical Conference (formed in 1872). The Civil War caused a north/south division in several denominations, and Lutherans were no exception. The General Synod, South was formed in 1862 when it seemed that the Confederacy might become a permanent political reality. Among the newly arrived immigrants in the Midwest, there was general opposition to slavery, although C. F. W. Walther of the Missouri Synod held, in opposition to the Abolitionist movement, that "slavery in itself" could not be condemned as a sin on biblical grounds. Some pastors in the Norwegian Synod agreed with the Missouri Synod on theological grounds, although the majority of lay members were abolitionists and signed up in large numbers to serve in the Union Army. As late as 1868 the issue was still being debated, although obviously the issue was no longer slavery but the interpretation and authority of the Bible. The debate, at the outset of the war, led the Norwegian Synod to pull out of Concordia Seminary in Saint Louis and to establish its own seminary at Halfway Creek, Wisconsin, in 1862.[50]

At the same time as the sectional divisions in the United States were causing ecclesiastical divisions, the confessional debates were causing schism. As part of his proposal to form a grand Evangelical Alliance, S. S. Schmucker introduced his *Definite Platform* with its American Recension of the Augsburg Confession to the General Synod in 1855.[51] The mere fact that such an issue was being discussed caused the more confessionally grounded midwestern immigrants to form their own synodical organizations. It caused an actual schism in the General Synod. The issuance of the *Definite Platform* had not caused the Ministerium of Pennsylvania to secede from the General Synod, but the withdrawal of the Scandinavian synods, the admission of the liberal Melanchthon Synod and the Franckean Synod, and the split occasioned by the Civil War caused the Ministerium of Pennsylvania to withdraw. It had already withdrawn from the Gettysburg Seminary and established its own seminary in Philadelphia (at Mt. Airy) in 1864 over the issue of the selection of a new president to succeed the retiring Dr. Schmucker. The General Council was constituted in Fort Wayne, Indiana, in 1867 by thirteen synods, including the Scandinavian Augustana Synod. The struggle over confessional principles led to the withdrawal of several midwestern synods, and the council was pushed to define its conditions for altar and pulpit fellowship. It needed to steer a path between the "unionism" from which many German Lutherans had escaped and which was implied in the *Definite Platform*, on the one hand, and a tendency to close communion to any who were not members of a particular congregation or synod, on the other hand. The discussion resulted in the Akron Rule, adopted in 1872, and reaffirmed as the Galesburg Rule in 1872.

---

[50] See Clifford Nelson, *The Lutherans in North America*, op. cit., 238–47.

[51] For a comparison of the texts of the Augsburg Confession (1530) and its American Recension (1855), see ibid., 222–3.

The rule is: (1) Lutheran pulpits are for Lutheran ministers only and Lutheran altars are for Lutheran communicants only; (2) the exceptions to the rule belong to the sphere of privilege, not of right; (3) the determination of the exceptions is to be made in consonance with these principles, by the conscientious judgment of pastors, as the case arises.[52]

One of the first acts of the General Council was to address the need for a liturgy and church book that reflected the confessional and liturgical recovery in Europe. Beale Melanchthon Schmucker, the confessionally minded and liturgically interested son of S. S. Schmucker, took the lead in efforts to restore in America the Reformation Lutheran liturgical and hymnological heritage. Schmucker, Charles Porterfield Krauth, and Joseph A. Seiss focused their attention on worship in English. A new German-language liturgy had been prepared in 1855 that reflected the liturgical retrieval in Germany. This served as the basis of *A Liturgy for the Use of the English Lutheran Church* (1860). But the real breakthrough toward a restored Lutheran liturgy and hymnal, to which occasional services were later added, was the *Church Book* prepared for the newly formed General Council of the Evangelical Lutheran Church (1868).[53] The influence of Beale M. Schmucker was also to be seen in the revised *Book of Worship* of the General Synod, South (1867) and in an improved Service of the old General Synod (the Washington Service, 1869).[54] These efforts set the stage for the cooperative work of the General Council, the General Synod, and the United Synod of the South leading to the preparation and adoption of the Common Service of 1888.

Interestingly, Muhlenberg's old idea of "one church, one book" was revived in the United Synod of the South by Dr. John Bachman, the venerable pastor of Saint John's Church in Charleston. His proposal was adopted by the Synod at its meeting in Staunton, Virginia, in 1876. In 1878 the Synod instructed its fraternal delegates to the General Council and the General Synod, North "to inquire whether these Bodies will be willing to appoint a committee to co-operate with a similar committee appointed by this Synod for the purpose of preparing a 'Service Book.'"[55] The General Council, meeting in Zanesville, Ohio, in 1879, "consented to co-operate provided that the Rule which shall decide all questions arising in its preparation shall be: The common consent of the pure Lutheran liturgies of the sixteenth century, and when there is not an entire agreement among them the consent of the largest number of greatest weight."[56]

The General Synod was skeptical "as to the acceptability of any basis which it might suggest for a Common 'Service Book,'" but was willing to appoint a committee "to confer with the General Synod South and with any other committee appointed for this purpose in order to ascertain whether an agreement upon any common basis is practicable."[57] Edward T. Horn published an article in the *Lutheran Quarterly Review*, entitled

---

[52] Ibid., 237.

[53] See Henry E. Jacobs, "The Making of the Church Book," *Lutheran Church Review* XXXI (1912), 597–622.

[54] See Reed, chapter 8.

[55] Ibid., 183.

[56] Ibid.

[57] Ibid., 183–4.

"Feasibility of a Service for all English-speaking Lutherans," which took the rule proposed by the General Council as a text and demonstrated something of the consensus of the Reformation church orders that would make the application of the Rule feasible.[58] In 1882 the General Synod, South accepted the Rule and in 1883 the General Synod, North responded to the desire of many of its own pastors for a liturgy "more in harmony with the historic Books of Worship," suspended the publication of more copies of its own worship book, and declared its willingness to work on a common service.

Actual work began in April 1884, when Drs. Schmucker, E. J. Wolf, S. A. Repass, and Pastors T. W. Dosh, George U. Wenner, and Edward T. Horn met in Horn's study in Charleston, South Carolina, to established working principles. The full "Joint Committee on a Common Service Book" was held in the library of the Philadelphia Seminary in May 1885. Dr. Schmucker was elected chair, and Pastor Horn was elected secretary. After each meeting of the Joint Committee, the progress of the work was forwarded to the synodical bodies; and suggested emendations were considered by the Joint Committee at its next meeting.[59]

Edward T. Horn reported that already at its May 1885 meeting, the Joint Committee was able to adopt and forward to its parent bodies "the parts and order of the Normal Lutheran Service," as follows:[60]

> Introit
> Kyrie
> Gloria
> Collect
> Epistle
> Alleluia
> Gospel
> Creed
> Sermon
> General Prayer
> Preface
> Sanctus and Hosanna
> Exhortation to Communicants
> Lord's Prayer and Words of Institution or Words of Institution and
>   Lord's Prayer
> Agnus Dei
> Distribution
> Collect of Thanksgiving
> Benediction

As *additions*, not as integral parts of the historical Service, the Committee proposed (Phila. 1885; *Harrisburg Report*, p. 4) and the General Bodies approved:

---

[58] Edward T. Horn, "Feasibility of a Service for all English-speaking Lutherans," *Lutheran Quarterly Review*, New Series, XI (1881), 163–78.

[59] Reed, 185ff., provides detailed descriptions of the work-in-progress drawn from the unpublished Memoirs of Dr. Henry E. Jacobs.

[60] Edward T. Horn, "The Lutheran Sources of the Common Service," *Lutheran Quarterly Review* XXI (1891), 244.

1. *At the beginning*: a hymn of invocation of the Holy Ghost; the words, In the name of the Father, and of the Son, and of the Holy Ghost; and the confession of sins;
2. *After the Creed*: the principal hymn; and
3. *After the General Prayer*: another hymn.[61]

Minor additions were made in the final preparation of the Service: the collection, the Pax, the words of dismissal after the distribution, the Nunc dimittis and the Benedicamus.[62]

Each of the main parts and the major and minor additions had to have some attestation in the "pure Lutheran liturgies" of the sixteenth century. The addition of hymns constituted no major issue. The major issues to be considered in the communion service were the use of a preparatory office of confession of sins, since some of the weightiest Lutheran Reformation church orders lacked this; the juxtaposition of the words of institution and the Lord's Prayer, since weighty sources disagreed in the order, and the inclusion of the Nunc dimittis as a post-communion canticle, since it was attested only in some north German church orders. It was considered that Lutherans had become used to a confession of sins and declaration of grace and the Common Service could not be without this; that the sources that placed the Lord's Prayer before the words of institution seemed "of greater weight" than the opposite arrangement; and that the Nunc dimittis could be provided as an option. In the literature that followed the publication of the Common Service by the three synodical bodies in 1888, the sources of the service were thoroughly explained, as Horn did in his exhaustive article on "The Lutheran Sources of the Common Service."[63] The fact that the Joint Committee drew upon the texts of the Creeds, the Lord's Prayers, the canticles, and many of the collects and prayers in the *Book of Common Prayer* was justified by Henry E. Jacobs on the grounds that the Thomas Cranmer had drawn upon the Lutheran church orders in the preparation of the Edwardian Prayer Books (especially 1549), and now that Lutherans were ready to worship and pray in English they could receive back these texts in worthy English translations.[64]

The finished text of the Order of Service, with and without communion, plus Matins, Vespers, and the Litany, with all their propers, were delivered to the three church bodies in 1888. The United Synod of the South, which had initiated the process, immediately published the Common Service in its *Book of Worship* in 1888. There was some controversy in the General Synod. James W. Richard, the liturgics professor at Gettysburg Seminary, questioned whether the rule had been followed in every particular, whether it was possible to follow it, and therefore whether the Common Service ought to be imposed on congregations.[65] George U. Wenner answered by describing the procedure used by the Joint Committee: "After the Normal Service had thus been found, certain

---

[61] Ibid., 248.

[62] Ibid., 249.

[63] Ibid., 217–56.

[64] See Henry Eyster Jacobs, *The Lutheran Movement in England during the Reigns of Henry VIII and Edward VI and Its Literary Monuments* (Philadelphia: General Council Publication House, 1908), 206–313.

[65] James W. Richard, "The Liturgical Question," *Lutheran Quarterly* XX (1890), 103–85.

changes were made by way of adaptation and on the basis of mutual concessions among the several Bodies. These changes were long and carefully considered, and were finally approved by the entire Joint Committee, and by the General Bodies."[66]

The result of this disagreement was that when the General Synod published its *Book of Worship* in 1888, it continued to print its 1869 Washington Service with the Common Service, thus giving congregations an option.[67] The Council did not get its *Church Book* published until 1892 because, unfortunately, Beale Schmucker, running to catch a train to Philadelphia on October 15, 1888, complete manuscript of the Common Service in his handbag, died from overexertion. The shock of Schmucker's death immobilized the General Council's committee for a time, and then with one eye on opposition to the Common Service in some part of the General Synod, tampered with the text to make it more like its 1868 *Church Book*.[68] The result, as the young Luther D. Reed pointed out in one of his early articles, was that the Common Service was not quite "common"; there were three official variants. Not surprising, in a comparison of the three versions with the original manuscript, he found that the United Synod of the South had remained closest to the received text.[69]

While it seems natural to set texts basically drawn from the *Book of Common Prayer* to Anglican chant, there was some desire to provide plain chant settings such as those associated with the old Lutheran liturgies in Europe. A significant effort in that direction was provided by *The Choral Service Book* by Harry G. Archer and Luther D. Reed (1901).[70] This handsomely printed book provided "Authentic Plain Song Intonations and Responses for the Order of Morning Service, the Orders of Matins and Vespers, the Litany and the Suffrages of the Common Service." Archer and Reed, in their preface, extolled "the quality of absolute churchliness" that plainsong possesses. As there is a distinctive liturgy of the church, which defines it over against the world, so that liturgy expresses itself in distinctive forms of architecture, art, literature, worship, and music. "The historical Plain Song Liturgical Music is as distinctively ecclesiastical in essential character and in effect as the Liturgy itself. Its very presence in the sanctuary is a forceful protest against diseased craving for dramatic display and sensational individualism in

---

[66] George U. Wenner, "An Answer to 'The Liturgical Question'," *Lutheran Quarterly* XX (1890), 312.

[67] The *Book of Worship with Hymns and Tunes*, Published by the General Synod of the Evangelical Lutheran Church in the United States (Philadelphia: Lutheran Publication Society, 1899) included the "Washington Services" on pp. 9ff. and the Common Service on pp. 19ff. The "Morning Service" (pp. 9ff.) consisted of the following hodge-podge of an order: Invocation and call to worship, Gloria Patri, confession of sins, Kyrie, prayer for forgiveness, Apostles' Creed, Gloria in excelsis, reading of scripture, hymn, prayer, hymn, collection, sermon, the Lord's Prayer, hymn, and benediction.

[68] The *Church Book, for the use of Evangelical Lutheran Congregations, by authority of the General Council of the Evangelical Lutheran Church in America. With Music* (Philadelphia: J. K. Shryock, 1897) was dedicated "To the Memory of Charles Porterfield Krauth and Beale Melanchthon Schmucker, Life-long Friends, whose Learning and Piety were Devoted to Purifying and Ennobling the Worship of the Church they Loved."

[69] Luther D. Reed, "The Standard Manuscript of the Common Service, and Variata Editions," *Lutheran Church Review* XX (1901), 459–73.

[70] *The Choral Service Book*, ed. by Harry G. Archer and Luther D. Reed (Philadelphia: The United Lutheran Publication House, 1901).

pulpit, pew, or choir."[71] So much in demand was this book that a second edition was published in its first year. It was followed in 1907 by *The Psalter and Canticles Pointed for Chanting to Gregorian Psalm Tones*.[72]

The Joint Committee continued its work until 1906, producing new translations of the Augsburg Confession and Luther's Small Catechism and working toward a common hymnal. As cooperation grew, the General Synod amended its constitution in 1913 to acknowledge the unaltered Augsburg Confession "as a correct exhibition of the faith and doctrine of our Church." The General Council was increasingly embarrassed by its tampering with the text of the Common Service, and in 1909 issued a call to the other church bodies to cooperate in the publication of a *Common Service Book with Hymnal*. Work began on this project in 1910, with Luther D. Reed serving as secretary of the Joint Committee and of all the subcommittees.[73] The *Common Service Book with Hymnal* was published in 1917, the quadricentennial anniversary of the Reformation. The excitement over the publication of this joint book contributed greatly to the merger of the General Council, the General Synod, and the United Synod of the South in 1918 to form the United Lutheran Church in America.

The first edition of the *Common Service Book* contained two musical settings for the Service, Matins, and Vespers—Anglican chant and plainchant. (The plainchant setting was dropped from the second edition, much to Reed's disappointment, to make room for more occasional services, such as baptism, confirmation, marriage, and burial.) A separate section of propers for Sundays and festivals included full provision for introits, collects, epistles, graduals, and gospels for the entire church year. The hymnal contained 578 hymn texts. The tunes, in the first two editions, were published with four-part harmonizations, but above the texts in the European style to facilitate the interchangeability of text and tune. There must have been numerous complaints, because in the third edition one or more stanzas of text were printed between the staves.[74]

The quality of the Common Service commended itself to other Lutheran groups. The first group to adopt it outside of the three that had worked on it was the English Evangelical Lutheran Synod of Missouri and Other States, which printed the Service, Matins, and Vespers in its *Evangelical Lutheran Hymn-Book* (Baltimore, 1893). This synod merged with the German Missouri Synod in 1911, in which it continued as the English District; and its *Evangelical Lutheran Hymn-Book* became the official English worship book and hymnal of the Missouri Synod in 1912.[75] Unfortunately, this book was

---

[71] Ibid., xxxiii–xxxiv.

[72] *The Psalter and Canticles Pointed for Chanting to the Gregorian Psalm Tones*, ed. by Harry G. Archer and Luther D. Reed, with an introduction by D. H. Geissinger (New York: The Christian Literature Co., 1907).

[73] This work of this Joint Committee is described in Reed, 200–4.

[74] *Common Service Book of the Lutheran Church* (Philadelphia: The Board of Publication of the United Lutheran Church in America, 1919).

[75] German-speaking Missouri Synod congregations used a modified Saxon Agenda, which depended on chorales more than on the historic liturgical texts. While the English District of the Missouri Synod was liturgically strong, the German congregations tended to be liturgically weak (having eschewed the superior Liturgy of King Friedrich Wilhelm III as a product of Unionism).

published without copyright notice,[76] so that when the Norwegian synods included the Common Service in *The Lutheran Hymnary* in 1913 credit was given to the Missouri Synod (which was true for the tunes, but not for the texts!).

As the *Common Service Book* led to the merger that created the United Lutheran Church in America, so *The Lutheran Hymnary* led to the merger of the Norwegian Synod, the Hauge Synod, and the United Norwegian Church in America in 1917 to form the Norwegian Lutheran Church of America. *The Lutheran Hymnary* included the texts of the Common Service, with tunes from Missouri's *Evangelical Lutheran Hymn-Book*, as well as the English translation of the Danish-Norwegian Service of 1887–1889. It is unlikely, however, that the Common Service was widely used in Norwegian congregations. The preference was for the English translation of the Norwegian liturgy, in which the collects, Lord's Prayer, words of institution, and benediction were all chanted by the minister. This was a pattern in Scandinavian worship books. The Swedish Augustana Synod, although a member of the General Council, did not adopt its *Church Book* (1892)—probably because most of its congregations worshiped in Swedish. In 1905 the Augustana Synod published an English translation of the Swedish Liturgy of 1895; but not until 1925 did the Augustana Synod include the Common Service as an option along with the 1905 Swedish-based liturgy in its *Hymnal and Order of Service*. In the *Hymnal for Church and Home* published by the two Danish synods in 1927, the Common Service was pasted into the liturgical section and was not printed in the book itself until 1953. Finally, we would note that Iowa Synod used the Common Service for its English-language liturgy, published in the *Wartburg Hymnal* in 1918. Its German-speaking congregations used the *Agende* of Wilhelm Loehe, which gave them a strong liturgical tradition. When the Iowa Synod, the Joint Synod of Ohio, and the Buffalo Synod merged in 1930 to form the American Lutheran Church, its *American Lutheran Hymnal* provided only the Common Service. Some smaller synodical bodies did not publish separate worship books in English, but allowed their congregations to use what was available. So, as George Muenich summarized, "It may be safely said that the Common Service was in general use in nearly all English-speaking Lutheran congregations in the U. S. and Canada by 1945, the year work began which resulted in the *Service Book and Hymnal* [1958]."[77]

Muenich has aptly called this achievement "the triumph of restorationism." This is largely accurate, as concerns the liturgical orders. But we must not forget that the liturgical revival was a reaction to Rationalism, Pietism, and Revivalism, whose fires were never completely smothered. Thus these liturgical orders with all their provisions were seldom used as their framers envisioned, since strains of Rationalism, Pietism, and Revivalism continued to flourish in areas of Lutheran church life.

---

[76] Reed, 176, n. 9 complains about this habit of Missouri Synod publishers up to and including *The Lutheran Hymnal* of 1941; in particular Reed chafed over the republication by Kahmer in Baltimore in 1906 of much of *The Choral Service Book* without permission or credit.

[77] George R. Muenich, "The Victory of Restorationism—The Common Service, 1888–1958" (Published privately by Luther-Northwestern Seminary, 1984, as part of a manuscript textbook in liturgics edited by Patrick Keifert), 33. See also Frank C. Senn, "The Achievement of the Common Service: Reflections on the Occasion of Its Centennial Anniversary," *dialog* 27 (Fall 1988), 291–4.

❦ THE RETRIEVAL OF OLD CHURCH MUSIC

At the time Klaus Harms issued his Ninety-Five Theses against Rationalism in 1817, church music was everywhere at a low ebb. With the promulgation of the Prussian liturgy, which was largely the personal achievement of King Friedrich Wilhelm III, there was an effort to provide it with an appropriate musical setting. The Agendas published in 1821 and 1822, however, were far from a return to the liturgical music of the Reformation. They represented a mixture of idioms, including Lutheran intonation formulas, Gregorian chant, and even Russian church music from Dimitri Bortnjansky (the Orthodox music director of the Russian court chapel); and, in any event, responsorial singing by the congregation was inadequately provided (it had also become a lost art). As early as 1823 the king granted permission to have the responses read by the cantor, teacher, or even the sexton. Only after 1843 were efforts made to have the responses sung by the congregation with organ accompaniment to provide support. This became the general style of Lutheran liturgical chant, although those interested in the revival of Gregorian chant preferred unaccompanied singing since the style of organ playing in the nineteenth century tended to be ponderous.[78]

At the same time as efforts were being made to retrieve plainsong liturgical settings, the Reformation hymns were being studied and put back into use. There were efforts to produce a common hymnal for the Protestant churches of Germany. Investigation showed that only about a half-dozen hymns from the Reformation could be found in all the hymnals surveyed. A conference of representatives of the highest Protestant church authorities in Germany met in Eisenach in 1852 and compiled a *Deutsches Evangelisches Kirchen-Gesangbuch* of 150 basic hymns. This "Eisenach basic hymnal" was incorporated into the Bavarian hymnal of 1854 and into the hymnals of a few small *Landeskirchen*; but the resistance of the laity to both the tunes (with their original melodies and rhythms) and the texts was formidable. They were too thoroughly imbued with Romantic notions of church music—it should be slow, somber, quiet, and dignified—and with Rationalist theology to appreciate the sprightly character of the old chorales or their dogmatic teachings. It should be noted that this resistance also came from the church music professionals. Georg Feder records these reactions:

Moritz Hauptmann, cantor at Saint Thomas's, thought the even-note chorale to be more "dignified"; the Thuringian organist F. Kuehmstedt opposed the restoration efforts in the 1850s with the syllogism that "rhythm is essentially nothing but organized time," while the chorale and the church were to lead man to eternity and to God. Friedrich Schneider (1852) went so far as to call rhythmical singing "a deplorable desecration and profanation of the sacred."[79]

It was obvious that musical forces were needed that could lead congregational singing and that would also be a force for change against the entrenched views of the professionals. In Saxony there were unsuccessful efforts to revive the old *Kantoreien* in the

---

[78] See Georg Feder, "Decline and Restoration," in Blume, ed., *Protestant Church Music*, op. cit., 377–8.

[79] Ibid., 380.

1830s. A more promising approach was King Friedrich Wilhelm IV's reorganization of the Berlin cathedral choir of men and boys in 1843 into a salaried group. This was based on the a cappella Russian court choir in Saint Petersburg. The success of this group prompted other cathedral or court choirs to be organized. But these professional choirs could not be implemented in every parish church. As late as 1885 there were few trained church choirs. The five churches in the city of Augsburg, for example, had one choir that rotated among these parishes.[80] At best parishes could draw from the volunteer singing societies that flourished in cities and towns. Sometimes these were men's choirs; sometimes they were women's choirs. There was also a revival of instrumental participation in church services (after the Enlightenment had discouraged it) with the interesting movement of "brass choirs" that followed the development of professional church choirs in the 1840s and 1850s. The provision of professional parish musical leadership was slower in coming, since the usual director of the parish choir was the cantor who served both as church organist and elementary school teacher. Furthermore, while few of the practicing church musicians understood the liturgical requirements of the music they were producing, most clergyman lacked any understanding of the liturgical role church music could play and therefore failed to encourage it.[81]

What style should church music exemplify? There were those who advocated unaccompanied singing. They took as their models the Russian church music with which the Prussians were in contact on their Eastern front and the Catholic Saint Cecelia Societies, which were dedicated to the music of Palestrina and his contemporaries. The growing ideal of a cappella singing is reflected in the paid choirs of men and boys that flourished in the mid-nineteenth century. But after Mendelssohn's celebrated 1829 revival of J. S. Bach's *St. Matthew Passion*, there were those who felt that Bach represented the apex of Protestant church music, which should serve as the ideal toward which church music should strive. This created quite a controversy. Schoeberlein and Winterfeld believed that the sixteenth and early seventeenth centuries represented the classical period of Protestant church music, and that solo singing (particularly in an operatic style) should be eliminated; that choral music (as the ideal voice of the church) should be restricted to antiphonal singing with the congregation or responsorial singing with the minister; and that Bach's works were more artful than edifying, and better suited to the concert hall than to the sanctuary.[82] The supporters of the works of J. S. Bach therefore had to renounce the devotional view of church music nurtured by the Enlightenment and Romanticism in order to get Bach's liturgical music, already being performed in concert halls, back into church services. Interestingly, theologians began to take note of the works of Bach and claim him as their own. He even came to be called the "fifth evangelist" because of his passions and gospel-oriented cantatas.[83]

Winterfeld, as early as 1848, raised the question of whether composers would only imitate the styles of glorified historical figures or find a new voice based on these

---

[80] See Edwin Liemohn, *Organ and Choir in Protestant Worship*, op. cit., 95.

[81] Feder, 388.

[82] Ibid., 390.

[83] Ibid., 392.

models. The fact is that little church music from the nineteenth century is regularly performed today. But very little of it was written, and the best examples come from composers who were more concerned with religious music than with church music as such. The Prussian king entrusted Felix Mendelssohn (1809–1847) with the direction of the Berlin cathedral choir. While he had an interest in the possibility of the revival of church music, he saw no possibility for it to flourish within the Prussian liturgy (letter to Pastor Bauer, 1835). While he wrote a cappella works for the Berlin choir, he was more interested in instrumentally accompanied choral music.[84] Johannes Brahms (1833–1897), on the other hand, was much more attracted to a cappella motet-writing. He composed thirteen motets and other a cappella works for the women's choir and other choirs he conducted during his career. The Bach historian, Philipp Spitta, made accessible to Brahms not only the works of J. S. Bach but also the organ music of Samuel Scheidt and the choral music of Heinrich Schütz. Brahms was able to draw upon these historical sources in a creative way. Thus while he was even farther from being a church composer than Mendelssohn, his interest in the old German Lutheran music made a significant contribution to the revival of church music as such.[85]

A similar interest in reviving older liturgical music based on Gregorian chant or the polyphonic music of Palestrina was promoted by the Roman Catholic Saint Cecelia Society. The aim of this society was to contend against the operatic-style music that continued to flourish in the Roman Catholic Church under the influence of such composers as Hertor Berlioz, Franz Liszt (who took minor orders), Charles Gounod (who intended to become a priest), César Franck, and Camille Saint-Saëns. Brahm's Roman Catholic contemporary in Vienna, Anton Bruckner (1824–1896), was, like Brahms, attracted to the a cappella motet as a partisan of the Saint Cecelia Society, although these works are not as well known as his masses.

If little choral music was being written for church services, there was even less new organ music for church services. Mendelssohn, Robert Schumann (1810–1856), and Joseph Rheinberger (1839–1901) each wrote a few organ works that could be considered usable in worship. Rheinberger was actually an organist at the Saint Michael's Church in Munich. At the end of his life Brahms published eleven Chorale Preludes (1896) on well-known German hymns of the sixteenth and seventeenth centuries. Anton Bruckner, who was a celebrated organist and who also had a church music background, left few works in this area (although organ textures influenced the scoring of his monumental symphonies).

There was a great renaissance of organ music in general and of organ music for church services in France toward the end of the nineteenth century. The great organ composers who contributed to this renaissance included the Belgian-born César Franck (1822–1890), who was organist of Sainte-Clotilde Church in Paris, Felix Alexander Guilmant (1837–1911), Charles-Marie Widor (1844–1937), organist at Sainte-Sulpice in Paris, Louis Vierne (1870–1937), the blind organist of Notre Dame Cathedral in Paris,

[84] Ibid., 396.
[85] See Adam Adrio, "Renewal and Rejuvenation," in *Protestant Church Music*, 408.

and Marcel Dupré (1886–1971), Widor's successor at Sainte-Sulpice. The organization of church music in France provided for three positions in major churches: the *organiste titulaire*, an assistant/apprentice organist who became a *survivancier* of his teacher (often succeeding him on the titular organist's retirement or death), and the master of the choirs. Often two organs were built in the church—the great organ and the choir organ. It had become customary for the titular organist to provide music at the offertory and the elevation of the mass, and at entrance and exit processions if there were such. A *sortie* after the mass or office provided the occasion for a virtuostic postlude. The choir organist accompanied the choir, especially in the singing of Gregorian chant.[86] Of all of these organists, Guilmant was perhaps the most conscious of being a church musician. The full title of his Opus 65 is *The Liturgical Organist, a Collection of Pieces based on Liturgical Chants, for Use in the Church, Composed for Organ (or Harmonium)*. All sixty pieces in *L'Organiste Liturgique* are based on chant; all are suitable for a church service. They reflect the impact of the plainsong revival of the Solesmes Benedictines.[87]

Perhaps the most influential of these organists was Widor, both as titular organist at the celebrated Church of Sainte-Sulpice and as a professor of organ at the Paris Conservatory. Saint-Sulpice was both a parish church and a seminary for the training of priests. Its choir consisted of twenty-four boys, ten men, and two players of serpents (curved horns with a bassoon-like sound) or double-basses. In 1862 murals in the Chapelle des Anges—*Heliodorus driven from the Temple* and *Jacob wrestling with the Angel*—were painted by Eugène Delacroix. In the same year, Cliquot's 1781 *Grand Orgue* in the west gallery was rebuilt by Cavaillé-Coll, with 118 stops and nearly 7,000 pipes laid out in seven storeys.[88] For a time Gabriel Fauré was appointed *Petit Organiste*, and he and Widor engaged in friendly contests of improvisation on their respective instruments, of which the congregation remained unaware.

Widor was a champion in the revival of interest in the organ music of J. S. Bach in France, which had already begun earlier in the century in the work of Alexandre-Pierre-Francois Boëly (1785–1858) and Jack Nikolaas Lemmens (1823–1881). One of Widor's most celebrated pupils, Albert Schweitzer, helped him to appreciate the fact that Bach's chorale preludes were not just models of counterpoint, but tone-paintings of the hymn-texts. Widor, in turn, encouraged the brilliant young theologian-musician to give his historical, hymnological, and theological insights into Bach's music wider currency, and the result was the publication of Schweitzer's *J. S. Bach: le musicien-poête*, first published in French in 1905, then expanded in the German and English editions (1908, 1911, respectively).[89] Widor and Schweitzer together helped to promote Bach's accessibility as

---

[86] See Orpha Ochse, *Organists and Organ Playing in Nineteenth Century France and Belgium*, op. cit., ch. XII on "Organ and Liturgy" (pp. 121ff.).

[87] See Edward Zimmerman and Lawrence Archbold, "Why Should We Not Do the Same with Our Catholic Melodies?" in *French Organ Music: From the Revolution to Franck and Widor*, ed. by Lawrence Archbold and William J. Peterson (University of Rochester Press, 1995), 201ff.

[88] See Andrew Thomson, *Widor: The Life and Times of Charles-Marie Widor, 1844–1937* (Oxford University Press, 1987), ch. 3 on "Saint-Sulpice" (pp. 17ff.).

[89] See Albert Schweitzer, *J. S. Bach*, Eng. trans. by Ernest Newman, 2 vols. (New York: Dover Publications, Inc., 1966).

a universal rather than as a confessional composer. Perhaps the high point of their professional relationship was the Widor-Schweitzer collaboration on an urtext edition of Bach's organ works, beginning in 1911. Only the first five volumes were completed under their joint efforts because in 1913 Schweitzer left Europe to found a mission hospital in Lambarene, Gabon, West Africa.[90]

Scandinavian church music fared poorly throughout much of the nineteenth century because Scandinavian national music was not well developed. It was heavily dependent on German musical influence, either because Germans were recruited to provide musical leadership or because Scandinavian students studied in Germany. The situation in Denmark was abysmal in the first half of the nineteenth century. The Niels Schioerring Chorale Book of 1783 that remained in use was heavily influenced by Rationalism. We have seen, however, that the hymns of Grundtvig provided a stimulus to the composition of more folk-like hymns by A. P. Berggren for inclusion in the 1855 Hymnbook. Many of these hymns were first published as sacred solos, and this was noted in the hymnbook.[91] There were virtually no professional choirs, although choirs composed of schoolchildren helped to lead congregational singing and probably rendered the Grundtvig hymns better than German-schooled professionals might have done.

The same situation existed in Norway as in Denmark since the hymn and chorale books had been the same in both countries. But since Norway was transferred to Sweden after the Napoleonic Wars, the Church of Norway ceased to be administered by the Church of Denmark and acquired more independence. The first chorale book for Norwegian organists was prepared in 1838 by O. A. Lindeman, the organist at Our Lady's Church in Trondheim. The hymns were set in the even-note rhythmic pattern so typical of the German books of the time. Congregational singing was at a low ebb, and some blamed it on the introduction of the organ and the choirs into the churches. But O. A. Lindeman's son, Ludwig Lindeman, organist at Our Savior's Church in Christiana (Oslo), advocated enlivening the tunes by the use of dotted rhythms and by replacing fermatas with short rests. He published another chorale book in 1871 in which he tried to rectify his father's shortcomings by providing the hymns with greater rhythmic and harmonic variety. As in Denmark, a few folk-type hymns were included. Lindeman actually wrote the tune that came to be associated with one of Grundtvig's most popular hymns, "Built on a rock the church doth stand."[92]

The Swedish counterpart to O. A. Lindeman was J. C. F. Haeffner, a German who was organist at the German Church in Stockholm as well as director of the Stockholm Opera and a court musician. His 1808 Chorale Book used melodies from recently published German chorale books. Like its models, it used even-note rhythms and ignored the rhythmic variety of Scandinavian hymns. There was great resistance to the use of this book among the Swedes, who regarded it as an innovation.[93] As in Denmark and Norway,

[90] See Thomson, 69–73.

[91] See Torben Schousboe, "Protestant Church Music in Scandinavia," in *Protestant Church Music*, 622–3.

[92] See O. M. Sandvik, *Norsk Koralhistoria* (Oslo: H. Aschehoug, 1930), 36–8. Six different tunes by Ludwig Lindeman are included in *LBW*.

[93] Liemohn, 98.

about 1860 there were movements toward reform of the church's tunes that resulted in a number of church music books. Some were conservative revisions of the Haeffner Chorale Book. Others imitated Ludwig Lindeman's book in Norway. Some tried to re-include the hymn versions from the 1697 hymnbook. The most radical was the Anjou and Törnwall book of 1882, which used rhythmically free arrangements without bar lines. The use of so many different chorale books (about a dozen in all) resulted in a lack of uniformity in church song, and efforts were made in the early twentieth century to produce an authorized chorale book that could be used throughout the whole country. The provisional book published in 1921 included examples of all the foregoing styles, including use of triple time, dotted rhythms, changing meters, Swedish folk melodies, and mission songs. However, *Den svenska Koralboken I–II* (authorized in 1939 to accompany the new hymnbook of 1937) was a reaction to all this in favor of the Haeffner tradition. Corresponding Finnish chorale books in 1904 and 1944 showed a spirit of national pride by including Finnish sacred songs as well as Swedish-based chorales in the 1697 style—which eventually found their way back into Swedish hymn singing in H. Göransson's *Koralmusik* (1957).[94]

German church music also exerted an influence in England, although in the English situation for the better. As Handel had made a great impression on the English a hundred years before him, so Mendelssohn took England by storm on his several visits, where he became a favorite of Queen Victoria and her German consort, Prince Albert. Some of Mendelssohn's church music was composed for Anglican services: two Magnificats and Nunc dimittis, a Te Deum and Jubilate, and a half-dozen English anthems. It is not difficult to see why Mendelssohn made such an impression on the English. The only church composer of any distinction in England since the death of Handel in 1759 was Samuel Sebastian Wesley (1810–1876), son of Samuel Wesley and grandson of Charles Wesley the hymnwriter. S. S. Wesley was a partisan of the high church movements emanating from Oxford and Cambridge. His enthusiasm for a choral eucharist led to a study of the works of earlier English composers. He was also an English pioneer in the Bach renaissance. While his organ writing is undistinguished (many English-made organs had pedal boards of only one or two octaves), the choral sonorities of his anthems are suited to the spatial dimensions of the soaring Gothic churches in which he worked and lose a great deal if performed in other settings.[95] Somewhat lesser figures in the production of Anglican service music were Henry Smart (1813–1879), John Goss (1800–1880), and John Stainer (1840–1901). In Eric Routley's opinion, "Victorian church music . . . can be described as music which occasionally rises to greatness, often achieves a serviceable character, but which is prone to diverge from even the serviceable ideal in the directions either of supreme tedium or of shameless vulgarity."[96]

In this climate the famous *Hymns Ancient and Modern* first appeared (1861). Although this hymnal was important for recovering a number of plainsong hymns (the

---

[94] See Schousboe, 627–8.

[95] See Watkins Shaw, "Church Music in England," in *Protestant Church Music*, 720.

[96] Eric Routley, *Church Music and Theology* (Philadelphia: Muhlenberg Press, 1959), 180.

translations of Greek and Latin hymns of John Mason Neale are important) and Reformation chorales in English translation (the translations of Catherine Winkworth are especially noteworthy and enduring), many of the vigorous "west gallery" tunes were deleted from the hymn repertory and the sentimental part-songs of John Bacchus Dykes (1823–1876) predominated.[97] In the period between 1860 and 1890 sentimentalism increased—the result of lesser composers utilizing the romantic musical expressions of not only Mendelssohn and Schumann, but of Liszt and Wagner, but always with much less telling effect. Routley notes the number of times the most telling phrase in Liszt's *Liebestrom* appears in part-songs and hymn tunes such as "Just As I Am" by Joseph Barnby (1838–1896).[98]

The chief figures in Anglican church music in the late Victorian era and into the twentieth century are Sir Charles Hubert Hastings Parry (1848–1918), Charles Villiers Stanford (1852–1924), and Charles Wood (1866–1926), who were well-rounded professional composers before they began writing music for the church and therefore brought a competence with them that was not found in those who were only church musicians. Wood composed more than thirty anthems and several choral services. Stanford composed five settings of the daily services, which energized Anglican cathedral music at the time. Parry composed ceremonial music rather than cathedral music (e.g., the coronation anthem, *I Was Glad*), although several of his hymn tunes have enjoyed enduring use (e.g., *Rustington, Laudate Dominum, Repton, Intercessor*). Ralph Vaughan Williams (1872–1958), perhaps England's greatest modern composer, composed practically no church music in the narrow sense, but made an important contribution to twentieth-century hymnody as the editor of *The English Hymnal* (1906), including several hymn tunes of his own (including *Sine nomine* and *Down Ampney*).[99] The influence of this book was limited due to its high church tone, but that reflected the editor of *The English Hymnal*, Percy Dearmer (author of *The Parson's Handbook*), not Vaughan Williams. Nevertheless, the musical renaissance brought about in England by Vaughan Williams and Gustav Holst helped a genuine church musician, like Martin Shaw (1875–1958), to clear away Victorian sentimentality in English church music. Shaw was co-editor with Vaughan Williams of *Songs of Praise* (1925; revised 1931) and the *Oxford Book of Carols* (1928, with subsequent revisions), as well as the composer of numerous anthems and hymn tunes.

German and English music in general had an influence on American church music in the early nineteenth century. Church musicians in America during the Romantic era eschewed the unschooled contributions of early American composers such as William Billings (1746–1800), who started out as a tanner, Daniel Read (1757–1836), a comb maker, and Oliver Holden (1765–1844), a carpenter, and turned to European masters. Lowell Mason (1792–1872), William B. Bradbury (1816–1868), Isaac B. Woodbury (1819–1858 [who started life as a blacksmith]), and George F. Root (1820–1895) all went to Europe and came back as "scientific" musicians. Already during the War of 1812 there

---

[97] Ibid., 728. Four tunes by Dykes are included in *LBW*.

[98] Routley, *Music Leadership in the Church*, op. cit., 41. Five tunes by Barnby are included in *LBW*.

[99] Sixteen original tunes or harmonizations by Vaughn Williams are included in *LBW*.

was a curious anti-American trend in such collections of anthems as *A Volume of Sacred Musick containing Thirty Anthems selected from the works of Handel, Purcel* [sic]*, Croft and other eminent European authors* (Newburyport, Massachusetts, 1814).

Mason was the most prominent church composer in nineteenth-century America. Cashing in on the interest in European music, he arranged hymn tunes from Beethoven excerpts in his *Boston Handel and Haydn Society Collection of Church Music* (Boston, 1822). A number of hymn tunes by great composers came into hymnals in this way, including "Joy to the World" (text: Isaac Watts, tune: Handel) and "Hark! The Herald Angels Sing" (text: Charles Wesley; tune: Mendelssohn).[100] Having learned the precepts of "correct" German harmony, Mason pumped out many hymn tunes that nevertheless survive in current hymnals, including "Wesley" ("Hail to the brightness"), "Bolston" ("Blest be the tie that binds"), "Missionary Hymn' ("From Greenland's icy mountains"), "Watchman" ("Watchman, tell us of the night"), "Harwell" ("Glorious things of thee are spoken"), "Henley" ("We would see Jesus"), "Hamburg" ("When I survey the wondrous cross"), and "Olivet" ("My faith looks up to thee").[101] These tunes endure because, in spite of Mason's Germanic pretensions, they sound American. Mason was American in spite of himself. He approached church music with a pragmatism unknown in Europe. Among his requisites for a good congregational tune were these listed by Robert Stevenson: "simplicity of intervals and rhythm; range not exceeding an octave or ninth, with D as the preferable upper limit and nothing ever above E."[102] For someone as much enamored of German music as Mason, these restrictions eliminated the whole chorale repertoire from classical Lutheranism; neither the original tunes with their syncopations nor the Bach harmonizations were satisfactory. Concerning the latter Mason wrote: "Congregations might as well undertake to sing Beethoven's Mass No. 2, as these chorals, with all sorts of complicated and difficult harmony parts."[103] Mason accepted the amended harmonizations of Conrad Kocher (1786–1872) to make "the harmony as simple as possible" since "the knowledge and taste of the public cannot be forced." He published volume after volume of choir music based on European sources, but like some of "robber barons" in nineteenth-century America, he helped himself freely to European music not protected by international copyright laws while warning other American publishers that "this property extends both to music and to words or poetry."[104]

While northern American church music bowed to the European cultural imperialism imposed by Mason and Hastings, other sections of the country built on the native American repertory. The most noteworthy collections of folk-like tunes were included in Ananias Davisson's *Kentucky Harmony* (1815–1816), David L. Clayton's *Virginia Harmony* (1831), and William Walker's *Southern Harmony* (published in four editions,

---

[100] Toward the end of the nineteenth century a chorus from Handel's *Judas Maccabaeus* provided the setting for Edward Budry's "Thine Is the Glory" and the "Ode to Joy" from Beethoven's Ninth Symphony provided the setting for Henry Van Dyke's "Joyful, Joyful We Adore Thee."

[101] There are three hymn tunes by Lowell Mason in *LBW*.

[102] Robert Stevenson, "Protestant Music in America," in *Protestant Church Music*, 676.

[103] Cited in ibid.

[104] Ibid.

1835–1854), which sold 600,000 copies. In his epochal study of *Spiritual Folk Songs of America*, George Pullen Jackson divided the repertory of the rural books for whites into: (1) religious ballads, with "Poor Wayfaring Stranger" as one of fifty-one examples; (2) folk hymns, with "Holy Manna" and "Pisgah" as two examples among ninety-eight; and (3) "spiritual songs," with "Roll, Jordan, Roll" and "Old-time Religion" as two examples among 101.[105] This third type flourished especially in the revivals generated by the Second Great Awakening and the millennial surge of the 1840s. It was this type that appealed most deeply to African Americans. In *White and Negro Spirituals* (1943), Jackson documented his assertion that the Negro spirituals were based on white revival songs with 114 parallels, including even such famous spirituals as "Go Down, Moses," "Go Tell It on the Mountain," "Roll, Jordan," and "Were You There When They Crucified My Lord." Convinced by this wealth of evidence, Jackson summarized: "The Negroes' spirituals were, up to comparatively recent times, adopted from the stock of tunes and texts which originated in the white man's revivals." Since this revival music was derived from a known folk music tradition, said Jackson, "we may conclude then, and with a high degree of certainty, that the African-American has been a potent factor in the carrying on of the Celtic-English-American's folk songs."[106]

Music has been an important aspect of revivalism. Every great evangelist had a musician on the team. Charles Finney used Thomas Hastings (1784–1872), to whom we owe such hymn tunes as "Toplady" (1830, "Rock of Ages") and "Zion" (1830, "Guide me, O thou great Jehovah"). Dwight L. Moody employed Ira B. Sankey, to whom we owe "Hold the Fort, For I Am Coming." Billy Graham continued this tradition with the musical team of Cliff Barrows and George Beverly Shea, who popularized the Swedish folk hymn, "O store Gud," in Stuart Hine's translation, "How Great Thou Art." The revival meetings often employed soloists, quartets, octets, or whole choirs, along with instrumental bands or pipe organs where available. It is amazing how quickly gospel quartets, choirs, and pipe organs found a place in churches from which they had previously been banned, once the techniques of revivalism were embraced.

By the middle of the nineteenth century, American denominations were already dividing along social lines: upper class/middle class/lower class, urban/rural, settled/frontier, and so forth. The kind of music sung in these settings reflected the social background of the congregation. Those congregations that were upwardly mobile and established especially in the northeast looked to Europe in the way of Lowell Mason; those which were lower class, rural, southern, or frontier turned to the revival songs. Sometimes there was a curious mixture of the two, such as at the Broadway Tabernacle in New York City where Bradbury poured out "Just As I Am" (1849), "Sweet Hour of Prayer" (1860), and "He Leadeth Me" (1864), as well as cantatas such as *Esther*, which, in its solo passages, could imitate the bravura of Bellini's operas.

Lutheranism represented a different and unique situation in American hymnody and church music. Although congregations that worshiped in English along the

---

[105] Ibid., 679.
[106] Ibid., 679–80.

Atlantic seaboard adopted both the revival hymns and Anglican Victorian hymnody, they represented a minority of Lutherans in the United States in the nineteenth century. In the German cultural cocoon of Pennsylvania, Lutheran congregations even in the General Synod and the General Council continued to worship in German and were not much affected by English hymnody. The millions of Lutheran immigrants pouring into the Midwest brought their hymnody with them from their countries of origin. These might include spiritual folk songs generated by the pietistic revivals in Norway, Sweden, and Finland, such as "Behold, A Host Arrayed in White" (*LBW* 314), "With God as Our Friend" (*LBW* 371), "Children of the Heavenly Father" (*LBW* 474), "Arise, My Soul, Arise!" (*LBW* 516), as well as the charming Christmas songs "Your Little Ones, Dear Lord" (*LBW* 52) and "When Christmas Morn Is Dawning" (*LBW* 59). They also included the German chorales that were in the common repertoire in Lutheran churches in Europe as well as those chorales that were unique to Scandinavian churches. These hymns, by such authors as Kingo, Lanstadt, and Brorson, with the melodies of Ludvig Lindemann were heavily represented in Scandinavian books such as *The Lutheran Hymnary* and *The Augustana Hymnal*. Some German tunes were also used in the non-syncopated versions. On the other hand, the syncopated settings of the German chorales were a staple of *The Lutheran Hymnal* (1941) of the Synodical Conference, which was used in congregations of the Missouri and Wisconsin Synods.

These songs and hymns were sung without regard to class or social distinction. If denominationalism in Britain and America came to represent the segregation of Christians along class lines, Lutherans simply were not a part of it by virtue of not being an Anglo-American religious group. They were, moreover, congregated in rural and urban areas in most parts of the country from the settled east to the western frontier and therefore embraced people in various economic and social situations. But as Lutherans became more integrated into American society during the twentieth century and lost their European roots, they began to take on more of the characteristics of an American denomination in hymnody and church music as in other aspects of church life.

❦ THE GOTHIC REVIVAL

The revival of Gothic architecture was a hallmark of romanticism. But, especially in America, the neo-Gothic church was not the only kind of church building being erected. Liturgical restoration was up against the revival movements that spun out of the Great Awakenings and that, James White says without exaggeration, have affected almost every aspect of modern American Protestantism.[107] Not the least of revivalism's influences on American Protestantism was its impact on the church building. As White notes, preaching was central to revival meetings, and the personality of the preacher was crucial to revivalistic preaching. "Many great revivalist preachers preferred a small desk-like pulpit big enough to hold only their notes. But they relished a large platform on which to make sorties in all directions as they pleaded for conversions."[108]

---

[107] James F. White, *Protestant Worship: Traditions in Transition*, op. cit., 171.
[108] James F. White, *Protestant Worship and Church Architecture* (New York: Oxford University Press, 1964), 124.

Church buildings influenced by Revivalism thus had small desk-like pulpits centrally placed on large platforms that also contained seats for song leaders and guest ministers. Since the purpose of revivalistic worship was to make an impact on the worshipers, features previously eschewed in Reformed and Puritan traditions were restored: organs, choirs, and stained glass windows. The choir was and is typically arranged in a semicircular seating pattern behind the pulpit platform. This concert hall arrangement speaks of the choir's role: It is not present just to support congregational singing but to perform for the congregation. This concert hall arrangement is typical of many Methodist and most Baptist and community-styled churches. It speaks of a worship style that is deficient by Reformation standards. The congregation is less an assembly than an audience and the role of the sacraments is minimalized. The communion table is usually placed on the floor below the pulpit in an unprominent position. In Baptist churches, the baptismal pool is located behind the pulpit or the choir and is closed off by a curtain when not in use.

But the other great influence on Protestant architecture in the nineteenth century was the Gothic revival. We have seen that the Gothic revival movement originated in the work of a group of undergraduates at Cambridge University in the 1840s who banded together as the Cambridge Camden Society "to promote the study of Ecclesiastical Architecture and Antiquities, and the restoration of mutilated Architectural remains."[109] These students were convinced that the Middle Ages represented the height of Christian piety and worship, and set about to restore and replicate medieval church buildings. The Cambridge movement prevailed through the writings of John Mason Neale, Benjamin Webb, and others, and may be viewed in tandem with the more theologically oriented Oxford "High Church" movement. As a result, it became de rigueur for Anglo-Catholic churches to have high altars, divided chancels, rood screens, and all of the "symbols" of the medieval church building (even those that had once served totally practical purposes, like the heavy lids over baptismal fonts that kept people out of the water who might use it for superstitious purposes). This arrangement was imposed on even the smallest parish churches. Whereas in cathedral or collegiate churches, the whole congregation served as the "choir," now the choir was added to the congregation and often usurped the congregation's liturgical role, rendering the people more passive in worship than they actually were even in the Middle Ages.

The real triumph of Gothic revival in America was the work of the Anglo-Catholic architect, Ralph Adams Cram (1863–1942), who built churches for most of the major Protestant denominations. He believed that Gothic was the style best suited to Catholic worship and at first was reluctant to build such churches for Protestants. But by the time he was done, Gothic churches with large chancels became popular among Methodists, Presbyterians, Congregationalists, and Unitarians as well as Episcopalians. Even Georgian buildings had to have deep chancels, high altars, and divided choirs. As Cram put, "Not in the barren and ugly meeting-house of the Puritans . . . were men most easily lifted out of themselves into spiritual communion with God . . . but where they

---

[109] James F. White, *The Cambridge Movement: The Ecclesiologists and the Gothic Revival* (Cambridge: Cambridge University Press, 1962).

were surrounded by the dim shadows of mysterious aisles . . . where was always . . . the still atmosphere of prayer and praise."[110] The operative word here is "atmosphere." Previous church buildings were erected to accommodate the Christian assembly and its liturgical functions. Under Romanticism, church buildings had to evoke a certain "atmosphere," which could not help but inject the element of subjectivity into the design and building of churches.

This subjectivism was further championed by the Unitarian Von Ogden Vogt, who found that "the intimations of Gothic building . . . are not chiefly intellectual . . . but emotional and mystical."[111] Removed from its association with Catholicism, bereft of statues of saints to fill niches and to surround worshipers with a sense of "the communion of saints," Gothic churches were eagerly built by Protestants who regarded the architectural style as a stimulus to mystical transport away from things secular and toward things spiritual.

While the Gothic church building seems to be the very opposite kind of structure from the auditorium of the revivalists, it fostered the same attitude toward worship: an individualistic piety that has little appreciation of the corporate dimension of worship or of liturgy as "the public work of the people of God." In both cases the acts of worship were performed for the people by the clergy and choirs occupying the liturgical centers, and such acts were calculated to elicit an emotional response whether the means used was a rousing choir anthem or a whiff of incense.

We might note that many Protestant worship leaders and church architects have instinctively realized the limitations of the Gothic revival building for the needs of Protestant worship. This is evident in several modifications of the basic design. The pulpit must be more centrally located than would be the case in a typical Gothic church. So while the pulpit in a medieval Gothic church might have wound around a pillar in the nave, pulpits in neo-Gothic churches were typically located in the chancel (so that no worshiper would have to turn his or her back on the altar in order to see the preacher). And the choir cannot adequately perform modern church anthems in a divided chancel. Monks and canons could sing psalm tones antiphonally to one another without much overt direction, but a choir singing more complex, polyphonic pieces needing musical direction must be able to see the director. So the choir stalls have sometimes been modified subtly to provide choir riser formations and choir directors have had to stand in front of the congregation as a conductor would stand in front of a concert audience. Or, where the choir director directed from the organ console, systems of mirrors had to be designed so that choir and director could see one another.

Many "great church" building designs are really a blending of the Gothic revival church and the auditorium. But the basic problem with both designs, or a blending of the two, from the standpoint of liturgy and ecclesiology, is not their impracticalities but rather their poor ability to express or realize the church as the assembly gathered to do its public

---

[110] Ralph Adams Cram, *Church Building: A Study of the Principles of Architecture in their Relation to the Church*, 3rd ed. (Boston: Marshall Jones Company, 1924), 89.

[111] Von Ogden Vogt, *Art and Religion* (New Haven: Yale University Press, 1921), 189.

work of proclaiming the word and celebrating the sacrament. The auditorium turns the congregation into an audience, and the Gothic church scatters it throughout a long, narrow nave or into nooks and crannies. It is not surprising that Gothic has not been the preferred architectural style of the modern liturgical movement with its concept of the liturgy as the "work of the people."

🍇 THE CHURCH BUILDING AS A HOUSE OF PRAYER

The church building must be designed to serve the needs of the congregation and its liturgy. But a use of the building that emerged in the nineteenth century, and that has not been well served by liturgical renewal in the twentieth century, is to make available a space for individual Christian devotion and meditation. Most of our modern urban places, crowded and intrusive as they are, do not provide quiet places where the individual can experience solitude and personal communion with God. If the Gothic church has not been conducive to communal worship, it has more than adequately provided a space conducive to private devotions and side chapels for small group worship. The Gothic church, more than any other style of church architecture, has replicated the function of the Jerusalem Temple to be "a house of prayer for all peoples" (Isaiah 56:7).

H. Sedlmayr, in his book on "the origins of the cathedrals," makes a case that the church building is not only a house for the earthly church. It also conveys a vision of the heavenly city, the new Jerusalem descending from heaven (Revelation 21). While the Baroque church building presented the heavenly city as an ethereal realm of clouds and light, the ancient Christian basilica presented the heavenly city by replicating the earthly city, complete with the city gates at the facade, the city streets of the arcade in the aisle of the nave, the emperor's palace, and the throne room. The early medieval Romanesque building reflected the strong walls and towers of a fortress, which was reminiscent of the medieval idea of the heavenly city. But the Gothic style evoked the heavenly city both as an otherworldly vision and as the firm reality of the faith journey. The combination of massiveness and weightlessness in the Gothic building suggested the city "coming down out of heaven." The Gothic church both pointed upward toward eschatological fulfillment and downward toward eschatological anticipation. In the Gothic heavenly city there were not only the "many mansions" of John 14 but also the common residence for all.[112]

No matter what one thinks of Sedlmayr's religious-poetic vision, it does support the practical idea of the church building as a place for personal edification as well as for the public work of the community of faith. The church building is like a town that has both public gathering places and private residences. The building must be large enough to accommodate festive gatherings, which requires a certain amount of open floor space for processions and walking about, and also suited to private devotion and small group worship, which might be accommodated in side chapels. A certain flexibility is evident in some nineteenth-century Gothic revival church buildings, especially in Europe, in that the pews of the previous centuries were often replaced with easily moved chairs.

---

[112] See H. Sedlmayr, *Die Entstehung der Kathedrale* (Emmendingen, 1950), 95f., 112f., 163f.

In discussing the need of the church building to transcend its immediate cultural surroundings if it is to convey a sense of being a sacred space, Gunnar Rosendal of the Church of Sweden argued that the church building cannot merely reflect the spirit of the times. This does not mean that the church building cannot be identified with the architectural styles of its time period, or be constructed using the building material found in its surrounding place. But it does mean that the very style of the church building ought to point beyond its time and place, in the direction of something more universal and eternal.[113] Rosendal pointed out how twelfth-century churches in Upland (such as those at Gamla Uppsala and Orbyhus), built by medieval people of stone from the hills or clay from the plains to express their view of life, are still meaningful today as they continue to minister to spiritual needs and realities. He also noted that the altars in these old churches are not book-laden reading desks, are not obscured by large and ornate railings, are not mere protrusions from the east wall, and are not depreciated architecturally by altar paintings or reredoses.[114] They emphasize the functionality of a table on which the Lord's Supper is placed. The altar-table is the center of action, but not of devotion. That purpose is served by the triumphant crucifix, suspended from the vaulting above the altar-table, and eliciting from worshipers a Sursum corda.

❧ ART AND VESTMENTS

The crucifix raises the issue of church art as a focus of devotion. Peter Brunner eschewed the pedagogical role of liturgical art championed by Luther (in his arguments for retaining liturgical art against iconoclasts who would have abolished it). It is the task of preaching to teach. Liturgical art, says Brunner, "fulfills its function if it aids in the proper pneumatic administration of worship; and not the least of these functions is that it be of assistance in prayer."[115]

"This function," admits Brunner, "places the stamp of the symbolic on the picture." The divine can only be made discernible through the symbol. The symbol draws one away from the object itself and to that which it represents. The advantage of symbolic representation as opposed to pictorial representation can be seen in that, during the Middle Ages, pictures of the Virgin Mary were looked upon as though they were the Mother of God herself, and people bowed to them as they entered or left the church building. Several stories are told about Lutheran congregants in Germany or Denmark who bow to a plain wall out of habit long after the picture of the Virgin has been whitewashed. The Eastern icon has the advantage of being symbolic rather than pictorial art, and thereby avoids the danger of idolatry. The cross, of course, is the central symbol of Christian devotion. All crosses, no matter how they are styled, are representations of an ancient Roman instrument of execution. But it is a symbol that does not require antiquarian reproduction; it can be as contemporary as one wishes.

---

[113] See Gunnar Rosendal, *Kapellbygge och kyrkorestauration* (Osby, 1945), 9.

[114] Ibid., 26ff.

[115] Peter Brunner, *Worship in the Name of Jesus*, op. cit., 281.

This is not true of the body which might be placed on the cross. While Christianity has tolerated the depiction of Christ because of his humanity (since divinity cannot be pictorially represented without violating the prohibition against graven images in the Decalogue), not every portrayal of Christ is suitable liturgical art. As in music, a distinction must be made between liturgical art and religious art. For example, a painting such as Leonardo da Vinci's "The Last Supper" focuses on the psychological aspects of the characters in the scene, particularly the agitation prompted by Jesus' prediction of betrayal and the disciples' earnest question, "Is it I?" The painting is in agreement with New Testament narrative; but the portrayal is psychological rather than biblical or dogmatic. In such portrayals, wrote Ildefons Herwegen, the object of faith (e.g., the institution of the Lord's Supper) is no longer the decisive focus; rather the psychological analysis intrudes.[116] This may be great religious art; but it is not satisfactory as liturgical art. Liturgical art draws its subjects from the liturgy itself and the mystery of redemption that is the content of the liturgical celebration.

By the same token, art that strains for originality or that seeks to shock is unsuitable for liturgical or devotional purposes. Art often does this by being timely or contextual. Christ may be portrayed in a certain life situation (e.g., a factory worker, a refugee, a peasant) or be given certain ethnic qualities (e.g., African, Chinese, Norwegian). Works that call attention to themselves because of their shock value are not pointing beyond themselves in a symbolic way. Works that are too self-consciously contemporary become quickly "dated" and may be scorned in only a few years. Liturgical art, like architecture, should have a timeless and enduring quality. On the other hand, liturgical art, like the liturgy itself, must be evocative, and art that is merely conventional or utterly banal will not do. In the absence of competent liturgical artists, therefore, it might be best to have whitewashed walls as the artistic backdrop for the event of the real presence. As Brunner suggested, "In certain situations this voluntary abstention may furnish the only fertile soil for a rebirth of the function of the plastic arts in worship."[117]

Textile arts also have a place in liturgical worship along with the plastic arts.[118] The historic vestments of the church, which were generally shortened during the Baroque era, were lengthened again during the Gothic revival.[119] The cotta was restored to the knee-length surplice in Anglican and American Lutheran use. In Scandinavian and Slovak Lutheran churches, a full ankle-length surplice was worn. Stoles were also lengthened during the Gothic revival and were commonly decorated with three crosses: one in the middle (at the back of the neck) and one at each end. The stole was the same color as the chasuble, and again the Gothic revival led to the restoration of the ample chasuble as

[116] Ildefons Herwegen, *Christliche Kunst und Mysterium* (Münster, 1929), 28ff.

[117] Brunner, 281.

[118] See Frances Morris, "English Embroideries," *The Bulletin of the Metropolitan Museum of Art* XXIV (1929).

[119] See Christa C. Mayer-Thurman, ed., *Raiment for the Lord's Service: A Thousand Years of Western Vestments* (The Art Institute of Chicago, 1975); Cyril E. Pocknee, *Liturgical Vesture: Its Origin and Development* (London: A. R. Mowbray, 1960).

[120] See Gilbert Cope, art. "Vestments," in J. G. Davies, ed., *The Westminster Dictionary of Worship* (Philadelphia: Westminster Press, 1972), 365–83.

opposed to the Baroque fiddleback chasuble.[120] The revival of Gothic vestments occurred mostly in the Anglican communion and in Scandinavian Lutheranism. Roman Catholicism was slow to abandon Baroque-styled vestments except in some liturgical centers (especially monasteries). In American Lutheranism a revival of any kind of liturgical vestments would not occur until the twentieth century, and then the tendency was to follow Episcopal Church practice.

During the Gothic revival there was also a desire to provide altar hangings and antependia on reading desks and pulpits in the same liturgical color as the vestments of the clergy. Victorian commercial interests were mobilized to provide matching sets of stoles, maniples, chasubles, tunics, dalmatics, and copes as well as altar paraments and antependia all in the "correct" liturgical colors for Anglo-Catholic and Roman Catholic parishes. This commercial interest helped a great deal in standardizing liturgical colors during the nineteenth century. Previously a great deal of variability could be detected in liturgical colors. The chart below lists the preferred colors of the Gothic revival, with other options from earlier traditions (including the Roman Missal of Pope Pius V, 1570)[121] as indicated (//).

> Advent to Christmas Eve—violet/rose on Gaudate // blue/black
> Christmas to Epiphany—white/gold
> Sundays after the Epiphany—green
> Septuagesima to Ash Wednesday—violet/black on Ash Wednesday // blue/black
> During Lent—violet/rose on Laetare // veiling of colors/earth tones
> Passion Sunday to Palm Sunday—violet // Red/rose
> Maundy Thursday—violet/white // red/rose
> Easter—white/gold
> Pentecost—red
> Trinity—white/gold
> Sundays after Trinity—green
> Ordinary weekdays—green
> Blessed Virgin Mary—white // red
> Apostles, evangelists, martyrs—red
> Saints other than martyrs—white
> Baptisms—white
> Confirmations—red
> Marriage—white
> Ordinations—white
> Funeral—violet // blue/black
> Dedication of a church—white

Lutherans were latecomers to the use of paraments. The previous practice had been to cover the altar with white linens. When Lutherans adopted the scheme of liturgical colors they tended to follow the first option in the above list, except for the occasional services; for those services the color of the day or season was specified, except for ordinations and dedications of churches, which usually prescribed red. Black was not widely used as a liturgical color, rose was seldom used, but blue was commonly used in Sweden in lieu of

---

[121] See Gilbert Cope, art. "Colours, Liturgical," in *The Westminster Dictionary of Christian Worship*, 139–42.

violet for Advent and Lent and has become a preferred color for Advent (to symbolize hope) rather than violet (the color of penitence) in American Lutheran usage.

While the Gothic revival strove for "correctness" as far as this was possible (which meant endorsing the color scheme of the Missal of Pius V), the modern liturgical movement has appreciated the emotional impact of colors and has used them more according to the "mood" of the day, season, or event rather than because of rubrical requirements. This development can be taken as a paradigmatic illustration of the difference between liturgical restoration, beginning in the Age of Romance, and liturgical renewal inspired by the modern liturgical movement. The liturgical movement has not been interested just in repristination of old liturgies, customs, and traditions, but in the adaptation and renewal of these historic forms and practices to the exigencies of modern life.

CHAPTER 17

The Modern Liturgical Movement

Tʜᴇ ɪɴᴛʀᴜsɪᴠᴇ ᴛʜʀᴜsᴛ ᴏғ so-called modernism into literature and the arts in the aftermath of the First World War may obscure the simultaneous survival of romanticism. In music, for example, late romantics like Jean Sibelius and Serge Rachmaninoff flourished contemporaneously with Igor Stravinsky and Arnold Schoenberg. Likewise, William Butler Yeats and Robert Frost wrote poetry contemporaneously with T. S. Eliot and Ezra Pound. The so-called modernists in art, architecture, design, music, and literature seemed radical because they took reality apart in order to probe its essence or to explore the realms of instinct and the irrational. But the antiromantic sensibilities of such figures as the architect Walter Gropius, the painter Pablo Picasso, the composer Igor Stravinsky, the novelist James Joyce, the poet T. S. Eliot, the critic Gertrude Stein, and others should not obscure the fact that these artists also had a great interest in tradition and that some of them were even labeled primitivists or neo-classicists. The upheavals of the twentieth century—unprecedented world wars, Communist revolutions, totalitarian regimes, technological and communications revolutions, the crumbling of venerated value systems, and so forth—either encouraged nostalgia for a simpler, more humane past or fostered primitivism as a mirror of the condition to which it seemed that modern Western civilization was returning. If there was a "debunking" of tradition after World War I, especially the most recent history (such as Lytton Strachey's *Eminent Victorians* in 1918), it was to recover a more genuine sense of tradition.[1]

---

[1] Michael Kammen, *Mystic Chords of Memory: The Transformation of Tradition in American Culture* (New York: Alfred K. Knopf, 1991), 299ff.

"Debunking" had its theological corollaries in the historical-critical study of the Bible, in Rudolf Bultmann's proposal for "demythologizing" the New Testament proclamation, and in the critical study of church history and liturgical texts and praxis. The object was to get at the "original meaning" of a text or the "original intention" of tradition in a way that would make it applicable to the contemporary situation. This was accomplished by peeling away later layers of tradition or interpretation to get at some supposed central core. The flourishing of neo-orthodox theology in the great dogmatic systems of Karl Barth and Karl Rahner and in the theological ethics of Dietrich Bonhoeffer and Emil Brunner can be viewed as a similar concern to get behind romantic idealism to the essence of Christian revelation and truth. To a great extent these neo-orthodox theological systems were also an application of historical-critical studies of the thought of Thomas Aquinas, Martin Luther, John Calvin, John Wesley, and others. The great liturgists of the first half of the twentieth century were also primarily historians: Josef Jungmann (Roman Catholic), Gregory Dix (Anglican), Luther D. Reed (Lutheran), William D. Maxwell (Presbyterian), and J. Ernest Rattenbury (Methodist).

Since Romanticism was eschewed but not entirely overcome, the historical-critical study of the tradition simply led to the idealization of a new "golden age" among liturgists—the patristic period.[2] Dom Guéranger of Solesmes, as we saw, thought that it was necessary to go back to the Middle Ages to recover authentic Catholic liturgy. A hundred years later Dom Herwegen of Maria Laach Abbey was showing that the Middle Ages had already begun to overlay the Catholic liturgy with devotional elements and fanciful allegorical interpretations that were foreign to its original conceptions. Many liturgists looked for some elusive apostolic model from which all later liturgies derived.[3] This search was hampered by the lack of texts. But Gregory Dix enabled this search for an original model to overcome the objections of lack of documentary evidence by proposing that the *sequence of ritual actions* rather than texts is what has come down to us from the apostolic church. While he recognized the diversity of texts and customs in the eucharistic celebration of the early church, he believed that they fit into common patterns of actions which he called "the shape of the liturgy."

> The outline—the Shape of the Liturgy—is still everywhere the same in all our sources, right back into the earliest period on which we can yet speak with certainty, the earlier half of the second century. There is even good reason to think that this outline—the Shape—of the Liturgy is of genuinely apostolic tradition.[4]

Liturgical studies went hand-in-hand with patristic studies (as in the translation of texts in *Sources chrétiennes*). The study of ancient sources aroused an interest in the retrieval of ancient liturgical practices, such as the celebration of the mass facing the people across the altar-table, the offertory procession of the faithful, the epiclesis in the

---

[2] See Ernest B. Koenker, *The Liturgical Renaissance in the Roman Catholic Church*, op. cit., 80ff.

[3] See Paul Bradshaw, *The Search for the Origins of Christian Worship* (London: S.P.C.K./New York: Oxford University Press, 1990).

[4] Gregory Dix, *The Shape of the Liturgy*, op. cit., 5.

eucharistic prayer, the rites of Holy Week, the communal and initiatory character of baptism, and the public and communal celebration of the Divine Office. These desiderata of liturgists were a pastoral response to the challenges of the individualism and utilitarianism of modern Western culture and the spiritual needs of modern Western people, especially the need for true community in the face of urbanism, mass culture and media, and changing or crumbling institutions.

Roman Catholic officials resisted what they regarded as efforts at repristinating antiquity.[5] Pope Pius XII warned the Benedictine abbots meeting in Rome in September 1947 against belittling private and popular devotions in their enthusiasm for retrieval the public and communal prayer of the ancient church.[6] Two months later, in November 1947, the pontiff issued his famous encyclical, *Mediator Dei*, in which he sought to rein in the enthusiasm of the liturgical renewalists for things ancient. He defended recent definitions of doctrine and developments in practice that had evolved in modern times under the guidance of the Holy Spirit, and strongly suggested that "No sincere Catholic . . . could disregard existing laws in order to revert to the decrees that are found in the most ancient sources of canon law. Similarly in regard to the liturgy, it is a zeal both unwise and misguided that would go back to ancient rites and customs and repudiate the new regulations which under God's wise Providence have been introduced to meet altered conditions."[7] The pontiff counseled liturgical renewalists against any antiquarian reaction that would simply rid the liturgy of all modern developments. The encyclical ends with a series of warnings, applied to various countries and circumstances, that had the effect of seeming to condemn such marks of the liturgical movement as table-altars, depictions of Christ as King without the marks of his suffering, the attack on private masses and the demeaning of private and popular devotions. But on the whole *Mediator Dei* has been taken as an endorsement of the pastoral aspect of the liturgical movement that sought to make liturgy a living reality in the lives of the faithful.[8] It also precipitated debate that would lead to agitation for reform, including arguments for the use of the vernacular, which appeared in numerous liturgical journals,[9] but which were also answered by well-argued defenses of the use of Latin.[10]

Because liturgical renewalists (Protestants as well as Roman Catholics) often found themselves at odds with both the leadership of the church and with popular piety, and because their proposals involved a thoroughgoing critique of modern Western society and the complacent relationship of the church to that society, the liturgical movement was regarded as elitist. But it was a protest from *within* the church, by some of its most

---

[5] See Monsignor Goellner, "Monitum de vitandis exaggerationibus in re liturgia," *Periodica de re morali canonica liturgia* (Rome: Apud Pontificium Universitatem Gregorianum, 1938), XXVII (1937), 164.

[6] "A Papal Warning About Liturgical Excesses," *Homiletic and Pastoral Review* XLVIII, Part 1, 289–91.

[7] Pius XII, *Mediator Dei*. English trans. in *Christian Worship* (London: Catholic Truth Society, n.d.), 546.

[8] This was the positive assessment of Louis Bouyer in *Liturgical Piety*, English trans. (Notre Dame, Ind.: University of Notre Dame Press, 1954).

[9] The entire issue No. 11 of *Le Maison-Dieu* was devoted to "Langues et traductions liturgiques."

[10] See Mary Perkins Ryan, "Our Language of Praise," *Proceedings of the National Liturgical Week* (The Liturgical Conference, 1942), 121–35.

ardent pastors and theologians. The fact that opposition caused devotees of the movement to band together into liturgical societies, armed with their own journals, provides a
good argument for Ernest Koenker's labeling of this movement as a *collegium pietatis*.[11]
Like the evangelical pietists of an earlier time, these liturgical reformers sought the renewal of the church from a source of spiritual power. Unlike the earlier pietists they did
not seek renewal through the exercises of conventicles at the margins of the church's life
but from the public expression of the church's life: liturgy defined in the documents of
the Second Vatican Council as "the public work of the people of God."

Groups on the margins of the church have often served as agents of spiritual renewal. The monasteries have played this role at various times in Christian history, and
they were in the forefront of the liturgical movement with historical research, theological
reflections, and pastoral implementations. The liturgical movement gained wider adherence as its cause was taken up by various liturgical conferences, institutes, and societies in
the Roman Catholic, Anglican, Lutheran, Methodist, and Reformed churches before the
work of liturgical reform and renewal was endorsed by the Second Vatican Council and
implemented up by official liturgical commissions. We will review these movements in
the monasteries and in the liturgical conferences, institutes, and societies, and look at one
significant prelude to liturgical renewal in the American Lutheran churches, before we
look at the *Constitution on the Sacred Liturgy*, which served as a catalyst for genuine reform and ecumenical cooperation in the revision of rites in both Roman Catholic and
Protestant churches.

❧ THE WORK OF THE MONASTIC SCHOOLS

In the last chapter we referred to the work of Dom Guéranger and the Solesmes
movement. Dom Guéranger laid the groundwork for a genuine liturgical spirituality by
proposing the liturgy of the church as the model of all Christian prayer. But at the same
time we said that this could not be taken as the beginning of the modern liturgical movement, because its aims were quite different. The Solesmes movement sought a recovery
of medieval ritual whereas the modern liturgical movement has been a recovery of the
corporate character of the liturgy as "the work of the people."

The beginning of the modern liturgical movement is sometimes dated to the
first Liturgical Week held at Louvain, Belgium, in 1911. One of the "insiders" of the liturgical movement, Dom Bernard Botte, places the beginning with the report given by Dom
Lambert Beauduin (1873–1960) of the Mont-César Monastery on the participation of the
faithful in worship to the Malines Conference in 1909.[12] The learned Dom Lambert, who
had experience as a secular priest among the working class before he became a Benedictine, was the leader of this movement, and the monasteries of Mont César, Maredsous,
and Saint André were its centers. Koenker, however, places the beginning of the movement at the first Liturgical Week held for laypeople at Maria Laach Abbey in Germany

---

[11] Koenker, 6.

[12] See Bernard Botte, *From Silence to Participation: An Insider's View of Liturgical Renewal*, trans. by John
Sullivan (Washington, D.C.: The Pastoral Press, 1988), 10.

during Holy Week 1914,[13] because this was the first effort to reach directly to the lay people. The leader of this center was Abbot Ildefons Herwegen (1874–1946). There is no doubt, however, that the Benedictine monasteries were at the forefront of the modern liturgical movement. The debate only concerns which one.

The monasteries were appropriate places for liturgical renewal to first flourish in the Roman Catholic Church, because they were communities primarily concerned with worship and they enjoyed a certain amount of self-rule. The Benedictine monasteries of Belgium provided the cradle in which the modern liturgical movement was nurtured. But it was an international movement from the start. In the nineteenth century two brothers named Wolters, who were priests of Cologne, became Benedictines and took the names Dom Maur and Dom Placid. They made their novitiate at Solemnes with Dom Guéranger. They reacted to the Enlightenment in typical Romantic fashion, but went beyond Guéranger's medievalism by developing an interest in the early church fathers. Dom Placid, the younger brother, was elected abbot of the newly founded monastery of Maredsous in Belgium. It was at this monastery in 1882 that the first complete translation of the Roman Missal for the use of the laity was accomplished, amid much controversy. One of its members, Dom Gérard van Caloen, attracted some notoriety at the Liturgical Congress held in Liège in 1883 by advocating the reception of communion during mass. After this he founded the first liturgical review, *Le Messager des fidèles*, which later became the scholarly journal *La Revue bénédictine* under the editorial leadership of Dom Germain Morin. Mardsous founded the monastery of Mont-César at Louvain, which became a liturgical center under Dom Lambert Beauduin. Also Dom Gérard van Caloen established a house at Saint-André, Lophem, near Brussels. From this latter house were published vernacular missals and the *Bulletin liturgique et paroissial*.

At the Catholic Conference at Malines in 1909, Dom Lambert set out the aims and program of the liturgical movement, with the full approval of Cardinal Mercier. These desiderata included: (1) the translation of the Roman Missal, and its promotion among the laity as their chief devotional book; (2) the cultivation of a liturgical piety through the recitation of Compline in the home and the encouragement of attendance at the parochial mass and Vespers; (3) the cultivation of Gregorian chant, in conformity with the *Motu proprio* of Pope Pius X; and (4) the encouragement of annual retreats for parish choirs in some center of liturgical life such as a Benedictine monastery.

In spite of the work of the Belgian monasteries, it was at Maria Laach Abbey in the German Rhineland that the modern liturgical movement first flourished in full force, with its research into patristic liturgy and its development of the theory of the *Kultmysterium*. It was here that the first Liturgical Week was held for lay people during Holy Week 1914. At this conference the first dialogue mass was celebrated in Germany (it had already been done in Belgium), which sent shock waves throughout German Catholicism.[14]

---

[13] Koenker, 12.

[14] See Dom Damasus Winzen, "Progress and Tradition in Maria Laach Art," *Liturgical Arts* X (1941), 20.

Monasteries had the luxury of engaging in a kind of disinterested liturgical research. The Abbey of Maria Laach was one of the primary centers of liturgical scholarship, and the liturgical leaders of this community were Abbot Ildefons Herwegen and Dom Odo Casel (1886–1948). Herwegen was the founder of the series *Ecclesia orans* in 1918, of which the first issue was Romano Guardini's *Vom Geist der Liturgie* (*The Spirit of the Liturgy*)[15] and the annual *Jahrbuch für Liturgiewissenschft* (first published in 1921).[16] Herwegen's great contribution was to show, contra Guéranger, that the Middle Ages was not the high point of liturgical development, but that during this period the liturgy had been laid over with subjective and dramatic elements inspired by allegorical commentaries on the mass that were essentially foreign to its early development. The *Jahrbuch* was carried on by the monk Odo Casel, who was the most original thinker of the group. In *Das christliche Kultmysterium* (1932) and numerous articles he developed a perspective on the theological understanding of the liturgy and the sacraments on the basis of the theology of the church fathers and the history of religions, which will be explicated in the next section.

The work of the somewhat aristocratic and intellectual Maria Laach Abbey was popularized in Austria through the work of Dr. Pius Parsch (1884–1945), Augustinian Canon of Klosterneuburg near Vienna. Through his Bible studies, devotional literature, commentaries, and the periodical that he founded, *Lebe mit der Kirche* (later called *Bibel und Liturgie*), Pius Parsch made Klosterneuburg and his *Volksliturgisches Apostolat* centers of a liturgical movement that taught that a living understanding of the Roman liturgy could be deepened and enriched by a greater knowledge of the Bible. Parsch disseminated this probing of the biblical base of the church's liturgy through his "Leaflet Missal" and the five-volume work, *Das Jahr des Heiles* (translated into English as *The Church's Year of Grace*).[17]

The liturgical movement was brought to America as early as the mid-1920s by Dom Virgil Michel (1890–1938) of Saint John's Benedictine Abbey in Collegeville, Minnesota. He founded the journal *Orate Fratres* in Advent 1925; its name changed to *Worship* in 1951. Michel combined liturgical knowledge, acquired firsthand from visits to monasteries in Belgium, Germany, and Austria, with social action. The liturgical movement faced an uphill battle in every place where it was introduced; but in America the situation was especially difficult owing to a huge country and an immigrant church. But Michel was able to attract diligent co-workers, including the Jesuit scholar Gerard Ellard (1894–1963) at Saint Louis University, and Fr. Martin Hellriegel (1890–1981), pastor of Holy Cross Parish in Saint Louis. Perhaps the most colorful of Michel's co-workers was Hans Anscar Reinhold (1897–1968), an immigrant from Germany in 1935, who wrote the "Timely Tracts" column in *Orate Fratres* from 1938 to 1954. Reinhold was a brilliant, if

---

[15] See Romano Guardini, *The Church and the Catholic and the Spirit of the Liturgy,* trans. by Ada Lane (New York: Sheed and Ward, 1953), 119–211. Guardini was the first to see liturgy as a form of spontaneous play that creates its own world.

[16] The Jahrbuch ceased publication in 1941, but resumed in 1950 as the *Archiv für Liturgiewissenschaft*.

[17] Pius Parsch, *The Church's Year of Grace*, Vols. I–V, trans. by William G. Heidt, O.S.B. (Collegeville: The Liturgical Press, 1957).

sometimes acerbic, writer, who championed the cause (which he called *The Cause*) of worship in the vernacular.[18] Michel's successor as editor of *Worship* was Fr. Godfrey Diekmann (until 1963), who also served as vice president of The Liturgical Conference and a *peritus* on the liturgy commission of the Second Vatican Council.[19] Editorial work on *Worship* continued to be carried out by other monks of Saint John's Abbey, including the late Michael Marx, and by Aelred Tegels. The Liturgical Press at Saint John's Abbey and University at Collegeville has made available not only monographs by American liturgists but also translations of significant European liturgical monographs.

☙ THE THEOLOGY OF THE MYSTERY

The modern liturgical movement was successful as a reforming movement in the church because it addressed the needs and longings of Western society and was broadly based with many leaders of great stature. But like the Reformation of the sixteenth century, it also operated with a theology that provided the reason and imperative for the practical work of reform. A theology of the liturgy and the sacraments emerged in the work of the Swedish Lutheran Bishop Yngve Brilioth and the monk of Maria Laach Abbey, Dom Odo Casel. Both exerted a profound influence on the liturgical movement.

Brilioth's great book, *Nattvarden i evangeliskt gudstjänstliv* (originally published in Swedish in 1926 and translated into English in 1930 by A.G. Hebert as *Eucharistic Faith and Practice, Evangelical and Catholic*), was an example of a true liturgical theology since it derived theological meanings from the liturgy itself. Brilioth explored four major strands of eucharistic meaning that are rooted in the institution of the Lord's Supper and are more or less constantly present throughout the history of eucharistic celebration: thanksgiving (eucharistia), communion or fellowship (koinonia), commemoration or memorial, and sacrifice. To these he added the dimension of Mystery, "which embraces and united all the others, and bridges the gap between the one act of the Savior and the innumerable eucharists in which that act is apprehended in the experience of faith, and its benefits appropriated."[20]

Thanksgiving is expressed principally, though not exclusively, in the great prayer said by the presider over the bread and wine in which all of God's gifts are acknowledged as gifts of grace. Communion is both a partaking of the elements consecrated by thanksgiving and the expression of fellowship with all the faithful people of Christ who share in the Lord's Supper. Commemoration is the historical aspect of the eucharist in which we remember everything that led up to the cross of Christ in salvation history and everything that results from the life-giving passion and resurrection of Christ. While the meal itself commemorates the saving cross of Christ, it needs the readings of the synaxis to put it into

---

[18] See *H.A.R.: The Autobiography of Father Reinhold* (New York: Herder and Herder, 1968).

[19] See Kathleen Hughes, "The History and Hopes of the Liturgical Movement: A Tribute on the Twenty-Fifth Anniversary of the Constitution on the Sacred Liturgy," *Proceedings of the Annual Meeting of the North American Academy of Liturgy*, Nashville, Tenn. 2–5 January 1989 (Valparaiso, Ind.: Valparaiso University, 1989), 5–26. See also her biography of Godfrey Diekmann, O.S.B., *A Monk's Tale* (Collegeville: The Liturgical Press, 1991).

[20] Brilioth, *Eucharistic Faith and Practice*, op. cit., 17.

the context of salvation history. Sacrifice is the self-offering of the church when it assembles to celebrate the eucharist, expressed through its offering of gifts. It is surprising even now to find Brilioth, a Protestant, understanding sacrifice in this way; but it shows that he derived his theology of the eucharist from liturgical data.

Brilioth insisted that it was impossible to reduce any of the great historical forms of the eucharist to one of these meanings, or to a set of meanings in some logical combination. Further, he said that any period in history in which a tendency arose to so reduce eucharistic meaning to such a simplification or logical ordering could be shown by this very fact to be a period of eucharistic decay. Obviously, the medieval period emphasized commemoration and sacrifice to the relative neglect of thanksgiving and communion. The Reformation reacted by emphasizing thanksgiving and communion and diminishing the commemorative and sacrificial aspects of the eucharist. What enables all four elements to be held together, and deepens each one of them, is the reality of Mystery, or the real presence of Christ. Conversely, as Brilioth saw it, the idea of Mystery itself is preserved from magic only by being joined with these four aspects of eucharistic meaning. Then the focus of the eucharist is not just on the eucharistic elements. If Mystery is seen in relation to thanksgiving, communion, commemoration, and sacrifice, and Mystery pervades these four aspects of eucharistic meaning, then thanksgiving is our acknowledgment of all the good gifts received in Christ. Partaking of the holy things is sharing in Christ himself; the saving events in history commemorated in the liturgy are the saving reality of the present as well, and the substance of all Christian sacrifice is the one sacrifice of Christ.

While Brilioth's study contributed to the enrichment of eucharistic understanding, Dom Odo Casel's patristic-based theological reflections breathed new life into ancient concepts such as mysterium, memoria, illuminatio, invocatio, and commemoratio. His *Mysterientheologie* ("mystery theology") infused profound meaning into the church year, the rites of initiation, and the eucharist. These ideas were spread throughout articles published in the fifteen volumes of the *Jahrbuch für Liturgiewissenschaft*, which Casel edited; in *Die Liturgie als Mysterienfeier*;[21] in his *Das Christliche Kultmysterium*, which was a straightforward, popular presentation of mystery theology;[22] and in *Das Christliche Opfermysterium*, left unfinished at the time of Casel's death, but edited and published posthumously by Dom Viktor Warnach.

The basic ideas of the mystery theology can be simply summarized, although they are based on solid, scholarly research into the writings of the fathers and the history of religions.[23] For Casel, "mystery" was not just some truth that lay beyond human reason, but the profound reality underlying all Christian celebrations and commemorations:

---

[21] Odo Casel, *Die Liturgie als Mysterienfeier*, in *Ecclesia Orans*, Vol. IX (Freiburg im Breisgau: Herder and Co., 1923).

[22] See Odo Casel, *Das christliche Kultmysterium* (Regensburg: F. Pustet, 1932); English trans. *The Mystery of Christian Worship and Other Writings*, ed. by Burkhard Neunheuser, O.S.B. (Westminster, Md.: The Newman Press; and London: Darton, Longman & Todd, 1932 for Part I, 1959 for Part II, 1962 for this translation).

[23] Summaries of the mystery theology are given in Bouyer, *Liturgical Piety*, 86ff. and Koenker, chapter VIII.

the presence of Christ through his Spirit in his paschal triumph. But to understand the mystery of God as a concrete reality, Casel's theology required Catholics to get behind the Aristoteleanism of scholastic theology to the Neo-platonism of the Greek fathers. It required a reappropriation of the idea that images and objects participate in a prototype, which alone possesses reality. The concrete image or the tangible object is real only to the extent that it participates in the reality of the prototype and leads us to that reality when we participate in it. It should be noted that this is the concept that lies behind the use of icons in the Byzantine churches, which is why icons are not regarded as "just pictures." It should also be noted that this is the concept of symbol developed in the theology of Paul Tillich—the symbol participates in the reality to which it points. What the symbols, sacraments, rites and ceremonies of the church point to, in Casel's view, is the divine reality, hidden yet communicated.

The mystery means, first of all therefore, God's being as God is in himself, infinitely above the world yet by grace dwelling within his creatures, "at once transcendent and immanent." While God's glory may be reflected in the things of the earth, it is most marvelously revealed in the Word made flesh—in Christ. And since Christ is no longer visibly present among us, "What was visible in the Lord has passed over into the mysteries [i.e., the sacraments]," as Saint Leo the Great put it. While the mystery of God is ineffable, beyond understanding or utterance, it is made accessible and tangible in the sacraments (which the Greeks called "the mysteries").[24] A Lutheran will immediately recognize in this idea a similarity with Martin Luther's teaching about God being simultaneously "hidden and revealed" in Christ, in the word and in the sacraments.[25] In fact, we will see the possibilities that the mystery theology afforded ecumenical convergence.

Casel taught, on the basis of his interpretation of the letters of Paul, that salvation consists of participating in the mystery of Christ—of sharing in his death and resurrection. We do not benefit from the saving act of God in Christ by remaining outside of it. Rather, what was realized in Christ must be realized in us. This does not mean just accepting the teachings of Christ or even making a decision for Christ; it means reliving the death and resurrection of Christ by participating in the sacraments, which commemorate the passover of Christ. In other words, the way to participate in Christ's death and resurrection is to be baptized into Christ's death and resurrection (Rom. 6:3ff.; Col. 3:1–4) and to share his life in the eucharist. This makes sacramental liturgy the central and most essential activity of the Christian religion, the center of the church's life and the most indispensable concern of the individual Christian.[26]

At this point that Casel introduced a concept that became absolutely crucial to his liturgical theology: the biblical and patristic understanding of anamnesis. In the liturgical commemoration the unique, historical, unrepeatable, saving mystery of Christ is represented. The repraesentatio (*Gegenwärtigsetzung*) of Christ occurs not just in the confection of the sacramental body and blood of Christ in the eucharist, but in the whole

---

[24] *The Mystery of Christian Worship*, 1–8.

[25] See Wilhelm Stählin, *The Mystery of God*, trans. by R. Birch Hoyle (St. Louis: Concordia Publishing House, 1964).

[26] *The Mystery of Christian Worship*, 9ff.

liturgical celebration. The passion and death, resurrection and ascension of Christ are made present for us, and we participate in them, not only in the sacramental celebrations but also as they are unfolded in the course of the church year and in the observance of the Lord's Day.[27]

It should also be noted that this idea of liturgical re-presentation had profound implications for the doctrine of eucharistic sacrifice, since it was then possible to speak of the presence of the once-for-all sacrifice of the cross in the eucharist with its saving benefits. This idea offered the possibilities of an ecumenical breakthrough on this controverted issue as it was embraced by Lutheran theologians such as Gustav Aulén in *Eucharist and Sacrifice* (originally published in 1956 as *För eder utgiven: En bok om nattvardens offermotiv*) and Peter Brunner in *Worship in the Name of Jesus* (originally published in 1951 as part of the first volume of *Leitourgia: Handbuch des evangelischen Gottesdienstes*). The Faith and Order Commission of the World Council of Churches, in 1951, saw in this theology of liturgical re-presentation "great possibilities for future development" and regarded it as "perhaps . . . the most promising approach" toward "understanding between Roman Catholic and non-Roman Churches."[28] Thirty years later the Ecumenical Working Group of Protestant and Catholic Theologians in Germany engaged in a study of "The Sacrifice of Jesus Christ and its Presence in the Church" in honor of Odo Casel.[29]

In developing the concept of repraesentatio, Casel turned to the mystery cults of the ancient Hellenistic world and found in them a ritual model that helps explain what liturgy is and does.[30] It is important to understand the scholarly context in which Casel developed his theory of the relationship between the pagan mysteries and the Christian sacraments. In Germany, in the early twentieth century, the "history of comparative religions" school tried to interpret the Old and New Testaments and early Christianity within the framework of the religions of the ancient Near East, and especially the mystery religions that were contemporary with early Christianity. Richard Reitzenstein, in *Die hellenistische Mysterienreligionen* (Leipzig, 1910) and Wilhelm Bousset, in *Kyrios Christos* (Göttingen, 1921), saw Christianity cast in the common mold of the mystery religions. Hans Lietzmann, in *Messe und Herrenmahl* (1926), contrasted Jesus' last supper with his disciples, based on Jewish family meals and recorded in the Gospel of Mark, with Paul's supposed invention of a Christian sacramental meal modeled on the Hellenistic mystery cults.[31] These ideas were popularized in France by Alfred Loisy, in *Les mystères païens et*

---

[27] Ibid., 63ff.

[28] *Ways of Worship: The Report of a Theological Commission of Faith and Order,* ed. by P. Edwall, E. Hayman, and W. Maxwell (London, 1951), 33.

[29] *Das Opfer Jesu Christi und seine Gegenwart in der Kirche. Klärungen zum Opfercharakter des Herrenmahles,* Dialog der Kirchen 3, ed. by Karl Lehmann and Edmund Schlink (Freiburg/Göttingen, 1983).

[30] Ibid., 50ff.

[31] To a great extent, Yngve Brilioth's 1930 work, *Eucharistic Faith and Practice: Evangelical and Catholic,* op. cit., was written against Lietzmann, to show that the various aspects of eucharistic meaning (e.g., thanksgiving, fellowship, commemoration, sacrifice) are not mutually exclusive, that the dimension of mystery, or the real presence of Christ, pervades all aspects of eucharistic meaning, and that mystery is therefore as much present in the synoptic accounts as in Paul.

le mystère chrétien (2nd ed., Paris, 1930). Casel, having also done research in the mystery cults, proposed that the pagan mysteries could be viewed as a providential preparation for the Christian revelation, and therefore he did not think it surprising that Paul or the church fathers would borrow many concepts from these cults. In any event, even though the forms and concepts of the pagan mysteries might be similar to the Christian sacraments, the unique content of the Christian sacraments is the Pascha of Christ. It is noteworthy that Odo Casel himself passed over with Christ when he died at the Easter Vigil in 1948, just after he had sung "The light of Christ." Nothing could have been more fitting, since he had helped to recover the paschal mystery as the core meaning of the Christian liturgy.[32]

Since Casel's death, Louis Bouyer has probed further into the connection between the pagan mysteries and the Christian sacraments. He has seen that Christian sacramental practice is far more dependent on antecedent Jewish practices than on Hellenistic ones. He even suggested that students of comparative religion have had a tendency to impose Christian concepts on the pagan cults, as Alfred Loisy did.[33] They have failed to see that the pagan rites were rites, pure and simple, on which later philosophers imposed meaning. But the mystery of which Paul speaks is not a rite that was formerly known by everyone but which has become a secret; it is the divine plan of salvation formerly hidden in the mind of God but now revealed in the proclamation of the cross of Christ. Nevertheless, while Bouyer disputed any putative influence of pagan mystery religions on the Christian sacraments, he did apply the insights of historians of religion like Mircea Eliade and the reflections of depth psychologists like Carl-Gustav Jung to the study of sacraments and symbols. He opened the door for liturgists to explore more wide-ranging ways of understanding the role of myth and ritual by reference to the work done by cultural anthropologists.[34]

Liturgical investigation of human ritual has raised the question of participation in ritual action. Casel's understanding of participation in the liturgy tolerated a more passive stance for the faithful than the modern liturgical movement has desired. He was more interested in the inward quality of participation than in the outward expressions of it. Yet concern for greater understanding of the liturgy led to concern for more intelligible rites, especially in the face of the breakdown of Christendom and the emergence of a secularized society. By 1964, the eminent liturgist Romano Guardini was raising the radical question that has haunted liturgical renewalists ever since. He asked:

> Is not the liturgical act . . . so bound up with historical background—antique or medieval or baroque—that it would be more honest to give it up altogether? Would it not be better to admit that man in this industrial and scientific age, with its sociological structure, is no longer capable of the liturgical act? And instead of talking about renewal, ought we not to consider how best to celebrate

---

[32] See Irmgard Pahl, "The Paschal Mystery in Its Central Meaning for the Shape of the Liturgy," *Studia Liturgica* 26 (1996), 16–38.

[33] Louis Bouyer, *Liturgical Piety*, op. cit., 90ff.; *Rite and Man*, op. cit., 123ff.

[34] See *The Roots of Ritual*, a Symposium sponsored by the Murphy Center for Liturgical Research at the University of Notre Dame, ed. by James D. Shaughnessy (Grand Rapids: William B. Eerdmans, 1973).

the sacred mysteries so that the modern man can grasp their meaning through his own approach to truth?[35]

It was becoming evident, through historical research, that the domination of the liturgy by the clergy was an aberration, that the action of worship belonged to all the people, and that secular influences were exposing the lifelessness of much conventional worship. Without denying the essential insights into the nature of liturgy and its role in the life of the church provided in the mystery theology of Odo Casel, leaders of the modern liturgical movement were intent on working for more active participation in the liturgy by the faithful and liturgical reforms to make this participation possible. The pastoral phase of the liturgical movement gained great momentum as it moved outside of monastic communities and was pursued in conferences, institutes, and societies.

❧ LITURGICAL CONFERENCES, INSTITUTES, AND SOCIETIES

The Reformation in the sixteenth century elicited widespread and immediate support by communicating directly with the public through printed materials, sermons, and professorships in the universities. The modern liturgical movement followed the same course of getting its message out to the clergy and people of the church and thereby influencing the work of reform and revision that would be undertaken by official liturgical committees. The path-breaking work of the monasteries was disseminated into the wider church through well-attended conferences, congresses, and institutes; and by the work of associations, clubs, centers, and societies that studied the liturgy, published tracts and monographs, conducted conferences and workshops, and modeled liturgical celebrations. These conferences, institutes, and societies were the political engines that drove the ideas of renewal toward official acts of reform.

Maria Laach Abbey remained a center of the liturgical movement with its publications (the *Jahrbuch* and later the *Archiv für Liturgiewissenschaft* and the monograph series, *Ecclesia Orans*), its academy of patristic studies, and its center for sacred art. A comparable center in France was the Centre de Pastorale Liturgique, which had a more pastoral focus than Maria Laach but also encouraged scientific research into the liturgy. The Centre also established the *Institut supérieur de liturgie* in co-sponsorship with the Abbey of Mont-César, at the Institut Catholique in Paris. On the whole the Centre is more interested in making a pastoral impact through its public meetings and liturgical weeks and its popular illustrated periodical, *Fêtes et Saisons*. Its more scholarly publications are the quarterly, *La Maison-Dieu*, and the monograph series, *Lex Orandi*.

In spite of a number of prominent Roman Catholic liturgists in Great Britain during the twentieth century (from Edmund Bishop through J. G. Crichton), there has been virtually no Roman Catholic liturgical renewal movement in Great Britain comparable to the movements in Belgium, Germany, Austria, and France. The reason for this lies in the unique situation of Roman Catholicism in Great Britain: it remained the primary

---

[35] Romano Guardini, quoted by Clement J. McNaspy, S.J., *Our Changing Liturgy* (Garden City: Doubleday Image Books, 1967), 13–4.

expression of pre-Reformation Christianity and has generally profited from maintaining a conservative liturgical ethos. The Protestant churches have harbored intense anti-Catholic feelings, which has hindered liturgical renewal even in the Church of England. Moreover, most of those interested in liturgical renewal in the Church of England emigrated into Anglo-Catholicism and embraced a pre-Reformation ethos similar to that of Roman Catholicism.

Within the Church of England, the Alcuin Club has long been dedicated to the scholarly study of orders of service in the *Book of Common Prayer*. The Henry Bradshaw Society has been devoted to scholarly studies on Christian worship in general. Significant contributions have been made to the relationship between liturgical renewal and Christian mission in society by A. G. Hebert, in *Liturgy and Society* (1935), Alfred Shands, in *The Liturgical Movement and the Local Church* (1959), Bishop John A. T. Robinson, in *Liturgy Coming to Life* (1960), and J. G. Davies, in *Worship and Mission* (1966). Nonconformist churches have been wary of liturgy as a result of their Puritan backgrounds, and also because an antiliturgical stance differentiates them from the Church of England. In Ireland, however, annual liturgical conferences for clergy have been held at the Glenstal Abbey since the end of World War II, which have promoted the ideas of the liturgical movement.

The great contribution to liturgical reform in England came from the work of Dom Gregory Dix of Nashdom Abbey. His proposal that the fourfold shape of the eucharistic liturgy—offertory, consecration, fraction, distribution—derives from the actions of Jesus at the last supper—taking the bread and wine, giving thanks over them, breaking the bread, and giving the elements to the disciples—influenced the revisions of the liturgies of several churches. The widespread acceptance of Dix's paradigm was not without its theological and liturgical critics.[36]

A lively liturgical movement has flourished in the Roman Catholic Church in the United States. We have mentioned the leadership of Saint John's Abbey in Collegeville, Minnesota, under Virgil Michel, Hans Anscar Reinhold, and Godfrey Diekmann. The first Liturgical Day was held at Saint John's Abbey in 1929. This was expanded into national Liturgical Weeks, the first of which was held in Chicago in 1940 under the sponsorship of the Benedictine Liturgical Conference. In 1943 the Benedictines passed the planning of these Weeks to an independent board known as The Liturgical Conference. The Liturgical Conference's annual Liturgical Weeks attracted thousands of participants each year, reaching a high point in the 1960s when 14,000 attended the Week in Philadelphia in 1963 and 20,000 attended the Week in Saint Louis in 1964. When the Liturgical Weeks were no longer held after the 1960s, the Conference continued to publish tracts, manuals, a quarterly journal entitled *Liturgy,* and a monthly periodical called *Homily Service.* Names associated with the literary productions of The Liturgical Conference in the 1960s and 1970s were Fr. Robert Hovda, who authored a number of

---

[36] See Oliver K. Olson, "Contemporary Trends in Liturgy Viewed from the Perspective of Classical Lutheran Theology," *Lutheran Quarterly* 26 (1974), 110–57, and, more recently, Bryan D. Spinks, "Mis-Shapen: Gregory Dix and the Four-Action Shape of the Liturgy," *Lutheran Quarterly* (new series) 4 (1990), 161–77.

manuals on implementing the goals of the liturgical movement and who popularized such concepts as "assembly" and "presiding minister," and Fr. Gerard Sloyan, who promoted the preaching of lectionary-based homilies within the Roman Catholic mass. The Liturgical Conference became ecumenical in 1979 when it merged with the Lutheran Society for Worship, Music, and the Arts, and since then has included on its board of directors members of several denominational traditions.

It was also necessary to provide places where Americans could study the liturgy as a serious academic pursuit. As early as 1941 Fr. Reynold Hillenbrand, a priest of the archdiocese of Chicago, organized a summer school program in liturgical studies at Saint Mary of the Lake Seminary in Mundelein, taught by such men as Godfrey Diekmann, Gerard Ellard, Martin Hellriegel, and A. R. Reinhold. In the summer of 1947, the first actual degree program in liturgical studies was established at the University of Notre Dame by Michael Mathis, C.S.C. (1885–1960).[37] This led to the establishment of the graduate program in Liturgical Studies at Notre Dame in 1965. To this program Fr. Mathis invited the most prominent European liturgists, such as Joseph Jungmann, Louis Bouyer, Jean Daniélou, and Johannes Hofinger. Many of their lectures were published in book form by the University of Notre Dame Press, including Bouyer's *Liturgical Piety*, Daniélou's *The Bible and the Liturgy*, and Jungmann's *The Early Liturgy to the Time of Gregory the Great*. To date, more than fifty doctoral dissertations have been written in the Notre Dame program. The Murphy Center for Liturgical Research was established at Notre Dame, which held annual conferences and published several collections of lectures from those conclaves.[38] The Murphy Center was replaced by the Center for Pastoral Liturgy, which has published several journals and digests. The experiments in actual worship as well as research conducted by faculty and graduate students in the Liturgical Studies program also had practical consequences in some official worship books. For example, efforts at retrieving the ancient cathedral office, under the leadership of Dr. William G. Storey and his graduate students, contributed greatly to the shape of the office of Vespers in *Lutheran Book of Worship* and also the use of psalter collects.[39]

The liturgical movement in the American Roman Catholic Church, in terms of its leading figures, was at first a veritable invasion from Germany. But there had also been a significant liturgical movement within the Lutheran churches in Germany. Liturgical renewal was stimulated in German Lutheranism at the end of the nineteenth century by Erlangen professors Adolf Harless, Johann W. F. Hoefling, and Theodosius Harnack. After the turn of the century professors Friedrich Heiler, Rudolf Otto, Hans Lietzmann,

---

[37] See Robert Kennedy, *Michael Mathis: An American Liturgical Pioneer* (Washington: The Pastoral Press, 1987).

[38] *The Roots of Ritual*, ed. by James D. Shaughnessy (Grand Rapids: William B. Eerdmans, 1973). Another volume of papers published by the Murphy Center for Liturgical Research was *Made, Not Born: New Perspectives on Christian Initiation and the Catechumenate* (Notre Dame, Ind.: University of Notre Dame Press, 1976).

[39] See *Morning Praise and Evensong*, ed. by William G. Storey, Frank Quinn, O.P., and David Wright, O.P. (Notre Dame, Ind.: Fides, 1973). The research into and experimentation with the divine office on the campus of the University of Notre Dame is related in Frank C. Senn, *The Pastor As Worship Leader: A Manual for Corporate Worship* (Minneapolis: Augsburg Publishing House, 1977), chapter 2.

Friedrich Spitta, and Julius Smend gave the liturgical movement spiritual depth and theological direction. The next generation of German Lutheran liturgical leaders applied this substantial historical and theological work to the pastoral phase of the liturgical movement. Cantor Friedrich Buchholz worked to achieve a "German Gregorianism," a restoration of church chant for congregational singing. Bishop Wilhelm Stählin, Karl Bernhard Ritter, and Wilhelm Thomas worked particularly in and through the *Evangelische Michaelsbruderschaft* (Evangelical Brotherhood of Saint Michael), founded in 1931, to foster an "inner renewal of the church" and devoted themselves to a "creative reorganization" of the liturgy, using the liturgical tradition as a point of departure. The Brotherhood did not believe in mere repristination of the historic liturgy, but in a creative adaptation of the traditional rites and orders. Stählin summarized the aims of this German evangelical liturgical movement as follows: "the overthrow of subjectivism, an orientation to the early church, the reinstatement of the whole worship service, a renewal of the evangelical proclamation of the Gospel, and the re-establishment of the eucharistic purpose of the sacrament of the altar."[40] A high point of the evangelical liturgical movement in Germany was the establishment of the Lutheran Liturgical Conference of Germany. Under the leadership of Christhard Mahrenholz, the scholars and church leaders who made up this conference endeavored to produce a common service for all the Lutheran churches of Germany, based on the historic liturgy. They also devoted a careful study to the worship of the ancient church. This work began to bear consequences in the 1950s in the new Agendas that were published in the various Landeskirchen, especially Saxony, Bavaria, and the Rhineland-Westphalia.

In Sweden the leading liturgical scholars in the early twentieth century were bishops: Eduard Rodhe, Yngve Brilioth, Bo Giertz, and Olof Herrlin, as well as Gustaf Aulén, who lent his inestimable theological reputation to the "liturgical renaissance" and the "evangelical catholic revival."[41] The pastoral figure, Dr. Gunnar Rosendal, aroused great interest in liturgical renewal, especially among students. The Sigtuna Foundation, with its folk high school, humanistic gymnasium, library, chapel, and hospice, has been a place through which many workers have tried "to bring the church to the people" and "to revive the immanent catholicity of the Swedish church." This theological and pastoral work culminated in the Swedish Mass of 1942, which eschewed the rationalistic elements of the 1819 *Manual* and recovered elements from the Reformation church order and the pre-Reformation liturgy. It was provided, for example, with complete musical settings based on plainsong chants. The inclusion of a eucharistic prayer in this mass-liturgy, brief though it was, was a sign of the influence of the modern liturgical scholarship within the Church of Sweden. It made an effort to bring elements of anamnesis and epiclesis into the eucharistic order. This prayer has been included as an option in the Service of Holy Communion in *Lutheran Book of Worship* (# 33).

---

[40] Rudolf Stählin, "Die Wiedergewinnung der Liturgie in der evangelischen Kirche," in *Leitourgia,* I (Kassel, 1955), 74ff.

[41] See Gustaf Aulén, "The Catholicity of Lutheranism: A Contribution to the Ecumenical Discussion," in *World Lutheranism of Today* (Geneva, 1950), 3–20.

In the United States, the Lutheran Liturgical Association flourished from 1898 to 1905. The papers from its monthly meetings, published in its annual *Memoirs*, still serve as a valuable source of information about historic Lutheran liturgies. We have cited articles published in the *Memoirs of the Lutheran Liturgical Association*. Increasingly Luther D. Reed (1873–1972) became the leader of this largely United Lutheran Church in America-dominated branch of the liturgical movement. Its strategy was to convince people that they could find in the Common Service a beautiful and dignified form of worship that was liturgically and psychologically balanced, catholic in spirit yet truly Lutheran.[42] Paul Z. Strodach (1876–1942) was a colleague of Reed's at the Philadelphia Seminary and also an influential figure.[43] The proximity of these leaders to centers of the Episcopal Church, and their commitment to the Common Service, may have disposed these leaders to borrow styles of church architecture and church music, models of ceremony, and types of vestments from the Anglican tradition. Reed and Strodach strongly recommended the cassock, surplice, and stole as standard vestments for Lutheran ministers, and also introduced choir and acolyte cassocks and cottas. They stressed moderation in matters of ceremonial, but absolute fidelity to the rubrics of the liturgical orders.

The other stream of the Lutheran liturgical movement was based in the Lutheran Church—Missouri Synod. The Society of Saint James was founded in Hoboken, New Jersey, in 1925, with Pastor Berthold von Schenk as its president. Their journal was *Pro Ecclesia Lutherana*, and the name indicated their concern. They had no Common Service around which to rally, but they also did not have to overcome the ravages of Rationalism and Revivalism. The articles in *Pro Ecclesia* do not argue for a beautiful and dignified liturgy, but for the catholicity of Lutheranism and its liturgical life. The Society of Saint James was more expansive in its appropriation of traditional Catholic vestments and ceremonies than Reed and Strodach had been. Albs, stoles, and chasubles were recommended, and incense and Sanctus bells were introduced in some parishes. When selecting vestments, Arthur Carl Piepkorn (1907–1973), professor of systematic theology at Concordia Seminary, Saint Louis, advised seminarians that they should choose a surplice to wear over cassock or gown that is "as long and at least as full as a good alb," since it was "etymologically just an alb made full enough to go over *(super)* a fur coat *(pelliceae)*."[44] Contrary to Luther Reed and the proposal of the Augustana Synod to recommend cassock, surplice, and stole (or stole over the gown), Piepkorn recommended as "first and most desireable [*sic*] . . . the restoration of the full Eucharistic vestments (cassock, amice, alb, cincture, stole, chasuble, and maniple) with cassock, surplice, and scarf (or stole for Sacramental and quasi-Sacramental offices . . .) for non-Eucharistic offices, a cope for solemn services, and a biretta and cope for out-of-doors." Failing that, "The second combination is cassock, alb, and chasuble, a use preserved by the Churches of Denmark and Norway." The stole, in his opinion, should not be reinstated until the Eucharistic

---

[42] The final expression of this movement is found in Luther D. Reed, *Worship: A Study of Corporate Devotion* (Philadelphia: Muhlenberg Press, 1959).

[43] See Paul Z. Strodach, *A Manual in Worship* (Philadelphia: Muhlenberg Press, 1946).

[44] Arthur Carl Piepkorn, "When Selecting a Vestment," *The Seminarian* (St. Louis: Concordia Seminary, March 1938).

vestments are reinstated.[45] The erudite Piepkorn assumed the intellectual leadership of this part of the Lutheran liturgical movement.[46]

Pro Ecclesia gave way to another journal, *Una Sancta* (1943–1967), which, like *Orate Fratres/Worship*, increasingly projected a vision of the liturgy as a source for social renewal as well as church renewal. *Una Sancta* was revived as an annual number of the quarterly journal *Lutheran Forum*, published by the American Lutheran Publicity Bureau.

The annual Institute of Liturgical Studies at Valparaiso University in Indiana, attracting hundreds of participants at annual conferences for nearly fifty years now, became a forum from which the original aims of the Saint James Society could be disseminated to a wider audience, and be enriched by inter-Lutheran participation and ecumenical contact.

Similar institutes and societies have flourished in other denominational traditions. Among them are Associated Parishes, an Episcopal Church fellowship with headquarters in Washington, D.C.; the Order of Saint Luke, a liturgical society within the United Methodist Church dating from 1948; the United Methodist Society for Worship, founded in 1975; and the Church Service Society within the Presbyterian Church.

Several societies devoted to the promotion of liturgical scholarship have been formed. Among them are the ecumenical Societas Liturgica, an international society that holds biennial week-long meetings, and the interfaith North American Academy of Liturgy, established in 1975, which is a professional society of liturgical scholars. Societas Liturgica operates in a more European manner with the presentation of major addresses and responses and case studies. The focus of the annual meetings of the North American Academy of Liturgy is the work done in seminar groups that continue from year to year. The papers of the Societas meeting are published in *Studia Liturgica* and the work of the NAAL is published in its *Proceedings*.

🍇 A High Point of Restorationism: Prelude to Renewal

In the middle of twentieth century, Lutherans in North America had the opportunity to take the first steps toward producing a liturgical rite that reflected the visions of the modern liturgical movement. We saw in the last chapter that the Common Service had been adopted by a number of Lutheran church bodies in the United States and Canada. The United Lutheran Church in America's (ULCA) *Common Service Book* committee began working on a revision of the *Common Service Book* in 1936, and submitted its final report to the convention of the ULCA in 1944. But instead of adopting the report, the convention adopted a resolution seeking the fullest cooperation with other church bodies in producing a common Lutheran hymnal (since the Common Service was included in the worship books of a number of church bodies). The Lutheran Church— Missouri Synod declined the invitation on the grounds that it had just published *The*

---

[45] Arthur Carl Piepkorn, "An Inquiry and Answer," *Una Sancta* VII/1 (1951), 22f.

[46] See Arthur C. Piepkorn, *The Church: Selected Writings*, ed. and Introduction by Michael P. Plekon and William S. Wiecher (Delhi, N.Y.: ALPB Books, 1993).

Lutheran Hymnal (1941). Other bodies, representing about two-thirds of Lutherans in North America, did respond positively, however; and at a meeting in Pittsburgh on June 23, 1945 the Joint Commission on the Hymnal was organized, with Dr. Luther Reed as its permanent chairman.[47] Work proceeded so well that in 1946 an exploratory conference was held to see if work could also be done on a common liturgy. Because of variations in the Common Service from one book to another, it was agreed that this work should be undertaken, but that the Common Service should serve as the basis. This time invitations were sent out to all Lutheran church bodies in North America; again the Missouri Synod declined.

For the next decade representatives of eight Lutheran church bodies worked on a common liturgy and a common hymnal (there were two joint commissions).[48] The *Service Book and Hymnal of the Lutheran Church in America* began rolling off the press on March 17, 1958.[49] The *SBH* was produced in a kind of cooperative climate as a pan-Lutheran project, and within four years the eight Lutheran bodies that cooperated on the Joint Commissions on the Liturgy and on the Hymnal were merged into two: the American Lutheran Church in 1960[50] and the Lutheran Church in America in 1962.[51]

The *Service Book and Hymnal* was a book admirably suited for its cultural and ecclesiastical context. Michael Kammen writes that "for approximately a full generation, beginning in the mid-1950s, 'heritage' has been one of the key words in American culture."[52] James F. White relates that the dominant interest in worship in the period after World War II was "recovering our heritage."[53] The *SBH* was clearly the apex of a hundred-year effort in American Lutheranism to recover the heritage of the Reformation church orders. But it was also the fitting product of a Lutheranism self-consciously moving out of its ethnic enclaves and striving under the energetic leadership of Franklin Clark Fry, president of the United Lutheran Church in America and later of the merged

---

[47] Reed, *The Lutheran Liturgy,* op. cit., 205ff., gives a detailed account of the work on the Common Liturgy.

[48] For an "insider's" view of the process see Edward T. Horn, III, "Preparation of the Service Book and Hymnal," in Edgar S. Brown, Jr., ed., *Liturgical Reconnaissance: Papers Presented at the Inter-Lutheran Consultation on Worship* (Philadelphia: Fortress Press, 1968), 91–101.

[49] *Service Book and Hymnal of the Lutheran Church in America* (Minneapolis: Augsburg Publishing House; Rock Island, Ill.: Augustana Book Concern; Blair, Nebraska: Lutheran Publishing House; Hancock, Michigan: Finnish Lutheran Book Concern; Philadelphia: United Lutheran Publication House; Columbus, Ohio: Wartburg Press, 1958).

[50] The merger that created the A.L.C. in 1960 included the American Lutheran Church (1930 merger of the Iowa, Ohio, and Buffalo Synods), the Evangelical Lutheran Church (Norwegian merger), and the United Evangelical Lutheran Church (Inner Mission Danes). The Lutheran Free Church (Haugian Norwegians) joined the A.L.C. in 1963.

[51] The L.C.A. was created in 1962 by a merger of the American Evangelical Lutheran Church (Grundtvigian Danes), the Augustana Evangelical Lutheran Church (Swedes), the Finnish Evangelical Lutheran Church in America, and the United Lutheran Church in America (predominantly eastern and Americanized Germans).

[52] Michael Kammen, *Mystic Chords of Memory,* op. cit., 621.

[53] James F. White, *Christian Worship in Transition* (Nashville: Abingdon, 1976), 82. Dieter Georgi, "The Interest in Life of Jesus Theology as a Paradigm for the Social History of Biblical Criticism," *Harvard Theological Review* 85 (1992), 51–83, makes the case that the New Quest for the historical Jesus and the restoration of the bourgeoisie in the United States and Germany after World War II is not coincidental.

Lutheran Church in America, to become a mainline Protestant denomination taking its place alongside other mainline denominations in America.

Thus, the *SBH* can be regarded as the high-water mark in the tide of liturgical recovery. But the Common Liturgy in the *SBH* was not just another version of the Common Service. The Common Service was based on the consensus of the pure Lutheran church orders of the sixteenth century. Even in this, the Common Service was not just a repristination of sixteenth-century liturgical style. The fact that the Common Service gave to the congregation what would have been sung by choirs in the classical Lutheran church orders (e.g., the Gloria rather than the chorale "All glory be to God on high") indicates the influence of the more participatory American cultural context. It anticipated the renewal of the concept of liturgy as "the work of the people" in the modern liturgical movement.[54] The Common Liturgy was indeed based on the Common Service; but it also shows the telltale marks of the modern liturgical movement. The preface to the liturgy admits that as

> our Churches in America have come more fully to appreciate each other, they have also discovered through deepened scholarship and broader fellowship, the rich treasury of ecumenical liturgy, especially in the ancient Greek tradition antedating the Roman rite from which European usage has been derived. A vision clearer than was sometimes possible in the turmoil of the Reformation controversy has revealed the enduring value of some elements which were lost temporarily in the sixteenth century reconstruction of the liturgy, as, for example, the proper use of the Prayer of Thanksgiving and the essential meaning of the term 'catholic' in the creeds. . . . The Common Liturgy is rooted in the developed worship of the ancient and medieval Christian Church, both East and West, and grounded on the historic German, Scandinavian, and American uses of the post-reformation centuries.[55]

In addition to new collects and prayers, the ancient bidding prayer from the Good Friday Liturgy, propers for Holy Saturday and Holy Innocents, and additional Introits and Graduals, the following inclusions are noted:

> The Litany of Peace from the Byzantine liturgy of John Chrysostom (the first four petitions and conclusion) as an alternative to the sixfold Kyrie;
>
> A complete series of Old Testament readings (which, although optional, soon enjoyed widespread use because the three readings were printed on lectionary insert sheets or on the backs of worship folders);
>
> A psalm or hymn version of a psalm after the Old Testament lesson (again optional, but not as widely used as the Old Testament lesson because psalmody was also included in the Introit and Gradual for the day);
>
> A congregational response to the petitions of the Prayer of the Church ("We beseech thee to hear us, good Lord");
>
> New eucharistic proper prefaces for Advent and All Saints Day;
>
> Most significantly, an original eucharistic prayer using quotations from classical eucharistic prayers, as well as the Scottish Anglican *Book of Common*

---

[54] See Frank C. Senn, "The Achievement of the Common Service," *dialog* 27 (1988), 291–4.

[55] *Service Book and Hymnal,* vii–viii.

Prayer and the Scottish Presbyterian *Book of Common Order*, but modeled on the West Syrian structure.[56]

About this prayer, composed largely by Luther Reed, Louis Bouyer wrote:

> It would be hard to be more ecumenical! But all of these elements, chosen with great discernment, have been molded into a composition that is as moderate as it is natural. In its brief simplicity this prayer has a concise fullness that we are not accustomed to seeing except in Christian antiquity. Here, as in the liturgy of the Church of South India, its eschatological orientation gives it a very primitive sound. Once again, this liturgy must be judged Catholic and orthodox to the extent that the traditional formulas it uses, with hardly an echo of the polemics of the Reformation, are in fact taken in their full and primary sense by the Church that uses them.[57]

This prayer, in slightly amended form, was incorporated into the Ministers Edition of *Lutheran Book of Worship* as Great Thanksgiving III.

The inclusion of a full eucharistic prayer, but with the option of using the words of institution alone, dictated a reversal of the order of the Common Service. The order after the Preface and Sanctus became: the Prayer of Thanksgiving, including the words of institution or words of institution alone, and then the Lord's Prayer, rather than the Lord's Prayer followed by the words of institution juxtaposed with the administration of the elements. More significantly, the Prayer of Thanksgiving was placed first, before the option of the words of institution alone, thus promoting it as the preferred option.

The Service, also called "The Communion," was provided with two musical settings in the pew edition of the *SBH*: an Anglican chant setting (based on the setting in the *Common Service Book*) and a continental plainsong setting arranged by Regina Fryxell of Augustana College in Rock Island, Illinois (the latter of which was adapted for use as the third setting of the Service of Holy Communion in *LBW*). A third setting based on Gregorian chant was published separately. Matins and Vespers were completely restored with full musical settings and propers. The Funeral Service, based on the Little Office of the Dead, with full musical provisions, is a veritable gem that ought not to be lost as the *SBH* fades into history. Thus, in spite of the continued use of Elizabethan/Jacobean English, the Common Liturgy of the *SBH* was a prelude to the liturgical revisions that would more fully reflect the proposals and purposes of the modern liturgical movement.

The *SBH* spelled the death of the ethnic rites inherited from immigrant Lutherans with its "catholic" liturgy and "ecumenical" hymnal. The hymnal was more inclusive of Anglo-American hymnody than many of the previous Lutheran hymnals had been, thus reaching out to the religious-cultural context of North American Lutheranism; it also included a number of plainsong hymns, which demonstrated its sense of continuity with the catholic tradition.

---

[56] Reed, *The Lutheran Liturgy*, op. cit., 356–7, gives the sources of this prayer.

[57] Bouyer, *Eucharist*, op. cit., 441–2.

The Constitution on the Sacred Liturgy

On January 25, 1959, less than a year after the *SBH* was published, Pope John XXIII announced his intention to convene a general council of the universal Roman Catholic Church to open the windows, as he put it, and let in fresh air. After extensive preparations, the Ecumenical and Universal Council Held in the Vatican Basilica, or the Second Vatican Ecumenical Council (as it is better known) opened on October 11, 1962, and lasted until December 8, 1965. To this council of the Roman Catholic Church were invited observers from Protestant and Eastern Orthodox churches and Jewish groups. These latter two groups declined to send observers, but representatives from more than forty Anglican, Baptist, Congregationalist, Disciples of Christ, Lutheran, Presbyterian, and other churches and groups were sent as delegate-observers. They freely entered into discussions in committees that met between official voting sessions.

It is no accident that the Constitution on the Sacred Liturgy was the first to be promulgated by the council. The modern liturgical movement, in both its scholarly and pastoral emphases, had elicited clerical and lay support in several countries. The detailed historical work of Fr. Joseph Jungmann, S.J., and scores of other scholars, made it possible to undertake reforms in line with the deepest traditions of the church. Five eminent liturgical scholars served on the preconciliar commission, of which Fr. A. Bugnini served as secretary, which drafted the initial text of the Constitution. From October 22 to November 13, 1962, the proposed text was debated in the council. On November 14, it was passed 2,162 to 46, and promulgated by Pope Paul VI (the former Cardinal Montini, archbishop of Milan), who had shown a special interest in the reform of the liturgy.

It is easy to wax effusive over (or, in the case of some, to lament) the results of the Constitution. Consequences are not the same as the document itself. The eminent canonist, Fr. Frederick McManus, showed the Constitution to be a carefully nuanced statement.[58] Thus, it carefully distinguishes between general principles and specific reforms of the Roman rite, especially since there were leaders of the council who used various Oriental rites. For example, provisions for vernacularization would apply only to the Roman rite, since Oriental liturgies were already in vernacular languages. Even so, contrary to popular impressions, the use of the Latin language for the Roman rite was not abolished; and vernacularizations are to be based on the Latin *editio typica*. The Constitution was a political document that shows the tendency of the Roman church to evolve teachings without repudiating what was taught previously. For example, the statement in I, 9 that the liturgy does not exhaust the entire activity of the church recalls the teaching of Pope Pius XII at the Assisi Conference in 1956; yet it also prepares the way for the statement that "the liturgy is the summit toward which the activity of the Church is directed" and "the fountain from which all her powers flow" (I, 10). The Constitution was not only a pastoral statement; it was also a juridical document emanating from the highest authority in the church—an ecumenical council convened by the pope. Thus, it not only

---

[58] See Frederick McManus, *Sacramental Liturgy* (New York: Herder and Herder, 1967). The text of the Constitution is in an appendix. See also Walter M. Abbott, S.J., *The Documents of Vatican II* (New York: Herder and Herder, 1966), 133ff.

called for the "full and active participation by all the people" in the rites of the church (I, 14); it also dealt with the education of liturgy professors (15), liturgical instruction in the seminaries (16) and in religious houses (17), the continuing education of clergy who were already serving in the ministry (18), and the instruction of the laity necessary to promote their full and active participation in the liturgy.

Just as the Council of Trent established principles that would be enacted later in concrete reforms, so the Constitution set down principles governing the practical reforms that would be carried out after the Council by the Consilium to Implement the Constitution. Nevertheless, the Constitution abounds in both general and specific recommendations for reform, which have as their objective "a general restoration of the liturgy itself" (21). The most consistent act of liturgical restoration in the Constitution is the promotion of the active participation of the people (30), and the rubrics are to take this into account (31). Since the faithful are to take an informed, active, and fruitful part in the rites, the liturgical books are to be reformed so that the rites may express their meanings more clearly. The rites are to display a noble simplicity, avoid useless repetitions, and not need much explanation (34). To the same end, "the treasures of the Bible are to be opened up more lavishly, so that richer fare may be provided for the faithful at the table of God's Word" (II, 51). Homilies are to be given, and should not be omitted at Sunday and festival masses (52). The "prayer of the faithful" is to be restored "in which the people are to take part" (53). "In Masses which are celebrated with the people, a suitable place may be allotted to their mother tongue," although it was left to local hierarchies to carry out this provision in an appropriate manner (54). The people are to receive communion at mass, and in certain instances "communion under both kinds may be granted when the bishops think fit, not only to clerics and religious, but also to the laity" (55). Permission was granted for concelebrations in certain cases and situations so as to reduce the number of private masses being celebrated (56).

In the chapter on the sacraments emphasis is again given to the need of the people to understand; and again the need for the use of the vernacular language was stressed (III, 63). The restoration of the catechumenate with its stages clearly marked by the successive rites (64), the stress laid on confirmation as a part of the rites of initiation (71), the statement that the anointing of the sick is to be so called and that it precedes viaticum (74), the permission to adapt marriage rites to local traditions (75), and the promised reform of the rites of penance and of funerals are all signs that the council appreciated the deficiencies of the 1614 *Rituale Romanum*.

The council was more explicit about the reform of the breviary. The Constitution established Lauds and Vespers as the principal offices of the hours and decreed that they be so celebrated (chapter IV). The office of Prime was abolished. Terce, Sext, and None remain, but in private celebrations one of them may be chosen for recitation and the other two omitted. Matins could still remain a nocturnal choir office, but could also be privately recited at any convenient time of the day. Weekly recitation of the psalter was abolished and the psalms were to be distributed over a longer period of time. This was perhaps the weakest chapter in the Constitution, since it was not able to overcome the clericalization of the Divine Office to make the prayer offices truly popular.

The chapter on the liturgical year (V) emphasized the preeminence of the temporal cycle over the sanctoral. The number of commemorations in the sanctoral cycle was to be reduced so that only those saints appear in the general calendar of the Roman rite who are of universal importance; and those of local interest are to be commemorated only where there is special reason for their veneration. Under no circumstances should a saint's day replace the Sunday office; and even the ferial Office should predominate over the commemoration of a saint. The Lord's Day is the church's original feast day as the day of resurrection, and nothing must take precedence over this day (106). The Lenten season is to stress the twofold aspects of preparation for baptism and a penitential spirit (109). "During Lent, penance should not be only internal and individual but also external and social" (110).

The Constitution concluded with chapters on Sacred Music (VI) and Sacred Art and Sacred Furnishings (VII). Composers and artists are to be encouraged to create proper vehicles for the expression of the liturgy. While a variety of musical forms and instruments may be admitted into the liturgy, Gregorian chant and pipe organs still retain premier places. While the church should still be a patron of the arts, care must be taken to maintain the integrity of the liturgy and the true spirit of devotion.

The concrete results of the Constitution in specific instances of liturgical revision will be detailed in the next chapter. Here we would simply note, by way of conclusion, that the Constitution set in motion principles that would govern not only liturgical revision, but also liturgical renewal. These principles include: the "full and active participation of the people" in ways appropriate to the priesthood of all believers; the adaptation of the Roman liturgy to local cultures (even to the point of adapting pagan rituals of initiation to Christian usage in par. 65); the centrality of scripture in terms of the place given to readings in the liturgical rites and the restoration of preaching; and the reform of the calendar so as to emphasize the paschal mystery. The reform of the calendar provided the most ecumenical note in the Constitution: the proviso in its appendix that a fixed day can be set for Easter if that could receive the consent of "the brethren who are not in Communion with the Apostolic See."

The Constitution on the Sacred Liturgy espoused the aims of the modern liturgical movement, but perhaps with an emphasis on "modern" that not all leaders in the liturgical movement would have endorsed. Thirty years after the promulgation of the Constitution we have the historical hindsight to recognize that while the Constitution called for the "full, conscious, and active participation" of the faithful "which is demanded by the very nature of the liturgy" and to which the Christian people have the right and duty "by reason of their baptism" (I, 14), in effect it adopted the humanist view of the sixteenth-century reformers that religious truth requires verbal intelligibility, and the Rationalist view of the Enlightenment that edification of the people requires "noble simplicity." For the most part, the Constitution itself avoided the recommendation of verbal pedagogy for the good of the uneducated, such as we find in Reformation and Enlightenment liturgies. But this was made up for by the practice of narrative liturgies during the time in which the reformed Roman mass was being introduced. The commentators (usually lay readers standing at a lectern) tended to attract attention to themselves that should have been given to the liturgical action and ministers; and in their expositions no allowance was made for the ineffable, the mysterious, the obscure, or for silence. The mass became an object lesson for the commentary. Thankfully that practice has waned (although one still finds on occasion "narrative eucharists" in which a commentator explains each part of the service in the interest of helping worshipers understand it).

In reaction to this heavy injection of didacticism into the liturgy, the tendency has been to take seriously Jungmann's statement that "Mass properly celebrated is itself the best catechesis."[59] If the mass were celebrated with dignity and grace, a sense of mystery in worship would be preserved. That sense has not always been maintained in the styles in which the reformed liturgies have been celebrated. Not surprisingly, many Catholic faithful do not find the reformed liturgies compelling or even edifying. So perhaps this section should end with the observation that if more attention had been given to Chapters VI and VII, on Sacred Music and Sacred Art, respectively, the liturgical reforms might have fostered the kind of restoration of the liturgy that the Constitution truly desired.

🍇 LITURGICAL WORK IN AN ECUMENICAL CONTEXT

The Second Vatican Council was truly ecumenical. While it was a world meeting of the bishops of the Roman Catholic Church, seldom have the views of ecumenical observers to a denominational meeting been so eagerly sought. The doctrinal emphases of the council, such as the primacy of grace, the centrality of the scriptures in the life of the church, the view of the church as the people of God, the revitalization of the priesthood of the baptized, and the need of the church to take seriously inculturation in pursuit of the mission of the gospel, challenged the Reformation churches to take seriously their own reforming heritages. The council sparked a great interest in ecumenical cooperation in an area in which it had not occurred previously—in liturgical reform.

Protestants had already had some experience of working and studying interdenominationally in the nineteenth century in Missionary societies, in the YMCA, the YWCA, the Student Volunteer movement, and the Student Christian movement. These initiatives flourished in the twentieth century in the Life and Work movement, the Faith and Order movement, and conciliarism (local, regional, national, and the World Councils of Churches, the latter of which included Eastern Orthodox churches as members). Roman Catholics also began to participate in conciliar work and in numerous bilateral dialogues. It is not surprising that almost from the outset the modern liturgical movement became ecumenical. The ecumenical movement made appreciative contact between the churches possible at a time when common cultural challenges required similar pastoral strategies.

Protestants as well as Roman Catholics were looking for means of combating modern individualism and social disintegration with practices that would foster a sense of community. Liturgical renewalists had an instinct for the role ritual and symbols could

---

[59] Josef A. Jungmann, *The Mass: An Historical, Theological, and Pastoral Survey,* trans. by Julian Fernandes, S.J., ed. by Mary Ellen Evans (Collegeville: The Liturgical Press, 1976), 263.

play in providing community cohesion and identity.[60] Protestants and Roman Catholics alike employed this instinct to promote a more frequent celebration of and participation in the eucharistic meal and also encouraged more vigorous congregational singing.

But what songs should be sung? The period of the 1960s and 1970s were marked by cultural pluralism. The Civil Rights movement of the 1960s and the anti-Vietnam War protests of 1966–1976 tore apart any consensus that might have existed previously, not just concerning politics but also concerning lifestyle. It seemed as if everything from sexual morality to hair style was subject to individual choice. Society was becoming more sensitive to various forms of discrimination: racism, sexism, ageism, and so forth. This prompted, at first, an assertion of one's identity, leading inevitably to a search for the "roots" of one's identity: racial, ethnic, sexual, and so forth. Alex Haley's *Roots*, published as a book in 1976 and viewed by tens of millions as a television series in 1977, was symptomatic of this phenomenon. The positive impact that *Roots* had on African Americans was incalculable; but it also sent other Americans on a quest to discover their own "roots." Thus, once again, the situation was ripe for a serious consideration of liturgical reform that simultaneously probed the tradition and addressed contemporary culture. But cultural pluralism made the publication of hardback worship books very problematic. It would have been difficult in the 1970s to achieve any consensus in matters of language or music. In an unprecedented situation, in which radical changes were occurring in society and radical reforms were being proposed in the churches, it seemed wise to produce a series of "trial services," as they were called in the Episcopal Church, to test what the ordinary worshipers would find meaningful, or at least tolerable. Marion Hatchett has called this "the period of paperback liturgies."[61]

Many of the mainline Western churches were working on liturgical revisions at the same time, and they did more than just look over one another's shoulders. Official ecumenical liturgical consultations have been organized, beginning with the International Consultation on English Texts (ICET) in 1969 by representatives of Roman Catholic and Protestant churches from about ten English-speaking countries. ICET worked on texts of the Lord's Prayer, Apostles' Creed, Nicene Creed, Kyrie, Gloria, Sursum Corda dialogue and Sanctus, Agnus Dei, and other liturgical canticles such as the Magnificat, Nunc dimittis, and Benedictus. These were published as *Prayers We Have in Common* in 1970, and then revised in 1972 and again in 1975.[62] These common texts have been included in various worship books of the participating churches, although not without amendment. For example, the Roman mass has included the ICET text of the doxology but not the

---

[60] La Maison-Dieu, Vol. XX, is devoted to "Valeur permanente du symbolisme" which prepared the way for a deeper appreciation of symbolism in rites, gestures, music, etc. The Notre Dame symposium on *The Roots of Ritual* opened the door to the contribution of cultural anthropologists to the study of liturgy. The Notre Dame Center for Pastoral Liturgy sponsored another symposium in 1992, entitled "Reclaiming our Rites," the papers of which were published in *Studia Liturgica* vol. 23, No. 1 (1993). The Center's publication, *Liturgy Digest* vol. 1, No. 1 (1993) revisited "The Roots of Ritual."

[61] Marion J. Hatchett, *Sanctifying Life, Time, and Space: An Introduction to Liturgical Study* (New York: The Seabury Press, 1976), 160ff.

[62] *Prayers We Have in Common* (Philadelphia: Fortress Press, 1970; enlarged and revised 1972; 2nd rev. ed. 1975).

petitions of the Lord's Prayer; and the Inter-Lutheran Commission on Worship altered the ICET text of the Apostles' Creed to retain "he descended into hell" in place of "he descended to the dead."[63]

A less-publicized body was the Consultation on Ecumenical Hymnody, which reviewed hymns in North American hymnals to determine which hymn texts and tunes could be recommended for retention in new hymnals. This required making decisions on the best translation and the marriage of text and tune, since common hymn texts are often given different tunes in different hymnals. A final list of 230 hymns was approved in 1971 and recommended to the churches.[64]

Among the most significant ecumenical borrowings were the Protestant adaptations of the Roman Catholic *Ordo Lectionum Missae* (1969 and 1980), which provided three lessons and a responsorial psalm for each Sunday and festival over a three-year cycle.[65] This lectionary cycle, with its church year calendar, was adopted, with alterations, by the Episcopal Church in *Prayer Book Studies 19: The Church Year* (1970), by the Presbyterian churches in the *Worshipbook* (1970), and by the Lutheran churches in *Contemporary Worship 6: The Church Year Calendar and Lectionary* (1973). It has since been included in the *Book of Common Prayer* (1979), *Lutheran Book of Worship* (1978), as well as in new worship books of the United Church of Christ (using the Presbyterian version), the Christian Church (Disciples of Christ), the United Methodist Church, the Presbyterian Church (U.S.A.), the United Church of Canada, and the Anglican Church of Canada. Homily preparation helps such as Fortress Press's *Proclamation* series and The Liturgical Conference's *Homily Service* have undoubtedly helped to shore up the use of the three-year lectionary in churches that have traditionally not followed a lectionary system. The adoption of the three-year lectionary for Sundays and festivals, however, required the adoption of the church year calendar, so that the major feast days (Christmas, Epiphany, Easter, Ascension, Pentecost) and the pivotal cycles of Advent-Christmas and Lent-Easter have secured a place in Protestant churches that these seasons had not had heretofore.

In 1978 the Consultation on Common Texts (CCT) undertook a review and revision of the three-year so-called Ecumenical Lectionary in an attempt to reconcile differences in the lectionaries of the various churches, to provide for greater selections of Old Testament narratives during the time after Pentecost, and to provide for the adjustment of the readings during the Sundays after Pentecost by eliminating excess readings at the beginning of the Pentecost season (as the Roman Catholics, Episcopalians, and Methodists do) rather than at the end of the Pentecost season (as the Lutherans and Presbyterians have done). There was also concern among Protestants that the Roman

---

[63] Eugene Brand, *"The Lutheran Book of Worship at 'Mid-life,'"* *Lutheran Forum* 27 (1993), 19, confides that this was to placate Missouri Synod objections, although it did not prevent the Missouri Synod's last-minute withdrawal of support for *LBW*. On the other hand, the "harrowing of hell" is a vibrant aspect of the Christus Victor view of the atonement, which the church may be richer for having. The mid-section of the Apostles' Creed, including "he descended into hell," seems to be based on 1 Peter 3:18–22.

[64] Items with an asterisk in the Index of the First Lines of Hymns in *Lutheran Book of Worship* are hymns recommended by the Consultation on Ecumenical Hymnody.

[65] See Claude Wiéner, "The Roman Catholic Eucharistic Lectionary," *Studia Liturgica* 21/1 (1991), 2–13.

lectionary was a eucharistic lectionary (hence the gospel is the "controlling" reading and the pericopes tend to be brief), whereas the Sunday worship of most Protestant churches (the Disciples of Christ excepted) tends to be noneucharistic—a Service of the Word with a major role for the sermon. The CCT proposal was published as the *Common Lectionary 1983*, which gave an expanded role to the Old Testament readings on the Sundays after Pentecost.[66] After several years of trial use and reaction, the CCT published a *Revised Common Lectionary* (1992), which has been included in new United Methodist and Presbyterian worship books, and approved for use in the Evangelical Lutheran Church in Canada in 1994, the Evangelical Lutheran Church in America in 1995, and in the Episcopal Church in dioceses in which the bishop gives approval.

Even the principle of a three-year ecumenical or common lectionary has not been adopted by the Protestant churches in Europe. They have consistently chosen to revise the one-year historic lectionary with supplemental preaching texts. The United Lutheran Church in Germany retains the one-year historic lectionary with a six-year cycle of preaching texts on which pastors are to base their sermons.[67] A Joint Liturgical Group (JLG) in Great Britain, whose membership is drawn from Roman Catholic, Anglican, Reformed, Methodist, and Baptist churches, worked on another ecumenical lectionary system for the use of the churches in those countries that follow a thematic approach rather than *lectio continua*.[68] This lectionary depends on the revised church year calendar proposed by the JLG, which pivots around Christmas, Easter, and Pentecost. Probably the unique feature of this calendar is the proposal of a nine-week pre-Christmas series that includes such pre-incarnation themes as creation and fall, the covenant of preservation (Noah), the election of God's people (Abraham), and the promise of redemption (Moses). It is evident in this system that the gospel is no longer necessarily the "controlling" reading.

In any event, a formidable ecumenical consensus has been achieved in the liturgical work of the period since about 1969. In addition to the worldwide use of the Roman Catholic rites, those churches which have published English-language worship books have had an impact even in non-English-speaking parts of the world because English tends to be the world's second language. In regional denominational or ecumenical conferences in parts of Africa and Asia, for example, English is used in order to overcome the multiplicity of local languages. English-language worship materials from such resources as the *Book of Common Prayer* (1979), *Lutheran Book of Worship* (1978), the *United Methodist Hymnal* (1989) and *The Presbyterian Hymnal* (1990) are used at regional and

---

[66] *Common Lectionary: The Lectionary Proposed by the Consultation on Common Texts* (New York: Church Hymnal Corporation, 1982). Apologists for this lectionary revision include Horace T. Allen, Jr., "The Promise of the Common Lectionary," *Accent on Worship* 3:2 (1985), 4, 8; "Common Lectionary: Origins, Assumptions, and Issues," *Studia Liturgica* 21/1 (1991), 14–30; and Hans Boehringer, "The Other New Lectionary," *Lutheran Forum* 18 (1984), 27–8; "The Common Lectionary," *Word and World* X/1 (1990), 27–32.

[67] See Karl-Heinrich Bieritz, "The Order of Readings and Sermon Texts for the German Lutheran Church," *Studia Liturgica* 21/1 (1991), 37–51.

[68] See Donald Gray, "The Contribution of the Joint Liturgical Group to the Search for an Ecumenical Lectionary," *Studia Liturgica* 21, No. 1 (1991), 31–6.

international church meetings, and they will influence liturgical developments in the younger churches just as surely as Roman liturgical materials influenced trans-Alpine liturgical books in the early Middle Ages. This makes the ecumenical liturgical consensus very important for the worldwide church at the end of the twentieth century. The specific content of this consensus will be explored in the next chapter, along with challenges to this consensus that have emerged from within the very circles that have nurtured it. But here we must affirm that nothing will advance Christian unity more than common liturgical orders and texts through which a common experience of God is encountered in the arena of public worship.

CHAPTER 18

Liturgical Revision
and Renewal

Ｉｎ the last quarter of the twentieth century, a massive ecumenical consensus has emerged concerning the forms and content of Christian liturgy in the Roman Catholic and Reformation churches as a result of the impact of the modern liturgical movement. Scholars and pastoral leaders inspired by the movement gained places on official liturgical commissions. As a result, worship books developed along similar lines and in an ecumenical context. A common shape of the liturgy of word and meal may be observed in the liturgical orders provided in the new worship books of these traditions. Ecumenical dialogue has produced convergence on issues in eucharistic theology that were formerly church-dividing. The worshiping communities that use these books also observe a common pattern in the church year calendar and the Roman Catholic Church and several North American Protestant churches use variant forms of a common three-year lectionary. This ecumenical lectionary (derived from the Roman *Ordo Lectionum*) and the common lectionary based upon it was not the only gift of a renewed Roman Catholicism to Protestant worship. The Roman Catholic Rite of Christian Initiation of Adults has had some limited impact on processes of Christian initiation and faith formation in other traditions. New attention has also been given to the initiation and faith formation of children. Rites of passage have been revised along similar lines in the Roman Catholic and mainline Protestant traditions. Hymnals reflect a shared body of hymnody, each one appropriating the best of several traditions. The modern liturgical movement has profoundly influenced the design of liturgical environment or worship space. In spite of this enormous consensus, however, all of the churches are being challenged on issues of inculturation, inclusive language, and reaching the unchurched. In this concluding chapter we will lay out the consensus that has emerged, and also consider the cultural challenges to this consensus.

🍇 WORSHIP BOOKS SINCE C. 1969

Our first task is to survey the array of official worship books that have been developed and authorized in Western churches, particularly in North America, which stand in the Western catholic tradition. It is difficult to chose a year with which to begin this survey, but about 1969 was when these new worship books began to emerge.

Experimentation in liturgical renewal was beginning already during the time in which the Second Vatican Council was meeting. An "interim" liturgy was implemented in Advent of 1964, in which the people were invited to recite or sing the choral texts of the mass (e.g., Gloria, Creed) and the dialogues, the prayers of the faithful were introduced after the Creed, and some of the prayers at the foot of the altar and the "last Gospel" were suppressed.[1] Liturgical experimentation was accelerated as a result of the ecumenical experiences of worship and celebration during the Civil Rights and anti-Vietnam War movements during the 1960s. These celebrations brought music of a folk and popular character into worship services.[2] There were also efforts to revitalize the singing of psalms in Christian worship through translations that recovered the musicalities of Hebrew verse set to modern psalms tones, such as those composed by Joseph Gelineau for the Taizé Community in France and translated into English.[3] Unofficial experiments with liturgical texts appeared in Roman Catholic circles about 1968–1970,[4] including *The Experimental Liturgy Book*.[5] 1969 was the year when the first official "experimental liturgy books" began to appear, such as the *Worship Supplement* of the Lutheran Church–Missouri Synod. In Advent of 1969 the *Missale Romanum: Editio Typica* was promulgated.

The fruits of the Constitution on the Sacred Liturgy and the Instruction for the Implementation of the Constitution of 1967 began to show during the next ten years in the Roman Catholic Church. Once a Latin editio typica text was approved by the Consilium for the Implementation of the Constitution (merged into the Congregation for Divine Worship in 1969, renamed the Congregation for the Sacraments and Divine Worship in 1975), the text was sent to international commissions for preparing translations into

---

[1] See W. Baraúna, ed., *The Liturgy of Vatican II*, 2 Vols. (Chicago, 1966).

[2] An early example is Ewald Bash and John Ylvisaker, *Songs for Today* (Minneapolis: The American Lutheran Church, 1963)—with many such collections to follow.

[3] There have been collections of 30, 24, and all 150 psalms and 12 canticles using the text of the Jerusalem Bible and set by Joseph Gelineau published by G.I.A. Publications in Chicago.

[4] The prayer and hymn collection of Huub Oosterhuis, *In het Voorbijgaan* (Utrecht: Ambo, 1968) was published in two volumes in English translation: *Prayers, Poems & Songs*, trans. by David Smith (New York: Herder and Herder, 1970) and *Open Your Hearts*, trans. by David Smith (New York: Herder and Herder, 1971). See also Jean-Thierry Maertens, Marguerite de Bilde et al., *Livre de la prière* (Paris: Editions du Centurion, 1969).

[5] Robert F. Hoey, *The Experimental Liturgy Book* (New York: Herder and Herder, 1969).

different languages. The International Commission on English in the Liturgy (ICEL) has been responsible for preparing English translations of Roman orders for use in eleven nations. An episcopal board representing the national bishops' conferences in each of these countries oversees the work of translation and approves the final product. But this in turn must by affirmed by Rome and approved by the national conference of bishops. ICEL paved the way for the work of Protestant liturgical revision since Roman Catholics were not bound to traditional English texts (often in Elizabethan style) and were free to experiment with English prose.

The chief Roman Catholic liturgical books have been the Roman Missal (1970), which includes the Sacramentary and the Lectionary;[6] the Liturgy of the Hours (1971), which has been the least successful of the Roman Catholic liturgical reforms because of its reliance on the monastic model; and the Rite of Initiation of Adults (1972), which has been the most radical of the Roman Catholic liturgical and pastoral reforms. The final products have been typically farmed out to commercial publishers, and therefore the Roman Missal, Sacramentary, Lectionary, Ritual, Pontifical, and so forth, are published in different editions.[7] The Roman Catholic Church does not authorize an official hymnal, so various hymnals are used in Roman Catholic worship.

The Episcopal Church in the U.S.A. had been involved in the work of liturgical revision since 1950, when the first in the series of *Prayer Book Studies* was published. This was twenty-five years after work stopped on the 1928 Prayer Book. Ultimately twenty-eight volumes of *Prayer Book Studies* would be published, which serve now as a chronicle of liturgical scholarship and evolving ideas of renewal during the whole period between 1950 and 1975. Some of these studies resulted in *Services for Trial Use* in 1970; *Authorized Services* in 1973; and *The Draft Proposed Book of Common Prayer* in 1976. After three years of trial use the American *Book of Common Prayer* was approved by the General Convention and authorized for use in 1979.[8] *The Hymnal 1982* replaced *The Hymnal 1940*, and contains service music as well as hymns.[9] Completing the collection of authorized worship books for use in the Episcopal Church is *The Book of Occasional Services*, published concurrently with the *BCP* in 1979.[10]

Close examination of the content of the major denominational worship books is not possible here. Detailed commentaries exist for several of the major books, and these are listed in the bibliography. However, each worship book has several unique features that are worth highlighting here. One unique feature of the *BCP* is that it includes prayers and rites in both traditional and contemporary English speech. Thus, Morning Prayer and Evening Prayer and the Holy Eucharist appear as Rite One (traditional

---

[6] The International Consultation on English Texts (ICET) published the definitive English language version of *The Roman Missal*, the *Roman Sacramentary*, and *The Roman Lectionary* in 1973.

[7] The most frequently cited English editions are *The Sacramentary* (New York: Catholic Book Publishing Co., 1973, 1985), *The Roman Missal: Lectionary for the Mass* (Collegeville: The Liturgical Press, 1970), *The Roman Missal: Sacramentary for the Mass* (Collegeville: The Liturgical Press, 1974), and *The Rites* (New York: Pueblo Publishing Co., 1976, 1983.)

[8] *The Book of Common Prayer* (New York: The Church Hymnal Corporation, 1979).

[9] *The Hymnal 1982* (New York: The Church Hymnal Corporation, 1985).

[10] *The Book of Occasional Services* (New York: The Church Hymnal Corporation, 1979).

language) and Rite Two (contemporary language). The eucharistic prayer in Rite One is also the traditional American Prayer Book eucharistic prayer. Four new eucharistic prayers are provided for Rite Two. There are also six forms for the prayer of the church in contemporary English. Other sacramental rites included in the *BCP* are in contemporary English. There are proper liturgies for Ash Wednesday, Palm Sunday, Maundy Thursday, Good Friday, Holy Saturday, and the Great Vigil of Easter. The importance of baptism in Christian life and worship has been reclaimed by placing the Order for Holy Baptism before the Holy Eucharist in the content of the Prayer Book, and not with the Pastoral Offices.

Even though the *Service Book and Hymnal* was only a few years old, Lutherans began working on a new worship book at the invitation of President Oliver Harms of the Lutheran Church–Missouri Synod, in 1966, to form an Inter-Lutheran Commission on Worship (ILCW), which he extended to the American Lutheran Church and the Lutheran Church in America.[11] *The Lutheran Hymnal* used by the Missouri and Wisconsin Synods (partners in the Synodical Conference) was twenty-five years old in 1966 and in need of revision. It should be understood that in 1966 no widespread dissatisfaction with the *SBH* had surfaced. But the Lutheran Church in America, as the heir of the Muhlenberg tradition, was committed to the ideal of one Lutheran worship book and one Lutheran church organization in North America; and this invitation from the Missouri Synod was too good to pass up.[12] Moreover, the Lutheran Church in America was in a position to give leadership to the organization of inter-Lutheran liturgical work since it was the first denomination to have a full-time staff person in worship. The first incumbent of that office was Dr. Edgar S. Brown, Jr. The Lutheran Church in America had already been publishing supplemental material to the *SBH* under the authority of its Commission on Worship.[13]

The Commission on Worship of the Lutheran Church–Missouri Synod had also been at work. The first decision of the Inter-Lutheran Commission on Worship was to agree to the publication of the paperback *Worship Supplement*, reflecting the work already done by the Commission on Worship of the Missouri Synod, in 1969.[14] The ILCW began to publish its own paperback *Contemporary Worship* series in 1969.[15] This was a slim collection of new hymns; the Service of Holy Communion followed in 1970. The

---

[11] The story of the Inter-Lutheran Commission on Worship is told in Philip H. Pfatteicher, *Commentary on the Lutheran Book of Worship* (Minneapolis: Augsburg Fortress, 1990), 4–11. Since this book is a companion to Pfatteicher, the story of the ILCW will not be repeated here.

[12] See W. Kent Gilbert, *Commitment to Unity: A History of the Lutheran Church in America* (Philadelphia: Fortress Press, 1980), 226–7, 317–9.

[13] *The Occasional Services* (Minneapolis: Augsburg, 1962); *Holy Week and Easter: Liturgical Orders Supplementing the Service Book and Hymnal* (Philadelphia: Fortress, 1964).

[14] *Worship Supplement*. Authorized by the Commission on Worship of the Lutheran Church–Missouri Synod and the Synod of Evangelical Lutheran Churches (St. Louis and London: Concordia Publishing House, 1969).

[15] See Pfatteicher, *Commentary on the Lutheran Book of Worship*, 8; also Eugene L. Brand, "The ILCW: Dimensions of Its Task," *dialog* 14 (1975), 90–6. See also "A Background Paper for a Theological Review of Materials Produced by the Inter-Lutheran Commission on Worship" prepared by William G. Rusch in January 1977, for the review of ILCW materials by the faculties of the Lutheran theological seminaries.

pluralism of the age was reflected in the fact that the *Worship Supplement* included three different orders for the Holy Eucharist with three eucharistic prayers (including a contemporary translation of the Anaphora of Hippolytus) and three different orders for a Service of Prayer and Preaching. While *Contemporary Worship 2: The Holy Communion* provided only one order and text, the texts were set to four different musical settings ranging from a type of church chant to folk music. Music has been important in the Lutheran liturgical tradition, so two of the ten *Contemporary Worship* booklets were collections of hymns. In all, ten booklets were published in the *Contemporary Worship* series, the last being a collection of Great Thanksgivings.

The work of the ILCW led to the approval and publication of *Lutheran Book of Worship* in 1978.[16] *LBW* was authorized for use in the American Lutheran Church, the Lutheran Church in America, and the Association of Evangelical Lutheran Churches, which merged in 1988 to form the Evangelical Lutheran Church in America, as well as in the Evangelical Lutheran Church of Canada, which merged with the Canadian section of the Lutheran Church in America in 1987 to form the Evangelical Lutheran Church in Canada. At its 1977 convention, however, the Lutheran Church–Missouri Synod withheld its approval of *LBW* and proceeded in 1979 with work on its own version, *Lutheran Worship* (1982),[17] although many Missouri Synod congregations adopted *LBW* in the years before *LW* was published.

Lutheran Book of Worship was published in two editions: the Pew Edition and the Ministers Edition. Additional materials in the ministers book that are not in the pew book are the notes on the liturgy, proper liturgies for Ash Wednesday, Palm Sunday, Maundy Thursday, Good Friday, and the Easter Vigil, additional eucharistic prayers (including the Anaphora of Hippolytus), the complete psalter with a psalter collect for each psalm, and extra hymnological indexes for worship planning. The ministers book lacks the hymnal. The orders that are ecumenically noteworthy are those for Holy Baptism, which uses baptism in Hippolytus's *Apostolic Tradition* as a model, Morning Prayer, with its concluding Paschal Blessing for Sundays, and Evening Prayer, with its Lucernarium.

Lutheran Worship was a compromise that included revised versions in contemporary English of the Service of Holy Communion (Divine Service I), Matins and Vespers from *The Lutheran Hymnal* as well as versions of the Service of Holy Communion (Divine Service II, with two musical settings), Morning Prayer and Evening Prayer from *LBW*. Divine Service III in *LW* is comparable to the Chorale Service in *LBW*, both of which were based on the tradition of Luther's *Deutsche Messe*. *LW* follows the order of the German Mass more faithfully than *LBW*, since *LBW* was concerned to use the

---

[16] *Lutheran Book of Worship* (Minneapolis: Augsburg Publishing House; and Philadelphia: Board of Publication, Lutheran Church in America, 1978) is the generic name covering several books that compose the complete liturgical corpus: the Pew Edition, the Ministers Edition (in two formats: the Altar Book and a Desk Edition), the *Accompaniment Edition Liturgy* and the *Organist Edition Hymns*.

[17] The final report of the Review Committee, *Report and Recommendations of the Special Hymnal Review Committee* (St. Louis: The Lutheran Church–Missouri Synod, n.d.), recommended to the Missouri Synod that *LBW* be accepted with modifications, and then after summarizing those suggested modifications provided forty pages of detailed commentary on them. This became the basis for work on *Lutheran Worship* (St. Louis: Concordia Publishing House, 1982).

chorales as a musical setting but keep the order of the Service of Holy Communion as it is otherwise given. The two musical settings of Divine Service II and the musical settings of Morning Prayer and Evening Prayer are the same as the comparable musical settings in *LBW*, with a few slight modifications in melodic lines (which surely trips users of one book who have occasion to use the other). In the Service of Holy Communion *LW* follows the Common Service order by placing the Lord's Prayer before the words of institution. Unlike *LBW*, it does not provide full eucharistic prayers. This is lamentable within an ecclesial body that first explored and tested eucharistic prayers within American Lutheranism.[18] Instead, *LW* provides a prayer between the Sanctus and the Lord's Prayer that is really a type of prayer for worthy communion. Divine Service I uses a version of the post-Sanctus prayer found in *Agenda I* (1955) of the United Lutheran Church in Germany. Divine Service II uses a version of the post-Sanctus prayer in the Swedish Mass of 1942, as does *LBW*. However, the *LBW* version is a more literal translation of the Swedish prayer. Divine Service I provides a chant-setting for the Words of Institution, based on the setting Luther provided in his German Mass.[19] *LW* provides a complete set of revised introits and graduals for use with Divine Service I, and its own revisions of both the historic one-year lectionary and of the ecumenical three-year lectionary. Like *LBW*, *LW* appears in a ministers or altar book that contains fuller provisions than the pew edition, including notes on the liturgy, the complete psalter, and additional indexes. Charles Evanson was undoubtedly correct in assessing that "*Lutheran Worship* is a cautious move forward for the Missouri Synod."[20]

Companion volumes have accompanied both *LBW* and *LW*. *Occasional Services: A Companion to Lutheran Book of Worship* was published in 1982.[21] Occasional services for use in the Missouri Synod were published in *Lutheran Worship: Little Agenda* in 1985.[22] Quasi-official hymnal companions and interpretative commentaries have also been published for both worship books.

The 400,000-member Wisconsin Evangelical Lutheran Synod had shared *The Lutheran Hymnal* with the Missouri Synod, but it was not prepared to adopt *LBW* or *LW*. Its roots were deeply pietistic, and while it had embraced the kind of orthodox theology practiced in the Missouri Synod it had not produced the kind of liturgical leaders who could exert the profound influence of a Luther D. Reed or an Arthur Carl Piepkorn. Worship leaders of this synod knew that they must have a more contemporary worship book, but felt that they should build carefully on the principles enshrined in *The Lutheran Hymnal*. After several years of careful study and work the worship committee produced *Christian Worship: A Lutheran Hymnal* (1993). In addition to an updating of

---

[18] See Arthur Carl Piepkorn and Howard R. Kunkle, "The Eucharistic Prayer," *Una Sancta* VI, No. 5 (1946), 6–22, which appeared a year before the first edition of Luther D. Reed, *The Lutheran Liturgy* (Philadelphia: Muhlenberg Press, 1947), which also proposed a full eucharistic prayer.

[19] *Lutheran Worship*, 150.

[20] Charles J. Evanson, "*Lutheran Worship* At 'Mid-Life,'" *Lutheran Forum* 27, No. 4 (November, 1993), 25–7.

[21] *Occasional Services: A Companion to Lutheran Book of Worship* (Philadelphia: Board of Publications of the Lutheran Church in America and Minneapolis: Augsburg Publishing House, 1982).

[22] *Lutheran Worship: Little Agenda* (St. Louis: Concordia Publishing House, 1985).

the Common Service, and new settings of Matins and Vespers, *CW* provided a new liturgical order, "Service of Word and Sacrament." For translations of the Nicene Creed and many of the liturgical canticles, *CW* uses the translations of the English Language Liturgical Consultation. Some musical settings of canticles were borrowed from other Lutheran worship books. The hymn anthology expanded beyond sixteenth-century German hymnody into eighteenth- and nineteenth-century English and American hymnody. *CW* thus seeks to move the Wisconsin Synod in a more catholic and ecumenical direction.

The integral role of music in Lutheran worship is indicated by the fact that Lutheran worship books continue to be two books in one: service books and hymnals. Unlike other traditions, Lutheran service music is printed in place within the liturgical orders. While this may seem like a principle that limits the development of additional liturgical settings, it does ensure that liturgies will be sung. Nevertheless, additional settings of the liturgies have been composed, and settings of proper Alleluia and Offertory verses have also been written for choirs. The hymn collections include a broad spectrum of hymns from different periods and traditions, but they also include an ample selection of vigorous old Lutheran chorales. Additional musical settings of the liturgy and hymn collections have been made available by the publishing houses. Paperback collections published by Augsburg Publishing House have aimed at providing folk and gospel settings of the liturgy and songs that are more inclusive of African American, Hispanic, and other cultural contributions, as well as new hymns that are being composed.[23]

The United Methodist Church published new editions of *The Methodist Hymnal* and *The Book of Worship* in 1965, just at the time the Constitution on the Sacred Liturgy was being promulgated. Like the Lutheran *SBH*, the language of the *Book of Worship* was Cranmerian and it reflected more the Reformation heritage than the modern liturgical movement. The Commission on Worship tried to move pastors and congregations in the direction of liturgical renewal through its *Companion to the Book of Worship* and *Companion to the Hymnal* in 1970, but these were never widely used. During the 1970s the Methodist church followed the paperback route by publishing the *Ventures in Worship* series, the *Alternate Rituals* series, and finally seventeen volumes in the *Supplemental Worship Resource* series. After many revisions of these "trial services," the definitive *United Methodist Hymnal* was published in 1989.[24] This was primarily a book for the people; *The United Methodist Book of Worship* was published in 1992 for the use of worship leaders.[25] Unlike the *Presbyterian Hymnal*, discussed below, there is a considerable body of liturgical orders and texts in the *United Methodist Hymnal*, including services of word and table and "Services of the Baptismal Covenant" (orders for infant and adult baptism, confirmation, reception into membership, and reaffirmation of the baptismal covenant) as well as a psalter of 100 psalms appointed for singing based on the

---

[23] Early examples include *Songs for the Journey* (Minneapolis: Augsburg Publishing House, 1985) and *Songs of the People* (Minneapolis: Augsburg Publishing House, 1986).

[24] *The United Methodist Hymnal: Book of United Methodist Worship* (Nashville: The United Methodist Publishing House, 1989).

[25] *The United Methodist Book of Worship* (Nashville: The United Methodist Publishing House, 1992).

New Revised Standard Version of the Bible. The Revised Common Lectionary provides the Sundays readings and psalmody for United Methodist worship.

One of the unique features of United Methodist liturgical development has been the proliferation of eucharistic prayers—twenty-two in *At the Lord's Table*.[26] The United Methodist worship executive, Hoyt Hickman, shared these texts with the eucharistic prayer seminar group of the North American Academy of Liturgy and received helpful ecumenical critique. Fifteen eucharistic prayers are provided in the *United Methodist Book of Worship*, varying according to season and occasion; two additional eucharistic prayers are included in the marriage and burial liturgies. "In services without Communion, thanks are given for God's mighty acts in Jesus Christ." In these cases, the eucharistic prayers can be used without including the words of institution and the epiclesis on the bread and cup. Some material is included in the *Book of Worship* that is not in the *Hymnal*.

Joint work on worship materials has promoted unity in the Presbyterian church as it has in the Lutheran church. The *Directory for Worship* adopted in 1961 replaced the 1644 *Westminster Directory*. A 1964 leaflet, Service for the Lord's Day, and the *Book of Common Worship—Provisional Services* in 1966, prepared the way for *The Worshipbook—Services* in 1970. At this point Elizabethan English had vanished entirely, although new sensibilities regarding inclusive language had not been observed. This liturgical material was incorporated into the *Worshipbook—Services and Hymns* in 1972. For the first time, American Presbyterians had a single pew book containing all the liturgical texts, service music, and hymns. But by 1974 the sexist language of the Presbyterian liturgical material was challenged in the General Assembly. While it was considered too expensive to revise a book that had been published only two years previously, supplemental liturgical resources were developed over the next fifteen years, culminating in *The Presbyterian Hymnal* in 1990[27] and the *Book of Common Worship* in 1993.[28]

Very little liturgical textual material is included in the *Presbyterian Hymnal*, although it does contain the outline for the Service for the Lord's Day and a section of service music. The texts are in the *Book of Common Worship*. This book still provides a kind of directory of worship: Basic Movement of the Service for the Lord's Day (pp. 33–45), followed by the same Outline of the Service for the Lord's Day found in the *Presbyterian Hymnal*. Then follows The Service for the Lord's Day: Order with Liturgical Texts (pp. 48–85). Then Additional Texts for the Service for the Lord's Day are provided, followed by Resources for the Liturgical Year, Baptism and Reaffirmation of the Baptismal Covenant, Daily Prayer, The Psalms, Prayers for Various Occasions (including the Great Litany), Christian Marriage, The Funeral, Pastoral Liturgies, and Calendar and Lectionaries. This is a compendious liturgical resource reflecting the ecumenical liturgical consensus of the past century. While the Service for the Lord's Day is envisioned to be a complete service of word and sacrament, provision is also made for the Service for the Lord's Day without communion (the Ante-communion) and it remains to be seen

---

[26] *At the Lord's Table*. Supplemental Worship Resource 9 (Nashville: Abingdon, 1981).

[27] *The Presbyterian Hymnal* (Louisville: Westminster/John Knox Press, 1990).

[28] *Book of Common Worship* (Louisville: Westminster/John Knox Press, 1993).

whether modern Presbyterians will be as resistant to weekly communion as the Reformed churches have historically been. On the other hand, there has been widespread acceptance of the three-year lectionary. There is no doubt that this has greatly enriched preaching in a tradition that was already noted for its substantial pulpiteering.

Finally, we would note that significant liturgical work has been done in the United Church of Christ, which is a merger of the Congregationalist Church, representing the heritage of New England Puritanism, and the Evangelical and Reformed Church, representing the heritage of the Prussian Union Church. These unlikely partners, from the standpoint of liturgy and polity, produced a *Book of Worship: United Church of Christ* in 1986.[29] This book seeks to move United Church of Christ congregations toward a use of the catholic shape of liturgy and the three-year lectionary. The *Book of Worship* also includes a selection of ancient creeds, Reformation confessions, and contemporary statements of faith that are used in worship and at other times. The order for baptism, for example, in the *Book of Worship*, and now also in *The New Century Hymnal*, offers a responsive version of the Apostles' Creed. The only authority this book has, however, in a church that values evangelical freedom, congregational autonomy, and liberty of conscience is its usefulness in expressing the various worship traditions of this "united and uniting church." The creedal statements serve as testimonies to the apostolic faith handed down through the ages, but not as confessional tests of faith. This stance has allowed worship leaders in the United Church of Christ to utilize more inclusive language (often of a controversial nature) than in the more confessional traditions.

🍇 THE SHAPE OF LITURGY

It has been said that if the covers were removed from the major worship books of the late twentieth century, it would be difficult to tell which book belongs to which church body. This may be an overstatement, but it does reflect the fact that the liturgical orders in these books follow a common "shape" and that many of the texts in these services are the common translations of ICET. Much liturgical commentary in the twentieth century has been based on the premise that there is a pattern in liturgical worship that goes back to early descriptions of the liturgy, such as that in Justin Martyr's *Apology* I, 67.[30] This basic shape comprises what has come to be seen as a four movement structure of gathering, the word, the meal, and the dismissal. As we have seen, devotional and ceremonial elements have been added to the core elements in the liturgy without obscuring its basic shape. It suffices to provide a comparative outline of the Roman Catholic, Lutheran, Episcopal, Methodist, and Presbyterian liturgies to indicate the remarkable similarities among the revised liturgies as a result of the consensus on the shape of the liturgy across a broad confessional spectrum. In the following chart, parentheses indicate optional or interchangeable elements.

---

[29] *The Book of Worship: United Church of Christ* (New York: United Church of Christ, 1986).

[30] In addition to Dix, *The Shape of the Liturgy*, see Anton Baumstark, *Comparative Liturgy*, English trans. (London: Mowbray, 1958), who proposed that structures were the surest grounds for comparing liturgical traditions.

ROMAN MISSAL 1969	LUTHERAN BOOK OF WORSHIP 1978	BOOK OF COMMON PRAYER 1977
The Order of Mass	*The Holy Communion*	*The Holy Eucharist*
Entrance Psalm	(Brief Order for Confession)	(Hymn, Psalm, or Anthem)
Invocation and Greeting		(Penitential Rite)
	Entrance Hymn	(Hymn, psalm, or anthem)
Penitential Rite	Apostolic Greeting	Greeting and Collect
(Kyrie)	(Kyrie)	(Gloria or Kyrie or Trisagion)
(Gloria)	(Gloria or Worthy is Christ or Hymn)	
Salutation and	Salutation and	Salutation and
Collect for the Day	Prayer of the Day	Collect of the Day
First Lesson	First Lesson	First Lesson
Psalmody	Psalmody	(Psalm, hymn, or anthem)
Second Lesson	Second Lesson	Second Lesson
Alleluia Verse	Alleluia Verse	(Psalm, hymn, or anthem)
Gospel	Gospel	Gospel
Homily	Sermon	Sermon
	Silent Reflection	
	Hymn of the Day	
Nicene Creed	Nicene or Apostles' Creed	Nicene Creed
Intercessions	Prayers of the Church	Prayers of the People
	(Confession of Sin)	(Confession of Sin)
	Greeting of Peace	The Peace
Offering	Offering	Offertory Sentence
Offertory Song	Offertory Verse	Offertory Procession
Offertory Prayers	Offertory Prayer	
Preface and Sanctus	Preface and Sanctus	Preface and Sanctus
Canon (9 options)	Great Thanksgiving (5 options) or Words of Institution	Great Thanksgiving (4 options)
Lord's Prayer	Lord's Prayer	Lord's Prayer
Peace of the Lord		Breaking of the Bread
Lamb of God	Communion	Communion
Communion	(Lamb of God or	(Hymns, psalms, or anthems)
(Communion songs)	other hymns)	
Silent Reflection	Post-Communion Song	
Post-Communion Prayer	Post-Communion Prayer	Post-Communion Prayer
	Silent Reflection	
Benediction and Dismissal	Benediction and Dismissal	Blessing and Dismissal

The common shape of liturgy in these five traditions is more remarkable than the differences. Even the commonly experienced differences in liturgical order disappear with a close reading of the rubrics. For example, in practice the Service of Holy Communion in *LBW* is usually preceded by the Brief Order for Confession and Forgiveness whereas the Episcopal Eucharist, in frequent practice, includes a prayer of

THE METHODIST HYMNAL 1989	BOOK OF COMMON WORSHIP 1993
Service of Word and Table	*Service for the Lord's Day*
Gathering	Call to Worship
Greeting	Prayer of the Day
Hymn of Praise	Hymn of Praise
Opening Prayer	Confession and Pardon
	(The Peace)
(Act of Praise)	Canticle, Psalm, Hymn, or Spiritual
Prayer for Illumination	Prayer for Illumination
Scripture Lesson	First Reading
(Psalm)	Psalm
(Scripture Lesson)	Second Reading
Hymn or Song	(Anthem, Hymn, Psalm, Canticle or
	Spiritual)
Gospel Lesson	Gospel Reading
Sermon	Sermon
(Occasional Service)	Affirmation of Faith
The Apostles' Creed	(Pastoral Rite of the Church)
Concerns and Prayers	Prayers of the People
Invitation to the Table	
Confession and Pardon	
The Peace	(The Peace)
Offering	Offering
(Hymn, Psalm, or Anthem)	
	Invitation to the Table
Great Thanksgiving	Great Thanksgiving
The Lord's Prayer	Lord's Prayer
Breaking of Bread	Breaking of Bread
Giving the Bread and Cup	Communion of the People
Post-Communion Prayer	
Hymn or Song	Hymn, Spiritual, Canticle, or Psalm
Dismissal with Blessing	Charge and Blessing
Going Forth	

confession with an absolution at the end of the intercessions. The Methodist Service of Word and Table includes Confession and Pardon after the intercessions and before the Peace. However, the Brief Order for Confession and Forgiveness in *LBW* may be omitted and a prayer of confession may be included in the intercessions; and the *BCP* provides A Penitential Order "for use at the beginning of the liturgy, or as a separate service." A matter of difference may be noted, however, in the fact that the Brief Order for Confession and Forgiveness is intended to precede the actual Service of Holy Communion, as a preparatory office, whereas the penitential rite is now integrated with the entrance rite in the Roman Mass, the Episcopal Eucharist, and the Presbyterian Service for the Lord's Day. In the Lutheran Service this represents a survival of the location of the prayers at the foot of the altar before the introit for the day. Another dissimilarity is that in the Roman Order of Mass, the old position of the peace before the communion is retained whereas in the other liturgies the peace is shared before the offertory. Here again, however, a rubric in *LBW* allows the peace to be shared before the communion, as in the Roman rite.

These liturgies also allow for flexibility in the entrance rite. It is not envisioned that the Kyrie and Canticle of Praise will both be used on all days and occasions. Traditionally, the canticle of praise has been omitted during the penitential seasons of Advent and Lent; the Kyrie may be omitted during Christmas and Easter; and the canticle chosen will depend on the day or season (e.g., "Glory to God in the highest" during Christmas–Epiphany, "Worthy is Christ" during Easter, the Thrice-Holy hymn during the Sundays after Pentecost). The flexibility built into the new liturgical orders requires that ministers and worship leaders know the rubrics and also be sensitive to the needs both of the occasion and of the assembly.[31]

The liturgy of the word is remarkably similar in all of these orders. Readings from the Hebrew Bible and psalmody have secured an immovable place in the new lectionaries as the salvation-historical context of the Christ-event proclaimed in the epistle and gospel. The sermon follows directly from the gospel and its preceding readings and obviously should be based on the readings rather than on some point of dogma or on a "topic" of the minister's choosing. The juxtaposition of readings and sermon will probably do much to encourage biblically based preaching and discourage topical or dogmatic preaching. The Lutheran tradition of a proper hymn of the day allows also for a musical proclamation of the word. The hymn may precede or follow the sermon, or engulf it. A litany form of the intercessions and thanksgivings has replaced the old general or pastoral prayers in all of these traditions, which brings the people verbally into the prayers of the people. It is envisioned that the intercessions and thanksgivings will be related to both the lectionary and the specific concerns of the local assembly.[32]

One of the controversial features of the revised liturgies has been the Gregory Dix-inspired revival of the offertory of the faithful in which the laity present the gifts of bread and wine, along with other gifts, to the presiding minister at the offertory.[33] Those

---

[31] Frank C. Senn, *The Pastor as Worship Leader*, op. cit., was written to inculcate the idea that rubrics must be applied with knowledge of the tradition and pastoral sensitivity to the local assembly and its environment.

[32] A model for this kind of praying is provided in Gail Ramshaw, ed., *Intercessions for the Christian People* (New York: Pueblo Publishing House, 1988).

[33] See Alfred Shands, *The Liturgical Movement and the Local Church* (New York: Morehouse-Barlow Co., 1965), 105ff.

who espoused this action saw it as a way of connecting liturgy with actual life in the world.[34] While the action gained wide acceptance in Anglican and Roman Catholic practice, it has not been without its theological and liturgical critics. The former Archbishop of Canterbury, Michael Ramsey, warned of "a shallow and romantic sort of Pelagianism" in the revived offertory procession and its emphasis on the self-offering of the people; "for we cannot, and we dare not, offer aught of our own apart from the one sacrifice of the Lamb of God."[35] Eric Mascall was also critical of the development of offertory theology as dangerously misleading unless it were qualified by the recognition that the produce of the earth, manufactured by human beings into bread and wine, partake of the fallenness of the creation and needs to be transformed by inclusion in the self-offering of Christ.[36] Colin Buchanan was far more critical of the restored offertory rite, charging that

> (1) The preparation of the elements is not an instituted act; (2) The word "offertory" is inappropriate in relation to the elements; (3) Collecting of alms has no relation to preparing the elements; (4) The use of 1 Chron. 29 ought to be confined to the collections of money; (5) The use of any words about the bread and wine prior to the Thanksgiving is misleading; (6) We do not need redundant processions in order to encourage active lay participation in the liturgy.[37]

W. Jardine Grisbrooke, after an exhaustive theological and liturgical analysis of the offertory, concluded that the offertory procession is an artificial construct that is theologically misleading and liturgically clumsy. He suggested instead the Eastern Orthodox practice of the people presenting their offerings at some convenient place when they arrive at church and the deacon taking from these offerings what is needed for the eucharist and bringing them to the altar before the Great Thanksgiving. Grisbrooke was willing to grant the use of an offertory prayer, provided that it did not anticipate the oblation in the anaphora.[38] What these European critics may not recognize in terms of the American context is the need to counter the prevalence of a creation-escaping, world-denying gnostic spirituality, one that devalues the material world. Gordon Lathrop has advocated "the recovery of the use of the Sunday collection primarily or even only for the poor."[39] During the collection, bread and wine from the material creation are also placed on the table. The offertory has also become a place for recognizing vocations and the exercise of gifts within the liturgical assembly and in the life and mission of the congregation, which

---

[34] See John A. T. Robinson, *Liturgy Coming to Life* (Philadelphia: The Westminster Press, 1960), 62.

[35] Michael Ramsey, "The Parish Communion," in *Durham Essays and Addresses* (London: S.P.C.K., 1956), 18.

[36] See the essay on "The Eucharist and the Order of Creation" appended to Eric L. Mascall, *Corpus Christi* (London: Longmans, 1953), 178–85.

[37] Colin Buchanan, *The End of the Offertory: An Anglican Study.* Grove Liturgy Study No. 14 (Bramcote: Grove Books, 1978), 38–40.

[38] W. Jardine Grisbrooke, "Oblation at the Eucharist, II. The Liturgical Issues," *Studia Liturgica* IV, No. 1 (1965), 37–50.

[39] See Gordon Lathrop, *Holy Things*, 156.

serves the needs of churches in North America and elsewhere that rely on the volunteer ministries of the laity.[40]

The books of each tradition now provide several eucharistic prayers.[41] The Roman rite led the way in the proliferation of eucharistic prayers when Pope Paul VI made the decision that in the reformed Roman rite the historic Roman canon would be slightly revised and supplemented with additional eucharistic prayers drawing on other Eastern and Western traditions. The nine prayers in the Roman rite include two for masses of reconciliation and three for masses with children. There has been a preference for the shape of the West Syrian anaphora in the eucharistic prayers in the new worship books. Component parts of these eucharistic prayers include: introductory dialogue, preface, Sanctus, post-Sanctus bridge or salvation history narration leading to the institution narrative, anamnesis, epiclesis, intercessions and commemorations, and concluding doxology.[42] Differences between the eucharistic prayers of the various traditions—for example, the double epiclesis in the Roman prayers, concerns over whether to place the epiclesis on the gifts before or after the institution narrative, the resistance to the language of sacrifice in the Lutheran prayers, the reticence to include commemorations of the saints and intercessions in the Protestant prayers, as well as the invariable use of the West Syrian shape—reflect the state of liturgical and theological scholarship at the time these prayers were developed. As a result of ecumenical dialogue and further liturgical study, drafting committees might be able to move beyond these confessional impasses as work continues on the writing of eucharistic prayers. It is also possible that church bodies would be willing to accept eucharistic prayers that follow a variety of structures and traditions, such as those that have been included in the 1986 Swedish Church Manual.[43] Liturgists at the end of the twentieth century are coming to recognize that eucharistic origins were more diverse than the liturgical historians of the early twentieth century were willing to admit. For example, it would seem that a bipartite structure of thanksgiving-supplication is even older in the eucharistic tradition than the tripartite structure of praise-remembrance-supplication.[44] There is a need to interest liturgical commissions in experimenting with various eucharistic structures rooted in the tradition. The future shape of the liturgy may call for greater diversity to serve more diverse human needs.[45]

---

[40] See the Order for the Recognition of Ministries in the Congregation in *Occasional Services: A Companion to Lutheran Book of Worship*, 143ff.

[41] See Frank C. Senn, ed., *New Eucharistic Prayers: An Analysis of Their Development and Structure* (Mahwah, N.J.: Paulist Press, 1987).

[42] See W. Jardine Grisbrooke, art. "Anaphora," in J. G. Davies, ed., *The Westminster Dictionary of Worship* (Philadelphia: The Westminster Press, 1972), 10–7; John Barry Ryan, art. "Eucharistic Prayers," in Peter E. Fink, S.J., *The New Dictionary of Sacramental Worship* (Collegeville: The Liturgical Press, 1990), 451–9.

[43] *Den svenska kyrkohandboken*, I (Stockholm: Verbum, 1987), 144–55.

[44] See Thomas J. Talley, "The Eucharistic Prayer of the Ancient Church According to Recent Research, Results and Reflections," *Studia Liturgica* 11 (1976), 138–58; Frank C. Senn, "Toward a Different Anaphora Structure," *Worship* 58 (1984), 346–58.

[45] See Paul F. Bradshaw, "The Homogenization of Christian Liturgy—Ancient and Modern: Presidential Address," *Studia Liturgica* 26 (1996), 1–15.

Finally, we would note that all of the revised rites emphasize the act of dismissal or sending forth at the end of the eucharistic liturgy. The dismissal rite usually includes: a post-communion prayer (which sometimes incorporates the idea of being sent from the table into the world), a benediction, an optional recessional or closing hymn, and words of dismissal and response. There has been a desire to see the relationship between liturgy and life, between worship and evangelism, between the word and the sacrament and the mission of the church.[46]

🍇 ECUMENICAL CONVERGENCE ON EUCHARISTIC THEOLOGY

Not only has a common shape of the eucharistic liturgy emerged in the worship books used in Roman Catholic, Anglican, Lutheran, Methodist, and Presbyterian churches, but through patient ecumenical dialogue these ecclesial traditions have also achieved consensus on points of eucharistic theology that were once considered church-dividing. It is reasonable to suppose that liturgical homogenization among the denominational traditions provided at least a context in which doctrinal convergence could be fostered.[47] Bilateral and multilateral dialogues have been the most fruitful aspects of the ecumenical movement, and these began in the 1960s simultaneously with the movement for liturgical renewal. The most controverted aspects of eucharistic theology in the past, namely, the presence of Christ in the eucharist and the eucharistic sacrifice, have received attention in the dialogues and resulted in formulations that transcend historical impasses.

It is beyond the scope of this work to survey all the dialogues that have taken place both internationally and in the United States with regard to eucharistic doctrines.[48] Here we would draw reference to the conclusions reached in Anglican–Roman Catholic and Lutheran–Roman Catholic dialogues, in the historic Leuenberg Concordat between the German Lutheran and Reformed churches, and to the World Council of Churches Faith and Order Commission document, "Baptism, Eucharist, and Ministry" (BEM), which has been in the process of "reception" by the churches of the world.

Work on the eucharistic presence of Christ by Roman Catholic theologians in the 1960s tried to advance beyond an exclusive identification of Christ's body and blood with the species of bread and wine. In an effort to supplement, if not replace, exclusive reliance on transubstantiation (changed substance or essence) to explain what happens in the eucharist, terms such as "transignification" (changed meaning) and "transfinalization"

---

[46] See Alfred Shands, *The Liturgical Movement and the Local Church*, especially chapters 3–5; J. G. Davies, *Worship and Mission* (London: SCM Press, 1966); Frank C. Senn, *The Witness of the Worshiping Community: Liturgy and the Practice of Evangelism* (Mahwah, N.J.: Paulist Press, 1993); Mark Olson, Frank Senn, Jann Fullenwieder, *Open Questions in Worship* 3: *How does worship evangelize?*, ed. by Gordon Lathrop (Minneapolis: Augsburg Fortress, 1995).

[47] See Paul Bradshaw and Bryan Spinks, eds., *Liturgy in Dialogue* (London: S.P.C.K., 1993).

[48] Leonard Swidler, ed., *The Eucharist in Ecumenical Dialogue*, preface by William Cardinal Baum (New York and Paramus: Paulist Press, 1976), was a dialogue sponsored by the *Journal of Ecumenical Studies* that involved Catholic dialogue on the eucharist with Orthodox, Anglican, Lutheran, Reformed, Methodist, Baptist, and Jewish partners.

(changed purpose) were proposed.[49] This was an attempt to relate eucharistic theology to the framework of human meaning, rather than to the framework of physical structures, by drawing upon the phenomenology of a meal rather than Aristotelean metaphysics. What one encounters in a shared meal is the *presence of other persons* and not just the food-elements that are consumed. The personal presence of those who share the meal provides or changes the meaning or the purpose of the meal. On this basis, the presence of Christ in the eucharistic meal determines the meaning and purpose of the meal.

These views of the "personal presence" of Christ in the eucharistic action influenced the dialogues on the eucharist. So, for example, the international Anglican-Roman Catholic dialogue affirms that Christ's "true presence [is] effectually signified by the bread and wine which, in this mystery, becomes his body and blood." The bread and wine mediate the personal presence that they signify, but do so because they become what they were not before: Christ's body and blood. The dialoguers agreed that this change occurs during the eucharistic prayer. But rather than pinpoint a "moment of change" as the scholastic theologians had done, they saw the whole eucharistic action as effecting a comprehensive and manifold personal presence of Christ to his community.[50]

The same idea of a "personal presence" of Christ, combined with a shift of emphasis from objects to events, provided a way to move beyond the historic Lutheran–Reformed impasse on the Lord's Supper in the Leuenberg Concordat of 1973. In the brief formulations offered in the Agreement, the historic Lutheran concern for the "objective" presence of Christ in the sacrament and the Reformed concern for the spiritual affect of the eucharistic action are both affirmed, with the conclusion that the two sides should no longer condemn one another.

18. In the Lord's Supper the risen Jesus Christ imparts himself in his body and blood, given up for all, through his word of promise with bread and wine. He thus gives himself unreservedly to all who receive the bread and wine; faith receives the Lord's Supper for salvation, unfaith for judgment.

19. We cannot separate communion with Jesus Christ in his body and blood from the act of eating and drinking. To be concerned about the manner of Christ's presence in the Lord's Supper in abstraction from this act is to run the risk of obscuring the meaning of the Lord's Supper.

20. Where such a consensus exists between the churches, the condemnations pronounced by the Reformation confessions are inapplicable to the doctrinal position of these churches.[51]

It should be noted the removal of condemnations is applicable "where such a consensus exists between the churches." If this consensus is to serve as a basis for

---

[49] See Eduard Schillebeeckx, *The Eucharist*, Eng. trans. (New York: Sheed and Ward, 1968), chapter 2; Joseph Powers, *Eucharistic Theology* (New York: Herder and Herder, 1967), chapter 4.

[50] Anglican-Roman Catholic International Commission, *Eucharistic Doctrine* (1971), 6–7; *Elucidation* (1979), 6.

[51] The text of the Concordat is in the appendix to *The Leuenberg Agreement and Lutheran-Reformed Relationships: Evaluations by North American and European Theologians*, ed. by William G. Rusch and Daniel F. Martensen (Minneapolis: Augsburg, 1989), 149.

Lutheran–Reformed fellowship, churches must sign on to the Agreement. So far nearly eighty churches in the Reformation tradition have done so. It must also be admitted that the conclusions proffered in this ecclesiastical-political document are not as rigorous as the conclusions reached in the German Lutheran–Roman Catholic theological dialogue. That document affirms that "The exalted Lord becomes present in the Supper, in his sacrificed body and blood, with his deity and his humanity, through his word of promise, in the meal-gifts of bread and wine, in the power of the Holy Spirit, for the reception of the congregation."[52]

We might also note that the "Joint Statement on Eucharistic Presence," drafted by the second round of the Lutheran–Episcopal Dialogue in the U.S.A., speaks of the presence of Christ within the liturgical context of the commanded eucharistic celebration, but nevertheless maintains, in very confessional language, that

> According to his word of promise, Christ's very body broken on the cross and his very blood shed for the forgiveness of our sins are present, distributed and received, as a means of partaking here and now of the fruit of that atoning sacrifice. This is also the presence of the risen and glorified Christ who pleads for us before the throne of God. It is not our faith that effects this presence of our Lord, but by the faith we have received, the blessings of the Lord's suffering, death, and resurrection are sealed to us until he comes again in glory.[53]

This Joint Statement also spoke of the role of the Holy Spirit in bringing about the "fruits of communion" (a reference to the epiclesis), which include the manifestation of the church as the body of Christ in the world and the forgiveness of sins as the power of new life (with reference to both Luther's Small Catechism and the *Book of the Common Prayer*). It also appeals to the eschatological dimension of the sacrament as an anticipation of the oneness of all creation under the reign of Christ and as a basis for intercommunion now. The Joint Statements in this dialogue series became the basis for the agreement of "interim eucharistic sharing" enacted by the Episcopal Church and three American Lutheran church bodies in 1982.

The most celebrated result of ecumenical discussion has been the Faith and Order document, "Baptism, Eucharist, and Ministry" (1982). BEM speaks of the eucharist as thanksgiving to the Father, as anamnesis or memorial of Christ, as invocation of the Spirit, as communion of the faithful, and as meal of the kingdom. Under the section concerning the anamnesis or memorial of Christ, the document affirms that "the eucharistic meal is the sacrament of the body and blood of Christ, the sacrament of his real presence." Then it specifies that, while Christ fulfills his promise to be present always with his own in a variety of ways,

> Christ's mode of presence in the eucharist is unique. Jesus said over the bread and wine of the eucharist: 'This is my body . . . this is my blood . . .' What Christ

---

[52] Arbeitsgruppe der deutschen Bischofskonferenz und der Kirchenleitung der Vereinigten Evangelisch-lutherischen Kirche Deutschlands, *Kirchengemeinschaft im Wort und Sakrament* (Paderborn: Bonifatius-Druckerei, 1984), 122.

[53] The Report of the Lutheran-Episcopal Dialogue Second Series 1976–1980, *Lutheran-Episcopal Dialogue: Report and Recommendations* (Cincinnati: Forward Movement Press, 1981), 27.

declares is true, and this truth is fulfilled every time the eucharist is celebrated. The Church confesses Christ's real, living and active presence in the eucharist. While Christ's real presence in the eucharist does not depend on the faith of the individual, all agree that to discern the body and blood of Christ, faith is required.[54]

Here again it is affirmed that Christ's "real presence" in the eucharist is a personal "living and active" presence; that his presence is experienced in the meal; and that somehow "body and blood" and "real presence" coincide. How the "real presence" relates to "body and blood" is left unspecified. The commentary simply observes that "many churches believe that by the words of Jesus and by the power of the Holy Spirit, the bread and wine of the eucharist become, in a real though mysterious manner, the body and blood of the risen Christ. . . . Some other churches . . . do not link that presence so definitely with the signs of bread and wine."[55]

The churches are in the process of "receiving" this document by responding on how it reflects their own faith. It would seem that most of the official responses concern what is *not said* rather than what is said. For example, the Roman Catholic responses to "Baptism, Eucharist, and Ministry" and to the Roman Catholic dialogues with Anglicans and Lutherans raise the question of "the duration of the presence . . . and the necessity of veneration which follows therefrom."[56] To this objection, it should be possible for Lutherans and Anglicans to affirm without difficulty that a personal presence still requires "embodiment," which in the eucharist is associated with the bread and wine,[57] and for Roman Catholics to admit that the "reverent disposal" of the consecrated elements, which is generally practiced by Anglicans and Lutherans in some ways, does not necessitate the kind of veneration practices that have had a history in Roman Catholic devotion. The Lutheran World Federation-sponsored Dialogue with the Roman Catholic Church on the eucharist states, after commending the use of the consecrated elements for the communion of the sick:

> Regarding eucharistic adoration, Catholics should be watchful that their practice does not contradict the common conviction of the meal character of the Eucharist. They should also be conscious of the fact that in the Orthodox Churches, for example, other forms of eucharistic piety exist without their eucharistic faith being questioned (by Rome). Lutherans for their part should consider "that adoration of the reserved sacrament" not only "has been very much a part of Catholic life and a meaningful form of devotion to Catholics for

---

[54] *Baptism, Eucharist and Ministry*, Faith and Order Paper No. 111 (Geneva: World Council of Churches, 1982), Eucharist, par. 13, p. 12.

[55] Ibid.

[56] The Secretariat for the Promotion of Christian Unity, with the Congregation for the Faith, *Response to "Baptism, Eucharist and Ministry"* (1987), III.B.2; Cipriano Vagaggini, "Observations au sujet du document de 1978 de la commission mixte catholique-luthérienne sur l'eucharistie," *Documentation Catholique* (1979), 34; Congregation for the Faith, "Observations on the ARCIC Final Report," *Origins* 11 (182), 754.

[57] See Robert W. Jenson, *Unbaptized God: The Basic Flaw in Ecumenical Theology* (Minneapolis: Fortress, 1992), 31ff.

many centuries," but that also for them "as long as Christ remains sacramentally present, worship, reverence and adoration are appropriate."[58]

Reformers and papalists in the sixteenth century hurled more searing invectives at one another concerning the sacrifice of the mass than concerning the doctrine of transubstantiation. We saw in the last chapter the extent to which the Casel-inspired appeal to the biblical and patristic understanding of anamnesis as sacramental re-presentation helped to overcome the ecumenical impasse over the eucharistic sacrifice. The international Anglican–Roman Catholic Dialogue asserts that "the notion of memorial as understood in the Passover celebration of the time of Christ—that is, the making effective in the present of an event of the past—has opened the way to a clearer understanding of the relationship between Christ's sacrifice and the Eucharist."[59] This ARCIC statement was quoted in the international Lutheran–Roman Catholic Dialogue, which then continued:

> In the memorial celebration . . . more happens than that past events are brought to mind by the power of recall. . . . The decisive point is not that what is past is called to mind, but that the Lord calls his people into his presence and confronts them with his salvation. In this creative act of God, the salvation event from the past becomes the offer of salvation for the present and the promise of salvation for the future.[60]

The Lutheran–Roman Catholic Dialogue in the U.S.A. also depended heavily on this understanding of sacramental re-presentation.

> Lutherans have often understood Roman Catholics to say that the Mass adds to Calvary, is a "re-doing" of Calvary and by this have implied that the one sacrifice of Christ is defective and incomplete. Catholics agreed that some of the language used in the sixteenth century by Catholics could be so interpreted. Lutherans agree that it was this . . . which brought about the strenuous objections of Luther and the Lutheran Confessions. Now we can agree that this is not what Roman Catholics intend to say. The sacrifice of Christ is complete and unalterable and cannot be supplemented or completed by any subsequent action. . . .
>
> Catholics have used the word "re-presentation," not in the sense of doing again, but in the sense of "presenting again." Lutherans can wholeheartedly agree. It was agreed that the unrepeatable sacrifice which was, now is in the Eucharist.[61]

This breakthrough went a long way toward resolving the issue of the benefits of the mass. There are no benefits apart from the presence of the once-for-all propitiatory sacrifice of Christ by which sins are forgiven and reconciliation with God is achieved. If the mass has any efficacy in this regard at all, it is because it is sacramentally united to the once-for-all sacrifice of Christ, not because it is an additional sacrifice. This consensus has

---

[58] Lutheran–Roman Catholic Joint Commission, *The Eucharist* (Geneva: Lutheran World Federation, 1980), 19.

[59] International Anglican–Roman Catholic Dialogue, *Eucharistic Doctrine* (1971), 5.

[60] International Lutheran–Roman Catholic Dialogue, *The Eucharist* (1978), 36.

[61] Kent S. Knutson, "Eucharist as Sacrifice," in *Lutherans and Catholics in Dialogue*, III: *The Eucharist as Sacrifice*, ed. by Paul Empie and T. Austin Murphy (Minneapolis: Augsburg, 1974), 13.

been possible because of the reclamation of the sacramental idea that was lost in the theology and praxis of the late Middle Ages.

But the issue of the sacramental presence of the sacrifice of Christ is not the only one dealt with in discussions concerning the eucharistic sacrifice. Far more problematic is the fact that the language of the classical eucharistic prayers includes the offering of the church: "Remembering . . . we offer." In what sense does the church offer its gifts or itself at the eucharist? Here we need to realize that language of sacrifice in human phenomenology is complicated and polysemous. It conveys several meanings simultaneously. It may be pointed out first, that sacrifices are forms of prayer that are offered with gestures and tokens of appreciation ("we offer from the many gifts you have given us"); second, that prayers as sacrifices are offered as expressions of praise and thanksgiving in acknowledgment of gifts also received (a point on which Catholics and Protestants never disagreed concerning the eucharist); and third, that all Christian prayer is offered by appealing to the meritorious sacrifice of Christ.

Yet this does not resolve all issues. Protestants are not comfortable with Roman Catholic language about the eucharist as the church's sacrifice. Yet, subsumed under Roman Catholic language about the eucharist as the sacrifice of the church, is concern over *who* offers the eucharistic sacrifice. Protestants would declare that Christ alone, as our high priest, offers his own sacrifice and the sacrifice of his church to God the Father. Without necessarily disagreeing with this, Roman Catholics would point out that the priests of the church act *in persona Christi* (in the role of Christ) at the eucharist.

The Lutheran–Roman Catholic Dialogue in the U.S.A. ended round three on "The Eucharist as Sacrifice" with a list of unresolved issues, all of which turned out to be about the ministry of the church.[62] The foreword to the report of the next round of Dialogue stated that after achieving such notable results on the eucharistic presence and sacrifice, it "seemed natural to take up as the next point the question of intercommunion. A weekend of conversation . . . quickly revealed that one could not even discuss the matter without considering the key question of a valid ministry in relation to the administration of the Sacrament."[63]

Ecumenical dialogue has had to sort out the relationship between ordained ministry in the church and the priesthood of all believers, the practice of ordination and the meaning of the charism bestowed by the laying on hands, ordination into the apostolic succession and the role of the historic episcopate within this succession, and—in the case of the Roman Catholic Church—communion with the Church of Rome. These issues are connected with dialogue on the eucharist because the eucharist is the expression of church fellowship. Historically the links of eucharistic fellowship have been established by bishops who are in communion with one another.

Each of these issues is theoretically resolvable in ecumenical dialogue. But they are not discussible within the scope of this work. I would simply note, at least as far as this

---

[62] Ibid., 198.

[63] *Lutherans and Catholics in Dialogue*, IV: *Eucharist and Ministry*, ed. by Paul Empie and T. Austin Murphy (Minneapolis: Augsburg, 1974), Foreword.

Lutheran is concerned, that there should be no disagreement from a confessional perspective that there exists in the church a ministry and office of the word and the sacraments; that this ministry is not simply an exercise of the priesthood of all believers, but exists by God's call and institution to preach to and preside over the sacramental celebrations of the church; that the incumbents of this ministerial office are set apart by a rite of ordination to stand in persona Christi in the pulpit and at the table, preferably by a bishop in historic succession who is also in communion with other bishops, including the bishop of Rome.[64] Stating this as a theoretical possibility, of course, is far easier than working out the details, although the Concordat of Agreement between the Episcopal Church and the Evangelical Lutheran Church in America provides one model.

❦ THE CHURCH YEAR CALENDAR AND LECTIONARY

The material for the preaching of the word, and the readings that fill out the eucharistic memorial, are contained in the lectionary, which forms the content of the liturgy of the word. Provision is made in each order given above for three readings and a responsorial psalm as well as other musical responses or acclamations between the lessons. What is even more remarkable is that on any given Sunday, at least during the seasons of Advent, Christmas, Epiphany, Lent, and Easter, the lections will be substantially the same in all these traditions. This has encouraged both lectionary-based preaching and ecumenical homiletical resources.[65]

One of the most far-reaching reforms of the Second Vatican Council was the revision of the church year calendar and lectionary. The Constitution on the Sacred Liturgy V:106–111 established a number of objectives. Sunday was to receive primary emphasis as "the original feast day." The *Proprium de tempore* was declared to be of greater importance than the *Proprium de Sanctis*. Many of the saints days were relegated to local observance and a few were consigned to oblivion. After the Sundays, the seasons of the church year were to be emphasized according to the principle that the two main cycles in the church year are Advent–Christmas and Lent–Easter, with Sundays after the Epiphany and after Pentecost being "ordinary" (Sundays per annum). The Consilium that implemented the Constitution developed a three-year lectionary for Sunday and festival masses according to a revolutionary proposal that Year A would follow primarily the Gospel of Matthew, Year B the Gospel of Mark, and Year C the Gospel of Luke, with readings from the Gospel of John during the Christmas and Easter seasons in all three years and supplementing the readings from Mark in Year B. An Old Testament series of readings was developed for the First Lesson of the mass to correlate typologically or in terms of prophecy/fulfillment with the Gospel reading, except during Easter when each year the First Lesson readings would be from the Book of Acts. A psalm or portion of a psalm was selected as a response to the Old Testament reading. It could also be related to

---

[64] See Jenson, *Unbaptized God*, 47ff.

[65] Three of the better lectionary-based ecumenically marketed homiletical helps are *Homily Service* (Silver Spring, Md.: The Liturgical Conference); the *Proclamation* series (Minneapolis: Augsburg Fortress); and *Emphasis* (Lima, Ohio: C.S.S. Publishing Co.).

the Gospel since there was some thematic connection between the First Lesson and the Gospel. The Second Lesson would be a reading from a New Testament epistle. During the festival cycles these readings would also correlate thematically with the First Lesson and the Gospel. During the Sundays per annum, however, the epistles would be read sequentially, as the Gospels are. Each year, on the Sundays after the Epiphany, the readings are from 1 Corinthians. But then, in Year A, Second Lesson readings are from Romans, Philippians, and 1 Thessalonians; in Year B, Second Lesson readings are from 2 Corinthians, Ephesians, James, and Hebrews 2–10 (Heb. 1 is read on Christmas Day); and in Year C, Second Lesson readings are from Galatians, Colossians, Hebrews 11–13, Philemon, 1 and 2 Timothy, and 2 Thessalonians.[66]

The Consilium for the Implementation of the Constitution admitted six observers from non-Roman Catholic churches to its deliberations in 1966. As a result, the reformed Roman Catholic calendar and lectionary became an influential model for calendar and lectionary revision in other churches. As a result, the Roman church year calendar and lectionary were adapted in Anglican/Episcopal, Evangelical Lutheran, United Methodist, United Presbyterian, and other churches in the United States and Canada.

Most of the Roman calendar proposals were accepted by the non-Roman churches. The pre-Lenten Sundays were dropped. Anglicans, Lutherans, and Methodists preferred to treat Epiphany as a season rather than as ordinary Sundays, and the Transfiguration was located on the Sunday before Ash Wednesday to provide a climax to Epiphany and a prelude to Lent-Easter. This necessitated finding another set of readings on the second Sunday in Lent, since the Roman lectionary observed the Transfiguration on that day. Easter was implemented as a fifty-day season, so that Ascensiontide was also dropped (although Anglicans and Lutherans continued to observe Ascension Day). The most varied Sundays in terms of pericope selections are in the time after Pentecost. *LBW* assigned particular readings to each Sunday, rather than following a strict lectio continua pattern. As a result, in a year with a brief Epiphany season some readings (e.g., sixth through ninth Sundays after the Epiphany) are not used. After Pentecost it is inevitable that the readings in these several traditions will be out of sync by several weeks. There have also been different decisions about the end of the church year, whether to let the Sundays keeping running up until Christ the King Sunday (thus possibly losing several sets of readings at the end of the year) or assigning the last three sets of readings to be used on the last three Sundays in order to retain the end-of-the-year eschatological thrust (thus losing some sets of readings before the last three Sundays).

Two other factors have affected the adaptation and implementation of the Roman Lectionary in the Protestant traditions. The Protestant lectionaries have preferred not to skip verses in a chapter, as the Roman Lectionary does. Thus, on Maundy Thursday the Lesson is Exodus 12:1–14 rather than Exodus 12:1–8, 11–14. The need not to skip verses in the psalmody is even more important for Episcopalians, Lutherans, Methodists, and Presbyterians, since the congregations have the capability of opening the worship

---

[66] See Claude Wiéner, "The Roman Catholic Eucharistic Lectionary," *Studia Liturgica* 21, No. 1 (1991), 2–13.

books and singing the responsorial psalm from the book. A second observation is that the Protestant lectionaries have either not accepted readings from the Apocrypha or have provided alternative selections as an option to the apocryphal reading. Most Protestant lectern or pulpit Bibles do not include apocryphal books because the Calvinist confessions defined a 66-book canon of scripture. The Lutheran confessions, on the other hand, never defined the canon of scripture, and Luther's German Bible included the Apocrypha. In spite of this, Missouri Synod representatives on the ILCW resisted including readings from the Apocrypha, so that the only ones in *LBW* are in the Easter Vigil (Baruch 3:9–37 and the Song of the Three Children from the apocryphal portion of the book of Daniel).

The supposed consensus on the lectionary became less of a consensus when the Consultation on Common Texts attempted to develop a truly Common Lectionary by reconciling the differences indicated above. In their deliberations, however, the CCT ended up with another radical proposal: that during the "ordinary" Sundays there be continuous readings from Old Testament books in order to provide greater exposure to the Hebrew Scriptures and more narrative possibilities for preaching.[67] The CCT was listening to many voices that had been raised, including within the Roman Catholic Church, for greater attention to the Hebrew Scriptures. Eugene J. Fisher also argued against the use of a typological and prophecy/fulfillment hermeneutic in the Ecumenical Lectionary as disrespectful to the Hebrew Bible, although he recognized that a balance must be struck between the triumphalism implied in continuity and the Marcionism implied in discontinuity.[68] Thus, on the Sundays after Pentecost during Year A, the Common Lectionary Old Testament readings would include sequential lections from Genesis 12ff., Exodus, Ruth; during Year B readings would be sequential lections from 1 and 2 Samuel, Wisdom literature, Genesis 2–3; during Year C readings would be sequential lections from 1 and 2 Kings, Jeremiah, Ezekiel, Hosea, and eight of the minor prophets. This is clearly an idea that is congenial to the Reformed tradition with its practice of reading and preaching through the Bible chapter by chapter, but it was not congenial to the Evangelical Lutheran Church in America or to the Episcopal Church, which preferred Old Testament readings to be typologically related to the gospels.

As a result of this disagreement, the CCT went back to work and produced the Revised Common Lectionary in 1988, which has provided for two approaches to the Old Testament readings on "Sundays during the Year": either a continuous reading of certain books or a pericope system. In this revised form the Common Lectionary was included in the *United Methodist Book of Worship* (1992) and the Presbyterian *Book of Common Worship* (1993). The Revised Common Lectionary was also approved for use in the Evangelical Lutheran Church in Canada (ELCIC) (1994) and then in the Evangelical Lutheran Church in America (ELCA) (1995) and in the Episcopal Church (1995), with the permission of the diocesan bishop. Interestingly, the ELCIC opted for the continuous

---

[67] See Horace T. Allen, Jr., *"Common Lectionary*: Origins, Assumptions, and Issues," *Studia Liturgica* 21, No. 1 (1991), 14–30.

[68] Eugene J. Fisher, "Continuity and Discontinuity in the Scripture Readings," *Liturgy* (May 1978), 30–7.

reading of Old Testament books and narratives during ordinary time and the ELCA opted for the pericope approach to the Old Testament readings. Most importantly, Lutherans who use the Revised Common Lectionary will be synchronized during ordinary time with other Christians who use it by designating sets of propers to be used within certain calendar dates: for example, Proper 10 on the Sunday between June 5 and 11. In this system, extra propers will be omitted on the Sundays immediately after Pentecost and Trinity Sunday rather than at the end of the church year. Thus, a full eschatological emphasis is restored to the month of November between All Saints Sunday and Christ the King Sunday, which will glide into the eschatological season of Advent. In effect, this restores the original Gallican six-week Advent season.

Adoption of the Revised Common Lectionary in these churches, however, does not create a truly common lectionary among the churches. As of this writing, the Roman Catholic Church has not officially embraced the Revised Common Lectionary, although it is still based on the Roman Lectionary. German Lutherans from the time of the promulgation of the *Ordo Lectionum Missae* have expressed regret at the Roman Catholic departure from the medieval cycle of readings (the "historic one-year lectionary") instead of just revising it and adding an Old Testament reading and psalm. (Both *LBW* and *LW* provide a revision of the one-year series as well as the three-year series, although the one-year series is rarely used.) Wilhelm Gundert claims that this historic medieval lectionary already constituted an ecumenical lectionary for the Western church.[69] The unwillingness of the European Lutherans to adopt a form of the *Ordo Lectionum Missae* divided them from North American Lutherans, who did.[70] In the same way, the Episcopal Church departed from the Church of England in its willingness to adapt the *Ordo Lectionum Missae*. As indicated in the last chapter, the Joint Liturgical Group in Great Britain and Ireland has also worked ecumenically in those countries to achieve a common lectionary for their churches.[71] Finally, there is the feminist critique of all the lectionaries for lack of stories about women in the Bible, but especially of the Common Lectionary for its heavy emphasis on such male figures as Abraham, Isaac, Jacob, Moses, David, and Solomon in the semi-continuous Old Testament readings. In its revised form, however, the CCT made an effort to include stories about women in the Revised Common Lectionary and to avoid the so-called texts of terror that show the suffering of women.[72]

Changes have occurred in the sanctoral cycle as well as the temporal cycle in the revised church year calendars. Probably the greatest change in the Roman calendar was the reduction in the number of saints days. The calendar of Pius V in 1568 reduced the number to about 150, but new additions in subsequent centuries ran the list up to 338. The Roman calendar after Vatican II had only thirty-three feast days (including feasts of the Lord), with sixty-three obligatory and ninety-five optional commemorations. The feast

---

[69] Wilhelm Gundert, "Das neue katholische Messlektionar," *Lutherische Monatschrifte* 8 (1969), 595–9.

[70] See Karl-Heinrich Bieritz, "The Order of Readings and Sermon Texts for the German Lutheran Church," *Studia Liturgica* 21, No. 1 (1991), 37–51.

[71] See Donald Gray, "The Contribution of the Joint Liturgical Group to the Search for an Ecumenical Lectionary," *Studia Liturgica* 21, No. 1 (1991), 31–6.

[72] See Phyllis Trible, *Texts of Terror* (Philadelphia: Fortress Press, 1982).

days, almost entirely limited to New Testament saints, compare with the lesser festivals in the *BCP* and *LBW*. The *BCP* added seven "red letter" days to the saints days Episcopalians already had; *LBW* added three or four lesser festivals to what had been observed in the *SBH*. Both *BCP* and *LBW* include Holy Cross Day. The *BCP* includes propers for American Independence Day and *LBW* retains Reformation Day. Two lesser festivals in the *BCP* and *LBW* that are not in the Roman calendar are the Confession of Saint Peter (January 18) and Saint James the Brother of our Lord (October 23). Both *BCP* and *LBW* provide a list of optional commemorations beyond the New Testament saints: 124 in the *LBW* and 151 in the *BCP* (although a perusal will show the Lutheran list to be more ecumenical).

These commemorations provide a way of exposing Christians within these traditions to a greater awareness of witnesses to the Christian faith in different times and places by providing examples of Christian faithfulness. The commemorations of the saints serve to nurture the faith and encourage the witness of contemporary Christians.[73] Some days are observed with civil or ecumenical support. For example, the birthday of Martin Luther King, Jr. (January 15) has been observed as a national holiday, and Saint Patrick's Day (March 17) has also become something of a civic festival. Other days have acquired ecclesiastical significance. For example, the days of the Confession of Saint Peter (January 18) and the Conversion of Saint Paul (January 25) straddle of Week of Prayer for Christian unity, and are sometimes observed ecumenically. Other days have become associated with popular causes. For example, the Day of Saint Francis of Assisi (October 4) has been observed with ecological themes (e.g., the Canticle of the Sun) and the blessings of animals, and Saint Luke's Day (October 15) has become a day on which to emphasize the healing ministry of the church. All Saints Day (November 1) has become, in Protestant practice, an occasion on which to remember all the faithful departed of the parish during the past year, and it is usually celebrated on the Sunday after November 1 because the festival of the Reformation is celebrated on the Sunday before October 31, its appointed day in the calendar.

❧ THE RITES OF CHRISTIAN INITIATION

The massive missionary endeavors in the twentieth century in Africa, Asia, Polynesia, and Latin America, and the need to reevangelize whole portions of Europe and continue the evangelization of populations in North America, have fortuitously collided with the efforts to reform liturgical rites by reviewing ancient texts and practices. These seemingly disparate concerns resulted in the retrieval of the ancient practices of Christian initiation in a way that addressed the missionary and evangelistic needs of the church in the twentieth century. There had been galvanizing debates over the appropriateness of continuing the practice of infant baptism, with its implied cultural captivity of

---

[73] See Philip H. Pfatteicher, *Festivals and Commemorations: Handbook to the Calendar in Lutheran Book of Worship* (Minneapolis: Augsburg Publishing House, 1980); also the brief descriptions of those included in the lesser festivals and commemorations in Philip H. Pfatteicher and Carlos R. Messerli, *Manual on the Liturgy: Lutheran Book of Worship* (Minneapolis: Augsburg Publishing House, 1979), 33–76.

the sacrament, in modern secular society between Karl Barth[74] and Oscar Cullmann[75] in the Reformed church, and debates over the relationships between the separate rites of initiation—baptism, confirmation, first communion—between Gregory Dix[76] and G. W. H. Lampe[77] in the Church of England. There was nothing like this kind of research and reflection in the Roman Catholic Church until after the Second Vatican Council, when the subcommittee charged with revising the rites of initiation, headed by Balthasar Fischer of Trier,[78] held a series of consultations between 1967 and 1970. The result, however, was not just a revision of the rites of the baptism of infants (1969), confirmation (1971), and the initiation of adults (1972), but a complete overhaul of Catholic initiation policy. The Rite of the Christian Initiation of Adults (RCIA) became the most radical liturgical reform to emanate from the Consilium to Implement the Constitution on the Sacred Liturgy.[79]

The RCIA has attempted nothing less than the repristination of the awe-inspiring rites of initiation in the ancient church, as described in the *Apostolic Tradition* of Hippolytus, the writings of Tertullian, the church orders of the fourth and fifth centuries, and the mystagogical homilies of the great bishops of antiquity. It has projected initiation in four stages, each marked by major and minor ritual transitions:[80]

> *Precatechumenate* — a period of inquiry and seeking with informal opportunities for discussion with clergy and informed lay persons;

> *Catechumenate* — marked by a rite of acceptance into the order of catechumens followed by catechumenal classes with intentional, but experientially oriented, instruction;

> *Period of purification and enlightenment* — marked by a rite of election or enrollment of names (usually at the beginning of Lent) and scrutinies on the third, fourth, and fifth Sundays in Lent during which the Creed and the Lord's Prayer are presented, and culminating in the sacraments of initiation: baptism, confirmation, and first communion (celebrated together at the Easter Vigil); and

> *Post-baptismal catechesis or mystagogy* — when the newly baptized are given formal instruction on the meaning of the sacraments they have just experienced.

Kavanagh and others have seen in the RCIA a process by which to take seriously the ancient dictim of Tertullian of Carthage that "Christians are made, not born," and to

---

[74] Karl Barth, *The Teaching of the Church Regarding Baptism*, trans. by E. A. Payne (London: SCM Press, 1948).

[75] Oscar Cullmann, *Baptism in the New Testament*, trans. J. K. S. Reid (London: SCM Press, 1950).

[76] Gregory Dix, *The Theology of Confirmation in Relation to Baptism* (London: Dacre Press, 1946).

[77] G. W. H. Lampe, *The Seal of the Spirit. A Study in the Doctrine of Baptism and Confirmation in the New Testament and in the Fathers*, 2nd ed. (London: S.P.C.K., 1967).

[78] See Balthasar Fischer, "Baptismal Exorcism in the Catholic Baptismal Rites after Vatican II," *Studia Liturgica* 10 (1974), 48–55.

[79] Aidan Kavanagh, *The Shape of Baptism: The Rite of Christian Initiation* (New York: Pueblo Publishing Co., 1978), 102ff.

[80] See *The Rites of the Catholic Church*, English trans. prepared by The International Commission on English in the Liturgy (New York: Pueblo Publishing House, 1976), 13ff.

be serious about the need for conversion and catechesis.[81] Indeed, the RCIA launched a major reconsideration of the relationship between initiation and conversion.[82]

Not surprisingly, the RCIA was not implemented in local communities as quickly as the reformed Order and Celebration of Mass. It required a whole new understanding of ritual processes and pedagogical models than had been previously available to liturgists, pastors, and catechists.[83] Parishes have had to understand catechesis as what Kavanagh calls "conversion therapy," which requires less exposure to rational content than experiential engagement in the community's rites, life, and mission.[84]

It has taken even longer for the shape of baptism delineated in the RCIA to be implemented in non-Roman Catholic churches. We should note, however, that the basic structure of Christian initiation—a period of inquiry, a rite of election or enrollment into the catechumenate, the time of catechesis or instruction, the celebration of the unified rites of baptism, confirmation, and first communion, and the period of post-baptismal mystagogia—was delineated in the Notes on the first order in *Occasional Services: Lutheran Book of Worship*, "Enrollment of Candidates for Baptism";[85] and the Order for Holy Baptism in *LBW* had already restored the "form and matter" of confirmation—the prayer for the Holy Spirit with the laying on of hands and the anointing—to the post-baptismal ceremonies. More recently Lutherans in North America have begun developing an adult catechumenate process, first by the Evangelical Lutheran Church in Canada in it *Living Witnesses* series (1992) and later by the Evangelical Lutheran Church in America with its *Welcome to Christ* resources (1997).[86]

The Lutheran resources have drawn not only on the RCIA, but also on The Catechumenal Process developed by the Office of Evangelism Ministries of the

---

[81] See *Made, Not Born. New Perspectives on Christian Initiation and the Catechumenate*, from The Murphy Center for Liturgical Research (Notre Dame, Ind., and London: University of Notre Dame Press, 1976), which includes essays by Aidan Kavanagh, Reginald H. Fuller, Robert M. Grant, Nathan D. Mitchell, Daniel B. Stevick, Ralph A. Keifer, and Robert W. Hovda—Episcopalians as well as Roman Catholics.

[82] See Lawrence J. Johnson, ed., *Initiation and Conversion* (Collegeville: The Liturgical Press, 1985), a collection of major presentations given at the 1984 National Meeting of the Federation of Diocesan Liturgical Commissions by Regis Duffy, O.F.M., James D. Shaughnessy, Barbara O'Dea, D.W., and James Lopresti, S.J.

[83] See the symposium on the R.C.I.A. in *Worship*, the 1982 Meeting of the North American Academy of Liturgy, Vol. 56, No. 4 (July 1982), with an address by Raymond Kemp and responses by Marl Searle, Ralph A. Keifer, and James W. Fowler.

[84] See Michael W. Merriman, *The Baptismal Mystery and the Catechumenate* (New York: The Church Hymnal Corporation, 1990), which includes addresses given by Richard Norris, Aidan Kavanagh, L. Wm. Countryman, Gail Ramshaw, Michael W. Merriman, Roger J. White, Walter L. Guettsche, and Robert Brooks at the National Liturgical Conference of the Episcopal Church at Grace Cathedral in San Francisco, 1988.

[85] *Occasional Services: A Companion to Lutheran Book of Worship*, 15.

[86] See *Living Witnesses: The Adult Catechumenate. Preparing Adults for Baptism and Ministry in the Church*, by Frederick P. Ludolph (Winnipeg: Evangelical Lutheran Church in Canada, 1992). Other resources in the series includes *Congregational Prayers to Accompany the Catechumenal Process*, by Gordon W. Lathrop (1992); *A Manual for the Catechumenal Process*, by Cynthia Halmarson (1994); and *Praying the Catechism: A Journey of Prayer and Meditation*, by Don Johnson (1995). *Welcome to Christ* contains three volumes: *A Lutheran Introduction to the Catechumenate, A Lutheran Catechetical Guide*, and *Lutheran Rites for the Catechumenate* (Minneapolis: Augsburg Fortress, 1997).

Episcopal Church in the United States of America.[87] The advance made in the Episcopal program has been to recognize that three processes of initiation need to occur simultaneously in North American parishes: the preparation of adults for Holy Baptism; the preparation of baptized persons for affirmation of the baptismal covenant; and the preparation of parents for the baptism of infants and young children. While the latter is still the most common need in parishes, there is a great influx into churches of persons who were baptized as infants and confirmed as adolescents who dropped out of church life during their teenage or college-age years. The Episcopal Catechumenal Process envisions these three forms of preparation occurring simultaneously.[88] The integration of the confirmation ministry for young people into the catechumenal process is also a possibility.

Initiation means incorporating a person by special processes and ceremonies into a community. Initiates are given a new identity, and they develop a sense of belonging in a process in which they make their own the traditions and values of the group. This is what the process of conversion is all about. The churches have been slow to take seriously the need for conversion, catechesis, and initiation in a world that is increasingly "post-Christian."

As long as it has taken to digest the reality of the current missionary situation of the Western churches, the churches have been even slower in recognizing that conversion, catechesis, and initiation applies to children as well as adults. Children baptized as infants have generally waited until the confirmation ministry during their adolescent years to experience any real conversion and initiation into the community of faith. But there are those who see the need for this kind of faith formation in baptized children even before the traditional age for confirmation (adolescence). They hold that children should be exposed less to religious education than to the experiences of ritual and relationships within the Christian community.[89] The idea is to include children as fully as possible into the life of the church, at their own level of capability. They should be engaged as fully as possible in the church's liturgy and they should have adults beyond those in their own family who can serve as faith-models. Nevertheless, the preparation of children for liturgical and sacramental participation in the community is best done in the Christian family, with materials and support provided by the faith community. This includes preparation for participation in Holy Communion. Many Western churches are moving toward an earlier age of first communion; some are even restoring first communion to the time of baptism as the logical expression of the goal of Christian initiation, which is incorporation into the central fellowship of the church at the Lord's Table. The inclusion of children in

---

[87] *The Catechumenal Process: Adult Initiation and Formation for Christian Life and Ministry* (New York: The Church Hymnal Corporation, 1990).

[88] For a fuller discussion of these three simultaneous processes of Christian initiation see Frank C. Senn, *The Witness of the Worshiping Community: Liturgy and the Practice of Evangelism* (Mahwah, N.J.: Paulist Press, 1993), 134ff.

[89] See Robert D. Duggan and Maureen A. Kelly, *The Christian Initiation of Children* (New York/Mahwah, N.J.: Paulist Press, 1991).

the celebration and reception of Holy Communion was the subject of a study under the auspices of the Faith and Order Commission of the World Council of Churches.[90]

Confirmation has remained a rite in search of a meaning.[91] Churches that practice the baptism of infants and young children, except for the Orthodox, have continued to be concerned that there be some rite by which adolescents or young adults may publicly affirm their baptism, after a period of catechetical instruction. In *LBW*, confirmation is one of the purposes of the rite of Affirmation of Baptism (the other two being reception into membership from other denominations and restoration to membership).[92] Catholic (and Anglo-Catholic) theology held that the gift of the Holy Spirit is given in the sacrament of confirmation. But this seems to qualify the Trinitarian fullness of baptism. In many of the Protestant churches confirmation had been a prerequisite for first communion. But many critics pointed out that this seemed to undermine Holy Communion as a sacrament of grace by giving the impression that it is a sacrament of achievement. Since the 1970s first communion has been separated from confirmation. As the age for first communion has been steadily lowered, the age for confirmation has been steadily increased into the early high school years.

The movement toward an older age of confirmation suggests some rationales for retaining the rite of confirmation. It provides an opportunity for the public profession of the faith of the church by those who were baptized in earlier years, after a period of exploration of this faith with those who are competent to guide this kind of study. Certainly the probing of meaning requires something more than rote memorization of the catechism, although fixing essential Christian texts in one's memory has its pedagogical and spiritual values. Confirmation provides an opportunity for youth and young adults to identify personally and publicly with the life and mission of the community of faith. This also provides a rationale for the involvement of the bishop in the rite of confirmation, in churches that have an episcopal polity, since the bishop represents the whole local church in its life and mission. There is a growing sense that being confirmed should be a decision that is personally made, when the catechetical instruction is completed, without the kind of familial and cultural pressures that used to be imposed on adolescents to be confirmed in earlier times. Some young people may decide, at the end of the confirmation ministry, not to be confirmed—at least not at that time. The question nags, however: When is someone capable of making a mature decision of faith? It is evident that the rite of confirmation will not be abandoned; it is also evident that we will not arrive at a satisfactory rationale for having it. It will remain in limbo as neither a rite of initiation into the church, since candidates for this rite are already baptized and communing Christians, nor as a rite of passage into adulthood, since there are questions about the competence of adolescents to make mature decisions.

---

[90] . . . *And Do Not Hinder Them. An Ecumenical Plea for the Admission of Children to the Eucharist*, ed. by Geiko Müller-Fahrenholz. Faith and Order Paper No. 109 (Geneva: World Council of Churches, 1982).

[91] See Frank C. Quinn, "Confirmation Reconsidered: Rite and Meaning," *Worship* 59 (1986), 354–70.

[92] *LBW*, 198–201. "Confirmation" was first construed as one of several purposes of Reaffirmation of Baptism in the ILCW's *Contemporary Worship 8: Reaffirmation of Baptism* (1975). See Frank C. Senn, "An End for Confirmation?" *Currents in Theology and Mission* 3 (1976), 45–52.

🍇 RITES OF PASSAGE

Marriage

True celebrations of maturity are rites that involve vocation, such as marriage, ordination and commissioning to ministry, and profession of religious vows. Marriage has always been both a social and a religious observance, with both civil and ecclesiastical implications. It has also been thoroughly embedded in the culture of a people, with cultural assumptions and mores determining its practice. The church has more or less "baptized" the marriage practices of a given society, though imposing its own meanings on the institution. In the societies of Christendom in Europe church law and civil law often intertwined in the regulation of marriage. In the societies of North America, especially in the United States, marriage has been totally secularized under state laws, as far as its legal ramifications are concerned. But couples still seek out churches for their wedding ceremonies and clergy are accorded the privilege of serving as magistrates for the occasion by license from the state. Churches still impose their own internal disciplines on marriage, as far as their members are concerned, especially those churches for whom marriage is regarded as a sacrament, such as the Roman Catholic and Orthodox churches. This allows priests, with the backing of the hierarchy and canon law, to enforce the disciplines of the church governing marriage. Protestants, who have regarded marriage as an order of creation rather than as a sacrament of the church, have been less able to enforce "marriage guidelines" adopted by pastors and congregations. The pluralism of American society has strained both canon law and "guidelines" as couples present all sorts of combinations of circumstances for ecumenical and interfaith marriages. The high frequency of divorce in Western societies also present clergy with the problems of sequential marriages, which strains theologies of marriage, canon law, and church discipline. However, in the interests of pastoral care, and even evangelism among the unchurched or tentatively churched, many pastors are willing to work with couples who present situations that challenge the preferred practices of the churches.[93]

Probably the majority of weddings in North America involve partners of different faith backgrounds. In most cases the marriage orders in the worship books of particular traditions are adapted to fit the circumstances. As part of marriage preparation, couples often choose readings, music, and special ceremonies under the guidance of their pastor. Nondenominational resources[94] and ecumenical marriage services have also been developed.[95] The selection of music for weddings remains a tense and controverted exercise since many brides and grooms want to bring music from their own realm of experience into what is essentially a worship service, and this is resisted by many pastors and church musicians. The preference for love songs and readings about love reflects the fact

---

[93] See William H. Willimon, *Worship as Pastoral Care* (Nashville: Abingdon, 1979), the chapter on the marriage service.

[94] David Glusker and Peter Misner, *Words for Your Wedding* (San Francisco: Harper, 1986) includes five denominational marriage services with additional textual options.

[95] See the Consultation on Common Texts, *A Christian Celebration of Marriage: An Ecumenical Liturgy* (Minneapolis: Augsburg Fortress, 1995).

that marriage has come to be seen as a public expression of loving commitment between a man and a woman rather than as a public expression of fidelity to each other "no matter what" "until death parts us," for which examples of God's faithfulness to his people and expressions of reliance on God's grace would be appropriate.

In contemporary practice the betrothal rite, which used to be performed on the church porch, has been amalgamated into the marriage rite itself, performed before the altar. An elaborate entrance rite is now planned to bring the bride into the sanctuary, accompanied by her bridesmaids and escorted by her father or a close substitute, to her waiting groom and his groomsmen. The idea of the father "giving over" the bride to the groom no longer ritualizes a legal transfer of property; but in spite of ideas of equality of the sexes the practice is slow to be abandoned—by the brides. Sometimes the bridal couple simply enters together. The rest of typical marriage rites include an opening prayer, scripture readings and a brief homily, the exchange of promises and rings, an announcement of the marriage, thanksgivings and intercessions, and a blessing of the couple. Increasingly in Protestant practice, the eucharist is celebrated at the weddings of church members. A eucharistic context is taken for granted in Roman Catholic marriage practice, although a rite for celebrating marriage outside the eucharist is provided. Communion is open to all who are eligible to receive the sacrament.

Ordination

The Roman Catholic rites for the ordination of bishops, priests, and deacons were revised in 1968.[96] There has been an effort to achieve greater uniformity in the structure of the rites of ordination to the three ministries. Whereas formerly the rite of ordination was located in different places within the order of mass depending on the office (deacons before the gospel so that they could then proclaim the gospel, priests and bishops before the offertory so that they could then offer the sacrifice of the mass), the revised ordination rites all take place after the gospel. The candidates for ordination are presented, and then a homily and an examination of the candidates follow. At the ordination of a bishop the hymn "Veni, Creator Spiritus" is sung. Candidates for presbyteral and diaconal ordination promise obedience to the bishop and his successors. Then a litany is sung, prayer is offered for the candidates, and all the laying on of hands follows in silence. All bishops present lay hands on the new bishop and all presbyters present may join the bishop in laying hands on the new presbyter. The consecration prayer follows the laying on of hands. Then the vestments and insignia of office are presented to the ordinands. A new bishop is presented with a gospel book, ring, miter, and pastoral staff. The hands of new presbyters are anointed with oil before they are presented with the gifts of bread and wine, which have been brought to the bishop by the faithful. Deacons are presented with the gospel book. If a new bishop is ordained in his own cathedral, he assumes presidency of the eucharist. Otherwise the consecrating bishop continues to preside and the new

---

[96] See Ordination of Deacons, Ordination of a Deacon; Ordination of Priests, Ordination of a Priest; Ordination of Bishops, Ordination of a Bishop, *Roman Pontifical*, I (Washington, D.C.: International Commission on English in the Liturgy, 1978), 155–254.

bishop joins the concelebrants at the altar. New priests concelebrate with the presiding bishop. Deacons exercise their role in the liturgy.

The revised rite of the Episcopal Church shares many similar features with the Roman rite in terms of striving for a common shape of ordination to the three ministries.[97] All three are called "ordination," including the rite for bishops (which used to be called "consecration"). The ordination rite occurs in the same locations in the eucharistic liturgy. However, in the Episcopal order the presentation of the candidates (with opportunity for the consent of the people) occurs at the beginning of the liturgy, before the ministry of the word. After the Nicene Creed the examination of the candidate occurs and the singing of "Veni, Creator Spiritus" or "Veni, Sancte Spiritus." After a period of silent prayer, the consecration prayer is offered and the laying on of hands occurs at the epicletic section of the prayer. In the rite of ordination a similar eucharistic prayer, modeled on that for the ordination of a bishop in Hippolytus's *Apostolic Tradition*, is said for each ministry, with different petitions in each version depending on the job description of the ministry. Following the ordination prayer the ordinands are vested according to their ministerial order and a Bible is presented to members of each order.

There had been an effort to achieve a similar uniformity of structure in the Orders for the Installation of a Bishop, the Ordination of a Pastor, and the Setting Apart or Consecration of a Deaconess in American Lutheran rites.[98] However, lack of agreement in the doctrine of the ministry militated against this solution.[99] Bishops in the Evangelical Lutheran Church in America and its predecessor bodies have not been understood as other than pastors with wider jurisdictional responsibilities, and therefore there could be no sense of "ordaining" them to the episcopal office. On the other hand, there is a similar structure for the orders of the ordination of a pastor and the setting apart of a deaconess; both use prayers of thanksgiving as the form of consecration; and in both cases there are similarities with the comparable consecration prayers for priests and deacons in the Episcopal Ordinal.[100] The acclamation or approval of the people is not joined to the presentation of the candidates in the Lutheran orders; it occurs at the end of the order. In every case, however, the rite takes place within the Service of Holy Communion after the sermon and hymn of the day.

The new ordination rites of the United Methodist Church follow those of the Episcopal Church very closely.[101] The presentation of candidates for the ordination of elders occurs at the beginning of the service. After the liturgy of the word there is an address to and examination of the candidates, which is followed by prayer and the singing of a hymn to the Holy Spirit. The laying on of hands takes place during the consecration

---

[97] The Ordination of a Bishop, The Ordination of a Priest, The Ordination of a Deacon, *The Book of Common Prayer*, 511–55.

[98] See *Occasional Services*, Ordination, 192ff.; Setting Apart of a Deaconess, 210ff.; Installation of a Bishop, 218ff.

[99] See Frank C. Senn, "Ordination Rites as a Source of Ecclesiology," *dialog* 27 (1988), 40–7.

[100] See Philip Pfatteicher, *Commentary on the Occasional Services*, 193–4, 209–10, 214–5.

[101] See *The United Methodist Book of Worship* (Nashville: United Methodist Publishing House, 1992), 652–713.

prayer, which is a reworking of the comparable prayer in the Episcopal Ordinal. Then a Bible is presented to the new elder, and a stole, chalice and paten if desired. Unlike the Roman Catholic, Episcopal, and Lutheran orders, the Methodist ordination service may conclude without the celebration of Holy Communion although the context of the eucharistic liturgy is presumed as normative.

Thus we see an ecumenical consensus also in the shape of the ordination rites of the different churches. This liturgical consensus has contributed to the statements on ordination and the threefold ministries of bishops, presbyters, and deacons in the Faith and Order Statement on Baptism, Eucharist, and Ministry. BEM regards ordination to ministry as a continuing expression of the apostolic commissioning of the risen Lord Jesus Christ (#39), as the action of God the Holy Spirit in the church (#40), accomplished by the imposition of hands by those who have been previously ordained in office and exercise oversight of the ministries of the church (#41), but nevertheless expressing the will and action of the whole community of faith who pray for the gift of the Holy Spirit for the one the community has chosen to be a minister in the church (#42). While God the Holy Spirit operates with freedom in the epiclesis, ordination is a sign performed in faith by the church (#43), trusting in the command and promise of Christ (as Melanchthon pointed out in *Apology* 13, in stating his reason for calling ordination a sacrament). The rite of ordination is performed in faith that the required charism of office has been already given to the ordaining minister and that it will be received by the ordinand, and therefore the new ministers "enter into a collegial relationship with other ordained ministers" (#44). Hence the new minister is spoken of being in an order of bishops, presbyters, or deacons. This historic, threefold ministry is commended by BEM to the whole church.

Reconciliation

In previous chapters we have treated penance in juxtaposition with baptism, since it is theologically and pastorally a second or subsequent forgiveness related to the primary forgiveness of sins in Holy Baptism. Penance has also been practiced as a gateway to Holy Communion, both as a means of spiritual preparation for receiving the sacrament and as a form of church discipline in terms of "fencing the table." But in modern times it has also acquired a kind of independent status as a rite related to personal spiritual discipline and the spiritual health of the Christian community.[102] Because penance, often now construed as the sacrament of reconciliation, is used as a form of pastoral care rather than as a form of church discipline, and therefore in conjunction with the spiritual crises of life, I am treating it here as a rite of passage.[103]

The reform of penance emanating from the Second Vatican Council emphasized the ecclesial and social dimension of this sacrament, and focused on the reconciliation of individuals, families, or fractions who are estranged from one another and from

---

[102] See Dietrich Bonhoeffer, *Life Together*, trans. by John W. Doberstein (New York and Evanston: Harper and Row, 1954) and Martin E. Marty, *The Hidden Discipline* (St. Louis: Concordia, 1962).

[103] See E. Thurneysen, *Die Lehre von der Seelsorge* (Zürich, 1946).

the community of faith.[104] The rites of penance included three forms: individual confession to a priest, reconciliation of several penitents with individual confession and absolution, and reconciliation of several penitents with confession and absolution.[105] Even individual confession stressed the social dimensions of penance by removing the transaction from a booth and placing the confessor and the penitent face to face for a dialogue, with the use of scripture and recitation of psalmody. The other two forms of reconciliation place confession and absolution after a liturgy of the word.

There are comparable orders in *LBW*.[106] The Order for Individual Confession and Forgiveness provides an opportunity for dialogue between the penitent and the pastor, the sharing of scripture, the recitation of psalmody, and the laying on of hands in conjunction with the absolution. The Order for Corporate Confession and Forgiveness is a service of the word with preaching, leading to a general confession of sins and absolution, with the option of individual absolution with the laying on of hands. This order may serve the historic purpose of communal preparation for Holy Communion, but it is doubtful that it can serve more extensive processes of conversion and reconciliation.[107]

The Roman Catholic faithful, by and large, have been confused about the "sacrament of reconciliation" and the Lutheran faithful have not been encouraged or given the opportunities to use the forms of the so-called third sacrament in the Orders for Corporate and Individual Confession and Forgiveness. Their primary use of Confession and Forgiveness remains the Brief Order, which usually precedes the Service of Holy Communion. Penance, or absolution (as Lutherans prefer to call it), remains, in the words of Larry Mick, a "once and future sacrament."[108]

Anointing of the Sick

Penance or absolution has played a role in the ministry to the sick. Indeed, the story of Jesus' healing of the paralytic in Mark 2:1–12 connects the forgiveness of sins with healing. As we saw in medieval rites of visitation of the sick, individual confession was one of the pastoral practices, along with the anointing and communion of the sick. In modern times too facile a connection between sin and disease has been eschewed. On the other hand, interest in holistic medicine, awareness of the relationship between lifestyle and disease, and the impact of the environment on health provides reasons to reconsider this biblical connection.

In contemporary society there has been a great deal of interest in health and wellness. As churches have searched their traditions for ways of ministering to the sick in a time when modern medicine has reduced the likelihood of "untimely death" due to catastrophic diseases or illness, but there is still a great desire for the ministry of healing,

---

[104] See James Dallen, *The Reconciling Community: The Rite of Penance* (New York: Pueblo Publishing Co., 1986).

[105] *The Rites of the Catholic Church* (New York: Pueblo Publishing Co., 1976), 337–64, 365–75, 376–9.

[106] *LBW*, 193–7. See also *Lutheran Worship—Agenda* (St. Louis: Concordia, 1984), 137–44.

[107] See Beverley A. Nitschke, "Confession and Forgiveness: The Continuing Agenda," *Worship* 68 (1996), 353–68.

[108] Lawrence E. Mick, *Penance: The Once and Future Sacrament* (Collegeville: The Liturgical Press, 1988).

they have come to see the ancient practice of anointing the sick as a means of proclaiming by a "visible word" God's will for the wholeness of creation. Recovering this practice has necessitated overcoming the Protestant antipathy to extreme unction, as practiced in the medieval church, and the Roman Catholic use of the ancient practice of anointing of the sick (James 5:14–15) only *in extremis*. The mainline churches have also had to carefully distinguish their practices of anointing and prayers for the healing of the sick from Pentecostal or "charismatic" practice, with its expectations of miraculous healings. This caution was necessitated by the fact that interest in sacramental healing coincided with the charismatic renewal movement in the mainline Protestant and Roman Catholic churches, which reached a high point in the 1960s and 1970s.

The anointing of the sick (as opposed to extreme unction, or "the last rites") reentered mainline Christian practice in the twentieth century through the Episcopal churches. Rites of unction were included in the 1928 revised edition of the *Book of Common Prayer* of the American Episcopal Church and the 1929 Prayer Book of the Scottish Episcopal Church. The 1962 revised Prayer Book of the Anglican Church of Canada also included an order for the anointing of the sick. Studies of rites of healing[109] in several mainline Protestant denominations and the Roman Catholic Church during the 1960s and 1970s led to the appearance of rites of anointing the sick in these churches in the 1970s and 1980s.[110]

Studies based on and promoting these rites have noted the connection between sin and sickness throughout the Bible, the anointing of prophets, priests, and kings in the Old Testament as a form of consecration, that Jesus' title, "the Christ," means "the anointed one," that oil is a type of the Holy Spirit, that Jesus commissioned his disciples to anoint with oil when they healed the sick (Mark 6:13), and that the practice of anointing for healing apparently became established in some early churches (James 5:14).[111]

Funerals and Burial of the Dead

Up until the advent of modern times, death was a reality with which societies and individuals had to deal. Perhaps sometimes death was dealt with too realistically. But since the Enlightenment, Western society has become progressively death-denying. The resurgence of the Greek notion of the immortal soul took the sting out of death. Contributing to the denial of death was the institution of the funeral home and embalming practices, in which the corpse could be made to look like someone asleep, and also the fact that many people die in hospitals and other institutions, out of the sight and experience of their families and friends. These cultural notions and experiences, combined with

---

[109] See Karl Rahner, *The Anointing of the Sick* (Denville, N.J.: Dimension Books, 1970); Morton T. Kelsey, *Healing and Christianity in Ancient Thought and Modern Times* (New York: Harper and Row, 1973).

[110] See *The Rites of the Catholic Church*, Vol. 2 (New York: Pueblo Publishing, 1980); *The Book of Common Prayer According to the Use of The Episcopal Church*, 453–61; *Occasional Services: Lutheran Book of Worship*, 89–102; *The United Methodist Book of Worship*, 613–30.

[111] See James L. Empereur, *The Message of the Sacraments*, Vol. 7: *Prophetic Anointing: God's Call to the Sick, the Elderly, and the Dying* (Wilmington, Del.: Michael Glazier, 1982); Charles W. Gusmer, *And You Visited Me: Sacramental Ministry to the Sick and Dying* (New York: Pueblo Publishing, 1984); Peter E. Fink, *Alternative Futures for Worship*, Vol. 7: *Anointing of the Sick* (Collegeville: Liturgical Press, 1988).

the growing practice of cremation, have made it difficult for the church to proclaim the gospel of the resurrection of Jesus, the expectation of the resurrection of the dead, and the hope of everlasting life.

In order to reclaim its proclamation, the contemporary churches have instituted practices designed to shore up the Christian proclamation by giving communities of faith and their ministers more control over the rites of death.[112] First and foremost, it is important to celebrate funerals in church buildings rather than in funeral homes. This is the place in which the congregation is used to gathering for worship and can more easily "own" the liturgy of death. In this setting it is possible to celebrate the full liturgy of Christian death, which in the revised rites of several churches is a form of the liturgy of the word and the eucharistic meal. Second, and just as important, the pastor or priest should preach at the funeral, using the texts read in the funeral service. This gives the community's preacher an opportunity to teach the biblical view of the reality of life and death. Third, the eucharist can be celebrated as a foretaste of the feast to come—the marriage supper of the Lamb in the kingdom of God—if this would be appropriate for the family of the deceased (that is, if they are faithful church members). Fourth, funerals held in the church building can use music and songs that invite congregational participation. Mourners often have "requests" that are usually honored by the officiating clergy. But these requests can be supplemented, if need be, by other songs which make a clearer proclamation of the gospel, if such is needed. Fifth, various Christian symbols can be used, such as the lighted paschal candle placed at the coffin as a reminder of baptism into the death and resurrection of Christ; a cross placed on or near the coffin, also as a reminder of one's baptism into Christ; a Bible placed on or near the coffin to symbolize the deceased's fidelity to the word of God. Sixth, the color white can be used—perhaps the parish's Easter array—to connect the Christian funeral with the proclamation of the resurrection of Christ. Seventh, there can be an immediate movement from the place of the funeral to the place of interment, suggesting that the funeral procession is a part of the ritual itself and not an interruption of the service. The procession itself can be symbolic of the Christian pilgrimage to the heavenly Jerusalem. Eighth, the coffin with the corpse should be interred in the presence of the witnesses, if that is feasible, with the proclamation of "the sure and certain hope of the resurrection to eternal life."

🍇 LITURGICAL ENVIRONMENT

We have seen that the main thrust of the liturgical movement of the twentieth century has been to recover a sense of the church as the mystical body of Christ, convened in an assembly for word and sacrament in which it performs its public work or leitourgia before the world. The liturgical movement has called for a greater sense of community in worship and an active participation in the rites of the church by the laity.

---

[112] See Richard Rutherford, *The Death of a Christian: The Rite of Funerals*, rev. ed. (New York: Pueblo Publishing Co., 1990), and *The Order of Christian Funerals: An Invitation to Pastoral Care* (Collegeville, Minn.: The Liturgical Press, 1990); also Virginia Sloyan, *A Sourcebook About Christian Death* (Chicago: Liturgy Training Publications, 1990).

These aims have had an impact on church architecture. Indeed, without an alteration of existing spaces or the construction of new spaces that would facilitate these goals, the major concerns of the liturgical movement would have been thwarted.

After World War II, it was necessary to rebuild many church buildings that had been destroyed by the war. Two German architects, Dominikus Boehm and Rudolf Schwartz, led the way in building churches that were austere, and in which the focus was on the liturgical action rather than on devotional objects.[113] After Vatican II, the Instruction on Implementing the Constitution on the Sacred Liturgy mandated a free-standing altar-table so that the priest could celebrate the eucharist facing the people. This led to the placement of a basilican-style presidential chair behind the altar, the removal of the tabernacle from the former high altar, the use of a simple ambo for the reading of scripture, the closure of side chapels, and the cessation of private masses with the emphasis on the community mass.

Architecture that expresses the goals of the liturgical renewal of the church is not that which simply provides more streamlined uses of contemporary materials, such as glass, steel, and concrete, but that which emphasizes the role of the assembly. Auditorium buildings continue to be built, especially by Evangelicals and Pentecostals. The auditorium design is preferred by "church growth"-oriented parishes and megachurches that either emphasize the "entertainment" factor in worship or that continue the frontier revival tradition in high-tech dress, such as the Garden Grove Community Church in Anaheim, California (the Crystal Cathedral) and Willow Creek Community Church in Barrington, Illinois. Neo-Gothic churches continue to be built also, although using contemporary designs such as the Cathedral at Coventry, England, and the Chapel at Valparaiso University in Indiana. Countless suburban A-frame buildings can also be classed as contemporary neo-Gothic.

There have been many contemporary experiments in building churches.[114] The work of Edward A. Sovik should be singled out. He has been concerned to provide space for worship in which the assembly and its functions are primary. Cognizant of the experiments with the Protestant meeting houses of the seventeenth and eighteenth centuries, and aware of the patristic ideal of the modern liturgical movement, Sovik has been building churches that are multipurpose in use but that also provide a room of generous proportions for the congregation's liturgical celebrations called a centrum. It should be clearly understood that this room is not a sanctuary, or a nave, or even a eucharistic hall such as some contemporary Roman Catholics have built; but a meeting place for people in which they can accomplish various liturgical tasks. To say that the room is multipurpose does not mean that it can serve every imaginable purpose; but it can accommodate such varied activities as worship, concerts, dramas, and sometimes even meals. It can do this because the furniture arrangement is flexible. Sovik advocates chairs rather than

---

[113] See Frederik Dubuyst, *Modern Architecture and Christian Celebration* (Richmond: John Knox Press, 1968), 24.

[114] A number of them are discussed in James F. White, *Protestant Worship and Church Architecture*, op. cit., 143ff. White continued the survey of "The Church Architecture of Change" beyond 1964 in *Christian Worship in Transition*, op. cit., chapter VIII, 143ff.

pews, modular platforms that can be arranged according to need, portable altar-tables and ambos. The only items in a Sovik church that are permanent fixtures in the centrum are the large baptismal pools with flowing water and pipe organs.[115] Among celebrated examples of Sovik's buildings are Our Savior's Lutheran Church in Jackson, Minnesota; Trinity Lutheran Church in Princeton, Minnesota; and Trinity United Methodist Church in Charles City, Iowa (this latter noted for its spacious concourse that facilitates the gathering of people before and after worship in the centrum).

One of the paradigms of contemporary Christian life is that of the servant ministry of Jesus Christ. Dietrich Bonhoeffer held that "in the incarnation God makes himself known as him who wishes to exist not for himself but 'for us'. Consequently, in view of the incarnation of God, to live as man before God can mean only to exist not for oneself but for God and for others."[116] Gibson Winter suggested that this insight must result in a new idea of the church. The idea of the church as a cultic community and the idea of the church as a confessing fellowship must now be replaced by the idea of the church as servant. "The Church as cultic community exercised its authority by replacing the disorder of the world with its own order. The Church as confessing fellowship embodied a sanctified life within the elect community and exercised its obedience in the world. The Church as servanthood of the laity is the discernment of the New [Humanity] within the structures of the world's life."[117]

Sovik has also picked up the paradigm of the incarnation and the social implications of the gospel in his theories of church architecture. If the church building is not a "house of God" but a "house of the people of God," and if God's people are servants in the world, then their building must reflect their servanthood.[118] Architecture as a technology needs to meet the demands of a modern shelter for people, which can be complex indeed. It must address traffic patterns, pedestrian flow, zoning and building codes, local standards of space usage, the arrangement of mechanical equipment, heating and cooling systems, kitchen and plumbing fixtures, as well as structural design and building materials.

Yet good architecture is not accomplished by just by solving technical problems. Architecture is also an art and as such communicates ideas. It does not do this just by being pleasing to the senses in its overall design and specific decorations. It makes a statement about the community that uses the building. Architecture is a form of witness. It witnesses to how the congregation serves God in its cultic life and in its ministries. It witnesses to how the congregation serves each other and the community surrounding the church building. It does this by providing spaces that do what needs to be done in them, that does not so overwhelm people that the building is inhospitable, and by using materials that are authentic and true to its character. A building will not witness to authenticity by employing cosmetics: for example, plaster painted to look like stone, veneer or plywood surfaces that pretend to be solid wood, plastic flooring that imitates slate. Indeed,

[115] E. A. Sovik, *Architecture for Worship* (Minneapolis: Augsburg Publishing House, 1973), 67ff.

[116] Dietrich Bonhoeffer, *Ethics*, ed. and trans. Eberhard Bethge (New York: Macmillan, 1955), 297.

[117] Gibson Winter, *The New Creation as Metropolis* (New York: Macmillan, 1963), 100.

[118] Sovik, 41ff.

since churches must be places of public accommodation, these kinds of materials are not practical because they will not hold up under long-term use. Church buildings should be constructed of brick, stone, and wood. Worship spaces should not be carpeted, except perhaps for a decorative carpet in front of or under the holy table. Every effort must be made to achieve balanced acoustics that are conducive to both speaking and singing.

A church building will not look "churchy," any more than Gothic churches were somehow more ecclesiastical-looking than the buildings that surrounded them in the Gothic age. An example of a non-"churchy"-looking church that nevertheless serves the its congregation's liturgical and social needs is Christ the Mediator Lutheran Church on the south side of Chicago. It is a modest building in a high-rise neighborhood. Like the buildings of Mies van der Rohe on the campus of the Illinois Institute of Technology a few blocks away, Christ the Mediator has a simple shape, simply framed, with a minimum of permanent internal divisions. Accepting the probability of change, the building looks neither new nor old; it does not try to imitate ecclesiastical structures of the past, nor does it make an effort to be contemporary. The only two spaces in the building that make any impression are the baptistery, which juts out toward the street corner on which the building is situated; and the altar space, which is the only portion of the building that can be considered "high and lifted up." The congregation, organized in 1960, has intentionally made the sacramental life the focus of its life together. Otherwise, there is a nave that allows people to "come and see" without overly exposing themselves, and a simple fellowship hall that can serve as a hospitality center. In other words, the building provides as much interaction as visitors may desire. The building does not overwhelm. But it does provide a sense of sacrality in the sacramental centers that goes beyond the sheer functionality of Sovik's buildings. This brings us to a final consideration: the church building as a "holy place."

Reformation Protestantism, and Protestantism in general, has eschewed the idea of the church building as a house of God. It is a shelter for the congregation. It is a meeting place for the assembly for word and sacrament. But this has not eliminated the popular attitude toward the church building as a "holy place." Indeed, one may observe an attitude of quiet reverence even in many Protestant church buildings. Nor has this behavior been discouraged. On the contrary, it is usually expected that quiet meditation will be maintained in the worship space before the service begins.

If the church building is not regarded as a house of God, in what sense may it be regarded as a "holy place"? A place is "holy" because it has been the location of an epiphany of the deity—a theophany. This has happened in buildings erected for worship. God's word has been proclaimed and the sacraments of Christ have been celebrated. Christ's presence has been experienced in word and sacrament, and through these means of grace a holy people have been formed. The evidence of faith active in acts of ministry is frequently deposited in church buildings, the houses of the church.

The remains of the holy people, the saints, are sometimes also deposited in the church building. We remember that the earliest buildings erected specifically for Christian worship were located over the tombs of the martyrs. Later on the remains of martyrs and saints were deposited in church buildings, particularly in the altars. Church grounds in both Europe and America have served as burial places of baptized Christians.

The church building deserves respect because it is a place where God's presence has been manifested in sacramental acts and in the lives and witness of God's people. The evidence of God's people in mission should be present in the church building through the display of artifacts and art works (and not just through denominational propaganda!). If new buildings, such as those erected by Sovik and company, are relatively void of artifacts and art works, this is not out of a puritanical resistance to such items; but rather so that items that are appropriate and meaningful to the local community of faith can be collected over a period of years, just as in our own homes we collect items over a period of years that are important to our family life and are accordingly put on display. Among those items displayed in our homes are pictures of family members. This argues for collections of icons of the saints in which we may be surrounded by the whole communion of saints as we do our liturgy.

Some church buildings become so representative of the culture of a local community that they acquire special status in the community beyond their evangelical use as a place of assembly for word and sacrament. When the primary purpose of the church building is obscured, the Protestant principle comes into play to critique the use of the space. Otherwise, the catholic substance of the church building as a house for the whole people of God, and a depository for items testifying to instances of Christian witness, should be affirmed.

CONTEMPORARY LITURGICAL CHALLENGES

Inculturation

There is no doubt that liturgy has been influenced by the culture of the people who have performed it in every stage of its development.[119] There are no aspects of Christian liturgy that are not derived from the various cultures through which it has passed in its historical evolution (e.g., Jewish meals, Greek rhetoric, Roman models of leadership, Byzantine court ceremonial, Mediterranean solstice festivals, etc.). Each of these cultural expressions has been transformed by use in Christian observance to contribute toward the formation of an ecclesiastical culture.[120] When missionaries bring their faith and practice to a new country, it is first necessary to "adapt" this faith and practice to local forms of cultural expression, since the missionary's faith and practice, rooted in the assumptions and expressions of a particular culture, cannot simply be replicated in the new location. "Adaptation" represents a cautious approach, however, since it is necessary to avoid religious (i.e., non-Christian) sensibilities rooted in the new culture in which the gospel is being proclaimed and celebrated. After a while the issue of inculturation is raised.

---

[119] See Frank C. Senn, *Christian Worship and its Cultural Setting* (Philadelphia: Fortress Press, 1983), especially chapter 3.

[120] See Anscar J. Chupungco, *Cultural Adaptation of the Liturgy* (New York: Paulist Press, 1982).

Inculturation (also called "contextualization" or "indigenization") has been a major concern in the Roman Catholic Church ever since the Constitution on the Sacred Liturgy opened the door to vernacularization. Because the Roman Catholic Church has had a concern to maintain ecclesiastical unity within a worldwide communion by appeal to the universal pastorate of the bishop of Rome, the initial efforts in reaching out to various cultures have been to adapt local cultural expressions to the Roman rite. But increasingly adaptation *(aptatio)* has been replaced by inculturation *(inculturatio)*, in which local forms replace the Roman archetype.[121]

The Pastoral Constitution of the Church in the Modern World began the movement from adaptation to inculturation by urging an appreciation of indigenous cultures. Inculturation was actually mandated in The Decree on the Missionary Activity of the Church *(Ad Gentes)*, which sees "seeds of the Word" *(semina Verbi)* being planted in every culture in which the gospel is proclaimed and celebrated. Pope John Paul II took up this analogy to the incarnation in his encyclical on missions, *Redemptoris Missio*. The pope wrote of introducing different cultures into the church, enriching the church's life with culturally embedded values and forms of expression. "Through inculturation the Church gives the Gospel body *(corporat)* in different cultures and at the same time leads peoples with their own cultures into its own community."[122] Yet there is still concern in the papal letter to place a safeguard on the processes of inculturation by urging adherence to the principles of remaining faithful to the gospel (understood here as the deposit of faith) and of remaining in communion with the universal church (specifically the Roman See). The 1994 instruction of the Congregation for Divine Worship and the Discipline of Sacraments on Inculturation and the Roman Liturgy builds on the pope's encyclical to provide guidelines for liturgical inculturation, but "within the unity of the Roman Rite."[123] This clearly indicates that, at least in the area of liturgy and culture, there is still a tension between "inculturation" and "adaptation."[124] The Roman ordo must be maintained even if indigenous texts and ceremonies are used. Gordon Lathrop, serving on the Lutheran World Federation Study Group dealing with Worship and Culture, has also asked, in a more hopeful vein, whether "the shape of the liturgy" cannot serve as "a framework for contextualization."[125]

Adaptation involves translation of texts and utilization of local forms of expression (e.g., music, art, architecture) within the forms and orders brought to a local culture by missionaries. True inculturation means replacing these forms and orders with indigenous forms and orders as well as linguistic and artistic expressions indigenous to the local

---

[121] See G. A. Arbuckle, "Inculturation not Adaptation: Time to Change Terminology," *Worship* 60 (1986), 511–20.

[122] John Paul II, "Litterae Encyclicae de perenni vi mandati missionalis," *AAS* LXXXIII (1990), 300 (no. 52).

[123] The Official Latin text of the instruction is "De Liturgia romana et inculturatione," *Notitiae* 30 (29 March 1994), 80–115. The English text appeared under the title *Inculturation of the Liturgy within the Roman Rite* (Vatican City: Vatican Press, 1994).

[124] See David N. Power, "Liturgy and Culture Revisited," *Worship* 69 (1995), 225–43.

[125] Gordon Lathrop, "The Shape of the Liturgy: A Framework for Contextualization," in *Christian Worship: Unity in Cultural Diversity*, ed. by S. Anita Stauffer (Geneva: Lutheran World Federation, 1996), 67–75.

culture. The difference might be illustrated with these examples. Adaptation means using some form of wheat bread and grape wine in the eucharist other than the products with which the missionaries were familiar in, say, Europe or North America. Inculturation means replacing wheat bread and grape wine entirely with local products, such as corn bread, rice wine, or even tea, in places in Africa and Asia where wheat and grapes are not always available. This might seem inconsequential, except that, theologically, the practice raises the question of how close subsequent Christian observance must be to the original institution of the sacrament, to the extent that can be known, since Christianity's saving gospel is rooted in actual historical events.[126] Or, again, the usual order places the liturgy of the word before the liturgy of the meal. But there may be cultural contexts in which it seems more logical to intermingle Bible readings and table talk with the liturgy of the meal, as indeed is the case in the Jewish Passover Seder (Ordo). That would rub up against a liturgical tradition that is at least as old as Justin Martyr and has acquired a theo-logic in terms of the distinction between the liturgy of the catechumens and the liturgy of the faithful.

It is noteworthy that Protestant churches have not been as excited to move to-ward inculturation as the Roman Catholic Church. While the Roman Catholic docu-ments speak of embodying the gospel in different cultures, the Lutheran World Federation study, *Worship and Culture in Dialogue*,[127] allows that the gospel may need to stand over against or at least alongside different cultures—including (perhaps espe-cially) cultures that have historically "hosted" Christianity (Christendom). Of the various models for relating the gospel to culture devised by H. Richard Niebuhr, the one that comes closest to describing the Lutheran approach is "Christ and culture in paradox."[128] This model regards culture as a reflection of the human condition: basically good because it is an expression of human creativity reflecting the *imago Dei* yet marred by the fall into sin and subject to evil. The concern is not to identify the gospel too closely with any par-ticular culture so that it may affirm what is good and criticize what is evil in each culture. In its Nairobi Report, the Lutheran World Federation study group suggested that wor-ship relates to culture in at least four ways.[129] The liturgy is *transcultural* in that it in-cludes orders and symbols that witness to the church as a worldwide communio. It is *contextual* in that it always admits the use of natural or cultural elements in worship in each locality. It is *countercultural* in that the gospel it proclaims and celebrates always holds out the vision of an alternative worldview and lifestyle. It is *cross-cultural* in that it uses expressions from different cultures.

The issue of inculturation has loomed in importance in non-Western societies and younger churches because of the need to disentangle Christianity from the Western

---

[126] See the discussion in Geoffrey Wainwright, *Doxology*, op. cit., 363–4. It might be noted that wheat and grapes did not grow in Scandinavia, yet efforts were made to continue using wheat-bread and grape-wine in continuity with the tradition.

[127] *Worship and Culture in Dialogue*. Reports of International Consultations in Cartigny, Switzerland, 1993 and Hong Kong, 1994, ed. by S. Anita Stauffer (The Lutheran World Federation: Geneva, 1994).

[128] See H. Richard Niebuhr, *Christ and Culture* (New York: Harper and Row, 1951).

[129] *Christian Worship: Unity in Cultural Diversity*, 14ff.

culture imposed during the period of colonialization and domination, during which local forms of cultural expressions were suppressed by the churches. It must be recognized that the issue of inculturation is complicated by the fact that pagan religious sensibilities are attached to many cultural practices, and that conversion sometimes means eschewing the culture in which one was reared. But after a time it seems religiously "safe" to revisit indigenous cultural expressions. Some proposed forms of inculturation in Christian liturgy include African initiation rites[130] and ways of honoring ancestors;[131] Indian forms of greeting and hospitality;[132] the style of the Japanese tea ceremony;[133] and American Indian/Alaska Native ways of showing oneness with the earth.[134] Employing cultural expressions that are rooted in paganism (as many Western customs originally were) requires a pastoral assessment of the congregation's maturity in faith and a kind of "baptism" of the practice so that it is clearly serving the evangelical purpose of proclaiming the gospel of Jesus Christ.

In addition to models of adaptation and inculturation, there is the phenomenon of cross-cultural or multicultural liturgy in which expressions from foreign or minority cultures within a dominant culture are given expression in the liturgy. This has been an especially important issue in the pluralistic culture of North America. As the church has "included" people of various ethnic backgrounds within its membership, it has had to find ways of including the cultural expressions of the various subcultures within its worship.[135] This is not an easy task because the dominant group does not easily surrender its forms of expression or reach out to "include" expressions from other groups. Lutherans in North America became "Americanized," in part, by including English and American hymns in their hymnals. This was not a foregone conclusion at the beginning of the twentieth century, when some Lutherans argued that it was not possible to articulate Lutheran doctrines in languages other than German and Latin. Since the beginning of the twentieth century, most mainline Protestant (white) denominations have included African American spirituals, such as "Were You There" and "Go Tell It on the Mountain," in their hymnals. More recently, gospel songs from the African American religious culture as well as Spanish-language songs from the Hispanic culture have been sung in predominantly European American liturgical assemblies. New hymnals published in North America include representative samplings of songs from Hispanic and African American religious

---

[130] See C. Mubengayi Lwakale, *Initiation africaine et initiation chrétienne* (Leopoldville [Kinshasa]: Editions du C. E. P., 1966); B. Burki, "Traditional Initiation in Africa," *Studia Liturgica* 12 (1977), 201–6.

[131] See H. Sawyer, *Creative Evangelism: Towards a new Christian encounter with Africa* (London: Lutterworth Press, 1968), especially chapter 5 ("A Fresh Liturgical Approach").

[132] See J. R. Chandran and W. Q. Lash, eds., *Christian Worship in India* (Bangalore: CLS, 1961).

[133] See Joseph Keenan, "Tea and Eucharist," *Worship* 56 (1976), 365–84.

[134] See Hilaire Valiquette, "Pueblos and Catholicism," *Proceedings of the North American Academy of Liturgy, Annual Meeting Albuquerque, NM 2–5 January 1993* (Valparaiso, Ind.: Valparaiso University, 1993), 17–33, with extensive bibliography on pp. 32–3.

[135] See Mark R. Francis, C.S.V., *Liturgy in a Multi-Cultural Community* (Collegeville: The Liturgical Press, 1991).

traditions, as well as songs from the global church.[136] These hymnals help to promote multicultural expressions in the liturgies of local assemblies.

The issue of the relation of liturgy to culture is a challenge not only in societies that have not been historically Christian, but also in those that have hosted a Christianized culture. The estrangement of Western secular society from the life of the church since the Enlightenment has prompted many critics to speak of a "post-Christian culture."[137] The major artists of Western societies, who give expression to culture, have flourished outside of the church since the Enlightenment. J. S. Bach may well have been the last major composer to earn a living in the church, although a number of later "secular" composers successfully wrote music for the church. Yet the arts have played an important role in building bridges between the community of faith and the secular society in which Christians live. Theologians such as Paul Tillich[138] and Joseph Sittler[139] devoted much attention to the relation between Christian thought, the arts, and culture, and perceived the fact that liturgy is the arena of mediation between the world and faith, and between nature and grace. Although noted especially for his acute sensitivity to the messages and methods of contemporary poets, Sittler also pointed out ways in which contemporary architecture assigns greater prominence to the world of nature by its use of texture, light, and color. He believed that in the setting of a contemporary church building, the doctrine of creation could take on new meaning as it is celebrated in creed and hymn, prayer and proclamation.[140] In James White's assessment, "In the 1950s and 1960s, most of the better examples of church architecture built in America were for Missouri Synod Lutheran congregations, largely guided by the faculty of Concordia Seminary in Saint Louis."[141]

The same Lutheran openness to the expressions of culture has been displayed in the area of church music. There has been a renaissance of church music in the twentieth century, especially in Germany.[142] It has built on the foundation of the liturgiological and musicological research that began in the late nineteenth century and led to the restoration of forms of church music from the past, such as chorale preludes, motets, cantatas, passions, and so forth. The great romantic composers who generated this interest in the past were Johannes Brahms and Max Reger (1873–1916). The restoration of past forms and styles in church music owes much to Brahm's disciple, Heinrich Freiherr von

---

[136] For a quality example of this kind of collection see *Gather,* 2nd ed., ed. by Robert J. Bastastini and Michael A. Cymbala (Chicago: GIA Publications, Inc., 1994), which is an expansion of *Gather* (1st ed.).

[137] See Gabriel Vahanian, *The Death of God: The Culture of Our Post-Christian Era* (New York: George Braziller, 1957).

[138] See Paul Tillich, *Theology of Culture* (New York: Oxford University Press, 1959).

[139] See Joseph Sittler, *Essays on Nature and Grace* (Philadelphia: Fortress Press, 1972); but more especially his address, "Dogma and Doxa," in Mandus Egge, ed., *Worship: Good News in Action* (Minneapolis: Augsburg Publishing House, 1973), 7–23.

[140] See Joseph Sittler, "A Hammer, the Incarnation, and Architecture," in *The Christian Century* LXXIV, No. 13 (1957), 394–5; "The Matrix of Form in Church Architecture," in Finley Eversole, ed., *Christian Faith and the Contemporary Arts* (Nashville: Abingdon Press, 1962); and "Faith and Form," in *The Anguish of Preaching* (Philadelphia: Fortress Press, 1966), 43–65.

[141] James F. White, *Protestant Worship: Traditions in Transition*, op. cit., 55.

[142] See Adam Adrio, "Renewal and Rejuvenation," in Blume, ed., *Protestant Church Music*, op. cit., 405–506.

Herzogenberg (1843–1900) and to Reger's contemporary, Arnold Mendelssohn. In the church motets of both composers the influence of Heinrich Schütz is discernible. Standing more between liturgy and culture was Heinrich Kaminski (1886–1946), who struggled against late romantic idioms to develop a unique polyphonic style based on older models. Beginning in the 1920s more exciting choral and organ compositions for church services were being composed by Kurt Thomas, Ernst Pepping, and Hugo Distler (1908–1942). After World War II the major German church composers were H. F. Micheelsen and Jan Bender, who continued the reliance on Schütz-inspired styles during the first half of the twentieth century, and Hans Werner Zimmermann, who juxtaposed elements of the polyphonic motet with jazz.

This renewal of church music in Germany was transferred to North American Lutheranism, where it was propagated by a host of well-trained organists and church musicians serving as cantors of larger parishes, such as Paul Manz, or on the faculties of Lutheran colleges, beginning with F. Melius Christiansen at Saint Olaf College and his sons Paul and Olaf. Richard Hillert and Carl Schalk, on the faculty of Concordia University, River Forest, Illinois, have led the way in composing liturgical settings and choral music based on this contemporary classical style. Gracia Grindal has argued that the liturgical music and hymnody in *LBW* pervasively reflects the modern, antiromantic biases of this generation of Lutheran church musicians.[143] There has been a turning, especially in pietistic circles where subjective feelings are a criterion for judging worship, toward more neo-romantic, lyrical expressions from composers like Marty Haugen, who provided a setting of Holy Communion for the *Hymnal Supplement 1991* as well as the Holden Evening Prayer.

The liturgical traditions we have been considering are largely European in origin. It is understandable that African Americans and other people becoming acutely aware of their own cultural history might look for ways to express their traditions within the historic Christian liturgy.[144] African American worship has a complex history in that it was first practiced by evangelized slaves who often had to meet clandestinely with their preachers.[145] Worship was a source of renewal and hope for an oppressed people; in their gatherings for worship black slaves could pass on, from one generation to another, styles of praying and singing brought from Africa. At the same time, black worship was as much affected as white worship by the format of worship at the camp meetings of the early nineteenth century. A basic pattern common to revival or "frontier" worship is practiced

---

[143] Gracia Grindal, "To Translate Is to Betray: Trying to Hand the Lutheran Tradition On," *dialog* 33 (1994), 183–90.

[144] See Robert Michael Franklin, "Defiant Spirituality: Worship and Formation in the Black Churches," in *Proceedings of the North American Academy of Liturgy, Annual Meeting Washington, D.C., 2–5 January 1992* (Valparaiso, Ind.: Valparaiso University, 1992), 15–23.

[145] See Melva Wilson Costen, "African-American Worship," in Robert E. Webber, ed., *The Complete Library of Christian Worship: Volume 2, Twenty Centuries of Christian Worship* (Nashville: Star Song Publishing Group, 1994), 89–95. Lester B. Scherer, *Slavery and the Churches in Early America, 1619–1818* (Grand Rapids: Eerdmans Publishing Co., 1975), provides a scholarly account of the evangelization process of black slaves and examples of the oppressive sermonizing and baptismal vows required of slaves, which gives insight into the need for separate worship spaces and rituals among the African Americans in early America.

in many black churches: gathering with songs of praise; sharing testimonies; calls to confession of sins and professions of faith; sharing concerns, which lead to thanksgivings, intercessions, and prayers for healing; proclaiming the word and preaching; responding to the word of God (invitation to discipleship); baptism and the Lord's Supper (when scheduled); and sending forth in God's name.[146] The prevalence of this pattern of worship complicates efforts to incorporate African American styles of worship into orders of worship used in predominantly European American denominations.[147] The African American Catholic hymnal, *Lead Me, Guide Me* (G.I.A. Publications), has proven to be a useful resource in several liturgical denominations as well as Roman Catholic.

At the same time as black styles of worship are being incorporated into predominantly white denominations, in the traditional African American churches there are criticisms of utilizing "white styles." A kind of antiquarianism is implied in this critique, although the need of historically oppressed peoples to return to their roots must be appreciated. Already in 1818 Bishop Richard Allen, the founder of the African Methodist Episcopal Church, published a hymnal for the exclusive use of his black congregation in which he collected 314 hymns and spirituals that would have a special appeal to his members.[148] The use of hymns and spirituals has been diminishing in black worship in favor of choir-led gospel music. Zora Neale Hurston has criticized the use of the standards of the professional recording artist instead of the moans and sounds of the people in "the sanctified church."[149]

The "return to roots" that was popularized by Alex Haley's *Roots* and the television series by that name in the 1970s[150] presents us with a peculiar use of history, and an example of a unique American religiosity that is common to both European Americans and African Americans. This religiosity wants to connect with origins without the need to deal with the intervening historical experiences. In the opinion of the critic Harold Bloom, "One of the grand myths of the American Religion is the restoration of the Primitive Church, which probably never existed."[151] The concept of the "myth of the Primitive Church" uses "myth" in a way congenial with Eliade's use of the term since it implies a condition that existed before the "fall" into history. Implicit in the idea of a "return to roots" is the assumption that all intervening history between one's origins and one's present time has been a negative development. In this sense the "American Religion," as Bloom describes it, partakes of qualities found in ancient Gnosticism.

---

[146] See Melva Wilson Costen, "Models of Renewing Worship: African-American Worship," in Robert E. Webber, ed., *The Complete Library of Christian Worship: Volume 3, The Renewal of Sunday Worship* (Nashville: Star Song Publishing Group, 1993), 131–5.

[147] See Clarence Joseph Rivers, ed., *This Far by Faith: American Worship and Its African Roots* (Washington, D.C.: National Office of Black Catholics, 1977), for the collection of major papers presented during a conference in 1977 on "Worship and Spirituality in the Black Community." For example of integration of a black style into a historic order of worship see John L. Heinemeier, "Class or Mass: Some Thoughts on Black Lutheran Liturgy," *Lutheran Forum* 25/2 (1991), 32–4.

[148] The latest edition is *The Hymnal: African Methodist Episcopal Church* (1984).

[149] See Zora Neale Hurston, *The Sanctified Church* (Berkeley: Turtle Island Press, 1981).

[150] See Michael Kammen, *Mystic Chords of Memory*, 641–5.

[151] Harold Bloom, *The American Religion*, 40.

Alienated from nature, history, community, institutions, and authorities, Americans practice a religion that is enthusiastic, experiential, personal, and subjective. It also tends to be antisacramental, antihistorical, antiinstitutional, and anticlerical. Beyond an interest in (prehistoric) origins, American religionists are, by and large, only interested in the Bible. They are biblicistic in a way in which even the Protestant reformers would have found unacceptable, since the Christianity of the reformers (as of the fathers) is a religion of creeds, church orders, liturgies, and polities as well as a religion of the book. This is why Bloom regards the "American Religion" as "post-Christian"—not in the sense of the European "post-Christian" secular culture, but in the sense that American Christianity is only in tenuous continuity with historical Christianity. This situation presents a special challenge to churches that are committed to the use of the historic liturgy and to the claims of historic confessions of faith. This situation explains why the use of this liturgy or details of the catholic liturgical heritage cannot be defended with appeals to historical use. Down deep, most Americans would view that as a reason to discard the practice. It explains why there is a grass roots ecumenism that is impatient with the more cautious ecumenical negotiations of the confessional traditions. Many American laypeople simply share a common religious sensibility.

The religious sensibility of Western culture presents a special challenge to the observance of the church year, with its cycle of historical commemorations. Church festivals and commemorations must contend against secularized versions of these festivals or against civil and cultural observances. As examples of the former, we note that Christmas (the Nativity of our Lord) continues to compete with the winter solstice celebrations throughout the world and that, in northern European countries, the Nativity of Saint John the Baptist has been all but eclipsed by the midsummer nature celebrations. In the United States, civil holidays such as New Year's Day, Memorial Day, Independence Day, and Labor Day, along with self-congratulatory festivals invented by the Protestant churches early in the twentieth century, such as Mother's Day, Children's Day, Father's Day, and Rally Day, compete with the church year calendar, to the extent that it is observed. The liturgical churches have resisted the impact of these days more than the free churches, but not entirely. Sometimes the civil and liturgical festivals collide, as when Mother's Day or Memorial Day bump up against the Day of Pentecost. The church's usual strategy has been, on the one hand, to capitalize on what remains of the Christian cultural legacy in a post-Christian society; and, on the other hand, to baptize or transform civil or cultural observances. These strategies have not been totally successful, since they send mixed signals. For example, the pastor may deemphasize Mother's Day by focusing on the role of Mary, the Mother of our Lord; the congregation still thinks that it is observing Mother's Day.

Jews and Moslems in North America have managed to maintain observance of their holy days in a cultural context in which social support for their festivals and days of devotion is lacking. But it might be too facile to suggest that Christians consult with Jewish and Moslem leaders and congregations to learn how to compete with the secular culture in order to practice a religious discipline. The liability that faces catholic Christianity is that it has to contend against a religiosity that retains only a tenuous connection with historical Christianity, yet regards itself as Christian. This situation presents a serious challenge to calls for inculturation in America, since the American mission field presents a religious sensibility that is as much in need of conversion into the catholic faith as any non-Christian mission field.

The Feminist Critique

Among the cultural challenges to liturgy, the feminist critique deserves special attention because it challenges the theological content of the liturgy.

The liturgical movement peaked in the 1960s and 1970s, just when the women's liberation movement was gaining momentum. Liturgical reforms of this period reflected the concerns of women for economic and social equality with men. Efforts to make the liturgy more "inclusive" of women and men included the elimination of gender-specific references as regards the human community and liturgical assembly. There were some initial efforts to discover more "gender-inclusive" images and metaphors of God for use in liturgical prayers and hymns. Attempts at the use of inclusive language, especially as concerns the human community, are evident in the authorized worship books of the late 1970s, such as *Lutheran Book of Worship* and *Book of Common Prayer according to the Use of the Episcopal Church*, although most feminists would think that these efforts are now woefully inadequate. The Inclusive Language Lectionary and the New Revised Standard Version of the Bible have provided a more gender-inclusive reading of the sacred texts, but there has also been a criticism of the lack of readings depicting women's experiences in the lectionaries.[152] Even more significant than inclusive language and images, however, have been efforts to secure visible roles for women in the liturgy as presiding and assisting ministers. The increasing number of women liturgical leaders, both ordained and lay, has also made the liturgy itself as a "public work of the people" more gender-inclusive.[153]

The use of more gender-inclusive language with which to address God has been an especially vexing issue. Gail Ramshaw has guided the church in the direction of "de-genderizing" God by proposing that personal pronouns be eliminated as far as possible in God-language, that verbs be used more than nouns, and that the "myth of the crown" be reformed so that "sovereign" be used instead of "king" and "dominion" in place of "kingdom."[154]

It has to be admitted that theological concerns and preferred language styles in the 1970s have exacerbated the problem of God language by accentuating address to God as "Father" beyond what it had been in the Western liturgical tradition and by requiring

---

[152] See Marjorie Procter-Smith, "Images of Women in the Lectionary," in Elizabeth Schüssler Fiorenza and Mary Collins, eds., *Women: Invisible in Church and Theology.* Consilium 182 (Edinburgh: T & T Clark Ltd., 1985), 51–62.

[153] I use the term "gender-inclusiveness" because of its widespread use in current parlance. However, gender is really a grammatical construction and concerns pronominal/verbal agreement. Where references are made to men and women in biological terms, the word "sex" (as in "sexual-inclusiveness") ought to be used.

[154] See Gail Ramshaw, *God Beyond Gender: Feminist Christian God-Language* (Minneapolis: Fortress Press, 1995).

the recurring use of the pronoun "he" because of the stylistic preference for indicative sentences. Thus, in order to foster a more familiar and less forbidding approach to God, the relational name of "Father" was preferred in prayers to the traditional Latin *Deus* or *Omnipotens Deus* or *Domine,* which are common in the classical Latin collects, and which have a certain gender-neutrality about them. Or again, the translations of the Creeds broke up paragraph-long sentences into shorter sentences of an indicative character (especially in the second article concerning the Son of God), declaring over and over again "He was conceived . . . He suffered . . . He descended . . . He rose . . . He ascended . . . He will come . . ." whereas the Latin and older English versions use the relative pronoun "Who," in a series of dependent clauses.

Nevertheless, trinitarian language has been a tough nut to crack. Some have argued that the imposition of the masculine name of God in baptism (i.e., Father, Son, and Holy Spirit) marginalizes women in their very reception of the covenant of grace.[155] But proposals to substitute "Creator, Redeemer, and Sanctifier" for the Name of the Father, the Son, and the Holy Spirit have been found inadequate for several reasons. (1) There is nothing specific in such a description of God. There is no god worth being a god who is not confessed to be a creator, a redeemer, and a sanctifier. (2) The Father alone within the Holy Trinity cannot be identified as the "Creator" since the Spirit and the Logos were also the agents of creation (Gen. 1:1; John 1:1). (3) In classical trinitarian confessions the Son is not created, but "begotten"; and the Spirit "proceeds from the Father" ("and the Son"—a source of disagreement between the Orthodox East and the Catholic West). (4) These terms are not names and they do not convey the relational character of the Holy Trinity as a community of persons who brings into being a community of faith. (5) The names of the Father, the Son, and the Holy Spirit are rooted in biblical narratives. Jesus calls God his "Father" in consequence of being designated as "Son" by the heavenly voice in the stories of his baptism and transfiguration. The "Spirit" is the bond between the Father and the Son imparted to human beings as the advocate of the truth of this revelation. In keeping with those narratives Ramshaw proposes the substitution of "Abba, Servant, and Paraclete" for "Father, Son, and Holy Spirit" as a gender-inclusive way of honoring the biblically rooted doctrine of the Trinity.[156]

Others have argued that even gender-inclusive language is inadequate to women's concerns because it does not help to overcome notions of the maleness of God embedded in our cultural assumptions and images of God. Marjorie Procter-Smith has proposed that what is needed is "emancipatory" God-language that helps to liberate women from the suppression brought about by living in a patriarchal culture.[157] Some women, especially in the Roman Catholic Church, finding official resistance to the inclusion of women in the ministries and work of the church, have banded together in supportive spirituality groups known as Women-church. Spearheaded by Rosemary Radford

---

[155] See Ruth C. Duck, *Gender and the Name of God: The Trinitarian Baptismal Formula* (New York: Pilgrim Press, 1991).

[156] Gail Ramshaw, "Naming the Trinity: Orthodoxy and Inclusivity," *Worship* 60 (1986), 491–8.

[157] Marjorie Procter-Smith, *In Her Own Rite: Constructing Feminist Liturgical Tradition* (Nashville: Abingdon, 1990), 85ff.

Ruether, these groups began "to take the shaping of the symbolic universe into their own hands."[158] These groups used the term "God/dess" to signify the oneness of divinity even as it honors the feminine and masculine forms of the word for the divine. Reuther, along with others, has pointed out that "Spirit" in both Hebrew (*ruach*) and Greek (*pneuma*) is feminine and that the feminine *sophia* (wisdom) is referred to by Jesus in Matthew 11:18–19.[159] There have been experiments in praying to Sophia. Perhaps the most controversial was at the worship event that took place at the RE-imagining Conference held in Minneapolis on November 4–7, 1993.[160] The closing worship service of this ecumenical event included the following prayer in a kind of communion service that included the sharing of milk and honey.

> Our maker Sophia, we are women in your image: With the hot blood of our wombs we give form to new life. With the courage of our convictions we pour out our life blood for justice. Sophia, creator God, let your milk and honey flow, shower us with your love. Our sweet Sophia, we are women in your image: With nectar between our thighs we invite a lover, we birth a child; with our warm body fluids we remind the world of its pleasures and sensations. Our guide, Sophia, we are women in your image: With our moist mouths we kiss away a tear, we smile encouragement, we prophesy a full humanity to all peoples.

The Judaeo-Christian tradition has been wary of attributing sexual characteristics to God, especially in reaction to ancient fertility rites that identified the deity with the creation or to ancient Gnostics who regularly worshiped the divine dyad: "God the Father/ God the Mother."[161] Catherine Mowry LaCugna has also objected to stereotyping the Spirit's activities according to culture-determined roles for women. "Nor should we give the impression that the Father and the Son are masculine, and the Spirit feminine; a Trinity that is predominantly (two-thirds) male with one female person implies that Father and Son are, or should be imaged, solely as masculine. Further, since the Spirit is always third, the association of feminine imagery solely with the Spirit would reinforce the subordination of women in church and society."[162]

Criticizing Christian worship in word and sacrament that "is in large measure shaped by an androcentric agenda which fosters relationships of domination and oppression," June C. Goudey proposes the development of "worship which, from its inception, has been rooted in communal life and ordered by the Spirit of Jesus the Christ."[163] Drawing upon models of feminist psychology that deal with "internalized" oppression by

---

[158] Rosemary Radford Ruether, *Women-Church: Theology and Practice of Feminist Liturgical Communities* (San Francisco: Harper and Row, 1985), 2.

[159] See Rosemary Radford Ruether, *Sexism and God-Talk: Toward a Feminist Theology* (Boston: Beacon Press, 1983), 58–61.

[160] This controversial conference was described perhaps most dispassionately in "A Controverted Conference," *The Christian Century* 111:5 (February 16, 1994), 160–2.

[161] Elaine Pagels, *The Gnostic Gospels* (New York: Random House Vintage Books, 1989), 48ff.

[162] Catherine Mowry LaCugna, "Freeing the Christian Imagination," *dialog* 33 (1994), 194. These comments confuse gender with sexuality; "Spirit" may be feminine without being female. The Trinity is neither male nor female.

[163] June C. Goudey, *Proceedings of the North American Academy of Liturgy, 1993,* op. cit., 89.

helping women to "take back their strength," and that propose a "self-in-relation" theory that "makes connections count," she offers a vision of a kind of worship that enables women to "claim their wholeness." Such worship "models inclusivity in all its aspects; openly celebrates embodiment; is participatory without being manipulative; fosters a relational sense of self which enhances mutuality between participants; allows for shared leadership; expands the canon of sacred texts, gestures and music; and holds women's stories/experiences as sacred stories."[164]

Feminist theory and praxis has not appealed to all women in the church. As it becomes more extreme, there are bound to be reactions. But it needs to be affirmed that the feminist critique has produced some positive contributions to liturgical renewal. Images of God in the Bible have been discovered that have not been utilized before. Women in the Bible and in the Christian tradition have come to be seen as models of faith, of whom the Mary the Mother of our Lord has always been preeminent. Liturgical planning has sought to include women and children in terms of their own needs, which inculcates a sense of the church as the "family of God" in which each member is equally cared for. Drawing upon a provocative distinction by Ronald Grimes,[165] Lesley A. Northup has argued that male-dominated liturgy requires space that is vertical and cultivates attitudes that are hierarchical, whereas female-dominated liturgy uses space that is horizontal (e.g., circular) and cultivates attitudes that are egalitarian and inclusive.[166] In these ways, even if worship of the mother goddess is rejected as neo-pagan and incompatible with the Christian worship of God, the feminist critique has affected liturgy in the mainline churches for years to come.

Reaching the Unchurched

A third major challenge to traditional liturgy comes from the so-called church growth movement. This movement, ostensibly in the name of evangelism (or the recruitment of church members from an increasingly unchurched population), not only challenges the style and content of the liturgy, but advocates the abolition of "traditional" liturgy altogether as the primary vehicle of the church's public celebrations.[167] "A generation of seekers"[168] absent from church since their youth or not raised in it at all, purportedly finds the traditional forms of ceremony, music, and even texts opaque, unattractive, and a barrier to reassimilation into church life. Megachurches boasting thousands of members, which resemble college campuses or shopping malls, and which are usually named "Community Church of . . ." so as not to scare away potential attendees with

---

[164] Ibid., 93.

[165] Ronald Grimes, "Liturgical Supinity, Liturgical Erectitude," *Studia Liturgica* 23 (1993), 51–69.

[166] Lesley A. Northup, "Claiming Horizontal Space: Women's Religious Rituals," *Studia Liturgica* 25 (1995), 86–102.

[167] Literature generated by this movement is not extensive because it relies more on high-touch/high-tech approaches to communication through workshops and videos, on-site visits and demonstrations. For a description of worship at Willow Creek Community Church in South Barrington, Illinois, see *The Complete Library of Christian Worship: Volume 3, The Renewal of Sunday Worship*, 124–7.

[168] See Wade Clark Roof, *A Generation of Seekers: The Spiritual Journeys of the Baby Boom Generation* (San Francisco: Harper and Row, 1992).

doctrinaire-sounding denominational labels, do not offer a "traditional liturgy" as the main attraction on Sunday morning, unless it is one option among other "contemporary services."[169] Instead, they offer "seeker services" that feature rock music at worship services, dramatizations, interviews, testimonies, and upbeat messages (instead of sermons), which draw on popular psychology to give lessons on overcoming addictions or negative thinking. Addiction and recovery have virtually replaced sin and grace as theological categories. Practitioners of this kind of celebrational encounter with the unchurched do not hesitate to refer to their efforts as entertainment evangelism.[170] There is no doubt that worship leaders have learned much from television communication,[171] and they even provide large TV screens in their auditoriums so that attendees reared on television can view the celebration from various angles. This generation grew up with TV, and it relates more to visual images than to printed texts.

Sunday morning worship in "growth-oriented" churches is given over to celebrational encounters with the unchurched. In spite of the use of high-tech media, the typical "seeker service" is really a form of the old frontier or revival pattern of worship with a gathering including songs, testimonies, concerns, and prayers, followed by the reading of scripture and preaching, and a response to the word. In the contemporary megachurch the response involves post-service discussion and invitations to join classes and groups rather than an explicit invitation to discipleship. "Growth-oriented" churches provide small groups for every imaginable need. It seems that the baby boomer generation, which is directly targeted in the marketing strategies of these churches, has a great deal of self-confidence that nevertheless needs to be shored up. According to Wade Clark Roof's sociological survey, eighty-six percent say that if you believe in yourself, there is almost no limit to what you can do. This self-confidence underlies an increasing demand for therapeutic services, from various forms of counseling to self-help support groups, since they believe that they can "get it together" within themselves; and it underlies their reported tolerance of people who are different from themselves in race, creed, or lifestyle.

In spite of the seeming "liberal" approach and attitudes that flourish in suburban megachurches, these churches are essentially conservative evangelical congregations. The Willow Creek Community Church in Barrington, Illinois, is related to the conservative evangelical tradition associated with Wheaton College. Classes in "Christianity 101" and support groups lead to "believers' worship," which occurs on Wednesday or Thursday nights. The format of "believers' worship" in this tradition may not be too different from the format on Sunday morning, except that the "message" is more explicitly evangelical and emphasizes the power and help that believers have in God. Sometimes the Lord's Supper is celebrated as a source of this power.

One cannot fault such churches for building on their own tradition of revivalism. The challenge to liturgical worship comes from the fact that congregations of mainline

---

169 "Traditional" services at the Crystal Cathedral (Garden Grove Community Church) in Anaheim, California, and at the Willow Creek Community Church in Barrington, Illinois, are held on weekdays rather than Sundays.

170 See Walter P. Kallestad, "Entertainment Evangelism," *The Lutheran* 3 (May 23, 1990), 17ff.

171 See Quentin J. Schultze, *Televangelism and American Culture—The Business of Popular Religion* (Grand Rapids: Baker Book House, 1991).

denominations turn to such traditions as models for their own growth and, in the name of evangelism, offer "alternative services," "contemporary worship," or "creative liturgies."[172] Yet, these celebrations, too, like those in the megachurches, follow the patterns of frontier worship. Charles Finney, with his "new measures," is the church growth movement's church father. Ingredients of "alternative worship services" include: a warm-up medley of songs performed by choirs with such names as "Hosanna! Singers" or "Celebration Alive! Singers" (as in the Rationalist liturgies of the early nineteenth century, many exclamation marks are used); dramatizations of Bible stories either by church drama groups or children from the church school; songs with simple "praise and glory" choruses that the congregation is invited to sing; and the "sermon message" given by an unvested preacher (sometimes even in shirt sleeves, like the revivalists of yesteryear) with a soft-cover Bible in hand. Communion services resemble those of the Rationalist liturgies reported in chapter fifteen.

The communion service below, published by Worship Alive! of Tempe, Arizona, is an example.[173] While the publisher provides a different liturgical text for every Sunday, the services tend to follow a regular order. In this particular text for the Epiphany season, after the gathering of the offering, during which the song "Take my life and let it be" is sung, the "prayers of the parish" are offered and the Lord's Prayer is said. Then:

> *Pastor*: Following the will of the Lord has never been easy. Satan is around every corner, waiting to deceive us, mock our faith, and pull us from the family of God. We need strength to overcome and renewal in our faith. Today Jesus stands before us with an invitation to come to Him, to lay down our wills and make His will our own; to taste and touch Him, and be filled with love that strengthens us for every situation in life.

> *Song*:　Take my will and make it Thine;
> 　　　　it shall be no longer mine.
> 　　　　Take my heart, it is Your own;
> 　　　　it shall be Your royal throne.

> *Pastor*: Before you is a table the Lord has prepared. The bread, His body, and the wine, His blood, are the nourishment we need for daily living, for spiritual wholeness. Jesus invites you to dine with him—listen to His call to you:

> The Words of Consecration of the Bread and Wine

> *Pastor*: The mercy and love of the Lord await you in this meal. Come to the table and be filled with all that is good, and may His peace be with you and in you now and forever. Amen.

> *Song*:　Take my love: my Lord, I pour
> 　　　　at Your feet its treasure store;
> 　　　　Take myself and I will be
> 　　　　ever, only, all for thee.

> Welcome to the Table of the Lord
> Blessing (based on Heb. 13:20)
> Closing Song: "I have decided to follow Jesus"

---

[172] See Frank C. Senn, "'Worship Alive': An Analysis and Critique of Alternative Worship Services," *Worship* 69 (1995), 194–224.

[173] *1993 Worship Alive!* The Fellowship Ministries, 6202 S. Maple, Suite 121, Tempe, AZ 85283.

Several observations may be made about this order of celebration. First, a perusal of a number of Worship Alive! resources indicates that the order of Holy Communion is as invariable as that in any traditional order. Even creative liturgists rub up against the common human limitation that there are only so many ways to do or say a thing, and that once a satisfactory form is found one continues to work within it. Second, while the theology or piety reflected in alternative worship services is not unchristian, it is deficient from the perspective of orthodoxia. It is deficient because it is Jesus-oriented devotion, but it is not grounded in trinitarian worship. All the classical texts of the liturgy that are trinitarian are omitted from alternative worship, including "Glory to God in the highest," the ecumenical Creeds, and the Great Thanksgiving. It is further deficient because it appeals to the response of the individual rather than to the corporate mission of the church. One wonders who these services are really for. The truly "unchurched" would surely find the references in these services as opaque as those in a traditional liturgy since these services still use biblical and liturgical allusions that the genuinely unchurched would not grasp. What the truly unchurched genuinely need is a liturgy of the catechumens. The services described here appeal to evangelical Christians who come out of pietistic backgrounds and do not like liturgical formalism (failing to discern that that is exactly what these or similar orders provide).

Fellowship Ministries claims to be selling its alternative worship services to more than 300 Lutheran congregations. They are only one of dozens of liturgical entrepreneurs marketing their wares to congregations within the mainline denominations. Some commercially produced resources are within the liturgical mainstream, such as G.I.A.'s *Hymnal Supplement*.[174] Others are only tenuously correlated with the liturgical tradition. The entrepreneurial approach to providing worship resources represents a significant kind of liturgical movement in its own right, since entrepreneurs operate independently of any ecclesiastical authority and outside of the canonical boundaries that have traditionally characterized liturgy as the public and representative work of the church.

The question is whether this kind of "alternative worship" represents the wave of the future. I am not confident that the leadership of mainline denominations, which have been experiencing serious membership hemorrhaging since the late 1960s, will resist the temptation to encourage congregations to "buy into" this kind of worship. And parochial clergy and lay leaders may conclude that there is some correlation between these liturgical orders, the style in which they are done (especially the use of popular music), and the high attendance that they may experience, without inquiring into other factors that have a bearing on worship attendance, such as the demographics of the parish community, congregational programs, or the hospitality extended to visitors. My assessment is that history is not on the side of this kind of worship. First, the modern worldview on which this kind

---

[174] *Hymnal Supplement 1991* (Chicago: GIA Publications, 1991) presents itself as a "supplement" to *LBW*. It does not scrupulously follow the texts of the *LBW* Service of Holy Communion, but it does have a pleasing Marty Haugen setting of the liturgy and a good anthology of psalm settings and hymns that are not contained in *LBW*.

of worship depends—the worldview of the Enlightenment—is in various stages of disintegration. We will discuss this further in the epilogue. Second, the baby boomers' sense of limitless possibility is running up against the oldest form of human limitation: mortality, in such guises as AIDS, ethnic cleansing, and ecological disaster. This might prompt people to look for deeper answers to the questions of life and more varied forms of prayer than are provided in "seeker services" or "alternative liturgies." Third, the children of unchurched baby boomers who have not been brought up in a churchly tradition do not have the same reasons or need to react negatively to this tradition as their parents did. They may be more interested in experiencing "traditional worship" if and when they do visit churches, and they may find it compelling. It is noteworthy that with no marketing and virtually no evangelism programs, Eastern Orthodox churches in America are experiencing a phenomenal growth in membership from non-ethnic converts. Many of these converts to Eastern Orthodoxy have come out of evangelical or mainline Protestant backgrounds. They are looking for a richer experience of worship than what is provided by worship that appeals purely to emotional catharsis or rational reflection. The issue is finally whether the churches that have remained faithful to the evangelical proclamation and the catholic liturgical heritage can offer meaningful responses to the disquieting realities people are facing as we complete one millennium and begin another, and something that addresses the human desire for a window to transcendence.

In the meantime, it may be necessary for the churches to gain more control over their own liturgical assemblies by providing the variety of formats for public worship that seem to be needed in our pluralistic culture. Here we might note, by way of example, that the 1986 Service Book of the Church of Sweden provides six different forms of the Sunday service: three with eucharist (solemn high mass, simplified mass, and family mass), and three without eucharist (again: solemn, simplified, and family). The decision of which service to use at what time is made by the priest and the parish council together. Churches that have only recently published definitive, hardbound worship books will not want to throw them out in order to produce new books, but "trial services" can once again be made available to congregations that will provide valuable experience leading to new, definitive books in the twenty-first century. The Division for Congregational Ministries of the Evangelical Lutheran Church in America has produced a worship resource under the title *With One Voice* (Pew Edition, Accompaniment Edition, Leaders Edition) that serves as a supplement to *Lutheran Book of Worship*. It contains two settings of the communion service (the same order as in *LBW*, but with ELLC translations of ecumenical Creeds available in the book and some modest "updating" of texts for gender-inclusive purposes), some additional eucharistic prayers and a listing of the readings for the three-year Revised Common Lectionary in the Leaders Edition, as well as an anthology of about two hundred multicultural hymns and songs embracing Gregorian chant, Bach chorale-settings, jazz, folk music, Victorian hymns, praise choruses, liturgical ostinatos from Taizé, and elements of Eastern and Western rite.

It can be argued that ritually resourceful worship leaders can provide the same variety using the resources afforded in the authorized worship books of the mainline

American denominations.[175] But it must be admitted that these resources have not always been user-friendly to pastors and other worship leaders, and the denominations have not provided the continuing education opportunities that will enable leaders to use these resources creatively. For example, in its most revolutionary proposal, *LBW* provided a role in each service for lay assisting ministers, but left it up to parish pastors (who themselves may have been in need of extensive training for their new role as "presiding minister"[176]) to provide the training necessary for lay persons to carry out the role of assisting minister. In contrast, many dioceses in Sweden have been training the laity to assume ministerial roles in the liturgy. In the diocese of Linköping alone, some 1,500 lay persons were trained to serve as assisting ministers. It is obvious that there have been many missed opportunities in the introduction of new worship books to communicate their vision of the liturgy as a corporate event involving a number of roles in the assembly.[177] Church growth enthusiasts are not shy about modeling worship styles. We are in need of liturgical models that can be observed and emulated.

Liturgical instruction in the parish has been largely hit and miss, but people can learn much about the liturgy just by attending it—if it is done well. It simply is not all that difficult to learn to worship liturgically, especially if the liturgy is repeated consistently week after week. There are many who have come from so-called nonliturgical backgrounds who have learned the liturgy and have grown to appreciate it. Furthermore, the liturgy is not all that unappealing to the unchurched if it is celebrated in a compelling way, with knowledge and sensitivity; if the presider keeps the service "flowing"[178] and avoids imposing himself or herself on the event with personal interjections and nervous mannerisms; if the assisting ministers know how to read and walk in public and display a reverence in handling holy things; if the acolytes appear well trained and genuinely helpful to other ministers and people; if the congregation responds robustly to words and gestures; if the choirs and musicians provide leadership that facilitates rather than replaces the congregation's singing; if the ushers serve as hospitable hosts who welcome strangers and provide useful cues for the movement of people into, through, and out of the assembly; if the word proclaimed in the readings and sermon and enacted in the sacramental signs "moves the heart" of the worshipers both toward God and toward the community of faith;[179] and if the core events of the church's liturgy become life-orienting.

---

[175] This is the thrust of the proposal of Patrick Keifert, *Welcoming the Stranger: A Public Theology of Worship and Evangelism* (Minneapolis: Fortress Press, 1992), who finally pleads for an imaginative, energetic, engaging rendition of the church's traditional liturgy.

[176] One of the most important handbooks for presiders remains Robert W. Hovda, *Strong, Loving and Wise: Presiding in Liturgy* (Washington, D.C.: The Liturgical Conference, 1976).

[177] Underused in Lutheran congregations was Ralph Van Loon, *Parish Worship Handbook*, ed. by S. Anita Stauffer (Philadelphia: Parish Life Press, 1979). The Liturgical Conference continues to provide useful resources for the local liturgical assembly. See most notably *Liturgy: We Proclaim*, Vol. 11, No. 1 (Washington, D.C.: The Liturgical Conference, 1993).

[178] The idea of flow as that which makes a sequence of actions appear natural and unforced is based on the pioneering psychological work of Mihaly Csikszentmihalyi, *Beyond Boredom and Anxiety* (San Francisco: Jossey-Bass, 1975).

[179] See Michael B. Aune, *To Move the Heart: Philip Melanchthon's Rhetorical View of Rite and Its Implications for Contemporary Ritual Theory* (San Francisco: Christian Universities Press, 1994).

Epilogue:
Postmodern Liturgy

W E HAVE TRAVELED THE distance of Judeo-Christian history in narrating the story of Christian liturgy. After the modern liturgical movement, with its proposals for the retrieval of historic rites and reform of the liturgy, and the revision of existing rites and agendas for the renewal of the churches' worship, where do we go? What comes after "modern"? The answer, of course, is "postmodernism."

Many critics, especially in literature and the arts, have spoken of postmodernism in the sense of a rejection of Rationalism and Romanticism. This was already the sensibility of the so-called modernism in the arts in the early twentieth century, so that postmodernism really comprehends both "modernism" and "postmodernism" in the arts. For example, the primitivism for which postmodernism has been known was already being expressed in the music of Stravinsky and the art of Picasso. The liturgical movement, too, had an interest in getting behind the Reformation and the Middle Ages to the worship of the ancient church. The tribalism and ethnocentricity that has been a characteristic of postmodern art has had its liturgical corollary in liturgies for special groups (e.g., women, children, baby boomers, generation X, etc.) and in concerns for multiculturalism.

The fact that these interests and concerns are not embraced everywhere by everyone should alert us to the fact that to speak of postmodernism is not simply to identify a historical period after the so-called modern era. To speak of modernism and post-modernism as historical periods presumes that there was also a period that can be regarded as pre-modern. History cannot be so neatly divided. Furthermore, the beliefs and values associated with Rationalism and Romanticism, that is, with classical liberalism and the repristination of tradition, continue to flourish also in religion.[1] Moreover, an acceptable definition of postmodernism has eluded the critics.[2] It seems, rather, to be a sensibility in the arts and literature, in philosophy and even in science, that rejects the worldview of the Enlightenment and Idealism, but without necessarily putting something positive in its place. If we ask, therefore, what follows modernity in Western intellectual history, we have to say: "nothing."

"Nothing" is meant here in the technical sense of "nihilism." Most of those who talk about postmodernism are belated disciples of Friedrich Nietzsche, who saw Western civilization collapsing into a moral abyss as a result of its functional atheism. The eighteenth-century philosophers had retained the idea of God and immortality as the necessary conditions for a moral life. But by the end of the nineteenth century, Nietzsche saw that God had been killed off by Enlightened society and that everything immoral was now permitted. He suggested that the only way for civilization to survive is for humankind to become its own god so that its actions will be "beyond good and evil." Out of the hollow "last man" would emerge the "superman."[3]

Part of Nietzsche's apocalyptic vision has been realized: the decadence of Western civilization and its "hollow men" were discerned by artistic figures already at the beginning of the twentieth century. One thinks especially of the work of James Joyce and T. S. Eliot, of Jean-Paul Sartre and Günter Grass, of Samuel Beckett and Eugene Ionesco. These literary figures rejected the modern world, that is, the world of the Enlightenment and Idealism. Nietzsche's contemporary, an equally prophetic figure, Gustav Mahler, bid a long farewell to the world of reason and romance in his Ninth Symphony (1910). The process of the disintegration of the modern world has continued during the course of the twentieth century as civilization has plunged into the nihilism of which Nietzsche prophesied; but his prophesies of an emerging freedom in a world of supermen have not been fulfilled. Therefore, as Robert Jenson has suggested, "the Western world is now 'post'-modern in the sense that modernity is dying all around us, it is not 'post'-modern in the sense that any new thing is yet replacing it."[4]

The present situation is that the modern world, built on a sense of critical reason and romantic idealism, is falling apart. Walter Lippmann spoke of "the acids of modernity," but it is modernity itself that has been eaten away by its own acids. Modernity was

---

[1] This is admitted by George A. Lindbeck, *The Nature of Doctrine: Religion and Theology in a Postliberal Age* (Philadelphia: The Westminster Press, 1984). Nevertheless, he proposes a postliberal "cultural-linguistic" alternative to the orthodox "cognitive-propositional" approach to religion and the liberal "experiential-expressive" model. This "alternative" takes seriously the particularities of religious narratives and rituals without concluding that other religions are in error or seeking a common essence behind the symbols of every religion.

[2] See Linda Hutcheon, *The Politics of Postmodernism* (London and New York: Routledge, 1989), 11ff.

[3] See Friedrich Nietzsche, *Thus Spake Zarathustra*, especially Part III; in *The Philosophy of Nietzsche* (New York: Modern Library, 1954); also *The Genealogy of Morals* in *The Birth of Tragedy and the Genealogy of Morals*, trans. by Francis Golffing (Garden City: Doubleday and Company, 1956), 147ff.

[4] Robert W. Jenson, "How the World Lost Its Story," *First Things*, No. 38 (October 1993), 19.

built on an intellectual and moral capital that has been spent. It presupposed life had a purpose and that history had a direction. But since Kant, transcendentalists of every sort have been liberated from theology. The direction of life and history, in nineteenth-century Darwinian terms, was based on "natural selection" and "the survival of the fittest." Building on this notion, Oswald Spengler spoke of a "Faustian man" who is locked in an endless strife with his world to overcome all natural obstacles; and Goethe's Faust, unlike Christopher Marlowe's Dr. Faustus, finally prevails. But the experience of our century is that people are more like Richard Strauss's anti-hero, *Till Eulenspielgel*, than like Faust or even the American can-do hero, Horatio Alger; and real life in our time has been experienced more like the absurd characters in Beckett's *Waiting for Godot*[5] than like Shakespeare's tragic figures (King Lear, Othello), whose reasons for suffering can at least be known by the audience. We have assumed that life and history have a narrative direction. But that has broken down in modern fiction and dramas, which narrate events that would make no sense in the real world or which do not arrange the bits and pieces of the story in any classically coherent way (a favorite device in avante garde cinema). Postmodern theorists, like Jean-Francois Lyotard, argue that the "meta-narrative" of the Enlightenment, as Jürgen Habermas called it, has been liquidated by history, for example, by the experience of Nazism, of concentration camps, of the Jewish holocaust, of communist pogroms and capitalist technoscience that has changed our understanding of knowledge; and that there can no longer be any grand totalizing narratives, only smaller narrative units that seek no universalizing legitimation.[6] This rejection of the quest for a "meta-narrative" is based on the assumption that we no longer have a narratable world. The narratable world, with its sense of linear development, collapsed with the demise of the doctrine of progress.

The narrative myth of modernism was based largely on the scientific worldview of the Enlightenment. During the course of the nineteenth century the story line was filled in with the dogma of evolution. Romanticism represented only an exception to the view that civilization had progressed to the point of experiencing "the best of all possible worlds"; romantics still looked for a golden age in the past to redeem a deficient present. In the twentieth century, however, that narration has broken down as the doctrine of progress has been discredited not only by devastating historical experiences but by science itself. The doctrine of progress was basically an eighteenth-century notion that human life would get better and better because of scientific and technological achievement ("better living through chemistry" was a popular advertising slogan of the 1950s). It flourished into the twentieth century principally through Marxism, whose philosophy was called "scientific materialism"; the ersatz philosophy or religion of scientism, whose devotees believe that the scientific method can provide the only kind of authentic knowledge that is liberating and therefore salvatory; and in America, which avoided the devastations of world wars, the long economic decline experienced by Europe since World War I, and

---

[5] Samuel Beckett, *Waiting for Godot*, trans. from the French by the author (New York: Grove Press, 1954).
[6] See Jean-Francois Lyotard, *The Postmodern Condition: A Report on Knowledge*, trans. by Geoff Bennington and Brian Massumi (Minneapolis: University of Minnesota Press, 1984).

the experience of totalitarianism. Marxism has now collapsed, and scientism is challenged by scientists such as Günther Stent (a molecular geneticist), who asserted:

> Contrary to expectation, it has turned out that the growth of our knowledge about nature has not made it any easier to reach rational decisions regarding man's fate. Instead, whereas the technological consequences of scientific progress have rendered the making of such decisions evermore pressing and their effects evermore grave, the intellectual consequences of scientific progress have made us aware of the difficulty, if not impossibility, of foreseeing the long-range results of our actions, while at the same time destroying the foundations for our judgment of their value.[7]

Even North America for the first time is apprehending the specter of limitations and social failure, although the optimistic baby boomer generation surveyed by Wade Clark Roof still believes overwhelmingly (86 percent) that one can do just about anything if one believes in oneself.[8] The generation following does not seem so confident of this.

The general culture, at the end of the twentieth century, has caught up with the artistic prophets from earlier in the century. In our cities and suburbs, classrooms and churches, we find people who have no coherent sense of history, nor a desire to acquire one. Their sense of living only for the moment with no meaningful tradition on which to build and no destiny of promise toward which to move is expressed in the raw nihilism of countless heavy metal rock lyrics (which are derivative from the beatnik poets of the 1960s). While many might recite mantras about the need to "get my life together," they do not and cannot understand their lives in a narrative sense. They cannot imagine that they are immersed in a tradition that provides meaning and that they have a responsibility to pass on to the next generation. So much is the historical memory obliterated from the consciousness that sometimes memories are even invented to give meaning to dysfunctional lives.[9] We should also note that non-Western cultures and religions do not share this notion that life must make sense and that history has meaning and direction, which may explain the fascination for Eastern religions such as Zen Buddhism and the emergence of "New Age" cults. This is a cop-out from the problem of history altogether, since history requires a retrievable memory and a sense of destiny. But the "American religion," as described by critic Harold Bloom, has a basic gnostic core that emphasizes the saving knowledge that comes from a personal relationship with Jesus or an inerrant Bible and thereby escapes the ambiguities and frustrations of history by seeking the god within. Bloom advises that "mere Gnosticism does not lend itself to communal worship, though doubtless that has been ventured, at one time and place or another."[10]

---

[7] Gunther S. Stent, *Paradoxes of Progress* (San Francisco: W. H. Freeman and Company, 1978), 1.

[8] See Wade Clark Roof, *A Generation of Seekers* (San Francisco: Harper and Row, 1993), 108–9.

[9] This is a very controversial assertion, but the question of memory—whether it is true or false—must concern the historian. On the emerging concern about a "false memory syndrome" see Paul R. McHugh, "Psychiatric Misadventures," *The American Scholar* (1992), esp. pp. 504–10, and Leon Jaroff, "Lies of the Mind," *Time* (November 29, 1993), 52–9.

[10] Harold Bloom, *Omens of Millennium: The Gnosis of Angel, Dreams, and Resurrection* (New York: Riverhead Books, 1996), 27.

This puts historical Christianity in an untenable cultural situation because it proclaims a salvation event that happened in history. There is a minimum historical awareness that is required to tell the story of salvation and to proclaim the promised destiny of the people of God. The church's mission is to tell the biblical story to the world and to enact it before God in worship. How does the church pursue this mission in a world that lacks narrative coherence? If, in the past, the church could correlate its mission with the culture's general quest for certainty, or its use of reason to construct a worldview, or its romantic yearning for an ideal society, or its liberal agenda for social reform, how does the church correlate its mission to proclaim a historical gospel with the nihilism of the postmodern world or the gnosticism of the "American Religion"? How does it voice the hope of the fulfillment of life in God's kingdom in a world that has experienced, on the one hand, the Holocaust, genocide, and mass starvation, and the contentments of suburbia, on the other?

One answer is that it proclaims the theology of the cross as a message affirming God's identification with a situation of failure and God-forsakenness. Particularly with the demise of the doctrine of progress after the devastating experiences of two world wars, the disastrous experiments in Fascist and Marxist totalitarianism, the threat of nuclear annihilation, and the nearly irreparable damage done to the environment, the church cannot afford to equate the gospel with "positive thinking"; nor is a triumphalistic faith tolerable.[11] When the notion that the world is getting better and better through scientific and technological progress has been discredited, modernity is left resourceless and has no way of renewing itself. Sooner or later even optimistic Americans are going to accept the evidence of humanity's follies, the limitations of progress, and the insufficiency of subjectivity. In the meantime, many who harbor suspicions about the basic goodness of humanity and those who are the victims of "progress" still attend houses of worship. The liturgical corollary to the gospel of the cross is the prayer of lament.

Lament points to that within the life and history of the people of God that betrays the hope of the promises of God. Some recent studies of the Jewish background of the Christian eucharistic prayer have turned to the *todah* (thanksgiving) tradition in the Old Testament rather than to the Birkat ha-Mazon.[12] It has been noted that, in this tradition, there is room for the insertion of intercession and even the confession of sins. In the psalms especially, thanksgiving is also able to encompass lament. David Power has drawn on this tradition to show how faith is able to name the suffering or the ideology that oppresses, and is thereby energized.[13] He has experimented with writing eucharistic prayers that incorporate the element of lament.[14] Greater exposure to the element of

---

[11] See Douglas John Hall, *Lighten our Darkness: Toward an Indigenous Theology of the Cross* (Philadelphia: The Westminster Press, 1976).

[12] See especially C. Giraudo, *La Struttura Letteraria della Preghiera Eucaristica* (Rome: Biblical Institute Press, 1981).

[13] See David N. Power, "When to Worship Is to Lament," in *Worship: Culture and Theology* (Washington, D.C.: The Pastoral Press, 1990), 155–73.

[14] See David N. Power, "The Eucharistic Prayer: Another Look," in Frank C. Senn, ed., *New Eucharistic Prayers*, op. cit., 251–5 and *The Eucharistic Mystery: Revitalizing the Tradition* (New York: Crossroads, 1995), 336–7.

lament in psalms, hymns, and prayer might provide optimistic worshipers with a more realistic assessment of the human situation and offer those who have experienced personal defeat in a success-ridden society an opportunity to "cry out for the resurrection of their lives."[15]

A faithful proclaiming of the gospel of the cross is called for in the church's mission to Western society; but it is insufficient as a total response to the postmodern situation. It establishes a point of contact in which people can see how God identifies with humanity in its suffering and weakness; that is comforting, in the biblical sense of strengthening. But the church must provide what people lack in order to offer meaning for their lives: a narratable world—a worldview that provides coherent meaning and a way of enacting it. If the world has come apart in postmodern nihilism, the church must redo the world. It must provide an aimless present with a usable past and a hope-filled future.[16] It should be noted that the church has done this before, most notably in the period of late antiquity in which the pessimistic assessment of a world-city in decline, experienced in "the fall of Rome," was met head-on by an alternate vision of reality, expressed formidably in Augustine's *City of God*. This required a relocation of the "golden age" from the beginning of history (e.g., the glorious founding of Rome) to its end (the consummation of the kingdom of God); and therefore a reorientation of focus from etiology to eschatology. And if we face in our society's religiosity a gnostic tendency to seek to escape from the threats of natural decay, temporal limitations, and political responsibility, this can be at least countered with attention to the sacramental life, the historic liturgy, and traditional ecclesiastical polity.[17]

T. S. Eliot, who surveyed the "wasteland" of the postmodern world,[18] also proposed "The Idea of a Christian Society." He saw a choice "between the formation of a new Christian culture, and the acceptance of a pagan one."[19] He thought that, given that choice, "the only hopeful course for a society which would thrive and continue its creative activity in the arts of civilization, is to become Christian."[20] I am not as pessimistic as Eliot that civilization cannot thrive without being Christian. In our global village we are quite aware of non-Christian civilizations that are thriving, such as Japan's. Nor would I want the culture of Christendom to be retrieved or replicated; the identification of the gospel with any human culture undermines the mission of the gospel to address all human societies. The mission of the gospel succeeds best if the gospel stands over against societies rather than becoming enmeshed in them. But there is a sense in which Eliot's proposal might be seriously reconsidered: the church constitutes a society "called out" of

---

[15] A phrase from the alternate Great Thanksgiving in *Lutheran Book of Worship*, Ministers Edition, 223. See also David Power, "Liturgy, Memory and the Absence of God," *Worship* 57 (1983), 326–9.

[16] See Robert W. Jenson, *Story and Promise* (Philadelphia: Fortress Press, 1972), who developed the idea that it is the church's constitutive task to tell the biblical narrative to the world in proclamation and to God in worship.

[17] See Philip J. Lee, *Against the Protestant Gnostics* (Oxford University Press, 1987).

[18] See T. S. Eliot, *The Waste Land and Other Poems* (New York: Harcourt, Brace and World, 1934; Harvest Book Ed.), 27–54.

[19] T. S. Eliot, *Christianity and Culture* (New York: Harcourt, Brace and Company, Harvest Book, n.d.), 10.

[20] Ibid., 19.

the world; and as a society it generates its own culture, its own worldview and way of life (what anthropologists call myth and ritual). A church that takes the historic Christian cultus seriously, implements it and lives from it, will inevitably generate a Christian culture.[21]

The church may be the only institution left in Western society that maintains continuity with tradition. That continuity is embodied in the church's historic liturgy. It would be faithless both to the gospel and to the catholic tradition to fail to maintain that continuity; but it is also evident that the task of communicating this sense of continuity to the church's members requires a massive effort in formation. New members will have to be painstakingly initiated into the community of faith and its traditions. The modern liturgical movement has been recovering the idea of baptism as a rite of initiation. Initiation implies the need to be formed and incorporated into a society with its own perspective on reality and its own way of life. This is a society that may sometimes live uncomfortably within the society of "this world," since its narration of reality may at times conflict with secular society's understanding of reality. Robert Webber and Rodney Clapp point out the elementary observation that "baptism initiates the individual into a community that takes its identity from the death and resurrection of Christ. With a new identity, the Christian is reoriented to the world."[22] William H. Willimon adds: "All of the church's worship, including baptism, is the communal assertion and therefore cultivation of an alternative construction of society. At what point the church's alternative construction of society leads to conflict with our nonbelieving neighbors depends, of course, upon the neighbors."[23]

What kind of response our neighbors' actions might call from us Christians is best left to ethicists such as John Howard Yoder and Stanley Hauerwas.[24] Our concern here is with the formation of an "alternative construction of society" in the assembly for word and sacrament, and with how the liturgical life conducted in this assembly can provide its members with the usable past and hopeful future that postmodern secular society no longer provides. Whether there is a spillover into secular society that exerts a transformative effect on that society depends on how convinced and convincing Christians are of the validity of their experience of the alternative society of the church. It is to the experience of that alternative society, formed and expressed in the liturgy of the church, that we must attend. The presupposition here is that the church's liturgy must be intact, and presented in its fullness, if it is to offer an alternative view of reality.[25] The church has to

---

[21] I am not here concerned with the possible relationships between the Christian cultus and the culture of the world theologically delineated in different models in H. Richard Niebuhr, *Christ and Culture* (New York: Harper and Row, 1951). For that see my book, *Christian Worship and Its Cultural Setting* (Philadelphia: Fortress Press, 1983), 90–4; also Geoffrey Wainwright, *Doxology*, op. cit., 388ff. Here I am concerned only with the development of a liturgical culture within the church.

[22] Robert E. Webber and Rodney Clapp, *People of the Truth* (San Francisco: Harper and Row, 1988), 75.

[23] William H. Willimon, *Peculiar Speech: Preaching to the Baptized* (Grand Rapids: William B. Eerdmans, 1992), 107.

[24] See John Howard Yoder, *The Politics of Jesus* (Grand Rapids: William B. Eerdmans, 1972) and Stanley Hauerwas, *Resident Aliens* (Nashville: Abingdon, 1989).

[25] This was the thrust of my book, *The Witness of the Worshiping Community* (Mahwah, N.J.: Paulist Press, 1993).

proclaim the biblical story clearly and critically to a world that has lost its story, and articulate in its assembly the eschatological hope that provides an option to the nihilism of postmodernity.

First, then, the story. The narration that makes sense of the world is found in the church's canonical book, the Bible. From the stories of beginnings in Genesis—the beginnings of the world, the beginnings of God's people—through the formation of God's people in the experience of slavery and exodus, through the efforts of God to keep the people faithful by means of the ministries of priests, kings, and prophets, through the final redemption of that people and the world itself in the sacrificial death and vindicating resurrection of Jesus the Christ, through the proclamation of this good news of resurrection and redemption in Christ in the mission of the apostles and the church, to the final consummation of all things in the divine kingdom of love, the Bible narrates a view of reality. Unfortunately, it cannot be presumed that the unchurched (and many of the churched) any longer have any acquaintance with this book or its stories; nor that they have any overarching sense of the biblical narrative in its entirety. If the unchurched are to be "churched," they must be exposed to this book, its stories, and its narrative scheme. Liturgy cannot bear the sole weight of this educational task; this is why the church has practiced catechesis. But the need to immerse Christians in the biblical story also requires that scripture be read, sung, and expounded in the public assembly in the systematic way provided by the church year lectionary with its readings and psalmody.

It can no longer be assumed that this is done in all Christian churches. Church services that are aimed at reaching the unchurched take their cue from television, which, as Neil Postman has observed, presents everything—even world events and religion—in the form of entertainment.[26] William H. Willimon commented:

> When the pulpit takes its cues from TV, argument, reason, refutation and exposition are jettisoned in favor of stories and drama. If it can't amuse, it can't be said. Therefore we emphasize preaching as storytelling, drama in preaching, a sermon as a story, the preacher as storyteller.[27]

Storytelling has become the vogue in homiletics instruction.[28] It appeals to the example of Jesus, who used parables to indicate what "the kingdom of God is like." Preaching as storytelling is not just the preacher telling one's personal story, in the form of a testimony or example; it is also, like the parables of Jesus, an attempt to invent or utilize stories that can illustrate the gospel. In "church growth" practice the "message" may sometimes even be a drama or play. In contrast to this, however, the apostolic preaching reported in the Book of Acts or exemplified in the apostolic epistles tells only one story: the story of God's mighty acts in Christ Jesus. True evangelical preaching proclaims Christ, and the whole biblical story is the setting for the Christ-event.

---

[26] See Neil Postman, *Amusing Ourselves to Death* (New York: Viking Press, 1985).

[27] William H. Willimon, "Preaching: Entertainment or Exposition?" *The Christian Century* (February 28, 1990), 206.

[28] For an early example of this emphasis in homiletics see Edmund Steimle, Morris Niedenthal, and Charles Rice, *Preaching as Storytelling* (Philadelphia: Fortress Press, 1981).

Many sermons these days, like postmodern novels, cinema, or MTV, string together disconnected images and stories without any discernible structure or transition, and aim to elicit an emotional response rather than to help form a worldview. Willimon comments:

> People are confused and lethargic not simply because they are tired of hearing the gospel or because they have never really been emotionally gripped by it, but also because they are confused. They have not heard the gospel in a way that provokes a thoughtful, basement-to-attic reappraisal of themselves and their world. Behind our drift toward preaching as entertainment lies the anachronistic assumption that our culture is so congenial to the gospel that the gospel can be evoked into consciousness by a touching story or two. I'd claim that in neo-pagan North America the gospel is so odd that at times one must explain it to people, expound it, exposit it, go through it point by point.[29]

Sermons are not the only liturgical forms that piece together the Bible's story. Hymns have been used as instructional devices as well as expressions of devotion at least since the hymns ascribed to Ambrose of Milan in the fourth century. Congregational participation in the liturgy was fostered by the singing of the office hymns in the cathedrals of antiquity, in the vernacular prose sequences of the medieval mass, in the songs and carols that accompanied paraliturgical devotions in late medieval and post-Tridentine Catholicism, in the explosion of hymns and chorales in the Lutheran reformation, in the development of the metrical psalms in the Reformed tradition, and in the further development of hymnody in post-Reformation Protestantism. Up until the influence of Pietism and Revivalism in the eighteenth century, hymn texts primarily rehearsed the story of salvation and reinforced doctrine. The more personal and subjective lyrics of pietistic hymns and revival songs can be regarded as the ancestors of the kind of contemporary Christian songs that have been in vogue since the 1960s: the pep rally-type folk songs of the 1960s and 1970s ("We are one in the Spirit," "Sons of God"), the "Voice of God" songs of the 1970s and 1980s that gave God a "softer image" ("On eagle's wings," "Be not afraid"), and the "glory and praise" songs of the 1980s and 1990s that, with a soft rock character, have all but expelled any music in the church that sounds "churchy." Through two centuries, from evangelical pietism to contemporary Christian music, the emphasis has been on one's personal relationship to Jesus or God rather than on what God has done for all humanity in the cross and resurrection of Christ. Not only has the image of a "community of salvation" been lost in the texts, but the difficulty of the intervals and rhythms in the tunes, and the increasing reliance on electronic instruments (e.g., organs, keyboards, guitars, basses, etc.), has lost the community in actuality, since the employment of popular musical styles in worship has diminished the level and vigor of congregational singing. Using songs that can only be effectively rendered by soloists, choirs, or combos contributes further to the idea of worship as entertainment. While the situation had been far worse in contemporary American Roman Catholicism than in mainline Protestant congregations, which still rely heavily on sturdy classical hymns meant for

---

[29] Willimon, *art. cit.*

congregational singing, the Catholic folk tradition is being rapidly imported into Protestant worship and could accomplish the same consequences: killing congregational participation and doing little to increase biblical or doctrinal literacy.[30]

The antidote to this, it would seem, is to encourage a multipronged offensive that would look very much like what the Constitution on the Sacred Liturgy of the Second Vatican Council called for, but that has not been implemented in America. The offensive would include "the teaching and practice of music in the seminaries" (to ensure competent and knowledgeable pastoral leadership); the encouragement of congregational singing "to contribute to the active participation which is rightfully theirs" (for which hymns and songs with a proven track record of promoting vigorous singing should be given pride of place); the development of choirs and the use of "other kinds of sacred music, especially polyphony" that "accord with the spirit of the liturgical action" (for which competent musicians trained as church musicians are needed); the revitalization of Gregorian chant (which has a proven track record of being a truly "catholic" form of church music, transcending cultural differences); the employment of songs of the people from their own culture (blended, as it is said nowadays, with church chant and classical hymns); the use of pipe organs and other instruments that "accord with the dignity of the temple, and truly contribute to the edification of the people"; and the encouragement of composers to set texts for worship that are "drawn chiefly from holy Scripture and from liturgical sources."[31]

The Creed is a condensed form of the biblical story. Creative liturgies that provide creative affirmations of faith instead of the ecumenical creeds risk not telling the whole story, and so may lose the true evangelical proclamation; or they may tell it in a way that lacks the consensus of the whole church, and therefore may lose the catholic connection.

The eucharistic prayer was a condensed form of the biblical story before the creeds found a secure place in the order of service. The eucharistic meal needs to be set in the context of the whole story of creation, redemption and sanctification by the will of the Father, through the work of the Son, realized in the community created by the Holy Spirit. For this meal focuses on bread and wine drawn from the gifts of creation; it regards the eating of the bread and the sharing of the cup as signs proclaiming the Lord Jesus' death until he comes; and it anticipates the heavenly banquet by virtue of the coming again of this Lord in his body and blood. Any coming of the Crucified and Risen One brings judgment and vindication, and therefore the community must be prepared to eat and drink together in the Lord's presence in a worthy manner—reconciled with the Lord and with each other (see 1 Cor. 11:27–32).[32]

---

[30] See Thomas Day, *Why Catholics Can't Sing: The Culture of Catholicism and the Triumph of Bad Taste* (New York: The Crossroad Publishing Co., 1995).

[31] *Constitution on the Sacred Liturgy*, chapter VI. See also "The Snowbird Statement on Catholic Liturgical Music" (November 1, 1995), adopted by a group of Catholic parish and cathedral musicians meeting at The Madeleine Institute in Salt Lake City, Utah.

[32] See Frank C. Senn, "Structures of Penance and the Ministry of Reconciliation," *Lutheran Quarterly* XXV (1973), 270–83; more recently, Beverley A. Nitschke, "Confession and Forgiveness: The Continuing Agenda," *Worship* 68 (1994), 353–68.

The eucharist combines what Jenson calls "story and promise" as an explication of the gospel. The eucharistic prayer rehearses the story of salvation and the sharing of the meal enacts the promised destiny of God's people. Perhaps the most significant recovery of eucharistic meaning in the twentieth century has been the recovery of the eschatological dimension of the eucharist. The eucharistic meal in the early church was not just a historical reenactment of what took place "in the night in which he was betrayed," but it was the celebration of the presence of the Crucified and Risen One with his failed disciples with the gift of forgiveness and reconciliation.[33]

The eschatological meanings of the eucharist in the early church include the antepast of heaven—feasting in the kingdom of God;[34] the remembrance of the saving acts of God in Christ (anamnesis) combined with an urgent plea (maranatha) to the one who comes in judgment and grace;[35] and the idea of the church as the firstfruits of the kingdom,[36] which was expressed liturgically in the eucharistic oblation with its sense of the self-offering of the priestly people of God.[37] These eschatological ideas were expressed in action and gesture as well as in texts: in the inclusiveness of the meal fellowship (Jew and Greek, men and women, slave and free); in the eastward liturgical orientation in anticipation of the appearance or parousia of the Sun of righteousness; and in the icon of Christ the Universal Ruler above the table in the apse or dome.

The church is an assembly "called out" of the world in order to enact in the midst of "this world" "the life of the world to come." It does so by celebrating the eucharist as an eschatological event (the Lord's Supper) by virtue of the presence of the Crucified and Risen One who reigns as Lord and comes again as judge. It does so on the day of resurrection (the Lord's Day) in order to express the tension between the time of "this world" and the "fullness of time" in the eschatological presence of Christ and his kingdom. The church gathers around the Lord's table not so much because its individual members need the benefits of the gift of communion, but because the church itself—convened by the word—is constituted as the Lord's people in the Lord's Supper, and is sent from the meal into the world in the abiding presence of Christ through his Spirit to proclaim the gospel to the whole creation (Mark 16:15-16) and all the nations (Matt. 28:16–20).

The liturgies of the church have consistently looked upon the Lord's Supper as a foretaste of the marriage feast of the Lamb (Rev. 19:6–7). This has been expressed most particularly in post-communion prayers in the Western rite, which regard Holy Communion as a "pledge," "promise," or "prefiguration" of the heavenly banquet. The Eastern liturgies, on the other hand, express the idea that the eucharist is already a participation in the heavenly feast. If the liturgy is, as Alexander Schmemann said, "the

---

[33] See Norman Perrin, *Recovering the Teaching of Jesus* (New York: Harper and Row, 1967), 107.

[34] See Matthew 8:11; Luke 13:29; also Luke 6:21a and Matthew 5:6.

[35] See 1 Corinthians 11:26, 16:22; *Didache* 10:6; and the *Benedictus qui venit* of Matthew 21:9 added to the Sanctus-hymn.

[36] See Romans 8:29; Colossians 1:18; 1 Corinthians 15:20; James 1:18.

[37] See Geoffrey Wainwright, *Eucharist and Eschatology* (New York: Oxford University Press, 1981).

journey of the church into the dimension of the kingdom,"[38] the eucharist is the point of arrival in which the parousia of Christ is experienced.[39] Something of this sense of realized eschatology in the eucharist is indicated by the use of the Song of Simeon (the Nunc dimittis) as the post-communion canticle in the Lutheran rite. "My own eyes have seen the salvation which you have prepared in the sight of every people; a light to reveal you to the nations and the glory of your people Israel." A similar text in the Byzantine liturgy proclaims: "We have seen the true Light, we have partaken of the Holy Spirit."

The eschatological vision may sometimes be dim inside the church, but the sense of the eschaton is entirely missing outside the church. If the whole liturgy is a "journey into the dimension of the Kingdom," the way must be more pictorially portrayed for modern seekers, catechumens, and believers. Faith comes from what is heard, not from what is seen. But in addressing the biblical story and promise to a generation reared on the visual images of television more than the printed texts of books, sight must be employed to assist hearing. It is, after all, a promised chief mark of the eschaton that hearing will be accompanied by glorious sight. Here we would note the need for art and artifacts in the worship space—the icons of Eastern Orthodox liturgy; the statuary of Western medieval churches; the pictures and symbols in stained glass; or at least banners hanging on the walls or suspended from the rafters, illustrating aspects of the story of salvation (but without the sloganeering that often appears on banners).[40] The event is also musical—texts are sung—because music injects the ecstasy of eternity into the historical moment. Worshipers will be enchanted when there are sounds to be heard, colors to be seen, textures to be felt, odors to be smelled, breads and wines to be tasted, and when all these sensual experiences are correlated in such a way that they are consonant with one another rather than disjunctive and disruptive.[41]

Liturgy in this postmodern world must aim for enchantment, not entertainment. Entertainment is a major facet of our culture. But entertainment as a cultural model is inadequate to the mission of the gospel because it works best when it leaves one satisfied with oneself and one's world. Enchantment, on the other hand, casts a spell that leads one from a drab world to another, brighter, more interesting world. This may be accomplished more through processions, lights, incense, chants, and a visually rich environment than through texts alone (although rhetorically elevated prose would be more of a help in enchanting worshipers than the banalities of didactic and rational discourse to which we are often subjected in so-called contemporary liturgies).

So we end where we began: with the recognition that the celebration of liturgy is meant to be primarily a symbolic activity. That experience is frustrated (and worshipers will find the liturgy to be finally banal) if liturgists attend as exclusively as they have up

[38] Alexander Schmemann, *For the Life of the World* (St. Vladimir's Seminary Press, 1973), 26.

[39] See Boris Bobrinsky, "Worship and the Ascension of Christ," in Michael J. Taylor, ed., *Liturgical Renewal in the Churches* (Baltimore–Dublin: Helicon Press, 1967), 144ff.

[40] See James Notebaart, "Shaping the Environment of Celebration: Art, Design for Visual Order and Beauty," *Living Worship* Vol. 10, No. 2 (Washington, D.C.: The Liturgical Conference, 1974).

[41] See Nelson Goodman, *The Language of Art: An Approach to a Theory of Symbols* (Indianapolis: Hackett Publishing Company, 1976).

until now to doctrinal precision or textual accuracy or political ideology. The role of symbols is not to convey doctrine, to translate ancient texts or to promote ideology; it is to provoke an encounter between God and his people. This does not mean that doctrine is unimportant. But it does mean that even to call creeds "symbols" is to suggest that they have more to do with establishing the *identity* of the community of faith than with providing a set of intellectual propositions. It is more important that orthodox Christians know that they recite the Nicene Creed to identify with the orthodox faith than that they know from the outset what *homoousios* means—just as, by analogy, it is more important for an army to recognize its flag than to know what its colors symbolize. Equipped with a distinctive sense of identity, a community of faith can constantly evaluate its relationships with God and with other communities and assess its call and mission in the light of these relationships. As its identity is challenged it will probe the meaning of its symbols to enter more deeply into what they represent. So, for example, when contemporary concerns challenge the name of the Trinity, Christians will explore the significance of the divine name. They will learn that the mystery of God cannot be exhausted by the name of the Father, the Son, and the Holy Spirit; but also that we cannot avoid the divine self-disclosures that have been recorded in the biblical narratives.

Concomitant with the reappropriation of symbols is the realization that a community that has a sturdy sense of identity will not likely celebrate itself poorly by doing its liturgy haphazardly. A community with a poor sense of identity will not promote itself with any degree of confidence. A community that knows what it believes and is secure in its tradition will perform its public work with a degree of certainty that commends it to others who are also looking for meaning in their lives and an opportunity to grow in their awareness of God. These are the issues our liturgical assemblies must be working on before we resume the inevitable task of liturgical revision. Doing liturgy in a postmodern world requires that we return to basics. In rediscovering the liturgy as "the school of the church,"[42] we will acquire a sense of who we are as God's people, how we are formed into the body of Christ by the word of God and the sacraments of Christ, and what this implies for our communal relationship to this world in which we live and move and have our being.

---

[42] See Philip H. Pfatteicher, *The School of the Church. Worship and Christian Formation* (Valley Forge: Trinity Press, 1995).

Bibliography:
For Further Study

THIS IS A BIBLIOGRAPHY of important liturgical studies and primary sources, mostly, but not exclusively, in English. For critical editions of many primary sources see the notes to the chapters. Not all studies noted in the chapters are included here, and some studies are included here that are not cited in the notes to the chapters. Some of these works are relevant to more than one category, but they are listed only once and in the category for which they seem primarily appropriate.

Introductions to Liturgical Study

Baumstark, Anton. *Comparative Liturgy*. Rev. by B. Botte. Trans. F.L. Cross. London: A.R. Mowbray, 1958. An older work that served as a pioneer in liturgiological methodology.

Hatchett, Marion J. *Sanctifying Life, Time, and Space. An Introduction to Liturgical Study*. New York: The Seabury Press, 1976. A survey of historical periods by literary type organized according to Eliade's differentiation of rites for the sanctification of life, time, and space.

Jones, Cheslyn, Geoffrey Wainwright, Edward Yarnold, and Paul Bradshaw, eds. *The Study of Liturgy*. Rev. ed. Oxford: Oxford University Press, 1992. An encyclopedic work mostly by British scholars that surveys the history and theology of particular liturgical rites.

Leiturgia, Handbuch des evangelischen Gottesdienstes. 5 vols. Kassel: Johannes Stauda Verlag, 1954–70. Significant historical and theological essays on various liturgical orders and rites by such liturgical and dogmatic theologians as Peter Brunner, Georg Kretschmar, Christoph Mahrenholz, and Edmund Schlink.

Schmidt-Lauber, Hans-Christoph and Karl-Heinz Bieritz, eds. *Handbuch der Liturgik: Liturgiewissenschaft in Theologie und Praxis der Kirche*. Göttingen: Vandenhoeck and Ruprecht, 1995.

Senn, Frank C. *Christian Worship and Its Cultural Setting*. Philadelphia: Fortress Press, 1983. An introduction to issues in pastoral liturgics that relates liturgical study to cultural anthropology.

Underhill, Evelyn. *Worship*. New York: Harper Torchbook, 1957. Originally published in 1936. A classic in liturgical spirituality. Underhill regards worship as the human response to the eternal.

Verheul, A. *Introduction to the Liturgy: Towards a Theology of Worship*. Trans. Collegeville: The Liturgical Press, 1968. Shows the theological dimensions implicit in the various liturgical orders and rites.

White, James F. *Introduction to Christian Worship*. Rev. ed. Nashville: Abingdon Press, 1990. An introduction to liturgical study according to ritual categories of time, space, word, sign, initiation and reconciliation, eucharist, and passage.

———. *Documents of Christian Worship. Descriptive and Interpretive Sources*. Louisville: Westminster/John Knox Press, 1991. An anthology of primary sources that should accompany White's *Introduction to Christian Worship*.

Ritual Studies, Myths, and Symbols

d'Aquili, Eugene, C.D. Laughlin, and J. McManus, eds. *The Spectrum of Ritual*. New York: Columbia University Press, 1979. A collection of essays essential for understanding the biogenetic basis and origins of ritual and religious belief.

Bell, Catherine. *Ritual Theory, Ritual Practice*. New York: Oxford University Press, 1992. Explores ritual as a way of acting that is distinct from other ways of acting.

Bouyer, Louis. *Rite and Man. Natural Sacredness and Christian Liturgy*. Trans. M. Joseph Costelloe, S.J. Notre Dame, Ind.: University of Notre Dame Press, 1963. A pioneering use of comparative religion and depth psychology in liturgical study.

Chauvet, Louise-Marie. *Symbol and Sacrament—A Sacramental Reinterpretation of Christian Experience*. Collegeville: The Liturgical Press, 1995.

Collins, Mary. *Worship: Renewal to Practice*. Washington, D.C.: The Pastoral Press, 1987. Several essays in this collection make important contributions to ritual studies.

Cooke, Bernard J. *The Distancing of God: The Ambiguity of Symbol in History and Theology*. Minneapolis: Fortress Press, 1990.

Douglas, Mary. *Natural Symbols. Exploration in Cosmology*. New York: Random House Vintage Books, 1970, 1973. An important thesis that the ritual use of the physical body is determined by the social body.

Eliade, Mircea. *The Sacred and the Profane. The Nature of Religion*. Trans. Willard R. Trask. New York and Evanston: Harper Torchbooks, 1957. Explores myth and ritual according to the categories of the sanctification of sacred space, sacred time, the sacredness of nature, and the sanctified life.

Grimes, Ronald L. *Beginnings in Ritual Studies*. Washington, D.C.: University Press of America, 1982.

———. *Research in Ritual Studies*. Metuchen, N.J.: Scarecrow Press and The American Theological Library Association, 1985. Contains a "programmatic essay" and an extended bibliography.

Journal of Ritual Studies. Department of Religious Studies, University of Pittsburgh (1987–present). Many articles are of interest to liturgists.

Jung, Carl Gustav. *Man and His Symbols*. New York: Dell Publishing Company, 1964; reprint, 1968. A popular version of Jung's general philosophy of archetypes and his distinction between sign and symbol.

Pieper, Josef. *In Tune with the World. A Theory of Festivity*. Trans. Richard and Clare Winston. Chicago: Franciscan Herald Press, 1973. A philosophical and anthropological study of the conditions needed for true festivity that also exposes pseudo-festivals in their harness and sinister forms.

Power, David N. *Unsearchable Riches: The Symbolic Nature of Liturgy*. New York: Pueblo Publishing Co., 1984. Written to show the need to relate liturgical theory and practice to cultural symbols.

Procter-Smith, Marjorie. *In Her Own Rite: Constructing Feminist Liturgical Tradition*. Nashville: Abingdon Press, 1990. An important contribution to feminist ritual study and liturgical praxis. The author distinguishes between "inclusive" and "emancipatory" God-language.

Schechner, Richard. *Between Theatre and Anthropology*. Philadelphia: University of Pennsylvannia Press, 1985. An exploration of "a world of colliding cultures" in which no performance of ritual or theatre can claim absolute or privileged status.

Shaughnessay, James, ed. *The Roots of Ritual*. Grand Rapids: William B. Eerdmans, 1973. Arguments by authors from various disciplines regarding the importance of ritual in the modern world.

Studia Liturgica 23:1 (1993). This issue has important articles on ritual and liturgics by Catherine Bell, Ronald Grimes, Lawrence Hoffman, Aidan Kavanagh, and Roy Rappaport.

Turner, Victor. *The Ritual Process: Structure and Anti-structure*. Chicago: Aldine Publishing Company, 1969. Important anthropological study of liminality and the conditions that foster communitas.

Liturgical Theologies

Bouyer, Louis. *Liturgical Piety*. Notre Dame, Ind.: University of Notre Dame Press, 1954.

Brunner, Peter. *Worship in the Name of Jesus*. Trans. M.H. Bertram. St. Louis: Concordia Publishing House, 1968. Originally published in *Liturgia, Handbuch des evangelischen Gottesdienst*, vol. I. Arguably the most important contemporary evangelical theology of worship.

Casel, Odo. *The Mystery of Christian Worship and Other Writings*. Ed. by Burkhard Neunheuser. Trans. I.T. Hale. London: Darton, Longman and Todd and Westminster, Md.: The Newman Press, 1962. Originally published in 1932.

Corbon, Jean. *The Wellspring of Worship*. Foreword by Edward J. Kilmartin, S.J. Trans.by Matthew J. O'Connell. New York and Mahwah, N.J.: Paulist Press, 1988. Originally published in 1980.

Fagerberg, David. *What Is Liturgical Theology?* Collegeville: The Liturgical Press, 1992.

Hoon, Paul Waitman. *The Integrity of Worship: Ecumenical and Pastoral Studies in Liturgical Theology*. Nashville and New York: Abingdon Press, 1971. A pastoral liturgics firmly anchored in the theological character of worship addressed to the Holy Trinity and determined by christology.

Irwin, Kevin. *Context and Text: Method in Liturgical Theology*. Collegeville: The Liturgical Press, 1994.

Kavanagh, Aidan. *On Liturgical Theology*. New York: Pueblo Publishing Co., 1984.

Kilmartin, Edward J., S.J. *Christian Liturgy*, Vol. I. *Systematic Theology of Liturgy*. Kansas City, Mo.: Sheed and Ward, 1988.

Lathrop, Gordon W. *Holy Things: A Liturgical Theology*. Minneapolis: Fortress Press, 1993.

Saliers, Don E. *Worship as Theology: Foretast of Glory Divine*. Nashville: Abingdon Press, 1994.

Schmemann, Alexander. *For the Life of the World*. New York: St. Vladimir's Seminary Press, 1973. Originally published for the National Student Christian Federation in 1963 as a study book.

———. *Introduction to Liturgical Theology*. London: The Faith Press and Portland, Maine: The American Orthodox Press, 1966. Reprinted by St. Vladimir's Seminary Press.

Vagaggini, C. *Theological Dimensions of the Liturgy*. Trans. Collegeville: The Liturgical Press, 1976.

Von Allmen, J.J. *Worship: Its Theology and Practice*. English trans. New York: Oxford University Press, 1965.

Wainwright, Geoffrey. *Doxology. The Praise of God in Worship, Doctrine, and Life*. New York: Oxford University Press, 1980. A systematic theology using liturgy as its "controlling principle."

General Histories of the Liturgy

Dix, Gregory. *The Shape of the Liturgy*. Additional notes by Paul V. Marshall. New York: The Seabury Press, 1982. Originally published in London: Dacre Press, 1945. In spite of challenges to Dix's theses and newer data, this remains one of the most coherently sweeping histories of the liturgy yet written.

Eisenhofer, Ludwig and Joseph Lechner. *The Liturgy of the Roman Rite*. Trans. A.J. and E.F. Peeler. New York: Herder and Herder, 1961. A commentary on the early sources of the Roman liturgy.

Jungmann, Joseph A. *The Mass of the Roman Rite: Its Origins and Development* [*Missarum Sollemnia*], I and II. Trans. Francis A. Brunner. New York and Westminster, Md.: Christian Classics, 1986. First published in English in 1951, 1955. The most detailed commentary on every part of the mass.

Klauser, Theodore. *A Short History of the Western Liturgy. An Account and Some Reflections*. Trans. John Halliburton. London: Oxford University Press, 1969. First published in German in 1965.

Maxwell, William D. *An Outline of Christian Worship: Its Developments and Forms*. London: Oxford University Press, 1936. Reissued as *History of Christian Worship*. Grand Rapids: Baker Book House, 1982. Especially good on Reformed liturgical orders.

Thompson, Bard. *Liturgies of the Western Church*. Cleveland: World Publishing Company, 1961; Philadelphia: Fortress Press, 1980. Especially good on Protestant liturgies from Luther through Wesley.

Wegman, Herman. *Christian Worship in East and West. A Study Guide to Liturgical History*. Trans. Gordon Lathrop. New York: Pueblo Publishing Co., 1985. Originally published in 1976. Pays attention to the relationship between cult and culture. It substantially ends with the Reformation era.

White, James F. *A Brief History of Christian Worship*. Nashville: Abingdon Press, 1993. The most succinct history of the liturgy available.

Particular Areas in Liturgical History

Jewish Liturgy

Bokser, Baruch M. *The Origins of the Seder*. Berkeley: University of California Press, 1984.

Bradshaw, Paul F. and Lawrence A. Hoffman, eds. *The Making of Jewish and Christian Worship*. Notre Dame, Ind.: University of Notre Dame Press, 1991.

DiSante, Carmine. *Jewish Prayer. The Origins of Christian Liturgy*. Trans. Matthew J. O'Connell. New York and Mahwah, N.J.: Paulist Press, 1991. Originally published in 1985.

Dugmore, C. W. *The Influence of the Synagogue Upon the Divine Office*. Westminster: The Faith Press, 1964. Originally published in 1937.

Fisher, Eugene J., ed. *The Jewish Roots of Christian Liturgy*. New York and Mahwah, N.J.: Paulist Press, 1990.

Hoffman, Lawrence A. *The Canonization of the Synagogue Service*. Notre Dame, Ind.: University of Notre Dame Press, 1979.

————., ed. *The Land of Israel: Jewish Perspectives*. Notre Dame, Ind.: University of Notre Dame Press, 1986.

Idlesohn, A. Z. *Jewish Liturgy and Its Development*. New York: Schocken Books, 1967. Originally published in 1932.

Schauss, Hayyim. *Guide to Jewish Holy Days: History and Observance*. Trans. Samuel Jaffe. New York: Schocken Books, 1962. Originally published in 1938.

Werner, Eric. *The Sacred Bridge: Liturgical Parallels in Synagogue and Early Church*. 2 volumes. Vol. 1: New York: Schocken Books, 1970; originally published in 1959. Vol. 2: New York, KTAV Publishing House, 1984.

Early Christian Worship

Bacciocchi, Samuele. *From Sabbath to Sunday: A Historical Investigation of the Rise of Sunday Observance in Early Christianity*. Rome: Pontifical Gregorian University, 1977.

Bradshaw, Paul F. *The Search for the Origins of Christian Worship: Sources and Methods for the Study of Early Liturgy*. New York and Oxford: Oxford University Press, 1992.

Brightman, F. E., and C. E. Hammond. *Liturgies Eastern and Western*. Vol. I, *Eastern Liturgies*. Oxford: Clarendon Press, 1896. Note: Vol. II was never published.

Cullmann, Oscar. *Early Christian Worship*. Studies in Biblical Theology No. 10. London: SCM Press, 1953.

Daly, Robert. *The Origins of the Christian Doctrine of Sacrifice*. Philadelphia: Fortress Press, 1978.

Deiss, Lucien, ed. *Springtime of the Liturgy: Liturgical Texts of the First Four Centuries*. Collegeville: The Liturgical Press, 1979.

Delling, D. Gerhard. *Worship in the New Testament*. Trans. Percy Scott. Philadelphia: Westminster Press, 1962.

Hahn, Ferdinand. *The Worship of the Early Church*. Trans. David E. Green. Introduction by John Reumann. Philadelphia: Fortress Press, 1973. Originally published in 1968.

Jungmann, Josef A. *The Early Liturgy to the Time of Gregory the Great*. Liturgical Studies VI. Trans. Francis A. Brunner. Notre Dame, Ind.: University of Notre Dame Press, 1959.

Moule, C. F. D. *Worship in the New Testament*. Ecumenical Studies in Worship No. 9. Richmond: John Knox Press, 1961.

Shepherd, Massey H. *The Paschal Liturgy and the Apocalpyse*. Ecumenical Studies in Liturgy No. 6. Richmond: John Knox Press, 1960.

Ancient Church Orders and Patristic Liturgy

Audet, J.-P. *La Didaché. Instructions des apôtres*. Paris, 1958.

Baldovin, John F. *Liturgy in Ancient Jerusalem*. Alcuin Club/Grove Liturgical Study 9. Bramcote, Notts.: Grove Books, 1989.

———. "The Urban Character of Christian Worship." *Orientalia Christiana Periodica* 228 (1987): 119–41.

Bishop, W. C. "The African Rite." *Journal of Theological Studies* XIII (1912): 250–79.

Botte, Bernard. *La Tradition apostolique de saint Hippolyte*. 4th ed. Münster, 1972.

Bradshaw, Paul F. *The Canons of Hippolytus*. Alcuin Club/Grove Liturgical Study 2. Bramcote, Notts.: Grove Books, 1987.

Bradshaw, Paul F, with Maxwell Johnson, L. Edward Phillips, and Grant Sperry White. *The Apostolic Tradition*. Minneapolis: Fortress Press, forthcoming.

Brock, Sebastian, and Michael Vasey. *The Liturgical Portions of the Didascalia*. Grove Liturgical Study 29. Bramcote, Notts.: Grove Books, 1982.

Cuming, G. J. *Hippolytus. A Text for Students*. Grove Liturgical Study 8. Bramcote, Notts.: Grove Books, 1976.

———. *Essays on Hippolytus*. Bramcote, Notts.: Grove Books, 1978.

Daniélou, Jean. *The Bible and the Liturgy*. English trans. Notre Dame, Ind.: University of Notre Dame Press, 1956.

Dix, Gregory. *The Treatise on the Apostolic Tradition of St. Hippolytus of Rome*. Preface and corrections by Henry Chadwick. London: S.P.C.K., 1968. Originally published in 1937.

Donaldson, James. *Constitutions of the Holy Apostles*. New York, 1926. Originally published in Edinburgh, 1886.

Grisbrooke, W. Jardine. *The Liturgical Portions of the Apostolic Constitutions. A Textbook for Students*. Alcuin Club/Grove Liturgical Study 13–14. Bramcote, Notts.: Grove Books, 1990.

Hanssens, J. M. *La Liturgie d'Hippolyte*. Vol. I.: Rome, 1959; 2nd ed., 1965. Vol. II: Rome, 1970.

Jeanes, Gordon. *Early Origins of the Roman Rite*. Alcuin Club/Grove Liturgical Study 20. Bramcote, Notts.: Grove Books, 1991.

Mateos, Juan, S. J. "The Evolution of the Byzantine Liturgy." *John XXIII Lectures*, Vol. 1. New York: Fordham University John XXIII Center for Eastern Christian Studies, 1966.

Niederwimmer, K., *The Didache*. Trans. Linda M. Maloney. Minneapolis: Fortress Press, forthcoming October 1998.

Schultz, Hans-Joachim. *The Byzantine Liturgy: Symbolic Structure and Faith Expression*. Trans. by Matthew J. O'Connell. English edition introduction by Robert J. Taft. New York: Pueblo Publishing Co., 1986.

Sperry-White, Grant. *The Testamentum Domini: A Textbook for Students*. Alcuin Club/Grove Liturgical Study 19. Bramcote, Notts.: Grove Books, 1991.

Taft, Robert. *The Great Entrance: A History of the Transfer of Gifts and Other Preanaphoral Rites of the Liturgy of St. John Chrysostom*. 2nd ed. Rome: Pontificium Institutum Studiorum Orientalium, 1975.

Van der Meer, Ferdinand. *Augustine the Bishop*. Trans. B. Battershaw and G. R. Lamb. London: Sheed and Ward, 1961. Available in Christian Classics reprint. See especially Parts 2, 3, and 4, which deal respectively with the cultus, preaching, and popular piety in the North African church and in Augustine's practice.

Van Olst, E. H. *The Bible and the Liturgy*. Trans. Grand Rapids: Eerdmans, 1991.

Vööbus, Arthur. *The Didascalia Apostolorum in Syriac with English Translation*. *Corpus Scriptorum Christianorum Orientalium* 401, 402, 407, 408; *Scriptores Syri* 175, 176, 179, 180. Louvain, 1979.

———. *Liturgical Material in the Didache*. Stockholm: Estonian Theological Society in Exile, 1968.

Wilkinson, John. *Egeria's Travels*. 2nd ed. London, 1981. Originally published in 1971. Contains invaluable archaeological information on Christian Jerusalem in the post-Constantinian era.

Wybrew, Hugh. *The Orthodox Liturgy: The Development of the Eucharistic Liturgy in the Byzantine Rite*. Crestwood, N.Y.: St. Vladimir's Seminary Press, 1990.

Western Medieval Liturgy

Beck, H. G. J. *The Pastoral Cure of Souls in Southeast France during the Fifth Century*. Rome, 1950.

Bishop, Edmund. *Liturgica Historica. Papers on the Liturgy and Religious Life of the Western Church*. Oxford: Clarendon Press, 1918.

Bishop, Edmund, and C. L. Feltoe. *The Mozarabic and Ambrosian Rites*. Alcuin Clun Tracts XV. London, 1910.

Ellard, Gerald. *Master Alcuin, Liturgist*. Chicago: Henry Regnery, 1956.

Harper, John. *The Forms and Orders of Western Liturgy from the Tenth to the Eighteenth Century*. Oxford: Clarendon Press, 1991.

King, Archdale A. *Liturgies of the Primartial Sees*. London, New York, Toronto, 1957.

Porter, W. S. *The Gallican Rite*. London, 1958.

Van Dijk, S. J. P., and Joan Hazeldon Walker. *The Origins of the Modern Roman Liturgy: The Liturgy of the Papal Court and the Franciscan Order in the Thirteenth Century*. London: Darton, Longman, and Todd, 1960.

Vogel, Cyrille. *Medieval Liturgy: An Introduction to the Sources*. Trans. and revised by William Storey and Niels Rasmussen. Washington: Pastoral Press, 1986. Originally published in French in 1970.

Warren, F. E. *Liturgy and Ritual of the Celtic Church*. Oxford, 1881.

Wilson, H. A. *The Gelasian Sacramentary*. Oxford, 1894.

Reformation Liturgy

Bergendoff, Conrad. *Olavus Petri and the Ecclesiastical Transformation in Sweden 1521–1552*. Philadelphia: Fortress Press, 1965. Originally published in 1928.

Bornert, René. *La réforme protestant du culte a Strassbourg au XVIe siècle (1523–1598): Approche sociologique et interpretation théologique*. Leiden: E. J. Brill, 1981.

Cuming, G. J. *A History of Anglican Liturgy*. 2nd ed. London: Macmillan, 1982.

Dugmore, C. W. *The Mass and the English Reformers*. London: Macmillan, 1958.

First and Second Prayer Books of Edward VI. Introduction by Douglas Harrison. Everyman's Library No. 448. London: Dent and New York: Dutton, 1910. Last reprinted 1968.

Jacobs, Henry Eyster. *The Lutheran Movement in England during the reigns of Henry VIII and Edward VI and Its Literary Monuments*. Rev. ed. Philadelphia: General Council Publication House, 1908.

Luther, Martin. *Luther's Works*. American Edition. Vol. 53, *Liturgy and Hymns*. Ed. by Ulrich S. Leupold. Philadelphia: Fortress Press, 1965.

Meyer, Hans Bernhard. *Luther und die Messe*. Paderborn, 1965.

More About Luther. Martin Luther Lectures, Vol. 2. Decorah, Iowa: Luther College Press, 1958. Buried treasure here! The three major essays in this volume by Jaroslav Pelikan, "Luther and the Liturgy"; by Regin Prenter, "Luther on Word and Sacrament"; and by Herman A. Preus, "The Christian and the Church," are unsurpassed in their treatment of these topics.

Old, Hughes Oliphant. *The Patristic Roots of Reformed Worship*. Zurich: Theologischer Verlag, 1975.

————. *Worship: Guides to the Reformed Tradition*. Altanta: John Knox Press, 1984.

Reed, Luther D. *The Lutheran Liturgy*. 2nd ed. Philadelphia: Fortress Press, 1959. While the longer second half of this classic is a commentary on the Common Liturgy of the *Service Book and Hymnal* of 1958, the historical sections on the Reformation church orders and the development of the Common Service in nineteenth-century American Lutheranism are enduring contributions.

Richter, Aemelius, ed. *Die evangelischen Kirchenordnungen des sechzehnten Jahrhunderts*. Weimar: Landindustriecomptoir, 1846. 2nd ed. Leipzig: Günther, 1871.

Schmidt-Clausing, F. *Zwingli als Liturgiker*. Göttingen, 1952.

Sehling, Emil, ed. *Die evangelischen Kirchenordungen des XVI. Jahrhunderts*, Vols. 1–5; Leipzig: Reisland, 1902–1913. Vol. 6ff.: Tübingen: Mohr, 1955ff.

Serenius, Sigtrygg. *Liturgia svecanae ecclesiae catholicae et orthodoxae conformis: En liturgiehistorisk undersökning med särskild hänsyn till struktur och förlagor*. Åbo, Finland: Åbo Akademi, 1966.

Smend, Julius. *Die evangelischen deutschen Messen bis zu Luthers Deutscher Messe*. Göttingen, 1896; reprinted 1967.

Vajta, Vilmos. *Luther on Worship*. Philadelphia: Fortress Press, 1958. English language abridgment of the original German: *Theologie des Gottesdienstes bei Luther*. Goettingen: Vanderhoeck und Ruprecht, 1952.

Van der Pol, G. J. *Martin Bucer's Liturgical Ideas*. Groningen: Van Gorcum, 1954.

Whitaker, E. C. *Martin Bucer and the Book of Common Prayer*. Alcuin Club Collections No. 55. Great Wakering: Mayhew-McCrimmon, 1974.

Yelverton, Eric E. *An Archbishhop of the Reformation, Laurentius Petri Nericius, Archbishop of Uppsala, 1531–73. A Study of His Liturgical Projects*. Minneapolis: Ausgburg Publishing House, 1959.

————. *The Manual of Olavus Petri, 1529*. London: S.P.C.K., 1953.

————. *The Mass in Sweden. Its Development from the Latin Rite from 1531 to 1917*. Henry Bradshaw Society, Vol. 57. London, 1920.

Post-Reformation Liturgy (17th to 19th Centuries)

Adams, Doug. *Meeting House to Camp Meeting: Toward a History of American Free Church Worship from 1620 to 1835*. Saratoga, N.Y.: Modern Liturgy Resource Publications, 1981.

Barkley, John M. *The Worship of the Reformed Church*. Richmond: John Knox Press, 1967.

Berry, Mary Frances, and John W. Blassingame. *Long Memory: The Black Experience in America*. New York: Oxford University Press, 1982. Especially relevant to liturgical studies is chapter 3, "Family and Church: Enduring Institutions."

Bishop, John. *Methodist Worship in Relation to Free Church Worship*. New York: Scholars Studies Press, 1975.

Davies, Horton. *Worship and Theology in England*. 5 vols. Princeton: Princeton University Press, 1961–1970. Updated in a 3-volume edition published in Grand Rapids: Eerdmans, 1996.

———. *The Worship of the English Puritans*. London: Dacre Press, 1948.

Donnelly, Marion C. *The New England Meeting House of the Seventeenth Century*. Middletown, Conn.: Wesley University, 1968.

Earle, Alice Morse. *The Sabbath in Puritan New England*. Lima, Ohio: CSS Press, 1996. A look at the entire Sunday experience in New England congregations.

Hatchett, Marion. *The Making of the First American Book of Common Prayer*. New York: Seabury Press, 1982.

Horn, Edward Traille. "The Lutheran Sources of the Common Service." *Lutheran Quarterly* 21 (1891): 239–68.

Jacobs, Henry Eyster. "The Making of the *Church Book*." *Lutheran Church Review* 31 (1912): 597–622.

Kalb, Friedrich. *Theology of Worship in Seventeenth-Century Lutheranism*. St. Louis: Concordia Publishing House, 1965.

Melton, Julius. *Presbyterian Worship in America: Changing Patterns Since 1787*. Richmond: John Knox Press, 1967.

Nichols, James Hasting. *Corporate Worship in the Reformed Tradition*. Philadelphia: Westminster Press, 1968.

Porter, Harry Boone. *Jeremy Taylor, Liturgist*. Alcuin Club Collections No. 61. London: S.P.C.K., 1979.

Rivers, Clarence Joseph, ed. *This Far by Faith: American Worship and Its African Roots*. Papers from the 1977 Conference on "Worship and Spirituality in the Black Community." Washington, D.C.: National Office of Black Catholics, 1977.

Stiller, Günther. *Johann Sebastian Bach and Liturgical Life in Leipzig*. Ed. by Robin A. Leaver. Trans. Herbert J. A. Bouman, Daniel F. Poellot, Hilton C. Oswald. St. Louis: Concordia Publishing House, 1984. Originally published in 1970.

Swindler, Leonard. *Aufklaerung Catholicism 1780–1850: Liturgical and Other Reforms in the Catholic Aufklaerung*. AAR Studies in Religion No. 17. Missoula: Scholars Press, 1978.

Weaver, F. Ellen. "The Neo-Gallican Liturgies Revisited." *Studia Liturgia* 16 (1986–87).

Weil, Louis. *Sacraments and Liturgy: The Outward Signs*. Oxford: Basil Blackwell, 1983. A study of the Oxford movement and the sacramental faith and practice of its principal protagonists.

White, James F. *The Cambridge Movement*. Cambridge: Cambridge University Press, 1979.

————. *Protestant Worship: Traditions in Transition*. Louisville: Westminster/John Knox Press, 1989.

————. *Roman Catholic Worship: Trent to Today*. New York and Mahwah, N.J.: Paulist Press, 1995.

Modern Liturgical Movement

Botte, Bernard. *From Silence to Participation. An Insider's View of Liturgical Renewal*. Trans. John Sullivan. Washington, D.C.: The Pastoral Press, 1988. Originally published in 1977. A personal look at the history of liturgical renewal in the Roman Catholic Church from one who contributed profoundly to it.

Hughes, Kathleen. *The Monk's Tale*. Collegeville: The Liturgical Press, 1992. A lovingly told biography of Godfrey Diekman, O.S.B.

Koenker, Ernest B. *The Liturgical Renaissance in the Roman Catholic Church*. St. Louis: Concordia Publishing House, 1966. First published in Chicago: University of Chicago Press, 1954. Perhaps the most well-documented study of the Roman Catholic liturgical movement.

McManus, Frederick R. *Sacramental Liturgy*. New York: Herder and Herder, 1967. Exegesis of the Constitution on the Sacred Liturgy.

Meeks, Blair Gilmer, ed. *The Landscape of Praise. Readings in Liturgical Renewal*. Valley Forge, Pa.: Trinity Press International, 1996. A collection of articles that first apppeared in *Liturgy*, the Journal of The Liturgical Conference, by forty-seven authors who have been leading liturgical movers and thinkers.

Robinson, John A. T. *Liturgy Coming to Life*. Philadelphia: The Westminster Press, 1960. A manifesto of liturgical renewal that exploded on the scene in the 1960s and was enormously influential among nonliturgical scholars.

Sacerdotal Communities of Saint-Severin of Paris and Saint-Joseph of Nice, The. *The Liturgical Movement*. Trans. Lancelot Sheppard. New York: Hawthorn Books, 1964.

Shands, Alfred. *The Liturgical Movement and the Local Church*. Rev. ed. New York: Morehouse-Barlow, 1965.

Shepherd, Lancelot, ed. *The People Worship: A History of the Liturgical Movement*. New York: Hawthorn Books, 1967.

Taylor, Michael J., ed. *Liturgical Renewal in the Christian Churches*. Baltimore-Dublin: Helicon, 1967.

Wainwright, Geoffrey. *Worship With One Accord: Where Liturgy and Ecumenism Embrace*. New York: Oxford University Press, 1997.

Webber, Robert E. *Signs of Wonder*. Nashville: Abbott Martyrn Press, 1992.

White, James F. *Christian Worship in Transition*. Nashville: Abingdon, 1976.

History and Theology of Specific Rites
Eucharistic Liturgy and Theology

Ahlberg, Bo. *Laurentius Petris nattvardsuppfattning*. Studia Theologica Lundensia 26. Lund: CWK Gleerup, 1964.

Aulén, Gustav. *Eucharist and Sacrifice*. Trans. Eric H. Wahlstrom. Edinburgh: Oliver and Boyd and Philadelphia: Muhlenberg Press, 1958.

Borgen, Ole E. *John Wesley on the Sacraments: A Theological Study*. Nashville: Abingdon, 1972.

Bouyer, Louis. *Eucharist: Theology and Spirituality of the Eucharistic Prayer*. Trans. Charles U. Quinn. Notre Dame, Ind.: University of Notre Dame Press, 1968. This work remains unsurpassed in its historical sweep of eucharistic prayers.

Bowmer, John C. *The Sacrament of the Lord's Supper in Early Methodism*. Fort Worth: Dominion Press, 1951.

Brilioth, Yngve. *Eucharistic Faith and Practice, Evangelical and Catholic*. Abridged and trans. A. G. Hebert. London: S.P.C.K., 1965. First published in Swedish in 1926; first English edition published in 1930.

Buxton, Richard F. *Eucharist and Institution Narrative. A Study in the Roman and Anglican traditions of the Consecration of the Eucharist from the Eighth to the Twentieth Centuries*. Alcuin Club Collections No. 58. Great Wakering: Mayhew-McCrimmon, 1976.

Clark, Francis. *Eucharistic Sacrifice and the Reformation*. 2nd ed. Oxford: Oxford University Press, 1967.

Elert, Werner. *Eucharist and Church Fellowship in the First Four Centuries*. Trans. N. E. Nagel. St. Louis: Concordia Publishing House, 1966. Originally published in German in 1954.

Foley, Edward. *From Age to Age: How Christians Celebrated the Eucharist*. Chicago: Liturgy Training Publications, 1991.

Hänggi, Anton, and Irmgard Pahl. *Prex Eucharistica. Textus e Variis Liturgiis Antuioribus Selecti*. Fribourg: Fribourg University Press, 1968.

Jasper, R. C. D., and G. J. Cuming. *Prayers of the Eucharist: Early and Reformed*. 3rd ed, revised and enlarged. New York: Pueblo Publishing Co., 1987.

Jeremias, Joachim. *The Eucharistic Words of Jesus*. Trans. Norman Perrin. London: SCM Press, 1966; Philadelphia: Fortress Press, 1977. This work has become a classic.

Kavanagh, Aidan. *The Concept of Eucharistic Memorial in the Canon Revisions of Thomas Cranmer, Archbishop of Canterbury 1533–1556*. St. Meinrad Archabbey: Abbey Press, 1964.

King, Archdale A. *Eucharistic Reservation in the Western Church*. New York: Sheed and Ward, 1965.

Lietzmann, Hans. *Mass and Lord's Supper: A Study in the History of the Liturgy*. Trans. with appendices by Dorthea H. G. Reeve. Leiden: Brill, 1979.

Ligier, Louis. "The Origins of the Eucharistic Prayer: From the Last Supper to the Eucharist." *Studia Liturgica* 9 (1973) 161–85.

Macy, Gary. *The Banquet's Wisdom: A Short History of the Theologies of the Lord's Supper*. New York and Mahwah, N.J.: Paulist Press, 1992.

————. *The Theologies of the Eucharist in the Early Scholastic Period: A Study of the Salvific Function of the Sacrament according to the Theologians, c. 1080–1220*. Oxford: Clarendon Press, 1984.

Mazza, Enrico. *The Eucharistic Prayers of the Roman Rite*. Trans. Matthew J. O'Connell. New York: Pueblo Publishing Co., 1986.

————. *The Origins of the Eucharistic Prayer*. Trans. Ronald E. Lane. Collegeville: The Liturgical Press, 1995.

McCue, James F. "The Doctrine of Transubstantiation from Berengar through Trent." *Harvard Theological Review* 61 (1968): 385–430.

McDonnell, Kilian. *John Calvin, the Church, and the Eucharist*. Princeton: Princeton University Press, 1967.

McKenna, John H. *Eucharist and Holy Spirit. The Eucharistic Epiclesis in 20th Century Theology*. Alcuin Club Collections No. 57. Great Wakering: Mayhew-McCrimmon, 1975.

Mitchell, Nathan. *Cult and Controversy: The Worship of the Eucharist Outside Mass*. New York: Pueblo Publishing Co., 1982.

Pahl, Irmgard. *Coena Domini*, vol. I. Spicilegium Friburgense 29. Fribourg: Fribourg University Press, 1983. Texts of Reformation eucharistic prayers and rites.

Power, David N. *The Eucharistic Mystery: Revitalizing the Tradition*. New York: The Crossroad Publishing Company, 1992.

———. *The Sacrifice We Offer: The Tridentine Dogma and Its Reinterpretation*. Edinburgh: T. and T. Clark; New York: The Crossroad Publishing Company, 1987.

Powers, Joseph M. *Eucharistic Theology*. New York: Seabury Press, 1967.

Rattenbury, J. Ernest. *The Eucharistic Hymns of John and Charles Wesley*. London: Epworth Press, 1964.

Rempel, John D. *The Lord's Supper in Anabaptism*. Scottsdale, Pa.: Herald Press, 1993.

Reumann, John H. P. *The Supper of the Lord: The New Testament, Ecumenical Dialogues, and Faith and Order on the Eucharist*. Philadelphia: Fortress Press, 1985.

Rordorf, Willy, et al. *The Eucharist of the Early Christians*. Trans. Matthew J. O'Connell. New York: Pueblo Publishing Co., 1978.

Rubin, Miri. *Corpus Christi: The Eucharist in Late Medieval Culture*. Cambridge: Cambridge University Press, 1991.

Ryan, John Barry. *The Eucharistic Prayer. A Study in Contemporary Liturgy*. New York/Paramus/Toronto: Paulist Press, 1974.

Sasse, Hermann. *This Is My Body. Luther's Contention for the Real Presence in the Sacrament of the Altar*. Minneapolis: Augsburg Publishing House, 1959. In spite of its polemical thrust, this remains the most thorough presentation of the intra-Reformation controversy over the real presence of Christ in the sacrament.

Schillebeeckx, Edward. *The Eucharist*. Trans. N. D. Smith. New York: Sheed and Ward, 1968.

Schmemann, Alexander. *The Eucharist: Sacrament of the Kingdom*. New York: St. Vladimir's Seminary Press, 1988.

Seasoltz, Kevin, ed. *Living Bread, Saving Cup*. Collegeville: The Liturgical Press, 1987. A collection of articles that first appeared in *Worship*.

Senn, Frank C. "Frequency of Celebration and Reception of Holy Communion in Protestantism." *Proceedings of the North American Academy of Liturgy. Annual Meeting, St. Louis, Mo., 2–5 January 1990*. Valparaiso, Ind.: Valparaiso University, 1990, pp. 98–118.

———. "Holy Communion Outside the Assembly: Two Models." *Proceedings of the Annual Meeting of the North American Academy of Liturgy, Nashville, Tenn., 2–5 January 1989*. Valparaiso, Ind.: Valparaiso University, 1989, pp. 190–210.

———. "Liturgia svecanae ecclesiae: An Attempt at Eucharistic Restoration during the Swedish Reformation." *Studia Liturgica* 14 (1980–1981): 20–36.

———. "Martin Luther's Revision of the Eucharistic Canon in the *Formula Missae* of 1523." *Concordia Theological Monthly* 44/2 (1973): 101–18.

————., ed. *New Eucharistic Prayers: An Ecumenical Study of Their Development and Structure.* Mahwah, N.J.: Paulist Press, 1987.

————. "Toward a Different Anaphora Structure." *Worship* 58/4 (1984): 346–58.

Spinks, Bryan D. *Freedom or Order: The Eucharistic Liturgy in English Congregationalism.* New York: Pilgrim Press, 1984.

————. *Luther's Liturgical Criteria and His Reform of the Canon of the Mass.* Grove Liturgical Study No. 30. Bramcote, Notts.: Grove Books, 1982.

————. *The Sanctus in the Eucharistic Prayer.* Cambridge: Cambridge University Press, 1991.

Stevenson, Kenneth. *Eucharist and Offering.* New York: Pueblo Publishing Co., 1986.

Talley, Thomas. "The Eucharistic Prayer of the Ancient Church According to Recent Research: Results and Reflections." *Studia Liturgica* 11 (1976): 138–58. Also "From *Berakah* to *Eucharistia*: A Reopening Question." *Worship* 50 (1976): 115–37. Talley's reexploring of the early eucharistic tradition served to challenge the hegemony of the West Syrian anaphoral structure as a model for new eucharistic prayers.

Thurian, Max, and Geoffrey Wainwright. *Baptism and Eucharist: Ecumenical Convergence in Celebration.* Faith and Order Paper No. 117. Geneva: World Council of Churches and Grand Rapids: William B. Eerdmans, 1983. An anthology of historic and contemporary liturgical texts.

————. *The Eucharistic Memorial.* 2 vols. Trans. J. G. Davies. London: Lutterworth Press and Richmond: John Knox Press, 1961.

Wainwright, Geoffrey. *Eucharist and Eschatology.* London and New York: Oxford University Press, 1981.

Wisløff, Carl F. *The Gift of Communion. Luther's Controversy with Rome on Eucharistic Sacrifice.* Trans. Joseph M. Shaw. Minneapolis: Augsburg Publishing House, 1964. Important for distinguishing between Luther's and Melanchthon's critique of the sacrifice of the mass.

Rites of Christian Initiation

Aland, Kurt. *Did the Early Church Baptize Infants?* Trans. G. R. Beasley-Murray. Philadelphia: The Westminster Press, 1963.

Austin, Gerard. *Anointing with the Spirit. The Rite of Confirmation: The Use of Oil and Chrism.* Studies in the Reformed Rites of the Catholic Church, vol. III. New York: Pueblo Publishing Co., 1985.

Beasley-Murray, G. R. *Baptism in the New Testament.* New York: Macmillan, 1962.

Brand, Eugene L. "Baptism and Communion of Infants: A Lutheran View." *Worship* 50 (1976): 29–42.

Cross, F. L. *I Peter: A Paschal Liturgy.* London: Mowbray, 1954.

Cullmann, Oscar. *Baptism in the New Testament.* Trans. J. K. S. Reid. London: SCM Press, 1950.

Dix, Gregory. *The Theology of Confirmation in Relation to Baptism.* London: Dacre Press, 1946.

Fisher, J. D. C. *Confirmation Then and Now.* Alcuin Club Collections No. 60. London: S.P.C.K., 1978.

————. *Christian Initiation: Baptism in the Medieval West.* Alcuin Club Collections No. 51. London: S.P.C.K., 1965.

————. *Christian Initiation: The Reformation Period.* Alcuin Club Collections No. 51. London: S.P.C.K., 1970.

Hamman, André, ed. *Baptism: Ancient Liturgies and Patristic Texts*. Staten Island: Alba House, 1967.

Holeton, David R. *Infant Communion—Then and Now*. Grove Liturgical Study No. 27. Bramcote, Notts: Grove Books, 1981.

Jagger, Peter. *Christian Initiation 1552–1969. Rites of Baptism and Confirmation Since the Reformation Period*. Alcuin Club Collection No. 52. London: S.P.C.K., 1972.

Jeremias, Joachim. *Infant Baptism in the First Four Centuries*. Trans. D. Cairns. Philadelphia: Westminster Press, 1962.

Kavanagh, Aidan. *Confirmation: Origins and Reform*. New York: Pueblo Publishing Co., 1988.

———. *The Shape of Baptism: The Rite of Christian Initiation*. Studies in the Reformed Rites of the Catholic Church, vol. I. New York: Pueblo Publishing Co., 1978. An insightful survey of the early tradition and a strategic vision of the renewal of Christian initiation and community by means of the Rite of Christian Initiation of Adults.

Kretschmar, Georg. "Recent Research on Christian Initiation." *Studia Liturgica* 12 (1977): 87–103.

Lampe, G. W. H. *The Seal of the Spirit: A Study in the Doctrine of Baptism and Confirmation in the New Testament and the Fathers*. Rev. ed. London: S.P.C.K., 1967.

Made, Not Born. New Perspectives on Christian Initiation and the Catechumenate. Ed. by the Murphy Center for Liturgical Research. Notre Dame, Ind.: University of Notre Dame Press, 1976.

Mitchell, Leonel L. *Baptismal Anointing*. Alcuin Club Collections No. 48. London: S.P.C.K., 1966.

Neunheuser, Burkhard. *Baptism and Confirmation*. Trans. J. Hughes. New York: Herder and Herder, 1964.

Old, Hughes Oliphant. *The Shaping of the Reformed Baptismal Rite in the Sixteenth Century*. Grand Rapids: Eerdmans, 1992.

Repp, Arthur. *Confirmation in the Lutheran Church*. St. Louis: Concordia Publishing House, 1964.

Schlink, Edmund. *The Doctrine of Baptism*. Trans. St. Louis: Concordia Publishing House, 1972.

Schmemann, Alexander. *Of Water and the Spirit*. New York: St. Vladimir's Seminary Press, 1974.

Schnackenburg, Rudolf. *Baptism in the Thought of St. Paul: A Study in Pauline Theology*. Trans. G. R. Beasley-Murray. New York: Herder, 1964.

Searle, Mark. *Christening: The Making of Christians*. Collegeville: The Liturgical Press, 1980.

Senn, Frank C. "An End for Confirmation?" *Currents in Theology and Mission* 3/1 (1976): 45–52.

Wainwright, Geoffrey. *Christian Initiation*. Richmond: John Knox Press, 1969.

Whitaker, E. C. *The Baptismal Liturgy*. Studies in Christian Worship V. London: The Faith Press, 1965.

———. *Documents of the Baptismal Liturgy*. 2nd ed. London: S.P.C.K., 1970.

Yarnold, Edward. *The Awe-inspiring Rites of Initiation: Baptismal Homilies of the Fourth Century*. 2nd ed. Collegeville: The Liturgical Press, 1994.

Penitential Rites

Bieler, Ludwig, ed. *The Irish Penitentials*. Dublin: Irish Institute for Advanced Studies, 1963.

Bouman, Walter R. "Confession and Absolution in the Eucharistic Liturgy." *Lutheran Quarterly* 26 (1974): 204–20.

Collins, Mary, and David Power. *The Fate of Confession*. Concilium 190. Edinburgh: T. and T. Clark, 1987.

Crichton, J. D. *The Ministry of Reconciliation*. London: Geoffrey Chapman, 1974.

Dallen, James. *The Reconciling Community: The Rite of Penance*. New York: Pueblo Publishing Co., 1986.

Gunstone, J. T. A. *The Liturgy of Penance*. London: The Faith Press, 1966.

———. *A History of the Cure of Souls*. New York: Harper and Row, 1965.

McNeill, John T. A., and Helena M. Garner. *Medieval Handbooks of Penance*. New York: Columbia University Press, 1938. Reprint New York: Octagon Books, 1965.

Palmer, Paul F. *Sacraments and Forgiveness*. Westminster, Md.: Newman Press, 1959.

Poschmann, Bernhard. *Penance and the Anointing of the Sick*. Trans. and rev. by Francis Courtney, S.J. New York: Herder and Herder, 1964.

Resonance 1/2 and 2/1 (1965/66). An issue devoted to "Penance: The Ministry of Reconciliation." Introduction by Aidan Kavanagh.

Senn, Frank C. "Structures of Penance and the Ministry of Reconciliation." *Lutheran Quarterly* 35 (1973): 270–83.

Studia Liturgica 18:1 (1988). An issue devoted to penance in contemporary scholarship and practice.

Thurian, Max. *Confession*. Trans. London: SCM Press, 1958.

Watkins, Oscar D. *A History of Penance*. 2 vols. New York: Longmans, Green, 1920. Reprint 1960.

The Church Year Calendar and Lectionary

Adam, Adolf. *The Liturgical Year*. Trans. Matthew J. O'Connell. New York: Pueblo Publishing Co., 1981.

Beckwith, Roger T. "The Origin of the Festivals of Easter and Whitsun." *Studia Liturgica* 13 (1979): 1–20.

Brown, Peter. *The Cult of the Saints: Its Rise and Function in Latin Christianity*. London: SCM Press, 1961; Chicago: University of Chicago, 1982.

Butler's Lives of the Saints. New Full Edition. 12 vols. Ed. Paul Burn. Collegeville: The Liturgical Press. (1995–).

Cowley, Patrick. *Advent: Its Liturgical Significance*. London: Faith Press, 1960.

Davies, J. Gordon, *Holy Week: A Short History*. Ecumenical Studies in Worship No. 11. Richmond: John Knox Press, 1963.

Gunstone, John A. T. *Christmas and Epiphany*. London: Faith Press, 1967.

———. *The Feast of Pentecost*. London: Faith Press, 1967.

Hickman, Hoyt, Don E. Saliers, Lawrence Hull Stookey, and James F. White. The New *Handbook of the Christian Year*. Nashville: Abingdon Press, 1992.

Klein, Terrance W. "Advent and the Evangelical Struggle for Cultural Symbols." *Worship* 69/6 (1995): 538–56.

Maertens, Thierry. *A Feast in Honor of Yahweh*. Trans. K. Sullivan. Notre Dame, Ind.: Fides Press, 1965.

McArthur, A. A. *The Christian Year and Lectionary Reform*. London: SCM Press, 1958.

Pfatteicher, Philip J. *Festivals and Commemorations: Handbook to the Calendar in the Lutheran Book of Worship*. Minneapolis: Augsburg Publishing House, 1980. Historical introduction to each day in the *LBW* calendar with a devotional selection and a listing of propers.

Regan, Patrick. "The Fifty Days and the Fiftieth Day." *Worship* 55 (1981): 194–218.

———. "The Three Days and the Forty Days." *Worship* 54 (1980): 2–18.

Roll, Susan K. *Toward the Origins of Christmas*. Tilburg, The Netherlands: Kok Pharos Publishing House, 1995.

Rordorf, Willy. *Sunday: The History of the Day of Rest and Worship in the Earliest Centuries of the Christian Church*. Trans. A. A. K. Graham. Philadelphia: The Westminster Press and London: SCM Press, 1968.

Sloyan, Gerard S. "The Bible as the Book of the Church." *Worship* 60 (1986): 9–21.

Talley, Thomas J. *The Origins of the Liturgical Year*. Emended 2nd ed. New York: Pueblo Publishing Co., 1991.

Tyrer, John Walton. *Historical Survey of Holy Week: Its Services and Ceremonial*. London: Oxford University Press, 1932.

Weiser, Francis X. *Handbook of Christian Feasts and Customs: The Year of the Lord in Liturgy and Folklore*. New York: Harcourt, Brace, and World, 1952.

Wilson, Stephen, ed. *Saints and Their Cults: Studies in Religious Sociology, Folklore, and History*. Cambridge and New York: Cambridge University Press, 1983.

Ordination Rites

Bradshaw, Paul F. *History of the Anglican Ordinal*. Alcuin Club Collections No. 53. London: S.P.C.K., 1971.

———. *Ordination Rites of the Ancient Churches of East and West*. New York: Pueblo Publishing Co., 1990.

Cooke, Bernard. *Ministry to Word and Sacraments: History and Theology*. Philadelphia: Fortress Press, 1976.

Fink, Peter E. "The Sacrament of Orders: Some Liturgical Reflections." *Liturgy* 56 (1982): 482–502.

Porter, H. Boone. *Ordination Prayers of the Ancient Western Churches*. Alcuin Club Collections No. 49. London: S.P.C.K., 1967.

Quere, Ralph W. "The Spirit and the Gifts Are Ours: Imparting or Imploring the Spirit in Ordination Rites?" *Lutheran Quarterly* 27 (1975): 322–46.

Studia Liturgica 13:2, 3, 4 (1979). "Ordination Rites. Papers read at the 1979 Congress of Societas Liturgica."

Rites of Passage

Gusmer, Charles W. *The Ministry of Healing in the Church of England. An Ecumenical-Liturgical Study*. Alcuin Club Collections No. 56. Great Wakering: Mayhew-McCrimmon, 1974.

James, Edwin O. *Marriage Customs Through the Ages*. New York: Collier, 1965.

Paxton, Frederick S. *Christianizing Death: The Creation of a Ritual Process in Early Medieval Europe.* Ithaca: Cornell University Press, 1990.

Rowell, Geoffrey. *The Liturgy of Christian Burial: An Introductory Survey of the Historical Development of Christian Burial Rites.* Alcuin Club No. 59. London: S.P.C.K., 1977.

Rutherford, Richard. *The Death of a Christian: The Rite of Funerals.* Rev. ed. Studies in the Reformed Rites of the Catholic Church 7. New York: Pueblo Publishing Co., 1990.

Stevenson, Kenneth. *Nuptual Blessing: A Study of Christian Marriage Rites.* Alcuin Club Collections 64. New York: Oxford University Press, 1983.

Wagner, Johannes, ed. *Reforming the Rites of Death.* Concilium 32. New York: Paulist Press, 1968.

Divine Office

Bradshaw, Paul F. *Daily Prayer in the Early Church: A Study of the Origin and Early Development of the Divine Office.* Alcuin Club Collections 63. London: S.P.C.K., 1981.

Fischer, Balthasar. "The Common Prayer of Congregation and Family in the Ancient Church." *Studia Liturgica* 10 (1974): 106–24.

Grisbrooke, W. Jardine. "A Contemporary Liturgical Problem: The Divine Office." *Studia Liturgica* 9:3 (1971–72): 129–68; 9:1–3 (1973): 1–18, 81–106.

Guiver, George. *Company of Voices: Daily Prayer and the People of God.* Collegeville: The Liturgical Press, 1988.

Jeremias, Joachim. *The Prayers of Jesus.* Trans. Naperville, Ill.: A.R. Allenson, 1974.

Mateos, Juan. "The Morning and Evening Office." *Worship* 42 (1968): 31–47.

———. "The Origins of the Divine Office." *Worship* 41 (1967): 477–85.

———. "La vigil cathedrale chez Egerie." *Orientalia Christiana Periodica* 27 (1961): 281–312.

Ratcliff, E. C. "The Choir Offices." In W. K. Lowther Clarke and Charles Harris, eds., *Liturgy and Worship.* London: S.P.C.K., 1932, pp. 257–95.

Salmon, Pierre. *The Breviary through the Centuries.* Trans. Sister David Mary, S.N.J.M. Collegeville: The Liturgical Press, 1962.

Storey, William G. "The Liturgy of the Hours: Principle and Practice." *Worship* 46 (1972): 194–203.

Studia Liturgica 10 (1975). The entire issue is devoted to the theme of Common Prayer.

Taft, Robert. *The Liturgy of the Hours in the Christian East: Origins, Meaning, Place in the Life of the Church.* Cochin, Kerala (India): KCM Press, 1984.

———. *The Liturgy of the Hours in East and West: The Origins of the Divine Office and Its Meaning for Today.* Collegeville: The Liturgical Press, 1986.

Wallwork, N. "The Psalter and the Divine Office." *Studia Liturgica* 12/1 (1977): 46–64.

Liturgical Arts

Architecture and Art

Aldershaw, G.W.O., and Frederick Etchells. *The Architectural Setting of Anglican Worship.* London: Faber and Faber, 1948.

Bouyer, Louis. *Liturgy and Architecture.* Notre Dame, Ind.: University of Notre Dame Press, 1967.

Cannon-Brookes, P. and C. *Baroque Churches*. London: Paul Hamlyn, 1969.

Davies, J.G. *The Architectural Setting of Baptism*. London: Barrie and Rockliff, 1962.

Dendy, D.R. *The Use of Lights in Christian Worship*. Alcuin Club Collections No. 41. London: S.P.C.K., 1959.

Duby, Georges. *The Age of the Cathedrals: Art and Society, 980–1420*. Trans. Eleanor Levieux and Barbara Thompson. Chicago: University of Chicago Press, 1981.

Edwards, David L. *The Cathedrals of Britain*. Wilton, Conn.: Morehouse Publishing, 1989. Good introductory material, discussion of master builders of different eras, and historical sketches of each of Britain's cathedrals, with excellent photographs.

Eire, Carlos M.N. *War Against the Idols: The Reformation of Worship from Erasmus to Calvin*. Cambridge: Cambridge University Press, 1986.

Grabar, Andre. *Christian Iconography: A Study of its Origins*. Princeton: Princeton University Press, 1986.

Maldonado, Luis, and David Power, eds. *Symbol and Art in Worship*. Concilium 132. New York: Seabury Press, 1980.

Panofsky, Erwin. *Gothic Architecture and Scholasticism*. New York: World Publishing Company, 1957.

Sovik, E.A. *Architecture for Worship*. Minneapolis: Augsburg Publishing House, 1973.

Stauffer, S. Anita. *On Baptismal Fonts: Ancient and Modern*. The Alcuin Club and the Group for Renewal of Christian Worship (GROW). Bramcott, Notts.: Grove Books, 1992.

Van der Leeuw, Gerhardus. *Sacred and Profane Beauty: The Holy in Art*. Trans.. New York: Holt, Rinehart, and Winston, 1963.

Van der Meer, Ferdinand. *Early Christian Art*. English trans. London: Faber and Faber, 1959. Originally published in Dutch.

Von Simson, Otto. *The Gothic Cathedral. Origins of Gothic Architecture and the Medieval Concept of Order*. 3rd ed. Princeton: Princeton University Press, 1979.

White, James F. *Protestant Worship and Church Architecture*. New York: Oxford University Press, 1964.

White, L. Michael. *The Social Origin of Christian Architecture*. Vol. 1, *Building God's House in the Roman World: Architectural Adaptation among Pagans, Jews, and Christians*. Vol. 2, *Texts and Monuments for the Christian Domus Ecclesiae in its Environment*. Valley Forge, Pa.: Trinity Press International, 1996.

White, Susan J. *Art, Architecture, and Liturgical Reform*. New York: Pueblo Publishing Co., 1990.

Music in Worship

Apel, Willi. *Gregorian Chant*. Bloomington, Ind.: Indiana University Press, 1958. Foundational study of Western medieval chant.

Ashton, Samuel. *Music in Worship*. New York: The Pilgrim Press, 1943.

Benson, Louis F. *The English Hymn*. Richmond: John Knox Press, 1962.

Blume, Friedrich, with Ludwig Finscher, Georg Feder, Adam Adrio, Walter Blankenburg, Torben Schousboe, Robert Stevenson, and Watkins Shaw. *Protestant Church Music: A History.* Foreword by Paul Henry Lang. English trans. of portions originally published in German as *Geschichte der Evangelischen Kirchenmusic.* New York: W.W. Norton, 1974. The single most important historical work for serious students of Protestant church music.

Buszin, Walter E. "Luther on Music." *The Musical Quarterly* 32/1 (1946): 80–97. A classic essay on the subject by the premier American Lutheran musicologist of the previous generation.

––––––. "Johann Walther: Composer, Pioneer, and Luther's Musical Consultant." *The Musical Heritage of the Church.* The Valparaiso Church Music Series, III. St. Louis: Concordia Publishing House, 1947, pp. 78–110.

Douglas, Winfred. *Church Music in History and Practice.* New York: Scribner's, 1962.

Ellingwood, Leonard. *The History of American Church Music.* Rev. ed. New York: Da Capo Press, 1970.

Etherington, Charles L. *Protestant Worship Music: Its History and Practice.* Westport, Conn.: Greenwood Press, 1978. Reprint of 1962 edition.

Fellerer, Karl Gustav. *The History of Catholic Church Music.* Trans. Francis A. Brunner. Baltimore: Helicon Press, 1961. Valuable survey of Catholic composers, but little information on liturgical practice.

Fellowes, Edmund H. *English Cathedral Music.* London: Methuen and Company, Ltd., 1969.

Foley, Edward, Capuchin. *Foundations of Christian Music: The Music of Pre-Constantinian Christianity.* Collegeville: The Liturgical Press, 1994.

––––––. *Ritual Music: Studies in Liturgical Musicology.* Beltsville, Md.: The Pastoral Press, 1995.

Frost, Maurice. *English and Scottish Psalm and Hymn Tunes.* London: Oxford University Press, 1953.

Gelineau, Joseph. *Voices and Instruments in Christian Worship: Principles, Laws, Applications.* Trans. Collegeville: The Liturgical Press, 1964.

Halter, Carl, and Carl Schalk, eds. *A Handbook of Church Music.* St. Louis: Concordia Publishing House, 1978.

Hiley, David. *Western Plainchant.* New York: Oxford University Press, 1993.

Hoffman, Lawrence A., and Janet Walton, eds. *Sacred Sound and Social Change: Liturgical Music in Jewish and Christian Experience.* Notre Dame, Ind.: University of Notre Dame Press, 1992.

Irwin, Joyce. *Neither Voice nor Heart: German Lutheran Theology of Music in the Age of the Baroque.* New York: Peter Lang, 1993.

LeHuray, Peter. *Music and the Reformation in England 1549–1660.* London: Herbert Jenkins, 1967.

Liemohn, Edwin. *The Chorale Through Four Hundred Years.* Philadelphia: Muhlenberg Press, 1953.

Liemohn, Edwin. *Organ and Choir in Protestant Worship.* Philadelphia: Fortress Press, 1968.

Long, Kenneth R. *The Music of the English Church.* Toronto: Hodder and Stoughton, 1971.

Lovelace, Austin C., and William C. Rice. *Music and Worship in the Church.* Rev. ed. Nashville: Abingdon Press, 1976.

McKinnon, James. *Music in Early Christian Literature.* New York: Cambridge University Press, 1987.

Mopson, J. Wendell, Jr. *The Ministry of Music in the Black Church*. Valley Forge, Pa.: Judson Press, 1984.

Quasten, Johannes. *Music and Worship in Pagan and Christian Antiquity*. Trans. Boniface Ramsey, O.P. Washington, D.C.: National Association of Pastoral Musicians, 1983. First German edition published in 1929.

Rice, William C. *A Concise History of Church Music*. Nashville: Abingdon Press, 1964.

Riedel, Johannes, ed. *Cantors at the Crossroads. Essays on Church Music in Honor of Walter E. Buszin*. St. Louis: Concordia Publishing House, 1967.

Routley, Erik. *The Church and Music: An Inquiry into the History, the Nature, and the Scope of Christian Judgment on Music*. Rev. ed. London: Gerald Duckworth and Company, Ltd., 1967.

Schalk, Carl. *Key Words in Church Music*. St. Louis: Concordia Publishing House, 1978.

Schweitzer, Albert. *J. S. Bach*. 2 vols. Trans. Ernest Newman. New York: Macmillan, 1950; New York: Dover Publications, Inc., 1966. Originally published in French in 1905; expanded and published in German in 1908. The preface to the German edition was written by Schweitzer's organ teacher, Charles Marie Widor.

Soehngen, Oskar. *Theologie der Musik*. Kassel: Johannes Stauda Verlag, 1967.

Spencer, Jon Michael. *Black Hymnody: A Hymnological History of the African-American Church*. Knoxville: University of Tennessee Press, 1992.

Squire, Russel N. *Church Music: Music and Hymnological Developments in Western Christianity*. St. Louis: Bethany Press, 1962.

Steere, Dwight. *Music in Protestant Worship*. Atlanta: John Knox Press, 1960.

Stevens, Dennis. *Tudor Church Music*. New York: Da Capo Press, 1973. Reprint of 1955 edition.

Temperley, Nicholas. *The Music of the English Parish Church*. 2 vols. Cambridge: Cambridge University Press, 1979.

Watson, J. R. *The English Hymn*. London and New York: Oxford University Press, 1997. A major work on the English hymn to be published in 1997.

Wilson-Dickson, Andrew. *The Story of Christian Music*. Oxford: Lion Publishing Company, 1992; Minneapolis: Fortress Press, 1997.

Winter, Miriam Therese. *Why Sing? Toward a Theology of Catholic Church Music*. Washington, D.C.: The Pastoral Press, 1984.

Liturgical Performance

Day, Thomas. *Why Catholics Can't Sing. The Culture of Catholicism and the Triumph of Bad Taste*. New York: Crossroad, 1990. In spite of its informal style, this is a penetrating analysis of problems with American Catholic liturgy, ritualization, and singing from several angles; applicable also to many Protestant situations!

Fortesque, Adrian, and J. B. O'Connell. *The Ceremonies of the Roman Rite Described*, 12. Rev. ed. London: Burns and Oates, 1962. A classic manual for celebrating the Tridentine Roman Mass.

Hoffman, Lawrence A. *The Art of Public Prayer. Not for Clergy Only*. Washington, D.C.: The Pastoral Press, 1988.

Hovda, Robert. *Strong, Loving, and Wise: Presiding in Liturgy*. Washington, D.C.: The Liturgical Conference, 1977. Reprinted by The Liturgical Press. More than a manual, this work projects a virtual spirituality of presiding in liturgy.

Huffman, Walter C., and S. Anita Stauffer. *Where We Worship*. Minneapolis: Augsburg Publishing House; Philadelphia: Board of Publication, Lutheran Church in America; St. Louis: Concordia Publishing House, 1987. Study book and leader's guide editions.

Kavanagh, Aidan. *Elements of Rite. A Handbook of Liturgical Style*. New York: Pueblo Publishing Co., 1982. Full of pithy aphorisms based on sound scholarship and unerring liturgical sensibility.

Lang, Paul H, D. *Ceremony and Celebration*. St. Louis: Concordia Publishing House, 1965. A ceremonial manual appropriate to the rubrics of liturgical restorationism, which had reached a high point in Lutheranism by the 1950s and 1960s. It is an approach to rubrics guided strictly by Lutheran theological sensitivities and appeal to historical precedent.

Lawrence, Joy E., and John A. Ferguson, eds. *A Musician's Guide to Church Music*. Foreword by Paul Manz. New York: The Pilgrim Press, 1981.

Liturgy: We Proclaim. Journal of the Liturgical Conference, 11/1 (1993). A manual-like volume that shows every aspect of proclamation in the liturgical assembly.

Perham, Michael. *The Eucharist*. Alcuin Club Manual No. 1. London: S.P.C.K., 1978.

Pfatteicher, Philip H., and Carlos Messerli. *Manual on the Liturgy: Lutheran Book of Worship*. Minneapolis: Augsburg Publishing House, 1979.

Roles in the Liturgical Assembly. Papers from the Twenty-third Saint Serge Liturgical Conference. Trans. Matthew J. O'Connell. New York: Pueblo Publishing Co., 1977.

Routley, Erik. *Music Leadership in the Church: A Conversation Chiefly with My American Friends*. Nashville: Abingdon Press, 1967.

Senn, Frank C. *The Pastor As Worship Leader. A Manual for Corporate Worship*. 2nd ed. Minneapolis: Augsburg Publishing House, 1977. Perhaps noteworthy for its insistence on the differentiation of liturgical roles—a new idea to Lutherans and almost every other Western tradition in the 1970s.

Westermeyer, Paul. *The Church Musician*. Rev. ed. Foreword by Martin E. Marty. Minneapolis: Augsburg Fortress, 1997.

Contemporary Worship Books with Related Commentaries

Episcopal

The Book of Common Prayer and Administration of the Sacraments and Other Rites and Ceremonies of the Church . . . According to the Use of The Episcopal Church. The Church Hymnal Corporation and The Seabury Press, 1977; authorized 1979.

Glover, Raymond F., ed. *Hymnal 1982 Companion*. New York: The Church Hymnal Corporation, 1995.

Hatchett, Marion. *Commentary on the American Prayer Book*. New York: Seabury Press, 1980.

The Hymnal 1982 According to the Use of The Episcopal Church. New York: The Church Hymnal Corporation, 1985.

Price, Charles P., and Louis Weil. *Liturgy for Living*. The Church's Teaching Series. New York: The Seabury Press, 1979.

Lutheran

Christian Worship: A Lutheran Hymnal. Milwaukee: Northwestern Publishing House, 1993.

Erneuerte Agende. Hannover: Lutherisches Verlagshaus, and Bielefeld: Luther-Verlag, 1990. This new agenda or worship book is approved for use in the Evangelical Lutheran Church in Germany and the Evangelical Church of the Union.

Lutheran Book of Worship. Minneapolis: Augsburg Publishing House, and Philaelphia: Board of Publication, Lutheran Church in America, 1978. Published in two editions: Ministers Edition (Altar version and desk version) and Pew Edition.

Lutheran Worship. St. Louis: Concordia Publishing House, 1982.

Nilsson, Nils-Henrik. *Gudstjänst i Svenska Kyrkan: En praktisk handledning*. Stockholm: Svenska Kyrkans Information, 1994.

Occasional Services: Lutheran Book of Worship. Minneapolis: Augsburg Publishing House, and Philadelphia: Board of Publication, Lutheran Church in America, 1982.

Pfatteicher, Philip H. *Commentary on the Lutheran Book of Worship: Lutheran Liturgy in Its Ecumenical Context*. Minneapolis: Augsburg Fortress, 1990.

———. *Commentary on the Occasional Services*. Philadelphia: Fortress Press, 1983.

Precht, Fred L., ed. *Commentary on Lutheran Worship*. St. Louis: Concordia Publishing House, 1992.

Stulken, Marilyn K. *Hymnal Companion to the Lutheran Book of Worship*. Philadelphia: Fortress Press, 1981.

Den Svenska Kyrkohandboken, I. Stockholm: Verbum Förlag, 1987. This is the authorized manual or agenda of the Church of Sweden.

Den Svenska Psalmboken. Stockholm: Petra Bokförlag, 1987.

Roman Catholic

Keifer, Ralph A. *To Give Thanks and Praise: General Instruction of the Roman Missal*. With Commentary for Musicians and Priests. Washington, D.C.: National Association of Pastoral Musicians, 1980.

Patino, J., ed. *The New Order of Mass*. Official text of *Instruction*, English Version and Commentary. Trans. the Monks of Mount Angel Abbey. Collegeville: The Liturgical Press, 1970.

The Rites of the Catholic Church. Vols. 1 and 2. New York: Pueblo Publishing Co., 1976.

The Roman Missal: Lectionary for Mass. Collegeville: The Liturgical Press, 1970.

The Roman Missal: The Sacramentary. New York: Catholic Book Publishing Company, 1973, 1985. English trans. by the International Consultation on English in the Liturgy [ICEL].

See the Studies in the Reformed Rites of the Catholic Church series published by Pueblo Publishing Co.

United Methodist

Hickman, Hoyt, ed. *The Worship Resources of the United Methodist Hymnal*. Nashville: Abingdon Press, 1994.

———. *Worshipping with United Methodists: A Guide for Pastor and Church Leaders*. Nashville: Abingdon Press, 1996.

The United Methodist Book of Worship. Nashville: The United Methodist Publishing House, 1992.

The United Methodist Hymnal: Book of United Methodist Worship. Nashville: The United Methodist Publishing House, 1989.

United Presbyterian

Book of Common Worship. Louisville: Westminster/John Knox Press, 1993. Prepared for the Presbyterian Church (U.S.A.) and the Cumberland Presbyterian Church.

The Presbyterian Hymnal: Hymns, Psalms, and Spiritual Songs. Louisville: Westminster/John Knox Press, 1990.

Reference Works

Altaner, Berthold. *Patrology*. 2nd ed. Trans. Hilda C. Graef. New York: Herder and Herder, 1961.

Brinkhoff, L., et al., eds. *Liturgisch Woordenboek*. Roermond, the Netherlands, 1958–1968; Supplement, 1970.

Cabrol, F. and H. Leclercq, eds. *Dictionnaire d'Archeologie chrétienne et de Liturgie*. Paris, 1907–1953.

Cross, F. L., and E. A. Livingstone, eds. *The Oxford Dictionary of the Christian Church*. 3rd ed. London: Oxford University Press, 1997.

Davies, J. G., ed. *The New Westminster Dictionary of Worship*. Philadelphia: The Westminster Press, 1986.

Fink, Peter E., S.J., ed. *The New Dictionary of Sacramental Worship*. A Michael Glazier Book. Collegeville: The Liturgical Press, 1990.

Hillerbrand, Hans J., ed. *The Oxford Encyclopedia of the Reformation*. 4 vols. New York and Oxford: Oxford University Press, 1996.

Klauser, Theodore, ed. *Reallexicon für Antike und Christentum*. Stuttgart, 1950ff.

Pfatteicher, Philip H. *A Dictionary of Liturgical Terms*. Valley Forge, Pa.: Trinity Press International, 1991.

Van der Meer, F. *Atlas of Western Civilization*. 2nd rev. ed. London and New York: Oxford University Press, 1960.

Van der Meer, F., and C. Mohrmann. *Atlas of the Early Christian World*. London and New York: Oxford University Press, 1959.

Van Loon, Ralph, and S. Anita Stauffer. *Worship Wordbook: A Practical Guide for Parish Worship*. Minneapolis: Augsburg Fortress, 1995.

Webber, Robert E., ed. *The Complete Library of Christian Worship*. Nashville: Star Song Publishing Group, 1993. Vol. 1: *The Biblical Foundations of Christian Worship;* Vol. 2: *Twenty Centuries of Christian Worship;* Vol. 3: *The Renewal of Sunday Worship;* Vol. 4 (in two books): *Music and the Arts in Christian Worship;* Vol. 5: *The Services of the Christian Year;* Vol. 6: *The Sacred Actions of Christian Worship;* Vol. 7: *The Ministries of Christian Worship*.

Index

SUBJECT

Index
PERSONS

Index

BIBLICAL REFERENCES AND DOCUMENTS

Non-Canonical Writings

Ancient Church Orders and Liturgical Sources